ECONOMICS:
A NEW INTRODUCTION

About the author

Hugh Stretton studied law and classics at Melbourne University, history at Oxford University, and economics and other social sciences as a visiting fellow at Princeton University. He has been a Fellow and Dean of Balliol College, Oxford. He has taught at Smith College, Massachusetts and at the University of Adelaide as Professor of History, then Reader, and then Research Fellow in Economics. He is a Fellow of the Australian Academies of the Humanities and the Social Sciences. For seventeen years he was deputy chairman of a public enterprise as it developed town centres, supplied commercial and industrial land, buildings and credit to the private sector, and built approximately 3000 houses a year.

Hugh Stretton is the author of *The Political Sciences: General Principles of Selection in Social Science and History* (1969), *Ideas for Australian Cities* (1970), *Housing and Government* (1974), *Capitalism, Socialism and the Environment* (1976), *Urban Planning in Rich and Poor Countries* (1978), *Political Essays* (1987), and with Lionel Orchard, *Public Goods, Public Enterprise, Public Choice: Theoretical Foundations of the Contemporary Attack on Government* (1994).

ECONOMICS:
A NEW INTRODUCTION

Hugh Stretton

Pluto Press

LONDON · STERLING, VIRGINIA

First published 1999 by Pluto Press
345 Archway Road, London N6 5AA
and 22883 Quicksilver Drive, Sterling, VA 20166–2012, USA

Revised edition 2000

www.plutobooks.com

British Library Cataloguing in Publication Data
A catalogue record for this book is available from the British Library

ISBN 0 7453 1536 4 hbk
ISBN 0 7453 1531 3 pbk

Library of Congress Cataloging in Publication Data
Stretton, Hugh.
   Economics : a new curriculum / Hugh Stretton.
      p. cm.
   Includes bibliographical references and index.
   ISBN 0–7453–1531–3
   1. Economics. I. Title.
HB171.5.S924   2000
   330—dc21   99–13960
                                                     CIP

09   08   07   06   05   04   03   02   01   00
10   9   8   7   6   5   4   3   2

Typeset in Australia
Printed in the European Union by Antony Rowe, Chippenham, England

to

Paul Streeten

Contents

Introduction

The rich democracies have economic troubles. Their uses of the environment are still far short of sustainable. They have obstinate unemployment and increasingly insecure employment. Some have unbalanced trade and payments and escalating foreign debt. Because women's new equalities are incomplete they cause stress and over-work to many women. In English-speaking countries a century of progress to greater equality has lately been reversed, and aid to poorer countries has declined.

The resort to deregulation, privatization and smaller government since the 1970s proves to have been a mistaken response to the new troubles, and an active cause of some of them. Economists share responsibility for that 'right turn' in economic policy. Without their expert authority it is hard to believe that the various political and business groups who drive the new strategy could have persuaded majorities to support it, or tolerate it, for so long.

Many able economists now attack the offending theories and the education which perpetuates them. This text offers them a new course-book for their students, and (I hope) some further reinforcement for their reasoning. It draws on elements of postKeynesian, green and feminist thought. But in the institutionalist tradition, its focus is on economic life and all workable ways of understanding it, rather than any one body of theory. It differs from comparable textbooks in the following ways.

Philosophy of science Bad economic theory can cause as much suffering and death as bad medicine or engineering can. Medical students must spend a year at chemistry and biology before they meet any medicine. Engineers must establish their maths and physics before they learn to design bridges or computers. I believe it is just as important for economists to begin by mastering two preliminaries: the intrinsic difficulties of a science of thoughtful, many-purposed, self-changing, conflict-ridden social activity; and some profound historical changes, in process now, to which economists' theories need to respond. Current 'Economics One' courses tend to neglect those two foundations or get them wrong. The first quarter of this text is devoted to them.

Values Economics is value-structured and controversial chiefly because it deals with such complex activity that its simplifications are necessarily selective. The text explains at length, with great care, why that is so, and why distinctions between 'positive' and 'normative' economics are unhelpful. (They may apply to many items of fact and opinion, but never to whole analyses of complex activity.) Economists need to understand the relations between their true-or-false factual knowledge, their unavoidably selective causal explanations, and the values and social purposes which have to shape the selective and imaginative elements of their work.

Theory Like other human activity, economic activity has complex motivation. It varies with cultural and political circumstances and changing technology. It is both repetitive and inventive, cooperative and conflict-ridden. It can change while we study it, sometimes because we study it. Such activity is not best studied by the use of a single comprehensive timeless monomotivational axiomatic/deductive theory whose users further limit their understanding, wherever they can, by replacing the more informative language of the economic actors with the less informative language of mathematics. Understanding economics is more like understanding politics or history or psychology than it is like understanding physics. It is best to use all the methods that will work. The text encourages students to measure and count and calculate, to trace complex causal networks, to understand the 'counter-factual' assumptions of their causal analyses, to understand economic actors' minds, to imagine the likely effects of alternative policies and institutional arrangements, and to gain vicarious experience by reading about diverse economic systems and ways of doing things. The emphasis is on investigative skills, and instrumental uses of whatever theory or experience helps with the case in hand.

But graduates with unorthodox beliefs risk professional disapproval and job discrimination. For confidence and self-defence they need to understand thoroughly the reasons for and against their non-conforming beliefs and the opposing orthodoxies. When it was proposed to simplify this text by removing most of the debate about neoclassical theory to another book, publishers' readers who want their students to use this text insisted that it stay as an essential of the education which the book offers.

History Through the centuries since classical and neoclassical theory were conceived there have been developments. The advanced economies now produce enough, if it were appropriately distributed, to keep all their people in secure comfort. They have had the first two or three generations of full democracy. Half their real incomes now come from sources other than paid work. They are radically reforming women's rights and opportunities. They lead in depleting and polluting the world's natural resources. Some are now increasing their inequalities: in the richest of them, as GDP continues to grow, the real incomes of the poorest third or so of the people now decline. In these circumstances it may make sense for further growth to take its place among, and often after, a number of other collective purposes. The text invites students to consider the implications of these and other historical changes for economists' criteria of productive and allocative efficiency, and for the desirable scope and uses of democratic governments' economic powers.

Three sectors The twentieth century saw increasing production by public enterprises and households. Together they now produce about half of the advanced economies' goods and services. The text treats modern economies as mixed economies with public, private and household producers. The three sectors operate on partly different principles. They call for partly different analysis. Their performance needs to be judged by partly different criteria. The text deals with them accordingly. It emphasizes the intricate trade and interdependence between them, and reviews better and worse ways of allocating resources between them.

Strategies There are chapters on the usual macroeconomic subjects - economic structure, trade and exchange, money and credit, inflation, employment. But they are followed by six chapters about economic strategies which may be appropriate for countries in different situations with different resources and capacities. Particular conditions may be better bases for strategic policy-making than theoretical preferences for bigger or smaller government, free trade or protection, open or boundaried financial systems, and so on.

Persuasion There is some attention to professional and everyday styles of economic argument and persuasion. Students need not conclude, because the work is intrinsically controversial, that 'there's no truth, anything goes'. There are more and less truthful, fair, coherent, logical, and helpful or misleading kinds of advocacy. Students are urged to avoid wilful deception and other dirty tricks, and to detect them in others. (Examples make opportunities for some fun.) But they are also urged to be sensitive - rather than routinely credulous or routinely cynical - about the relations, which vary widely in real life, between people's material interests, their professed and unspoken beliefs, and their selfish, disinterested and altruistic behavior.

Working time A course based on this text should probably extend over three or four semesters for undergraduates who must study two or three other subjects at the same time, or a year for those who can give it half their time, or one semester for graduate students from other disciplines who can give it their whole time. Other readers can find their way to chapters which interest them, and tolerate the painstaking exposition of familiar material which a course for beginners has to include.

Acknowledgements

I thank my informal economics teachers. The first of them was Paul Streeten, fellow-student, colleague, mentor and friend. Watching the late Thomas Balogh's relations with four British governments was a livelier education in political economy than most books offer. Geoff Harcourt mixes inspiration, instruction and practical help with unworldly generosity. Peter Riach has been specially helpful to this present book. I thank Peter Karmel, Ken and Amirah Inglis, David Donnison and Kay Carmichael, Andrew Graham, John Langmore, Clive Hamilton, Max Neutze and Patrick Troy, as exemplars: able professionals who speak and write plain language to the citizens whose conditions of life in rich and poor countries they work to improve.

This book owes much to Ivan Szelényi for his experienced understanding of Eastern Europe during and since its communist years, and the role of dissident intellectuals in those dangerous times; to Kyoko Sheridan for the history and prospects of Japan's government of its economy; to Ian Halkett, Cedric Pugh, Rod Lawrence and Riaz Hassan for exemplary research into relations between people and their houses; to Lionel Orchard for his urban philosophy and his astringent reading of public choice theory; to Paul Chapman for critical advice about industrial clusters and other subjects; to David Robertson, digital gambler on horses and currencies who is wonderfully unlike those reproved in this book; and to Don DeBats, Ric De Angelis and more others than I can remember for telling me what to read in their fields.

I thank Robert Heilbroner, Edward Nell and Victoria Chick for criticism of earlier drafts. Michael Keaney, Geoff Hodgson, John Hillard, Alison Kirk and Lucy Heller know well what I owe to their encouragement.

Paul Edwards and the late Alex Ramsay were chief executives of a public enterprise which developed and traded commercial and industrial property and public and private houses on a big scale over a wide region. Edwards had done as well in the private as in the public sector. Both were masters at the intricate trade and competition between the sectors, and at exploiting for good public purposes the salutary influence which each sector can have on the other's efficiency and social performance. For that central theme of this text readers can thank those two and Don Dunstan, the head of government who made my opportunity to work with them.

I thank the Australian Research Council, Mark Wootton of the Poola Foundation, Harold Wilkinson of the Oikoumene Foundation and an anonymous donor for financial support. I thank my hosts for a year at the University of York where the project was conceived. I am deeply grateful for ten research years in the school of Economics at the University of Adelaide, with help of many kinds from John Hatch, Jonathan Pincus, Richard Pomfret, Sue Richardson, Colin Rogers, Tom Sheridan and other staff. I am deeply indebted to the goodwill and magical skills of Les Howard, exemplary research librarian in the Barr Smith Library.

As always, I thank my family. Tolerant children put up with broken schooling and years away from home. They gave me my first computer and made me use it. Whatever their private thoughts about this project, they have generously encouraged it. Most of what the text says about shared incomes and women's options is inspired by my good and clever sister Bid. And as the preface to my first book said, for intellectual as well as domestic reasons, 'speaking of clever and good, my wife Pat enabled this book to be written.' Now as then, I thank her most of all.

H.S.

Part One

STUDYING ECONOMICS

1

What you can know, what you can't know

Economics is about questions like these:

- How have modern economic systems developed? How do they grow and change? Why do they differ as widely as they do – from peasant to post-industrial, from static to fast-changing, from poor to rich?

- In your own country what material resources do the people have, and what skill and organization to use them? *How* do they use them – what goods and services, and waste and pollution, do they produce? By what methods – from housework and small farms and corner shops to transnational corporations?

- Who gets what? How are wealth and income distributed? Land and housing space? Health and education and opportunity? How equally or unequally are those things distributed or shared between women and men? Between richer and poorer households? Between races? Between generations?

- How are the work and the products and people's shares of them determined? What mixture of force, persuasion, hard bargaining, consumers' choice, friendly cooperation and unselfish generosity decides *what* to produce, *how*, and for *whom?*

- How does economic life relate to the rest of life? Is the economic system an important cause or effect of a society's freedoms, equalities and inequalities, gender relations, culture, quality of life, environmental care?

- Why do people disagree so incurably about their economic systems and policies? Which of the disagreements express conflicts of interest? Right-or-wrong disputes about the facts? Disagreed values and priorities?

There are not many knock-down, true-or-false answers to those questions (or there would not be such disagreements). The fact is that economic life is complicated and shot through with conflicts and uncertainties, so the science which studies it can't be a simple expertise, agreed by all. It deals with hard facts but also with conflicting interests and disagreed social values and purposes. Some economists – mostly men – see it as the science of 'choice under scarcity' as we decide the best array of material goods we can get from our limited resources and productive capacities. Some want it to be a branch of the environmental science which studies how to conserve resources for our grandchildren, and for continuing human life on earth. Some – especially women – see it as the study of provisioning: of the nurture and cooperation by which we supply each others' material needs and organize our mutual care and interdependence. And there are others with other concerns.

Economics is thus – like other social sciences – part study and part debate. An expert, many-sided, continuously changing debate. A mixture of science and social philosophy and politics.

This course of study aims to introduce you to that debate, and make you skilful at it. You will find it tough and confusing at times. But it is rewarding, as one of the world's great debates. It has technical fascinations. It rewards practical skills as well as talents for theory. And it is important: it affects the way the world works.

So if you are serious about it you must face the fact that you need quite a tough, complicated, controversial education.

A hard subject, but ...

One thing which makes economics a hard subject is that economic beliefs and disagreements are part of economic life. They are 'working parts' of the economic system. They cause things to happen. That is because people act according to what they believe. If people change their economic beliefs, that may cause them to change their economic behavior, and that may change the way the economic system works. To understand how an economic system works you therefore need to know (among other things) how the people *think* it works. That includes understanding how they disagree about it. People with powerful economic influence – government leaders, business leaders, labor leaders, voters in national elections – don't only disagree about how the economy *ought* to work. They often also disagree about how it *does* work – about what is causing what, here and now.

Textbooks also disagree. One feature of this textbook is that it emphasizes the practical importance of economic beliefs and disagreements in the actual work-ing of the economic system. That is why the whole of Part One – Chapters 1 to 7 – is about general problems of economic knowledge. Then each of the next five Parts will include passages about its own particular problems of knowledge. What do the actors in the econ-omy – governments, investors, labor leaders, etc. – *think* they are doing, and how do the economists who study their behaviour *understand* what they are doing?

That means that for many students this first Part will be the most unfamiliar and difficult part of the whole course of study. Two things may help you to cope with that:

First, this opening chapter will presently give you an easy start.

Second, you *can* then skip Chapters 2 to 7, and start work at Chapter 8 on the substantial economics of Part Two.

I believe that learning to understand the nature and variety of economic disagreements – the subject of Chapters 2 to 7 – is a basic part of your economic edu-cation. In the end, you will need it if you want to be a skilled contender in the great debate. But 'in the end' may suit you better than a hard beginning would. In that case, start by working your way through the solid economics of Parts Two to Five. Then come back to Part One, to make sure you understand the nature of economists' disagreements, before you read Part Six, which is about some major policy questions in the great debate.

... an easy start

Whatever you decide to do when you come to Chapter 2, you can now relax for a bit. This first chapter won't put you to work, it is more of an advertisement for the work to come. It offers some first impressions: of the range of things you will study, the variety of methods you will need to use, the uncertain and changeable ele-ments as well as the more stable elements of a lot of eco-nomic knowledge. Most of the blurred detail that flicks by in this chapter you will meet again later in orderly, learnable form. So read this chapter straight through. Don't mind if it is confusing, it is meant to be. None of it is for hard learning.

We even start with fiction – a simple tale to illustrate some of the range of activity that economists study. Read it for fun. To keep your mind ticking over, just try to notice two things as you go:

Notice what a troublesome mixture of facts, proba-bilities, uncertainties and unknowns the business people in the story have to cope with.

Notice that the story sticks to what those business competitors need to know. Would you want to include any additional facts, or trace any different chains of cause and effect, if you were telling any of the other par-ties what they needed to know about the problem? The government, for example? Or the husbands, wives and children of the workers in the story?

MAKE A BETTER MOUSETRAP AND THE WORLD WILL BEAT A PATH TO YOUR DOOR

So said Ralph Waldo Emerson about a hundred and fifty years ago, meaning to encourage inventors.

Now imagine a day in the life of a modern mousetrap manufacturer.

To keep things simple, suppose that his mousetrap factory is a small workshop in a small country, perhaps Norway or New Zealand. The owner works with two employees, a metalworker and a woodworker. The metalworker shapes the springs and strikers out of steel wire. (Her union is proud that it admitted women before the British metalworkers did – but it took forty more years to get them equal pay). The wood-worker cuts wooden bases for the traps and fixes the metal parts onto them. The owner sees to buying the raw materials, packing and selling the fin-ished traps and freighting them to supermarkets and hardware stores.

He also keeps the accounts. We won't print them here – the money values keep changing with inflation, and they would soon be out of date. But we can indicate a basic relation between what the business owner spends and what he gets. For every $100 he spends on wages and materials and other costs of production, he sells traps for $150. That may look like a big profit margin. But the government takes nearly half of it as company tax. The rest is the owner's income, and the government takes a quarter of *that* as personal income tax. Since the business is only making 1000 mousetraps a week, that's a modest income – better than wages, for the long hours the owner labors at the business, but not much better.

This morning the owner faces a business decision. A new automated metal-shaping machine has come onto the market, designed for small workshops like his. Should he buy one? With a little ingenuity the machine could be programmed to turn out one-piece all-metal mousetraps and it could make 2000 of them a week which would double the present output. The metalwork-er could learn to set and feed the machine. The wood-worker would no longer be needed. The savings on wood and woodworker's wages would cover the cost of the extra metal and electric power.

So with no increase in day-by-day costs it looks as if production could be doubled. If the new traps still sold at the old price, each $100 of cost which used to produce traps worth $150 would produce twice as many traps, i.e. it would produce traps to sell for $300. Work through that and you will find that the rate of profit has soared from 50 per cent on turnover to 200 per cent. Income goes up fourfold! BONANZA! Reach for the chequebook, order the machine ...

Wait a minute. The machine costs money to buy, more money than our man has got. To buy it he will need a bank loan. Repaying the loan with interest over the working life of the machine will add $50 to every $100 of the other costs. So what? If $150 costs will produce $300 sales that is still two or three times the present rate of profit. So hurry to the bank, buy the machine ...

And go broke, quite likely. Before he hurries to the bank and buys the machine the prudent mousetrap manufacturer will consider at least the following:

Mice are not doing too well in modern life. They appear to have achieved Zero Population Growth. They still bother enough people to create a national demand for a couple of thousand traps a week, but no more. (That's two thousand *new* traps – nobody knows how many times each trap is used before it rusts up or wears out). Our manufacturer supplies half the national demand. The other half is supplied by the conservative country-town firm of McTavish, run on a shoestring by its founder's granddaughter. If our man doubles his output, who will buy the extra thousand traps a week?

Answer: the machine can halve the price of producing each trap. So cut prices. The low prices will attract enough of McTavish's customers to put her out of business. Our machine can then supply the whole national demand for 2000 traps a week.

What if McTavish buys a machine too? After a price-cutting war the two of them may end up each selling the same thousand traps as before, but with half-idle machines, half the former income because of the halved prices, and a whole load of debt to repay.

Find out what McTavish intends to do? No, you can't, because (1) she doesn't know herself yet, and (2) what she does will depend on what her competitor does, and her competitor is still waiting to see what *she* will do.

Why don't the two of them merge? If they formed one firm they could buy one machine and keep it fully employed. Furthermore he could work the machine while she did the packing and selling, so they could sack the metalworkers as well as the woodworkers – *two* people could produce the traps that *six* people produce now. It they could go on selling the new traps at the old prices, they could make some real monopoly profits. Lush incomes for both partners, swimming pools and private schools for his children and her grandchildren ...

And why go on paying all that company tax? They could employ themselves for wages, and raise the wages high enough to use up all the sales revenue. On paper the firm would then break even, showing no profit. Company tax is on profits, so no profit would mean no company tax. The partners would still have to pay income tax on their wages, but their winnings would only be taxed once (instead of twice at present, once as company profit and then as personal income). The company might even provide them with cars and pay their phone bills, so that those items would be entirely tax free. There is more real take-home income to be gained by reconstructing those tax liabilities than by (say) improving productive efficiency to add ten per cent to output or cut ten per cent off costs.

The tax tricks might work, but alas the merger won't. Our man's wife won't leave her city job, McTavish won't leave her children and grandchildren. Neither firm will move so the merger is not practical. Besides, it would not be a safe monopoly. Some enterprising stranger would see his chance, buy a machine, cut prices, restore competition – and they would all be back with under-used machines and big debts.

But use some imagination. Why accept the market limit of 2000 traps a week? Can't the public be conned into buying more traps? Cutting the price won't do it – there are only so many mice to catch, and catching them is not the kind of pleasure people will buy more of just because its price goes down. But some artful psychology might change that. Some people are already so rich or squeamish that when they trap a mouse they can't face the ghoulish business of extracting its corpse from the trap, so they throw the trap and mouse away together and set a new trap for the next mouse. How could more of the customers be persuaded to do that? Suppose that (1) the retail price of the new traps was cut by a third, but (2) they were marketed only in plastic packs of three, and (3) presented as *New, Hygienic, DISPOS-ABLE*. They could be made well and truly disposable – more costs could be saved by setting the machine to make an extra-cheap trap that would only snap once and could not be re-set or re-used. The customers would then be spending altogether *more* money to buy *more* traps to catch *the same number* of mice. How many suckers would fall for it? Hard to predict.

So far, our manufacturer has no debts. That has some business advantages, especially in uncertain times. If mousetrap sales decline for any reason (such as an economic recession, or a drought which causes a mouse recession) he can cut most of his costs in step with his declining sales. He can buy less wood and wire, put his workers on short time and wages, maybe do more of the work himself. That way, making 500 traps won't cost much more per trap than making 1000 would. Halving the sales will halve his income, but *only* halve it. Worse things than that can happen if he buys the expensive machine. Once bought, he cannot then cut *its* costs week by week. If it is bought with borrowed money, weekly debt repayments will be the same however little work the machine does. So if sales decline, anything the owner can save on wages and materials will be a smaller proportion of his total costs than it would have been without the machine. If he earns less than it takes to keep up the debt payments he will go broke. But on the other hand if he doesn't buy the machine McTavish may buy one and put him out of business by undercutting his prices. What to do?

Another anxiety: The government calls mousetraps 'manufactured goods' and this country protects its manufactures from foreign competition. It has what is known as a 25 per cent *ad valorem* tariff on most of them. That means that if anyone buys a foreign mousetrap for a dollar and imports it, he has to pay the government a tax of 25 cents – so that once inside the country, that $1 mousetrap effectively costs $1.25, so $1.25 is the wholesale cost our man and McTavish have to compete with. What if the government stops listening to the Chamber of Manufactures which supports the tariff, and starts listening instead to the Chamber of Commerce which favors free trade? If the government abolishes the tariff, both mousetrap makers may be put out of business by a flood of cheap-labor mousetraps from China. Who will defend the mousetrap tariff? Mousetrap manufacturers do not contribute a lot

of votes or funds to the political parties, they are not what is known as an influential lobby. (But the metalworkers union is a big lobby, and a powerful supporter of the tariff. Think twice about sacking those metalworkers?)

More anxieties: who knows what will be invented next? Amalgamated Pharmaceutical may come up with an effective mouse poison that does not poison anything else. Brandnew Biotechnics may come up with a mouse-specific virus to decimate mice like myxomatosis once decimated rabbits. Friends of the Earth may persuade the government to declare mice an Endangered Species, and outlaw mouse-trapping. If any of those disasters happens, mousetrap manufacturers don't want to be caught with a lot of expensive capital equipment and debts. Things have changed since Ralph Waldo Emerson. Make a better mousetrap and the world may bankrupt you next week.

And so on. That is only a sample of the possibilities the small business owners may have to worry about. It scarcely begins on the possibilities the government may need to worry about, or the two male woodworkers' wives and children may need to worry about.

WHAT YOU CAN KNOW, WHAT YOU CAN'T KNOW

So what? Is economic life a pure lottery? Or can research and experience improve our understanding and control of it?

It is certainly not a *pure* lottery. When that business man is considering whether to buy the new machine, he knows a lot about the business. He knows more than any novice would know. He can predict many things better than a toss of a coin would do.

But there are also enough uncertainties and unknowns to ensure that nobody can *predict for certain* which course of action will pay the investor best. He can't predict that. The technologists of the new machinery can't. Economists can't. However expert and well-informed they are, their 'forward knowledge' is usually a mixture of some certainties, some probabilities, some uncertainties, some unknowns. The mixture varies from case to case – some aspects of economic life are more predictable than others. Some negatives – things that *cannot* happen – are sure enough. But what *will* happen is seldom perfectly predictable. Moreover, as we will see in Chapter 2, uncertainty beforehand about *what* will happen is often followed by disagreement afterwards about *why* it happened.

So your knowledge can vary greatly in its degree of certainty.

As you begin learning economics it is also important to grasp the mixed and diverse nature of the information with which you will have to work. It is so important that we will now rub it in three times over by sorting out some of the facts of the mousetrap case in three different ways, just to emphasize their diversity. They could of course be classified in plenty of other ways besides these three – but for present purposes three will do. We will classify them –

(1) according to how certain or uncertain the knowledge can be;

(2) according to the different ways of knowing what causes what; and

(3) according to who wants to know – i.e. whose fortunes the economist chooses to follow. Does she want to trace the likely effects of the proposed new investment on the manufacturer, or the consumers, or the workers, or their partners and children – or on more general social facts such as the total value of national output, or the distribution of wealth and income?

Remember that you are not expected to learn these lists in detail. Just read them through as reminders that economics has to include a great mixture of different *kinds* of knowledge – knowledge of quantities and qualities and causal relations; physical facts, institutional rules, human purposes and feelings; and so on.

Measuring, estimating, understanding, judging, guessing

First, consider the mixture of certain and uncertain knowledge, and unavoidable ignorance, with which the mousetrap manufacturer has to face the future and decide what to do.

He knows exactly – or surely enough for practical business purposes:

- how the new machine works, what it can make, what it costs to buy

- what he can borrow to buy the machine – though not how the rate of interest may vary through the life of the loan

- the laws and regulations his business has to comply with

- the costs, output, takings and taxes of his business last year.

He knows roughly – at least for a year or two ahead:

- what the machine will cost to run

- the wage rates he will probably have to pay his workers

- the prices he will probably have to pay for his materials

- who are the main wholesalers of his traps

- the number of traps the nation will probably buy if the design and prices of the traps don't change

- the tax reductions he can probably get away with, and those he probably can't.

He can guess – uncertainly, but still better than by tossing a coin:

- how many of the present traps might sell at lower prices

- how many new disposable traps might sell at lower prices

- how advertising might affect sales

- how unlikely the Free Trade party is to win the next national election and abolish the tariff.

He cannot know

- what next year's weather or epidemics may do to the mouse population

- what new business aids or taxes the government may introduce

- what McTavish will do next

- what the next technical inventions will be

- what the international exchanges will do next

Notice that the *uncertainties often reduce the practical value of the certainties*. Knowing the size of the national market is less use if you don't know whether it will continue to be protected from foreign competition. Knowing exactly what the new machine can make, at what cost, is less use if you can't predict how many of the new traps the public will buy. And so on.

CAUSE AND EFFECT: HOW DO YOU KNOW WHAT CAUSES WHAT?

A lot of the manufacturer's knowledge consists of knowing what is likely to cause what – i.e. he has to know about a lot of *causal relations*. The causal relations are of many different kinds, just as they are in daily life. The point to notice for our purposes is that *different kinds of causal relations* often have to be *known by different methods*.

Start with an example from daily life. Suppose you buy a bad pie and it makes you sick.

How do you know it was the pie that made you sick?

That takes technical knowledge of the physical working of the body.

Who caused the pie to be bad? The butcher, the cook, the retailer? To answer that, you may have to mix technical knowledge with some legal or ethical judgment. Technical: When and how did the poison or bacteria get into the pie? Ethical: Whose business was it to see that did not happen? Whose mistake or carelessness let it happen? Even if the butcher supplied the bad meat, perhaps the cook could be expected to notice it but the retailer could not. So the butcher and the cook caused your trouble but the retailer did not.

Whoever did it, what caused him to do it? It may help if you understand his situation. (Was he over-worked that day? Lost his spectacles? Refrigerator broken down?) You can understand how you yourself might respond to external facts like that, without know-ing what went on in the other person's mind. But if he did not respond as you think you would, or as you think most people would, you may need to find out (if you can) what *actually* went on in his mind. (Was he flustered? Inattentive to what he was doing? Was he positively trying to poison you?)

At each step of the process from bad meat to bad digestion, particular causes produced particular effects. You can see that there is a sequence of causal relations. But you can also see that a number of different *kinds* of causal relations have to be understood by different *methods*. The methods range from technical knowledge of physical processes and knowledge of social customs and situations to legal or ethical judgments of responsi-bility and psychological understanding of people's thoughts and feelings. Different causal relations have to be known by different methods of observation, under-standing and choice. The diversity is extremely impor-tant for economic science. There will be more about it in Chapter 3.

Meanwhile, back to the mousetrap business. Running a business is more complicated than buying a pie, but the same principles apply – you need to know what causes what. The mousetrap manufacturer needs to understand causal relations of many kinds. Some of them – like how the new machine works in a technical way – he can leave to other experts. But there are plenty of causal relations which he needs to under-stand for himself. Here is a list of some of the methods – the kinds of observation and reasoning and under-standing – that he must use. (Again, you need not learn the list in detail. Just notice how diverse the methods are.)

Simple arithmetic shows how –

- doubling one manufacturer's output will increase the national output of mousetraps by 50 per cent
- halving the cost of production (without reducing the selling price) could increase profit on turnover by 300 per cent.
- the debt on the new machine could kill the business if weekly sales declined by half or more.

Regular association, chiefly in experience with other products, shows that –

- lower prices often increase the quantity sold
- advertising often increases the quantity sold.

Knowing rules and regulations tells how –

- cutting *some* costs won't improve profits. For exam-ple failing to provide a staff lavatory or accident insurance or proper company accounts will cause the government to close the factory
- failure to pay regular wage rates will cause the metalworkers union to close the factory.

Understanding people's thoughts and feelings shows –

- why lower prices by themselves may not increase mousetrap sales
- what sort of advertising may have most effect
- why the two producers will not combine their opera-tions in a single firm or partnership.

Notice that the relations between particular causes and effects are often known by more than one method at once. *Example*: Suppose you have observed that as a general rule, with many goods, more advertising is usu-ally followed by more sales. That means you have observed a *regular association* between advertising and sales. You may also notice that the relation is changing over the years as people learn to respond to advertising in more sophisticated ways – i.e. you have a *historical explanation* showing how a particular causal relation is changing over time. To check whether the usual link between advertising and sales holds for the particular case of mousetrap sales, you may *study the situation* of people who are bothered by mice, and ask yourself whether it would make sense for them to buy more traps. You may then check your reasoning by asking some of the people about their purposes and tactics when they are trapping mice, and about their feelings when disposing of dead mice. Thus you get to *under-stand their thoughts and feelings*. If all that leads you to guess that a particular style of advertising might persuade some of them to buy more traps, you may give that idea a trial by *controlled experiment*. How? Choose two similar regions which have so far had similar mousetrap sales. Advertise in one region but not in the other. Watch for any difference in sales. (But keep a sharp eye out for any *other* causes, such as a local plague of cats or health inspectors, which may be disturbing your experiment by affecting sales in either of the two regions.)

Whatever you finally learn about the effects of advertising on mousetrap sales, you will have discovered it by a wide variety of methods, some fairly precise and reliable, some quite rough and *un*reliable. This may seem messy but it is unavoidable. The diversity is in the nature of the causal relations themselves. That is why economic science can't replace that wide variety of methods by any single super-scientific method. For example you can't understand all causal relations by statistical inference alone – that method is not the best way to understand human reasoning and motivation. The social forces at work in a modern economy are so many and complicated that you can rarely run properly controlled experiments. You certainly can't describe all the causal relations in mathematical language, or deduce them all from a few axioms like Newton's Laws of Motion.

What *can* economists do? They can work to improve each of the methods. Measure the quantities more accurately. Refine the statistical analyses. Improve the historical explanations. Learn more about the political and legal and social conditions of economic life. Perceive the human motives more acutely. And so on. Improving your understanding of economics is like improving your understanding of politics or marriage or daily life. You need to broaden your understanding, not narrow it.

Conclusion: For the best knowledge of economic causes and effects, use all the relevant methods in all appropriate ways.

Yes, but *which* causes and *which* effects?

That all depends on why you want to know – or on *who* wants to know.

CAUSE AND EFFECT: WHO WANTS TO KNOW?

Our story so far has been told strictly from the mousetrap manufacturer's point of view. It has only included the facts which the manufacturer needs to know. It has left out a lot of things that other people might need to know.

In the next chapter we will see that people with different interests might want quite different explanations

of the changes in the mousetrap business. They might want to explore different *causes* of those changes.

Here, to keep the example simple, we can ask a question about *effects*. We have been told that there is a new machine which promises a major technological change in the mousetrap industry. *Question*: What will be the economic effects of that technological change?

Our story has already tried to answer that question as well as the many uncertainties of the case allowed. But it only answered the question for the manufacturer. It included only the effects likely to affect *his* fortunes. It did not include everything that other people might need to know for *their* purposes. For example:

The workers need to know the firm's accounts and business prospects, in order to judge how hard to bargain for whatever the firm can afford to give them in the way of higher wages, shorter hours, better working conditions. If their jobs are threatened, they need to know their rights under any relevant laws and industrial agreements. They need to know what alternative jobs there may be for their skills – or what opportunities there are to acquire other skills. Do they face life on the unemployment dole, and if so, on what conditions?

The workers' families may want to know where any alternative jobs are likely to be. Will the new technology cause them to move house, change schools, lose old friends and neighbors? One metalworker supports a retired husband; they could move, but metal work for a woman past fifty is hard to find. Both woodworkers have wives and small children. One of the wives keeps house and cares for the children because she likes the work, and believes in that division of labor with her partner. The other does the same for different reasons: she could be out earning if they lived in reach of her parents, who would mind the children, but where the parents live there is no work for her husband. If the two men lose their jobs, can they find others without moving house? Could the women find local jobs, or would they also have to move house to earn? Until those and other questions are answered, they can't know what the economic effects of the new mousetrap technology will be for them.

The national government may scarcely notice the tiny mousetrap industry. But it does want the industry's figures to be included in many national accounts: for example in total national output, in total industrial production, in the small-business share of industrial production, in the small-business shares of *national* employment and *industrial* employment and *regional* employment and *tariff-protected* employment – and so on. It needs that information to estimate the effects of its economic policies and to plan future policies – policies which may have powerful effects on the mousetrap industry even though the government scarcely knows it is there.

The local government may want to know quite different effects of any changes in the industry. What sort of location will it need? What pollution will it create? What local traffic will it generate? What gas, power, water supplies and sewerage will it demand? And so on.

Notice that some of the information and analysis is useful to everybody. But in addition to that common pool of knowledge, many of the parties need further information, or different kinds of analysis, for particular purposes. That's normal – it rarely happens that a single analysis can meet all the information needs of all the people involved. It is natural that investors want the information that helps them to estimate risks and rates of profit. Workers want to know about jobs, wages, working conditions. Their spouses want to know about jobs, housing options, schools, neighborhood services. National governments want one range of information, local governments want another range. They all have different interests so they ask different questions. Even when they ask the same question – like 'What will be the effects of new technology?' – they often want different answers.

Notice that they don't only want different information. They often also want it differently organized. For example, several parties may want to know what the new technology will do to employment. But one (perhaps the national government) wants the effects on employment to be totalled up. Another wants them broken down by sex to see the effects on (say) women's chances of part-time work. Another wants the figures broken down by region, to see the effects on local government revenue, or on local housing and services. And so on. People with different interests not only need different facts. They often also need different classifications and analyses of those facts.

So if investors, workers, workers' partners and children, national and local governments should all ask 'What will be the economic effects of technological changes in the mousetrap industry?', they may all want different answers.

Remember that they all want *true* answers. They don't want any false facts or wishful thinking. They don't want inconsistent or contradictory answers. But they do want *different* answers.

Sometimes, if the issues are very simple, an econo-mist may be able to meet all the parties' needs with a single survey of the relevant economic effects. But more often she can't do that. There is *some* common knowledge useful to everybody but over and above that, each party needs some additional facts and some different kinds of analysis.

Self-verifying and self-falsifying beliefs

People with different working interests who therefore need different selections and arrangements of information are one source of disagreements in economics – but not the only source. Experts can also disagree about the facts. They can disagree about what causes what. And they can disagree in some beliefs which look like plain statements of facts or causal relations, but which have the awkward quality that they come true if people believe in them, or alternatively prove false if people believe in them.

Examples:

If people believe that inflation will continue (i.e. prices will keep rising, the value of money will keep falling) they may act accordingly. Producers raise prices because they expect that their costs will continue to rise. Workers demand higher wages because they expect that prices will continue to rise. Lenders raise interest rates to cover the expected rate of inflation. *Because they all do those things* the inflation continues. The belief that it will continue has caused it to continue. The belief is *self-verifying*, it makes itself come true.

Similarly if enough people believe an economic depression is coming, they may act accordingly. Businessmen stop investing. Shops run their stocks down. Consumers spend less and save more for the hard times ahead. Together those actions *cause* a depression. Thus the belief causes the event which makes the belief come true.

But consider this third example. People observed that their bank managers were prudent with money and imposed strict standards of prudence on borrowers. After a generation of that reassuring experience it seemed sensible to ask 'Why should governments regulate such prudent people, who know their business so well and do it so conservatively?' So from the 1970s governments deregulated them. The bankers responded by expanding credit two or three times faster than before. They fuelled inflation. They financed the most extravagant office-building boom and slump of the century. They enticed the poor people of the third world into crippling debt. They turned the international exchanges into a casino in which gambling transactions outnumber trade and investment transactions many times over.

The bankers had indeed been prudent for a generation, but – it turned out – that was because they were strictly regulated by prudent governments. As long as people doubted their prudence and therefore regulated them, they behaved prudently. As soon as people came to believe that they were inherently prudent, and therefore freed them, they used the freedom to show how false the belief was. Just as there can be self-verifying beliefs, there can also be self-falsifying beliefs.

So there are paradoxes, of kinds that don't usually afflict natural sciences. If a belief *causes* events which prove it true, that is not the same as a scientific proof that the belief was true in the first place. It may not have been true, it may just have been persuasive. So if people are divided between two contradictory beliefs – i.e. beliefs which cannot both be true – there may sometimes be no scientific way to test which belief *is* true; and if one of the beliefs *comes* true, that may not prove that the other was necessarily false.

Remember that we are talking about the special class of self-verifying and self-falsifying beliefs. Not all beliefs are like that – economic life has plenty of hard facts and relationships which stay the same whatever you believe about them. You can't *usually* make things come true just by believing them or persuading others to believe them. But true or false, what people believe about the economic facts affects what people do, and therefore how the system works. So self-verifying and self-falsifying beliefs are not the only beliefs that can affect the way the economy works. True beliefs and false beliefs can both affect people's market behavior and governments' policies, and thus how well the economy works, and how its benefits are distributed.

Do you begin to understand what it means to say that beliefs are working parts of economic systems? It means that you cannot simply study the system from outside, in an uninterfering way, like most natural scientists can study their subjects. Your understanding of the system is *part of the system*, it can affect the way the system works. Get used to the idea. We will return to it often.

CONCLUSIONS

You were encouraged to relax and read straight through this first chapter, to get a general impression of some of the complexities and uncertainties of economic life, and the problems of studying it. The details didn't matter, so don't worry if they didn't stick. You will meet the arguments again. They will be slowed down, spaced out,

learnable. So don't worry if they are swimming confusingly round in your head at this stage.

Most of the chapters ahead will end with regular aids to learning and revision, including exercises for you to work at. But for this introductory chapter some broad conclusions will do.

Six numbered conclusions follow. Experts will recognize them. They stand for a particular approach to economics. It is an historical, institutional, practical approach. It is aimed at the needs of the working world, rather than the conventions of academic learning. It tries to teach you, as far as book-learning can, the skills and sensitivities you will actually need to use as an economist working for business, labor, government, political parties or civic movements for reform or conservation in a modern mixed economy.

The emphasis is on skills and sensitivities rather than 'principles'. This is because I don't believe there are many unchanging 'principles of economics' which you can learn by heart and apply in all cases. Too many of the principles keep changing because economic organization and behavior keep changing.

Besides changing over time, the 'principles' also vary a good deal from place to place, from industry to industry, from market to market. What you need is the ability to find *what* principles are at work in particular countries, industries, markets, at particular times, and in what directions they are changing.

So besides a changing stock of principles you also need a lot of adaptable skills – like a footballer does, or a car-driver in difficult traffic, or a politician. Adaptable abilities, responding intelligently to changing and uncertain situations as well as to familiar ones. The following conclusions sum up the main reasons why, to be effective, economic expertise needs to be like that.

SUMMARY

1. Economic beliefs are working parts of economic systems. The systems change as beliefs about them change, and beliefs change as the systems do.

2. Though 'economic system' is a useful phrase it can also be a deceptive one. The economic activity of a society is not an independent system. It is continually affected by political, social and intellectual forces as well as by purely economic forces. As an economist you must be prepared to trace networks of cause and effect and interdependence wherever they lead. If you look *only* at economic causes you may not be much good at explaining or predicting economic *effects* – a 'pure' economist is a wilfully ignorant economist!

3. What causes what? In the business of producing and distributing a society's material goods and services there are causal relations of many different kinds, which have to be understood by different methods. The methods include simple counting and measuring and arithmetic; statistical inference and judgment of probabilities; technical and social understanding of many different economic processes; knowing about institutions and their rules and routines; understanding people's thoughts and feelings. Such diverse *kinds* of causal relations, and such diverse *ways of knowing* what causes what, cannot be reduced to any single form. For example you can't deduce the working of the economic system from a few axioms about economic motivation. You can't discover all the causal relations by statistical methods. You can't describe many of the causal relations mathematically.

4. All economic theory and all economic analysis have to be *selective*. Many technical considerations guide the selections. But they also have to be guided by social purposes. Different people with different interests and values often have different social purposes, and always will. So economics is an *intrinsically* controversial subject, like marriage or politics: no amount of science can ever make us all agree about it. So understanding the different kinds of economic disagreement is often an essential part of understanding the working of the economic system itself.

5. Now put together Conclusion No. 1 and Conclusion No. 4, and you get this most uncomfortable conclusion of all: In studying any modern economy you are studying (1) *a system of material production and distribution* which is also (2) *a system for organizing and carrying on many social conflicts*. Those conflicts are often won by the parties whose beliefs about them manage to prevail. So, often enough, *economic analyses and the theories which shape them are themselves weapons in the conflicts which they analyse*. That makes them all the more likely to be controversial and disagreed.

6. This course of study is no exception. Nor is any other textbook, or class curriculum. They are all unavoidably selective, unavoidably persuasive, shaped more by some social values and purposes than by others. Pretences of perfect neutrality are *all* false pretences. At the end of Part One I will return to this subject. You are entitled to know what an author thinks his values and purposes are and how he thinks they have shaped his book. I do my best to declare the conscious values and purposes which have shaped this book, and some beliefs about the right relations between teachers' and students' values, at the end of Chapter 7.

As you have been reminded before, there is also plenty of *un*controversial economics. There are many straightforward measuring and accounting tasks. There are many physical facts and processes to be studied which don't occasion much disagreement. But the minute you ask *what causes what*, or *why* things happen as they do, or how they might be changed – i.e. the minute you ask the central and challenging economic questions – you are back with the six conclusions above: with an uncertain, controversial science of an unstable, conflict-ridden economic system.

So if you are a character who likes to make your way through a predictable world with a cut-and-dried science to guide you, you are not going to like economics much. (You might shift to analytical chemistry, or surveying.) If on the other hand you like the arts and skills and excitements of political and intellectual combat, you may enjoy economics anywhere from cheerfully to diabolically.

But don't write it off – at least not yet – as too confusing for you. The next six chapters will lead you by the hand over a lot of the ground you just raced over so rapidly. It is not all as confusing as it seems at first sight. Economic life has many uncertainties, economic science has many disagreements – but there are better and worse ways of coping with them.

Now read on.

2

Causes and effects (1) the need to select

There's an old tale about a woman walking a new pig home from market. She comes to a stile. The pig won't jump over it. She tells her dog to bully the pig but the dog won't. She tells her stick to beat the dog, but the stick won't. She tries everything else she can think of, and she can think of plenty, as you will see. But none of them works. You can gather whose help she has been asking for, from her complaints at not getting it –

> *Butcher won't kill ox,*
> *Ox won't drink water,*
> *Water won't quench fire,*
> *Fire won't burn stick,*
> *Stick won't beat dog,*
> *Dog won't bite pig,*
> *Pig won't jump over the stile,*
> *And I shall never get home to my supper tonight.*

Question: What *caused* her to go hungry? The pig? The dog? The butcher?

This chapter is about how we decide what causes what in economic life. How do economists study and theorize about the relations between cause and effect? In particular, how do they choose *which* causal relations to study?

But first –

Hard learning starts here

After a chapter of easy reading it is time to change gear. The following chapters introduce ways of thinking about economic life while knowing two unnerving things: that some of the life is wilful and unpredictable, and that economists are bound to disagree about some of it. That is not just ignorance or human error, it is in the nature of the subject and our purposes in studying it.

The argument is not hard to follow step by step. But as a whole it is complex and partly unfamiliar. Give it your whole attention and take your time with it. If it is still confusing, you can skip to Part Two and return to these chapters later. But their themes recur throughout the course of study, so master them now if you can.

FACTS, VALUES, SELECTIONS

Philosophers may think the first two of the following definitions are too simple, but most economists use them, and so can we.

Facts are truths about the objective world. You make *positive* statements about them. All competent observers of the same facts should agree about them.

Values are the subjective bases of belief and opinion: of preferences, likes and dislikes, moral and ethical codes and judgments. You make *normative* statements of them. They are not factually true-or-false, or provable. People naturally disagree about them, as they do about religion and politics.

Selections in social science are mostly *valuations choosing facts*. Facts can't choose themselves. So which facts do you choose to notice? By which characteristics do you choose to recognize them, group them, separate them or total them up? The purposes of your study must decide – and your purposes express social values. Your purposes and selections, and therefore your science as a whole, are necessarily *value-structured*.

Suppose three observers consider Mr Gordon Sumner. The first says 'I see a white middle-aged English multi-millionaire.' The next says 'I see an ex-schoolteacher with dyed blond hair who campaigns for human rights and forest conservation.' The third says 'I see Sting, first famous as lead singer and songwriter for The Police.' Those are all true facts. Objective, positive, not a value in sight. But are they neutral, value-free observers? Of course they are not. Their values – i.e. their different purposes, preferences, judgments of what is interesting or important – lead them to notice or select *different* true facts.

To study complicated economic activity you have to select and simplify. Most economic theories abstract and model relationships which the theorists select as important. Important for what? Important by what criteria? Important to whose interests? Only your values – or *someone's* values – can guide those selections coherently. They cannot select themselves.

So here is a first professional disagreement. Some economics texts tell you the difference between positive facts and normative values, then say they will offer you facts only: positive economics, not normative economics. I disagree. Their 'positive' work is every bit as selective as yours or mine. However factual, their theory and information is shaped throughout by the social assumptions and values which necessarily guide their selections. It could not be otherwise – the facts and simplifications cannot choose themselves.

Before you decide who is right, here are five chapters about *how* economists select.

WHICH CAUSES, WHICH EFFECTS?

In social and economic life the causal relations are extremely complicated. 'Everything depends on everything else.' So *which* causal relations should economists study?

A great many of the serious disagreements between economists are not about facts at all. They are about these questions of selection.

Consider a simple example. In our mousetrap story, the two producers between them were manufacturing two thousand old-style wood-and-wire mousetraps each week – a hundred thousand a year. Let's call that output of traps an economic effect, and ask what causes it.

Obviously a large number of conditions have to be present to produce that effect. To mention only a very few of them: There has to be a demand for the traps. For that, there have to be mice and there have to be people. The people have to have money to spend on traps. And they have to have a culture which teaches them to keep mice out of their barns and kitchens.

To supply the traps there has to be a history of mousetrap design and development. There has to be a supply of suitable wood, and woodworking tools and skills. There has to be a supply of steel wire.

To supply steel wire of that springy strength there have to be coal mines, iron mines, a steel mill, and advanced technical knowledge of metallurgy.

And so on. That's only a beginning, a small sample, of the long list of *necessary conditions*. Any one of these conditions may be regarded as a *cause* of the annual output of traps. If you doubt it, try removing one of the necessary conditions. For example, suppose the mice all die off. Or there is a strike at the steel mill, and no steel wire. Or instead of being in an industrial society we are in a primitive culture without any manufacturing technology. Or a society whose religion prohibits killing animals. In *any* of those conditions, modern mousetraps will not be produced.

Are you bothered by the language of 'causes' and 'necessary conditions?' Should we really treat all the necessary conditions for manufacturing mousetraps as *causes* of the output of mousetraps? Can't we distinguish mere necessary conditions from active causes? I don't believe it matters much how you label the various

kinds of causes. A reason for thinking it does not matter comes later in this chapter – you can suspend your misgivings until then.

Scientific laws and selective explanations

If economics is a science, why does it have to pick and choose which causes and effects to include in selective explanations? Why can't it run on scientific laws which say plainly what causes what?

Sometimes it can. For example many texts offer you a *law of demand*. It says: *The lower the price of a commodity, the more of it consumers will tend to buy.*

If you are in business selling something, can you rely on that law? For some goods in some markets at some times you can. But which goods, which markets, which times? *Only detailed selective explanations, case by case, can tell you that.*

For example the 'law of demand' does not usually hold for low-priced mousetraps. Nor for any products which households do not happen to want. If you are selling carrots, it is true that you may *often* sell more by lowering the price. But not *always*. Not if other carrot farmers lower their prices further than you do. Not if competitors offer parsnips more alluring than your carrots. Not if you drop your price after the shoppers have spent all their money. Not if you are selling at some inconspicuous place where the shoppers don't notice your carrots. Not if there has been a health warning against carrots in the morning paper.

And so on – innumerable conditions are necessary for you to sell more carrots by lowering the price. I mean *innumerable* – you can never keep them all in mind, or specify them all. If you take care of the half-dozen hazards listed in the previous paragraph, your law can still be broken by other hazards you didn't think to specify. (Fire, earthquake, industrial disputes. It is Halloween in the US and people only want pumpkins. It is St Patrick's day in Ireland and people won't buy orange vegetables, only green ones.)

Economists commonly cope with these difficulties by saying their laws will hold *ceteris paribus*. 'Ceteris paribus' means, roughly, 'other things being equal', or 'as long as nothing else changes'.

On the one hand that is a simple way to say something about *one* of the influences that may be at work in a complicated situation (e.g. the possible influence of a price change). On the other hand it states only one of innumerable conditions which have to be present for the law to hold, i.e. for sales to respond to price changes as the law predicts they will. In real life *some* other things are nearly always changing.

One of the lessons of Chapter 1 was that most economic activity is a complicated mixture of regular and irregular processes and events. Economic laws may describe the regular ones, but only selective explanations can describe the irregular ones. And you may often need a selective causal explanation to tell you *whether* a particular law is likely to hold, or *which* laws are likely to hold, in any particular case.

'Everything depends on everything else': endless chains of cause and effect, seamless webs of interdependence

The economic life of a modern society is very complicated. The effects which economists study have innumerable necessary conditions or causes. To emphasize how complicated the life is, and how complicated its causal relations are, it may be helpful to draw a rough distinction between the present causes and the past causes of economic effects.
Like this:

- To produce any economic effect there has to be a sufficient set of necessary conditions or 'present causes'. For example to produce wire-spring mousetraps the conditions have to include a supply of wire from a steel mill.

- Each necessary condition in its turn has *its* necessary conditions or 'present causes'. For example a great many conditions have to be present for a society to have a modern steel mill.

- To produce those many conditions, and to produce the mill itself, there must also have been a past history of developing the technology, educating the skilled people, investing in the industry, designing and building the mill, and so on.

Summary: Any economic effect has both present and past causes. And each of those causes is itself an effect of other present and past causes.

If you fancy jargon you can call the sequences in which effects follow causes through time 'diachronic causation' (means 'through time'). And you can call mutual or simultaneous causal relations 'synchronic causation' (means 'at the same time').

I don't think the jargon helps. But whatever you call them, notice that causal relations of both kinds are *endless*. Chains of cause and effect reach back and back through history, they don't start at any particular date. Similarly the present conditions for any economic effect depend in turn on *their* necessary conditions, which depend on *theirs* – and so on, through the whole causal network of social and economic life. The inter-dependence is continuous. 'Everything depends on everything else.'

THE NEED TO SELECT

Faced with that endless complexity of causal relations, nobody can ever know them all.

So which of them do economists study? *Which* causes, *which* effects, *which* interrelations?

Answer: They can only study a limited number of *selected* causes, *selected* effects, *selected* causal relations. All social and economic theory and causal analysis has to be selective.

Next question: How do economists choose which causes, effects and relationships they will study? What principles of selection do they use?

Answer: They use many different principles. Economists with different specialist interests select differently. And economists with different social values and political purposes select differently. They select different links in the endless chains of causation. They select different items from the sets of necessary conditions. And *their different principles of selection are at the root of many of the fundamental disagreements in economics.*

Many of the disagreements are inevitable. No appeal to the facts, no amount of better research, can get rid of them. In a social science like economics you cannot expect universal scientific agreement. You cannot expect it because (1) you can never trace and specify the whole pattern of causation, i.e. *all* the innumerable necessary conditions, and *all* the links in *all* the historical chains of cause and effect that produced those necessary conditions. So you always have to select. But (2) there cannot be any perfectly neutral or 'purely scientific' principle of selection. The reason why there can't be is simple: What part of the causal pattern you need to know about depends on *why* you want to know – it depends on what you want the knowledge *for*, what you want it to enable people to *do*. You have to make your selections in the light of your purposes in studying the subject. But in any society, however peaceful and co-operative it may be, some interests always conflict with others, some social values are disagreed. And those different interests and purposes often call for different principles of selection in the analysis of patterns of cause and effect in social and economic life.

- Objection: Social *life* may be full of conflicts, but surely *science* can have agreed purposes? However economists may differ in their social values *as citizens*, surely they can agree that *as economists* they will look for nothing but the objective truth?

- Answer: Yes, scientists should look for nothing but the truth. But the truth *about what?* About *which* social facts, *which* of their (innumerable) causes, *which* of their (innumerable) effects? Truth is a fundamental principle of science, but it is not a principle of selection. Except for preferring truth to falsehood, it is no help to economists' problems of selection. More about this in Chapter 3.

Summary *Economic theory and analysis have to be selective. Their selections have to be guided by their social purposes. Different social purposes must often shape different – and disagreed – theories and analyses.*

That's it: the most important item in your economic education. This chapter and the next just spell it out in detail, with some of its practical implications.

The relation between *social purposes* and *scientific selection* is basic to your understanding of economics. It is so important that we will now repeat it three times over, in three different ways, through three practical examples, starting with the simplest. First, that bad pie you met in Chapter 1. Second, the mousetrap business. Third (in Chapter 3) a hot controversy from the real world – what causes inflation?

Example: the bad pie

The bad pie caused a bellyache, remember? But here some experts appear to be disagreeing about what caused the bellyache:

Doctor: Bacteria called salmonella caused the bellyache.

Lawyer: The unhygienic butcher and the careless cook caused the bellyache.

Health Inspector: Their shops had not been inspected for years. Slack administration of public health regulations caused the bellyache.

They are all speaking nothing but the objective truth. They don't disagree about any of the facts. They don't disagree about any of the causal relations. They merely *select* differently. Each chooses a different necessary condition, and calls it 'the cause'.

Why do they select differently? Partly because they happen to have different expertise. But chiefly because they have different kinds of action in mind – different policies for dealing with bellyaches.

The doctor focuses on the particular infection which should have been prevented.

The lawyer focuses on the people who have a duty not to let microbes into the food.

The health inspector focuses on one of the conditions which determine how much care those people take – how carefully they do their work.

Thus each expert selects one of the necessary conditions – the one that is relevant to the kind of policy that interests her or him – and calls that one 'the cause'. In this case the three chosen causes happen to be links in a chain or sequence of causation. If we make solid arrows ━━▶ mean 'cause' and dotted ┈┈▶ mean 'select', we can make a diagram:

Inspector:	**Lawyer:**	**Doctor:**
Let's do something about this	*Let's do something about this*	*Let's do something about this*
↓	↓	↓
Slack administration ━▶	Careless butcher and cook ━▶	Salmonella in pie ━▶ Bellyache

Now notice two things:

(1) It would *not* be sensible for the three experts to start contradicting each other, the inspector saying 'Slack administration was the *sole* cause of the bellyache', the lawyer saying 'No, no, it was the workers' carelessness' and the doctor saying 'You're both wrong, it was the salmonella.' If they disagree at all, it is not really about *causes*, it is about *policy*. Should we clean up the food supply by better inspection, or by re-educating the butcher and the cook? Or just cure the bellyache with the right pill? Their selective causal analyses have been guided, quite rationally, by their different social purposes.

(2) Remember we are only talking about different *selections*. Of course there can be other kinds of disagreement. If someone says 'It wasn't salmonella, it was streptococcus', that is a disagreement about *facts*. If someone says the bellyache was caused by nervous strain, or by the astrological fact that the planet Venus was ascendant at the time, that would be a disagreement about a *causal relation*. In principle it should be possible to resolve those disagreements by better research, i.e. by finding who is right and who is wrong about the causal process.

The summary at the end of this chapter will tell you that you need to develop this important skill: to know, when economists disagree, whether they are disagreeing about facts, or about causal processes, or about the social purposes which guide the selection of facts and causal relations in their analyses.

Now we repeat the same lesson with a second example.

Example: the mousetrap business

We could ask any number of cause-and-effect questions about that imaginary country and its mousetrap industry. Let us simply ask what causes the country to have a mousetrap industry at all. Why doesn't it import whatever mousetraps it needs? Why does it make its own, when so many other countries don't?

Here are some answers – some 'causal analyses':

Businessman: Because we have enterprising business men and women with the capital, courage and know-how to start and carry on such businesses.

Labor Leader: Because we have skilled productive workers to actually make the traps.

Professor: Because we have a productive 'public sector' – schools to educate the managers and workers, universities to research the metallurgy for the steel mill and the physics for automating the new machine.

This time the analysts are not selecting particular links from some chain of causes and effects through time. They are selecting different 'present and active' causes from the many which have to be simultaneously present:

Those three conditions are themselves a narrow selection. Many more conditions besides those have to be present to produce factory industry – we listed dozens more a few pages back, and even that was a limited selection.

Each of these analysts is focusing on the condition they know best, the one that gives them their living, or the one they think most important for the pupose in hand. Once again they are all selecting true facts and real causal relations. There is no necessary contradiction between them – as long as no one is foolish enough to say that 'his' cause alone is *sufficient* to produce the industry, without the presence of the others.

People are rarely *that* foolish. They don't think the industry could exist without those other conditions. But they do often think 'their' chosen condition is more important, and the other conditions are less important. A

common way of saying so is to say 'Yours are admittedly *necessary conditions*. But mine is the *cause*.' (Or the main cause, or the effective cause.)

'Causes' and 'necessary conditions'

Earlier, you were promised an argument against accepting any serious distinctions between 'causes' and 'necessary conditions'. Here it is:

It is possible to classify causes or conditions for particular effects in any number of ways. For example, you can distinguish *past* from *present* causes, or *variable* from *stable* causes, or causes which *can be manipulated* from causes which *cannot*. Those and many other possible classifications may be useful at times for particular purposes. But most writers who insist on separating 'causes' from 'conditions' are simply separating the factors they personally want to focus on from the factors they don't. That may be a practical judgment – 'This is a factor we can manipulate'. Or it may be a policy judgment – 'This is the factor we *ought* to manipulate.' It may be both – 'This is the set of factors we *can and should* try to control'. In each case the choice of factors is guided by some *purpose*. There is no intrinsic, factual difference between a 'cause' and a 'necessary condition' – it often depends on whether you want to 'use it' or 'leave it alone'.

For example it would not really make much sense for (say) the mousetrap manufacturer to say 'Education and research and a skilled work force are merely *necessary conditions* for factory industry. It's the business people who actually make it happen – they're the real *cause*.' The truth is that all four of those factors – education, research, skill, business initiative – and dozens of other conditions too are equally necessary, and they *all* have to be present before any *one* of them can contribute to production.

Conclusions Most distinctions between different categories of causes and conditions are simply practical. They follow from the particular purposes of the inquiry, and they are likely to vary from case to case as those purposes vary. 'Conditions' for one purpose are 'causes' for another. This is rational and right. It is how causal analyses ought to be shaped. No better way is available. But the guiding purposes are by nature likely to be controversial. So don't let anyone bluff you into accepting that their purposes and selections have any special privileges over yours or anyone else's.

This theme is so important that it is worth reinforcing it with one more example.

SELECTIVE CAUSAL ANALYSIS IN PRACTICE

Suppose that a country which has so far imported its mousetraps thinks it might be good to make its own. The government asks you, an economist, to advise on the conditions in which such an industry could be made to flourish. That calls for a selective causal analysis. You rightly select your analysis to tell the government what it needs to know, i.e. you let the *social purpose of the inquiry* guide the selection of your causal analysis. Though it may not say so in so many words, your report sorts out the relevant causal forces and relations into, roughly, three categories:

(1) The causal relations we should concentrate on, because they are the ones we can use. Perhaps: 'If you want your country to manufacture mousetraps, you need to do three things, which amount to working on three causal relations: (1) Find an able business entrepreneur. (2) Provide him or her with $200,000 of capital. (3) Put a 25 per cent tariff on imported traps. Do those things, and the rest should follow.'

(2) But the rest will *not* follow unless a lot of other necessary conditions are present, and it may be wise to mention *some* of these – any that may vary, or be overlooked, etc. Perhaps: 'For the above causal process to operate as described, there must of course be law and order, general economic prosperity, some skilled woodworkers and metalworkers available, a market demand for at least 100,000 traps a year, and a reliable supply of steel wire.'

(3) Of course innumerable other conditions also have to be present – from international peace, through a supply of electric power, to a cat population too lazy to do its proper duty. You could not sufficiently specify *all* such conditions, and you don't waste time trying. You take them for granted, leave them asleep, don't mention them. Or perhaps you acknowledge their existence with some broad collective phrase, saying that the conditions you *have* specified should be sufficient to produce the desired effect 'if all goes well', or 'in normal circumstances', or 'as long as there are no unexpected disturbances'. People will forgive you if your otherwise-accurate analysis is shattered by a war or an earthquake, or some sudden technological breakthrough.

So for the particular purposes of this analysis you have sorted out (1) some important causal relations, (2) some others which need watching, and (3) a larger number of (unspecified) conditions which also affect the business but can safely be neglected.

But remember that if the purposes of the inquiry were different you might well reshuffle a lot of those items into different categories. The purpose above was to state conditions for the *existence* of the industry. Suppose you were asked instead about the *efficiency* of the industry. In that case you might well take for granted some of the factors which were selected as important in the earlier analysis. For example you might take for granted the supply of financial capital (which was important for getting the industry started) and focus instead on *the cost and performance of physical capital*, because *efficiency* depends on using the equipment whose total purchase and operating costs are least per unit of output. (That is not always the most up-to-date equipment. It may be economically efficient to go on using older gear because it is paid for, so allows the lowest-cost output.) Or you might take for granted the *supply* of skilled labor and ask about its *price* per unit of output, because that also affects the industry's efficiency. And so on throughout the causal analysis – different social purposes, expressed in different purposes of inquiry, will focus your attention on different parts of the causal pattern. The point is this: Whether (say) the supply of finance is

(a) central to your causal analysis, or
(b) a necessary condition to keep in mind, or
(c) a normal fact of economic life which can be 'assumed' and left out of the analysis altogether

– is a choice which is not determined by any intrinsic characteristic of finance, or its causal relations with industry. It is determined by the purpose of the inquiry: by who wants to know, why they want to know, what they want to use the knowledge for.

Don't forget that we are only talking about the selection of causal relations. Your purposes of inquiry don't determine what actually causes what out there in the world. They just determine which of those innumerable causal relations you choose to trace and measure, and include in your analysis.

SUMMARY

1. *What causes what* in economic life is very complicated. There are seamless webs of interdependence here and now, and endless chains of cause and effect through time.

2. No analysis of what causes what in a general way, or of what causes any particular economic effect, can be complete or sufficient, if that means specifying all relevant direct and indirect causes. All analysis has to be selective.

3. Scientific laws of the type 'A fall in the price of a commodity will increase the demand for it' are no

exception. Such laws are never universal or sufficient. They select and state one or a few of the many conditions necessary to produce the specified effect; they are only true in conditions which they never sufficiently specify. They are as selective as any other analyses of causal relations have to be.

4. In choosing which causal relations to investigate and include in an analysis an economist can only be guided by the social purposes of the work. Who wants to know? What do they hope to use the knowledge for?

For that purpose, which causal relations do they need to understand?

5. The purposes need not necessarily express the economist's personal values. They may reflect her client's purposes – for example if she works for a firm or a labor union or government, or designs a course of study for students. But some such social purposes – her own or those she chooses to represent – must guide her selections if the causal analyses are to be coherent and useful.

EXERCISES

1. A firm employs a worker to mine asbestos. Soon after he leaves the job he dies of the lung disease asbestosis. To decide what caused his death you ask (a) the manager of the firm, (b) a labor leader, (c) a doctor who specializes in diseases of the lung, and (d) a doctor who is a government public health officer. Letting none of them say anything untrue, sketch their likely answers.

2. An industrial dispute leads to a strike. Write short analyses of the causes of the strike by (a) the employer, (b) the workers' leader, and (c) a fair-minded arbitrator. Then answer the following questions 3 and 4.

3. Between the three accounts you've written, sort out any disagreements. Which of the disagreements are about facts, which are about the causal force or effect of particular factors, and which are disagreements about which causes should be mentioned and included in the analysis, i.e. disagreed selections?

4. If you prefer the arbitrator's analysis to the other two, answer this: is it technically better, e.g. because it includes more causes, truer facts, etc.? Or is it morally or politically better, because its selection and allocations of causal responsibility are more just and fair-minded? (Or how much of each advantage does it have?)

5. How do you think wages ought to be fixed in a mousetrap industry – i.e. what causes should determine wage levels in that industry? Write a note of what you think the considerations ought to be, as if you are an arbitrator recommending a wage rate. Don't get your instructor to read the note. Put it away where you won't lose it, and pull it out and read it yourself some months (or terms, or semesters) from now, when you've worked your way through future chapters on wage-fixing, the pricing of products and the distribution of income.

3

Causes and effects (2) how to select

Chapter 2 explained why economists have to select – because the patterns of cause and effect in social and economic life are so complicated that they rule out any total or 'sufficient' analysis of what causes what.

This chapter and the next are about *how* economists select their causal analyses: how they *do* select, how they *should* select, and some ways in which they should take care *not* to select.

You already considered the general nature of selective causal analysis. This chapter first illustrates that theme with the question 'What causes inflation?' then recalls some earlier items:

- disagreement about *facts*, about *causal relations*, and about the *selection* of causal analyses
- diverse *kinds* of causal relations and the diverse *ways of knowing* them
- the difference between two kinds of bias: your guiding social *values and purposes* (which you can't do without) and biased *misrepresentation of facts* (which you should certainly do without).

From those lines of argument you will then be offered some conclusions: some general ways in which you *should* select and shape your causal analyses, and some particular ways in which you should *not* select and shape them.

Example: what causes inflation?

Inflation means a general rise in prices or (same thing) a decline in the value and purchasing power of money. Though the following example is from real life it is still drastically simplified. Don't take it as a proper introduction to the subject of inflation – that will come later in the course.

We will presently introduce four theorists who favor four different approaches to the problem of inflation. Here first is some of the information available to them all.

Inflation is already happening. Most people expect it to continue, though they would like it to stop. Prices rise unevenly but continuously. Government statisticians monitor the prices, and publish price indexes which tell the public the precise rate at which the purchasing power of money is falling. Suppose that the indexes show that it has fallen 10 per cent in the last year. To restore the real value of their wages, workers demand 10 per cent more money wages. That is reasonable, and anyway it could be enforced by industrial action, so most employers concede it. To pay it, many of them have to borrow from their banks. By means you will learn about later, the banks create the extra money and lend it to them. The employers eventually repay those loans, and continue to cover the new wage costs, by raising the prices of the goods and services they produce. Soon the government statisticians notice those price rises, and publish new indexes to tell the public exactly how much further the value of money has fallen. The workers respond by demanding another wage rise ... and around we go again.

There is thus a vicious circle of causation – rising wages cause rising prices which cause rising wages which cause rising prices, and so on.

(Earlier we used a similar example to illustrate a self-verifying belief: because people *expected* inflation to continue they *caused* it to continue. In that example people acted to anticipate future inflation, in this present example they act in response to past inflation. In practice they often do a bit of both.)

SELECTIVE CAUSAL ANALYSIS: SENSIBLE AND SILLY WAYS TO DISAGREE

Faced with that vicious circle – or spiral, since it is continuously inflating the currency – we can sort out (1) a sensible way and (2) a silly way to debate the practical problem which the vicious circle poses.

The sensible way is to debate *what to do*. What *could* the workers or the employers or the government do? What *should* they do? If there are conflicting interests at stake, whose interests should prevail over whose? There may not be agreed answers to the last two questions – but that is nevertheless the sensible way to debate the problem.

The silly way is to recommend whichever action you favor by the method of asserting that *inflation has only one cause*, namely the one you want to attack. If you are that sort of single-causer, you will probably dismiss all the other causes as mere necessary conditions, or as effects of the inflation rather than causes of it. (In circular causation, all the forces are effects as well as causes. Pick any one of them, and it is easy to show either that it is the cause of all the others, or that it is an innocent effect of one or more of the others.)

We will now illustrate sensible and silly ways in which four people might argue for different policies to combat inflation. Remember that we are simplifying grossly just to show some principles – serious study of inflation and rival theories about it will come later in the course.

Also remember that in these examples 'sensible argument' does not necessarily mean that a sensible *policy* is being recommended. It just means that a sensible way of arguing and of using causal analysis is being employed.

- **A middle-of-the-road economist** thinks the best way to break the vicious circle would be to stop the wage rises. Government, employers and labor unions should try to achieve that by negotiating a strong incomes policy. If wages can be stabilized, the money supply and the price level should stabilize themselves as a result.

  That's a sensible way to argue. But it would be silly to assert that wage pressure is the sole cause of inflation.

- **A conservative economist** does not believe the government can or should regulate incomes. Instead, it should break the vicious circle by controlling the rate at which the banks create extra money. Then (he argues) people will soon learn that higher wages merely reduce employment and higher prices merely reduce sales, and they will stop pressing for such rises.

  That's a sensible way to argue. But it is silly to assert that the money supply is the sole cause of inflation.

- **A radical economist** is against both those proposals – wage controls usually reduce real wages and tight money creates unemployment, and both are unfair to workers. Instead, the government should break the vicious circle by controlling profits and prices.

  That's a sensible way to argue. But it would be silly to assert that capitalist exploitation through excessive profits and prices is the sole cause of inflation.

- **A cunning politician** says to hell with *all* those proposals. Wage controls madden the workers, price controls madden business leaders, tight money maddens nearly everybody, and it's terrible bad politics

to madden *anybody* if you can help it. What we should do instead is fiddle the index. (Of course he does not say fiddle it, he says 'correct its damaging distortions'.) The government should tell its statisticians to stop counting any price rises that happen to be caused by foreigners, international exchange rates, taxes, bad weather and other Acts of God. What is left in the index after those items are excluded will show only a small rise in the price level. So the workers will only demand small pay rises. Let's break the vicious circle by 'correcting' the price index.

Whatever you think of that policy, it is candidly argued. But it would be silly to assert that monitoring prices and publishing the price index is the main cause of inflation.

For those who like diagrams, here are the sensible forms of those four proposals:

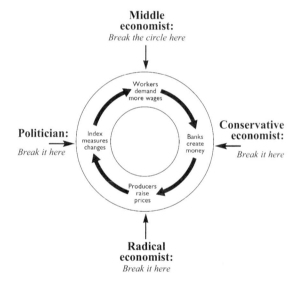

Each debater is recommending a particular approach: 'Work on *this* item, because it influences these others.' But notice that the principle is much the same if the debater is recommending *no* action. He may say 'Don't try to regulate wages or prices – you'll do more harm than good.' Or he may say 'Don't tamper with this pattern of causal relations at all, because you can't predict what effects your action may have.'

In either case the advice needs to be based on a selective causal analysis. That means an analysis of the causal relations which seem relevant to the purpose in hand. Those may be –

the forces which chiefly affect your interests;

the variable forces you need to guard against;

the variable forces you can work on;

the permanent conditions which limit your options;

and so on. However elaborate it may be, any such analysis is still selective and should not pretend to be otherwise.

But what about our own account of the vicious circle – the one back on page 19? We seem to have been treating that as a comprehensive analysis of the causes of inflation, from which our various experts have been choosing their selective analyses. Doesn't our vicious circle of four interacting processes show all the causes of inflation?

It certainly does not. It selects and simplifies drastically. For some of its principles of selection you must read ahead in Chapter 52. But plenty of omissions are already plain to see. For example the sketch does not show what the government's budget policy, or tax changes, or import prices are contributing to inflation. It does not show how or why the banks create extra money when it's wanted. Or who they create it *for* – how much for government, how much for other employers, how much for housing loans, how much for consumer credit. How the extra money is created, and who gets it, can affect the rate of inflation in a number of ways. It can also help to determine who gains and who loses by the inflation. That in turn can affect the overall rate of inflation. And so on – the actual causal relations are very intricate, and our 'vicious circle' sketch has selected and simplified ruthlessly.

Second, our sketch suggests that each item in the circle is the only cause of the next. But in fact, changes in the value of money as indicated in the index are only one of many things that may prompt workers to demand higher wages. Higher wages are by no means the only cause of increases in the money supply. Increases in the money supply can cause prices to rise, but so can many other things. The price changes in our sketch, i.e. those which result from wage changes, are not the only price changes which cause changes in the price index. Many prices which have little or nothing to do with wage levels or other costs of production also affect the index – for example 'shortage' prices, 'glut' prices, monopoly prices, government-subsidized prices, the foreign prices of goods we import, international exchange rates, etc.

Third, *all* of those causes – the ones we put into our circle and the ones we left out – were produced by *other* causes, which in turn were produced by others again, and so on. Anywhere along those networks of cause and

effect there may be relevant items. There may be items whose behaviour affects the rate or the process of inflation. There may be points where governments could intervene to affect the inflation. And so on. But very little indeed of that endless web of causal relations was included in our simple analysis.

That sketch of a vicious circle of four causes of inflation is itself an example. It was chosen for a particular teaching purpose and serves that purpose. It is a true, relevant and useful causal analysis – but it is still a highly selective one.

Now recall some earlier themes, to draw together a range of considerations you need to have in mind in selecting your own causal analyses.

THREE KINDS OF DISAGREEMENT

In this chapter so far we have been talking about disagreed *selection* in causal analysis – the disagreements that happen when people with different purposes choose to focus on different selections of the forces at work, different parts of the causal pattern. Those disagreements usually arise from basic differences of value and purpose – political differences which may be clarified but can't usually be resolved by research. Neither side can 'prove' its selections by scientific tests.

But don't forget that people disagree about other things too. They can disagree about the facts, and they can disagree about the causal relations. In real-life debates about inflation they often disagree about both.

For example inflation-watchers sometimes disagree about how much money is circulating in the economy, or how fast it is circulating. That is a disagreement about *facts*. In principle it could be resolved by accurate measurement (however difficult that may be in practice).

Some economists don't agree that wage rises have any effect on the rate of inflation. Others don't agree that unemployment has much effect in restraining inflation. Those are disagreements about the causal relations themselves, i.e. about the *existence* or *force* of the link between cause and effect.

Now bring those two kinds of disagreement together with the disagreements about selection that we have been describing – for example the disagreements between the politician and economists in our sketch of the vicious circle. You will then have a disagreed *fact*, a disagreed *causal relation* and a disagreed *selection*:

- **Fact** Did the money supply increase by $100 million or $200 million this month?

- **Causation** Do wage increases affect the rate of inflation or do they not? (Always? Sometimes? This time? Never?)

- **Selection** Should our causal analysis emphasize the wage pressures, or the monetary pressures, or the price-setting processes, or the effects of indexation? Or should it select other causes altogether, such as the 'revolution of rising aspirations', from the complicated social and historical forces which have produced the vicious circle of wage and price changes?

Those three are the commonest kinds of disagreement in economics. Learn to tell them apart. It is not always easy – as we will see later, the three sometimes impersonate each other in various ways. But most of the time for most working purposes you can tell them apart, and it is often important to do so.

Now remember this from Chapter 1 –

TYPES OF CAUSAL RELATION AND WAYS OF KNOWING THEM

If you want to know what causes what in economic life you have to investigate causal relations of many different kinds. Causal relations of different kinds may have to be understood by different methods. For example –

- **Arithmetic** shows how individual flows of money or goods add up to produce aggregate effects.

- **Statistical analysis** may sometimes help to prove or disprove causal relations hypothesized by other means. But its main use is to find the *magnitude* of effects. Lowering the price of a commodity often increases its sales. You may know that causal relation by understanding the minds and motives of the buyers. But to find *how much* change in price causes *how much* change in sales you may need some statistical analysis.

- **Knowing institutional structures and rules and routines** is necessary for understanding the large amount of economic behaviour which is organized by institutions with their own working rules – public and private firms, banks, trade unions, government departments, etc.

- **Understanding physical mechanisms and processes** may usually be the business of other experts rather than economists. But economists need to know (for example) how weather affects farm output, how particular technologies dictate the scale and organization of particular industries, etc.

- **Understanding situations** in which people find themselves may show you what decides them to

act as they do. But you often also need to know how *they* perceived their options, and decided what to do. So –

- **Understanding people's thoughts, feelings, values, purposes, choices, etc.,** is the heart of most useful causal analysis in the social sciences. People act as they do because they think and feel and believe as they do. You can rarely know *all* their relevant thoughts and feelings, or know *any* of their thoughts and feelings with perfect certainty. But if you understand them as well as you can you should be ahead of any experts who understand them less well, or not at all.

- **Historical explanations** tell how major economic conflicts are won or lost or compromised, and how economic systems and institutions grow and change.

Those ways of seeing, understanding and connecting have widely varying accuracy and objectivity. Some of them are precise and others are rough and ready with wide margins of error. But each is the best or only way of knowing *some* of the important causal forces and relations at work in modern economic systems. So as long as you use each method intelligently, for its appropriate purpose, you can know more by using them all than you can ever know if you only use a few of them. Scientific types who measure the flows of goods and money but won't try to understand the people's minds and purposes will know less economics than they *could* know. Artistic types who understand like anything, but can't count or measure, will also know less than they could. People who use all the methods competently will usually know most and do best.

CAUSATION AND COMMON SENSE

This chapter has not told you anything mysterious. On the contrary, to know what causes what, economists need to analyse causes and effects in much the same way as we do in everyday life. They have to pick their way over the infinitely complicated networks of social and economic interdependence, selecting the links they need to study for particular purposes. Their causal knowledge is always incomplete. It is always selective. It should always be selected with its purposes and uses in mind.

So what we have been anatomizing are not exotic scientific procedures. They are the many and various kinds of causal knowledge that we use in everyday life. Science can improve some of those methods in detail but it can't afford to discard any of them.

If you doubt that, study economists when they are off

duty, coping with their private business or social or family problems. They don't use a lot of jargon or algebra *then*. They use all the methods that work. They measure and count, accurately where it matters. They know all about any relevant rules and regulations and institutional structures. They make judgments (often subjective, likely to be disagreed) about their own and other people's best interests, their options and opportunities, their rights and duties. They understand people as shrewdly as they can, judging which way they may jump under pressure, judging what to expect of each of them.

And they know very well that if they deliberately did without some of that knowledge they would not understand or manage their business any better, they would know less and do worse. I believe (though some economists do not believe it) that the same goes for our professional understanding of the larger economy. To know most and do best, we should use all the means there are.

That diversified knowledge cannot all be objective. Some of it (like understanding people, or judging what their effective options are) has unavoidably subjective or uncertain elements. All of it has to be selected, in the light of the economists' purposes.

In practice there can often be plenty of overlap – plenty of common methods and shared information, as there is in politics. But as in politics, there can never be an entirely unanimous economics, or a neutral or value-free economics. Does that mean that all economics is biased – that there can never be a single authoritative economic science?

Yes, it does mean that. But it does NOT mean you can fudge the facts and figures to suit your prejudices. You must learn the difference between two meanings of 'bias'.

Faith, values, moral principles, chosen purposes

Values and chosen social purposes have to guide the questions you ask, and your selection and arrangement of economic facts and relationships. You cannot do without some guiding values and purposes, so don't try.

Your work can still be just, fair-minded, sympathetic. If you understand and respect more than one side of an argument or conflict of interests, and judge it by reference to legal or moral or other principles rather than your own self-interest or personal or racial or gendered feelings, you may claim to be impartial. But just, fair-minded, sympathetic and impartial are wholly or partly moral words: they signify particular values or moral principles.

Some values and purposes are more admirable, desirable, sociable, loveable than others – but those also are statements of values or preference rather than fact. Nobody's values are authoritative. Value judgments cannot be proved right or wrong by reference to facts or logical reasoning alone. They have to be judged by reference to other values. People are always likely – and entitled – to disagree about them. That is why you are in an unavoidably controversial science.

Technical bias

This stands for falsifying or misrepresenting facts. For example you may select unrepresentative samples in order to deceive readers about the population which the samples purport to represent. Don't do it. It is true that some of the facts and relationships you study cannot be known with perfect objectivity, but you should work as truthfully as the facts allow.

How can you tell one kind from the other? The simplest test is to ask whether an unbiased alternative is logically possible.

A bowling ball with a metal weight off-centre in it will not usually roll straight. It is biased. The same ball without the off-centred weight *will* roll straight: an unbiased alternative is possible.

Examples To illustrate the difference between (unavoidable) social values and (avoidable) factual misrepresentation, here are two *proper* ways and then two *improper* ways for social values to shape economic analyses –

1. Three economists care about particular inequalities, which they regard as injustices, in the distribution of income.
   The first economist suspects that workers are not getting their fair share of income. She shapes an analysis to compare the wage share of national income with the profit share which goes to landowners and capitalists.
   The second economist suspects that women are not getting their fair share of income. She shapes an analysis to compare men's incomes with women's incomes, and includes systematic sampling of the wages men and women get for identical work.
   The third economist suspects that old people, disabled people and other pensioners are not getting fair shares. She shapes an analysis to show two things: How much income is transferred each year through taxes and pensions from those in work to those on pensions; and which classes of people gain and

which classes lose from those transfers, not just year by year but over their whole working and pensioned lifetimes.

Those are three proper uses of values to guide technical work. Each analysis is 'biased' to show particular distributions, but shows them objectively. There is no 'unbiased' alternative – no way of analysing the distribution of income to show simultaneously the shares that go to all imaginable categories of people.

2. You care about the harmful effects of unemployment. So you design an analysis to show how government policies affect the amount of unemployment, tracing and measuring the effects as accurately as the facts allow.

That's a proper use of your values to guide your technical work. Economists with different values may respond (just as properly) by analysing the effects of the same government policies on (say) economic growth or environmental pollution. There can then be useful debates about the comparative importance of those various effects.

Once again, there is no *unbiased* way to decide whether effects on employment, growth, pollution (or a dozen other things) are the most important effects of particular government policies.

Now compare two examples of ways in which your values should *not* be allowed to bias your technical work –

3. You care about the harmful effects of unemployment. So you double-count and fudge the facts to allege that four million workers are unemployed, when in fact only two million are.

Social bias has been allowed to cause technical bias. You should not do it. Even if it has what your values judge to be good effects, e.g. by frightening the government into improving its policies, it is still dishonest science and dishonest politics and you should not do it.

4. You care about the harmful effects of unemployment, and you want to scare people into doing more about it by persuading them that unemployment is increasing dangerously fast. But you don't want to be caught telling lies. So you publish an analysis which shows that five per cent more workers are unemployed this midsummer than were unemployed six months ago. The statistics are accurate. You have not told any lies. And five per cent in six months is indeed an alarming rate of increase. Readers can work out for themselves that it means

ten per cent a year.

But what you have *not* told those readers is that the midsummer figures are always high. Many people choose the summer break as a time to change jobs. The official employment offices allow school leavers to register the day they leave school although very few of them will actually find work until after the summer break. So the midsummer figures are usually about six per cent higher than the previous midwinter figures. In 'seasonally adjusted' terms this year's five per cent difference between midwinter and midsummer actually indicates a slight *fall* in round-the-year unemployment.

An unbiased alternative to your biased analysis was available. You could have disclosed the usual relation between winter and summer figures, or you could have used seasonally adjusted figures. Social bias has been allowed to cause technical bias, wrongly. And that is only one of many ways in which true facts can be misused to mislead people.

Unhappily you can't always draw such a clear line between avoidable and unavoidable bias, or between factual bias and social bias. Consider an example. Suppose that a labor representative sets out to discredit some business policies by presenting a biased sample of employers' behaviour. One critic says the sample misrepresents the facts (a technical judgment about its truth). Another critic says the sample was selected unfairly (a moral judgment about its justice). They are both right. The distinction can be difficult.

And there are other hard cases. But don't let the hard cases put you off recognizing the distinction. Remember that honest economics is still unavoidably, and often controversially, selective. The best you can do is to make clear the purposes which guide your selections, get the facts as true as you can, make any samples as fairly representative as you can. (And if others fall short of these high principles, expose their tricks as effectively as you can.)

RIGHT AND WRONG PRINCIPLES OF SELECTION IN CAUSAL ANALYSIS:

(1) RIGHT PRINCIPLES

You cannot know all the causes of anything. But you can often know the causes which matter for particular purposes. It is rational to let those purposes guide the selection of your causal analyses and explanations.

How? Use your common sense. Who wants the information? What do they want it for? Is it to allow action for particular purposes? Is it to expose particular causal relations for moral or political judgment? Whatever it is *for*, select and shape it usefully for *that*. (*Question*: What if the purpose is to deceive? *Answer*: The values which guide your working purposes also have to set your standards of honesty.)

Letting your purposes guide your selections does not mean that you should select in a one-eyed or wilfully misleading way. As far as possible you should know what you're doing. Be aware of the range of things you are leaving out. Make your purposes and principles of selection clear. Know what other investigators with other purposes might want to include instead.

You are in a plural society. You may often want to work for plural purposes. You may shape an analysis to satisfy a broad curiosity, or to serve a wide range of business or policy options. That may call for multi-purposed analysis. Your selections can be extensive, they can be complicated, they can be broad-minded. They can shape analyses to serve consensual purposes, or to serve a wide range of the purposes, including conflicting purposes, to be found in your society. But they are still selections. Don't dream of a single, all-purpose analysis: you can never include *all* the causes or *all* the effects of anything.

So how do you tell a good analysis from a bad one? Do economic analyses express nothing but their authors' controversial values?

No, economic analyses link those values to plenty of technical work and objective information. To assess any analysis of causes and effects you must usually apply two tests –

1. *What values and purposes shaped this analysis?* Do I agree with the values? Do I share the purposes? If not, do I nevertheless find them important or interesting? Which groups in our plural society have those purposes and need this sort of analysis to serve them?

2. *Is this a technically truthful and well-selected analysis for those purposes?* Does it trace the main causal relations which folk with those purposes need to know? Does it do its technical work well – does it do its sampling correctly, does it count and measure accurately, does it get its facts right, does it reason logically?

Finally, remember to use all your faculties and all appropriate methods, to understand causal relations of all kinds. Don't ban from science any rational methods of observation and understanding that you would trust in daily life.

(2) WRONG PRINCIPLES

Meet a new word: 'scientistic'. It stands for mistaken imitations of science.

Physics is a powerfully successful science. So what should economists learn from physics? They should learn to use the scientific methods *which fit their particular problems and subject matter* – as physicists do. That's scientific.

What should economists not copy from physics? They should not copy its particular methods. Physicists do not study the structure of atoms or the motions of planets by using the methods of (say) linguistics or animal ecology. Nor should economists study economic behaviour by trying to use the methods of physics. Trying to look scientific in that irrational way is 'scientistic'.

Unhappily there has been a good deal of scientistic work in economics. Learn to recognize it, and avoid it in your own work. Scientistic economists commonly use or recommend one or more of five principles of selection, which can be summed up as selecting for *discipline, objectivity, certainty, mathematical appearances,* and *regularity*. For purposes of understanding, managing or predicting economic life, each of them is an irrational principle of selection. In detail –

I Work within the discipline

Some economists think they should study economic facts and relationships alone. They should explain economic performance by reference to its purely economic causes, not to any political, social, psychological or other causes (except perhaps government interference) that may be at work. Those should be left to academic departments of political science, sociology, psychology, etc.

What's wrong with that? What is wrong with it is that you will understand less than you *could*, about what causes what. Economic performance is affected critically by many political and social and cultural conditions. But people in the other academic disciplines rarely ask *your* questions or let your purposes shape their analyses of political or social influences on economic performance. So if you, as economist, systematically neglect those influences, you are likely to know less and do worse than economists who *do* study them. Their understanding of the political and social conditions may be less than perfect but it is usually better than nothing, better than deliberate ignorance.

It is crippling to define the discipline of economics

as the study of economic facts and relationships *alone*. Better definitions: (1) Economists study the causes of economic performance, wherever those causes are to be found. Or (2) Economics is the discipline which asks economic questions – but it need not confine itself to economic answers.

2 Select for certainty

'Stick to what you can prove.' *No* – but grasp a clear distinction: (1) If there are two ways of knowing something and one of them is more certain than the other, it is rational to choose the surer method. Measuring quantities is better than guessing them. But (2) if a number of different causes contribute to producing an economic effect, it is not necessarily rational to confine your analysis to the causes you can know most certainly. The changing wages and prices (which you can measure accurately) may not tell you as much about the causes of inflation as the wage-bargainers' and price-setters' psychology (which you can only understand imperfectly). If two economists measure the wage and price movements, and one of them *also* does her imperfect best to understand the people's psychology, that one is likely to know more and do better than the other.

Don't fall into the 'all or nothing' trap of thinking that if you don't know something certainly you don't know it at all. You know what to expect of people you know well much better than you know what to expect of strangers you meet on the street, though you don't have perfect knowledge of either. There is a very wide range of useful knowledge between mathematical certainty on the one hand and romantic fiction or superstition on the other.

3 Keep your work objective

No. The arguments for and against are like the arguments about certainty. There are some causal relations you can know objectively. When measurable flows of goods or money combine to produce aggregate effects, the measurements and the arithmetic can be objective. All competent observers will agree about them. But other causal relations cannot be known so objectively. You can rarely be quite objective about the reasons why people choose and act as they do. It involves judging what actual options they have, or believe they have, and which elements in their situation have most influence on their choices. There are always subjective elements in those judgments. But knowing why people act as they do, and what might lead them to act differently, is at the heart of causal knowledge in economics. Knowing what

causes what is *mostly* knowing why people act as they do.

As before, if there are alternative ways of knowing the same thing it is right to choose the more objective way – measuring is better than guessing. But that is different from making objectivity a principle of selection, which is what you do if you shape your causal analysis to include only what you can actually measure, and dismiss other forces (however important) which require some human understanding.

If you 'select for objectivity', how do you explain inflation? You probably say the money supply or the wage or price movements cause it. You don't ask what determines the money supply or the wage and price movements because that would lead you to human choices and actions. You could actually understand those human choices quite *well* if you wanted to – but not quite *objectively*. So you leave any serious understanding of them out of your analysis. You therefore know less and do worse than someone who *does* study the springs of that behaviour, however imperfectly.

That smarter student who does study the human behaviour – why does she want to include such uncertain, unstable stuff in her analysis? She does it because her social purposes, rather than any overriding preference for objectivity, are telling her which links in the causal pattern it may be most fruitful to understand.

4 Be as mathematical as possible

Some texts urge you to use as much maths as you can because it is a rigorous language whose meaning and implications are always clear. (But are they? Paul Streeten observes that 'mathematics is also fuzzy. The fuzziness arises not from the deductive process, which is rigorous, but from the identification of a symbol with a real thing.' Suppose a mathematical analyst of inflation has l stand for the annual change in labor costs and i for the annual rate of inflation. Which direct, indirect and external costs of employing workers count as labor costs? Which tax, import, exchange and distributional effects on prices are netted out of the analyst's measure of inflation? If those choices are necessarily arbitrary and open to disagreement the analysis is equally fuzzy in plain language and in mathematical language.)

By all means use maths where it serves your working purposes. But don't make it a principle of selection – don't shape your analyses by selecting causal relations which happen to allow some use of maths, and omitting causal relations which don't.

Most of the reasons for this are in the following Chapter 4. Briefly, mathematical language is poor language for describing causal relations themselves. If you limit yourself to causal relations which happen to produce regular mathematical relations between measurable flows of goods or money you will understand too little about economic life. So little, that what a preference for maths tends to do in practice is this: it switches attention away from the real world altogether, onto abstract models of *imaginary* economic systems. The imaginary systems are not designed chiefly to simulate real economic life, they are designed chiefly to allow mathematical notation and deductive mathematical reasoning. Quite early in the mathematical transformation of academic economics John Maynard Keynes, whose own degree was in mathematics, complained that 'Too large a proportion of recent 'mathematical' economics are merely concoctions, as imprecise as the initial assumptions they rest on, which allow the author to lose sight of the complexities and interdependencies of the real world in a maze of pretentious and unhelpful symbols.'

(We will deal later in the book with some attempts of a different kind: attempts to build extremely complicated and *realistic* models of the working of particular national economic systems, for purposes of economic forecasting.)

Long ago, the eminent economist Alfred Marshall stated a basic objection to most mathematical modelling of economic activity: 'In my view every economic fact whether or not it is of such a nature as to be expressed in numbers, stands in relation as cause and effect to many other facts, and since it NEVER happens that all of them can be expressed in numbers, the application of exact mathematical methods to those which can is nearly always waste of time, while in the large majority of cases it is positively misleading ... ' (Letter to A.L.Bowley, 3 March 1901).

5 Focus on regularities

Begin with a distinction:

It makes sense to search for any reliable regularities of economic behaviour. Knowing them will help you to predict (or manage or control) economic activity. But –

It does not make sense to make regularity a principle of selection in causal analysis – i.e. to pay more attention to regular causes and relations than to irregular ones.

'Selecting for regularity' may restrict your analysis to relations between things which are regularly associated – relations which are discovered or proven chiefly by statistical methods. That rules out a lot of other things which can have powerful economic effects: conflicts of interest and the ways they are fought out; business and government decisions of some potent kinds; inventions and innovations; changing institutional forms and rules and purposes; general historical changes; and above all, changing beliefs.

Remember that if you want to know as much as you can about what causes what in economic life, and if you want to pick the causal relations it is most important to know, all those scientistic principles of selection are irrational. If you let any of them guide your work instead of letting your social values and purposes guide it you will not know most and do best, you will usually know less and do worse.

MEN AND WOMEN

This text is arguing that it is good science as well as common sense to use all the helpful and workable ways of understanding what causes what in economic life. The argument gets special force from the experience of women economists, of whom there are still disgracefully few. Many of those few identify scientistic thought simply as masculine thought. Sue Richardson asks –

> In this masculine way of knowing, where are the metaphors, stories, experiences, imagination, feeling, words, values, real living? These are dismissed as soft and unrigorous and unscientific, but in fact they colour much of what economists actually do, especially when they get to policy recommendations. But in man-made economics it is necessary to pretend otherwise. This pretence is bad science. It is deceptive, so the uses of these other ways of knowing are not open and acknowledged and capable of being examined. And to the extent that it is real and not a pretence, then it denies the use of ways of knowing which are important and insightful and ought to be used.
> – *Economic Papers* 17, 1, March 1998, p.39

There are three accusations in that short paragraph. The men who command the profession don't try to know as much as they could and should know about economic life. They conceal the role of their values in shaping their work. And if they actually believe and act on their mistaken pretences of objectivity, they can know even less about their subject.

This is a main theme of this course. To be useful, economists need to use all the workable ways of understanding economic life. They need to perceive qualities as well as measure quantities. They need to understand causal relations in the thoughts and intentions of the economic actors, not just in regular associations between flows of money and goods. They need to know about the unpaid household and voluntary work which is more than a third of all work, and a condition of much of the quality and productivity of the paid work. They need to study what determines people's experience of work, which can be as important to their productivity as their wage incentives are, and as important to their happiness as their leisure and consumption are.

Those concerns are absent from neoclassical theory and are discouraged by many leaders of the profession. The best way to cure that might well be to have equal numbers of women in the profession - but surveys suggest that the behaviour which they could reform is what chiefly deters them from enrolling in economics courses, or persisting if they do enrol. The general competence of the profession, as well as questions of equal opportunity and fair employment, make this a serious issue. We will return to it in Chapter 10 with some lessons which rich countries can learn from women's roles in the economic development of poor countries, and in Chapter 18 about the schools of economic thought which compete for influence in the rich democracies.

SUMMARY

1. To know what causes what – i.e. to understand how economic systems work in a general way, or to know what causes particular economic effects – start by asking who wants to know, and what they hope to use the knowledge for. That may mean knowing your own values and purposes, or it may mean knowing the values and purposes of people you choose to work for.

2. Use your common sense (and all you've got of brains and ingenuity and experience) to decide which causal relations it would be most useful to know for

those purposes. Direct your studies accordingly and in the light of what you find, select and shape your analysis accordingly.

3. Whatever you want to find out, use the best methods available. But don't reverse that relation – don't let preference for particular methods determine what you will try to find out. Don't look only for whatever you happen to be able to find most easily or most accurately.

4. Of course there are some things you can't find out by any method, and there are some methods so unreliable they are not worth using at all – they don't promise any net gain on ignorance. To that extent methods do affect what you decide to look for. But wherever the best available methods offer *some* net gain over ignorance, use them. Imperfect knowledge of important causal relations may be more use than perfect knowledge of unimportant ones. Don't be like the drunk who is cited in all methodology books, who loses a coin in one street but searches for it in a different street because the light is better there.

5. When people disagree about what causes what, analyse their disagreements. Do they have different values and purposes which make them interested in different parts of the causal pattern? Or do they share common purposes but disagree about which causal relations they need to know for those purposes? (Those two are disagreed *selections*.) Or are they disagreeing about the causal relations themselves? Or are they disagreeing about other facts of the situation? (In principle those last two are factual disagreements which could be resolved by research – though that is not always so easy in practice.)

EXERCISES

1. Suggest examples you have not met in this text, of disagreements about economic *facts*, about *causal relations*, and about the *selection* of causes in causal analyses.

2. Think of an economic effect whose causes you need to know for some purpose – and whose relevant causes cannot be understood without some *arithmetic*, some understanding of people's *motives and intentions*, and some knowledge of *rules and regulations*.

3. Parsnips are very cheap at the wholesale market this morning. That's surprising because carrots are scarce and dear, and that usually drives the price of parsnips up too, as more people try to buy them as 'carrot substitutes'. As an exercise your teacher asks you to explain why parsnips are nevertheless going cheap, and you come up with this:

   > Parsnips are in season. It has been a good season so there are plenty of them. A hot weekend is forecast and a lot of people are planning picnics or cold salads rather than hot vegetables – the morning paper had half a page of salad recipes. It also reported an industrial dispute that has stopped the local cannery buying anything this week. Any excess of supply over demand tends to push prices further down on Friday than other days because sellers want to clear their stocks – the market rules don't allow perishables to stay in the place over weekends.

   There you have a selective causal analysis. Now notice which of the causal relations are regular enough to have been predicted from economic laws, and which ones can be known without any subjective understanding of people's tastes. Then (1) rewrite the analysis to leave out any irregular or once-only causes. (2) Rewrite it to leave out anything that cannot be known quite certainly and objectively.

4. Make sure you understand the difference between the two ways of thinking in the following pairs –

A $\rightarrow$ B (A causes B)	A = 2B (Whatever causes them, there is a regular mathematical relation between A and B.)
Rightly, try to know any fact or causal relations by the surest and most objective method that the nature of the fact or relation allow.	Wrongly, try to confine your study to things you can know accurately and objectively, neglecting any other forces at work in the economy.
Rightly, avoid technical bias when unbiased observation and representation are possible.	Wrongly, try to ban any social values and purposes from your work. Select your causal analyses instead by preferring particular types of causal relations – e.g. regular relations, quantitative relations, statistical relations.
Rightly, describe any regularities you find in economic behavior and do your best to specify the conditions in which they are likely to occur. But in analysing particular economic problems and processes be equally alert for the 'regular' and 'irregular' forces at work.	Wrongly, confine your economic studies to the regular elements in economic behavior – for fear that if you notice the unique or uncertain or changing elements too, you may be accused of abandoning economic science for history or 'mere ad hocery'.

Recognizing those differences needs to become second nature to you – an intellectual habit, a routine professional skill. It will be time well spent now if you go over the pairs above, or the longer lists of 'scientistic principles of selection' earlier in this chapter, and fit them with as many practical examples as you can. Imaginary examples, daily-life examples, morning-newspaper examples, economic examples. Practise on anything that comes your way. Practise until it is *habitual* to recognize the difference between a biased sample and a rational selection-for-a-purpose. And to recognize the purposes and the selections. And to get the facts as objective as you can without falling into the trap of 'selecting for objectivity'. And so on.

4

Explanations and equations

The last chapter was about the problems of selection you face because you can't trace all the causes or all the effects of anything. This chapter is about problems you face because the system you study keeps changing.

Other sciences are luckier. Physicists can accumulate knowledge of (say) the structure of atoms because that structure is not changing. Its regular parts and relationships can be described in sets of equations. The equations are worth having. They allow accurate prediction of the behavior of matter because (1) the atoms don't change their ways of their own accord, and (2) they don't start acting differently when they read a new physics textbook.

Similarly if people sought wealth and income in a sufficiently uniform unchanging way their economic nature might be described in a few axioms from which it might be possible to deduce what they would do in any circumstances, and thus model their economic activity in a science like physics. (Like simple nineteenth-century physics, modern physicists will tell you.) But people differ from each other, learn by doing, change their ways and their economic institutions. They fight over what to do, and who gets what, sometimes with unpredicted effects which none of the contenders intended. The weapons they use include rival economic theories.

There are some regular economic relations which allow rigorous theory to predict what will happen in particular circumstances. But rather more of any useful theory has to be of the kinds that enrich your experience and improve your investigative skills – warn you what to look for, what to check, what to guard against – in a wide range of situations. And much of that understanding of changing economic processes and institutions, and of people's beliefs and aims and conflicts, has to be expressed in words, in selective causal analyses of one kind or another. They are commonly called *explanations* and for convenience this text will often call them that from now on.

This chapter is about relations between explanations and equations – or between language and mathematics – in economics.

The relations you study keep changing

Back in Chapter 3 we sketched a vicious circle of forces which can push inflation along. Recall: rising prices push up wages, rising wages push prices up. Extra money is created to pay the higher wages and prices. Price indexes and daily shopping tell everybody how fast the inflation is happening, and keep them pushing the treadmill around as they all try to keep up.

You were warned that the sketch selected and simplified a few forces from the complicated processes of real economic life. Now notice something else about it: the sketch said nothing about *where* or *when* its vicious circle of forces might operate. In fact it has operated very variably – strongly at some times and places, scarcely at all at other times and places. Where it does operate, the wages and prices rise at varying rates, driving varying rates of inflation. And there is no regular ratio between the wage changes and the price changes. That is because the changes are determined each time by bargaining and business decisions and public policy-making, and those are not reliably repetitive forms of behavior.

Two examples:

1. When the OPEC oil-producing nations first jacked up world oil prices, British workers tried to restore their lost purchasing power by a wage rise. That was not possible, so the rise which they fought for and got was mostly inflationary, it did not restore their former purchasing power. German workers meanwhile accepted that the loss to OPEC could not be restored by wage changes and they accepted the loss without inflationary bargaining.

2. Through the 1970s and 1980s Australian inflation fluctuated a good deal – but the wage and price changes had different ratios every year, whatever time-lags the accountants allowed for.

Does the ratio keep changing because wages are influenced by other things as well as prices – is a steady 'price effect on wages' being masked by the effects of other more variable influences on wages? Probably, but the price effect itself may also vary, because wage bargainers are adaptable, inventive humans, and so are the politicians who make the relevant economic and industrial policies. So there is always likely to be *some* relation between price and wage changes, but it is an irregular relation. And just as the ratios vary, so do the time-lags, insofar as you can measure them at all. (There are continuous price changes. How do you know whether this month's wage changes were triggered by the price changes that happened last month, or last year, or the year before – or by other causes? The effects can even precede the causes, if people raise their prices or wage demands to cover *anticipated* increases in wage costs or prices.)

Two conclusions about relations between wage and price changes: (1) The study of economics should teach you that there is *likely* to be a causal relation between the two. So be alert to look for it in particular cases. But (2) the relation is too variable to be reliably modelled or predicted by any equation or rule of thumb.

A great many causal relations in economic life have that general character.

EXPLANATIONS AND EQUATIONS

'Explanation' is a broad term, and explanations may do other things besides analysing relations between causes and effects. But we are using the word as shorthand for selective causal analysis. For that purpose, an explanation may survey some necessary conditions of the activity to be explained. It may describe relevant institutions, rules, procedures. It may explain people's reasons for what they do. One way or another it aims to tell what causes what, by what means.

Economics books include a lot of explanations. Many of them also include a lot of equations. What is the relation between the equations and the explanations?

A short answer is that explanations describe causal relations and equations state quantitative relations. Equations don't tell you what causes what. But if you already know that A causes B (in our causal notation, AgB), then an equation may tell you *how much* of A is regularly accompanied by *how much* of B. (Perhaps A = 2B.)

Beginners often misunderstand these relations between explanations and equations, so it is worth taking time over them.

We can begin with an example freely adapted from a rival textbook. Suppose researchers believe they have observed a regular relation between what a particular household earns and what it spends. Here are three statements about that relation: an explanation, a graph, and an equation:

An explanation

When there is no income the family stays alive by spending $2000 a year on bare necessities. They spend savings, or borrow, or sell assets. When there is some income, out of every dollar of disposable income (i.e. income remaining after taxes and $2,000 spent on necessities) the family spends 80 cents on consumption goods.

A graph

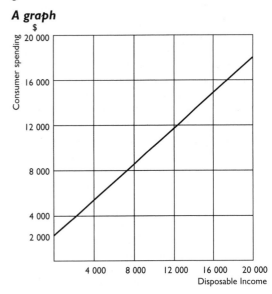

Figure 4.1 A relation between a family's income and its consumer spending

An equation

C = 2000 + 0.8Y

where C is consumer spending and Y is disposable income.

Now compare those statements. They all tell you the quantitative relation between income and consumer spending (one by arithmetic, one by geometry, one by algebra). The explanation adds some causal information: except for $2000 spent on necessities the income determines the spending, not the other way round. The graph and the equation don't tell you that.

Equations don't tell you what causes what

C = 2000 + 0.8Y does not tell you whether Y determines C, or C determines Y, or some third force determines them both and keeps them in that relation to each other. Thus equations are rarely much use without causal explanations. But they sometimes tempt people to assume, or theorize, the explanation without investigating it. As a frivolous example –

> Suppose that I know nothing about the relation between earning and spending except that they are regularly associated as the equation describes. If C (consumption expenditure) = 2000 + 0.8Y, I reason that it must follow that Y (income) = 1.25C – 2000. If that is so, I should be able to earn more by spending more. I have already earned and spent $2000 this year, but these days there are plenty of ways of spending money you have not yet earned. So I go on a shopping spree and charge up and take home $2000 of goods I can't pay for. Then I pour a long drink from my new stock of liquor, put a CD on my new sound system, stretch out on my new chaise-longue, and idly wait for the extra $2500 of income to flow in as promised by the equation.

What actually flow in after some time-lag are bailiffs with repossession orders to teach me the hard way that equations tell you nothing about causal relations (though they may usefully add quantities to causal explanations).

In real life this particular equation is more likely to fit the average behavior of all households than their individual behavior. But that average behavior does vary over time and from country to country. It is often important to know what proportions of income a society is currently saving and spending, but the current proportions are not necessarily a reliable guide to future behavior, and they tend to become less reliable with economic growth, as ways of providing for old age change, and rising proportions of spending are not on predictable necessities but are open to changing tastes and choices.

Beware of black boxes

If you mistake an equation for a causal explanation, i.e. if you think A = 2B means A g 2B, you have the simplest form of black box theory.

'Black box' is a common name for any theory that tells you what to expect without telling you why. It purports to tell you what causes what without telling you *how*, i.e. without describing the causal process or mechanism. A dictionary definition –

> A black theory attempts to relate input to output in a system by a formal description of the transformation rules that link the two but without stating the nature of the process that embodies or gives realization to these rules.

Because I am not a radio engineer, a radio receiver is a black box to me. I know what inputs cause what outputs: if I supply electric power and turn the dials in particular ways, I'll hear words and music. But I don't understand how or why. I don't know what goes on inside the box. But a radio receiver is not a black box to an engineer who *does* understand what goes on inside the box.

The usual basis of a black box theory is a *correlation* or *covariance* – two or more things are observed to vary in some regular relation to each other. In itself that does not prove anything about causal relations, and the words 'correlation' and 'covariance' do not imply anything about causal relations. But if things are observed to vary together, it may be tempting to theorize that one causes the other. Do it carelessly without studying and understanding the actual causal forces or processes, and you have a black box theory.

In the last example above it was observed (correctly, let's assume for the moment) that extra income regularly exceeded extra spending by 25 per cent. On that correlation you saw me build a black box theory – the theory that expenditure could determine income, so that spending more would cause income to increase.

That example was frivolous. But economics suffers from serious black box theories from time to time. They don't *have* to be wrong, but they too easily can be.

Suppose you observe that two economic items (like income and saving, or the money supply and inflation) appear to vary together in a regular way. Call them C and E. Whenever C changes, E follows a year or so later. Black-boxing, you theorize that C causes E. But their simple covariance is actually consistent with any one of four explanations:

1. C causes E and will go on doing so. In that case the black box theory is true and reliable.

2. C has caused E up to now but you can't rely on it. The causal link happens to be a habit of behavior which the relevant people could decide to change any day. In the 1960s Swedes abruptly saved less. In the 1990s Japanese abruptly saved more.

3. C does not cause E, nor does E cause C. Manipulating one of them won't have any effect on the other. They have varied together because each has been independently determined by a third force.

4. C and E have no causal relations at all. Their varying together has been a simple coincidence and may cease any day.

Troubles of the fourth kind – accidental correlations – are not uncommon in economics. Huge volumes of statistical series are kept these days, and a computer search of them can often turn up accidental covariances which don't arise from causal relations at all. In a fierce argument about the causes of English inflation in the 1970s one sceptical contributor reported that there was a closer correlation between the rate of inflation in Britain and the preceding incidence of dysentery in Scotland than between the rate of inflation and the rate of growth of the money supply. The figures were authentic, the correlation was genuine and its statistical significance was very high. A government which believed (as some texts advise) that statistically significant correlation is the *only* way to know what causes what would have concluded that British inflation could best be attacked through Scottish bowels.

Fertile doubts about causal relations

Equations don't tell you what causes what so we scarcely need to compare them with explanations as ways of stating causal relations.

However, some scholars try to use regression equations and some related statistical methods to discover what causes what. They have not discovered any positive causal relations that were not already known by other means. The best they can sometimes do is to estimate the probability that the other methods of understanding have got the relations right. Believers in those recursive mathematical methods think the methods need further development. I think that their use is severely limited by the subject matter, i.e. by the nature of the causal relations in social and economic life.

But other statistical work can apply some stringent tests to causal analysis. If it can't positively discover or prove causal relations, it can help to *disprove* them. If statistical studies show no regular relation between A and B, it is unlikely that A is regularly causing B. In that way statistics can prompt fertile doubts about causal relations which have been understood – or misunderstood – by other means.

Capital punishment is a famous case. Theorists of the understanding kind thought they understood how fear of death would deter people from killing. But most statistical studies of countries with and without capital punishment, and of countries before and after they abolished capital punishment, have shown no regular relation between the number of murders and the presence or absence of capital punishment.

Does that prove that capital punishment has no deterrent effect? Certainly not. But it makes it likely that the fear of being killed has much the same deterrent effect as the fear of being jailed, which is the alternative in all

the statistical studies so far. (There are no societies with *no* punishments for murder, so all the statistical studies can do is compare one deterrent with another.)

Conclusion Statistics cannot prove that A causes B – but they may help to disprove it if it is untrue. But don't confuse two functions of the statistical services. They may not tell you *why* things happen. But don't let that lead you to underrate their importance. Their main and indispensable function is to tell you *what* happens. Government and other statistical offices keep the national accounts. They monitor and measure how much of what is produced, from what resources, at what prices, how the products are distributed, and a host of other things: they are the richest single source of the economist's information.

Fertile doubts about forecasts

A common kind of predictive question asks if present regularities and trends are likely to continue, or to change. For questions of that kind, explanations and statistical information tend to have different 'early warning' or 'doubt-provoking' qualities.

Some changes of direction appear first in the figures – in unexpected changes in monthly or quarterly indexes, consumer spending figures, import/export figures, employment and unemployment figures. Statistical surprises prompt investigations and explanations. Sometimes it happens the other way around; changes in behavior can be forecast before their effects show in the figures. Thus analysts may guess how spending and saving may respond to tax changes, how birthrates may respond to workforce changes, how labor leaders may respond to wage cuts, and so on.

Examples of each method correcting the other:

(1) There is rising inflation. Considering the likely human response to that, a thinker makes a forecast.

Thinker Under inflation, property maintains its value but money loses value. Rational people will convert their money into goods. They will spend or invest. Expect a decline in saving and bank deposits.

Statistician No – successive quarterly returns show household spending *down* and savings and bank deposits *up* since the inflation began.

Thus provoked, the thinker does what he should have done in the first place. He investigates the causal process by asking a sample of households why they are banking so much money. He learns that most household saving is to buy specific things. Inflation raises their money prices, so forces more saving – for house, car, holidays, school outfits and so on. Thus inflation makes them save *more* than they would do if prices were stable. Statistical information has thus prompted research and explanation.

The reverse relation can also happen:

(2) Begin with an individual example. George and Martha have shared bed and board for twenty years past. George has been away about seven days a year on business trips, Martha has been away about half as often as that to visit her mother or help sick friends. Will that pattern continue? See how the local statistician and the local gossip approach that question:

Statistician They have shared bed and board for 7112 of the last 7300 nights. Tests of statistical significance show that there is very little chance that those were 7112 random coincidences. That gives very high probability to their continuing association.

Gossip I happen to know that they're bored with each other, George is arranging to go off with Desiree, Martha intends to stop housekeeping and start a business, and a land agent has been engaged to put the matrimonial home on the market. Of course you never know for sure until it happens – but I'd give their continuing association about one chance in twenty.

There are collective equivalents of that homely tale. Mass behavior can change in response to changing circumstances, sometimes in unexpectedly thoughtful or wilful ways. National rates of saving and spending have changed abruptly. Powerful changes of mind and changing patterns of conflict and consensus are occurring in gender relations, in environmental behavior and policy, in prevailing patterns of greed and generosity, in tax and welfare and international aid policies, and in prevailing

ideas of the economic role of government. Much may depend on the intelligence and goodwill with which we anticipate these changing values and intentions, and deal with the economic dangers and opportunities which they bring.

SUMMARY

1. Steady quantitative relationships between flows of money or goods can conveniently be expressed mathematically.

2. It is better to count and measure quantities than to guess them.

3. Equations do not tell you what causes what.

4. As with the relations between George and Martha or between Scotch dysentery and English inflation, statistical associations and inferences are only as good as the causal understanding they are built on, but they may offer useful correction to mistaken causal explanations.

5. An economics which strains to be mathematical, preferring algebra to language wherever possible, is likely to discover less and make more mistakes than an understanding economics which uses quantitative methods to get its quantities and regular correlations right, but uses all possible ways of understanding human intentions and behavior to explain what causes what. It is for that technical reason, rather than to make the work easier, that this text has more detailed explanation of more diverse case studies, and less mathematical or axiomatic reasoning, than most other general introductions to economics have.

EXERCISE

Think of some practical examples, not included in this chapter, of causal questions which would best be answered by statistical methods; some which would best be answered by investigating the situations, incentives and purposeful activities of a sample of the people involved; and some which might best be answered by combining those methods.

5

The controversial language of economics

THE CHOICE OF IDENTITIES

Observing anything takes two: the observer and the thing observed. What you see depends on what you are looking at but it also depends on your eyesight. That is more than just physical eyesight. It is an educated and selective eyesight. It understands and recognizes some things but not others.

Three people can look at the same country landscape and 'see' it differently. A poet sees a romantic setting for rustic lads and lasses. A painter sees interesting patterns of form and colour. A farmer sees Jersey cows doing poorly on unsuitable pasture. We all observe the world through 'perceptual screens' which – to some extent at least – select and shape what we see.

Among other things we have in mind a set of identities: things we recognize and have names for. Where a stranger from Mars might look at our landscape and see only some chunky shapes, a flat space and some brown things moving, our educated earthdwellers' eyesight recognizes a *farmhouse*, a *field*, a *Jersey herd* – familiar identities all.

Economists have to decide what identities they will recognize and use. They may use a lot of society's concepts – 'farm', 'field', 'Jersey herd'. They add language of their own if they want to use concepts which the people they are studying don't use – 'national product', 'marginal utility', 'consumer durables'. As with other choices of theory and method, the choice of concepts reflects the economists' social and technical purposes. So it can be controversial.

Identities and the relations between them

Notice the obvious link between the *identities you choose to use* and *the relations you can study*.

If the smallest economic identity you recognize is households, you cannot study relations within households. To study those you have to disaggregate households and group their members according to the roles, and the relations between them, that you want to study. You may recognize men and women and children, and earners and household workers and dependants, then investigate their divisions of labor, each group's contribution to national output, their shares of influence and income, the services that they do or don't do for one

another – or whatever else you think important about their household economy.

Besides taking whole institutions apart in that way, you can also add things up or put parts together to identify new 'wholes'. For example, suppose that firms have been perceived as employing people with a wide range of skills – scientists, programmers, office cleaners and so on – who use a wide range of equipment – laboratories, computers, buckets and mops – in their work. Economists decide to identify all the equipment as *capital* and all the workers as *labor*. That allows you to study some new aggregates, and relations between them. You may for example calculate capital/labor ratios, meaning how much of each are being used in production. You may calculate how much of the reward of production is going to the workers and how much to the capital-owners: what the *wage share* and *profit share* are in a particular firm. You may go on to compare the wage shares and profit shares in different firms, or in different industries, or between national economic systems; and you can see how the shares change (or don't) over time. What you find may improve your technical understanding of what causes what. It may affect judgments about the justice of different class shares of wealth and income. But it depends on choosing to use the collective identities 'capital' and 'labor'.

No one set of identities is likely to suit everybody. We saw earlier how different purposes help to select different causal analyses. Part of that process is the choice of the identities the analyst will use – the wholes and the parts, and the particular kinds of action and qualities of behavior, that will figure in her economic analysis.

Right, Left and Centre

When different economists use different language, the reason is often technical: they happen to be investigating different things. It may also be value-based: they have different social purposes in mind. In relating economists' methodological choices to their social purposes, this text will often draw examples from the traditional political categories of Left and Right. But each of those terms is commonly used in wildly different ways – Left for anything from cautious social democracy to communist dictatorship, Right for anything from cautious conservatism to fascist dictatorship. This note is to let you know that in this text the words generally signify attitudes to inequalities of wealth and income. Some people favor greater or less equality for its own sake. Others favor greater or less equality as means to other ends, such as productive efficiency or the reduction of poverty. (There are hard choices for the Left if it is ever true that greater equality may reduce productivity, and for the Right if greater equality may increase productivity.) Whatever their reasons, this text generally uses Right for those who want greater inequality than exists in their society, Left for those who want greater equality, and Centre or middle-of-the-road for those who don't want much change in either direction.

Now begin your direct study of the subject by learning some of its working language.

A CONTROVERSIAL BOUNDARY OF ECONOMICS

Economists have traditionally begun their definitions with a simple picture of a worker *(labor)* using a plough *(capital)* on a field *(land)* to grow corn *(a commodity)*. That whole process is *production*. Eating the corn is then *consumption*. The people pay for what they consume out of their *incomes*. The worker earns *wages*. The owner of the plough earns *profits*. The owner of the land earns *rent*. (A farmer working his own plough on his own land collects all three.)

We will presently introduce those traditional terms, and others. But there is first a question which affects the meaning of many of them. The question is not about economic life, it is about how much of that life economists should study. What should be the boundary of economics?

Think of the long chain of processes and exchanges that produce your dinner.

Farms grow animals and crops and vegetables. Commercial services transport them, process them and get them to your local shops. You buy them, take them home on foot or by bus or bike or in the family car. You store and refrigerate them, then prepare them and cook them for dinner.

Traditionally, economists have lost interest *at the moment when you leave the local shop*. They study the commercial work but not the household work. (They would study the household work if you paid a servant to do it.) National accounts sometimes value and count the output of subsistence farming, or the (imputed) rent of owner-occupied houses. But with those exceptions economics has traditionally been confined to things exchanged for money i.e. *paid* work and *marketed* goods and services.

That leaves out most housework, transport by private cars and bikes, do-it-yourself work, charitable and other voluntary work and various kinds of neighborly cooperation.

There are ways of measuring and comparing the amount and value of the 'paid' and 'unpaid' work. Different measures estimate the unpaid contribution in an advanced modern economy at between a third and three fifths of the whole. When the traditional boundary of economics excludes that unpaid contribution – chiefly the household contribution – it thus excludes a third or more of the productive activity of a modern industrial society.

Deciding how much of that process to study is a *choice*. The economic facts don't dictate it, the economist's values do. If either boundary suits the social purposes of your work, use it. If not, don't.

This course of study will disregard the traditional or 'narrow' boundary wherever it can. The author's reasons? I believe (1) the unpaid sectors of the economy are important for what they produce, how they produce it, and how they distribute it; and (2) the working relations *between* the paid and unpaid sectors are important for the productivity of both of them.

You must nevertheless cope with the institutional effects of the traditional boundary. (Remember Chapter 1: economic beliefs are working parts of the economic systems you study.) Many of the accounts and statistics which you will need to use will measure the paid activities only. Others will estimate the volumes or values of unpaid goods and services. Some comprehensive accounts will include both. So get into the habit of

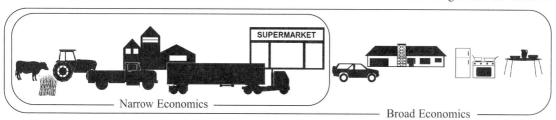

Figure 5.1 The scope of economics

noticing what you are being offered, and how it has been measured or estimated.

The boundary also affects the meaning of some of the words economists use. For example when you drive home with your groceries and cook your dinner, a 'broad' economist calls the driving and cooking activity *production,* while an economist working within the traditional boundary calls it *consumption.* The broad economist calls your car and your kitchen cooker *capital* or *producer goods.* The traditional economist would only call them capital or producer goods if their products were marketed for money, i.e. if the car belonged to a cab-driver and the cooker belonged to a restaurant. But if they belong to you (a *consumer* by definition, if you're not paid for driving or cooking) those productive machines are traditionally called *consumer durables.* Do you see how the economists' choices of boundary can lead them to classify identical goods and activities in opposite ways – how they can actually reverse the meanings of basic economic concepts like *production* and *consumption?*

Notice that the disagreements are – as usual – about purposes, selections, desirable classifications. They are *not* true-or-false disagreements about the objective facts.

Disagreed selections run through a lot of the language (or jargon) of economics, as we will now see. We can follow tradition in at least one way, by beginning our definitions with *land, labor* and *capital.*

LAND

Land is shorthand for the gifts of nature: material resources men can use without first working to produce them. Earth, air, water, weather, sunlight, minerals, natural forests, the power of tides.

Land may be a handy word for those resources. But before it can signify economic resources – usable resources – it has to include some social as well as physical meaning. Nowadays planning and zoning and environmental laws define what you can do with your land. There is a sense in which they tell you *what* your land is – a nature reserve, a crop-growing acre, a residential allotment, a city office site? Some countries say you own any minerals under your land, other countries say you don't. (In some, the government owns the minerals. In some, whoever discovers the minerals owns them.) Some classes of English landowners once owned all the local birdlife, whether it was shot on or off their private acres.

Those rules change from time to time and from place to place. You can see them as regulating what you may do with your land. Or you can see them as defining what your land *is.* The rules can be more important than the natural characteristics of the land. Manhattan Island once changed hands for some coins and blankets and trinkets. Now an acre of it may have very little cash value, or it may have billion-dollar value, according to its zoning. Political action can determine which. Quicker fortunes are made from land by manipulating its zoning than by growing anything on it by honest toil.

So when you buy land now you buy *physical resources.* You buy a *social location* at which to live or do business. And you buy what may prove to be a changeable set of rights and duties. All three affect the land's economic uses and market value.

LABOR

Economists tend to use 'labor' ambiguously for the work and the worker.

Some economists have treated people, and therefore their capacity to work, as a natural resource like land. Others insist that people are *produced* much as other products are – if you doubt it, ask parents who work and spend to feed and clothe and socialize children through their first twelve or twenty years. Or ask the governments and taxpayers and teachers who provide the schools that equip them with many of their working skills.

Whether you think people are economic products, or just grow naturally like Topsy, is their *labor* a commodity like beans and butter? Can you buy and sell it?

One answer says you can, but wherever slavery has been outlawed you are not allowed to. Humans must not be bought and sold, they can only be 'rented' for wages.

Another answer chooses to distinguish people (who cannot be sold) from the work they do (which can). If I employ you I buy your labor. If I buy something you have made I buy the labor you put into it. So economists talk of labor *markets,* with wages and salaries and fees as labor's *price.* This text will argue that employing people is partly similar to buying market goods from them, but partly different, and the differences are such that we will understand the relation better if we use other language for it, rather than thinking of it as a market.

There are other disagreements if you ask who is paid and who is not, and what is work and what is play.

Who is paid? We noticed that a third or more of the productive work of a modern society is done at home, or among friends, or by voluntary work for charities. Plenty of it is actually paid for. Housewives rarely starve. They receive income in cash or kind, however fair or unfair their shares of whole household income. But their work does not earn a formal wage so most economists, and most national accounts, do not record it.

If you choose, instead, to *include* unpaid productive work in your economic analysis, that choice forces you to face some further choices. What is work and what is not?

An amateur football champion turns pro. He goes on playing as before, with all the same joy in the game. Has an unchanged activity changed from 'play' into 'work'? If parents help to coach school teams, are they working while their pupils are playing? There are fine lines between work and recreation. And pleasure and pain are no help: some recreation (camping out in bad weather, breaking limbs in rough sports) is miserably painful, some work (Handel composing his Hallelujah chorus) is pure joy.

So if a broad economics wants to include unpaid work, *what* unpaid activity should it count as work? There is no simple answer. (That is one reason why so many economists work within the traditional 'paid work' boundary, however unsatisfactory they find it.) As 'broad' economists we must *choose* what to count as work. There will be some rough-and-ready choices. Then there will be more rough-and-ready choices to estimate the amount and value of the unpaid work. All we can do is make the choices and estimates as sensible – and also as clear – as we can.

CAPITAL

'Capital' is a word with many meanings, some of them much disputed. We can start with some of the more detailed and less contentious meanings.

Fixed capital Modern productivity depends on complicated divisions of labor and manufacturing processes. To turn raw materials into (say) an automobile or a digital watch, many skills must use many machines to process the materials in many ways. The raw materials come in one way or another from 'land'. The skills are 'labor'. The rest is 'capital': factories, machinery, equipment, power generators, warehouses, roads and rails and pipes and wires. Those long-lasting productive items are variously known as *fixed capital, capital goods* and *producer goods*.

Although all those items wear out in time, they can be distinguished from things which are transformed or consumed in the process of production – things like raw materials, fuel, electric power. Those are commonly called *intermediate goods* to distinguish them from

long-lasting *producer goods* on the one hand, and goods for final consumption *(consumer goods)* on the other.

A short definition of capital and intermediate goods: *Produced goods used for further production.*

Working capital To make cars or watches you need more than fixed capital (factories, machines). Production takes *time*. Long before you have any finished cars or watches to sell you have to be buying materials and power *(intermediate goods)*, paying wages, and meeting other costs of production (rent, insurance, taxes). To meet those costs before you get any revenue from sales you need money as *working capital*.

So far, this language is acceptable to most economists.

Human capital To make cars or watches you need more than fixed and working capital. You also need the will and the skill to use them. Most economists call that capacity to work *human capital*. Can it be deliberately produced, like other capital? In some conditions that can be difficult. Cultures which fit people for elaborately organized production tend to be slow historical growths. Some poor as well as rich countries have such cultures. But some tribal societies' members are unpromising factory labor, and some economically advanced societies produce more adaptable modern workers than others do – North American culture seems to allow better organization and management than South American cultures do, for example.

But where the culture allows, there is a sense in which individuals and national societies *can* invest in human capital. Anything which improves people's health and strength and useful skill is likely to improve their productivity. Spend time and money getting an engineering degree, and you add to your own and your society's productive capacity. The society does the same in a collective way when it builds and staffs the engineering school. You may even be able to calculate rough rates of return on those investments. How much more will you earn with the engineering degree than without it? How much more will the society produce with that engineering school than without it?

The idea of human capital has attracted two kinds of criticism. Some economists think the concept overlaps confusingly with the concepts of labor and skill. So they call the material forms of knowledge – the books and accumulated technical knowledge – capital. But when the knowledge and skills are embodied in people they prefer to speak of skilled labor.

Other objections come from critics who fear that if education is seen as productive investment it will be funded according to its financial rates of return. Engineering schools will do well. But it is hard to prove financial rates of return to education in the humanities and social sciences, so their funding – and their cultural and civilizing functions – may suffer at the hands of materialistic accountants and policy-makers.

This text counts those cultural and civilizing functions as productive, just as it counts the cultural and civilizing functions of households as productive. So it will treat people's skills and capacities, both marketable and non-marketable, as human capital.

Public, private and household capital

Recall the process that produces your dinner. This time, focus on the capital items and notice who commonly owns them in a modern mixed economy.

Government owns the agricultural research institutes, the educational services, and the roads and perhaps the rails that bear the transport. Private capitalists own the farm, the trucks, the food-processing factories, the wholesale and retail stores. Households own or rent the house, and own the home-delivery car, the kitchen refrigerator and cooker, the pots and pans and table and chairs.

The three contributions vary with what you happen to be eating – private capitalists contribute more to your roast meat than to the fruit you pick from your own tree. But if you trace most home-cooked dinners back to their sources you will find that the three 'sectors' are capitalized in the reverse of their order above. The household has most capital per dinner served; the food supply industries have a little less; the government has less again, though still a substantial share. All three kinds of capital are needed to produce your modern dinner.

Notice that you can't always equate the *type of capital* with the *type of ownership*. Each type of capital can be owned by each type of owner. Most roads and bridges are public but there are some private and household roads and bridges. Most factories are owned by private shareholders but some – like most European steelmakers and some French and British carmakers before the recent privatizations – are publicly owned. Households own refrigerators and cookers, but so do capitalist hotels, non-profit colleges, public hospitals. Houses – the biggest item of household capital – may be owned by their occupiers or by private landlords or by public landlords. When you meet accounts of total public, private and household capital, notice which way they've been classified – by who owns them, or by what they typically produce.

Right and Left language for classifying capital

Although all economists recognize the existence of public and private and household capital, they don't all use the same names for those categories. Here in the left-hand column they are named as in this book. In the right-hand column are alternative names for them.

PUBLIC CAPITAL = INFRASTRUCTURE
PRIVATE CAPITAL = CAPITAL
HOUSEHOLD CAPITAL = HOUSING, CONSUMER DURABLES

EXERCISE

Before you read on, can you work out why the Left and Right columns may be ideologically Left and Right too?

The right-hand column names private profit-seeking capital – 'capitalist' capital – as the only real capital. Does it matter? It does if the language is persuasive. (Beliefs about the economic system are working parts of the system.)

In this case there are mixed technical and social reasons for preferring one language or the other. There are technical disagreements about what produces what. And there are conflicts of interest and social purpose. Here are first some conservative or 'Right' reasons for preferring the language in the right-hand column, and then some Left reasons for preferring the language in the left-hand column:

Some Right reasons for preferring the language on the right There will be more and richer private capitalists the more private capital there is. So there is a capitalist class interest in persuading people and governments to keep as much capital as possible in private ownership.

Many people on the Right assert, often falsely, that private capital is more productive than public or household capital. It will help to persuade public and governments of this if the *products* of public and household capital are as far as possible left out of the national accounts. Public and household capital will then look unproductive. If they're not even *called* capital, people won't even *expect* them to be productive.

Many people rightly associate the accumulation of capital with productivity and growth. If the language persuades them to see private capital as the main or only productive capital they may be persuaded that there is a collective interest – a consensual, classless interest – in keeping as much capital as possible in private hands.

Another deception follows, often unconsciously. Firms, and stock exchanges, and the private sector as a whole through its peak associations, give publicity to the rates of return to private capital. But almost every private enterprise also uses public capital: roads and bridges, research and educational capital, statistical and other information services' capital, and so on. Almost every private return is a return on the use of some private *and some public capital.* So accounts of private rates of return systematically exaggerate the productivity of private capital and conceal the productivity of public capital. The deception is surer if the public capital is not perceived as capital at all, but as infrastructure.

So – I think consciously with some but unconsciously with most – it suits private enterprisers to use other words for public and household capital. If public buildings, roads and rails and bridges, schools and hospitals, law courts and police stations are called infrastructure that identifies their functions as secondary – mere necessary conditions for private enterprise to do the actual production. (If you don't remember why people identify 'necessary conditions' in that prejudicial way, revise Chapter 2.) People are thus encouraged to think they need public investment only to facilitate private production (or for welfare purposes, which may be defined as not productive at all).

Similarly if household capital is called *housing* and *consumer durables,* and its productive use is called consumption, its share of capital resources can also be described (falsely but persuasively) as unproductive.

Some Left reasons for preferring the language on the left Most people don't own private capital or share in its profits. So majorities may have a class interest in keeping as much capital as possible in public or household ownership, as long as it is productive in those hands. Most households will be poorer in the long run if they have to pay rent to private landlords, i.e. if they don't own their household capital or rent it 'at cost' from a public landlord. So they need language which keeps people aware of the options by calling the stuff *capital* whoever owns it.

There is no reason to believe that capital is necessarily more productive in private ownership than in public or household ownership. As noticed earlier, household capital tends to average about as productive as private capital. Modern equipment makes household labor much more productive than it used to be.

The aim of policy should be to distribute capital to the public, private and household sectors in complementary proportions. If (for example) capital is distributed efficiently to workplace, home and neighborhood, many people can put in many more hours of productive work than they could do if productive work were possible only at the commercial workplace. The most productive countries accordingly have mixed economies, and their economic growth for at least a century up to the 1970s saw a steady increase in the proportions of capital in public and household ownership.

All this is easiest to understand, and the policy options are clearest, if productive capital is called capital whoever owns it. So *public capital, private capital,* and *household capital* – the language of the left-hand column on page 39 – will usually be used in this course of study. Students who disagree can translate as they wish.

Rent, interest, profit: capital owners' rewards

Notice that 'capital' is used interchangeably of solid assets (factories, machines) and the money to buy them. A person who owns a factory and a person with a million dollars to invest are both capitalists.

Just as the capital can take many forms, so can its earnings. Own a business, and you make *profits.* Buy shares in a company, and its profits provide you with *dividends.* Lend your money or buy bonds or debentures, and you can earn *interest.* Lease your land or buildings, and you can collect *rent.* If the things you own increase their value – i.e. if the market prices of your land or shares or works of art increase while you own them – you make *capital gains.* You will learn all that language, and more, when you study the detailed organization of the economic system. Here it will do to describe the assets collectively as capital, and everything they earn as capital owners' rewards.

It is when they see capital 'whole' in relation to its economic functions and rewards that economists' values prompt some of their deepest disagreements. Some of the disagreements are technical – about facts, or what causes what. But many of them are not. The theorists see accurately enough the things they choose to see. But they choose to emphasize different aspects of the facts and industrial relations.

Consider: A capitalist hires and equips a worker to produce useful goods to sell to a consumer. Which elements of that process do your social values identify as its most important elements?

- An observer with one set of values sees capital and labor cooperating to meet the consumer's needs.

- Another observer sees the capitalist creating employment and thus helping to distribute income.

- Another sees him getting more work from the worker than he pays for, or getting a higher price from the consumer than he needs to cover his costs, or both: he's an exploiter.

- Another sees him owning and directing productive resources which might alternatively be owned and directed by the workers or by the consumers, who might put the resources to different uses: he's an allocator of resources, a policy-maker.

There is no necessary disagreement about the facts or what causes what between those four observers. They merely select differently because they put different values on different effects of the capitalist's activity.

With those different judgments of the capitalists' roles go different justifications of their rewards. Some ideologists see them as rewards for waiting: for consuming less now in order to consume more later. Some see them as rewards for allocating capital resources to their most productive uses. Some see them as legalized plunder: rights to unearned income, created by the laws of property. (Marx defined capital as 'power over the labor of others'.) The disagreements are distilled in the question 'Do capitalists give or take?' Contribute land and capital to production, or simply take unearned income from the fact of ownership?

We will return to the question in chapters on economists' alternative models of mixed economies.

How much capital? If you don't know what capital is worth, you can't know what rate of profit it is earning, or how much capital your business or your country has got, or how fast it is accumulating. But it is hard stuff to measure. Consider:

If you lend $1 million at 10 per cent annual interest, and there is no inflation, then there is no doubt what your capital is worth and what it is earning for you.

But if you invest in almost any other way there is likely to be some doubt about one or more of the relevant figures. Suppose you spend $1 million on a factory, machinery, raw materials and wages and start producing mousetraps for sale. In the first year the business makes $100,000 profit. You are earning 10 per cent on the money you spent. But are you earning 10 per cent on the capital you now have? If you were to sell your factory and second-hand machines piecemeal and add the working capital the firm has in the bank, you might only have $800,000. Does that mean your $100,000 profit represents 12.5 per cent profit on $800,000 of capital? But you have patented your traps and they are selling well, so if you were to sell the business as a going concern you might well get $1,250,000. Does

that mean your $100,000 profit is only an 8 per cent return on $1,250,000 of capital? Or does it mean your $100,000 trading profit plus your $250,000 capital gain shows 35 per cent profit on your original $1 million investment? Whichever way you choose to calculate it you can't be sure of the actual rate because if you did sell the machinery or the whole business the price would depend on market conditions at the time. If your firm's shares are quoted on the stock exchange, then every time the share prices rise or fall the value of your capital changes, and so does your rate of profit on it.

So there is a measurement problem. At the moment when you invest, you know the value of the capital but you don't yet know what it will earn. By the time you know what it is earning, you no longer know what the capital is worth. So although *capital value* and its *percentage rate of return* are important to many people – investors, forecasters, tax gatherers, keepers of national accounts – they are often uncertain and open to disagreement.

Economists get over the difficulty as best they can. They use going rates of interest – i.e. the rates you can get if you lend money *today*. They use rough approximations of capital value. The law specifies particular ways of keeping accounts for some particular purposes. But plenty of those concerned – owners and managers, taxpayers and tax gatherers, employers and employees – have conflicting interests. Some may want the earning rate to look high, for example to impress clients or attract new capital. Others may want the earning rate to look low, for example to minimize tax or to resist wage demands. If they can, they will choose their methods of calculation accordingly.

Conclusion Capital is often hard to value. Rates of profit are often a matter of opinion. Don't necessarily accept either without finding out how they have been calculated.

WEALTH AND INCOME

Wealth is what you *own*, income is what you *earn* or receive unearned as property income, as an owner of capital. Your *stock* of capital is wealth, your *flow* of salary, wages, pension, profits, dividends, rent or interest is income.

In borderline cases it can be hard to draw the line between the two. The distinction matters for a number of reasons. You may need to know how much you can safely consume while maintaining your capital intact so that future income and consumption can be maintained. Nationally, it can be important for resource and environmental policy. If mining companies mine and sell exhaustible resources, are they earning income or selling irreplaceable capital?

The distinction also matters for tax reasons. Disguising income as capital is one main method of tax avoidance. If capital gains are to count as income, *when* do they count? When they happen – when the wine aging in your cellars has increased its market value by another dollar a bottle? Or only when you sell it and realize the gain? ('Realize' means turn into money in hand.)

Income in cash or kind? Remember the controversial boundary of economics. Income certainly includes your inflow of money from wages, pension, dividends, interest, rent. You may also get income in kind: free meals at work, use of a company car, and so on. You may produce income in kind for yourself: fruit from your garden, mileage in your car, hot meals from your kitchen.

Tax collectors count some kinds of income in kind from employers. Some countries tax the employees who receive those benefits, some tax the employers who provide them, some tax neither.

Most national accounts count money incomes only, plus a very few other items. Some add estimates of the value of food that subsistence farmers produce for themselves. Some add the 'imputed' rent of owner-occupied houses. None count the unmarketed goods and services which households produce for themselves.

Real income You will meet two or three meanings. 'Real' often means purchasing power, so real income can mean money income adjusted for inflation. If your wage rises 12 per cent through a year which sees 10 per cent inflation, your *nominal* income has risen 12 per cent while your *real* income has risen 2 per cent. But 'real income' is sometimes used to mean your whole income including money, income in kind, and goods and services you produce for yourself: i.e. your whole flow of material goods and services from all sources. And those two meanings may be combined. Take money income, add the estimated money value of the in-kind and home-produced items, and adjust the total for inflation. You can then follow, from year to year, the stable or changing value of your income from all sources.

PRODUCTION AND CONSUMPTION

There are plain meanings of production and consumption. Farmers and bakers *produce* bread. Households *consume* it.

Does that mean that (except for waste) production equals consumption? Not at any particular time. To see why not, learn another identity:

Inventories Sometimes products don't sell immediately. Producers and wholesalers and retailers store them. If production runs ahead of consumption, goods accumulate in store. If consumption exceeds production, the stocks dwindle.

Firms keep accounts of their stocks – detailed lists of the goods in their warehouses and stores. The lists are called inventories. For firms and industries and for the economy as a whole, economists often use *inventories* as a general word for the fluctuating stock of unsold products.

Producers also consume, consumers also produce People sometimes write as if producers only produce and consumers only consume. Producers and consumers are mostly the same people, so the simplification has them producing only at work and consuming only at leisure. In practice people do some of both most of the time, and in most of their institutions. Workers eat and drink and wear out their clothes at work, i.e. they consume at work. At home and at leisure they produce quite a lot of what they consume – households do a third or more of all economic production.

Controversial boundaries of production and consumption So far, 'produce' and 'consume' have simple physical meanings. But economists have complicated them in a number of ways. Those who use the narrowest boundary of economics often distinguish production from consumption by reference to *the last sale* of a product. From the farm through the mill to the supermarket, flour is being *produced*. Once retailed to a household it is being *consumed,* however long the cook labors to turn it into however many cakes. Broad economists see the household work as productive. Narrow economists don't. Nor do most of the national accounts you will use. For them, the final retail sale – the last time goods exchange for money – is taken as concluding the process of production. Also (with allowance for exports and imports, and for inventories of goods awaiting sale) the retail sales measure the whole value of goods produced and consumed in the economy.

That 'narrow' approach has one advantage. The retail sales are easier to monitor and measure than the household activities are. The statistician can know what flour was sold, for what price. It would take more trouble to monitor the household's work and estimate the money value of its output. But the narrow view also has disadvantages, especially if economists insist on classifying *all* economic activity as either production or consumption. Consider these effects of that choice of analytical identities –

Picnic Standing over your campfire eating a charred chop with one hand and cooking two more with the other, you appear to be both producing and consuming. But the last retail sale is past, so the national accounts must see you consuming with both hands.

Piano When you play *(labor)* the piano *(capital)* to make *(produce)* music *(a product)* for your own pleasure *(consumption)* it is not really very helpful to analyse out the 'productive' and 'consumptive' elements of what you're at. It would be more sensible to say you are well *occupied.*

Producing or consuming children? Paid nannies, orphanages, kindergartens, day care and other paid services to children count as productive. But what about households' unpaid services?

Some economists select the fact that parents are producing the next generation of workers. Their future employers can't yet be identified or made to pay, so the state helps to pay for the service through child allowances, tax remissions, etc. Those payments need not be seen as measures of social compassion or redistribution. They are payments to the producers of a socially useful product – namely, the next generation of workers.

Others' values prompt different views. They judge that parents are sufficiently rewarded by the pleasure, and perhaps the support in their old age, that their children afford them. The work and expenditures of child care are the price they pay for those advantages.

Ideologies of production and consumption

Choosing to call all household activity 'consumption' is doubly prejudicial. It conceals and treats as valueless most of the productive work that has traditionally been done by women. And it limits the questions which economists can ask – and tends to limit them in a conservative way.

Households vary greatly in their productivity. Some 'consume' most of the time – eating fast food and watching television. Others produce a great deal for themselves. Some produce for others as well as for themselves.

Are those always free choices? No. Some households can get all the productive space, time and capital they want. Some households can't – even the richest societies leave a quarter or more of their households

short of the household space and equipment to make and do all the things they would like to make and do. That is an important issue. First, it affects national efficiency: is the available land and capital distributed between public, private and household sectors in the most productive way? Second, it is both a cause and an effect of the distribution of wealth and whole income between classes, households and individuals.

Like other production, most household production uses land, labor and capital. Economists who are concerned about productivity and about equalities will want to research questions like these:

- Is the household sector of the economy getting the *space* it needs – the housing and workshop space, and the private or communal land – to do all the do-it-yourself production that households would like to do?

- Is the household sector getting an appropriate share of *capital,* in competition with the public and private sectors of the economy?

- Is household capital distributed as productively as possible *between* households? And *within* households? (Which members of the household have cars? Bikes? Rooms of their own? Work space, tool kits, hobby gear?)

- How do women, children and men share the household work?

- How do households *decide* what to buy ready-made for money, and what to produce for themselves? Are the systems of housing, finance and income distribution giving them effective choices between doing without, buying ready-made, and equipping themselves to produce for themselves?

You cannot research those questions effectively if you choose to define all household activity as consumption. If you do that you have to call identical activities 'production' or 'consumption' according to how they're paid for. You have to say that driving to work, cooking a dinner, cleaning and laundering, building a bookshelf, playing football, teaching a child or making love is *production* if it's paid for, but *consumption* if it's not. More precisely you have to call it production if any payment comes as a commercial wage or price, but consumption if the payment comes informally as income sharing between the members of the household. Conclusions:

1. This course of study will usually call household and other unpaid production *production.*

2. We will use the other, narrower language when necessary, for example when using narrow-based statistics.

3. We need not necessarily classify all activity as either production or consumption. There are many activities like home gardening or playing the piano or entertaining friends in which people use economic resources in creative ways so that we *could* say they are simultaneously producing and consuming. But it may often be simpler to say they are *well occupied.*

GOODS AND BADS

You can't always produce things you want without also producing other things, good or bad. Wheat comes with chaff, peas come with pods, electric power comes with pollution. To describe these effects economists speak of costs, products, by-products, and externalities or neighborhood effects.

Suppose a factory produces (1) mousetraps, (2) sawdust, and (3) smoke. The mousetraps sell for money so they're *products.*. If the sawdust fetches a price for some commercial use it is a *by*-product. It is a by-product because it is an effect of making mousetraps – you would not build the factory just to produce the sawdust. (But if the sawdust is useless and you have to pay for its disposal, that's an ordinary *cost* of production.)

Externalities If the smoke pours freely over the near neighbors and adds to their cleaning expenses and doctors' bills that is also a cost, but for them rather than for you. Economists call it an *external diseconomy.* If the smoke also discourages mosquitos, or colors the sunsets enjoyably for more distant neighbors, that is an *external economy.* Good and bad effects which the producer neither pays for nor is paid for are collectively called *externalities* or *neighborhood effects.*

But if the law makes you contain your factory smoke or pay for any damage it does to neighbors, that cost becomes an ordinary cost of production, like rubbish disposal. If you could charge the viewers a fee for those technicolor sunsets, it would cease to be either externality or cost and become a by-product.

MEASURES OF NATIONAL PRODUCT

There are three common ways of measuring total national money income, or paid-for output, for a specified period. One of them adds up all the money incomes derived from economic activity. One adds up the market prices of finished goods, i.e investment goods and consumption goods but excluding intermediate goods to avoid double counting. It adjusts for taxes concealed in product prices, subtracts spending on imports, and adds the value of exports. A third method values output industry by industry to arrive at its totals. The three are alternative ways of arriving at the familiar measures:

- **Gross domestic product (GDP)** The money value of the year's output of finished goods and services.
- **Gross national product (GNP)** Gross domestic product adjusted for net income from foreign economic relations.
- **Net national product** Gross national product minus the amount lost through the same period by capital consumption, i.e. the wearing out and obsolescence of capital goods.
- **Whole national product** The paid-for product (as above) plus the value added by household and other unpaid work. This is a 'broad' economist's view of national product.

MEASURES OF WELFARE

The measures of national income and product have shortcomings which economists of all schools of thought acknowledge. Those measures count the production of wastes and then the costs of cleaning them up. They don't subtract for mess that is not cleaned up. They don't count leisure, or many of the productive and enjoyable uses people make of it. If the same goods and services were produced by a 40-hour week in one country and a 30-hour week in another, or with great harm to the people's health in one and no harm in another, GNP would be the same in both.

So various ways of valuing 'measured economic welfare' (MEW) or 'net economic welfare'(NEW) have been proposed. They are calculated like this:

Start with GNP.
Add the value of unpaid production, as for *whole national product.*
Add a value for leisure.
Subtract defence expenditure.
Subtract the dirtying-and-cleaning-up elements of GNP.
Subtract for mess which the economic system creates but does *not* clean up: pollution, crowded roads, crime, anxiety, alienation.

That seems to offer a better measure of useful output. But there are two difficulties.

First, it is hard to decide what to add and subtract. If you add for leisure, do you subtract for unemployment, i.e. for unwanted leisure? If one country has expensive water treatment to remove natural impurities from its water supply and another country has it to remove manmade pollutants, do you add the cost to one country's net economic welfare but subtract it from the other's? And how do you arrive at money values for the unmarketed items – how much congestion is as bad as how much pollution, and how much leisure would compensate for either? With arbitrary choices like those to make, people are unlikely to accept the result as an agreed or objective measure of welfare.

Second, these may be useful measures of economic *product.* But do they measure economic *welfare?.*

Their authors think so. But Left economists do not agree that welfare can be measured regardless of the distribution of the economic benefits. Consider two countries with the same per capita GNP but one with greater inequalities than the other. Suppose that the first has oil or cattle millionaires, and also poor peasants and unemployed or underpaid townspeople living in shanty towns without clean water, sanitation or enough to eat. In the second country (Norway, perhaps) the people collectively own the oil, there are fewer millionaires, and the poorest people are well fed and comfortably housed with access to good education and health services. Like GNP, some of the measures of economic welfare may show those countries as equally well off.

Common sense says that the better distribution of capital, income and services in the second country means that the same GNP produces more welfare there. Many orthodox economists do not accept that. They profess the philosophical belief that you cannot quantify or compare the welfare which a dollar of income gives to different users. Then in their theorizing and welfare accounting they assume – inconsistently – that a dollar buys the *same* amount of welfare whoever gets it and spends it. You will meet both sides of the argument in later chapters. Meanwhile there are various ways of modifying the measures to reflect national patterns of equality and inequality, and of environmental prudence. Examples of two kinds:

American and European researchers have developed Indexes of Sustainable Economic Welfare and Genuine Progress Indicators. The Australia Institute publishes a more carefully detailed Genuine Progress Indicator whose twenty five components include income and its distribution, net capital growth and various private and communal uses of public capital and services, the value of household and community work, and the costs – estimated by various means – of a long list of bads including unemployment, overwork, crime, transport and industrial accidents, air and water pollution, land degradation, loss of old-growth forests, depletion of non-renewable sources of energy, ozone depletion and climate change.

Some development economists have focused on basic needs and developed means of measuring and comparing the real income and welfare of the poorest people (rather than the average income, or degrees of inequality, of the whole population) in different countries. Among the poorer members of the poorer societies, money income alone can be deceptive. Its value depends on what it will buy. It won't keep children alive if there is no clean water supply, or educate them if there are no schools. In Chapter 10 you will meet arguments for using (especially in developing countries) three indicators which correlate quite well with a number of others: purchasing power per head, life expectancy, and literacy. A United Nations agency has combined them in a Human Development Index, published for all the world's nations in the annual Human Development Report of the UN Development Programme. In 1997 the World Bank began annual publication of a set of nearly 600 World Development Indicators for all but about forty of the world's nations.

A dilemma ...

There is an awkward problem with efforts to improve the measures of national income and welfare. As the measures get better in one way, they tend to get worse in another. They may get better as indicators of economic and social health. But they get less objective, and harder to measure reliably. The nearer they get to a fair and sensitive measure of national economic performance, the more scope there is for disagreement about their methods of measurement. For criticism of some of their methods of measurement, see Partha Dasgupta, *An Inquiry into Well-Being and Destitution* (1993).

That is one reason why most national accounts stick to GNP. What it chooses to measure can be measured fairly objectively. Does that make it an objective measure of economic welfare? No, for at least two reasons: (1) It only measures selected products – the paid and not the unpaid ones. (2) It adds up dissimilar things like food, motor cars and nights at the opera. It does so by valuing them all at the prices people pay for them. But those prices depend on distributions of wealth and income. They may also depend on patterns of monopoly and competition among producers, and on changeable government policies. Those conditions vary from time to time and place to place. So the totals of national product are not strictly comparable over time, or from nation to nation. Nor do similar totals necessarily indicate levels of welfare in the everyday sense of the word, especially between societies with different scales and patterns of inequality.

... and three responses

Faced with that dilemma, experts tend to respond in one of three ways.

Many settle for GNP. Besides being fairly reliable, long-standing statistical series allow it to be calculated a long way back into the past for many countries. Its supporters don't worry too much about the unpaid activity it leaves out, because they think that what it does record is often quite a good indicator of what it does not record – higher GNP, signifying more paid production, usually means there is also more unpaid production, from bigger and better-equipped houses, more car owners, more leisure, etc.

Some who don't trust GNP for many purposes use alternative aggregate measures like NEW and others listed earlier.

Others either distrust *any* quantitative indicators of qualities of life, or believe that they are best used together with more specific information. The best totals and indexes still depend on disputable judgments of what items to include and what values to put on some of them. So this third group tend (especially when dealing with developed countries) to use GNP *plus* accounts of whatever else seems relevant for the purpose in hand, but *without* combining them in a single index. For example to compare British and Japanese performance, they may start with GNP then add independent information about working and leisure hours, housing space and equipment, neighborhood facilities, travel patterns, health and education. They will put their conclusions into words as well as figures: Japanese produce more manufactured goods and more job security, British have bigger houses and gardens and more accessible country recreation. Japanese travel farther to work longer hours in more congested cities – but live a little longer. And so on. That sort of report can be more informative than index figures of welfare-per-head can be. It exposes more of the reporter's choices and value judgments, and it tells readers more of what they need to know to make those judgments for themselves. (In Chapter 14 this difference between indexes and more detailed assessments of welfare will reappear as the much-debated difference between *cost-benefit analyses* and *impact statements* as aids to policy-making.)

The third of those approaches is the one you will most often meet in this course of study. The reasons for

that choice are summarized in the next chapter, so they need not be summarized here.

A CHECK-LIST

Here is a check-list of words discussed in this chapter. Turn back and revise any whose meanings are not clear to you. Then try the exercises – they give you some practice at recognizing what purposes may lie behind particular choices of words and meaning.

Land
    natural resources
Labor
    the work or the worker
    paid or unpaid
Capital
    fixed capital
    working capital
    human capital
    public capital (infrastructure?)
    private capital
    household capital (housing and consumer durables?)
rent, interest, profits
    as rewards for waiting?
    as rewards for efficient allocation?
    as gains by exploitation?
Wealth
Income
Capital gain
'Nominal' and 'real' values
Production
    paid and unpaid
    products
    by-products
    costs
    externalities
Measures of national performance
    gross domestic product (GDP)
    gross national product (GNP)
    net national product (NNP)
    whole national product
    net or measured economic welfare
    human development index (HDI)

EXERCISES

1. Revise the bit of theory which began this chapter – the choice of identities, page 35. Recall the question 'Were the bad pie and the bellyache caused by the slovenly workers *or* by Amalgamated Foods *or* by the private capitalist sector of the economy?' Think through the reasons why (i) facts by themselves can't answer that question, and (ii) the three suggested answers are all true and compatible with each other.

2. What considerations might lead you to call your car or your kitchen cooker (i) household capital, (ii) consumer durables, or (iii) uproductive assets?

3. Suppose a restaurant kitchen produces a lot of meat and vegetable scraps. Can you think of different circumstances (for example different uses for the scraps) in which those scraps would be called (i) products, (ii) by-products, (iii) costs, and (iv) externalities?

4. Recall the reasons for seeing capital-owners' rewards as rewards for waiting, or as rewards for efficient allocation of capital, or as gains from exploiting other people's labor. To what extent do those different views represent –

   (i)   disagreements about the facts – i.e. what capital-owners actually do, and what their motives actually are?

   (ii) true accounts of three different kinds of investments?

   (iii) different beliefs – perhaps based on different values – as to which of the purposes and effects of capitalist investment are the most important ones?

5. Remember how economists who define the economic system to include unpaid production will call the kitchen cooker 'productive capital', but those who define the system to exclude unpaid production may call the kitchen cooker a 'consumer durable'. Now see if you can think of two or three other examples of classifications which fit with particular views of the scope of economics, or the boundaries of the economic system.

6

Efficiency, welfare and the scope of economics

We begin with some more items of controversial language. An economic system is presumably good or bad according to the efficiency with which it contributes to people's welfare by meeting their economic demands. But what do economists mean by *efficiency, welfare* and *demand,* and how do they measure or judge them?

EFFICIENCY

GNP (gross national product) and other measures try to measure *how much* we produce. We can also ask *how efficiently* we produce it.

Common sense says it is efficient to produce at least cost: to get most output from given input, or to produce given output from least input.

- **Efficient workers** The shearer who cleanly shears most sheep per 40-hour week is the most efficient.

- **Efficient machines** The generator which produces most electric power from each ton of fuel is the most efficient.

- **Efficient firms** Given equal resources, the firm which produces the greatest value of goods and makes most profit is the most efficient.

- **Efficient economic systems** The country which produces most of what its people want with given resources of land, labor and capital is the most efficient.

- **Discovery and invention** In the previous definition, 'given resources' is usually taken to mean the resources which people know they have and know how to use. Pre-industrial economies were less efficient than they could have been with steam or atomic power, but it seems unreasonable to reproach them for not having yet invented those productive aids. Nevertheless *some* pride or regret may be reasonable. Examples:

Until about the fourteenth century AD, Chinese science and technology were comparable to European. But their further development, and the business use of them, then lagged far behind European progress. Historians tend to ascribe that to some religious and cultural constraints, and their enforcement by imperial Chinese governments which (for example) gave private business low status and little or no help, and for long periods prohibited foreign exploration and trade.

Should the West be proud of its better performance? Perhaps – but through those inventive centuries Western societies chose to develop and put to scientific and economic use only half of the exceptional individual talents available to them. They worked their women hard at farm and household and other trades. They allowed some scope to women writers and decorative artists. But they made scarcely any use of women's capacities for science, technical invention, business initiative and management, politics, public administration or higher education. Most of the paid occupations open to them had low pay and status, however high the skills that some of them demanded. Enough exceptional women nevertheless distinguished themselves in science and the arts, for at least two centuries before any women won the vote, to leave no real excuse for the generations of intelligent, inventive men who continued to undervalue and obstruct the development of so much human capital.

So far, so good. That commonsense idea of efficiency is a valuable one, worth using for many purposes. But it only works in that simple way when it is applied to conveniently simple facts. If the facts or the purposes of the test are complicated, efficiency is apt to become controversial.

VALUE JUDGMENTS AND MEASURES OF EFFICIENCY

If you measure efficiency by more than one criterion, you have to decide how much weight to give to each of the criteria. The facts can't do that for you. It takes a value judgment, and that value judgment will be built into your measure of efficiency.

Earlier, you read this: 'Common sense says it is efficient to get a given output from the least input.' But what does 'least input' mean? Does it mean least raw materials? Least work? Least expenditure? You have to decide. Consider a couple of examples:

Efficient at what? We are choosing a new power generator. Do we want to get electricity from least fuel?

Or with least labor? Or counting the capital costs and the fuel costs and the labor costs, do we want electricity from least expenditure? There are already three criteria, which may favor three different generators. And we can add three more if one environmentalist says 'Power with least pollution' and two others say 'Tidal powered generators and solar powered generators cost more, but they are socially efficient because they spare exhaustible fuels for other uses. So a *less efficient* way of generating electricity may allow a *more efficient* whole supply of energy.'

Efficient for whom? Earlier, we said the most efficient firm was the one which 'produces most goods from given resources and makes most profit'. But what if the firm which produces most goods is not the one which makes most profit? Suppose Firm A produces most goods, but most of the benefit of that efficiency goes in high wages to its workers and low prices to its customers. Meanwhile Firm B produces less goods but manages to pay lower wages and charge higher prices and so make more profit. Firm A is the most efficient producer. Firm B is the most efficient earner. Which is the most efficient firm? That depends on whose interest you have in mind – the workers', the customers' or the shareholders'. Shareholders may think Firm B has the most efficient *management.* But that is a matter of opinion: is the first duty of management to produce or to earn? It is also a matter of opinion which firm has the most efficient labor. Is it the one with the most output *per worker,* or the one with the most output *per labor cost,* i.e. per dollar of wages paid?

Most tests of efficiency require some value judgments. They can be made into objective tests by precise specifications: output of *what* per input of *what.* But that merely shifts the conflicts of interest and the necessary value judgments from the conduct of the test to the choice and design of the test.

This principle applies to judgments of many other things besides efficiency. You will presently see that it applies to economists' judgments of welfare. But first, there is a prior question about *demand.* One test of efficiency, and of welfare, is to ask if the economy is producing what the citizens actually want. But how do you know what they want, or which of their wants the economic system ought to supply?

WANTS AND DEMANDS

People *want* all sorts of things. Nutritionists, doctors, psychologists, educators and others know a good deal about what people *need.* But in economists' language

people are only said to *demand* things which they are willing and able to pay for.

There may be *latent* or *potential* demand for things people would buy if they could afford them. Only when they are willing and able to buy – 'cash in hand' – do economists speak of *effective demand.*

If people are willing and able to buy particular goods but can't do so because the government bans the goods or the producers fail to supply them, that may be called *frustrated demand.*

This is not controversial language. But it is language for a controversial subject. There is much disagreement about the questions economists should ask about demand. Once again, what should be the scope and boundary of economics? Here is a preview of some questions about wants and demands that you will meet in later chapters:

Unlimited wants? Economists have traditionally assumed that people's wants are unlimited. Given more income, they will always think of something to spend it on. Economic growth won't come to a grinding halt one day with folk saying 'That's enough. We don't want any more'.

But the tradition which assumed unlimited wants also assumed unlimited natural resources. Now that we are polluting the environment and using up exhaustible resources, environmentalists ask: 'Does demand *have* to grow without limit? Shouldn't we settle for a sufficient standard of living and stop demanding more?'

To stop demand growing we would need to know what makes it grow, and study *how* to stop it.

Revealed preferences? Economists have traditionally taken people's particular tastes and preferences as 'given'. They observe *what* people demand; they study *how* economic systems meet those demands by producing goods and services and distributing income.

But should we also study how the wants and tastes and preferences are created? How the people's demands are formed? By their natural appetites, their culture, their education? By persuasion and advertising? Do most people decide what they want in an independent, autonomous way? Or do advertisers and others brainwash people into 'demanding' what it suits producers to sell them?

Take that question a step further. If you study how wants are created or influenced, you extend your view of what the economic system produces. By education, advertising and displaying its wares, it produces demands. It also produces goods and services to supply the demands. So there are three questions you can ask about the system's performance:

- What wants and demands does it encourage?
- What supplies (goods and services) does it produce?
- How good or bad is the fit between the demands and the supplies?

That suggests, next, a third controversial question about economists' treatment of demand.

GOOD AND BAD DEMANDS

Should economic systems be judged by the wants they generate as well as by the wants they satisfy? That is not an academic question. It bothers a wide range of thinkers these days.

Environmentalists don't only worry about the demand for more and more goods. They also worry about preferences for worse rather than better goods. Could people be persuaded to demand goods with less packaging? Movies with less violence? Cars with less horse-power? Could they demand fewer cars and more bikes? Fewer speedboats and more sailing boats? Could they hunt and shoot with fewer guns and more cameras?

Feminists worry about the way advertisers and women's magazines shape women's conceptions of their roles, their tastes and anxieties – and their housing demands and shopping lists.

Many people worry about the commercial encouragement of styles of 'competition', 'enterprise' and 'success' that might alternatively be called conflict, greed and ostentation – keeping up with the Joneses, and doing down the Joneses, by increasingly expensive and soul-destroying means. For example, here is a modern name for an old subject of concern:

Positional goods Competitive systems encourage people to compete – i.e. to get ahead of others, not just to get enough for themselves. If the competition is for who comes top, few can win and many must be frustrated. But that is what people try for if they come to value their position on the social ladder more than the other things their incomes buy them. They don't just want sufficient income – they want a top income *however high the top happens to be.* They don't just want a capacious, productive house at a convenient address – they want a house that tells the world they are top people, at an exclusive address that only top people can afford. They don't just want a reliable car, they want a limo or one of the rarer Ferraris. They don't just want beautiful pictures on their walls, they want originals.

To the extent that a social and economic system gives people that positional motivation, it creates demands which *no* output of goods and services can ever satisfy. No increase in productivity can increase the proportion of incomes in the top 1 or 10 per cent, or the goods which only the top 1 or 10 per cent can have.

That means that *to the extent that people value position above other things,* more productivity cannot improve the efficiency with which the economic system supplies what people want.

Is that good or bad?

Some people think capitalism can't survive without continuous economic growth. They welcome the competitive spirit because it seems to guarantee the continuous growth of demand – however rich people get, they will still want more.

Others think that self-frustrating 'treadmill competition' does more harm than good. It makes people anxious and unhappy. It tends to encourage the worst rather than the best human propensities. It degrades a society's culture. It rules out economic restraint and prudent environmental management at a time when the world needs those policies as never before.

Remember: positional demand can only be satisfied by exclusive goods. The finest Ferrari won't satisfy such a buyer unless he also knows there will be very few like it. Do you see what that means? His 'consumer demand' is a double-headed one. It is a demand *both* to buy something for himself *and* to limit other people's options. That is just one example of a general feature of economic demand to which we will now turn.

WHAT RANGE OF CHOICE DO YOU WANT?

Grasp a basic difference between two meanings of 'consumer sovereignty':

Choosing options People choose what they want from the range of goods and services which the economic system offers them.

Choosing option sets People prefer one pattern of options to another. They want to influence the range of choice and the types of option which the system offers to its individual members.

Sometimes those two are complementary. There is no conflict between them if some consumers simply want an additional option and producers respond by supplying it. Every year there are personal computers with new capacities, more software, more computer games: more things to choose from, more options in the set.

But other choices are not like that. Options can conflict with one another. Things which *you* want may rule out things which I want. Buyers may want to restrict other people's options, and they certainly want their own options to be restricted. So there is conflict and controversy about what goods and services should be offered in the market: i.e. what the *option set* should be. Examples:

- A few good options are better than any number of bad ones. Whenever it is technically difficult for consumers to tell the difference between good and bad goods, they themselves want their options to be restricted. They don't want to be offered *any* poisoned food, tubercular milk, wrongly-labelled drugs, fraudulent stocks and shares, quack doctors, or unsafe buildings and bridges.

- Options for some people may directly or indirectly damage other people. Guns available to all may bring death to some. So may printed or broadcast incitements to rape, murder, arson, theft – or 'positional ambition'. There is nothing necessarily unreasonable in some citizens wanting to influence other citizens' demands, or the supplies available to them.

- Some options rule out others. Example: If most city people do *not* have the option of owning private cars, most of them *can* have the option of low-priced efficient public transport. But if (say) two thirds have the option of private transport, then it is likely (in most patterns of settlement) that nobody can have the option of low-priced efficient public transport. (They may have low-priced *inefficient* public transport if government subsidizes it. But government is less likely to do that if two thirds of its electors don't want that option.)

We will return to this later, to study relations between people's option sets as consumers and as producers: is a wide choice of attractive consumer goods worth having if it makes for a narrow choice of unattractive jobs?

Conclusions about demand

1. Demand for goods and services is determined partly by individual choices and partly by collective choices (and of course, by individual and collective capacity to pay). Both types of choice are open to plenty of influence. Both can pose conflicts of interest and policy problems.

2. Economists consequently need to study how tastes and preferences are formed, including preferences for some option sets rather than others. They need to understand how the structure of demand is affected 'by influence as well as income, and by law as well as choice'.

3. It is reasonable to judge and compare the performance of economic systems by (i) the demands they generate, (ii) the supplies they produce, and (iii) the relations between the two.

But those are not the only things by which economic systems can be judged. Read on.

WELFARE

Economists have given this word two different meanings.

Welfare as in 'welfare state' is a common word for the money allowances and social services which modern governments provide for their citizens: pensions for the aged, the sick, the unemployed, widows, lone parents and others; child allowances, student allowances; health and educational and other services of many kinds. *The welfare bill* is a loose term for the whole cost of those provisions. *The welfare population* is a loose term for everybody living on one or other of those pensions. *The welfare state* sometimes means the governmental apparatus which supplies the welfare provisions; at other times it means the whole society of which the welfare provisions are a part. For the second meaning some think *the welfare society* is a better term.

But none of that is what *welfare economists* typically study. *Welfare economics* has traditionally meant the study of the general efficiency with which the economic system serves its members. Is it producing *as much as* it could, with existing productive resources? Is it producing what its members *most want*? Is it producing *the correct proportions* of the things people want?

Question: Could a smaller GNP possibly do more good – give the people more welfare – than a larger GNP? Could *less* goods and services per head be better than *more* goods and services?
Answer: Yes.
Question: How?
Answer: Suppose the smaller GNP consists entirely of correct proportions of the things people most desire, including nourishing food that is also good to eat; long-lasting household equipment; attractive, fashionable, well-made clothing; efficient public services where they are most needed; and so on. Meanwhile a neighboring country's bigger GNP includes dull, unhealthy food, less stylish and less durable household goods, ill-fitting shoes, last year's fashions; together with new reservoirs where there is no rain to fill them and new bus routes where nobody wants to travel.

By any test the second country's larger output is doing less good. It is not using its resources efficiently to supply what its citizens want. It is doing less than it could for their welfare. It could easily improve some people's fortunes without hurting others, or using any additional resources, simply by making shoes that fit instead of shoes that don't, and so on.

But any test of economic performance is a narrow test if it looks only at the supply of goods and services. An economic system affects people's welfare in more ways than that.

Changing measures of efficiency and welfare

Remember the account of selective causal analysis in Chapters 2 and 3. You can never trace all the effects of something as complicated as a modern economic system. Even among the effects which you *can* trace, you have to decide which you think are the most important, and what weight to give to each of them.

It used to be common to judge national economic performance chiefly by the size and growth of GNP. That made some sense back in the days when most people lived hard and poor, and the most important economic task was to raise basic standards of living to tolerable levels. A lot of the world is still in that condition, but the developed countries are not: they are rich enough now to allow all their people long life in secure comfort. If they fail to do that, it is from bad distribution, not from lack of productive capacity. Nearly a century ago the eminent economist Arthur Pigou was already arguing that insofar as welfare depended on income it depended not only on the amount of national income but also on its distribution, and its stability: on the shares people got, and their confidence that their incomes would continue.

But having achieved high productivity the developed countries are generating other troubles. Inflation. Pollution. Endangered species, exhaustible resources. Technological changes which threaten to cause rising unemployment. Population changes which threaten new conflicts between falling numbers of earners and rising numbers of pensioners. Policy changes which increase inequalities for the first time in more than a century. Drugs, boredom, new kinds of crime and disorder.

So even if it used to be sensible to judge the economy chiefly by the quantity of goods and services it produced, it may not be so sensible now.

Economic ingredients of welfare in rich countries

If you want to know what a rich country's economic system is contributing to the welfare of its people, it is reasonable to ask *at least* these questions:

- What GNP per head does the economy produce?

- What whole national product (GNP plus unpaid production) does the economy produce?

- How equally or unequally does it distribute wealth and income?

- On what principles are unequal shares distributed? Do wealth and high income mostly reward invention and enterprise and hard work? Or do they mostly reward tax avoidance, monopoly and lucky inheritance? What shares of income go to non-earners: old, sick, unemployed? Lone parents, widowed housewives? How good and how well distributed are the welfare services?

- What main economic conflicts are there? In those conflicts, how are political and economic strength and bargaining power distributed?

- How fair or unfair, happy or unhappy, are gender relations? What does their quality owe to the economic system?

- What does the economic system contribute to the people's desirable rights and freedoms? To their security from crime and domestic violence? To their protection from racist, pornographic, drug-peddling or other criminal incitements?

- Who own the mass media? How persuasive are they? What side(s) are they on?

- Is there full employment? Jobs for all competent workers? Part-time or casual work for those who want it?

- How wide and interesting is the variety of skills and occupations open to the people? Must most workers choose between (say) farm labor and mining guano, as in some island economies – or are there also opportunities for people who would like to be (say) violin makers, airline pilots, mathematicians, potters, safari guides, film directors, social workers, carpenters, programmers, dancers, advertising executives – even economists?

- Given the variety of occupations, is the work mostly as good as it could be – as safe, as interesting, as sociable, as satisfying as it could be? Are the proportions of dull, dirty and dangerous jobs as low as they could be? Is it easy to be independent and self-employed if you want to be? If you don't, how good or bad are industrial relations between employers and employees? How much industrial democracy or 'participant management' is there and how well is it working?

- How well is capital allocated between public and private and household production? Are there good, accessible, fairly distributed public services? Is capital available to the more efficient, productive, innovative public and private enterprises? Can households and other unpaid, voluntary or cooperative producers get the capital they need in order to be as productive as they are willing and able to be?

- How healthy and long-lived are the people?

- How well-educated are the people?

- How well – and for whose advantage – are the human settlements laid out? For example do people average long or short journeys to work, to services, to town or city centres? Do they have good access to outdoor and country recreations?

- What range and variety of recreations can people enjoy *without* spending much money?

- How good or bad is the economy's environmental management? How clean or dirty are the air and water? How prudent is the management of pesticides, herbicides, dangerous wastes? What conservation is there of wilderness, of species, of cohesive neighborhoods, of historically interesting buildings, precincts, landscapes?

- Hardest of all to judge: how good or bad are the relations between the society's economy and its culture? What patterns of demand does the economic system generate? What patterns of economic motivation does the culture encourage? How much activity is motivated by self-interest, how much by cooperative interest, how much by duty, generosity, fun? From the interaction of the economy and the culture, what quality of life do the people suffer or enjoy?

Could you measure all those effects, then add them up to make a measure or index of total welfare? Of course not. We are back where Part One began, with three kinds of uncertainty or disagreement:

Facts Many of those effects can't be measured. For example power, bargaining strength, conflicts of interest, and the quality of education are all *facts,* but very few of them can be precisely measured.

Causes There is room for a good deal of disagreement about what causes what. Many things on the list

are both causes and effects of the prevailing economic system. For example the media influence people's opinions (as critics allege) and also reflect those opinions (as media-owners allege). Neither effect can be precisely measured.

Values What do you define as 'goods' and 'bads' in assessing welfare? Especially when gains for some people mean losses for others? Many of that long list of economic effects could be counted as good or bad – i.e. as adding to welfare or reducing it – only by controversial value judgments.

We saw earlier that there can't be a purely objective measure of the general efficiency of an economic system. For similar reasons there can't be a purely objective measure of economic welfare. But judgments have to be made – to understand the system, to manage it, to conserve or improve it, to arrive at and act on the many collective decisions without which the system cannot work at all, or democratically. So there is work for your values as well as your skills.

CONCLUSIONS

Most of these chapters end with their own summaries. This one ends instead by summarizing some broad conclusions from all the work done so far.

1. Economists decide the scope and boundaries of their studies. They decide what to investigate, and what to take as given. They choose a working language: a set of identities, a pattern of wholes and parts whose relationships they will study.

2. Those choices can't be determined by the facts alone. They also have to be guided by economists' social values and purposes of study.

3. Economists with different values and purposes may choose to recognize different facts and qualities, and different wholes and parts, in the economic activity they study. For the different identities they recognize, they need different language. (There is usually also a good deal of common language, which all parties find it convenient to use.)

4. Economic beliefs and disagreements are working parts of economic life. To understand the working of economic systems you may often need to be 'multilingual'. You need to recognize which points of view, which values, which selections are built into the reports and expert opinions you hear. The language which individual economists choose to use can often tell you a lot about their purposes and the schools of thought they represent.

5. Like any other economic document, this course of study is shaped by its author's choices. There is an explanation of those choices in the next chapter. The text will use appropriate language for its purposes. But one purpose is to teach you some of the other languages of the marketplace. So these opening chapters have not recommended a definitive 'language of economics'. Instead they have introduced some common terms and some of their common meanings. And they have shown how different purposes of study, though equally truthful about facts, may often *need* different analytical methods, abstracting and simplifying different elements of economic life, breaking it down into different wholes and parts, naming some of them differently or giving their common names different meanings.

From now on it gets easier

Up to this point the chapters of Part One have described the confusing, conflicting, many-voiced nature of economics. They have deliberately heaped difficulty on difficulty. Conflicting interests and purposes. Conflicting values. Warring principles of selection. A babel of languages – things with alternative names, words with alternative meanings.

It was necessary to lead you this far into the confusion. Only if you understand its nature can you learn to cope with it.

But deep enough is far enough. Imagine you're wading across a wide, rough river. Step by step you go deeper into faster currents. Ankle-deep, knee-deep, waist-deep. But there comes a point where the river bed you're treading begins to rise again, the current eases, you're past half way and making your way up and out. Speaking of murder rather than methodology, Macbeth recognized the moment when he was –

> Stept in so far that, should I wade no more,
> Returning were as tedious as go o'er.

That is where you are now, fellow-worker. In philosophy up to your neck – but from now on you are on your way up and out. You know enough about the confusing nature of economics. Now you can start learning the skills you need to cope with it.

7

Skills and values you will need

What skills will you need? That may depend on what sort of work you want to do. There is work in business and government for types who like objective measuring and calculating and accounting. There is selective, analytical, controversial work for those who advise business, labor, government or independent movements and organizations in their policy-making, and their lobbying and bargaining activities. There is cross-cultural work – agonizing, sad-dening, heart-warming – in international aid. There is speculative work for economic theorists and philoso-phers. There is work for inventive people who can design new institutional forms and ways of doing things. There is plenty of work for teachers. In politics and journalism and broadcasting there is work for inves-tigators, good simplifiers, good writers.

So by all means go for the kind of work you like best, and concentrate on developing the particular skills you will need for it.

Here is a short list of some of the general kinds of skill and background knowledge you may need, depending on the kind of work you do:

Know the institutions

You need to know how economic activity is organized: the structure and rules and procedures of the relevant institutions, from government departments and transna-tional corporations all the way down to family farms, corner shops, households.

How much of that has to be learned on the job? How much can you learn in advance from books? How much from *this* book?

There are vast numbers of economic institutions and rules and regulations. Many are not described in books at all, except perhaps their own rulebooks or annual reports. If you need to know your local land zoning or clean air regulations, or the work of your local public housing agency or Egg Marketing Board, or the details of your Companies Act or consumer protection laws – then you need local knowledge, learned on the job.

There is more to read about major economic institu-tions. Specialist books and reports can tell you a lot about your country's departments of government, its central bank, its tariff and trade policies, its tax system,

its labor organization, and so on. There are many useful surveys, for example from the World Bank, the International Monetary Fund (IMF), the Bank of International Settlements (BIS), the United Nations (UN), the European Union (EU) and the Organization for Economic Cooperation and Development (OECD), which compare industries and economic institutions of different countries.

This course of study is for use in a number of coun-tries so it can't describe your national institutions in any detail. (It will sometimes list books that do so.) Instead it will sketch a range of institutional forms and rules which different countries and different industries have used at different times to organize their economic activ-ities. So when you come to study (say) your country's banking system, you must do it from local sources. But this book can help by outlining (1) the usual functions of the main types of banks, (2) the range of public and private ownership and control under which banks have operated at different times, and (3) main issues in cur-rent debates about the best structure and management of national banking systems.

Counting, measuring, sampling, monitoring

Most economics involves quantities, and you must learn to get them right. However good your reasoning or analysis may be, you will still go wrong if the basic facts and figures you are analysing are wrong.

In most economists' work, the way to get the quanti-ties right is to know what accounts are kept by business and government, where to find them, how reliable they are, and how to use them without mistakes.

Households, firms and government departments need to know for their own purposes what business they are doing. Households may not keep written accounts but business firms and government departments do. Many of their accounts have to be kept and published in forms specified by law. Some industries also have to make regular returns to government statistical offices. How many workers are unemployed this week? How much did banks lend this month? How many sheep went to slaughter this quarter? How many houses got built this year? Somewhere a government department is col-lecting regular returns from every firm and service concerned, and periodically totalling them. So depending on your field of work, you will learn your way around your national accounts, and the many statistical series published by the World Bank, the UN, the EU and the OECD.

Households don't keep such systematic accounts, and except for tax purposes governments don't demand regular reports from them. But their economic activity is important for many purposes. Economists have various ways of monitoring it. Where households deal with business or government, the business or government records may serve. Banks tell government daily totals of the deposits they have and the personal loans and housing loans they are making. Firms tell government their sales volumes. Public enterprises and services tell government what water and gas and power and welfare services they are supplying to households. And so on. Many totals of household activity can be calculated from those non-household sources.

But a lot of important household information does not come that way. It has to be gathered independently, directly from the households. How much of their own (unpaid) production are households doing? What goods and services are they producing? How do the people in the households share the work? How do they share the products? How do those household activities correlate with household income, and with the numbers, age, sex, education (etc.) of household members? For that sort of information it is usually necessary to conduct special-purpose surveys. The government surveys everyone every five or ten years in the census. But the census is infrequent, it is expensive, and it can't ask many of the innumerable household questions which researchers want answered for many purposes. So most household information has to come from sample surveys. Researchers ask questions of selected samples of the population – a few hundred for some purposes, thousands or hundreds of thousands for other purposes – and draw conclusions about the whole population which the samples represent.

In those and other fact-finding activities, try to develop the habit of finding your way to the *best* source of the facts and figures you need. Don't guess if you can look it up. Don't approximate if you can measure it exactly. Don't accept other people's totals and summaries as gospel – if in doubt, cross-check, replicate the calculations, and so on.

But also, use your common sense. Don't waste time niggling at details which don't matter for the purpose in hand. Does this paragraph contradict the last one, which said 'Get it *right*'? Yes and no. Good investigators

develop an experienced instinct for what to accept at face value and what to suspect, check, replicate. Some bit of the picture doesn't fit – or perhaps it fits *too* smoothly – and alarm bells ring. A great man in another discipline said 'What you need is an instinct for how it *could not* have happened.' Which line in the company accounts to question. Which total in the national accounts to break down into components. Which market survey looks odd enough for you to demand to see the original questionnaire. And so on. Textbooks can't teach this flair. You will discover you have it, or not, on the job. But the 'batteries of possibilities' which we will presently introduce may help you.

THE MAIN TASKS: INVESTIGATING, FORE-CASTING, PLANNING, ANALYSING, EXPLAINING

So far this chapter has been about fact-finding skills: knowing the institutions and their rules and procedures; measuring, monitoring, sampling the stocks and flows of money and goods; keeping accounts. That is the hard labor of knowing *what* is happening in the economic system. Most of it could be done without economists – though economists have designed many of the national accounts. Knowing how and why those facts are happening is harder.

1. You need to know what to look for. It helps to be aware of the range of possibilities: the alternative things that might be happening in given circumstances.

2. You need to understand the purposeful and selective nature of most economic argument and explanation.

3. You need to know what you yourself are doing: what factual knowledge, values and selections are shaping your economic understanding.

Part One of this course has introduced 2 and 3. You should be able to sort out the objective facts and figures, the controversial values and the purposeful selections in your own and other people's work. The chapters to come will exercise that skill again and again.

Item 1 – knowing where to look, and what to look for – is the next subject.

Batteries

I don't believe there is any single set of principles, or master-model of economic behavior, which can guide your investigations in all cases.

Instead, this course of study offers you a different device. You have read of doctors or detectives or other investigators applying 'a battery of tests'. This course will offer you batteries of possibilities, or of questions to ask, for a range of subjects.

You have met some of them already. On page 4, eleven uncertainties that may face an investor in new technology. On page 22, seven types of causal relation. On page 44, seven alternative ways of measuring national product. And so on.

Notice that the batteries list things of different kinds: alternative kinds of causation, alternative policies for governments to adopt, alternative methods of study. To indicate the range of batteries you will meet, and the variety of uses they are designed to serve, here is a double-decker: a battery of batteries:

- **Alternative principles of action** How people may perform particular tasks or behave in particular circumstances. *Example:* Firms have to price their products. In Chapter 34 you will find eight ways that private firms may do it; in Chapter 38 eleven ways that public firms may do it.

- **Alternative structures** Alternative ways of organizing particular economic activities. *Example:* In Chapter 28, alternative kinds of public, private, cooperative and unincorporated firms and associations.

- **Alternative strategies** Examples of alternative aims and 'policy packages' for national societies, governments, public and private firms, households, individuals.

- **Alternative tactics** Different ways of implementing public or private policies. *Examples:* In Chapter 17, alternative ways for governments to control pollution. In Chapters 33 and 34, alternative modes of competition between private firms.

- **Aids to causal analysis (1)** Likely effects to look out for in particular conditions, *Examples:* In Chapter 50, possible effects of rising interest rates on ten kinds of investments; in Chapter 51, a dozen likely effects of an under-regulated world capital market.

- **Aids to causal analysis (2)** Methods. *Examples:* On page 22 seven types of causal relation and causal knowledge. On pages 25–27 five irrational principles of selection which you should usually avoid when making selective causal analyses.

Lists like those can help you in a number of ways. They alert you to things to look for: forces which *may* be at work, effects which *may* follow. They alert you to risks, possibilities, alternative strategies and tactics. If you are designing an institution or a policy, they tell you some of the options the world has tried – the known ways and means of doing the kind of business you have in mind.

The 'batteries' are also meant to alert you to their own limitations. Most of them are open-ended. They do no more than list examples of the options or possibilities you may need to consider. They can rarely be complete, listing all possibilities. (Nobody can list in advance *all* the known ways of (say) stimulating investment, or *all* the effects that may follow from (say) a change in interest rates.) You need an education that alerts you to the range of likely effects – but also warns you to look beyond those likely effects for any unlikely ones. You should not usually predict in a dogmatic way. You must not let any 'battery of possibilities' *limit* what you look for. Whatever has happened in other cases, be alert for any local peculiarities in *your* case. Be inventive, where necessary. Be alert for any unusual or inventive behavior which may add one more to the possibilities.

Theory and practice, or education and experience?

This chapter is advising you to be an open-minded, observant, investigative kind of economist. One who can rarely predict or deduce what *must* be happening in the economic system, but who is quick and good at finding out what *is* happening, and at judging risks and possibilities.

This is controversial advice. To see why, consider two contrasting models of theory and practice – or education and experience.

A determinate science As in physics or engineering, *theory* states universal principles. It models basic forces and relationships which are thought to underlie and determine the apparent confusion and diversity of day-to-day life.

Armed with that sort of theory, *practice* has three elements. (1) You must learn how to identify and recognize those underlying forces. (2) You must learn about life's imperfections – i.e. how real life differs in detail from the theoretical model. (3) You can then use the theory to predict economic behavior. You can deduce what probably *is* happening and predict what probably *will* happen in the economy, and where necessary control it.

Thus some economists hope to use theory much as physicists or engineers do – though with some practical allowance for life's many imperfections.

A social science Others believe that much of the confusion and diversity of economic life is not just apparent, it is real. Economic activity is often irregular. It keeps changing. It has conflicts and uncertainties. Much of it is not determined by underlying forces of a reliably regular kind, so cannot be understood by the kind of theory that physicists or engineers use. Instead of that sort of theory, what you need is experienced skill. You have to know a great deal in a factual way. But you must also be able to adapt flexibly to changing facts, and cope with risks and conflicts and uncertainties, much as business people and politicians do.

Academic education can contribute three things to that sort of skill. (1) It can teach you to measure and count and calculate and keep accounts accurately. (2) It can substitute for experience by detailing many of the commoner variants of economic life, in 'batteries of possibilities'. (3) It can identify and describe many of the warring interests and values that contend in the economic arena. That can help you to understand *them*. And it can help you to sort out *your own* purposes, and arrive at coherent values to shape your work.

So in this 'social' model, theory chiefly does two things. It offers summaries of experience, as short cuts to help you to develop experienced skills. And it involves you in the great debates about social values and purposes, and the economic policies they call for.

This course of study offers more of that second, 'social' model than of the first. Less pure theory, more practical, adaptable skills. But as all these chapters have emphasized, economic skills can't be neutral. You need coherent purposes and principles of selection to shape your work, or the work will be incoherent. So what can teachers and textbooks do to help you develop coherent values?

WHOSE VALUES?

Your values are your own. That is part of the human condition. Glory in it, regret it, or be driven to distraction by it, but get used to it. It is inescapable.

You may apply your own values directly in your study and analysis of economic problems, in all the ways that have been described in these chapters.

Alternatively you may choose to draw your working values from one of at least two other sources.

You may work for clients, as a doctor or a lawyer does. In that case you may use the clients' values to shape your work. You choose language, questions, principles of selection and so on, with an eye to the interests and values of the corporation, or labor union, or newspaper, or poor people in poor countries, or whoever else you have chosen to work for. (Like a doctor or lawyer you may also insist on some professional values of your own. You may only deal in true facts, representative samples, honest arguments, etc.)

As a third alternative you may accept whatever values and principles of selection happen to be built into the theory and method of economics which you learned in class. You may do that consciously, if you recognize what those values are, and agree with them (or decide to act as if you do!). Or you may do it unconsciously, if you don't know they are there – i.e. if you make the mistake of thinking that the theory and method of economics which you were taught are neutral techniques, chosen without any reference to social values or purposes.

Except for that 'unconscious' case, for simplicity we can call all those alternatives *your* values, in that wherever they come from *you* choose to apply them in your work.

Reasoning about values

Some texts say your values are somehow 'given' and can't be improved by education – or not by your economic education. Any attempt to improve them would be a wanton interference with your democratic rights and personal independence. Or it would amount to preaching at you.

In that view, your values are not reasoned beliefs. They are emotions, desires or items of religious faith which have nothing to do with reason. You believe them or you don't. People with opposing values can merely assert them, or fight about them – there can be no useful reasoning about them.

Many philosophers, on the other hand, believe that rational discussion and reflection on your own and others' values are vital to your general education, the development of your own values, and your economic expertise. For at least these reasons:

- You need to know and understand other people's values. You will understand many economic arguments and analyses better if you know what values shaped them and what purposes they were designed to serve. You may also want to judge how *well* their values shaped them – i.e. how well or badly they serve their own purposes in a technical way.

- Understanding a wide range of values – which in practice means understanding the values of a wide variety of people – is an important aid to arriving at your own, and to criticizing and reconsidering your own values.

- For many reasons, both personal and professional, it can matter how coherent your values are. Do they fit together to allow a coherent view of life and social justice? Or do they trouble you with internal strains and contradictions? (Or are they full of contradictions which don't trouble you in the slightest bit – but which make you a chaotic character or an incoherent economist?)

Notice that your 'value set' can have two distinct kinds of incoherence. Your values may contradict one another in a direct logical way. (You are absolutely, categorically *against* (1) racism, (2) blacks, and (3) dogmatic attitudes.) Or they may conflict in a more indirect way, as follows.

- Values which don't contradict each other in a logical way may nevertheless have conflicting effects when they are applied in practical life. *Example:* Suppose you put high value on both economic equality and economic efficiency. You would like society to have more of both. Now consider two policies: (1) Faced with unemployment, your government increases welfare allowances to poor people in a way that has two effects: it makes society more equal, and by restoring effective demand and full employment it also improves economic efficiency. So your values 'fit' without conflict. But at the same time (2) the government cuts taxes on high income in the hope of improving investors' and managers' incentives to work efficiently. That increases *in*equality. Many of the people who value both equality and efficiency will recognize some practical conflict between the two, and simply decide (with more reference to their values) how much less of which is worth how much more of the other. That means they adjust their *policies.* But their *values* remain as before, favoring all the equality and efficiency they can get.

But to that same conflict of values, other people may respond differently. Suppose there are three researchers who all, to begin with, put the same high values on equality and efficiency. They face an incentives policy (cutting taxes on high incomes) which seems to put their values into conflict. They respond in three different ways –

- *The first researcher* is upset by such a conflict between two things she values highly. She decides to review the technical evidence for believing that such a conflict exists. She does some research (which you will meet later). It shows that tax cuts usually have no effect on the work of 80 per cent of the people concerned. They induce about 10 per cent to work longer hours, and they induce another 10 per cent or so to work shorter hours. The tax cuts are thus likely to have little or no net effect on efficiency.

The researcher's values have prompted her to look more carefully at the facts, and she is happy to find there is not much practical conflict between her chosen purposes after all.

- *The second researcher* is led to question the value he puts on equality and efficiency. He decides to investigate a sample of high earners to see what they actually do to deserve their high earnings. He chooses the city land-dealing and office-building industry. His researches show that it is a fairly anti-social industry – the more efficiently it prospers, the more urban congestion and pollution the citizens seem to suffer – so he revises the value he puts on individual and corporate efficiency. He also finds that the investors and their executives are into corruption and tax evasion like pigs at a trough. So he revises the value he puts on equality. He says 'I'm shocked at how much those sharks earn. We should double their taxes. I'm keener than ever for more equality.'

In this case, new facts have led the researcher to revise both his values.

- *The third researcher* likewise decides to see what high earners actually do to deserve their high earnings. But she goes to a different industry, and the facts she finds there lead her to different conclusions. She says 'I'm shocked at how little we pay our medical researchers. Their talents are rare and valuable. Their work lengthens life and reduces suffering for countless millions of people – but they earn less than many of the doctors who use their discoveries. Their work is vital, but it can't be for the money that they do it – most of them could earn more in medical practice or other occupations. Tax cuts won't affect their work. But they deserve higher pay as a matter of justice. I now favor more inequality than I did – we *ought* to pay high incomes to our best and most productive people.'

Once again the facts have led the researcher to change her values – though this time in a different direction.

Educating your values

Those examples illustrate a fundamental relation between facts and values, in daily life as well as in economic science. People's values help to shape their selective understanding of the world. In turn, that factual understanding prompts them to review and refine their values. Revised values then select and shape revised views of the facts ... and so on. It is a continuous process of mutual criticism.

So how can this course of study help you to educate your values?

The text will draw your attention, again and again on subject after subject, to the purposes which shape particular analyses, and to the types of analysis which serve particular purposes best. There will be exercises to develop and test your skill at perceiving those connections yourself.

In fields where *persuasion* is a main method of economic action, we will see how statistics, selective causal analysis, and other ways of 'arranging the facts' can be shaped to persuade people. Sometimes it is done honestly, sometimes dishonestly. Sometimes the persuasion is aimed at moving people's feelings and values. Sometimes it tries to shape their understanding of the facts and causal relations. You need to perceive what is going on in those debates. You will be offered plenty of examples, and exercises.

On many subjects, the text will outline policy debates. It will then help you to analyse them, sorting out the self-interests, the social values and purposes, the selective principles and the factual beliefs of the contending parties.

Now and then, especially towards the end of the course in Part Six, you will be asked to consider some key values quite directly. Which freedoms do you value most, and why? Which equalities? Which principles of social justice do you think are best? Now that you know how wealth and income and work and opportunity *are* distributed in your society, how do you think they *ought* to be distributed?

To be a useful economist, you have to see that the value judgments which select and shape your questions and analyses and explanations are coherent. So you need to keep your values and purposes out in the daylight, open to criticism and review – by you, by others, and by the facts you find. *You won't know what you are doing* if you don't know the part your values play in doing it. So debating the rights and wrongs of economic life, and the values and ethical beliefs by which you judge those rights and wrongs, will not be a waste of your time. I believe it is a vital part of your economic education.

Students' and teachers' values

You are learning a controversial, value-structured subject. How can *your* values direct your work if a teacher's values have shaped your course of study?

As a student your main business is to develop skills. That means learning to think and to do things, rather than remembering the contents of textbooks. Unfortunately, encouraged by mass methods of teaching, too many students spend too much time reading books and hearing lectures and too little time exercising their skills: solving problems, researching, writing. Teachers should certainly lead you to good sources of the book-learning you need. But their main business should be like teaching (say) driving, or clinical medicine. They should show you how to do things. They should set tasks for you. They should study how you do the exercises – and analyse, criticize, educate and encourage the skill with which you do them.

That calls for some individual tuition. I hope you are getting it. No lectures or textbooks can substitute for it. Do your assignments come back with bare marks on them? No useful comments, no chance to discuss them with your instructor? If that is happening, find out how many assignments she has to attend to each year. If it is less than a couple of hundred, complain that you are being neglected. If spurned, think about organizing. But if she is genuinely overworked, forgive her: some institutions and some of the governments which under-fund them make good teaching too hard.

Discrimination? Some professional readers who advised against publishing this book complained that its old-fashioned idea of individual tutorial attention to students' work is impractical and out of date.

Even in economics it is not out of date in the best universities. In rich countries it is nowhere out of date in the teaching of skills which people think actually matter. Medical schools make their students watch, and do, more clinical work than ever, all of it under individual supervision. Poor law schools don't, but the best law schools do, give plenty of individual attention to students' assignments and moot practice. Good schools of engineering, architecture, painting, sculpture, music, drama and dance likewise attend regularly or continuously to the quality of their individual students' work. Those are skills which respectable universities treat with respect, because poor performance is either dangerous to life, or visible and open to hurtful professional and public criticism. So as the numbers in tertiary education rise and their funding per head declines, the cuts tend to come disproportionately from the quality of teaching in the humanities and social sciences.

It may be true, though no excuse, that bad education in sociology or English literature kills fewer people than incompetent physicians or surgeons might kill. But the directions of much neoclassical economic theory and of much national and international economic policy through the last twenty years have contributed to absolute poverty and death in some poor countries, and relative poverty and insecurity in rich countries, on a scale to rival any effects of poor doctoring or engineering.

Economists can do great good or harm to the world. Their skills and values matter, and are intrinsically controversial. They need as much hands-on practice and individual criticism and guidance as apprentices to other dangerous professions do.

Power sharing? Whatever the method of teaching, whose values should determine what you learn to do and how you do it – yours or your teachers'?

The answer has to be some of both.

You can't avoid *some* elements of 'teacher in command'. Teachers have to define tasks, decide criteria of assessment, impose standards of accuracy and honesty. More important, they have to educate your skills. Every time you finish an assignment your teacher has to judge the skill, style, economy, balance, perception and originality with which you have worked. She can't judge those qualities in a purely technical way. She has to mix technical and value judgements all the time.

So teachers can't help applying some values of their own in their efforts to develop students' skills. What they *can* do is to put a high value on their students' independence and self-determination. I want my students to get what *they* want, to develop in directions *they* choose, to become efficient agents of *their* social purposes. (Within limits, of course. If they want to learn to cheat and deceive, or restore eighteenth-century inequalities, they can go to some other shop.)

A competent teacher in a controversial social science should be able to tell an excellent conservative essay or analysis from a poor one, and mark them accordingly. She should be equally able to tell an excellent Marxist exercise from a poor one, an excellent feminist exercise from a poor one, an excellent employers' case from a poor one – and so on. She should be willing and able to judge how well a student's work is serving that student's values and purposes. Those judgments are not always easy and they are often controversial. But that is what teachers in a free society should try for.

It requires that teachers and students know what they are doing. An inexcusable number of academic social scientists are still teaching as 'objective fact' or as 'purely technical theory and analysis' beliefs and methods which are shaped throughout by concealed or unconscious values. When that happens, teachers think they are disciplining students to use rigorous methods

correctly when they are actually disciplining them to accept quite controversial, value-structured ideologies.

If you meet that sort of brainwashing you are entitled to resist it.

But watch it, fellow worker. Don't use this line of argument as a routine excuse for bad work. When your instructor tells you what is wrong with your work that earned it a 'D', don't assume that he is just expressing his reactionary values.

And don't expect too much. As a teacher I respect your values and encourage your independence. But my values inevitably shape a lot of my efforts to help you. I have to ask you questions, set you tasks, suggest sources and methods you might use. I can't leave all that to you – you would be ignorant or unadventurous at some of it. I am useful *because* I can challenge you in ways you might not have discovered for yourself: because I can analyse and criticize your work from other points of view than your own.

The relations between students' and teachers' values should ideally be like their personal relations: considerate, sympathetic, generous. But they can't always be perfect. When they are not, reflect that there is safety in numbers. You need not get all your education from one teacher. Do your best to see that you don't get it all from one school of thought either, or from one discipline.

Author's values

As for teachers, so for textbooks. What values are shaping this textbook and the course of study it offers?

You are certainly entitled to know. But you should not really need to ask. If you have learned what these seven chapters have tried to teach you, the values which helped to select and arrange what you are reading should be plain to your educated eye, page by page as you go.

But you are entitled to a 'declaration of values' by the author, so here it is, in four parts:

Motherhood values I am for peace rather than war, and cooperation wherever possible. (But freedom sometimes has to be fought for, and competition works better than cooperation for some purposes.) I am for democracy, free speech and assembly, due process of law, the standard civil liberties. I value opportunities for personal diversity, individuality and self-expression; so I value a shared culture which encourages *individual* difference and non-conformity. The more the big bureaucracies of business and government can be humanized, the better: small is beautiful wherever it works well. One place it needs to work well is the household. Households not only do a third or more of economic production. They also do a lot to shape the character, skills and moralities of the children they bring up. Their resources for the task are important, and have been unduly neglected by most economists. But although upbringing is important, childhood should not be treated merely as a preparation for adult life. It can be a good, bad or indifferent experience in itself, and economic policies can have important effects on it. Young or old, each year of life should have equal value.

Economic concerns I am for more equality within and between nations, more satisfying work, more active recreations, and less 'consumerist' brainwashing than we have now. For all who want to earn – and for some though by no means all who don't – earned incomes are better than doles. If changing conditions call for radical kinds of work-creation and work-sharing, we should work hard to provide them.

We should be thoughtful about the directions of economic development: about what we produce as well as how we distribute it. In rich countries at least three values conflict with any policy of undiscriminating market-directed 'growth regardless'. There are severe resource and environmental problems. There are gross international inequalities which call for various kinds of restraint in the rich countries, and intelligent international aid. And there is mounting evidence that the rich countries have now passed the threshold above which more material income does not increase the sum of human happiness. Materially those societies now have more to gain by better distribution than by further growth. Socially most of their people have more to gain by secure employment in good company than by any addition to national output that is expected (rightly or wrongly) to be won by turning rising numbers of them into increasingly anxious competitors for increasingly insecure jobs.

Capitalism or socialism? Are these capitalist or socialist values? I think that is a wrong question. Developed modern economies are mixed economies in at least four senses:

• They mix public and private and cooperative and household *ownership* of the means of production.

• They mix public and private and cooperative and household *work* in the processes of production.

• To distribute wealth and income and goods and services, they mix market methods, administrative distribution, and household and cooperative and voluntary distribution.

• The fourth 'mixture' deserves a heading of its own:

Human nature and culture All those institutions run on mixtures of motive: desires for money, power, security, respect, love, and other people's welfare; individual gain, class gain, mutual service, self-sacrifice; national, racial, religious, corporate, family and other loyalties. Hear Andrew Graham, who spent many years in the Prime Minister's economic policy unit at 10 Downing Street and rose to lead it, reflecting on the mistakes of his successors there:

> There always is a social element to people's behavior as well as an economic element. The extent to which individuals are partly motivated by economic incentives, and partly by social commitments, social obligations, loyalty to institutions and obligations to others, is extremely important and is a factor that was greatly underestimated in the whole shift towards the market-oriented economy in the late 1980s. You can see this mistake most dramatically in areas of the public sector – nursing, education, police – where people go into these professions partly out of commitment to the activities themselves. Yet in the 1980s people in these jobs have been almost attacked for having such a commitment. Indeed they have been regarded as stupid if they didn't quite respond as economists wanted them to, for example to performance-related pay or to greater inequality in the distribution of income. What we have seen is people acting in ways that many economists find surprising – though of course they ought not to have been surprised. As a result, the market-oriented reforms haven't worked anything like as well as people who advocated them expected.

– Reported in Michael Kandiah and Anthony Seldon (eds), *Ideas and Think-Tanks in Contemporary Britain* (1996)

No economic system could possibly run on universal selfishness. Nor on universal duty, universal love, or any other single motive. And debating the mix of types of ownership and motivation, trying to improve it, and adapting it to changing conditions, are central concerns of economic policy. (Should we nationalize this industry? Privatize that one? Try public/private competition in this third one? Pay doctors by the year, by the number of patients, or by the unit of service? Re-distribute the care of handicapped people between home, local services and public institutions? Replace commercial blood-banks by voluntary ones? Pay parents for parenting – or only pay poor parents or sole parents for parenting? And so on.) So I think economists should be attentive students of the changing mixtures of motivation, and the alternative patterns of incentive, on which economic institutions can actually run.

It was impractical to expect that a socialist economy could run efficiently on one type of ownership, with a limited range of cooperative, dutiful or obedient motivation. It was equally mistaken to build Western economic theories on the assumption that 'economic man' always acts with single-minded selfishness and that it is socially efficient for him to do so. In fact twentieth-century capitalist development was accompanied by increasingly generous welfare provisions, and a steady shift of economic activity out of profit-seeking ownership into the public and household sectors. Within the private capitalist sector, moreover, many successful firms have found that good human relations can be as important as money in motivating good work; and the more competitive a firm wants to be, the more cooperative with the firm and with one another it may need its workers to be.

Similarly in the structures of mixed economies there is continual experiment and change in the distribution of work to the public and private sectors, to independent institutions and to households. Some public services are owned and managed by public agencies, some are owned and managed by franchised private firms, some are publicly owned and privately managed. Some public hospitals have private wards for some fee-paying patients, some private hospitals serve public patients financed by Medicare. Government pays some households to care for their infirm members. Independent universities are financed by mixtures of government grant, private endowment, contract research, patented discoveries, and student fees. Private contractors compete to build public buildings. Public and private generators compete to feed power into the national grid. And so on.

So in place of any dominant capitalist or socialist assumptions, this course of study aims to equip you to understand the intricate working relations between the public, private, independent and household sectors of mixed economies, and – in the light of your social values and technical understanding – to be an effective critic, defender or improver of the mix.

You can fool some of the people all the time, and all the people some of the time ... Writing a textbook as long as this one is grinding hard work. Since I already earn more income than I need, why bother? Here is a personal explanation:

I work part-time in various policy-making branches of government. They employ some excellent econo-mists. But also, some bad ones. As representative samples, I have heard economists pressing the following beliefs, often successfully, on business and government and sometimes on organized labor:

- Monetary restraint alone will stop inflation and then revive employment – *in conditions in which it won't do either.*
- Reducing public investment will increase private investment – *when in fact it will reduce private investment.*
- Free trade and exchange will make our manufacturers efficient – *when in our particular circumstances it will put too many of them out of business, increase long-term unemployment, and wreck our balance of payments.*
- Cutting wages would increase employment – *when it would not.*
- Shifting taxes off the rich onto the poor will induce the rich to employ more of the poor – *which it will not.*
- A freer capital market will allow more people to buy their houses – *when in fact it will allow fewer people to buy their houses.*
- Rent controls always hurt tenants – *when in many circumstances they can greatly help tenants.*

In all those cases, in my opinion, people have been fooled by mistaken or misused economic theories. Beliefs are working parts of economic systems, and some of those mistakes have had cruel human costs. Poor people stay poor, willing workers can't get work, productive capacities lie idle. Landlords get needlessly richer (which does not lead them to improve the supply of cheap rental housing). Politicians march fearlessly in wrong directions.

Most of the mistakes are not ignorant laymen's mistakes, they are professional economists' mistakes. It is maddening to watch. It drives some experienced hands to drink, it drives others to write textbooks. Whatever your values, the overriding purpose of this course of study is to help you to be a *competent* economist: to know what you are doing, who you are doing it for, who it may help and who it may hurt.

SUMMARY

1. You will need to know the structure and function and working rules of many economic institutions. You may often have to learn about them from local sources, or on the job.

2. Learn to get quantities right – by careful research, observation, counting, calculating, etc. (But never assume that what you cannot count does not count, or matters less than the measurable elements of the situation.)

3. Learn how households, firms, governments and others keep their accounts; where to find the accessible accounts; and what can and cannot be derived from them. (They have many traps for the unwary.)

4. You may need some statistical training, especially if you want to work at economic sampling and surveying, or use others' surveys competently.

5. The skills you need in order to find, analyse and explain what causes what in economic life are too complicated to summarize. Among other aids, this text will offer, on many subjects, 'batteries of possibilities' to look for. Working experience will further extend the range of things you are alert to notice and investigate. Deductive master-theories have limited uses. You more often need theory that summarizes experience and improves investigative skills.

6. Much of your work will have to be selective. Your principles of selection have to relate both to the nature of the facts and to your social philosophy and working purposes which for simplicity we have called values. To guide your selections you can use your own values, or your clients' values, or (as long as you know what you are doing) the values which one or another school of economic thought has built into its professional language and methods.

7. Because values and conflicts about them have the force they do in both economic life and economic analysis, your professional education should include a good deal of discussion, comparison and interrelation of values: how different values fit or don't fit with one another; how your values and your understanding of economic processes can affect each other and respond to each other; how particular sets of values work out when they are applied in economic policy and practice; and what your own values and purposes prompt you to accept and reject from the offerings of teachers and textbooks.

Part Two

ECONOMIC GROWTH AND CHANGE

8

Understanding growth and change

There was a time – before people learned to farm, before the axe or the wheel, before the steam engine or the computer – when by our modern standards *all* humans were poor.

Today a billion or more are still poor, with a bare minimum of food and shelter and next to no formal education or health care, averaging 50 years or less of life.

A billion are climbing out of the worst poverty.

Perhaps two billion live in frugal comfort.

And a billion or so are now comparatively rich: well fed and housed and educated, with powered services, worldwide communications and rich and varied recreations, averaging more than 70 years of life.

By processes of economic growth, history has thus produced gross differences between rich and poor countries, and also large inequalities within most countries. The wealth and inequalities are vital facts of modern life, and also the root of many of its conflicts. So here begin eleven chapters about past, present and future economic growth and change. *Past:* How the richer countries of the world have developed their high productivity. *Present:* How poorer countries are developing their economies, or trying to. *Future:* What options may be opened to choice in future economic development, especially in the rich countries which have no pathfinders to follow.

Why study growth first?

Why study economic growth so early in your course? Why learn how systems *change* before you learn how systems *work*? Two reasons:

Skill The skill you need as an economist is skill at understanding changing systems. Before you start learning methods of detailed analysis, it is important to grasp that the systems you analyse may be changing as you study them. (Many of their members will certainly be *trying* to change them, in various directions with varying success.) You need to be aware of the processes of change and alert to adapt your methods to them.

Judgment 'Judgment' is what you need for tasks and problems which are partly measurable and predictable and partly not. Recall the perils of the mousetrap business – economic life is full of problems which mix some certainties or probabilities with some *un*certainties. You need to recognize which of those elements are which.

That calls for mixtures of knowledge, skill, choice and guesswork – and the wider your knowledge of diverse systems and their problems, the better your judgment may be.

Knowledge of past times and other systems is a kind of extended experience. It can help you to recognize what is local or changeable in your economic system, and what is universal and perhaps permanent. Two examples:

Institutional alternatives Suppose your rich mixed economy happens to have private banks and public airlines. Do you conclude that it is in the nature of banks to be privately owned, and of airlines to be publicly owned? Or has experience proved that those are always the best forms of ownership for them? Or could you just as well have efficient *public* banks and *private* airlines? If your experience is broad you will know that the world has efficient public banks, efficient private banks, efficient public airlines and efficient private airlines. Also inefficient examples of all four. Knowing what works in other systems may not prove what will work best in your system, but it can improve your judgment of the possibilities.

Theoretical expectations An example of which you will be reminded a number of times in this course: In 1974 industrial countries suddenly had to pay sharply increased prices for their oil imports, which had the effect of raising many other prices. British workers responded by pushing up their money wages, which fuelled inflation. German workers did not. Should British economists conclude that import price changes *automatically* cause widespread wage changes? Should German economists conclude that they don't? If each knows about the other's history they are more likely to see those responses as workers' *choices*, conditioned by the workers' particular historical experience and beliefs – and perhaps capable of changing in response to further experience or education.

To summarize: You study the history and diversity of economic systems early in your course to learn something about (1) what has been common to most economic systems, (2) what has differed from system to system, and (3) how systems grow and change. Those lessons should help you to judge which methods of analysis to apply to which tasks. They should make you wary of unduly rigid theories and models, and alert to adapt your methods to local conditions and to changing economic organization and behavior.

Growth of what?

In Chapter 5 you met disagreements about what should count as economic output, and therefore as national product: Marketable goods and services? Plus household and other Do-It-Yourself production? Minus pollution and clean-up costs?

It is not only the measures that vary. National economies vary greatly not only in the rates at which they grow but also in the industries which they develop, the material goods and services which they offer their people, and the equalities and inequalities and the experience of work and social life which they offer. The economists who created the Human Development Index enjoyed contrasting its ranking of the world's national economies with the order in which GNP ranked them. Table 8.1 adapts an example from the 1994 United Nations *Human Development Report*.

PATHS or MODELS or HISTORIES OF GROWTH?

Path Should you look for some regular stages of economic growth, as the usual or only path from

national poverty to w

Model Should you try regular dynamics of grow forces *make* it happen?

History What if different forces n ently in different countries at diff economic growth may have to be un tailed research and historical explanation

We can imagine a world in which there n conflict between those three approaches. S there was only one workable path of economic gr You could learn that path. Suppose that regu dynamic forces, the same in every case, make economic systems grow in that particular way. You could model those forces. But suppose that nations had different local conditions and resources, which determined whether and when and how strongly those 'regular dynamic forces' would operate. Local conditions would thus allow some national economics to grow quickly, some more slowly, and some not at all. Then you would need historical explanations to explain how far forward or backward each nation was, along the regular path of growth.

So in that imaginary world, *history* would tell you when and why certain *regular forces* caused particular countries to grow at particular rates through the *regular*

Country	GNP per capita (US$)	HDI value (Best = 1)	HDI rank (in world)	Life expectancy (years)	Adult literacy (%)	Baby deaths (per 1000 live births)
GNP per capita around $400 to $500						
Sri Lanka	500	0.665	90	71.2	89	24
Nicaragua	400	0.583	106	65.4	78	53
Pakistan	400	0.393	132	58.3	36	99
Guinea	500	0.191	173	43.9	27	135
GNP per capita around $2,300 to $2,600						
Chile	2,360	0.848	38	71.9	94	17
Malaysia	2,520	0.794	57	70.4	80	14
South Africa	2,540	0.650	93	62.2	80	53
Iraq	2,550	0.614	100	65.7	63	59

Table 8.1 Similar income (GNP), different human development index (HDI), 1991/92

The Human Development Index is criticized for some faulty fact-finding, but corrections might not much reduce the overall scale of differences between countries with similar money incomes.

real world
ny different
nas been no
st as history
should make
possible paths
societies with
are likely to be
d technological
y under govern-
fferent strategies.
owth continuously
uccessful national
conditions and the
... which the next modernization
.. attempted. Trying to become the first or
second country in the world to produce steel or atomic
energy is a very different task from trying to become the
twentieth or thirtieth country to produce such things.
Economic growth is history – at least *partly* unique in
each historical era, and in each national case.

Models that work and models that don't

So you can't know all about economic development by
learning one dynamic model and one historical path.

But that does not mean that all talk of paths and
models is nonsense. A particular country at a particular
time may well find itself developing in a particular way,
with forces at work which it makes sense for economists
to model. It may *find* itself on such a path – or it may try
to *set* itself on a chosen path.

Many modern governments have development
strategies. They plan related patterns of saving and
spending, research and education, public and private
investment, free and regulated trade. They decide what
economic activity to manage and what to leave to
market forces, with the purpose of developing the
national economy in particular directions. To know
what they are doing and to give effect to their plans – to
pull the right levers, to get the quantities right – their
economists may do their best to model the complicated
forces which they are trying, directly and indirectly, to
manipulate.

In *Income Distribution, Inflation and Growth:
Lectures on structuralist macroeconomic theory* (1991)
and *The Rocky Road to Reform: Adjustment, income
distribution and growth in the developing world* (1993)
Lance Taylor explores the mathematical modelling not
of general principles of growth but of individual countries' unique conditions and development strategies.

Even with those he finds that there are commonly *some*
conditions and processes which can't usefully be
modelled: only institutional description and historical
explanation can represent them properly. Those are
good books. If you like maths, make time to read
Income Distribution, Inflation and Growth; if not, try to
read at least Taylor's chapters and some of the case
studies in *The Rocky Road*.

Thus to understand and act on the forces at work *in a
particular economic system at a particular time* it may
often be useful to model them in some way. But it is
important to remember how specific such models are
likely to be to particular times and conditions.
Otherwise you may mistake particular models for
general truths, and try to apply them in conditions they
don't fit. What happens then? In case you don't know it
already, hear the tale of Epaminondas.

Epaminondas was a little boy whose mammy went
out to work each day. One morning she told him to
go to a farm while she was at work, and fetch half a
dozen eggs. He stuffed the eggs in his pockets and
got home with no whole eggs and his pants in a
terrible mess.

'That's no way to carry them' his mammy said.
'You should carry them carefully in a string bag.'

Next day she sent him for a pound of farm butter.
It was a hot day and the butter all melted and ran out
of the string bag he carried it in.

'Idiot' said his mammy, 'you should have cooled
it under water in the stream, then brought it home
wrapped in wet leaves.'

Next day he heard that his aunt had a puppy for
him. He wrapped it in wet leaves and cooled it in the
stream and drowned the poor thing.

'You should have tied a string around its neck and
led it along behind you' his mammy said.

Next day she sent him to the butcher for a leg of
mutton. He tied a string around it and dragged it
home, followed by most of the neighborhood's dogs.
What was left of it wasn't worth roasting so she
made it into pies and set them out on the doorstep to
cool. Before she went out she warned him – 'Mind
how you step on those pies, now.' So he took care to
step on every one of them.

Epaminondas was applying models to tasks and conditions which they did not fit. Notice *three* ways models
can mislead:

- The model may be wrong in the first place. For
  example wrapping it in wet leaves may actually be a
  bad way to carry butter.

- Conditions may change. Even if wet leaves was a good method once, the streams are polluted nowadays, and refrigeration and plastic bags are available. The wet-leaves model is *outmoded*.

- You may apply models to wrong tasks or in wrong conditions, as Epaminondas did.

There is a sense in which every attempt to repeat an historical success or to learn by example is making a model of a particular case or series of similar cases. To illustrate, and to help you remember the point, we can translate the old fable into (equally fanciful) economic terms. Imagine that Epaminondas grows up and becomes first Prime Minister of a new African nation when it becomes independent of British colonial rule. He wants to induce economic growth in his uneducated, unskilled, undeveloped country. His British colonial education has taught him that back in the 1770s some Britons invented ways of making cloth with simple steam-powered machinery which could mostly be fed and minded by uneducated, unskilled workers. The machinery multiplied the output of the average textile worker by 5 or 10, which contributed handsomely to British economic growth. 'That's how the British started on their way to wealth when *they* were comparatively poor and uneducated' says Epaminondas two hundred years later; 'that's the model to put us on that same path.' So he goes looking for engineers who can build steam engines to those old 1770 designs.

You can see what is wrong with that plan. The 1780 model won't work in the changed conditions of 1980. If the cloth is for export, or to compete with imported cloths in an unprotected home market, a deliberately antique industry can't compete with other nations' modern machinery and skilled workers. Even if the cloth is for a protected home market, there are now better easy-to-use machines than those old museum pieces.

You may think that fictitious example is far-fetched. But something like that 'wrong model choice' did occur in the competitive national development of the nineteenth century. There is a fuller account of it in Chapter 11; here, a brief note will do.

A British mistake

Britain developed the first effective steam-powered machinery in the 1780s, and quickly forged ahead to become 'the workshop of the world'. But some features of that early success misled British governments and economists for the best part of a century afterwards. First, they had an effective monopoly of the new machinery for a generation or more – so if they used it inefficiently it didn't matter too much, there being few competitors. Second, it happened that most of the scientists and engineers who invented the machinery had been educated, and done their research, in schools and universities which were not financed by government. Third, the tradesmen who maintained the new machinery and the foremen who managed the factories were practical men trained on the job, and most of the workers had little or no education and needed less skill than the handicraft workers they replaced. So the world's first industrial revolution *seemed* to show that –

- technological revolutions come without government aid; and

- the higher the technology, the less skill the workers need.

Thinking they had a winning model, British governments accordingly adopted economic policies of free trade and small government. They provided no public primary education until the 1870s, no technical or commercial education until the twentieth century, no publicly funded scientific or industrial research. (And the upper-class minorities who *were* highly educated tended to avoid manufacturing industry and make careers in finance or trade or government instead.)

Intelligent competitors

German and American business and government leaders saw that the model of 'higher technology with lower skills' had worked for a country with a monopoly of the steam engine in 1780, but it was likely to be a wrong model for the technical and competitive conditions of 1880. Accordingly German and American governments, including state and local governments, soon forged ahead of the British in providing universal schooling, and higher education and research in technical colleges and institutes. With those public aids German and American firms, rather than British, led the next round of industrial development with science-based and highly-skilled revolutions in the chemical, metallurgical, optical and electrical industries. Instead of copying a *past* model of economic growth, they had reasoned their way to an inventive new model.

Changing conditions

That new model in its turn may be outmoded. Consider: most of the countries which are now rich have contrived industrial revolutions. At some stage of their development they have created the mills and factories to manufacture ships, machinery, rails and rolling stock for railways, cars, refrigerators and washing machines, textiles, paper, tools and kitchen gear and mousetraps. Many of those productions use steel. So early in their industrial development most of those countries built steel mills. For a century or two, to about 1970, factory industry seemed to be the great producer and employer for developing countries, and the base for industrial development was the capacity to produce steel.

But since then, three things have changed. (1) The development of computers and robots means that manufacturing employs fewer and fewer people; (2) plastics and other metals have replaced steel for some purposes; so (3) there is a glut of steel. The world has built more steel mills than it needs, so that many mills are running below capacity, losing money and cutting prices so that a developing country can import cheaper steel than it can hope to make for itself.

So *now*, if a poor peasant country is trying to develop its economy early in the twenty first century, should it set out to employ a third or more of its workers in manufacturing, as used to be possible? Should it begin that development by building steel mills? Those industries can be more productive than ever, but their modern forms employ fewer and fewer people. How will the rest of the people earn income to buy the output of the factories? In short, will one more old-style industrial revolution produce one more comfortably rich country like (say) France or Canada – or in today's changing conditions, might it produce a disaster worthy of Epaminondas?

The folly of Epaminondas or the wisdom of experience?

This chapter seems to be contradicting itself. First it urged you to understand economic growth by studying as many historical cases as you can. Then the Epaminondas fable told you to distrust that sort of experience as a guide to action: models from past times and other systems are unlikely to work in your present time and place.

Which to believe? Is experience a good guide? Or does it mislead you into making 'model mistakes' – melting the butter, drowning the puppy, or building more bankrupt steel mills in a world with too many steel mills already?

Experience is generally the best guide.

Models of growth are necessarily selective, like most other statements of economic cause and effect. They cannot state all the conditions which have to be present for their specified cause(s) to have their intended effect(s). The best defence against misusing them –

against letting them shape business strategies or government policies in conditions in which they won't work as intended – is experience of similar problems. That may be personal experience, but a lot of it is likely to be other people's experience which you learn about by listening, reading and research. What initiatives are firms or governments currently taking in the relevant field, with what success or failure? What efforts have succeeded or failed in the past, in your own or other countries, in what conditions, for what reasons? Knowing about others' experience extends your capacity to notice the traps and complexities of your own situation, and to judge how best to cope with them.

CONCLUSIONS

1. Economic growth is not a regular progress along a regular path propelled by a few easily-modelled dynamic forces. Growth is history, and like other processes of historical change it is likely to be somewhat different every time. It has to be understood by selective causal explanation each time – but the explanations may well show universal as well as local factors at work, with similarities as well as differences between growth at different times and in different countries.

2. The better you understand the complicated nature of the processes of economic growth – processes which include physical operations, quantitative flows and accumulations, social conflict and cooperation, institutional arrangements, patterns of belief and culture, etc. – the better you are likely to be at judging which factors and conditions are the important ones for the purposes you have in mind in your particular historical circumstances.

3. The more case histories you know, the more you know of the actual variety of past and present patterns of growth and change, the better you are likely to be (if you are bright) at judging development possibilities, and at choosing strategies to fit the relevant conditions, rather than (like Epaminondas) strategies which don't fit and won't work.

The following chapters will try those last two approaches in turn. Chapters 9 and 10 are about the *general* wisdom which economists have tried to distil from recent experience of economic development: experience which has driven them from simple models which tried to explain growth as a product of a very few factors (saving, investment, technology) to more and more comprehensive historical explanations. Chapter 11 uses particular case histories to illustrate a variety of different 'ways to wealth' in the development of countries that are now rich. The remaining chapters of Part Two are then about some problems of *future* development which are likely to arise from historical changes which are in process *now*.

A book to read Instead of exercises to end this chapter, I suggest you read a great book. W. Arthur Lewis wrote his *Theory of Economic Growth* more than 40 years ago. In some respects it has dated, but it has not been bettered. Some of the policies which looked promising then have since proved disappointing; and the growth which Lewis set out to explain was the narrow effect of growth of GNP per head. But there is nothing narrow about his guide to the conditions which *can* affect economic growth: conditions which range from population and physical resources through forms of political and economic organization to patterns of belief, culture, motivation and morality. The book is two classics at once: a classic of economic theory, and a classic of historical explanation. It is beautifully written in plain language anyone can understand. Make time to read it now, if you can.

9

Theories of economic growth

The last chapter insisted (and Chapter 11's case histories will illustrate) that the nations of the world do not have identical economic histories.

Nevertheless generations of economists have searched for regular causes of growth and tried to model them. Most of the simple theories of growth that have attracted notice have focused on a few genuinely necessary conditions of growth – but claimed too much for those few. You have met that way of thinking before. Remember the rival explanations of inflation, back in Chapter 3? Four theorists with different social purposes each selected a different contributing cause of inflation and treated it as the main cause, and the one which government should manipulate if it wanted to control inflation.

Many theories of economic growth have had that character. They select a few genuinely relevant conditions of economic growth – and neglect a lot of other, equally necessary conditions including the variable factors which account for the many differences between national histories of growth. They say, for example, that growth is sufficiently caused by specialization and division of labor, *or* by saving and capital formation, *or* by technical invention, or by some two or three of such factors.

In real life, economic growth is never sufficiently caused or explained by so few factors. So why have theorists kept on offering such narrow selections? There have been motives of three kinds, all of which you have met before:

Scientistic Economists who yearn for a regular predictive science like physics may look for a few factors or relationships which seem to occur in all cases of growth, and to generalize them (wrongly) as *the* dynamics of growth – the sufficient cause of it. (For what is wrong with 'selecting for regularity' like that, revise Chapter 3).

Practical Current troubles attract attention. If a country has persistent foreign exchange difficulties, its economists may look hard for links between export earnings and growth. For other topical reasons there may be times when they focus on links between war and growth, inflation and growth, and so on.

Political As for 'practical' but with more emphasis on conflicting values and interests. Capitalists may try to show that tax advantages for capitalists bring advantages for everyone else too by stimulating national economic growth. Labor leaders may show how high wages and full employment sustain the consumer demand which is a necessary condition of growth. I would like society to be somewhat more equal than it is, so I look for ways in which improving equalities can help growth. (Those author's values help to select the case histories you will meet in Chapter 11.)

Remember what you have learned about relations between theorists' values and their selections. Selections are not necessarily bad and theories are not necessarily wrong because they are purposeful. All selections and simplifications need to be shaped by their working purposes. Even narrow selections may be appropriate in particular cases. For example an economist may judge that her country's conditions are right for successful growth except for one or two missing factors – so she rightly focuses on those one or two. But there needs to be continuous awareness of (1) the values and purposes which shape the selective theories, (2) conflicts of interest and purpose which may generate rival theories (each too often claiming to be the one true science) and (3) the tests of truth and practicality which theories meet when they are applied to prediction and policy-making. Except as propaganda, purposeful theories don't serve their purposes if they don't *work*.

The following sketches of past and present theories are necessarily brief and simplified.

MERCANTILISTS

The new monarchies which shaped the European nation states from the 16th to the 18th centuries were powerful in two ways. They developed strong central government over their own territories; and they secured those territories chiefly by winning wars. They competed with each other in war, trade, imperial expansion, or all three. Their experience generated an array of economic beliefs – some theoretical, some practical, some discordant with one another – for which 'mercantilist' is a collective label.

Mercantilists were, above all, *political* economists.

They saw close relations between wealth and power. They thought that economic activity needed a good deal of careful government.

The relations between wealth and power were mutual. *Wealth could increase power*. Governments with good revenues could rule securely. Richer countries could usually beat poorer countries in war. Reciprocally, *power could increase wealth*. Strong nations could acquire natural resources, profitable ports, export markets and other advantages by conquering or colonizing. The more powerful they were the more they could hope to regulate international trade to their national advantage. They could protect their industries from competitive imports. They could confine their overseas trade and their colonies' trade to their own nationals' ships. They could force weaker nations to sign unequal commercial treaties with them.

Mercantilists attached great importance to the balance of trade. If a nation earned more by its exports than it paid for its imports it would gain a net inflow of money. In those days money meant chiefly gold and silver. Some 'bullionists' valued it simply as spending money, specially useful for financing foreign wars. Other mercantilists had other advantages in mind. Exports could have a double effect on employment and economic growth. Directly, producing for export employed people and distributed income to them. Indirectly, their spending then added to the domestic demand which kept others employed. By contrast, imports employed nobody directly, and by directing spending abroad they reduced effective demand for other home-produced goods. Most mercantilists saw some value in international specialization and trade. They did not want government to ban imports altogether. But they did want government to protect particular industries, and to protect the national balance of exports over imports.

James Steuart

Suppose for example that an established industry is threatened by a new supply of cheaper goods from abroad. What should government do? In *An Inquiry into the Principles of Political Economy* (1767) the able mercantilist James Steuart considered three aspects of that question. First, jobs and incomes are threatened. Second, the increase of imports may affect the national trade balance. Third, should government aim at full employment and a favourable balance of payments with a *larger* or with a *smaller* volume of trade – i.e. should it cut imports down to the current level of exports, or should it try to expand exports to balance the threatened

increase of imports?

If all else failed Steuart thought the jobs and the trading balance should be protected by restricting the imports. But *only* if all else failed. Government should first see whether the threatened workers could switch to making some more competitive product whose export could balance the new imports. It should bargain with the foreign government to admit those English exports, as a condition of England's admitting the foreign nation's exports. If all that could be achieved, free trade was best.

But free trade was not always or automatically best. Steuart understood the likely effects of free trade between traders of unequal strength. His understanding was common sense to many statesmen and business men, but he was a century or two ahead of most economic theorists. He grasped that in any trading exchange there is a dual quality, *both* a common interest *and* a conflict of interest:

- There must be *some* advantage for each party or they won't make the exchange.

- But there is no guarantee that the advantages they get will be of equal value.

If one bargainer is tougher than the other, or more skilful or better equipped, or richer so that he can hold out longer, or if he has a monopoly, or if he has political influence to rig the rules of trade to his own advantage, he is likely to get the best of the bargain. So free trade between unequals tends to increase their inequalities. Free trade is therefore a rational policy for winners, rather than for everybody. The German writer Friedrich List was almost alone among economic theorists when he argued this in the 1840s, and the British economist Thomas Balogh and others were still a minority when they argued it from the 1940s. Steuart was anticipating their perceptions when he wrote in 1767 –

> A laborious, oeconomical, and sagacious nation, such as I suppose our traders to be, will be able to profit of many circumstances, which would infallibly turn to the disadvantage of others less expert in commerce, with whom she trades.

But . . .

The best mercantilists were right enough about many of the economic realities of their time. Their beliefs have continued to shape many national policies to this day. But there were nevertheless practical and theoretical objections to their theory of growth as a whole:

- Their principles were often applied badly in practice.

Governments were quick to introduce new trade restrictions and taxes but slow to dismantle old ones which had outlived their usefulness. By 1800 Britain had accumulated an expensive complexity of hundreds of detailed import duties and regulations, some of them centuries old, many serving no useful purpose. Smuggling and corruption were accordingly rife – and sensible, in many cases.

• There was plenty of conflict between the notional 'national interest' and particular business interests. Tariffs were too often introduced or continued by strictly self-interested lobbying and political horse-trading by the interests concerned. So the 'protected' population, denied cheap imports, may often have paid more than necessary for the products of less efficient home industries, *without* much gain in full employment or national self-reliance.

• Mercantilists were right to warn against chronic trade deficits, but wrong to look for chronic surpluses. In a world with limited supplies of gold and silver for international payments, a country which accumulated too much of that scarce currency might well lose export markets as its beggared neighbors lost their capacity to pay.

• Mercantilists generally exaggerated the importance of international trade. Economic growth could come by increasing productivity for export – but it could just as well come by increasing productivity for home consumption. Some mercantilists understood how a nation's external links, through trade or conquest, could help full employment and productivity at home. But they neglected other aids to growth – purely internal ways of improving home productivity for home consumption.

CLASSICAL ECONOMISTS

'Classical' is a modern label for a succession of writers who gave new directions to economic theory at the time of the first industrial revolution, the steam-engine revolution that began in Britain in the 1770s. The most notable were Adam Smith (1723-90), David Ricardo (1772-1823) and Thomas Malthus (1766-1834).

The mercantilists had been theorists of a *state-aided commercial* capitalism: a muscle-powered and wind-powered economy of farming, handcraft manufacturing, and world wide trading and fighting and colonizing for profit.

By contrast, the classical economists have been described as the theorists of free-trading industrial capitalism. When they wrote, there were actually two economic transformations under way. In the English countryside state-aided enclosures were perfecting conditions for efficient capitalist farming. In town, water-powered then steam-powered machinery was beginning to revolutionize manufacturing productivity. For a generation or two Britain had a near-monopoly of the new technology. While that lasted, British manufacturers scarcely needed protection in their home markets, and Britain was a likely winner from any freeing of trade abroad.

Adam Smith

A third revolution – an intellectual one – began with the publication in 1776 of the most famous of all economics books, Adam Smith's *Inquiry into the Nature and Causes of the Wealth of Nations*. In that book Smith argued that economic growth came chiefly from three causes: (1) the division and specialization of labor, (2) technical invention, especially of labor-saving machinery, and (3) the accumulation of capital financed from capitalist profits.

He instanced the manufacture of pins. If a worker makes one pin after another, changing his tools and materials for each successive stage of the job, he is slow at the work. But in an efficient pin factory 'one man draws out the wire, another straights it, a third cuts it, a fourth points it, a fifth grinds it at the top for receiving the head..' and so on through about eighteen specialized operations. By those means the output of pins per worker can be multiplied several times.

The division of labor (Smith said) allows gains of three kinds. Specialized workers can increase their skill or speed. They can save the time they used to spend in moving from one task to the next. And it is the breaking down of the productive process into many parts that allows parts of it to be mechanized, by 'the invention of a great number of machines which facilitate and abridge labour, and enable one man to do the work of many'.

As in the pin factory, so on a national and international scale: specialization and exchange can increase productivity. They allow invention, and the most efficient use of resources, and therefore growth. But (Smith argued) people and nations cannot specialize unless they can freely exchange their specialities: trade must not be hindered by government taxes or regulations. If people are free to use and exchange their labor and resources as each thinks best, it should follow – as if ordered by a benign 'hidden hand' – that resources will be used most efficiently to produce the array of goods that the people most desire to have. At home and abroad, between individuals and firms and nations, Adam Smith was a free trader.

So far so good. But where will the capital come from? Who will build the pin factory, buy the machines, and pay the workers' wages before any money comes in from selling the pins? How fast will the necessary capital accumulate? Specialization, invention and growth can't proceed without capital accumulation.

Class shares

To explain the accumulation of capital the classical economists devised a model of three social classes and their economic relations with each other. To constitute their model they selected and simplified some class relations from the capitalist countryside rather than the factory town. In Adam Smith's words (with 'stock' meaning capital) –

> The whole annual produce of the land and labour of every country ... naturally divides itself ... into three parts: the rent of land, the wages of labour, and the profits of stock; and constitutes a revenue to three different orders of people.

Workers get subsistence *wages*, enough to keep them alive and working. Surplus output above that is divided between *profit* to the capitalist farmer, and the *rent* he pays his landlord. Smith's model assumed that workers must spend all their wages to keep alive; landlords are drones who spend all their rents on high living; only capitalists save to provide next season's wages and seed corn, and invest to improve farms, build factories, buy machines. So capital accumulation depends on what share the capitalist gets of the surplus the workers produce. The less the landlord gets as rent, the more the capitalist can keep as profit. The more profit he gets and invests, the more his accumulating capital will increase each worker's productivity, and the more economic growth there will therefore be.

But the growth will be for the capitalists and landlords. Smith thought employers would usually keep wages down to bare subsistence, so workers could not expect much benefit from economic growth.

Limits to growth

Oddly it was Adam Smith writing in the 1770s before the steam revolution had much industrial effect who was optimistic about technical invention and mechanized factory production. A generation later Malthus and Ricardo stuck to the old 'three-class farm' as their model of the national economy despite the fact that the steam engine was revolutionizing productivity

under their noses. From their model they deduced that relations between people and land were likely to limit economic growth in the following direct and indirect ways.

A growing population could keep up its output per head only if there was unlimited land, so that extra workers and extra capital could find extra land to work. But in most of Britain and Europe they could not. The good land was already in use. As additional labor and capital were applied to existing farmland or poorer marginal land, each worker had less or worse land to work. Output per acre might rise (from more intensive cultivation) but output per worker must fall. Similarly as more capital was applied to less land, total output might rise but there would be less output per unit of capital.

That was bad enough, but there was worse. As rising numbers of people competed for the limited land the landowners would be able to exact more rent. That would leave less profit, so the capitalists would have less to invest.

Moreover physical capital is not everlasting. It wears out or gets used up. The more of it you have, the more you must save and spend each year to maintain what you have before you can actually add to it. So in a mature economy the rate of saving may be *above* the rate required to maintain existing capital stocks, in which case there can be some continuing growth. Or it may just *maintain* existing capital, but provide no growth. Or it may fall *below* that, causing negative growth as some capital wears out without replacement, and productivity per worker declines.

Summary

With individual differences, the classical economists thought this about economic growth:

- Unhindered specialization and exchange, technical invention and the profit/rent split would together determine the rate of any growth.

- Most of the benefits of growth would go to landlords and capitalists; workers' incomes were unlikely to rise much above subsistence.

- Growth would be self-limiting in the following way: As population rose on limited land each worker would produce less. After paying subsistence wages there would therefore be less surplus to divide between capitalist and landlord, and the landlord would get more of it. Capitalists would get a *falling* share of a *falling* surplus, and would invest less.

- The system might stabilize at a level at which (1) the

wage level would keep existing numbers alive, but no more; and (2) the rate of profit would maintain existing capital, but not increase it.

But ...

Before you read on, try an exercise of your own. Consider the modern world of rich and poor countries; then with your two centuries of hindsight consider the classical economists' choice of their farm model as a selective explanation of economic growth. If it does not sufficiently explain the growth that has occurred, why doesn't it? Does it mistake the causes and conditions of growth? Or include too few of them? Or lump too many different things together in its concepts of 'land', 'labor' and 'capital'? Does it assume the causes of growth are more regular and unvarying than they really are?

The classical theorists were good critics of the mercantilists' obsession with foreign trade. They asked important questions about the distribution of income between unequal classes. But for explaining economic growth their simplifications were bad ones. They selected too few of the factors which helped or hindered growth, and they were mistaken about the usual effects of some of those few. So their model was deceptive in their own day, and later history has not developed as the model led them to expect.

- Science and technology have revolutionized productivity more than even Adam Smith hoped. But that high-tech productivity depends on many more cultural and social and political conditions than Smith thought to specify, so the same technical knowledge can have very different uses and effects in different societies. Among other conditions for using it productively, government has to provide research and education, power and transport and public services, and ever-more-complicated regulation of the ever-more-complicated processes and organization of production and distribution.

- The social classes have not behaved at all as the classical theorists expected. Instead of rent taking a rising share of farm output it has nearly everywhere taken a falling share. Where there has been substantial economic growth, wage earners *have* eventually got a share of it. Contrary to the classical expectations, *all* classes save and invest. (Besides other investments, wage-earners' savings have provided most of the housing, home equipment and private cars that constitute a third or more of the productive capital of the richer countries.)

- Free trade has not lived up to classical expectations.

Locally, the division and specialization of labor which Adam Smith wanted has depended sometimes on free exchange, but at other times on local or national protection. Nationally, many free-trading countries have stayed poor or achieved slower growth than many of their protected competitors. Adam Smith was right about some bad protective practices but he was wrong about free trade as a universal principle. What matters is *what* industries the government helps, for what reasons, by what means, for whose benefit.

Policies

The classical economists thought growth and wealth would come from policies of (1) free trade, (2) small government, and (3) unaided private enterprise; and that (4) the workers would get very little of any increased output. They turned out to be wrong – some or all of the time – on all four counts.

MARX

Is it worth knowing about Marx now that communism is dead? Yes, for three reasons.

- His theories helped to split and weaken the Left for nearly a century. Without his influence the social-democratic reform of capitalism might have achieved either more or less than it did. Perhaps more, from the greater strength of a united democratic Left. Perhaps less, without the threat of communist revolution if capitalism was *not* reformed.

- Some of his shrewd observation and analysis of capitalist business is still worth having, and it had significant effects on the development of economic theory. Some of the authors of neoclassical theory developed it as a defensive response to Marx's attack on capitalism. Some Marxist insights survive in contemporary post-Keynesian theory.

- In the current drive to the Right – to smaller government, meaner welfare and steeper inequality – Western leaders may be following some seriously mistaken theory. Relating bad theory to its practical ill effects is a valuable part of your education, whether the theory comes from Right, Left or Centre. A misjudgment at the heart of Marx's theory shares responsibility for some of the twentieth century's worst horrors. It is well worth half an hour's work – over the next few pages – to understand that mistake, as an example of how simple some fatal mistakes can be.

Karl Marx (1818-1883) developed his system of

economic belief and analysis in many books and papers over more than forty years, and finally in the three volumes of *Capital*. The first volume of *Capital* appeared in 1867. The second (1885) and third (1894) were edited from his papers by Engels after Marx's death. His voluminous work is like the bible: many and various interpretations have been put on its many and complex themes. What follows is one severe simplification of his theory of economic growth and change.

The prime mover of economic growth (Marx believed) is human ingenuity. People are restless and inventive. They keep improving – and sometimes revolutionizing – their methods of production.

Changing means of production (the spear, the spade, the steam engine: therefore hunting, farming, manufacturing) need appropriate forms of organization. Nomadic hunters work best in tribes. Settled farmers need laws about land ownership. Warring societies need systems of military service and command. And so on – in Marx's language the *forces* of production (resources, tools, know-how) have to be matched by appropriate *relations* of production (how production is organized, who commands it, with what rights and powers, etc.)

The relations of production are full of conflict. When new methods of production demand new forms of organization, old ruling classes may cling to power until they are ousted by political revolution. And in all past and present systems there have been conflicts of interest between the ruling class and the ruled. Only in the classless socialist society of the future (Marx predicted) would such conflicts cease.

Meanwhile change is continuous. Each historical system by degrees prepares the conditions for the next. Better than any other theorist, Marx understood that economists have to study changing systems.

Capitalism

To understand the capitalist phase of history Marx began with the classical economists' analysis of social classes. Adam Smith had observed that workers produced a surplus above their own subsistence needs, and most of the surplus went to landlords and capitalists. Ricardo asked what exactly determined the landlords' and capitalists' respective shares. Marx asked why there was a surplus in the first place: why would workers first produce a surplus, then part with it?

Answer: because the ruling class would starve them or hang them if they didn't. Marx usually lumped landlords and capitalists together as the capitalist ruling class. That class owned the means of production (land, buildings, tools, seed-corn, etc.) Without using those means of production the workers could not produce anything at all. The ruling class allowed the workers to use the means of production to produce for their own subsistence *only* if they also produced a surplus and handed it over.

Why did workers put up with such exploitation? For two reasons. First, the government made them put up with it. The state was an instrument of the ruling class. It wrote the property and labor laws, and enforced them. Second, when they bargained about wages, the capitalists were usually strong and the workers weak. Employers could hold out longer than workers who had no reserves of money or food. A number of factors, including labor-saving inventions and periodical slumps, produced unemployment and maintained what Marx called 'the industrial reserve army of unemployed', so that workers had to compete with one another for what jobs there were, and employers could generally bid their wages down near to bare subsistence.

Capitalists also competed with one another. That kept them efficient, because only the efficient survived. It motivated them to save and invest their profits, rather than spending them on consumption – and again, those who saved most would survive the competition best. So in the system as a whole, capital accumulated and productivity increased. Marx thought the capitalist system although cruel had been brilliantly productive. Also progressive: it had achieved the greatest growth of productivity and wealth in human history.

But Marx thought it also had internal contradictions which would eventually destroy it.

Contradictions

Marx expected that the processes of *competition* and *capital accumulation* would together produce a *falling rate of profit* for capitalists, a *rising rate of exploitation* of workers, and periodical *slumps* of increasing severity. The following is a much-simplified version of his reasoning, step by step:

1. Capitalists compete against each other chiefly by offering consumers more for less. If you are a capitalist, improving your product or cutting its selling price must cut your profit margin, unless you can cut your costs of production.

2. There are two main ways to cut costs of production. You can invest more capital to make each worker more productive; or you can cut wages, though not below subsistence.

3. Increasing your capital eventually saves labor. One way or another that tends to create unemployment. Either the extra capital allows you to produce the

same with less labor (so you sack some workers); or you manage to produce and sell more, in which case some less efficient competitor loses sales (and has to sack some workers). The unemployment keeps the workers anxious about their jobs and helps employers to keep wages down.

4. As capital accumulates Marx thought it must depress both profit rates and wage rates. Translated into modern terms his reasons were as follows. There are capital costs and wage costs of production. By the time production gets under way the capital costs are fixed – the land, buildings, machinery, etc. have been bought and their costs cannot now be reduced. The variable costs are chiefly the wages you must pay day by day. So if you meet competition and have to cut costs, it must chiefly be from those wages.

Now see, in Figures 9.1 and 9.2, how Marx expects capital accumulation to reduce your room for manoeuvre. As (say) an old charcoal-burning ironworks (1) is developed with more capital into a coke-fired works (2) and then into a modern steel mill (3), watch what happens to two ratios: the ratio of fixed capital costs to variable wage costs, and the ratio of wages to total costs. Do the Figure 9.1 exercise and you will see why Marx expected economic growth to immiserate the workers. It is in the most advanced, most productive firm that any given price cut requires the biggest wage cut.

As for the firm (Marx thought) so for the capitalist system: the accumulation of capital and growth of productivity will tend to force wages *down*. When wages 'bottom' at bare subsistence, price-cutting competition will have to bite into profit rates. As profits decline there will be less surplus to invest, so growth will slow down, perhaps stop. There seemed to be a contradiction: capital accumulation both *produces* economic growth, and *arrests* it.

Or does it? Suppose that instead of selling cheaper to the consumers the capitalists increase their prices to allow their costs to *rise* a little. See Figure 9.2 for the possibilities which *that* creates.

A given price rise can finance a bigger and bigger wage rise as capital accumulates. Alternatively a given wage rise can hurt the consumers less and less as capital accumulates. For example a 10 per cent wage rise has to add 8 per cent to the primitive industry's prices but it need only add 2 per cent to the advanced industry's prices. The more advanced the industry (or the whole economic system) the *easier* is the relation between wages and prices. The changing ratio between fixed capital costs and variable wage costs, which Marx

thought must force wages downwards, can actually make it easier to raise them. If intelligent, inventive capitalists and workers and governments perceived that, wouldn't they find ways to share the benefits of capital growth and rescue the system from breakdown?

Even Marx sometimes thought that they might – some of his later writings expressed doubts about his earlier reasoning. We will return to the question presently. But first notice some other reasons why he expected capitalism to arrest its own growth and break down.

Boom and slump

Marx expected periodical slumps of increasing severity. If there were periods of full employment and labor shortage, wages might rise for a time. With high wages the workers' spending would ensure effective demand for the goods they produced. But the high wages would meanwhile leave employers with less profit. So they would invest less, and the demand for capital goods (buildings, machines, etc.) would fall, bringing unemployment again.

Alternatively a period of low wages might allow high rates of profit. Capitalists would save, invest, and accumulate capital. But at the same time the low wages would reduce the workers' demand for consumer goods. Capitalists cannot go on producing goods they cannot sell, so the rapidly increasing productive capacity would soon be under-used. Profits would fall, investment would dwindle, unemployment would increase, to bring another slump.

Thus Marx saw a chronic contradiction between production and consumption. The conditions which increased productive capacity would reduce consumption; conditions which encouraged consumption would discourage the growth of productive capacity. The actions and reactions took time, so instead of the contrary tendencies coming into a stable balance, there would be alternating booms and slumps.

These short-term instabilities of the system would be intensified by the long-term tendencies to lower profits and harsher pressures on labor which we noted earlier. 'The ultimate reason for all real crises always remains the poverty and restricted consumption of the masses as opposed to the drive of capitalist production to develop the productive forces.' (*Capital*, III, p.472) Capitalist growth must eventually reach a stage at which –

- technical development and capital accumulation have produced great productive capacity; but

- the internal contradictions of capitalism are seriously restricting the use of that productive capacity; and

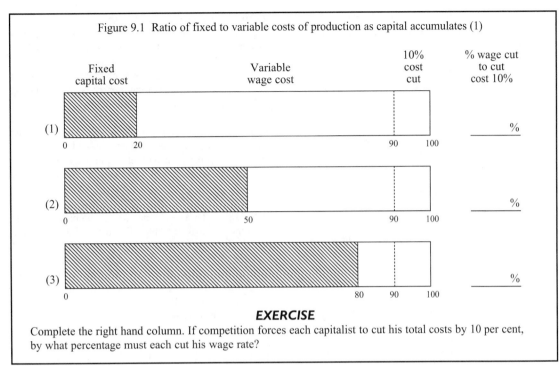

Figure 9.1 Ratio of fixed to variable costs of production as capital accumulates (1)

EXERCISE

Complete the right hand column. If competition forces each capitalist to cut his total costs by 10 per cent, by what percentage must each cut his wage rate?

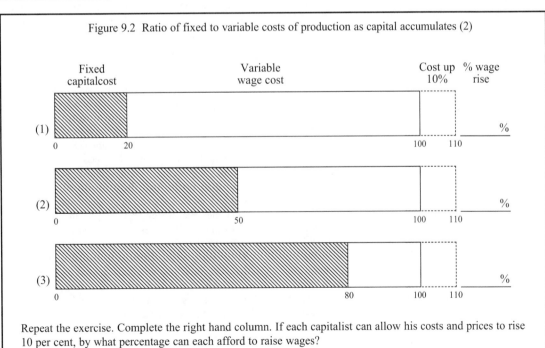

Figure 9.2 Ratio of fixed to variable costs of production as capital accumulates (2)

Repeat the exercise. Complete the right hand column. If each capitalist can allow his costs and prices to rise 10 per cent, by what percentage can each afford to raise wages?

- the masses find their sufferings intolerable, and realise that (unlike poverty in earlier, less productive times) the sufferings are now unnecessary.

That is the time for a proletarian revolution to abolish the private ownership of the means of production and create a classless socialist society. Then capital can cease to mean 'power over the labor of others'. Exploitation can give way to co-operation. Production for profit can give way to production for use. The productive capacity which is capitalism's great historical achievement can at last be fully and continuously employed, as collective social decisions instead of the profit motive determine what to produce and how to distribute it.

But . . .

A century later capitalism is still here. It now seems more likely to destroy itself by nuclear war or global pollution than by the contradictions Marx described.

In the mature capitalist countries it is true that growth has slowed and booms and slumps continue. But profit rates, though they fluctuate, show no general downward trend. The workers *have* shared in the benefits of economic growth, though unevenly at different times and in different countries. Marx turns out to have been right about some particular trends but wrong in a general way: the system survives, much changed and continuing to change. I think he underestimated the adaptive, inventive capacities of capitalists, workers and governments alike.

Moreover it was not in mature capitalist countries that socialist revolutions succeeded. They succeeded in poor peasant countries, then were imposed on some more advanced East European countries by foreign force. They were governed by dictatorships with varying amounts of terror. Their socialist economies grew, but sluggishly, and were soon falling behind the Western mixed economies. Their governments eventually decided to recreate capitalist private sectors, and (in Russia and East Europe) democratic government. The troubles of that transformation will occupy one of the last chapters of this course of study.

Should we therefore forget Marx? No, for a number of reasons. Beliefs are working parts, and it would be hard to understand the Russian or Chinese communist revolutions or their economic policies without knowing what their leaders drew from Marx's work. Elsewhere in the world, despite Marx's misjudgment of capitalist capacities, his followers have kept alive the classical economists' concern with class interests and capitalist distributions of wealth and income through a century when neoclassical theory diverted many economists'

attention from those subjects. And not only capitalist distributions – Ivan Szelényi and George Konrád, dissident intellectuals in communist Hungary, reported (in *The Intellectuals on the Road to Class Power*, 1979) how they discovered a new respect for Marx as they asked what surplus value Hungarian workers were producing, and what mechanisms and distributions of power were determining which groups got what shares of it. Interest in those issues has revived in old as well as new capitalist economies since their governments shifted to the Right, and their declining inequalities began to increase again, through the last quarter of the twentieth century.

NEOCLASSICAL ECONOMISTS

In the 1870s it was as if classical economics had come to a fork in the road. While Marx directed it to the Left, others directed it to the Right. In books published between 1871 and 1890 four writers – the Englishmen W.S. Jevons (1835-82) and Alfred Marshall (1842-1924), the Austrian Carl Menger (1840-1921) and the Swiss Leon Walras (1834-1910) – laid the foundations of what is now called neoclassical economic theory. With many elaborations and internal disagreements it is still the most widely held economic theory in the world. You will meet it often in this course of study. Here a short sketch of it will do, because unlike classical and Marxist theory it is not primarily about growth. It claims to tell how capitalist economies work rather than why they change.

Basic neoclassical theory

Like other theorists the neoclassics selected a few relationships from complicated real life, and modelled those few only. They focused on sales and exchanges: on markets. They set out to explain how prices are arrived at for finished goods, and also for the factors of production – the land and labor and capital that are used to produce the finished goods. They theorized as follows.

To the marketplace, people bring whatever they can contribute to production: their labor, and any land or capital they chance to own. In the marketplace they find out (1) the prices they can get for their productive services, and (2) the prices of all the consumer goods and services their incomes can then buy for them.

In the light of those prices, individuals decide their preferences: how they will contribute to production, and how they will spend the incomes their contributions earn. Their preferences adjust to the prices, and the prices keep adjusting to the preferences revealed in their spending.

Neoclassical theory purports to explain (1) how each price is arrived at between buyer and seller, and (2) how the prices affect each other.

The selective causal explanations at the heart of the theory are basically these:

Demand and supply The cheaper carrots are, the more consumers will tend to buy – but the less producers will tend to supply. So at any particular time there is only one price at which the amount supplied and the amount demanded are the same. Prices and quantities tend toward that equilibrium. At the same time the quantities and prices of different goods affect each other, because people have only so much to spend and if they buy more carrots they will usually demand less parsnips. In the economic system as a whole, supply (determined by the costs and difficulties of production) interacts with demand (determined by people's tastes and how much they have to spend) to determine how society's productive resources are used, to produce what mix of commodities at what prices.

Diminishing marginal utility The first bite of the carrot is usually the best. By the third or fifth carrot you have had enough or you are longing for a change to parsnips, even if they cost more. The more you have of a commodity (the theory says) the less willing you will usually be to pay for any more of it. And (for reasons which can wait) what you are willing to pay for the last carrot you buy is likely to be the price you pay for *all* the carrots you buy that day.

Factor prices and the distribution of income Suppose that to grow an extra ton of carrots the grower will have to spend an extra $1,000 on his 'factors of production', i.e. on land, labor, transport, etc. If the extra carrots will sell for $1,100 he will grow them; if they will only fetch $900, he won't. Suppose he does expect to get $1,100 for his last, marginal ton. If he finds he can get the necessary factors of production for $1,000, two things follow: (1) He will produce the carrots, unless he can get a higher profit on his $1,000 capital by using it to produce something else; and (2) the $1,000 he pays to the factors will reward them for their productive contribution. With reasoning you will meet later, the neoclassical theorists went on to argue that each one of the factors would get what it (or he or she) contributed to the market value of the finished goods. Rent would reflect what the land contributed, wages would reflect what the workers contributed, the grower's $100 profit would reflect what the use of his capital contributed.

The theory thus offers to explain two things: how prices are arrived at, and how income is distributed. If wages rise above subsistence that is not the puzzle it was to classical theorists. Workers get what their work contributes to the market value of the product. As their productivity increases, so do their incomes.

If objections to that theory occur to you (as I think they should) save them for later. First, what did the theory say about growth and change?

Neoclassical theories of growth

Remember the classical theory of a growing population on limited land? The growing population makes more and more workers per acre. That means less land per worker. So as population increases (the theory said) *gross output* and *output per acre* may increase (from more intense cultivation) but *output per worker* will fall (because each worker has less land to work with). So income per head will fall, which will eventually limit population numbers.

The neoclassics did four new things. (1) They switched the emphasis from land to capital. (2) They tried to explain the rate at which people saved and capital accumulated. (3) They introduced the factor-price theory of the distribution of income. (4) They applied the idea of diminishing marginal productivity to each productive factor in relation to others.

Saving and spending We can begin with the second of those items. What determines how much people save?

(Here first is a non-neoclassical answer: People wish to live as long as their physical nature allows. Property owners and wage earners alike need to save for sickness and old age, and to make provision for widows and children. So if they can, they save in order to spread their spending over time. There are also other reasons for saving, for example to buy big things like house or car, or to have more to spend at the expensive stages of life.)

So people would save a good deal even if there were no additional reward for doing it. Neoclassical theory does not acknowledge that. It makes the odd assumption that people desire to consume all their resources *now*. They will only save for later if they are rewarded for doing it. Profits, interest and rent – the returns to capital – are to be understood as *rewards for waiting*.

So what determines how much people save? Answer: the relation between the rate of interest and their personal time discounts. I will abstain from eating a hundred dollars of candy *now* only if I'm promised a hundred and five dollars' worth next year (or a hundred and four, or a hundred and six, depending on my personal price for waiting). The theory implies that people don't save because they want to spend later, they only save if it allows them to spend *more* later.

So the rate of saving reflects a relation between two

preferences. The *lower* the return to capital, the lower the producers' profits, the cheaper the products are: it's good to spend now. The *higher* the return to capital, the dearer products are now, and the more inducement there is to save. Between those two inducements, people decide what mix of spending and saving will maximize their material satisfactions. But if they save too much, productive capacity will rise faster than its output can sell (because there won't be enough spending to buy all the output). Then profits will fall, there will be less inducement to save, and people will save less and spend more. If they save too little and spend too much, there will be buoyant demand for goods, prices will rise, producers will offer higher interest or dividends to attract more capital, so people will save more and spend less. They should soon arrive at the equilibrium rates at which they will accumulate capital just as fast as their spending can consume its output.

(What is wrong with the theory? As usual, it is mono-causal: of all the many considerations that determine how people save and spend, it assumes that only two – the rival attractions of spending now, or earning the rate of interest – determine their behavior.)

Growth slows down Unless there is technological progress (neoclassical theory says) economic growth will cause a declining rate of return to investment, and therefore a declining rate of capital accumulation and economic growth. The reasons for expecting this tendency can be simply stated in either of two ways:

- As capital accumulates, each unit of it must have less land and less labor to work with. So it will add less to output. At the same time it will have made each worker more productive (because each worker has more capital to work with) and it will have made labor scarcer 'per unit of capital', so the factor price of labor will rise – i.e., wages will rise. Meanwhile as capital accumulates and its marginal productivity declines the factor price of all capital will fall – i.e. the rate of profit and interest will fall. Growth will slow down and eventually stop.

- An alternative neoclassical way of expressing the same expectations: With given amounts of land and labor and technical knowledge there is a limited amount of productive investment that *could* be made, to arrive at the saturation point at which all land and labor is working with the most productive known technology. As fast as capitalists can accumulate funds they make the possible investments. They naturally begin (the theory says) with the most profitable investments, which are assumed to be the most

productive. Over time they work their way down the list of possible investments, each less profitable/productive than the last. As they go down the list the return to new investment falls and so the average return to all capital falls. Eventually all existing knowledge is fully applied to all the production to which it can profitably be applied, so growth stops. Growth turns out to have been a temporary phase, continuing only as long as the society still had *known but unused* investment possibilities.

(What's wrong with that? First, for reasons that can wait, you can't always assume that the most profitable investments are the most productive. Second, you certainly can't assume that the most profitable investments can always be made first. What if a break-even railway has to be built before a profitable timber mill can start? Or break-even housing and services for the workforce have to be built before a profitable petroleum refinery can start? Or non-profit schools and universities have to be built and run at high cost for many years to impart existing technical knowledge before profitable high-tech industries can be staffed? There is *no* reliable relation whatever between the necessary order and complementarity of investments, and their profitability.)

And historically, rates of profit and rates of growth have not declined as the theory says they should.

Learning and invention Neoclassics try to rescue that simple theory by adding one further causal factor. They say the simple theory only applies to an uninventive world with a fixed stock of technical knowledge. In the modern world people are constantly inventing better ways to make better mousetraps. So instead of marginal investors buying more of the same old machines they can buy better ones which produce more per dollar invested.

Therefore neoclassics say: Learning and invention may speed up economic growth as fast or faster than declining marginal productivity slows it.

Can you check that belief by measuring the two tendencies? In practice no, for several reasons. You can't isolate those two factors from all the others that affect economic growth. You can't quantify learning and invention, or most of their effects. You may be able to measure a new machine's immediate effect on output – but not its longer-term and wider-spreading effects. It is hard to sort out which bits of old and new plant have contributed how much to the value of finished products. And there is no uncontroversial way to measure the present value of capital created by past investment, to allow you to measure the average return on all capital.

Common sense says that invention and education are

powerful causes of economic growth, which in turn often stimulates invention and education. But the processes are not strictly measurable, and they happen differently in different historical cases and conditions.

Capital and growth With or without technical innovation, many economists continued for a long time to see capital accumulation as the main cause or mechanism of growth. Two of them (Roy Harrod in 1948 and E.D. Domar in 1957) offered a two-cause model of the process. They believed the rate of growth should follow from (1) the rate at which a nation saved, and (2) the productivity of the capital which the savings provided.

The proportion of income that a nation saves (and spends on capital goods rather than on consumption) can be shown as a *savings/income ratio*. The value of capital can be related to the value of the goods it produces per year in a *capital/output ratio*. Divide the first ratio by the second (Harrod and Domar said) and the result should tell you the annual rate of economic growth.

In practice it doesn't Economic output and economic growth never depend on investment alone. They always depend on other factors as well. Many of the other factors vary independently of the investment. As contributors to growth, how do you separate the effects of investment from the effects of health, education, skill, motivation, organization and management, effective demand?

Practical applications However bad the theory, beliefs are working parts. Through the 1950s and 1960s, versions of the Harrod/Domar model were sold to the governments of many poor countries. Their economic planners were persuaded to believe among other things that they must *increase saving*, chiefly from steeper *profits and rents and taxes*, chiefly by *cutting current consumption*, chiefly consumption by already-poor *peasants*.

And how should the extra savings be invested? Heavy industry had the most productive capital/output ratio. Agricultural investment had a poorer ratio. Housing appeared to have the poorest – not surprising since the theorists chose not to count most of the real output of housing capital. So investment should be directed away from housing and subsistence farming, into large-scale capitalist farming and (best of all) heavy industry. One best-selling text said that steel mills had a capital/output ratio *eight times* more productive than investment in housing.

That was mostly wrong. It was technically mistaken about what causes what, as well as socially reactionary. For many reasons. Here are a few of the reasons:

The industries of a modern economic system *complement* each other more than they can substitute for each other. The 'high output' industries need the services of many 'low-output' industries so that the system needs both. Most industries produce supplies or services for other industries or for workers in other industries. Except for some export-import purposes, the proportions of a country's component industries can't vary very far from their needs for mutual service. Imagine a country which built *all* steel mills and *no* mines or transport to serve the mills, and *no* houses or food supplies for the steel workers. There would not only be no food, shelter or transport, there would be no steel either. It is rarely practical to bias a developing country's investment towards high-output industries at the expense of others. The real need is to improve productivity 'across the board'.

Similarly it was wrong to see consumption and investment as simple alternatives. They also can sometimes be complements rather than alternatives, especially in poor countries. Poor and under-employed people can often increase consumption and saving *together* more readily than they can provide savings if their consumption is cut. Not only is the extra consumption compatible with extra saving; it may also increase output and growth by other means than investment, for example by improving workers' health and skill and motivation, and by increasing effective demand for the nation's output.

It was wrong to assume that only capitalists and governments can save. Peasants can save and invest, especially if their property laws and institutions allow the investment to take the form of their own labor improving their land for their own benefit rather than for the benefit of capitalists or landlords. Urban workers, employed as well as unemployed, can save and invest if they can use their non-earning time to build their own houses and neighborhood services on sites to which they can have secure tenure.

A more equal distribution of land to peasants can and often does help economic growth more than harsher exploitation of the peasants can. (There can be contrary effects when changes in farming techniques require more capital or larger holdings. But there is no *general* rule that bigger holdings and harsher exploitation of labor are always more productive.)

It was wrong to believe that 'social investment' in housing and living conditions would slow economic growth by diverting investment away from high-output industries. Countries which have directly improved the housing and living conditions of peasants and urban workers have in many cases achieved both more and better growth than countries which have not.

Through the 1960s the governments of Hong Kong and Singapore ensured that the world's highest-ever proportions of national income were invested in building new housing. Those rates of housing investment were accompanied by *the world's highest-ever recorded rates of economic growth*. Neither country had yet built any steel mills.

Free trade In 1948 Paul Samuelson argued, on assumptions widely accepted by neoclassical economists, that free trade should have the effect of equalizing the world's wages, i.e. wages for similar work done in different countries. With *some* continuing differences (because countries might specialize in different industries) that should tend to equalize income and standards of living in all countries. Here was another single-factor theory of economic growth.

Marxists and others led by A.G. Frank alleged an opposite relation: intercourse between rich and poor countries was chiefly exploitive. It made the rich richer and was the main cause of the poor staying poor. That theory predicted the real history of the post-war decades almost as badly as Samuelson's did. In fact some busy trading countries grew richer and others did not; some sparse traders grew richer and others stayed poor.

Between those two schools of thought but earlier than either, Thomas Balogh and other pragmatic institutional economists had observed that free trade and investment between unequal countries has often tended to increase their inequalities – but it does so as a net result of complex processes *some* of which have, or could be made to have, the contrary effect of reducing inequalities. Governments should learn to distinguish the helpful from the unhelpful relations, and discriminate accordingly in their trade and development policies.

KEYNESIAN EXPECTATIONS

This heading has a double meaning: what John Maynard Keynes (1883-1946) expected to happen, and what he believed would cause it to happen. You will find some essentials of his reasoning in Chapter 18. There are two reasons for deferring our main consideration of it until then. He did not say much directly about economic growth, but his followers think freely about it. And many of their thoughts accord with the historical and institutional views to be reviewed next in Chapter 10. Here, the briefest note about Keynesian views of growth will suffice.

Keynesians don't always agree what the essentials of Keynes' theory were. Here is one impression of its implications for the understanding of economic growth, in the narrow meaning of growth of GDP.

A national economy's level of unemployment or full employment is influenced chiefly by its levels of investment and aggregate demand. Those two affect each other in circular ways. How much firms invest depends on what demand they expect for their products. Demand depends on what consumers have to spend, which depends on their total income. That depends on how many of them are employed, which depends on how much investors are investing – which depends on how much demand they expect. How much demand they expect also depends a good deal on how much investment they expect, i.e. on what each investor guesses that most of the other investors will do. A main effect of this understanding of the process is that Keynesians do not expect that market forces will necessarily arrive at the precise proportions of investment and consumer spending which will provide and maintain full employment.

Meanwhile *possibilities* of economic growth are determined by many and various conditions: technological progress, human capital including entrepreneurial spirit, attitudes to work, cultural capacities for competition and cooperation, and so on. But how fully those possibilities are realized depends chiefly on how fully and continuously the economy is employed. Unaided market forces cannot be trusted to keep it fully employed. That also requires government action to sustain investors' confidence, their access to capital funds, and consumers' after-tax income.

Thus Keynes' main contribution to understanding growth was his contribution to understanding what determined investment and employment, and therefore the rates at which national economies actually realized their possibilities of growth. As to the many technical and cultural and institutional conditions which shaped those possibilities, there was no distinct Keynesian theory. Keynesians were as free as anyone else – and freer than many Marxist and neoclassical theorists – to think about the conditions and processes of economic development and growth, as discussed in the next chapter.

SUMMARY: SIMPLE THEORIES GIVE WAY TO COMPLICATED EXPERIENCE

All theories which ascribed growth to one or a few causes have failed the tests of experience.

For a decade or two from 1945 most neoclassical and Marxist theorists agreed in seeing saving and investment as the keys to growth. But saving looked difficult for poor countries if it had to come by cutting their already-low consumption. It might also be hard for poor countries to turn savings into productive capital (power generators, petroleum refineries, vehicles etc.) They were not equipped to produce such goods, or (in many cases) to earn enough foreign exchange to buy and import them. So here seemed to be an effective way for rich countries to help poor countries. By international aid and/or international private investment they could supply the missing savings and where necessary the missing capital goods.

So there was international aid and investment, especially in public capital and in private mining and industries. Some of it served its intended purposes well. But some aid was filched by venal officials and businessmen in the receiving countries. Some equipment was installed but inefficiently used. Some got as far as the wharves or building sites in the receiving countries and rusted there. It became apparent that saving and investment were not the *only* 'missing components' or 'barriers to development'.

As one barrier was overcome, others appeared to block the path. As one missing component was supplied, other components were missed. One single-barrier theory, or missing-component theory, succeeded another. Step by step, learning by experience, orthodox thinkers came to understand what Arthur Lewis and plenty of institutional economists and practical people had understood from the beginning: There is not *one* path of growth. A country's own path is rarely blocked by *one* barrier only. In most cases – but always varying with the particular circumstances – economic growth is likely to be affected by *at least* the following:

- Natural resources
- Appropriate government
- Education
- Health care
- Birth control
- Appropriate technology
- Appropriate skill and know-how
- Entrepreneurship and tolerance of innovation
- Work culture
- Saving and investment
- Foreign exchange
- External markets and terms of trade

But are those conditions together *sufficient* to ensure growth – will a twelve-factor growth model work where a one-factor or two-factor model won't? No. Some of those conditions are not measurable. All of them together don't guarantee any particular rate or direction of growth.

And on the other hand some undemocratic oil-rich states have achieved very high GNP per head *without* a number of those 'necessary' conditions, and with their social and economic systems still undeveloped, in many respects, for many of their suffering citizens.

FIRST CONCLUSION: ECONOMIC SYSTEMS ARE NOT MACHINES OR TREES OR BABIES

Mechanical *models* of growth fail because economic growth is not mechanical. It is not a process by which a few specifiable inputs regularly produce predictable outputs.

Theories which generalize a single *path of growth* or a regular sequence of *stages of growth* fail because economic growth is not like organic growth. It has elements of belief, choice and invention. It often involves conflicts. Rates and directions of change can depend on who wins and who loses. Economic growth is not predetermined – not even 'predetermined given congenial conditions' – like the growth of a genetically programmed plant or animal.

Moreover each successful national and international development is likely to alter the conditions, and therefore the possibilities, for others. Growth can actually close the path it has taken – winners can kick the ladder down – so some *intrinsic* irregularity has to be expected.

If follows that you cannot simply model growth, or simply fuel it. Putting (say) capital investment or international aid or free trade or neoclassical economic theory into a national economic system is not like putting fuel into an engine, fertiliser into a field, an acorn into the ground, or food into a child.

SECOND CONCLUSION: GROWTH IS HISTORY

The fact is that 'growth' is a misleading metaphor. Economic development is *history*: complex, inventive, conflict-ridden, partly repetitive but partly different every time. And 'differently different' – you can't always foresee *which* elements of the process will continue as before, and which will vary next time.

In more than two thousand years since Greek historians and philosophers began the search, historians have not discovered any reliably regular models or paths of historical change. Instead of simple or rigid theories of change, what the best historians have in their heads as they research the relevant facts are very complicated expectations, alternative possibilities, and lessons of experience.

Think for yourself. Suppose you want to understand

the history of England. Or the history of warfare. Or the history of childhood. Or the history of any other complex human activities and institutions. You don't reach for some mechanical, single-cause theory of growth, or some predetermined path of growth. You know better.

As for England, or warfare, or childhood, or any other complex human activity, so for economic life: you should know better. The history of economic activity, like the history of other human activities, tends to be difficult to understand without historical explanation. As in the examples of causal explanation that you met in Part One of this course, the causal explanations should usually be chosen and shaped with reference to the nature of the facts and the purposes of the inquiry. Social theories and historical explanations can be broader or narrower, more or less comprehensive – but they can never be *exhaustive* or *sufficient*; they can never serve *all* the possible purposes of inquiry. They can only offer 'a purposeful selection of relationships it is useful to know'.

As for explanation, so for action. If governments want to stimulate or give direction to economic development they need to apply the mixed methods we anatomized in Part One. They have to *measure* physical and financial stocks and flows; *model* some physical processes like the transformation of given inputs of coal and iron ore into given outputs of smoke and ash and steel; *model* some financial processes, where those processes happen to be regular and predictable; *understand* people and their institutions; *learn the rules and procedures* of relevant institutions; *decide* which causal chains and conditions and processes they will try to trace and which they won't; *design* coherent policies; *judge* how people are likely to respond to the policies –

including what conflicts there may be and who may win or lose or stalemate them. They must judge what government agents can be *made* to do, what other people may be *persuaded* to do, what market motivations can or cannot be *relied on* to do. And they must judge which of those methods to use for which tasks: when to trust regular models or rules of thumb, when on the other hand to expect changes, and study the changing minds and situations of the decision-makers more directly.

If you do that sort of work you are likely to be abler and wiser the more you know of the world's working experience of economic development. Simple theories of growth don't work, any more than simple theories of history work. But some economic strategies work, just as some political or social strategies work, if they are well designed for their particular conditions. And the world is steadily accumulating experience which should improve the skill and awareness with which governments approach their problems of development. (*Should* improve – but the plainest lessons of experience can still be mistaken by unwilling or unskilled observers.)

What next?

From here, your course of study branches: first to some more theory, then to the past practice of development, then to its future problems.

Chapter 10 introduces a school of economists who have always treated economic growth as history.

Chapter 11 surveys a number of national histories to see how widely patterns of development have varied in the past.

Six chapters then explore current processes and directions of historical change which pose problems for future economic theory and practice.

EXERCISES

1. Take four blank pages. Head each page with the name of one school of thought: Mercantilist, Classical, Marxist, Neoclassical. Divide each page into two columns. Use the columns to summarize the pros and cons of each approach to economic growth, i.e. make your own summaries, in headings or short notes, of what you see as the main strengths and uses (in one column) and the main shortcomings (in the other column) of mercantilist, classical, Marxist and neoclassical theories of growth.

2. Turn back to the list of twelve conditions of growth on page 85. For at least six of those items (and for all of them, if you like) do these two exercises:
   (i) Consider each item singly. Sketch some conditions in which it could fail to affect economic growth. (For example, sketch some conditions in which increased investment might not increase growth.)
   (ii) Sketch some conditions in which there could be growth without the item. (For example, sketch some means by which, in certain conditions, there could be growth without additional investment.)

10

Institutional studies of economic development

Besides their pure theorists, most schools of economic thought also have more practical members – economists who may or may not contribute to the development of theory, but who approach real-life economic problems with less confidence in their theoretical models and more attention to the facts of each case. Some economists go further, to build that practical concern into the theory itself. Instead of theory which tries to model universal principles of economic behavior, they rely on bits of the regular theories where they fit, but also on distilled experience, batteries of possibilities to look for in particular circumstances, questions to ask and investigative methods of answering them. They may expect economic behavior to have many regularities – but also to vary from time to time, place to place, industry to industry. Their focus is on economic life: on the economic actors and their actual opportunities, incentives, purposes, choices. The previous chapter introduced mercantilist, classical, Marxist, neoclassical and Keynesian economists. Now meet a fifth school, whose principles have – broadly speaking – shaped this course of study.

INSTITUTIONAL ECONOMISTS

Political, historical and institutional are rough-and-ready labels for a range of economists who have philosophical and practical objections to 'pure' economics, i.e. to any economics which studies only the *economic* causes of economic performance, or only causes of the kind that are modelled in one or another general economic theory. 'Institutional' is an inadequate collective label for them, but is customary, so we use it. Their differences from 'pure' or 'narrow' economists can be characterized in various ways:

- To explain economic effects pure theorists try to select causes which are (1) economic, and (2) components of their regular models – i.e. they select both for *discipline* and for *regularity*, as described back in Chapter 3. By contrast, institutional economists relate economic effects to whichever of their economic, social, political or other causes it would be useful to know for the purpose in hand.

- Institutional economists study economic activity as part of a society's whole social and political life. Pure economists try to *abstract* economic systems *from* their social surroundings, and imagine how they might work for 'purely economic' people.

- Pure economists try to build a 'hard' science appropriate to a regular world. Institutionalists try for the different science and skills that cope best with a changing, partly uncertain, often *ir*regular world.

- Pure economists say 'Of course we know that real-life economic systems vary, from each other and from any ideal model. But it is economical to describe their variations by *reference to* and *differentiation from* a pure model. Using a pure competitive market model for the purpose allows (1) quick and clear description of the real-life variations and (2) valuable criticism of their imperfections and inefficiencies.' Institutionalists respond: 'Each country's economy may need some of its own theory, its own models, its own useful simplifications. If you insist on describing all varieties by differentiation from one master-model you inevitably build a bias in favor of that master-model into all your work. A double bias, both technical and political.'

- Some institutionalists add: 'Your pure competitive market model is not a timeless model of an ideally efficient economic system. On the contrary we think it is a socially reactionary and technically obsolete model. It was shaped by the interests and values of the rich in conditions which prevailed in the richer capitalist countries from about the 1860s to the 1930s. For the values and interests of *other* classes, and the changing conditions the world *now* faces, we think it is socially undesirable and technically misleading to try to understand real economic life by differentiation from *that* old master-model.'

- But institutional economists don't have a rival master-model. They don't believe in such things. Particular models for particular purposes, yes. But one model for all purposes, no.

But remember how this chapter opened. There are practical, institutional thinkers in all theoretical schools. One outstanding warning against type-casting economists by their theoretical commitments alone is Arthur Lewis, author of *Theory of Economic Growth* which I hope you have read by now. In chapter 5 of that book in 1955 he offered a simple model of economic growth as a function of saving and investment – a model acceptable to the purest neoclassical theorists, and since partly discredited, then partly rehabilitated again, by practical experience. But in the same book he also set out the broadest of all accounts of the manifold political, social, cultural, religious and institutional conditions that are likely to affect any strategy of growth. Thus he earned his Nobel prize as a leader in *both* theoretical schools.

Values and interests

The nature of the institutional approach does not tie it to any particular ideology or set of social values. Institutional methods, shaped by appropriate values in each case, could in principle serve the purposes of anyone from far-Right conservative to far-Left revolutionary. But in practice most institutional economists have had three general characteristics.

First, they have been democratic and reformist: neither revolutionary nor conservative, but practical improvers anywhere from the moderate Left to the middle of the road. Appropriate experts for the mixed economies of modern welfare states, or for poorer countries striving for development.

Second, the institutional school has supplied some outstanding economic philosophers and methodologists. Gunnar Myrdal and Paul Streeten have led the world in analysing the irreducible role which values play in social and economic understanding. They are detailed and effective critics of neoclassical 'value-blindness'. They developed much of the scientific self-knowledge you were offered in Part One of this course. And they have pioneered, in a range of fruitful ways, the conscious and rational inter-relation of values, theory, research, and social and economic policy.

Third, the open-minded characteristics of the institutional approach have obvious technical advantages for studying *strange* or *changing* economic systems. Societies with under-developed economies facing radical challenges are likely to be served best by economists whose philosophy positively encourages them to discard, replace or adapt their theories and methods as often as changing realities and social purposes require.

Through the rest of Part Two we will look first at some strange and then at some changing subjects. In this chapter, some institutional economists' contributions to problems of economic development outside the rich West, and some lessons for the West which they have learned from those studies. In the next, examples of diverse patterns of development in the past history of the

rich countries. Then some chapters about new problems which those countries face now and in the next few decades: decades when you (young economist) will be looking to practise your craft.

Theory and experience

In sixty years since the second World War economists of all schools have learned a lot about the problems of poor countries trying to develop in the wake of countries which are already rich. In *Development Perspectives* (1981) and *Thinking about Development* (1995) Paul Streeten has summed up six shifts of perception since the 1940s. Further simplified, they are:

1. A shift away from believing that poor countries can necessarily follow rich countries along the same path of growth. In a number of ways the power and competitive strength of the rich may now block that path. But alternative paths may be open to choice, with or without conflict.

2. A shift of aim from simple growth of GNP per head to the things that growth is supposed to achieve, with a corresponding shift of economic analysis from high abstraction and aggregation to concreteness and disaggregation. What does that mean? It means less attention to totals like GNP, national rates of saving and capital formation, etc. It means more attention to particulars such as the incomes of particular groups; the work available in particular regions; provisions for vulnerable groups of women, children, migrants, ethnic minorities, etc.; and the supply of the necessities of life to the poorest people. In Streeten's words 'it became clear that measured income and its growth is only a part of basic needs. Adequate nutrition and safe water at hand, continuing employment, secure and adequate livelihoods for the self-employed, more and better schooling for their children, better preventive medical services, adequate shelter, cheap transport ... would figure on the list of urgently felt needs of poor people ...

    'In addition to those specific 'economic' objectives, a new emphasis was laid on 'non-material' needs ... such as self-determination, self-reliance, political freedom and security, participation in making the decisions that affect workers and citizens, national and cultural identity, and a sense of purpose in life and work – needs which 'in addition to being valued in their own right may [also] be the conditions for meeting material needs.' (*Development Perspectives*, p. 110).

3. A shift from problems of national growth towards

global problems common to rich and poor countries alike: population numbers, resource limits, pollution and environmental quality.

4. A shift from believing in harmony of interests (Adam Smith's 'hidden hand' bringing social good from individual competition, and national benefits from international division-of-labor and trade) to recognizing conflicts of interest: conflicts for possession of scarce resources; conflicts over international prices and terms of trade; class conflicts for power and wealth both within and between nations; etc.

5. A shift from treating the Third World as one, i.e. as a group of similar countries with similar problems, to recognizing many and growing differences between country and country, and the problems they face.

6. A shift from optimism to pessimism about poor countries' development prospects, and the help they can expect from rich countries and international agencies. For many poor countries the tasks and problems of development have proved to be tougher than expected. Many of their ruling classes have proved to be nastier than expected. Trade with the rich world has been less helpful than expected. International aid has proved less effective than expected, and for that and other reasons the rich countries have been reducing its volume. And (as the previous chapter emphasized) some of the economic theories which rich countries have exported to poor countries have done them more harm than good.

Many of those shifts were led by institutional economists and they were all in the direction of more open-minded practical approaches to development problems. Three samples follow: a perceptive local observation; a great book and its treatment of a particular development problem; and a great institution created by a researcher in response to what he met, and took the trouble to understand, in the working life of some poor women in a very poor village.

POLLY HILL'S COCOA FARMERS

Polly Hill may have had some helpful genes – her mother was Maynard Keynes' sister and her father was a brilliant natural scientist. Working as an anthropologist in tropical West Africa in the 1950s she studied some cocoa farmers whom economists supposed were local people using traditional techniques. She found that they were migrants. Their methods were new to the district. There were two groups of them, who had come from different origins. The two differed radically from each other, and from the local people of the district, in their family organization and systems of inheritance, but both

cultures were compatible with their similar farming methods, as the local people's were not. Any strategy for agrarian development in that region needed to be based on understanding *those people in that region*, not the universal human robots of the general theoretical models.

From her first book on the cocoa farmers in 1956, Polly Hill battled to persuade development economists to study and understand the family and community and intellectual life, as well as the work, of the people whose economic systems and development prospects concerned them. Many of them did learn a good deal of what she wanted to teach them, some from her writing and others from their own experience. But she never thought they had learned enough. Thirty years after her first book she was still telling them, in *Development Economists on Trial: The Anthropological Case for a Prosecution* (1986), to learn more about the social life of any people whose economic activity they wanted to understand.

GUNNAR MYRDAL'S ASIAN DRAMA

A great many lessons of experience were spelled out by Gunnar Myrdal and associates in *Asian Drama: An Inquiry into the Poverty of Nations* (3 vols., 1968). The book reported a seven-year study of the development problems of South Asia: Pakistan, India, Sri Lanka, Burma, Thailand, Laos, Cambodia, Vietnam, Malaya, Indonesia and the Philippines. It exemplifies the institutional approach to economic problems. It is 'self-aware', exposing and discussing its own values and methods. It treats the diverse economic problems of the area in their diverse social and political contexts. It includes the most extensive and detailed study of the effects of applying Western neoclassical economic theories to societies they don't fit. I don't suggest you read it as you have read Arthur Lewis's *Theory of Economic Growth*, because *Asian Drama* is three volumes and 2284 pages long. But you can try Part One (pp. 37-125) on the values and methods employed, then read the detailed Table of Contents to find some chapters on subjects that interest you. A sample follows. Never mind its being thirty years old. It is a superb example of how an economist should approach a development problem in a particular society, at a particular time, aware that the society and the problem are changing, and ready to replace old theory which does not fit the time and place with new theory which does.

For example: Indian farming

Myrdal and his colleagues found that the links between industrial and agricultural development had often been neglected, and the importance of agricultural development under-rated. They also found that Western concepts of employment and unemployment did not fit most undeveloped countries' village life. So instead of studying 'employment' and 'unemployment', they studied 'labor utilization': not just who had paid jobs and who did not, but what work was done, by whom, how efficiently, for whose benefit, whether in paid employment or not.

After some post-war improvement Indian agriculture had stagnated while population numbers continued to grow. The limits to output were not technical. The methods in use were primitive and open to many improvements, but those primitive methods themselves were being under-used. The land was under-used because the existing labor was under-used.

Western economic theory and farming technique suggested that producing more would require less labor. For India, that was not true: India had large technical possibilities of producing more by applying more labor. But the obstructions were many. They included:

- Settled habits of short hours of not-very-hard work.

- Caste and cultural and educational values which discouraged many people from manual work as undignified and degrading.

- Local pride combined with Western theory to discourage proper understanding of the under-utilization of labor, and the social conditions and beliefs that cause it. Western theory and research tend to focus on agricultural technique and organization, because European people respond well to new technical opportunities. Indian theory and research needed to focus instead on social and attitudinal problems, because there was already a good deal of under-used technical potentiality, and the hard problems were the human ones.

- Technical knowledge is still needed – but some Western science (like some Western economic theory) can be misused in ways that actually discourage better science. Indians found it easy to import Western agricultural science and education, so they were slow to develop their own. It followed that little was known about Indian climate, soil, crops, livestock, etc. When imported techniques were applied ignorantly – for example when fertilizers were applied on European principles to Indian soils which had not been analysed – the results were often disappointing. *That discredited 'science' and made it even harder to persuade people to get the soils analysed.* (Myrdal was a connoisseur of circular causation.)

- As with science, so with technology. Progressive Indian policy-makers looked to Western practice for technical guidance. But Western farming techniques are intensely labor-saving. They may not help societies which need to occupy and feed as many people as possible in their rural villages. Americans and some Europeans want most grain per acre with *least* labor; in India the same yield with *most* labor may be best for most people.

And there were other hindrances to progress. Many Indian peasants suffered from oppressive moneylenders or landlords. War and independence and communal strife helped to get rid of many of the moneylenders and some of the landlords, but a drastic general land reform was still needed if the people who actually worked the land were to have clear, debt-free ownership of it.

Governments went some little way in land reform. Holdings were bought from some landlords – but usually sold to others. Some limits were placed on the size of the individual holdings. Some regulations were designed to protect laborers and sharecroppers. But many of those changes were evaded or otherwise ineffective. And there was no general confiscation or redistribution of land to make its ownership either much more equal, or much more productive, than before.

The need for some radical redistribution had been widely acknowledged – so why didn't it happen? Rich and poor both helped to prevent it, for different reasons. There was a natural conservative alliance against it. Absentee landlords (including many politicians, public servants and other influential people) and the bigger landowners in the villages combined to oppose reforms. On the other side, the poor generally *failed* to combine. They might agree what land should be *taken* – but to which of them should it then be *given*, in what shares, on what principles? There could be plenty of disagreement about that. So the conservatives tended to be united and the potential radicals divided. There was not very much redistribution, and what there was tended to be from one landlord to another.

There was also an ideological problem. Educated radicals – 'Delhi radicals' – who were ready to cancel moneylenders' rights and confiscate landlords' land were mostly socialists. Their socialism made them aware of the need to redistribute land. It made them willing to do it by confiscation if need be. But the same socialist beliefs made most of them oppose *any* private ownership of the land. They did not want to equalize the ownership of land by distributing it to small individual holdings (which was what most landless peasants wanted). Socialists wanted cooperative farming. Most poor peasants did not understand or did not want cooperative farming. In not wanting it they proved to be right enough, because conservatives made sure that most farm cooperation in India should be cooperation among land-lords and capitalists. Like joint share-holders, owners pooled resources to exploit laborers and sharecroppers much as before. Thus socialist ideas were misused, and were rightly unpopular with the poor people they were meant to help.

So much for cooperation in private farming. Could it do better in the public sector – for example in communal public works? As an early lesson of experience, econo-mists of all schools tended to agree in three related beliefs: (1) Indian villages had plenty of spare labor that should be put to work. So (2) saving and capital invest-ment need not require any reduction of the standard of living, because (3) without reducing anyone's consump-tion, spare labor could be put to work creating productive capital.

How could labor alone, or almost alone, create produc-tive capital? Myrdal summed up 'the type of additional labor input that can be considered "investment" because it promises to raise future yields and hence produce a sustained increase in employment.' It calls for –

> the mobilization of labor to build roads, bridges, irri-gation canals and drainage ditches, wells, tanks, and soil conservation terraces . . . and to work on affore-station, pasture improvement, and the construction of warehouses for storing crops and farm supplies. These "investment" activities are all highly labor-intensive and require few resources to complement labor beyond those locally available; many of them can be expected to raise yields fairly quickly. But they presuppose collective action, as the scale of effort required surpasses the immediate interests or resources of individual families. Other suggested uses of the villagers' spare time are ... construction of schools, dispensaries, village privies, gutters, and clean wells for drinking water and other household uses, paving of village streets to end dust and mud, improving the houses, manufacturing simple furni-ture, killing rats, or merely washing the children and keeping flies away from their eyes. It is generally recognized that these undertakings in the service of consumption can also be productive.
> – *Asian Drama*, p. 1357

Nevertheless writing in 1965 Myrdal had to report that 'every effort to mobilize and organize under-utilized labor for investment purposes has been a failure or near-failure'. Why? Such labor can be voluntary, or

compulsory, or wage-paid. When villagers are asked to *volunteer* work they don't do much. They think too many of the benefits will go to their betters, who don't do any voluntary work at all. *Compulsory* labor usually fails for a similar reason. Too many people simply refuse to work because they think manual work is beneath them – and if they won't work, others won't work either. If *wages* are offered for communal work, somebody richer than the laborer must be taxed to pay the wages. The taxation is resisted. 'Even when the ultimate benefits of the investments would be reaped mainly by the upper strata of landowners, the initial taxation would have to be redistributional in character', i.e. it would have to take money from those who have it and give it as wages to those who don't. Myrdal concluded:

> Such a scheme would be resisted politically the more effectively since at both the village and the state levels the power belongs to those who would have to make the most sacrifices, at least initially. Ultimately the difficulty in mobilizing idle laborers for construc-tive work is rooted in the inegalitarian structure of the villages and the national community. In an egalitarian rural society it would be much more natural and feasible to insist that all should work in the common interest.   – *Asian Drama*, p. 1362.

For those and other reasons he concluded that twenty years of Indian independence had seen very limited agri-cultural progress, most of it for the benefit of those in least need. 'Perhaps the most conspicuous result ... has been the strengthening of the upper strata in the villages and a corresponding reduction in the position of share-croppers and landless laborers in the lower strata of rural society. All the significant policy measures for agricul-tural uplift adopted by the governments – whether technological or institutional – have tended to shift the power balance of the rural structure in favor of the priv-ileged classes.'

What to do now? Myrdal insisted that the problems belonged to an historical process, not a static system. What happens in one decade affects what is possible in the next. Conditions had changed, so options and possi-bilities had changed, from what they might have been twenty years earlier:

> The political consequences of the postwar trend of events are far-reaching. The evidence suggests that the opportune moment for a radical reshaping of the agrarian structure has passed. Sweeping changes might perhaps have been accomplished in the revolu-tionary environment of the immediate post-war and post-independence years. But if consent for a funda-

mental change in property and tenancy rights might have been won then, it is not possible now.

– Asian Drama, p. 1367

What is possible now? For Myrdal's advice in detail you must read pages 1366-84 of *Asian Drama*. Briefly, he suggested three lines of action:

• However reluctantly, governments should accept the strength of the village capitalists as a fact of life, and try to make capitalist agriculture more productive. They should stop dreaming of socialist agriculture. They should also stop talking about it, so that the existing owners could feel secure, and improve their farms without fear of future confiscations.

• Some existing regulation of land ownership could be strengthened and extended. Individuals should only be allowed to own what they would live on and cultivate. Existing absentee owners could not be dispossessed, but there should be no further purchases by absentees.

• It might be possible to give landless laborers small plots of their own, in private ownership. To be politically possible, the plots would have to be very small, too small to support a laborer or stop him working for others for wages. But even from tiny 'kitchen gardens' Myrdal hoped for three good effects: (1) Private plots would motivate work and output *additional* to whatever the laborers did for their employers, i.e. it would motivate some economic growth. (2) If laborers were seen to work some land of their own as well as employers' land, that might help to dignify manual labor and reduce its stigma. (3) In a country too poor to afford monetary welfare (pensions, doles, etc.) kitchen gardens could provide people with some welfare 'in kind' to fall back on in hard times.

Myrdal did not think it very likely that even those mild policies would be adopted. But if they were, he thought they would increase farm output, and reduce inequalities a little. They might also bring some better feeling to the villages, and soften some class and caste hostilities.

Thirty years later his pessimism appears to have been justified. *Some* reforms have made *some* progress in *some* Indian provinces. But over much of the country, attempts at reform by redistribution have been defeated by mixtures of conservative resistance, administrative failure and popular inertia.

It is time to remind you of the purpose of this sample from *Asian Drama*. It is not to make you an expert in some past problems of Indian agriculture, but just to illustrate some institutional economists' methods.

Myrdal's *values* shaped his purposes. Here his *purpose* was economic: to find ways to increase output and reduce poverty in Indian villages. The *analysis* therefore extends to economic, political, social and cultural conditions, conditions *selected* because they seemed likely to help or hinder desirable kinds of development. Some Western economic theory about what-causes-what is used, where it fits. Some is discarded because it does not fit. Quite a lot is not just discarded but explicitly condemned, because if Indians continue to believe it they will persist with inappropriate or self-defeating policies, including policies which purport to reduce inequalities but actually increase them.

MUHAMMAD YUNUS' ASIAN ENTERPRISE

Muhammad Yunus was an academic. Studying the life of a poor village in 1976, he and one of his students found 42 very poor people who worked independently at various trades but had to borrow small sums at extortionate rates from traders and moneylenders to buy their working materials. He divided £17 between them, then decided that they needed an institution rather than a personal lender. Step by step he founded the Grameen Bank which was formally incorporated in 1982. It accepts savings from poor people, and lends without security to those of them who need working capital with which to earn.

I was not trying to become a moneylender ... all I really wanted was to solve an immediate problem: the problem of poverty which humiliates and denigrates everything that a human being stands for.

We did not know anything about how to run a bank for the poor, so we had to learn from scratch. I wanted to cover all aspects of rural lives such as trading, small manufacturing, retailing and even selling from door to door ... Our clients do not need to show how large their savings are and how much wealth they have, they need to prove how poor they are, how little savings they have.

To my amazement and surprise the repayment of loans by people who borrow without collateral is much better than those whose borrowings are secured by enormous assets. Indeed, more than 98 per cent of our loans are repaid because the poor know this is the only opportunity they have to break out of their poverty. .

Now we have more than 12,000 employees and 1,112 branches in Bangladesh. The staff meet more than 2,300,000 borrowers face to face each week, on their doorstep. Each month we lend out more than

$35 million in tiny loans. At the same time, almost, a similar amount comes back to us in repayments.

Gradually we focused almost exclusively on lending to women. If the goals of economic development include improved standards of living, removal of poverty, access to dignified employment, and reduction in inequality, then it is quite natural to start with women. They constitute the majority of the poor, the unemployed and the economically and socially disadvantaged. And since they were closer to the children, women were also our key to the future of Bangladesh.

This was not easy. The first and most formidable opposition came from the husbands. Next the mullahs. Then the professional people, and even government officials.

– Muhammad Yunus, in the *Guardian Weekly*,
8 November 1998

In rich as well as poor countries there is a lot of argument about relations between inequality and economic growth. That subject also tends to be better understood, industry by industry and country by country, by open-minded investigators than by strong-minded theorists of either the Left or the Right – as follows.

GROWTH AND INEQUALITY

Economists disagree about relations between economic growth and the distribution of wealth and income. Does the growth affect the distribution, or the distribution affect the growth? Does growth tend to increase or reduce inequalities? If governments want to stimulate growth should they begin by redistributing income upwards, from the poor who won't otherwise save at all to the capitalists who alone will invest the savings? Or downwards, to give poor people the means of investing to make their labor more effective? Or should they redistribute bit by bit as growth proceeds? Or wait till the country is rich and can afford tax-and-welfare transfers from its rich to its poor? Or leave the distribution of wealth and income to look after themselves? There has been theoretical support for each of those strategies.

There has also been practical experience of more than one of them. Radical land reforms helped Japan's and Taiwan's growth and reduced their inequalities after World War Two. But in other conditions opposite relations have prevailed. To make full use of the new crops and techniques known as 'the green revolution', small land holdings have been consolidated into larger holdings in a number of countries. There, rich peasants are richer and some poor peasants are poorer than before and GNP has been increased by means which *increased*

inequalities. Those are a few examples of many – both downward and upward redistributions have at times helped growth, and there have also been 'neutral' cases. You can find examples of all three in Lance Taylor (ed.) *The Rocky Road to Reform* (1993). The links between growth and distribution tend to be different in each case. But they are often open to collective choice *if the people realise that they have a choice*, which may require that they disregard some of their economists. There is nothing necessarily impractical about designing policies to combine growth with greater equality, or (for example in rich but environmentally threatened countries) policies to improve equalities *without* further growth.

DEVELOPMENT AND BASIC NEEDS

In 1976 the International Labor Organization published a basic needs strategy in *Employment, Growth and Basic Needs: A One-World Problem* (ILO, Geneva). The World Bank began studies whose conclusions were reported by Paul Streeten and others in *First Things First: Meeting basic human needs in the developing countries* (1981). That book explained the ends and means of a basic needs strategy. It reviewed arguments for and against it, and related it to economic growth, population growth and other aspects of development.

The theorists start from a mixture of old and new beliefs:

First, poor people don't *only* need money income. They also need to be able to spend it on essentials. They can't buy clean water if there isn't any. They can't buy better health and education if there are no health services or schools. And so on – some of the things they want may be supplied in a market way, but others may not be.

Second, economists' traditional distinctions between consumption and investment don't always fit poor conditions. In rich countries food and drink and housing and many health and education services are seen as consumption goods. But in poor countries those same things can often do what capital goods do in rich countries: they can increase productivity. Clean water, sufficient food and shelter and basic education and health services can turn weak, sick, apathetic, ignorant and unproductive people into strong, healthy, willing, knowledgeable and productive people.

Third, it has been conventional to rely on economic growth to reduce population growth. As people earn more income, they tend to have fewer children. But which *particular* effects of the higher income lead them to limit their families? Could those *particular* conditions be provided sooner, to limit population sooner than general economic growth can limit it?

Essentially, basic needs theorists argue that some particular elements of economic development are more urgent than others – so we should try to develop those elements immediately and directly, instead of waiting for the general growth of income to produce them. This strategy need not hinder broader development, and can be designed to help it.

> The hypothesis of the basic needs approach is that a set of selective policies makes it possible to satisfy the basic human needs of the whole population at levels of income per head substantially below those required by a less discriminating strategy of all-round income growth – and it is therefore possible to satisfy these needs sooner. Attacking the evils of hunger, malnutrition, disease, and illiteracy with precision will eradicate (or at least ameliorate) these evils with fewer resources (or sooner) than would the round-about method of raising incomes.

Reducing poverty is good in itself. Doing it in a selective, accurate way can also economize resources and help more general development.

> A combined operation for providing an appropriately selected package of basic needs (water, sewerage, nutrition, and health) economizes on the use of resources and improves the impact because of link-ages, complementarities, and interdependencies between different sectors.
>
> – *First Things First*, pp. 37-39.

Linkages Those 'linkages, complementarities and interdependencies' are important for a number of reasons.

First, the necessary policies don't have reliable independent effects. The effects of each depend on the presence of others. Water without drainage can do more harm than good. Clean water and sanitation don't achieve much unless people are educated in hygiene. Health services don't achieve much unless clean water and adequate food are available. Good food does more good if gastroenteric diseases are prevented. Schools achieve more if the children are healthy, health services achieve more if the children are educated. And so on – the mix and coordination of the basic provisions are most important. Good coordination can reduce the costs of some of the services, and increase the productivity of all of them.

Besides needing to be supplied *together*, the basic provisions can also reinforce each other *in sequence*, over time. Streeten offers a particular example, then an indication of the general kind of selective causal analysis

that is required:

> First, knowledge of hygienic practices improves health. In particular, the education of mothers improves the health of their children. Second, education that raises productivity increases the resources available for meeting basic needs and improving health status. Healthy people, especially children, have a greater capacity for learning, which reinforces the impact of education on health and on productivity ... higher productivity and earning power and better education encourage family planning; family planning improves nutrition; nutrition improves health; and better health improves attitudes towards family planning. The cumulative and reciprocal nature of these processes shows that policy interventions will have multiplier effects.
>
> The general point is that policies have direct and indirect effects; some reinforce the basic needs objective, others frustrate it. Nutrition policies improve nutrition; health policies, health; and education policies, education. But nutrition policies also affect health and education, as well as the earning power of the poor; health policies affect nutrition, education, and earning power; and education policies affect nutrition, health, and earning power. It may also be that these policies, and the improved productivity of the poor, contribute to the incomes of the better-off. Moneylenders, employers, public officials, and foreign companies may benefit from these improvements, either directly or indirectly. Each of these linkages has a time dimension, so that better education of the poor may lead to higher productivity and to increased incomes of employers, which in turn may give rise to more jobs for the poor. A fully articulated basic needs strategy would have to assess these indirect effects and linkages through time and evolve a set of policies in the light of the basic needs objective.   – *First Things First*, pp. 50-1

For economists, thinking in that way can do two useful things. It can *disaggregate* analysis, and *integrate* policy-making.

First, it calls for more detailed and concrete economic analysis. Instead of dealing in 'abstract aggregations' like Gross National Product, it looks to the actual material conditions of life of particular people: women, children, old people, sick people, unskilled people, and so on. In doing that it returns economics to its original purpose of improving people's living conditions. And it builds a value explicitly into the method of analysis: a concern for the poorest people, and a judgment that goods and services which meet basic needs are more important than goods and services which meet further wants beyond those basic needs.

Second – besides achieving a more concrete and detailed analysis – Streeten claims that a basic needs approach has considerable organizing and integrating power, both politically and intellectually. Conventional approaches tend to deal separately with apparently unconnected problems to do with energy, environmental pollution, scarce raw materials, appropriate technology, healthy and sociable patterns of consumption, urbanization, international trade, international dominance and dependance, and the treatment of transnational corporations. A basic needs approach can link them rather better than a simple concern with growth can do; and it can generate policies which integrate action about them.

FACE TO FACE

The best economists of poor countries' development problems have studied and understood the problems face to face in the lives and work of the people, often including the poorest people. Some of them, like Muhammad Yunus, have grown up in developing countries. Some, like Gunnar Myrdal, have been Western researchers in those countries. Both have done their best to understand what the people want, their actual opportunities and conflicts and frustrations, what they know and what they don't know how to do, and what they might learn to do. That personal fieldwork can have compound good effects. It does not attract economists whose chief interests are in mathematical theory and in writing articles for refereed journals. It exposes a lot of that theory as trivial, irrelevant or positively misleading about real economic life. It tends to attract researchers with some care and liking for the people whose life they study. It leaves them in no doubt about the importance of household resources, unpaid work, children's upbringing and education, women's economic roles, and the value of women's perceptions of economic problems.

Those elements of the researchers' choices and experience have been specially important because most of the researchers have so far been men. The best of them have learned not only how women live and work and how vitally they contribute to development but also – to some extent, where there are real gender differences – how women *think* about economic life.

Some of the best development economists also work at rich countries' problems. When they do, what they have learned from poor women in developing countries serves as a kind of reverse international aid. It can improve economists' approaches to economic systems at every stage of development from poorest to richest. It is not just for equal opportunity within the profession that the rich democracies need at least half their economists to be women. Simple competence, better principles of selection in causal analysis, a better understanding of many elements of economic experience, better judgment of the uses and misuses of coercion and competition and cooperation in economic life, more attention to the concerns and potentialities of women students, and the impulse and the necessary numbers to contest the misconceived scientist domination of the profession, all demand it.

This argument will be resumed, mostly by women economists, at the conclusion of Chapter 18.

BELIEFS ARE WORKING PARTS, AND ALSO WEAPONS

It is worth noticing, now and then, how warring theories and policy proposals confront one another in practice, not in the course of research but in policy-making and public persuasion.

In debates about international aid and strategies for developing countries there are often complicated conflicts of real and pretended interests. Usually no poor people from either world are present at the debates: neither the poor countries' poor nor the rich countries' workers. Within the research institutes and international agencies and across the negotiating tables, rich politicians and administrators and economists from rich countries face comparatively rich but often much less secure politicians and administrators and economists from poor countries.

Some from both worlds are honest unselfish people trying to help the poor of the poor countries by effective means.

Some from both worlds are honest unselfish people trying to help the poor by technically mistaken and ineffective or counter-effective means.

Some are looking after what they see as general interests of the rich: for example to keep labor weak, to restrict the scope of government, to keep as much economic activity as possible in private capitalist hands.

Some are looking after specific rich interests: markets for particular products, opportunities for particular banks, advantages for particular firms, jobs for selves and friends.

So things like this happen:

Somebody observes that most people in the poor countries are poor and asks what keeps them poor. Are they kept poor chiefly by their own shortcomings, or chiefly by their own rich, or chiefly by the rich of the rich countries?

The rich of the poor countries are sometimes the most reactionary and least democratic of all the debaters around the table. But some of them profess the more-or-less-Marxist belief that the rich industrial countries *alone* keep the poor countries poor – and are now proposing to make sure of it by tying 'basic needs' strings to any international aid they offer. Some Left voices from both worlds agree with that, and join in opposing tied aid. Thus Left and Right are in unnatural alliance, and the poor of the poor countries are likely to suffer from it.

Meanwhile two other groups of Leftish democrats from rich countries adopt different tactics. They recognize that the poor of some poor countries can expect little or no good from the Rightist dictators and ruling groups who govern them. So one group tries to tie international aid to basic needs, and police it so that it actually reaches the poor it is intended for. Rich representatives of those poor countries holler 'Imperialism' and protest against such infringements of sovereignty. The other group of Leftish democrats wants to avoid that response, and honestly believes in respecting the developing countries' independence. So they propose to switch aid from countries which neglect basic needs to others whose governments (voluntarily, independently) try to meet their people's basic needs. Rich and poor from the countries which would lose aid unite in protest. They are demanding aid which would mostly go to the rich in some of the worst governed societies in the world – but they are telling rich capitalist countries not to 'tie' their aid, so they may well get applause and support from some of the Left in both 'worlds'.

Stop. What is all this confusing babble doing here, in a course of study which is supposed to be making economics *clear* to you? Answer: honest disclosure. To be an effective economist you must learn to see through ideological smokescreens to the interests contending in the smoke. And not only the selfish class and corporate interests. It is just as important to recognize the honest contenders: the humane conservatives, the genuine reformers, the effective administrators of aid programs who can be found among the representatives of both the rich and the poor countries. And while you are sorting out the interests, you also need to be sorting out the intellectual ammunition they are using: the more and less accurate facts and figures; the true beliefs, the mistaken beliefs, the pretended beliefs, and the self-fulfilling or self-defeating beliefs, about what causes what. However hair-raising, that is what a great deal of the most important persuasion and negotiation and policy-making is like. Get used to it, it's your trade.

And good does come of it, if the good contenders don't tire. More basic needs are met. Children are healthier. Women are freer. People are better housed and equipped. They can do more for themselves and one another. They read more, know more about the world, enjoy more arts and recreations.

Even without much economic growth, Sri Lankans live twenty years longer than their grandparents did. In the forty five poorest countries in the world, the (often imperfect) records suggest that between 1960 and 1995 average expectation of life increased by fifteen years. Infant mortality halved. Where fewer than a quarter of the people had access to safe water, more than half have it now. Where a third were literate, half are literate now. GDP per person appears to have doubled.

In the seventeen best-performing poor countries life expectancy rose from 58.5 to 70.5 years between 1960 and 1992. Baby deaths fell from 83 to 30 per 1000 births. Productivity and real income more than doubled, and if you could count all the unaccounted production it probably trebled.

You may decide that those effects are worth working for.

SUMMARY

This is not so much a summary of this chapter as a reminder of its purposes.

1. It introduced institutional economists, their attention to the political and social context of economic activity, and their adaptable, open-minded methods. They include scholars like Myrdal and Streeten who are institutionalists by methodological choice, and others like Arthur Lewis whose different theoretical equipment has not hindered them from dealing in practical, open-minded ways with changing economic realities.

2. The chapter showed how the understanding of economic development can change with accumulating experience – and how it needs to change as economic systems themselves change, and their methods and possibilities of development change, over time.

3. It argued that we need more women economists, to balance the prevailing men's values and to combat or reform some of them.

4. You have been reminded yet again that these lessons don't only apply to the study of growth and development. Whatever economic activity you study, never forget that (i) it may be affected in many ways by its historical and institutional context, and (ii) it may be changing as you study it, sometimes *because* you study it.

EXERCISES

First student: This chapter has been a great relief. If open minds, competent accounting, experienced common sense and humane purposes are economists' best equipment, our work promises to be more useful to humankind than if it continues to be shaped by theories of the kind that have recently been shaping most of it.

Second student: This chapter, like most of this course so far, is recommending a general retreat from serious social science and professional skill to uneducated anecdotal assertions and opinions shaped by economists' subjective prejudices. At best, undisciplined journalism. At worst, dangerous rubbish.

Either –

1. Defend the first or the second student's judgment of this book's first ten chapters. If you are also studying law and intending to make your living at it, defend them both (in different briefs).

Or –

2. Chapter 9's sketches of mercantilist, classical, Marxist and neoclassical theories were each followed by an assessment of their advantages and limitations. Do the same, at about the same length, for this chapter's recommendations – as the author (perhaps significantly?) has not done.

11

Some economic histories

Treat all but the last part of this chapter as easy reading. It is a string of historical sketches. The message is important but not difficult.

Chapter 10 concluded that 'growth is history'. The process of economic development has differed over time and from country to country. There is much to be learned by studying it but it can't be sufficiently explained by any single theory or single set of historical forces.

This chapter's purpose is to illustrate some of the range and limits of variation in the development of modern mixed economies. The contents have been selected chiefly to show similarities and differences in –

- the order of development of agriculture, industries and services;
- main sources of innovation;
- the role of government; and
- the 'mix' of the mixed economy.

The sketches are grouped. First, two densely populated countries developing as specialized industrial processors and exporters: Britain industrializing from 1750, Japan from 1870. Second, emigrant European societies making contrasting uses of abundant natural resources to yield the world's highest average incomes at the time: the USA and Australia from the 1860s to 1890. Third, the diverse development strategies of six rich countries – the USA, France, Sweden, Australia, Japan and Britain – through the 'long boom' from 1950 to 1973. Fourth, the historic change of direction since the 1970s as the rich countries' growth slowed, English-speaking governments moved sharply to the Right, and over much of the developed Western world the century-long progress to greater equality was reversed. Inequalities began to increase again, and some Right forces were suspected of contriving a global counter-attack against the democracies' powers of self-government.

INDUSTRIALIZATION : BRITAIN AND JAPAN

BRITAIN FROM 1750

Britain is rightly famous for the steam revolution, because steam power revolutionized industrial productivity. But many elements of a technical and commercial revolution were well advanced, and in good shape to exploit the steam engine, before James Watt's engine became available in the 1770s. Radical agricultural reorganization was under way in a country which already had advanced coal, metal, textile, building, shipbuilding and shipping industries, worldwide trade, and aggressively commercial foreign and colonial policies.

In agriculture some innovative landowners had been importing or developing better plant and animal strains and breeding methods, new farm tools, better drainage and fertilizers, new crop rotation and soil management. By the 1750s methods existed which could substantially increase output per head and per acre wherever farmland could be consolidated into substantial capitalist farms. In the next eighty years about 6m. acres – up to half the land in some midland counties, nearly a fifth of England altogether – were enclosed by Act of Parliament, and more by landowners' private agree-

ments, with considerable coercion of smallholders, tenants and laborers. The new farming employed about as many people as before, but its greater productivity helped to feed a fast-growing population whose increase supplied labor to the developing towns and industries. About half the nation's workers farmed in 1750, less than a quarter a century later.

There was already a good deal of industry. Wool and cloth were processed in town workshops and tens of thousands of peasant households, by an industry whose biggest operators employed as many as five hundred hands and used shipping, warehousing and banking services from North America to the East Indies. Coal was mined and marketed on a big scale. There were also metal mining and smelting, metalworking, shipbuilding, rope and sailmaking, timber trades, furniture making, coachbuilding, papermaking and printing, glasswork and pottery, brewing and saltmaking. People were building what are still England's most prized country and town houses. Civil engineers were improving their skills with turnpike roads, docks and harbors and river and canal navigations. Water and wind power had allowed the development of some simple industrial machinery which was easily adaptable to steam power when it came. Altogether the technical and commercial conditions were such that when effective steam engines were developed they could be applied readily in coal mining, then in milling and smelting, then most spectacularly in textile manufacture, machine-making, and water and rail transport.

Many things contributed to accelerating industrial development through the second half of the eighteenth century. Historians have explored the sources of political stability, internal unity and commercial freedom; business optimism and acceptance of hard work and high risks; expanding markets and transport to reach them; and the sources of raw materials, labor and capital. All those conditions were needed. But for our present comparative purposes, notice two contributors: the innovative engineers and businessmen, and the activities of government.

Innovators

Many of the leading industrial innovators had a number of things in common. They were able improvers and organizers rather than brilliant inventors (there had been other steam engines before James Watt's). They were sons of skilled tradesmen or business people. They grew up in provincial towns, in Nonconformist families whose members did not belong to the Church of England. With some self-educated exceptions they went to day schools and learned useful modern subjects. Nonconformists were barred from parliament, from most jobs in the government's civil and military services, and from learning or teaching at English universities. But they could go into business. There has been much debate about the economic influence of the Nonconformist churches and about relations, if any, between 'the protestant ethic and the spirit of capitalism'. Whatever direct effects there may have been on the beliefs and motivation of the early industrialists, there was also an important indirect effect, in that their nonconformity barred them from orthodox upper-class upbringing. Barred from the fashionable schools and universities, they founded their own schools – modest day-schools teaching subjects and skills useful to trades and business people – and sent their young men on to Scottish or continental universities, or straight from school into business.

What difference did it make? Compare the upbringing of a nonconformist boy with the upbringing of someone 'born to lead' in that century. A privileged son of the aristocracy, gentry or one of the established professions was likely to grow up among people with no special interest in business, and often some contempt for it. While still a child he was likely to leave family life and the company of women for a more or less brutal boarding school, then an all-male university whose teachers were all unmarried clergymen. He would be schooled in Greek and Latin language and literature, some mathematics and theology, perhaps some law. The corporate life and culture of his teachers and peers was likely to encourage public, military, literary or pleasure-loving ambitions appropriate to a choice of careers on the land or in government, the armed services, the established church or perhaps the law. And the upbringing did its best to instil a conservative respect for the political and social order, and established ways of doing things. It did produce some innovators – but not many, and rarely in business or engineering.

Until the religious tests were repealed in the nineteenth century that conservative upbringing was not available to outsiders. Some Scots and Irish and all Jews and Nonconformists were excluded from it. Instead, a bright son of well-off English Congregationalists or other Nonconformists was likely to grow up among merchants, craftsmen or other business people. He was likely to live at home, in company with adults as well as children, women as well as men, workers and servants as well as owners. At day school he would learn English and modern languages, mathematics and some natural science, book-keeping and some commercial law. Most of his career chances would then be in private enterprise of some kind. And because of the way that limitation was imposed on him, and the beliefs he met at home and school, he was unlikely to have much respect for the established church, its claims to authority, its members' privileges, or the political regime which enforced them. However stern his family or business discipline might or might not be, he was unlikely to be conservative or conformist in other ways. Altogether it would be hard to imagine a more effective way to produce constructive innovators in a conservative society. Constructive innovators rather than rebels, for two reasons. They were not a desperately frustrated class: there was scope and hope for them in business. And if they did well and wanted to join the establishment, they could. A successful merchant or manufacturer or engineer could join the Church of England, buy a manor, buy a seat in Parliament, marry his children to gentry. Robert Peel, Conservative Prime Minister from 1841, was a grandson of England's first calico printer.

Government

Eighteenth century governments did not do much directly, but did a lot indirectly, to develop manufacturing industry. An economic historian sums up what they did *not* do:

> Compared with countries like France, Prussia, or even Russia in the eighteenth century, and with the process of industrialization in all other countries in later times (including the United States) ... industrialization in Britain ... was not the result of deliberate government policy sponsoring industrial progress. The state did very little indeed to promote industrial innovations as an act of policy, to stimulate productive investment (except via its military expenditures) ... It did not conduct enterprise itself on any scale, certainly not in strategic areas of industrial growth and innovation, limiting its direct commitments to a handful of naval dockyards (producing specialized warships and very active only in wartime), gunpowder mills and ordnance works such as Woolwich Arsenal. The state did not set out energetically to attract foreign capital or foreign skills. It was reluctant to accept responsibility on a national scale for meeting the social investment consequent upon industrialization and urbanization (at least until the 1840s) – either the social investment needed to aid economic growth or to cope with its consequences: effective local government, city improvement, health, sanitation, education. It did not even concern itself much with establishing the usual infrastructure of planning, financing or organizing the financing of roads, canals, railways or public utilities like docks.
>
> – Peter Mathias, *The First Industrial Nation*, 2nd ed. (1983) 31-2

And Mathias goes on to suggest that some of the things the government *did* do, to regulate trade, banking, company structures and internal migration may have positively hindered industrialization.

But intentionally or not they also did some helpful things:

They made war for twenty of the steam engine's first forty years. In some of those years the government spent 28 per cent of British national income, not far from the proportion which American governments spent in the 1990s; and in some years new public investment may have exceeded new private. Other governments – foes as well as friends – bought textiles, arms and equipment from British suppliers. Though public enterprise was mostly confined as Mathias says

to shipbuilding and weaponry, it was significant in quantity and inventiveness. A century before Henry Ford thought of the moving assembly line Mark Brunel had one working in a British government pulley-block factory.

That was not the only profitable war. More than a century of conquest, coercive treaty-making, Navigation Acts and effective mercantilist policies had made Britain and its colonies the world's richest internal free-trade area. Much of its external trade was confined to its own ships and required to pass through British ports. Those extensive activities must have contributed in many indirect ways to the market, the capital resources and the business experience of British industry, though how much can't now be calculated.

At home, cheap decentralized government maintained internal peace and security. It worked well for men of property. Most magistrates were local proprietors. Private Acts of Parliament empowered proprietors to enclose land or acquire routes and rights for roads, canals, railways and drainage schemes. State power was thus available for many private business purposes, usually on the investors' rather than the government's initiative. (You will presently see that that was also the American, but not the European or Japanese, model.) Labor organization and collective bargaining were banned. So (less effectively) were the emigration of skilled workers and the export of some patented machinery.

In short, governments gave landowners and businessmen much of what they asked for: aggressive expansion abroad, an open market at home, tariff and patent protection, coercive powers over the land and labor they needed. What government did *not* do was to think ahead of the businessmen, to provide the aids to development which depended on public rather than private initiative: education and technical training, scientific and technical research, the transport and urban services that come best from public suppliers, effective company law, and a professional public service. The success of the steam revolution lulled British governments and businessmen into thinking that business could go on growing without those public aids. Britain's lack of a thoughtful public service and public education and science left the better-served Germans and Americans to lead in much of the next industrial phase – the chemical, metallurgical, optical, electrical and automotive developments which required more advanced technology.

Could the government of the first industrial nation be expected to foresee those needs and provide for them?

Some contemporaries thought so. Robert Owen, a successful cottonspinner, showed that a model factory and town could run as profitably as their most ruthless competitors. His example was widely famous, but not much followed. He wanted factory reform, urban reform and educational reform to generalize his standards. There is no reason to think they could not have succeeded. French and Germans already had abler public services and bigger, better coordinated public investment programs. Americans and Germans soon had more widespread public education and support for science.

Leadership lost

Those were shortcomings of governments elected by less than a tenth of the people. They were curable. In due course government was democratized. Provisions for industrial safety, health, education and welfare were introduced. After 1945 there was some public ownership of major industries. But long before that Britain had lost its industrial leadership, chiefly to the USA.

Why? Half the reasons lay in the Americans' superior resources and performance. The other half – the slower growth of British productivity – had (among others) causes of two general kinds. People misread some lessons of the steam revolution. And in a number of ways England's class culture was hostile to continuing industrial leadership.

The steam revolution could too easily be seen as a triumph of unaided private enterprise. It was easy to generalize that experience and conclude in practice, as the classical economists were arguing in theory, that free trade, minimal government and unaided private enterprise were the way to go.

It was a compound mistake. First, more active government could have made a better job of the steam revolution. Second, that revolution was not in fact unaided. Besides help from public developments and demands in wartime, it also used plenty of science. Some of the science had been developed earlier by Boyle and Newton and others at home and abroad on public salaries. Watt developed his engine as a skilled instrument maker trained and employed in the physics department of Glasgow University whose professors helped him considerably. Many of the English entrepreneurs and engineers were well educated themselves and had help from Priestley and other scientists. But at that time the central government did not finance the schools or universities or most of the scientists, and could conclude that their education and funding need not be public responsibilities. As for the innovators, so for the workers: the use of unskilled labor by the first

factories turned out to be a bad guide to later needs. German public servants and American businessmen and politicians were much quicker than the British to predict, and supply, the public research, technical education and mass education that further technical progress would require.

Some of the British neglect of those needs came to be encouraged by the industrial owners and managers themselves. A complicated social history of the changing character of owners and managers of many of the bigger British firms may be simplified – *much* simplified – as follows. As sketched earlier, many of the early industrialists were able, well-educated boys brought up in business families. In the firms they founded or inherited they themselves were the owners, managers and innovators. Who succeeded them? In Germany and (especially) the USA their sons and grandsons or other successors were of their own kind, perhaps with the additional benefit of better technical or business education at one of the new technical universities or land-grant colleges. And families which could not supply educated management for their firms knew what sort of educated management they needed to hire – or they sold their firms.

Successful English industrialists tended to send their sons, instead, to join the upper class. In the class culture of the time that would usually distance them from any active, expert or inventive management of manufacturing or service industries. The boys went to private boarding schools, misleadingly called public schools, some of whose characteristics were sketched earlier. If they went into business at all, as some did, it tended to be business that could be done in London offices or sometimes overseas, rather than in the grimy industrial north: banking, insurance, stockbroking, property dealing, – or sometimes, directing northern industries ineptly from London offices.

The 'class transformation' of the sons tended to do double harm to their fathers' industries. The sons did not supply expert, enterprising direction themselves. And they did not hire others likely to supply it either. Instead they tended to trust their fathers' faithful servants, or successors like them: pragmatic overseers, trained chiefly by long experience on the job, who knew every detail of the business. They had been serviceable managers for enterprising directors. Without enterprising direction they tended to stick to the routines they knew. Some of them were ingenious improvers in practical and technical ways, but those talents tended to be wasted without expert, enterprising direction.

Besides tending to be amateur or absent, the direction could also be dulled by some other class effects. Individually, absentee gentleman-owners tended to be averse from both risk and saving, which meant averse from radical re-equipment or changes of product or strategy. Nor did pragmatic, unimaginative managers recommend such upheavals if they could help it. The owners wanted reliable unearned incomes to sustain their lifestyles. As long as markets could be found for the regular products of the old machinery and management, gentlemen let them continue. And markets could often be found. British industry expanded 'laterally', exporting its traditional wares – textiles, pottery, hardware, steam engines, rails and locomotives – to wider and wider areas of Europe, Asia, North and South America and the overseas empire. Germans and Americans meanwhile pioneered the new high-tech industries.

Gentlemen might not manage factories but they did manage the financial institutions. In that capacity they switched a rising proportion of British investment away from manufacturing and away from Britain. There was some risky overseas investment in cattle, sheep, mining, railroads; some investment in urban property, utilities and financial services in developing countries overseas; and increasingly, safe lending to foreign and colonial governments. Capital which might have equipped British industry to build (say) the early electric locomotives and generators went instead to build more and more miles of steam railway in Australia or Argentina.

Of course there were many exceptions. Britain pioneered some of the new technology, copied more of it, and by one means or another got some share of most of the new industries. It continued to produce some excellent individual scientists and inventors. It also got some benefits of *not* having a fully commercial or technological culture or upper class. By the twentieth century the quality of British writing, publishing and broadcasting; the institutional arrangements for music and drama; the quantity and quality of education in the humanities; the early development of welfare theory and practice; the conservation of the countryside; the invention of so many of the world's sports and games – all those might perhaps have done worse if business had been doing better, and business values had more influence. Whether the industrial decline was necessary to those civilized achievements is open to argument. But the decline was real. Through much of the twentieth century the rate of investment in British industry ran well below the American rate, per dollar of national income or per head of population.

Summary

For comparative purposes, notice half a dozen characteristics of Britain's steam revolution and its aftermath:

1. Various political, social and economic developments gave eighteenth-century Britain an exceptional source of inventive entrepreneurs.

2. British government helped indirectly to create many of the market and institutional conditions for the early industrialization.

3. It did not then give the industrialists much direct help.

4. It was backward in providing the science, technical training and mass education which later industrial development needed.

5. It was backward in protecting workers and consumers from industrial ill effects, and in civilizing their urban living conditions.

6. After the dissenters' steam revolution, British class culture worked increasingly to deprive British industry of enterprising investment and management.

Now compare the first hundred years of Japanese industrialization a century later. The Japanese performed much like the British at items 2 and 5 above – but very differently at items 1, 3, 4 and 6.

JAPAN FROM 1868

For a century before and after the appearance of James Watt's steam engine Japan remained a conservative feudal society. It was deliberately secluded from the outside world. Its Emperor was holy but powerless; the country was governed by a central military command and bureaucracy and about two hundred local feudal lords. It had a formal class structure of samurai, peasants, artisans, and merchants, in that order of status.

In the 1850s American and European coercion opened the country to foreign trade. In 1868 a group of young samurai overthrew the central government by coup d'etat and took its place. They abolished the feudal structures of government and the legal class divisions. Formally they restored the power of the Emperor (hence the name 'Meiji restoration'). In fact they ruled in his name. The Diet (parliament) which they presently created was also powerless. The conservative feudal dictatorship had thus been replaced by a modernizing group dictatorship, which began with some success to modernize the Japanese economy and defence capacity. After the Second World War a brief American dictatorship established democratic government, under which the country achieved very fast economic growth indeed. In one century from 1868, Japan caught up with two centuries of British industrial growth. We can compare in turn the resources they started with; their sources of innovative and entrepreneurial talent; and the role of government in their industrial growth.

Resources

What did the new Japanese regime inherit? Materially it had climate, sea and fisheries similar to the British, and a similar capacity to feed itself, but only just. It had some mineral resources but much less than the British, especially of coal and iron. Socially there was a homogeneous, orderly, peaceful community with common language and culture, and powerful traditions of authority, obedience, and national and group and family solidarity.

Feudal Japan was already heavily populated. It had well developed agriculture, mostly of rice, both land-intensive and labor-intensive, with considerable investment in reclaiming and extending cultivable land. A big fishing industry provided food and agricultural fertiliser. Silk, embroidery, pottery and other crafts and decorative arts flourished. For its time and type it was a skilled and well educated society: Learning was revered, the ruling class had elaborate traditional education, the merchants were rational calculators and good book-keepers, many peasants attended temple schools and nearly half were literate. But there was little to match the new European technology of the eighteenth and nineteenth centuries: no machinery, no railed transport, no steam engines. When an early Japanese modernizer got himself a European ship-building manual and followed its instructions to build a ship, he found afterwards that it was a seventeenth-century book so he had a brand new two-hundred-year-old European ship.

Those existing economic activities, institutions and skills were one part of Japan's modernizing resources. Equally important were the people's values, culture and class structure. On the one hand they were intensely conformist, revering age and traditional authority and established ways of doing things. On the other hand they had traditions of hard work, honesty and cooperative endeavor. Their culture might not encourage much individual competition but it allowed plenty of national and team competition.

The class structure and culture also had both promising and unpromising potentialities.

The samurai, about 7 per cent of the population, had become 'soldiers without war' and without an indepen-

dent economic base either. Some were rich but many were not. Unlike most European ruling classes they were not regular landowners with rents or farm management to live on. The feudal authorities paid them (unequally and often inadequately) from tax revenues, to serve as soldiers, bureaucrats and teachers. They were thus a kind of salaried aristocracy and intelligentsia, cultural leaders with a strict, somewhat military code of behavior, and not much practical economic skill or experience. They led the 1868 revolution and were appropriate bureaucrats and teachers for the new Japan – but that would not employ them all, and they did not look like promising entrepreneurs or business managers.

Most of the peasant class, in Japan as anywhere else, worked hard for the little subsistence left to them after heavy taxation. Only a few grew rich as landowners or specialist producers. Similarly the artisans – the third feudal class – were mostly hard workers in family trades, with very few rich enough to see themselves as 'businessmen'.

The merchants, fourth and lowest in status, seemed at first sight to be the society's likeliest entrepreneurs and modernizers. They traded much of the country produce, feeding and supplying the cities. They managed and marketed the great flow of rice which was the main element of the feudal tax system. They organized trade in silk, pottery and other craft products. They managed the coastal shipping which was the main mode of heavy and long-distance transport. Besides marketing fish for food they had developed a big trade in dried fish as fertiliser. In their own way many of them were efficient. They were good book-keepers. The bigger merchant houses, though keeping to the family form, had good managerial standards and would often adopt outsiders if their own sons were not competent. Some houses – most famously the chain-store house of Mitsui founded in the seventeenth century – had great wealth and large-scale organization.

Mitsui and some others were effective innovators after 1868. But disappointingly, most of the merchants were not, or if they were, they were led to it by others rather than their own initiatives. Where their old trades could continue they carried them on. But their class did not supply many of the entrepreneurs of new industries. Why so unadaptable? Under the old regime they had become very specialized, and strictly regulated by their guilds. They traded within established rights and routines and market shares, without much competition. They supplied the feudal authorities, lent them money, got monopolies and other favors from them. After 1868 those functions, the rice-tax business and their guild

structures were all swept away, and when the feudal
lords lost their governing powers most of their debts to
the merchants were cancelled. Many merchants failed
altogether, and only a few took much advantage of the
new regime's novel opportunities. Historians suggest
that they had been too thoroughly feudalized and
conservatized, then too roughly treated when the feudal
structures were dismantled, to respond actively to risky
new opportunities.

The samurai

The samurai were also a feudal class with strong traditional values, and with the additional disadvantage of
having no obvious economic role in a new Japan. But
where the merchants had been a despised class with
little cause for self-confidence the samurai could think
of themselves as natural leaders. Those of them who
made or supported the coup d'etat had been made rebel-
lious by patriotism, fear of foreign conquest, and feudal
contradictions between their high status and their low
pay. If they could revolutionize government, they were
bold enough to think they could surely revolutionize
business, however ignorant of it they were to begin
with. Some of their early attempts to turn surplus
samurai into small businessmen had high failure rates.
But in bigger business they did more than any other
class to modernize the economy. To begin with – in
strong contrast to the British experience – they did more
of it as public servants than as private businessmen. But
not as socialists: they deliberately used the power and
resources of government to create a private capitalist
economy. The new breed of business managers who
succeeded the first generation in the 1890s were not
apprentice sons of business houses, in the English style.
They were sons of the leading class, graduated from the
leading universities. Surveyed in 1924, 40 per cent of
them were of samurai origin. One remarkable achievement of the samurai class as a whole had been to make
themselves over to new and radically different social
roles and purposes.

The role of government

After early blunders and confusions and changes of
course, the new leaders' successful methods may be
summed up under half a dozen heads.

First they abolished all feudal powers and privileges
of class and introduced legal equality, freedom of movement and occupation and business activity, and
individual instead of family property ownership: the
standard Western legal conditions. Government
continued to pay the samurai salaries for ten years then

paid them off with government bonds. They taxed the
peasants so unmercifully that they did not have to tax
others much. Democracy remained a vague promise for
the future.

Second, they worked at their own and the nation's
beliefs and values. They made ingenious mixtures of old
and new belief, using some traditional allegiances to
overcome others. When told in the Emperor's name to
abandon tradition and modernize, *tradition* required
them to obey. Japan must westernize, but in a Japanese
way. It must equal or excel the barbarians in productivity and war, but with superior purpose. Entrepreneurs
should excel for the sake of ancestors and Emperor and
nation, rather than for individual enrichment: Japan's
superior spirit should enable it to develop capitalist
wealth and power without capitalist corruptions.
Japanese capitalists soon enough developed western
capitalist motivation – and corruptions – but traditional
forces had much to do with their transformation.

Third, the modernizers revolutionized education and
its social role. They founded schools for all, and general
and technical universities. Within one generation the
nation was wholly literate. Higher education became
both the normal preparation and the competitive test for
high office in government and business alike, and also
for social status. Graduates entered government and
business above non-graduates and on higher pay scales.
By the turn of the century most of the upper ranks of the
public service were graduates, half of them from the
University of Tokyo. (A century later the proportions
have scarcely changed.) A standard track to the top in
private business was by way of university then some
years in public service before 'descending' to high rank
and fast advancement in a private firm.

Did the hot educational competition mean equal
opportunity for all? No, because access to the education
was by no means equal. Most university people were
children of bureaucrats, business or professional people
or landowners. But the educational experience had
important effects on them. It put the same sort of people
– often friends and fellow-students – at the head of
government and business. Some of the individual
competition between them was over by the time their
academic results determined their privileged track in
government or business, so within those organizations
individual competition could be muted, and cooperation
easier. So although higher education was mostly
confined to an upper class, the experience of it did a
good deal for the quality, commitment and performance
of that class.

Fourth, all concerned were encouraged to learn all

they could from the West. Leaders travelled – soon after the revolution a big group of national leaders toured the world for two years. There were generous travelling scholarships for students. Foreign experts were imported freely to Japan. One American laid the foundations of Japanese banking, another did the same for insurance. At one time the departments of government had more than 500 foreign experts on pay in Japan, many serving private as well as public enterprises. Feelings about the foreigners varied. Japanese tended to embrace a lot of Western fashion and culture through the 1880s then recoil from some of it in the 1890s. But the introduction of Western technology continued steadily, much of it at government initiative, or expense, or both.

Fifth, government did a lot quite directly to create or modernize financial and industrial enterprises. The travellers had been impressed by Bismarck's Germany, where a traditional military monarchy was modernizing the economy 'from above', taught by the economist List who had argued that late industrializers must use state power to protect their infant industries. Treaties forced on Japan forbade tariff protection. So the Japanese government offered Japan's private enterprises everything else: subsidies, tax holidays, loan guarantees, assured purchase of products, Western experts at public expense. At times it was hard to tell Mitsui and the Ministry of Finance apart – Mitsui did many contract services for the government, and the government let Mitsui profiteer on its supplies and services to government, especially in wartime. More respectably, eminent ex-public servants acted as private sector 'starters', designing new enterprises and finding capital, managers and markets for them. Private banking, insurance, paper-making, ship-building, cotton manufacture and other industries all benefited in that way. And where aids to private enterprise were not effective, government started the enterprises itself. Some, like the main railways, it kept as permanent public services. But most it sold. Public servants would found corporations in new industries, often with Western expertise, run them for a while, write off their establishment costs and any debts and losses, then sell them to private buyers – some to the likes of Mitsui, some to the new private entrepreneurs, some to public servants taking the opportunity to 'go private', some to widespread share ownership. The public managers were often adventurous but inexperienced, building businesses but losing money. The terms of sale were often favorable to the point of corruption. Government lost money but some able businessmen got hold of good enterprises by those means. Most of the public creations were in private hands by the 1880s.

Sixth, there was what came to be known as the Japan system or Japan management of labor. The first decades of fast growth took leading industries ahead of the supply of skilled labor. Wages rose as firms competed for scarce skills. There was job-hopping as skilled workers moved from firm to firm, shopping for better wages and conditions. The efficiency as well as the wage costs of production suffered as employers lost human capital in the form of skills learned on the job and specific to the needs and procedures of particular employers. What to do? There were government proposals to peg the wages of skilled workers and regulate their mobility between employers. Employers disliked that prospect. One of them could have been a clone of Robert Owen at New Lanark a century before. He was Muto Sanji, born in 1867, the young managing director of a cotton-spinning business. He had been taught and strongly influenced by a leading intellectual of the business revolution – Fukuzawa Yukichi, whom you will meet in Chapter 30's debates about the purposes of private firms. Muto developed a solution to the double problem of training and retaining the skills he needed, and restraining their wage costs. He introduced in-house training programs within his factories. To retain the workers whom he trained and at the same time restrain their wage demands he offered them – subject to good performance – a range of benefits: lifetime employment; promotion by seniority, partly as an inducement to stay and partly to allow trustful cooperation between workers; patient consultation with managers about the organization of their work; and some beginnings of 'company welfare' for themselves and their families. Muto's initial purpose was to improve the performance and restrain the costs of his own firm. But on the basis of its success he developed a management philosophy which linked his industrial relations to the purposes and prosperity of the nation, its firms, and their employees.

Fifty years into its steam revolution the British government had taken no interest in Robert Owen's reform of industrial relations and company welfare at New Lanark, and although it was widely known it was not copied by other firms. Fifty years into Japan's steam revolution a century later, the government welcomed Muto's initiative and many big companies copied it. Their skilled workers gained security and respect. Employers gained good cooperative service for comparatively low pay. The nation got its distinctive system of labor and company welfare. But a majority of workers – unskilled, seasonal and casual workers and almost all women workers – remained outside the new system, getting the low pay without the accompanying benefits, contributing to steady economic growth of which they continued to get very little share. *All* Robert Owen's New Lanark workers , including many women, got company education and company housing.

The 'Japanese miracle'

In sixty years the Meiji 'great leap forward' took Japan from a feudal agricultural country to one with a developed industrial sector capable of building its own battleships and locomotives, with – overall – about a third of Britain's measured productivity per head. There was then another, more spectacular leap forward after 1945, under American rule then under Japan's first democracy. In thirty years Japan overtook and passed Britain's GNP per head, and began to supply substantial elements of Britain's high technology.

That leap also was led by government. An Australian designed and the Americans effected a great land reform, transferring absent-owned land to its tenant farmers. They purged a whole generation of Japan's senior political and business leaders. The Ministry of International Trade and Industry – the famous MITI – was re-established in 1948 and staffed, after the Americans left in 1952, with very able, single-minded young graduates (mostly in law and politics rather than economics). There was incessant three-cornered discussion between bureaucrats, political leaders and businessmen to arrive at 'consensual' policies; but most industrial development policies began with MITI planning and were implemented under MITI guidance and regulation.

The policy-makers reasoned that Japan had an able, well educated population but lacked natural resources, capital and technology. They decided to concentrate new capital and technology in industries capable of selling abroad as well as at home, to earn the means of importing what they lacked. In two respects they took a line of their own. They would not let foreign transnationals introduce the new capital and technology; Japanese must buy, import or develop it themselves. And instead of developing industries chiefly to save foreign exchange by replacing imports – a common strategy for late industrializers – they would for the time being ration imports. So as key industries for development they chose capital-intensive, technology-intensive potential exporters: iron and steel, petrochemicals, electrics, automobiles, industrial machinery. MITI rationed and allocated essential imports. That incidentally protected Japanese industry from competitive

imports, without tariffs. MITI supervised contracts for foreign technology. It facilitated the creation of new firms and industries, and influenced the supply and allocation of new capital. In old industries – textiles, lumber, chemicals, shipping – it encouraged technical modernization, division of labor and specialization, mergers and 'rationalization cartels'. Amending or evading the anti-monopoly rules which the Americans had bequeathed, MITI went out for size: besides any technical economies of scale Japanese firms should be as big and powerful in the marketplace as their international competitors.

From the 1970s there was increasing criticism of the 'economic miracle' and MITI's policies, especially for their effects of monopoly, pollution, and domestic privation. 'Growth regardless' had produced some over-investment and over-capacity, and now some oligopolist behavior as big firms and groups began to use their strength against Japanese as well as foreign interests. There was some pollution and environmental degradation. And public and household investment had been starved. Japanese households might have more to spend than British, but they had smaller, poorer but (in the cities) higher-priced houses in which to produce for themselves and enjoy their leisure. Their neighborhoods, like their houses, were short of outdoor space and communal capital. In the big cities many workers travelled long distances to work, and work was expected to absorb most of their interest and energy. Women and children got too little of husbands' and fathers' time and attention.

In 1978 Seichiro Saito interviewed a group of MITI leaders who had joined as elite graduates in 1952 and worked zealously at the economic miracle. Twenty five years on, at the height of their power, with the miracle accomplished, many of them were uneasy, unconfident, newly uncertain about their own and Japan's directions. But they were still thinking ahead. They were joining with other branches of government in disciplining some of the oligopolist misbehavior and some of the environmental performance of Japanese industry. They were encouraging the removal of some heavy industries to other Asian locations, and the growth of Japanese investment in the United States.

New troubles afflicted the economy. Through the 1980s the government relaxed the public supervision of Japan's banks. The banks responded by financing a destructive boom and bust in city land prices. It left a number of them technically insolvent, needing public rescue. Worldwide deregulation meanwhile brought fluctuating exchange rates and interest rates and large-scale gambling on the fluctuations. Banks and other industries faced alarming new risks. Anxiously, the Japanese people responded by spending less and saving more, expecting hard times. Demand for consumption goods languished. The government tried to restore it by increasing consumers' disposable income. The consumers saved more still. Growth slowed, and open and concealed unemployment increased, as Japan suffered an apparently permanent recession through the 1990s.

Against that background MITI's state of mind was surveyed again. Kyoko Sheridan had graduated in Japan then emigrated to work in Western universities. In 1996 she interviewed a sample of MITI officers representing all age-groups from new recruits to retired leaders, and including some of the few women who are now rising in the MITI ranks. MITI's role now relies more on persuasion and less on command than it used to do. But in the developing global economy its officers expect an expanding role for government, rather than the dwindling role which many English-speaking governments expect. They want Japan to be a helpful and respected leader in the world economy. Some of them hope that Japan will show the way to an Asian model of capitalism distinct from the Western model. They regret the current Americanizing tendencies of some Japanese business and culture. Within Japan some of them want to improve the conditions of household and family life. That is partly for the benefit of Japanese women, but it also reflects a concern to conserve the sources of Japan's hardworking and cooperative 'culture of achievement'.

Time will tell how effective their new visions prove to be. But they still exemplify the habits of mind of MITI's early leaders – and of Myrdal's approach to Swedish, American and Asian economic problems, and of other economists of the historical/institutional school. Government can often be an effective force for good in economic development, especially if its policies reflect particular national conditions and capacities rather than general economic theories. Most MITI officers have not been economics graduates. Sheridan thinks that helps to explain their success. She worries about the likely influence of the rising number of Japanese economists who now go to American graduate schools.

CONTRASTS

You can usefully compare many elements of Britain's and Japan's industrial transformations. Here we are comparing only two: their entrepreneurs, and the role of government through the first century of industrial development.

Enterprise Britain had a 'natural' source of entrepreneurs: a business class with habits of hard work, links with their country's leading scientists, wide business experience, and a tradition of dissent and self-help. Japan had to develop a business class from unlikely-looking material. A feudal ruling class managed to adapt and transform its traditional values and authority, and was one of the world's first to introduce a common university education for leaders of government and business alike.

Further comparisons would show that Russia, France, Germany and the United States all mixed some each of those British and Japanese methods, and some each of their own, as they industrialized with varying speed and success. There has been no one regular best source of business innovators and developers. It is important to have them. Countries which lack them need not wring their hands, they can perhaps take heart from the Japanese example and set about producing them.

Government In Britain, government could well have done more for the industrial revolution. It could have contrived earlier improvements of banking and commercial and company and bankruptcy law, factory regulation, local government and public services in the industrial cities. Those were all practicable at the time and could have improved both the efficiency and the humanity of the industrial transformation. In the next round of technological innovation, earlier and better public education and scientific and technical research and training might have helped; also perhaps some responsive industrial protection in an increasingly protectionist world, and some public regulation of the export of British capital. An earlier creation of a modern civil service might have brought earlier action on those fronts. With hindsight, the fact that the first industrial revolution happened without much direct government aid or direction does not make a strong case for that abstinence.

By contrast, both the Japanese 'leaps forward' were led by government. (So was the disastrous change of course to war and defeat from 1931 to 1945.) The postwar leap forward, in which government concentrated on stimulating and directing the private production of market goods to the exclusion of much public production or social provision is now one of the world's leading examples of fast and super-competitive economic growth. How much of it might have happened in a market way without public direction? Perhaps some but certainly not all of it. That may also be true of its social and household costs.

So if you ever believed that government direction (1) always hinders efficiency and growth, or (2) always has socialist aims and effects, remember the Japanese case. Stupid government can hinder, intelligent government can greatly help private economic performance. And government can be anywhere from socialist to 'more capitalist than the capitalists'. If Japanese resources had been allocated since 1945 more by market forces and local preferences and less by central government, Japan might now look a bit more British or socialist: it might have a little less heavy industrial and export capacity, pollution, and measured GNP, but bigger houses, more public and private gardens, more neighborhood space and public services, and more family time together. (But those effects might also have been achieved by different government rather than less government.) Government can do a lot about the pace and direction of economic development – if voters and consumers want it, investors and workers cooperate, skills and resources are available, and other necessary conditions allow.

NATURAL WEALTH :
AMERICA AND AUSTRALIA 1860-1890

By 1860 the British were still industrial leaders but Americans and Australians were richer. We will notice some similarities and some striking contrasts between the American and Australian economies, to see by what different means the same measured incomes per head could be produced.

Similarities: Both societies were of British or other European people who brought developed economic capacities to areas of abundant land and natural resources which they took by force from native populations. They farmed to support themselves, and hunted and fished and mined to export naturally-occurring primary products: fur, timber, whale and seal products, gold, copper, flax, copra. Increasingly through the nineteenth century they also farmed for export: wool, grain, and after refrigerated ships were developed, meat. Both populations grew rapidly from natural increase and continuing immigration. Both built substantial cities. Both built rail networks, and proceeded (in different ways and at different rates) to industrialize. Most of the time both societies perceived themselves to be short of both capital and labor. The demand for labor kept wages high by European standards. The demand for capital led both societies to save and to import capital to invest at higher rates than were usual elsewhere. Americans invested about 20 per cent of their annual product and Australians were close behind. As far as can now be calculated from imperfect records they had about the same GNP per head, and it was the world's highest.

Differences: The following differences are selected to show what diverse means could produce similar income and growth from similar resources at that time.

Scale

The two countries had comparable land areas but much more of the American continent was fertile and habit- able. Americans outnumbered Australians 35:1 in 1860, 20:1 in 1890. (Between those dates Americans doubled from 31.5m to 63m, Australians more than trebled from 0.8 to 3m.) The American numbers made one of the world's big internal markets. The few Australians were scattered over six self-governing colonies, some of them taxing trade with the others.

Economic maturity

By 1860 the United States had accumulated substantial public, private and household capital: old-established Eastern cities, well-equipped farms, some heavy manufacturing capacity, 30,000 miles of railroad, housing and schools and churches for most of the white population. By contrast, three quarters of the white Australians had been in the country less than ten years. Nearly half were still in bark huts or shanties or tents. They were just beginning their first railways, importing every rail and spike 12,000 miles from Britain, and had very little manufacturing capacity.

Both economies were less 'mature' than the British: more occupied with primary production, less industrialized. Australia – still grossly short of houses and piped water and paved roads, let alone steam engines – was way behind America. How could primitive Australia and semi-developed America have similar income per head, both higher than British income per head?

Historians offer rival or overlapping explanations of that achievement. Here is one selection of relevant conditions and causes. More than half the Australians had come with recent gold rushes. They were an abnormally young, male, energetic population with few non-working dependants. Besides farming, building and simple manufacturing for their own support they took advantage of their new terrain to produce and export gold, copper, wool, grain, and various products of

Pacific whaling and trading. For a decade or two the gold and wool came with comparatively little investment, though both became capital-intensive later. The early gold was won by many diggers, spreading modest wealth widely. It paid for plentiful imports, kept demand buoyant which kept everybody employed, and financed many small farms and businesses. Meanwhile some of the steady build-up of capital in the wool business happened without much saving or investment – it came easily by the natural increase of flocks. So wages were high, wealth and income widely shared, and government very democratic. In those conditions the people devoted a lot of capital – some of it saved, some of it brought in by immigrants, a lot of it borrowed from Britain – to building good houses, communications and public institutions.

Americans had most of those advantages, with a different pattern of primary products. They had a longer and larger accumulation of public, private and household capital. And they invested heavily in fast-growing, inventive, heavily protected manufacturing, mostly for their own needs rather than for export.

The profit motive

More of the American allocation of capital resources was for profit, more of the Australian was not.

(Be careful of the distinction. It refers to the primary purpose(s) of investment decisions rather than to their effects. Thus a private investor who tries but fails to make profits is still a profit-seeking investor. A public railroad is a non-profit investment, whether it runs at a profit or a loss, if profit was not the government's main motive for building it. Public buildings are non-profit investments whether or not the government hires profit-seeking contractors to build them. Household capital in private houses, cars, etc., is for use without profit, except that the following comparisons class residential investment by landlords as profit-seeking, and by owner-occupiers as non-profit. Notice that the distinction is not between selfish and unselfish, and is not always between individual and collective decisions. Some private investors may be more interested in productive achievement than in profits. Plenty of non-profit investment is self-interested in one way or another.)

Why use the profit/non-profit distinction at all? Chiefly because you will meet it often in arguments about the best way to allocate productive resources. Some ideologists think the most profitable uses of resources are usually the most productive, so most investment is best left to profit-seeking market forces. Others have thought that planned allocation by collective decision could be more efficient or equitable, or both. I believe that relations between individual and collective choice, between profit and non-profit motivation, and between economic efficiency and equity, are more complex than such simple generalizations allow. Remember post-war Japan: planned allocation of resources by MITI bureaucrats was *combined* with a good deal of market competition by profit-seeking firms for shares of the allocated resources. Other variations, both successful in their time, are illustrated in these nineteenth century U.S./Australian comparisons. On the one hand market forces failed to provide Australia with railways: collective non-profit investment had to do that. On the other hand market forces allocated a high proportion of Australian savings to non-profit owner-occupied housing. Consider the U.S./Australian contrasts with those complications in mind.

The following comparisons simplify by assuming: (i) Private investment is for profit, public and household investment (where it is for household rather than business use) are not. (ii) That includes railways. (iii) Housing built for landlords is investment for profit, housing built for owner-occupiers is for non-profit use. (iv) From imperfect data it is estimated that two thirds of American and one third of Australian housing investment through these decades was profit-seeking. (v) Percentages of national product invested for profit and non-profit use have been averaged for the U.S. for the years 1869-1890 (to keep clear of the war between the States), and for Australia for 1860-1890. (vi) The first comparison omits consumer durables. The second comparison includes them as non-profit household investment.

Percentage of national product allocated to profit-seeking and non-profit investment, excluding consumer durables, 1860/69 – 1890.

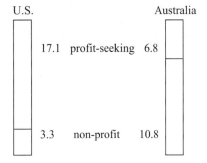

Percentage of national product allocated to profit-seeking and non-profit investment, including consumer durables, 1860/69 – 1890.

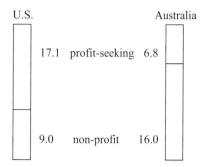

Figure 11.1 Profit-seeking proportions of US and Australian investment, 1860/69 – 1890

Equality and productivity

Americans began to give some land and rights back to their Indians long before Australians did much for their Aborigines. But among the immigrant populations, Australian wealth and income appear to have been distributed more equally than American. Labor being scarce tended to fetch high wages in both countries. But Australian governments gave workers earlier and better legislative protection from their employers. And there were proportionately more American rich chiefly because America had more private capital.

Australians could produce high income with less private capital for a number of reasons. The early decades of goldmining and woolgrowing were extremely productive per unit of capital and labor employed. Some other trades also yielded good income to young, mobile workers without much capital. As Australian manufacturing developed it made many fewer millionaires than American manufacturing did. It was mostly small-scale, primitive and labor-intensive: food processing, shoemaking and dressmaking, carpentry and brickmaking and blacksmithing. Some Australians got rich from growing wool, mining, overseas trading. A few got rich from speculative land dealing. But there were few big urban landlords and no oilmen, steelmakers, big inventive manufacturers, or equivalents of the private railroad promoters to whom American governments gave away seven per cent of the land surface of the United States. In Australia by comparison with the USA (i) more of the nation's income came from low-capital activities, (ii) more of the productive capital was owned by government, and (iii) more of the residential capital was owned by the households using it.

So Australian capitalists were fewer and averaged less rich than American. In their conflicts with labor they were consequently weaker, and got less help from government. Australian unions managed to organize a higher proportion of the workforce, earlier, than American unions did. American labor decided not to put a party of its own into politics. Australian labor did so, successfully – the party formed the world's first Labor government in Queensland in 1899 and was strong in the first decades of national government after 1901. Then and since it has helped to industrialize the country behind protective tariffs, and to develop elaborate public institutional machinery for industrial arbitration and wage-fixing. In the USA, stronger capital and weaker labor tended to be self-perpetuating. American government gave employers rather more legal and police protection than it gave their workers. Besides being tougher sometimes, American management has probably been, on average, more able and more enterprising than Australian. So by comparison, American firms have found it easier to re-equip, change direction, shed labor, shift location, close plants.

By 1980 Australian GNP per head had slipped to tenth or twelfth on the world table. Critics say the industrial and political muscle of organized labor helped mediocre managers to fossilize Australian manufacturing and prevent its modernization. Defenders think the critics exaggerate. For twenty years now the poorest third of Australian workers have earned more than their U.S. equivalents. A 1991 study found Australian workers still more productive per hour than Japanese – Australians produce a little less per year by working shorter hours and taking longer holidays. Some of the protected job security may have been worth its costs for many social reasons. And there were other benefits. GNP omits the effects of generous and fairly shared household space and capital. Australia is still one of the more equal and comfortable countries, with workers better protected than American workers are.

THE LONG BOOM 1950 – 1973

After the Second World War the Western democracies enjoyed a generation of stability, full employment and steady economic growth. Income rose to allow most workers what their parents would have seen as middle-class standards of living, and bit by bit the modern structure of welfare incomes and services was built. It was an important passage of history because it appeared to reconcile majorities of workers to the principles if not all the details of their mixed economies. Capitalism finally won. But it had help. The capitalism which won was extensively regulated. It used substantial public capital and services. Other public services educated the workforce, kept it healthy, and provided it with income through illness, unemployment and old age. Governments expanded the public services to business and to households steadily enough to employ the rising proportion of workers whom the increasingly productive, labor-saving private sector could not employ. Public enterprises and services and well-equipped households together produced half or more of the democracies' material goods and services.

Western socialist parties, in their parliamentary role, had contributed to those achievements. Democratic socialists, and in practice many Western communists, became moderate reformers of their mixed economies, with no serious prospect of achieving the Marxist aim of full public ownership of the means of production, distribution and exchange. That aim *was* achieved by Russian power in the countries of Eastern Europe and by independent revolution in China. Its economic performance was unimpressive and it was governed by oppressive dictatorships. So for negative as well as positive reasons, socialist support in the West declined. At the beginning of the long boom a British Labor government was nationalizing major industries and it seemed possible that revolutionary socialist parties might win electoral majorities and govern in France and Italy. Thirty years later those parties, far from endangering private capitalism, were defending the status quo of the mixed economies against active 'new Right' efforts to privatize their public industries and dismantle some of their welfare provisions.

Once again we will list similarities and differences in the economic policy and performance of a number of countries, to notice the range of variation in their methods of development through the long boom.

COMMON EXPERIENCE

The advanced Western economies had these things among others in common:

Full employment Governments believed they could manage their economies to maintain full employment. In English-speaking countries – though not so widely in the US – the belief was reinforced by Keynesian theory. In *The General Theory of Employment Interest and Money* (1936) John Maynard Keynes had launched one simple and one complicated argument. The simple one explained how (i) left to itself, a capitalist economy could easily leave some of its productive resources unemployed, but (ii) some quite moderate government action could adjust the system to operate with continuous full employment. The complicated argument, which need not concern us here, was designed to show economists why their traditional theoretical reasons for expecting full employment to come naturally were mistaken.

At the heart of Keynes' simple argument was the observation that business directors would invest (or not), produce more (or less), and employ all (or fewer than all) the available workers, according to how much output they could expect to sell, and how confidently they could expect to sell it. Government could influence those expectations partly by adjusting the amount of disposable income which consumers had to spend, but chiefly by influencing investment more directly, for example by adjusting the amount of public investment, and the amount of credit available to private investors.

To this day, Keynesians and others still debate the causes of those two or three decades of full employment through the long boom. Was direct government influence on disposable income and investment chiefly responsible? Or did the belief that Keynesian governments would act if necessary stimulate enough confident private investment to maintain full employment *without* much government action? Or did the special historical circumstances – the imperative need and popular demand for postwar reconstruction and social reform – drive that generation of public and private investors to employ all the resources they could lay their hands on? That third explanation was specially persuasive in the non-English-speaking countries. In Japan and much of Western Europe there were traditions of strong central government and public enterprise, much of it contrived by broadly educated, untheoretical public servants rather than economists, and not much influenced either by Keynes or by the earlier theories which he attacked.

From whatever pattern of causes of those three kinds,

the advanced Western economies enjoyed full or nearly full employment throughout the long boom, and Japan achieved it about 1960 and continued it thereafter.

Besides national economic management there was also some international management. Through the 1950s most countries controlled the uses of the foreign exchange they earned and the US dollars they were lent or given as international aid. International agreements in the 1940s established a system of fixed financial exchange rates, with the World Bank and International Monetary Fund to ease their working. The system operated until its main elements broke down early in the 1970s. There were also some agreed rules – not always observed – for national trade policies.

Leaders and followers All the developed countries (except Britain at times) maintained high rates of saving and investment. Most of the others saved harder and grew faster than the US. The US was both the main technological leader and the most fully developed, i.e. more of its industries were near to their current technological frontiers; so opportunities for additional investment above the level needed to maintain existing capital depended a good deal on inventive progress. By contrast 'follower' countries were doubly backward. Technical progress was easier for them because they could import rather than invent new methods. And 'lateral' development was easier because they had more backward or undeveloped industries to be modernized. So they had greater investment opportunities. Thus when Japan was investing at twice the US rate and growing at three or four times the US rate, that did not necessarily signify performance of superior quality. Catching up was technically easier than leading. Japan also had two other advantages, one apparent and one real. First it modernized with an extreme bias for (measured) private capitalist productivity rather than (unmeasured or less measured) household and communal productivity, so the official accounts exaggerate the real difference between Japanese and other Western rates of growth. Second, Japan and Germany were not allowed to spend on defence, and their security came to depend on the victor countries' defence investment and spending. That slowed the growth of useful productivity in the victor countries and allowed it to grow faster in Germany and Japan.

Technology All the developed countries continued to modernize and mechanize their agriculture, and regulate and protect it. Farming employed steadily fewer workers and produced steadily more output. In manufacturing, changing technology allowed steadily

declining numbers to produce steadily increasing output. So also in transport and trading: container ships, articulated trucks and mechanized handling enabled fewer people to move more goods. Supermarket methods enabled fewer people to retail more goods. In computerized banks and insurance offices fewer people handled more money and accounts. All governments stimulated and subsidized house-building, which also grew more efficient as more of its components were factory-produced. Household productivity increased as more people got better houses, domestic equipment, network energy, and private cars. Many also got more time to make more use of that Do-It-Yourself (DIY) capital, because of shorter hours and longer holidays in their paid jobs.

Economic growth Thus fast growth of output and income per head were achieved by a combination of –

- full employment
- public rationing and regulation of the uses of some main physical and financial resources
- research, invention and technological progress
- the extension of current technology to more countries, industries, firms and households
- rising levels of education and skill, and
- some higher participation in paid work.

From 1950 to 1970 the growth of Gross Domestic Product in the dozen richest countries averaged 4.7 per cent per year. Some countries grew faster than others, so some climbed and some slipped down the rank order of income per head. But generally they all moved nearer to full productive use of the world's available technical knowledge, and in doing that, followers tended to catch up with leaders: the dozen richest were more closely 'bunched' in 1970 than they had been in 1939 or 1950.

Equalities One use of the rising output was to provide household investment which extended some common material living standards to majorities who had never had them before. Even if working-class incomes were no nearer than before to those above them, the classes now had more material conditions in common. Many had cars, and nearly all had refrigerators, washing machines, and nearly-identical standards of food and health and hygiene. Some theorists wondered whether that would 'bourgeoisify' the workers in political and cultural ways. It certainly did so in material ways: by the 1970s most employed workers' households had the kind of housing, equipment and spending money which only a well-off middle-class household – perhaps one

European household in every four or five – had before 1950.

Those middle and higher incomes had also increased. Faster or slower than the working-class incomes – was there now greater or less equality of income? It depends on criteria of equality – on what changes you think matter most. Most scholars agree that inequalities of income declined until the 1970s and have since been stable or increased again. But there were differences between countries, and in the fortunes of particular groups of rich and poor.

Welfare Whatever the primary inequalities were, those decades saw the creation of most of the modern apparatus of welfare. Before 1939 most industrial countries had means-tested old age pensions, some public hospitals and clinics for the sick poor, and short-term aids – more in kind than money – for some categories of unemployed. By 1970 most of those countries had universal public health service or insurance; much-improved income support and home-help and other services for the aged; regular public incomes for most of the sick, handicapped and unemployed, and in some countries for many students and single parents; family allowances and daycare and other services for people with children; and personal social services for a wide range of needs.

What did those services do for equalities? There is some disagreement. Undoubtedly some *income* was transferred from the richest class to the poorest. But many of the *services*, especially in health and higher education, were used more by people with middle and higher incomes than by those with low incomes. Since the services were financed by some indirect taxation of everyone, some direct taxation of many, and some progressive taxation of the rich, they tended to transfer real income from both ends of the income scale to the middle. But whatever the effect on proportional equalities, the new welfare improved many of the poorest incomes and living conditions, and thus the working efficiency of the people as a whole.

This is a suitable point at which to turn from the similarities of the leading industrial economies through the long boom to some of their differences. Remember that these sketches are not balanced economic histories. They are notes to show *some* ways in which methods and paths of national development have varied in recent times.

France

France had a long tradition of strong central government by a powerful public service, ambitious public enter-prise, and weak, conservative and heavily protected private industry. In 1945 many of the old masters of business and government had been discredited during the war and the German occupation of France. The patriots who took over the public service were also able to take over some more of French industry: the coal mines, the Renault company, the major banks and insurance companies were added to the railways, canals, power suppliers and other enterprises that the government already owned. They then developed a new style of 'indicative' national economic planning similar in some ways to MITI's industrial planning in Japan. Using formal powers, informal influence and extensive public ownership, the planners went to work with two main purposes: to re-equip and modernize French industry, and to negotiate an integrated European economy. The integration had at least three purposes: to end any further possibility of internal war in Europe; to build an economic system to match the scale and strength of the American and Russian systems; and to bring competitive pressure to bear in modernizing French industry – but in a controlled way, without exposing France as a free-trader in a protectionist world.

They succeeded. International action began in the coal and steel industries, and in 1957 the Treaty of Rome began the gradual integration of the European Economic Community. From 1945 to 1960 France recorded its fastest-ever economic growth. Measured GNP per head overtook British about 1960 and was among the world leaders by the 1980s.

For our present comparative purposes, notice these features of the French performance:

* There was strong central planning and a good deal of informal support and direction of industrial develop-ment. Far from a 'dead hand of government' inhibiting a vigorous private sector, the public servants worked through many failures and frustra-tions to break old routines and protections and induce more energetic, adventurous performance by both private and public enterprises.

* Agriculture was modernized, but with continuing high protection and price supports. The protection was partly for vote-winning purposes but partly also for purposes of physical and social conservation which will be noticed in Chapter 16 – plenty of city as well as country voters did not want to turn the French countryside into a depopulated 'American prairie'.

* Through the years of fastest growth about a fifth of all French industry, including as much as half of

heavy industry, was owned by government, and half or more of all new investment was provided or controlled by public institutions. When a bigger private share was encouraged after 1960, the government continued to limit and regulate any foreign ownership of French industry.

- Differences in productive efficiency tend to have been between the protected and the unprotected sectors, rather than between the public and private sectors. Some public enterprises, for example in car-making and sea and air transport, have been at least as efficient as their private French and foreign competitors.

- The extensive state planning, ownership and control were not generally used for socialist or equalizing purposes. Their uses were frequently opposed by organized labor and the socialist parties who were the main political opposition. Though in the post-war years there was less private capital ownership than in comparable countries, incomes were at least as unequal as in those countries.

Thus France has contradicted beliefs, widely held by both Left and Right, that private capitalists are the main agents of inequality, and public ownership and economic power the main agents of greater equality. In democratic France, (i) greater public economic power than in most other rich democracies has been used to keep incomes at least as unequal as in those more capitalist countries; and (ii) this has been contrived rather more by public employees and professional people than by private capitalists.

But don't make a general rule of that relation between public power and private inequality. Compare Sweden and Australia, which used similar central economic powers through the long boom, but in contrasting ways, and with some different effects. Their strategies are the subject of later chapters, so for the present comparative purpose short notes on their differences will do.

Sweden

Swedish manufacturing had prospered under liberal 'small government' before the depression of the 1930s. The Swedish Social Democratic Labor Party decided that it could not win elections while it stood for socialist public ownership, or with the support of blue-collar workers alone. So it switched to a strategy of equality *without* public ownership. It made alliances with Sweden's farmers and later with white-collar wage-earners, won power in 1932 and governed for most of the next sixty eight years.

Meanwhile the unions brought 70 per cent of white collar and 90 per cent of blue collar workers into the most effective national labor organization in the world. At the employers' request, a periodical central negotiation fixed general wage levels. And the unions' rather than the political party's economists were for some decades the main authors of Sweden's economic strategy. Its main elements were –

- *Solidarity* By central wage-bargaining labor should work for more equality among wage earners as well as between wage earners and others. Workers in similar jobs should not be paid unequally because some happened to be in less efficient firms. Sweden should get rid of less efficient firms.

- *Full employment* High wages, with other national policies, should maintain effective demand and full employment.

- *Growth* Full employment at high wages could fuel inflation – so labor should bargain for wage levels which the economy could really pay, and keep those levels rising by 'going for growth'.

- *Investment* Investors got some help from specialist public and public/private banks. There was strict public regulation of the private banks, the movement of capital funds in and out of Sweden, and any foreign ownership of Swedish enterprises.

- *Labor policy* Basically labor said 'We want high wages. So we want firms efficient enough to pay them. We will see they *do* pay – but we will also do everything necessary to keep them efficient.' Workers should willingly go wherever they could be most productively employed. They should not try to perpetuate existing jobs by getting government to protect or subsidize failing industries. Instead they should welcome the re-direction of capital and labor to industries which *could* pay high and rising wages.

- *Free trade and progressive taxation* Most public revenue should come from direct progressive taxes on income and wealth. Besides improving equalities that should have two other effects. Free-trading, duty-free imports would keep prices down and the purchasing power of wages up. And they would help growth by forcing inefficient industries to reform or close.

- *Welfare* By the 1950s Sweden was an industrial leader and wages were approaching the world's best. What next? As in most of Western Europe, but most generously in Sweden, the welfare system was extended to meet a wider range of needs and especially to provide high, earnings-related, inflation-proof pensions. Wage and salary earners would retire on up to 80 per cent of their working incomes. That and other developments made Sweden the first mixed economy to put more than half of its national income through its public budget.

Though successful for half a century, the strategy had some shortcomings and political and social costs. By the 1970s they were troublesome enough to bring some conflict and re-thinking of the strategy itself. We will pick up the story later in the course.

Australia

Though Australia and Sweden took radically different paths they have similar interest as small populations trying unusual economic strategies. Sweden is the extreme case of a small country specializing: importing freely, and developing only the manufactures that could win export markets. Australia was the opposite case of a small country trying to do everything: a sort of pint-sized United States trying to be as self-sufficient as possible by manufacturing a very wide range of goods for its own use. Through the long boom it continued to export staples – wool, grain, meat, minerals – and to import specialized and high-quality manufactures. But behind protective tariffs it developed a wide range of bulk manufacturing, supplying many of its own needs for steel, aluminium, plastics, chemicals, paper, ships, farm and railway machinery, cars, household equipment, textiles, clothing, furniture, and processed food and drink. Most of the products cost more than imports would have cost, and could not compete as exports. Growth was only average. Parts of Europe were passing Australia by in measured GNP, though probably not in household capital and productivity. But as suggested earlier, Australia was still a comfortably rich country. Its long-boom record of very full employment, high social and household investment, quite high public ownership, and protected, diversified manufacturing adds one more to the list of alternative paths to national growth and wealth.

The United States

The U.S. economy grew slowly but nevertheless stayed ahead, as evidence that a more market-reliant economy could produce as efficiently as the more deliberately directed ones. The achievement was unspecialized and comprehensive. A skilful, highly educated population with abundant land and natural resources had used tariff and other protection to develop a very wide range of industries, so the economy was unusually self-sufficient, trading comparatively little with the rest of the world (though investing in many parts of it). Business had strong influence with government and used it to get protection, subsidies, contracts and franchises for public works and services. The protection of industry and agriculture do not seem to have done much harm to their productive efficiency. That may have owed something to the large size of the national market, to an inventive, acquisitive, competitive culture, and perhaps to other causes. At the same time government was more active in the economy than it has since become. Until various dates in the 1970s it acted as a kind of central banker to the Western world. It regulated rates of exchange and capital transactions with other currencies. Within the U.S. it regulated the rate of interest at which banks could lend, and the operations of the savings institutions. It was active in schemes of urban renewal. It improved some social services and income supports through the Kennedy/Johnston welfare programs in the 1960s. But the United States was still in most respects the least planned of the Western economies, the most unequal, and the richest.

The United Kingdom

British GNP per head had increased nearly fourfold since 1870 – but it was third in the world in 1890, sixth in 1950, and about fifteenth by 1970. Why did it grow less fast than others?

Business and labor tended to blame each other. Britain had strong unions, but unlike the Swedish unions they tended to be defensive and protective – in effect conservative, using their muscle to preserve existing jobs from import competition, from structural change, from job-shedding modernization. Britain saved too little and invested too much of it either overseas or in other things than manufacturing, so although it depended as vitally as Sweden or Japan on exporting manufactured goods to competitive markets it failed to keep enough of its manufacturing capacity up to date and competitive. As we noted earlier, there may also have been some class and cultural reasons for some shortage of skill and enterprise in the manufacturing industries. If the ablest people went into business at all, they tended to choose finance or retailing or the media rather than manufacturing – and what they most liked to finance did not always include competitive manufacturing industries with quick-changing technology, long investment lead-times and low rates of return.

COMPARISONS

Remember that this is easy reading – don't be snowed by the details.

Begin with some aspects of the postwar performance of Japan, France and Sweden. All had some deliberate central planning of the general directions of economic development, and strong public influence on their levels and patterns of investment. In all three the planning and direction were done chiefly by an elite, highly educated public service. In France and Japan that elite answered to governments of the moderate Right, in Sweden to governments of the Left. In Japan the policies were mostly conceived by the public servants; in France by politicians and public servants; in Sweden by economists of the labor movement. France had a lot of public ownership, Japan and Sweden comparatively little. Sweden and France had earlier and bigger welfare provisions than Japan.

There are other similarities and contrasts if you turn from the planners to the non-planners, i.e. to countries in which business interests had more influence on government and – for that or other reasons – government put more trust in the market allocation of resources, and gave less deliberate direction to the economy, except to provide tariffs and subsidies desired by business. Obvious examples are the United States and – to some degree, after its return to more conservative government in 1951 – Britain. Both economies grew through the long boom, but not as fast as Japan, France, Germany or Australia did.

Among developed countries the fast growth and rising productivity were accompanied by democratic government, internal law and order, and high levels of investment, education and research. There the positive similarities seem to end. National population and natural resources, economic structure and the amount and kind of national economic planning all varied widely. So did patterns of trade, trade policies, public and private ownership, labor organization, distributions of political and industrial strength, and (to a lesser extent) inequalities of wealth and income.

Some limits of variation can be observed. Through the last years of the boom, our sample of six countries (the US, the UK, Japan, France, Sweden and Australia) were investing between 16 and 32 per cent of their income. They traded between 9 and 30 per cent of their output. None put much less than a third or much more than a half of its income through its public budget. The richest one per cent of their people got between 5 and 8 per cent of their income; the richest twenty per cent got between 38 and 50 per cent; the poorest twenty per cent got 6 per cent or less. Inequalities of wealth were greater than inequalities of income, and varied more from country to country.

Thus fast growth and full employment have been consistent with quite a wide range of national economic structures and strategies. If growth were the only test, there does not seem to have been any one clearly-best strategy. It was possible to have economic growth with rising or with declining inequality. It was possible to combine either rising or declining inequality with either greater or less productive efficiency. Much depended on the design of the policies and the skill with which they were applied, and on the culture and other national conditions in which they had to operate. But – subject to those conditions – policies to maximize economic efficiency and growth do not necessarily dictate particular distributional policies, or vice versa, though the two are likely to affect each other in various ways and need to be designed with their mutual effects in mind.

At the same time a successful economic and social strategy has to be more than a collection of separate 'best policies' – a 'best policy' about central planning, a 'best policy' about trade, a 'best policy' about public and private ownership, and so on. The policies need to hang together. Any search for a best strategy for chosen purposes should compare whole strategies rather than just their component parts one by one. We will compare half a dozen of them at the end of this course of study.

RIGHT TURN 1970 – 2000

To understand what followed the long boom you must first understand what ended it.

Many forces combined to end it. Since most of them are still at work you will study them in depth and detail through later chapters. But a short preview of them now can serve three purposes:

• to explain why the boom ended;

• to introduce a number of problems which have troubled the leading economies ever since; and

• to explain why the governments of most English-speaking countries shifted their economic policies sharply to the Right through the 1980s.

Hard learning

This passage of history is important. It introduces the world we live in now: the world in which you will begin your work as an economist in the twenty-first century. The following account of it focuses selectively on current directions of change. It is in relation to those processes of change – and the possible alternatives to them, and the warring forces which are contending to direct them – that you will have to decide what matters most to you: what to work for, whose interests to work for, what visions and principles should guide you, in your professional life.

So treat this final part of this chapter as hard learning. It sketches an explanation of this current phase of Western history. It is an explanation which has strongly influenced the design of this course of study. However you eventually judge it, please take time and care to understand it.

To help the hard learning, a summary comes at the beginning rather than the end of the explanation, to map its structure for you before you start working through its parts.

SUMMARY

At various dates from late in the 1960s onwards –

1. Continuing growth and full employment led governments to dismantle some of the controls which were actually contributing to the growth and full employment. (Because the controls had been associated with temporary war organization or postwar reconstruction their value as permanent aids to growth and stability was not widely understood.)

2. Some effects of technological progress and economic growth began to generate structural and transitional unemployment.

3. Competition for shares of income (with some other causes) generated rising rates of inflation, and in some countries continued to do so as unemployment increased.

4. Unemployment, inflation, policy changes and other factors combined to revive the tendency to periodical boom and slump in the rich economies; slow their economic growth; increase their public welfare costs; and consequently sharpen political conflicts about their levels of welfare and taxation.

5. Those troubles began to discredit the economic theories and public policies which had accompanied the long boom. The prevailing national and international strategies seemed to need some repair or replacement.

6. *Repair?* Plenty of people of the Left and Centre wanted to repair the social-democratic management of the mixed economy. The means might include restoring stricter controls of banking and credit and of trade and exchange; restoring full employment by developing labor-intensive green industries and by some further improvement of labor-intensive education, health and welfare services; price and income policies to restrain inflationary competition for shares of income; progressive taxation and some further reduction of inequalities.

7. *Replacement?* Many people on the Right – including some each of rich people, business people, libertarians, conservative politicians and neoclassical economists – had always opposed the Keynesian beliefs and policies, and some of them regretted the equalizing tendencies of the postwar developments. They took advantage of the troubles noted in 2, 3, 4 and 5 above to step up campaigns for a return to pre-Keynesian neoclassical theory, smaller government, greater business freedom and bargaining strength against labor, lower and less progressive taxes, meaner welfare and steeper inequality.

8. Which side would win – and how, and why? The main mass supporters of the Left and Centre policies were blue-collar workers and other low earners, plus quite big minorities of middle class people whose humane social values and feelings of national solidarity had been formed by the experience of deep depression and total war. But they were declining proportions of the voters and of the influential elite. The fast growth of incomes, of household capital and of helpful public services was increasing the numbers of contented and potentially conservative

voters. And the elite schooled in depression and war and Keynesian economics was giving way to a well-off generation who had led liberation movements and other campaigns against government in the 1960s, then lost faith in economic policies which betrayed expectations by allowing the simultaneous rise of inflation and unemployment. In English-speaking countries all the main political parties shifted their economic policies some way to the Right, but except in the United States the new levels of unemployment persisted. A number of West European countries held onto their social-democratic policies – but without effective repair. They also suffered heavy unemployment, and paid high taxes to finance its welfare costs.

9. Where Right policies prevailed, new links were developed between the democracies' foreign economic policies and their internal economic policies. Freer trade, deregulated banking and international financial dealings, the growth of transnational corporations, and the Asian tigers' development of competitive manufacturing combined to allow the world to develop towards a single global economy. Within the rich democracies Right campaigners, including many economists with faith in free market forces, began to frighten their societies with predictions of falling investment and growth, and rising unemployment and poverty, if they did not become more internationally competitive. To become more competitive they were advised that they must continue to privatize public business and deregulate private business. And they must cut their lowest wages, working conditions, taxes and welfare standards down to match those of the low-paid competitors to whom the new free trade was exposing them.

10. There was thus a critical sequence of steps to the Right. Inflation and unemployment discredited the Keynesian regime. Decisions to deregulate trade and exchange exposed Western economies to new low-wage and high-tech competitors, and further unemployment. Together those conditions weakened resistance to the next steps to the Right: the attacks on workers' rights, wage and welfare levels, progressive taxation and other egalitarian achievements of the historic first century of male democracy and the first half-century of full democracy. The drive towards a single global economy in which no government could expect to protect its own economy or people – a drive which the radical, *laissez-faire* division of the Right now depicted as 'inevitable' and 'irresistible' – began to look like a capitalist counter-attack against democracy itself.

That is a bare outline of what I believe were some main causes of the shift of English-speaking governments' economic policies to the Right, i.e. towards steeper inequalities, through the last quarter of the century. Try to keep the structure of the explanation in mind – without necessarily accepting it – as you now work your way through more of its detail and argument.

TECHNOLOGY AND EMPLOYMENT

The main engine of fast economic growth through the long boom was technological progress in farming, manufacturing, transport, communications, information processing, and household productivity. In many branches of those industries, rising output was produced by declining numbers of workers.

Full employment nevertheless continued for a generation because people spent rising proportions of their rising incomes on labor-intensive services. Some of those were market services (hairdressing and other personal services, private child care, restaurant and takeaway meals, commercial recreations, holiday travel and tourism). Some – especially education, health and welfare services – were partly or wholly financed from taxation. So as fast as the technically advancing industries shed workers, the expanding labor-intensive services employed them.

But that complementary relation between labor-shedding and labor-intensive industries was a phase rather than a permanent trend in the changing structure of demand. There were a number of reasons why it could not continue forever:

*   The price inducements point the wrong way. Products of job-shedding industries get relatively cheaper and tend to attract more demand, while labor-intensive services get relatively dearer and tend to attract less demand.

*   Faced with rising prices for labor-intensive market services, the technical revolution in household capital equips people to do more things for themselves. Washing machines, dishwashers, vacuum cleaners, hair-dryers get steadily cheaper and – with much less household labor than the work used to take – they replace commercial services and domestic servants.

*   Some of the services themselves begin to benefit from technical progress, and shed labor as they mechanize and computerize. That leaves a falling proportion of labor-intensive services to pick up the workers shed by a rising proportion of labor-saving industries and services.

As labor-saving industries improve their productivity and lower their prices, and labor-intensive industries raise their relative prices, there is no reason to expect that people as consumers and citizens will always adjust their spending and tax-paying to keep both sectors fully employed. In most of the rich countries they ceased to do so through the 1970s. And even if their demands could in principle have kept all workers employed, that did not happen in practice, for the following reasons.

Aggregate demand fell below full-employment levels as some English-speaking governments and some others responded to inflation, rising welfare costs, and the return to neoclassical theory, by cutting public investment and services. That directly cut demand for investment goods. By reducing public employment it reduced total earned income. That reduced household demand for investment goods, and for consumer goods and services. Many governments raised interest rates to discourage private investment. Some cut aggregate demand further by reducing their budget deficits. So it was fair to blame governments for some of the new unemployment.

But not for all of it: other causes were also at work.

Changing technology, changing skills The lead times and retraining required for any big reallocation of labor between declining and growing industries can increase levels of both temporary and permanent unemployment. It takes time to turn unwanted farm laborers into plumbers or hairdressers – and employers wanting plumbers or hairdressers may prefer younger recruits if they can get them. There can be similar intervals of unemployment for surplus assembly-line workers, pen-and-ink account-keepers, middle managers, 'down-sized' public servants; and if they lose their jobs in middle age because of declining demand for their skills, their unemployment is often permanent. Thus technical progress can *directly* change both the required skills and the required proportions of each of them; and it can change their employment *indirectly* as its effects on productivity and prices cause shifts in the demand for particular goods and services, and therefore for particular skills.

Structural unemployment, transitional unemployment If the available skills don't match the skills which employers need to hire, or if the available workers live too far away from the available jobs, the consequent unemployment is called *structural*. If it is curable – if the unemployed workers can be re-trained, or if the next generation can be appropriately educated, or if the available workers can move to where the jobs are, or the jobs move to where the workers are – then the structural unemployment may be *transitional*.

Economists have generally believed that *all* structural unemployment is transitional, because technological progress has never yet brought a permanent reduction of available employment. But that reading of history may be misleading. The twentieth-century progress of the leading economies has equipped them, *for the first time ever*, to keep all their people in material comfort and security. Their people responded at first by working steadily shorter hours: they want much less consumption than they could now have if they worked their grandparents' hours.

Nevertheless there has not been much pressure to cut the working week to less than thirty five hours, or to cut the working year to less than eleven months, or to cut the working life-time to less than forty years; and there is mounting evidence of the positive value of work itself to most workers. There is also some pressure – and there may soon be more – to limit material output and consumption in the rich countries for environmental reasons. So the amount of employment that people want may conceivably cease to fit the particular pattern of output and consumption that they want. *Any* amount of the goods they want may be produced (with jobless growth) by fewer hours of paid work than they want. That may make opportunities for some people to monopolize the scarce employment and force unemployment on others, rather than rationing whatever employment there is to allow all willing workers to have shares of it.

It may be too soon to judge whether technological progress will force some permanent unemployment or under-employment. But it does seem to be causing some permanent increase of temporary and transitional unemployment.

INFLATION

Some early Keynesians had warned Keynes that full employment would fuel inflation as workers' bargaining strength increased and employers competed for scarce labor. It did so, though at such different rates in different countries that it was wrong to see it as an *automatic* effect of full employment. Other causes also operated:

- Tax changes which raised prices, monopolists who raised prices, exchange rates which raised import prices, could all prompt workers to defend their real incomes by demanding wage rises which in turn would cause prices to rise again.

- Banks, especially as governments began to weaken or mismanage their regulation, could create too much credit for investors or consumers or both, so that demand for goods and services ran ahead of supply and pushed prices up.

- Governments could similarly inflate demand by allowing too big a gap between their public spending and the money they withdrew from the economy by taxation.

By the 1970s inflation was upsetting everyone's theoretical expectations by continuing (and sometimes accelerating) through periods of slack investment, slack demand and rising unemployment. Inflationary pricing and wage-bargaining had become habitual – producers raising prices to recoup the last wage rises, workers demanding wage rises to match others' wage rises or the last price rises, and so on. Some of it had also become anticipatory. People pushed up wages and prices because they rightly expected further inflation. They wanted compensation as it happened, not after months or years of time-lag and loss.

COMPOUND EFFECTS

In the private sector

As some technological unemployment developed it began to have 'chain' or multiplier effects. Unemployment slowed the growth of wage income and total household investment and consumer spending. Together with anxiety about inflation, that depressed investors' spirits and lowered their self-fulfilling expectations of continuing expansion. So some of them invested less, i.e. they bought less capital and intermediate goods. Producers of those goods consequently bought less materials and components and employed fewer workers. Household income and spending slowed further or actually fell as unemployment spread, and private investment and employment followed household spending down. Thus technological unemployment triggered some further unemployment of the kind that had traditionally occurred during periodical recessions.

In the public sector

Both some successes of the long boom and its eventual ending increased government's financial obligations.

Successes: Collectively, people voted to use some of their rising income to improve public education and health services, and the provision of income and public services to old, invalid and unemployed people, and to some parents and others. The new provisions did not cost too much when they were introduced after World War Two in conditions of full employment, mid-century technology and mid-century medical practice. But those conditions were changing:

- Public costs increased as medical science and the new welfare provisions enabled people to live longer, and therefore need more care, after they stopped earning.

- The costs increased more dramatically as heavy investment in medical research revolutionized the technology of preventive and curative medicine. Through the third quarter of the century that revolution doubled the percentage of national income (from about 4 to about 8 per cent) which could be spent effectively, without waste, on medical services to maximize people's health and length of life. (Countries whose health services are more wastefully organized and paid for are now spending up to 14 per cent of national income on them.)

- Public costs rose further as technological progress in a wide range of industries and services called for new skills, and therefore more public education for the workforce. Many people also sought more education for its own sake, as one of the goods on which they chose to spend some of their rising income.

The health, educational and welfare improvements were rightly popular, and for a while the technical progress which made them possible also took care of their costs. Fast economic growth expanded the 'revenue base', i.e. the flows of income and goods and services on which taxes were levied. So fixed tax *rates* brought in rising revenue. Slow rates of inflation had similar effects, as 'bracket creep' moved earners to higher rates of income tax. So the growth of public revenue was politically tolerable. (If people with rising incomes buy more market goods with some traditional rates of tax concealed in the market prices, they pay more tax but don't complain about it. As rising incomes and slow inflation take them into higher income tax brackets they may grumble a bit – but progressive income tax has been a fact of life for several generations, and as long as the rates at each income level don't rise there are unlikely to be tax revolts in Europe, Britain or the Commonwealth countries.)

But a change – with new political dilemmas and opportunities – came with the onset of heavy unemployment in the 1970s.

Troubles As the long boom faltered, rising unemployment increased the amount of income which had to be transferred to unemployed people and their dependants. Thus (as with medicine and education) another welfare promise began to cost more than its creators had expected. And this was a harder promise to keep, for two reasons. First, it was not a promise to the big numbers who benefited from better health and education. The unemployed were only ten percent or so of the workforce. And with the end of the boom the 'natural' growth of public revenue had slowed or stopped, and bigger public spending could well require higher tax *rates* to which many tax payers were likely to object.

Politicians certainly expected tax increases to be unpopular. They tried hard not to introduce new taxes or higher rates. They denounced opponents who introduced, or proposed, or were suspected of considering higher taxes. They attacked each others' tax performance so fiercely that they almost certainly strengthened the tax resistance that they were afraid of, as year by year, insistently, opposing parties told their electors that taxes collected or contemplated by their opponents were needlessly high and wasteful and could be cut without any loss of the services they financed. Governments began to finance rising health and welfare costs and income transfers by cutting other public services. They cut where cuts could be disguised (often dishonestly) as aids to efficiency. They cut welfare benefits where they could stigmatize the losers (truthfully or not) as layabouts or welfare cheats. And they began to cut public investment; to privatize public services; and to dissave (i.e. spend capital) by selling public assets and using the proceeds to finance current services.

Public-private interactions In the short run most of the public cuts reduced employment, income, and economic growth. By reducing the number of public employees they reduced total income, spending and demand. They also reduced the public sector's output of goods and services. Where those were 'final' goods, their loss reduced national output directly. Where they were inputs to private production the cuts could reduce private output or increase its costs. Where public services were privatized the new owners or contractors usually reduced the numbers they employed, with similar effects on total demand. Lower rates of public investment cut public purchases from private suppliers. Private investment and employment in the affected industries declined, or failed to grow, accordingly.

As investment, employment and the rate of growth declined, so did the growth of the revenue. So public costs increased faster than public revenue. In some of the English-speaking countries, politicians responded with *more* cuts, privatizations and asset sales, with further depressing effects.

CROSSROADS

Twentieth century technical progress had thus brought a revolution in productivity and potential affluence for all.

But it had also created problems which scarcely any economists had foreseen. It had created necessary new roles for the public sector – but divisive conflicts about how to perform and finance them. It had brought changes to some traditional areas of conflict and co-operation: between business and government, between business and labor, between men and women, between humans and their natural environment. How should the first generation of mature welfare democracies respond to those problems?

A variety of answers to that question have been proposed since the 1970s. From the debates about them we can distil a coherent Left Centre strategy and a coherent Right strategy. They indicate about how far to the Left and to the Right political leaders have been able, at times, to attract substantial support – though never yet majority support. Actual policies, some more coherent than others, have developed between those extremes.

The two strategies are worth noticing for a number reasons. First, why has neither of them attracted decisive support – although one promises full employment, better environmental care and more equality, and the other has the high authority of the Organization for Economic Cooperation and Development, whose owners and members are the governments of the twenty four richest democracies? See for yourselves.

A Left Centre strategy

There were socialists, Keynesian social democrats, labor leaders, feminists, environmental reformers, and some middle-of-the-road liberals and conservatives who wanted to *repair* the postwar social-democratic strategy, some favoring more radical repairs than others.

Some wanted to combine full employment with low inflation by restraining prices and incomes, whether by public controls or by negotiation between government and the peak organizations of business and labor. Some wanted to restore full employment by rationing employment, i.e. by shortening the working week or year or the working lifetime. Others wanted to restore full employment by continuing to expand labor-intensive public services, especially social and educational and environmental services. Some, less ambitious, accepted some unemployment as a necessary price to pay for desirable business freedom and for the restraint of inflation. But they wanted good welfare services and income transfers for the unemployed. They thus took unemployment seriously, but wanted to treat it as a social rather than an economic problem.

Most of those who wanted to restore full employment also had social purposes in mind. Besides increasing employment, expanded neighborhood services could improve the lives of many old, infirm and handicapped people, and also the lives of the family members, mostly women, who had to care for them. Mentally ill and handicapped people who had been 'de-institutionalized' by cost-cutting governments had all too often been thrown out of their accustomed institutions and friendships and care to take their chances in squalid boarding houses. Better-financed services could return them to better and safer care. Women's and men's job opportunities could be more nearly equalized by better child-care services. To keep other options open there could also be more public support for full-time parents and for those wanting re-training to return to paid work after parenting.

There could be similar links between employment and environmental policy. Forests needed replanting. Soil conservation called for some replanting, and other labor-intensive work. A great many buildings needed to have their insulation improved and some of their heating and powered equipment replaced. In some industries and services and household work there was room for some return from machine power to muscle power.

Finance? Some of the new services could be marketed, and pay for themselves. Full employment would expand the tax base and the revenue from existing tax rates. Social-democratic governments could make bolder use of budget deficits, and have public banks finance public investment. Where more tax revenue was needed, bold reformers wanted to restore earlier rates of progressive tax on high incomes. More pragmatic politicians wanted to raise what they needed by taxing a wide range of goods and services. They could still make those taxes mildly progressive by exempting basic food and rent, and taxing luxury goods at high rates.

Sources of strength and weakness There was some support for that sort of social-democratic program in many of the rich countries. But where major parties tried to adopt elements of it (as at different times in France and Sweden) they were beaten in national elections, or by hostile market reprisals, or by internal party disagreements. In most countries no major party adopted much of the program. The traditional Labor and Social-Democratic parties were being led to the Right and offering more low-tax, market-trusting policies. So national electors did not have many opportunities to choose effective social-democratic remedies for the new economic troubles.

Why were leaders of the Left and the social-democratic Centre so reluctant to attempt a radical repair of the thirty-year-old social-democratic strategy? It was partly because efforts to repair it could so easily be attacked as merely continuing a strategy which had ceased to work.

Proposals for more public employment could be attacked as promising higher taxes to finance inefficient 'make-work'. If they did restore full employment, wouldn't it be as inflationary as before? If government tried to suppress inflation by controlling wages and prices, wouldn't that hinder efficient competition and block the vital price mechanisms of the market economy? More regulation, public employment and taxation were easily attacked as socialist, and therefore oppressive and inefficient, at a time when the communist governments themselves were acknowledging the inefficiency of their socialist economies. Five or ten years of unemployment and inflation had helped people to forget that many of the democracies' 'socialist' devices had been essential conditions of the fast growth and high efficiency of the golden age of capitalism through the long boom.

There were also some paradoxical effects of the popular radicalism – the student radicalism and 'street radicalism' – of the 1960s. It had some Left elements, especially in attitudes to conscription and to the Vietnam war. But its main focus was on black rights, students' rights, women's rights, free speech and sexual liberation – many of them conceived as rights against government, and sometimes against majority rule.

So into the 1980s three things – some class effects of economic growth, a generation change, and an intellectual reaction – joined in changing the political balance of the English-speaking countries:

- Economic growth had increased the numbers of comparatively comfortable and conservative voters and reduced the numbers of traditional working-class supporters of Labor and Social-Democratic parties.

- Among the educated middle-class people who supply important elements of professional service and leadership to the Left and Centre there was some cultural change. The generation which had experienced the economic breakdown and human suffering of the Great Depression and then the shared sacrifices and class cooperation of the Second World War had responded by developing the institutions of the fully employed welfare society. Through the 1970s it was handing over to a generation brought up in comparative affluence and security, liberated in self-expressive, self-assertive ways through the 1960s, and taught to distrust government rather than to use it confidently as a constructive and compassionate force for good.

- Through the same years there was a steady increase in the number of economists in business and government, and in the number who returned from Keynesian to neoclassical beliefs. (They said they were disillusioned by the breakdown of the Keynesian system. Post-Keynesians accused them of helping to cause the breakdown by encouraging governments to end their national and international financial controls and other necessary public services.) By the 1980s, post-Keynesian and other economists who wanted to rebuild the public management of the mixed economies were outnumbered and outgunned in the English-speaking countries by those who believed that more market freedom would deliver better economic performance than more government could.

And as those class, generational and intellectual changes weakened the political Left and Centre, they positively strengthened their Right opponents.

A Right strategy

In its full-blooded form the new Right analysis goes like this:

The rich democracies face an increasingly open and competitive world economy. To survive in it they need radical reform. Market forces must be freed to stimulate and discipline the private sector, which is the productive sector, to match world standards of efficiency. Public employment and spending must be cut to release resources for productive use. Public regulation must be reduced wherever it hinders enterprise. In open economies facing both tough competition and rapid technological change the necessary incentives will need to include steeper inequalities of income, and insecure employment. To meet the new industrial competition Western workers, especially those with low skills, must be willing to work Asian hours under Asian discipline for Asian wages. To drive their wages down, the unemployed must constantly compete for their jobs. To drive that competition, there must be no comfortable welfare alternative to work.

The strategy was spelled out very clearly in the 1995 OECD *Economic Outlook*. It is quoted at length in Chapter 56 of this book. For present purposes, here is a preview.

The aim should be 'high economic growth with sustained increases in employment and productivity'. That can only be achieved in 'open competitive markets, which put producers under continuous pressures to improve efficiency and to innovate'. Harsh transitional effects on groups and individuals should not be allowed to slow the opening of the markets.

International as well as national business must be freed. 'Further productivity growth and an efficient allocation of the world's real resources will also depend on the free movement of financial resources' through 'globalised and liberalised financial markets.' To avoid any government distortion of market forces, insolvent banks should be allowed to fail and ruin their creditors too. There should be no restraint of the banks' new gambling activities. Trade in goods and services, like the trade in money, should be entirely free.

There must be no Keynesian deficit budgeting to sustain effective demand and employment. National governments must balance their budgets, chiefly by spending less. They can cut some public services and privatize others. And 'a fundamental reassessment of social transfers is required'. Rising numbers of old people are wanting more public help. Don't give it to them. Instead, cut what they already get. Raise the pension age, cut the pension itself, lower the asset and income levels which disqualify people from the pension. Also disqualify more of the other people who are currently entitled to public incomes – the unemployed, invalids, lone parents and others – and reduce the incomes of those who do continue to be entitled.

One purpose of those cuts is to cut public costs and taxation. Another is to drive the unemployed to work for low enough wages to attract investors to employ them. To achieve that, governments need only stop protecting workers and consumers. They should repeal all tariffs, open their markets to all comers, and thus open their workers to worldwide wage competition. And they must repeal any minimum wage regulation, ban collective bargaining, and avoid unnecessary consumer protection. Together those measures can be expected 'to make wage and price formation more responsive to market conditions and speed the adjustment to changing price signals'. That market discipline can shape and enforce a more productive performance than any government can hope to contrive.

Who wants that program?

Some rich people, some business leaders, some conservative politicians, some neoclassical economists, and some individuals in all social classes had always opposed the development of the fully employed welfare society. Others came to oppose it when it began to malfunction with rising inflation and unemployment. Some of those who want the full Right program have moral as well as economic objections to the welfare society. They think it taxes high incomes at rates which unjustly punish the most productive people, and amount to confiscation of property (which is prohibited in most of the democracies' constitutions). And it seduces the unemployed and other poor with public incomes which sap their independence and self-reliance and willingness to work – and consequently reduce their enjoyment of life as well as their societies' productivity.

The program attracts the usual mixture of self-interested, disinterested and public-spirited support. Most of the economists who recommend it presumably believe in it for technical reasons whatever their moral view of it, and think that it promises higher world income, less inequality between rich and poor countries, and in the long run a better life for poor as well as rich, than could be achieved by any other strategy.

Some potential winners from the strategy are honest believers in its social as well as its individual promise. Some are fairly thoughtless believers in whatever serves their interests. Some are cynics who don't believe in its advertised benefits but pretend to because it serves their interests, or because they expect its policies to prevail and as politicians they want to be on the winning side. And many ordinary people trust their societies' leaders and experts and suppose they must be right when so many of them warn about the hazards of the global economy and advise that smaller government, lower taxes and lower wages will induce economic growth and prevent even higher unemployment.

At the time, the strategy was attacked as cruel: greater efficiency and faster growth would not be worth achieving at such human cost. Twenty years on, the criticism focuses on the program's incompetence, and on the faults of the theory which shaped it. Except to reduce inflation, none of its promises of better performance have been fulfilled. Evidence of its failure and reasons for its failure are reviewed in Part Six of this course.

HALF RIGHT

Most of the recommended financial freedoms were completed through the 1980s. Governments varied widely in the extent to which they deregulated other industries and markets, and privatized their public services. No government cut its welfare incomes and services as severely as the OECD economists recommended. In the policies which they did introduce, retain, adjust, chop-and-change or abandon through the last quarter of the century, each country had its own history. We can notice some contrasts between three groups: continental European countries, the United Kingdom and some Commonwealth countries, and the

United States.

Western European governments did some cost-cutting, but did not stray very far from their established middle-of-the-road social democratic strategies. Nor did they repair those strategies effectively to restore full employment. They continued to invest in good public infrastructure to support their private farming and manufacturing. They continued to regulate business and its labor relations in considerable detail. The detail increased as governments adjusted their codes to comply with European Union requirements. They freed their trade with each other but not with the rest of the world. Many of them joined in introducing the Union's common currency. And most of them kept most of their welfare and superannuation promises. To meet their rising costs they continued to budget 45 per cent or thereabouts of national income. Though Europe had the developed world's highest unemployment, its richer countries generally took the best care of their poorer members.

A Conservative government in Britain and Labor governments in Australia and New Zealand moved their economic policies sharply to the Right through the 1980s. They privatized power, water, rail and bus utilities, and sold their public airlines. They cut taxes, chiefly on the rich, and financed the cuts chiefly by taxing mass consumption goods, cutting public services and selling public assets. They reduced some regulation of business, but also repaired some in response to business scandals and (in Britain) to European requirements. Through the 1980s British output and labor productivity grew at much the same comparatively slow rate as they had done through the long boom. The outstanding difference through the last quarter of the century has been persistent unemployment, at rates which have generally run somewhere between the higher West European rates and the lower US rate. Trade Unions are weaker, workers have lost some legal rights and job security, and most minimum wage laws have been repealed. But average wages have generally kept up with economic growth.

The United States already had much of the Right program. The public sector produced less of the national product, and less of the national income passed through public hands, than in any other rich country. Many public utilities had long been privately owned. Private firms produced most defence goods. Wealth was more widely owned than in some countries, but income was distributed more unequally than in any other developed economy.

Through the 1980s a Republican President and a Democratic Congress arrived at an odd mixture of economic policies.

Financial deregulation was well advanced before Reagan's election. As an early effect of it, his government had to rescue some of the world's biggest banks from incompetent losses. It also had to rescue a great many of the smallest banks, as managers of tens of thousands of local savings banks used their new freedom to lose or steal an estimated $460 billion of their depositors' money, all guaranteed by the government and repayable by US taxpayers.

The President had promised a conservative fiscal policy with balanced budgets, but delivered a very liberal one with big tax cuts and budget deficits. There was also a great increase in American borrowing from foreigners, much of it by sale of Treasury bonds so that the debt was denominated in US dollars and any exchange risks were with the lenders. In ten years the world's biggest creditor nation became its biggest debtor. Some of the easy money financed big defence investment. Most of the rest of it financed buoyant consumer spending from middle and upper incomes, rather than investment. Some of the spending was on services to households – services which can expand with more labor but not much more investment (mow our lawn, clean our house, shovel our snow, mind our kids, massage our bodies or spirits). Some business employment could also expand without much new investment (advertising, financial advice and services, gambling on share prices and interest rates and exchange rates). Not for the first time, American energy and ingenuity seemed to defy theory, this time by expanding business activity and employment in step with the rising numbers in the workforce but with surprisingly little growth of saving, investment or productivity.

Critics thus observed a double irony. In the heartland of business influence on government a conservative government was sustaining aggregate demand and comparatively high employment by Keynesian attention to consumer spending. But instead of Keynesian encouragements to new investors, the rich were simply getting a fast-rising share of the national income. And they were *not* investing much of it in new productive capacity in the U.S.

For many Americans through the same years there was an historic reversal of the traditional progress to higher living standards and greater equality. Since the 1970s the wage rates and incomes of the poorest third or more of American workers have been falling. They declined in relation to other incomes, and they declined absolutely, buying 12 or 15 per cent less goods and services in 1995 than they bought in 1975. Those are averages – the worst losses exceed 25 per cent. By official measures, 14 per cent of American children were in poverty in 1979, 23 per cent were in poverty in 1993. Meanwhile the top 1 per cent, 5 per cent and 10 per cent of earners took rising shares of national income as the poorest half took falling shares. In *Peddling Prosperity: Economic Sense and Nonsense in the Age of Diminished Expectations* (1990) Paul Krugman calculated how much of the rise in average family income between 1977 and 1989 went to different quintiles and percentiles of families. The poorest 40 percent lost income through those years. Who gained it? Krugman finds the answer to that question 'quite startling: 70 percent of the rise in average family income went to the top 1 percent' (pp.135-7). Executive plunder continues to outstrip all other pay growth. Inequality between the richest tenth and the poorest half of Americans is back to roughly where it was sixty years ago.

For twenty years rising inequality did not appear to have the incentive effects on productivity that Right theorists predicted. US rates of saving, investment and productivity growth still lagged behind those of Japan, the European leaders, Britain, Canada and Australia – countries whose workers' real wages continued to grow with occasional interruptions, and whose executive rewards lagged far behind the Americans'. But US performance recovered through the 1990s. A cyclical upswing? A new golden age achieved by the Right strategy? If you're wondering, make time for James K. Galbraith, *Created Unequal: The Crisis in American Pay (1998)*.

Global inequalities Fast economic growth rescued some East Asians and others from poverty. Experts disagree about relations between the richest and poorest countries. The United Nations' 1999 *Human Development Report,* using statistical methods which tend to over-rate the differences, showed a steep increase of inequality between the richest 20 per cent and the poorest 20 per cent of the world's people between 1960 and the 1990s. World Bank, International Monetary Fund and other calculators, comparing purchasing power by methods which tend to under-rate inequalities, showed a small reduction of those inequalities over those years. But the poorest people still lacked many basic necessities of life. International aid to them declined. And many poor countries' water, soil, forests and fisheries continued to be depleted or degraded.

Global inefficiencies The direct and indirect influence of Western financial deregulation on some of the most successful and some of the least successful developing countries was illustrated vividly in the East Asian financial crisis of 1997-8. Through the 1980s Japan joined the Western leaders, and led the less developed

East Asian countries, in freeing the region's banks from much of their public regulation. Japanese banks responded by financing a wild inflation of city property prices. When that boom collapsed the government had to rescue a number of insolvent banks. Korean banks used their new freedom, with government encouragement, to borrow from foreign (chiefly American) banks and on-lend to Korean manufacturers to continue Korea's fast industrialization. Optimistic investors created some surplus capacity and under-employment. American and other lenders meanwhile financed various developments in Thailand, Malaysia and Indonesia. Then abruptly in 1997 the Western lenders began to call in their Asian loans, and at the same time to 'sell down' the borrowers' currencies to levels which made the service and repayment of the loans very difficult for Korea and Thailand and Malaysia and impossible for Indonesia. The International Monetary Fund was asked to help. It made conditions. The indebted countries' trade, banking and exchange must be further deregulated. Their governments must balance their budgets and deflate their currencies, chiefly by cutting their public services. The Fund managers eventually conceded that those cruel and counter-productive policies were 'mistaken'. But by the time they did so, Indonesia's currency was exchanging at 20 per cent of its former value. Vital import flows had ceased. The country's public services, including its minimal social services, were breaking down. Millions of the poorest people, especially the poorest children, suffered terrible increases of poverty, starvation and death.

Neoclassical imagination of the effects of government To put the question as sensationally as I believe it deserves, what had economic theory to do with those children's deaths?

In Chapter 51 you will meet a discussion of the general contribution of economic theory to the Right turn through the last quarter of the century. Here, a preview of one element of it.

Recall the neoclassical model of a self-adjusting national or global economy. People act in their own interests. Market mechanisms harness that self-interested behavior to the common good in three vital ways. They allocate resources efficiently to maximize the economy's output. They tend to keep the system running in a stable equilibrium. And they pay landowners, capitalists and workers the value of their individual contributions to output.

As the sufficient causes of those benign effects the theory selects some impersonal market mechanisms. Consciously or not, users of the theory can all too easily assume that *if an economic system is working well, it must be those mechanisms which are causing it to do so.* So no other causal explanation is needed. Serious investigation is only needed if the system is working badly. (Analysts must then discover or imagine what particular market failure or government intervention is preventing the system from performing as modelled.) What the theory does *not* encourage its users to understand is the necessary role of government in the market mechanisms themselves if they are to work at their best. The government often needs to be quite intricate, and tailored to the peculiarities of particular markets and industries. (You will meet diverse examples in Chapter 42.)

It was that short cut – 'If the economy is working well it must be working according to our model of it' – that led many neoclassical economists to misjudge the government of the leading economies, first through the 'golden age' of the 1950s and 1960s, and then in the troubled 1970s. In the golden age they did not so much mistake what the social democratic policies were causing, as what they were preventing. They were not seen as preventing the anti-social behavior or the market failures which had originally occasioned their introduction. Nor were they seen as preventing the new kinds of misbehavior that bankers and others might invent (and did invent) if deregulation freed them. As long as full employment, fast growth and low inflation continued through the golden age, neoclassical economists too easily assumed that the market mechanisms themselves, theorized as needing little or no government, were the sufficient causes of the good performance. And in the bad times that followed, the same theorists could identify any continuing regulation of business as *preventing* the 'pure' market mechanisms from doing their theoretical duty of maximizing efficiency and growth.

Thus that generation perpetuated the neoclassical mistake of opposing 'market' and 'government' as alternative modes of choice and principles of organization – instead of understanding how much of the market freedom and efficiency which they rightly value depends on appropriate government of the markets and industries concerned.

Part Six of this course will review evidence for the generally poorer performance of Western economies and the world economy since the Right turn. The summary of this Chapter's explanation of the reasons for the Right turn is back on pages 117-18.

WHY HISTORY?

Recall the purposes of this historical chapter. It was designed to link two lines of study –

- up to now: the general nature of economic activity, and ways of investigating and understanding it;

- next: processes of change at work in the world now, and conflicts about their directions, which should prompt economists to re-think some of their social purposes and professional theories and methods.

Well-researched and well-written histories are good reminders of varieties of causation which economists tend to neglect as too uncertain or irregular for a regular quantitative science: political conflict and consensus, institutional forms and rules, means of coercion and persuasion, effects of equal and unequal bargaining power, effects of culture and prevailing beliefs, and complexities of human motivation. Those can all affect the chances of particular economic strategies. That is equally true of active and of passive strategies – of strong planning, or strong faith in uninfluenced market forces, or any combination of the two. Any national strategy needs to fit its country's capacities: its particular pattern of natural resources, trading opportunities, physical and human capital, and so on. Especially the human resources: the character, education, skills, expectations, work culture, propensity to compete or co-operate (and so on) of the people, including their likely capacity to arrive at a coherent economic strategy and stick to it.

It is to nourish that sort of imagination and judgment that some deep and broad historical knowledge is valuable. 'Deep' means thorough, thoughtful, explanatory histories. 'Broad' means histories of a wide range of countries, industries, institutions and economic behavior. History is vicarious experience. Like other social experience, what you distil from it is necessarily selective. It doesn't yield many cut-and-dried scientific laws of human behavior. But experienced thought is still, often, better than inexperienced. And it is not necessarily more conservative or less inventive. Knowing more about what has and has not been tried, and has failed or succeeded, can open your mind to new possibilities as it closes off others. Knowing more about the world's diverse experience makes some thinkers more cautious, but it makes others bolder.

Don't be content with this chapter's few and short historical sketches. Make time to read some of the best economic histories – perhaps one or two or three of these:

David Landes *The unbound Prometheus: Technological change and industrial development in Western Europe from 1750 to the present* Cambridge University Press 1969; or (though perhaps not quite as good) his *The Wealth and Poverty of Nations: Why some are so rich and some so poor* N.Y.: W. W. Norton 1998

Eric Jones *The European Miracle: environments, economies and geopolities in the history of Europe and Asia* Cambridge University Press 2nd ed. 1987

Eric Hobsbawm *The Age of Extremes: The short twentieth century 1914 – 1991* London: Michael Joseph 1994

Fernand Braudel *Capitalism and Material Life 1400 – 1800* (1967) English edition Weidenfeld & Nicolson 1973

Clive Ponting *A Green History of the World* London 1991, U.S. 1992, Penguin Books 1993

Lewis Mumford *The City in History: Its origins, its transformations and its prospects* London: Secker & Warburg 1961

Bridget Hill *Women, Work and Sexual Politics in Eighteenth-Century England* Oxford: Blackwell 1989

Joan W. Scott *The glassworkers of Carmaux: French craftsmen and political action in a nineteenth century city* Harvard University Press 1974

Louise A. Tilly and Joan W Scott *Women, work and family* N.Y.: Methuen 1987

Joan Hoff *Law, gender and injustice: A legal history of U.S. women* New York University Press 1991

Jonathan R.T. Hughes and Louis P. Cain *American Economic History* N.Y.: Harper Collins 4th ed. 1993

Gary M. Walton and Hugh Rockoff *History of the American Economy* N.Y. Harcourt Brace Jovanovich 6th ed. 1990

Christopher Hill *Reformation to Industrial Revolution 1530 – 1780* in the Pelican Economic History of England, Penguin Books 1969

Charles Wilson *England's apprenticeship 1603 – 1763* 2nd ed., N.Y.: Longman 1984

Peter Mathias *The first industrial nation: An economic history of Britain 1700 – 1914* 2nd ed. London & N.Y.: Methuen 1983

Peter Gatrell *The Tsarist economy 1850 – 1917* London: Batsford 1986

Alec Nove *Economic history of the USSR 1917 – 1991* 3rd ed. Penguin Books 1992.

Kyoko Sheridan *Governing the Japanese economy* Cambridge: Polity Press 1993

Mark Elvin *The pattern of the Chinese past* London: Eyre Methuen 1973

History and theory combine on a grand scale to relate historically changing systems to the kinds of theory and analysis they call for, in –

Edward J. Nell *The general theory of transformational change* Cambridge University Press 1997

EXERCISES

Here are two national economic strategists, each a devout believer in some simple principles:

Right thinker The aim should be to maximize productivity. The method should be to leave production and distribution as far as possible to the free play of market forces.

Government should supply defence, law and order, roads and bridges, water and sewerage, elementary education and welfare. Other public services (gas and electricity, telecommunications, health, higher education, broadcasting, etc.) should be left to private enterprise, franchised where necessary, and expected to pay their way. Government should control the money supply, as the sufficient way to prevent inflation. Beyond that the strategy is simple: least-possible government, and therefore least-possible taxation and public borrowing, leaving production to private enterprise, with perfectly free trade and least-possible regulation of business. The trade and business freedoms will ensure maximum competition, which in turn will ensure the best use of resources, the most efficient production, the closest attention to consumers' demands, and the highest material satisfaction all round.

The single aim of maximizing GNP is sufficient, not because other things don't matter, but because the liberal strategy allows other needs to look after themselves. If wages and prices and working conditions are left to the market, people will earn what their productive contribution is worth. Most people will insure against sickness and accident and save for retirement. For those who fail to do so there should be welfare provision, but it should be such that nobody will prefer it to honest work.

Left thinker The aim should be wealth for the benefit of all in an equal, cooperative society.

Capitalist production is for profit, is exploitive, and generates all significant inequalities. Capitalists are also prone to pollute, to export capital, to consume capital, to live as idle unproductive rentiers, and other antisocial offences. By contrast socialist production is for use, is non-exploitive, and allows income to be distributed on equitable, democratically determined principles. Being for use rather than profit it can also be neighborly, non-pollutant, and careful of its workers' safety and rights.

Since revolutionary change is not politically possible, a socialist strategy in a mixed economy should aim to increase the socialist elements in the mix gradually, by all lawful methods of industrial and democratic political action. That means increasing the elements of central economic planning, public ownership, and the redistribution of income by progressive tax and welfare provisions. In the remaining private capitalist sector there should be strict public regulation of business, and strong labor organization, bargaining for the best possible conditions and the highest wages. High wage shares should shave profit margins, limit capitalist expansion, and encourage the changeover to public enterprise.

Economic growth does not have to be the first purpose of the strategy, because it will be a natural effect of it. As public planning and ownership increase and incomes become more equal, class conflict will give way to co-operation; and a healthier, happier, better motivated, more co-operative population, producing for their own use instead of their class enemies' profit, will inevitably be more productive.

Exercise You are a historian. Write a thoughtful letter to each of those theorists. On this occasion you need not quarrel with their values, or pick holes in their logic, whatever your own views. Just tell each of them what you think they might learn, for their own purposes, from some historical study.

(Be careful. You can tell them plenty about the actual historical experience of the 'regular' or 'inevitable' associations they seem to be relying on, e.g. between free trade and fast growth, or between public ownership and workers' rights. But don't fall into the trap of assuming that history is finished, i.e. that past experience exhausts the possibilities, or that anything that has failed once can never succeed.)

NEW DIRECTIONS

12

Changing modes of production and sources of income

Part Two is exploring ways in which economic systems change as they develop, and may call for changing methods of analysis and understanding. In the last four chapters, past experience. In the next seven, present and potential causes and processes of change in the advanced mixed economies. How may economists' theories and practices need to respond to

- changing proportions of public, private and household production ?

- changing sources of individual income ?

- changing demands for goods and for employment, with some new misfits between the goods that people want, the work that they want to do, and the productive capital that they have?

- changing divisions of labor between men and women at home and in paid work?

- resource and environmental problems, some of which pose –

- new conflicts of interest between classes, nations, and generations?

This chapter is about changes which come in the normal course of economic development, with growing wealth and experience. As incomes grow and lifestyles change there are likely to be changes in economic systems and structures, some of which may call for changes in economists' theories and methods. For example:

- Basic needs take proportionately less of income, so more income is open to discretionary saving and spending.

- The proportions of farming, manufacturing and service work and output change.

- The proportions of public, private and household work and output change.

- The proportions of earning and non-earning years in most lifetimes change.

- Methods of distributing wealth and income may change as the non-earning years increase, and as beliefs about rights and claims to income change.

We will look in turn at those changes, then at some profound problems which they pose for economic theory, education and policy.

THE GROWTH OF PUBLIC AND HOUSEHOLD PRODUCTION

Basic and discretionary wants

In their spending, people generally have to look after some basic needs first. The poorest people have to spend most of their incomes or working time getting food, and enough clothing and shelter to keep the weather out. When they can afford more than that they buy *better* food and clothes, and start accumulating domestic capital: better houses and furniture; piped water and network power; books, radio, TV, computers; mechanical cleaners, washers, polishers, mowers, drills, saws; refrigerators, space heaters and coolers; skateboards, bikes, motorbikes, cars; pools, saunas, jacuzzi; yachts, aircraft, second and third houses. They also spend more on services: health services and education, hairdressing, entertainments, eating out, travel and holidays.

Our present purpose is to notice three effects of those changing demands. They alter and often increase economic uncertainties. They are supplied by changing patterns of industries and services. And they are supplied by changing proportions of public, private and household production.

Uncertainties

Some uncertainties can be reduced by economic development. Poor peasant societies may suffer flood damage and crop failures from bouts of bad weather. Output may be reduced unexpectedly by epidemics of human, animal or plant diseases or parasites. Societies which depend heavily on exporting staple crops or minerals may suffer from volatile world prices. Those uncertainties usually diminish with economic growth.

But other uncertainties increase. The basic reason is that rising income increases the proportion of saving and spending that is *discretionary* rather than *necessary*. From predictable spending on food and necessaries people progress to choosing between more and more diverse options. The widening choices are both individual and social.

After basic needs are met, there are wider choices for any further household income. Should we consume more? (Fancier food and dearer liquor?) Should we switch from household to commercial services? (Eat out more?) Or from public to private services? (Less buses, more cabs?) Save for later by methods which add to private capital? (Buy stocks and shares?) Or improve our household capital? (Buy a car?) When and how? (Run the old car another year, or replace it now? Replace it with an imported car, or a home-built one?) Multiplied by millions of households, those choices can have large short-term effects on national economic performance: on effective demand and levels of employment; on interest rates and house-buying capacities; on import/export balances and foreign exchange requirements.

There are similar collective choices. How much of their expanding income will the democracies choose to invest in roads and bridges, public buildings, national museums and art galleries? How much will they choose to spend on public services – on health, education, defence, law and order? Some of the political choices are as unpredictable as some of the household choices are.

Conclusion As rising proportions of spending and saving become 'choosey', able to fluctuate with changing tastes and beliefs and consumer confidence, so do aggregate saving and spending become less stable, harder to forecast surely, and harder (with present institutions) for governments to manage or adapt to.

Economic growth also affects economic structure, changing the mix of goods and services which the economic system is equipped to produce, and its ways of producing them. Two ways of analysing the structural effects are outlined in the next two sections.

PRODUCTIVE DIVISIONS: FARMS, FACTORIES, SERVICES

Economists have long observed that as incomes grow, people spend changing proportions of income on farm products, on manufactured goods, and on services. The industries which chiefly produce those things have traditionally been classified as *Primary* (farming, fishing, mining), *Secondary* (manufacturing) and *Tertiary* (services).

Those sectors are not independent producers of finished goods. Each uses some of the output of the other two. But using those rough classifications (and neglecting some of the historical variations you met in Chapter 11) the modern history of the rich countries' economic development has often been sketched like this:

An agrarian revolution (as in England in the eighteenth century) makes farming more efficient. Farms produce more, but employ less labor.

Some of the surplus labor goes to work in new factories and workshops, and people spend rising proportions of their rising incomes on manufactured goods.

Manufacturing in its turn grows more efficient. It produces more but employs less labor.

Some of the surplus labor goes to staff new services – but some of the services in their turn grow more efficient, and employ fewer people.

All those processes continue. The farms don't stop modernizing when the factories start. While computers are revolutionizing banking, farms and factories and households are also continuing to innovate, produce more, and shed labor. What will the surplus labor do next? Economists have profound disagreements about that question. We will return to it in Chapter 13. Until it is answered, economic systems are likely to work worse than they did through the long boom.

MODES OF PRODUCTION: PUBLIC, PRIVATE, HOUSEHOLD

Now recall that other familiar analysis which classifies production according to who owns the capital. Common usage says that governments or other public-interest institutions own the *public sector*. Capitalists (from multimillionaires to your local plumber and newsagent) own the *private sector*. Households own or rent the capital of the *household* sector. Some theorists prefer to call these 'modes', and speak of public, private and household *modes of production*. This course uses both terms: the private sector uses the private mode of production, and so on.

The two analyses don't match. The primary, secondary and tertiary divisions of industry don't respectively use the public, private and household modes of production. In mixed economies each mode does a bit of the work of each sector. (*Primary division*: Subsistence farming and gardening are household business, most farming for market is private, some research and experimental farming is public. *Secondary division*: There are public and private manufacturers (Renault and Fiat); and DIY carpenters, boatbuilders, etc., making things for themselves in the household mode. *Tertiary division*: There are public services, private services and plenty of mutual service between family members. Moreover services to all three divisions are provided by all three modes – see if you can think of examples of the nine mode-to-division and six mode-to-mode flows.)

Historically, how do the changing shares of the primary, secondary and tertiary industries relate to the shares of work done by the public, private and domestic sectors? That can't be answered precisely. There are different answers for shares of *working time* and shares of *output*. Some of the boundaries between sectors are rough. Most estimates of housework and other DIY activities are rough. But best-guessing with the information available, the distribution of working time in an average modern mixed economy may be 45-50 per cent private, 40-45 per cent household and 10-15 per cent public.

The private sector stimulates the others' growth in two ways.

First, the more technically advanced private industry becomes, the more it tends to demand and get public services as inputs to private production.

Second, the private sector has been improving its manufacturing productivity more than its service productivity. Prices of more-efficient manufactures have therefore been falling relative to prices of many less-efficient private sector services. (TV sets are cheaper but theatre tickets are dearer. Cookers are cheaper but restaurant meals are dearer. Cars are cheaper but taxi rides are dearer. Motor mowers are cheaper but commercial gardening services are dearer. And so on.) The price changes encourage households to stop buying commercial services and instead to invest, i.e. to buy manufactured capital equipment with which they can produce more goods and services for themselves. That in turn prompts them to demand more public investment – for example power stations to power their new domestic equipment, better roads for more private motoring. Thus the highest productivity gains in the private sector

have tended to expand the other sectors' shares of work and output.

Figures 12.1 and 2 show how the household revolution happened in the United States where (with Canada and Australia) it happened first. In 1900, households invested 4 or 5 per cent of GNP. Private enterprises invested 14 or 15 per cent, i.e. three times as much as households did. Sixty years later private enterprises were investing about 7 per cent of GNP, households 10 or 11 per cent: the household sector had become (and remains to this day) a bigger investor than the private sector.

If we omit the effects of two world wars and the great depression of the 1930s, Figure 12.2 can be simplified to show that through its historical development from a mostly-private capitalist economy to a mixed economy, the US continued to invest a fairly constant proportion of GNP in creating 'tangible' capital (buildings, equipment, etc.). But in the course of the household revolution through the first half of the twentieth century, about half of the flow of private investment was replaced by public and household investment. There was also a fourfold increase in the rate of 'intangible' investment in education, training and research to create knowledge and skill, or human capital. Add that to the tangible investment, and you can see that as the private sector cut its share of investment by half, the US economy as a whole increased its rate of investment by half.

Other mixed economies took the same path, with higher percentages of public investment in Britain and most of Western Europe. Nearly every household is now an actual or potential investor, deciding from time to time whether and when to spend or save spare income, and replace or increase its physical capital. When the necessities of life are paid for, what should the next $1000 buy – a dishwasher, a video recorder, a holiday, $1000 off the mortgage debt, $1000 added to superannuation savings – or more day-by-day consumption of food and drink and entertainment?

As incomes grow, those freedoms tend to increase. Household investment grows bigger, and more variable. The variations hit the other sectors of the economy, where their uncertainty may be compounded, for this reason: much of the variable household demand is for built or manufactured goods. Builders and manufacturers are also investors – *but with longer lead-times than the household investors' lead-times*. Many of them can't wait and see what households will demand next month or next year – if they want to supply those demands they

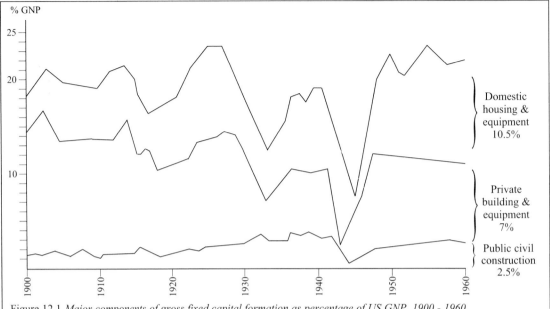

Figure 12.1 *Major components of gross fixed capital formation as percentage of US GNP, 1900 - 1960*
Source: F. Thomas Juster, *Household capital formation and financing, 1897 - 1962,* National Bureau of Economic research 1966. By omitting public equipment and military spending the chart understates public investment.

must anticipate them. That means that private sector investment decisions depend partly on guessing future household investment decisions. Because the household demands are variable and hard to predict, the suppliers sometimes guess right, sometimes guess wrong and sometimes all guess differently. Wondering how many people will decide to trade their cars or washers next year, some manufacturers increase productive capacity; some produce ahead of demand and fill their warehouses; some cut investment and output and wait for sales to empty their warehouses.

So the household fluctuations are not simply transmitted to the national totals of investment and employment and output. They are sometimes offset and sometimes increased by the private sector's investment and production decisions, which add further to national uncertainties – even the booms and slumps become less predictable.

And through the twentieth century the household fluctuations have been increasing. The National Bureau of Economic Research study cited above measured not only the relative volume of private and household investment, but also their absolute and relative fluctuation: how far each varied, in boom and slump, from its own long-term growth path. There have been large historical changes through the twentieth century.

Before 1914 private investment was larger than household investment, and it also fluctuated more, both absolutely and relatively. So the national variation in private investment was about four times the variation in household investment. Since 1945 household investment has become absolutely greater, and private investment has become less variable, i.e. more like household investment in its percentage variation. Together those changes have made total household investment variations about 40 per cent greater than private investment variations. The private and household variations obviously affect each other, but not regularly enough for reliable prediction. Sometimes they move together to intensify effects of boom or slump. At other times they offset each other. So relations between the sectors tend to be *more important* but *less predictable* than they used to be when most household spending was on necessities, and most investment was by profit-seeking firms.

Conclusion Economic growth allows households to acquire more capital. That can increase their productivity and reduce some household risks and uncertainties. But it tends to increase some national economic uncertainties, and irregular fluctuations in investment and employment.

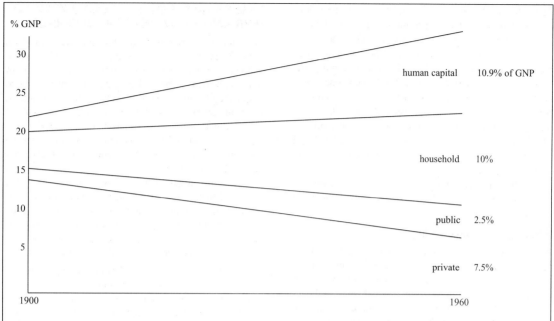

Figure 12.2 *Long-term trends in private, public and domestic investment and human capital investment as percentages of US GNP, 1900 - 1960.*

THE GROWTH OF NON-MARKET INCOMES

This chapter is listing ways in which developed economies change in the ordinary course of economic growth. So far we have noticed how rising productivity and changing wants affect the organization of production. Next are some changing ways of distributing income.

Theme

The proportion of incomes earned in competitive markets is declining and the proportion of incomes determined in other ways is increasing. As the proportions change, market theories of the distribution of income need to be supplemented by explanations of other kinds.

We will use two conventional but controversial distinctions: between market and non-market incomes, and between earned and transferred incomes. Why controversial? Orthodox economists have traditionally seen the supply of land, labor and capital, and the demand for them, determining their prices (i.e. rents, wages, interest and profits) in an ordinary supply-and-demand way. Dissenters suspect that force, custom, biased law and

unequal bargaining strength, rather than free and equal market exchanges, determine many of the incomes. But for the present purpose we can accept that –

Market incomes consist of rent, interest, dividends, wages and fees earned in the private sector.

Non-market incomes are all other incomes: public servants' wages; incomes transferred by governments, for example from taxpayers to pensioners; and incomes transferred from people's earning years to their non-earning years by institutional means (i.e. otherwise than by individual saving and investment, which would yield market income).

The distinction can't be clear-cut. Market incomes are affected by many public policies and non-market incomes may be market-related in various ways, as when public employers pay market rates for the skills they hire. But although the distinction is rough, we will use it because it sheds light on an important problem of economic theory.

People can also disagree about distinctions between

'earned' income and 'transferred' income. Convention-ally (and in most national accounts) wages are said to be *earned* from employers, pensions are said to be *trans-ferred* from earners to non-earners. The distinction may suggest that earners work for their incomes and deserve them, but that pensioners don't. But the pensioners may reflect that they worked and earned and paid taxes for forty or fifty years, which earned them the well-deserved pensions they get now – and that pensions for war veterans, and living allowances for students and single parents, may be earned by harder work than many wage-earners do.

For this chapter's purposes we will nevertheless use the conventional distinction between earned income and transferred income.

Earning and non-earning

Most adults work, but not all of them earn. Many non-earners supply income 'in kind' to earners, in the form of household goods and services. Many earners provide money income to non-earners, whether directly as housekeeping or pocket money, or indirectly through taxes which finance other people's pensions, child allowances, etc.

So there are some people who work and earn; some (housewives, students) who work but don't earn; some (owners living on rent, interest or dividends from prop-erty managed by others) who earn without working, and some (children, invalids) who neither work nor earn.

If you stop and think about it – not about the defin-itions this time but about the detailed distribution of the work, the earned incomes, the unearned incomes, and the relations between them – you can see that it is a system which *works*, after a fashion: it keeps most people fed and clothed and housed, however unequal-ly, and it keeps some of them satisfied. But there is nothing inevitable or holy about it. Other distributions of work and money income can readily be imagined. Socialists and others have long questioned the distrib-ution of work and income between workers and capi-talists. Feminists have long questioned the distribution of work and income between men and women. Nowadays three other relations are also being ques-tioned:

- Who owes what income to young people: to children, to those who work at caring for them, and to young adult students?
- Who owes what income to unemployed people?
- Who owes what income to retired people?

TRANSFERRING INCOME FROM YEAR TO YEAR AND FROM PERSON TO PERSON

To complicate the problem, income transfers from people's earning years to their non-earning years go backwards as well as forwards in time. Earners save for their retirement. They also repay income received before they began to earn, as they pay taxes to support the next generation's child care, education, student living allowances, and so on. But for the present pur-pose we can simplify by focusing on 'forward' transfers from the working years when people earn to the later years when they don't.

Questions about income transfers have become active political issues. But how you choose to state the questions tends to bias the answers you get, so it is good to be clear about the values and reasoning which shape your perception of the questions. For example here are two ways of understanding exactly the same facts:

- I am likely to live longer than my grandparents did. Compared with them I am lucky to have a longer education before I start earning and a longer retire-ment after I stop. So I need to transfer more income than they did, from my earning years to my non-earning years. That's no hardship, since growing productivity means that in real terms I earn two or three times as much as they did. But transferring income over twenty and forty years is risky for indi-vidual investors, so I would be glad if a reliable pub-lic institution would do it for me.

- The welfare burden is becoming intolerable. A steadily declining number of productive workers is having to support a steadily increasing number of unproductive pensioners. The aging population structure shows that the dependent proportion will continue to grow: it is already 15 per cent of all households, and the way we're going it may approach 25 per cent by the year 2020. The long-suf-fering producers simply won't stand for it. Tax revolts are only the beginning – the real need is to dismantle most of the welfare state.

It is important that you be clear – and as an economist, teach your society to be clear – about the *common facts* and the *conflicting values* which underlie disagreements of that sort.

Remember, from Part One, why all analysis is nec-essarily selective. Unavoidably, its language and cate-gories have to be designed to notice some phenomena and not others.

I left some questions open by labelling the section before this one EARNING AND NON-EARNING.

That might refer to the earning years and the non-earning years that occur in every earner's lifetime. Or it might refer to people who earn and other people who don't. That ambiguity is what underlies those two apparently contradictory accounts of income transfers to pensioners.

Now slow down and take care. Prepare to explore the relations between those two analyses. Their relations are more complicated and interesting than may appear at first sight. Step by step:

Read the two again.

The first says, correctly, that I forego some income through my earning years in order to have income in my retirement.

The second notices, correctly, that transferring rights to money income *over time* can't help affecting the distribution of real income (goods and services) *between people*.

When I save to pay taxes or contribute to a superannuation fund during my earning years, that does not normally mean that society produces that much less goods and services. It normally means that someone else gets the goods and services which I would have got if I had spent that fraction of income instead of saving it. Twenty or forty years later, having transferred that *right to income* over time, I receive it in the form of a pension and spend it. Then I get some goods and services produced by others, which might otherwise have been consumed by others.

Notice three things about the process:

1. When I save, I consume less than I produce. My saving thus affects the distribution of goods and services at that date. Someone else may get *more* than they produce.

2. When I draw my pension and spend it, I affect the distribution of goods and services at *that* date: I consume more than I produce, some others consume less than they produce.

3. I have not transferred real goods and services from one year to the other – I did not bake bread twenty years ago and store it in a warehouse to eat after I retired. What I have transferred from one year to another is a *right* to income.

We will presently return to the question how the right to income is transferred. But first, concentrate on the two ways of perceiving the transfer at the time when I receive it as pension. (1) It is a transfer of my own income which I earned and saved in earlier years. (2) It is a transfer this year from some other earner to me.

How do they differ? Each selects *one* cause or necessary condition of my getting the income. (1) I have to be entitled to it. True. (2) Since I am not doing paid work, others have to produce some or all of the real income I get. True. In context and depending on its purpose, either explanation may be reasonable. (Or unreasonable – we will presently sample some of the unreasonable uses that people make of such selective explanations.)

We can now explore some relations between the distribution of rights to income over time, and the distribution of income between people.

Misfits between transfers over time and transfers between persons

Here is a simple model of a changing economic system.

Imagine a society with a stable population of 6, not counting children whom we will ignore. We also ignore holidays and assume a 12-month working year. When our history begins, each member works for 50 years from age 10 to 60, then retires and dies 10 years later at 70. For simplicity it is an equal society: members get equal wages then equal pensions, and all die at the same age. To begin with, the currency unit is what a worker produces in a month, though that will change with increasing productivity.

Stage 1

Producing 12 units a year, each worker draws 11 units as current income and puts 1 unit into a pension fund. Arithmetically that will accumulate 50 units by the time the worker retires, to provide a 5-unit pension for 10 years. Meanwhile the 'saved' unit of output goes from each of the 5 workers to provide the present pensioner with his 5-unit pension. Thus the transfer of rights over time neatly fits the transfer of output between persons.

How should you understand that system, and how should you institutionalize it?

There are alternatives.

If you like selfishness, self-help and individual independence – or if without liking those motives you nevertheless think them the most reliable – you can see each worker as saving for his or her old age. The appropriate institutional form is a private superannuation fund.

If you prefer co-operation and mutual aid, you can see the workers as donating income to the pensioner, confident that others' generosity will pension them in their turn. The simplest institutional form for that is for the government to pay public pensions from taxation.

By either method the distribution of income is the same; and here are the National Accounts:

Output		Income	
5 workers x 12 units	60	5 workers x 11-unit wage	55
		1 retired x 5-unit pension	5
National Product:	60	*National Income:*	60

Stage 2

Progress without growth. As a result of educational and medical changes people now work only 40 years, from age 20 to 60, then survive 20 years to die at 80. So instead of 5 workers and 1 pensioner at any date there are now 4 workers and 2 pensioners. Workers save harder during their shorter working life to finance their longer retirement. Each year they draw 10 units of income and save 2. Over 40 years that accumulates enough to pay 4-unit pensions for 20 years. The standard of living has fallen: take-home wages are down from 11 units to 10 per year, pensions are down from 5 units to 4 per year, whole life incomes are down from 600 to 480. But the transfers over time still accord with the transfers between persons. National Accounts:

Output		Income	
4 workers x 12 units	48	4 workers x 10-unit wage	40
		2 retired x 4-unit pension	8
National Product:	48	*National Income:*	48

Stage 3

Economic growth. Better health and education combine with technical progress to increase productivity by 25 per cent. Workers now produce 15 units each per year. Should they draw 12 as current income and save 3? That will entitle them to 6-unit pensions for 20 years. But it will meanwhile provide pensions of 6 units to each of the present pensioners, whose past savings only entitle them to 4-unit pensions. Should they get past or present standards of living? Private pension funds may give them one of those options, public pensions may give them the other – social decisions are needed. There are arguments about those decisions, but they are not too bitter, because the conflict is for shares of a gain, not a loss.

Stage 4a

Declining population, no growth. For cultural and environmental reasons people halve the number of children born in each generation, and stop economic growth. Sixty years after those changes, the last member of the last 'big' generation retires. At that date there are as many pensioners as ever but only half as many workers as there used to be. Our model population has fallen from 6 to 4: 2 workers with 2 pensioners to

provide for.

This is *very* divisive. The present pensioners saved 3 units a year all their working lives to entitle themselves to 6-unit pensions. The present workers would like to do the same. But the figures don't fit. Instead of national accounts of output and income, here are National Accounts of Output and *Income Claims*:

Output		Income	
2 workers x 15 units	30	2 workers x 12-unit wage	24
		2 retired x 6-unit pension	12
National Product:	30	*National Income:*	36

With the present ratio of workers to pensioners the practical options lie somewhere between (1) maintaining the regular wage but halving the pension entitlements, and (2) honoring the pension entitlements but halving the wage. Option 1 would cheat the present pensioners of half their savings. Option 2 could be seen as halving the wages of workers whose productivity had not fallen at all – or as forcing workers to save twice what they should need to save to provide themselves with standard pensions.

Stage 4b

Declining population, continuing growth. Suppose that the environmental restraints were overcome by alternative technology. The declining population increases productivity per worker by a further 20 per cent. The National Accounts show:

Output		Income	
2 workers x 18 units	36	2 workers x 12-unit wage	24
		2 retired x 6-unit pension	12
National Product:	36	*National Income:*	36

That may seem fair to the pensioners, since everyone has the same income as before. But the workers may reasonably protest. Why should they get *no* benefit of a 20 percent rise in productivity? Why should they hand over a third of their incomes to pensioners who only saved a fifth of theirs? Why should they save more than the value of the pensions they want in their retirement? Economic growth may have softened the conflict between the generations, but it has not improved the fit between current output and the members' desired transfers of income over time.

Stage 5

Real Life. In contemporary life, transfers over time are subject to at least three further complications. We need not elaborate them here – two of them are the subjects of the next two chapters. But a brief list of them will fill out your picture of the practical and theoretical problems which are likely to accompany growing demands to transfer income over time.

Growth as a choice Environmental problems may make economic growth a matter of collective choice, rather than the unquestioned purpose it has tended to be for a century past. Each generation may be conscious of deciding what share of limited resources – and of dangerous rubbish – it should leave to its successors. Collective decisions about *how much* to produce will complicate decisions about how to distribute the product.

Technology and the future of work Technical change may reduce the demand for paid work. That may pose more collective choices: for example, whether to ration what paid work there is, or to tax it to finance pensions to the permanent unemployed. Either choice will subject the distribution of income to a further element of social and political decision.

Comparing transfers Rich countries already pay pensions or allowances to people who have not previously earned or saved any pension entitlement – for example to unemployed and sick and disabled people, to students, to lone parents and some widows. Where those allowances coexist with pensions which *are* related to past savings or contributions, people are apt to compare the two. 'Why should students or unemployed get more (or get less) than old age pensioners?' The existence of incomes *perceived as transferred between persons* is likely to influence the interpretation of entitlements to incomes *perceived as transferred over time*, especially if those entitlements are already being questioned or reinterpreted because of changes in productivity or population structure.

ALTERNATIVE WAYS OF TRANSFERRING RIGHTS TO INCOME OVER TIME

We have been reviewing some changing *conditions* in which rights to income are transferred over time. We now turn to some *methods* by which such transfers can be made. The choice of method can have substantial effects on what the receivers of transferred income actually get, and on the general distribution of income of which their incomes are part.

First there is the obvious market method. If you want to save for your old age, you can do it yourself. While you earn you can save and invest, then after you retire you can live on your dividends and/or spend your capital.

That is not reliable as a national system now that affluent societies have decided that everybody should have some income in old age and nobody, however improvident they have been, should starve to death. Self-help is unreliable. Some people never earn so can't save. Some earners are too poor to save. Some don't choose to save. Some (especially spouses) make off with other people's savings. Some savers lose their savings in bad investments. And individual savers have no insurance against dying either too early or too late: you may die at 40 leaving a brood of dependant children, or you may retire at 60, spend your life's savings by 75, but live on to 90.

Because of those hazards, affluent societies have developed a number of more reliable methods of providing income to the aged. As you read through the following examples, notice two things about each of them: (1) How is the method of transferring claims to income *over time* likely to affect the distribution of income *between people*? (2) To what extent does the amount of income received by the transferee depend on market forces, and to what extent does it depend on public and institutional policies? In the first example (private superannuation, which comes nearest to a market method of transferring income over time) we will add a third question: how far will the relevant public policies depend on people's beliefs, or choice of economic theories?

Private superannuation

While you earn you can contribute to a private life insurance and superannuation fund. The fund managers invest your contribution to earn income for the fund. When you retire you draw income from the fund. How you do so depends on the contract you have with the fund. You may take your benefit as a lump sum, then spend or invest it as you like. Or you may draw a pension or annuity. That may cease when you die, or when your surviving spouse dies, or when any dependent children who survive you have grown up – there are many alternative schemes.

Depending on the details of the scheme, the amount of income you manage to transfer from your earning years to your retirement is likely to depend on (1) how much you earned as a worker; (2) how much of your earnings (including any employer's contribution to your superannuation) you paid into the fund; (3) how much if any of that saving the government exempted from income tax; (4) how profitably the fund was invested, how its directors judge its future risks, and how much they judge they can therefore afford to pay you; (5) what corporate taxes or exemptions the government applies to the fund's income; and (6) the form in which you elect to take your lump sum or pension or annuity.

The amount of income you get in your retirement is thus influenced by public policies, especially taxation, but it is still basically a market income: it is savings from your earned income, plus rent, dividends or interest earned by those savings.

Now recall what you learned about *relations between transfers over time and transfers between persons.* Suppose that population changes produce a misfit between the income claims of a retired generation and the claims of the generation which is still earning. How will private superannuation, as a market method of making transfers over time, resolve the conflict between the generations?

Consider the 'worst case' which appeared as Stage 4A on page 136. A sudden fall in the birthrate produces, for a time, big numbers in retirement but smaller numbers working and earning. The retired people have saved through their working years, and the managers of their superannuation funds have invested their savings in stocks and shares. Will those investments now give the pensioners back the real value they saved, plus whatever income the savings have earned?

Probably not. The retired have become capitalists, but the decline in the working population means that the society now has too much capital per worker, or (same thing) too few workers per unit of capital. Market theory expects that market forces will therefore work as follows. Too much capital is chasing too few workers. Labor is relatively scarce, so its price will rise. Wages will take a rising share of output, leaving a declining profit share for the capitalist pensioners. Meanwhile with fewer earners saving for their old age there is less total saving each year. So there is less demand for stocks and shares, including the stocks and shares owned by the superannuation funds. The market price of stocks and shares declines.

Those effects of the population change tend to work against the pensioners. Their capital values are likely to shrink, and so may the rate of return on what remains. People who suffer such losses through no fault of their own may look to their politicians to do something about the harsh way the market has treated them.

There may then be disagreements.

Market theorists may argue that the pensioner-capitalists and the worker-earners are each getting the market value of the endowments they currently contribute to production. The low profit share will motivate

people to let the stock of capital run down until it matches the reduced supply of labor. Market forces are thus restoring productive efficiency.

Institutional economists may argue that over their lifetimes each generation brings the same endowments to market: works as hard, saves as prudently, confides its capital to expert management. Therefore their whole-life rewards should ideally be similar proportions of the national income to which their work contributed. But if declining population and output rule that out, it is neither fair nor efficient to let one transitional generation bear the whole of the loss.

A market process which has that effect ought to be corrected or (better) replaced. A system which makes everyone's provision for their old age depend on fluctuating wage and profit shares is a bad system. When claims conflict, people should be able to decide in a collective political way what distribution of income would be fair and efficient in the circumstances.

Those theorists disagree about the way in which income transfers over time *ought* to be related to transfers between people. The final distribution of income – in any year, and between generations – will depend on which theory prevails with government and its electors.

Public superannuation

If you work for the government, or if you live in a country which offers a public superannuation scheme to all its citizens, you may contribute specified taxes or contributions while you earn, then draw income from the scheme when you retire. Most national schemes relate the amount of the pension to the amounts that you earned and contributed – but by formulae which differ widely from scheme to scheme. No national scheme confines its pensions to those who have contributed. (Too many non-contributors would starve.) Some schemes pay a basic pension to everyone, plus supplementary amounts related to pensioners' former earnings or contributions. Some schemes bias that relation, for example to reduce inequalities by letting pro-rata benefits decline as earnings rise.

Methods of financing such public schemes vary. Some put contributions into investment funds, others don't. But the pensioners have rights to specified incomes, from taxation if necessary, and don't depend on what the funds may earn. Pensions from such schemes depend chiefly on political decisions.

Pensions financed from taxation

Simplest of all are public pensions financed from general taxation rather than from specific superannuation contributions. Most countries which pay such pensions means-test them, to go only to people who are short of other income. Because there is no direct link between the taxes you pay while you are earning and the pension you draw when you retire, this system tends to be seen as transferring income from earners to others, rather than as transferring earners' own incomes over time. That may invite more political conflict than a market method would; but it may cope better with generational misfits, because neither earners nor pensioners have particular entitlements, and year by year the national income has to be divided between them by political judgments of what seems fair 'all things considered'. (Of course that may be what seems fair to ruling classes or electoral majorities.)

A rose by any other name might smell even sweeter ...

The postwar British pension is a hybrid. A basic pension is financed from taxation and paid to everyone of pensionable age, rich and poor alike. But the transfer of income is disguised as contributory superannuation by naming a part of everyone's income tax a 'National Insurance' contribution.

Why such cosmetics? The designers of the scheme wanted people to pay the tax without complaint, and accept the pension without shame. Neither pensioners nor taxpayers should see pensioners as 'living on welfare', or as living on income transferred from others. They should all see themselves as providing for their own old age with prudence, independence and self-respect. There need be no welfare stigma and no class wars or tax revolts if the annual transfer of income from taxpayers to pensioners was perceived by both of them as transferring income over time, rather than as transferring income from person to person or class to class.

Class divisions

Australia for some years offered two options of public assistance to retired people. (1) A means-tested public pension was financed from taxation and paid to all old people who had no other income. Alternatively, (2) many white-collar workers could contribute along with their employers to private superannuation funds, which would then pay them pensions or capital sums in their retirement. The contributors, their employers and the funds were allowed large tax exemptions.

In practice the means-tested public pension took comparatively good care of the poorest people, but the scheme as a whole had two unfair effects. On average, the private superannuants got more tax revenue (negatively, by the tax exemption of their own and their employers' contributions) than the public pensioners received as pensions, so the scheme as a whole increased inequalities. But that effect was concealed. The superannuants were entitled to their pensions as capitalists living on interest and dividends, while the public pensioners were visibly living 'on welfare'.

That list does not exhaust the ways of transferring rights to income over time. It says nothing about the incomes which support young people before they can earn, lone parents, incapacitated people, and others. But it serves to show once again how transfers over time unavoidably affect the distribution of income between people; and how most transfers over time depend on public and institutional policies as well as, or instead of, depending on market processes.

Conclusions

As social beliefs and political and institutional policies have increasing effects on the distribution of income, I believe economists should respond in at least these ways:

1. Theories and explanations of the distribution of income should give due weight to the non-market as well as the market forces that determine the distribution.

2. Economists should work, as part of their professional duty, to improve the quality of the public and political debates about the distribution of income: the clarity and consistency, and the honesty and self-knowledge, with which the debates are carried on.

3. As economists set about understanding alternative criteria of distributive justice, alternative criteria of economic efficiency, and the complex relations between the two, the economists' values must necessarily shape their selections and analyses. They can't help being *contenders in*, as well as *analysts of*, the debates and conflicts about distribution. They should be explicit about that and not try to conceal it.

EXERCISE

As more incomes are determined by political and institutional decisions, more people have to argue their income claims. The arguments range from simple 'Gimme' to complicated social philosophies. They rely on a wide (and sometimes wild) variety of technical and ethical assumptions.

Economists need to understand the nature of those arguments, the relations between their technical and political elements, and the ways in which both their technical and their political elements are selected and shaped by the debaters' interests and values.

As an expert economist you may be called on to elucidate the arguments: to 'analyse the analyses'. You can require true rather than false facts, accurate rather than inaccurate quantities. But you can't require 'true' selections – selective explanations and analyses have to be criticized as consistent or inconsistent, honest or deceptive, fair or unfair, useful or useless for particular purposes. When you criticize people's income claims, are you straying from economics into other disciplines? No, you are analysing some of the causes which determine the distribution of an increasing proportion of incomes.

Now try your hand at the three that follow. They're all cheats. Write short notes about the selective tricks they're playing.

1. John Q. Snide qualified as an accountant but never practised because he inherited a modest fortune, moved to a tax haven and devoted his life to golf and good dinners. He is outraged when his native country starts taxing its expatriates' investments – why should he be forced to finance, among other things, doles to unemployed youth who don't work or earn or pay taxes, and are parasites in a country he does not even live in?

2. While John Q. Thick is earning he pays taxes which (among other things) finance other people's pensions. He complains about supporting those idle layabouts. When he retires and draws the same pension he believes his lifetime of taxpaying entitles him to it: it's a return of his own earned income, owing nothing to anyone else's toil.

3. John Q. Smart contributed 6 per cent of his salary and his employer contributed a further 12 per cent – both tax-exempt at the time – to a superannuation fund from which he now draws his pension. When he passed from earning to drawing a pension he did not switch from one explanation to another as Thick did. Smart is consistent. He opposes all welfare taxes and pensions. He joins the tax revolt and tells the world, in words you met a few pages back, that 'the welfare burden is becoming intolerable... Fewer and fewer productive workers are supporting more and more unproductive pensioners... Why didn't those proletarian layabouts save for their old age like I did – why should I have to finance my pension *then pay taxes to finance theirs too?* It really is time we dismantled the welfare state and put the parasites back to work.'

This chapter has argued that a shift from market incomes to incomes determined chiefly by political and institutional means would call for changes in economic theory and explanation. The reasoning is fine, but do the facts call for it? Is the proportion of pensioners and other 'transferees' actually increasing? Is the proportion of public employees actually increasing? It's time for facts and figures.

SOURCES OF INCOME IN MODERN MIXED ECONOMIES

Up to natural biological limits it has usually happened that with advanced economic development, people average more years of education before they start earning, and live longer in retirement after they stop. So in the lifetime of most full-time workers, economic growth brings fewer earning years and more non-earning years.

It does not *necessarily* follow that the proportion of earners in the population declines. The proportion earning at any date depends on a number of things:

- The ages at which workers enter the paid workforce, leave it, and die.

- The age structure of the population. A growing population may have many children but few pensioners. A declining population may have many pensioners but few children.

- Participation in the paid workforce, i.e. the number of *potential* earners who *actually* earn. In practice this varies chiefly with (1) the proportion of women who want paid work, and (2) the level of employment and unemployment for those of both sexes who want paid work. (Remember that most unemployment figures are of unemployment among people recorded as seeking paid jobs. So with (say) 54 per cent of the population in paid jobs there may in principle be 'full employment' if only that number want jobs – but 10 per cent unemployment if 60 per cent want jobs. If rising proportions are looking for jobs, employment and unemployment can both increase at once.)

Year by year through the third quarter of the twentieth century in most of the developed countries, men stayed longer at school before starting to earn and lived longer after retiring. That steadily reduced their ratio of earning to non-earning years. But through the same period rising proportions of women were entering the paid workforce for rising proportions of their lifetimes. Some European countries also increased their ratios of earners by importing migrant workers without their dependants.

When more housewives went out and got paid jobs, did that mean that women worked more hours altogether?

Women who did paid jobs as well as housework certainly worked longer, and probably harder because they 'compressed' the housework. The effect could be moderated in three ways: (1) Some men began to do a little more of the housework. (2) More of the paid jobs were part-time. (3) Labor-saving domestic equipment could cut houseworking time.

Could but often did not, as far as the imperfect records show. Housewives without paid jobs had averaged 7 or 8 daily hours of housework. Housewives *with* paid jobs had averaged 4 or 5 hours of housework. Total houseworking hours have been reduced as women moved from the one group to the other. But they do *not* appear to have been reduced *within* either group. Women with jobs still average 4 or 5 hours of housework; women without jobs still average 7 or 8. Women have not used the revolution in domestic equipment and productivity to reduce work. They have used it to increase output, i.e. to produce more and better domestic goods and services.

Rising household productivity not only improves work and output at home. It also has two large effects on the output of the paid sectors.

First, some paid workers have switched from domestic service to other industries. The middle classes do more of their own housework and employ fewer domestic servants than they once did. So many of the paid workers who would once have been domestic servants now do other jobs in the paid economy (though sometimes providing similar services, as cooks, cleaners, waiters, drivers, gardeners, etc.)

Second, more than half of all married women have added to their total working hours and output by taking paid jobs. Where less than 20 per cent had paid jobs in 1950, about 60 per cent have paid jobs now.

The accumulation of household capital has thus contributed both directly and indirectly to real economic growth: directly by increasing household output, and indirectly by freeing labor to work in other sectors of the economy.

Government as paymaster By 1982 the public/private proportions of employment in the rich democracies ranged from 38 per cent public / 62 per cent private in Sweden, through 33 / 66 in France and 26 / 74 in Germany, to 19 per cent public and 81 per cent private in the United States.

With rising numbers of pensioners and unemployed, about twice as many people drew public transfer incomes as earned public wages. Averaging the figures for Britain, France, Germany and Italy (and omitting all household transfers and self-support) government had become the source of more incomes than the private sector. Private employment provided 48 per cent of incomes, public employment 18 per cent, and public income transfers 34 per cent.

Incomes in the 1990s In 1992/3 in the 23 countries that the World Bank classified as high-income countries there were –

828 million people, of whom
555m. were aged between 15 and 64, of whom
380m. were in the workforce; but with about 10 per cent of them unemployed,
340m. – about 40 per cent of the population – were actually earning.

Among the 60 per cent who were not earning, about

25 per cent of the population lived on public income transfers, and
35 per cent of the population lived on household income transfers and unmarketed output.

(Data from Richard Rose, *Public Employment in Western Nations* (1985) pp.11, 43-5 and *World Bank, World Development Report 1994* pp. 210-11)

Households get money incomes from employment or public income transfers, then transfer some of it in cash and kind to their non-earning members. Some earning and non-earning members may work to produce household output, which all members share. (One-person households can neglect this analysis!).

Now guess (for lack of better sources) that 2 per cent of people (other than those who have retired) live entirely on unearned private income without also working.

And guess that some privatizing and public job-shedding will continue for a few more years. On those assumptions the people of the rich countries are likely to start the next millennium with public, private and household incomes in roughly these proportions:

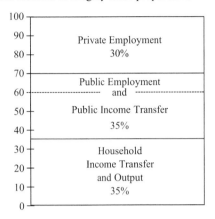

IMPLICATIONS FOR ECONOMIC THEORY

It takes selective causal analysis to explain why income is distributed as it is, because so many forces affect its distribution. Neoclassical economists have traditionally preferred 'pure' explanations which link wages to the supply and demand for labor, and to the value which workers contribute to the value of output. Those relations are still important; but (1) they were always affected by other forces as well, for example by balances of bargaining power, and prevailing ideas about wage justice and relativities; (2) the market relations themselves are increasingly affected by public policies, and (3) market incomes are a declining minority of all incomes. A useful understanding of the distribution of income now has to take account of tax policies, the regulation of industry and industrial relations, wage-bargaining and wage-setting institutions, the design and volume of public income transfers, changing claims to income and ideas of wage justice, changing ideas of the value of the work itself to the worker, and many conflicts of interest and ideology whose outcomes affect the public and institutional policies.

Consciously or not, many economists have assumed that – whatever else they may achieve – most of those institutional arrangements reduce the productive efficiency with which market forces would otherwise allocate resources and reward the contributors to production. Evidence that this is the worst of all the profession's theoretical mistakes is reviewed in Chapter 54 of this course. Preview it now if you like, and you can have it in mind throughout the course.

13

Technology

This is a two-part chapter on the effects of technical changes on (1) employment and (2) the distribution of information. Previews:

Employment Technical progress is transforming many processes of production and distribution. But it has different effects on different industries and services. The differences are of two general kinds –

Technical changes affect productive processes in two ways:

- Some technical change is capital-saving. Cheaper capital equipment can be used to produce the same output as before.

- Some technical change is labor-saving. New equipment (whether cheaper or dearer than the gear it replaces) enables fewer workers to produce the same output as before.

- Some technical changes have both effects.

Industries differ in their possibilities of technical improvement. For example –

- Steelmaking uses dearer capital but fewer workers to produce a given output.

- Many computing processes are using cheaper capital equipment and fewer workers than before to process information.

- Medical services use dearer capital and more labor to care for the health of given numbers of people.

Taken together, what are those directions of technical change doing to our levels of employment and unemployment, and what new policy problems may they pose for government? Then as a case study, the second part of the chapter considers –

Information technology What may the information superhighway do to our life and economy, and what policy problems does it pose for national and international government?

TECHNOLOGY AND EMPLOYMENT

The previous chapter closed with information about the sources of income of the whole population. Return, now, from the whole population to the paid workforce: those who have paid employment, or would have it if they could get it. In the advanced economies recorded unemployment now ranges from about 6 to 12 per cent of the workforce. Real unemployment is higher. (Some part-time workers want more time or full time. Some governments don't include in the workforce, or count as unemployed, anyone who has never been employed, or anyone who has been unemployed for more than a year. Some people who want work are too discouraged to keep looking for it, so are counted as having left, or never joined, the workforce.)

Is a return to full employment likely? If not, it may be for one of these reasons:

- The economic system is capable of employing every willing worker if it is properly managed, but government is neglecting or mismanaging it.

- The unemployment is technological or structural. If the economic system was producing all it could there would still be some people unemployed. There is a misfit between the skills the system demands and the skills it produces, so that there are both vacant jobs and unemployed workers.

- The trouble is social. The people don't want all the products and by-products which the system could produce at full capacity. So it has to run below capacity, with some workers unemployed. There is a misfit between the goods the system can produce, the wants which the society generates, and the amount of paid work which the people want to do.

Skip the first of those possibilities – the management of the economy for full employment comes later in the course. Here, look at questions of the second and third kind. Are machines replacing workers in ways which may leave some willing workers permanently unemployed? Are people's wants developing so that producing what they want as consumers may not create all the paid jobs they want as workers?

Experts disagree about those questions. And if the pessimists are right and some permanent unemployment threatens, there will also be disagreements about what to do about it. Change the system to restore full employment? Change the system to share out what employment there is? Accept the system and transfer adequate income to the unemployed? Accept the system and *don't* transfer adequate income to the unemployed? Re-educate people to blur the distinction between work and leisure, so that employed and unemployed alike may be well occupied, with adequate income and self-respect?

These are partly diagnostic, predictive questions: what is causing present unemployment and how are the causes and effects of unemployment changing or likely to change? But they are partly also policy questions: which of the causes of unemployment would you choose to attack, and by what means?

The relations between different kinds of unemployment also create problems in ordering this course of study, for the usual reason that you can't study everything at once. You will meet causes of short-term cyclical unemployment, transitional unemployment and 'mismanaged' unemployment at various later stages of the course. Until you have done that work you may not be fully equipped for the business of telling one kind of unemployment from another. Nevertheless it is expedient to notice some long-term trends now while you are surveying ways in which the leading economies may be changing over time. So here is a simple introduction to the subject and its problems, many of which you will study more thoroughly later on. It starts with a reminder that in one skill you should already be better equipped than some of the experts in the field.

Methodology

This is difficult, so slow down and take care.

Remember that causal analysis is *both* factual *and* selective.

Disagreements between analysts may be factual: the alleged causes or conditions did not in fact influence the alleged effect. Or they may be selective: of the innumerable conditions which did influence the effect, different selections may interest analysts with different purposes.

Keep that model in mind as you study different types of unemployment. Because it is important, here is the methodological lesson twice more, first in pure and then in practical form.

In principle Types of unemployment are defined by what is thought to cause them. What is thought to cause them is always a *selection* of their necessary causes and conditions. So you should keep in mind: (1) *Truth*: did condition A really contribute to causing effect E, or did it in fact have nothing to do with it? (2) *Selection*: of the innumerable conditions which had to be present to pro-

duce effect E, which one(s) is it useful to analyse, and perhaps operate on in practice?

But cause and cure are not necessarily related in that simple way. So also remember that (3) things can be over-caused. Conditions A, B and C may each be sufficient to cause effect E – so removing only one or two of them won't prevent the effect E from occurring. (4) The conditions you select to explain an effect – those which satisfy your curiosity about why it happened – may not be the ones you would prefer to manipulate in order to alter or prevent the effect. Perhaps adding condition A to the pre-existing conditions B, C, D, was what triggered effect E, so A was the immediate cause of E; but to reverse E it may be better to operate on one of those other necessary conditions B, C, D, etc.

In practice Suppose the invention and installation of a new labor-saving machine disemploys some workers. The following analyses may all be truthful about the facts and their causal relations. They are numbered for later reference:

1. You select the new machinery as the cause of the unemployment. That identifies the effect as *technological* unemployment, and suggests that it could be prevented by regulating the introduction of new technology.

2. You select the fact that the workers lost their jobs in a specialized industrial region which offers few other jobs for their particular skills in reach of their homes. There is a misfit between the location of their fixed household capital and the location of the industrial capital elsewhere in the country which could employ them. So you identify *regional* unemployment which is one kind of *structural* unemployment. It could be attacked by locating new industries in the region, or by enabling workers and their families to move house.

3. You observe that there are jobs offering in the region, but for skills which the disemployed workmen do not have. Some of those workers could not acquire those skills however hard they tried. You identify another kind of *structural* unemployment: there is a misfit between the skills the economy demands, and the skills it has generated. Some reform of the system of education and training is needed.

4. Some of the disemployed workers *could* acquire the needed skills, given some time and help. You identify *transitional* unemployment. What is needed is a retraining scheme with temporary income support.

5. You select, as cause, the fact that it was during a recession that the new machinery was introduced and the workers lost their jobs. In buoyant years there would be jobs for their skills, even in this region. You identify cyclical unemployment. Time will cure it, but the government could help with measures to stimulate demand and investment.

6. The government does not stimulate demand by the means you recommend because for other reasons it believes in strictly restraining the money supply. Its policies perpetuate the unemployment, which you therefore identify as *mismanaged* or *monetarist* unemployment. The cure for that is a change of policy (and perhaps of government).

7. You believe that if the unemployed offered to work for lower pay – say, at jobbing gardening or window-cleaning – more people would demand those services and the unemployed would be employed. Because the workers won't work for lower pay you identify *voluntary* unemployment. It should be cured by cutting the dole and welfare allowances so that people will prefer *any* paid work to unemployment.

Each analyst selects causes which suggest the kind of action s/he would like to see. Could you improve on those narrow explanations? Yes, by combining them to offer a more comprehensive analysis which would expose a range of alternative policies for consideration.

But *wait!* (as they used to cry in the best melodramas). Are *all* classifications of unemployment, and disagreements about it, of that purely selective kind?

Certainly not. The facts in the above example chance to be consistent with those seven alternative analyses.

That happens often enough in real economic life – but by no means always. Unemployment also occurs in ways which do *not* fit one or more of those analyses. If some of the facts were different, each of those identifications of a particular type of unemployment could be disputed on factual as well as selective grounds. Examples: Some new machinery employs more rather than fewer workers. Some workers are disemployed by new technology during cyclical booms rather than recessions. Workers who live within reach of a wide range of occupations don't often suffer regional unemployment. Voluntary unemployment is a much-misunderstood phenomenon which usually affects which people are unemployed, rather than how many are. Campaigns to drive the unemployed back to work by cutting wages and welfare may merely displace some workers by others, or it may discourage investment and create unemployment by cutting total wage income and aggregate demand.

Identifying particular types of unemployment, defined by particular causes, usually depends on some each of hard facts, value-based selections, and less-than-certain predictions. Keep that in mind as you return to the main subject in hand, to consider whether the advanced economies are changing in ways which threaten heavier unemployment, and therefore harder problems in occupying people and distributing income to them.

But before you return, here is an exercise. Don't just read it, do it, for two reasons. It will dust off and limber up the methodological skills you learned earlier. And it may boost your confidence to find that you have skills that some expert economists still lack.

EXERCISE

Read this passage from S.G. Peitchinis, *Computer Technology and Employment, Retrospect and Prospect*, 1983, p. 17

Advocates of technological change would argue that technological changes cause displacement and replacement; destroy and create; they do not cause unemployment. To the extent that some people become and remain unemployed for long, the causes will be found in inadequate training facilities and programmes, inability or lack of desire on the part of workers to move, preferences for work that is not available, and inadequate demand relative to the productive capacity of the economy. Concerns should be directed to these causes and not towards technological changes.

Write a page or two to sort out the elements of (1) observation, (2) selection, (3) prediction, and (4) social purpose which appear to underlie the belief that 'technological changes ... do not cause unemployment' and the recommendation that 'concerns should be directed to other causes and not towards technological change'.

Disagreements

While the long boom lasted it seemed that technical progress had brought us from primitive hunting and gathering to our present affluence with increasing leisure but without any permanent increase of unemployment. Will that progress continue, or do we face a qualitative change, brought on by technology which breaks the link between maximum output and full employment? Has a critical proportion of the productive system now achieved 'jobless growth', a technical capacity to increase output indefinitely, to meet *any* growth of effective demand, without employing all who want to earn? These are difficult questions because they are partly about future choices, choices not yet taken. There is wide professional disagreement about them. It ranges over (at least) this spectrum:

• Technical progress may cause unemployment which government cannot prevent.

• Technical progress tends to cause unemployment which however government can prevent.

• Technical progress would not cause more than transitional unemployment if market mechanisms (prices, wages, labor mobility) were free to respond to the technical changes. But unemployment may be caused by government, labor unions or others interfering with the operation of those market forces.

• Technical progress does not cause unemployment at all. It creates at least as many skills and jobs as it displaces.

Each of those is a direction in which *someone* thinks the advanced economies may be developing. This chapter outlines their reasons: reasons why technical change may cause unemployment; reasons why it may not; alternative governmental approaches to the problem; and some reasons for and against wanting to maintain full employment.

WHY TECHNICAL PROGRESS MIGHT INCREASE UNEMPLOYMENT

Start with the simplest reasons, most of which you already know.

Recall the historical 'march through the sectors' as technical progress transformed agriculture, manufacturing, transport and services in turn.

Agriculture has steadily shed labor while increasing output.

Manufacturing first increased its workforce but is now reducing it while continuing to increase output.

Technical progress in domestic equipment increases the productivity of unpaid housework and DIY activities, but by equipping households to take over work formerly done by private services it also reduces some paid employment.

In many private services – mass transport, banking and office work, supermarket retailing, audio and video broadcasting and reproduction of film, music, spectator sports and some educational and training material – technical progress is allowing less labor to provide more service.

In many public services wages keep up with national growth but for technical reasons productivity does not. (Judges are paid more but hear no more cases than before. School teachers are paid more but teach no more pupils than before.) So the unit costs of service rise: it costs more per case, per pupil, per client in social work and counselling services, per patient in public health services. For political and other reasons, tax-resistance may limit the further growth of public employment.

It seems to follow that the decline of employment in agriculture, industry, transport and the mechanized and computerized private services can be replaced *only* by expanding employment in the remaining labor-intensive private services: private health and counselling services, hairdressing, hotels and restaurants, tourism, individual lessons in anything from violin through golf to self-assertion, and other labor-intensive entertainments and recreational services.

Will demand for those services expand enough to soak up all the labor shed by other sectors? On the one hand the labor-intensive private services suffer as the public services do from rising relative costs. That may deter customers from buying them – many of them are non-essentials which people can easily do without – or it may encourage their replacement by do-it-yourself alternatives. On the other hand people can afford more expensive services if they want to, from the rising incomes that come from technical progress and rising productivity in the other sectors.

But even if it proves to be true (as orthodox economic theories assume) that wants are unlimited, so that people will continue to spend a steady proportion of their rising incomes, it need not follow that *they will direct enough of their spending to labor-intensive services to maintain full employment*. What if their preferences run to home equipment and other manufactured goods, networked information and other automated services, broadcast and recorded film and music and spectator sports and other reproducible entertainment – most of which for technical reasons can now increase output by 'jobless growth'?

Worse, what if spending goes to capital-saving industries, i.e. industries in which technical progress not only gets more output from less labor, but also gets more output from less capital? (Not only is electronic technology more productive than the electromechanical technology it replaced; it is also cheaper to make. So instead of more investment producing more output, *less* investment produces more output.) You will presently learn that technological optimists expect some of the labor-shedding effects of new technology to be offset by the extra jobs required to produce the new technology. But to the extent that new technology is capital-saving *and* labor-saving, *both* in its production *and* in its output, the loss of jobs may be dramatic.

Those pessimistic assumptions can be relaxed in many ways and still not promise 'natural' full employment. Suppose that people's wants do increase with income, do not prompt much capital-saving investment, and do demand enough labor-intensive services to re-employ any labor shed by the technically-advanced sectors. And suppose that within those advanced sectors any unemployment is transitional and temporary. There may still be too *much* 'transition' from too fast and bumpy a rate of technical change. There may always be a lot of people temporarily out of work, and therefore a high permanent level of unemployment. (Note: a permanent level of unemployment, not a level of permanent unemployment.) That may happen if technical changes are too many and frequent, and of a kind which require workers to re-train or move house, so that each transition takes time and trouble.

Fast technical change can also increase competitive risks and therefore employment risks, especially in industries exposed to international competition. Employment in Swiss watchmaking, British shipbuilding, US manufacture of TV and radio sets, has been drastically cut by technical advances in other countries. In some industries, such insecurity may become chronic.

Government

If for those or other reasons technical progress threatens permanent unemployment, governments may intervene. This is not the place to describe how – the macroeconomic management of national economies is for study later. But inasmuch as that management aims to maintain full employment by manipulating national levels of investment and consumer demand, there may be reasons why it cannot always counter the disemploying effects of technical change.

Some of the hindrances arise independently of the technical changes. Governments may believe (rightly or wrongly) that measures to maintain employment would risk higher inflation or adverse trade balances. Other hindrances may arise from the nature of the technical changes. The usual macroeconomic measures can't do much about transitional unemployment – measures to stimulate aggregate demand won't employ workers immediately if the workers must first retrain or move house. Nor will such measures work with the longer-lasting unemployment which may occur if changes in an industry's productivity release such large numbers of workers that they can't be re-employed in other industries until there have been some years of new investment to expand those other industries. That is structural unemployment from capital shortage. Structural unemployment can also arise from shortages of critical skills, if there are sudden changes to the pattern of skills which industries, or the whole economy, demand. (Analogy: If the building industry is short of bricklayers it can't employ its plumbers and electricians; if it is short of skilled trades it can't employ unskilled workers however far they offer to lower their wages.) Such effects may occur as industries are automated, and (for example) can't employ keyboard operators until they also have programmers, or other high skills which take years of higher education to produce.

If those structural troubles come, they won't yield to ordinary macroeconomic management. It does not follow that governments will be helpless – but they may face changed economic systems which call for inventive new kinds of management.

Technology policies Besides having employment policies, governments also have technology policies which may affect employment. These policies don't always fit easily into traditional party patterns. For example there can be misgivings in all parties about technical change. Some manufacturers want to keep on using old plant, some workers want to preserve existing jobs, some conservationists distrust most technical change. Some social-democratic governments require new technology to be introduced by negotiated agreement with the workers concerned, and with income support and any necessary retraining for those displaced. That can discourage modernizing investment, and cause business failure and unemployment if it advantages foreign competitors. On the other hand time spent in negotiating workers' consent and cooperation may yield the most efficient use of new technology.

There are also tensions on the Right. Some say it's a cut-throat world in which technical leaders do well and laggards don't, and it is vital to be quick off the mark.

So all hindrances to technical progress are bad. Besides funding basic research, governments should give tax and other aids to innovative enterprises, cut tariffs to expose backward industries to challenging competition, and fight any Luddite opposition to technical progress by organized labor. But some experienced managers fear that such ruthless policies may not only cause technological unemployment, but may also provoke such labor resistance that they actually retard technical change.

Time lags Pessimists fear that policy-makers may be lulled into an unguarded acceptance of technical change by certain delayed-action effects.

When new technology is developed, investors begin by buying new plant. While they are doing that, there is increased employment: the old plant continues to employ the old workforce, and there is additional work to produce the new capital goods. It is some time later – when the demand for new capital goods has been met and the new plant is in place and operating – that there may be a double loss of jobs. The producers of capital goods are looking for work again; and the new plant is shedding some of the workers that the old, less-productive plant used to employ.

Pessimists reflect on the end of the long boom. After the Second World War, the boom ran for a quarter of a century because it took as long as that first to replace war losses then to equip a majority of all the advanced countries' households with the new household technology of hot-and-cold plumbed and powered housing, car, refrigerator, washing and cleaning machinery, television, record and tape and video gear, and (for many) new standards of decor and furniture. Before 1940, well-off minorities had that scale of domestic capital; through the long boom, rising productivity allowed most households to get it. But when most households *had* got it, and the capital-goods producers were reverting to a replacement volume of output, the boom ended. That was helped by a number of other factors, but they coincided with a basic levelling-off of the demand which had sustained the boom. If people still spent as much as before it was now on other things, leaving some of the 'boom' structure of capital and skills unemployed. Most advanced countries have had a tenth or more of their workforce unemployed since the 1970s. (The US is an outstanding exception. But the reasons for its lower unemployment are widely disagreed, and can wait until you meet them later in the course.)

We are into a similar cycle with the microelectronic and robotic revolution. But pessimists fear that there is a critical difference. The long boom was chiefly equip-

ping *households*, i.e. it was revolutionizing the productivity of household producers rather than paid producers. That had some indirect effects on paid employment – it freed women to go out to paid work, and it transferred some service activities from the private to the household sector. But as households doubled their productivity they did not sack half their members. And a main part of the indirect effect on paid employment was to increase the number of workers rather than to reduce the number of jobs.

The electronic revolution is different. It improves household productivity in various ways but its biggest effect is to revolutionize productivity in a wide range of manufacturing and service industries – industries where labor-saving innovation can cost jobs. The household-goods revolution was completed by the 1970s and there has been a permanent 10 per cent or so of unemployment ever since. In its turn the microelectronic revolution may have done most of its work in twenty or thirty years, and its effects on employment may be more severe for two reasons: (1) Its technology allows substantial capital saving. That means that labor-saving improvements of productivity can be achieved by less investment in cheaper plant whose own production uses less labor than it took to produce the plant it replaces. (2) Unlike the household equipment revolution, most of the labor saving this time is in areas of paid employment rather than household activity.

Governments have not managed to restore full employment since the completion of the household goods revolution. There are still no agreed policies for restoring it after the microelectronic revolution. One reason for that failure is the optimistic belief that present unemployment must be from other causes, and won't increase. So if the pessimists are correct, the optimists and their economic theories are among the causes of present and potential structural unemployment.

In that view government need not be helpless. But we should recognize that the economic system is changing. Besides ordinary macroeconomic management, it may now require additional, innovative action to contrive full or fairly shared employment.

Nightmare

To rest your brain for a minute, and help you to remember the heart of the pessimists' argument, here are two ways of summing it up.

Model Imagine an advanced economic system with only three members, two Workers and an unemployed member called Scruff. The system is so technically advanced that the Workers jointly own and work a Universal Machine which has such artificial intelligence and robotic capacities that with a skilled operator it can produce comparatively cheaply most of the goods and services that people want, either producing them directly, or producing equipment with which people can make and do things for themselves.

The Workers simply don't need Scruff, and there is no way that dealing with him can make them any happier or better provided than they are already. He is not bright enough to work the Machine, or rich enough to invest in one of his own, and anyway the Workers would not want to work any shorter hours than they already do. Scruff offers personal services: can he earn a bit by entertaining them, digging their gardens, cutting their hair? But their videos and holo-grams can reproduce the world's finest entertain-ment, they like to dig their own gardens, and the Machine makes cheap home-hairdressing gear with a computerized auto-design-and-styling capacity with which they do their own hair better than Scruff could do it. Desperate, he offers to work for *any* wages, down to bare subsistence. But anything he can do for bare subsistence the Machine can do for less – or else it is something the customers don't want because they prefer to spend their incomes on other things which, it happens, can be done best by the Machine or by themselves. Poor Scruff is soon so shabby and resentful and unlikeable that they would not *want* personal services from him. They resent the extra hour they have to run the Machine to produce a wel-fare income for him. ('That's what keeps him idle' they theorize; 'if he had to work to live he would soon find something to do.') Altogether they don't want him, can't use him and wish he wasn't there.

Analogy The employed members of a rich society may develop a sufficient life and economic system for themselves. Their relations with the unemployed may then come to resemble relations between a rich and a poor country – say, France and Bangladesh – which have little occasion to trade with one another. The rich don't exploit the poor, they simply don't need them – and may not feel they owe them much aid, either.

Remember the point of the nightmare. It is not the age-old fear of scarcity or famine, the fear that the system of production may break down. It is a new nightmare, that even with ample production the system of *distribution* may break down. Poverty in the midst of plenty: on your doorstep, instead of away out of sight in the third world.

WHY TECHNICAL PROGRESS MIGHT NOT INCREASE UNEMPLOYMENT

Optimists say:

First, it never has. Temporarily yes, permanently no. In the long historical progress from primitive poverty to modern affluence, one technical advance after another has increased the productivity of labor. That has often put people out of work, and old skills out of use. But people have never yet failed to find other things for the displaced workers to produce, with old or new skills. Either human wants are *naturally* unlimited, or modern societies *generate* wants at least as fast as they develop the productive capacity to supply them.

So if productive capacity is under-used and willing workers are out of work, optimists look for causes which are temporary and curable. Any technological or structural unemployment must be transitional. Seasonal, cyclical or government-induced unemployment are, or ought to be, temporary. Technical changes may indeed cause industries to reorganize, workers to re-train or migrate. If the changes come thick and fast – as once with the steam revolution and now perhaps with micro-electronics – the dislocations and adjustments may be bumpy for a generation or two. But in the long run peo-ple will divide the gains from rising productivity as they have always done, between working less and consuming more. There is no reason in history, human nature or capitalist organization (optimists say) to fear that whole societies will *want to produce more than they want to consume*, which is what 'structural unemployment' amounts to.

Least of all should pessimists fear that people may run out of material wants. The universal presence of inequalities should be enough to convince anyone of that. At every stage of historical development there have been inequalities. Many of the poorer people have been willing, if it should become practicable, to have incomes like their richer neighbors have; and the richest have not usually been against getting richer still. Rising output may well saturate *particular* demands (for food, televi-sion sets, lavatory seats) but to saturate *all* material wants, so that for example *nobody wants any of what anyone richer has got*, seems absolutely unlikely.

Besides their improbable forecasts of future develop-ments, the pessimists also make some mistakes about the past.

Work shifts

Historically the advanced economies appear to have made the technological 'march through the sectors' described earlier, shedding labor from farming and manufacturing as they modernized. But that simple story exaggerates the loss of jobs in both sectors. Some of those jobs were not lost, they merely shifted into other accounting classifications. Farm and factory now employ fewer hands but they buy more inputs from other industries which consequently employ more hands.

It happens like this: When manufacturers organized their businesses themselves and had their own employees clean their factories and offices, cart rubbish away, estimate markets for new products then design them and write and place their advertising, those employees were classified by national account-keepers as being in manufacturing employment. Nowadays a lot of that work is contracted out to specialist firms. Much the same folk may be doing the work but they do it now as employees of cleaning and waste disposal firms, management consultants, freelance designers, market research and advertising firms – so they are now classed as being in service employment. Similarly when apprentices learned from skilled workers on the job, teachers and pupils were both in manufacturing employment; if the skills are now learned in technical colleges the instructors are service workers and the pupils are not classed as employed at all.

Some of those sector shifts are labor-saving but many are not. Specialist cleaners and waste-disposers tend to perform their functions with less hands than before, but management consultants, market researchers, advertisers and others tend to employ more people than the manufacturers used to employ for those functions. So the whole workforce engaged in producing manufactured goods and getting them to their consumers may not have fallen as far as the accounts suggest. Some jobs have been shed but others have merely shifted to other employers and other classifications.

So also for agriculture. Stephen Peitchinis calculated that US agriculture may not actually have shed any labor for thirty years past:

'Employment in agriculture has fallen significantly ... but the decrease has been perhaps more than offset by increases of employment in enterprises, institutions and activities functionally related to agriculture, such as manufacturing farm machinery and equipment; distributing machinery, equipment and supplies; manufacturing fertilisers and chemical products used in agriculture; agricultural research activities, and farm consultative services of all kinds; and governmental and institutional departments and agencies ... If all those are counted, employment in

agriculture did not decrease; the industrial and occupational structure of employment changed. Millions of farm workers who worked with hand-operated implements and used animals in work activities became industrial, commercial and service workers, in activities related to agriculture.'

Computer Technology and Employment, p. 146

Between optimists' and pessimists' expectations that revised information is inconclusive. There was less job-shedding than appeared, but there was still jobless growth, and not all of the rising productivity went to raise standards of living. US agricultural productivity increased threefold in thirty years – and occasioned radical government measures to restrict output. Some of the 'under-employed over-capacity' which the pessimists feared did indeed seem to be developing, if more slowly than expected.

Work sharing

Some potential unemployment was avoided by what may alternatively be called voluntary work-sharing, or changing preferences for work and leisure. Most people, over their lifetimes, did less hours of paid work than their fathers had done. They started work older and retired younger. Between 1951 and 1981 the weekly hours expected of full time workers in the USA fell about 10 per cent and the hours actually worked fell perhaps 20 per cent. The hours worked per year fell further still. There were more statutory holidays, longer annual holidays, more discretionary leave, maternity leave, sick leave, and time off for education and training. There was some increase in part-time self-employment, and part-time employment rose from about 8 per cent to about 14 per cent of all employment. Altogether more than a third of the increase of jobs was offset by a fall in the hours worked per job.

That progressive trend reversed, for the poorest third or so of full-time American workers, about 1980. They have since earned declining wage rates and real incomes for *increasing* hours of work, as economic growth continues but inequalities increase. But notice some aspects of the preceding 30 years.

There was some voluntary job-sharing. It is hard to know how much because the records don't show how many of the part-timers would have preferred full-time jobs. But willingly or not, people were taking *some* of the benefit of rising productivity in higher income and *some* in greater leisure or household working time. Higher household productivity per hour worked was freeing more women to look for full or part-time employment. How much of that movement from home to paid work was for the money and how much for the other attractions of employment? Not much is known – and the best research might still leave some uncertainty about the mixture of motives. The important thing is that there was some convergence, as paid workers used some of their rising productivity to do *less* paid work, and household workers used some of their rising productivity to do *more* paid work. That suggests that rising numbers of those who have real choice are looking for short, flexible hours of paid employment, over fewer months of the year and fewer years of life than full-time workers used to do, but more than most married women in advanced economies used to do.

We will presently consider the possibility that for more and more people in these societies a fundamental assumption of economic life and economic theory may be changing. It has traditionally been assumed that people balance goods and leisure (as desirable) against the work it takes to earn them (as undesirable). What if people come to desire positive amounts of all three, each independently desirable – the thirty hours of work and human company just as desirable an effect of employment as the pay and the goods it buys? There will be opportunity to think through some implications of that. But first notice the third and strongest kind of evidence for the optimists' case.

Old and new products

The optimists' best evidence is the historical record of the growth of consumption. As fast as technical change has improved productivity, people have bought the increasing product, and thus kept each other employed. *Process* innovation (new ways of producing existing goods and services) has allowed them to buy *more; product* innovation (producing new goods and services) has allowed them to buy *different.* You should not need a textbook to tell you what people buy nowadays that your grandparents either could not afford or had not invented. Here's a sample list to illustrate various types of innovation:

- *More and better:* Bigger, better-equipped houses. Better cars. Better distribution of 'old' products from revolutions in transport, storage, retailing; fruit out of season from glasshouses, special storages, or flown from other latitudes. Year-round output of battery farming where the farmer makes the seasons. As fast as supermarkets shed labor from 'basic' retailing, labor-intensive round-the-clock shops multiply, selling food, crafts, specialties.
- *Seduction of the innocent*, or commercializing the uncommercial: Sports and games which once used simple equipment (bat, ball, old clothes) are more elaborately clothed and equipped. Suddenly joggers need tracksuit, pedometer, stopwatch. Golfers used to carry five clubs in a bag, but see what their electric buggies carry now. English canalsides used to be lined on Sundays by folk with a few shillings' worth of hook, line and sinker, failing to catch fish. Now they sit there with four or five hundred pounds' worth of metal and plastic gear and six colors of bait, still failing to catch fish.
- *Re-valuing the past:* The richer people become from quick-changing technology, the more many of them value antiquity and permanence: new industries spring up to supply roots, heritage, wilderness. There is mushroom growth of labor-intensive crafts, skilled restoration of buildings and works of art, museums and monuments, camping and canoeing and sailing and hunting gear; and accommodation and tourist trades to go with them.
- *Lifestyles:* Kids leave their parents' houses to live elsewhere, so more new housing is built and equipped, and more old housing under-occupied. As people take longer holidays away from home more tourist accommodation and services are produced for them. So there is more 'built space' per head, more beds and plumbing and equipment, more employment in producing and servicing 'homes away from home' – and some re-switching back from household self-service to paid services.
- *Fashion* is the most spectacular and labor-intensive way of getting people to throw things away before they wear out: clothes, decor, hairstyles, cars, etc.
- *New products:* Electronic games. Word processors, home computers, and the many new things people do with them. Home recording and reproduction of film and music. Unexpected new employment as more hours of the day demand to be filled with music without boring repetition – so more groups than you can count, more musicologists rediscovering more early baroque composers than your parents knew existed. Moog music, electronic art and design.
- *Old age* is a very labor-intensive, employment-creating new product. Excellent for the suppliers: the more of it they can produce by extending the customers' lives, the more labor-intensive it is to maintain. Home nursing and nursing homes, medical care and medical hardware, physiological and pharmaceutical research, drug production and distribution,

offers of immortality ranging from religion to refrigeration. As a captive, self-sustaining market, old age beats even addictive drugs like alcohol and tobacco. So much so that – along with education – it deserves a section of its own.

Education and health care have big but ambiguous, perhaps dangerous, implications for the future of employment.

(A note from the author: Both these developments have technological causes, so they belong in this chapter. But their effects on employment also depend on people's shopping and saving and tax-paying choices, so they belong in the following chapter about people's changing wants. Since the technical changes come first and the choices follow, the analysis can begin here. It concerns vital and divisive questions of economic policy, so hard learning would be appropriate – but the learning is not hard. The conflicts of interest and belief may be difficult to resolve, but they are easy to understand.)

The more advanced our culture and technology, the more education we need, most of it before we start earning.

The more advanced our medical science, the more we can do to prolong our old age after we stop.

Education and health care happen to be labor-intensive services. So their further development should in principle (i) increase the number of jobs, (ii) keep people at school for longer and retired for longer, and thus (iii) reduce the proportion of the population who want jobs. The unemployment problem solved?

Yes in principle. In practice there are problems. Because you need most of the education before you start earning and most of the health care after you stop earning, you are not well placed to pay for either of them, or to pay for your own support while you enjoy them. You need to transfer a lot of income over time. For your own support you need some household income transfer (from parents) before you start earning and some public or private income transfer (by age pension or superannuation) to support you in retirement. And you need income transfers from your own and perhaps from other people's earning years to finance the educational and medical services, whether by tax-financed public services or by individual insurance.

Hence the paradox:

On the one hand there is no doubt that most people want at least as much education and health care as they currently get, and they are likely to want any additional years of life and good health that medical advances may offer them.

On the other hand the current shift of opinion and policy to the Right threatens to frustrate those demands. The loudest business, political and professional voices are urging people to vote for less taxation and smaller government, meaning less or worse public services, and less public help with transferring income over time.

Be sure that you grasp the double reason for the contradiction:

(1) Even if there is no further increase in the health and educational share of national output – i.e. if those services grow at the same rate as the rest of the output grows – they must take a *rising* share of the nation's labor, and therefore its spending. That is because they are more labor-intensive than the average of the rest of the economy, and their productivity rises more slowly; so to increase their output at the *same* rate as the rest of the economy they need a *rising* share of labor, and therefore a rising proportion of all spending. Because most health care and education have to be collectively financed, that also means that taxation or insurance must take a rising share of national income, and individual market spending a smaller share. That need not mean that you buy less market goods. With continuing economic growth you do more shopping and bring home more goods every year. But they cost you a declining proportion of your money as their relative prices decline.

(2) The spending shift is even greater if – as in the last half-century – people want to *increase* the health and educational share of output, because of rising economic and cultural demand for education, and the rate at which medical science increases the health services it can offer.

The problem was dramatised in a pictorial way by William J. Baumol in a short article in 1993:

'In an economy in which productivity is growing in almost every sector and declining in none, consumers can have more of *every* good and service ... To achieve this goal, society must change the *proportions* of its income that it devotes to the different products. It is a fiscal illusion that underlies the view that consumers as a group cannot afford to pay the rising costs of education, health care, and other such services.

'But over the longer run, the size of the required transfer of income is startling. . . We will now see what would be entailed if: 1) the *real* prices of education and health care were to continue to grow at their current rates for 50 years; 2) overall U.S. productivity were to rise for that period at its historic rate of (approximately) 2 per cent; and 3) real educational and health care outputs were to maintain an unchanged share of GNP – that is, the economy were to produce more education, health care and everything else, in their current relative proportions.'

– William J Baumol, 'Health care, education and the cost disease: a looming crisis for public choice', *Public Choice 77*, 1993, pp. 23-5.

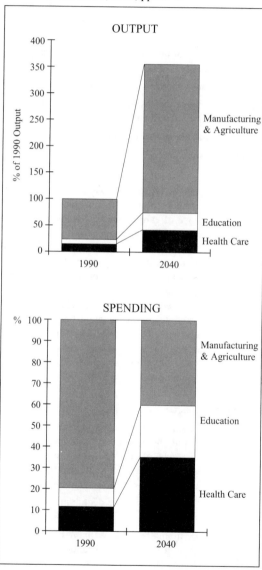

Figure 13.1 Hypothetical changes in U.S. output and spending, 1990-2040, derived from William J Baumol,, *Public Choice 77*, 1993, pp. 24-5.

The figures are not forecasts, they are hypothetical projections of present rates of growth. The OUTPUT figure shows 50 years of (notional) economic growth, with total output, and each component of output, growing to just over three and a half times their volume in 1990. The SPENDING figure shows the shift of resources and spending that would be required to maintain the health and educational share of total output at the same 20 per cent as in 1990. That 20 per cent of real output now takes nearly 60 per cent of the workforce, and of spending – but people are *also* buying three and a half times the volume of other goods that they were buying fifty years earlier.

These changing relations between sector productivity and prices, and the widespread misunderstanding of them, are at the root of some of the most destructive conflicts in economically advanced countries – and they are conflicts that are not gentled but made worse by further economic progress as long as the misunderstandings continue. So treat these pages as critically important: read them – or go to William Baumol's article and read that – as often and carefully as it takes to learn the real relationships beyond mistake or forgetting.

Why? Because all those insistent voices which urge us to cap taxes and cut government spending are actually demanding some combination of two changes which they rarely admit to: a steady *reduction* of the health and educational share of output, and a steady reduction of poorer people's access to them. That is not only inequitable, it must also slow the growth of productivity in the technically progressive sectors of the economy – they will do less well with unhealthy, under-educated, resentful workers.

Notice that Baumol was careful to write of consumers 'as a group' when he demonstrated that they could have more of *both* farm and factory products *and* education and health services despite their changing prices. But how will the poorest third of US earners fare in that fifty-year exercise, if their incomes and real purchasing power continue to *decline* with economic growth, as they have been doing for most of the last twenty years?

SUMMARY

Methodology

1. Like most explanations, explanations of unemployment are necessarily selective. Each analyst tends to select the causes of unemployment which suggest the kind(s) of policy which that analyst favors. S/he may then identify the *type* of unemployment by reference

to those causes. So explanations and identifications of unemployment, and policies for dealing with it, should face the usual double tests. Are their factual elements true? Are their selective elements desirable – what values and whose interests do they serve? Structural, technological, transitional, cyclical, mismanaged and voluntary unemployment are not necessarily exclusive categories. Depending on the facts of the case, unemployment *may* have any number of those characteristics at once.

Technical change

2. *The march through the sectors:* Farming, manufacturing, housework, and now many services, have shed labor in turn as technical progress increased their productivity. Some of the changes are deceptive, where labor is not shed but merely reclassified as 'service'; but much of the labor-saving is real. Will demand for the remaining (or new) labor-*intensive* goods and services grow fast enough to employ all the labor which the labor-*saving* industries don't want?

3. *Selective demand:* Even if demand continues to grow it may be biased toward labor-saving and capital-saving rather than labor-intensive products. Tastes may dictate that. So may market forces, as follows.

4. *Relative prices:* Labor-saving improvements tend to allow lower prices and higher wages. Less productive industries then have to offer higher wages to attract and retain the labor they need, and their workers want some share of the higher wages for reasons of equality. Thus both market forces and organized bargaining tend to spread the wage gains, so that as the technically advancing industries lower their prices, the technically static industries have to raise theirs. Relative prices change (kitchen gadgets are cheaper, domestic service is dearer, etc.). If that attracts demand away from the dearer products towards the cheaper products, and if technical progress in the advancing industries allows them to meet the rising demand by jobless growth, there may be jobless growth in the economy as a whole. Make sure you grasp how rising productivity in *part* of the economy might thus limit employment in *all* of it. But that effect may be avoided if rising income and changing tastes lead people to increase their demands for labor-intensive products (higher education, health services, fast fashion changes, handcrafted goods) despite their relative prices.

5. *Public employment* does not escape the relative price effect. Some labor-intensive public services – teaching, nursing, social work, policy-making – don't allow much labor-saving mechanization. So as wages rise, *unchanging* levels of service require *rising* taxation. Public resistance to taxation (or politicians' fear of it) may limit the numbers government can employ.

6. *Time lags:* Public and policy-makers may be lulled by the time lag which commonly delays the labor-saving effects of new technology until re-equipment is far advanced.

Faced with those choices and uncertainties –

Optimists expect that as technical progress increases our productivity we will continue to –

- invent desirable new goods and services,
- consume more, and
- work less.

Optimists expect us to do so in ways which need not cause permanent unemployment. If people each choose their own balance of earning-and-spending, household work and leisure, market mechanisms should continue to give us, individually and collectively, the balance of increasing income and increasing leisure that we want. Except for the usual income transfers to retired people and welfare transfers to people who genuinely can't work, our main means of distributing income can continue to be market wages, profit, interest and rent.

Alternatively, green optimists hope that radical environmental reform will include some return to energy-saving and labor-intensive methods of production in enough industries to restore and sustain full employment.

Pessimists expect:

- Structural unemployment tends to be time-lagged. Some structural unemployment has come as part of the current levels of unemployment in advanced economies, and unless we act to prevent it, more will come as the electronic-robotic revolution matures.

- There are social reasons why people may **choose** to limit the growth of output. They may include –

- the reasons, dramatized by William Baumol, why people may limit the growth of labor-intensive services which they genuinely want if the services have to be financed from taxation or public insurance.

- There are resource and environmental reasons why people may be *compelled* to limit output.

If output is limited for any of those reasons, employment may come to be valued as a scarce good. Whether because they like the occupation or because they want the income, people with jobs may want no further reduction of working hours or years. If productivity continues to rise, a dwindling majority may hang onto the jobs, leaving a growing minority unemployed. It would then take radical public action to distribute income tolerably, whether by ever-increasing welfare transfers or (preferably) by rationing employment to give everyone a fair share of it.

Gloomy optimists and hopeful pessimists?

This chapter has been about *technological* optimists and pessimists, in the narrow context of expectations about future employment. The labels are convenient, but many intelligent people have complex and conditional expectations which can't be categorized so crudely. Notice especially that the labels don't necessarily indicate *social* judgments. For example some people accept the optimistic forecasts but dislike them. They expect that is how the future will be – but think it will be achieved by increasing manipulation of people's wants and competitive/conformist anxieties, to induce them to produce and consume more and more junk they would be better without, and to perpetuate acquisitive materialist attitudes we would all be better without. Acquisitive values made sense in conditions of scarcity. They still do wherever people are still poor. But advanced societies should

be using their abundant productivity to shed those values, not to perpetuate them. They should be helping others, rather than helping themselves to further material growth. In short the technical optimists' future may be judged a socially rotten future.

Reciprocally, some technical pessimists are social optimists. They think the rich societies should shed those aggressively greedy values. They are not likely to shed them while growth and full employment continue to come easily. But where sweet reason fails to turn people away from 'mindless materialism', hard facts of unemployment and dwindling resources and increasing pollution may succeed. People may be driven to adopt good new economic principles – green, compassionate, frugal – if the bad old principles actually cease to work.

That goes beyond summarizing what you have read, to foreshadow what comes next. So far you have been exploring the possibility that technical progress may continue to expand output – but may increase productivity even faster, so that it *limits employment.*

The following chapters discuss the possibility that employment may be limited because people deliberately decide to *limit output,* for social or environmental reasons. Social reasons of several kinds in the next three chapters. Environmental reasons after that. But first, consider some effects of changing technology on other things besides employment. The information revolution is an outstanding example.

THE INFORMATION SUPERHIGHWAY

The digital and communications revolution is transforming some of the production and much of the transmission of information.

Terminology To distinguish two uses of the technology, analysts give different meanings to 'data' and 'information'. The revolution in processing, storing and transmitting data has profound effects on production and employment. Robots replace people on assembly lines. There is electronic accounting, banking, EFTPOS (electronic funds transfer at point of sale) in shops and supermarkets. Integral activities can be sprinkled around the world to wherever each component comes cheapest. A European airline does its accounting in Bombay, some American doctors have their typing done in Bangalore: data flows between continents as quickly as it used to pass from hand to hand within one office. But those miracles don't tell people anything they would not otherwise know. This course will often be concerned with those effects of data-processing on production and employment. But here, focus on its effects

on the distribution of information: on what it enables people to know that they would not know without it.

Also remember what computerspeak has done to the meaning of 'information'. Traditionally it distinguished fact from fiction or guesswork. Now it means anything that a mind (and increasingly, a smart machine) can see, hear, read and understand: facts and fictions, games and visual arts, music and movies, news and persuasions.

Technology To transmit information of all those kinds there are the existing telephone networks and radio and TV transmitters, and now new cable networks and satellites. There are also old and new techniques of transmission. The old networks used 'circuit switching', the new technology uses 'packet switching'. Wire and optical fibre networks can carry either; but for packet switching the networks have to be equipped with router computers. Packet switching allows much more traffic on any line: it economizes cable. Circuit switching connects the sender of each message directly to its receiver, as traditional telephones do: it economizes computing equipment. In the 1970s the computing equipment became cheaper than the amount of cable that it saved, and packet switching became the preferred mode for most of the growth of the superhighway.

Cable networks and satellites are expensive. Once installed they can now carry floods of information very cheaply at very high speeds. That tends to make them natural monopolies. A lot of the old and new gear is owned by a few big investors who can control and charge for its use. Where the telephone networks were public some of them are being privatized.

Next, some of the companies which own the means of transmission already own some of the information they carry, and are moving to own more of it by merging with its present owners: newspaper and TV news services; financial and other specialized information services; much broadcast entertainment; and much of the world's accumulated stock of film, video and recorded music. The expensive infrastructure encourages concentrated ownership and control. Owners may choose to transmit a wide variety of products into a variety of markets. They may open their channels to use by others. But there are also possibilities of monopoly pricing and political and cultural influence.

Small local networks (like your university's or your government's internal telephone network) can still be comparatively cheap to establish. The Internet grew by developing links between them. Most of its components were developed by public or independent non-profit institutions. A worldwide multitude of national, regional and local networks now communicate with each other by use of a common protocol (TCP/IP: Transmission Control Protocol / Internet Protocol).

Two further developments have opposite implications for the Internet. First, experts expect a single fully integrated network to be developed before long. It should function as a 'people's superhighway' capable of carrying digitized print, sound and moving pictures from anywhere to anywhere, open to anyone who wants to contribute information to it or draw information from it, carrying fast-growing flows of e-mail, tapping rich sources of stored information in government, libraries and museums, and in danger only of rising congestion.

But technology has meanwhile developed to allow contributors to the Internet to restrict access to their contributions. What have come to be called 'intranets' can be used to sell information to paying customers. So the private control of information which is already possible for owners of the big cable and satellite infrastructure can now extend into the Internet too.

How important may these developments prove to be?

Information as a commodity

Considered as stuff to produce and buy and sell, information has some special qualities.

Reputation Once you know something, you no longer need to buy it. So how do you know what information is worth buying, and for how much? Newspapers, magazines, TV news services, film producers build reputations: people learn what to expect from each of them, and how much of it to trust, including whose advertising to trust, which book and film reviewers to trust, and so on. A reputation for truth, good judgment and fair dealing can be a valuable asset and source of private sales or public influence.

Power Many public and private enterprises and institutions control particular stocks and flows of information and can decide what to publish and what to conceal, or what to offer to some but not to other users.

Influence Besides suffering from what they don't know, people are influenced by what they do know. Information affects their preferences for public and private and household goods, their values and the way they vote. Information can also affect its own market, i.e. the sort of information people want and the sources from which they prefer to get it.

Community The quality of democratic life depends in many ways on the common knowledge that the people share. Some homogeneous societies share a great deal. (That can sometimes be oppressive.) Some multicultural societies have richer stocks and flows of information but share less of it: more of it is fragmented, local, multi-lingual. (That can be fascinating but divisive.) A society's common knowledge comes from innumerable past and present sources and is maintained and renewed by daily flows of print, radio, TV and conversation. The substance and quality of that information is very likely to affect the scope and quality of the common knowledge, for better or worse.

Those characteristics of information have always been important in the democracies, and the flow of information has always been a subject of law and policy. Who should own newspapers, publishers, broadcasters? How and by whom should the information they carry be regulated? Besides the private production and distribution of information for profit, what public supplies of information should there be? And what opportunities for the citizens to go public – in local news items, letters to the editor, talk-back radio, TV chat shows? The information superhighway poses some of the same questions, but also some new ones, and some old ones in new forms.

Policy questions

The technology can be used in a variety of ways. How to use it calls for important public and commercial decisions. One way to sort them out is to look in turn at questions of –

- the broad, long-term purposes of information policy
- the possibilities of monopoly, competition and consumer sovereignty
- the public role in regulating the information which the superhighway carries
- the public role in supplying information to the superhighway.

VISIONS

Americans led in developing the new technology, and they were early in thinking about its best uses. There is a continuing debate about the rival claims of entertainment and democracy.

An entertainment model The superhighway could deliver more of exactly the kind of entertainment you want, exactly when you want it. Every kind of music, drama, games, interview and chat shows and other 'infotainment'. Scores of channels showing programmed movies and videos. Others showing them on demand to individual receivers. Some transmissions free to the receivers, paid for by advertisers. Some paid by subscribers to the channel. Some paid by the hour or by the item. Consumer sovereignty could thus have new force and accuracy, with people shopping as they do in supermarkets for exactly what they want and can afford, and with suppliers responding. This model tends to attract infrastructure investment in traditional and satellite broadcasting, and in narrowband one-way uses of cable. As in other markets, the consumers' spending choices (and their viewing choices of any free-to-air broadcasts) sufficiently indicate their preferences.

A democracy model Citizens could be wiser and better informed with more and better broadcast news, current affairs and public debate about political, social and economic issues. The Internet could offer the resources of libraries, museums, art galleries, research centres and government departments. People and their representative organizations could put their opinions of business and government, and their demands on both, onto the net. And their conversations with each other could be cheaper and easier than ever, by telephone, videophone, fax and e-mail.

This model needs more broadband cable to carry information both ways than the entertainment model needs. It needs government or cooperative action to finance the open, two-way elements of the infrastructure. And it can benefit greatly from cooperation by the institutions which do or could supply information to the net.

Education can find uses for both models. Private satellites which transmit mass entertainment can be paid to carry, also, elements of 'top-down' education: courses of lectures with related videos, for example. But teleconference tutorials and other conversations between students and teachers need two-way cable. (There is an interesting irony in the most elite education – one-to-one with your professor, with *her* responding to *your* work most of the time – needing the most democratic technology.) But for students' own work the greatest improvement should come from individual access to the internet resources proposed for the democracy model. There is promising cooperation among universities to allow worldwide e-mail. U.S. universities are furthest forward in putting research and teaching resources onto the net.

In a broader way, you may want the entertainment and informative uses of the superhighway to offer some leadership as well as consumer sovereignty. Governments introduced free compulsory education before the children (or some of their parents) asked for it. They did it partly to make people more productive, partly to enrich their culture, partly to equip them to make more knowledgeable use of their democratic rights. Those can well be among the uses of the new technology now.

MONOPOLY AND COMPETITION, PRIVATIZATION AND DEREGULATION

The full possibilities of the new technology coincided with the political 'Right turn' of many of the rich democracies through the last quarter of the century. Whatever outcomes they hoped for, governments wanted the new business to be market business rather than public business wherever possible. Specifically,

- they wanted private investors to finance the expensive new satellite and cable infrastructure;
- they wanted open access to the new channels, without very clearly specifying what 'open' should mean;
- they wanted competition both between many producers of information and between its carriers; and
- they expected to encourage competition by

deregulating the old and new media as far as possible.

Competition between carriers National telephone networks already existed and could carry a lot of the new traffic, if allowed. Each satellite was hugely expensive and could be equipped to reflect many simultaneous signals. Both techniques made for natural monopolies. Two cables past every house, or two underemployed satellites side by side in the sky, could be as uneconomical as two waterpipes down every street. To create competing carriers it was usually necessary to ban the telephone networks from carrying anything except telephone calls, and sometimes to give new competitors some monopolist business of their own. Competition could thus require more rather than less regulation, and even with public help new commercial competitors with the big carriers were hard to establish. Most of the small new networks were created by public or independent institutions for their own purposes.

There are also conflicts between national and international policy. As international networks are negotiated, governments want their national carriers to be as strong and influential as possible. That is at odds with efforts to have internal competitors cut them down to size, or with deregulation which allows foreigners to buy them.

Competition between producers also has some problems. The big media companies have economies of scale and considerable market and political strength. It would be difficult for governments to dismember them. And deregulation won't enable competitors to dismember them – it is more likely to allow them to defeat or take over the competitors.

Might producers and carriers compete for profit shares? Tendencies to monopoly are reinforced by the spread of digitation from print to sound and video. That offers further economies of scale to firms which own both press and TV, and to owners who both produce and carry information. So why did experts advise their governments that with the new technology the producers and the carriers of information would be independent of each other? "Because car drivers don't own the highways", one of them is said to have said. There would be no savings if the drivers did own the highways. But with packet-switching transmission of digitized information there *are* gains for firms which own print and TV media, own the satellites and cables which transmit their products, and can bar competitors from using their channels.

Conclusions It may be hard to prevent firms, especially multinationals, from owning newspapers *and* TV

and other information services. It may be impossible to prevent such owners from launching satellites from one of the dozen countries which have launching facilities, then controlling their use by technical means. But a national government *can* control the laying and use of cable in its territory. When public networks are privatized or private networks are created, government can require that the information they carry for publication comply with accepted standards. And like railways, private cable networks need government authority to establish their routes. In exchange they can be required to carry a specified range of public information and services free of charge. But after the networks are in place it may be hard to impose new obligations on them. So prudent governments need to act at the strategic times. They are not helped by the persistent coupling of 'privatization and deregulation' in current campaigns for smaller government and less tax. As with other profitable public services and natural monopolies, privatization tends to call for *more* regulation, and in the long run for more tax.

PUBLIC ROLES

Countries with different cultures and institutional capacities are likely to develop different policies. Two examples:

English-speaking countries are open to more foreign transmissions to the mass of their people than are countries with languages of their own. The English speakers may find it harder to preserve whatever they have of distinctive national cultures. Countries with their own languages can choose more freely what foreign news and entertainment they make accessible by the languages their schools teach, and by the need to translate, subtitle or dub foreign news, TV and video.

Within the English-speaking world, Britain and Canada and Australia have more and better public broadcasting than the U.S. does. But American universities are ahead of the rest of the world in developing the Internet and making massive resources easily accessible on it. Different strategies for the educative and democratic uses of the superhighway may thus be appropriate for countries with different institutional traditions.

But there are decisions which they must all take, by choice or neglect, about the roles of their public institutions.

Regulating the channels As noted already, new or privatized cable networks need government authority for their use of public streets. Government can attach conditions, especially when the networks are first created or privatized. To keep new channels open to many users it is reasonable to require that they create margins of spare two-way capacity, open to desirable community uses. Similar conditions can be attached to any corporate mergers between producers and carriers of information which need government permission. There may also be a role for government in coordinating the private operators' negotiation of technical standards and protocols to keep their channels compatible with each other.

Regulating the information There is a lot of existing law about what may and may not be published: what is criminal because it offends national security or public decency or privacy, or because it aids or incites crime; what is open to civil action because it harms other people's property, business or reputation; and so on. Some of the rules vary according to the mode and circumstances of publication: different laws or conventions apply to publication in newspapers, radio, TV, scientific and technical texts, and private communications. Which of those existing codes should apply to information put onto the Internet for any surfer of any age to see at any hour of the day or night in any country and time zones? Should it meet newspaper standards, or live theatre standards, or TV Children's Hour standards? What rules should apply to paid-for or other restricted channels which any buyer or subscriber can see, so that they are not as private as (say) telephone conversations or first-class mail? Can restricted access protect instructions for making atom bombs, traceless poisons, perfect crimes, sadistic pleasures? These and other questions may be decided by judges if the business is left to them, by legislators, by official regulators, by international negotiation, or by default where rules prove to be unenforceable. But they have to be decided somehow.

A British example

If the policy problems of the superhighway interest you, you can learn a lot about them from the papers in B. Kahin and E. Wilson (eds) *National Information Infrastructure Initiatives: Vision and Policy Design* (1997) and from Andrew Graham and Gavyn Davies, *Broadcasting Society and Policy in the Multimedia Age* (1997). Graham, senior economist at Balliol College, Oxford, was economic adviser to two Prime Ministers. Most of this chapter's treatment of the superhighway is drawn gratefully from that and other papers of his, and it can end with some conclusions which he draws from the British experience.

The government's intentions From 1979 to 1997 a Conservative government tried hard to get the Information Superhighway to develop in a market way. The carriers and most of the producers of news and entertainment should be privately owned. They should be many and competitive, with the competition driven by a general privatization and deregulation of the industry. Producers' shares should reflect the consumers' responses to the services they were offered.

In 1984 the government privatized Telecom's national telephone network. It licensed Mercury as a privileged competitor with Telecom. A Cable and Broadcasting Act established the legal conditions for new private cable networks to carry pay-TV and anything else (except telephone service) that could pay its way on the superhighway. Thirteen operators were licensed. None of them made much progress. In 1991 their prospects revived when they were allowed to offer telephone service.

The people's responses Britain thus became the only country in the world which allowed cable companies to offer telephones but did not allow the national telephone network to carry cable TV. Four years later there were a dozen active cable companies and cables in reach of five million households – but only one in five of those households had chosen to connect to the cables. People still got most of their TV from the old publicly-owned free-to-air broadcasters. Commercial TV attracted only a sixth of people's watching time, which was still half as much again as they spent reading newspapers. A striking 1993 comparison of the twelve biggest media producers showed that the BBC used 17.5 percent of total revenue to attract nearly 45 percent of the consumers' media time. People spent ten times as much on buying and hiring videos as on cable services. The time and the spending which they devoted to the new superhighway channels lagged behind other West European and far behind American levels. Merely permitting competition, and then privileging or subsidizing some of it, had not so far made much difference to the people's continuing preferences for the world's best public broadcasting.

It nevertheless seemed likely that as the market policies were modified to improve the private operators' incentives, they would have more of their intended effects:

- commercial TV, advertiser-paid or user-paid, would increase its market share, with its infrastructure and programs owned by a few big operators some of whom also owned newspapers.

- their influence, together with continuing pressures to cap or cut taxes, might well move government to reduce the BBC's funds and scope, as Australian governments under similar pressures were doing to their public broadcasters.

• public institutions' contributions to the Internet would continue to be patchy and uncoordinated, and the other stuff accumulating on the net would continue to have a wide and confusing range of interest, reliability and reputation. (A Californian professor said 'We've all heard that a million monkeys banging on a million typewriters will eventually reproduce the entire works of Shakespeare. Now, thanks to the Internet, we know this is not true'.)

However well they had used the old broadcasting channels, Britain's public institutions were missing new opportunities to contribute valuably to the nation's intellectual and artistic and civic life.

A social-democratic alternative

Government might give the public institutions their best opportunities in the new competitive conditions by combining six policies:

1. The great public broadcasters should continue without any reduction of their money, scope or political independence.

2. Rather than lowering their standards to meet the new competition they should do their best to set the competitive standards. In 1988, half way through the Conservative regime, a House of Commons committee had declared that (in Andrew Graham's summary) 'from its outset, British broadcasting has been dominated by the principles of public service broadcasting. This has implied a strong concern that broadcasting should be used for the national good rather than for the benefit of particular interest groups; it should be universal in its reach, free at the point of use, free from government intervention in its day-to-day affairs and in the content of its programs and committed to informing and educating as well as entertainment and to promoting quality programs with high technical and artistic standards that extend the public taste rather than take it as given.' And the responsible Minister added that 'these principles were expected to guide the commercial channels as much as the BBC'.

Those arguments conflicted directly with the idea that broadcasting policy should simply express consumer sovereignty. But they were forced on a privatizing government by massive public support for the public broadcasters: *the consumers* did not appear to want much commercial, user-paid consumer sovereignty. Eight

years later in evidence to another Parliamentary committee Graham recommended a set of policies to give effect to the earlier committee's aspirations. The traditional public broadcasting should continue. By contract and regulation the new private competitors should be required to carry some public-interest programs. And for the public use of the new technology he suggested four items to complete a six-point program:

3. Complementary to the private sector's provision of information on the one hand and the multiplicity of individuals providing information free as now on the Internet, there should be a set of public (or quasi-public) institutions responsible for collecting, organising and disseminating high quality public domain information using the new technology that the Information Superhighway makes possible.

4. These institutions should include public service broadcasters, public libraries, public museums, universities (plus the publishing businesses of the universities), schools, hospitals, and bodies such as the Citizens Advice Bureaus as well as charitable organisations and central and local government.

5. This public domain information should be financed via 'top-slicing'. This involves taking a small fraction of the budgets of all Government departments, or all universities, or all libraries and deploying it centrally. It has been used most effectively to finance the UK's infrastructure in the form of JANET (the Joint Academic Network) and now of SuperJANET. What is now required … is that the same should be done for content.

6. Common knowledge should be further buttressed by ensuring that public service broadcasts should be available to all and by all means.

Together those policies would continue the traditional public free-to-air broadcasting. They would make available to anyone with a computer the resources of a wide range of public and independent institutions – and through the regulatory offices, the annual public reports of all private-sector companies. That might chiefly interest professional people – when these policies were proposed fewer than a third of British households had computers. But there were computers in the offices of all political parties, labor unions, tenants' associations and other mass organizations. Through them, and to rising numbers of households directly, the superhighway services could extend and strengthen the effect which education, public broadcasting and the press had long had on the society's common knowledge.

Common knowledge Graham reminds you why it matters:

To think about the relationship between information and democracy it is necessary to appreciate the importance of 'common knowledge' – what everybody knows that everybody knows. We take the existence of such knowledge largely for granted. However, it plays a role in society that is more profound and more important than at first it seems. It is more profound because *any* debate requires *some* common knowledge (you have to agree what you are debating) and because in modern societies the media is one major way in which common knowledge is *created*. It is more important because almost all agreements on solutions to problems require the *extension* of common knowledge. This is a precondition for the solution of many coordination policies in democratic societies. How the Information Superhighway will affect common knowledge is therefore a matter of central importance.

– House of Lords Select Committee on Science and Technology, Subcommittee on Information Superhighway: Applications in Society, April 1996.

SUMMARY

The summary of this chapter's treatment of technology and employment is back on pp. 153-155. Here we summarize its treatment of the Information Superhighway.

• **The new technology** is expensive, but once installed it allows high volumes of information to be stored, made accessible, and transmitted cheaply over any distance through open or restricted one-way or two-way channels.

• **Concentration** is likely. Relations between the high capital and low running costs make for economies of scale, and monopolist or oligopolist ownership and control of the new channels; and that may be joined with the concentrated ownership of a lot of the entertainment and news services that the channels will transmit. However –

• **Regulation** Private installation of much of the necessary infrastructure needs government aid or permission, so some public obligations can be imposed on the investors by contract as well as by ordinary regulation.

• **Public and private competitive prospects** depend partly on existing national capacities and institutions, including the presence or absence of strong popular public broadcasting. British broadcasting may limit the market for the various kinds of pay-TV. But in all countries the technology offers promising cultural, educational and democratic returns to modest investment to make available on the superhighway the existing information stocks and services of government departments, universities, public libraries, museums and other institutions.

For analysis of the economic impact and potentiality of the superhighway a good source is Neil Barrett, *The State of the Cybernation* (1996).

14

Wants

We are reviewing ways in which economic systems are or may be changing. This chapter asks how people's wants may be developing, with effects on employment and on social and economic policies.

The world abounds with simple stereotypes of 'what people really want'. 'People are basically generous.' 'People are basically selfish.' 'All they want is money.' 'What they want is power.' Economists also have their simplicities – 'It is safe to assume that, subject to risk and leisure preferences, what economic actors want is to maximize income over time.'

Two things are wrong with such gereralizations. Individual wants vary so widely that it is usually wrong to suggest that people all want the same sort of thing. And most of them individually have diverse wants and mixed motives and complicated moralities. To study wants and identify their effects for predictive or policy-making purposes it is as well to keep at least these complexities in mind:

- People have wants as *producers,* as *consumers,* and more generally as *citizens,* i.e. as members of a society whose general qualities matter to them. Those wants all have force, and affect one another in varying ways.

- In each of those capacities people's wants relate both to particular objects, and to option sets. What I get for myself is not all that I want. I also want there to be a range of options to choose from (and for my children to choose from). I want to live in a society made interesting by the range of occupations and products it offers (i.e. by both its work options and its shopping options.) I also want its economic system to have better rather than worse moral qualities, with option sets which encourage better rather than worse behavior.

- There are selfish wants. (I want to earn, and as enjoyably as possible.) There are disinterested wants. (I want the economy to run efficiently, justly, enjoyably, for all its members.) There are generous wants. (People give to others, work for others, work for nothing, reform institutions to their own disadvantage.) Good economic systems make productive use of *each kind of motivation,* and may perhaps also affect the balance between them. The scope for each and the relations between them are a subject which economists have unduly neglected.

- Many people and interests (some selfish, some disinterested, some generous) contend to *shape* people's wants: parents, teachers, preachers, producers, traders, advertisers, politicians, and so on. The *distribution, use* and *effect* of that *persuasive power* is a critical part of any economic system. So is the system's capacity or lack of capacity to develop some independence and autonomy – some capacity to think for themselves – in the people who are the persuaders' targets. It is quite wrong to write off all persuaders equally, as enemies of individual independence. Individual independence is a social product which has to be built into people, just as much as its opposites do.

ENOUGH?

You already know why many thinkers expect a continuation of 'business as usual': past trends will continue, wants will expand at least as fast as output, economic growth will continue with no more than normal unemployment.

You also know one set of reasons for doubting that forecast, or at least keeping an open mind about it: technical progress may produce various kinds of structural unemployment, and a need for inventive new public policies to maintain full or fairly shared employment.

Now consider a second set of reasons for doubting the 'business as usual' forecast. People may respond to rising productivity by deliberately limiting their wants, and producing less than they could. As with technological unemployment, that might create a need for new employment policies.

The idea of a no-growth, steady-state economy already inspires a good deal of research and persuasion in rich countries. It is the program of some Green parties, some Communitarians and others, and attracts significant numbers of votes. If it prevails, the strongest reasons will probably be the resource and environmental reasons. But independently of those there may also be reasons in the experience of affluent life: not so much costs of affluence, as disillusion with its benefits. We will notice reasons of five kinds under the headings of junk, boredom, congestion, positional goods, and the erosion of necessary morals.

Junk Half a century ago in *The Ecstasy of Owen Muir* (1954) Ring Lardner had his hero invent something that looked like a cigarette lighter, but when you hit its trigger it popped up a safety match for you to strike in the ordinary way. To sell this item it had to be displayed alongside the cash register so that it could be bought within seconds of being demonstrated. With any time at all for reflection, people would have more sense.

Affluent societies produce and consume a good deal of worthless junk. (That cigarette lighter. Excessive packaging. Air conditioning in temperate climates. Fattening industries which create markets for slimming industries. Americans buy more psychiatric and other therapeutic services – including pet psychiatry – than Europeans do, some of them creating and perpetuating the anxieties they offer to cure.)

Some of the products we don't need are needless elaborations of products we do need. We do want toothbrushes, golf courses, cars. But *electric* toothbrushes, *powered* golf buggies, *automatic* gearboxes? Advocates of the simple life observe that some rich as well as poor car-buyers still choose to change their own gears, just as they choose to dig their own gardens and tie their own bow ties. Discriminating abstinence from affordable technical advances may spread to more people and products, and eventually to popular misgivings about continuing economic growth.

Boredom A quarter of a century ago in *The Joyless Economy, An inquiry into human satisfaction and consumer dissatisfaction* (1976) Tibor Scitovsky asked why economic growth appeared to do so little for American happiness. Through the fast growth of income and spending through the long boom, periodical polls showed happiness peaking then beginning to decline before any signs that the boom was ending. What is it about Americans' life and culture, Scitovsky wondered, that allows them to increase their consumption without any gain in satisfaction or happiness?

He argued that most modern growth of productivity has come from technical advances which exploit economies of scale, i.e. from mechanized mass production of standardized goods and services. That has the secondary effect of changing relative prices, and through them consumer preferences, so that people are encouraged to buy more and more standardized products and less and less individually crafted products. The standardized goods tend to be doubly boring. They are boring in themselves because standardized. And they tend to be goods which increase the boring comfort instead of the pleasing novelty of life. But habitual values drive people to save time, save energy, save trouble, save money, and therefore welcome every technical advance which offers to save some more of those things. That tends to encourage passive recreation: hearing music instead of making it, watching sport instead of playing it.

But there is no *need* for well-off people to be bored. They can make daily life interesting if they want to, and many do. Whether from reading books like Scitovsky's, or from their own reflections on the experience of processed entertainment, they may well develop more skilful and intelligent ways of enjoying themselves. What economic effects might follow? Two different ones, with opposite effects on employment, seem likely. Skilful, active pleasure-seekers may do more for themselves in ways (like walking, cycling, cooking, spending time over sociable meals, meeting at friends' houses, reading books, appreciating high arts and practising amateur arts and crafts, organizing and fund-raising and politicking for good causes) which do comparatively little for consumer demand or paid employment. But alternatively skilful pleasure-seekers may come to demand more diverse, less standardized commercial products (more model changes and fashion changes), more aids to active recreation (more ski schools, riding schools, yachts and climbing and camping gear and holiday hotels), more individually crafted products (paintings, hand-woven ties, craft pottery), and more meals out, and hours at cafes and pubs. Those are mostly demands for labor-intensive goods and services. If wants shift in those directions, away from mass-manufactured comforts, then slower measured economic growth may still maintain plenty of paid employment.

Community? Besides those choices between passive or active, boring or interesting lifestyles, there is a third question about the effects of rising national income on people's wants. When most people are materially comfortable, will they become more selfish or less? How many will relax their competitive and acquisitive anxieties and welcome more generous or cooperative or simply more restful social arrangements? Having enough, will they be readier to support fairer work sharing, or other means of further reducing inequalities? Optimists hope so. Pessimists don't. Precisely because it is easy to believe that everyone has enough now and losers are taken care of, winners may feel freer than ever to compete for the fruits of growth and enjoy their success without misgiving.

Some of them have since gone further than that, as it has turned out. It did not occur to Scitovsky writing in 1976 that the winners would actually turn on the losers and begin to take back the civilizing margins of income and welfare and job security that a century of democracy and economic growth had won for them.

Perhaps that counter-attack on the losers – the winners' 'Right turn' in the English-speaking countries – was prompted by some unexpected frustrations. Here comes an argument that rising national income can make single-minded self-enrichment less satisfying for rising numbers of individual winners.

Self-limiting gains?

Fred Hirsch's *Social Limits to Growth* (1976) appeared in the same year as Scitovsky's *Joyless Economy.* Hirsch argued that the good things which people expect of economic growth and rising income may be limited by (1) congestion, (2) a sterile kind of competition, and (3) some corrosion of morale.

Congestion Economic growth may give more people access to the good things of life but at the same time degrade some of those things, whether for snobbish/exclusive reasons or by simple physical crowding. Before proceeding to serious argument about it, rest your mind with two homely examples.

On a summer holiday long ago I climbed a Cumbrian peak and stayed on the summit for an hour – one beautiful unforgettable hour of solitary grandeur in that mountain landscape. Thirty years later my children climbed that peak, along with a continuous stream of others (of all shapes and sizes, they said, from toddlers to grannies. One of them had her knitting.) Forty feet below the summit they had to queue to wait for their turn to step up, in groups of four, to the top for a minute or two. No silence or solitude or time for reflection. No long, unhurried drenching of the senses in the beauty of the place. No awestruck imagination of what it must have been like to be first on Everest. The joy that people could once have there is a lesser joy now. The reasons for that are in themselves good reasons. The place has not been spoiled or vandalized, and the crowding is not a population effect – the population of Britain has grown very little in those thirty years. But many more of the people now have time, money and means to get to the mountains at weekends; and many more share in what used to be an exclusive upper-class culture which prompts people to climb mountains for pleasure and discover how rich the pleasure can be.

As in the country, so in the city. Millions get to work in London by train, tube, bus, or on foot. A generation ago a few got there more quickly and comfortably by car, some chauffeur-driven. Now, the many who drive to work are slowed, traffic-jammed, exhaust-polluted, and left behind by masked cyclists passing between the lines of stopped cars. Public as well as private transport suffers as the congestion slows buses too. Others as well as travellers suffer as the government knocks down more houses to build more roads. *Both* the privileged *and* the unprivileged may be worse off.

And over time, some of both have been cheated. They were led to believe that hard work, high ability or lucky inheritance could get them access to mountain solitudes and chauffeured limousines. Their frustrations now are not caused by rising expectations, but by the declining value of the prizes.

But by no means all of the products of economic growth have those self-limiting or self-defeating qualities. Only their own tastes limit the amounts of fine food and drink people can consume, the music they can hear, the films they can watch, the fashions they can buy, the perfume they can wear, the art and decoration they can apply to their houses. Consumption of those and many other products is not limited or degraded by rising numbers of users.

But some of the goods can lose their charm for serious competitors who want to get right to the top. What *real* winners want to be seen wearing Chanel 5 or Charvet ties now that tens of thousands do?

Positional goods Hirsch's second theme is that some of the things that winners want may be in absolutely short supply. He calls them positional goods. However many compete in a race, only one can win first prize. However many compete for an income in the top ten per cent of incomes, only one earner in ten can succeed. And that is still true *at any level of national income, after any amount of economic growth.* Hirsch and Scitovsky believed, and some of the American 'happiness' polls seemed to confirm, that above a certain level of material comfort and security, people are more concerned about rank than about income. In Britain and Europe that might be social or intellectual or artistic or aristocratic rank. In America (these American observers thought) it was more often income rank. But if people value only their place in the rank order of incomes, no further effort or income growth can increase total happiness. If everyone stands on tiptoe, nobody sees any better. (But as in some other anxious competitions, they may all get sore feet.)

Economic implications How are congestion and the pursuit of positional goods likely to affect economic performance? Much simplified, this was Hirsch's view of the possibilities:

1. In the historical process of growth from poverty to affluence it does not matter that competition for positional goods cannot increase the supply of positional goods, because it can and does increase the output of other goods, by keeping top people hard at work. Positional competition ensures continuing growth even when people might otherwise feel they had enough, and could relax.

2. So what is new? Hirsch argues that with growing affluence and crowding, demand for positional goods intensifies while positional goods (being absolutely limited while other output grows) are a falling proportion of the goods available, so there is rising frustration.

3. Rising numbers of the people may therefore tire of the treadmill pursuit of goods which most of them can't have, and which also have declining value (from congestion and other causes) for those who *do* have them. What is likely to follow?

4. Growth may continue, but with rising frustration and unhappiness.

5. Alternatively people may stop contending for what they realise can't be had. In that case economic growth may slow down and perhaps stop. Continuing technical progress may continue to reduce the labor required to produce a level output. So there will be rising unemployment, and conflict and unhappiness from that cause.

What can optimists make of that gloomy analysis?

They can bring together an obvious criticism of the argument about positional goods, and Hirsch's own elaboration of the argument about crowding. In turn –

Positional goods in a plural society may have quite different effects if there is in fact not a shortage but an abundance of them.

In an income-ranked society most workers take *some* steps up their occupational ladders as they grow older, and that progress may satisfy the 'positional' desires of many of them: as time goes by their incomes and their rank both improve and they can look down to see how far they have come instead of looking up to see how low they still are.

More important: affluent democracies develop a huge number and variety of ranked positions and prizes. They can produce 'positional goods' almost without limit. If you can't get to be head of government or a captain of industry you may still rise high in insurance-sales

contests, golf tournaments, beauty contests, rose-growing, budgerigar shows, stamp collecting. You may win prizes in their competitions, you may win office in their organizations (as chair, secretary, treasurer, instructor, referee). If you crave team membership rather than individual distinction you can play in a team or sing in a choir. If vicarious victories will do, you can support a champion football team. And so on. Some pony clubs arrange their gymkhanas so that every competitor wins a ribbon for *something*. It is not inconceivable that a pluralist society might offer *some* positional goods to nearly everyone.

Congestion also has happier uses than those this chapter has so far noticed. My satisfaction with the mountain view or the drive to the London office may depend on other people *not* being there. But my pleasure in the local cafe or pub or street festival may depend on other people *being* there. A lot of the pleasures of a successful life are sociable pleasures. That is the next step in Hirsch's argument:

> As the level of average consumption rises, an increasing proportion of consumption takes on a social as well as an individual aspect. That is to say, the satisfaction that individuals derive from goods and services depends in increasing measure not only on their own consumption but on consumption by others as well.   – *Social Limits to Growth*, p. 2.

He concludes that we should set less store by individual income as either the motivator or the main reward of economic activity. The activity itself is as important to many people's personal development and happiness as the income it earns, as long as the income suffices. We should moderate the competition for ever-increasing consumption, and the unjustified expectations of the joy it will buy, by reducing the inequalities of income for which people are driven or enticed to compete.

Up to this point the argument is not necessarily an argument for greater generosity. People may well continue as selfish as before, but if so, they need to learn that they will serve their own interests better, and have more joy of them, by learning to cooperate more and share more of their consumption with others.

But there is a second half to Hirsch's argument. It suggests that individual self-seeking is in worse trouble than that. Rational self-interest, the traditional fuel of capitalism, may now be corroding it.

NECESSARY MORALITY

Some built-in individual and social morality is a necessary condition of almost any economic system. It is specially necessary to the efficiency of a complicated, pluralist, market economy. Such a decentralized system, with millions of daily actions and transactions, has to rely on most of the people most of the time willingly behaving themselves: telling the truth, giving fair measure, keeping promises and contracts, observing customary obligations, working reliably, cooperating sensibly, not cheating or stealing.

Those requirements certainly have to be reinforced by formal law and enforcement, or the bad will prey on the good and the good be diverted from production to self-defence, to the point of anarchy and breakdown. But it is a great mistake to conclude from that hard fact of life that legal enforcement will work *without* a social morality. It is impossible to supervise all or most of a modern society's actions and transactions; and if it *were* possible, what would guarantee the honesty of such an army of supervisors? If everybody including the police and government will steal whenever they can get away with it, then they will mostly get away with it, and there will be very little economic efficiency. 'Internal' morality and 'external' enforcement are necessary to each other, and both are necessary conditions of orderly society. Law enforcement cannot *replace* a substantial social morality.

On the contrary, its function is to reinforce the morality and protect the people who abide by it – as most people most of the time in most societies want to do.

There is a simple reason why voluntary or customary good behavior helps economic efficiency: it is cheap. Bad behavior has costs, and institutional measures to prevent it have costs. There are direct costs of surveillance, regulation, reporting and auditing, physical security, trial and imprisonment. And there are indirect costs for business as increasingly complicated regulation complicates productive processes and raises their costs. Mutual trust, with least formality and least paperwork, is quickest and best wherever you can rely on it. So the *nature and quality* of a society's moral order, and the *level of habitual compliance* with it – the level of good behavior – are critical elements, and conditions of efficiency, in any economic system.

But the economic systems themselves are not usually the main producers of the morality on which they rely (though they affect it, by the motivation and opportunities and temptations which they offer). What are the main sources of the necessary morality? Here are three answers. They complement rather than contradict each other, as each focuses on a different element in the conditioning of good behavior.

Adam Smith believed that an economic system motivated chiefly by individual self-interest must rely, and generally *could* rely, on people pursuing their interests by honest exchange rather than by force or fraud. Before he wrote *The Wealth of Nations* he wrote the *Theory of Moral Sentiments.* He observed as a fact that love of others is as natural as love of self. People are born with both. Where circumstances and their interests allow, they generally like to behave well to others: altruism is one of their pleasures. Smith was also well aware of people's villainous propensities, and of the need to reinforce their moral impulses with social and legal sanctions. But to the question 'What makes most of the people behave well most of the time?' his answer was 'The nature they are born with.'

Fred Hirsch thought that capitalist societies inherited moral standards and habits generated by earlier social and economic conditions. There had previously been a slow-changing rural society, with small-scale, guild-regulated town industries. Individuals tended to have a recognized trade and economic role, with traditional rights and duties. They lived and worked in such small, settled communities that mutual observation and social pressure did most of any necessary enforcement. But law, custom and religious belief 'internalized' a good deal of the morality, so that it operated with less external enforcement than it takes to keep people well-behaved these days.

(I think Hirsch's history was partly romantic. In the eighteenth century, public and private coercion were widespread and often savage. 'Victorian' morality, with a puritan emphasis on hard work and abstemious living, tended to develop *with* industrial capitalism. But Hirsch was right enough about the shift from informal to formal law and order: from mutual observation and social control in settled communities, to professional policing in the mobile, anonymous, mass life of the industrial cities.)

Some modern observers see current moralities as coming neither from birth nor from the distant past. Instead they see continuous competition for influence between the sectors of the mixed economy. Profit-seekers say 'Earn and spend all you can. Don't worry about other people. Market forces – the 'hidden hand' – will ensure that intelligent self-interest will serve everyone best. If you *must* indulge in dutiful or altruistic feelings, your social duty is really to look to your own interests and leave other people to look after theirs.' While the private sector urges that, in deed if not always in word, the household and public sectors urge otherwise. Mothers and fathers – partly from love, partly for self-preservation – try to teach their children to be honest and peaceful and fair at home. Teachers, preachers, public broadcasters, social reformers and other non-profit-seeking voices recommend just-and-generous social moralities. In brief, the profit-seekers say 'Look after yourself', while the rest say 'Be fair; do as you would be done by'. If it is true that capitalism needs an external supply of morality, the suppliers nowadays are in the household and public sectors: roughly speaking, parents and teachers. The argument obviously misrepresents real life – some parents teach their children to be go-getters, many private firms demand high standards of honesty, loyalty and care of their employees, not all public servants have generous philosophies. But however fair or unfair to the sectors, the point of the argument is that public and private morality are social products, continuously created and re-created by contending social forces.

Those arguments are about the *sources* of good behavior, or lack of it, in affluent societies. But the heart of the argument is that wherever the necessary morality comes from, capitalist practice is now eroding it. In three ways: by persuasion, practice, and infectious example.

Commercial persuasion Technical advances are increasing the 'media saturation' of daily life and its saturation by advertising. There is argument about the actual effect of advertising on voting and spending, but not about its effect – to the extent that it is free from public control and public competitors – in degrading programs and fragmenting people's attention. Control of the more influential media is increasingly concentrated in the hands of a few super-rich individuals. Satellite transmission may eventually remove their broadcasting from any effective public control at all. And their influence may combine with other Right pressures to induce governments to deregulate the media and to commercialize and sell off any remaining public broadcasting.

Business practice grows more inventively selfish. Directors take for themselves rising multiples of the average incomes they pay their employees. Many public regulations and many private contracts grow more elaborate and detailed (and time-consuming and expensive) as more ingenious evasions and malpractices have to be specifically prohibited. There are growth industries in loopholing the law, re-designing accounts to reduce tax liability, frustrating the intentions of land-use and planning regulation, and so on. Firms locate their head offices or their 'profit centres' offshore, or in tax havens, to avoid taxation or control by the countries in

which they operate or are owned. These trends are all rational if the business of individuals, and of firms' directors and managers, is to maximize wealth and income to the limit the law allows, and to the limit to which the law can be frustrated or avoided. If it is the duty of a corporate officer to cut costs where he can, then rationally it is his duty to cut tax exposure where he can, to offset taxable gains by buying tax losses, to heap obligations onto a subsidiary then bankrupt or sell it, to offload waste disposal costs onto neighbors or public agencies, and so on. Firms which don't do those things may lose in competition with firms which do. Officers who do such things successfully may be promoted over officers who don't. The practices are increasingly complicated but Hirsch's point about them is simple: explicit law and contract are having to replace implicit morality, and the result is often evil and nearly always expensive and (by any sensible criteria) inefficient:

> the principle of self-interest is incomplete as a social organizing device. It operates effectively only in tandem with some supporting social principle . .[In trying] to erect an increasingly explicit social organization without a supporting social morality . . the foundations of the market system have been weakened while its general behavioural norm of acting on the criterion of self-interest has won ever-widening acceptance. – *Social Limits to Growth*, p. 12

Business principles That 'ever-widening acceptance' is infectious. It infects domestic life, professional ethics, government. If the norm in business is ingenious and ruthless self-service to the limit the law can be twisted to allow, some others besides businessmen will want to exploit such profitable ethics. Breadwinners learn to desert unwanted parents, lovers, spouses, children. Affluent societies have rising numbers of single-parent families, and grandparents in nursing homes. Sports and games are commercialized to enrich their champions, promoters, and the advertisers who exploit them. Leading lawyers and accountants make a new industry of tax-avoidance, and take much higher pay than the tax officers they are hired to outwit.

Hirsch was specially concerned about the infection of government. The more amoral business and the professions become, the more they need legal regulation. But – Hirsch asked – 'Why expect the controllers, alone, to abstain from maximizing their individual advantage?' If ruthless self-service is regarded as efficient in private business, why should public business managers and public service leaders work for half or a quarter of the pay that leading doctors and lawyers and corporate executives take? Some critics despair of honest govern-ment and become privatizers and deregulators. The whole idea of self-restraint and moral behavior is busily discredited by those who profit by doing without it. Orthodox economic theories idealize rational self-interest and market freedoms. Liberationists stigmatize morality as elderly, religious, wowserish, oppressive. So – unless other pressures prevail over those ones – the more the ruthless self-interest increases the need for public regulation, the less or worse regulation there tends to be.

The extent of these 'immoralizing' effects cannot be measured. Nor can the extent to which they are offset by reverse effects, for example by further improvements in welfare, in the regulation of business, and in public support for both. (There can be simultaneous increases in rich tax avoidance and in helpful aids for the disabled – the moral trend is rarely all one way.) But the fact that the moral qualities of social and economic life cannot be quantified does not make them unimportant. They are valuable for their own sakes, and in many industries and services they are critical conditions for good economic performance, in both meanings of good.

Morality and employment

If law is replacing morality as Hirsch suggests – if more legalism, regulation and small-print contracts are need-ed to enforce fair dealing – that may add some jobs for lawyers, accountants, tax officers and others.

But most relations between 'necessary morality' and employment are likely to be political and indirect. If majorities genuinely value full employment, govern-ments will try harder to achieve it, and people will be more willing to accept any costs of achieving it. If peo-ple are persuaded to believe that full employment is not attainable or not desirable, governments may not try for it. Worse, they may find positive uses for unemploy-ment.

Since the 1970s unemployment has increased in most affluent societies. There is widespread disagree-ment as to how to reduce it, and whether to try. There is more argument than there used to be against the welfare state and the policies of full employment, and in favor of explicitly selfish and liberationist social philosophies. Openly or not, some economists, employers and others welcome substantial unemployment because they think it disciplines the workers and restrains inflation, and thus serves good economic purposes. Others are per-suaded that whatever its value, full employment is no longer achievable and substantial numbers of unem-ployed may always need some public income.

But for most people work is much the most satisfac-tory source of income. It occupies people. It usually interests them. It contributes a great deal to the devel-opment of their social as well as their working skills. Even of the capital-owners who could afford not to work, most choose to work. On average, employed peo-ple enjoy their leisure much more than the unemployed do. Evidence of the high importance of work to human development and happiness is marshalled by Robert Lane in *The Market Experience* (1991), a book whose message you will meet at length in later chapters. Unless their employment is unusually unpleasant or insecure, the evidence suggests that working and earn-ing allow most workers, most of the time, to feel wanted, respected, productive, independent. Those sat-isfactions tend to be greater the less fear there is of unemployment.

Older inequalities If this chapter has over-empha-sized the effects of financial inequality and excessive competition for money income, that may be because much of it is written with Scitovsky's and Hirsch's and more recent critics' American experience in mind. There were other inequalities in Thomas Balogh's mem-ory when he wrote *The Irrelevance of Conventional Economics* (1982). Before he became an eminent econ-omist and adviser to British Prime Ministers Balogh had grown up as a subject of the Habsburg Empire and worked in Hungary when a Magyar aristocracy ruled it, then in Germany in deep depression on the eve of Hitler's rise to power. Notice the human and class rela-tions which made *him* celebrate full employment:

> Full employment not only makes domestic help scarce but it generally removes the need for servility, and thus alters the way of life, the relationship between classes...[So it is] not merely a means to higher production and faster expansion. It is also an aim in itself, weakening the dominance of men over men, dissolving the master-servant relation. It is the greatest engine for the attainment by all of human dignity and greater equality, and not merely in respect of incomes and consumption, important as those may be... Human dignity and satisfaction are incompatible with unemployment, even if the fear of penury had been completely eliminated by the social services – as it has not. The knowledge that a man fulfils a role in the community, that he has a positive function to perform, has a value which no system of social security, however lavish, can provide.
> *The Irrelevance of Conventional Economics*, pp. 47, 76

Unemployment can have profound effects on the

employed as well as the unemployed. I hope you will think hard, morally as well as technically, when you meet proposals that we should accept some unemployment as a normal aid to national economic management and persuade democratic majorities that they should not want full employment.

FIRST SUMMARY

You are offered two summaries of this chapter. This first one is orderly. The second one will be more realistic.

1. People have wants as producers, as consumers and as citizens. Each of the three can influence the others, and affect the working of the economy.

2. *Influence* Many parties – public, private and domestic; interested and disinterested – contend to influence people's wants. It is idle to think that people's wants could or should be *un*influenced. It takes at least as much educational effort to produce discriminating people who think for themselves as it takes to produce consumers programmed to vote and spend as directed by political and commercial persuaders.

3. *Happiness* In affluent societies individual income gains may tend to increase individual happiness while total income gains don't increase total happiness. Happiness may relate more to income security and perhaps to income rank than to the quantity of income. If further growth can't increase total happiness it remains possible that some better distribution of income might increase it, and reduce anxieties about income rank. (And of course many other things than income affect happiness.)

4. *Morality* Exclusively self-interested, amoral behavior may reduce both happiness and economic efficiency in a number of ways. Total self-seeking tends to be less satisfying than do human mixtures of self-interested, cooperative and altruistic activity. If a decline of voluntary and customary self-restraint in economic life makes more formal regulation and policing necessary, that may increase costs, reduce efficiency and reduce the satisfaction which a given level of output gives to people as producers, consumers and citizens. Too much 'rational self-interest' may thus be irrational. As they come to understand these contradictions, some people may care less for further growth, and be readier to limit it for social or environmental reasons. Others may try to 'moralize' the system by nationalizing some of the offending industries, or by improving the distribu-

tion of income – measures which need not restrict employment as 'no-growth' policies might.

5. *Orthodox possibilities* Whether by nature or nurture people may continue to develop wants for goods and services whose production can keep all willing workers employed.

6. *Possible problems* Technical progress may take productivity ahead of demand, especially where capital-saving inventions allow rising output from less of *both* capital *and* labor. There may be some recoil from waste, junk, excessive energy use, excessive packaging, the frustrating pursuit of positional goods, or other treadmill activity. Work may be attractive enough for workers to want no further reduction of working hours or working life, no further part-timing or work sharing. Those in work may want to monopolize what employment there is. For those or other reasons there may tend to be significant unemployment.

Those tendencies may or may not lead to effective public action to restore full or fairly shared employment. Techniques for doing that will be discussed in chapters on national policy.

SECOND SUMMARY

Reminders We are reviewing processes of change: ways in which developed mixed economies are or may be changing. For purposes of study we have to review causes of change one by one. But in real life they all operate at once, and act and react on each other, so outcomes can't be predicted simply by totalling up their individual effects. Some of the action and reaction is between people, as they coerce or persuade or bargain with each other. Some is *within* people, as individuals sort out their values and interests and views of the world, deciding what they want, what to believe, what to do. Some effects are predictable: if the current consumption of oil continues it must eventually exhaust the world's supplies. Others are not: will people act to conserve oil, will they invent adequate substitutes for it? There are enough intrinsic uncertainties to make most positive long-term forecasting uncertain.

The form of this second summary is chosen to emphasize three themes: (i) economic futures are partly unpredictable because they are partly open to be chosen, argued, fought over; (ii) the conflicts of purpose and belief are partly between people but partly also within people; and (iii) you yourself inescapably, by act or omission, are one of the contenders. What follow are sketches of half a dozen economic actors. They are chosen to sample people with diverse incomes, occupations, wants, beliefs, etc. But they are not fully or reliably representative – not all teachers are like the Greens, not all tycoons want what Robinson wants, and plenty of real-life interests and beliefs are not represented at all among the six. Treat them as easy reading, but seriously meant: one more reminder of how and where 'impersonal economic forces' actually collide and interact. They are real people, only the names are fictitious.

Contenders

- **Smith** drives a public bus. As a worker she would like more pay. As a consumer she mostly wants basic goods at low prices. But more than higher pay or lower prices she values her job security. Besides a sufficient income and a pension it secures her husband and her in a house they are just managing to buy, in a neighborhood they like, in reach of his (less secure) job, near to kin and friends and a school their children like. However well she and her husband understood (say) Swedish labor policies they might well not want them: the higher pay and material standards would not be worth the risks Swedish workers face of forced mobility, with uprooting and re-training and moving house, and trying once more to find two jobs in reach of each other. She votes for moderate union officers who oppose privatizing the buses, avoid industrial conflicts, and support 'social contract' incomes policies. She believes the union leaders who say that decent wages and conditions have always depended on union solidarity. She believes the moderate politicians who say full employment depends on income policies. She believes the Right newspapers who say greedy unions cause inflation and unemployment. She's for solidarity, security and full employment, and she's not greedy.

- **Brown** is a mechanic. He works shifts, maintaining machinery in a textile mill. His housing and consumer preferences matter less for our purposes than his attitude to employers, an attitude which the employers call militant and rapacious. He is a shop steward of his (old, big, traditionally militant) union. He believes in keeping employers under continuous pressure. Workers should use their collective power to the limit, to extract the maximum possible pay, perquisites, working conditions and short hours. They should press all the time, as opportunities offer, for marginal gains, administrative relaxations and reinterpretations and so on, as well as for big gains at the periodical 'wage rounds'. When moderates argue

for restraint, to avoid inflation, and to allow reasonable profit levels for reinvestment and other long-term reasons, Brown argues as follows: The employers' power, backed by the class power of the government and the media, is more than enough to maintain profit levels. Moreover the profits are consumed, exported, or invested in speculative property more often than they are re-invested in industry. (He's British.) If any *are* invested in industry it is usually to shed labor, then use the surrounding unemployment to increase pressure on the remaining workforce. As industrially, so also politically: Brown opposes all social contracts, income controls or 'policies of consensus'. In those policies the wage restraints are always real and the restraints on prices, profits and rich incomes are mostly phoney. Brown thinks workers should fight public employers and government almost as hard as they fight private employers. They should resist taxation at least as hard as the rich resist it. If that limits welfare, Brown is unmoved. First, it could just as well limit defence spending or some of the 'upward welfare' the rich get from government. Second, a lot of welfare is designed to buy compliance to an exploitive economic system, and Brown would rather see the unemployed and underpaid poor and angry. Though he doesn't put it that way, he believes workers should optimize by all workable means, like anyone else.

- **John Green** is a school teacher with strong green values. He's into ecology, nuclear disarmament, solar power, conserving wilderness. As a consumer he wants much the same things as Smith does, plus books, newspapers, and camping gear for his own, his pupils' and his family's holidays. His household uses very little fast food, personal services, tourist services: they're great DIY buffs. As a producer Green is devoted and generous: gives his pupils good value, with more after-school and weekend and vacation services than his contract requires. He also does more with and for his wife and children than many men do. As an employee he is less concerned about pay than about conditions of work: class sizes, library back-up, preparation time, and intellectual freedom from direction by bureaucrats or (within reason) parents. He agrees that teachers are underpaid, supports his union's efforts to put that right, and sees that he gets the pay and promotions due to him by the rules of the system. But he would be genuinely glad to change the system; and he works for, votes for, and would readily accept change towards a more equal, co-operative, steady-state economy even if it paid him less.

- **Jane Green** is like her husband in many respects but more conservative in some. She lost a brother to heroin and she worries for her children's safety from that and other commercial hazards. She sees no good whatever in the pornography and drug trades, or in most of the videos, electronic games or cheap amusement parlors that attract young people and turn them into zombies. She would ban soft as well as hard porn, censor books, movies, TV and video more restrictively than now, and stop all advertising of alcohol and tobacco. She does not think such restraints would conflict with free speech or liberal values. The dangerous and degrading products merely displace better uses of time and resources, and allow the nastiest capitalists to seduce and exploit the most disadvantaged and vulnerable customers. The products are full of incitement to crime, mostly by men against women and children. We should reverse the onus of proof which will only ban goods after they have established a market and done visible damage. Instead, all goods should have to be licensed in advance by consumer-protection officers who should generally be women. Parents and teachers should do their best to proof children against the degrading kinds of exploitation of consumers, but their efforts should be reinforced, not contradicted, by the law and management of the marketplace. Jane Green agrees with the Left in favoring democratic socialism. She agrees with the Greens about environmental reform. She agrees with the Feminists about equal pay, abortion, contraception and reforming the rape laws. She agrees with the conservative Festival of Light and Moral Majority about censorship and the protection of children and family life. (It is a coherent program for which there would be wide support if male politicians only realised it.)

- **Jones** is a tenured Professor of Economics with a salary in the top 1 per cent of earned incomes, additional income as author and consultant, and an indexed pension for his life and the life of his widow if he leaves one. As his income grows he invests more of it, mostly in real estate for tax-avoiding capital gain. Beyond that his spending runs to fine art and furniture, expensive cars and foreign holidays. His expertise, from which flow much of his income, reputation and work-satisfaction, is built on economic theory which 'assumes that, subject to risk and leisure preferences, economic actors act to maximize

income over time'. They also know their own interests best and should not have their products or purchases regulated by government. Jones would abolish censorship, legalize all drugs, minimize the public regulation of business, and privatize existing public enterprises where possible. He concedes the need for a welfare safety net for the casualties of the system, but as long as that is there, he believes that somewhat steeper inequalities would improve motivation, productivity and national output, and be in everyone's interest in the long run. 'More Ferraris and more bikes would be no bad thing.' His last article was an elegant demonstration that current unemployment could be classified as natural or voluntary without remainder. His current research, funded by a private nursing-home consortium, is into privatizing welfare. Given adequate health insurance and a guaranteed minimum income administered through the tax office, people could buy the services they actually want from competitive private suppliers, and most of the public bureaucracies could be dismantled. Jones teaches what he believes, and derides any other beliefs, to large lecture classes and about twenty tutorial pupils each year. The bright ones go, in roughly equal numbers, into business, government and journalism.

- **Robinson** is a tycoon whose energies have turned a small inherited fortune into a huge multinational one. By ownership and other means he effectively controls newspapers, government-licensed TV and radio stations, a government-franchised lottery, a government-franchised airline, and he has interests in a government-licensed bank and in mines which depend on government export licenses. He lives comfortably but that can't be what he chiefly wants or he would have retired long ago to become a full-time consumer. What he appears to want is to win, expand his capital, keep personal control of all of it, support what strike him as good causes in the world if they are compatible with those prior aims, and live decently as a family man. Among his ways of winning he was a pioneer of greenmailing, a style of corporate raiding which profited the raider whether his takeover bids succeeded or failed. (That's illegal now.) Where there are markets for elite newspapers, he provides good ones. Where readers like reports of sex, violence and cruelty to children to be really vivid, he outdoes all competition. What sort of economic system does he want? On the one hand he encourages privatization and wants as much enterprise as possible to be in private profit-seeking hands. On the other hand a lot of his own success comes from private uses of government power. Wherever he acquires media influential enough to interest politicians, he sooner or later gets financial favors from governments: licences, franchises, advantageous loans from public banks, exemptions from anti-trust or media monopoly or foreign-ownership rules. His main interest for our present purpose is that he and a few others like him are concentrating media ownership and broadcast entertainment in ever fewer and richer hands. In 1945 a British Labor government which promised to nationalize a number of private industries was elected against the advice of 80 per cent of the country's national newspapers, but with its only broadcaster – a public monopoly – giving equal time to the two parties. Could social-democratic initiatives do as well as that now, with such powerful opponents standing to lose so much?

The world has many more types than those six – including *conservative* workers, *anti-censorship* feminists, *socialist* professors, *fair-minded* newspaper proprietors, *repentant* billionaires and many other interested and disinterested contenders. Those six are merely reminders that the directions of economic development do not depend only on impersonal historical or market forces, they also depend on who wins how much of what, in continuing political conflicts and compromises – and also on the many unforeseen effects of those conflicts, the muddled outcomes which nobody planned or intended.

EXERCISE

List some more contenders. Sketch what you know of the beliefs, purposes and possible influence of half a dozen of your acquaintances, as they may bear on the future of employment.

Compulsory: Include yourself in the set.

15

Childhood

Two ways to start this chapter:

1. Think about your mum and dad. How they brought you up, what you cost them in love and money and freedom. What sort of childhood they gave you, how you have so far rewarded them. What sort of character you are, with what capacities and opportunities for happiness. Do you hope to do the same for a kid or two of your own, or do it differently, or do without children?

2. Most of the differences between richer and poorer societies, and between better and worse societies at any level of wealth or poverty, are built into their people: their skills and ability to learn, their competitive and cooperative impulses, their will to work and play, their affection or dislike or indifference for one another, their capacity for a happy or anxious or miserable experience of life. Most of those qualities, or the capacity to acquire them, are instilled into them or elicited from them in childhood. Economic performance, individual and national, depends on them. And the technological element in economic growth keeps demanding longer and more complex education, and longer and more expensive dependence on parents. Economists need to notice these trends.

The best accounts of children's experience may always be found in fiction and biography. But social research now suggests that your chances of adult competence and happiness tend to vary not only with your parents' personal qualities but also with their occupational and sexual choices. On average, with many individual exceptions, and with disputable judgments about who should count as well-brought-up adults, research in a number of disciplines seems to suggest that -

- Children's best chances are with parents living happily together with them throughout their childhood, with one or other parent on hand or accessible through most of their out-of-school hours.

- Next best seem to be parents who both earn, but arrange day care by someone as permanent and dependable in the children's world as themselves.

- Next, a group who are likely to be good but stressed

parents: two earners without a permanent daytime substitute, perhaps with pre-school infants in crowded ten-hour daycare with changing staff; or a lone parent with enough income to care full-time for children, or with a nanny or granny to do it while the parent earns.

- Last, an unhappy lot: couples who are both permanently unemployed; earners anxious about changing and unreliable child care; parents with dangerous or changing resident partners; criminal, alcoholic, drug-addicted or other incapacitated parents; children brought up in institutions.

Those are no more than tendencies. Parents in the last group do bring up some successful people. Happy marriages do bring up some troubled or troublesome people. But children's average chances seem to vary significantly with their parents' relations to each other and to employment.

The first option on the list commonly has one parent sharing the other's income while giving a decade or two to housekeeping, children and (often) unpaid school and neighborhood activities. By a small margin over the next alternative, that tends to bring up the highest proportion of happy and workable adults. By a big margin it also presents the most troublesome dilemmas to many parents. Other dilemmas, especially for government, are posed by the last group of troubled parents and children.

None of these problems is wholly economic. But they all have economic elements, many of which are changing with economic growth, with women's changing roles, with changing relations between business and government, and with conflicting social values and purposes. The economic and policy problems will demand attention through your working years. A range of effects on productivity, social justice and personal happiness may depend on how they are resolved. Hence this chapter.

WHOSE PROBLEM?

Many people enjoy childhood and remember it happily. Many think that bringing up children is one of the best things they do. For both, the experience is one of life's greatest goods, besides being necessary for the production of other goods.

But parents' and children's relations with one another also pose conflicts of interest: between parents and children, between mothers and fathers, between parenting work and other work. And in rich countries upbringing is expensive: how should its costs be distributed between parents, their employers, taxpayers and any others? Conflicts about that issue are often also about how good the upbringing can afford to be, and how far its quality should or should not vary with parents' capacity and willingness to pay, and with children's intellectual and other differences. Childless taxpayers ask why they should subsidize other people's brats when they have contributed neither to their number nor to the environmental costs of over-population. (Answers: because (i) qualities of their society which they do enjoy and profit by – its culture, productivity, interesting diversity, law and order – depend on how its people are brought up, and (ii) if they want to live on after they stop earning they need a younger generation to feed and doctor and service them. If they don't contribute labor to bringing up that generation they should certainly help to finance the hardworking parents who do. Besides working longer hours, those parents may also forgo income one way or another – by staying home or by hiring help – to do it well.)

Which is to say that bringing up children is not just a parents' problem or a women's problem, it is everyone's business. It presents broad problems of justice and efficiency, and of equity between many groups, especially between social classes, between parents and others, and between women and men. That is the theme of the two feminist books cited in the next section.

SAME DIFFERENCE

One strand in the history of feminist thought has been debate about the likeness or difference between women and men. Do their similarities justify identical political rights and economic roles? Are their differences (other than child-bearing) natural, or are they socially imposed? In *Same Difference: Feminism and Sexual Difference* (1990) Carol Bacchi traces the history of the debate. The changing balance of belief has tended to reflect the practical possibilities of reform at particular times and places. Sometimes there was more to be gained by asserting the similarities between women and men, at other times by asserting their differences. But Bacchi concludes that it is an unhelpful debate, for a number of reasons.

As a women's debate about women's rights it tends to encourage conservative men to dismiss reproduction and upbringing from serious political consideration.

Male political philosophers continue to theorize about individual rights in societies of independent, fully formed adults. They *ought* to treat the creation and formation of those adults, and of their capacities for independence, as one of the main social and economic tasks, and as everyone's business rather than women's business. Making gender questions the primary focus of debate 'is an inappropriate way of thinking about important social issues, such as how society is to reproduce itself and the kind of society in which we wish to live'. In considering their collective social tasks and purposes, people have to take into account the particular needs and capacities of a great many particular groups: children before they join the workforce, unemployed members of the workforce, old people after they leave it; physically and mentally handicapped people; people in specially difficult or valuable or dangerous occupations who need special incentives or protection or regulation; and so on. Particular needs or capacities of women, or of women in some occupations, or at some stages of their lives, are among the many groups who may need some special legal or institutional provisions. So are a great many activities in which people's rights and capacities are *not* affected by their sex. Rival generalizations asserting some uniform sameness between all men and all women, or uniform differences between them, are not good foundations for social thought or policy.

The philosopher Elizabeth Wolgast reminds us that such general beliefs can be positively harmful. In the vision of a society whose citizens must compete on equal terms, with identical individual rights, 'anomalies appear. In such a society the elderly and frail must compete with the young and strong, men compete with their child-bearing wives, the handicapped compete with the well-endowed. . . The problems of this picture have not deterred social and economic thinkers from using it, even though it is at center a picture of ruthless egoism and unconcern for others.' *(The Grammar of Justice,* 1987, pp. 15, 18-19). In real life equal rights are not the only necessary or important rights:

> Some rights depend on individual differences, on accidents of fortune, on talents, or on other features that distinguish people. These rights are special or differential ones: among them are the right of a blind person to use of a white cane, the right of a veteran to burial at public expense, the right of an indigent to government assistance, the right of a fatherless child to public support. Many rights are of this kind. They are not rights for everyone but rights only for those who qualify, and most of them have a presumptive basis in needs . . . The two kinds of rights, equal and

differential (or special) work quite differently. With regard to an equal right, taking a person's individual qualities into account may constitute discrimination. But with special rights, they *must* be taken into account, for these rights are based on human differences. – Elizabeth Wolgast, *Equality and the Rights of Women* (1980) pp. 41-2.

Can any one principle justify rights of both kinds? Wolgast thinks not. We reason from different foundations to rules to fit different problems. There can be difficult choices, sometimes, between the general and the special rules. But we must face and cope with those difficulties, because civilized societies could not possibly do without rules and roles of both kinds.

JUSTICE AND GENDER

Since the democracies are necessarily laced with rights and policies of both kinds, Wolgast sees no good reason why all the rules affecting gender or the care of children should be of the equal and uniform kind and none be of the differential kind. There is more than one tolerable way for two people to divide the work of earning and keeping house. Wolgast agrees with the many feminists who see bearing and bringing up children as 'a fair part of what life is about', to be embraced and enjoyed, not regretted as a chore. Men should do more of it. That can be good for men, good for women's work loads and career opportunities, probably good for the children. But there is more than one good way to do it. Half a dozen ways are presently sketched, all of which should be open to parents' choice.

Feminists who value some distinctive qualities of women also fear that uniform rules and a unisex culture would in practice force ambitious women to compete with men on men's traditional terms. But if the point of empowering women is to bring their distinctive capacities to bear in business, government and intellectual life, the distinctive qualities should not have to be discarded on the way to the top. And if one purpose of empowering women is to reform men they may respond better to feminine women than to women imitating men.

There is an interesting example of women's influence in the early history of socialist thought. Socialist ideas and language were born between – roughly – the 1790s and the 1840s. Among its creators were Irish, English and French women, including Anna Wheeler, Fanny Wright, Emma Martin and Flora Tristan. They wrote about family and communal life as well as about paid work in industry. There is no room here to detail their contributions, but their visions of reform included personal freedom, self-government, and tolerable conditions of life for men and women and children, young and old, at home as well as at work. At work there should be more shared ownership of business, safer conditions, and equal pay for equal work by men and women. At home there should be more equal conditions of housing and community life, and full equality between men and women whatever their divisions of labor. Thus they aspired to four kinds of equality: class equality at work, class equality in home and neighborhood, sex equality at work, and sex equality at home. A brutal effect of Marx's takeover of the socialist movement through the second half of the century, reinforced by the growth of mostly-male trade unions, was to exclude three of those four aspirations from serious socialist thought for a century. Equality came to mean equality only among men and only in paid employment, and paid employment became the only meaning of work. In returning to those earlier women's concerns, twentieth century feminists often had as little help from the Marxist Left as from the conservative Right.

Twentieth century experience has also brought some feminist second thoughts about income-sharing. Eight hours at the jam factory or plucking chickens plus five hours of housework and child care, even if the housework and child care are fairly shared, does not make for the happiest childhood or parenthood: three full-time jobs can be too many for two people. So there has lately developed some overlap on the subject of income-sharing between some feminists and the anti-feminist women who defend the traditional division of labor between men who earn and women who keep house. All feminists condemn that as a *compulsory* role for married women. But if it can be freely chosen, it offers women one more option (whether as the earning or the non-earning partner) than they would otherwise have. And it is a popular option. Recent polls suggest, for example, that more than half of British women would rather not be earning while they bring up children.

Women who stop earning to raise children have usually finished doing that with about half their life still ahead of them. Many return to paid work. But some who choose not to do that have made sharing a partner's income a way to freedom rather than captivity. Many women's local or national political careers have depended, at least for a while, on income sharing. Some independent charities get more of their work done by volunteers supported by their parents or spouses than by paid workers. Some countries' primary schools depend on parent volunteers for a variety of services. Commercially, few people of either sex who have to earn a living can risk trying to do it by freelance writing, painting, composing or other crafts, or by grazing mohair or breeding warmbloods, or starting suburban coffee shops or boutiques. Income sharing allows all sorts of otherwise intolerable risks, artistic or commercial. If ever unemployment has to be attacked by rationing paid work, income sharing between willing partners may offer specially desirable freedoms and opportunities. But women need some insurance if they are the non-earning partners. While there are children, they need an alternative income if the shared income fails. When the children can spare them – or if either partner ends the partnership – they need a payable trade they can return to, if possible without any penalty for having been away.

Thus four advantages are claimed for having many common roles and rules but also some differential ones, for women and men who want them. There may be some innate differences between the sexes which would make a unisex regime oppressive. A free society should allow its members to decide and negotiate their relations and divisions of labor. Some of women's distinctive qualities are socially valuable and will be more so as greater equality and some differential opportunities increase their influence. And – subject to the justice of the arrangements – some sex and gender differences can contribute to the joy and interest of life. Elizabeth Wolgast concludes:

> In the absence of a compelling reason against them, it seems reasonable to suppose that sex roles in some form or other are tolerable. What is needed is not their abolition or their amalgamation to a single androgynous role, but adjustments within them. In many respects adjustment is needed to make the roles more similar. [Many present differences are falsely based, unjust, and must go.] But to say that grown women are generally somewhat easier with children than men, somewhat more expressive of feelings, more understanding of other's feelings, more demonstrative, and somewhat less competitive, is not clearly false. Nor are the consequences for sex roles clearly negligible. Some differences between the sexes, their nature, temperament, and roles, may actually be a nice thing.
>
> – *Equality and the Rights of Women*, p. 124-5

DIVISIONS OF LABOR

Here are ten alternatives. Parents can choose any of the first five or six, or be landed, willing or not, with one of the last four or five.

1. Both parents earn, but one stops earning for as long as the children need care during working hours.

2. One parent earns, the other never does, and provides most of the care while there are children.

3. Both parents earn part-time while there are children, with timetables which allow them to take turns with the children.

4. Both parents earn. Other people are paid to mind their children during their working hours (public child-care, employers' child-care, commercial child-care, a private nanny).

5. Both parents earn. Unpaid kin or friends mind their children during their working hours.

6. A parent lives with a non-parent partner, with any of the above divisions of labor.

7. Neither parent earns. They both look for work but can't find any, and share the care of the children; or one looks for work and the other does not, but provides most care of the children.

8. A lone parent lives on transferred income from the absent parent or government, and brings up the children full-time.

9. A lone parent earns, and others (paid or unpaid) look after the children during working hours.

10. Children of dead, absent or incompetent parents are brought up by foster parents or in institutions.

And there should be another, catch-all category for children whose grown-up company changes – once or twice or often, unhappily or dangerously or sometimes for the better – during their childhood.

Children are brought up in each of those ways, including the worst of them. A good society should do what it can to make good upbringing possible for all of them. The worse the conditions, the more the community as a whole has to fear from the long-lasting ill effects of bad upbringing. Any effective aids to lone, unemployed, invalid, hard-up or otherwise handicapped parents are justified by everyone's self-interest, as well as by compassion for the suffering parents and children.

The rest of this chapter reviews in turn –

- some possible directions of reform to adapt the task of bringing up children to changing economic and social conditions

- some dilemmas in designing policies for that purpose

- reminders of a range of other policies (about housing, employment, industrial relations, taxation, etc.) which can also affect children's upbringing

- some damage which globalization and smaller government seem likely to do to children's chances, and through them to human capital and economic efficiency.

DIRECTIONS OF REFORM

Parenting is affected in many ways by the feminist reforms which are already under way – though not all progressing very fast – in most rich democracies: equal pay and opportunity in employment, including access to traditionally male occupations; paid or unpaid maternity and paternity leave for short or long periods; public day-care for children; employer-financed day-care; commercial day-care; family day-care. There are women's health services, and safe houses or shelters for endangered women and children. Welfare services are empowered to protect children from dangerous parents or other minders. Most rich countries pay a public income – subject to various conditions and means-tests – to lone parents who forego earning to care full-time for their children.

Many of the services are understaffed, out of reach of many of their potential users, provided by some but not other employers and some but not other local governments. Equal pay and opportunity in employment are nowhere complete or available in all occupations. Progress toward them has varied chiefly with governments' means of enforcing them. The desired re-education of men, and feminization of culture, still have far to go. But all these elements of a feminist program have achieved *some* official status and *some* progress, though some of them are now in danger from the drift of economic policy to the Right in many countries.

But those reforms still leave two big gaps. People should ideally be able to choose freely, without much financial pressure either way, whether or not to have children; whether or not to stop earning in order to look after them; and whether to share income with a partner in a more permanent way without anxiety or social disapproval. The choices ought to be open to both sexes, though at present more women than men are likely to take advantage of some of them. And they ought to be open to people with low as well as high incomes. For those purposes there really need to be two further reforms: (i) a parenting wage, and (ii) better ways back into employment for parents who leave the paid workforce for some years to bring up children. Both are unlikely in the present political climate. But notes about them follow in case the climate changes, or you would like to help it to change.

A parenting wage

Many countries pay a public income to lone parents who give full time to their young children. The income tends to be low, means-tested, and not available to a parent sharing the income of the other parent or anyone else. (One of its ill effects is therefore to encourage hard-up or de facto couples to live apart.) Many parents' and children's lives could be improved if a full wage were paid, recognized and respected as *earned* income, and available to any full-time parent whether living alone or with another wage-earner. (Should it be available to two parents each earning half-time?) Public and political opinion might demand some limitations: perhaps means tests where the full-time parent's partner has income above a basic or average wage, and a limit on the age at which children could entitle a parent to the wage.

However it was limited the scheme would be expensive. But it would reduce other public spending on child care. Depending on economic circumstances it could reduce unemployment and its public and private costs. It might well reduce public as well as human costs by reducing the tendency of lone and unemployed parents, prisoners' wives, widowed or deserted fathers with children, women who cannot afford to get rid of dangerous partners, and other vulnerable parents, to bring up more illiterate, uncooperative, unemployed, unhealthy and criminal adults than (on average) secure parents bring up.

In some circumstances such a wage may motivate people to have children they would not otherwise choose to have. You may judge that enabling responsible people to have much-desired children is so valuable that it outweighs the harm done if a few people are prompted to have children they would not otherwise want. Research has found very few of such deliberate income-seeking births. They are mostly 'conceived' by propagandists against welfare provisions. But the possibility can be used very effectively by opponents of public aid to poor children. A lone parent's allowance may also affect some parents' decisions to desert or not to desert each other and their children. But the good effects of that kind may well outnumber the bad ones.

These are troublesome, sometimes heart-rending, dilemmas. Any policy, including no policy, must do some harm as well as the good it does. I don't believe the difficulties should deter us from acting to improve people's career and parenting options, especially women's options. Every member of society has an interest in the upbringing of all its children, especially those with the poorest parents. But the policies can be troublesome and vulnerable, like the people they are designed to serve. In *Equality and the Rights of Women* (p. 117) Elizabeth Wolgast quotes the biologist Mary Midgley on the human species –

> We are fairly aggressive, yet we want company and depend on long-term enterprises. We love those around us and need their love, yet we want independence and need to wander. We are restlessly curious and meddling, but long for permanence. Unlike many primates, we do have a tendency to pair-formation, but it is an incomplete one, and gives us a lot of trouble.

Returning to employment after years as a full-time parent In most occupations, people who return to work after long absence are disadvantaged, especially in their prospects of pay, promotion and responsibility. The more ambitious and well-qualified they are, and the higher it is possible to rise in their occupations, the more they risk losing by taking time away with children.

A revolution in the prospects of re-entry to paid employment might achieve a number of good things. It could employ ex-parents more justly, and often more productively. It would allow freer, better-balanced choices to parents considering whether to interrupt their careers. If it encouraged more of them to do so, more children could benefit from full-time, unstressed parental company. If technological progress reduces available employment and prompts some rationing of it, more well-supported full-time parenting will be welcome. It will be doubly welcome if it reduces the inequality and the stressful parenting that result when well-off couples with children both earn, leaving poorer children's parents both unemployed. On the other hand if environmental necessities force some return to *more* work (to conserve scarce resources, economize energy, reduce pollution) that is likely to mean more and harder work at home as well as in employment, and lower material standards of living. Different policies may then be needed if parents and children are to be protected from the stresses to be expected when two people try to do three jobs, with two of the jobs paying less than they did and all three demanding longer hours than they did.

Many aids to re-entry to the workforce – training courses, equal opportunity and affirmative action policies, job-finding services – already exist for some occupations or are offered by some employers. But we could surely do better. Understanding of the problem might be improved by a research proposal published in Lionel Orchard and Robert Dare (eds) *Markets, Morals and Public Policy* (1989). It called for an expert, detailed (and therefore expensive) survey of the hun-

dreds of occupations in an advanced economy to distinguish the skills and experience which each occupation actually uses from other considerations which influence employers' personnel policies: for example age, sex, length of service; academic qualifications which are not actually the source of the relevant skills; preferences which employers may exercise for equitable or incentive reasons, or by agreement with unions – and so on. What is needed is a distinction between *functional* requirements (which of the applicants for this job could actually do it?) and institutional ways of deciding which of the competent applicants to hire or promote. With expert consultation in each case, investigators could try to discover of each occupation –

- whether it is functionally possible, ignoring any institutional barriers, for someone once competent in the occupation to return to it after (say) ten years away, given one or two years of re-training where necessary;

- what institutional, non-functional barriers to re-entry there currently are; for example –

- whether any pay or power differentials which come with length of service are there for functional reasons, or for other reasons – perhaps equitable or incentive or hard-bargained or merely customary reasons; and

- if there are functional skills which cannot survive a long break, whether they could be maintained, through the break, by some weekly hours of part-time work, and whether the industry currently offers such work.

The grounds for such judgments would vary from occupation to occupation. Some quite factual judgments are possible. Plenty of bus drivers, school teachers and shopkeepers have returned to work successfully after long absences. No neurosurgeons, virtuoso trumpeters or jumbo pilots have, or are likely to. Some occupations are difficult to judge, especially if their future technology is unpredictable. But it should be possible to reach reasonable conclusions about perhaps eight or nine occupations of every ten. And (guessing *without* benefit of such research) it would not be surprising to find some such result as this:

- 15 – 20% of occupations cannot be re-entered after a decade away, but in some of them the necessary skills could be maintained by part-time work

- about 30% can, but require a year or two of re-training

- about 30% can, with little or no re-training

- 15 – 20% may often be done better by people with diverse experience than by those whose whole working life has been in the same occupation.

The last group exist because some jobs burn out some of their long-serving workers, and many jobs can benefit from parenting or worldly experience of various kinds. In the public sector police, clergy, historians and economists and other social scientists, consumer protection and equal opportunity officers, politicians and some public servants, and in the private sector many writers, actors and artists, market researchers, advertisers, marketing and sales staff, personnel officers and administrators are among those who may be better for some experience outside those occupations. If other things are equal between two 40-year-old social workers, school teachers, family court judges, children's book authors or editors or publishers, the one who has brought up children may well do better than the one who has not (though, as always, there will be individual exceptions).

For each group of occupations the investigators should also report any non-functional barriers to re-entry, suggest how they might be overcome, map the interests which might obstruct such reform, and consider whether, and how, improvement might be negotiated, or enforced by law.

Such research might have a number of uses. People who knew they wanted children, and wanted themselves or a partner or both to give plenty of time to the children, might choose their occupations (and sometimes perhaps their partners) with the re-entry possibilities as well as all the other considerations in mind. Nationally, policy-makers could know more about re-entry problems and possibilities. The array of non-functional barriers, and hindrances to the career paths of parents who return after years with children, could be better known both by the parents and by the long-serving workers, many of them also parents, with whom returning parents may have to compete. The knowledge could perhaps be persuasive, and improve the climate for reforms, the design of reforms, and the chances of popular and political support for them.

OTHER POLICIES

Obviously, many other economic conditions and policies affect the experience of children and the parents who bring them up. Some of those conditions and policies are changing or seem likely to change. Brief reminders:

Employment, housing, health, education, neighborhood Prevailing levels of employment and unemployment, the security of employment, and the degree of wage equality or inequality affect the conditions of childhood. So do housing and banking policies which affect what housing and private land families can afford, and how securely they can occupy them. So does the cost and accessibility of health services and the quality and cost (and class structure, if any) of school education. So does the public provision of neighborhood space and facilities for children.

Public and commercial influence The twentieth century saw a massive increase in public and commercial communication to children through press, radio, cinema, TV, video and computer screens. Children learn much more than earlier generations could know about the world and its people – especially what they look like and sound like. Besides all the trivial things they can see quite a lot of good children's and educational broadcasting and other useful and interesting information. Incessant advertising encourages them to spend and consume – but many of the soaps and sitcoms and some of the crime and adventure stories encourage traditional virtues and family values, and wit and fun and knockabout humor.

Until now there has been some censorship, and disagreement about it. Technical progress may soon make it harder to control what children can see and hear, or (what may be more important for children's well-being) what their predators can see and hear on special cable or satellite channels. Who should try to censor it? The classical liberal philosophy tends to focus on the civic and market rights of fully-formed adults, leaving any necessary protection of children to their minders. In that spirit the new broadcasters are arguing that their output should be censored, if at all, by its receivers, not by its transmitters or government. Experienced parents and their children may both think that parents' attempts to control what their children watch tend to be more oppressive and less effective than the public censorship of film and broadcasting has usually been.

Globalization is a subject of later chapters. It is a program to create private corporate rights to trade, invest, lend or borrow money and buy and own property anywhere in the world without much hindrance by national governments. It would bar governments from most of the common methods of helping or protecting their national industries and employment. It is a winners' program promoted chiefly by some business interests, governments and neoclassical economists in Europe and the United States. One of its purposes is to intensify international competition for jobs. Together with other Right policies it is likely to maintain some unemployment in the rich countries and reduce the wage rates of their lower-paid workers, and reduce the proportions of secure employment.

That threatens the time and material resources of poor parents. It may keep some of them unwillingly unemployed. It may drive some couples to both work, or to work longer hours, when one or both would rather spend more time with their children. Changing jobs may force changes of address which break children's school and neighborhood attachments and friendships. Where mortgage interest has to be paid at international market rates rather than at nationally controlled rates, fewer couples can buy houses, or buy them while they have young children.

Poor, insecure, ill-equipped or neglected upbringing is a cruelty to children which a good society's economic policies should not encourage. It also tends to increase the numbers who grow up anxious or unconfident or illiterate or unco-operative, and less happy or productive than they might otherwise have been. These effects rarely figure in employers' or governments' or economists' analyses or discussions of economic policy. You can try to change that, if you think it should change, in your working life as an economist. (Or of course as a politician, public servant or business tycoon.)

Postscript: I am wrong. Business leaders *have* begun to worry about childhood. They are finding that it is bad for business. *Fortune* magazine has just reported that big American corporations, led by Coca Cola and BellSouth, now prefer to hire young men and women without wives, husbands or children. Another U.S. survey has found higher average incomes and more promotions for male managers with wives who attend to all that domestic stuff and do not earn. In an Australian report Don Edgar finds that the new leaner management tends to mean overloaded management:

> White-collar workers have no penalty rates to cover overtime and employers find it easier to work them harder than to put on more people to do the work. What this leaves is a workforce both exhausted and overstressed. Change is so rapid that insecurity rules, fear is rampant, bosses can get away with demands that would have been impossible just a few years ago.

> The demands of this new economy wreak havoc on family routines that are the bulwark of childhood.

That is one more reason for adding effects on childhood to the list of things to be aware of, and alert for, in economic observation, analysis and policy-making. Effects on children's experience, on parents' experience, and through them on human capital and happiness. Routinely, habitually, professionally, alert. And when necessary, argumentative – coldly when that will work best, passionately when that will.

That is this chapter's message and sufficient conclusion.

16

Threatened social capital

Here come two chapters about endangered resources. Some of them need protection from market forces. Some need protection from misguided government. Some need both. In the next chapter, the natural environment. In this chapter, two human creations: physical capital (heritage buildings, fine city parks and squares, picturesque villages, well-kept countryside); and valuable social institutions and qualities of culture and community life which may be threatened by technological or economic changes.

These subjects belong in an economists' course of study because they often complicate economic analysis – or *ought* to complicate it. They represent things which people want but cannot achieve by individual market spending, or they are public assets which are threatened by conflicts of private interest. Economists need to have them in mind in debates about many questions of economic efficiency and welfare.

CONSERVING MAN-MADE STRUCTURES

People conserve buildings, streets, neighborhoods, and sometimes whole towns or man-made landscapes, for a variety of reasons.

The old things may simply be beautiful.

They may exemplify the history of design, or the work of particular designers.

They may be valued for their historical associations. (In this hall the Declaration of Independence was signed. In this church people have worshipped for ten centuries. In this house Milton wrote or Leonardo painted or Anne Frank lived in hiding.)

Undistinguished buildings may be valued as evidence about past ways of life and work – as documents of social history. People preserve prehistoric huts, Roman camps, medieval villages, ordinary buildings of every age and style. Eighteenth century ironworks have been reconstructed in Shropshire. The eighteenth century town of Williamsburg has been reconstructed in Maryland.

Most of the items mentioned so far lend themselves to one or another kind of 'museum' preservation. They can be bought and cared for and put on show as public works or commercial exhibits. They don't present any special problems to economists.

But people also want to conserve assets on bigger scale, including assets in ordinary private ownership and in ordinary working use. Without turning them into museum pieces, conservationists want good old buildings to be continued in use rather than demolished and replaced. Neighborhoods defend themselves from property developers' and highway builders' bulldozers. Planning regulations may require new buildings to conform in scale and style with the older buildings around them. Taxes can be designed to make it more profitable to preserve existing buildings than to replace them. Thus conservationist values may be built into the general control of building and land uses which now prevails in one form or another in most developed countries.

Regulating what owners may do with their land has various purposes including the efficient functioning of traffic and transport systems and other public services. But the commonest purpose is one which can equally well be called conservationist or conservative: when people choose a place to live or to locate a business, they want to know that the character of the place won't change for the worse. If they buy a house and plant a garden they may want to stay for life, or if they move they will want to sell the property for at least as much as it cost them. So they need to know that nobody can build a glue boiler or a panel-beating shop or a tower block next door. Meanwhile investors looking for sites for glue boilers and panel-beating shops and tower blocks need to know where they *will* be tolerated. So in principle, zoning land for compatible uses can help all parties, however badly it has sometimes been done in practice.

Zoning concerns economists in particular ways. They help to plan it, as experts in the quantities of land likely to be needed for the different kinds of use. And they must take account of it in analysing how land markets work.

There are also more general questions. What are the social costs and benefits of urban conservation? If governments compel the conservation of buildings whose owners would rather demolish them, the owners believe they lose something. Is the sum of their losses the social cost of conservation? Does such public interference with private rights and market forces necessarily leave the whole society materially poorer than it might otherwise have been? Not necessarily, for reasons of economy, diversity, and time, as follows.

Economy

A + B > B. If you add a new building to a sound old one, you have two. If you demolish the old one to make room for the new one you only have one. Part of your spending has merely restored what you already had, so the net addition has cost more than it need have cost. Of course some old buildings are rotten or unusable and have to go, and some locations are so valuable that it makes sense to replace small old buildings with big new ones, to give the benefit of the location to more people. But wherever the old structures are sound and usable, a society which manages to build what it needs with the least destruction of old fabric will get the most 'built space' for its money. Won't market forces see to that? No – later chapters will explain why land markets don't work with that sort of social efficiency. Owners can often make most money soonest by demolishing old buildings which others could still use and the society would do well to conserve. (It helps the efficiency of any city if there is room in and around its central places for poor as well as rich people to live, for cheap trades paying low rents, and for marginal or uncommercial cultural activities like fringe theatre, arts and crafts, secondhand books, cheap meeting places.) Conserving old urban fabric is not just a matter of regulating the demolition of individual buildings. It needs strategies of urban growth which do not generate too much commercial competition for scarce central space.

Diversity

This is another effect of the same economical policy of adding new buildings without demolishing old ones. Compare the (imaginary) histories of city A and city B:

> Through the centuries city A keeps its centre in the same place. As needs and techniques change, buildings are replaced accordingly. For example the metropolis grows so that its centre has to serve the central needs of ever-increasing numbers. The small town hall is replaced by a bigger one, the small church is replaced by a big cathedral, the low office buildings are replaced by taller ones. Then more growth brings further numbers – but also a decline in churchgoing and attendance at civic meetings. So the big town hall is replaced by a convention centre and the big cathedral is replaced by a small church, leaving space for an expansion of the office centre. And so on. In each century the metropolis has an entirely modern centre. It continually demolishes and

replaces its past.

> City B lets its central activities grow by addition rather than replacement. As needs and techniques change it builds new town halls and cathedrals and office buildings on new ground, keeping many of the old buildings and finding uses for them. Instead of one central place it therefore develops (over the centuries) a network of central places – as London, Paris and Rome have done. As one urban planning text puts it: 'New York has destroyed its past. London has preserved examples of everything it has been through three centuries. Paris preserves the middle ages, Rome some of the Roman Empire and patches of most things since. Which is more diverse? A range of age affords the cheapest, most innocent, most beautiful of all physical diversities; and fast-growing populations, doubling their urban fabric every generation with full monotony of age and style, are always likely to have welcome uses for the old buildings they manage to preserve.'

Old churches house new arts and crafts. New trades and services find cheap space in old back streets. Old riverside warehouses are converted into fashionable apartments. Thus economic growth does contradictory things. It replaces old structures then – too late – generates new uses for them. There is thus a presumption in favor of conserving more old buildings, streets, neighborhoods and townscapes than current market forces will preserve. Of course conservers need to discriminate. Not many people would want to exchange Georgian squares or Parisian boulevards for the older fabric which they replaced. But there is often a case for conserving more of a growing city's fabric than unhindered market forces would conserve. And because A+B>B, the case for some deliberate public conservation is often 'hard', i.e. it is a rational economic case. It does not always depend on preferring other, non-material values to economic values.

CONSERVING SOCIAL RELATIONS AND INSTITUTIONS

Settled communities accumulate informal social capital which sometimes needs to be conserved by public policy. It can be seen as a social equivalent of the individual knowledge and skills which constitute human capital. It consists of people's local knowledge, their experienced expectations of one another, their informal systems of mutual aid and exchange.

Such local social networks are often dependent on (1) patterns of paid employment and (2) the physical form and layout and communication patterns of town or country. Because of that interdependence, economists should do their best to understand relations between the economic, physical and social dimensions of local life. If they don't, they may mislead policy-makers: simple economic optimizing, by public or private investors, can too easily win economic gains for some at unreasonable social cost to others.

Here follow four examples. You need not learn all their local details. Just be sure you can see how unduly narrow economic analysis could prompt policies with disproportionate social costs.

An English example

From 1945 British governments began some major urban redevelopments with three main purposes. They were to repair wartime bomb damage. They were to restrain the outward sprawl of the bigger cities. And they were to demolish and replace bad old slum housing.

New towns were built to receive some of the displaced city-dwellers. Wholesale demolitions began in working-class quarters of some of the old cities, especially the East End of London. Good buildings were bulldozed along with bad in order to clear big sites, to allow comprehensive replanning on new principles and on large scale. Whether the old residents liked it or not, they had to move. Some did like it but many did not. Some moved into new walk-up flats or housing towers nearby. Others departed to other parts of town, to other cities, to New Towns, or to migrate overseas. Neighbors parted, brothers and sisters lost touch, old people found themselves a long way from married daughters they used to see nearly every day.

In 1954 Michael Young and Peter Willmott began to study some social effects of the physical destruction of the people's habitat. Their first findings appeared in 1957 in *Family and Kinship in East London*. In the working-class neighborhood of Bethnal Green – i.e. not in some slow-changing country village but in one of the world's biggest cities alongside one of the world's busiest ports – they found things which greatly surprised them. More than half of their sample of those who lived there had been born there. There were many links between kinship and community life, employment and economic life. 'Far from the family excluding ties to outsiders, it acts as an important means of promoting them. When a person has relatives in the borough, as most people do, each of those relatives is a go-between with other people in the district. His brother's friends are his acquaintances, if not his friends; his grandmoth-

er's neighbours so well known as almost to be his own. The kindred are . . a bridge between the individual and the community.' (p.81). Above all there were networks of family and friendship through which women helped each other to endure the behavior of governments, landlords, employers and (often) their own menfolk.

Those informal networks flourished easily in the close mixture of industry and warehouses and shops, and terrace and tenement housing with front doors and windows opening onto common pavements, and back yards abutting each other. If wholesale bulldozing of the buildings dispersed the people, the networks suffered. If the dispersal was to distant suburbs or gigantic housing towers, the networks were hard to rebuild. 'If the purpose of rehousing is to meet human needs, not as they are judged by others but as people themselves assess their own' the authors said, means must be found to 'enable the city to be rebuilt without squandering the fruits of social cohesion'. They offered excellent advice as to how that might be done. For ten years or more very little notice was taken of it. Forty years on, with many of the towers demolished and their social and economic costs well known, that advice is worth reprinting yet again: 'The sense of loyalty to each other amongst the inhabitants of a place like Bethnal Green is not due to buildings. It is due far more to ties of kinship and friendship which connect the *people* of one household to the *people* of another. In such a district community spirit does not have to be fostered, it is already there. If the authorities regard that spirit as a social asset worth preserving, they will not uproot more people, but build the new houses around the social groups to which they already belong.' (p.166)

Thirty years after Young and Willmott began their research, Alice Coleman finished hers. Where Young and Willmott studied the effects of destroying the old habitat, Coleman and her colleagues at King's College, London, studied the effects of the new habitat. The results were published in Alice Coleman and others, *Utopia on Trial: Vision and Reality in Planned Housing* (1985). The research was thorough, the conclusions devastating. Without regard for the residents' wishes, bureaucrats had created a habitat of massive apartment blocks and towers standing in semi-public, mostly unusable land. They were more expensive to build and to maintain than house-and-garden forms are. Most of them did not even save land. The housing alienated its residents, grossly restricted their domestic productivity, de-skilled them, bored them, impoverished the quality of their child and adult lives, and drove abnormal proportions of them to mental depression, vandalism and crime. The planners had poured scorn on notions of 'physical determinism'. They prove to have been dreadfully wrong. Tower-building continued for ten years after Young and Willmott's book appeared. It ceased before Alice Coleman's book appeared, and demolition of the towers began soon after it appeared.

Forty years after the original Bethnal Green study, Young and colleagues began a new study of the same area. In the last twenty years many immigrants have arrived from Bangladesh. They will soon be a majority of the local population. Coping with this influx, the housing authorities continued to make mistakes. Bangladeshi families were too often housed on their own without like families around them. Thus isolated, they have been easy targets for white racial prejudice. Only gradually have the authorities come to house them in groups of connected families. In 1999 the advice offered so long before was finally adopted, at least in part. Some priority is now given to extended families, brown and white, whose members in different generations want to live close together.

Meanwhile be careful what you conclude from the first study. The old slums were bomb-damaged and physically neglected. Private landlords could not repair or replace them at rents the people could afford. Public action *was* needed. But it could and should have repaired a good deal of the old fabric, reduced its crowding, and patched it with new housing of similar sociable style. So don't be doctrinaire. In those London conditions market forces were not very helpful and public actions were positively harmful. Better government has since improved them both – but with more help from sociologists and geographers than from economists.

An American example

Jane Jacobs lived in Hudson Street in New York city. In the 1950s city engineers planned a new urban highway which would cut through the street and destroy most of it. Defending her patch, Jane Jacobs wrote *The Death and Life of Great American Cities* (1960). At the heart of her argument and her urban philosophy was a finely detailed observation of the daily life of her street: a complex, interesting, economically efficient and socially valuable life, which depended critically on the physical fabric of the neighborhood and the continuity of its social history.

It was a short street, mostly built up to three or four floors, with buildings of diverse ages, many with shops or workshops at street level and apartments above. The close mixture of shops, workshops and apartments was efficient. The shops supplied the local residents' and workers' daily needs. That base of local custom allowed some of the businesses to specialize and attract customers from further afield, which in turn provided a wider range of goods and services to the locals. The street had the classical efficiencies of a good marketplace. It also had great social strength and efficiency. The street was safe because it was under such continuous and knowledgeable observation. Its residents, shopkeepers, daily visitors and strangers made up a familiar, mutually helpful and continuously interesting social life.

That complicated, continuous life is valuable to most of the people who share it. Its interest and safeties and efficiencies – Jane Jacobs believed – depend on (1) its fabric of new and old, cheap and dear buildings which accommodate such a variety of people and activities, and (2) its social continuity. Its complex mixture of activities and division of labor have developed slowly over time, with people and businesses adapting in very detailed ways to one another's presence and custom. From time to time households and businesses leave the street, others come to take their places, old people die, babies are born – but the changes happen bit by bit, one at a time, so that the complicated social system is never drastically upset. Piecemeal changes and long-term trends alike can be assimilated into a social system characterized by good mutual service, mutual knowledge, and a strong sense of identity. Those social assets are slow to grow. They are valuable. They are fragile. They should not be shattered and the people dispersed, either by large public works or by large private redevelopments.

Whether or not she knew it at the time, Jane Jacobs was rediscovering a classical conservative philosophy. A hundred and seventy years earlier, in his *Reflections on the Revolution in France* (1790), Edmund Burke argued in a similar way about society as a whole. A civilized society (he said) was a slow-growing, complicated structure. It should be understood as a complicated division of labor, a complicated structure of institutions, and an extremely complicated set of social roles and mutual expectations. Individuals learn particular roles in family, business, social and political life. They learn particular relations with the many different role-players they meet – how to deal with elderly aunts, different kinds of employers, friendly neighbors, unfriendly neighbors, salespersons, post office clerks, strangers in the street, welcome lovers, unwelcome lovers, and many more. They learn what to expect of each, and what each will expect of them. It takes centuries of detailed social trial and error to build such a system (Burke believed) and it takes twenty years or more of growing up and formal and informal education for each individual to learn how to live in it. There is no quick way to create such a structure or to replace it if you smash it up: no possibility of 'instant complexity'.

So on a national scale Edmund Burke was against smashing the social system by political revolution, and on a neighborhood scale Jane Jacobs was against smashing it by wholesale demolition and replacement of its streets and buildings. Public investors should plan their roads with care for more things than motorists' costs and benefits. Private developers should not be able to profit by disrupting settled neighborhoods. As a basis for urban investment, narrow economic analysis (e.g. of transport benefits, or property developers' profits) should be replaced by more extensive analysis of more of the interests concerned.

Those slow-built social networks, and relaxed relations between neighbors and strangers, don't depend on the crowded city housing in which Young and Willmott and Jane Jacobs observed them. They flourish as strongly in well-established New Towns, in innumerable house-and-garden suburbs and other patterns of settlement which have reasonably secure housing and employment. Compare, next, two village and country-town cases. For different reasons the European Economic Community and communist Hungary adopted economic policies whose purposes included some positive conservation of *rural* society: keeping more people in the country than would be kept there by narrow considerations of agricultural efficiency. The West Europeans were trying to conserve some country life for its own sake. In Hungary it was conserved not for its own sake but for some new industrial purposes.

A West European example

As Europe's Common Agricultural Policy was originally negotiated it had three main purposes. It should encourage a technical revolution in agricultural productivity. It should ensure food supplies at steady and reasonable prices. And it should bring rural standards of living nearer to city standards, especially by improving the incomes of farmers and farm workers.

The 'levelling up' of rural standards of living was wanted for reasons of social justice, and also to reduce the drift of population to the cities. But there was potential conflict between the two aims of keeping the people in the country, and improving their incomes. The world's most cost-efficient farming was in the USA – but it had been achieved by getting rid of most of the farm population. In the American model, least labor and most mechanization produced output at least cost. Was

that the type of efficiency Europe should aim at? In 1960 the people-to-land relations compared like this:

	USA	European Community
Farm workers	3.1m	3.6m
Farm acres	400m	40m
Acres per farm worker	130	11

Should the reformers clear the way for an efficient 'European prairie' by moving nine tenths of the country people into town? No, for a number of reasons. (1) With abundant land America could afford to aim at lowest-cost production, which in practice meant maximum output *per worker*. With scarce land Europe might do best to use more labor to farm more intensively for maximum output *per acre*. (2) Europe was already highly industrialized; industry was already shedding labor in the course of its own technical advancement; so if the country population moved to town it might not find enough employment there. (3) Europe's country and village life was valued for its own sake, and for its services to a country landscape that was also valued. Precisely because they *were* numerous the country people had solid political influence, and majorities used it to protect rather than dismantle their way of life. But plenty of city people also valued the village life and landscape, for both interested and disinterested reasons, and supported the policy.

Thus it seemed desirable to displace as few as possible of the rural population. Nevertheless if their incomes were to improve, their farming techniques and organization would have to go *some* way in an American direction. For more than a decade the authorities did their best to modernize – but gently. They concentrated on improving agricultural techniques, on consolidating fewer and larger farms, and on compensating the displaced people in a variety of ways. Before Britain entered in 1972 the Community was 92 per cent self-sufficient in farm produce and embarrassed by surpluses of some products. Technical change had combined with measures of protection and subsidy to achieve a good deal of the desired convergence of town and country incomes. But they had also brought some 'American' effects: fewer farms, some people gone from the villages, others unemployed, and country cottages passing from local owners to tourists and city rich.

How much further should Europe go in those directions? Was it time to review the directions as well as the pace of agricultural change?

Some reformers believed it was time for agricultural

policy itself to give way to policy with broader purposes. The countryside had always had other uses besides farming, and the other uses became more important with economic growth. Growth helped to end the worst rural poverty, so the need to increase farm incomes was a little less urgent. It equipped more households with cars, for quick and easy transport between town and country. It increased the proportions of discretionary saving and spending. Together those changes brought a steadily increasing demand in town and country alike for country pleasures and recreations, and for the conservation of traditional country life and landscape. The widest support, from Left as well as Right, was attracted by conservative proposals that the Common Agricultural Policy should become an element of a more comprehensive rural policy:

> Our rural areas are not just places in which to produce food as quickly, cheaply, and efficiently as possible, they are a resource to be husbanded, to contribute as fully as possible to the overall well-being of our society. For a number of years now there has been a growing interest in the rural areas of our increasingly industrialised world and in the ways in which they enhance that indefinable 'quality of life' which few but the most hardened urbanites would deny. The activities of the countryside concern us all, in more than just the material sense, and it is essential that our rural resources be maintained in a state of social as well as economic health.

Agricultural policies have devastated rural societies in the past. In the fifteenth century English critics complained that 'the sheep had eaten the people'. In the eighteenth century, rational profit-seeking depopulated the Scottish highlands. One day in 1981 a Welsh hamlet of eighteen cottages lost its last resident – all eighteen now had absent English owners who would use them only in summer. With no caretaker left to mind them, Welsh nationalists burned them down. The conservative critics of the Common Agricultural Policy described two alternative futures to which they feared that a policy of uniformly large farms might lead: a prairie countryside with most of the people gone and most of the buildings in ruins, or a countryside populated by city commuters and holiday-makers with no real rural society.

They proposed, instead, a new range of rural policies. They would retain a proportion of small farms 'on which the big farmer of tomorrow can prove his skill and ability'. They would encourage some reafforestation. They would bring some new occupations to rural areas to replace lost agricultural jobs: new industries

and arts and crafts, and new services to recreation and leisure. In those and other ways they would modernize but still conserve a good deal of traditional country life and landscape.

Those critics were arguing that agricultural economics was no longer a sufficient basis for rural policy. With Europe nearly self-sufficient in food it was time for policies which would reconcile efficient farming with a number of other social purposes.

> An integrated rural policy must be directed to holding together rural communities . . . and any policy aimed at improving the efficiency of agriculture in isolation from society as a whole must be declared short-sighted. . . . Rural policy must take account of social as well as economic health. It must maintain the rural way of life, modernized perhaps, but nonetheless with its distinctive flavour, at the same time as it produces food efficiently. – Jim Scott-Hopkins and John Corrie, *Towards a Community Rural Policy,* 1979, 1-2

Since that was written the policy has over-succeeded. Technical improvement of expensive, intensive farming has generated mounting surpluses of food which Europe can dispose of only by export dumping. It is right to object to the dumping and demand that it cease. But it is wrong to demand that Europe's protection of its country life and landscape should cease. It needs to develop some new means of serving its old purposes. And it deserves more respect than it gets from the foreign critics who write it off as a squalid vote-catching device. Intelligent social thought had at least as much to do with it as electoral concerns did – and the electoral appeal was to civilized concerns of many town and country people, as well as to country pockets.

An East European example

Paradoxically it was as part of a program of fast industrialization that communist Hungary deliberately conserved a lot of its village life.

From the 1950s the new communist regime wanted to revolutionize Hungarian industry and agriculture as quickly as possible. The two aims were seen as complementary: agricultural modernization would release a lot of labor, which the industrial revolution would then employ. But if a million or more 'switched' workers and their families had to move house from their country villages to live in industrial cities there would need to be a third revolution: they would have to be provided with new housing and urban infrastructure and services in town, while their old village habitations went to waste.

The planners believed that housing and urban-service investment on that scale would divert resources away from factory investment and reduce economic growth. So they conceived the idea of building the factories in reach of the village people who would supply most of their labor. Geographically, Hungary happened to have a fairly even distribution of rural population, and of country towns. Industrialize those towns, the planners reasoned, and as farm workers switch to factory work they and their families can go on living where they have always lived. Workers can commute to town daily or, if their homes are too far away for that, they can lodge in town from Monday to Friday and go home to their wives and children and old folk at weekends. The industrializing towns will need *some* new housing and services for managers and skilled workers. But most labor can continue to live in the country. Village housing and services can continue in use. The village people can continue to build any houses they need by traditional methods, without state help. So factory investment can take the lion's share of national saving and capital formation.

That strategy was adopted. It produced, by the East European standards of the time, good industrial and agricultural progress. It also produced what Hungarian sociologists called 'under-urbanization', meaning more urban jobs than urban houses. By 1970 about 10 per cent of Hungarians were commuting daily or weekly from country to town, which meant that about a quarter of all Hungarians lived in households with a commuter. That caused hardship – some workers had to travel long distances or sleep away from home; the towns got most of the limited investment in state housing and services, so the villages were starved of capital for modernization. Increasingly, an urban middle class was exploiting a rural working class.

But there were also other effects. A lot of village life was conserved, and in some critical ways it was strengthened. And there were also some wholesome effects on industrial and class relations in the towns.

Traditionally, country people depend on farm income, and industrial workers depend on industrial jobs. Unusually, in Hungary's villages, more and more workers had access to either or both. That meant they could supplement one *from* the other, or play off one *against* the other. Industrial development steadily increased town employment and the town market for farm produce. Agricultural modernization increased farm output and farm wages. Both were pushed as hard as the planners could push them, so there were times when they competed quite actively for the available

labor. Moreover there were two kinds of farm income. State farms employed wage labor, but private small-holding and market gardening also continued, and supplied more than a quarter of Hungary's food.

So *because* they still lived in the country, many of the poorer industrial workers had options which their town-dwelling managers and overseers did not have. While the communist regime lasted nobody was allowed to bargain in any organized way for higher wages, but the villagers could often bargain silently by switching from state farms to town industries, or by switching from town industries to grow more tomatos at home or to work on state farms or at village trades. Through the 1970s, partly by those means, they achieved some real improvement in the comparative wage levels of unskilled industrial labor.

Some also improved their housing and household productivity. Most of the new state housing in the towns consisted of multi-storeyed flats without private land, built by heavy construction methods, in uniform style regardless of the tenants' individual tastes. But workers who could not get state housing continued to build in traditional forms by traditional methods. Those methods actually produce more house at less cost. The advantages come from building cottages on the ground instead of higher, heavier structures; from the wider range of materials that can be used; and from letting people decide what to build for themselves. Cottages with some private land are also more adaptable to spare-time trades, vegetable gardening and so on. So contrary to official expectations, private housebuilding increased its share of national housing construction, and with economic growth and rising incomes it sometimes produced more spacious and productive housing than state construction provided.

Thus the deliberate conservation of Hungarian village life had a number of unintended effects, some of which proved to be wholesome for many of the people concerned, and self-reinforcing.

ATTITUDES TO CHANGE AND CONSERVATION

The above were local examples of conservation. For a more general example you need only return to the previous chapter. How can we *conserve* conditions for secure and stimulating childhood while radically *changing* the rights and roles of women? More generally still, how can we combine personal freedom, individuality and inventiveness (liberal ideals) with the social supports, constraints, mutual obligations, and dutiful and affectionate bonds of family, community and teamwork which are necessary to social peace and economic productivity (conservative ideals)?

Is it incoherent to want to change some things and conserve others? Of course not. Then what should be your general attitude to change? Answer: you should not have a general attitude to change. There are two reasons for that. First, it is right to favor changes for the better and oppose changes for the worse, just as it is right to conserve good features of society and wrong to conserve bad ones. Second, change and conservation often depend on each other: one *requires* the other. To reduce pollution from vehicle exhausts it may be prudent to conserve existing rail networks, however under-used they currently are. To reduce unemployment and inequality it may be necessary to conserve the existing powers of national governments. At the same time – confusingly – to conserve the natural environment on which human life depends it may be necessary to change some of the purposes for which the powers of government are used.

Those are subjects of the following chapter on natural resources. A summary of themes about both social and natural conservation can wait until the end of that chapter.

EXERCISE

List - with brief indications of your reasons - one or two qualities of your society that you would like to conserve, and one or two qualities that you would like to change. Then list some economic policies which would serve the conservative or the reformist purposes or – best of all – both. Whose support would you hope to attract for the suggested policies?

17

Threatened natural resources

We have seen how technical progress and rising productivity are changing economic activity and economists' tasks. Environmental stress is likely to be the most forceful cause of further changes – radical changes if governments grapple with the problem, or worse changes if they don't. This chapter is about economists' tasks, rather than the scale and urgency of the environmental trouble itself. But the general nature of the trouble was distilled a generation ago in the title of a notable journal article:

THE TRAGEDY OF THE COMMONS

In a paper first published in *Science,* 162, in 1968, Gareth Hardin wrote -

> The tragedy of the commons develops in this way. Picture a pasture open to all. It is to be expected that each herdsman will try to keep as many cattle as possible on the commons. Such an arrangement may work reasonably satisfactorily for centuries because tribal wars, poaching, and disease keep the numbers of both man and beast well below the carrying capacity of the land. Finally, however, comes the day of reckoning, that is, the day when the long desired goal of social stability becomes a reality. At this point, the inherent logic of the commons remorselessly generates tragedy.

> As a rational being, each herdsman seeks to maximize his gain. Explicitly or implicitly, more or less consciously, he asks, "What is the utility *to me* of adding one more animal to my herd?" This utility has one negative and one positive component.

> 1. The positive component is a function of the increment of one animal. Since the herdsman receives all the proceeds from the sale of the additional animal, the positive utility is nearly +1.

> 2. The negative component is a function of the additional overgrazing created by one more animal. Since, however, the effects of overgrazing are shared by all the herdsmen, the negative utility for any particular decision-making herdsman is only a fraction of -1.

> Adding together the component partial utilities, the rational herdsman concludes that the only sensi-

> ble course for him to pursue is to add another animal to his herd. And another; and another. . . But this is the conclusion reached by each and every rational herdsman sharing a commons. Therein is the tragedy. Each man is locked into a system that compels him to increase his herd without limit – in a world that is limited. Ruin is the destination toward which all men rush, each pursuing his own best interest in a society that believes in the freedom of the commons. Freedom in a commons brings ruin to all.

Or it brings new work for government. To avert the tragedy, people have to limit their numbers and regulate their use of resources. A conserving society has to amend some of its ideas of individual freedom and social purpose. It has to change some of its economic organization. It has to meld its methods of economic and ecological analysis to equip its people and policymakers to know what they are doing locally, regionally, nationally and globally to the resources on which their survival depends. Among the new requirements –

- New kinds of resource accounting are needed.

- Conservation often means producing less than we could, i.e. it means a degree of 'voluntary scarcity'. Output must be determined by other things besides supply and demand and immediate need.

- Conservation calls for collective decisions about what may be produced, where, by which methods, using which resources. Those policies inevitably affect the distribution of wealth and income here and now, because in practice it is not possible to control *what* is produced without affecting *who gets it.* Theories and explanations of the distribution of income need to be amended accordingly.

- There must also be some deliberate distribution of income between generations. In relation to old age pensions you noticed that transferring *rights* to income over time affects the distribution of income between persons. Conserving physical resources for future use may be seen as transferring *real* income over time, which also affects the distribution of income between persons. Economists need to be able to analyse the relations between the time distributions and the class and individual distributions.

(Notice how these and other changes are complicating the work of economists who study the distribution of income and advise about income policies or conservation policies. The distribution of income as traditionally understood – i.e. the distribution of income between persons at any date – now needs to be related to (1) the relevant market forces; (2) any deliberate income controls which may be introduced to retrain inflation; (3) arrangements to transfer rights to income from people's earning to their non-earning years; and (4) any deliberate distribution of real income between generations. Each affects all the others to some degree. Explanations of the distribution of income must take account of those interrelations.)

The first part of this chapter will deal in turn with –

- population numbers
- the idea of 'deliberate scarcity' or 'enough is enough';
- relations between conservation and economic growth; and
- a classification of things which people may want to conserve.

The second part of the chapter, about who gets what, will deal with -

- relations between environmental policies and the distribution of wealth, income, employment and 'environmental enjoyment'; and
- the equity and efficiency of alternative methods of environmental management.

The chapter won't make you an expert environmental economist. It is here to show some further ways in which economists' theories and methods need to adapt to changes in the life which they concern.

WHAT TO CONSERVE, AND WHY

POPULATION

Some ecologists have argued that the increase of human numbers is the sufficient cause of most environmental troubles, and 'zero population growth' is their only cure. Farmers don't overstock their pastures; humans should not over-populate the earth.

That analogy is misleading. There are limits to what farm animals can eat but there are no such limits to humans' capacity to consume, transform or spoil the earth's resources. Environmental damage is a product of numbers x quantity and type of resource use per head. North Americans and Europeans 'consume', directly or indirectly, many times more material per head than South Asians do, so twenty or more South Asian births currently threaten less environmental damage than one Northern birth does. But those relations may change with the rich countries' policies, with South Asian economic growth, with changing technology, and with the degradation or exhaustion of existing resources.

Methodology

Human numbers are still important. Economists and demographers have long interested themselves in the causes of population growth, stability and decline. Many of their efforts to theorize those causes have been incompetent, for familiar scientist reasons. They have supposed that constant principles of human behavior would allow their social science to imitate the more formal, timeless and determinate branches of natural science; or they have supposed that theories of animal ecology could sufficiently explain and predict human behavior. The history of those blunders won't help you to understand human ecology, but it reinforces the methodological lessons of Part One, so a brief sketch of it follows.

People as rabbits Some classical economists led by Malthus (1766-1834) believed that people usually breed up to the available food supply. Unless 'moral restraint' leads them to marry later and copulate less, the masses can never expect much material progress. If they produce more, that will merely allow more babies to survive. Gross economic growth will not mean growth per head. *Example:* Through the eighteenth century the introduction of the potato enabled the Irish to double their food supply, and they responded by doubling their numbers. When disease destroyed the potato crop in 1846-7, starvation and emigration drastically reduced the population.

The next century of history belied that theory. The industrializing countries produced rising material standards for their people, who proceeded to breed *less*. The experts responded with a new theory. Like the old one, it asserted that population numbers responded automatically to the level of income – but in a different way. Industrializing countries (it said) 'jump' their population numbers from a stable low level to a stable high level in a way which can be represented like this –

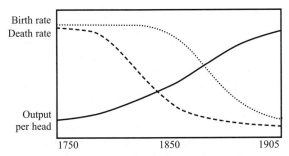

Birth rate
Death rate

Output
per head

1750   1850   1905

Figure 17.1 A mistaken theory of human ecology

This generation of experts theorized that in the old peasant societies women had all the babies they physically could, so the birth rate was at its natural physiological limit. The death rate was high too, from poverty and ignorance. High birth and death rates balanced each other and maintained a stable or very slow-growing population. Through the early stages of modernization the high birth rate continued but improvements in food supply and sanitation reduced the death rate, so there was rapid population growth. Then the steam engine made output grow even faster than population, so contrary to Malthus' expectations there was some growth of income per head and some improvement of the masses' material standards. After a time the birth rate began to fall. When it bottomed out at the same low level as the death rate, numbers were stable again. There had meanwhile been a big increase in population, and a permanent change in its age structure.

Guesswork Why did the birth rate behave like that? Guessing rather than researching, economists and demographers explained it as follows: Peasants breed freely because (1) they have no effective contraceptives, (2) children supply their farm and household labor, (3) they need children to care for them in old age, and (4) infant mortality is so high that it is necessary to have a lot of babies to be *sure* of having adult children.

With economic growth and urbanization those conditions change. (1) Contraceptive aids become available. (2) More of the babies survive so fewer need to be born to assure family continuity. (3) Children no longer supply their parents with cheap labor. Instead, rising aspirations make parents maintain children through long periods of education. (4) Public pensions are invented to provide for old age. Children who were once an asset become a luxury or a liability, so people have fewer of them.

Formal theory That historical explanation was unresearched and partly fictitious. (Some of the facts were

true but others, and some strands of the causal analysis, were not.) But theory (those unwary theorists believed) could be simpler: the *rate* of *population growth* is a function of the *stage* of *economic growth*. (Forget the human relations and intentions. The algebraic relation is all the smart theorist needs.)

Policy implications By deduction from that one-liner there was a policy implication for much of the Third World. Once modernization starts, cuts the death rate and unleashes the population explosion, it should be completed as quickly as possible to the mature stage at which it will cut the birth rate, stop the explosion and stabilize population again. If economic growth lags, i.e. if it fails to exceed the rate of population growth, there will be no growth of real income per head. The birth rate will not fall. The society will then face a Malthusian catastrophe: numbers will go on multiplying until sheer starvation stops them.

As late as the 1970s some ecologists and others were using that theory to oppose most international aid from rich to poor countries. They reasoned as follows: The world's physical resources are so limited that the Third World's two billion people can never achieve American/European standards of living. However hard they try for economic growth, resource limits will prevent their achieving the material standard at which the birth rate falls. Action which starts modernizing those societies will therefore start a population explosion which cannot be stopped by further economic growth. It will continue until it is stopped by mass starvation. It is kinder not to start such a process.

What was wrong with that theory?

First it was built on bad history. Research (mostly by historians, scarcely any by demographers or economists) has since shown that the peasant societies did not have uniformly high birth rates. Birth rates rose with modernization at some times and places. French birth rates on the other hand were already low before any significant modernization. The theorists were guessing some of the hard facts instead of researching them. They were also guessing rather than researching the people's reasons for having or not having children.

Second, if the theorized regularity was there at all, it was there because *people* were *choosing* to have or not to have babies. That sort of conscious reasoning and choosing can change. So even if the behavior is observed to be regular, it may be best to generalize it in human rather than abstract terms. Instead of saying

The rate of population growth is a function of the *stage of economic growth.*

it is safer to say

> Uneducated peasants expect children to increase their incomes. Educated city-dwellers expect children to cost them money. So as their incomes grow, as they learn to read and write, and as they move from country to town, most men and women choose to have fewer children.

Seeing that, historians may be prompted to check its past truth. Even if true of the past, economists can see how such behavior might change in changing conditions. Feminists can see how it might change if women got more control of reproduction. Policy-makers can judge how it might be encouraged to change by educational or other means. Stated in those human terms nobody need mistake it for an unchangeable economic law. About thoughtful behavior, language can communicate more than algebra can.

In the twentieth century the behavior has in fact been quite irregular. In the rich countries birth rates rise and fall, apparently responding in changing ways to war and peace, boom and slump, and changing patterns of culture, belief and family life. People learn from experience, foresee environmental troubles, change their social rules and private values, enjoy larger or smaller families. The 'net reproduction rate' in the US was twice as high in 1960 as it was in 1930 and in 1980. In France and Australia it fell about 30 per cent from the 1960s to the 1970s. Poor countries also varied their rates. The Chinese communist government at first encouraged population growth, then reversed its policy to impose a 'one-child' rule on Chinese women. Other persuasions and compulsions have been applied with some effect in India and elsewhere.

Faced with such fluctuations demographers now disaggregate and detail and qualify their forecasts more carefully. They study women of childbearing age. How many girl babies are they currently producing, how many may those girls in their turn produce? Though women can bear children for about forty years, most bear them during a much shorter phase of their lives, so demographers break the figures down by ten or five-year periods. From figures of those already born, with margins of uncertainty for possible war and migration and changing death rates, it is possible to calculate how many women will be aged 20 to 24, 25 to 29, 30 to 34, and so on, at future dates up to twenty years ahead.

Knowing that 'age-specific fertility' will tell you the reproductive *possibilities* at those dates. But it will not tell you what use the people will choose to make of those possibilities. In many developed countries there

was a low birth rate through the 1930s. There was consequently a shortage of potential mothers twenty years later. Did that reduce the 1950s birth rate? No, in many countries the rate *rose* in the 1950s – the fewer women had more babies each than their mothers had done. Those girl babies of the 1950s and 1960s reached childbearing age in the 1970s and 1980s. Instead of their numbers raising the birth rate, their choices lowered it: they averaged fewer babies each than their mothers had. They had easier means of contraception. There was rising unemployment, specially for their generation. There were rising anxieties about atomic and environmental damage. There was some pessimism about children's prospects. As feminist progress improved women's working and earning opportunities, more women preferred childless lifestyles.

Some theorists have since built those expectations into theories which predict a catastrophic collapse of world population. How long may it be before coal and oil and forest interests have experts tell us that there is consequently no further need for environmental restraint?

Conclusion

You've met it before and will meet it again: Good theories and generalizations about relations between social variables make clear what *kinds* of causation are involved. When the links are human choices, people who use the theory need to be alert to how conscious, and free or habitual or constrained, the choices are, and how possible it is that they may change.

DELIBERATE SCARCITY, OR 'ENOUGH IS ENOUGH'

Environmental plenty or scarcity, and safety or danger, are products of population x resource use per head. Public policy can try to control the numbers, or the use of resources, or both. You just considered the numbers. Now consider the deliberate conservation of resources.

Until recently it seemed safe to assume that people have generally wanted to produce as much as they reasonably could: they have wanted some best balance of income, work satisfaction and leisure. If for environmental reasons we are moving from that age-old state of involuntary scarcity to an historically new condition of deliberately chosen scarcity (or deliberately chosen sufficiency), that must bring substantial changes to some elements of economic motivation, management and policy-making. People will want expert help with a new range of policy choices. *How* should they go about deciding what should be produced, where, by which methods, from which resources? Exactly *how* should private market demand be related to public environmental policy? (There are many alternative ways of doing it.) Decisions which could once be taken by optimizing a single value – for example to yield most profit, or to produce most at given cost – must now be taken with an eye to multiple and often conflicting purposes.

Notice that such choices may be further complicated if there are other reasons besides environmental reasons for limiting material production. The previous chapter reviewed some of those other reasons. There is mounting evidence that for societies as a whole there may be a comparatively modest material standard of living above which more income does not generally increase human happiness. When people have abundant food and warmth, comfortable housing, a short working week and long annual holidays, secure pensions in retirement, generous education and health care, and diversely interesting recreations (but not necessarily expensive, mechanized or pollutant recreations) – i.e. when they have the average income achieved by the United States about 1950 and by most European countries at various dates since – then better *distribution* of wealth and income and welfare may increase happiness, but it seems unlikely that further growth of total income will do so. So why do people continue to work and compete for more? Perhaps they want to accumulate capital for greater individual security. (But secure superannuation should supply that.) Perhaps they are conditioned to see capital wealth, high income and conspicuous consumption as symbols of achievement. But other cultures have conditioned their people to look for other rewards and reassurances – perhaps a reformed culture could bring up less acquisitive, less competitive people, or people who competed in other, uncommercial ways. And such an alternative society might have human and social advantages as well as better resource conservation. The social reasons canvassed by Scitovsky, Hirsch and others might not be enough by themselves to induce a change of heart. But as we turn to environmental issues, remember that the *need* to limit production for resource and environmental reasons may be reinforced by some *desire* to limit it for social and cultural reasons.

New collective choices will not be universally agreed. Not everyone will agree that 'enough is enough'. As deliberate conservation develops, there will be conflicts about the desirable volume and composition of the national product. Those new conflicts will complicate the old competition for shares of the product. (If we must use less energy, *who* should use *how much* less? If we must produce it by more expensive methods,

who should pay? If we must close down pollutant industries, should we compensate owners who lose capital and workers who lose income?) So besides needing new analyses to assist the new collective choices, we may also need to amend our explanations of the distribution of wealth and income.

Here is the same theme in simpler form:

A fable Each summer a family rents a holiday cottage deep in a forest, without power or piped water. They have to carry water in buckets from a dammed stream half a mile away. So collectively they have to balance their desire for water against the labor of fetching it, and they have to resolve any conflicts about their individual shares of the work, and of the water.

In the course of economic development, upstream landowners divert so much water that the stream only flows in wintertime. Next summer our family arrives to find the dam already half empty. Now they have to take more complicated decisions. Besides balancing their need for water against the labor of fetching it, they also have to consider:

- Must they limit their consumption to spin out the supply over their two-week holiday?

- More families will follow them through the rest of the summer. How much water should they leave for their successors?

- What if they leave a generous supply, but the first successors are greedier and scoff the lot?

- *Social control (1):* Should they try to get the landlord to enforce fair rationing on all the tenants?

- *Social control (2):* Should they themselves take to fetching water in pairs, or see that children are always accompanied by adults, so that no member of the family can be suspected of secretly using more than a fair share?

- Should they wash in the dam (to conserve water) or wash in buckets then throw the bath-water away (to keep the dam clean for drinking)?

- Should the landlord reduce the rent because there is less water than there used to be – or should he *add* a charge for the water because it has become scarce?

- Or should they all say 'To hell with these complications. Let's use the water freely and hope for rain.' (They may pin their hopes to prayer and rain-dancing – or to a technical breakthrough in precipitating rain by cloud-seeding.)

You can see that their decisions are more complicated than they used to be. And because of that, economists'

tasks of advising, predicting or explaining their behavior are more complicated and perhaps more uncertain
than before.

CONSERVATION AND ECONOMIC GROWTH

Most conservation involves some deliberate restraint of
present consumption. But it does not follow that all conservation is at the cost of economic growth, or that all
growth degrades the environment. Relations between
growth and conservation are more variable than that.

In the fable you just read, the people responded to the
drought in a passive way by using less water. Suppose
now that they are more inventive than that. They go to
work to line the dam with clay to stop it leaking. They
roof it to stop it evaporating. They dig a well to get
ground water. They recycle some metal parts from a
junk yard to build a still to purify their bath water so that
it can be re-used. To fire the still they gather dead wood
from the forest floor. That reduces the risk of forest fires
and makes room for more live undergrowth, so even the
consumption of fuel conserves the forest rather than
degrading it.

Thus the people work to accumulate capital, increase
productivity, and increase their real income. They have
responded to drought with a burst of economic growth
which improves *both* conservation *and* material standards of living.

Suppose that instead of a recycled woodburning still
they bought a new oil-fired still whose sulphurous
smoke defoliated trees. They would then conserve one
renewable resource (water) but degrade two others (air
and forest) and deplete a finite, non-renewable resource
(oil).

Water and wood happen to be renewable resources.
When non-renewable resources are threatened, growth
and conservation may be harder to reconcile. With
man's technical capacity to transform matter limited as
it is at present, the world has only so much of coal, oil,
rare metals and other finite resources. Some kinds of
chemical and radioactive pollution are irreversible.
Genetic stocks of plant and animal species once lost
may be irreplaceable despite the new cloning possibilities. So there are plenty of real conflicts between
conservation and growth, and between conservation and
current rates of consumption *without* any further
growth.

Economists can help to clarify those conflicts in a
number of ways. But there are also larger disagreements. Extreme believers in Growth Regardless
confront extreme environmentalists who want to Stop

Growth Now and return to simple village life. Can economists contribute anything useful to those debates?

They can perhaps argue like this:

Conservation and growth have common aims. They
are both programs to provide for the material needs of
people in the future.

Believers in growth stress the *producible* resources
which future people will need. They will need physical
and human capital: buildings, machinery, infrastructure,
information systems, techniques, skills, education – all
products of economic growth.

Environmentalists stress the *exhaustible* resources
which the same future people will need. They will need
clean air, fertile soil, mineral fuels and metals, genetic
stocks of plant and animal species, unspoiled landscapes, habitable environments – all finite resources
which need conserving.

Relations between the two – between producible
resources and exhaustible resources – are not uniform,
they are diverse. For example –

- There can be direct conflict between the two. If
  growth increases the use of oil, the world's oil will
  run out sooner. If there is an international limit on
  whaling, the whale-based industries can't grow.

- The resources can complement each other. Oil-fired
  factories won't be productive if the oil runs out. But
  saved oil won't be usable if there is no industry to
  find, extract, process and transport it.

- The resources can be alternatives. Exhaustible oil
  and inexhaustible sunshine may be alternative
  sources of energy. (But it may require economic
  growth including some growth of oil-fired industries
  to develop the means of using the solar energy.)

- Growth may require conservation. The paper industry won't continue to grow if it doesn't replant its
  forests.

- Conservation may require growth. We could conserve energy by insulating buildings properly – but it
  would take some growth to produce the insulation.

- Relations between producible, renewable and
  exhaustible resources may be open to choice.
  Remember the drought-stricken family of our fable.
  They needed to distil water. One way of doing it
  would conserve both water and forest. An alternative
  way would conserve water by exhausting oil and
  degrading forest.

Moral: Beware of all-embracing, undiscriminating attitudes to growth or conservation. It may be wise to plan
prudently for the future, and to forego present con-

sumption for the benefit of future people. But to simply 'ban growth' may not be an effective way to do it. Effective long-term conservation does need to be based on more radical self-restraint than prevails now. It almost certainly depends on reducing the rich countries' material standards of living. But it also needs to be based on two kinds of detailed knowledge: (1) technical knowledge of industrial processes and their complicated chemical and other effects on producible, renewable, degradable and exhaustible resources; and (2) political understanding of *who* is expected to do without present resources for the benefit of *which* present and future people.

Choices

The world has long had examples of 'perfect fit' between systems of production and systems of conservation. 'Conservative Dutch farming' – as practised by many more people than the Dutch – does not degrade or deplete the land. It aims at the best annual output *that can be maintained indefinitely*. Trees are planted as trees are used; pasture is not over-stocked; arable land is cropped, rotated, fallowed and naturally fertilized to maintain perpetual fertility, and contour-ploughed to conserve water and avoid erosion. Drinking water comes from clean wells and streams, human and animal manures enrich the soil, controlled hunting keeps the wild game at useful levels.

But that model relation between people and land has not held for the world as a whole, or for most of its cities and industries. With accumulating damage from modern pesticides and herbicides and chemical fertilizers it no longer holds for farming either, over much of the world. Instead, the relation between the human race and its natural resources is perhaps in mid-passage between one historical condition and another.

In the past, people took deliberate care of many local resources, but with rare exceptions nobody kept count of total national stocks or the whole world's stocks of life-sustaining materials: air, water, mineral fuels and metals, soil, vegetation, animal life. In the future, human life on earth may come to depend on population control and on worldwide monitoring, management and rationing of physical resources. Just now we are somewhere between the first condition and the second.

The world's air has rising quantities of chemical and particle pollution. Its upper layers admit more harmful solar radiation than they did. Water and soil are accumulating metallic and other poisons, radioactivity, and forms of organic life which spoil the resources for human uses. Some of the mess is sewage but most of it is produced industrially. Some of it pollutes only the nations which produce it, but some pollutes neighboring nations or the whole globe.

There are many effective local environmental controls. There are some regional and national controls, with increasingly complicated and expensive attempts to regulate the processes, products and by-products of pollutant industries. There has been progress here and there: some cities have cleaner air, some rivers have cleaner water than they have had for generations. But on balance the pollution is ahead of the efforts to contain it. There are still very few effective international or world controls. And some of the national controls introduced through the third quarter of the century are already repealed, weakened or under attack. Recording the effective withdrawal of protection from some U.S. forests in 1995, two investigators contrasted the improving environmental behavior of American households with the deteriorating behavior of business and government –

> A quarter-century after the first Earth Day the corporate counter-attack launched in the late 1970s is nearly complete. As citizens virtuously warehouse their newspapers, seek redemption in glass and aluminium and recycle their direct mail pleas from mainstream environmental groups into properly labelled receptacles, they may be too busy acting locally to notice the national picture. – Alexander Cockburn & Ken Silverstein, *Washington Babylon,* 1996, p.247

Those authors perceived an American scandal. Earlier, in a paper called 'Economics of the coming space-ship Earth' (1966), Kenneth Boulding had predicted a more general change of direction. When people first perceived that their resources were running out, they would slow the degradation by developing new kinds of individual and collective self-restraint. But as the resources dwindled, succeeding generations would have a change of heart, and quicken the degradation by competing greedily for shares of what remained.

If American government is as corruptible as Cockburn and Silverstein believe, and America's international political and corporate influence continues – or if Boulding's misgivings about everyone's human nature are justified – there may not be much point in exploring the possible ends and means of environmental reform. But with those two as the likely alternatives to effective conservation, it's worth a try.

Tasks

What follows is a standard way of classifying the natural resources which people may want to conserve. As you read through the list, notice (1) how the introduction of deliberate resource management may affect traditional economic processes and policies, and (2) what changing tasks economists may face, both in planning and managing a conserving society and in explaining and judging its economic performance.

Exhaustible resources For example coal and oil. *Necessary information:* Geological knowledge of known and estimated reserves. Chemical and engineering knowledge of present and potential uses. Economic knowledge of costs and products of alternative uses, and comparative costs of using alternative resources. *Policies:* How fast should we use up the reserves? Nationally, should we try to use our own deposits first, or import all we can and conserve our own? Should we use oil only where there are no substitutes for it, or only where there are no good substitutes – i.e. should we use it only for plastics and aviation fuel? For public road transport? Private cars? Should we stop using it to propel ships and trains, heat buildings, generate electricity, for all of which there are alternative fuels? *Methods of control:* Taxing, pricing, regulating, rationing? How should the costs and benefits of control be distributed? *Conflicting purposes:* The immediate substitutes for oil are coal and atomic energy. They are more plentiful than oil but also more pollutant. Will our grandchildren prefer to be immobilized, poisoned, or irradiated?

Renewable resources For example, forests. *Necessary information:* Technical information about present acreage and composition; rates of growth of present species; current rates of depletion. Where and how forest could be extended. *Renewal:* (1) Simple replanting of present species on present acreage won't provide a perpetual resource – trees don't grow fast enough to keep up with current rates of consumption. (2) There is also some reversible pollution (for which, see next section). Some not-too-expensive changes to coal-fired and oil-fired industries could stop the destruction of forest by acid rain and other air-borne pollution. *Competing uses:* Forests perform important but imperfectly understood functions for the world's air supply. They also supply paper, building materials, plant and animal habitats, water catchments and many human recreations. Many of the uses are mutually compatible, but maintaining *all* the uses raises the costs of *some* of them. (For example clearfelling produces the cheapest pulp and building timber, but selective cutting, though more expensive, allows the forest's other uses to continue.) *Policies:* How should forest be owned and managed? How should its various users be allocated their shares of benefits and costs? Should the production and consumption of forest be brought into balance? By cutting consumption (by taxing, pricing, regulating, rationing?); by planting more forest (in place of which other land uses?); by planting faster-growing species (with some loss of habitat and recreational quality)? Or by what mix of those methods? Economists can contribute a good deal to that policy-making: costing, process analysis or input-output analysis, relations with complementary and alternative industries.

Reversible pollution For example, water. Human and industrial wastes, agricultural poisons and fertilizers, and the damming and diversion of natural watercourses have contributed to the pollution of rivers, lakes and groundwater. *Reversal:* Natural evaporation and rain are good purifiers. Techniques exist for removing sewage and other water-borne pollutants. Lakes and rivers have been cleaned up by preventive methods, by intercepting the wastes which used to be discharged into them. *Policies:* As before – how much cleaning up is worth its costs? How should its costs and benefits be distributed? For example which waste processing and disposal services should be private and which should be public, and should the public ones be financed from user charges or taxation?.

Irreversible pollution Examples: A global greenhouse effect from the increase of atmospheric carbon dioxide; a global ice age from the increase of atmospheric dust; other global dangers from decay of the ozone layer; local dangers from accumulating radioactivity, lead, asbestos, carcinogens, etc. *Policies:* There are technological risks to be judged, optimistic or pessimistic gambles to be taken. There are conflicts of national interest and generational interest. There are now effective international controls for a few of the worst pollutants, but so far there are more broken promises than concerted action about the greenhouse and ozone problems.

RECAPITULATION

This chapter is noticing a number of reasons why economists' theories and methods need to adapt to new environmental problems and conservationist purposes.

We first asked whether conservation and economic growth are simple alternatives. No – their relations can be quite complicated. Some kinds of growth require some conservation, some kinds of conservation would require some further economic growth. Alternative methods of production can have different environmental effects, alternative methods of conservation can have different effects on production. Relations between growth and conservation need to be studied in detail, case by case.

So do relations between conservation and population numbers. If birth rates and death rates were ever simply determined by economic conditions, they are no longer. Rich populations frequently vary their birth rates. Poor countries with similar GNP per head vary widely in their birth rates, death rates and expectations of life. Most rich countries still average longer life, lower birth rates and less population growth than most poor countries. But in both, deliberate individual and collective choices appear to be increasingly important in determining population, and long-term demographic forecasting is accordingly conditional and uncertain.

We have listed types of things which people may want to conserve. Exhaustible and renewable natural resources. Resources subject to reversible or irreversible spoiling. And in the previous chapter, heritage of arti-facts, buildings, townscapes, landscapes and social structures and continuities of town or country life, including conditions of family life which can make childhood enjoyable and help parents to bring up sociable, productive people.

Environmental stresses strengthen the case for broadening the basis on which we judge economic performance. Remember (whether or not you agree with it) the opinion that economic activity should be judged by reference to its effects on human capital, employment, the distribution of income and quality of life, and other important outcomes including the conservation of threatened resources, *as well as* by its output per head. These more complex judgments are harder to make. Not all their components can be measured. They cannot expect to be unanimous. But they are better for many purposes than the traditional cost-efficient or Pareto-efficient judgments are.

Conservation policies should be judged, like other policies, by as many as possible of their important effects. That holds for their aims, and also – our next subject – for their ways and means.

HOW TO CONSERVE, AND FOR WHOSE BENEFIT

From *what* to conserve we turn to *how* to conserve, at whose cost and for whose benefit. Remember that the purpose is still to notice how economists' tasks are changing. What theories and methods will help most to answer questions like these:

- If we want to conserve resource A, which way of doing it will cost least now? Cost least later? Cost least money, or least environmental damage? Be fairest? Increase or reduce inequalities? Favor men or favor women? Favor capital or favor labor? Favor the farmers or favor the townspeople? Lose least votes?

- If we try to conserve quantity A of resource B by methods C and D, how will the costs and benefits of that action be distributed to which classes and groups? How certain or uncertain are these expectations and if they prove to be wrong what are the foreseeable risks, and for whom?

TIME AND CLASS DISTRIBUTION OF THE COSTS AND BENEFITS OF CONSERVATION

Conservation affects the distribution of wealth and income. It is rarely possible to control the use of a resource without also affecting who gets what shares of it, at what cost or price. Examples:

- There are many alternative ways of conserving energy. Some ways would stop the rich wasting it. Some ways would stop the poor getting it, which might freeze or starve or immobilize them. Some ways would increase employment, some ways would reduce it. Some ways would increase industrial costs, some would chiefly affect necessaries, some would chiefly affect luxuries and recreations.

- There are many ways of conserving forest. Some would make forest owners and paper makers richer, others would make them poorer. Some would reduce newsprint, some would chiefly reduce newspaper advertising and needless packaging. Some would open the forests to hikers and holiday-makers, others would exclude them.

- There are many ways of conserving the layout and buildings of old city streets and neighbourhoods. Some ways conserve them for the people who already live in them. Some ways drive those people out and bring richer people in. Some (for example purchases for public housing) bring poor people in. Some methods cost the owners or residents money, others cost the taxpayers.

Time and class effects

Besides being distributed between *classes of people,* the costs and benefits of conservation are also distributed *over time.* Relations between the time and class distributions depend on the nature of the resources and the methods of conservation. Some resources can be conserved for perpetual use (clean air and water supplies, beautiful landscapes). Some are saved from consumption by some people now so that they can be consumed by other people later (oil, coal, other minerals). Some things are transferred from use by some people (now and later) to use by other people (now and later) as when government buys private land and opens it as a public park.

If things are running out, who should have what shares of them, now and later, until they are gone? Using exhaustible resources later is not necessarily better than using them now. It depends who gets them at either date. Poverty and premature death are as bad for poor people now as for their grandchildren later: except for its uncertainties, time does not alter most principles of distributive justice. Nor does exhaustibility. If exhaustible goods ought to be distributed fairly, so should any other life-saving or comforting goods, whether they are scarce because they are running out or because of ordinary costs of production.

Equal rationing at controlled prices (as practised in wartime) may wring more wellbeing from less material. It may buy time to develop substitutes. It may reserve scarce resources for essential uses, and prevent wasteful uses of them. But rationing by price, or by quota proportionately to past use, can mean that the poor get less now so that the rich can enjoy more for longer.

Many programs express genuinely unselfish desires to suffer more scarcity now in order to reserve resources for people not yet born. This can be compared with attempts to persuade rich countries to give international aid. The purpose is the same: to save strangers from hardship and early death. Half a century of passionate and expert effort has not persuaded any national population to give as much as 1 per cent of its output for that. On the face of it, intergenerational aid looks even less likely than international aid. The people to be helped are more remote. They are so far off in an imperfectly predictable future that we cannot be very sure about their needs, or that aid will actually reach them or do them much good. And if people do nevertheless become generous in that way, why should they give to unborn poor rather than to poor Africans or Javanese here and now? Many of these programs, though generous, are limited by national or family feeling.

Direct and indirect effects

Conservation of a particular resource often affects other distributions too. It may redistribute wealth by altering the ownership or value of private assets. It often redistributes income through its effects on employment. Conservation programs of different kinds can extinguish jobs, create jobs, relocate jobs and people, alter the safety or skill requirements of particular occupations.

Economists have to do their best to trace and measure that wide range of direct and indirect distributional effects of conservationist policies. They can apply some general principles but they usually also need detailed study of local facts. Suppose, for example, that two countries decide to conserve oil chiefly by taxing its use to raise its price. That policy can have different effects if the countries have different economic structures and levels of income:

The rich get more oil and the poor get less In Country A oil is used to fuel road, rail and air transport and to generate electricity. Homes are heated, water is heated and cooking is fuelled by oil directly, or by oil-fired electricity. The climate is cool-temperate and there are no cheap alternative energy sources. So when the price of oil rises, all the related costs rise. Rich people can afford the new prices and they reduce their consumption very little. (They save a little less, and spend a little less on luxuries, so some jobs disappear.) The poor spend mostly on necessaries. They cut their oil-related spending as much as they can bear, putting up with simpler cooking, colder houses, etc. So they get less of the scarce resource than they would have got at the old low price.

The rich get less oil and the poor get more Country B uses oil for much the same purposes but it is poorer, more unequal, more inventive, and has a colder climate. The poor live as tenants, mostly in cheaply built apartment blocks, and use public transport or old cars. The rich have the new cars, and own their houses and gardens. When the oil price soars, the rich adapt. They trade in their gas-guzzling cars for new, lightweight, fuel-efficient models. As before, they get their firms to buy most of their air tickets. They insulate and double-glaze their houses. They junk their electric and oil-fired stoves and water heaters and space heaters and replace them with solid-fuel systems burning cheap coke or wood, often with supplementary solar units. Thus they replace their household capital with equipment which halves their oil consumption and keeps their overall energy bills down.

The poor can't do any of those things. They can't get their landlords to insulate their housing properly, or to convert to solid-fuel or solar heating systems. Those with their own housing can't afford the capital costs of conversion. The poor must still get to work and services. They go by public transport, whose fares rise with the rising fuel costs. Or they drive their big old inefficient cars, because second-hand cars are all they can afford. Being poor, they have never used more power than they could help; in this cold country they dare not reduce their house-heat any further and they dare not stop travelling to work. So they pay the new oil prices in full and have that much less income left to spend on food and other necessaries.

So in this country the rich respond to the price rise by using less oil than they did. Oil supplies will last longer, the poor will get a *higher* proportion of them, and the poor will still be worse off.

Moral: keep your theories 'open' to changing realities, including human inventiveness. Be alert to test your generalizations against the facts of the case, directly researched.

> ### EXERCISE
>
> Can you think of an oil policy for Country B which would reduce both oil consumption and inequalities between rich and poor?

METHODS OF CONSERVATION

Threatened resources can be conserved in a variety of ways. Methods differ in how effectively they conserve the resource, and in the way they distribute the costs and benefits of conserving it. Some resources may be conserved by any of the alternative methods listed below. With others there may be fewer options – for example, fresh air can't be conserved by rationing it, or raising its price, or taking it into public ownership. Methods have to fit the nature of the resorce and the purpose of conserving it. But as policy-makers consider what to do in particular cases, they should have in mind such general alternatives as education, regulation, rationing, taxing and pricing and price-controlling, and appropriate ownership.

Education

If people know better they often do better. Education is specially effective where there are no conflicts of interest and where individual action is needed. For example

it is possible to reduce private heating costs, conserve fossil fuels and reduce air pollution by applying better heat insulation to houses and workplaces. People who know it are likelier to do it.

Though education tends to be most effective where there are no conflicts of interest it may also help where conflicts do exist. Environmental education works on people's social concerns and values. They learn to recognize environmental hazards, to worry about dwindling resources, to welcome environmental policies and tolerate their costs. They carry their litter out of parks and forests as a matter of citizens' pride or ramblers' expertise. In the long run parents and teachers may prove to be the most effective of all environmental reformers.

But where there are serious conflicts of interest, or where environmental management requires substantial organization or coordination, education alone will rarely suffice.

Regulation

Many environmental issues involve conflicts of interest which cannot be resolved by the market, i.e. by bargaining between those concerned. Examples –

- A scarce resource needs to be rationed, as in the tragedy of the commons. Appeals for voluntary restraint either don't work at all, or merely allow those who don't exercise restraint to win business at the expense of those who do.

- There are three ways for paper manufacturers to treat the forests which supply them with their raw material. (1) They can clearfell, and not replant for future generations. (2) They can clearfell, and replant. (3) They can fell selectively, so that the forest continues to serve other uses as well (and replants itself without assistance). The first method is the most antisocial and usually the cheapest. The third is best but usually dearest. Left to the market, the worst-behaved paper-makers will drive out the better-behaved.

- Manufacturers who pollute air and rivers can often under-sell those who contain and process their wastes properly. Once again the anti-social operators tend to drive out the better-behaved.

If such industries are to continue in competitive private ownership they need to be regulated, with the same rules applied impartially to all competitors. (Should such regulated competitors also be tariff-protected against imports from unregulated competitors abroad – perhaps competitors in poor countries whose governments believe they can't yet afford high environmental standards? You will meet that question in Chapter 49 on trade policy.)

Commerce and industry have long been regulated for many other purposes, so in principle there is nothing very new in regulating them for the purposes of resource and environmental management. Accordingly public authorities now regulate land uses, farm practices, the disposal of solid, liquid and airborn wastes, the use of chemical fertilizers and pesticides, the preservation of valued landscapes and townscapes and buildings, and other subjects of resource and environmental policy. The principle may be old, but the wider its uses the more work there is likely to be for economists. Regulating industries for environmental purposes is a difficult art to which economists contribute in at least four ways –

- **Resource accounting** Geologists and other specialists are the primary accountants of physical resources. But economists are needed to forecast demand for the resources, and to do the input-output analysis which estimates (for example) how much iron ore, coal and oil will provide how much public or private transport mileage to meet the likely demands of particular populations.

- **Costs of regulation** It costs public money to draft laws, get them known, and employ inspectors, accountants, prosecutors and magistrates to enforce them. There are often also private costs as firms hire staff to know the regulations and see that their procedures comply with them. Those immediate costs may be accountants' business, but it is economists' business to trace and measure the effects of regulation on employment, on the products and prices of the industries concerned, and on their suppliers and customers.

- **Distributional effects** Most environmental regulation has direct or indirect effects on the distribution of wealth, income, living costs, and access to environmental benefits. Economists should be able to trace those effects, measure those that are measurable, and estimate the likely distributional effects of new policies.

Rationing

Authorities may ration particular resources either *because* they are scarce, or to *keep* them scarce, i.e. to limit the rate at which finite or renewable resources are used. Everybody does it, not only governments. *Household examples:* Five-minute shower-baths to save hot water; one chocolate per child, to save either money

or teeth. *Corporate examples:* two uniforms a year for uniformed employees; rationed uses of company cars. *National examples:* Food and fuel rationing in wartime; water rationing during droughts. *International examples:* Fishing and whaling quotas; arms limitation treaties.

War and drought are temporary, but some environmental scarcities may be permanent. Will people resort to permanent rationing as a regular instrument of environmental policy? Will we ration finite, exhaustible resources such as oil, to spin them out over time or share them fairly between people? Will we ration slowly-renewable resources such as timber, to limit consumption to the rate at which the resource can be renewed? I think such policies may be adopted – so economists should learn the principles and problems of rationing.

Some sceptics disagree, for reasons of two kinds. First, they don't believe people will be sufficiently prudent or cooperative to accept permanent rationing even if there is genuine need for it. Second, some economists doubt the genuine need. They believe that if a resource is running out its price will rise, which will reduce demand for it and motivate people to look for substitutes or alternatives for it. *Example:* As the world's easily-accessible oil runs low its price will rise for two reasons: scarcity, and a resort to more and more expensive methods of production (oil from shale, oil from coal). Consumers will respond to the rising prices by using less and looking for alternatives. Investors will respond by researching and developing alternatives. Thus markets should respond to scarcities automatically, and more efficiently than administrative rationing is likely to do.

Real life does not follow that model very reliably. Even oil is wayward. As with other minerals it is not necessarily the cheaply-mined deposits that are discovered or mined first. For national reasons some expensive under-sea oilfields are already producing long before the world's cheaper resources are exhausted. Arabian, African and South American owners of many of the cheap fields are driven by their cash needs to oscillate between monopolist and competitive behavior. So world oil prices do not rise steadily as reserves diminish (as the model suggests they should); they jump and decline irregularly, and when they do increase it has so far been by monopolist choice rather than from scarcity or rising costs of production.

But whatever the force of the free-market argument, there are resources and processes to which it does not apply. For example –

- As in the tragedy of the commons there are resources whose unrestricted use will degrade the world for everyone. Burning fossil fuels may have a greenhouse effect on world temperatures. Rationing by international agreement and national action may be appropriate, for that as for other pollutant resources and processes.

- Unrestricted use may destroy genetic stocks. International agreements already regulate whaling. National game laws restrict hunting seasons and for some species ration the numbers taken. Rationing may be extended to more species.

- Some resources can be depleted without the rising costs or scarcity prices of the market model. The world's forests continue to be cut at steady costs, and their owners still compete to sell the dwindling remainder at low prices. Why don't some suppliers hold out for higher prices later? A few may do so – but for most, commercial horizons are much shorter than the time it takes to grow trees.

- Forests are only one of a larger class of resources which ought to be conserved for perpetual use (soil, fish, particular habitats) or for as long as possible (oil, coal, temperate world weather). Self-interested market motivation won't usually conserve or renew resources more than ten or twenty years ahead.

- Market distribution, i.e. rationing by price, may distribute essential resources very unequally, or with little regard to need, or with unreasonable profits to monopolist suppliers. There may then be moral, social, political reasons for rationing.

- Mixtures of rationing and market pricing are possible. In Canberra the government rations suburban land. Households are only allowed so much land per house. There is open marketing of allotments, so the biggest permitted sizes, at the most desired locations, fetch high prices – but nobody however rich is allowed two allotments around one house.

So there may be increasing use of permanent rationing. But its effectiveness, and the fairness and productivity of its effects, can vary widely with the nature of the resources being rationed, the methods employed, and the political and social culture of the society concerned. It is comparatively easy to ration big, visible items: cars and houses, for example. It is easy to ration network gas and electricity, because they are metered supplies from a monopoly supplier. Food and other fuels are easier to conceal, harder to ration. There are other difficulties with things that take diverse, non-standard forms – if you are rationing clothing, how much cotton cloth = how many woollen garments = how many leather shoes = how many plastic raincoats – and should bigger people get bigger rations?

Rationing is as much art as science. It requires judgments of people's honesty, motivation, tolerance, as well as technical choices. Is it better to ration a scarce resource at source (ration the mining or refining of oil?) or at final sale (ration gas-station sales to motorists?) or in use (install a sealed mileage meter in every car and have government officials read the meter twice a year?). Such decisions have to be taken with attention to the social and economic purposes of the rationing, the technicalities of the resources and their uses, the prevailing honesty and values of the people and the regulators, the administrative costs, and so on. And much may depend on the wisdom and skill with which such judgments are made.

Taxing

If government wants to conserve something we have seen how it may ban its use, *regulate* it, or *ration* it which may also entail *price-controlling* it. Now notice what may be achieved by taxing it.

Direct price controls are typically used to keep prices *down*. When governments want to limit consumption by pushing prices up they may do it by taxing. Such 'tax-pricing' has long been used for other purposes than conservation. Governments protect home industries by taxing and thus raising the prices of competing imports. They encourage sobriety and long life by taxing liquor and cigarettes.

Some economists would apply the principle wherever practicable to environmental management, basically by taxing the use of scarce resources and/or the emission of pollutants. The yield of such taxes may then be used positively to encourage better private behavior or to meet public environmental costs. For example all four of those purposes might be served if government taxed sales of fossil fuels (which would raise their prices, deter their use, make finite supplies last longer, and reduce local pollution and the world greenhouse effect) and used the tax yield to subsidize solar and wind and tide power and to finance research into other energy sources.

Arguments in favor: Such price changes can encourage desirable environmental behavior without reducing producers' and consumers' freedoms. As with other price changes, people can adapt in their own way and their own time, as suits each best, and market freedoms and efficiencies can continue. And such taxes can sometimes serve other good purposes too. Economists of the Australia Institute have proposed a carbon tax to replace an existing payroll tax. Together with other tax and regulatory changes that is designed to cut the country's greenhouse gas emissions by 40 per cent and its urban air pollution by 30 per cent within 20 years, and its unemployment by 25 per cent rather sooner.

One main objection to environmental taxes (described below) is that they tend to be regressive, costing poorer people bigger proportions of income than they cost richer people. But it may be possible, as in the Australian proposal, to offset that effect by other measures. And the environmental benefits themselves – stable climate and cleaner air and water – tend to be *progressive,* improving poorer people's health and living conditions more than richer people's.

Arguments against environmental taxation: There are questions of effectiveness and fairness. *Effectiveness:* Price changes may not be forceful enough. As this text keeps reminding you, when people decided to stop slavery, child labor, dangerous machinery, unhealthy workplaces, unsafe ships, adulterated food and liquor, they did not tax them, they banned them. Faced with (say) dearer energy many people may use as much as ever, pay more for it, and have less to spend on environmentally wholesome things. *Equity:* If you tax necessaries you cut most people's standard of living. Necessaries (heat, food, transport) take a bigger proportion of poor people's spending than of rich people's spending, so taxing them increases inequality. Rationing at controlled prices would be fairer.

Pollution may present different options. If it is taxed, the tax revenue rarely goes to compensate those who suffer from the pollution, though they may benefit from the cleaner environment. If it is banned, polluters may have to raise their prices by whatever it costs to clean up their methods of production. Depending on the products, that also may hit poor pensioner' budgets.

But effects can be complicated. *Example:* Suppose government allows a local paper factory to pour its wastes freely into public sewers. The heavy treatment costs are then paid by government out of progressive taxation. As compared with 'making the polluter pay' the winners and losers from the policy may be: *Winners:* Paper users, the factory's shareholders, and paper-making and sewage workers if their jobs depend on keeping the factory's costs down. *Losers:* Taxpayers (richer more than poorer); people elsewhere who might get paper-making profits and jobs if this factory closed; later generations who will inherit less forest. If paper was dearer and people paid correspondingly less taxes,

they might enjoy spending that margin of income on other things than paper. *Because* effects can be so complicated, economists should be equipped to trace them.

Ownership

Instead of bullying and cajoling others, perhaps government should do its own dirty work. There is a case for pubic ownership of some scarce resources, and public management of some pollutant and anti-pollutant processes.

When government tries to induce good environmental behavior by educating, regulating, rationing, price-controlling or taxing producers or consumers, there are many conflicts of interest. There may be heavy administrative costs. Government pays lawyers to draft regulations, firms pay lawyers to tell them how to comply with the rules or how to frustrate them. Government pays inspectors to inspect, some firms bribe some inspectors not to. Firms which manage to evade taxes or regulations undersell honest competitors. Cleaned-up industries in one country or neighborhood lose to dirtier competitors in less-regulated countries or neighborhoods. The costs and the quality of business and government may all suffer.

So there is a case for re-defining the problem. Government should stop asking 'How can we best discipline wasteful, improvident, pollutant, or otherwise antisocial producers?' Instead it should ask 'Which resources and processes can safely be left in competitive profit-seeking hands and which can not?' Where competitive profit-seeking conflicts with public environmental interests, it might best be replaced by public ownership of the resources or public management of production, or both.

Arguments in favor: It is as owners that governments can have the simplest, surest control of resources and industrial processes. Without cumbersome regulation and enforcement, or fear of evasion or legal resistance, public owners can decide what resources to use or conserve, what methods of production to use, how to process and dispose of wastes. If their governments wish, public corporations can fell the forests selectively, plant for future generations, leave the oil in the ground, charge pensioners half-price for power and public transport – losing money where necessary. In short government can control its own corporations more surely and with less resentment than it can control other people's; and it can often make them serve a wider range of social and environmental purposes than it can make private corporations serve. So what it should often do to recalcitrant resource-strippers or polluters is buy them.

Arguments against: Governments have contributed their share of waste and pollution. They have their own motives for bad behavior. Some politicians have short horizons. Some bureaucrats and public business managers are as tunnel-visioned as any profit-seeker. They build roads without care for young or old pedestrians. They build dams that drown precious wilderness. They build highest-yield, lowest-cost power systems without caring what environmental damage they do. They build public housing towers in which they would not dream of bringing up their own children. Some of them have such statutory powers to trample over private rights and public values that they are harder to discipline than private enterprises are.

So (some private enterprisers argue) the environment can't safely be trusted *either* to unrestrained profit-seekers *or* to over-powerful bureaucrats. Either works best when watched and checked by the other, as when private enterprises work under public scrutiny, each quick to tell press or parliament or courts if the other misbehaves.

But relations between private industries and their public regulators have a checkered history. The relation has often worked well. It has sometimes encouraged corruption. It has sometimes become 'cosy' – there are examples of the public watchdogs becoming uncritical friends and promoters of the industries they are supposed to discipline.

Independent institutional ownership can be better than either government or private ownership if you want to conserve a resource for one over-riding use or value. Wilderness, for example: if profit-seekers own it they may be tempted to log it, mine it, build resort hotels on it. If central government owns it, politicians and public servants may be tempted to mine it or dam it for public utility purposes or fence it in as an army firing range. If local government owns it, locals may use it for rubbish tips, off-road motorcycling, summer camping. If you want it to be managed with over-riding care for natural conservation it may be safest for Friends of the Earth or National Trusts to own it.

All types of ownership have their hazards. But they can all show examples of good performance, too. Reformers should study the successes and work for more like them. And instead of any general preference for public or private or independent ownership of critical resources and processes, policy-makers should ask detailed questions about each conservation problem in its social and political context. Wise governments do their best to decide which public/private/independent ownership or 'mix'

will work best in the particular local and national circumstances, case by case.

INTERNATIONAL POLICIES

The world needs some global environmental policies, and means of enforcing them, for a number of reasons.

All countries contribute to some global degradation, which will impact on them all. Besides contributing to those global problems, the rich countries also contribute to poorer countries' local troubles. Some poor countries have such corrupt or incompetent government that although they have suffered environmental harm from developed countries, their own environmental performance can sometimes be improved by tied aid from rich countries or by other international coercion.

There are international agreements for the reduction of CFC and greenhouse gas emissions, for the protection of some species, for some heritage conservation, and for other conservationist purposes. Some agreed programs and timetables have been fulfilled but many of them – so far – have not.

What to do　Most of what follows is based gratefully on Chapter 15 of Michael Jacobs, *The Green Economy.*

If self-interest, generosity and global prudence prompt rich democracies to help the developing countries' environmental performance, there are a number of things they can do:

- They can pay more for the farm and factory products they import from poor countries and thus help those countries to earn the foreign exchange they need without degrading their resources and living and working conditions. Unregulated markets can't achieve that. It calls for international agreements to pay appropriate prices for goods whose production meets specified health and environmental standards.

- Environmental aid can be added to existing flows of aid. Some independent organizations have pioneered 'debt for nature' swaps: poor countries conserve particular resources in exchange for some reduction of their debts. Governments could negotiate such deals on much bigger scale. Governments of poor countries resist that sort of tied aid as 'gringo greenmail', often resisting it most strongly where corrupt misuse of untied aid is most likely. Donors may be able to help by adding tied aid to existing aid, rather than by attaching new conditions to existing aid. And they can design environmental programs which also reduce poverty – governments don't like to be seen to refuse aid to their poorest people.

- Some of the governments can help by hard bargaining. Big developing countries, especially China and India, will add a lot to the pollution which rich countries suffer if they use coal, CFC and cheap old technology for their energy and refrigeration. But it is expensive for them to do otherwise, and without enough foreign exchange it may be impossible. They should bargain hard for Western aid in cash, some cancellation of debt, and free access to the latest technology, in exchange for limiting their contribution to global pollution.

How to pay An international levy on greenhouse emissions could finance programs to minimize the developing countries' emissions. Governments could raise the levy from carbon taxes and pay it to a U.N. agency for allocation to developing countries' environmental programs. But agreement on such a program might be hard to achieve, for a number of reasons.

There are free rider problems. Countries which do not sign the agreements or restrict their emissions will still benefit from the cleaner performance of those who do. Countries which sign but then fail to perform may be hard to discipline.

There are distributional problems. What principles should determine what share of environmental aid each rich country should contribute? What share of it each developing country should receive? What self-restraint each country should contribute to global self-restraint? Current greenhouse agreements call for percentage reductions of the volume of emissions in a base year, with some easier conditions for developing countries. But equal percentage reductions can work unfairly between richer and poorer countries with different needs for further development. They can work unfairly between countries like Japan which capped or cut their emissions earlier and more severely than countries like the US have yet done. They can work very unfairly between poor countries which have used up very few non-renewable resources and contributed very little to existing global pollution and countries which have done a lot of both. The sinks into which the rich countries have poured their harmful wastes are dangerously near to full. Newcomers, still poor, should surely have big shares of any remaining capacity.

Conflicting principles of fairness and equal sacrifice thus compound the self-interests which already make it hard for the nations to agree.

A best solution? There is an ideal solution, if the rich countries would agree to it. It is a clever mix of governmental and market allocation. A simple international agreement, renewed every two years or so, should fix equal greenhouse emission rights *per head of population,* and make them *saleable at market prices,* with some protection against cornering and monopoly-pricing them. Rich countries with high emissions would have to buy rights from poor countries with lower-than-permitted emissions. To the extent that rich countries could save energy by means that cost less than the permits cost, they would do that. So would poor countries, to gain foreign exchange by selling as many permits as possible. Thus (i) everybody would have incentives to improve environmental performance by both technical improvement and self-restraint, (ii) rich countries would pay most of the costs of abating dangers which they chiefly created, and (iii) the program would reduce both environmental harm and international inequalities.

Too good to come true? I think there might be majorities for it in many of the rich democracies – but not at present in their centres of government or corporate power. Meanwhile return to Michael Jacobs' summary of reasons why the rich countries should contrive and finance not only their own but also many of the poor countries' necessary environmental reforms:

> Industrialized countries are currently 'exporting unsustainability'. Sometimes this is very starkly obvious, as when toxic wastes are shipped to Third World countries for disposal. But it occurs on a much more widespread basis through the normal mechanisms of international trade. Environments in the South are often degraded in the process of producing primary commodities for export to the North. Fishing grounds are depleted, forests destroyed, soil eroded, wilderness areas despoiled. Even degradation caused by subsistence farming can often be traced back to the displacement of traditional communities onto more fragile, marginal land by landowners and governments oriented towards export. Meanwhile manufactured goods exported by Third World countries are kept cheap (in part) by waiving the environmental standards which would apply in the North. This has the effect of forcing Southern factory workers, neighbouring communities and local ecosystems to pay the cost – in ill-health and ecological damage – which the Northern consumer avoids.
>
> Even if policies are implemented which maintain environmental capacity in the North, therefore, sustainability cannot be said to be achieved so long as such degradation continues in the Third World. There is clearly a crucial international dimension to environmental economic policy *even for Northern*

countries considered alone; that is, without considering the equally reasonable demand of equity that the Third World should be assisted simply because it is poor.

This is an important conclusion. From the point of view of industrialized countries, measures which assist the South to achieve sustainable development will frequently look like 'aid' in one form or another. Given current inequalities, most actions designed to enhance Southern environments will involve costs to the North. But it seems much more appropriate to regard transfers to the South as compensations for environmental damage than simply as charitable gifts to alleviate poverty. If the reason that environments in the South are degraded is because of past and present demands placed on them by the North, the 'degrader pays' principle suggests that those who benefited should pay the costs. 'Aid' is then simply a way of internalising transnational externalities.

This is particularly true when global environmental issues such as the greenhouse effect and ozone depletion are considered. Here the inequality between North and South is not simply a question of wealth: that poor countries cannot afford to cut down their emissions of carbon dioxide and CFCs to the same degree as industrialized ones. It is that the global commons (such as the atmosphere) have not been equally damaged by all countries. If they are thought of as waste sinks of finite size, it is the North which has filled almost all the space in them so far. A reasonable principle for common resources is that all nations should have the opportunity to benefit equally from them. But if this is so, the poor countries should not have to reduce their emissions at all. At the very least, if they are to be encouraged to do so by the North, the North should pay the cost.

– *The Green Economy* pp. 181-2

ECONOMISTS' TASKS

Economists can help to clarify many of the technical and political options, and to bring together and order the diverse technical, political, social and economic information on which many environmental arguments and policy choices ought to be based. Examples:

Resource accounting

Geologists, biologists, chemists, engineers and others originate most information about the earth's natural resources and their potential industrial uses. Economists can study how the resource markets work, how prices are set, etc.; compare the direct production costs of using alternative resources and processes to produce given products; compare the direct costs of alternative methods of abating pollution, disposing of wastes, etc.; estimate future reserves and flows of threatened resources on alternative technical, market and policy assumptions.

Modern manufacturing tends to pass resources through many intermediate processes, and through many intermediate markets, from raw resource to finished product. Diverse resources have to be brought together in appropriate combinations at appropriate stages of their processing. How much of which metals, fuel, chemicals, etc., does it take to produce any specific basket of finished goods? What by-products and waste products do those processes spin off? Economists can develop input-output analyses for particular firms, industries and sectors, modelling the flows of resources through the successive stages of production, and comparing any technical substitutions that seem worth exploring. At their best (with adequate information and stable conditions) such analyses can help firms to arrive at least-cost methods of production, including methods of complying with environmental requirements. They can help policy-makers to compare the likely effects of alternative environmental policies on private and public costs, on employment, and perhaps on the distribution of some of the costs and benefits of environmental damage and policies to prevent it.

Cost-benefit analysis

Many public policies, including public investment decisions, have multiple purposes. In deciding on a new power source, for example, it can be argued that most power for least cost should not be the only consideration. Effects on employment, landscape, pollution and fuel reserves should also count. But *how much* damage to *whose* landscape is worth *how much* improvement in employment or energy costs? Or how would action to increase energy supply compare with action to economize energy use? Cost-benefit analysis was developed as an apparently objective, non-political approach to such choices. It differs from an ordinary investor's project appraisal because it counts effects on others' interests as well as the investor's own. The basic procedure is as follows –

1. Draw up a list of alternative projects: perhaps alternative ways to achieve a given end, perhaps alternative ways to use a given resource. (Build a road or a railway? Use a forest for defence and timber supply, or for recreation and water supply?)

2. List what you judge to be the important costs and benefits of each alternative, to the people who will be affected by it.

3. Quantify the costs and benefits as far as possible.

4. Value the costs and benefits, in money. Where they don't have market values (e.g. environmental quality, clean or dirty air and water, etc.) arrive at shadow prices for them.

5. Decide how future costs and benefits should compare with present ones. Should they rank equally, or should futures be discounted for distance and uncertainty? At the current rate of interest?

6. Bring all to account. The winner is the project with the biggest net surplus of benefits, or the highest rate of return to costs incurred. Projects with a net surplus of costs are not worth doing at all. If projects' net benefits or rates of return are below those available on other public investments there may be better uses for the resources concerned.

Though better for some projects than others, the cost-benefit procedure has severe shortcomings. We will return to them later, when studying public enterprises' principles of action. Briefly, the main objections are to false pretences of objectivity.

• *Selection* (1) Results depend on the choice of alternatives to be compared. Where the business is complex and the experts represent some interests rather than others, they may get the policies they want by comparing them with deliberately unpromising alternatives.

• *Selection* (2) Cost-benefit instruction books tell analysts to list *all* of each project's effects on *all* affected interests. In most cases that is impossible. (Revise Chapter 2 if you need to.) Consciously or not, analysts have to select *which* effects on *whose* interests they will bring to account. There may be no harm in that if they are fair-minded and make their principles of selection explicit. But it is wrong to depict the results as objective or exhaustive.

• *Shadow pricing* is open to a number of objections. Analysts try to price environmental quality by (for example) observing what effects pollution, noise or ugly views have on house prices and rents. They try to price life and death by observing what people spend on life insurance. But when the people themselves don't put prices on things like life, safety, clean air or natural beauty, they may have good reasons for not doing so. Pricing such things may imply that it is right to buy and sell them, or that it is right

that the rich should get as much of them as they can afford, and the poor as little as they can afford. (That objection holds to market as well as shadow pricing – see below.) Similarly with life and safety. Most life insurance is to ensure income, not to protect life. It has nothing to do with the value people put on (say) children's lives, or the non-monetary effects of death. If one policy alternative will kill more people than another, that fact is best known plainly, not concealed in a financial bottom line. To emphasize that ethical rules should not be subject to economic considerations, U.S. laws and court decisions have prohibited the use of cost-benefit analysis in some branches of environmental policy-making.

• *Distributional values:* Market prices and shadow prices alike are affected by the distribution of income. Valuing costs and benefits by their prices can accordingly give distributional bias to public policies. Rich house prices are much more sensitive to environmental quality than poor house prices are, simply because the rich have more to spend on such refinements. So a cost-benefit analysis which compares (say) alternative routes for a motorway, or sites for industrial development, may well show a greater net surplus of benefit for policies which protect or enhance the already-comfortable lives of fewer rich, than for alternatives which would protect or improve the less-comfortable lives of larger numbers of poorer people. Your values may or may not agree with doing that – but it is fraudulent to present it as an objective calculation of maximum community benefit.

Other biases can replace that last one. For example analysts can decide to put higher value on improving poor incomes or living conditions than on improving rich incomes or living conditions. They can decide to put higher value on increasing employment than on increasing GNP. One objection to biasing analyses in that way – an odd objection, but it has some force in practice – is that it may help to nourish the illusion that analyses which accept *existing* prices and distributions of wealth and income are somehow objective and non-political. (They're not, they just favor different interests.) A simpler objection is that it is better to show people the actual distributional effects of the alternatives they face, rather than concealing them (together with life and death and environmental quality, etc.) in a financial bottom line. If you agree with those objections you won't want the usual kind of cost-benefit analysis. Instead you will want something currently called impact analysis.

Impact statements

Most of what a cost-benefit analyst does is right. To clarify policy and investment options it is often right to compare some promising-looking alternatives. It is always right to forecast as many as you can of their more important effects. Wherever effects can be measured it is right to measure rather than guess them – numbers of people, amounts of money, effects on costs and prices, numbers of jobs gained or lost, hours of travel time saved, effects on resource reserves, parts per million of air or water pollution, and so on.

But having got the quantities as correct as they can, there are three further steps which impact analysts do not take. Where qualities matter they describe them, they don't substitute quantities for them. They don't try to price what the people themselves don't price. And they don't try to reduce all physical, social, distributional and generational effects to money values. Instead, a good impact statement describes expected effects in plain terms. It may summarize direct financial costs and returns; indirect effects on other investors; effects on public, private or domestic productivity, and on national product and balance of payments; the numbers of people who will gain or lose jobs, and perhaps the options which will face those who lose jobs; quantitative effects on measurable resources; qualitative effects on environmental beauty or ugliness, social relations, culture, law and order or any other qualities of life that are likely to be affected.

The main advantages of impact statements over cost-benefit analyses are (1) for most readers they are more informative, and (2) they expose their values plainly and allow readers to substitute their own values.

Analyses of either kind are made to be used by people with diverse and often conflicting interests. Impact statements can of course be shaped to serve some interests rather than others, just as they can be mistaken or dishonest. But good impact statements, researched and written with fair-minded attention to a wide range of the relevant interests, can enable readers with different interests and values to disagree with the selections which have shaped the analysis, and to give their own weights to effects on productivity, employment, income distribution, environmental quality, resource depletion, and so on. That adaptability makes them useful to a wide variety of users.

SUMMARY

Here is a brief list, some of it merely in headings, of the subjects which this and the previous chapter have introduced.

1. *The tragedy of the commons* threatens when effects of individual economic activity will exhaust resources or degrade the environment for others.

2. *Population* appears to be increasingly controllable. Scientific knowledge and economic growth have reduced death rates and allowed periods of fast population growth almost everywhere. It is not true that further economic growth is then the only way to stabilize numbers by inducing a corresponding fall in birth rates. Experience shows that cultural change, education, medical and social services and other public action can have strong effects on birth rates in poor as well as rich countries. Many rich and some poor countries are in sight of z.p.g. But stable population by itself will not solve many environmental problems. The use of resources matters just as much, and tends to be more damaging the richer the country.

3. *Deliberate scarcity:* Environmental and social reasons may prompt some individual or collective self-restraint of consumption. Such policies affect the distribution as well as the total of consumption, so they are likely to succeed or fail politically on their distributional as well as their environmrntal merits.

4. *Conservation and growth* have similar aims, to provide for the material needs of people in the future. Relations between them vary with the facts of the case. They may be mutually exclusive (more paper = less forest). Or growth may require conservation (in the long term more paper requires much replanting). Conservation may require growth (replanting requires investment, equipment, etc.). Alternative ways of conserving one resource may have diverse effects on others, so policies need to be as comprehensive or compatible as possible.

5. *Natural resources* may need to be conserved by local, regional, national or international action, depending on the facts of the case. Different principles may be applied to exhaustible and renewable resources, reversible and irreversible pollution.

6. *Man-made structures* may be worth conserving: landscapes, townscapes, buildings, streets, precincts. Museum conservation. 'Working' conservation. Building and land-use controls. Considerations of economy and diversity in the addition or replacement of urban structures. A presumption in favor of conserving more buildings than current market forces will conserve at any date.

7. *Social relations and institutions* may depend on conserving physical fabric. The value of slow-grown, settled communities and the case for protecting them from unwanted disturbance by public or private developers. English, American, West European and Hungarian examples of deliberate conservation of local social and economic structures.

8. *Time and class distribution* of the costs and benefits of conservation. Most deliberate conservation of common resources affects the distribution of their benefits, and sometimes the general distribution of wealth and income. There can be complex relations between time and class distributions: saving a resource for later use may transfer it from richer to poorer, poorer to richer, etc., depending on the methods employed. The certainty with which resources can be conserved also varies widely.

9. *Methods of conservation:* Advantages and disadvantages of education, regulation, rationing, taxing, public and private and trust ownership. National and international problems of global conservation.

10. *Economics: Particular:* There are tasks for economists in resource accounting, input/output analysis, the economics of environmental regulation, land-use control, recycling of old buildings. *General:* As more economic decision-making is motivated or regulated to consider collective environmental values, and interests other than the decision-makers' own, theoretical/deductive approaches to economic understanding may need to give way to more practical, institutional approaches.

A book to read Almost any economist beginning work in the twenty-first century is likely to need more understanding of environmental problems than this chapter (or any general introduction to economics) has had room to offer. Instead of a concluding exercise I recommend that you get your own copy of Michael Jacobs' *The Green Economy* (London: Pluto Press, 1991), read it now, and keep it by you for future reference.

18

The rich democracies now

Now stop the clock for a bit. Before you turn from the broad directions of historical change to the detailed working of economic systems here and now, this chapter offers you summaries of three elements of the work done so far.

First, the forces of change surveyed in the last six chapters and new problems which they pose.

Second, the economic structure and institutions with which the rich mixed economies face the new problems.

Third, the intellectual resources – especially the advice they get from economists – with which their people debate what to do next about their old and new economic problems.

New achievements, new troubles, new tasks

The twentieth century revolution in the leading economies' productivity has transformed their people's opportunities. If they could manage the economy and distribute its output well enough, they could all live in material comfort. Most of them could choose from a wide range of occupations, and collectively they could do a lot to make most work safe, satisfying and sociable. Households could have quite wide choices between buying ready-made goods and services and making and doing things for themselves. They could likewise choose from an interesting range of lifestyles and recreations.

Many of their people already enjoy many of those blessings. But some poverty, some unemployment, some anxious insecurity and many conflicts of interest and social purpose continue. Besides their humane achievements, democracy and economic growth have also brought new problems:

- Rising productivity has required more people to have more educated skills, and people have also chosen to spend more of their rising income on education for its own sake. So education occupies more years of life and costs a rising proportion of national income.

- Medical science develops increasingly expensive means of improving health and length of life, so people live longer after they stop earning, and spend a rising proportion of national income on health services.

- Technical change continues to lower the relative prices of farm and factory products and some services, and to raise the relative prices of education, health and other labor-intensive services.

- Some technical changes tend to create or maintain persistent unemployment. If there are no effective corrective policies, there are rising public costs of income transfers and welfare services to poor households.

- To finance the rising educational, medical and welfare costs, and the rising proportion of non-earning years in most people's lives, *rights* to income have to be transferred from people's earning years to their non-earning years. That requires transfers of *actual* income from people currently earning to children, old folk, invalids and unemployed and others not currently earning. The transfers can happen within families; or as unearned property income from savings or superannuation; or by public income transfers and services.

- Democracy and economic growth have together transformed women's living and working possibilities, and there is widespread disagreement about the best uses to make of the new opportunities.

- Rising income enables communities to afford both more destruction and more conservation of valued buildings, urban forms, townscapes and landscapes, and communal institutions – but there can be conflicts about what to conserve and at whose expense.

- Rising numbers of people, multiplied in the rich countries by rising consumption, pollution and waste per head, create environmental troubles on local, national and global scale, and for future as well as present people.

None of those problems can be resolved by unaided market forces. They all create new tasks for government. As the rich democracies face them, what resources do they bring to bear on the work – what skills, divisions of labor, economic institutions and beliefs?

DIVISIONS OF LABOR AND SOURCES OF INCOME

Look first at the 'mix' of the mixed economies as they completed their decades of fast growth through the long boom and began to suffer their new troubles:

- the proportions of farming, manufacturing and service employment

- the proportions of public, private and household work, and the working relations between them

- the proportions of public, private and household incomes

- the proportions of earned income, unearned property income, and transferred income

- the proportions of market and non-market incomes.

How are public, private and household production related?

Each produces for the others. Their relations would be easy to model if households simply traded factors of production to private enterprises in exchange for finished consumer goods (food, clothing, cars) and to public enterprises in exchange for finished public goods (justice, education, roads). Real relations are otherwise. If you're French, or old enough to remember the ownership history of the British car manufacturers, you should not have read the sentence before the last without objecting that some of the private cars are made by public firms and the public roads are often built by private contractors. On the way from raw material to final use, most products pass through many processes and many hands, often bouncing to and fro between the modes of production, and drawing components from all of them.

What can simplifiers and model-builders make of these complexities?

Most national accounts include, periodically, detailed input/output tables showing what each productive branch and division of the economy supplies to each. They usually have matrix form. Down the side the industrial divisions are listed as *producers;* across the top the same divisions are listed as *users.* So in the boxes of the matrix you can see (for example) how much metal, energy, transport, tooling, etc., goes into the manufacture of wire, then how the output of wire is distributed as inputs to the packaging, fencing and powerline industries . . and so on. Find yourself a set (for example in every tenth year of the EUROSTAT accounts) and browse over it to sharpen your sense of the complexity and interdependence of productive

processes. But you will find that the tables only record technical processes and physical flows; they don't identify the public, private or household status of the producers. In principle, with some very detailed information-gathering, you could stripe each box in the matrix with three colors, proportioned to indicate how much of its contents came from public, private and household producers. Some areas of the national matrix would be mostly red for 'public', some mostly blue for 'private', some mostly white for 'household'. Other areas would have tricolors in every box, variously proportioned. The irregularly dappled result would dramatize the intricacy and interdependence of the working relations between the three – but it would not *simplify* the reality much.

But *some* simple conclusions appear from the input/output tables:

- Each mode produces some each of capital goods, intermediate goods and consumption goods. Households do, private producers do, public producers do. (Make a 3 x 3 matrix with the three types of producer down the side and the three types of product across the top, and think of likely products for each of the nine boxes.)

- Each mode produces for each other one. Public producers supply goods and services to other public producers, to private producers and to households. So do private producers. So do households.

Relations between producers are intricate In the motoring example, *public* and *private* producers contributed to producing capital goods (cars and roads) and intermediate goods (fuel) for intensive use chiefly by *household* labor. The example is not necessarily representative -

- Public, private and household shares of the work may vary *from country to country.* In Japan or the USA for example there was less public and more private contribution to car-making.

- Shares vary *over time.* Fifteen years earlier, and again ten years later, Britain had no public carmakers.

- Shares vary *from product to product.* For example food tends to come chiefly from private producers and household cooks. Clothing tends to come ready-to-wear from private producers then gets mostly household cleaning and pressing. Education everywhere, and health services in Europe, are mostly public considered as 'final products'. But there are private elements in the terms on which doctors and others work for public services or are paid by public

WHO EARNS?

Which Europeans earned pay from employment or self-employment in 1981?

HOW DO AGRICULTURE, INDUSTRY, SERVICES AND HOUSEHOLDS SHARE THE WORK?

How was work distributed between productive activities?

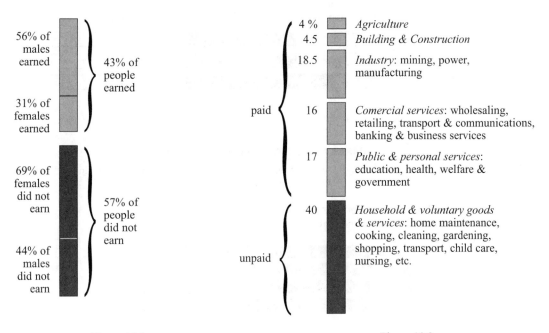

Figure 18.1   Figure 18.2

Notes on terms and sources:

Households are counted as unpaid producers. (When they produce for market they appear here, and in the EUROSTAT accounts, as private enterprises.) There are three ways of estimating the value of their unmarketed output. (1) Value it at the going commercial prices for the same goods and services. (2) Value the hours of work at current wage rates for similar work. (3) Compare the total hours of unpaid work with the total hours of paid work in the economy. Hundreds of estimates were surveyed by Luisella Goldschmidt- Clermont in *Unpaid work in the household,* Geneva: I.L.O., 1982, and there is discussion of them by Richard Rose in 'Getting By in three economies' in J-E. Lane (ed.) *State and Market: The politics of the public and the private,* London: Sage, 1985. In *Portrait of the Family within the Total Economy: A study in long-run dynamics, Australia 1788-1990,* Cambridge 1994, Graeme D. Snooks estimates that unpaid household contribution to real income in Australia from 1945 to 1990 averaged 34.2 per cent. That may underestimate it because women were paid less than men for

similar work, and because driving vehicles is included in the estimates of market work but not in the estimates of household work. In this text I have assumed that unpaid household work and other voluntary work in developed economies average about 40 per cent of all work. That probably conceals significant differences over time and between countries, but it is the best I can do.

Public enterprises are those whose capital does not belong, and whose profits if any cannot go, to individuals: government-owned firms and services, churches, universities and other non-profit institutions, and charities. *Government,* meaning the legislators and public servants engaged in governing, is generally included in estimates of public employment and the public sector, but not of public enterprise.

The source for Figures 18.1-4 is Richard Rose and others, *Public Employment in Western Nations,* 1985, Tables 1.1, 1.12, 1.16 and 1.17, adjusted to include assumed household work, output and income transfers.

HOW DO PUBLIC, PRIVATE AND HOUSEHOLD PRODUCERS SHARE THE WORK?

The public and private shares varied widely among the richest countries –

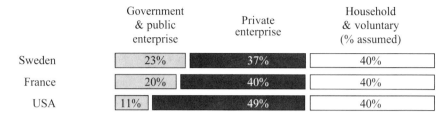

Figure 18.3

MARKET AND NON-MARKET INCOMES

Incomes from public and private enterprise and public income transfers, excluding transfers and in-kind income within households.

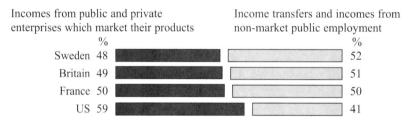

Figure 18.4

FOR EXAMPLE, WHO PRODUCED BRITISH AND FRENCH MOTORING IN 1985?

There were some public, some private and some household producers:

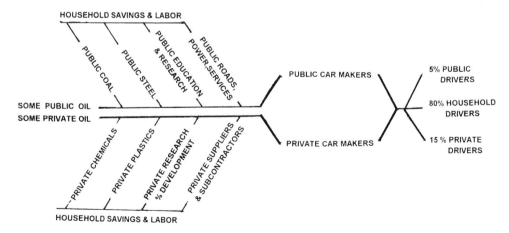

Figure 18.5 Sector contributions to British and French motoring before the British privatizations.

services. And the public services buy plenty of equipment and materials from private suppliers.

The main point is this: national totals of public, private and household work or output don't represent independent productive sectors. Whatever their 'final' goods and services, most productive processes draw numerous inputs from all three sectors, often in mixed order as in the motoring example above. Most of the working relations between them are market relations, i.e. people shopping around and buying and selling to each other. And the prices vary with degrees of competition or monopoly, differences of market strength and bargaining power, and direct and indirect effects of many government policies.

Notice a particular effect of that diversity -

Diverse pricing diversifies business opportunities
In an economy which mixes competitive, monopolist and political pricing, profit-seekers may seek advantage in a variety of ways. Depending on the nature and organization of their particular industries they may do best (1) by competing hard, (2) by working to protect themselves from competition, or (3) by manipulating their relations with non-competitors, including government. For some firms those may be alternative strategies. Others may manage all three at once. How? Think of a *big* firm, itself *oligopolist* and *protected from foreign competitors,* buying most of its inputs from *competitive*

suppliers, using *free* public scientific research and *subsidized* rail freight, selling *patented* products to *government* and also exporting (sometimes at different prices) to *unprotected* markets abroad. Too good to be true? No, those are possible conditions for makers of military and space hardware, nuclear power stations, pharmaceutical drugs. At the other extreme are industries which are mostly competitive from inputs to final sales. (Fresh and frozen vegetable supplies; house-building; hairdressing.)

Whatever the example, remember the principles. In mixed economies, enterprises may be able to advance their interests (whether profit-seeking interests or public interests) –

- by competing perfectly;

- by competing 'imperfectly' – over-persuading customers, developing superior financial and bargaining power, buying or breaking competitors, developing degrees of monopoly;

- by dealing advantageously with more-competitive and less-competitive others, for example by buying in competitive markets and selling in protected or monopolized markets;

- by getting help from government in any of its roles as public enterpriser, researcher, taxer, subsidizer, law-maker and regulator, free-trader or protectionist.

A summary and an exercise:

TWELVE WAYS TO DO WELL IN A MIXED ECONOMY

We have been summarizing some structural facts. Divisions of labor; numbers at work in the different modes of production; working relations between the modes and sectors; proportions of public, private and transferred incomes. It is time to draw that information together, and see what light it casts on alternative models of the economic system as a whole.

One way to do that is to list the *types of opportunity* which are offered by each *type of economic institution.* We can then see how rival economic theories treat those opportunities: which opportunities they model satisfactorily, which they treat unsatisfactorily, which they ignore.

It is quite important that you keep the following summary of opportunities in mind as you work through the rest of this chapter, and also at later stages of the course.

So to grab your attention, slow you down and encourage you to think, it is designed as both lesson and exercise.

As follows:

Continue to classify the economic institutions as (1) households, (2) private enterprises, and (3) public enterprises and government. Individually, enterprises of those kinds may have all sorts of purposes – to make profits and earn incomes, to make good products, to make households richer or happier or better occupied, to serve particular public interests, to serve particular ideas of social justice. But whatever they happen to want, one way to classify *their possible means of getting it* is this:

They may –

1. Work at their own performance, meaning the internal efficiency with which they use their time and existing resources.

2. Work at their relations with households with whom they deal.

3. Work at relations with private enterprises with whom they deal.

4. Work at relations with public enterprises and authorities with whom they deal.

Three types of institution with four chances each makes twelve types of opportunity altogether. We will now list those twelve. The text will suggest examples of each. Then it will leave space for you to add more examples.

The text's examples and yours between them can scarcely begin to review all or most of the possible opportunities. (Much of the rest of the course of study will be devoted to that.) Here the exercise is to help you to digest the lesson: the range and diversity of the ways to wealth, income and whatever else people want in contemporary mixed economies.

It should then be possible to see how rival models deal with that diversity, by noticing which models recognize which types of opportunity. You can try that as you go along, or return to it after you have worked through the description and criticism of alternative models later in the chapter.

A household

1. *By itself* it can make the best use of its time and resources.
   Examples: It can think up new recreations. Improve cooking and diet and eat better. Grow less lawn and more vegetables (or according to taste, more lawn and less vegetables). Using some inputs from other modes it can improve its domestic capital: learn housekeeping skills; build a games room, a workshop, a tree-house; go fishing.
   More examples:

2. *With other households* it can exchange baby-sitting, share holidays, jointly own a boat.
   More examples:

3. *With private enterprises* household members can look for jobs. They can shop shrewdly for private-sector products. Depending on their purposes they can look for the cheapest eggs from price-cutting producers – or they can buy free-range eggs and boycott battery producers, whether for their own sake or for the hens' sake. They can also agitate to bring government to bear on private producers, as noted below.
   More examples:

4. With public enterprises and government household members can look for public employment. They can agitate and vote for higher or lower taxes, pensions, welfare services, for themselves or for other citizens. They can press government to make local industries suppress their smoke, curfew their heavy traffic, pay bigger shares of local taxes.
   More examples:

A private enterprise

5. *By itself* it can manage better, waste less, cut costs, improve processes, attract its workers' loyalty, make a better mousetrap.
   More examples:

6. *With households* it can study to please them with old or new products. It can work to produce what they want or persuade them to want what it produces. It may supply domestic capital (cars, washing machines) or compete with their products (by running cabs, laundries). It can draw good workers from households, borrow their savings, lend them consumer credit. It can get customers to do more of the work, serving themselves or assembling products from kits – or find other customers who will pay to have the work done for them.
More examples:

7. *With other private enterprises* it can know its markets and exercise the classical competitive and market skills. It can buy its inputs from the most competitive suppliers. Depending on the nature of the industry that may mean anything from daily buying in open markets (to stock a local fruit or fish shop) to ten-year contracts at fixed prices (for coal and ore supplies to a steel mill). If the business sells its products to other businesses it may (i) compete for customers by offering best quality most reliably at lowest prices, or (ii) reduce competition by buying patents, advantageous locations, etc.; (iii) reduce competition by cartel agreements with competitors; (iv) borrow enough money or issue enough shares to buy the competitors, or (v) buy the customers, as when brewers buy hotels.
More examples:

8. *With public enterprises and government* a private enterprise may design its business and accounts to minimize taxation. Get power, water, sewerage, rail links, etc., as cheaply as possible from public suppli-

ers. Hire workers with publicly educated skills. Compete – by fair means or foul, as the system allows – for public contracts. Apply for mineral exploration leases, mining or logging or tourist concessions in national parks and forests. Buy land zoned rural and persuade the relevant authorities to re-zone it urban – or buy urban land zoned for three-storey houses and get it re-zoned for forty storey offices. If the nature of the business allows, encourage national or local governments to attract private investment by offering investors public land, soft loans, credit guarantees, industrial subsidies, tax holidays, permits to pollute.
More examples:

A public enterprise

9. *By itself* a public enterprise can do most of the things a private enterprise can do to improve its internal efficiency. It can also do things private enterprises may not be able to do. It can undertake very long term projects with no early returns. It can forego profits, run at a loss or give its products away, as its social purposes may require. (It may also, of course, abuse those possibilities to conceal inefficiencies.)
More examples

10. *To households* public enterprises can supply goods and services free, at cost, or at prices above or below cost, as policies require. *(From* the households, directly or indirectly, the policies are supposed to come by democratic process.) Public enterprises can help their customers to know and use their services. (Some public offices exist to help people in their battles with other public offices.) Fundamental social purposes – some consensual, some conflicting and

disagreed – are served by public action to distribute and redistribute income, to educate people, keep them healthy, regulate their living and working conditions, provide them with all the other standard services of government – and attract their votes. Getting the folk who provide the services to be reliably humane and helpful, as well as honest and efficient, in all their dealings with the people they are there to serve, is a central task of government. But it also depends on the prevailing values and culture from which the public employees come – i.e. on the households themselves.
More examples

11. *With private enterprises* government deals in its many roles as taxer, legislator and regulator, economic policy-maker, and in any of those roles it can try to advance public purposes by influencing private producers. Public services can affect private costs, locational choices, environmental performance. So can public purchases of private products, for example if the purchasers insist on buying from local rather than foreign producers, from equal-opportunity employers, or other 'good behavers'. Government serves some public purposes by protecting private enterprises, for example by tariff. It serves other public purposes by protecting people *from* private enterprises, and protecting private enterprises from one another, for example by factory acts, labor laws, pure food and drug laws, consumer protection services.
More examples:

12. *Public enterprises.* Governments can't and don't coordinate the whole public sector by simple command from above. Public enterprises develop their individual skills and policies, often with consider-

able independence. Relations between them can be as hard-bargained as market relations between private enterprises. Their success can depend on how well they deal with other public operators.
Example: A child-care service whose job is to find and help uncared-for or endangered children. It needs to negotiate the following kinds of cooperation, each of which may be resisted by the relevant agency for respectable reasons of its own. (i) Child-care needs adequate funding from Treasury – but Treasury sees a duty to restrain public spending wherever it can. (ii) To attract good people into social work requires good wage awards from public wage tribunals – but these tribunals face many competing claims, and demands for economy. (iii) All school teachers, public health officers and other welfare workers must reliably report signs of children at risk – but they may fear that doing so may damage their own clients' trust in them, dry up their sources of information, etc. (iv) Police and public law officers must report any relevant criminal records of people who apply for child-care jobs – but that offends widely-held concepts of privacy and civil rights.
More examples:

Now see how those various opportunities and working relations figure – or don't – in the democracies' debates about their economic policies.

SIMPLE MODELS OF MIXED ECONOMIES

People need simple understandings, or pictures, of their economic system for many purposes: to work in it, to vote policies for it, to make it intelligible rather than mysterious in a general way. Anything so complicated has to be understood through selections and simplifications of *some* kind. With many conflicting interests and values in society there are bound to be rival selections and simplifications. The simple general models developed by economists (often distilled from very complicated theories) have uses of at least these four kinds:

As explanations they offer selective causal explanations of selected functions of the economic system. For example one model may model some of the processes which determine what gets produced – how many cars, pizzas, heart transplants, country and western concerts. It may also model some of the processes which distribute wealth and income – the forces which make some people richer and others poorer. Another model mayfocus on different contributing causes of these same effects, or on different effects. For example it may model processes of technical change and growth – forces which make some societies richer than others.

As theories they offer means of 'moving from the known to the unknown', enabling people to predict future events and therefore influence them or adapt to them.

As theories they may also offer tests of efficiency, to help people answer such questions as 'Are we producing as much as our resources and technology allow?', and 'Are government's economic policies actually doing what they're meant to do?'

As recommendations they offer value judgments of economic systems and policies. Some do so explicitly. They all do so, explicitly or not, by choosing to model some elements and effects of the system rather than others.

Keep those uses in mind. Now consider some simple general models: a neoclassical model; a post-Keynesian, post-Marxist one which some might call a Cambridge model; and an institutional approach which reflects some of the special concerns of this course of study. The text will outline each model, then suggest some of its advantages and disadvantages, and notice some ways it may be used or abused in political and economic life.

A NEOCLASSICAL MODEL

In English-speaking countries this model shapes more university teaching of economics than the other models do. There are many divisions of opinion among its users, but most versions of it select the following as the basic principles of a market economy:

People have productive endowments. They own land, physical capital, money to lend or invest; and they can learn skills, and work.

In workplace and marketplace people trade what they *have* for what they *want.* They trade their land for rent, their capital for interest or dividends, their labor for wages. Then they trade the money they've earned for the goods and services they want to buy.

A few trade directly with other individuals or households. (They let a house for rent, run a local shop, practise as a local doctor or plumber.) But most people trade their endowments to firms, and buy their finished goods from firms.

Firms compete in factor markets to attract the capital, land and labor they need. They compete to use those means of production most efficiently, inventively, productively. They compete in goods-and-services markets to sell their products to consumers. The firms which produce most efficiently, i.e. which use factors of given value to produce goods of greatest value, are the ones which survive.

People thus express their individual preferences, and make the best of their individual endowments, in a double way. They get the best combination of risk and return for their land and capital, or sell their labor where they can get the work, wages, hours and conditions that suit them best. Then they spend their earnings on the basket of goods and services that suits them best.

The two markets – the *factor* markets for capital, land and labor, and the *goods* markets for consumer goods and services – depend jointly on each other and on people's tastes. People's spending choices depend on the relative prices of the goods and services offering, which in turn depend on what those goods and services cost to produce. Goods can't sell cheaper than the price of the factors used to produce them (or not for long, or their producers will go broke). Reciprocally, the factor prices depend on the finished goods prices: farmer, carter, miller, baker and retailer can't together pay more for their factors than the finished loaf of bread will fetch from its consumer.

That interdependence means that the amount and detailed composition of a society's material output – how many cars, shirts, pizzas, horse races, heart transplants – are determined jointly by the people's preferences as producers and as consumers. Collectively or individually, they can't *get* more than they *give.* But at any current level of technology, competition should sort out the more efficient from the less efficient firms so that the people get the *most possible* of what they *most want* in return for the productive contributions they are *able* and *willing* to make.

Paul Samuelson and others have sketched it as in Figure 18.1.

There remain two questions which are main subjects of neoclassical theory. How can you know that the incomes people get do actually represent the value of their productive contributions? And is the system really self-adjusting – left to itself, will it tend to run steadily with all willing factors fully employed?

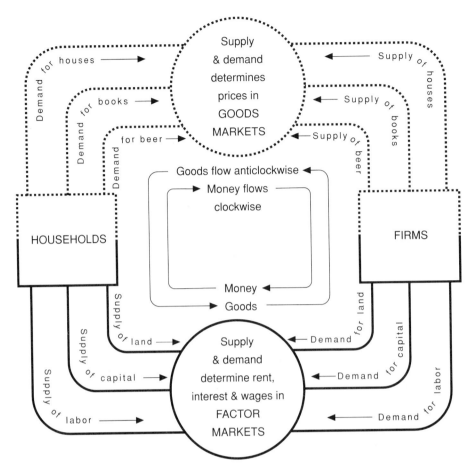

Figure 18.1 Goods and services flow anticlockwise. Factors of production go from households to firms along the lower loop, finished goods go from firms back to households along the upper loop. Money to pay for them flows clockwise. Prices are determined by supply and demand in goods markets on the upper loop, and in factor markets on the lower loop. Adapted from editions of Paul Samuelson, *Economics*, 1948-95 by permission of McGraw Hill.

Here it is again, simpler:

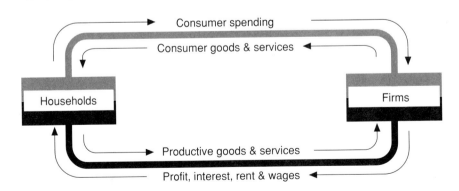

INCOMES AS FAIR EXCHANGES

The classical economists – Smith, Ricardo and others – remained puzzled about the class distribution of income. They knew why landlords got rent, capitalists got profits and workers got wages. But what determined *exactly how much* each got – what proportion of their joint product each got?

In the 1860's and 1870's neoclassical theorists (Jevons, Marshall, Walras and others) offered an answer, arrived at by the marginal analysis which is still orthodox now. In a sentence: add a dollar's worth of any one factor to an existing productive process, and if that increases output by a dollar's worth, you know the factor has earned its dollar, *and so have all the other units of that factor at that price.*

Think of a tenant farmer who hires all his factors of production: he rents land, hires machinery, employs workers. Each of the three factors is a necessary condition of any production at all. Do without any one of them, and output is nil. So when the three combine to raise a crop, how do you know *how much* of the sale value of the crop is due to *each one* of the factors? Does it even make sense to ask, since you can't have any output at all without combining all three?

Marginal theorists tell you to consider the factors one by one.

The farmer will rent more land as long as the next acre will add more to his output than it costs him in rent. But *with given capital and labor,* each additional acre will add less to output. That is because with each additional acre there will be less labor and machinery to work each acre, so there will be less yield per acre. When the next acre would 'break even' the farmer will stop expanding (or he will look for more workers or machinery rather than more land). Meanwhile the landlord will only *supply* more land if the rent from the farmer is more than any alternative tenant or land-use would pay. There is some further theory to show that if the land is all of the same quality the rent for the marginal acre – the one whose productive contribution just equals its rent – will tend to set the rent level for all the farmer's acres. So the supply and demand for land, interacting with the supply and demand for its products, determine the quantity and price of the land the farmer uses. The farmer gets the best return for his capital and enterprise. The land finds its most productive use. And the landlord gets what the land itself actually contributes to the value of the crop.

As with land, so with capital. The farmer hires more or better machinery until the next machine would merely break even. With given amounts of land and labor, the more machines he has the less land and labor there is per machine, and the less an additional machine will add to total output. At the same time the machine-suppliers will only supply him if they can't get a better return for their capital elsewhere.

So also with work. With given land and capital, labor has diminishing marginal productivity – the more workers there are, the less land and machinery there is for each hand to work. The farmer will go on hiring until the next worker would cost as much as he would contribute to output; the workers will only work for that farmer as long as he is offering the best wages and conditions they can get. All the wages on the farm (with variations for skill, etc.) will tend to be set by the marginal wage of the last worker hired. And the wage for each kind of skill will measure the contribution to the value of output of every worker using that skill. (Unequal pay for work of equal value upsets this theory, so women's experience makes nonsense of it.)

Thus *by pricing the effect on output of marginal increases of each factor with the other factors 'held',* marginal theorists claim to show how incomes, as factor prices, measure the factors' actual contributions to the market value of jointly produced goods. Simultaneously competition in the factor markets makes sure that capital and labor go to the firms which will pay highest for them. Put those two beliefs together, and it follows that when factors go to their *highest-paying uses,* they have thereby found their *most productive* uses. (Two objections: First, whatever the producer has to pay for each of his factors has to go onto his selling price. So it makes just as much sense to say that the factor prices indicate the market strength and bargaining power of the suppliers, rather than the value that each contributes to the product. Second, in this model 'most-productive' means whatever consumers will pay most for, with all their inequalities of wealth and income. Making a dollar's worth of mink-and-gold-plating counts as more productive than making ninety cents' worth of rusks and sterile nappies.)

What if firms don't actually know what they are doing? The farm example may be simple, but how does (say) an advertising agency or a restaurant or a shipbuilder measure the effect on vital revenue of hiring one more accounts clerk or office cleaner? Often enough the firm does not know – *but the theory says that does not necessarily matter.* What matters is that firms which *in fact* combine and economize factors more efficiently will out-compete and survive firms which do it less efficiently, whether the efficient choices come by correct calculation or happy accident. In a competitive system the fact that a firm survives should signify that its choices are efficient however they are arrived at. That means (in this model) that whether or not the managers know it, the successful firm must be paying its factors the value they actually add to its output – or must at least be getting nearer to it than less successful competitors are managing to do.

Tendencies to equilibrium

For any one product, supply and demand are said to be in equilibrium if suppliers will go on supplying current quantities, and buyers will go on buying current quantities, at current prices. But will market forces make for interdependent prices and quantities of all goods and services such that *the system as a whole* – not just the prices of all the individual goods and services – will tend to equilibrium, continuously self-adjusting like a plane on automatic pilot? And if so, will it necessarily be equilibrium at full employment? Or (as we asked in an earlier chapter) might the system tend to a stable equilibrium with some of its land, or some of its capital, or some of its willing workers unemployed? Those are subjects of advanced theory, and advanced disagreements.

JUDGING THE MODEL

The neoclassical users of the model are the first to warn you how far it differs from real economic life. The only activities it models are people trading their individual endowments, in equal exchanges, for the private market goods they individually want. But in real life people want public as well as private goods – roads as well as cars. Even the private goods can't be produced without varying amounts of public production and 'infrastructure'. Real life also sees plenty of departures from perfect competition and fair exchange. There are public and private monopolies. When employers pay men more than women for work of equal value, as they have done through most of history, the women get unfair exchanges for their work. So may the men, if the women are indirectly subsidizing them. There are environmental and other 'externalities' – i.e. effects on people who had no part in the transactions which caused them. There are gross inequalities of wealth, information and bargaining strength. From those and other causes have come the development of big government and big welfare. For a summary of these differences between life and the model by an eminent economist who has done much to link neoclassical microeconomics to Keynesian macroeconomics, you can read pages 30-37 of the fif-

teenth (1995) edition of Paul Samuelson and William D. Nordhaus, *Economics.*

Knowing all that, conservative economists still value the model and find uses for it. It is the basis of the methods they use to explain and predict how competitive markets work; to judge national economic efficiencies; and for many educational and ideological purposes. Much advanced neoclassical theory consists of theoretical and mathematical elaboration of the implications of the basic model. Much policy advice is based on the model's selective causal analysis, and its assumptions about what should count as efficient and productive.

Beliefs are working parts, and disagreements about this model and its relation to real economic life underlie a great many economic controversies, practical as well as theoretical. So it is important that you understand the model, and the common arguments about its virtues and vices and uses and abuses. In doing that you won't be wasting time on purely academic wrangles. You will be studying the real-life weapons – the means of persuasion, deception, bafflement, enlightenment – with which farmers and manufacturers, importers and exporters, borrowers and lenders, developers and conservationists, bosses and workers, Left and Right fight their battles or negotiate their compromises, especially when their fortunes depend on attracting public support and influencing government policies.

You will meet many fragments of controversy about the neoclassical model as you study particular subjects – the effects of rival beliefs on financial markets, wage bargaining, housing inequalities, tax policies, and so on. You will be better equipped for those particular arguments if you have a general understanding of the controversy as a whole. It is a wide-ranging, many-sided controversy. So take time and care with the following summary of its main ethical, theoretical and practical components. Remember that you are studying with double purpose: not only to arrive at beliefs of your own, but also to understand people with other beliefs so that you can deal with them perceptively and effectively. It is not enough to dismiss people you don't agree with as wrong. You also need to know what their beliefs may prompt them to do next, what persuasions they may or may not respond do, what agreements or alliances may or may not be possible.

So we will look in turn at some of the main ethical, theoretical and practical arguments about the neoclassical model.

Ethical arguments

Friends of the neoclassical model have two sharply

different views of its ethics. Positivists who think their economic science is value-free claim that the model merely explains how the economy works in an objective factual way, without any ethical assumptions or implications. Non-positivists disagree. If you can't remember why they disagree, revise Part One. *Any* such simple model is a highly selective causal explanation of how the economy works, and its selections can't help shaping and being shaped by social values and purposes.

More intelligent friends of the model acknowledge its ethics and defend them. Among the most important defences are these three:

- It is right that people should get what they give, i.e. get as income the value they contribute to output, so it is good to use a model which shows that sort of exchange to be efficient as well as fair.

- It is right that people themselves, rather than bureaucratic planners or politicians, should decide their working and spending preferences, so it is good to use a model which treats that 'individual sovereignty' as the efficient way to allocate resources.

- A model which encourages confidence in market methods can help freedom and democracy in more-than-economic ways. The less people think they need central powers and institutions to manage the economy, the less danger there is that they will create powers for economic purposes which can then be misused for oppressive political purposes.

Objections Critics think that directly or indirectly, in a variety of ways, the model is likely to encourage some bad behavior and discourage some good behavior.

Individual self-interest is the model's only productive motive. There will always be plenty of it and it is good, as the model suggests, to make productive use of it. But self-interested private market exchanges can't be relied on to produce public goods, or to produce safe and beautiful environments, or town and country conservation, or long-term resource conservation, or a fair or most-productive distribution of 'endowments', or a fair distribution of economic rights and opportunities and security. By ignoring all those economic goods the model implies that they are less important than the private market goods whose production it does model.

You have already met two ethical objections to the model's treatment of distributive justice. First it chooses to classify 'factors' in a way which gives the same productive status to (say) the coalminer doing dangerous work underground, and the idle share-owner doing nothing at all in exchange for his unearned property income. Why should they both count as contributing to production when the share-owner actually contributes nothing? Second, the model explains both their incomes as factor rewards, i.e. as the market value of the endowments they contribute to production. But it does not explain how they came by their endowments. Thus it directs its users' attention towards the element of fair exchange in factor markets (which makes capitalism look good) and away from the facts and causes of inequality (which make capitalism look bad).

Worst, the model leads some (though not all) of its users to reverse the Golden Rule: to applaud greed and positively discourage generosity. The reasoning goes like this. Individual choices operating through market mechanisms allocate resources most efficiently. Other ways of allocating resources are less efficient. They are less efficient because they can mistake or ignore people's real wants, and because they can escape the discipline of open-market competition. Political, administrative or charitable allocation and management are at best necessary evils. Public income transfers, welfare services and other collective efforts to improve the quality and justice of social life all include an element of *some people deciding what is good for other people.* That tends to be less free and efficient than letting people make their own choices as they do in market relations.

This reasoning implies that in practice, in economic life, concern for self is productive and good, and concern for others can be oppressive and bad. Thus the model can be used to reverse the central principle of most of the world's systems of ethical and moral belief.

Theoretical arguments

Would a 'pure' market economy be naturally competitive – or would it tend to develop monopolies, alliances and other uncompetitive behavior?

Would it be self-adjusting, tending always toward a stable equilibrium – or would its market forces cause it to fluctuate irregularly, or oscillate regularly, between boom and slump?

Would it tend to employ all willing factors and produce at full capacity – or might it leave willing capital and labor unemployed?

You can approach those questions pragmatically by seeing how market economies behave in real life. They are never as perfectly competitive as the model requires. But it may be hard to decide whether the imperfections are caused by the market forces themselves or by people and institutions interfering to block or distort the market forces.

An alternative approach – a theorist's approach – is

to study the internal logic of the competitive market model itself, to see whether the modelled conditions would necessarily determine the modelled results. If you *assume* an economic system in which individual actors act rationally to optimize their own interests, can you *deduce* that the result must necessarily be an efficient, competitive, fully employed economy with its market forces tending to keep it in stable equilibrium?

Rigorous neoclassical theorists long ago demonstrated that you can't – or certainly not from those few assumptions alone. So they went on to ask from *what* assumptions the modelled results *could* be deduced. What are the logically necessary conditions from which it could be predicted that a market economy would work as modelled?

There is a mass of theory on the subject. You don't need to know most of it, but here are some of its widely-agreed conclusions. For a perfectly efficient, competitive, fully employed economy to work as modelled the conditions would have to include these, none of which is always or reliably present in real life:

- The economic actors are assumed to be individual units (people or firms) acting rationally to optimize their own benefits.

- No operator must be big enough for his operations alone to affect prices significantly.

- To achieve the above condition, producers must have U-shaped costs. That means that firms may have *some* economies of scale – i.e. producing more may reduce costs per unit produced – but only up to a point, beyond which it must cost *more* per unit to produce more. Why? Because if costs continue to fall with rising output (economists say 'if there are continuous returns to scale') then bigger firms will regularly undersell smaller firms, and acquire them or put them out of business, *until each industry is monopolized by a single firm*. Then rational self-interest will lead that firm to restrict output, raise prices and take monopoly profits. Conclusion: the competitive market model won't work where there are continuous returns to scale.

- There must be diminishing marginal utility, with people willing to pay a bit less for each additional carrot they buy.

- There must not be much 'salted peanut' psychology (the more you eat the more you want) or 'irregular drunk' psychology (you want the fourth and fifth drink more desperately than either the first when you were sober or the tenth when you were zonked.)

- There must not be significant interdependence or indivisibility. *(Interdependence:* The usefulness of your car depends on how many other people have cars, how much the government spends on roads, how efficient the alternative public transport is, etc. *Indivisibility:* Some products are big things of which you must have all or nothing. There is no point in building half a power station. Households can't usually buy houses bit by bit. A railway with only the left-hand rails, or with all the rails but none of the rolling stock, may cost half as much as the whole outfit would cost but it can't do half the work the whole outfit can do.)

- All people and firms must have equal bargaining power – equal capacity to hold out or go elsewhere, equal expertise or capacity to hire expertise, etc.

- Everyone must be fully, truly and equally informed.

- There must be futures markets with known prices. (You must be able to buy and sell, *now*, goods to be transferred at correctly predicted prices at future dates.)

- Firms and individuals must not unequalize their bargaining power by acting together through cartels, labor unions, political lobbies etc.

- Productive agreements and processes must not affect people who are not willing parties to them. There must be no pollution, environmental degradation or other neighborhood effects or externalities.

In theorists' shorthand those conditions can be listed as atomistic optimizing individuals; individual impotence; no combination or coercion; 'convexity', with diminishing marginal utility and no interdependence or indivisibility; U-shaped costs; no externalities; future markets with known prices; constant or slow-changing tastes and beliefs; and everyone equally well and truly informed about everything that affects their interests.

Some other conditions are more controversial – some theorists think they are logically necessary to the model, others don't. They include two you've met before:

- There must be diminishing marginal utility of goods and services but *not* of wealth and income. All consumers' incomes and bids for goods and services must have – dollar for dollar – equal value. If the tycoon's capacity to pay for ostentatious luxuries is any more or less valuable than the single mum's capacity to pay for rusks and nappies, the model does not have the efficiencies it claims.

- Recall Fred Hirsch's *Social Limits to Growth*. The

increasing complexity of economic life may be increasing the self-defeating element in 'rational optimizing'. For the system to work as modelled, everyone must optimize by honest production and exchange, not by lying, cheating, stealing, coercing or combining to bargain from strength. But there is often more to be gained by misbehaving, and those who do can often under-sell and out-compete those who don't. That makes a case for public regulation – but that is more difficult in some industries than others, it tends to raise public and private costs, it can distort some competitive incentives, and it creates new opportunities for political favoritism or corruption. Conclusion: perfect competition may only be achievable if the competitors are schizophrenic, rationally self-interested in half their behavior but irrationally self-denying and public-spirited in the other half.

Many of those conditions are not present – or not always or reliably present – in real life. Some of the shortcomings of neoclassical theory reflect the shortcomings of the market behavior which it models. In *Whither Socialism* (1994) Joseph Stiglitz warns the ex-communist countries not to be fooled by the neoclassical description of market motivation and performance. If market agents are left to themselves, their prices and other market signals may be designed to mislead, they may be based on inadequate information or on unequal access to necessary information. Firms' directors and workers may act in their own rather than their shareholders' interests. Their efficiency may be hindered by shortages of public capital and goods and services which they need but cannot produce for themselves. That is specially likely where neoclassical theory is believed, and encourages politicians and their electors to cut the tax bill by starving the private sector of the public goods and the pervasive government that it needs. How profit-seekers may then misuse their market freedom was illustrated vividly in the East Asian financial crisis of 1997/8. Western and Asian bankers and fund managers did gross damage to a number of national economies, and to millions of their poorest people, by mixtures of greed, incompetence and panic which made cruel nonsense of the theory that the freer they were, the more accurately they would allocate the world's capital resources to their most productive uses.

So much for the theory. Time now for both sides' practical arguments.

Practical arguments

We can use a conventional classification to discuss the model's practical influence first on macroeconomic then on microeconomic policies. *Macroeconomics:* does this model help policy makers to manage national levels of employment, income and inflation? *Microeconomic:* does it help them to make good policies for particular firms, industries, markets, localities, or social groups?

Macroeconomics In its purest form the neoclassical model suggests that a market economy doesn't really need any national management. It should be self-adjusting. The market forces of supply and demand, operating through market prices, should attract productive resources to their highest-paying, most-productive uses as determined by the consumers' spending choices. Wherever there is over-supply, falling prices should switch resources to other uses; wherever there are shortages, rising prices should attract resources *from* other uses. Everyone with anything to sell – land, capital, labor, finished goods and services – will take the best price they can get. They will take it however low it is, because anything is better than nothing, so all markets will 'clear', leaving no willing factor unemployed and no product unsold. If it worked as modelled, the system should not need any macroeconomic management. If it *does* need management this model does not show why, or what the macroeconomic policies should be.

Historically capitalist systems have not worked as modelled. Many neoclassical economists came to accept Keynes' double argument that fluctuating investment could cause booms and slumps by varying national levels of income and effective demand, and that the tendencies to equilibrium that the system *did* have were as likely to arrive at under-employed equilibrium as at fully-employed equilibrium. For twenty years or so after 1945 governments seemed to have stabilized full employment by deliberate management. But new levels of inflation and unemployment have since ended that consensus. The neoclassical model, with or without Keynesian adjustments, no longer offers any generally accepted or proven way of explaining inflation and unemployment, or controlling them. Instead of one neoclassical model of those phenomena there are now many rival models.

Microeconomics In a detailed way the neoclassical model was not a bad fit when it was invented more than a century ago. Then most production was by more-or-less competitive firms and individuals. But a century later, how much of present economic activity does the old model fit?

- Recall the summaries a few pages back. By the end of the long boom the private capitalist share of paid production ranged from about 62 per cent in Sweden to about 81 per cent in the US. If unpaid production is included the private percentages fall to about 37 (Sweden) and 48 (US). Moreover not all of that private production is by competitive firms, and not all of its products are marketed to individuals exercising their consumer sovereignty as the model describes.

• Remember the sources of modern incomes. Omitting informal incomes to household dependents, and counting only formal money incomes, perhaps a third of British and West European incomes and perhaps half of American incomes come from competitive private enterprises producing for market as the model requires. The model does not explain the 58 per cent of Swedish incomes, the 55 or 56 per cent of British and French, or the 42 per cent of American incomes which, before the recent privatizations, came from public and other non-profit employers or government income transfers.

• Recall the twelve ways to do well in a mixed economy. Work through them again and you will find that a pure market model can only offer to explain the productive choices and income effects of four of the twelve (3, 5, 6 and 7 as they were numbered earlier in this chapter).

Next, to understand the working of the private sector it is not enough to understand its internal causation alone. You also need to know about its external relations – how it is taxed and regulated, how it trades with public suppliers, what free public goods and uses of public capital it gets, how its customers' purchasing power is affected by public distributions of income, how it is affected in other ways by the collective or conflicting social purposes of the society around it.

(Notice that this is equally true of the public sector. Just as *private* enterprise in a modern mixed economy can be very different from private enterprise in the mostly-private economy of a hundred years ago, so *public* activity in a mixed economy, with private competition and democratic government, can be very different from public activity in a communist 'command economy' with no private competition and with dictatorial government. Models drawn from Queen Victoria's Britain are misleading guides to the private sector of a modern mixed economy. Models drawn from Stalin's Russia are misleading guides to its public sector.)

Even for the private-sector activities which it does model, some of the neoclassical model's principles are simply wrong. And some are too general for practical use, and can therefore mislead believers who apply

them too generally. For example it is certainly useful to understand how supply, demand and prices affect each other in particular markets. But that does not require a general model of the economy, or even a 'pure' model of relations between supply, demand and prices. Those relations actually vary widely from market to market. For example there are critical differences between the working of markets for money, land, corn, pharmaceutical drugs, antiques and fresh fruit. Many of their peculiarities arise from the nature of the goods, the time they take to produce, their size or divisibility, their degree of interdependence or substitutability with other goods, the need (or not) for people to borrow to buy them. Many of the differences are not best understood as 'imperfections' or departures from an ideal model. When you study them in detail— later in this course of study, or in real life – you will find that 'pure' models of market forces can harm as well as help the understanding and management of particular markets.

Now take in a simple theoretical reason for being careful how you use *any* 'pure' models.

The theory of second best

Should second best try to copy best? Not necessarily – sometimes yes, sometimes no. Suppose for practical reasons you can't afford a Ferrari and have to settle for a Ford. But after buying the Ford you have *some* cash left. Can it help you to make the Ford a bit more like the Ferrari? Can you improve the Ford by substituting *some* Ferrari parts for its Ford parts? Sometimes, yes: a Ferrari paint-job can improve a Ford. Sometimes, no: a few Ferrari cog-wheels won't improve a Ford gear-box, they will jam it or strip it. A Ford has its own design principles and its own distinctive directions of improvement. In Ford gear-boxes, Ford parts are best.

So with economic systems. Suppose you think that a wholly private, unregulated, perfectly competitive economic system would be ideal. (I don't, and you may not, but let's suppose.) It is not achievable in practice for well-known reasons – because of the need for public goods, the tendencies to monopoly, the need to regulate operators who try anti-social methods of competition, and so on. So you settle for second best: a mixed economy with a substantial public sector and a good deal of regulation. Can you improve that second-best by making it *as like as possible* to the ideal model?

As with the Ford and Ferrari, sometimes yes, and sometimes no.

Example: In your mixed economy, piped water supply is a natural monopoly. Do you reason that if it can't be *competitive* as in the ideal model, at least it can get you half way there by being *private* and *unregulated* as in the model?

No, because an unregulated private monopoly of water supply is likely to be not second but fourth best – worse than either a regulated private monopoly or a public monopoly, both of which can be restrained from extorting monopoly prices.

As in the details, so also in the general structure of the economy: even if you think a wholly private competitive economy would be the ideal, it does not follow that the best mixed economy will be the one most like that ideal model, i.e. the one with the smallest public sector, the least regulation, etc. And it does not necessarily follow that that ideal model will be much help to the mixed economy's policy-makers. It may just as often mislead them. A mixed economy has its own principles and if it needs an ideal model at all, it needs one of its own.

CONCLUSION

People want public, private and household goods and services in proportions which vary over time with changing tastes and technology.

Those goods are produced, in proportions which also vary, by combinations of public, private and household production.

The people derive their incomes from property rights, from work, from formal income transfers by institutions and informal transfers by kin and others.

To understand why the mixtures are as they are, to predict how they may be changing, to decide as a policy-maker what mixtures would be best, and to understand the working of each part of the mix, it is not helpful to rely on a general model of the system which models *only* private goods and private production, and models *those* as if they were unaffected by the presence of government, public producers and public income transfers.

The way most textbooks present it and users use it, it is fair to call the simple neoclassical model a capitalists' or property-owners' model. You know why. It chooses to equate passive ownership and active work as similar 'endowments', similarly productive. It accepts the unequal distribution of capital ownership as 'given'. It puts no value on the productivity that is lost when households can't get adequate household capital, or use of public capital. It chooses criteria of economic efficiency which are indifferent to unlimited inequalities. The criteria are also biased in favor of what people want as consumers rather than what they want as paid and unpaid producers. It encourages a systematic preference for privately profitable production over other modes. And many of the economists and others who use the model are unconscious of the values which shape it, and believe – wrongly – that it is an objective, value-free representation of economic activity.

Next, compare a model with a similar limitation: it also models a private market economy without public or household production. But I think it is truer to what it does model; it gives more scope and importance to government; and most of its users are aware of the values and social preferences which have helped to shape the theory that they use.

A POST-MARXIST, POST-KEYNESIAN MODEL

Historical reminders:

The classical economists – Smith, Ricardo, and others – were interested in the class distribution of income. They knew why landlords got rent, capitalists got profits and workers got wages – but they could not decide what determined *exactly how much* each got.

In the 1860s neoclassics began to argue, as we have just seen, that they each get as income the amount they contribute to the market value of the goods which they jointly produce. It follows that their rewards should give them enough income to buy all that they jointly produce, and keep each other fully employed.

Marx argued differently. A part of workers' output has to go to the workers as a subsistence wage to keep them alive and breeding and bringing up their replacements. The rest of their output is surplus value. That's up for grabs. Who gets it – how it is split between capitalist and worker – is a subject of class conflict and is chiefly determined by relative strength and bargaining power. Marx thought the capitalists got most of it. But the fluctuating strength of the bargainers, plus some effects of technical progress and capital accumulation, caused regular booms and slumps. Those and other causes would eventually destroy capitalism.

Sixty years later neither story seemed to fit the facts of twentieth century capitalism. Marxist theory could not explain why the system survived, with workers getting substantial shares of surplus value as their incomes kept pace with economic growth. Neoclassical theory could not explain the system's booms and slumps and unemployment, least of all in the 1930s when plenty of people willing to work for bare subsistence wages were still unemployed.

New theory was needed. It came from widely scattered places, from institutional economists, modernizing Marxists and disillusioned neoclassics. It has since been distilled into simple general models like the one we will presently introduce. Because such models owe something each to classical theory, to Marx, and to new theory from the 1920s to the 1950s, they are variously labelled 'classical/Marxist', 'neoMarxist' or 'post-Keynesian'. For convenience we will call them post-Keynesian. You need not learn all the contributing theories, but for identification the leading contributors were John Maynard Keynes (English, 1883-1946), Gunnar Myrdal (Swedish, 1898-1987), Piero Sraffa (Italian, 1898-1983), Michal Kalecki (Polish, 1899-1970), Edward Chamberlin (American, 1899-1967), Joan Robinson (English, 1903-1983), Thomas Balogh (Hungarian 1905-1985) and Nicholas Kaldor (Hungarian, 1908-1986).

Some or all of those theorists thought real life differed from the neoclassical model in five critical respects:

- Imperfect competition is not just an occasional shortcoming of capitalist systems. Capitalist systems have some systematic tendencies to monopoly. (Sraffa, Robinson, Chamberlin, Kalecki.)

- Wage and profit shares are determined chiefly by bargaining strength. So wages don't necessarily reflect the value the worker produces. Profit is not a reward for the use of a given value of capital. On the contrary, it is the profit the capitalist manages to take that determines the value of his capital. (Kalecki, Robinson, Sraffa.)

- What capitalists choose to do with their profits (spend? invest? keep liquid?) is what chiefly determines the level of employment. (Keynes, Kalecki.) But -

- Investment has such uncertainties and time-lagged multiplier effects that investors are not likely to produce steady full employment. Left to itself capitalism has some natural instability. (Myrdal, Kalecki, Keynes, Sraffa.)

- There are means by which government can contrive full employment. (Keynes, Kalecki.)

- But steady full employment is likely to cause accelerating inflation unless there is also some public restraint of incomes. (Robinson, Kalecki, Balogh.)

The theorists had their differences. But except for Chamberlin who was more conservative than the others, most of their differences were about methods of analysis rather than about the way the economic system actually worked. The following model is simplified from the version offered in Joan Robinson and John Eatwell, *An Introduction to Modern Economics* (1973).

Summary in a sentence: Employment and growth are determined mainly by investors' decisions, but those are made with such uncertainty about the future, and such time-lagged and multiplier effects, that left to themselves they are as likely to cause booms and slumps or long-lasting unemployment as to cause stable full employment; and left to itself, any stable full employment is likely to cause accelerating inflation.

So as a first conclusion, government should not leave the economy to itself. To arrive at what it should do, post-Keynesians identify the basic forces at work in a capitalist economy as follows.

CAPITAL

A few of the people – commonly less than one in ten of them in Keynes' day – own most of the private capital. Not many owners allocate their capital to particular uses as in neoclassical models. Instead they own shares in firms, whose directors make most of the saving and investment decisions. Or they deposit their money with financial institutions (banks, superannuation funds, investment trusts) whose directors decide where to lend or invest it. Most productive private investment is by firms, out of profits or loans serviced from profits. And when firms borrow, it is not all from owners of funds. Quite a lot of it is money created for them by commercial banks.

Some capitalists (from Bill Gates to your local storekeeper) do run their own businesses. That's productive work and it deserves managers' rewards, whether those are fixed salaries or a share of profits. But whether owners or others do the work, the element of *ownership* does not in itself contribute anything to production. As Marx argued, it merely amounts to 'power over the labor of others': a property right to take unearned income from the output of others.

WAGES, PRICES AND PROFITS

Firms hire workers to produce goods and services for market. The firms may pay some rent for land, and some interest if they borrow money. But their main cost of production is wages – both their own wage bills, and the wage costs which are incorporated in the prices of the capital equipment, components and materials which they buy from others. *Money wages* are determined chiefly by bargaining strength, within limits set by custom, community standards and expectations, and capacity to pay. *Real wages* then depend on what the money wages will buy, i.e. on prices.

Some prices (for example for bulk commodities like corn, meat, wool) vary with supply and demand as in the neoclassical model, so that producers don't know what profit they will get until they go to market. But nowadays the prices of most goods are set by adding a profit mark-up to the costs of production. The forces of supply and demand are still at work – but at prices which are also affected by market strength. The profit mark-up over wage costs is what determines the wage share and the profit share of output. (You will presently see that the mark-up determines the wage share in a double way. It divides the immediate returns between profit and wages. And by setting prices, it determines what share of output the wages will actually buy.)

Degrees of monopoly

What determines how big the mark-up can be? That varies with the market strength of those concerned. How strong is the firm against labor, to keep wages down? How strong is it against competitors and consumers, to push prices up? Consider four limiting cases:

Strong, Strong Firms may be strong against labor and also against competitors and consumers – for example if they use unskilled, unorganized labor to produce a monopoly service that consumers can't do without.

Strong, Weak Firms may be strong enough against labor to get labor for low wages, but have their mark-ups shaved by consumer resistance and price-cutting competition from other firms.

Weak, Strong Firms may be weak against labor but strong against consumers, for example if they use scarce, skilled, strongly organized labor to produce patented products or monopoly services.

Weak, Weak Firms may have to pay high wages to strong labor, but shave their profit mark-ups to sell in hotly competitive markets.

Those four are extreme cases. In practice industries range from strong to weak against labor, and from monopolist to competitive against each other and the consumers, through all the degrees between the extremes. Small firms (local trades-people, village general stores) may have 'conditional' monopolies as long as they don't drive local custom away by pushing prices *too* high. Big firms may dominate as monopolists or oligopolists in industries which have high costs of entry or continuous returns to scale. Firms which own limited natural resources, or patented products, or brand names which customers have come to trust, may be able to price their products above their competitors' and still outsell them. Where substitutions are possible, monopolists may compete with one another: gas with electricity, buses with trains, one exclusive brand name with another.

A producer with some degree of monopoly can aim at a degree of monopoly pricing. What is monopoly pricing? With most goods, the higher the price, the less people are likely to buy. The lower the price, the more they are likely to buy. Market experience should reveal the price, and the profit mark-up *per unit* at which a firm's *total* profits are highest. Suppose for example that you are the only supplier of ice creams on a hot beach – but it is only a *degree* of monopoly, because there is a competitor not *too* far away, and people can do without ice creams altogether if they think the price is unreasonable. Your production costs are 10 cents per ice cream, with no economies of scale. You find that you can sell 1,000 a day at 20 cents, or 600 at 30 cents, or 300 at 40 cents. Work out which one will get you most *total* profit. That is the optimum monopoly price for your degree of monopoly. What does 'optimum' mean in this case? It means the price that will make you richest. Notice that it is not the price that yields most profit per ice cream. It is not the price that sells most ice creams. And it is not the price at which you would be making the most productive use of resources for your society.

Now remember how complex modern production is. Dozens of firms may have contributed materials, components and services to any finished product, each firm pricing its contribution according to its particular labor costs and its particular market strength. Each firm in the production chain totals its costs of capital, its labor costs and the costs of the materials or components that it buys, then adds a profit mark-up to arrive at the price at which it sells the developing product on to the next firm in the chain. Each firm's profit is thus part of the next firm's costs. So costs and profits early in the chain may be marked up many times before a final owner buys a finished product. A common effect of that (averaging widely different pricing in different industries) sees firms' mark-ups of 5 to 10 percent yielding total profit shares around 30 per cent and labor shares around 70 per cent, for whole industries and national economies. (There is an example near the end of Chapter 34 – turn to it now if you would like to see some figures.)

DYNAMIC INSTABILITY

So far, the model has offered a modern Marxist view of

the distribution of wealth and income through capitalists' and workers' competition for shares of surplus value. We now turn to questions of national economic management. What determines a capitalist economy's levels of investment, employment and inflation? Why do those levels fluctuate? Why isn't the system self-adjusting? Left to themselves, why *don't* market forces keep the system running smoothly with full employment, stable prices and no inflation?

Effective demand

Where does the spending money come from, to buy all the goods that are produced?

This model assumes that investment comes from the profit share. It assumes that workers don't save or invest on any significant scale; they spend their wages on consumer goods. But the wages of the workers who make the consumer goods are only 70 per cent or so of the selling price of those goods. So the workers who make them can only buy about 70 per cent of them. Who buys the rest?

Firms have the 30 per cent profit share. They distribute some of it (say, 10 of the 30 percent) as dividends to the capital owners, who spend it on consumer goods or investment goods. That disposes of another 10 per cent of the output of goods: 80 per cent sold, 20 per cent to go.

From the rest of the profit share (the 20 per cent of national income left after paying 10 per cent as dividend) firms can invest. To maintain existing output they must replace plant as it wears out. To expand production they must order new buildings, equipment, components and materials. Thus they can use the remaining profit share to buy the remaining 20 per cent of output.

They *can* do that. But *will* they?

Boom and slump

This is how employment and output can fluctuate:

Slump Various signs and portents make investors uncertain or pessimistic about the future. So they invest less, and keep some of their money handy to meet any trading losses. With less investment, the capital goods industries get fewer orders. They lay off some workers, who then have less to spend, so there is that much less demand for consumer goods. With falling sales, the producers of consumer goods find their output accumulating in their warehouses. So they cut output and lay off workers, which further reduces consumer demand. They also see how wise they were to cut investment, and they maybe cut it some more. That makes a further fall in orders for capital goods, more lay-offs, less consumer demand – and so on down the spiral into a general slump with heavy unemployment.

Boom Producers have overdone their cuts, taking output down *below* the reduced volume of sales. Warehouses are emptying. Some firms decide the time has come to increase output. Others have to resume investing whether they like it or not, just to stay in business, because through the slump they have let so much old plant run down and wear out. It may also happen that new products are invented – bicycles, cars, roller blades, VCRs, PCs – and industries start equipping themselves to meet predictable new demands. For those or other reasons, investment revives. Orders go to the capital goods industries. To meet the orders some of those industries also have to invest, ordering more machines to make machines. The capital goods producers hire more hands, whose wages begin to revive consumer demand. With rising demand, the producers of consumer goods also hire more hands (whose wages add to demand); they see how wise they were to invest; and if they decide the boom is going to last long enough to make it worth while, they may invest some more.

When the first orders for capital goods generate more demand for capital and consumer goods, that's called a multiplier. When the effects of higher income return to generate further investment by the original investors, that's called an accelerator. Over a year or two the multiplier and accelerator together can turn each dollar's worth of additional investment into several dollars' worth of additional wage income, effective demand, and output. (The actual magnitudes of multiplier and accelerator vary with circumstances.)

The boom may be self-limiting. Suppose the investors equip themselves fully to meet all the effective demand generated by the boom. Then – being fully equipped or over-equipped – they stop investing. Fewer orders go to the capital goods industries, which cut output, put off hands, pay less wages. That reduces effective demand for consumer goods, whose producers invest less still – and so on down the 'slump' spiral.

Alternatively the boom may overheat. Suppose firms demand more capital goods, and fully employed well-paid consumers demand more consumer goods, than the fully-employed system can physically produce. Too much money is chasing too few goods. Frustrated customers bid higher to get the goods they want. Producers find they can raise prices without losing sales. They do so, so there is demand-pull inflation. Workers respond. With rising prices reducing their purchasing power, and strong demand for their labor, they demand and get higher wages. That pushes up producers' costs and soon, consequently, their prices – so there is cost-push inflation.

Booms and slumps can have internal causes, as just described. They can also have external causes – for example sudden changes in export markets or import prices. So instability is likely, and is *natural to the system*. The system has no reliable self-stabilizing quality: levels of income and employment depend on innumerable independent investment decisions, taken with varying degrees of uncertainty and with variously time-lagged effects. There is no market mechanism or 'hidden hand' to stabilize the resulting total of investment.

What sort of mechanism *could* stabilize the whole volume of investment? It would have to work like this: If some firms increased their flow of investment, that would need to affect sales or prices in ways which motivated other firms to reduce their investment by corresponding amounts. Or if some firms decided to invest less, that must somehow cause others to invest more. In real life that sometimes happens – changes by some firms or industries are balanced by reverse changes in others. But destabilizing effects are equally possible. Strong investment may increase employment and income and effective demand as described in this model, and stimulate more investment. Or declining investment may reduce demand and further reduce investment, employment and income. Instead of negative feedback and self-adjustment, there is positive feedback and cumulative causation.

Tasks for government

If market forces can't maintain stable full employment, government should be able to do so. It controls public investment. Through its central banking, trade and corporate-tax policies it can influence private investment. Its income-tax and income-transfer policies can raise or lower the community's spendable income. Its sales taxes and tariff policies can raise or lower prices. It should keep those policies flexible, and flex them to restrain spending and investment when booms threaten to overheat, and to stimulate spending and investment when necessary to prevent unemployment. Government should maintain full employment by managing the levels of investment and effective demand.

That was Keynes' message. Most governments of developed mixed economies accepted it and tried with varying success to practise it from the 1940s through the 1960s. But increasingly from the 1970s they suffered rising levels of *both* inflation *and* unemployment. That happened – this model says – because governments and their economic advisers had accepted the Keynesian but not the post-Keynesian components of the model. What Robinson, Kalecki and Balogh argued soon after the appearance of Keynes' *General Theory* was this:

- Managed full employment is likely to have a self-destructive effect which must also be controlled if the full employment is to endure. Secure full employment alters a critical balance of power: it strengthens labor in its wage-bargaining with employers. Whether the bargaining is done centrally through national institutions (as used to happen in Sweden and Australia), or by strong unions industry by industry (as tends to happen in Britain), or in a market way as firms compete for scarce labor and workers shop around for the best offers (as tends to happen in the US), the result may be much the same: wages will rise faster than output. If wages do, so will prices. As prices rise, so again will wages, as workers act to maintain their real purchasing power.

- Workers don't have to be greedy to produce this effect. Economic growth comes from technical improvement in some industries but not others – typically in manufacturing but not in labor-intensive services like nursing or teaching. Where technical progress improves productivity, the workers have to get higher wages merely to maintain their wage share. That seems reasonable, so they seek and get wage rises. But with full employment, that may attract some workers and young recruits away from the occupations which do not have the benefit of technological progress. Workers in those occupations demand wage rises as a matter of comparative wage justice. That also is reasonable (or we would now be paying teachers and nurses the real wages they earned a century ago, less than the dole we now pay to the unemployed). To retain their labor and stay in business when other wages rise, employers of labor-intensive services have to raise their wages and therefore the selling prices of their services. When that happens in occupations which have had no increase in productivity, total wages and spending can rise faster than total output in the economy as a whole, with an inflationary effect on prices.

The fairest thing to do, and the effective way to prevent inflation, is to limit most wage increases to the rate of growth of productivity and total output in the economy as a whole. If there is full employment, market relations are unlikely to achieve that. It calls for some combination of public institutional restraint and prudent self-restraint of wages and prices. Both are easiest to contrive, and work best, where there is a culture of prudence and co-operation.

A political trade cycle? If governments try to manage full employment by Keynesian means only – by managing the levels of current investment and effective demand *without* effective price or income restraints – they may merely replace one pattern of boom and slump by another. It can happen like this:

The economic system itself tends to boom and slump for the reasons just noted.

There are also some cyclical tendencies in the economic policies of democratic governments which have to face elections every four or five years. Newly elected governments feel that they can if necessary do unpopular things which hurt people now but have good effects later. But as elections approach they want the economy to be looking good, and government tax and spending policies to be looking generous.

As Keynesian governments maintain full employment, tendencies to inflation will appear. We will presently see why there may also be balance-of-payments troubles. If the government has no price and income policies, all it can do to restrain the ill effects is to cut demand back to less than its full employment level. That is an unpopular effect, and it usually has to be contrived by unpopular means, for example by increasing taxes or interest rates, or both.

So democratic governments are tempted to stimulate the economy in election years, then restrain inflation by unpopular means after the elections. The heavier the cuts then, the more room there will be for a heart-warming upturn in the run-up to the next election a few years later.

Why can't such governments strike a happy medium that keeps the forces in stable balance? Because without price and income restraints, the only stable balance would be one with inflation restrained by substantial unemployment. When the post-Keynesian model was born in the 1940s governments which offered permanent unemployment would not have got elected at all. So for twenty years or more, governments tended to cope with the contradiction between full employment and stable wages and prices by applying the brakes after each election, then restoring free-spending full employment in time for the next election. Hence the 'political trade cycle' first predicted in the 1940s by Thomas Balogh and Michal Kalecki.

Stagflation The model then predicts three further effects of attempts to manage full employment. Anyone could predict the first of them – it is not special to this model – but it adds one more to the post-Keynesians' tasks for government.

• Managed full employment may worsen the foreign exchange problems of countries with difficult trade balances. Suppose, for example, that the British economy is underemployed and needs stimulating. The government acts to increase consumers' spendable income. But the consumers don't use all of the extra money to buy British, they spend some of it on imported goods. The government has thus increased British spending on imports without doing anything to increase foreign spending on British exports. So (i) some of the effective demand the government has created will not help British employment and output as it was meant to do; (ii) the extra imports may cause a trade and payment deficit; and (iii) if the trade and payment difficulties are left to the market, exchange rates may change with effects which hurt employment and financial stability within Britain. So some countries' trading patterns may dictate that managed full employment should be accompanied by import and exchange controls.

• In all countries, changes to the wage and profit shares won't *only* affect the distribution of income between workers and capitalists. They will also affect the amounts available for consumer spending and for investment, and may therefore affect future rates of growth and levels of employment in the system as a whole. That is to say, the *division* of the cake can affect the size of the cake. If workers achieve too high a wage share they may *lose* real income (by restraining investment). If firms achieve too high a profit share they may *lose* income for their owners (by leaving too little effective consumer demand). (Notice that this prediction assumes that investment is from profits, and that wages are spent on consumer goods. We will presently note that those assumptions may now be out of date.)

• For a number of reasons (which can wait) full employment is not likely to survive continuing high inflation. So whoever happens to be winning the running battle for wage and profit shares, the inflationary effect of the battle is likely to keep employment and income below their full potential. But the inflationary habits of behavior may continue, with wages chasing prices and prices chasing wages long after the death of the full employment which generated that behavior. Hence 'stagflation', the simultaneous occurrence of unemployment and inflation which Keynesian theory could not explain, but (post-Keynesians claim) this model can.

History and culture Economists of at least six nationalities contributed to post-Keynesian theory, but most of them were writing in, or about, English-speaking countries. Some of their assumptions about the motivation and behavior of business, labor and government were less true of some other countries. Germans and Japanese had suffered defeat and terrible bombing destruction in World War Two, and Germans had historical memories of a disastrous runaway inflation in 1923/4. As they rebuilt their cities and their economy after the war they tended to work harder, co-operate more, demand less, and avoid inflation by more self-restraint than their English-speaking equivalents did. The patterns of self-interest which post-Keynesians discerned in fully-employed capitalism were present in German and Japanese capitalism, but were better restrained for cultural and historical reasons. They may perhaps be more restrained in English-speaking countries now, after their experience of inflation through the 1970s and 1980s.

Conclusion Managed full employment may not work for long unless it is accompanied by some effective control and/or self-restraint of incomes and prices, and sometimes also some import and exchange controls.

Advantages of the model

I think this model has virtues of three general kinds. It is a better guide than neoclassical theory is to the amount and kind of government which market activities need; to the processes which determine levels of investment, employment and inflation; and to policies for influencing those levels. It is realistic about the common and conflicting interests of capitalists and workers in the private sector. And it models those private-sector relationships in a way which positively invites ethical and reformist thought about them.

Changing conflicts of interest Keynes and the early post-Keynesian theorists assumed that capital owners (not including home owners) were perhaps ten per cent of the population, and did all its saving and investing from their profit share. The rest of the people had an indirect interest in the profit share, in that it financed the investment which kept them employed and productive. But the owners did not invest the whole profit share, they spent quite a lot of it on luxurious living. So it was easy to see them as exploiters keeping the rest of the people poorer than they need have been.

In fact many wage-earners also saved. But they mostly deposited their savings in savings banks and building societies, which lent the savings to government or back to the savers to buy houses or other household capital, so their saving did not contribute much to what

the theorists counted as private capital ownership. That has since changed a good deal. Besides saving to buy household capital rising numbers of wage and salary earners now save anything from five to twenty per cent of their incomes through their own and their employers' contributions to superannuation funds. In some countries more than half of all households are accumulating capital which will provide property income to their members in old age. Those savings are a big source of investment, and are typically invested not by their owners but by professional fund managers. Instead of a society in which ten per cent exploited the rest, we may now be developing societies in which fifty or sixty per cent of wage earners accumulate some private capital and expect some property income through long years of retirement. They may lose to the profit share through their earning years, but in retirement they will pull interest, rent and profit from those still earning, including perhaps forty per cent who do not own their houses, have no superannuation, and will depend on tax-funded age pensions.

Likely political effects of those changing numbers?

On the one hand more voters than before, especially ageing voters with private superannuation, may vote for pro-business, anti-labor, anti-tax and anti-welfare policies, and this may already have contributed a little to the historical Right turn. On the other hand post-Keynesian theory does not encourage that shift as readily as most versions of neoclassical theory do. Post-Keynesians are readier to recognize the contributions of market strength, bargaining strength and political strength to overall wage and profit shares and to particular wage inequalities. They see more scope for government to stabilize investment by means which also allow low and stable rates of interest, and combine low unemployment with low inflation and with adequate welfare incomes and services. So voters who get their economic understanding from post-Keynesian economists may respond to the changing distribution of property income both more fairly and more effectively than do voters with more faith in *un*aided and *un*restrained market forces.

DISADVANTAGES OF THE MODEL

Who produces? Like the neoclassical model, this is basically a model of a private enterprise economy. Its households don't produce anything, or save, or invest, they only consume. Post-Keynesians see a more active role for government than many neoclassics do, but their model still shows government chiefly as a regulator and redistributor, not as a producer.

The model distinguishes between capital goods,

which are productive, and their owners who (if they don't work) are not. That encourages users of the model to disapprove of capital inequalities and unearned property incomes. So why doesn't it contrast both public and household capital ownership as 'innocent', allowing the productive use of capital goods without great capital inequalities or unearned incomes? Keynes looked forward, perhaps in a more visionary than practical way, to the 'socialization' of a good deal of investment, by which he may have meant more public influence on new investment rather than more public ownership of it. It is surprising that modern post-Keynesians don't take more interest in the public sector's capacity to produce with other aims than profit, to run monopolies which don't necessarily exploit their monopolist advantages, to provide competition in industries which would otherwise be open to private monopoly, to price services differently to people with different capacities to pay, or to provide jobs and incomes in areas, or at occupations, or to types of people, whom competitive profit-seekers could not employ. In practice many post-Keynesians do support those uses of public ownership and employment. But it is practical thought rather than their

distinctive theory which prompts them to. The theory has the negative virtue that it does not imply that such policies necessarily reduce economic efficiency. But it is reasonable to argue that economists with the social values that many post-Keynesians have should use models which draw attention to, rather than away from, the distinctive uses of public and household capital. They should be specially interested in relations between the productive effects and the distributive effects of different patterns of public, private and household capital ownership. To the extent that the financing of private and household investment is left to the market as neoclassical models recommend and post-Keynesian models (by omission) allow, some bad allocation is likely. Allocation between business and household investment may not be as productive as it could be. Nor may allocation between household and household. And allocation beteen landlords and owner-occupiers may be positively unproductive and unfair, increasing inequalities in ways which reduce productivity.

But it would not be difficult to extend post-Keynesian theory to have it deal satisfactorily with public and household production.

A THREE-SECTOR INSTITUTIONAL APPROACH

Now consider the approach to economic understanding that this text offers. 'Approach' rather than 'model', because it recommends that you do without a single master-model of economic systems. Plenty of thinkers in other disciplines – in history, political science, geography, sociology – do without them. But economists, especially as they are currently educated in English-speaking countries, tend to cling to their master-models so obstinately, and to feel so lost without one, that one eminent critic says, regretfully, that 'it takes a model to kick out a model'. You can treat this text's approach as another model if you like, but an anti-model or a multi-model might be a better name for it. Summarized in two sentences it says that your understanding of a society's economic activity is necessarily selective and therefore partly value-structured and intrinsically controversial. And what you study may be changing as you study it; so may your purposes in studying it; and so may the theories and methods of investigation that you will therefore need.

For use in rich democracies as the new century opens this approach takes account of the twentieth century growth of public, private and household productivity, public income transfers, and the opportunities summarized earlier as 'twelve ways to do well in

a mixed economy'. It takes account of the disagreed and changing purposes of economic activity as democracies become productive enough to keep all their people in secure comfort, and as they contemplate radical changes in the economic relations between men and women and children, between rich and poor countries, and between present and future generations and their natural environment. Within mixed economies it focuses on how resources are allocated to public, private and household producers; how they trade with each other and deal with government; and how wealth and income are distributed. Its selections and simplifications are shaped by many technical considerations and by the values which shape this course of study.

Here follow some main assumptions and recommendations of this approach, for comparison with those of the neoclassical and post-Keynesian approaches.

A MIXED ECONOMY

People want material goods and services. Besides the goods and services themselves, they want their production and distribution to serve other purposes too: purposes of freedom, security, enjoyment, self-expression, sociability, equality or inequality, justice, and so on.

People have many common and many conflicting interests and values. Their material interests and their values often influence each other but don't necessarily determine each other. People both shape and are shaped by their culture. Their culture does a good deal to shape their economic activity, and some of the economic activity is designed to sustain or change the culture. People work to sustain or change the culture – for example, to influence each others' wants and values – for both selfish and unselfish reasons. Economic theories are among their means of persuasion, so different groups may want differently-selective economic models and analyses.

Modes of production Most production needs some capital and organization. This approach classifies modes of production as household, private, and public, as defined earlier.

Motivating the modes It is a critical advantage of a mixed economy that it can get goods produced and distributed for a wide range of purposes as well as – and often together with – individual self-interest. It would be unworldly to depict households motivated only by love, public enterprises only by duty and private enterprises only by material self-interest. But speaking not of personal motivation but of institutional purposes it is a reasonable simplification to see household production for *use,* private production for *profit,* and public production for *multiple* economic and social purposes.

The diversity is good for *productivity:* compared with the single-sector private-enterprise economy of neoclassical and other models it can make productive use of a wider range of actual human motivation. It is good for *justice:* it provides transferred incomes, social services and household capital to large numbers of old, unemployed and poor people who could not get them from a private-sector-only economy. And it is good for the *quality of life,* including the opportunities for individual self-expression, because besides private employment it also offers a wide range of fulfilling work to people who like best to work within their families or neighborly groups, in charitable organizations, or in a public 'culture of service', for generous or cooperative rather than purely self-serving purposes.

But notice what this argument does *not* say. It does not say that all housework and public service are unselfish and all private employment is selfish. In reality there are selfish and generous, bossy and co-operative types everywhere – in households, in business and in government. Even if the average individual psychology does vary between the modes, the variations may not all be creditable to the household and public modes. Some

households, charities and public services offer opportunities to bullies and bigots; and private enterprise can often motivate selfish people to be more thoughtful and generous – more attentive to employers' or customers' wants – than they would be at home or in public service.

But however like or unlike the individual psychology may be, there are basic differences between the institutional constraints of the three modes of production. Households *can* produce cooperatively for use, as most public and private enterprises cannot. Public enterprises *can* (and many do) produce for multiple economic and social purposes. Private enterprises may give their customers excellent value for money, but it does usually have to be for money: competitive producers cannot behave much more generously than their competitors do, or they will go out of business. But their private status can often free them to respond quickly and inventively to changing technology and market conditions, and many executives, professionals and skilled tradespeople have found private employment more stimulating and satisfying than public.

Interdependence Each mode of production affects the performance of the others in both cooperative and competitive ways.

Cooperative: There is intricate trade between the sectors. This text will often remind you that we do not have a public sector producing all our public goods, a private sector producing all our market goods, and households sleeping in home-made bedding and cooking their dinners on home-made stoves. Each type of product (public goods, private goods, household goods) is produced with contributions from all three sectors. (Remember the example of the sector mix of British and French motoring in 1985.) Lots of public capital is used by producers in all three sectors. How family households bring up their children helps to determine how willingly and skilfully, and happily or unhappily, the grown children will work in all three sectors. Public and household producers' work is affected by the quality and price of the many goods and services which they must buy from private producers. And so on.

Competitive: The presence of each mode of production affects the performance of the others in various competitive ways. There may be less domestic oppression if women can escape it by going out to earn. There may be less public inefficiency where there is private competition and some threat or possibility of privatizing public services. There is less private exploitation of cheap labor where government regulates private enterprise, has public enterprises pay fair wages, and pays transfer incomes to the unemployed. There is less private exploitation of tenants where poor households can rent public housing or buy their own. And so on. (So private-sector-only models of the mixed economy may even misrepresent the private sector which they *do* model, by neglecting the other sectors' effects on it.)

Producers, consumers and voters are the same people People influence the whole sector-mix of the mixed economy, and their individual uses of public and private and household services, in a number of ways.

They demand private goods and services and some public goods and services in a market way by their spending and investment choices. They demand other public goods, and they ban or regulate many private goods, by voting and other political means. To the extent that their means allow, they decide what to make and do for themselves as household producers. But the economy as a whole gives most people much wider spending choices than working choices, and there is mounting evidence that in rich countries the quality of life at work is just as important to people's happiness as their quality of life at leisure and as consumers. For many purposes, concepts of economic efficiency should give due weight not only to costs of production and fair wage levels but also to the organization of work and the quality of workers' experience of it.

GOVERNMENT

Although it is common to lump government and public enterprises together as 'the public sector', government has important but partly different relations with the three productive sectors which it has to regulate. As a rough definition where it is helpful to distinguish them from one another, *public enterprises* produce goods and services, while *government* makes and enforces laws, regulates and taxes people, and transfers income.

Real governments are not single-minded. Within a modern democratic government many people and purposes are at work in a great many institutions, conflicting and competing as well as co-operating with one another. Setting aside those complexities and treating government not as a single will but as a type of activity, the functions of government in a mixed economy include these:

Mixing a manageable economy   Government does a good deal to determine the mix:

- It decides what collective public goods (roads, scientific research, clean air) should be produced.
- It decides what individual goods (education, welfare services) to produce and distribute free or below cost to individuals.

- It decides what ordinary market goods (posts, telecommunications, power, transport, coal, steel, manufactured goods) should be produced by public enterprises, and whether as monopolists or as competitors with private producers.
- It does a good deal to decide what the private sector can produce, by banning some industries, protecting others, regulating them all, providing or failing to provide the research and education and public services which particular industries need.
- By taxation and other means it has some influence (usually minor) on the distribution of wealth.
- It has major influence on the distribution of income through minimum wage policies, income and commodity taxes, income transfers, public housing and welfare policies.
- It has some influence, by educational provisions, political persuasion and other means, on the cultural determinants of economic belief and behavior.

People won't all agree what mix is best – what proportions of public, private and household production, with what patterns of regulation, would be best. Some of their interests and ideals conflict. They put different values on different freedoms and equalities, on productivity, on environmental care, and so on. They even measure some of those qualities differently. But there should be quite wide agreement that whatever its other effects a good sector mix should -

- allow people to be as productive as they are willing and able to be;
- allow all desirable freedoms of choice;
- protect things which majorities want to protect, such as workers' and consumers' health and safety, threatened resources, valued items of heritage; and
- give government effective means of managing full employment, low inflation and balanced foreign trade and exchange, and assuring appropriate allocation of resources to the three modes of production.

Managing a mixed economy How the industries, markets and other institutions of modern mixed economies work in detail, and need to be governed, are subjects of the next twenty eight chapters. Fourteen chapters then review the strategies by which they may try for full employment, low inflation, satisfying work, equitable distribution of income, and social and environmental reform and conservation in a conflict-ridden globalizing world economy. This already-exhausting chapter is not the place to preview all that.

SUMMARY

This course of study will encourage you to use items of neoclassical, post-Keynesian and other theory wherever they fit the facts and serve your purposes. Along with that uninhibited use of others' ideas, this adaptable historical and institutional three-sector approach has some theory of its own -

- If you recognize three modes of production, that encourages you to explore their different potentialities, the working relations between them, the alternative ways of doing things which they sometimes offer, and ways of allocating resources between and within them.

- If you do your best to understand the actual situations, beliefs and purposes of economic actors, you are likely to understand their activity better, and conceive better economic policies, than economists who deal only in hard facts and quantities.

- There are similarities between buyers' and sellers' *market* relations and employers' and workers' working relations, but there are also important differences. The differences make it more misleading than helpful to think of work relations as market relations. Economists should stop using the concept of a 'labor market'.

- Like other social activity, economic activity has such complicated patterns of cause and effect that causal analysis of it has to select, to simplify, and to guess. You can understand it best, and do it best, if you see it as having three ingredients: facts, which should be true; selections, which are likely to be disagreed by people with different values and social purposes; and causal relations, which you can only know by knowing what would have happened without the causes in question. But in practice you must often guess or imagine, rather than know for a fact, what would be happening if particular causes were not operating or were operating differently. Depending on the facts of the case, those imagined alternatives can be anywhere from obvious to quite uncertain: from easy to know to hard to guess with any confidence.

- There are various ways of arriving at the imagined alternatives on which knowledge of causal relations has to depend. Analysts can trace the causal processes themselves, doing their best to understand the minds and motives of the people concerned. They can compare historical studies, letting some countries' experience serve as instructive alternatives to others. They can look for statistical associations or dissociations, which suggest that particular phenomena may or may not be causally related. Or they can

be guided by their theories. Example: Neoclassical theory tells free traders that tariffs normally reduce the output and income of the protected economy. Other theories predict that there are circumstances in which well designed tariffs can make the protected economy *more* productive. This text will advise that you may need to know a lot of the local facts and potentialities before you can judge a particular tariff's effects with any confidence at all.

- There are uses for some maths and some professional jargon in economics. But the more its causal analysis can be done in plain language, the better it can usually protect its authors and its users from mistakes, especially 'scientistic' mistakes about the forces at work in the economy. The most important of those forces are commonly people's values, beliefs, purposes, changes of mind, and responses to economic and other constraints and opportunities.

- As political economists have long argued, economics is the discipline which asks economic questions but looks for the answers wherever they lie. Economists should explore whatever causes of economic effects it would be useful or interesting to know, wherever those causes are to be found in economic, social, cultural or political life, and in present or past time.

Advantages and disadvantages of an adaptable historical and institutional approach

The main disadvantage of this approach, as of this whole course of study, is its emphasis on the complexity and changeability of economic behavior. It does not promise many sure ways of predicting economic futures, especially in the middle and long terms. It does not even promise much better prediction as economists accumulate more theory. Instead it predicts that as economic organization and behavior change, economists' theories and methods are likely to obsolesce and need replacement. Prediction can perhaps be improved by developing better economic arrangements rather than better theories about them. (Or better theories will be those which design better arrangements, rather than merely improving our understanding of how present institutions work.)

As for economic science, so for social purposes. This adaptable approach does not offer simple, sufficient, consensual aims for national policy (where others may say 'most is best – it is in everybody's interest to maximize conventionally-measured output'). It says that the aims themselves, and the effective ways of achieving them, are likely to vary over time, with economic growth, with national cultures and political and business capacities.

The advantages of this approach are much the same as its disadvantages. It is more realistic and less misleading than the neoclassical model or any other timeless deductive theory with unrealistic assumptions about human nature and motivation. It accepts much post-Keynesian wisdom but adds to it as the facts of public and household production and interaction require. It emphasizes the need to study local facts and circumstances, and to expect economic behavior to vary considerably with time and place. So it suggests that economists' intellectual equipment should be less scientistic and more experienced and investigative than is currently orthodox. It should include batteries of possibilities: alternative kinds of purpose and performance to look for, and questions to ask and methods of investigation to use, in situations of many kinds.

Thus instead of offering a single master-model of economic systems and relationships and criteria of efficiency, usable by all economists for all purposes and claiming falsely to be objective and value-free, this approach insists that although economists' dealings with fact should always be truthful, and their causal connections should be as sure as the facts allow, their analyses are necessarily selective and – to that extent – value-structured and likely to be disagreed. So we must expect a plurality of theories and analyses.

That makes three reasons why economists should keep not one but a number of general models and theoretical approaches in mind. First, different problems and purposes, especially in different sectors of the economy, may call for different approaches. Second, conflicting values help to shape many of the public conflicts and professional disagreements with which, as an economist, you will have to deal.. Clarifying and debating the social, ethical and moral merits as well as the technical merits of contending analyses should be a regular part of your work. Third, to understand or predict or influence economic behavior you will often need to know how the economic actors think. You must do your best to understand their aims and expectations and the theoretical beliefs which underlie them, as well as knowing your own.

So, modestly, this approach suggests that it should not be the only model in your head.

Now compare it with another approach which arrives by a different route at very similar conclusions.

MEN AND WOMEN

In the United States in 1995 7.5 per cent of all professors of economics, and 5.4 per cent of those in the twenty leading economics departments, were women. In the United Kingdom in 1996 4.2 per cent of the professors of economics were women. Men thus outnumber women by fifteen or twenty to one in the leadership of a profession whose work is necessarily influenced by its members' values, and has significant influence on the distribution of income and work and leisure, including their distribution between women and men. What has that scandalous distribution of power to do with the choice and design of rival bodies of economic theory and education?

Male feminists are rarely popular with either sex, so let an able woman economist speak for her kind. I thank Dr. Sue Richardson for permission to quote at length from *Why do Women Make Hopeless Economists? (or Fail to Succeed Playing Man-Made Economics by Men's Rules)* in *Economic Papers 17,* 1, March 1998.

> To make women feel welcome in economics is important because it is fair and it will expand the opportunities for women and the potential recruits for economics. But that is just the beginning. It is highly likely that the inclusion of substantial numbers of women into the economists' fold will, as has happened with other disciplines, expand the range of questions and the analytical approaches used. Questions of particular interest to women, including the role of women in the economy, are more likely to be asked. . .

> Some examples of the questions which women may well wish to explore are:

> - discrimination
> - intersection between family and paid work
> - work as an experience, not just as a source of income
> - properly defined constraints and choices, to include cultural constraints and power relations (you will stay home and look after my children: it is demeaning for a man to do this)
> - government as an efficient substitute for the male head of household as a form of support for dependants (elderly, young children, disabled). . .

The Masculine Assumptions of Economics

The metropolitan centre of economics is occupied by a form of the discipline which aspires to be, and largely is, rigorous, analytical, deductive, logically impeccable and hard (why are men so keen to be *hard?).* In order to do this well, you need to be clever, and so it is a good way of establishing a hierarchy of esteem. But you do not need to be useful or knowledgeable about how the world works or imaginative or insightful.

The deductive character of masculine economics means that a whole elaborate edifice has been constructed on the foundation of a few assumptions about the way people behave in their economic life. Initially the assumptions and the deductions from them were adopted to see whether self-interested behaviour could, under certain conditions, lead to socially desirable results. It was, in effect, a formal logical test of [Adam] Smith's propositions about the efficacy of the invisible hand. But it became more than that. Masculine economics slipped from the insight that under certain tightly defined conditions, selfish, individual and egocentric behaviour *could* produce economically efficient outcomes, to the assumption that people, in their economic behaviour, are indeed selfish, individual and egocentric. These foundation assumptions of economics have rarely been explicitly tested to see whether they have much intersection with the way in which people actually feel and act in their economic lives. In Sen's words, "A specific concept of man is ingrained in the question itself, and there is no freedom to depart from this conception so long as one is engaged in answering this question. The realism of the chosen conception of man is simply not a part of this inquiry." [from Amartya Sen, 'Rational Fools: A Critique of the Behavioral Foundations of Economic Theory', *Philosophy and Public Affairs*, 6, 1977] . . .

Edgeworth asserted that "the first principle of Economics is that every agent is actuated only by self-interest". This proposition can be (and has been) made to be tautological – any action which is taken is preferred by the actor to the alternatives which are available to her, so it is self-interested. I find this depressing. It robs humanity of the possibility of noble behaviour. It means that we cannot distinguish morally or in other ways between the private and greedy person, the passionate believer in a cause, the person who devotes her life to the well-being of others. All are equally said to be acting in their own self-interest.

The proposition that all economic action is selfish diminishes humanity in a second way. It has been applied, by economists, to the effect that if the slightest whiff of self-interest can be detected in an action then that self-interest is assumed to be the whole of the motivation. In fact, motivations are multiple and complex. Altruism, duty, love, compassion and fellow feeling are among them.

But those motivations often need *some* reinforcement (though not necessarily dominant, direct or immediate) from self-interest. Only the saintly will be entirely guided by selfless motives. Thus some self-interest can nearly always be identified. And with a wave of the hand it is assumed by masculine economics to displace all other motivations.

The assumption that people are entirely selfish in their economic behaviour also rules out systematic inquiry into the extent to which selfish or other motivations are affected by context and the behaviour of others. If a person behaves altruistically and gets selfishness in return, then she will feel not moral but a mug. This issue is important to the crucial question: does a system which runs on and assumes selfishness increase the total quantum of selfish behaviour, because this is the norm and is rewarded, or does it diminish it because it economises on altruism, saving altruism for circumstances where selfishness is hostile to human well-being? Man-made economics does not explore these questions (though the occasional male economist/philosopher does) because preferences are assumed to be stable and exogenous, not determined by experience and environment, and motivations are fixed by assumption. As Sen puts it [in the paper cited above] the long debate about whether selfish behaviour guided by price signals and competition would promote the general good has dominated economics. "The limited nature of the query has had a decisive influence on the choice of economic models and the conception of human beings in them."

Compare that reasoning with the preceding summary of the principles which shape this course of study. The two agree about what is wrong with the rigorous, deductive master-models. They agree about the complex human nature and the diverse and changing purposes which actually shape economic activity. They agree about the equal importance of women's and men's roles in that activity; and about a good deal else. Dr Richardson agrees that there are personal exceptions to her characterization of masculine and feminine economics – some women are orthodox neoclassical economists, some men like Amartya Sen are not. As a male author I don't claim that this is a feminist text. But it encourages its users to work for a social democratic world in which – among other blessings – half the economists are women and the distinctive concerns of women have strong influence on economic education and policy. And it aims at the kind of economic education that I believe such a world would want.

Conclusion: a reminder of the political and social uses of economic master models

This chapter ends the philosophical and historical part of this course of study. Its exercises will presently test your skill at relating economic models and analyses to the social purposes which they can serve. We have devoted eighteen chapters, and perhaps half a year of your time, to developing that skill because it is a critically important one. The rich democracies face historic questions about the uses of their new affluence, their principles of justice, relations between men and women and children, the spoiling and exhaustion of the world's natural resources. Through your working lifetime a lot may depend on the economic self-knowledge or self-deception which experts offer, in simple understandable forms, to their societies' citizens. So here is a final summary of reasons why the warring economic theories matter, and may matter most in the simplified forms in which they reach the public.

Remember what the simple master-models do. They tell you what causes what in the economy, and they select and simplify what their authors judge to be the most important elements of economic activity. That means they first select the *effects* they will model. (National output? Its unequal distribution between classes? Between men and women? Rates of growth? unemployment? inflation? Rates of resource use and renewal, environmental care or spoiling? The allocation of resources for the upbringing and education of children?) Then they select which *causes* of those effects they will model. (The market exchanges? Inequalities of market strength and bargaining power which underlie the exchanges? Current knowledge and technology? The shaping of people's economic wants? The political conflicts and choices? Cultural determinants, including the prevailing economic theories?) And they select the *concepts and identities,* the methods of *measurement* and the criteria of *efficiency* which their models will use. Most of those choices necessarily call on the modellers' social values and purposes as well as their observation of facts and their judgment of causal relations.

So as a selector, each model directs attention to particular elements of economic activity: to particular kinds of causes of particular kinds of effects. That commonly suggests some particular range of policy options and limitations.

For example -

Suppose that shareholders and banks provide funds to a firm which builds a factory, buys materials and hires workers to manufacture washing machines to sell to shops which retail them for cash or credit to households whose women (mostly) use them to do the family laundry.

You know how different observers of those facts will – consciously or not – see different aspects of them and draw attention to different causes and effects of them. For example –

- Observer A sees an admirable economic system meeting everyone's needs and choices.

- B's sense of justice notices that the production is all for profit, the workers get less than the value they produce, so the capitalists get something for nothing.

- C likewise notices the relation between capital and labor but accepts it because she sees the profit share as a necessary source of investment and growth whose benefits go to everyone, however unequally.

- D notices how the sale price of the washing machine is split between profits, capital costs, high wages, and advertising costs. She suspects that all those winners – capitalists, workers and advertisers – overcharge the customers.

- E is a male feminist (they do exist) who sees simple patriarchal exploitation as mostly-male owners take all the unearned income, mostly-male workers take all the earned income, and most of the unpaid work (the household washing) is done by women.

All those differences are moral rather than technical. They are differently valued selections from the same bare facts and causal relations. They need not include (although they sometimes do also include) any factual or causal disagreement – any 'objective' disagreement – at all.

That is the sort of selective vision and valuation that pervades everyone's understanding of daily life. Among economists the analyses may be more complicated but the same selective principles apply. It is not hard to imagine how differently the rival models sketched in this chapter might dispose experts to perceive the facts of that laundering industry, and suggest what (if anything) government ought to do about it.

This course is about to change gear and become more practical and detailed. Many microeconomic chapters have to describe many particular economic institutions, markets and processes. Like any other descriptions these descriptions have to be selective and purposeful. The purpose is your education, but the information can't help being selected by my values. My values include respect for yours. This course aims to equip you to think your way to your own view of the world. To achieve that independence I believe you need to be able to do three things at once in much of your work:

- notice the underlying *purposes and selective principles* of the analyses you meet

- notice how the analysts arrive at their *causal conclusions* – i.e. having selected the causal areas and possibilities that they will investigate, by what means (and how reliably) do they decide what is actually or probably causing what?

- judge how true and representative the *facts* in the analysis are, or seem likely to be.
Try them now.

EXERCISE

Take all the questions as referring to modern mixed economies.

1. Three economists – a neoclassic, a post-Keynesian and a three-sector institutionalist, each of the kind sketched in this chapter – are asked to find out why sales of pornographic videos are increasing.

(A) What causes of the increase would you expect each to go looking for? If they found what they expected to find, what general kind of explanation of the increase might each offer?

(B) Your government wants some independent policy advice about the censorship, regulation or liberation of pornography. You have to write the brief which will ask the consultants for their proposals. What difference if any do you think it will make to the consultants' responses if you present the question as -

(i) a question from the Department of Justice about free speech and individual rights;

(ii) a question from the Departments of Health and Education about how consumers' tastes and market preferences are formed; or

(iii) a question from the Departments of Industrial Relations and Consumer Protection about the permissible exploitation of employees and consumers by the profit-seekers who produce pornography?

To add to the interest of the task, you may specify the gender of each brief-writer, or leave readers to discern that for themselves.

2. Our neoclassic, post-Keynesian and institutionalist economists are asked how they think that radio and television broadcasting would best be owned, financed and regulated. Sketch three likely answers.

3. Seven people are asked why their country has had more than 8 per cent of its workforce unemployed for more than 10 years. What can you guess about their general economic beliefs from their short answers?

- *Smith:* The workers are paid less than the value of what they produce. So there is not enough purchasing power to buy all they can produce. So there is chronic unemployment.

- *Smythe* My country's welfare incomes are so over-generous that some people prefer idling on the dole to working for a wage. The unemployment is voluntary – but the government's welfare policy is the real cause of it.

- *Jones:* They are unemployed because the married women have left home and taken their jobs.

- *Robinson:* My country's wage rates are fixed by public tribunals and enforced by strong unions.. There is unemployment because some of the rates are fixed too high for employers to afford. It doesn't matter whether the unemployed would be *willing* to work for less; the fact is they are not allowed to. To restore full employment we should deregulate the labor market.

- *Gray:* Inflation frightened the government into abandoning its commitment to full employment. It retreated from the taxing and spending policies which used to give people enough spending power to keep each other fully employed. We are back with 1930s unemployment because the government has returned to 1930s policies.

- *Brown:* Yes, but that is only half the story. The government cuts also have a more direct effect on employment. Industrially, we have had forty years of jobless growth – technical progress has allowed the private sector to increase output without increasing employment. All the job growth to employ the growing workforce has come by expanding public services. Since the 1970s the lurch to the Right and the tax revolt have stopped the growth of public services and begun to cut some of them. They have not kept up with the growth of the workforce, so there is chronic unemployment. It deserves to be called political unemployment.

- *Green:* No, it deserves to be called technological unemployment. The problem is created by jobless growth, and it could be cured if the system as a whole used fewer robots and more hands – i.e. if we deliberately used appropriate technology to produce a correct balance of output, employment and environmental conservation.

Part Three

DEMANDS FOR GOODS AND SERVICES

19

Dual demands: for goods and services, and for modes of supply

Here begin twenty seven chapters about the productive institutions: the demands they meet, how they're organized, where they get their capital and know-how, how they pay their workers, how they price their products, how the markets work, how wealth and income are distributed. Dignified title: the forces which determine the detailed composition and distribution of the national product. Short title: who makes what, when, how, and who gets it. Shortest title: microeconomics.

It's time to be your own watchdog

You will notice some change of style. The rest of the course of study is more matter-of-fact and less methodological than its first two parts have been. That is not because the methods don't matter. Theory and analysis still have to be selective. So the text continues to be value-structured, and where there are major conflicts of interest or belief it will still draw attention to them. But there are two reasons why it can get on with most of its business, from now on, without much methodological introspection. First, some of the subject matter allows it – there's a lot of information which can be presented in straightforward ways acceptable to most of the relevant interests. Second, if you are working your way through this course you should be a sophisticated reader – and detective – by now. The text need not digress so often to tell you what tricks it is up to: you should be noticing for yourself, routinely, what the assumptions and selective principles and guiding purposes of the analyses are.

DEMANDS FOR PUBLIC SUPPLIES, MARKET SUPPLIES AND HOUSEHOLD SUPPLIES

Economists have traditionally distinguished demands from wants. Demands are wants backed by purchasing power and willingness to pay. But that can only hold for demands for market goods, and market goods are nowadays only about half of all the goods and services demanded and supplied in mixed economies. So there are two *kinds* of demand:

• people want particular goods and services, and

• they want them supplied in particular ways.

That complicates economists' tasks. So does the fact that households' demands for goods and services gener-

ate producers' demands for raw materials, components and other intermediate goods. So begin by noting two distinctions:

• between demands for *goods and services* and demands for particular *modes of supply*, and

• between *primary* and *derived* demands.

As follows –

Mode of production and mode of supply You know how intricate the relations between public, private and household production are: inputs from each of them contribute to the production of most finished goods. Forget that complication now. Focus instead on the way people want particular goods *supplied* (regardless of how they may have been *produced*). Do people want them supplied as public goods? As market goods? Or as home-made, do-it-yourself household goods? Those involve different methods of payment. For public goods you (or others) pay taxes. For market goods you pay each item's purchase price. For household goods you pay in sweat (if you cook the dinner) or indirectly in money (if your money income supports whoever cooks the dinner) or not at all (if you give nothing but love, and sometimes not even that, to whoever cooks the dinner).

There are plenty of options. You can demand public or private education, health care, broadcast news and entertainment. To get about you can demand public trains and trams, public or private buses, private cabs, family cars, bikes, skateboards, rollerblades. You can eat restaurant, take-away, home-delivered or home-cooked meals.

Some of the choices don't make much difference to the demands that have traditionally interested economists. Public or private utilities may demand the same inputs, employ the same labor and supply power or water or rubbish-removal to the same customers at much the same prices. But other choices do affect the structure and performance of the paid economy. Household transport shifts demand from making buses to making cars; it shifts labor from driving buses to maintaining cars; it raises the unit costs of most public transport. Home cooking increases demand for cookbooks but reduces demand for restaurant services. And so on, to our next reminder –

Primary and derived demand Most demands on private producers – including demands for investment goods and intermediate goods – arise from households' demands for finished goods. Though they come last in the chain of production, the households' demands are called 'primary' because they generate the demand – therefore called 'derived' demand – for most of the other goods. Remember how long some of those 'derived' production chains are in a developed economy. Simple household choices can have extensive economic effects.

For example, order a sandwich. It doesn't matter whether you happen to be serving your country just now so it's supplied by an army cook (a public supplier), or whether it comes from a sandwich shop (a private supplier) or from your long-suffering mum (a household supplier). Any one of them has to demand bread, butter, ham, knives, and probably a refrigerator and other equipment, from other suppliers. Each of those demands has to be met by a separate chain of demand and supply. Trace just one of those many chains: the baker who supplies the bread has to demand flour from a miller, who has to demand wheat from a farmer, who has to demand fertilizer from a transnational corporation, which has to demand guano from some faraway islanders, who nowadays demand mechanical excavators and oil fuel from other transnationals – and so on. Your demand for the sandwich, with other demands like it, generates all the rest: the *derived* demands for raw materials, intermediate goods, capital goods and all.

The declining predictability of demand The demand for market supplies is about half of a rich society's demand for goods and services, depending on the precise mix of public, market and household supply in the society's economy. The remaining demand, for public and household supplies, tends to be imperfectly predictable, for reasons we have noted. Now recall that some of the public and domestic uncertainty can affect the predictability of demands for *market* supply. It happens because demands for public, household and market supplies are interdependent. As the less predictable demands for public and household supplies increase as proportions of all demand, they spread some of their uncertainties, partly to the derived demand for market goods, and partly by displacing some of the demand for market goods.

With those reminders, we can now look at the range and variety of theories of demand that have been developed for different purposes.

SELECTIVE THEORIES OF MARKET DEMAND

Theories and analyses should serve their users' purposes. Remember those simple lessons about the mousetrap business, the bad pie, the rival explanations of inflation. Similar choices face investigators who want to understand what disposes households to demand particular quantities of particular goods. Before reviewing some of the prevailing theories, here is a simple reminder of the reasons why, and ways in which, they are likely to differ from one another.

Suppose (for simplicity) that to predict how shoppers will make their spending choices, it is only necessary to know two causal chains which converge to determine their choices:

$$A1 \rightarrow A2 \rightarrow A3 \searrow$$
$$\qquad\qquad\qquad\qquad E$$
$$B1 \rightarrow B2 \rightarrow B3 \nearrow$$

E is the effect you want to predict, the customers' shopping choices. Suppose the As are a chain of causes and effects which determine the customers' tastes, and the Bs are a chain of causes and effects which determine the relevant prices. Suppose that A3 (current tastes) and B3 (current prices) are readily observable, and have reliably regular effects on E (consumer demand). When you see them change, to predict changes in E the theory you need is:

That's all you need if all you want to do with E is *predict* it. But suppose you want to *influence* it. (You're a business seeking more sales. You're a government wondering which commodities to tax. You're a reformer wanting to discourage tobacco-smoking.) You may need to extend the theory in two directions:

1. E has many other necessary conditions. They are omitted from the theory because they don't usually vary, so it is safe to neglect them. But some of them could be varied. One of them, for example, is the state of the law. Advertising cigarettes used to be lawful. That fact had not changed for centuries. Nevertheless it was a condition which reformers could work to change. Call it C. An anti-smoking reformer, looking for opportunities to act, wants this much theory:

2. Besides knowing more of the immediate causes of E, some theory-users may need to know what determines those immediate causes: what chains of cause and effect produce them. Business wants to know what influences consumers' tastes, so it can work to change them. Government wants to know how production costs affect the prices which affect demand, so it can know what it is doing when it taxes producers. The anti-smoking reformer needs to look beyond the only bit of law she has noticed so far. Smoking is lawful, which is one reason why the tobacco trade is lawful, which is one reason why its advertising is lawful. Is the reformer's best bet to get the government to regulate the smoking, the manufacture, or the advertising? The theory needs to expose each of those possibilities by modelling their relations to each other and to E. (Call them C1, C2 and C3.) What each user – businessman, tax man, reformer – wants is theory which models longer chains of causation. One of them may want to trace cause and effect back to the nearest opportunity to intervene. Another (the anti-smoker) may want to expose alternative points at which it might be possible to intervene.

3. Thus there are 'lateral' or 'synchronic' needs to know a particular range of immediate causes of the behavior of consumers' demand (E). And there are 'linear' or 'diachronic' needs to track back along some causal chains. Put them together, and business and government and our reformer might all be served by theory which selects and models this much of the complex real-life pattern of cause and effect:

Tastes: A1 ➞ A2 ➞ A3
Prices: B1 ➞ B2 ➞ B3 ➞ E: Effective
Laws: C1 ➞ C2 ➞ C3   demand

Remember that these diagrams simply indicate the scope of the relevant theories. Useful theory doesn't merely say where causal relations are likely to be, it says something about how they work. For example B3 ➞ E stands for theory which doesn't just say that prices influence demand. It tells you how to find out, for particular commodities, *how much* change in price is likely to cause *how much* change in demand.

Left and right theories of demand

In each of the purpose-built theories represented above, suppose that all the causal relations are truthfully represented, and they operate regularly enough to make these models of past causal relations useful guides to future causal relations. They serve different users by modelling different parts of the real-life pattern of causes and effects, but if they do it truthfully and usefully, there need be no conflict between them.

Yet there *is* rivalry and mutual criticism between theorists of market demand. Why should that be so? It is partly because there are some real questions of truth and reliability: some of the criticism is on good technical grounds. But it is also because the different users' needs which the theories aim to serve happen to connect with more divisive, sometimes passionate, differences of ideology and broad social purpose.

Right theory The neoclassical theory of demand selects prices, the consumers' incomes, and the consumers' tastes and preferences, as the determinants of demand. It models the influence of each of them, and shows how to measure and predict some of their effects (for example *how much* change in price or income will cause *how much* change in the demand for a particular commodity).

The theory thus emphasizes consumer sovereignty. It shows consumers deciding directly what will be produced, and indirectly how society's productive resources will be allocated to meet their demands most efficiently. That makes capitalism look good – the capitalists compete to do what the consumers want. In a mixed economy it makes the market sector look better – more individually democratic – than the public sector. Left critics think those persuasions influence people in ways which help to enlarge the profit-seeking sectors of mixed economies at the expense of other sectors, and thus tend to increase inequalities of wealth and power.

Left theory, marketing theory Left economists don't deny that prices, incomes and tastes influence demand. But they insist on asking what influences shape the consumers' tastes. *Answers:* (i) Producers do. In deciding what can and what can't be produced profitably, they determine the option sets from which consumers must choose. (ii) Producers do. By their advertising and salesmanship they persuade consumers what they should buy, often by methods of image-making and sub-conscious association which have very little to do with the quality or usefulness of the product. (iii) Producers do. Advertisers' persuasions go far beyond recommending particular commodities or brands. Their collective effect is to recommend the tastes, lifestyles and social values which dispose people to desire ever-increasing quantities of market goods, rather than public goods or less goods. (iv) Most tastes and preferences are social creations. They are shaped by the society's culture, customs, laws and institutions. Profit-seeking producers don't create people's tastes and preferences single-handed, but they exert much influence on many of them.

That selective causal explanation encourages two lines of thought. First, 'consumer sovereignty' is partly a producers' pretence. If producers are persuading people to demand goods which are personally or socially or environmentally harmful, if their advertising is undesirable (for example, degrading to women), or if they are simply devoting too much of national income to advertising, there need be nothing wrong with government doing something about it. In regulating products or their advertising, or educating consumers to be more discriminating, government need not be seen as infringing consumer sovereignty.

More generally, most demand is socially conditioned. There is no special virtue in having more and more of the conditioning done by self-interested profit-seekers. It may well be possible for democratic government and public enterprise and education to improve society by improving the demands which its people choose to make. A society's quality (remember) can depend as much on the kinds of demand it generates as on its capacity to satisfy them. It can depend on *not* producing, rather than producing, supplies to meet improvident or degrading or destructive demands.

Notice a paradoxical relation between the political attractions and the business uses of this approach to demand. Ideologically, neoclassical theory of consumer sovereignty has friendlier implications for private business than has this Leftist theory which depicts consumers as putty in producers' hands. But theory about how to mould the putty is the theory which business chiefly uses. Theory about producers' influence on consumers is welcome on the Left, but not much of it was developed by the Left. Some institutional economists have contributed to it. But most theorizing and research on how consumers think, and how advertisers and packagers can persuade them, has been done by psychologists, opinion pollsters and others working for capitalist employers in the specialized business of marketing and advertising research. Theory about the manipulation of demand is one of the few intellectual products that is of equal interest to capitalist business and its socialist critics!

The following chapters will survey (1) some main influences on consumers' tastes, (2) the essentials of the neoclassical theory of market demand, and (3) some ways of measuring the likely effects of income and price changes on demands for market goods.

CONCLUSIONS ABOUT DEMAND

1. People want particular goods and services for their own use.
2. They want the economic system to offer them particular option sets or ranges of choice.
3. They want goods and services to be supplied and paid for in particular ways, as public or market or home-made supplies.
4. These wants are partly individual. Looking to her own needs (for example) a person may know what goods and services she wants. She wants them to be included in the options the economy offers her. And for her own purposes she wants them supplied in particular ways. She may want to be her own driver (household supply), to shop for food and clothing (market supply) and to pay for education through taxes (public supply).
5. Besides being individual, many of the wants are partly or wholly social. People want to live in a society with particular qualities. For others as well as herself one citizen may favor the kind of society that includes individual shopping but tax-paid education and health services, while another would favor a society in which education and health care were also household or market goods. One citizen may want a society free of junk goods and commercial pressures to conform and compete and consume, while another thinks the commercial hype brings wealth and color that are worth their social costs. Among people who don't personally drink booze, smoke pot or watch pornography, some think the economy should offer shoppers those options while others think it should not. And so on.
6. The social purposes of people's economic demands are as important as their individual purposes. That may be increasingly so as collective problems of resource use and environmental policy intensify.
7. Many interests in a modern economy work to persuade people to adopt particular tastes or patterns of demand. They do so for a wide range of purposes – profit-seeking, social, religious. Persuading people is a big industry.
8. Consumer sovereignty need not be impaired by public persuasion, or no more than it is impaired by com-

mercial persuasion. Is it impaired if government regulates the goods that may be offered to the shoppers, or the way they may be advertised? Yes, if some consumers are frustrated by the regulation. But more may be frustrated without it, if they or their society are degraded by harmful goods or deceptive persuasions which they have made clear they don't want. Consumer sovereignty can't achieve miraculous consensus. It can't escape the conflicts of interest, and the ultimate resort to majority rule, which are part of any democratic sovereignty.

CONCLUSIONS ABOUT THEORIES AND EXPLANATIONS OF DEMAND

1. The patterns of demand which determine the respective shares of public supply, market supply and household supply in a national economic system offer more scope for historical explanation and political forecasting than for reliable economic theory and prediction.

2. Similarly *within* two of the three sectors. Some political demands are predictable, some are uncertain until the political battles are fought and won. Some household demand is regular, some is irregular as households decide how much to save and spend, what to buy and what to produce for themselves.

3. Many market demands are roughly predictable. But demands are so interrelated that uncertainties about demands for public and household supplies tend to make market demands less predictable than they once were. The uncertainties tend to increase with economic growth and rising income.

4. Neoclassical theory relates demand to prices, incomes and tastes. It traces some determinants of prices and incomes but not of tastes. It thus emphasizes the sovereignty of consumers.

5. While agreeing about price and income effects, many firms with products to sell and many Left economists focus on the influences which form people's tastes and, more generally, people's skill and capacity to choose. They thus emphasize producers' and others' influence upon consumers.

6. Though the mix may vary, and conflicting interests allow no mix to be best for everyone, the three modes of supply are all necessary and important to the people whose demands for goods and services it is your business as an economist to study and understand.

EXERCISES

Here is a question each for practical thinkers and philosophical thinkers:

1. Recalling earlier analyses of the mix of mixed economies, as well as this chapter's themes, write an essay on what you see as the comparative merits and best uses of public supply and market supply.

2. This chapter has distinguished demands which people make for individual purposes (shopping for their dinners) from those which they make for social purposes (when they opt for public tax-paid schools rather than private fee-paying schools). The chapter has been careful *not* to assert that the individual demands are all selfish (I may buy what the kids like for our dinner rather than what I like). And it has not suggested that the social demands are all altruistic (even if you have no children, it may still be for your own pleasure and profit rather than for other people's benefit that you want your society to be sure to educate all its members).

Exercise: Write an essay about the relations (or lack of them) that you personally see between (i) the individual and social purposes of people's demands for particular modes of supply, and (ii) the selfish and unselfish purposes of those demands.

20

How are wants and tastes formed?

The main purpose of this chapter is to remind you that although your tastes and preferences are your own, they are a good deal influenced by external constraints and persuasions. *Constraints* limit the range of things you feel free to like or choose. *Persuasions* work on the beliefs and tastes of the 'you' who do the choosing, so that if the persuaders succeed in persuading you, you do what they want you to do of your own free will as an independent, self-directed individual.

PERSUASION AND INDEPENDENCE

There is a philosophical problem which we should recognize, but need not necessarily resolve. Every human has to be nurtured from birth (or they would die) and brought up and educated *somehow*. You cannot become an adult without that upbringing. But the upbringing can't be neutral in the sense of leaving it entirely to you – the infant, unformed you – to decide, uninfluenced by anyone else, what sort of person you want to be, with what beliefs and tastes. Everyone is formed somehow by their upbringing, whether directly or by reaction against it. But that obvious truth does not deny your right, as soon as you are able, to act as an independent person making your own choices. You may well grow up to be critical of the conditions which formed you, sceptical of politicians' and advertisers' efforts to persuade you, and so on. You may also be capable of self-change: of reforming the self and the tastes and beliefs which others' persuasions have helped to form. The capacity to reject your upbringing may itself be a product of your upbringing. One serious question to ask about any culture is 'How independent and self-reliant are the people it brings up?' Another is 'How good or bad are the desires and expectations which it instils into its people?' Societies and economic systems (remember) should be judged as much by the wants they generate as by the wants they satisfy. *Conclusion:* there is no necessary conflict between (i) respecting people as independent beings responsible for their own beliefs and tastes and preferences; (ii) studying how they come by those beliefs and tastes and preferences; and (iii) adding your own persuasions, if you have something to sell or something to say, to all the other formative and persuasive influences to which your fellow citizens are exposed.

The kinds of constraint and persuasion which help to form people's tastes and economic preferences can be listed under half a dozen headings: (i) natural needs; (ii) law; (iii) culture; (iv) profit-seeking persuaders; (v) other persuaders and educators; and (vi) individuals themselves as self-reliant thinkers with whatever independence they have after exposure to influence of the first five kinds. Notes on the six can remind you of the modes of persuasion which economists should keep in mind when claims are made for consumer sovereignty on the one hand, or for the excessive power of advertising on the other.

NATURE

Universal human needs for food and drink, shelter, warmth and physical safety account for most consumer demand in poor countries, and underlie demands for basic goods in richer countries.

LAW

Law constrains demands, and may sometimes convince people not even to want the things it prohibits. (It is not respectable to desire slaves, cocaine or under-age prostitutes.) It also restricts your right to influence other people's tastes. (You may not advertise or incite the use of some prohibited goods.) Even when you are recommending lawful goods, the law may regulate how you go about it. Harmless pills made of chalk are lawful – but you must not advertise them as cures for cancer. Cigarettes are lawful – but you must not advertise them at all.

CULTURE

Cultural influences on economic wants range through a spectrum from force at one extreme to fads and fashions at the other. At the coercive end of the spectrum you will be banned from most employment and social life in most countries unless you wear pants, do something about your hair, and keep reasonably clean and odorless (or positively sweet-smelling). Those requirements dictate economic demands for pants, soap, combs, scissors or razors. Many more demands are conditioned by the range of lifestyles, housing, dress, food and drink, arts and recreations that the culture defines as acceptable, and encourages people to like. Some of the tastes it encourages persist (for pizzas, classical and jazz music, TV sitcoms). Others are quicker-changing (punk rock, black jeans, orange hair, lizards for pets).

On many of those demands the culture exerts a double influence, if its requirements are what some psychologists call 'internalized' by the people concerned. Some free spirits only wash and wear pants because they fear reprisals if they don't. The culture *constrains* them. Others wash and wear pants because they positively believe in doing so. The culture has *persuaded* them. (If they are deeply convinced, they may join Clean Living Campaigns to enforce the rule that even the freest spirits must wash and wear pants whether they like it or not.)

ADVERTISERS

Commercial persuaders include advertisers, sales promoters, marketing strategists, public relations services. 'Puffing is of various sorts' wrote the playwright Sheridan two centuries ago; 'the principal are, the puff direct – the puff preliminary – the puff collateral – the puff collusive, and the puff oblique, or puff by implication.'

Much research has tried to find out how much influence these persuaders have. Some, certainly; but it remains hard to measure precisely. Sam Wanamaker, a pioneer retailer and advertiser, used to say 'I know that half my advertising costs are wasted. But I can never find out which half.' A century later the complaint persists. If you know some algebra you can read a summary of efforts of great econometric sophistication to find out what, if anything, advertising does for British liquor sales, in Lester W. Johnson, 'Alternative Econometric Estimates of the Effect of Advertising on the Demand for Alcoholic Beverages in the United Kingdom' (*International Journal of Advertising*, 1985, 4, 19-25). Dr. Johnson concludes that 'beer advertising has a statistically significant effect on beer, as well as on wine, demand, while wine advertising has a statistically significant effect on wine, as well as on beer, demand. It appears that spirits advertising has no statistically significant effect on any of the three beverages. An additional result of our estimation is that total alcohol advertising does not have a statistically significant effect on total alcohol demand.' He reports that his conclusions differ substantially from those of three studies by other econometricians, though all four used the same raw data of prices, advertising outlays, and sales. 'Our results are surprisingly different from previous results in that we find significant effects of wine advertising and

no effects of spirits advertising, whereas, if anything, other studies found essentially the opposite ... We are not saying that our results are correct and the others mentioned are incorrect, but are pointing out that no definitive statement can be made as to the effect of advertising on individual alcoholic beverage classes or the demand for alcohol in the UK.' Wanamaker said it first, and shorter.

One thing that can be measured, though still with some uncertainty, is the amount rich countries spend on commercial persuasion. The uncertainty arises because advertising costs are not separated from broader classes of cost and output in most national accounts. So national estimates and international comparisons are based on independent studies whose data and methods vary quite widely. Items which some studies count and others don't include the taxes which advertisers pay, commission paid to advertising agencies, production costs of advertisements (as opposed to their payments for newspaper space, TV time, etc.), and the costs of direct mail advertising which are now between a fifth and a third of all advertising costs in rich countries. Conservative estimates show a threefold range, or thereabouts, in the proportions of national income which rich democracies spend on advertising. Sweden, France and Germany spend less than one per cent. Japan spends about one and a half, Britain about one and three quarters, and the United States between two and two and a half per cent, depending on what the researchers count. Other persuaders – the non-advertising contents of books, magazines, newspapers and broadcasting, and all levels of education – attract between four or five times as much spending (in the US) and ten times as much (in Sweden).

Whatever its share of the nation's spending and the people's attention, what does advertising aim to do? Most of it does one or more of four things.

1. It informs you. Many classified and other small ads simply tell you what is available, where, at what price. When I last searched the sources, British classified advertising was about 58 per cent in regional and local newspapers, 19 per cent in directories, 12 per cent in national newspapers, 9 per cent in business and trade journals, and 2 per cent elsewhere. 28 per cent of it was advertising jobs vacant or wanted, 21 per cent cars, 21 per cent houses and other property, and 30 per cent everything else. Not much consumerist brainwashing in all that. (*Source:* Advertising Association, *Advertising Expenditure in the UK:* 1983 Survey. Readers in Britain can find later issues of the survey.)

2. It persuades you to prefer one brand to another. Lux beats Brand X.

3. It persuades you to want more or different goods. You don't only need the best soap, you need *more* soap. Deodorants too. And the new seductive masculine perfumes for men. Recommending the brand and the product commonly go together. When such advertising was lawful, you could not recommend Alpine cigarettes against other brands without also recommending smoking against not smoking, especially if smoking Alpine was shown to bring good-looking boys and girls together on fresh green grass in woodland glades beside sparkling streams in magic springtime.

4. As advertisers recommend increasingly alluring houses, cars, furniture, clothing and adornment, food and drink, conducted tours and commercial recreations, they are unavoidably also urging people in a general way to get and spend all they can. Happiness comes by spending. More is better than less. Especially, buying and owning and enjoying more private market goods is better.

Governments spend a little – but not nearly as much as private advertisers spend – to persuade you to demand and pay for more and better schools, hospitals, public libraries, national parks, scientific research, and so on. And the little that government does to advertise those public goods may be contradicted by rival politicians' electoral promises to cut taxes, cut public spending, cut budget deficits, and deliver smaller government.

Most disagreement about the social effects of modern advertising focuses on three questions. Does advertising help producers to exploit consumers? Does it degrade people's values and aspirations? Does it help the mixed economy to survive by keeping demand up to growing productivity, or does it help it to self-destruct by stimulating short-sighted consumption instead of far-sighted environmental prudence?

Higher or lower prices ?

Does advertising help producers to exploit consumers? A monopoly view says yes, an efficiency view says no. Research suggests there are elements of both effects in many industries, with one or other effect dominant in some industries.

The monopoly view says that advertising costs have to go onto product prices. If heavy advertising entrenches a good brand image in consumers' minds they will pay more for it than for identical products without the

image. If heavy advertising is then a condition of launching competitive brands, that raises the cost of launching them, which further protects the established brands' monopoly. When the US Federal Trade Commission brought an anti-trust action against a nationwide supplier of reconstituted lemon juice, it brought the firm's own marketing plan into evidence. The plan included this:

> Although reconstituted lemon juice is virtually indistinguishable one brand from another, heavy emphasis on the ReaLemon brand name through media effort should create such memorability for the brand, that an almost imaginary superiority would exist in the mind of the consumer, a justification for paying the high price we are asking. (FTC vs Borden Inc., 92 FTC 669 (1978) Initial Decision p. 709)

That is the monopoly view. The efficiency view claims that advertising helps consumers in a number of ways. It informs them of their options and cuts their costs of finding what they want. By expanding demand and/or concentrating it on a few brands it allows economies of scale. That can cut costs of production and distribution, which can allow lower prices to consumers. Where advertising intensifies brand competition in competitive industries, it may make it harder for poor products to succeed, and may motivate all the competitors to improve their products.

In the ReaLemon case the court found that the company had more than 80 per cent of the market, advertised more heavily than its competitors, charged higher prices than they did, took excessive profits, and beat off new entrants to the industry by discriminatory price-cutting in their localities. The court took all that as evidence that the company both maintained and milked its near-monopoly by undesirable means. At a later hearing the court reversed its view of local price-cutting: if it banned price-cutting it would itself be supporting monopoly prices. There is no dispute that the company was a near-monopolist in its industry. But pro- and anti-advertisers still argue about the extent to which its monopoly power and pricing depended on its advertising.

Full employment or environmental doom?

The developed economies are now productive beyond any sensible judgment of need. You can remember earlier discussion of the implications of that. Will consumer demand keep growing as productivity grows? If so, are we in for more needless goods, throwaway junk, positional goods? If not – if demand levels off – do we face jobless growth with a constant national product produced by a declining workforce? More unemployed, more inequality, more conflict between winners and losers, increasing difficulty in distributing income to people whom the system can't employ? Or can we respond with deliberate work-sharing – instead of reducing the numbers in work, can rising productivity continue to reduce everyone's working hours?

People can agree to disagree about the merits of 'junk consumption' as long as the main things at stake are freedom, equality and full employment. But environmental dangers are different. Rich societies already begin to economize energy and replace some extravagant or pollutant methods of production; but they should undoubtedly be moving beyond that, changing direction to consume absolutely less than they currently do. Modern advertising and the interests it serves are formidable enemies of that: enemies of prudence, of fairness to future generations, of fairness to poorer competitors for the world's scarce or unspoiled resources. (But imagine how environmental reform might progress if the skill and resources of the advertising industry would work for it instead of against it. A few already do. Products advertise their non-pollutant effects and recycled packaging. Some public power suppliers who used to advertise to stimulate demand for power now campaign to persuade households and industries to use less of it.)

Advertising the system and the suppliers, as well as the supplies

Advertisers insist that advertising needs to be backed by salesmanship, sales promotion and investment in public relations – the puff collateral and the puff oblique or puff by implication. The disproportionate advertising of market goods rather than public goods has been backed in recent times by increasing spending on the private sector's public relations. Big firms finance PR services to improve their images as patriotic, productive, non-pollutant, socially responsible, friendly, *caring* capitalists. Whole industries do the same through their employers' associations (Farmer' Unions, Motor Traders' Associations, Chambers of Commerce and Manufactures). Economists set up private think tanks as profit-seeking firms which produce and sell economic theory and research in a market way. Some of them supply straightforward business information and advice. Others chiefly supply ideology: theoretical supports and persuasions for tax revolts, privatization, deregulation, and campaigns for smaller government.

Social values

Does the advertising of consumer goods degrade or enrich our culture and social values? I need not state the case against it, because it has been stated by better men. Jonathan Swift wrote 'We ate when we were not hungry, and drank without the provocation of thirst.' William Wordsworth wrote 'The world is too much with us. Late and soon, getting and spending, we lay waste our powers', and he called a lot of what we get and spend 'a sordid boon'. In *Culture and Environment* (1933) F.R. Leavis quoted others' opinions that 'Where the acquiring of things is a religion the offering of them is sacerdotal. To saddle the public with useless articles, to create an unnatural demand for them, to scrap the still sound article and purchase the ever less durable novelty, to keep the styles moving, such are the aims pursued with an almost missionary zeal. . . The material prosperity of modern civilization depends upon inducing people to buy what they do not want, and to want what they should not buy.'

In *The Affluent Society* (1958) J.K. Galbraith contrasted the 'private affluence and public squalor' which come of over-persuading people to prefer market goods to public goods. He summarized the direct and indirect effects of that sort of advertising in *Economics and the Public Purpose* (1973): 'The advertising of the individual automobile company seeks to win consumers from other makes. But the advertising of all together contributes to the conviction that happiness is associated with automobile ownership. Additionally ... it persuades people that the contemporary tendencies in automobile physiognomy and decoration are desirable, that those of the past are obsolete, eccentric or otherwise unworthy. Thus it encourages the general discarding of old vehicles and the purchase of new. Similarly, if one soap manufacturer can establish that white sheets are an index of womanly virtue, this virtue is rewarding to all soap and detergent manufacturers. If one manufacturer can make modest intoxication a mark of suave respectability, so it becomes for all makers of intoxicants. If one hairdressing contributes to successful seduction, then so may all. More important still, the aggregate of all such persuasion affirms in the most powerful possible manner that happiness is the result of the possession and use of goods and that [to that extent] happiness will be enhanced in proportion as more goods are produced and consumed.' (Penguin edition, p. 156)

There are contrary arguments of three kinds.

1. Some advertising encourages quite wholesome social values. Why shouldn't people be encouraged

to look nice and keep clean? There is more disagreement about advertisers' images of family life. Many feminists have objected to ads which idealized the traditional division of labor between earning husbands and stay-at-home housewives. Others, including some feminists, think that the emphasis on good housekeeping, generous care for others, and family affection and solidarity, encourages more good than bad values.

2. An argument which this text more than most should respect: commercial advertising may plug private rather than public goods, but it is not generally biased against household goods. A high proportion of the goods advertised consist of equipment and materials for use in household production. The images which recommend them are images of active, productive households. The people are cooking, serving, cleaning, laundering, caring for kids, meeting and socializing, making love, travelling, picnicking, playing sports and games. TV ads rarely depict people passively watching TV. Advertisers do recommend some TV dinners, and other ready-made alternatives to household products. They recommend leisure time activities which use market products rather than activities which don't. But the balance of their persuasions can't be accused of any general bias against household productivity.

3. Some advertising, chiefly on television, is interesting, entertaining, witty, beautiful. It is an art which some think worth having for its own sake. If you *have* to do the household laundry, is it good or bad that your chosen detergent puts you in mind of a million lemons bursting comically from telephone booths? If a student wants a Coke, does it brighten his unadventurous life to remember those thirsty kids descending from a passing plane on skateboards? Is your imagination really poorer for all the beautiful people and happy families, the beautifully photographed island beaches, sails in the sunset, highland streams and mountain splendors that the advertisers have planted in it? The socialist economies might have lasted longer with some of that color and fun.

Even if the advertisements themselves cheer people up, it may not follow that the values and aspirations which they encourage make people happier than they would otherwise be. Recent research by two American psychologists suggests that they do not. People who aspire to material wealth, fame and physical beauty and strive to achieve them average less happy than people who aspire to good human relationships, strive for those, and work to help their communities. Some economists' as well as some advertisers' assumptions need attention if those researchers are right. Read them if you are interested: Tim Kasser and Richard Ryan, 'A dark side of the American Dream: Correlates of financial success as a central life aspiration', *Journal of Personality and Social Psychology* 65, 1993, 410-22, and 'Further examining the American Dream', *Personality and Social Psychology* Bulletin 22, 1996, 280-7.

Consumers' views of advertising

Sample polls report the proportions of people who like and dislike particular advertisers, and advertising in general. They also report what people believe advertising does and does not achieve.

Western Europe (including the UK) spends about a quarter of the world's advertising money. Polled in the 1980s, about two thirds of Europeans (including higher proportions in Britain and lower proportions in France and Denmark) thought advertising was useful. Italian opinion worsened when television advertising began. British opinion of broadcast advertising has continued to improve. But neither its friends nor its critics think it matters much: it is not an important political issue for them.

Feelings have been both stronger and more hostile across the Atlantic. The US spends about half the world's advertising money. Eric J. Zanot surveyed the history of Americans' attitudes to advertising (in the *International Journal of Advertising*, 1984, 3, 3-15). From the beginning of polling through the 1930s and 1940s – before television – advertising was seen in a generally favorable light. Two thirds or more of respondents thought it was necessary, useful, and helped to improve standards of living. More than half thought it was becoming more truthful. Very few thought it led people to buy things they did not want or could not afford. But half or more believed it increased prices. Through the 1950s the broadly favorable attitudes continued, but majorities began to think that advertising did lead people to buy more than they should, and that some advertisements 'insulted their intelligence'.

Through the 1960s and 1970s American majorities turned against their advertisers. They continued to think advertising necessary. But rising numbers disliked its quality, its cultural effects and its untruthfulness. The proportion who believed that advertising led people to buy things they did not need or want rose from 20 per cent in the 1930s through 54 per cent in the 1960s to 71 per cent by 1980. Nastily, an earlier poll had asked the neighbors of advertising employees what sort of people the admen were (in 1961, before there were many adwomen). No neighbors thought them 'honest, straightforward'. Only 2 per cent thought their work benefited society. Only 4 per cent wanted their sister to marry one.

Advertisers noticed, and some connected the change with other changes. More of the women to whom they advertised were educated, employed and earning, often feminist. To sell to them, advertisers must amend their stereotypes of women-as-housewives. That connected with a change in advertising theory. It had been ortho-dox to believe that the ad should not compete with the product: it should not be so interesting or attractive that it took attention away from the product. It must grab attention (however brashly) but must not compete with the product for the customer's affections and desires. That was a recipe for irritating advertising, and profes-sionals knew it: 'We must irritate them a bit to get through to them'. But the new unpopularity prompted research into the causes of the unpopularity. Some of its findings suggested that the orthodoxy was wrong, and that more attractive ads could do more for sales.

If a switch from hard selling to pleasing and enter-taining the customers actually promised commercial gains, there was much to be said for it. Significantly it was said first by women. In *The Moving Target: What Every Marketer Should Know About Women* (1982) Rena Bartos, a Senior Vice-President of the biggest advertising transnational in the world, argued for adding a like/dislike test (testing customers' liking for the ad itself, independently of their feelings about the adver-tised product) as a routine component of market research and advertising decision. Both the customers' values and the technology of communication were changing. 'When advertising is invited into the viewers' homes, rather than attempting to crash its way into their consciousness, the industry will be forced to reconsider its definitions of advertising "effectiveness". As the media context changes [with two-way cable TV, for example] the dimension of liking could be a crucial cri-terion of advertising effectiveness. A happy by-product of the change could be greater consonance between a corporation's goals and purposes and public perceptions of its advertising brands. When positive emotional response becomes an essential sales tool, top manage-ments may find that they are not only selling their prod-ucts but they are improving the images of their brands and enhancing the credibility of their companies' repu-tations.' In short – though it is not how Rena Bartos might put it – they may rebuild both the detailed sales

influence and the general social influence that J.K. Galbraith complained of.

Do you as an economist need to pay as much attention to advertising as this long section of text is suggesting?

Yes, for two reasons. First, however hard it is to theorize or measure its effects exactly, commercial per-suasion is clearly a significant contributor to demand, and more generally to popular economic beliefs and policy preferences.

Second, the national differences within Europe and the American history of changing media and methods of advertising, changing popular judgments of it, and responsive changes in advertisers' strategies, are one more reminder that what you study may be changing as you study it. Economists cannot hope to discover and theorize, once and for all, what advertising contributes to demand. Instead you need to know how to find out what advertising is currently contributing to demand, and to economic beliefs and policies, at the particular times in the particular industries and countries that concern you. (Much of the evidence in this section has been from the 1980s and earlier. To update it, start by scanning the last ten years of the International Journal of Advertising, and of a national journal if your country has any.)

OTHER PERSUADERS

There are plenty of other persuaders. Some of them agree with the advertisers. For example there are inde-pendent economists who agree that the main measure of economic success is material output and growth, and that advertising stimulates both. Many also fear that unemployment must increase if demand does not keep up with the growth of productivity per head. (Both those beliefs tend to come naturally if you use a single-sector model of a private market economy as your basic means of understanding the economic system.) And there are others besides advertisers and economists who agree – whether or not as a result of commercial persuasion – that 'happiness will be enhanced in proportion as more goods are produced and consumed'. Are the advertisers and PR services *creating* those beliefs, or merely responding to them:? Some of both, obviously.

Other voices offer other messages, about the qualities of particular products and the general benefits of increasing consumption. The US Consumers' Union began in 1936. The British Consumers' Association launched its magazine *Which* in 1957. The Australian association followed with *Choice*. By the 1960s there was a European Bureau and an International Organization of national Consumers' Unions. The movement's research services and political activities don't necessarily discourage consumption but they aim to make products safer and better, and consumers better informed, more discriminating, and harder to fool. The services test and compare products. They tell their members, and the press and public, what they find. They bring public pressure and consumer resistance to bear on poor products and misleading advertising. They lobby governments for stricter regulation of advertising and product quality. Where appropriate they sue offending producers, or help their members to sue them. They began by concentrating on market goods, but many now also scrutinize public goods and bureaucratic behavior, and non-market products like noise and pollution. Modern consumer protection has achieved a good deal in its short life. Its direct information services tend to go to the well-off, well educated consumers who make up most of the unions' membership. But other people benefit from the greater care with product quality and advertising which many producers now take, and from the official consumer protection laws and services which most governments have now created.

Besides the new consumer protection agencies there are other services which work with similar aims. Public, independent and private sources publish wholesome advice about diet and exercise. There is a big market for books and magazines and newspaper columns which teach people how to be healthy, what to eat, what not to smoke, when not to drink, how to exercise, how to relax, how to avoid unwanted pregnancies, how to avoid the long list of diseases that are now known to be related to behavior.

The environmental movement offers some of the most direct and effective opposition to commercial advertising. Environmentalist activists, academics and public officials expose and attack the activities of pollutant and resource-using industries. Many also preach and teach against consumption itself: against economic growth as a collective aim, against output per head as a measure of economic efficiency, against wasteful and pollutant lifestyles, against business and political policies which put short-term prosperity before long-term environmental prudence. Some explore positive programs for simpler ways of life: they theorize how we could be as happy with less, or report on simpler societies which look as if they *are* happy with less. But the advertisers are still powerfully persuasive and have big shares of media space and time. If they are to be balanced by 'equal time' for other opinions it must be from the two sources which have some chance of getting as

much of the customers' attention as they do: home and school.

Home and school

This is not the place for an essay about the formative effects of home and school. Think over your own experience, compare what you know of friends' and relations' experience. Even within one national culture, or within one class culture, or within one ethnic culture, there can be wide differences between the particular tastes, and between the general attitudes to material possessions, which parents and teachers try to instil into the children they bring up. Many families encourage their children to be ambitious to get on, to earn and spend. But – if only for domestic peace and safety – they usually encourage some sharing and co-operation too. Most households cultivate some scepticism about seductive advertising and easy credit. At school, anti-commercial values and arguments usually get some space in the curriculum. So do some self-restraining approaches to diet and health. Besides those persuasions, the ordinary contents of scientific, social, literary and artistic education include many elements which can equip people to be more discriminating consumers. But not always more restrained consumers – more education tends to equip you to earn more income, so it can happen that the more you learn the more you spend.

Parents and teachers themselves are open to all the commercial and anti-commercial persuasions. They transmit plenty of beliefs and tastes from the society around them to the children they teach. But they also bring some thought of their own to their tasks. And the tasks themselves compel some reflection: when experience contradicts the TV commercials, experience sometimes wins. Children meanwhile arrive at conclusions of *their* own, not always the ones which advertisers, parents or teachers intended.

Out of that and much other experience comes quite a lot of 'anti-consumption' thought. Many people deliberately content themselves with whatever modest levels of income and spending they have. Some limit their consumption in order to save for their children. Some limit their consumption to give to charities at home or abroad. Left ideologists attack rich spending and commercial advertising. People on Left and Right alike distinguish good taste from bad taste, and shun some styles of consumption – including some they could afford if they wanted to – as extravagant, ostentatious, vulgar. The advertisers don't have it all their own way.

Shoppers also work

One important argument is omitted from this chapter
because you will meet it in a number of others. Briefly:
through much of their lives producers and consumers
are the same people, and their experience of work is as
important to their happiness as their shopping choices
are. But a market economy gives most people much
wider shopping choices than job choices. Employers
who compete to sell goods to them by competing to get
more and harder work from them in return for less pay
or security or job satisfaction are not necessarily catering for their actual tastes and preferences. Many of those
worker/shoppers might be happy to see a few less or
dearer goods in the shops if that would allow them some
better work options. I do not want my consumer tastes
to be 'sovereign' over my working opportunities. I want
a balance between the two, and that may well require
some collective action, by labor unions or government
or both, about the conditions of work.

Conclusions

You decide yours. Here are mine:

1. Tastes and preferences are neither wholly independent nor wholly created by advertisers and other persuaders.

2. However tastes are formed, consumer sovereignty is
a good principle of democratic society. It expresses a
proper respect for people's right to make their own
saving and spending choices. But it should apply
across the board – to the public goods people want
their taxes to buy, and the things they would like to
be equipped to do for themselves, as well as the market goods they buy when they go shopping. Respect
for consumer sovereignty should not justify any privilege for market goods over other goods, except to
the extent that the citizens actually express that preference in their voting and household choices.

3. Advertisers and other persuaders nevertheless exert a
double influence over people's choices. They influence particular choices by commending particular
goods. More important, to the extent that their persuasions are 'internalized' they influence the beliefs
and tastes and values of the choosers. They influence
general attitudes to consumption, especially to the
consumption of unnecessary goods and services
above and beyond what are needed for a comfortable, interesting and fulfilling life.

4. The intensified commercial persuasions have contributed to the two cruellest developments of recent
years in the rich democracies: the shift of opinion to
the Right which has reversed a century of progress to
greater compassion and equality; and the resistance
to effective environmental reform and collective
self-restraint in rich countries.

5. Evidence is accumulating (you've met some in Fred
Hirsch's, Tibor Scitovsky's and Robert Lane's
books) that the waste and excessive consumption in
those rich societies does nothing for their net human
happiness, so there is no balance of benefit for the
social and environmental costs of the self-indulgence.

6. Advertisers of market goods have more money to
spend, and command more media space and time,
than do advocates of uncommercial values, advocates of public goods, advocates of greater equality,
or advocates of environmental prudence. It seems
likely that many people's tastes and preferences will
be biased – to some degree, which can't be measured
– by that biased distribution of persuasive resources
and opportunities.

7. If the balance of persuasion is biased in that way,
there is a corresponding bias in any economic analysis which chooses not to notice the processes of persuasion. Analysis which accepts their effects as
'given' and starts from the revealed preferences
which they help to shape, cannot expose the possibility of different patterns of persuasion. It does not
encourage thought about what different persuasion
might achieve in the way of less consumerist values,
more public goods, more household self-sufficiency,
more material equality, more international aid or
more environmental prudence.

8. There need be nothing undemocratic or damaging to
consumer choice in public action to redress the balance of persuasion. Public radio and TV channels
which don't advertise leave their audiences as free
and sovereign as channels which do advertise.
Modern societies need plenty of informative advertising – but the more they get their general education
from home and school, work and play, books and
arts and music, and press and political debate, the
more sensible their spending and their long-term
economic and environmental policies are likely
to be.

EXERCISE

In countries with developed economies no government bans all advertising, but all governments regulate advertising. (Nowhere, nowadays, can you lawfully advertise chalk pills as cures for cancer.) In a long essay or extensive notes, set out the principles which you think should guide the regulation of advertising. What kinds of advertising, in what media, should government allow, with what requirements of truth, decency, or anything else? How might advertisers be protected from unfair or corrupt regulation? Should public suppliers and public-interest organizations and educators advertise more than they currently do? If so, how might their advertising be financed?

21

How do prices, incomes and tastes influence demand?

This chapter presents the essentials of the neoclassical theory of demand. Whatever its social bias and technical shortcomings, the theory is still serviceable for a number of practical and theoretical purposes. And whether or not you need to use it, you won't pass as an economist if you don't *know* it. So the time has come to learn it.

DEMAND THEORY

The theory classifies some immediate causes (or 'proximate conditions') which influence consumers' demands for market goods and services, and predicts their likely influence on the demands.

In what follows, *demand* means willingness to buy specific quantities of goods at specific prices. *Quantities* means flows, i.e. amounts demanded over periods of time, like hair appointments per month, or tonnes of potatoes per year. *Good(s)* means any marketed goods or services which consumers may buy.

This outline of the theory can begin and end with the same summary. The quantity of a good which a consumer demands is likely to be influenced by –

• the present and expected price of the good;

• the prices of other goods;

• the amount of the consumer's income; and

• the consumer's needs and tastes and preferences, including in most cases the diminishing marginal utility of the good for the consumer.

Together those conditions are likely to determine –

• the income elasticity and the price elasticity of the consumer's demand for the good.

We will unpack those items in turn, noticing how each of the conditions may affect demand for a product by individual consumers, and total demand for it by all consumers.

Price

For most goods there tends to be more demand the lower the price. Where market experience records how much of a product has been selling at each of a range of prices, the information can be expressed in a schedule or a graph. Those do not necessarily record how sales change with changing prices over time. The schedule and the curve are meant as snapshots: though demand schedules and curves are commonly based on market observations over time, what they predict is the cus-

Price per bushel (P)	Quantity demanded per day (Q)
$10	100 bushels
$8	120 bushels
$6	150 bushels
$4	200 bushels
$2	300 bushels

Table 21.1 Demand schedule for carrots

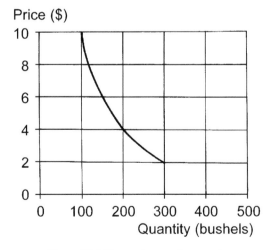

Figure 21.1 Demand curve for carrots

Price per bushel (P)	Quantity demanded before the change (D1)	Quantity demanded since the change (D2)
$10	100 bushels	160 bushels
$8	120 bushels	200 bushels
$6	150 bushels	250 bushels
$4	200 bushels	330 bushels
$2	300 bushels	500 bushels

Table 21.2 Demand schedules

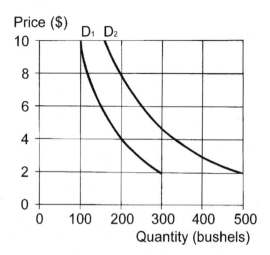

Figure 21.2 Demand curves

tomers' state of mind – their willingness to buy particular quantities at particular prices – at any *one* time. If the relations have held steadily in the past, they may continue to hold. Any day that suppliers charge $6 they can collectively expect to sell 150 bushels. Any day they want to sell altogether 150 bushels they had better price them at $6.

Now suppose that some strong stuff in a diet column of the local newspaper persuades people that carrots can do wonders for their vitality. Being keener on carrots than they were, they will tend to buy more at any given price. Market analysts will need a new demand schedule and demand curve. Above are the old and new schedules, and the old and new curves.

A number of things may have caused the greater demand for carrots. There may have been some persuasion, as in our example. Other vegetables may be dearer, shifting some demand to carrots. People may have come to market with more spending money. Whatever the cause, you need a new demand schedule and a new curve. You need them whenever demand changes for any other reason than a change in price. Economists get into the habit (I think it's a bad habit) of talking about the curve rather than the life it represents. Instead of saying 'Demand has changed because of a price change', they say ''There has been movement along the demand curve.' Instead of saying 'No, this change in demand has happened for other reasons', they say 'The curve has shifted' – to the right if demand has strengthened, to the left if it has weakened. But you may keep a clearer head for realities, and for the theory's limitations, if you generally think in real terms. Instead of ask-

ing 'Is this change in demand a *movement along* the curve, or a *shift of* the curve?' ask what is causing the change: a price change, an effect of advertising on people's preferences, a change in the amount they have to spend – or what?

Out in the marketplace, can you tell movements along the curve (effects of price changes) from shifts of the curve (effects of all other causes)? From the sales figures alone you often can't. Suppose that on Monday (M) 140 bushels of carrots sell at $8 a bushel. On Tuesday (T) 220 bushels sell at $5.80. On Wednesday (W) 330 bushels sell at $5.20. As shown on Figure 21.3,

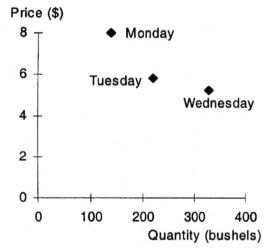

Figure 21.3 Changing prices and quantities

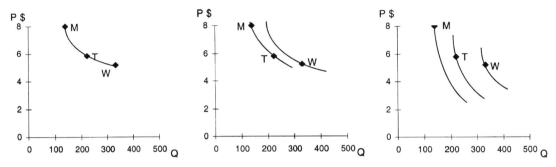

Figure 21.4 Alternative interpretations of Figure 21.3

those sales can't tell you whether you are facing a steady demand schedule or two or three quick-changing ones. It can't tell you which of the alternatives in Figure 21.4 to plot on your graph.

When changes in tastes, income, or the prices of other goods affect the demand for carrots (or 'shift the curve'), that does not mean that prices cease to affect it. The new passion for carrots may increase the demand for them at any given price. But demand will still respond to changes in price: price changes will merely move the demand along its new rather than its old curve.

Why do people tend to buy more of a commodity the cheaper it is? A basic reason is this: the cheaper it is, the less other goods they must do without to buy any given quantity of it. The cheaper it is, the less is its opportunity cost, i.e. its cost in other goods foregone. If smoked salmon were cheaper I would eat more of it, because if it were cheaper, eating it would require less sacrifice of other pleasures. For a meal of smoked salmon I would willingly go vegetarian for the rest of the day. But at present prices, to pay for a meal of smoked salmon I would have to go vegetarian for the rest of the week, and – with regret – I don't think it's worth it. A meal of salmon gives me as much joy as two sensible meals, but not as much joy as seven sensible meals.

Consumers' choices are not all between similar goods like alternative foods. Some people go hungry to buy concert tickets. Some people spend next to nothing on clothes so that they can afford to buy books or artists' materials. I spread my spending – or if I behaved as rationally as economic theorists would like me to, I *would* spread my spending – to get the most satisfying combination of goods and services that my money can buy. To my taste, how does one more mouthful of salmon per month compare with one more haircut per year? How does buying a toy for a child compare with sending a food parcel to Ethiopia? That depends on my

individual tastes and 'marginal utilities', which we will presently consider. But the options I must weigh – how much salmon would cost how many haircuts, what sort of toy would cost what sort of food parcel – depend on the relative prices of the goods.

Exceptions As the price of a good falls, demand for it usually increases, as some existing buyers buy more of it, and some newcomers enter the market – folk who could not afford it, or did not think it was worth it, at the higher price. When prices fall, demand is so likely to increase that economists have called that tendency 'the law of demand'. There are nevertheless some exceptions to it. As follows:

• *Expectations* The examples above were all of static calculation. (How much salmon do I want at today's price?) But people also think ahead and notice if prices seem likely to rise or fall. What do I do if the price of petrol falls one Tuesday when my tank is half empty? If I think the lower price is here to stay, I will refill the tank next Friday as usual. If I expect the price to bounce back up to normal tomorrow, I will top up the tank today. If I think today's price fall is the beginning of a continuing decline, I will delay refilling the tank for as long as possible, or until the falling price seems to have bottomed. Similarly if the price *rises* this Tuesday: I may buy less this week because I expect the price to fall next week, or I may buy more today because I expect the price to go on rising. Notice three things: (1) Price movements will only affect my total demand over time if they induce me to change my driving habits; but (2) in the short run, rising prices may reduce *or* increase demand, and falling prices may increase *or* reduce demand, depending on people's expectations; and (3) the expectations may be caused by the price movements themselves, or by information from other sources, or by both.

- *Natural limits* There are natural or social limits to the demand for some goods. People want only so many pounds of salt, boxes of matches and rolls of toilet paper. When they have all they can use, lower prices won't usually induce them to demand more.

- *Inferior goods* If some goods become cheaper, that may release income to be spent on dearer goods. Suppose you are addicted to twelve alcoholic drinks a week. You prefer whisky, but it costs $1.40 a shot. Beer is only $1. $12 a week is all you can afford for booze, so you spend it on twelve beers each week. Then a brewers' price war drops the price of a beer to 80 cents. Your $12 will now buy eight beers and four whiskies, so that is what you now drink. Cutting the price of beer by 20 per cent has reduced your demand for it by 33 per cent. Economists conclude that you regard beer as an 'inferior good'. (We will presently see that the same shift can happen without any price changes, if your income increases.)

- *Showing off* People buy some things to show what they can afford. A medium priced car could transport them comfortably but a Rolls Royce tells the world something about their wealth or importance (and critics may think, something about their social values). Because Rolls Royces are heavy and expensive to run, they don't appeal to people who want to economize their transport costs. They tend to appeal to people who want to be seen to have the world's most expensive car. So reducing their prices might not increase demand for them. The principle was expressed more than a century ago in a general theory of conspicuous expenditure in *Theory of the Leisure Class* by the institutional economist Thorstein Veblen.

- *Fooling people* Buying things because they look expensive may overlap with another reason why people sometimes prefer higher to lower prices. When it is technically difficult for buyers to judge the quality of goods, they may believe that the price indicates the quality. They may prefer expensive surgeons to cheaper ones, hoping for safer operations. They may prefer dearer torch batteries to cheaper ones, hoping they will last longer. If they get what they expect, they have simply preferred better goods to worse ones; that does not contradict the tendency for lower prices to increase demand for any one good. But people can be fooled, sometimes. There was a famous case of a hair conditioner so cheap that nobody trusted it – until its sales trebled when it trebled its price. The higher price itself may change the buyers' judg-ment of the product. It may help to change it further if it yields more sales revenue to finance more advertising. In cosmetics, pharmaceutical drugs, and a number of other fields it is not uncommon for dearer brands of an identical commodity to outsell cheaper brands, partly *because* they are dearer.

Under the last two items, notice that what matters is that the public price, and therefore the reputation of the product, should be high. The reputation is part of what the buyers buy. That may not stop individual buyers from getting it cheap if they can – as long as it is not *known* to be cheap. (But for light relief, work out how the theory fits the sharp operator who values *both* a reputation for wealth, *and* a reputation for clever dealing. He manages to beat the rules and buy his Rolls Royce duty-free through an offshore tax haven – then he *boasts* that he got it half price.)

When lower prices don't increase demand, or higher prices don't reduce it, it may be for any of those reasons: price expectations, natural limits to demand, inferior goods, buyers showing off, sellers fooling buyers. You need to keep all those possibilities in mind. But in real life most of them are rare. For most goods most of the time the 'law of demand' holds: lower prices attract more demand, higher prices attract less.

The world's shopkeepers did not need economists to tell them that. What they often need to know is *how much* change of price will cause *how much* change in demand, or *how much* increase of supply will cause prices to fall *how far*. You will presently learn, under *price elasticity of demand*, how that can sometimes be calculated. But first notice the other influences on demand, besides the price of the commodity itself, which are modelled in neoclassical theory.

Prices of other goods The demand for a good can be affected by the prices of other goods in three main ways.

- *Substitutes* Demand for a good may rise or fall without any change in its price if there are changes in the prices of goods which serve as alternatives or substitutes for it. If the price of carrots rises but the price of parsnips does not, some demand may shift from carrots to parsnips. If the price of carrots falls but the price of parsnips does not, some demand may shift from parsnips to carrots. (The shift of demand may then affect the price of parsnips – but that price change will be an effect, not a cause, of the shift in demand.)

- *Complements* Some things are commonly used together, so demands for them move together (rather than inversely as with demands for substitutes). If a change in the price of one complementary good increases or reduces demand for it, demand for the other(s) changes in the same direction. If a fall in the price of paint induces people to use more of it, demand for brushes is likely to increase without any change in their price. If cheaper petrol induces people to drive more miles, they will also demand more lubricating oil. If dearer petrol induces people to drive less miles the demand for lubricating oil will fall, and no amount of price-cutting will prevent it falling. Demand for complementary goods which are used together is sometimes called 'joint demand'.

• *Income effects* Price changes for some goods can affect demand for other goods if they leave consumers with more or less to spend on those other goods. Suppose the government raises the price of alcohol and tobacco by increasing the taxes on them. If they continue drinking and smoking as much as before, drinkers and smokers will have less to spend on other goods. Demand for those other goods will fall though their prices are unchanged. When some oil-producing countries combined in 1973 to force a big increase in the world price of oil, motorists responded by buying a little less petrol (a price effect, complying with the law of demand) and also a little less of other things whose prices had *not* changed (an income effect). Income effects follow when price changes affect demand by increasing or reducing customers' real incomes, i.e. the whole quantity of goods which their incomes can buy. They are special cases of the general relations between income and demand which are described under the next two headings.

The amount of income

Definitions: Remember that in conventional economic usage, 'real income' means purchasing power: what your income will actually buy. But elsewhere in this text real income has been defined as the purchasing power of your money income plus the goods and services you produce for yourself at home. For this exposition of neoclassical theory it is convenient to return to the conventional usage, so for the rest of this chapter real income means the purchasing power of your money income. That is determined by income *and* prices. If your wage rises 25 per cent and all prices rise 25 per cent your real income has not changed. If your wage rises 25 per cent and prices don't rise at all, your real income has risen 25 per cent. If your wage does not rise but prices rise 25 per cent, your real income has fallen by 20 per cent.

We can now ask what effects income can have on demand. Obviously, what consumers can demand is limited by what they have to spend.. Suppose a household's real income increases by 10 per cent. Will it then buy 10 per cent more of every one of the goods and services it was buying before the wage rise? That is unlikely. It may well buy less of some things (beer, because it can now afford whisky); the same amount as before of some things (matches, toilet paper); 10 per cent more of some things (steak, magazines); 100 per cent more of some things (four weeks away in summer instead of the two it could afford before); and some things it did not buy at all before (occasional opera tickets).

You have met some of those effects before as effects of price changes. They happen when price changes alter real incomes, which in turn affect demands. More generally, any change in real income – whatever its cause – may affect demand in one or more of the following ways.

Saving and spending When households' incomes change, they may decide to save more or less than before, and therefore to spend less or more. So the change in their total demand for consumer goods may not correspond to the change in their incomes. (What they save may still be spent, if their bank lends their savings to other consumers or investors; but there is no longer a direct link between the income change and the type of demand it may generate.) Can an increase of real income ever *reduce* a household's spending? Yes, if it prompts the people to change their economic strategy. Suppose, for example, that a family living in a rented house acquires a second earner, and thus a substantial increase in real income. It decides it can now aim at buying a house, and starts saving hard to accumulate enough deposit to attract a housing loan. Saving leaves less to spend, so as long as the saving continues, increasing the household's income has *reduced* its consumer spending. Suppose that when it has saved most of the intended deposit it loses one earner. The one remaining income is not enough to repay the early years of a housing loan, so the household won't be given a housing loan and can no longer hope to buy a house. So it stops saving, and consoles itself by beginning to spend its accumulated savings. A lower income has caused the household to *increase* its demand for consumer goods. Those inverse relations between income and demand can occur, but they are not usual, and their effects on national totals of saving and spending tend to be offset by the more normal behavior of most households. Nevertheless national proportions of saving and spending have changed, sometimes quite sharply in some countries. The changes may well have owed something to increasing income. But they have also been affected by changes in culture, by household investment choices, by changing systems of superannuation and systems of housing finance, and by expectations of inflation; i.e. by complex causation. If a recession brings a sharp fall in employment and income, it is predictable that demand for consumer goods will decline. But small changes in income no longer have reliably predictable effects on total consumer demand, either for an individual household or in the economy as a whole. Nor – as we shall now see – are the effects on demand the same for all goods and services.

Normal goods Demand for some goods tends to vary regularly with income. Economists call those 'normal goods'. We suggested magazines and superior foods as examples. As incomes rise, some existing buyers buy more of them, and some new buyers (who could not afford them before) start buying them. The list of goods which are treated this way may be different for each consumer, but nationally, experience identifies many goods and services for which demand tends to vary in regular relation to the society's total demand for all market goods and services. To the extent that total demand varies with income, so does demand for these normal goods.

Sufficient goods Some needs don't change with income (unless you are very poor). Enough is enough, however rich you become, of matches, toilet paper, salt, bread, and other basic commodities.

Inferior goods These also you have met already. As income increases, people buy less of some goods because they can afford better alternatives. Fewer sausages because they can afford steak. Less fast food because they can afford restaurant service. Less public transport because they can afford a car.

The distribution of income

Households with different incomes tend to demand partly-different baskets of goods. They all buy water, salt, matches, bread, and other basics. But as incomes rise, households don't only buy more of each item. They also buy some different items.

The poor buy more than the rich do of public transport, tabloid newspapers, hamburgers.

People with middle incomes buy more low and medium priced cars, fresh meat and vegetables, broadsheet newspapers, sensible woollens and tweeds.

The rich buy more expensive cars, expensive furniture, diamonds and silk, caviar and smoked salmon.

What proportions of goods of each kind a population

demands therefore depends on its distribution of income. Among affluent societies a more equal society, with few rich and few poor, demands more woollens and tweeds and good cotton prints; a less equal society, with more and richer rich and more and poorer poor, demands more cheap jeans and rayon tops and sausages and chips, and more silk and bespoke tailoring and smoked salmon and French brandy.

Tastes and preferences

How is the demand for marketed consumer goods affected by people's tastes and preferences? Most of the answer is obvious: people go shopping for things they want, not for things they don't want. Their wants are not sovereign – their tastes and preferences are modified by the goods and prices they find in the shops, and the amounts of money they have to spend. But however the tastes are formed, and however the preferences are modified by other conditions, the tastes are still powerful.

In practice some tastes are steadier than others. Steady needs and tastes ensure fairly steady demands for food, fuel, morning newspapers, commuter transport, and other items of habitual daily use.

For other things people don't go shopping with fixed 'demand schedules'. They go to town, or they go to the country or seaside on Sunday, with money in their pockets and a general willingness to have their attention caught, surprised, attracted by whoever can. Some tastes are impulsive and quick-changing. So in economists' jargon some demand curves shift – or come into and out of existence – more often than demand 'moves along' them. When traders are out to sell people lucky dips or paper hats or buskers' performances – or extortionate 'protection' which they positively don't want – the very idea of 'demand' may be inappropriate. The demands, sometimes insistent, come from the suppliers.

A more substantial misgiving about the role of tastes in the theory of demand is that analysts are tempted to use them, without actually investigating them, as residual causes of anything the rest of the theory fails to explain. The theory's other variables – the price of the commodity, the prices of other commodities, the consumers' incomes – are independently observed. It is by relating those independently observed variables to observed sales that theorists have been able to model the influence of prices and incomes on demand. So how can the influence of tastes on demand be modelled if the tastes are not independently observed? The role of tastes in neoclassical demand theory is really this: Effects which have not been predicted by reference to prices and incomes are not said to be random or unexplained.

Instead, they are said to be caused by changing tastes. Theoretically that's deplorable. But in a commonsense way there is something to be said for it. Economists theorizing in academic journals may stick to 'revealed preferences'. But economists working for operators in the marketplace – living the life they are concerned with, reading the papers, watching TV, aware of current fashions and advertising and other persuasions – know much more about current tastes than the theory requires, and apply what they know in commonsense ways. That includes knowing when careful study of the relations between past prices and sales is likely to help prediction, and when it is not. When it is, the traditional theory may be quite serviceable.

Finally, three ways of theorizing not about tastes themselves but about their effects on market demands. Meet utility theory, then indifference theory, then the concept of elasticity and some ways of measuring it.

UTILITY THEORY

Imagine a woman shopping for her family's dinner. What will they have tonight? Expensive steak then a cheap sweet – or a cheap first course then a treat of strawberries and cream? Economists wanting to model her choices may model what she *thinks* or what she *does*. Utility theorists guess how she *thinks* (she thinks a plate of steak promises more pleasure than a bowl of strawberries does). Indifference theorists try to stick to what she does. At what prices does she substitute how many strawberries for how much steak?

Utility theory assumes that all human pains and pleasures can be measured in a common currency rather like money. It assumes that a consumer can know (for example) that in the net satisfactions they yield, 3 nights of love = 20 salmon dinners = 1 new bike = avoiding 1 week of toothache. Call the common quality – the net of gain over pain – 'utility'. If you are observed to buy steak rather than strawberries we will theorize that steak gives you more utility than strawberries do. Does that say any more than that you prefer steak to strawberries? No, no more; it is just a different way of saying it. You can't see or measure the utility or prove that it exists. It is just a theoretical device. But it has an element of common sense: the shopper deliberating between steak-then-jelly and sausages-then-strawberries-and-cream probably *is* estimating which combination will give the family the best combination of nourishment and pleasure. There is less sense in imputing 'utility' to more serious choices – between helping yourself and helping others; between dull productive work and enjoyable unproductive work; between love and duty if they conflict.

Marginal utility For theoretical convenience we will return from steak to smoked salmon because salmon tends to come in smaller helpings, allowing second and even third helpings. The first helping is the best. Each helping after that gives a little less delight, though it does still add to the whole pleasure of the meal. The same is true of strawberries and cream. If I can only have one course I'll choose salmon. If I can have two courses I'll choose a plate of salmon then a dish of strawberries rather than two helpings of either. If three courses are possible I'll have two of salmon and one of strawberries. If four are possible, some cheese might be more desirable than either a third plate of salmon or a second dish of strawberries.

And so on. In the language of utility –

- Each good has diminishing marginal utility.

- As long as its marginal utility is still positive (i.e. up to the point where more would make the consumer sick) more of the good brings more *total* utility but diminishing *marginal* utility, as each increment of the good increases total utility by less than the last increment did.

- Marginal utilities can be compared. With a certain quantity of each (for example) the marginal utility of the next ounce of salmon may be equal to the marginal utility of the next five strawberries. In the light of her income limit and the relative prices of salmon and strawberries, the shopper can judge what mix of salmon and strawberries will yield most utility.

- She can do that by buying the quantities of salmon and strawberries that will ensure that the last dollar she spends on salmon buys the same marginal utility as the last dollar she spends on strawberries. She will maximize the utility of all her shopping if she apportions her spending so that *the last dollar's worth of every good she buys brings as much marginal utility as the last dollar's worth of every other good she buys*.

When the shopper gets it right she is said to be in 'consumer equilibrium'. As long as her income and the relevant prices don't change, and the household's tastes don't change, she is maximizing her household's utility and no change in her pattern of spending can increase it further. If income or prices or the household's preferences *do* change, she will need to adjust her buying, and the composition of her family's dinner, to restore the equal marginal utility of the last dollar's worth of every good she buys.

Contradictions Can that shopper know what will most please the other members of her household? She generally can, and you and I know that she can. But scientistic economists insist that she can't – that nobody can make objective *interpersonal comparisons of utility*, so the shopper cannot either compare or add up the utility which her purchases will yield to the different members of the household.. And even if their individual orders of preference were known, there is some genuinely rigorous theory which shows that no mathematical reasoning from those individual preferences can arrive at a policy which is 'objectively' best for the group as a whole: that always requires some value judgments. In the theory of demand as in other branches of neoclassical theory there is unresolved confusion between the beliefs that (i) nobody can make valid interpersonal judgments of utility, but (ii) an economic system in which each consumer derives equal utility from the marginal dollar's worth of each good and service that they buy will maximize its members' total utility; (iii) most goods have diminishing marginal utility for their purchasers, but (iv) there is no ground for believing in the diminishing marginal utility either of individual or of total income.

Substitution prices Notice an effect on shopping choices of the diminishing marginal utility of particular goods. You are shopping for that salmon and strawberry dinner. You get the proportions wrong – you buy too much salmon and too few strawberries. Because of their marginal utilities the diners would give up quite a lot of their salmon for a few more strawberries. If you make the opposite mistake and offer them too little salmon and too many strawberries they would give up quite a lot of strawberries for a little more salmon. Between the first mistake and the second –

• the market prices of salmon and strawberries have not changed; but for this group of diners –

• the strawberry price of salmon and the salmon price of strawberries have changed.

If you could watch shoppers with different marginal utilities shopping for their dinners, you might avoid the need to speculate about their subjective utilities by observing that they applied different substitution prices between one good and another. (You might in principle, however impossible it would be in practice.) Where does this different approach get you? It gets you into indifference theory.

INDIFFERENCE THEORY

Utility theory is quite understandable in words and figures without diagrams. So that is how it has been presented on the last page or two. But to expound indifference theory in words only, without any pictures, would be like trying to describe a spiral in words while sitting on your hands. So we will use the indifference theorists' geometry.

Imagine a household with fixed income and fixed tastes, spending its whole income on two goods only. Most expositions use food and clothing, but since we have come so far with salmon and strawberries we will stick to them. Our household is a single consumer with an income of $8 a day. He doesn't save or borrow. He spends it all on salmon and strawberries. Our only problem is to understand how he divides his spending between the two.

The budget line Salmon is $1 an ounce. Strawberries are 20 cents each. So an income of $8 will buy 8 ounces of salmon or 40 strawberries. Between those extremes, the budget line depicts the possible mixes that $8 will buy. Number of strawberries on the vertical axis, ounces of salmon on the horizontal axis:

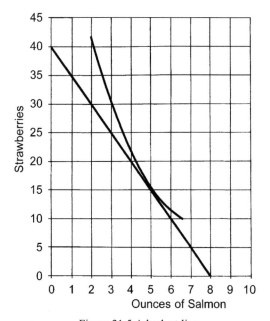

Figure 21.5 A budget line

$8 will buy 35 strawberries and 1 ounce of salmon; *or* 30 strawberries and 2 ounces of salmon; and so on. You didn't need a graph to work that out. But now consider how this character should spend his $8. With his particular marginal utilities the efficient mix happens to be 5 ounces of salmon (for $5) and 15 strawberries (for $3), because if he has them in those proportions the last ounce of salmon (for $1) yields the same pleasure as the last 5 strawberries (for $1).

But does that 'substitution price' mean that he would willingly trade an ounce less salmon for five more strawberries, and dine on 4 ounces of salmon and 20 strawberries? No – his diminishing marginal utilities mean that he would miss the lost ounce of salmon more than he would enjoy the extra strawberries. But more strawberries would add something – even at a diminishing marginal rate – to his pleasure. So there should be some quantity of strawberries that would compensate him for losing that fifth ounce of salmon. Seven, perhaps. But the next ounce after that – cutting the whole salmon ration back to 3 ounces – would cost 10 strawberries. Similarly for changes in the other direction. At 5 ounces of salmon and 15 strawberries he would not willingly trade 5 of his strawberries for another ounce of salmon, which would give him 6 ounces of salmon and 10 strawberries. To give up those 5 strawberries he would want perhaps 1 1/2 ounces of salmon. So here are four alternative dinners with equal attraction: (1) 3 ounces of salmon and 32 strawberries; (2) 4 ounces of salmon and 22 strawberries; (3) 5 ounces of salmon and 15 strawberries; (4) 6 1/2 ounces of salmon and 10 strawberries.

Those four meals may give the same pleasure but they don't come at the same price. Price them:

	Ounces of salmon at $3 an ounce	Strawberries at $1 for 5	Dinner price
(1)	3	32	$9.40
(2)	4	22	8.40
(3)	5	15	8.00
(4)	6.5	10	8.50

Now plot them with the budget line, and you will find as in Figure 21.6, an *indifference curve*. Any point on it represents a mix of salmon and strawberries that would satisfy you as much as the mix represented by any other point on the curve.

The changing slope of the curve represents the changing substitution rate between the two goods. If you read the quantities off the two axes, you can see that the top end of the curve shows (roughly) 10 strawberries = 1 ounce of salmon; the lower end shows (roughly) 3 strawberries = 1 ounce of salmon. Where the curve touches the budget line, its tangent is parallel to the budget line. There, *both* the indifference curve *and* the budget line say 5 strawberries = 1 ounce of salmon. Your personal substitution rate = the market substitution rate

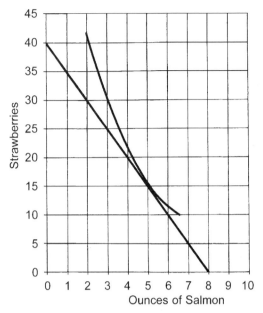

Figure 21.6 An indifference curve

at the current market prices. That's also the only point at which you can afford any of the mixes represented on this curve. It is the dinner your tastes will choose if $8 is what you have to spend. But as the mix changes to include more strawberries and less salmon, your tastes keep increasing the strawberry price of salmon. As the mix changes in the other direction, you increase the salmon price of strawberries. To express that common truth about human appetites –

- *Utility theory* says: when one good is scarce and another is plentiful, the marginal utility of the scarce good rises relative to the marginal utility of the plentiful good.

- *Indifference theory* says: the scarce good is observed to have greater substitution value. People are willing to pay more for it in other goods foregone.

Innumerable indifference curves can be drawn to represent the preferences of any one consumer – a more realistic consumer who wants not just two goods but scores of them. He can be observed choosing between alternative *bundles* of goods. Plot his ranking of all possible options, to produce a very large number of indifference curves, and you will have what indifference theorists call his indifference map, or indifference surface. Combine it with appropriate budget lines and it should show which bundle gives him best value for money, as judged by his tastes and preferences. The map can also show how his substitution prices will respond to changes in market prices. And from his observed spending choices, economists could in principle deduce what his preferences must be.

Can indifference theory tell shoppers or shopkeepers anything they don't know already? No. The theory was developed to allow economists to theorize about shoppers' behavior from their observed spending alone, without claiming to know anything about their utilities, i.e. their subjective purposes or feelings or reasoning. It was a case of 'selecting for objectivity'. It has little or no practical use in market analysis. I don't think you need it, but have included this short account of it so that you will recognize it if you meet it.

Summary

1. Begin with the summary with which this chapter began. The quantity of a good which a consumer demands is likely to be influenced by –

- the price of the good;

- the prices of other goods;

- the amount of the consumer's income; and

- the consumer's tastes and preferences, including in most cases the diminishing marginal utility of the good for the consumer.

2. The effects of prices, incomes and tastes on demand are more predictable for large numbers – for example, for the whole market demand for a broad category of goods, such as 'food' or 'clothing – than for individual consumers' choices of particular goods.

3. Whole market demand (as opposed to an individual consumer's demand) is influenced by the distribution as well as by the whole amount of consumers' income.

4. Neoclassical theory offers two ways of deducing the above relationships from simple assumptions about the consumers. *Utility theory* assumes that all the satisfactions which consumers get from goods can be called 'utility'. Each good tends to have diminishing marginal utility for each consumer. A consumer is shopping efficiently when the marginal utility of the last unit of each good she buys is equal to the marginal utility of the last unit of every other good she buys. Many theorists purport to believe that each person can compare his or her own utilities, but that 'interpersonal comparisons of utility' cannot be known. That means that you can know that the

millionaire gets less utility from a third bottle of champagne than from a second bottle, by observing that he doesn't buy the third. But you cannot know whether he gets more or less utility from his second bottle than a starving family gets from a square meal at the same price. (Believe that if you want to. I don't. Nor do most of the theorists in their real-life judgments about other people's pains and pleasures.)

5. *Indifference theory* was developed to avoid those speculations about people's feelings. Instead of comparing subjective utilities, it says that market observations can tell you any consumer's substitution rate between one commodity and another. *Utility theory* says that the more she already has of a commodity, the less utility she will get from a further unit of it. *Indifference theory* says that the more she already has of a commodity, the likelier she will be to spend her next dollar on something else. Her substitution rate between the commodities will vary with their prices, and the amount she already has of each. As with utility theory, this is a formal assumption to reason from. Economists don't actually measure individual consumers' substitution rates, and for whole markets 'measuring substitution rates' merely means recording the quantities and prices of all goods sold.

6. The theories arrive at similar conclusions about the likely effect on demand of prices and consumers' incomes and tastes. The likely relations between those four variables are as follows.

7. Any change in the price of a good is likely to have both an income effect and a substitution effect. *Income effect:* If the price of a good falls, buyers of that good have more real income to spend; if the price rises, they have less to spend. *Substitution effect:* If the price of a good falls, buyers are likely to buy more of it and (depending on the income effect) less or more or the same amount of other goods. If the price of a good rises, buyers are likely to buy less of it and (depending on the income effect) more or less or the same amount of other goods.

8. A rise in the demand for a good may be caused by –

- a fall in its price

- a rise in the price of a substitute

- a fall in the price of a complement

- a rise in total consumers' income

- a change in the distribution of consumers' income

- a change of taste in favor of the good, or its complements.

9. A fall in the demand for a good may be caused by –

- a rise in its price
- a fall in the price of a substitute
- a rise in the price of a complement
- a fall in total consumers' income
- a change in the distribution of consumers' income
- a decline of taste for the good, or its complements.

10. A rise in the price of a good may cause –

- a fall in demand for it
- a rise in demand for substitutes
- a fall in demand for complements
- a fall in the real income of consumers who buy any
  of the good

11. Now *you* complete the summary by filling in the
    remaining four-letter words. A fall in the price of a
    good may cause –

- a   in demand for it
- a   in demand for substitutes
- a   in demand for complements
- a   in the real income of consumers who buy any
               of the good.

CONCLUSIONS

We conclude with three critical questions. For educational purposes, what sort of social bias does the neoclassical
theory of demand encourage? Does it tell us anything
useful that experienced traders did not know already?
And in practical economic life, can the causes and effects
which it models be measured, for predictive purposes?

The need to select The neoclassical theory of
demand selects a certain effect (effective demand) and
models certain of its causes (prices, incomes, tastes).
Both choices are disagreed by other theorists with other
purposes – for example by Left theorists, marketing
experts, political and sociological theorists.

Selecting the effect The neoclassical theory of
demand aims to explain and predict effective demand,
i.e. consumers' willingness and capacity to buy particular quantities of particular goods at particular prices. It
does not aim to explain other effects of households'
wants and tastes and incomes. It models the effect of
unequal incomes on demand for cheap and expensive
goods, but it does not model the sufferings of people
who have wants they can't afford to satisfy. It does not

model the social or environmental effects of over-stim-
ulating people's desires for unnecessary goods, pollutant goods, positional goods. It does not model the fit or
misfit between the wants the system generates and the
wants it satisfies.

Other theorists with other purposes select otherwise.
Many Left theorists distinguish basic needs for necessary goods from 'induced' demands for luxuries, and
model the hardships of poor people who can't afford
enough necessary goods. Social psychologists, sociologists, criminologists and others focus on effects of the
fit or misfit between the wants and expectations which
an economic system generates and the wants and expectations which it satisfies. Some also theorize about the
goodness or badness of the wants the system generates,
and the goodness or badness of satisfying or not satisfying those wants. (Which is best? To restrict some freedoms in order to avoid generating demand for sadistic
pornography? To generate demand for it but ban supplies of it? Or to allow profit-seekers to generate
demand for it and supply the demand?)

Selecting causes of the effect Having selected
effective demand as the effect to be explained and predicted, neoclassical theory then selects certain causes of
that effect and models their influence on it. The selections show preferences for causes which emphasize the
sovereignty of consumers rather than any manipulation
of consumers. Demand is explained as an effect of
prices, incomes and tastes. Other parts of neoclassical
theory model some of the causes which determine the
prices and incomes. But they don't model any of the
causes which influence the tastes. They don't model
advertisers' efforts to influence tastes and preferences,
and they don't model the broader social forces which
determine how independent and sceptical or how ill-
informed and manipulable the 'sovereign' consumers
are in arriving at their tastes and preferences.

SOME SELECTIONS COMPARED

As in the two preceding chapters we are noticing how
neoclassics, Left economists, marketing experts and
others select and model different strands of the complex
pattern of causes and effects which surround the
demand for goods and services in real economic life. To
summarize their differences we can first map the part of
the pattern which each theorist chooses to model, then
assemble the parts into a more comprehensive (but still
selective) pattern of causal relations. That is a simple
way to relate the neoclassical theory to neighboring theories, and show what it does and does not aim to do.

Advertising and marketing experts theorize chiefly about the relations through which their clients can exert some influence:

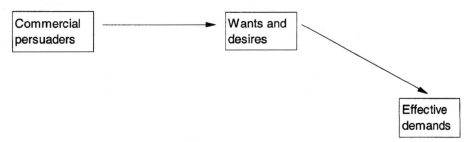

Environmentalists add links to both ends of the causal chain. Left environmentalists may trace it further left to show capitalism as a main cause of the commercial persuasions.

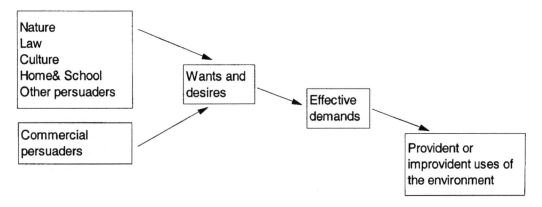

Sociologists, social psychologists and other students of social conflict and cohesion add some effects of frustrated desires and expectations as well as satisfied ones:

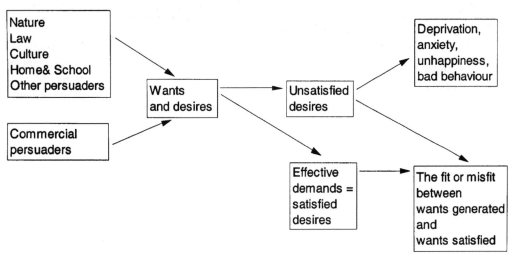

Left economists see demand created, but many needs frustrated, by the capitalist system:

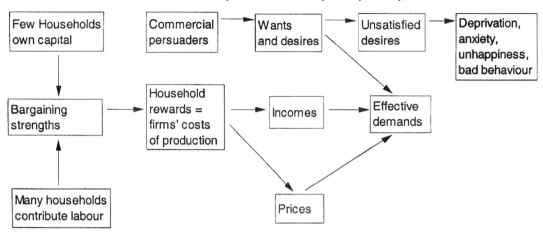

Now assemble them all, including the components of the neoclassical theory, perhaps as a guide to the range of interest of a 'broad' economist, who will focus on particular parts of the causal pattern as particular tasks require:

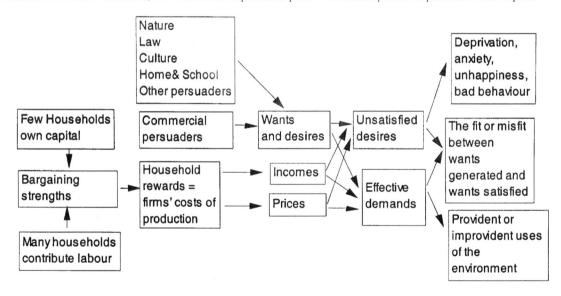

How useful is the neoclassical theory of demand? Opinions differ, even among neoclassical economists. The theory says what common sense has always known, that if the price of a commodity falls, people can afford to buy more of it (the income effect) and often want to buy more of it (the substitution effect).

Business people have the same understanding of relations between price and demand. But when they want expert help in forecasting or influencing demand, they tend to get it from market theorists and researchers who use psychological rather than economic theory, and who focus on the one demand condition which neoclassical theory takes as given, the formation of tastes and preferences. Among other things they distinguish habitual shopping for daily needs from thoughtful buying based on considered tastes and preferences, and from less rational kinds of impulsive buying and 'cheer-up' shopping. Different principles apply to each. For each, they try to discover how fear, affection, curiosity and imagination mix with economic rationality in shoppers' minds. They explore, sometimes in controlled experiments, the effects of different packaging, advertising and marketing techniques.

Market forecasters do have work for economists. They expect them to forecast population changes, rates of household formation, changes in national income and saving and spending and interest rates, effects of taxes on prices, and other processes which can affect consumer demand. Thus economists chiefly contribute some of their other skills, rather than their elaborations of utility theory or indifference theory, to the practical study of demand. Practical investigators of demand don't use theory which reduces the complexities of shoppers' minds and purposes to a simple pursuit of 'utility'. Even less do they use indifference theory, which was invented to avoid paying any attention to all to people's psychology. One frivolous critic mentioned that he was 'indifferent to these theories because they have so little practical utility'.

Nevertheless you need to be routinely alert to the possible relations, and aware of the likely relations, between prices, incomes, tastes and demands. Whether it is from common sense, market experience or the neoclassical theory of demand that you learn those relations, you need to keep them in mind. That is not because they can always provide determinate predictions of the effect of each variable on the others in particular cases. They often can't. But in practical work they can serve as a useful investigator's guide, i.e. as one of the 'batteries of possibilities', or lists of things to look for, which must be a main part of your profession-

al equipment. An economist who is routinely aware that a change in a commodity's price may also affect demand for substitutes and complements, and may have an income as well as a substitution effect, is likely to be a better student of demand than one who forgets to look for some of those effects.

Measuring and forecasting demand Firms have to decide how much of what to produce, how to price their products, or both. Governments have to decide how to tax and regulate economic activity. Both need to know what the elementary theory of demand offers to tell them, but they need to have it quantified. For particular goods or groups of goods in particular markets, if no change is expected in advertising or marketing techniques or other conditions, *how much* change in price will induce *how much* change in the quantities people will want to buy? *How much* change in households' spendable income will cause *how much* change in the quantities demanded of *which* goods? The questions occur in many practical forms. Producers need to know how far they can increase supplies without forcing prices down to unprofitable levels. If government thinks of doubling the tax on whisky for revenue rather than health reasons, it may want to know whether doubling the tax will fetch more revenue, or cut demand so far that the tax revenue will actually decline. If government thinks of cutting taxes to leave the population more spending money, it may want to know how much of the extra spending will be on imports for which the country is short of foreign exchange. And so on – the practical questions are plentiful and often important.

Answers may depend partly on things outside the scope of neoclassical theory, for example on expected responses to innovative advertising or political persuasion. But to the extent that they do depend on the influence of prices and incomes on demand, researchers must use market and census and other records to find out how responsive the demand in question has been, in the past, to changes in prices or incomes. The records may also show how regular or irregular the responsiveness has been and therefore how reliable it may be as a guide to future responses.

The degree of responsiveness is known as the elasticity of demand. Responsiveness to price changes is *price elasticity of demand*. Responsiveness to income changes is *income elasticity of demand*. If neoclassical theorists studied the formation of tastes and preferences, they might also have a concept of *persuasion elasticity of demand*. (Advertisers do.) Measuring the price elasticity and the income elasticity of demand is the subject of the next chapter. Modern market monitoring and record keeping have made it an effective aid to a range of business and government decision-making. It builds on the elementary theory of demand, but does not need advanced utility or indifference theory.

EXERCISES

1. Explain what is meant by the income effect and the substitution effect of a price change.

2. In what conditions, and how, can a consumer decide for herself how much income effect she will suffer from a particular price change?

3. The price of hamburgers goes up because the retailers' rents and wage bills rise, i.e. not because of any increase in raw material prices. Indicate by +, – or = whether demand for these items is likely to go up (+), down (-), or stay the same (=):

    > Raw minced beef
    >
    > Bread rolls
    >
    > Tomato sauce
    >
    > Takeaway chicken
    >
    > Ice cream

4. Specify possible (though perhaps unusual) conditions which could produce effects opposite to your + and – answers to Question 3. (For example, dearer hamburgers might not reduce demand for ketchup if the consumers' preferred substitute was hot dogs, or if the customers were so addicted to tomato sauce that when they switched from hamburgers to chicken they put ketchup on the chicken.)

5. Over a 5 year period the average real income of people living on welfare incomes does not change; the average real income of wage and salary earners rises 10 per cent; the average net worth of the richest 5 per cent of the population rises 25 per cent in real terms. Describe the likely +, – or = effects on demand for ten or more commodities, including some commodities used by each group.

6. Where possible, describe other demand conditions which (though perhaps unusual) might neutralize or reverse the + and – effects predicted in your answers to Question 5. (Perhaps the expected rise in demand for furs is reversed by a successful animal lib campaign. Perhaps old age and unemployment have increased so that a higher proportion of the population are on welfare incomes. And so on.)

7. If your answers to Questions 4 and 6 have not included one example each of naturally limited demand, inferior goods, price changes to complementary goods, price changes to substitutes, ostentatious spending, and shoppers mistakes, add answers to include an effect of each of those causes.

22

The elasticity of demand

By 'elasticity' economists mean responsiveness. Cutting the price of a product usually attracts more demand for it. But *how much* more? Increasing people's incomes usually leads them to demand more goods. But *how much* more, and of which goods?

Just as demand responds to price changes, so may supply. If the price of a good rises, suppliers may offer more of it. But *how much* more?

Meet three concepts of elasticity:

- The price elasticity of demand is a measure of how much the demand for a good changes in response to a change in its price (if nothing else changes).

- The income elasticity of demand is a measure of how much the demand for a good – or for all goods – changes in response to a change in consumers' incomes.

- The price elasticity of supply is a measure of how much the supply of a good changes in response to a change in its price.

All three have to be qualified by 'if nothing else changes'. When a number of forces operate at once it may be difficult to distinguish the effects of price or income changes from the effects of other causes. Even where other conditions are steady, the demand for some products (bread, butter) is more predictable than the demand for others (ice creams, sports cars) which may respond more to impulse, advertising or the weather. And you will meet other causes for caution in using the concept of elasticity. But first, what does it mean and how is it measured? We will illustrate from the price elasticity of demand, which is the measure that gets the most use.

THE PRICE ELASTICITY OF DEMAND

Producers often need to know what relations to expect between prices and the quantities they can sell. They study the past behavior of their markets to find answers to any of the following questions, which are all about the relation between changes in price and changes in quantity demanded:

- Will a *price cut* increase the volume of sales by enough to increase total revenue? Or by enough to yield the same revenue as before? Or by little enough to reduce total revenue? (You're selling 1000 pounds

of carrots a week at $1 a pound for a total $1000. If you halve the price, will consumers buy 3000 lb. for $1500? Or 2000 lb. for the same $1000 as before? Or 1500 lb. for only $750?)

- Will a *price increase* cut sales by little enough to yield an increase in total revenue? Or by an amount which yields the same revenue as before? Or by an amount which yields less total revenue than before?

- Will an *increase in supply* push prices down far enough to yield less total revenue than before? Or the same? Or more?

- Will a *cut in supply* push prices up to a level which yields more total revenue than before? Or the same? Or less?

Many producers are less interested in total revenue than in relations between their sales revenue and their costs of production. Suppose a producer has potential economies of scale. Producing more can cut the unit costs of the product. Will an increased supply cut market prices by less than it cuts the producer's costs? (Then the producer will be richer.) Or will the increased supply cut market prices by *more* than it cuts the producer's costs? (Then one more mousetrap-maker may bite the dust.) Notice that if prices rise further than costs do, or if costs fall further than prices do, it is quite possible for a producer to be better off – to be making more profit per unit and more total profit – despite a fall in total revenue.

So the question above can be re-stated with reference to profit margins rather than total revenue. Will a higher volume at a lower price have a bigger effect on revenue than on costs? Or a neutral effect? Or a smaller effect? Will a change to a lower volume at a higher price have a bigger effect on revenue than on costs, a neutral effect, or a smaller effect?

All those questions call for (among other things) estimates of price elasticities of demand. So economists have developed rough ways of naming and measuring them.

Classifying elasticity

- If a price cut brings such a big increase in sales that total revenue is greater than before, demand is said to be *elastic*.

• If a price cut brings a proportionate change in demand so that revenue is the same as before, demand is *unit-elastic*.

• If a price cut brings a less-than-proportionate increase in demand so that total revenue is less than before, demand is *inelastic*.

Suppose your local vegetable market is selling 1000 pounds of carrots a week at $1 a pound. Total revenue to the growers is $1 x 1000 = $1000. Now suppose the growers halve the price. If consumers respond by doubling their consumption, revenue will be 50 cents x 2000 = the same $1000 as before. Demand is *unit elastic*. If consumers treble their consumption, revenue will be 50 cents x 3000 = $1500. Demand is *elastic*. If sales only increase by half, revenue will be 50 cents x 1500 = $750. Demand is *inelastic*.

Notice three implications of the principle:

1. Symmetrical relations hold for price increases. If a price increase cuts demand more than proportionately, so that total revenue falls, demand is elastic. If a price increase cuts demand less than proportionately, so that total revenue increases, demand is inelastic.

2. The examples so far are of changes in price causing changes in demand. The same principles hold if the price changes come as effects of changes in the quantity supplied. If the growers have a glut of carrots and double the supply to the market, how far will the price have to fall to induce consumers to buy the doubled supply? If the price has to be halved, so that total revenue is the same as before, there is unit-elasticity of demand. If the price has to go lower still (so that doubling the supply actually cuts total revenue), demand is inelastic. If the price needs to fall by less than half, so that increasing the supply increases total revenue, the demand is elastic.

3. Notice that with inelastic demand, total revenue changes in the same direction as price. Cutting the price cuts total revenue. Raising the price increases total revenue. With elastic demand, total revenue changes in the opposite direction to price. Cutting the price increases total revenue. Raising the price cuts total revenue.

But suppliers don't just want to know whether a price change will increase or reduce their total revenue. They want to know by how much.

Measuring elasticity

The price elasticity of demand for a market good is defined as the percentage change in quantity demanded divided by the percentage change in price. Different theorists use different symbols for it: E, Ep or h (the Greek letter eta). Here, E will do.

$$E = \frac{\text{per cent rise in quantity demanded}}{\text{per cent cut in price}}$$

or

$$\frac{\text{per cent fall in quantity demanded}}{\text{per cent cut in price}}$$

For example –

• If price falls 10 per cent and demand rises 5 per cent, the price elasticity of demand is said to be $\frac{1}{2}$ or 0.5. Demand with that or any other elasticity less than 1 (E < 1) is inelastic.

• If price falls 10 per cent and demand rises 10 per cent, the price elasticity of demand is 1. E = 1. Elasticity is unitary.

• If price falls 10 per cent and demand rises 20 per cent, the price elasticity of demand is 2. With that or any other elasticity greater than 1 (E > 1) demand is elastic.

This method of measuring elasticity has some imperfections. It works better for small changes in price and quantity than for large ones, and it works better near the middle of the range than at the extremes of elasticity and inelasticity. Recall the alternative ways of measuring the percentage difference between two numbers. From 100 to 125 is a 25 per cent increase, but from 125 to 100 is only a 20 per cent decrease. Measurements of elasticity commonly relate a rise in price to a fall in demand, or vice versa. To avoid confusion it is customary to average the percentages in each case. If price or quantity has moved either way between 100 and 125, call the change the average of 25 per cent and 20 per cent, i.e. 22 $\frac{1}{2}$ per cent. So if (say) a price rise from $100 to $125 a ton cuts demand for potatoes from 1250 tons to 1000 tons, analysts of elasticity say that a 22 $\frac{1}{2}$ per cent rise in price has caused a 22 $\frac{1}{2}$ per cent fall in the quantity demanded. They will say the same with the causation reversed if a supply increase from 1000 to 1250 tons causes the price to fall from $125 to $100 a ton.

With many goods it is natural for the elasticity of demand to increase as prices rise, and decline as they fall. When prices are high, small increases can choke off a lot of the remaining demand. When prices are low and people are therefore getting all they want of the commodity, further price-cutting won't induce them to buy much more, so demand is relatively inelastic. But this tendency is exaggerated by the method of measuring elasticity. When a small quantity is selling at a high price, a small change in both quantity and price appears as a big percentage of the (small) quantity, but as a small percentage of the (big) price. Conversely at the other end of the range when a big quantity is selling at a low price, changes figure as a small percentage of the quantity but a large percentage of the price. To demonstrate, extend our old carrot demand schedule upward to show that only 10 bushels would sell if the price were $20, and only 20 bushels at $18. When the price changes from $20 to $18, a 10 per cent price cut adds 100 per cent to demand, showing extreme elasticity. But at the bottom of the scale (with 200 bushels selling at $4), if the same $2 price cut increased demand by the same 10 bushels, our method of measurement would show a 50 per cent price cut causing a 5 per cent increase in demand, with extreme inelasticity. If a new product comes onto the market, is popular, and sells at a constant price with rising sales keeping pace with the maker's productive capacity, it may be some time before the price elasticity of demand for it can be measured, or significant for business purposes.

So if you are calculating the elasticity of demand for particular goods for trading purposes, remember that the calculation may need to be quite local, in several senses. You may need sales information from the particular market concerned, for price changes at about the price levels concerned. Knowing how demand for carrots responded to price movements between $8 and $10 last week won't tell you how demand may respond to price movements between $4 and $6 this week. Elasticities recorded in summer may not tell you what to expect in winter. And any elasticities may fail to repeat themselves if other market conditions change: if the customers change cookbooks or diet books, or have more or less to spend, or if rival or complementary products change their prices.

Three further characteristics of price elasticities of demand are worth noting.

Necessaries, optional goods and luxuries There is relatively inelastic demand for things people can't do without: food, shelter, light and power, transport to work. If their prices go up, people tend to buy nearly as much as before, and cut other less necessary spending. Demand for luxuries tends to be more elastic. But the categories overlap. There are plain and fancy ways of meeting many basic needs, and demand for the fancy ways may be more elastic than demand for the plain ways. Where the supply of necessary goods is competitive, as with clothing, *inelastic* demand for a basic item (like underwear) may coexist with *highly elastic* demand for each competing brand. If you're making

(say) men's white cotton underwear, demand is likely to fall sharply if your prices rise much above your competitors', though the whole demand for underwear remains steady.

Broader and narrower categories of goods As in the clothing example, measures of elasticity may vary with the group or category of goods you choose to measure. Demand for carrots and demand for parsnips may fluctuate elastically, often at each other's expense, while the total demand for root vegetables is steady and inelastic. With some exceptions (like salt) elasticity tends to be higher the more narrowly products are defined, and lower the more broadly they are grouped.

So if you are asked 'How elastic is the demand for fresh vegetables?' *what* you calculate should depend on who wants to know, and for what purpose. Examples:

(1) The owner of the town marketplace wants to judge how far he can raise the stallholders' rents (which affect what they must charge for their vegetables) without cutting their total revenue (and their capacity to pay rent). High prices could prompt customers to buy less vegetables, or buy them elsewhere, or both. For this client's purposes you should calculate the price elasticity of the total demand for vegetables sold in his marketplace, from records of tonnage and prices and total revenue over the past year or two. He doesn't need to know the elasticities for particular vegetables.

(2) The government wants to know how much growers would suffer from a sales tax on vegetables. The tax would apply at all points of sale so there is no need to worry about driving buyers from place to place. You should calculate as for the market owner, but from records of vegetable sales throughout the government's territory, not just at one marketplace. (That's a counsel of perfection. In practice you use the best records you can find. Perhaps only one marketplace has kept any records. Perhaps there are national statistics but they were compiled by an under-staffed department from samples by a clerk who did all his sampling in that one marketplace.)

(3) Your client is a grower whose land and farming methods enable her to produce good crops very early or very late in each vegetable's season. She wants to know which vegetables will fetch the highest premium prices when they are scarce. That means those for which, at high price levels, demand is most inelastic. If the necessary market records exist you should (i) calculate elasticities for each vegetable, and (ii) calculate them for the periods in recent years in which the vegetable has been scarce and near the top of its seasonal price range.

Cross elasticity If goods are complements or substitutes for each other, demand for one may be related to demand for others. If cars become dearer there may be less demand for petrol (a complement) and more demand for public transport (a substitute). With some goods the relation is close. Wherever cement is demanded, so is clean building sand. Neither has much use without the other. But although bread and butter go together as complements, they are not as inseparable as cement and sand. Bread *can* be spread with other things; butter can go onto biscuits and into cakes. A change in the price of butter may affect demand for bread – but not as strongly or predictably as a change in the price of cement may affect demand for building sand.

When you come to study how prices are determined, how firms make their pricing decisions, and how governments make their taxing decisions, it will be clear that forecasting price elasticities of demand is important in many branches of business and government. But always start by asking who wants to know, and for what purpose. And always remember that other things besides price may be causing changes in demand: price elasticities of demand by themselves are not necessarily reliable forecasters of the demand there will be at particular prices.

Graphing elasticity

The price elasticity of demand for a product is represented by the slope of its demand curve. A steep curve, with big changes in price making small differences to the quantity people will buy, signifies inelastic demand. A flatter curve, with small changes in price producing big increases in demand, shows elastic demand. (But remember that the slope you see on the graph depends on the calibration of the axes, as well as the information which the graph represents. Read the figures as well as observing the gradient.)

Figure 22.1 shows elastic, unit-elastic, inelastic and variably elastic demand for four commodities, and indicates the price x quantity revenue (P x Q = R) for each of them at higher and lower prices. In the fourth example demand is elastic at prices above $4 a unit and inelastic at prices below $4. That is quite a common pattern in real life. At high prices people are easily put off: the stuff is unreasonably expensive and at those prices they can do without it. But at low prices they become unresponsive to price changes. Enough is enough, and no amount of 'something for nothing' will tempt them to take home much more than they can actually use.

THE INCOME ELASTICITY OF DEMAND

You have already met this phenomenon. It only remains to learn some formal language for it.

When you earn more you commonly spend more. But on which goods? You may spend less than before on beer, the same as before on salt, a little more on food, rather more on clothes, and a lot more on musical tapes and CDs. Those five will do to introduce the language of income elasticity of demand.

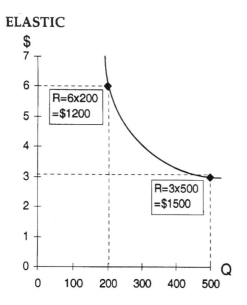

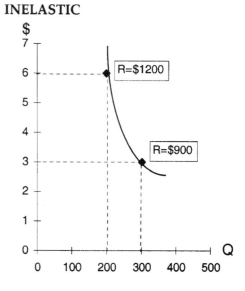

UNIT ELASTIC

VARIABLY ELASTIC

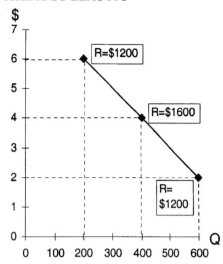

Figure 22.1 Price elasticities of demand for carrots, showing revenue (R) at higher and lower prices

Economists' usual symbol for income is Y. So income elasticity of demand is Ey.

Ey = percentage change in quantity demanded / percentage change in income

If a pay rise leads you to spend less on a commodity, your demand for it has negative income elasticity. If you spend the same as before on it, your demand has zero income elasticity. If your demand for it increases but by a smaller percentage than your income increases, your demand is income-inelastic. If your demand increases by the same percentage as your income does – which means that you spend a constant proportion of your income on the commodity – your demand for it has unit elasticity. If your demand increases by a larger percentage than your income does, your demand is income-elastic.

Hence the five goods in our example. When income rises 10 per cent –

Income %	Commodity	Quantity demanded %	Income elasticity of demand	
+10	Beer	–50	–5	Negative
+10	Salt	no change	0	Zero
+10	Food	+5	0.5	Inelastic
+10	Clothes	+10	1	Unit elastic
+10	Music	+50	5	Elastic

Table 22.1 Income elasticies of demand

You learned that price elasticity of demand can vary with the price level – for many goods, demand becomes elastic at high prices but inelastic at low prices. So also with income elasticity: your demand for a particular commodity may be more responsive to income changes at some levels of income than at others. Beer can provide an example. We will first graph it, then explain it. To let time as well as income run from left to right, Figure 22.2 (overleaf) puts quantity demanded on the vertical axis, and income on the horizontal.

B-B is your demand curve for beer, W-W for wine and whisky. Like other demand curves these can be read as indicating what an economist believes you would buy at any date given different levels of income. But we can also suppose that time runs from left to right at about an inch a year. On $100 a week in your first student year all you can afford to drink is water. That saintly life palls so you do some part-time earning and start some modest boozing. At $110 a week, one beer on Saturdays. At $160 a week, a beer every evening except Sunday. At $200 a week, one every evening and *two* on Sunday. From $100 to $200 a week your demand for the stuff has been income elastic. But enough is enough, you're no lush, and you go on drinking the same eight beers a week while your income doubles through the next two years. Income elasticity of demand is zero. But above $400 a week (into the big money as a graduate with a research fellowship) though you still don't get any drunker, you do grow more refined. Cheap beer

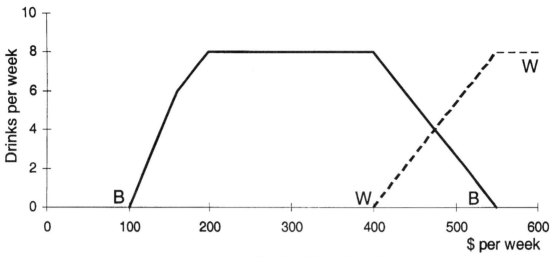

Figure 22.2 Income elasticity of demand over time

gives way to dearer wine and whisky.

As to that last phase, should we call beer an inferior good and say your demand for it now has negative income elasticity? Or should we guess that as you've matured, your tastes have changed? If you hear that question asked, be wary of econometricians, because the only way they can find out is to cut your income back to $100 then watch what you drink to drown your sorrow. A broad economist can probably find out by asking you. Or if his client is a brewer who wants the answer for millions of you, market researchers can probably find out by polling a sample of a few thousand of you. Whatever preferences they find, advertisers and other educators may be able to tell you what it would cost to persuade you to change some of them.

Moral: as always in economic analysis, keep your mind on the real reasons why people think and act as they do, as well as on the algebra and geometry with which (as in demand curves) it is sometimes convenient to symbolize them.

PRACTICAL USES OF MEASURES OF ELASTICITY

Price elasticities of demand chiefly concern producers and traders, and governments regulating or taxing production and trade, in the short run. They also matter to people who plan permanent institutions (like marketing boards or income equalization funds) whose purpose is to smooth out short-term fluctuations in prices and producers' incomes.

Examples:

Price equalization Good weather and bumper crops used to leave some farmers poorer than average years did, because demand for basic foodstuffs is price inelastic: small changes in the quantity supplied can cause big changes in price. That is for competitive reasons. If there is a glut of wheat, sellers bid the price a long way down as they compete for shares of the inadequate demand. If a bad season leaves wheat scarce, buyers with inelastic demands bid the price up high as they compete for shares of the scarce resource. So it used to happen that good seasons left consumers or middlemen rather than farmers better off; and in bad seasons farmers with average or better crops did well. It happens less often now, since cheap rail and sea transport made a world market for wheat: shortages in Britain are made up from North American prairies, shortages in Russia or China are supplied from Australia, because there is rarely bad weather everywhere at once. But fixing the old problem has created a new one, now that farmers *don't* get higher prices when their output falls. Instead of the weather causing consumers' costs of living to fluctuate, it causes farmers' incomes to fluctuate. If a good season in one region produces a local surplus, the surplus sells abroad at world prices and its producers do well. If a bad season then cuts their output, imports from the prairies keep prices down so farmers with poor crops get poor income. So governments provide subsidies, marketing boards, income equalization funds and other devices to smooth farm incomes from year to year.

Monopolist pricing Those are problems in competitive industries. In monopolist or oligopolist industries one or a few suppliers can decide the whole quantity to be supplied, or they can fix minimum prices and supply only what sells at those prices, or they can do some of both. Such industries may or may not fear anti-trust action by government, or effective action by independent organizations of consumers or environmentalists; so their price-and-quantity decisions may also have regard to political and public tolerances. But in all such calculations, the relevant price elasticities of demand are likely to be important. Optimal monopoly pricing, for the most profitable exploitation of monopolist market strength, depends critically on those elasticities.

Taxation Good forecasting of price elasticities is also needed for effective public taxing and regulating of production and trade. For public health purposes, can a tax on tobacco do much to reduce the consumption of tobacco? For public revenue purposes, how high can the tax go before it cuts demand so far that the total tax revenue declines? Both questions require forecasts of demand elasticities.

Tariff protection If a country such as Canada or Australia makes ordinary cars but imports luxury cars, what level of tariff will have what effect on the luxury imports? If the main aim of taxing the imports is to raise revenue from their rich buyers, the tariff should be set at the level that will yield most revenue. That is the level at which a further increase in price would turn the corner from inelastic demand (raising the price increases total revenue) to elastic demand (raising the price cuts total revenue). But the tariff may need to be higher than that (and the revenue accordingly less) if the government has different purposes – for example to encourage local manufacturing for purposes of full employment, or to cut imports because the country has balance-of-payments trouble from importing more than it exports.

Employment The income elasticity of demand also matters to more general judgments of macroeconomic policy. Suppose that government aims to increase employment by measures which give people more spending money. To get the amount right, it has to estimate how much of the additional income people will spend and how much they will save; how much of the additional spending will be on imported goods without much effect on local employment; and if the aim is to cut unemployment in specific regions or industries, how much of the spending will be on products of those regions or industries.

Uncertainties The income elasticities of demand are necessary information for many public and business judgments, but they may not be either sufficient or very

certain for the purpose. Remember that other causes may also be affecting demand. That applies not only to forecasts of future demand, but also to the original calculation of elasticities from past income and market records. Suppose you find, from the national accounts, that over (say) a three year period in which spendable income grew by 10 per cent there was (say) 2 per cent more spending on food, 10 per cent more on clothing, 20 per cent more on books and records, and 15 per cent more on total imports. You must not assume that those changes in demand were caused by the change in income alone. Changing tastes, changing propensities to save or spend and to buy ready-made or do-it-yourself, and changes in consumers' confidence, may all affect demand to mask effects of changing income. Changes in supply conditions and international terms of trade and exchange can also affect patterns of demand. Some of those effects can be isolated and separately measured, others cannot. So forecasts of the income elasticity of demand, though often worth making, may have double uncertainty. The calculation of elasticity from past records has elements of rough judgment and uncertainty because the effects of income changes can't be precisely separated from other influences on demand; and future responses to income changes may well vary from past patterns, because of other influences on demand.

THE ELASTICITY OF SUPPLY

This short section foreshadows work to be done at length later, on conditions of supply and relations between supply and demand.

Besides elasticities of demand, many of the business and policy judgments we have been considering must also take into account elasticities of supply: the capacity of producers to respond to changes in demand and price. But producers' capacities to respond vary widely with technical conditions of production. Consider:

- A supplier with a warehouse full of clothing or washing machines or video games may be able to meet an increased demand at an hour's or a day's notice.

- A manufacturer running his assembly lines at 80 per cent capacity may be able to increase production by 20 per cent at a few weeks' or months' notice.

- A steel industry working at full capacity may need two or three years' investment and plant expansion to increase its output.

- A country with no advanced manufacturing or engineering industries may take ten years or more to produce the flow of educated, work-experienced engineers – the human capital – which advanced manufacturing requires.

Just as different industries have different investment lead-times, so a single industry may have different lead-times for meeting demand increases of different scale. If demand for this book you are reading should increase a bit, bookshops can re-stock from the publisher's warehouse within a few days. If a sudden increase of demand sells out the current edition, it may take a month or two to reprint the book. If publishers foresee an increasing demand for this kind of economic writing, it may take some years to meet that demand: to find and commission authors to think out, research and write new manuscripts.

As for rising demand, so for falling demand. If demand declines, some producers and suppliers respond quickly by dropping their prices or cutting output, or both. It is no good catching and bringing to market more perishable fresh fish than the customers will buy. Other producers are slower to respond. Some (like some publishers) may stick to their fixed prices and accept fewer sales. Some (like many farmers) may continue to market all they can grow, and accept lower prices. Some producers of durable things like washing machines may guess that the dip in demand is temporary, and maintain *both* their prices *and* their volume of production, accumulating unsold stock in their warehouses against the expected revival of demand. When demand for public transport declines, one government may respond by cutting fares to try to entice people back onto the buses. A second government may respond by *raising* fares, hoping that relatively inelastic demand will allow them to pull the same total revenue as before from fewer customers. A third government may decide – for reasons of distributive justice, environmental prudence, or national economic efficiency – not to respond at all to the decline in demand, but to use some tax subsidy to continue the supply and prices of commuter transport as before.

For those and other reasons, supply curves tend to be less simple than demand curves. Changes in today's demand for fish, beef, books, houses, or steel may have different immediate effects on supply in those industries with their different techniques of production and storage. And within each industry there may be different effects next month, next year and next decade as today's investment decisions have their time-lagged effects through future years.

SUPPLY AND DEMAND

It should be clear by now that a variety of relations are possible between the demand conditions and the supply conditions for market goods. Even if we look only at elasticities of supply and demand, i.e. at the effect of price changes alone on producers' and consumers' decisions, any of these relations is possible:

Elastic demand can face elastic supply; unit elastic supply; steady inelastic supply; fluctuating inelastic supply; or zero elastic supply.

Unit elastic demand can face elastic supply; unit elastic supply; steady inelastic supply; fluctuating inelastic supply; zero elastic supply.

Inelastic demand can face elastic supply; unit elastic supply; steady inelastic supply; fluctuating inelastic supply; or zero elastic supply.

(Question: how can supply be inelastic, but still fluctuate? Answer: by fluctuating for reasons other than price. Output can vary with the weather, or it can be often but unpredictably interrupted by industrial disputes, while continuing to be relatively unresponsive to price changes.)

Now complicate those possibilities further by recalling some earlier lessons. Price elasticities of supply may have time lags from ten minutes to ten years. Derived demands, i.e. producers' demands for inputs, may have corresponding lags and lagged effects on other producers. Some supplies are chiefly designed to create or alter or reduce demands, whether by informing or persuading the customers or by offering them new products. Thus supply and demand can influence each other by other means as well as by price changes. It follows that many markets are more complicated than your local market for fresh fish or carrots. Their market forces can't all be understood as simple elasticities of demand and supply, expressed in demand and supply curves which intersect to determine the prices and quantities traded.

Meanwhile this account of demand needs to be matched by an account of supply. Part Three has reviewed a developed society's demands for goods and services and for particular modes of supply. Part Four will now review the means by which those demands are met: people's motives and capacities as producers, and the institutions – the households and voluntary organizations, the private enterprises and the public enterprises – in which they organize the production of goods and services.

Part Four

THE PRODUCTIVE INSTITUTIONS

- *HOUSEHOLDS*
- *PRIVATE ENTERPRISES*
- *PUBLIC ENTERPRISES*

23

People as producers

We continue to classify three kinds of productive institutions – households, private enterprises, public enterprises – in order to study the characteristic organization and operating principles of each, and their potentialities: what they generally can and can't produce. You need to know about them in order to –

- understand, and where possible predict, their behavior;

- know good from bad of each kind – what makes for better or worse performance in households, in private firms, in public enterprises; how poor performers of each kind may be improved; and

- know, for policy-making purposes, what each mode of production can and can't do: for example what might be the best mode or mix of modes for particular industries or services, or for particular countries with particular capacities and social purposes.

Parts of the study are technical. (What technology particular industries use, what scale and skills and divisions of labor the technology dictates, etc.) But more of the study is about motives: how do *they* (the owners) get *you* (a manager) to induce *me* (a worker) to work for *their* purposes rather than yours or mine, or in addition to yours and mine? How do the interests of all those parties as producers connect, or conflict, with their interests as consumers? So these chapters about the productive institutions begin with this short one about relations between institutional purposes and individual motivation.

Ways of characterizing productive institutions

Methodology: for many purposes this text will continue to treat households as producers for *use,* private enterprises as producers for *profit,* and public enterprises as producers for *collective* or *multiple* purposes. This present chapter is here to remind you of the intricate patterns of real-life motivation which underlie those simplifications, and to warn you not to misuse the simplifications or be misled by them.

First, as you doubtless noticed, the three characterizations are highly selective: they classify each type of institution by one only of the many characteristics it may have in real life.

For example plenty of public enterprises make profits, and some of them exist to enable private enterprises to make profits, so we could truthfully characterize many of them as 'producing for profit'. But because of the special social value of their capacity to produce for other purposes besides profit, they are classified here by their capacity to produce for collective – and often multiple – purposes.

Private enterprises can also be seen as multi-purposed. To make profits they commonly have to produce things their customers can use, and they must also pay their workers, pay their taxes, and meet public requirements of safety and honest dealing. If they don't serve those other purposes they won't achieve their own aims. So they could truthfully be characterized as producing for customers' use, workers' sustenance, owners' profit, and public purposes of health, safety and full employment – i.e. for multiple purposes. But profit-seeking affects their behavior and survival, and their society's distribution of work and wealth and income, so powerfully that 'profit-seeking' is widely accepted as the defining characteristic of private enterprise.

Household production could likewise be defined as multi-purposed. Household members produce for their own and one another's use – but also for friends and neighbors, for the pleasure of the work, to interest and educate children, to beat boredom, and so on. But what they produce for use rather than sale is a large fraction of all output; its distributive effects differ in important ways from those of most public or private production; and it has too often been neglected, or misrepresented as consumption rather than production. So when it needs simplification it is reasonable to simplify it as production for use.

INDIVIDUAL, INSTITUTIONAL AND NATIONAL PURPOSES

Social analysis would be simpler if people had the same purposes as the institutions in which they work – if household workers worked for nothing but love, private employees worked for nothing but money, public servants were motivated by nothing but duty. Of course the facts are otherwise. The people in each institution are ordinary mortals driven by varying mixtures of self-interest, love and duty – with anything from affection through indifference to hatred for the folk they work with, and anything from boredom to fascination with the work itself.

How work is motivated in mixed economies is nevertheless important for the reasons noted earlier. It affects productivity – well motivated producers are generally more productive than those who find their work dull or unrewarding, or see their employers, fellow workers or customers as enemies. It affects economic structure, as the motivational needs of different industries determine needs for public or private ownership or regulation. (Given their usual motives, can profit-seeking owners be trusted with dangerous trades or natural monopolies? Given their usual motives, can governments be trusted to own newspapers?) And it is part of the social order: the rewards and penalties and human relations which the productive institutions offer are among the forces which hold societies together (or tear them apart) and determine many of their qualities.

And the work itself is – for many people, much of the time – at least as valuable as its rewards. Robert Lane's *The Market Experience* (1991) has been cited already, and will be again. Among his conclusions from the mass of evidence he surveys is that work is a powerful and usually beneficent human developer. For most of us the experience of work, whether enjoyable or not, ranks with our parenting, education and adult family life in shaping our social as well as working skills, our relations with the people around us, our perceptions of ourselves and our confidence (or not) in our capacities and beliefs: 'the people we are'.

It matters. Two centuries of economic growth and less than one of fully democratic government have transformed the experience of work for the better, for most people in the advanced economies. But for twenty years now a powerful alliance of business, political and professorial voices has been pushing deregulatory and global policies which threaten to make work more individually competitive, anxious, insecure, and for many, more unsociable than it was a generation ago. Whatever the other effects of that change of direction – on productivity, growth, pay and inequalities – the effects on work itself, and through it on the character of the people and the quality of life away from work, deserve attention.

So it matters what patterns of motivation are at work in each sector. How much housework is pleasure or duty, cooperative or exploitive? Do public servants' conditions of employment encourage them to be lazy or energetic, cautious or inventive? Do private employers reward workers who cooperate with each other, or workers who compete with each other? Can a greedy, corner-cutting, tax-dodging, profit-seeking enterprise rely (as it may need to do) on finding opposite qualities – honesty, fairness, trust – in its workers or customers?

It matters how the sectors affect *each others'* motivation. What are welfare incomes doing to workers' and employers' incentives? Can firms do better by dodging taxes than by giving better service? Are private managers' rewards making public managers envious and eager for privatization?

It also matters what the economic incentives do to *the social system* in more general ways. There are reciprocal relations between a society's culture and its working conditions. A predominance of secure, relaxed, satisfying jobs may go with one sort of culture (in Australia?). More insecure and competitive jobs, evoking more energy, mobility, anxiety, may go with another (in the US?). Slavish labor by oppressed workers may go with yet another (in some poor countries). The links between the motivation of work and the quality of life make one more reason for distrusting GNP as a sufficient measure of an economic system's real productivity. Besides the other effects which the economic system produces – material goods and services, environmental effects, the primary distribution of income, the range of skills and occupations open to the people – the economic system can also affect social values and expectations: the society's general levels of envy and contentment, fairness and unfairness, security and anxiety. Those are important effects, however difficult to measure.

Mixed motives

You don't need telling yet again that the workers in a productive institution don't necessarily share the institution's or its owners' purposes. (Some mean folk work for charities, some anti-social types work in public services, plenty of workers want to earn for themselves rather than their employers, and so on.) So what? So the art of management – anywhere from charities through public services to Microsoft – includes finding ways to link the workers' purposes, by some means or other, to the institution's purposes.

Good management rarely achieves that by financial means only, i.e. by assuming that workers are motivated simply as income seekers. Workers do want money. They commonly want the rate for the job, they may look about for the best-paying jobs, they resist wage-lowering, some are ambitious to rise. But good management usually has to tap other motives too. Depending on the nature of the work it may, for example, contrive any of these –

- Interesting, challenging or otherwise pleasing tasks.
- Tasks with some wholeness or independence, so that workers can enjoy some pride of craft.
- Sociable roles in small working groups or teams; or in congenial relations with customers.
- A real concern to develop latent talent: managers spot promising workers, make educational and training and promotional opportunities for them, encourage and celebrate them. 'The firm is even prouder of its people than of its products.'
- A shared concern for excellence, both as a means (to the firm's profit and the worker's promotion) and as an end: as one of the joys of life.

Believe it or not, the fanciest of those rewards are sometimes achieved by producers of quite uninspiring goods and services. You may not swell with pride at producing (say) paper clips or toilet rolls or office cleaning services – but you can still be proud of your production technology, your clever programming, your imaginative marketing strategy, your personal way with the customers – and you can enjoy good teamwork, a 'happy ship', investment in *people*.

The Hawthorne experiments   In 1931 industrial psychologists at General Electric's Hawthorne plant experimented with the motivation of workers engaged in a dull, repetitive, manual task (nimble-fingered assembly of small electrical components). They isolated a group of six workers and proceeded to improve their material conditions one by one, measuring the effect of each change on their output. As wages, hours, rest periods, wall color and lighting were one by one improved, output duly increased.

But then as the improvements were one by one *taken away again*, output continued to increase. The researchers concluded that the workers produced more efficiently because of their growing solidarity as a group, and (especially) because of the respectful attention they were getting from the experimenters. (Critics of the experiment have since ascribed some of its unexpected effects to the influence of one leading personality among the six.) In the social sciences since then 'the Hawthorne effect' has meant the effect of observers on those they observe. But the experiment also showed how the motivation of work can vary, with the conventional financial incentives less powerful in some conditions than in others, even for the same people doing the same work.

At Hawthorne the products and processes were not interesting in themselves. When they *are* interesting – if the products can inspire the producers, or the producers can deal directly with customers they enjoy dealing with – then non-monetary motives may be even stronger. It can be good to be helping people – teaching, healing, mending, social-working – if the human encounters are satisfying and enjoyable. (But not if they're not.) It can be good to be part of an enterprise that makes good houses, furniture, clothes, cars, books, records, or anything else whose quality people recognize and value. (But not if the management is mean or oppressive.) While others are sweating thanklessly in run-of-the-mill automakers' paintshops, the robots that *your* team controls are putting fourteen superfine coats on superfine Porsches ...

Culture and motivation

Any society has some general culture of claims and expectations. The culture helps to shape what people want, what they think they are entitled to, what exchanges they judge to be fair or advantageous – for example, how much work is a fair exchange for how much money or goods. It thus helps to set wage levels and relativities, and other rewards that are accepted as motivating work. Thus the culture doesn't displace the forces of supply and demand, it helps to shape them. And it can vary widely over time and between societies.

Until very recent times, wherever men and women have done the same work with the same efficiency men have been paid more for it, even in quite unregulated labor markets, for example in the textile factories of the early industrial revolution, and in office work since. The roles of culture and government in determining that gender difference were explored by Lisa Peattie and Martin Rein in *Women's Claims: A study in political economy* (1983). They describe a basic relation between a society's culture and its economic motivation in a two-step argument. First, any culture includes beliefs – conscious or unconscious, agreed or disagreed – about what is natural, i.e.

> that which cannot be changed because it is in the order of things, outside the span of intervention. We may argue about the specific wage differences between janitors and professors, but it is typically regarded as only natural that professors should receive substantially higher wages than janitors, because professors' skills are in shorter supply, their acquisition requires a much longer investment in training, and their contribution to society is greater. We may argue about the circumstances under which it is appropriate for women to work, and the kinds of employment which they may appropriately enter, and we may argue about

the proper allocation of rights and responsibilities between husband and wife in the family, but most people consider it is only natural that the man should be both the main breadwinner and the family head because women naturally are best adapted to rearing children and men are able to earn better in the world of work outside. While both these examples deal with the division of labor and the division of reward, what they share more crucially for our purposes is the constraint imposed on negotiation and argument by the idea of the natural. (*Women's Claims*, p.1.)

What is not natural is artificial: the laws, institutions and ways of doing things that people recognize as deliberate social creations open to argument and open to deliberate change. The safest way to entrench your interests is to get them accepted as natural. The hardest part of a campaign for change is often to get natural things re-defined as artificial, i.e. as open to argument and deliberate reform.

Peattie and Rein then compare the rights to income in money or kind – the 'claims on consumption' – that arise within families, in private and public enterprises, and in welfare systems. Traditionally, family obligations and workers' wages have been seen as natural, but welfare entitlements as artificial. Peattie and Rein want to end that distinction. Historically, family and business structures are social creations just as governments and welfare systems are. Distinguishing particular claims as either natural or artificial is merely one of the devices people use in competing with one another for rights to wealth and income, or for rival principles of social justice. And what people regard as natural keeps changing. Once, they expected their children to support them in old age. Now they expect the government to do it. If public age pensions have changed from 'a dangerous experiment' to a natural right, so may other claims – for example workers' claims to own shares in the firms they work for, women's claims to equality at work, women's claims to equality at home. It is the history of cultural change, rather than a supply-and-demand labor market, which leads Peattie and Rein to 'treat "earnings from work" as one component in an institutionalized system of claims on consumption, along with other sets of claims generated in the kinship system (as in the case of wives, children) or against the state (as in the case of welfare).' (*Women's Claims*, p.20.)

FROM MARY TO MIDAS : A SPECTRUM OF MOTIVATION

The range and variety of motives for working can be illustrated from examples in my neighborhood. Look about and you can probably match them in yours. Only some names are fictitious:

1. Mary, a ragged pensioner, used to stay ragged because she spent half her pension on cheap butchers' meat and half her day wheeling it around the neighborhood in a battered pram to feed her clientele of cats. Some of them are well fed already – she does it for her own pleasure as much as their need. Whatever her motives, she gave away a higher proportion of her income than any of the local rich did, until – inspired by her example – the butcher began to give her meat for nothing.

2 Meals on Wheels. Per million of the province's people, 10 paid organizers assist 6,000 volunteers (each working one day per week or fortnight or month) to cook and deliver hot meals to about 3,000 old, sick and disabled people who can still live at home if they can get some home service. The customers pay about two thirds of the cost of the raw materials. The government pays the other third, saving itself the higher costs of institutionalizing many of the customers. The labor is a gift, mostly from pensioners and housewives, many of whom do it for the interest and the company as much as from concern for the customers.

3. For the motives which get four tenths or so of all production done by household labor, consult your own experience and acquaintance. It is not all love and generosity. There is also simple need for subsistence, work done for the joy of doing it, hardheaded exchange of services, one-sided exploitation, bored work by women who would rather be out earning, bullied and coerced work.

4. Wage and salary earners are the biggest group of earners in the neighborhood. They have their own spectrum of motivation. The worker on the car assembly line is both stressed and bored. He'll move when he can. So will a couple of insecurely employed laborers. Two public servants are ambitious to rise and to improve their pay and conditions; one seems more interested than the other in the work she does. A third left a private law practice to become a salaried legal aid lawyer, then left that for a precarious living as guitarist and song-writer in a group he formed. Some of the women workers are unambitious, glad of secure jobs and incomes, not much interested in the work they do: a hospital accounts clerk, a dental nurse, a school cleaner. Others like their work for its own sake – they expect the rate for the job, but don't much mind what the

rate is: a riding instructor, a graphic designer, a museum researcher, a woman who has been behind the counter at the local pastrycook's for thirty years and knows and likes the customers; and a judge. The judge lost income by leaving the bar for the bench, but she enjoyed her judicial authority and her role as a national leader and liberator of women. By my rough count, about a quarter of the wage and salary workers are in jobs that don't interest them, purely for the money. About a quarter do work they actively enjoy. The half (or so) in the middle quite enjoy their work, the people they work with, the customers they meet, or all three. Many of them specially value the security of their jobs and incomes, or specially regret their *in*security. The unhappiest workers, without exception, are the unemployed. Questioned, they rank the lack of money, lack of daily occupation and lack of hope as equal causes of their unhappiness.

5. There are family private enterprises: family farms, shops, restaurants. Heads of the households may deal fairly or unfairly with the family workers, who may work for fair wages; for bed and board and whatever pocket money they are allowed; to learn trades at which they may then earn for themselves; in hope of inheritance; from customary obedience, welcome or unwelcome; from fear for themselves or for other family members.

6. Self-employed work. Some is 'put out' at piece rates to contract workers. A lot of it is unskilled, uninteresting, low-paid and irregular: letter-boxing, assembling components, packing mail-order kits, picking fruit. Money is the main incentive. Some skilled trades are partly or wholly self-employed: painters, plumbers, electricians, doctors, dentists, lawyers, freelance designers, artists and performers. Many have skills which could alternatively find salaried employment. They choose to work independently because they like the independence, or earn more that way. Having chosen both the occupation and the independence they tend to be doing work they enjoy.

7. Single-minded money-makers. They may be single-minded because needy or greedy, or so hard up they will do any work to earn, or so eager for money that they really do apply their talents where and how they can earn most, sometimes for very long hours, regardless of the pleasures or pains of the work. To complete our spectrum of motivation with a worker with purely financial motives, meet Midas. He's a currency gambler for a bank. He is paid a salary plus a percentage of his gains. Making money is his pride and pleasure, his own single, satisfying measure of his skill and success.

Genius

The very highest skills seem to have quite irregular relations with money. On the one hand there are plenty of inventive business and professional people and artists and performers who work wherever they can earn most, like textbook optimizers. On the other hand there are many who don't. Picasso left paintings worth more than a billion dollars, most of which he never tried to sell, and would have painted just the same if their prices had done no more than feed him and buy his paint and canvas. Much of the best twentieth century painting, writing and serious musical composition has been done by people who could have earned more in advertising, pulp writing or commercial art. Most of the best twentieth century science has been done by salaried scientists with no great financial expectations. (When, as now, some computing and biotechnical scientists are offered quick fortunes, some seize them and others continue to work just as inventively without them.) Universities try to get the best out of young talent, and attract and hold proven talent, at least as much by the company and working conditions they offer as by the money they offer. Their inducements still tend to determine *where* the best people do their work rather than *what* they do or how hard they work at it. Genius has to eat, but beyond that is motivated by many other things besides, or instead of, money.

Grasshoppers and beavers

Nobody has managed to count how many modern workers are motivated chiefly by the money and hours, and how many just want a fair deal on those fronts and make most of their working choices for other reasons. Economists disagree sharply about the motivation they should assume most employers and employees to have. Here are rival beliefs, the first shared by many neoclassics, the second by many industrial psychologists and institutional economists:

Neoclassical: The labor market is much like other markets. Workers sell labor, employers buy it. Its prices are said to be determined by supply and demand for particular skills and by their marginal productivity. Where there are too few workers, wages will rise to attract more, and to compete for those there are. Where there are too many, wages will fall until some of the unemployed are hired and others switch to other trades or withdraw from the workforce, i.e. until supply and demand are in balance and the labor market 'clears'.

Institutional: In most modern industries the worker's skill is not like that. It is not a finished commodity with known productivity which the worker sells at a market price, motivated only by the money it will fetch. Most organized production requires a lot of learning on the job, some from the employer but most from fellow-workers. It requires continuous willing cooperation between workers. Productivity varies widely with the management's quality and the workers' motivation, and it varies with the morale of teams rather than individuals. Not much of each individual's duty to cooperate can be specified by the boss – indeed 'working to rule' can drastically *reduce* efficiency. Most of the cooperation has to be developed and sustained informally by the workers themselves.

How can that necessary teaching and learning and cooperation be motivated? Certainly not by auctioning the jobs from time to time to the lowest bidders, with every job up for grabs every time. Seniors won't teach juniors skills if the skills can then be used to take their jobs from them. Juniors may not cooperate if poor performance may get their seniors sacked and themselves promoted. Different ranks and trades cooperate best if their wage relativities are seen as fair, settled, and not open to undercutting or any other job-stealing. Employers know all this as well as workers do: willing teaching and learning and cooperation require job and wage securities which rule out dog-eat-dog competition between worker and worker. So what many neoclassics see as inefficient rigidities – fixed wage scales, secure tenure, regard for seniority – are in fact the efficient ways to motivate the cooperative training-on-the-job, and the continuous cooperation between workers, which efficient production requires in many industries. The alternative of auctioning labor at fluctuating supply-and-demand prices would be quite inefficient.

Does that rule out *any* stick-and-carrot or competitive motivation? No. First, workers are still sacked for misbehaving. Second, they compete for entry to firms. That's basically a competition for training opportunities leading to predictable careers. Third, there can be competition for promotion to vacancies and new posts. That need not do too much harm to the general cooperation because the competitors are not kicking each other *down* – one worker's promotion does not cause another's sacking or demotion.

As with promotion, so with innovation and technical progress. Secure employees who can expect to re-train and stay on through technical changes, and to earn more from the increased productivity which the changes bring, are motivated to welcome technical progress.

Insecure workers who must fear that new technology will have them replaced by juniors or outsiders with new skills are famously resistant to change.

Hence the paradox: stable employment often goes well with technical change, and insecure employment often does not. Lester Thurow, a pioneer in leading economists to recognize those relations, concluded: 'In setting wages, equity becomes important for efficiency. In practice, most production processes also require a degree of teamwork that can only be acquired through common on-the-job experiences, a high degree of internal harmony, and a substantial period of practice working together. Team and not individual productivity dominates industrial processes.' (*Dangerous Currents*, 1983, p.204)

Which of those rival models fits the facts? Both and neither. Each fits some people and jobs but not others. Plenty of work, for example by artists, evangelists, revolutionaries, and mothers caring for children, doesn't fit well with either. And the proportions are almost certainly changing. Since Thurow wrote *Dangerous Currents* the drive to 'downsize' many public and private organizations, and motivate their workers more directly by more immediate greed and fear, has brought mass dismissals and loss of job security in many firms and branches of government. Recall Andrew Graham's judgment of the ill effects of that, quoted earlier in Chapter 7.

The world still has plenty of individual selfishness. No business manager, politician or public administrator can afford to underestimate its force. Institutions, including public and charitable institutions, need to be designed to enlist it or restrain it, or both. Institutions' behavior can't usually be predicted without some knowledge of their members' self-interests. But it is nearly always a mistake to assume that acquisitive, material self-interest prevails over other purposes reliably enough to allow monocausal prediction of either individual or institutional behavior. For a vivid example, read the comparison of diverse and changing conditions of work, and satisfaction from work, in two Italian industries, in Paola Villa, *The structuring of labour markets* (1986).

Altogether there is very mixed and varied motivation of work in a modern mixed economy. To understand it and to manage or predict it for particular people or jobs or industries in particular societies at particular times you will generally need equal quantities of general theory (or experienced wisdom) and detailed local knowledge.

SUMMARY

Economic analysis must often distinguish institutions' purposes from their managers' and workers' purposes. Relations between the institutions' purposes and their members' motivation are important for many reasons of individual, corporate and national equity and efficiency. And they are widely variable, both within each productive sector and between them.

- It may be safe to assume that households produce chiefly for their own use, making their own choices between what to buy ready-made and what to produce for themselves. But you may need local knowledge to know how efficient they are, how they decide and motivate their members' shares of the work, and how they share the products.

- It may be safe to assume that private enterprises are profit seekers. But you may need local knowledge of their owners', managers' and workers' motivation, and of the prevailing culture, to know how conservative or adventurous they are likely to be, where they lie between satisficing and optimizing in their pursuit of profit, and where they lie between a single-minded pursuit of profit and a balanced concern for the interests of their owners, employees, customers, neighbors and national community.

- It may be safe to assume that public institutions have the aims they say they have. But you may need local knowledge of their politicians' and managers' and workers' motivation to know what other purposes they also serve, how they rank one purpose against another, and how well or badly they serve their various purposes.

Exercises on this subject can wait until you study each type of institution in more detail, through the following chapters.

HOUSEHOLDS

24

Household histories

Households producing for market belong in later chapters on private enterprise. Here we look at them as unpaid producers for their own use or for communal or charitable purposes. This and the following two chapters will

- sketch some history of western households;
- remind you of the household share of capital, work and output in modern mixed economies;
- explore some relations between household productivity and the public and private sectors, especially
- how households get their capital.

So be prepared for some revision as these chapters draw together material you have met before on widening household choices, and on household roles in mixed economies. There is also some overlap with future chapters on land and capital markets. The repetitions won't hurt if they reinforce your understanding of a sector too often neglected in economic theory and education. Reasons for taking it seriously are distilled in the opening pages of the best British book on housing policy:

House and home stand at the centre of people's lives, giving them a shelter for sleep and for half their waking activities, shielding them from the world yet admitting it in a controlled and selective fashion, and providing storage and a showcase for most of their possessions. Demands for housing are therefore complex and constantly changing as culture and living standards evolve and as families grow and disperse ...

Other goods generally have a limited range of uses and meanings: a spade is a spade is a spade. But a house is not just a dwelling. It confers a bundle of rights and duties which may be distributed in various ways among various people – the occupier, the owner, tenants and sub-tenants, and the authorities responsible for taxation, town planning and public health. There is the right to occupy the house; rights to sell, let, and sub-let it; rights to control the use which others make of it; rights to extend, demolish, rebuild and redecorate it; rights to benefit from tax concessions and subsidies; the right to hold an asset which generally retains its real value despite inflation; and the right to bequeath that asset to one's heirs. The duties attached to housing – duties to maintain it, and to pay various taxes on it, for example – can also take various forms and be distributed in various ways. Houses, moreover, are fixed to one place. With the house come the neighbours, the reputation of the neighbourhood, and the jobs, schools, doctors, shops and other opportunities within reach of that point on the map ...

Finally, the home provides the setting within which men and women develop their own domestic economy and domestic roles. With bigger and better-equipped houses, this domestic economy has grown increasingly productive. Women, defined in industrial societies as 'housewives', have generally been responsible for most of that production. But men and children contribute to it in changing ways, helping to produce domestic services, fresh fruit and vegetables, maintenance and repair work on the house, the motor car and other property of the household. What they can all do depends partly on the character of their housing.

Thus housing needs are neither simple nor self-evident. They are a collection of rights, opportunities, assets and attributes, about as complex, as liable to change and as difficult to define as needs for education, health and general prosperity.

– David Donnison and Claire Ungerson,
Housing Policy (1982) pp.11-12.

HISTORIES

This historical chapter is chiefly to remind you of three things. Households as producers have differed widely, changed over time, and still do. So do their internal relations – how income is shared, who does the domestic work, how its product is shared, who does the choosing. And domestic productivity is rarely independent; it commonly depends a good deal on households' relations with the public and private sectors.

Research into the history of the family is a growth industry, with some scholarly disagreements. Researchers have tended to generalize the history of 'the Western family' from studies of particular family types at particular times and places. As the evidence of diversity accumulated, one surveyor of the state of the art concluded that

> the one unambiguous fact which has emerged in the last twenty years is that there is no simple history of *the* Western family since the sixteenth century because there is not, nor ever has there been, a single family system. The West has always been characterised by diversity of family forms, by diversity of family functions and by diversity in attitudes to family relationships not only over time but at any one point in time ... Peasant families have typically differed markedly from merchant families and labouring families from aristocratic families. Peasants in eighteenth century north-west France differed from peasants in central France, and in Germany or Sweden marked differences could be found even between neighbouring communities. England perhaps alone appears to have been much more homogeneous.
>
> – Michael Anderson, *Approaches to the history of the Western family, 1500-1914* (1980).

And even in England there have been large class differences, and changes over time. So here follow fictitious but representative sketches of an English country household and a town household since the seventeenth century – with regular warnings (in italics) that these are only two strands of family history among many.

1650 Jack and Jill Farmer are peasants. They have customary tenure – rent free, but they can't sell it – of a two-roomed wood-and-daub cottage with a sleeping loft, thatched roof, rubble floor, open fireplace for warmth and cooking, water from a well, light from a wick in a dish of oil. Jill had six children, three survived. They grow grain on a couple of strips to which Jack inherited rights. He ploughs with a single furrow behind a borrowed ox. They all sow, reap and thresh by hand. They sell a third of the grain, pay a miller to grind a third for themselves, and save a third for next year's seed. Jill keeps a dozen fowls in the back yard. They

keep a cow on the common, milk her and sell some when she's in milk, buy milk when she's not, sell an occasional calf. Besides some income from the grain and livestock, they earn a bit from harvesting and doing odd jobs on the big enclosed farms in the neighborhood. They buy tools, clothes, shoes, salt, some bread when they run out of their own, cheese, occasional meat. One boy will inherit the cottage and land rights. The other will have to find some other living. The daughter will need to find a husband. Any of them may die any day – disease is mysterious, childbirth is dangerous, the average age of death is about 50, there are not many old folk to care for.

Joe and Jo Weaver meanwhile live in a bigger, better-built wood-and-daub house in town. At street level there's a loom room, a living room, pantry and store-room; up narrow stairs, attic bedrooms. Water from a town well, open fires for warmth and cooking, light from candles. Urine goes into the street, faeces are carted to the edge of town. Father, son, and an apprentice from another family weave woollen cloth. Wife Jo fetches the yarn, takes the cloth to market, earns a bit by occasional needlework. She also shops, cooks, washes, keeps the place clean, and makes most of the family's clothes. She teaches all those skills to her daughter, who may become as productive in a similar household when she marries, or in some richer household as a paid housekeeper, or on her own as a full-time seamstress.

Notice that, in varying proportions, both households have (1) some household capital, partly earned but mostly inherited; (2) some each of business income as a private enterprise, wages from working for others, and unpaid household output for their own use; and (3) both spouses working and earning, with some shared tasks but also many segregated, gender-specific tasks.

But seventeenth-century England also has (i) rich families in grand houses with armies of indoor and outdoor servants, private transport by coach-and-four, and households like small towns with privately employed artists, tutors, librarians, dressmakers, harnessmakers and other trades all producing for household use rather than for market; (ii) gentry, merchants and professional men in country and town with solid, comfortable houses, several servants, riding horses, and all necessary farm or trade equipment, bringing up sons to inherit, or to go off and earn in 'army, navy, church or state', with wives teaching daughters mostly housekeeping arts, but in some households reading and writing for pleasure, performing music, sharing with their menfolk in the management of the family business; (iii) many households in which men and women already move in what modern feminists call 'separate spheres', the women in domestic life at home, the men earning away from home, sometimes far away for long periods as sailors, merchants, carriers and carters, itinerant tradesmen; (iv) landless laborers earning poor wages, sleeping in hovels, eating chiefly bread and fat, unable to keep wife or children decently fed and sheltered unless they also earn somehow; (v) orphans, vagrants, fugitives and others with nowhere of their own to live, driven from parish to parish, whipped and ducked and locked in stocks for begging, poaching or not moving on, the men exposed to sudden abduction for service at sea, unattached women exposed to sexual abuse and sometimes to stoning or burning as witches – all folk with no households at all, or domestic productivity to speak of.

1750 – 1850 The heirs of Jack and Jill Farmer lost most of their land to an enclosure. (Major landowners got a private Act of Parliament to consolidate the commons and open-field strips into efficient capitalist farms. In exchange for the cropping and grazing rights he lost, Jack got a saleable title to his cottage.) The new enclosed farming was more productive, but the farmer and landlord took most benefit of that; as a wage laborer Jack's daily pay would rarely buy much more than a loaf of bread. He and Jill still got some eggs and potatoes from the cottage garden. Two generations of Jills got work which they and their children could do at home, as piece-rate spinners for a city wool merchant. But when textile manufacture was mechanized – first by water power then by steam – that work dwindled. Farmers had taken advantage of the women's earnings to pay below-subsistence wages to their husbands, and when the women's earnings dwindled many households became desperately poor. There were thefts from Jack and Jill's garden. Jack went poaching, risking death or transportation. Government responded variously. On the one hand it enforced game laws which made wild birds and animals the squire's property wherever they strayed, so it was a felony for Jack to catch a pigeon or rabbit in his own garden, or on a public roadside. As theft increased, the landowners' parliament trebled the number of offences that carried the death penalty. On the other hand some of the local magistrates who administered poor relief leapt a century ahead of their time in welfare policy. They pegged farm wages to bread prices and supplemented the wages from local taxes whenever they fell short; and they paid a dole to many unemployed. With that 'welfare net', and generally full

employment and high farm prices through the Napeoleonic wars, the Jack and Jill who lived through the first third of the nineteenth century did comparatively well. *Too* well, parliament thought – and abolished the dole incomes and cost-of-living wage supplements in 1834.

Meanwhile in town the heirs of Jo Weaver had a rougher passage. Joe foresaw the effects of steam power earlier than most wool weavers did. In 1800 he sold up, moved to one of the new black towns and started a small cotton mill. Like nine out of ten who tried that, he went bust and (in the days before government had instituted joint stock, limited liability or modern bankruptcy law) lost all he had and took some creditors down with him. Jo and their daughters got intermittent factory work. So did Joe, when he came out of debtors prison. Their combined wages were better than Jack's in the country but there was no cottage garden or game to poach or free firewood to gather. The Weavers lived in a couple of rooms in a back-to-back house. Besides rent they had to pay for all their sparse food, fuel, clothing and bedding. They slept on straw or cotton waste. They had a table and chairs, a cupboard and shelves, some pots and pans and lamps. Their town had no public sanitation or transport, no public schools, no public parks or gardens, no transfer incomes, no welfare outside the workhouse. Government was busily deregulating trade and industry, so factory workers had little or no protection from bad air, dangerous machinery, long hours or brutal overseers.

They were presently joined by Jack and Jill Farmer and their children, moving to town to look for work after Jack lost his job (to more labor-saving farm technology), and the rural economy had no more employment for Jill, or welfare for any of them.

Summary Through the first half of the nineteenth century the farm and factory revolutions made the Farmers and the Weavers more productive at work than their ancestors could be, but their wages did not yet give them much benefit of that growth. Government did less for them than for centuries before or since. Their household productivity of goods for their own use was lower than for centuries before and since.

As before, those two were not the only household types. (i) There were increasing numbers of grand households, enriched by gains from the farm and factory revolutions and the canal and railway revolutions, from supplying the greatly-expanded public sector through a long war, and from expanding overseas empire and trade. (ii) Though some factory

*industries and heavy industries took business away
from household producers, many other trades continued on household scale, with families living 'over
the shop' and parents passing on capital and skills to
their children, in households at least as productive
as the Farmers and Weavers had been in their hey-
day. (iii) As country women lost textile piece-work,
town women gained some. As clothmaking moved
into the factories and mass-produced cloth became
cheap, the ready-made garment industry was born,
and some of the garment-making was 'put out' at
piece rates to women working at home or in sweatshops nearby. Thus some women could still earn and
mind small children at the same time. (iv)
Nevertheless most earning by most women was still
before marriage or when there were no small
children to mind; and was in domestic service or
low-paid jobs at or near home – as boarding house
keepers, launderers, shopkeepers, carters, petty
traders. (v) There continued to be many itinerant or
homeless people with little or no domestic capital or
productivity.*

1850 – 1950 A revolution in household productivity
was made possible by great advances in technology,
private and public productivity, and government policy.

In the private sector the manufacturing revolution
produced powered sea and land transport, refrigerated
transport, air transport. For households it produced
cheap cloth, ready-made clothing, household linen and
furniture; bikes, motorbikes, cars; sewing and knitting
machines, washing machines, ice chests then refrigerators, telephones, radio. And from about 1850 it paid rising wages so that rising numbers of workers could buy
those new goods and services.

The public and private sectors provided mass public
transport by train, tram, bus. City workers used it to live
further from work, which in turn allowed them to have
more private space. Out of town, the suburbs were born.
In town, the housing grew less crowded. From the 1870s
government began to regulate the size as well as the
safety of new housing – in England tenement-building
ceased and most new houses were required to be self-
contained and to have some back yard space.

Thus the private and public sectors provided the
means for an internal economic revolution for a steadily increasing number of households.

The rich saw least change – the new pipes and wires
and machinery merely helped their servants to do the
cooking and cleaning and gardening and personal services that servants had always done for them; cars
replaced the horse-powered private transport they had

always had. The main benefits of the household revolution were for poorer households. People from tenements
got row houses with back yards. People from row houses with back yards got suburban houses and gardens.
People who used to travel only as far as they could walk
got public transport, bikes, cars. People whose parents
could not read began to read newspapers, magazines,
books from a mushroom growth of public and private
lending libraries. Shortening hours at work left time for
leisure and productive activity at home, and rising
wages bought the space, equipment and services to
make that time enjoyable or productive, or both.

The Farmers' and Weavers' family fortunes
diverged. The Farmer men labored on as factory hands,
carriers, pick-and-shovel workers. The Jack who
worked at the London docks from the 1830s earned
enough to spend some time and money at the pub on
pay nights. He wasn't the worst of husbands, but Jill's
labor provided most of their little domestic productivity. She washed their clothes in a kitchen tub, darned
and mended them by hand sewing, minded the children
when they were small and nursed them when they were
sick. She exchanged a good deal of mutual aid and
comfort with kin and neighbors in a chatty network that
served as an informal kind of women's cooperative
defence league, welfare net and job information service. (Her grand-daughters, often in the same old row
houses where they'd survived the blitz, were still
exchanging aid and comfort through similar networks
when sociologists surveyed family and kinship in east
London in the 1950s.) When the depression struck in
1929 the current Jill was at home caring for young children. Her husband spent five years out of work. They
put up with humiliating means tests to get a minimal
transfer income, on which they survived, with the help
of free schooling for the children and public hospital
clinics when they were sick.

Meanwhile the Weavers had done rather better.
Some of the boys became skilled workers in the new
metal industries, and one of them succeeded (where his
grandfather had failed) in starting a small business. Four
generations of the women had four kinds of earning and
domestic experience through the century. Jo who married in 1850 continued to do all the sewing and button-
holing work she had time for – sixty hours a week
before she married, twenty or thirty while she had small
children, fluctuating amounts later in life. Her daughter
who married a skilled worker in 1880 was the only one
of the four who never earned after she married, but
stayed at home cooking, cleaning, making and mending
clothes, gardening, rearing children, helping neighbors,

helping at church. Hers was the first Weaver household to have some books, board games, jigsaw puzzles, bicycles. (It was also the first to afford occasional train and tram fares, and to have free public libraries, museums, art galleries and high schools in reach.) There was next to no money to spend on luxuries or commercial entertainments. But the household was resourceful enough to keep breadwinner Joe contented through the lengthening evenings and weekends that came with the eight hour day and forty eight hour week at work. And it was resourceful enough to give its youngest, cleverest child what she needed to get through high school to medical school.

That daughter – the one who might have married about 1910 – faced a choice between career and marriage when it was nearly impossible for a professional woman to have both. She stayed single, got a medical degree and worked for forty years for modest pay as a general practitioner in a working class clinic in which she developed a strictly unofficial birth control clinic. Her bank lent her enough to buy a small house near her work. In it in her spare time she read a lot, listened to the gramophone in the 1920s and the wireless from the 1930s, tended a small garden, cooked for herself. She paid a woman two hours a day to shop, clean and launder for her. She went out sometimes to concerts and plays. Between the wars she had a small car, and spent summer holidays walking in the Lake District. She helped one of her nieces to become a doctor too – but with professional and household prospects very different from her own, as we will presently see.

As before, plenty of households differed from the Farmers' and Weavers'. Some people were homeless. Some were caravan gypsies. The age of the Big Cold Institutions had come: orphans lived in orphanages, child offenders in reformatories, adult offenders in the new long-term prisons, mentally ill people (and some people whose kin simply didn't want them) were held in public and private lunatic asylums. In England tenement building stopped but the old tenements survived and poor households continued to live in them. Rich households continued to employ many servants. Increasing numbers of parents confided their children's upbringing to nannies, governesses, boarding schools. With their households managed by butlers and housekeepers, some women with rich husbands had neither any earning nor any domestic work to do. There was as wide a range of household wealth and household productivity as ever. But whatever the inequalities,

technical progress in the public and private and domestic sectors had made possible a revolution in domestic productivity for the rising proportion of households who could afford to equip themselves with the new physical and human capital.

1950 – 1990 The next Jo qualified as a doctor in 1955, and married another doctor. Together they set up practice in a country town. (That made an interesting sector mix. Like private practitioners they worked from home, provided their own capital, and competed with rival practitioners for patients – but most of those they attracted were paid for by the government through the national health service.) Between them they earned and borrowed enough to buy a comfortable old house with a few acres of water-meadow. Since then they have worked from a new health centre in town, seen local patients at home in the evenings, and kept continuous touch with the practice office by radio bleeper and telephone. They're good, up-to-date doctors, training juniors and periodically re-training themselves.

Joe retired in 1985, before the big changes to the health service. Over the years, living fairly poor and cold at first, he and Jo have plumbed, warmed and furnished the old house. It includes a self-contained flat which they let rent-free in return for part-time household help. The house also has, by now, rich cultural resources: books, pictures, painting materials, piano and violin, musical records and tapes, radio and television and video gear; computers but no computer games; cards, chess, checkers, Monopoly and other board games; back-packs, camping equipment and ordnance maps of much of Britain and France; trunks of old clothes for dressing up. On different parts of the surrounding land Jo grows a beautiful flower garden, there is a small orchard, a neighbor share-farms vegetables for both households' use. There is a pasture for the old horse three generations rode. Sometimes he rested elsewhere while the home paddock fattened a bullock for market. In this beautiful place Jo and Joe have brought up four children, Jo working full time in the practice before they were born, half time or less while they were young, four fifths time since they grew up. They grew up healthy, well spoken, socially competent; prepared by the local day schools to get what higher education and professional training they wanted; speaking two or three languages; able to ride, drive, ski, skate, swim, sail. Especially sail. In their annual holidays Joe, Jo and any children who are free rent boats and sail the English channel, the Channel Islands and French coast, the Greek Islands – sailing with skill, hard work, much discomfort and occasional danger. The children grew up to be as productive at work as at leisure. One is a national campaigner for better health. One runs an inventive international charity. One runs the youth hostel she and her husband developed in an old French barn. One runs his own business in the City.

Jo and Joe are not rich by their own country's standards. Individually, neither is in the top five per cent of British earners. They earn less than general practitioners do in most other developed countries. They have used cheap old cars, sent their children to free day schools, worked and earned for twenty years before the old house was equipped to be warm in winter. Their exceptional household productivity comes from saving hard, spending next to nothing on 'consumer recreations', acquiring their own recreational capital instead, then using it with great energy. A lot of their household labor is itself recreation: rather than 'producing and consuming' they are better understood as 'well occupied'.

Meanwhile the Jack Farmer who had been unemployed through the 1930s depression returned from war service in 1945. For the rest of his working life he was employed, better paid than before, well served by the new health and welfare services. He and his wife got a walk-up Council flat and (half a mile away) a garden allotment – thirty feet square with a tool shed – with a hundred others on some waste land. There he could ruminate, grow vegetables, chat with other gardeners. In winter when the allotment was quiet he spent Saturday afternoons watching football. On Sundays he and Jill usually visited those of their children who lived in reach; and they were the first husband and wife of their line to frequent their local pub *together*. At home they had warmth, comfort, good food, friendly neighbors, low rent, secure tenure, a daily paper, radio and then TV full of fun and interest: a safe haven after all the years of unemployment and wartime crowding and 'rationed poverty'.

Those two did not live to see the adult life of their youngest grandchild. She was born in 1975 of a suffering mother and a violent father. She left home early to avoid incest. At an age when she might have married she had two children by a man who did not marry her and soon left her. She lived on the dole and child allowance. The children entitled her to a Council flat, but it was on one of the dangerous estates. Outdoors was a wasteland with obscene graffiti, unsafe for children by day and for her at night. The lifts stank of urine. Inside the all-electric flat there was minimal furniture, no telephone, and a TV which she and the children watched for six or eight hours a day. Most of the time she was too depressed to cook, and they lived on fast food brought

home in daylight and warmed up at night. She spent too much on cigarettes, got behind with bills, feared the power might be cut off one day for non-payment, and hoped she could hold out until the children were big enough for school and she could look for a job. One depressed day she travelled back to her home town to ask if her mother could take over the children for a while. Her mother dared not. Her father came home drunk and called her a slut. She went home and a few days before her twenty first birthday she killed her children and herself.

Those latest Weavers and Farmers mark some limits of productivity and poverty in contemporary households. Between the extremes there is great diversity, and continuing change. There are more small households. More young people leave their parents' houses to form households, often temporary, of their own. Old people live longer, mostly in households of their own. You will have noticed those trends. Now notice two others. The public and private sectors are shifting some work back into households.

In the private sector technical change is allowing some employers to return some productive processes from factory and office to households. Publishers, for example, have always been able to put out the reading and editing of manuscripts; since the print and computer revolutions the books can also be typeset and paged at home. Some of the shift is welcome all round: employers save accommodation and employee services, homebound people get work they could not otherwise get, with free timetables. But other shifts cut costs chiefly by replacing regular wage labor and collective bargaining with piecework at take-it-or-leave-it rates, without job or income security for the workers.

In the public sector the era of some at least of the Big Cold Institutions is passing as their inmates are returned to their homes, or to foster homes, or to homeless loafing and begging and stealing and sleeping on the streets. Some of the change is for good social and clinical reasons. Some is for cost-cutting, tax-cutting reasons. It's a blessing for children who move from orphanages to foster homes, or old folk who can stay on at home with visiting services instead of going into nursing homes. It's risky with some, for example schizophrenic youths turned out of hospitals without homes to go to. But however it affects the sufferers themselves it usually means less work for women in paid public employment and more work – often unpleasant, stressful, unrewarding work – for the unpaid wives and mothers and daughters who accept the sick, handicapped, demented or incontinent sufferers into their households, or visit them regularly to clean them up, make and mend for them, shop and run errands for them. The stress may extend from the unpaid workers to the others in their households who also help, exploit or depend on them. If the experience is unfamiliar to you, you can sample it painlessly, shit and ingratitude and all, by reading Doris Lessing's novels: The Diary of a Good Neighbor *and* If The Old Could, *republished together as* The Diaries of Jane Somers *(1984). For better proposals for old age in rich democracies, try Michael Young,* Life After Work: The arrival of the ageless society *(1991).*

Lessons of history Except for their names the latest Weaver household (the doctors) and the latest Farmer household (the mother and children who died) were not fictitious, they were real English households. Together with the women of Jane Somers' world, who work unpaid at caring for the chronically sick and old and incompetent, they represent the extremes of household productivity, unproductive poverty, and cruel exploitation which can coexist in a rich modern economy. That range of possibilities is what makes your study of the conditions of household productivity important.

THE HOUSEHOLD SHARE OF PRODUCTION IN A MODERN MIXED ECONOMY

Revision: As noted earlier, equipping households to produce copiously for their own use has altered the productive structure of the economy as a whole. Total domestic capital now runs close to the total of private sector capital. At 40 per cent or more of national product (depending how you count it) total household and other unpaid output of goods and services is not far behind total private sector output.

The shift to higher household production came earliest in North America and Australia. In 1900 annual US private investment in fixed capital (buildings and equipment) was about 14 per cent of GNP. By 1960 it was down to 7.5 per cent. Had the leading capitalist country really halved the proportion of income it saved and the proportion of output it devoted to creating productive capital? No: as you learned in Chapter 12, the proportion had actually increased, but there had been some

shift from private to public investment, a large shift from private to household investment, and a fourfold increase in education, research and other investment in human capital. Neither the household nor the human capital figured as productive capital in the regular national accounts. But the research which was the source of Figures 12.1 and 2 found that by 1960 public and private capital formation together were taking about 10 per cent of GNP; household capital formation about 10 per cent; and human capital about 10 per cent. Thus 30 per cent of national income was being saved: 30 per cent of output was of capital goods or human capacities to maintain or increase future output.

Notice how the growth of public, private, household and human capital have interacted to increase household productivity. As the technical means of production improve, public and private producers are able to give their workers higher pay and shorter hours. They can also produce more and better household capital equipment at lower prices. The rising wages enable households to buy the equipment, the shorter hours leave them time to use it. Human capital from better education improves their capacity to use it: it equips and motivates people to read a wider range of books and papers, acquire higher skills, manage more complicated equipment, enjoy a wider range of arts and more skilful and demanding recreations. In return such households can provide the public and private sectors with adaptable people to meet their increasingly complex human capital needs.

Thus historically there has been interaction between the growth of public, private and household productivity. The following chapters show that the interdependence continues. Households in modern societies can rarely be independent, self-reliant producers. To acquire the household capital they need, and to make productive use of it day by day, they also need flows of income and goods and services from the public and private sectors. So in a developed society the productivity of the household sector as a whole depends on (among other things) how the public and private sectors distribute wealth, income, credit and housing finance to households.

Those are the subjects of the next chapters. Summaries and exercises can wait until the last of these chapters on households as producers.

25

Household capital

More revision: Besides widening the range of consumer goods in the shops, technical progress has widened households' choices between buying ready-made goods and services, and alternatively producing for themselves.

Technical progress has brought the invention and mass manufacture of gas and electric cookers and heaters, refrigerators and air coolers, vacuum cleaners, washing machines, dishwashers; bikes and cars; cheap hand tools and power tools; magic new paints, adhesives and DIY materials; gramophones, radios, modern sound systems; cameras, home movie gear, television, videos, computers; electric razors, carving knives, hairdriers, toothbrushes, radio-controlled front gates and garage doors. And new transport systems (vertical and horizontal) allow people to work and shop in city centres while living in apartments forty floors above them, or in spacious houses and gardens – or modest cottages – in distant suburbs or countryside.

HOUSEHOLD INVESTMENT CHOICES

Technical progress thus gave households new options. They could equip themselves to produce more for themselves, and to replace some of the public and private sector services. (Buy a car and stop using the train?) Once equipped, the choices would recur day by day. (Ride the bus to work or drive the car? Cook dinner or buy fast food or ring for a pizza or dine out? Pay a commercial laundry to do the family washing, or do it yourself at a launderette, or wash it in a machine at home then dry it outdoors or in a powered drier?)

But the options which households actually have, between buying ready-made goods and services and equipping themselves to produce their own, still depend heavily on their relations with the public and private sectors, especially on how fully employed their employable members are and how rich or poor they are. So most of this chapter is about two questions:

1. **Income** and productivity: What relations may there be between a household's wealth and earned income and its household productivity?

2. **Capital** and productivity: How much of the capital which they use do household producers need to own?

Can public and private capital (public parks and playgrounds, communal workshops, private hire services) substitute for household capital? Who should own the main item of household capital, the house – its occupiers? A private landlord? A public landlord?

Income and household productivity

Some countries still have subsistence farmers who produce most of what they consume, with some local barter but very little money income or market dealing with other producers. But in developed economies researchers now generally find that for a majority of households, especially in the low and middle income range, income and household productivity tend to vary together, not inversely. There are wide individual variations but on average the more money households earn, the more they also make and do for themselves. The less they earn, the less they make and do for themselves. The poorest households who most need to supplement their incomes with output of their own are often those who produce least. So instead of offsetting inequalities of income, household production tends to compound them.

That is a cruel paradox, but there are straightforward economic reasons for it. It costs money to buy and equip houses and gardens. The more money, the better the equipment it can buy, the more productive it can make the household's labor.

Once bought, most household space and equipment also cost money to maintain and use: money for rates and taxes and licences; gas, power, petrol, oil, other fuels, mechanical servicing; seedlings, fertilizer, insecticides; pens, pencils, paper, paint, canvas; soap, detergent, scourers, polishes; wood, nails, screws, blades and bits, glue, paint; clay and glazes; cloth and thread; audio tapes, video and home computer software; film, printing paper, photographic chemicals; toymaking and modelling materials; food and vetting for pets; all sorts of spare parts and repairs and servicing.

So although households with wage-earners may have less time to spare for unpaid work than unemployed households have, the earning households nevertheless have overriding advantages. They can afford the capital and current costs of household production, so they have real choices between buying goods and services and producing their own. At many tasks their better equipment makes their labor more agreeable or more productive than the labor of worse-equipped households. That in turn may make the work more rewarding, and motivate them to do more of it.

Thus the paradox – that families which don't have earners also tend to do less at home – has solid economic causes. But it may also have social or psychological causes in particular cases. For some people unemployment is demoralizing. Some others are idle by nature: with them it may be the demoralization that causes the unemployment. Some who might once have been energetic are seduced by modern inventions – welfare incomes, push-button warmth, take-away food, television – into lazing about. Because such causes of inaction are difficult to know for certain, they tend to be subjects of ideological guesswork. Some Left ideologists think everybody wants to work, and all the unemployed would be productive at home as well as at work if only they could find jobs. Right ideologists object: plenty of people who were productive through their earning years continue to be productive at home after they retire, houseworking, gardening, making and mending, despite diminished income. Unemployment doesn't stop them, and that arouses suspicion that it may be sloth that keeps some of the other unemployed idle. But that in turn is hard to reconcile with the good working and earning record, through the mid-century decades of full employment, of the households from which those who are now unemployed have come.

Moreover the great increase of unemployment through the 1970s came as more of the population of working age tried to join the paid workforce. (Employment was increasing at the same time as unemployment was, remember?) The unemployment signified that *more* people, not less, wanted to work. And when they're denied paid work, lack of income rules out many kinds of unpaid production however willing the people are.

Who should own the capital that household producers use?

You just noted that going out to earn wages, and producing goods and services at home, are more often complements than alternatives. (Don't confuse that with a different relation. Producing something at home is often an alternative to buying it ready-made. But you first have to earn some money to have *either* of those options.) Now notice a similar relation between households' uses of their own and other capital.

Land and equipment Some of the space and equipment that households use can be domestic or private or public. (You can own books or borrow them from a library. You can own a car, rent a car or use cabs.) Cabs are used more daily hours than most private cars are. Public playgrounds are used by more kids than most back yards are. Would it therefore be efficient if public authorities and private hirers provided more of the capital that domestic producers use? At first sight, yes; but with further study, many of the public and household facilities turn out to function as complements rather than alternatives to each other.

The first systematic research into the relationship was done in Australia by Ian Halkett. It was designed to help policy makers with a particular question. Planners, economists and other experts have recurring disagreements about urban density. Should city dwellers live 'dense and high' in compact cities, without much private garden space but with short journeys to their work and recreations? Or should they be free to spread out to live in suburban house-and-garden style? Experts who favor the compact policy used to argue that people don't really need, or make much use of, their private gardens; they only have them for conformist reasons and because misguided planning regulations ban denser housing forms. Defenders of the suburbs respond by insisting that people do use and value their gardens, and know what they're doing when they choose their housing forms. The argument has practical interest because most deliberate attempts to make cities more compact increase their inequalities. (The 'compact' policies rarely stop well-off households owning as much space as they want, in town or in country retreats or both. But they commonly allow denser building in poorer neighborhoods. They raise land prices beyond the means of poorer homebuyers. And they build public housing dense and high, without private gardens. The disastrous forms of public housing built in Britain and the US from about 1950 to 1975 contrasted with the rising capacity of those countries' better-off households to buy houses and gardens of increasing size.) Though 'dense' theories have appealed to some Left as well as Right experts, the usual effect of dense policies is to redistribute shares of private urban space from poorer to richer households.

The opposing theories had been asserted for half a century without hard evidence of their truth or falsehood when Ian Halkett, a Canadian geographer working in Australia, began his research. By aerial photography, questionnaires and interviews he discovered how a large sample of suburban residents actually used their private land, and how and why they valued it. The results published in *The Quarter Acre Block* (1976) were overwhelmingly on the gardeners' side, and not only for suburban Australians. Immigrants from Europe were even keener for private land, had more of it, produced more from it and generally used it more intensively. Wherever they were born, most people made busy and varied uses of their gardens, sheds and workshops. Childless households used them nearly as much as families with children did. More than half the people averaged more than fifteen hours a week in their private outdoors. Most thought the benefits of suburban space were well worth their public and private costs.

Those findings were as garden city theorists had expected, and they had been anticipated by similar studies in the US. It was in a follow-up study that the surprising discoveries came. A local public housing agency reasoned that Halkett had proved what local space and equipment the people would use – but he had not proved that they needed to *own* all the space and equipment. How much of it could be sufficiently replaced by public facilities? Could denser residence be achieved without social loss if people had less private space but more shared resources? The agency was planning its first big tract of medium-density housing, in which some residents would occupy landless apartments and others would have row houses with smaller-than-usual back yards and no private front gardens. Some of the land thus saved would go to provide communal gardens, car parks, playgrounds, a waterfront beach, a craft and community centre, and a primary school designed for community uses at night and weekends. How well would those public provisions replace the lost private space? Might they serve even better, by encouraging more sociable and cooperative activity? Halkett was invited to find out. With his wife (a kindergartener) and their young children he rented the first house in the estate and moved in to study the developing community as a participant researcher.

We noted earlier that households who need to do most for themselves because they lack income tend in practice to be the ones who do least for themselves. Halkett now observed a second paradox: the people who 'should' make most use of public and communal resources, because they have least space and equipment of their own, tend in practice to make least use of the public resources. Deprive a family of resourceful house and garden and instead of going out more to public facilities they go out less, and to less active recreations. Give them resourceful houses and gardens and they go out more, use more public resources, and use them in more active ways.

There are obvious exceptions to these tendencies. Some well equipped people make less use of neighborhood resources (though that may be because their recreations take them further afield to city centres or countryside). Some families without land of their own spend a good deal of time in local playgrounds. People with their own swimming pools make less use of public pools. In some crowded urban quarters in the past, people without many material resources at home have enjoyed a regular social life at local pubs or clubs. But generally the tendency is as Halkett observed: the people who are better equipped at home are also busier away from home.

Once observed, the reasons for the tendency are not mysterious. People who grow things at home take a more knowledgeable interest in what they see in public gardens. People from homes with books are likelier to borrow more from public libraries. People who play music at home go to more live concerts. People who go out to learn carpentry, weaving, metalwork, leatherwork or other crafts need space at home to practise them. Pony clubbers need somewhere to keep ponies. And so on – some public and household resources are genuine alternatives, but many are complements to each other with the public resources used most where the households are best equipped, and the household resources most productive where the public supports are best.

Halkett's observations did not support *either* policies of privatization *or* their opposites. To the extent that the households he studied were representative it is not true that people with more household resources use less public resources; and it is not true that people with access to public resources don't need the complementary household resources. It is not true that well equipped homeowners 'privatize leisure' – turn their backs on the world, go out less, grow less sociable. In practice they tend to mix and socialize more than do people who lack a secure base and resources of their own.

You noticed earlier, in connection with urban conservation, that saving an old house from demolition can be as useful as building a new one. In a similar way good private income and public services can get existing housing and household equipment better used, by helping their owners to make more interesting or productive use of them. Halkett's 'participant' reports for the public housing enterprise were not published. In the following passage one of his associates illustrated the interdependence of public and household space and equipment by comparing similar households with different household resources and *consequently* access to more public resources.

> Meet two low-income families. Soon after they form households they have children. The women become full-time housewives, the households have only the men's wages. With hire-purchase debts and housing costs they don't have much to spare for expensive outings or entertainment. As the years go by the men may earn a bit more, the women may go back to

work, and eventually the kids will start earning; but the first ten years will be hard.

One family rents a walk-up flat. They do what they can in it. They read and draw and play table games; they play whatever outdoor games they can in streets and public parks. But most things out there you're not allowed to muck about with, and most of the entertainments away from home cost money, so except for swimming in the municipal pool they're in the flat a lot, sprawling around letting the commercial television channels persuade them to spend more on pop discs, computer games, personal freshness and aspirin. Whatever they manage to consume, they don't produce much.

The other family manages to get a low-deposit mortgage loan to buy a cottage in a garden with an old shed, and goes to work to use those resources, and those of a helpful neighborhood. Here's a short list of things they do at one time or another that they could not do, or not so freely, if they lived in a flat:

They grow fruit and flowers and vegetables. They design their garden, and redesign it now and then, especially when the kids go through the phase when they want plots of their own. They play in an inflatable pool when they're little and a canvas one when they're bigger. They keep paint and tools in the shed, partly to work on the house and bikes and the car when they have one, but mostly to make things. Things made in the shed over the years include shelves and cupboards for the house; some good toys made *for* the children and a lot of crazy constructions made *by* the children, often with second-hand bits of wood or metal or plastic that would otherwise go for rubbish; a tree house; dog kennels, rabbit hutches and cubby houses from packing cases that would have gone for rubbish.

Young and old see a good deal of their friends in the back garden, often doing things and enjoying themselves in ways that would not go so well in a public park. There are various pets at various times. The dogs help to exercise the humans in the parks, especially after the children have left home. And there are serious hobbies: painting, pottery, carpentry, fine roses to show. When members of the family need help with their amateur skills they can sometimes find it in neighbors' back yards where there are other unofficial industries, or at the local public library, or at the craft and trade classes and community workshops which flourish in the neighborhood *because* so many people have scope to practise crafts at home.

Notice that the second household's greater productivity comes partly from the *form and location* of their housing, an adaptable cottage and garden near good neighborhood services, and partly from their *tenure*. As owners they can alter the form and uses of the property more freely than a landlord might allow, and they maintain and add to it as they might not do if they were improving a landlord's asset rather than their own. We will presently see that they may also have more money than tenants would have for those improvements, and for the running costs of household production.

Does it follow that owning houses is always better than renting them? No, it depends on the households' particular needs, means, lifestyles and stages of household life.

Reasons for renting People who rent by choice – i.e. who could afford to buy their housing but choose not to – may have any of these reasons:

1. *Risk.* Landlords bear most of the financial risks of physical decay, cracking walls, leaking roofs, corroded pipes, blocked sewers, etc. Tenants also face risks – of insecure tenure, unreasonable rent increases, etc. – but may prefer them to owners' risks. And some of the tenants' risks can be reduced by appropriate contract terms, by public regulation of private landlords, or by public landlords.

2. *Chores.* Most landlords (depending on the terms of tenancy) maintain the place, paint and repair it, remember to insure it and pay its rates, and generally relieve tenants of a lot of owners' work and responsibility.

3. *Mobility.* Young or childless households may want to be footloose and free to move. Households whose earners' occupations compel them to move often may avoid trouble and risk by renting wherever they go.

4. *Lifestyle.* People whose work, recreations and social life keep them occupied away from home may want trouble-free housing, maintained by someone else, to use for little more than bed and breakfast.

5. *Age and infirmity.* Old and handicapped people may want trouble-free housing maintained by someone else. There are also hybrid tenures. From some institutions old people can buy housing units and own them for life – but with tenant services, and with ownership reverting to the institution when the occupants leave.

6. *Public housing.* Most public tenants have secure tenure and pay lower rents than average private rents.

Where the housing is in house-and-garden form, public tenants may have some of the advantages of homeowners.

7. *Public aids to tenants.* Government can do a good deal to reduce the disadvantages of renting. It can regulate building health and safety, and landlords' and tenants' rights. It can regulate private rents, or subsidize them by giving hard-up tenants rent allowances.

Those are all reasons for choosing to rent. But there are still many households who rent only because they can't afford to buy. Most of them face a cruel paradox: the more productive housing which they can't afford to own would cost them less than the *less* productive housing they are compelled to rent instead.

How can that be?

It is the single most important principle of household economics – so learn it well:

Who owns the house? Who pays for it? If owner-occupiers build or buy the house, it costs them

- the purchase price;
- interest on a housing loan, if they need one; and
- taxes and maintenance costs of the house for as long as they have it.

If on the other hand a landlord buys the house and lets it to the household, there are two ways of perceiving the financial effect. This is the pro-landlord way:

- The landlord invests capital in the house. He is no richer or poorer by doing that. Where he had (say) $100,000 of money he now has $100,000 worth of house.
- He charges the tenant enough rent to pay the annual taxes and maintenance costs of the house, plus some profit which is the rate of return on his capital investment.

The rate of return needs to be at least as high as the investor could get (with similar risks, etc.) in other industries, or he won't invest in housing and the tenant won't be housed. Suppose that the annual tax and maintenance costs total 2.5 per cent of the capital value, and the rate of profit is 5 per cent, so the rent the tenant pays is 7.5 per cent: $7,500 a year for a house worth $100,000.

If the household life is 40 years that annual 5 per cent of profit adds up to 200 per cent of the value of the house. So an alternative pro-tenant, anti-landlord way to see the same landlord-tenant relation is this:

Financially the landlord contributes nothing. The tenant's rent first repays the purchase price of the house then gives the landlord continuing profit through the remainder of the tenant's household life. For the household, the main differences between buying and renting the house are two:

- Renting costs more than twice as much over the life of the household; and
- it buys the capital asset for someone else.

Over household life, counting what they pay out for their housing and what they own at the end, the tenant may pay two or three times as much for the use of the house as the homebuyer does. If the landlord invests his profits the tenant's rent may buy him two or three houses, whose tenants will in turn buy him two or three more. Am I exaggerating? Not necessarily. My family and I have been tenants of a London landlady whose husband died leaving her one house and the price of one other. Twenty years later she owned forty, all bought with loans repaid or being repaid from tenants' rents.

Check the financial effects for yourself. (You need to know how – you may work one day for a property investor or a tenants' defence league.) Here's an example, then an exercise.

Example This example simplifies. It assumes there is no inflation (except of house prices, as specified). To allow a precise comparison it puts identical households into identical houses, one as owner and one as tenant. Each household earns $25,000 a year and pays a quarter of that in tax. Each occupies a house worth $75,000, i.e. worth three years' income at the start of their household life, but with its market value rising with urban growth altogether 20 per cent over the 40 years of household life. To maintain a house (repair and paint and insure it and pay its local rates) costs an average 2.5 per cent of its original value each year. If it is rented the rent is $120 a week which is a quarter of the household's gross income and a third of its income after tax. Per year it is about 8 per cent of the house's original value. Of that 8 per cent, 2.5 is landlord's tax and maintenance cost and 5.5 is the landlord's annual rent and rate of profit.

At the start of its household life one household manages to borrow $10,000 interest-free from the bride's parents and $65,000 as a housing loan from a bank, and buys its house. The first loan is repaid in five years and the bank loan in twenty, with interest at 3 per cent on the remaining debt each year. (That's real interest. When there is inflation, real interest is the difference between the rates of interest and inflation. It has often been less than 3 per cent when rates of inflation and nominal interest were high.)

The second household starts without any savings or well-off relatives. Paying a third of its after-tax income in rent, it never manages to save – over and above that rent – the deposit that would induce a bank to lend it enough to buy a house.

After 40 years of household life this is how the household totals compare:

Net housing costs

Homebuyer			Tenant		
Purchase price of house		$75,000	Rent		$240,000
Real interest on bank loan		20,000			
Maintenance		75,000			
Gross housing cost		170,000			
Less wealth acquired		90,000			
Net housing cost:	Total	80,000	Net housing cost:	Total	240,000
	Per year	2,000		Per year	6,000

Net worth

Homebuyer			Tenant		
Income (40 years x $25,000)		$1,000,000	Income (40 x $25,000)		$1,000,000
Less Tax	250,000		Less Tax	250,000	
House price	75,000		House rent	240,000	
Interest	20,000				490,000
Maintenance	75,000				
		420,000			
Income after tax and housing costs		580,000			
Plus house worth -		90,000			
Owner's net worth after tax and housing costs		670,000	Tenant's net worth after tax and housing costs		510,000

Landlord's gains

Suppose the landlord invests $10,000 of his own plus $65,000 from the same bank housing loan as our homebuyer uses. After repaying the loan the landlord then spends the rest on consumables, rather than reinvesting it. This is what his investment adds to his net worth over 40 years:

Rent received		240,000	
Wealth acquired		90,000	
Gross gain			330,000
Less	purchase price (75,000), interest (20,000) and maintenance (75,000) as for our homebuyer	170,000	
	Tax on the taxable part of the rent (interest and maintenance costs are tax-exempt)	40,000	
			210,000
Net gain			120,000

Over household life the homeowner's housing cost is about a third of the tenant's, and the homeowner's net worth after tax and housing costs is about a third higher than the tenant's.

The landlord's net gain of $120,000 represents an after-tax return of 1200 per cent, or 30 per cent per year, on the investment of $10,000. Alternatively if the landlord does not borrow, but invests $75,000 of his own to buy the house, then (with no interest and some consequent tax adjustments) the after-tax return is about 250 per cent, or 6.25 per cent per year. Compare that 6.25 per cent with the 39 per cent per year of the $10,000 investor, and you can see why property investors like to be 'highly geared', i.e. to use a little of their own money to attract a high proportion of borrowed money.

Who provides the landlord's $155,000 gain? The $15,000 from rising house prices will come from whoever next buys the house. The rest comes from the tenant. This is what the tenant's $250,000 rent does: It pays the landlord's loan interest ($20,000) and maintenance ($75,000), costs which it is reasonable for the occupier to pay for the use of the financial and physical capital which the house represents. Over and above those necessary costs the tenant buys the house for the landlord ($75,000) and transfers a further $110,000 of income to him. Together those two items transfer

$185,000 of wealth and income from the tenant to the landlord, who hands on $35,000 or $40,000 of it as tax to the government.

Equality and productivity If you think that tenant ought to be able to buy the house if she wants to, and if you favor greater equality and higher productivity for the whole society, you can argue like this:

If the government would lend or transfer $10,000 to the household, so that the household instead of the landlord could get the housing loan and buy the house, the household would not need to transfer $185,000 to the landlord and the government. Also, as owner the household might adapt and alter the house and use it more freely than it can do as tenant. With $110,000 more to spend it could afford the capital and current costs of more domestic production, and of keeping its members better occupied.

So if the landlord is richer than the household (as is usually though not always true) a cheap loan or 'downward' transfer of $10,000 could prevent an upward transfer of $185,000; reduce inequalities of wealth and income; and allow an increase of productivity.

In practice it is unusual to buy a house in the first year of household life. Try a slightly more realistic comparison, in which the homebuyer has to begin by saving a loan deposit, and ends as a homeowner *and* landlord:

EXERCISE

Household A with two earners earns altogether $50,000 a year. Household B has one earner earning $30,000. Income tax takes 25 per cent of income. Landlord's maintenance costs, and everybody's loan interest payments, can be subtracted from taxable income. Houses cost $90,000, apartments cost $60,000, their prices don't change, and there is no inflation. Annual rent is 10 per cent of capital value. Maintenance costs landlords 3 per cent of capital value (= 30 per cent of rent), but it only costs owner-occupiers 1.5 per cent because they use some of their own unpaid labor. Banks lend 90 per cent of the value of houses or apartments. The loans pay 3 per cent of real interest per year. You can cut some complexities and assume it adds a total of 30 per cent to loan repayments.

Household A starts by renting a house. Of the income left after paying tax and rent it saves 10 per cent until it has a 10 per cent deposit on a house. Then it stops renting, borrows, and buys a house. Its loan and interest repayments happen to equal the rent it formerly paid. It continues to save 10 per cent of income remaining after tax and loan repayments, until it can deposit 10 per cent and borrow 90 per cent of the price of an apartment, which it buys and commences to let for rent. Both loans are repaid before the end of its household life. Meanwhile household B spends its 40 years of household life as a tenant of an apartment. Assume that B's landlord (C) bought the apartment for cash, without borrowing, at the beginning of the period – but being richer than the other two, pays 35 per cent of his net rent income (after maintenance costs) in tax.

Calculate A's and B's net worth over household life after tax and housing costs. B has earned 60 per cent of the amount of wage income that A has earned. Does their net worth reduce or increase that degree of inequality, and by how much? What has C's investment added to his net worth after tax? (What has it *added*? Don't count the $60,000 he invested.)

That exercise, like the text example it followed, is unrealistic in a number of respects. It assumes a flat rate of income tax. Most income taxes are progressive, so that the marginal rates the households would pay or save on their housing dealings would be above their average tax rates. It deals in real interest rates. In practice most countries experience some inflation and use nominal interest rates. That produces a 'sloped credit' effect which you will study in later chapters on the management of capital markets. Sloped credit raises higher barriers against entry to home ownership than appear in our examples. And in real life most of the other specified conditions would be likely to vary through the life of a household or a housing loan, rather than holding steady to simplify your calculations.

But despite their simplifications those examples do not misrepresent the general nature of relations between owner-occupiers, tenants, landlords and financial institutions, or their effects on the distribution of wealth, income and household productivity. So it is important to know how the relevant markets and institutions determine what household capital resources particular households get or fail to get, and what the resources cost them.

HOW HOUSING CAPITAL IS ALLOCATED

The problem Housing is about 40 per cent of a developed economy's fixed capital and is used in the production of a third or more of final goods and services. Houses last longer than most other capital equipment, so that 40 per cent of total fixed capital is accumulated by allocating about 20 per cent of annual investment to housing. But that allocation can't be done efficiently (meaning most productively) *either* by the market principle which allocates most private capital *or* by the political and administrative principles which allocate most public capital. Different principles are needed. The remainder of this Chapter analyses the elements of the problem, suggests what principles should be applied to it, and describes a range of things, from good to bad, which have been done about it in developed mixed economies.

As they appear to the household seeking housing, the elements of the problem can be sorted out like this:

- To buy a house, the household may have to pay for two houses for a period of years.

- It must deal in two markets the first of which, the capital market, is not naturally efficient for the purpose.

- When there is inflation, conventionally managed capital markets deal in 'sloped credit' which is specially obstructive to the housing needs of households with low income.

We will trace the elements of the problem in that order.

A double bind Most households want housing as soon as they are formed. But houses cost two or three years' income. If you start saving to buy one, you must meanwhile rent another. That means paying for two houses at once. You might accumulate enough to buy one by saving (say) a quarter of your income for ten years. But if rent is taking a second quarter and income tax a third quarter of the income, that may not leave enough to live on. Most other things you want – car, fine furniture, dishwasher, video – you can do without while you save to buy them. But you can't do without some sort of housing from the day you leave your parents' house or college dormitory to form a *household* of your own. Conclusion: You either spend your life buying houses for landlords, or borrow to buy one of your own.

If you want to borrow and buy, you may still face a period of 'double bind'. In most countries banks and building societies won't lend the whole price of a house. Why not? Partly to ration whatever funds they have to lend; but chiefly to reduce their risks if you fail to repay. Left to themselves most banks and building societies would like you to deposit 20 or 30 per cent of the purchase price, and they will lend 70 or 80 per cent. With government aid and encouragement they may lend up to 90 per cent. But whether you have to contribute 30 per cent or 20 or 10 as an opening deposit, you must first save it. And if you are also paying rent while you save you are back in that double bind, paying for two houses at once. If you can afford to pay for one house, an efficient system should be able to house you while you do it. We will return later to some methods by which that can be done.

Meanwhile, how do people manage? Many put up with the double bind for long enough to save the necessary deposit. Some avoid the double bind by saving up a deposit while they are still members of other households, commonly their parents'. Some cadge or borrow the deposit from parents. Some borrow it, often at high interest, as a second loan additional to their main housing loan – repaying two loans at once need be no harder than paying for two houses at once. And many households save the deposit without hardship because they have more than one member earning. The double bind is tolerable if there is double income.

By one means or other in most rich societies nowadays a majority of households do manage to buy their housing. The proportions who do, and the stage of household life at which they manage to do it, vary over time and from country to country. But in countries in which 65 or 70 per cent of households own their housing, 50 or 60 per cent may borrow and buy. 10 or 15 per cent may be rich enough to buy a first house without borrowing. 10 or 15 per cent may not want to own their housing at any stage of their household lives. But in all countries, however rich, there remain somewhere between 15 and 25 per cent who would like to buy houses but cannot, and more who cannot buy their first houses as early in their household life as they would like. Most households could well afford to buy – over household life they will pay more in rent than it would cost them to buy. But the capital market allocates the necessary capital to landlords instead, with the effects outlined in the previous section. That tends to increase inequality and reduce household (and total) productivity. To the extent that an economic system withholds capital from households which could pay the going rate for it and use it productively, the system appears to be inefficient and inequitable. If orthodox economists perceived housing as productive capital they would diagnose a market failure. But a main cause of the failure is that the relevant market managers and economists do *not* perceive housing as productive capital. As we will now see.

Market failure in theory Recall some theory which is relevant here because it has practical effects on policy. (Beliefs are working parts.) For most economists, production ends at the last exchange of goods and services for money. Anything that happens after that is consumption. Households are said to 'organize consumption'. By definition, the equipment they use for that purpose can't be productive capital. So don't call it capital, call it housing and consumer durables.

You are already familiar with one effect of that choice. To know whether a car is capital or not, i.e. productive or not, you have to know whether its driver is paid to drive it. To know whether a cooker is capital you have to know whether it is in a restaurant or an owner-occupied household. A rented house has double identity: it is a consumer durable for the household in it, but it is capital earning rent for its landlord.

Now notice another effect. If you define household activity as consumption it will be appropriate to judge its efficiency by your theory of consumption, not your theory of production. To understand the effects of that you must recall some essentials of neoclassical theory. Here again are the bare bones:

As consumers, people have wants. As producers,

they have 'endowments' – capital or labor which they can contribute to production. Most production is done by firms. So to get what they want as consumers, people trade in two markets. They sell firms the use of their capital or labor in factor markets. They then use their earnings to buy the consumer goods they want in the 'final goods' markets.

The firms compete in both markets. They bid against each other in factor markets for the capital and labor they want, then compete for the consumers' dollars in the final goods markets. *The most efficient firms*, i.e. the ones which manage to use factors of given value to produce and sell goods of most value (as valued by the customers who buy them) *will be able to outbid their competitors for the use of the capital they want*. The firms which can use the capital most profitably are presumed to be the ones who can use it most productively. That market mechanism, by which consumers' choices determine the most productive allocation and use of a society's capital resources, is at the heart of neoclassical theory, and of capitalist efficiency as neoclassics define it.

That's the theory of production. The theory of consumption is simpler. It says that when people sell the use of their productive endowments, the money they get represents the value of their productive contribution. That determines the primary distribution of income and the amount each earner has to spend on consumables. The consumers themselves decide how to spend it. For whatever money they have to spend, they simply decide what basket of goods will be most useful and pleasing to them.

Now notice that the theory of production and the theory of consumption have different implications for the efficiency of the economic system as a whole. Neoclassics assume, with various hedges and fences which need not concern us here, that with given resources, more output is more efficient than less, regardless of how the product is distributed to the consumers. If people don't like the distribution of income they can have government redistribute it. So although there may be conflicts about shares of the cake, there is a common interest, shared by all, in the size of the cake. And to get maximum production, that common interest requires that most of the owners of capital don't use it themselves but (as shareholders or lenders) hire it out to be used by others: by the firms which pay most for it because they can produce most with it. There is a common interest in the most productive firms getting the capital.

So says the theory of production. But the theory of consumption does not suggest that there is any comparable common interest in individual consumers' choices. Except for some externalities (smoke if they buy smoky fuel, noise if they buy drums), how consumers spend their incomes is nobody's business but their own: it need not affect anyone else's interests, or any common interest of the whole society.

Do you begin to see why it matters whether you define housing and housing equipment as capital or as consumer durables?

If they are consumables or durables used in the course of consumption, they should go like other consumables to shoppers who can afford them and prefer them to the other consumables they might alternatively spend their money on. Their distribution can't affect productivity or total national output. National efficiency merely requires that there be genuine consumer sovereignty, with the least possible government interference with the people's freedom to choose.

But *if they are capital resources*, common interest and national efficiency require that they be allocated to households *in whatever distribution will get them used most productively*, to add most household product to the measured national product of the public and private sectors. Are poorer households currently underemploying their unpaid labor because they lack the equipment and income to employ it fully? Even if it is fully employed, is the labor less productive than it could be with better equipment? If better equipped, might those households produce more to increase both the real national product and their own shares of it? Here may be a 'hard' reason of efficiency, over and above the traditional reasons of justice or social compassion, for government to redistribute some wealth from richer to poorer households.

We will return to that question of policy. First, the heart of the analysis. Suppose we accept as plain fact that housing and domestic equipment are productive capital: bricks and mortar shelter us at home as well as in hotels, stoves cook our dinners as productively at home as in restaurants, cars transport us whoever drives them and whether firms or households own them; and so on. If those capital goods are nevertheless allocated to households as if they were consumer goods, i.e. on the principles which determine the distribution of consumer goods, what actual market failures and inefficiencies can we expect?

Market failure in practice The basic cause of failure was sketched earlier in our account of the allocation of capital between the sectors of the mixed economy. Recall: if capital is allocated efficiently to profit-seeking firms it is because *the profits from its use create the capacity to pay for it*. But unlike that private capital, household capital is used to produce goods and services which are not sold for money. So it cannot be money returns from the use of the capital which pay to acquire the capital. A household has to bid and pay for its capital with money from other sources altogether – typically with income from employment in the public or private sectors. That income does not come from, or depend on, the productive use of the household capital which it buys. So there is no causal connection between the household's capacity to use the capital, and its competitive capacity to get it and pay for it. An inactive old couple who happen to be rich may outbid (say) an industrious young family of six for funds, land and bricks and mortar which the poorer household would use much more productively. In the private sector unproductive firms can't bid resources away from productive firms like that. But with households, the classical link between market *allocation* and productive *use* of capital – the most basic capitalist efficiency – simply is not there.

To buy houses most households must deal in two markets (both of which you will study in later chapters): the money market for loans, and the real estate market for houses and land. In each, three kinds of competition can occur. In none of the three can market forces be relied on to allocate the capital resources efficiently.

1. *Household versus firm* When household producers compete with profit-seeking producers for scarce resources (as when households compete with firms for available loan funds or building resources) there is no reason to expect that the most productive user can necessarily bid highest and get the capital. Consequently on macroeconomic scale, market forces cannot be relied on to allocate capital between the sectors in the most productive way.

2. *Household versus household* When households compete with each other there is no reason to expect that the most productive user can necessarily bid highest and get the capital.

3. *Household versus landlord* When households compete with landlords, the households pay for the capital whoever wins and gets to own it. When the landlords win the households pay more, over time, often for less or worse housing, so both their productivity and their consumption are likely to be reduced. Whether national output falls may depend on what the landlords do with their gains.

Any of those three competitors can hinder households with low incomes from getting housing loans and buying houses which they would use productively. Where significant inflation prevails they also face a fourth and worse hindrance. It is called 'sloped credit' and you will study it at length in Chapter 53 on capital markets. Here it need only be sketched:

Housing loans under inflation When inflation sets in, lenders want something done to protect the real value of the capital they lend, especially when they lend it for long terms as they do for housing. They don't want to be repaid in inflated currency with less purchasing power than they lent. Most Western financial institutions have tried to protect them by adding the expected or actual rate of inflation to the rate of interest. As you will learn, the element of inflation in the rate of interest is not really interest at all, it is better understood as an early return of capital. That has a range of economic effects but the one that concerns us here is that it increases the initial rate of repayment – *real* repayment – of housing loans. In relation to average or below-average household incomes and capacities to pay, the increases can be prohibitive. Do some simple arithmetic and you will see why. Suppose a household borrows three years' income to buy a house, and can afford to pay a quarter of its annual income in loan repayments. Through the first years of repayment, to pay each percentage point of interest on that loan will take 3 per cent of income. At an interest rate of 4 per cent, interest takes 12 per cent of income leaving 13 per cent for repaying capital. At 8.3 per cent, interest absorbs the borrower's whole capacity to pay and there is no capital repayment. Above 8.3 per cent the household would be further in debt each year – but that is not likely to happen, because on those figures nobody would lend to the household in the first place.

Practical effects of theoretical disagreements

Such inefficient markets appear to need some better management. But beliefs are working parts, and policy choices depend on how the policy-makers choose to see the problem. Do they see houses as producers' or consumers' goods? Do they bother to analyse the relations between two competitions: competition between housing and other industries for resources, and competition for ownership of the housing? To illustrate what practical effects the theoretical differences can have, we can anticipate one of the policy devices to be listed later in the Chapter.

Investment incentives for landlords If housing shortages bring high rents, in a perfect market the high rents should cure the shortages. Seeing the high rents as high returns to capital, investors should switch from less profitable industries to build more rental housing. In practice that may not happen, for various reasons. There

are long time lags. It can take a year or two to build apartment blocks. Developed countries tend to have enough building capacity to add only two or three per cent to the housing stock each year, and it may take four or five years to attract and train more skilled building workers. But suppose that there appears to be some spare building capacity. Landlord-investors will explain that you can't expect shortage rents to attract new investment. The rents may fall within a few years, as soon as enough new housing is built to end the shortage – but returns to residential investment need to hold reliably for decades. 'What are really deterring investors', the investors may say, 'are unhelpful public policies. If government wants more rental housing it should cut landlords' taxes to make a *permanent* improvement in the return to residential investment.'

Faced with that suggestion, which is self-interested but may also be true, what should government believe? Should it assume that the promise of higher returns will increase the supply of housing, and eventually reduce its rents?

Not necessarily. Government should first study the local facts to get the best answers it can to these questions.

1. How much of their own money will the housing investors use, and how much will they borrow?

2. If they borrow, will it be from institutions like merchant banks or insurance companies which might not otherwise lend for housing or will it be from institutions like savings banks or building societies which would otherwise lend to homebuyers?

3. Will the investors build new housing or buy existing housing?

4. Will it follow that the investors add some rental housing to the whole supply of housing, without reducing the number of homeowning households? Or will they merely turn would-be owners into unwilling tenants, by intercepting funds and housing which would otherwise have gone to homebuyers?

If investors switch funds from (say) office building to apartment building, they may increase the supply of housing and reduce its rents, which may enable some households to increase their spendable income and their domestic productivity. But if the investors go to banks and building societies and bid funds away from homebuyers, then use the funds to bid land and labor and materials away from homebuyers, and use the bricks and mortar to build forms of housing which the households find less enjoyable and productive than the forms they would build for themselves, then the market failure is complete. The investors prosper by shifting households from the more productive, more equal class of owners to the less productive, less equal class of tenants. They also prosper by avoiding some of the taxes which the households as owners would have paid. Remember that these failures follow from leaving market forces to allocate productive capital whose output does not sell for money, so cannot finance the (more productive) households to outbid the (less productive) landlords.

Thus rental housing investment may improve household productivity, or reduce it, in proportions which are theoretically quite uncertain, and must be expected to vary with the local facts of each case. Here is a crude way to classify the possibilities:

	Build new housing	Buy old housing
Funds switched from other industries	+	−
Funds switched from other housing uses	−	−

New housing investment which falls in the top left square is likely to improve household productivity. In the other three squares it is at least as likely to reduce productivity and increase inequalities. So if government thinks to improve equality and productivity by reducing hindrances or offering inducements to rental housing investment, it should first see if detailed study of the local markets can predict how much of the relevant investment will be of the helpful kind.

Summary as before: Left to itself market competition cannot be relied on to divide capital resources efficiently between housing and other investment. It will not allocate housing efficiently between household and household. And it will not stop landlords pre-empting some housing whose users would rather buy it themselves.

So the market needs help. But how much help?

How much would be too much? How can governments decide how much capital to direct to housing?

The theory which identifies the inefficiencies of market allocation does not specify what allocations would be efficient. In practice interests conflict and no best-for-all solution can be expected. Determining a desirable level of housing investment is necessarily a task for political judgment. I suggest two principles to guide the judgment.

1. Observe your society's median housing standard, i.e. the standard of housing which households with the society's median income choose (on average) to pay for in a market way. Government can assume that it will be improving the society's household productivity, but will not be inducing inefficient over-investment in housing, if it acts to enable all households who want it to get housing up to the standard which households with median incomes typically buy.

2. Wherever possible, aids should strengthen rather than replace households' market bidding for resources, for two reasons: (i) to retain their capacity to choose for themselves and have their choices influence the design of the housing supplied; and (ii) to discipline the households. However assisted, their housing choices should still be at the expense of other spending to motivate efficient choices and discourage extravagance.

CONCLUSIONS

Market allocation is likely to be the most efficient way of allocating housing as long as there is strong public management of the supply of housing loans, with some subsidy where necessary.

Fairness, freedom of choice and household productivity seem likely to do best in the following conditions, which are unlikely to be wasteful since they can generally be met at levels of housing investment below those which have accompanied most of the fastest economic growth recorded by European and East Asian countries since 1945.

Most housing is built by competitive private and public suppliers and marketed to give its users effective individual choices, and thus a general market influence over the type and design of new housing.

Government manages the capital market so that households which want to buy houses do so, with aids to the poorest tapering to nothing at about the median levels of income and house value.

Private landlords (i) have public or cooperative competitors, and (ii) are regulated to require fair rents and conditions, and to discourage investors from bidding resources away from homebuyers and non-profit landlords.

How to put such principles into practice? The next chapter surveys what modern governments have done along those lines, and some further things they might do.

EXERCISE

The chapter has argued for effective housing options for 'households'. But conflicts of interest within households may rule out any unanimous optimizing choices for households which have more than one member. Members may disagree both about the goods and services they want and about the best way to get them. Suppose that in a family household with only one earner, it is the earner who decides how to spend the income, and that includes deciding what capital equipment the non-earners will get to work with. If the earner is male, will he use available investment spending to buy a power mower to speed up his lawnmowing, or a washing machine to speed up his wife's laundering, or bikes to speed up the children's journeys to school? Buy himself a grand car, or a cheap car each for his wife and himself? Build himself a workshop, or his children a tree house? Household choices can't always be optimal for every member, any more than national allocations of productive resources can be optimal for every household.

Write anything from a short statement of principles to a thoughtful essay about economic relations within family households. How should decisions be taken about investments in housing and equipment? About shares of paid work and household work? About caring for children and bringing them up? What if anything should law or public services do about the shares of power and work and spending within families?

26

Housing policies

BELIEFS AND INTERESTS

No government of a developed country has left housing entirely to market forces. All governments have acted to provide more housing, and to distribute it better, than market forces alone would do. But the policy makers have not usually thought they were acting to improve allocative efficiency and household productivity and real national income, as this text argues that they were generally doing. Instead they have seen their housing policies as social policies with economic costs: welfare policies to alleviate poverty, meet basic needs, and help the citizens to get something popular which majorities of them love to have. Some think adequate housing is not so much a consumer good as a citizens' right, so government has a duty (where necessary) to provide it. Whatever their reasoning, politicians have tended to see the task as 'spending on' rather than 'investing in' better housing. Many economists and some public servants who see housing as an aid to consumption rather than production have accused politicians of diverting resources from investment and growth into housing 'consumption' chiefly to curry favor with voters.

So influences of at least three kinds have converged on policy makers.

Their housing policies are seen as spending rather than investing (so don't spend too much). They are seen by some experts as distorting efficient markets rather than correcting inefficient ones (so don't interfere too much). Aids to homeowners have helped more well-off than hard-up households (so be a bit shamefaced about them). They ought to be matched by equivalent aids to tenants, but mass rent subsidies or public housing provisions cost the government more than aids to homebuyers do (and they may reach fewer swinging voters).

Second, are you sure you know what you're doing? There are uncertainties about who actually benefits from some of the policies. Do aids to homebuyers merely raise the prices that can be extracted from them for the money they borrow or the houses they buy? Or if the aids work, how many of them help well-off households who could do without them rather than those who could not buy houses without them? Do landlords capture rent

subsidies by raising their rents? Do tenants get any benefit from tax concessions to landlords?

Third, those questions of fact and principle are usually complicated by conflicts of sectional interest. Homebuyers want tax concessions for homebuyers, landlords want them for landlords, financial institutions want them for their depositors. Builders want aids to go to buyers of new houses rather than old ones. Local interests want public housing brought into or kept out of their neighborhoods. They all lobby the policy makers, and the policies they get incorporate varying mixtures of social principle, economic theory, electoral calculations and business patronage.

Those mixed origins account for the variety of housing policies, sometimes including inconsistent or contradictory policies, to be found in developed countries in recent times. We will list the main policy devices that governments have used. Some of their effects depend on the context of other policies and market conditions in which they are applied, so the shopping list of policy items is followed by sketches of some national housing strategies to show how the items have been combined in coherent (or sometimes incoherent) programs. Then follows a strategy you may favor if you recognize household capital and labor as productive.

But first, a reminder about the uses of this book

Before you read the next pages, remember that this is a course of study in practical, institutional economics. You have just read some suggested principles of housing policy. You are about to read some quite long and detailed lists of institutional devices by which such principles may be applied in practice. Through the rest of this book you will meet many such lists of practical alternatives and possibilities. Should you try to memorize them? No. Read them, noticing how the items do or don't relate to the relevant principles; then merely remember that the lists are there, for future reference. That lets you use this book for two distinct purposes. It is a source of principles and skills, to be learned and exercised. It is also a reference book, a manual to keep by you for practical use. For example you can reach for the book and look up the following lists if you find yourself advising a government or political party about housing policy options; or advising a homebuyers' or builders' association what to lobby for; or reviewing housing problems and policies as an economic journalist. So do read and understand the following lists, as an exercise in relating principles to policies. But there is no need to memorize them. Just remember where to find them if you need them.

Even by this book's standards this catalogue of housing policies is long, detailed and (you may well find) tedious. Its purpose is corrective. Texts which don't treat households as productive tend to neglect this subject, mistake its principles and neglect its practice. By act or omission they encourage their readers to support policies which leave many millions of hard-up people less productive, independent and happy than they could otherwise be. It is worth taking time and trouble to correct such mistakes.

AIDS TO HOMEBUYERS

Titles An English homebuyer may spend time and money having a lawyer search the back history of the title-to-ownership that she is buying, to see that the seller genuinely owns what he is purporting to sell, and that it is free of debt or other encumbrances. Most other governments in the developed world have introduced varieties of Torrens title (named after the Englishman who introduced it in Australia in 1858). Government keeps a map and register of land titles, each with its owner's name. Some also record any current debts or encumbrances on it. That is the only lawful title, and any member of the public can see it. Sales, and in some countries mortgage loans and other encumbrances, are not enforceable until registered on the title. So buyers can know, cheaply and quickly, what they are buying.

Building regulation Government regulates houses' structural safety, fire safety, plumbing and electrical standards, and sometimes dryness, ventilation and other health-related qualities. Some governments enforce the rules effectively, others don't. Some discourage substandard rental housing by rent-controlling it.

Planning regulation Government zones land for housing and other uses, chiefly to segregate incompatible uses. Some governments regulate the size, shape, height, population density, car-parking provisions, design style and other qualities of new housing. (*Here*, the planning authority may say, you may build apartment blocks up to 8 storeys, with up to 4 times the floor area that you have land area, as long as you have no more than 80 bedspaces per hectare and no less than 6 carspaces per 10 bedspaces...etc. Whereas *there*, you may only build family houses on garden blocks, of

which the house must cover less than half, with its front at least 5 metres from the street and its sides at least 2 metres from its side fences...etc.) Some residential land-use codes are very detailed. They aim to give households effective choices not only of house but also of street and neighborhood character. They work well for that good purpose if they are politically stable and long-lasting. They also have some actual or potential disadvantages (depending on your values). They can be designed to segregate richer from poorer residents, harmfully to the poorer ones. (They can even let rich households get their land cheaper than poor households get theirs.) And the effect of the zoning on land prices can allow fortunes to be made, if there is unstable or corrupt government, by buying land in low-use zones (like house-and-garden zones) then getting it rezoned for more profitable use (like building eight floors of apartments).

Taxation Governments do any or all of the following:

- Encourage lending to homebuyers by exempting from income tax the interest earned by depositors in housing finance institutions. This may be accompanied by a bulk tax on the institution's total deposits.

- Exempt homebuyers from income tax on the interest they pay on their housing loans.

- Charge residential owners lower property taxes than businesses pay.

- Among residential owners, charge owner-occupiers lower property taxes than landlords pay.

- Though not defined as taxation, public utilities' differential pricing policies can have similar aims and effects. In some countries households are charged more than business users, and in some countries less, for telephones, power, gas, water and sewerage, rubbish removal. Or the discrimination may be between household and household, for example where pensioners get services at cheaper rates.

- Tax imputed rent. Tenants pay rent from their taxed incomes for the use of their houses. But once their houses are paid for, owner-occupiers get the same day-to-day use of their houses for nothing. Some governments see the use of the house as an item of real income, which should accordingly be income-taxed. So they 'impute' a rent (by estimating what rent a tenant would pay for the house) and add it to the owner-occupier's taxable income. That is meant to achieve fairer taxation between homeowners and tenants, which it does. For the same purpose, those who favor taxing imputed rent also think homebuyers should pay their loan interest out of taxed income. Accordingly some governments income-tax both the income which pays loan interest, and imputed rent. That reduces inequities between homeowners and tenants. But it increases inequities between households and other producers. Commercial and industrial producers do not pay company tax or income tax on the income with which they pay their loan interest, or on the actual or imputed rent of any land and buildings they use. Government treats those outlays as costs of production, and taxes only the firms' profits and dividends. So if it income-taxes households on those items it discriminates against them. Buying and using any dollar's worth of productive property then costs households more than it would cost a profit-seeking business. That helps any business to outbid any household for available funds, and for any land or buildings open to alternative residential or business uses. Depending on the presence or absence of other tax policies (such as depreciation allowances and negative gearing, described below) it may also advantage landlords against households trying to buy houses. Thus policies intended to correct inequities between homeowners and tenants have the effect of *creating* inequities, and biasing capital allocations, between households and businesses. Conclusion: Instead of taxing the homeowners to reduce inequity between homeowners and tenants it would be better to help the tenants. How? Up to some reasonable limit, let them subtract their rent payments from their taxable incomes, as firms do. Help those who want to buy houses to buy them. And see below for some other aids to tenants.

Funds are needed (i) to build replacements and additions to the housing stock, and (ii) to finance changes of ownership. Proportions vary, but there are usually four or five sales of existing houses for every new house built. That means that of every four or five demands for funds, only one competes with other investors for real resources of labor, bricks and mortar, etc. So a simple way to see the system is this: (i) New house-building competes with other industries for investment funds and real resources; but (ii) the resale of existing houses does not use real resources or add to the housing stock, and to the extent that it uses borrowed money it can be seen as financed from a revolving fund – i.e. the total flows are *as if* the proceeds from selling existing houses are either spent on buying other houses or deposited with the institutions which lend for housing. If the whole available housing finance is too little, or too difficult for

households to borrow because of high deposit requirements or interest rates or sloped credit, then there may be housing shortages, and landlords are likely to outbid households for some of the housing the households would prefer to own. If on the other hand the loans available to households are too big and easy they may inflate land and housing prices harmfully. You know the reasons why market forces can't be trusted to get the allocations right, either between housing and other industries or between household and household. Some collective decisions are needed. If government wants the citizens to get the amount and quality of housing they want to pay for, it must see that financial institutions offer loans on terms which make them available to all the households who would rather pay for their housing by buying it than by renting it. No government has quite achieved that, but some have tried quite hard. Besides the tax measures listed above, their financial measures have included these:

- Grants. Government gives cash grants, to help meet deposit requirements, to households buying their first houses.

- Public savings banks or specialized housing banks attract household savings and lend them to homebuyers. If they can't attract enough deposits for their housing purposes, government may top up their funds from taxation, or selling government bonds, or by creating credit for the purpose.

- Private savings banks and building societies are given privileges not allowed to other banks – for example, to pay interest on ordinary deposit accounts or cheque accounts, when other banks are not allowed to do so – on condition that they lend to homebuyers. They may pay a 'bulk' tax which allows them to pay tax-free interest to their depositors, as some countries' post-office savings banks and British building societies do.

- Government provides mortgage loan insurance. Lenders who are insured against loss can be encouraged to lend at lower interest, or to households with lower incomes and deposits.

- Government may regulate the rates of interest that may be charged on housing loans. That usually also limits the rates the institutions can offer their depositors. If that is not to drive the depositors away, it may need to be accompanied by other measures: some compensating privileges (as above) for the institutions or their depositors; similar regulation of other interest rates, so that the housing rates have no special disadvantage; boundary controls to stop people from evading the national regulations by lending abroad to unregulated foreigners.

- Portfolio requirements. Financial institutions can be required to lend specified proportions of their funds for housing. Building societies have been required to lend only for housing; savings banks to lend only to government or for housing. Insurers and superannuation funds have earned tax concessions by lending specified proportions of their funds for housing or to government. Within those wholesale rules the institutions may be free to retail as they like, i.e. to decide how much to lend on what terms to which landlords or homebuyers. And borrowers are free to choose the housing they want, but are under the market discipline of borrowing and buying only what they can pay for. Bankers and orthodox economists used to condemn these regulations, and have got many of them repealed. But in most cases the regulations have coincided with record rates of house-building *and* record rates of recorded economic growth, and probably also with unusually fast growth of unrecorded household productivity.

- Secondary mortgage markets. Lending to homebuyers is a specialized and time-consuming business. With loans to buy existing houses the lender must check the title and value of the houses, and the buyers' capacities to pay. To lend for new houses the lender may also need to check building designs and estimates, see that they comply with building and planning regulations, then deal out the loan bit by bit to pay the builder as the stages of construction are completed. Savings banks, building societies and other housing finance institutions specialize in that work. But when the house is up and occupied, collecting the regular loan repayments is simpler, and in some countries the lender can 'sell' the loan to another investor for a lump sum, which can immediately be lent to the next homebuyer. Thus funds are attracted from investors (for example, superannuation funds) who from lack of retailing capacity would not otherwise lend for housing.

- Level instead of sloped credit. When lenders add the rate of inflation to the real interest rate on big long-term loans, that requires borrowers to make very high early repayments. That 'sloped credit' effect has excluded many potential homebuyers from the market in periods of substantial inflation. To reduce the slope, lenders may design 'low front' loans. Repayments start low and rise over time as the bor-

rower's income rises in step with inflation. If the early repayments are less than the annual interest bill, the deficit is added to the capital debt. That is called 'deficit financing': a few years into the repayment period you may owe more than you first borrowed, but you hope the inflation that caused the trouble will eventually cure it by inflating your income to allow a positive rate of repayment. Chapter 52, on inflation, will argue that it would often be better to avoid sloped credit altogether by indexing the capital debt, rather than the interest rate, to the rate of inflation.

Public housing aids to homebuyers Public housing can help to beat the double bind if it sets rent low enough to leave tenants some spare income from which to save homebuying deposits. But public housing can also be used to help homebuyers more directly:

- Public housing is sold to sitting tenants. To pay for it they may have to save and borrow like any other homebuyer; they may be given credit by the agency which sells them the house; their debt may be reduced by re-defining past rent payments as contributions to purchase; the sale price may be set below market price. If the sales to tenants aim at a permanent change in the ratio of tenants to homeowners, the proceeds may go to other government uses. But if renting then buying is to be a regular option for future generations of tenants, sale proceeds should go to build or buy more public housing to replace the stock sold.

- Public housing is rental-purchased. The household moves in as a tenant, but with an owner's freedom and obligation to maintain the house, and with a rent calculated like a loan repayment to buy the house over a period. At the end of the period rents cease and the tenant becomes the owner. If they leave before that, the landlord sells the house and gives them whatever share of the proceeds their rental-purchase payments have bought by that date. Because it offers ownership without any double bind or capital deposit, this can be the best way of all to extend ownership, without any public cost or subsidy, to households with low incomes. Question: Why use rental-purchase – why not lend the household the whole price of the house, to buy it in the ordinary way? Answer: If the household has no savings and a low or insecure income, both parties may feel safer with rental-purchase. A loan to a poor household for the whole price of a house is risky. If the borrower fails to pay, the procedure for repossessing and selling the house can be time-consuming and expensive. It is humiliating for the defaulter, and can formally bankrupt her if the house sells for less than the debt on it. So rental-purchase is safer for the agency selling the house, and acceptable to low-income households who won't risk borrowing to buy. At worst, to leave a house because you can no longer manage such a high rent is a prudent sacrifice, not a shameful default.

- Public agencies have usually offered only their own housing stock for rental-purchase. But buyers have wider choices if the rules allow them to go house-hunting in the open market. When they find a house which they like and can afford, the public agent buys it and lets it to them on rental-purchase, at a rent calculated to repay the government with interest over the rental-purchase period.

- Public suppliers sell houses on the open market in competition with private suppliers. They may do it for socialist reasons, to combine non-profit supply with buyers' market choices. They may do it simply to augment housing supply during housing shortages. They may do it for purposes of welfare or efficient allocation, if they can sell at lower prices on lower deposits to marginal homebuyers who can't afford the private suppliers' prices or terms. Public/private competition can help to keep the public suppliers economical and attentive to households' market preferences, which in turn may improve the public suppliers' design and choice of public rental housing. The competition can also discipline the private suppliers, especially where conditions tempt them to over-charge for the land they sell with their houses. A public supplier kept one Australian city's land unusually cheap for a generation by supplying a third or more of its new housing and land each year. He used to say that the competition between his public organization and his private competitors 'keeps *us* lean and *them* honest'.

AIDS TO TENANTS

Public rental housing has provided as much as 40 per cent of some developed countries' housing, and as little as 2 per cent of others'. It has taken a wide variety of forms from cottages to towers, and been allocated and managed on a wide variety of principles.

At worst, public rental housing has been expensive, ill-designed, segregated, stigmatized, bureaucratically mismanaged, socially degrading, doing next to nothing for the household productivity of its occupiers. It often

serves the poorest people worst where it is most accurately 'allocated to need', i.e. where welfare tenants who manage to find jobs and climb back above the breadline are evicted because they can no longer pass the public housing means test. Where public housing has had the urban planning aim of packing the working classes into towers and barracks in order to limit the lateral growth of cities (as in Britain through the third quarter of the twentieth century) its designers have often surrounded the barracks with so much barren space that it fails in its urban as well as its social and household purposes.

At best, public rental housing can house people well and helpfully. It need not segregate or stigmatize them, or penalize them when they prosper. It can give house and garden forms to those who want them and not to those who don't. It can allow more secure tenure than many private landlords provide. Government can subsidize its rents, or set them to cover costs, or set them to return profits to finance more public housing. Where demand for it exceeds supply it can be allocated (i.e. rationed) by waiting time or by judgments of relative need; at rents adjustable to changing capacities to pay; at locations which individual households need for working, educational, health or other reasons; and so on. Difficult judgments have to be made about tenants' rights, obligations to the landlord and each other, real or pretended hardships, rent arrears, requests to move house from one place to another, and so on. Good management can cope with most of those fairly and unoppressively. Many of those troubles tend to be less the more 'normal' the public housing is. It is generally best sprinkled down every street, indistinguishable from housing in any other tenure.

As with public housing for sale, public housing for rent can affect the private market around it. If public supply is effective at reducing general housing shortages and is available in significant quantities in acceptable forms at restrained rents, private competitors will find it hard to impose oppressive conditions or charge excessive rents.

Economics and ideology Does public housing improve welfare, equality, efficient allocation and productivity? Are the taxpayers doing the tenants a favor, or vice versa? Answers to those questions depend partly on facts. Do the rents repay the costs, including any loan interest costs, over time? If some tenants are subsidized, are they subsidized from tax revenue or from other tenants' rents (so that the poorest are subsidized by the next poorest)? Answers also depend on how long a view you take: the taxpayers may be losing now but gain in the long run. And answers may depend on the relative weight your values attach to the 'consumable' qualities of the housing and to its productivity. Where rent surpluses cover any individual rent reductions and total rents repay costs within the lifetime of the houses, as has happened where substantial public housing has existed through periods of full employment, the tenants don't owe the taxpayers anything. On the contrary, over time they buy big capital assets for the taxpayers, just as tenants do for private landlords.

But how should their rents be set? Ideologists in principle, and public housing managers in practice, face a dilemma. In the jargon of the trade they must choose between historic cost and current cost renting. Each embodies a good social principle – but the principles are incompatible.

Historic cost Believers in historic cost rent think a main purpose of public rental housing should be to pre-vent lifelong income transfers from tenants to landlords. Public tenants should get as many as possible of the financial advantages of homebuyers. Rents should be set to recover the cost of building the houses and the continuing costs of maintaining and managing them. But that should be all: that's what 'non-profit housing' should *mean*.

But under that rule, inequities will develop over time. With economic growth and inflation, new houses will have to pay higher rents than old ones pay. And the old houses don't keep their old tenants for ever. Suppose that two identical households with identical incomes move into public housing this year. By luck or locational preference one gets a 50-year-old house, the other gets a new house. Because the old one is solider or better located, the houses have identical market value. But with historical cost rents, the rent of the new house may be twice the rent of the old one, and that difference will persist through the lifetimes of the households. That's not fair. So people turn to the 'current cost' principle.

Average cost Regard the whole public housing stock as a collective resource. Total rent must cover total costs without profit, but it should be averaged over all tenants so that all contribute equally (or proportionately to their means and the value of their houses) and share equally in any necessary rent increases over time. Sounds fair? But over the generations the old houses will pay for themselves several times over, just as if they were yield-ing perpetual income to capitalist landlords; and tenants of old houses will be subsidizing new houses, whose tenants will accordingly be getting them below cost and not paying their way. What's fair about *that*? What

became of the principle that public tenants should each pay their way, but no more?

It is a true dilemma, with no neat or ideal solution. Most governments have started their public housing programs on the historic cost principle, then shifted to the average or current cost principle after a generation or so as the old/new inequities became obvious.

Cooperatives offer alternative forms of non-profit ownership. Tenants who can't get credit to buy houses individually can't usually get it collectively either, so most rental housing cooperatives are part-financed or guaranteed by government or major charities. A public housing agency may 'joint venture' with a cooperative, supplying the deposit money and credit guarantees which enable the cooperative to borrow most of its funds from private financial institutions. Advantages: the tenants may get more say in the management of their housing. By attracting private funds the public funds go further to fund more low-cost housing than they could fund on their own. Some Scandinavian cooperatives allow part of their members' rent payments to buy them equity shares in the cooperative, so they receive landlord services, have elements of self-management, and have some of the financial advantages of home ownership.

Public contracts with private landlords For com-bining public control with private funds to produce low-cost housing there is a range of possible public/private mixes. Starting from the public end there is public hous-ing built with funds which government borrows from private citizens and institutions. Cooperatives common-ly use some public funds to attract private funds, and have non-profit but non-government management. Fuller private ownership with lighter public control is achieved in Canada and some West European countries by contracts between government and private landlord-investors. The investors undertake to provide agreed forms of low cost housing at rents fixed by agreed for-mulae. In exchange, government gives them financial guarantees, planning permission, tax holidays, rent sub-sidies or other public aids.

Rent subsidies Suppose you are a lobbyist for private landlord interests, or you are a disinterested pol-icy-maker with more confidence in competitive private producers than in bureaucrats. Rather than use public capital to fund construction of public housing, why not use public revenue to fund the citizens to house them-selves independently like everyone else? How? By transferring income. Instead of bureaucrats building houses, have them identify the needy households and pay them rent allowances for as long as they need them. That lets the people find their own housing and pay for it in the ordinary way. If private landlords are not providing enough of it, believers in rent allowances hope that the stronger demand provided by the rent allowances will attract investors to build more of it.

This – i.e., accurately directed income transfer – is the compassionate conservative's commonest response to housing hardship. There is a lot to be said for it:

- It allows tenants the same choice, independence and dignity in their housing arrangements as everyone else. Also privacy – nobody need know they are getting public help.

- The housing may be better, if competition makes private landlords pay more attention to tenants' preferences than public landlords do.

- The help can start as soon as it is needed, whereas public housing often has long waiting lists.

- The help can stop when the need stops, whereas public housing once built is there to stay, and so are many of its tenants, long after they could afford to move out and pay private rents.

- Some public housing systems have established such strong tenant rights that nothing can be done about tenants who menace their neighbors' safety, property and peace of mind by bad behavior. Even if public landlords can evict offensive tenants they may not choose to, if eviction would remove the only available public housing aid from the suffering women and children in the offenders' households. For those households, rent allowances can divide responsibilities helpfully, especially if the allowances are paid wherever possible to women members of the households. Private landlords evict wrongdoers, but the rent allowance enables households to try again, sometimes without their offending members.

Some Left critics, some public landlords and some tenants' associations respond to those arguments with some or all of these:

- Public housing can give tenants more secure tenure and more reliable standards of maintenance than many private landlords do.

- Private landlording generally increases inequalities of wealth and income. Public housing generally reduces them.

- Private landlords rarely help tenants to become owners. Public landlords can offer them a range of aids to saving and buying, from low rents which allow them to save to rental-purchase which avoids the double bind altogether.

- If public housing rents are set to cover costs so that the housing pays its way there should be no objection to tenants staying as long as they like. If they lose income and need to be subsidized, rent reductions can be just as prompt, flexible and temporary as rent allowances to private tenants can be.

- If government and public opinion want them to be, public landlords can be as tough as private landlords with misbehaving tenants. Where necessary they can also move suffering women and children and conceal their new addresses from their persecutors. That sort of flight is harder if ill-treated women must do their own househunting, convince a new private landlord, offer a security deposit and rent in advance, etc.

- The private supply and pricing of rental housing is not always as responsive and competitive as the conservative policy assumes. War, migration, recovery from depression, or fast economic growth can push housing demand ahead of supply. It takes time to build houses, and more time to expand the capacity to build them (by training more skilled tradesmen, building more brickworks, etc.). Housing shortages, with high rents and crowding and profiteering, can continue for many years. Public landlords may not be able to increase the supply of housing in those conditions, but they can abstain from profiteering.

- Private rental housing of the kind provided by rational investors tends to have a systematic bias against family tenants, and against their preferred and most productive kinds of housing. For best returns investors tend to build blocks of flats. The rent they can get from a household depends a good deal on the proportion of earners in it. An income per bed is best of all. Two or three earners sharing an apartment can outbid a larger family depending on one breadwinner. So rental investors generally build for adults if they can. Scarcely anywhere in the twentieth century have they built house-and-garden forms of family housing for rent. The more rational the investors, the more they tend to build housing unhelpful to tenants with children; to prefer adult tenants; and to try for rents which working-class families with non-earning housewives, or lone parents with children, cannot afford. Public landlords can reverse all those policies, if governments want them to.

Most Left policy-makers in mixed economies are happy to leave the luxury, tourist, and other affluent rental housing markets to private enterprise. Many also welcome private competition through the middle and lower ranges of the market where public or cooperative landlords operate. But experience suggests that wholly private supply of rental housing, with rent allowances as the only public aids, will not provide the housing types or locations that many low-income households want and can use well; and with big numbers of subsidized tenants and no competition from public housing, landlords may well raise rents to take a share of the rent allowances. A conclusion: public rent allowances are a good safety net for a variety of tenants who can't find, don't like or are not acceptable to public landlords. But they work best, and can only work at all well, in combination with substantial public housing supply and aids to home-purchase.

Regulation   Landlords themselves often regulate crowding, subletting, noise, animals, and the uses that tenants can make of their housing. Governments regulate the physical condition of rental housing: its weatherproofing, fire exits, ventilation, plumbing and wiring, general state of repair. Modern regulations often extend to the conditions of tenancy: what landlords may lawfully take as security deposits and rent in advance; what rights they have to inspect the premises or otherwise invade tenants' privacy; what notice they must give if they want tenants to leave; what action they can take (such as seizing tenants' property) to recover unpaid rent. Some governments let landlords hold tenants' security deposits. Others don't – because it can be hard for tenants to recover them from dishonest landlords, deposits have to be held by public offices or other third parties. Equal opportunity laws try to prevent landlords from rejecting tenants on grounds of race, gender, family composition or physical disability. Most systems have landlord-tenant tribunals, as well as recourse to ordinary courts, to enforce the rules and resolve disputes about them. The rules were not introduced without good cause – you can read them as indicating what some landlords and tenants once did and might still do without them. But they would be cumbersome and expensive if they had to be actively enforced or disputed in many individual tenancies. In most systems they don't have to be: the rules are peacefully observed most of the time by most of the parties. So (unlike behavior on the roads, for example) it is not an expensive area of law and order. Nor is there usually much disagreement about the general principles of regulation.

But that is not true of the final item on this list of aids to tenants, which is hotly disputed, especially by economists, as follows.

Rent control   Most Economics textbooks which mention rent controls tell you this about them:

> Rent controls reduce the rate of return to housing investment. That deters investors and encourages them to switch their funds to other industries. That reduces the supply of new housing, and intensifies the shortage of housing. The excess of demand over supply pushes house prices and rents up. Rent controls can't really prevent that for long: with too many households competing for too few houses the richer households will soon be outbidding the poorer ones with offers of illegal 'key money' and black market rent. Existing landlords accept those gains. But as unlawful gains they are too risky to attract new investors, so the controls continue to discourage new supply. Rents therefore rise higher, and tenants are worse served, than they would have been without the controls. Conclusion: Rent controls don't help tenants, they hurt them.

In real life it ain't necessarily so. With honest administration, appropriate publicity and most tenants insisting on their rights, many governments have controlled rents quite effectively, sometimes for long periods. Their economic effects depend on the local facts of the case. For example:

1. Economists' objections to rent control do not apply if any shortfall in the private supply of rental housing is matched by a sufficient public supply.

2. If rents are controlled in wartime when new house building is banned, they prevent inflation and profiteering without any accompanying ill effects. Most economists accept the case for rent and price controls in the special conditions of wartime.

3. When there is persisting pressure of demand – for example from fast economic growth, immigration, or war damage – rents can be controlled (as in much of western Europe for 20 years or more after the second World War) at levels which are high enough to attract investment while preventing unreasonable profiteering. Most investors who build new rental housing are interested in reliable long-term returns. So they invest, or not, according to the normal long-term rent levels that they expect, and there need be no harm in imposing those levels immediately by regulation, to prevent windfall profits, and hardship to tenants, while the shortages continue.

4. Some governments define minimum acceptable standards for rental housing, and control the rents of substandard units for as long as they remain

substandard. That helps some tenants by improving their housing, and others by restraining their rents. It may hurt some by motivating their landlords to demolish their housing, or to do it up and rent it up beyond their means.

5. Rent controls can have important effects on the competition for housing resources, especially the competition between landlords and households for the ownership of the housing which – whoever owns it – the households will use and pay for. If rent controls discourage investors from switching funds from other industries to build new rental housing, that may harden the market against tenants and reduce some household productivity, as the orthodox theory expects. But it need not have that effect if it is accompanied by public action to maintain sufficient supply. If rent controls improve equalities between public and private tenants, and at the same time discourage private investors from competing with homebuyers for available funds and houses, that may enable more households to become owners, paying lower loan interest and house prices than they would otherwise have faced.

Conclusion: As with other incentives and disincentives for private landlords, the economic effects of rent controls are theoretically uncertain. To predict them you need local knowledge of the types of control, the market conditions in which they will be applied, and the other public policies that will accompany them.

Because they have costs, and because they have been and can be misused, rent controls are best avoided if possible, for example if market forces, aids to homebuyers, and supplies of public housing are together sufficient to discipline the private rental market in a competitive way. But there are other conditions in which they can combine with other housing policies to greatly improve the supply and distribution of housing, its ownership, and its productivity.

Taxation One way to help tenants would be to exempt their rent payments from income tax. When employees get rent-free housing from their employers, some countries do and some don't estimate its value and tax it as part of the tenant's income. No country has exempted all tenants from income tax on their rent payments. *Reasons for doing it*: It would reduce tenants' general disadvantages, and it would make fairer tax treatment of tenants and homeowners wherever the homeowners are not taxed on imputed rent of their houses. *Reasons against*: It would increase other inequalities. The higher the rent and the richer the ten-

ant, the bigger the concession. Rich tenants of penthouses would get big tax gifts, tenants too poor to pay income tax would get none. Means-tested rent subsidies are both cheaper and more effective.

AIDS TO LANDLORDS

Private landlords are a diverse lot. They range from financial institutions with agents managing large property holdings for them, through professional landlords who build apartment blocks, others who rack-rent old slums, to the salary earner who buys an apartment or two as an investment, and the tradesman who leaves his widow a pair of attached cottages for her to live in one chiefly on the rent from the other. Some national surveys also show quite a lot of rent-free tenants, mostly employees or kin of their landlords.

Of those diverse owners many but by no means all are chiefly interested in the rent. Some are more interested in capital effects: they buy in and out of property booms for capital gains, or they hold property as a safe way to protect capital value against inflation. Some hold property for some future use, and accept whatever rent they can get meanwhile. Some inherit property. Some use their own money to build or buy rental housing; others borrow, often heavily, and repay their loans (and thus buy their properties) from their tenants' rent. Some of the borrowers compete for funds with homebuyers; others borrow from sources not accessible to homebuyers.

It is difficult to design public policies which will have uniformly good effects on the behavior of such diverse landlords. A tax concession which induces one investor to add to the housing stock may induce another to outbid homebuyers for available funds and housing, and turn would-be owner-occupiers into unwilling tenants. A quality control which gets one slum improved may get another demolished. One landlord may pass public benefits on to tenants, another's market situation may allow him to pocket them. And so on – accurate public action tends to depend on good local knowledge, and the coordination of a number of public measures.

Measures which modern governments have tried include these:

Funds Government gives or (usually) lends money to private housing investors, commonly to top up funds from other sources. Dutch or German investors could once supply 10 per cent of the cost of new apartment blocks from their own money, borrow 70 per cent from private banks or pension funds, and borrow the remaining 20 per cent from government. The government may attach conditions, perhaps limiting the size and rents of the apartments to direct them to low or middle income earners. Some critics dislike helping profit-seeking landlords like that, and much of the European funding has gone to 'independent' rather than private landlords: i.e. to non-profit housing associations of various kinds.

Taxation Property taxes and income taxes can each be designed to affect investors' incentives.

Property taxes may be designed to attract or deter rental housing investment. To attract it, tax housing at lower rates than other property. Give new rental investors tax holidays, i.e. a few years at low or zero rates. To attract owner occupiers rather than landlords and tenants, tax rental housing at the same rate as other commercial property but tax owner-occupiers at a lower rate. That last arrangement tends to happen in districts where commercial and residential uses compete for scarce land, but an owner-occupiers' majority commands the local government.

Where the landlords have more influence with national government, government may allow them either or both of depreciation, and negative gearing – as follows.

Depreciation When you study taxation you will learn that most tax systems apply the principle that the costs of running a business are tax deductible, but the cost of buying it is not. You get no tax help to buy land; but the costs of sowing and harvesting grain are then deductible from the income you get from sale of the crop, to arrive at the profit income on which you pay income tax. With land which lasts for ever the distinction between capital purchase and running costs is clear. But with machinery and other capital items which wear out, most countries' tax collectors have been persuaded to treat the wearing out of capital items as a running cost deductible from taxable income. (Suppose you pay $100,000 for a truck. You get no tax help with that capital purchase. In its first year the truck earns you $80,000. From that revenue you subtract the $50,000 you spent on fuel and drivers' wages. You seem to have made $30,000 profit. But you expect the truck to wear out in five years, its resale value has already dropped $20,000, so you reckon that this year it has lost a fifth – $20,000 – of its value. You knock that off your taxable profit which comes down to $10,000, on which you pay income tax. The $20,000 worth of wear-out is known as depreciation. Over five years its tax treatment will get you tax exemption from the whole price of a replacement truck.)

Thus in principle you use taxed income (or capital

funds) to buy a capital asset in the first place, but maintaining and (indirectly) replacing it is treated thereafter as a tax-deductible running cost. How are buildings treated – like land, or like machinery? Most tax regimes treat them like land. Maintaining them is a deductible expense, replacing them is not. Owners can deduct maintenance costs from taxable income, but no depreciation. But there are solid gains for landlords if they are ever allowed to deduct both. So although properly maintained apartment blocks don't usually begin to lose value for a generation or more, governments wanting to encourage private rental investors may allow notional depreciation of their buildings for tax purposes. That may attract funds from other industries into rental housing investment. It may also encourage landlords who can get depreciation allowances to bid funds and building resources away from homebuyers who can't. The second tendency may be stronger if government also allows negative gearing.

Negative gearing Recall the case of the landlord who 'geared up' $10,000 of his own money with $65,000 of borrowed money to buy a $75,000 house, which he let to a tenant, whose rent over time repaid the loan and thus bought the house for the landlord. In that example the calculations were simplified by assuming that there was no inflation so the interest rate represents real interest. In real life the interest rate is likely to be higher because it includes an element of inflation. Suppose the landlord pays annual interest at 10 per cent, while netting only 6 per cent in rent income. He seems to be losing. But (i) he takes the whole 10 per cent interest payment off his taxable income, and (ii) the market value of the house is keeping pace with inflation and adding to his net worth as time goes by. There are two ways to see how he gains at the taxpayers' expense. (i) As conventionally understood, his year-by-year interest losses on the housing deal overflow to exempt part of his other income also from tax. (ii) If you understand sloped credit you will understand that the inflated interest rate is best understood as returning capital to the lender at the rate of inflation; so the landlord is beating a basic tax rule by getting tax exemption for part of the purchase of a capital asset.

Summary Negative gearing means buying assets with borrowed money in a way which allows an apparent loss on the interest costs of the transaction to reduce the taxation of the borrower's *other* income as well as the income from the new asset. It can be prevented if the law 'quarantines' each purchase and allows its costs to be set against its own income alone; or if the law treats real interest only (the interest rate minus the inflation rate) as a genuine business cost for tax purposes.

NATIONAL HOUSING STRATEGIES

You noticed how many of those policies for homebuyers, tenants and landlords can have different effects depending on the market conditions in which they are applied and the other policies which accompany them. It follows that to be effective, policy-makers can't simply pick and choose policies on the individual merits and likely effects of each policy. A set of compatible, mutually supporting policies needs to be combined in a coherent national strategy. To illustrate, sketches of five modern strategies follow. Only their main principles are indicated, so the sketches are greatly simplified.

The United States

The US has tried four main approaches in modern times: financial aids to home ownership; public housing; public demolition for private urban redevelopment; and experiments with housing allowances to private tenants. The aids to ownership are permanent. The other three are not so much complementary policies as successive failures to solve persisting problems.

Federal Acts of 1931-4 created national institutions to provide aids to home purchase which continue to this day. Public and private banks lend homebuyers up to 80 per cent of the value of their houses. The loans are for long terms with level repayments which include interest and capital repayments. (Since steady inflation set in some 'low start' loans have been designed to reduce the sloped credit effect.) Government provides mortgage loan insurance and guarantees (to protect lenders from defaulting borrowers) and a secondary mortgage market in which financial institutions which don't want to retail housing loans can buy them ready-made. Homebuyers' interest payments are deductible from taxable income. With these aids about two thirds of US households have become owner-occupiers.

Public housing is less than 2 per cent of US housing. It is strictly means-tested, for the very poor rather than for employed workers' households. Some of it is a poverty trap: if you get work and prosper, you are evicted. In *Housing in Capitalist Societies (1980)* Cedric Pugh characterized it: 'American public housing became identified with undesirable social consequences. It faced local and central political hostility; it accentuated segregation; it was highly stigmatized for its "welfare" image and its dominant use by blacks in some cities; it was confined to sites which other users did not want; it had some bureaucratic tendencies; and it

was relatively expensive. This imagery forced policy makers ... to use other methods to express social aims in housing.'

One of the other methods was urban renewal. From 1949 local governments could buy old buildings compulsorily, empty them and demolish them, sell the sites to private developers, and bill the federal government for most of any loss on the deal. Corrupt local officials could thus convey big federal subsidies to the private developers, and some did. Honest or not, the common effect of the projects was to replace cheap housing by dearer housing, and blacks by whites. Ideas are working parts, especially when they reinforce self-interests:

> During 1940-59 there was a massive migration of southern blacks to the northern industrial cities, and they settled in the inner urban areas. Their low incomes led them to crowd older sub-standard tenements and some inner-area housing. Simultaneously, the rising incomes among middle-class whites enabled them to move to lower-priced land and more spacious new housing in the outer suburban areas. Town planners interpreted this double migratory movement as a chain of 'blight' and 'flight' in a continuous pattern of urban decay. In effect, planners had a strong belief in the idea that bad housing attracted lower income groups, causing the flight of the middle classes. The low per-household expenditure on housing would then, so the theory concluded, result in a continuous deterioration of property, spreading into neighbouring areas. Renewal was thus seen as an imperative to reverse the blight and to apply structural surgery to correct urban obsolescence. These ideas grew out of some older theories developed by the Chicago school of human ecologists. The theory and its extensions are invalid...' In practice researchers found that 'the programme had displaced the poor and brought anguish to the urban blacks. Scarce low-income housing had been destroyed and the programme had diverted resources away from social housing to middle-income housing and commercial enterprise.'

> *– Housing in Capitalist Societies*, 249

Some local authorities turned from demolishing old housing to doing it up, sometimes to use as public housing. Researchers found that sort of rehabilitation to be – in the US – the most effective way for public funds to improve poor people's housing.

The federal government next financed a lot of research into possible uses of housing allowances. Who should get them, what would they cost, how should they be administered? Would tenants spend them on housing or other things? Would landlords raise rents to pre-empt their tenants' allowances? Several million tenants now benefit from a number of schemes, but there are still no general allowances for all poor American tenants.

Between poor tenants at the bottom of the income scale and well-off tenants and owners in its top two thirds, a third 'housing class' developed. By the 1970s about 40 million Americans – one household in every five – were living as owners, part-owners or tenants in shelter which the law did not formally define as houses. Some had shanties, some had caravans, many had pre-fabricated transportable houses which are houses by anyone else's standards but don't qualify for US mort-gage loans. Because their ownership can be separated from the ownership of the land they stand on, and they don't qualify for long-term low-interest housing loans, they have to be bought on hire purchase at higher rates of interest. They lose value over time faster than solid houses do. Many of them pay rent to landlords for their land. So like private tenants, some dwellers in caravans and transportables pay more for their housing over time than home-owners do.

Despite the amount of research and debate they have attracted, American housing policies have not fitted together with each other or with other welfare policies in any coherent or long-lasting way. With abundant land, income, and aids to ownership the US is amply supplied with housing, with as much 'built space' per head as any country in the world. But both the houses and their costs are distributed in ways which tend to increase rather than reduce inequalities from other causes. The resources do less than they could for the productivity of many of the poorest quarter or so of American households.

Britain

The UK had fast city growth and much overcrowding of unhealthy slums through the nineteenth century. Those conditions prompted well-informed debates about hous-ing hardships and what government might do about them. Three approaches were seriously considered. First, some social workers wanted government to help in modernizing the slums and thinning out their occupa-tion. (Proposed in the 1870s, that got its first practical government support a century later in the 1970s.) Second, conservative philanthropists showed how to mix public and private funds to finance independent non-profit housing at rents the workers could afford. (That principle has since produced tens of millions of affordable rental apartments – but in north-west Europe,

not in Britain.) Third, radicals and then socialists want-ed public rental housing entirely financed, built and managed by government. In Britain it was the radical proposal that won, to be implemented from 1919 to 1980 by governments of all parties. So British housing development through most of the twentieth century was shaped by five main policies:

First, the national government subsidized local gov-ernments to build public rental housing on a scale which made public housing a quarter of all British housing by 1958 and 30 per cent by 1968. From 1961 some similar subsidies also went to independent non-profit housing associations.

Second, wartime rent controls introduced in 1915 were continued permanently in one form or another on all but the most expensive private rental housing. Rents were pegged at levels which discouraged much new building. Private landlords chiefly crowded poor people into old houses, often without much maintenance or modernization.

Third, from 1930 to the 1960s a 'government bull-dozer' was at work. Central government subsidized local governments' compulsory purchase, demolition and replacement of the cities' older and poorer quarters. A lot of private rental housing was replaced by public housing by that means.

Fourth, there were moderate aids to home ownership. On the one hand town planning policies were quite help-ful to the development of house and garden suburbs, rent controls deterred private landlords from bidding against homebuyers for resources, and homebuyers' interest payments were tax deductible. On the other hand local property taxes were quite high, and until 1964 homeowners were taxed on imputed rents of their houses, though generally at low rates.

Fifth, Britain built about forty New Towns, each coherently planned and developed by a public corpora-tion. Some served as overflow 'dormitories' for big cities, but they all tried, many successfully, to attract industrial and commercial investors to employ their res-idents.

Together those policies could make a coherent national housing strategy. They would encourage home ownership, but tax it fairly. They would keep private rents low until most private rental housing was either sold to homebuyers (which the rent controls encouraged it to be) or replaced by new public housing of good quality. New Towns and other decentralizing policies would distribute town life and employment economical-ly, to discourage the overgrowth and congestion of the big cities.

So why have those apparently coherent and progressive policies since attracted strong criticism? Among the reasons are three. (1) The strategy assumed that English class relations made class-structured housing appropriate. The middle and upper classes could be homeowners, the working class could be public tenants in visibly different housing in segregated estates. (2) There was more compulsory displacement and demolition than there need have been. Dispersing settled communities hurt many people in their family, social and working relations, and potentially attractive old neighborhoods were often replaced by arid, less attractive ones. (3) For two critical decades from 1954, theorists persuaded the central government to encourage local authorities to build public housing in the form of towers and barracks: not houses, but massive blocks of 'units' without individuality or private land. Some childless households enjoy the view from the towers but for most, the housing defies the users' needs and preferences. It cost more in money, land and bricks and mortar than their preferred housing forms need have cost, and its degrading social effects are opposite to those predicted by the theorists responsible for it. Generous economic provisions were wrecked by bad planning and design. To learn just how bad the planning, design and social effects were, read Alice Coleman, *Utopia on Trial: Vision and Reality in Planned Housing* (1985).

What Alice Coleman found in the decades of planning that she investigated so shocked her that she recommended that government get out of the housing business altogether. I think that was a great mistake. The 'barracks' housing she rightly condemns (and is now rightly helping to demolish) was never as much as a tenth of Britain's housing stock. Much of the rest is among the world's best: capacious, well serviced and equipped, most of it with private gardens. Most of the public housing built before 1955 and some built since has the semi-detached or terraced form which many homebuyers were choosing at the time, and many still like best. It is adaptable to owner-occupation and much of it has lately been sold to its tenants.

Sweden, West Germany and the Netherlands

Though there were detailed differences, some common principles guided the housing performance of these countries after the Second World War. The common policies reflected some common conditions. The countries have cold climates, so gardens are usable for less of the year. Apartment blocks can be cheaper to heat than separate houses, and apartment housing had long been common in the towns. In 1945 the countries were desperately short of housing, Sweden because of fast industrialization and migration from country to town and the others because of wartime damage and cessation of building. Sweden and Germany had public services accustomed to strong central government with some capacity for economic planning. Those conditions don't necessarily determine particular housing policies – in similar conditions Norway chose different policies throughout the period, and the three countries themselves have since changed direction. But the conditions help to explain the choice of mid-century policies. The main policies were: (i) to have public developers provide most new urban land; (ii) to mix public and private funds to finance large quantities of non-profit or limited-profit apartment housing at affordable rents; (iii) to regulate all rents; (iv) to correct any consequent anomalies or inequities by paying housing allowances, selectively, where necessary; and (v) to use planning and land policies, or high land prices, or both, to discourage house-and-garden development and home ownership in the cities.

A typical development by a non-profit housing association or cooperative might borrow 70 per cent of its funds on first mortgage from a private life assurance company or pension fund, and the rest on second mortgage from government. In practice that second loan amounts to a government guarantee to the private lenders, so they lend at low, risk-free interest rates. What interest and repayment the government requires for its loan has varied with time and place, but has generally conveyed enough subsidy to allow the housing to be offered at affordable rents. In Germany, which has both a non-profit sector and a big private rental sector, the private landlords may get less government loans but they get other public aids. Rent regulation is at levels which allow reasonable returns to investors, and the government allows large tax concessions for notional depreciation.

Whether in its non-profit or its profit-seeking form this approach has some advantages for all parties. The government gets credit for helping housing development without itself taking on the troubles of a bureaucratic landlord. Households get housing of good quality at restrained rents from independent local landlords who are either strictly regulated, or have no motive for rack-renting or otherwise exploiting them. The private lenders get safe, long-term, government-guaranteed investments very useful to managers of superannuation and pension funds. The non-profit developers may have some unpaid directors and may be motivated by some considerations of public interest; but they also provide work and income for salaried managers and staff, professional designers and profit-seeking building contractors. North western Europe has had no difficulty in motivating efficient performance by non-profit, non-government housing developers.

That approach to housing supply has been supported by two complementary policies. First, there has been public control or regulation of private rents throughout. (It has seen bigger allocations of private savings, of national investment, and of national product, to rental housing than were made in any country which lacked rent controls. So much for economists' theory about the effects of rent controls!) Second, as non-profit housing accumulated over the years it developed problems sketched earlier: dilemmas between historic-cost and current-cost renting with inequities between old and new tenants, and between tenants of non-profit and profit-seeking landlords. Some of the anomalies have been reduced by adjusting the rent-setting and rent-regulating rules. But the three countries have also introduced housing allowances, paid selectively to disadvantaged tenants. The allowances supplement and correct the effects of subsidized housing supply, they don't replace it.

To assess that strategy we can begin by comparing its apartment-building to the British production of towers and barracks. In almost all ways it seems to me that the Europeans win. They built in traditional styles in which their towns had always been built. Some of their bigger, more bureaucratic landlords built some big bureaucratic blocks or estates, but those were exceptions. Most of north western Europe's subsidized and non-profit housing looks like and mixes with its other housing, old and new. European cities have richer and poorer quarters but their inequalities are 'continuous': most of them are not divided by the single, striking British division between 'Council estates' and the rest. Many of the cooperatives allow tenants' rents to buy them shares of ownership which can be sold or bequeathed, and they allow some tenant participation in the management of the housing. Finally the mix of public and private funds which finances so much of the housing in all tenures makes less occasion for political backlash against the costs of the program than public funding of public housing has occasioned in some other countries.

Altogether these countries appear to have arrived at sensible ways of meeting – or compromising between – the three theoretical requirements proposed earlier in this Chapter. Recall them:

- Because household production can't finance the purchase of household capital, households can't necessarily get efficient allocations of housing by market

means alone. Public action is needed to improve on market allocation, both between household and household and between housing and other kinds of investment.

- But the public action should strengthen, rather than replace, households' market choices. Households, not public administrators, know best what type, design, location and tenure of housing they individually want.

- To avoid waste and freeloading, the public aids should be such that the households' choices are still under some market discipline, i.e. the more housing they opt for, the less they will have left to spend on other things.

Now see how the Swedish/German/Dutch strategy meets those requirements. Government adds substantial subsidies, ultimately from tax revenue, to the market provision of funds for housing. The aids are available in diverse forms as capital grants or loans, tax concessions, or income allowances. They are available to subsidize both the supply of housing and the capacity to pay for it. In allocating them the government sets both minimum housing standards, and the incomes which the poorest households should have left after paying for their housing. That meets the need to supply a necessary minimum of capital to all households, regardless of their capacity to pay. Above that minimum some market discipline applies: to get better housing you have to pay more, but through the middle range of income and house-value the household payments are still supplemented by some subsidy. It is like power-assisted steering – the subsidies are applied to empower and strengthen the households' own choices.

Considered simply as a system of capital allocation the result is partly efficient: it improves the national allocation of housing while leaving households as the best judges of how much income they want to trade for what sort of housing. Partly it is inefficient: there can still be low-income households who could make productive use of more housing and equipment than they can afford, and richer households who choose to pay for more and better than they need. But in the dilemma between market allocation of housing (which can't be efficient by itself) and administrative allocation by bureaucrats (which can't either) this 'Dutch compromise' mixes the two in a way that chiefly 'gears up' the households' own market choices. Also – in a rough way, with exceptions – it manages to reduce the ratio of subsidy to housing costs as households' incomes rise, without dividing the nation into two distinct housing classes in the cutting way that the British system does.

Those are valuable qualities. But the strategy also had two disadvantages. They related not to households' capacities to choose, but to the range of alternatives from which they could choose, i.e. the option set which they faced. As authors and subsidizers of the strategy the governments had strong influences on the forms and tenures of the new housing. For most of it they chose apartment forms and rental tenure. While shortages continued, the millions on the long waiting lists did not complain much about either, but welcomed whatever they could get. But after a quarter of a century the shortages were overcome; fast economic growth had doubled average real incomes and capacities to pay: and revolutions in travel, television and advertising had affected many town-dwellers' lifestyles and aspirations. Many of them wanted more and different domestic space, for new kinds of storage, equipment, activity. Early in the 1970s all three governments were surprised by surpluses of unwanted new urban apartments. At the same time the political parties – especially the Social Democrats who had long-standing ideological objections to home-owners, and houses with gardens – learned that rising numbers of middle- and low-income voters now wanted houses with gardens, and wanted to own them. The political and market signals reinforced each other. In Sweden, houses with gardens were 32 per cent of new dwellings built in 1971. By 1976 they were 70 per cent; and in the Netherlands they were 78 per cent.

These countries had been more flexible than most in adapting their *policies* to changing conditions. But they now found that they had spent a generation building *housing forms* which are very difficult to adapt to changing demands. Households with rising income and changing wants can alter or enlarge most houses on the ground. But they can't do much of that to most apartments. If they want to use income from the growth of public and private productivity to increase their household productivity – to give children separate bedsitters, or adults and children separate living rooms, to add a games room, a workshop, a boat storage or a double garage – they may have to move house. But where will they move to if their country has a basic misfit between its old unadaptable housing stock and its new housing wants? In Stockholm in 1980 houses and apartments of similar size cost about the same. Apartments were available on demand, but there was a ten-year wait for houses with gardens.

The citizens had been ahead of their governments in coming to regret that they did not have the more adapt-able, expandable kinds of housing that Americans, Australians and Norwegians had. They did not want the American 'slum or caravan' way of housing their poorer households. So what strategies had produced the more equal and adaptable Australian and Norwegian stocks of houses and gardens?

Australia

In 1945 about 50 per cent of Australia's households owned their houses; about 10 per cent were living unwillingly in shared accommodation or huts or camps; and most of the rest were tenants, many of them in the old slum cottages in inner industrial suburbs of the State capital cities which had housed most of the urban working classes since the cities were built in the previous century.

New policies were introduced by Labor governments in the 1940s and modified by conservative governments through the 1950s. They were effective. Within 20 years most of the housing shortage was over; about 85 per cent of households had houses with gardens; and home ownership was the highest in the developed world. That was achieved by a good 'fit' between national financial policy and housing policy. Public savings banks, independent building societies and later some private savings banks organized household savings into long-term loans to governments or for housing. Interest rates on housing loans were regulated as part of a general regulation of all bank interest rates. A low rate of inflation trailed a low rate of interest to keep the real interest rate below 1 per cent for thirty five years. There were portfolio requirements: savings banks alone were allowed to pay interest on ordinary deposit accounts, and in return were required to lend specified proportions of their funds directly, or indirectly through government, for housing. Homebuyers' interest payments were exempt from income tax. Those measures, without any positive subsidy, sufficed to finance three quarters or more of the country's house and garden development. The remaining quarter or so was assisted, still with very little subsidy, by some versatile public measures. Government funded non-profit building societies or State banks to make housing loans on low deposits to homebuyers with low incomes. And it funded State agencies to build public housing, initially about 20 per cent of all new housing, mostly in house and garden form. Much of the public housing could be either rented or rental-purchased, as its tenants preferred or could afford.

There were regional variations. Some States extended the public housing business to compete with private enterprises in building houses for sale in the open market. Other States built some regrettable housing towers into their biggest cities. Though public housing eventually included a good mix of owners and tenants, a lot of it was in large segregated estates. Some of the estates were poorly serviced, some were in reach of too few jobs for their residents. Some worked well until the great increase of unemployment and lone parenting in the 1970s began to turn them into 'welfare ghettos'. Intellectuals included them in their general denunciations of Australia's uninteresting suburbia. Nevertheless the measures sketched above allowed a high proportion of the Australian families who could not afford to buy houses without some help to use one of three public aids. They could rent a flat or a house and garden from a public landlord. They could rental-purchase a house and garden from the public housing stock. Or they could borrow on specially easy terms to buy a house on the open market.

While it lasted that strategy achieved, with remarkably little subsidy, three creditable things. In 15 years from 1951 to 1966 home ownership rose from 50 to 70 per cent of households, with (now) 85 per cent of retired people owning their houses. Most public housing customers could choose the kind of housing and the tenure that they preferred. And Australia distributed private urban land and housing space more equally than it distributed wealth, income, education or almost anything else – and (with New Zealand) more equally than any other developed country did.

Much of that strategy has since been abandoned (I think cruelly) with the shift of both political parties to the Right. But could the unique housing performance of the 1950s and 1960s have been given some better, longer-lasting financial and political basis? The country which has come nearest to combining Australian housing forms and tenures with European financing principles is Norway.

Norway

Together with Britain, Belgium, Switzerland and the Netherlands, Norway has Europe's biggest houses, and most housing space per head. Among those leaders Norway distributes individual or cooperative housing ownership to the highest proportion of its people. Those are effects of three long-standing policies.

In 1894 government founded a Housing Loan Fund. Its form and function have changed more than once to become, in modern times, the national Housing Bank and Smallholders' Bank.

In 1916 the Norwegian Labor Party adopted a housing policy which included public land development in

towns, public housing where necessary, rent control where necessary, support for cooperative housing, and – generations before any other party of the Left – support for home ownership. That helped to keep the party in power for most of the century.

Through the 1920s and 1930s some public housing and some cooperative housing were built. The cooperatives were more popular, and took over most of the public housing from 1946.

Though details change from time to time with changing conditions, the main elements of the strategy through most of the century have been these:

- The public housing banks are financed chiefly by selling bonds to the private savings banks. The citizens deposit their savings in the private banks and get some of them back as public housing loans. It is an unusual division of labor, but it gives government direct control of lending policy, and an easy means of subsidizing it where desired. The public banks lend for housing in all tenures, i.e. to homebuyers, cooperatives and private landlords, under only one restriction: they limit the size and value of houses and apartments that can be built with their funds. They finance about three quarters of Norway's new housing construction. Loans to homebuyers are at affordable interest but have generally been for no more than 70 or 75 per cent of the houses' value. Households find the rest as they can – from inheritance, savings, family loans, or second-mortgage loans from private banks. 25 or 30 per cent is a big deposit requirement, so for marginal households buying a house is harder than it would be in English-speaking countries. But unlike the English-speaking countries, the next alternative to individual ownership still includes an element of ownership.

- Households who can't or don't want to buy houses can qualify by waiting-time to join a housing cooperative. That gets them housed, usually in an apartment block. They can vote for the directors of their cooperative, and share in the management of their own block. The cooperative owns their apartment, but their rent buys them an equity share in the cooperative. When they leave they can give or bequeath the apartment to kin, or sell their share back to the cooperative for cash. So cooperative housing avoids the double bind, and allows part of members' rent payments to double as capital savings.

Into the 1980s the richest quarter or so of Norwegian housing was privately financed. The remaining 75 per cent was financed by the public banks. 75 per cent of those publicly financed dwellings were houses with gardens. About 60 per cent of them were for homebuyers, 23 per cent for cooperatives, 9 per cent for private landlords, the rest for other residential institutions.

Other policies deal even-handedly with the three main tenures. Housing allowances are available to hard-up households in all tenures, and are set so that private rents, cooperative rents and homebuyers' loan repayments are all linked to household incomes, on a sliding scale which leaves the poorest households to spend 15 per cent of their incomes on housing costs, with the public allowance decreasing as income increases until the rents or repayments take 20 per cent of income. In all tenures, interest payments are tax exempt. But rent is not, and homeowners pay tax on imputed rent. That amounts to a capital tax. But housing capital pays at only 30 per cent of the rate for commercial and industrial capital.

All those policies are adjustable, and have been adapted from time to time to inflation, rising incomes, and changing tastes. But the strategy as a whole has held for a long time, sustained by generally stable and popular financial and housing institutions. Norway achieves quite high home ownership. With one exception noted below it enables people to get the kind of housing they want. The kind most of them want is the house-and-garden kind most expandable and adaptable to rising income and changing tastes. And the distribution of both housing space and housing costs is exceptionally fair and egalitarian.

Have those unusually generous arrangements diverted resources from more productive uses? There can be no certain answers to that, but there are some indications. The comparative costs of building different housing forms vary from country to country, but houses on the ground generally yield more usable floor space per unit of building cost than multi-storeyed apartments do. Norway does not devote higher proportions of national income or capital formation to housing than her neighbors do. But she appears to use the resources more efficiently. The houses are bigger (but they're for bigger households). They meet more households' real preferences. Because of that, and because of their gardens, they probably allow more household production. And more of them are adaptable to changing wants over time.

Norway and Sweden represent Europe's extremes in the effects of their housing arrangements on their national accounts. Norway has fewer, bigger family households, typically in big houses with gardens. Sweden has more and smaller households, with many more of them in comparatively small apartments. A higher proportion of Norwegians (about 25 per cent) also have holiday houses or cabins in the country. So both at home and on holiday, Norwegians do more of their own cooking, laundering, making-and-mending; Swedes more often eat out, use commercial services, have tradesmen do their making-and-mending. So more of the Swedish activity is exchanged for money and appears in the national accounts. Because of their large manufacturing sector Swedes have been richer per head than Norwegians through most of the century – but not as *much* richer as the national accounts showed. To a lesser degree the same may be true of comparisons between Norway's accounts and those of Germany and the Netherlands. With or without allowance for that bias the accounts show Norway's postwar economic growth as fast as the European average, and faster since Norway's offshore oil began to flow in the 1970s.

If Norway's housing strategy has been the best in the developed world, has it been the best possible? I don't think so, for two reasons. First, the deposit requirements for home purchase have been unnecessarily high, excluding quite a lot of households – perhaps 10 to 15 per cent of all households – who would have preferred to buy houses. Was that a necessary rationing of scarce resources? No, the resources they might have had by borrowing for themselves were conveyed to them instead by the cooperatives borrowing and building for them. Second, when they turned to the cooperatives many of them did not get their preferred kind of housing. Until the 1970s the cooperative movement ran with a particular division of labor. A cooperative developer planned and built the housing, then handed it over to the association which would own and manage it. The cooperative *members* – the households who would occupy the housing and take part in its management – were the last to arrive, and had too little influence on the choice of housing type and design. They had *some* influence, because there was some competition for their custom between one cooperative and another, and between cooperative and other tenures. So the developers had to design acceptable housing. But in practice, especially in the big cities, as long as the housing shortages lasted the cooperative developers were often as bureaucratic, and attentive to architectural fashion rather that residents' preferences, as the public housing authorities who were building towers and barracks in other countries. About 1975 when most housing shortages were at last overcome, and Swedes and Germans and Dutch were rebelling against their apartment-block housing forms, Norwegian cooperative members began to do likewise, and to insist that they be identified and consulted at the design stage of their housing production. But by that time a fifth or so of Norwegian town-dwellers, who tended to be the poorer fifth of them, were in well-built, long-lasting apartment blocks which would be part of the national housing stock for a long time to come. Norway distributes indoor housing space as equally as Australia does, and housing costs and taxes more equally. But while it lasted the postwar Australian strategy distributed household land more equally than Norway did, and met more of its households' preferences for housing type and tenure.

UTOPIA

After half a century or more of large-scale trial and error in those and other countries, what might a contemporary government now learn about housing strategy? It can't arrive at a technically best and perfectly consensual strategy, because interests conflict. (Private landlords want one policy, homebuyers want another; poor households want more housing equality, some rich households want less; some lifestyles think a dense city is worth its costs, others think house-and-garden suburbia is worth its costs; and so on.) But what strategy might (i) seem fairest to yours or my values, (ii) make the most productive allocation of capital between household and household and between housing and other investment, and (iii) at the same time attract support of a sufficient majority of voters?

Answers must vary from country to country because they must adapt to cultural and political differences and to the existing stock of housing and distribution of ownership. But here follows a sample strategy built on the two bases sketched in this chapter: the perception that household capital is productive, and the practical lessons to be learned from the good, bad and indifferent housing policies which rich democracies tried at one time or another through the twentieth century. The strategy could well be linked with urban land policies you will meet when you study land markets, and it assumes that government regulates banks, insurers, pension funds and other financial institutions in ways you will meet when you study the management of capital markets. Here are the housing essentials:

1. There is a public housing bank. Financial institutions are required to lend specified proportions of their funds on specified terms for housing, or to fund the public bank to the same extent. Its funds may be augmented if necessary by credit created for the purpose by the National Reserve Bank.

2. Mortgage loans on the specified terms are available to homebuyers, cooperatives, public and other non-profit landlords, but not to profit-seeking landlords (who must use open-market finance if they need to borrow).

3. The specified terms include a regulated interest rate, a borrowers' choice between sloped repayment and level repayment, and a limit on the value of the houses or apartments financed. The limit is set to exclude the richest quarter or so of houses. (Extravagant housing should not have benefit of restrained interest rates; but it is desirable that a majority of households, not just a 'welfare' minority, should regard the regulated service as normal, use and value it for themselves or in prospect for their children, and support it politically.)

4. Rental purchase of houses from the open market or from public housing stock is available from public landlords funded for the purpose by the housing bank.

5. The public landlords can also supply housing for sale or rent where there is unsatisfied demand for it; and they supply housing, mostly managed by others, for women's and children's shelters and for transient and homeless people and other groups with special needs.

6. Households which want apartments with landlords' maintenance services can get them from public or private landlords, from housing cooperatives, or by buying or rental-purchasing apartments on a strata title or condominium basis. (Strata or condominium title means that you own your particular apartment, and are also a voting and rent-paying member of a company which provides services and external maintenance to the building as a whole.)

7. Means-tested housing allowances are available to some of the households with incomes in the bottom 25 per cent of household incomes. The allowances are designed to limit their housing costs to 20 per cent of income, as long as their housing choices comply with house-value limits which prevent the use of the allowances as blank cheques to acquire expensive housing.

8. Interest payments on housing loans are exempt from income tax. There is no taxation of imputed rent. If the society has a capital tax, housing pays 1 per cent per annum (less than half the general rate) but most housing escapes it because the base exemption (i.e. the amount of capital any tax-payer can own free of

capital tax) is set above the average value of a family house.

9. The whole allocation of capital to housing is limited by political judgments which affect households' market choices. The limits are imposed, and adjusted as necessary from time to time, by government setting (i) the price limit on housing units for which housing loans can be made; (ii) the amount of deposit required of borrowers; (iii) the rate of interest on housing loans; (iv) the portfolio requirements and other financial provisions which determine the quantity of funds available for housing loans on regulated terms; and (v) the amount of any public housing supply. In some conditions the limits may force some rationing of the available resources. More political decisions must then decide between rationing by price (e.g. by raising deposit requirements or interest rates), or by waiting time, judgments of need, or other means. Outside the regulated system, market forces can safety determine how much additional household saving and business borrowing are applied to housing investment by private landlords and rich homebuyers.

27

Households : a summary

This chapter summarizes the main themes of the last three.

1. Historically the functions of households in producing for market, producing for themselves, socializing and skilling their children, and keeping their members well occupied, have varied greatly with economic growth, changing technology, and changing social and economic organization. The functions continue to change. Some of the directions of change are open to collective choice, so theoretical beliefs which affect the choices are important.

2. With economic and technological growth households individually get wider choices of household equipment, and choices between buying ready-made goods and services and producing for themselves. Because of the ways in which households' spending and investing behavior responds to those wider choices, economic growth tends to increase the amount of fluctuation and uncertainty in national economic activity and employment.

3. Household investing and spending choices would be more predictable if they were regularly determined as economic choices are in economic theory, for example by the relative prices of commercial services and household equipment, the technical productivity of the household equipment, and the household's earning capacity. But those expectations become uncertain if the equipment has other functions (such as ostentatious waste or display) besides its primary use; if the household work has positive attractions; or if households have internal conflicts of interest about money and household work and parents' duty to children.

4. In developed mixed economies a mass of middle-income households now have reasonable capacities to save, borrow and invest, so they have effective housing choices, and choices between buying ready-made goods and services and producing for themselves. Nevertheless their market choices do not necessarily achieve the most efficient allocation of capital resources, for reasons summarized in the next paragraph; and towards the top and bottom of the income scale there tend to be perverse relations between households' need to produce for themselves and their capacity to do so. Beyond a certain point rich households don't increase their household work or output much however much housing and other gear they acquire. And many poor households who most need household output nevertheless produce very little for themselves, from lack of income, household capital, private space, morale, or all four.

5. The main reasons why unaided market forces cannot be trusted to allocate household capital efficiently are these:

   • *A pure inefficiency* Because household output does not earn money, it cannot pay for the capital it uses, or for its own running costs. So there is no efficient link between the ability to use capital productively and the ability to acquire it. Both depend chiefly on income from other sources.

   • *A double bind* Households need housing from the day they are formed. If they are formed without prior saving, and have to rent one house while they save to buy another, they are paying for two houses through a stage of household life when it is hard enough to pay for one. But if they don't do that, they face –

   • *A rent trap* For equivalent houses rent is usually lower than mortgage payments are through the early years of purchase. But renting costs more than buying does over household life (or there would be no profit-seeking landlords) and for many households it provides less satisfactory housing. For people who want secure tenure of houses with gardens, most countries' landlord-investors don't offer either secure tenure or houses with gardens. Private landlords do provide needed services for some households. But there is inefficient allocation wherever landlords outbid households for the ownership of housing resources which the households would rather borrow and buy for themselves. When that happens the unwilling tenants commonly get less, and less adaptable, housing than the same money would buy them as owners. And over household life they are left with less income to spend on making productive use of their household time and capital.

6. Public institutions can be excellent allocators of housing money and credit. But large-scale government design and allocation of the housing itself tends to be at least as inefficient as unaided market allocation. Some small-scale, locally based public housing agencies have served their tenants well, but big public institutions operating on big scale have made many more bad than good choices of housing. The reasons include these:

- *Choice* Households generally know, better than bureaucrats could, what housing they want. Up to whatever limit they can afford they will generally do best if they can search and choose from all the housing stock available on the market.

- *Diversity* The housing stock may never fit present wants perfectly, because at any date most of it was built at past dates to meet past wants. But it is likely to come nearer to matching the diversity of present wants if (i) plenty of it was originally designed to meet households' real wants in a market way, and (ii) plenty of it is in forms which are alterable to meet the changing wants of successive occupiers. If enough of the national stock has those qualities, then the addition of some public housing may extend rather than restrict its useful diversity, especially if the public housing providers are local, and living among their tenants. Good additions to the housing stock should certainly be possible now that there has been a century's experience of the difference between good and bad public housing design. But there still tends to be an insensitive lack of diversity in most big public projects.

- *Competition* A sufficient supply of public, cooperative or other non-profit housing can discipline private land and housing prices. It can also allow rent control, where circumstances make that desirable, without perverse effects on housing supply and prices.

- *Economy* If government makes housing free, or if there is no link between the amount of it that people are entitled to and the price they have to pay for it, some inefficient allocation is likely. People who don't need their whole entitlement may nevertheless insist on taking it; people who could make good use of more than their entitlement may be prevented from getting it. Either may happen when public housing agencies decide

the house you will get by counting your children, but fix the rent you will pay as a percentage of your income. 'From each according to his capacity, to each according to his need' is an honorable principle, and does no great harm in practice when applied to the distribution of basic public housing to hard-up households. But if the principle were extended to the administrative allocation of housing to all or most of a modern population, as some socialist theorists have proposed, there would probably be a good deal of both bad design and inefficient allocation. There is much to be said for an element of market discipline, as well as market choice, in households' housing and equipment choices.

7. The objections to public allocation of houses don't hold against public banking or other aids to the supply of housing finance, as long as elements of market discipline continue to motivate households to economize their housing demands.

8. What housing strategy do these considerations suggest? Conflicts of interest make it likely that any strategy will be disagreed. So will any way of measuring or judging what is the most productive allocation of capital between households, and between household and other uses. But that uncertainty does not justify leaving allocation to market forces with the market failures listed in (5) above. Common sense suggests that government's best and most popular course may be (i) to see that the nation's poorest housing is at least safe, healthy, and of a standard to allow its occupants to hold their heads up as respectable members of society, and (ii) to enable all competent households to have effective choices of the main housing types and tenures.

9. To achieve those ends, public landlords should supply sufficient quantities of the types of rental housing that people want but private investors don't supply. But for most households government need only manage the financial system to provide a sufficient flow of housing loans on affordable terms to households, cooperatives and non-profit landlords. The public aid can be tapered to give most help, at least proportionately, to those with least income and most need, and to give less help the higher the households' income.

10. The direction of affordable funds to housing is both assisted and limited by political judgments which decide how far to gear up the households' housing

choices and capacities to pay. The national allocation of resources to housing is thus limited by a mixture of political and market choice.

11. As mixed economies grow and change, alternative directions of development may be open to households as productive institutions. They are likely to be linked to alternative aspirations for individual and family life. In the 1960s (for example) there was a 'Swedish vision', part socialist and part hedonist, of small households forming and reforming as individuals' interests and affections changed, operating sociably from city apartments, substituting public or commercial services for many traditional household tasks including a good deal of child care. From the 1970s that expectation was contradicted (or proven to be a short phase in most people's young adult lives) by growing political and market demands for household ownership of houses with individuality, and gardens. There has also been some revival of interest in traditional, stable, productive family life.

12. Voters, politicians and administrators who shape policies which affect family life should keep in mind those alternative directions of change, and the divisions of interest and opinion about them, including these divisions:

- Different household members can have conflicting interests in household productivity: in choices between buying ready-made services and producing for themselves, and in distributing the work and benefit of producing for themselves.

- There can be conflicts between the interests of children, the interests of those who chiefly care for them, and the collective interest in the quality of human company and human capital which households bring up.

- People who hate *either* capitalist exploitation and alienation *or* socialist bureaucracy and alienation (or both) may see household production-for-use as the freest, least exploitive, least alienating,

most expressive and satisfying mode of production. But –

- households can also be large exploiters of women's labor, and –

- they may become worse exploiters, if private enterprises manage to replace more regular employment by low-paid piece-work done by workers at home, and if government returns more caring from paid public services to be done instead by unpaid workers, mostly women in charitable services or at home.

- So some reformers want to reduce people's dependence on their households. How? Keep moving in the 'Swedish direction' towards smaller households, with all adult members going out to work and earn, and commercial services supplying most meals, recreations, housework and child care. But –

- other reformers value the warmth and solidarity and productivity of the traditional family household and want better conditions for it. Alternatives: (1) Fairer shares of housework and child care within the household, with more part-time earning by both parents and generous public child allowances. (2) For those who prefer the traditional division of labor while there are children, there is need for a new and genuine equality between the parent who earns away from home and the parent who does most of the work of the household and care of the children. For genuine equality the public aids would need to include a full wage and status for a parent who stays home with children; effective aids to retraining and returning to paid work after parenting, as described in our chapter on childhood; and a genuine recognition that bringing up secure, sociable, skilful, energetic children is a condition of all other productivity.

EXERCISE

Which of the conflicts of interest and opinion listed in item 12 above are irreducible, so that public policies cannot resolve them or must choose between them, with the options open to households and their members being shaped and limited accordingly?

Which on the other hand are interests which could all be served by societies which tolerated diverse relations and divisions of labor within families, offered a wide range of public aids to the care of children and old people, offered diverse types and tenures of private and public housing, and so on?

Which if any of those diverse options which *could* be offered should *not* be offered, in your opinion? Your reasons?

PRIVATE ENTERPRISES

28

Business powers

Here begin nine chapters about –

- business organization and powers
- how firms work, including
- how they get their capital and technology
- how they engage and manage their workers
- how they keep accounts
- how they know their costs
- how they price their products
- how they take each other over
- the range and variety of their directors' purposes, and
- their relations with government and public policy.

This first chapter is about the creation and regulation of their business powers.

THE ORGANIZATION OF WORK

Relations between producers can be classified as *organized* relations or *market* relations.

A restaurant manager *plans and organizes* the day's work: plans a menu, organizes shoppers and kitchen hands and cooks and waiters to contribute their necessary services at the necessary times and places.

But she doesn't have to organize the farmers, truckers, and shopkeepers who supply the fresh meat and vegetables the restaurant needs. For those, she goes shopping. *Market relations* are all she needs with those contributors to her final product.

Some divisions of labor can be coordinated by either method. Example: One winemaker grows his own grapes and sells his wine from his cellar door. Thus he *organizes* the working relations between growing the grapes, making the wine, and selling it. Another winemaker shops around for the grapes he needs, and sells his product to wine merchants. Thus instead of organized relations he relies on *market relations* between the

vineyards, the winery, and the shops.

Organization and market relations are not mutually exclusive: there can be 'organized market relations'. If a carmaker buys components from many small suppliers, they all have to meet strict requirements of design, quality and timetable. Their market relations don't make much difference to the amount of organized coordination there would be if the carmaking firm itself manufactured the components. The same holds for other big operators who can alternatively employ all the labor they use, or have independent contractors employ it. Office builders have cranes hoisting ten-tonne girders and skips of concrete a hundred metres above crowded city streets. The builders must arrange for the new building's structure, cladding, plumbing, wiring, fireproofing and air-conditioning elements to be installed in correct order, according to plan, with frequent independent inspections between one operation and the next to comply with contract requirements, insurance requirements, Building Act and fire and safety requirements. To get all that right, the amount of managerial authority and organization has to be much the same whether the workers are employed by one firm or by a dozen subcontractors.

How does the builder decide whether to employ all the workers he needs, or deal with them in a market way as independent contractors? A simple answer was theorized by Ronald Coase in 1937. Bureaucratic coordination within the firm has costs (planners', administrators', personnel officers' salaries, office gear, rent for office space). Market relations (shopping around, assessing and comparing rival suppliers, calling and comparing tenders, writing contracts, enforcing them) also have costs. For each bit of coordination it is rational to choose whichever is the cheaper alternative. If the organization costs would be lower than the market costs, expand the firm to employ the necessary capital and labor. If the market costs would be lower, buy the inputs from other firms. The theory neglected some other considerations, for example considerations of bargaining and political strength. But it had the merit of emphasizing that even within the private sector, market relations are only one of the means of coordination (or there would be no firms).

The mixture of market and bureaucratic coordination varies from industry to industry, but the bureaucratic share of the whole task of coordination is not diminishing with economic growth. Some firms are now bigger than some national governments in the amount of business they do and the number of people they employ. Market relations *between* firms are not reducing the need for bureaucratic powers *within* firms.

This chapter is about the forms those powers take in private enterprises: how the rights and powers of owners and managers are created, and how they are regulated in a never-ending battle to prevent dishonest and anti-social uses of corporate powers without hindering their honest productive uses.

BUSINESS OWNERSHIP

There are three basic forms of private business ownership: individual proprietors, partnerships, and companies. The three give owners and managers different powers and duties. The greatest number of businesses still have individual owners. The greatest volume of business is nowadays done by companies. Here follow brief descriptions of each of the three forms.

Individual proprietors

Anyone can do business as a private individual. You can earn by producing goods for sale, offering services, or drawing rent from property, just as lawfully as you can earn wages from an employer. You can be an employer yourself. Producing goods and services for sale rather than for your own use doesn't necessarily require any change of legal status.

More than half of all private enterprises still have this simple form. It has been the traditional form of most family farms, hotels and boarding houses and restaurants, small shops and workshops, and the many providers of professional, trade, and personal services who work independently for fees rather than as employees for wages: your neighborhood doctor, plumber, electrician, hairdresser. The advantages of doing business as an ordinary citizen are cheapness, simplicity, privacy and independence.

Individual proprietors may still have to comply with plenty of regulation. Farmers must obey rules about land use, chemical pollution, plant and animal diseases, clean handling of meat and milk, and so on. Shops and restaurants have their cleanliness and sometimes their trading hours regulated. Anyone who employs workers may have to insure them, withhold tax from their wages, provide regulated or union-negotiated wages and working conditions. Any business must keep full enough accounts to satisfy tax authorities. And so on – to know and obey all the rules, many individual enterprises nowadays have to hire help from lawyers and accountants. But their organization and accounting can still be simpler and freer from red tape than if they were in partnership, or incorporated as companies.

Individual proprietorship nevertheless has disadvantages. The owner has unlimited liability for any debts of the business. If your business fails, owing more than it can pay, you may lose not only the money you put into the business but also anything else you own: your family house and savings, for example. And in a family business there can be conflicts between the owner and other family members.

If you want to have this simplest kind of ownership and control but have more than one person share it, you may form a partnership.

Partnerships

Partnership extends the conditions of individual proprietorship to more than one proprietor. A spoken or written agreement defines the partners' relations to one another, but their collective relation to the outside world remains much the same as that of an individual proprietor.

Partnership can work well for two kinds of business. It works when a small number of people pool their money and labor to run a business to which they are all committed in a reasonably permanent way. And it can work, sometimes on a bigger scale, for professionals who deal independently with their clients but share some office space and staff, or other services. Doctors, lawyers, architects, accountants and some other 'consultant' professionals have traditionally worked in partnership (though many are now preferring to incorporate as companies). Any partner can end the partnership at any time. Partners can't usually sell their shares – if one partner dies or departs, the partnerships ends. Its assets may need to be valued to determine the departing member's share. If the others want to continue the business they must make a new partnership agreement.

The main disadvantage is the same as for individual proprietors, but with more possibilities of conflict. Like individual proprietors, partners have unlimited liability for the partnership's debts. If all goes well, each partner should only have to pay his pro-rata share of any debt. But if some partners can't pay, the others must, and (like individual proprietors) they may lose their other possessions as well as whatever they have invested in the business. Understandably, rich investors with a lot to lose are often reluctant to confide resources to poor partners with less to lose.

Continental Europe long ago developed partnerships with limited liability. Some English-speaking countries have allowed 'sleeping' partners, who invest but don't work in the business, to limit their losses to the money they invest. But generally, if owners of businesses want to be sure that they can lose no more than they invest, they do best to form companies rather than partnerships.

So why don't all partnerships turn themselves into companies? First, with power to end the partnership at any time, a partner has greater bargaining strength than a minority shareholder in a company has. Second, forming a company may get you double-taxed, as will soon be explained. Third, the company form can cost time and money, and sometimes some business freedom, as will also be explained.

Companies

In developing the legal form of the limited company, government has created three vital conditions of large-scale capitalist organization: corporate identity, joint stock, and limited liability.

Corporate Identity The firm exists independently of its owners. Government registers each firm and gives it status as a 'legal person'. Though shareholders own it, it is legally distinct from them – if they all die at once, the firm is still there. Directors and managers speak and act for the firm, but they also are distinct from it, and their relations with it are regulated by law. The firm can sue and be sued, break laws and be punished (though it can't go to jail). Each firm has a constitution – its memorandum and articles of association which define its objects and powers.

Joint stock allows many investors to pool their resources under single management. When a firm is founded, investors own shares of it in proportion to the capital they contribute to it. If the firm earns, they draw whatever dividend per share the directors decide to pay each year. At shareholders' meetings they elect the firm's directors, receive its accounts, and vote on some questions of policy, for example whether and how to raise more capital. Shares in public companies (you'll presently learn the meaning of 'public' in this context)

are freely saleable through stock exchanges or by private sales.

Limited liability The principle is simple: unlike individuals or most partners, company shareholders can only lose what they invest. If you buy a $1 share, that $1 is all you can lose. If a firm loses all its shareholders' money and still has debts it can't pay, the further losers are its creditors, not its owners.

Why is limited liability a good principle? Because it encourages enterprise. It allows entrepreneurs to raise risk capital from investors who would never trust them with it if that meant risking the rest of the investors' property as well. Limited liability has been a vital condition of large-scale capitalist enterprise and growth.

But it is also a potentially dangerous principle, because it can be misused for all sorts of unfair or fraudulent purposes. Together with corporate identity and joint stock, its uses need to be strictly regulated.

Public and private companies In this context 'public' does not mean government-owned. Public companies are companies which offer their shares to the public. Raising money from strangers, with limited liability, is open to so much abuse that public companies have to be strictly regulated. The regulation has costs for both the government and the companies, and it can constrain the companies' business freedoms in various ways.

To avoid some of those costs and constraints, a simpler company form is available in most countries. If a group of investors have enough capital of their own and don't need to offer shares for sale to the public, but if they want the advantages of joint stock and limited liability, they may form a private company. (It is variously called a 'private' company, a 'proprietary' company, an 'exempt' company, and in the US a 'close' company.) It is presumed that such investors can keep control of their resources without much public help – they are often the directors as well as the owners of the enterprise. They don't need to be regulated to protect them from themselves. Because they don't offer shares to strangers, they don't have to submit a prospectus for government approval. Because they are not using strangers' funds, they don't have to publish their annual accounts. Because their shares can't be traded on stock exchanges, they are not troubled by share-trading regulations.

They work well for small businesses, and are cheaper and simpler to manage than public companies are.

Disadvantages Being a company has some disadvantages for the company and its owners. There are also some potential disadvantages for societies which allow joint stock companies with limited liability.

- *Double tax.* Most countries tax company profits. Only the profit remaining after tax is available to be distributed as dividend income, on which shareholders then pay income tax. Some companies and shareholders manage to avoid that effect, lawfully or not, by ingenious 'creative accounting'. Some countries don't income-tax dividend income from companies which have paid company tax. But the world still has quite a lot of double taxation of company earnings. That's one reason why many small businesses continue as individuals or partnerships, doing without the limited liability they could have as companies.

- *Other people's money.* In joint stock companies, directors and managers commonly manage other people's money. They can all too easily mismanage it. When they do, limited liability can allow the costs of mismanagement to be shifted from the owners and managers of the company to innocent third parties, for example to unpaid creditors or ill-served consumers. Experience proves that taxpayers, shareholders, creditors and consumers need elaborate protection from the abuse of their powers by dishonest or inefficient managers of other people's money. The need for protection leads directly to the third main disadvantage of the company form of organization –

- *Red tape.* Regulation to prevent inefficiency and dishonesty can impose costs on all enterprises, including all the efficient and honest ones, and on taxpayers. There are public costs as government hires lawyers and accountants to do the regulating. There are corporate costs as companies hire lawyers and accountants to keep the elaborate accounts and submit the detailed returns which the regulators require. There are corporate costs as some companies hire *more* lawyers and accountants to find ways through or around the regulations which honest companies are obeying. And there are costs in time and efficiency as well as money as honest companies are compelled to adopt the less-than-efficient methods and routines which dishonest operators have prompted the regulators to require. As we will now see.

WHY REGULATE CORPORATE BEHAVIOR?

The public company with corporate identity, joint stock and limited liability, owned by large numbers of shareholders who are strangers to each other, and buying most of its inputs and selling its products in a market way, has proved to be an extraordinarily efficient and adaptable institution for marshalling resources and producing goods in industries whose technical conditions call for substantial capital and organization.

But corporate identity, joint stock and limited liability can easily be misused. For example –

How to cheat creditors Form a company with next-to-no capital, owned and directed by you and a few mates. Buy goods on credit and sell them for cash. Pay yourself and your mates half the cash as directors' fees and the other half as shareholders' dividends. Then wind up the company. (That means close it down.) The suckers who sold you goods on credit have probably lost their money. In principle they can sue the directors as directors, though not as shareholders. In principle the public authorities may charge the directors with criminal offences. But in practice the creditors' chances of recovering their losses are not promising.

How to cheat owners Print a plausible prospectus to persuade investors that a new company directed by you and your mates will be profitable. Sell $2m. of shares. Use half a million of the money to do some of the proposed business, for appearances' sake and to avoid charges of fraud. Use another half million to keep the shareholders quiet by paying them two or three annual dividends. (Don't tell them they are getting some of their capital back, rather than honestly earned profits.) Over the same two or three years pay the remaining million to yourself and mates as directors' fees. When the money is all gone, resign and leave the company. You've taken the shareholders for a million. If the government responds by legislating against that kind of fraud, try this kind:

How to cheat owners next time As before, attract $2m. of capital to a new company to be run by three of your mates. Also found a second company (RIPOFF Inc.) with only $100 capital, wholly owned by three other mates. The companies trade with each other. The first company trades unskilfully, RIPOFF trades skilfully, so within a year or two the first company has lost $1m. to RIPOFF. That is so disgraceful that the first company's 'incompetent' directors resign. RIPOFF then winds up and distributes its assets to its owners and their mates – who, as before, have taken a million from unwary shareholders.

How to cheat taxpayers Suppose you earn a big income as (say) a surgeon. You register a company and have it employ you as a salaried surgeon. The company collects the usual high fees from your patients, but pays you a low wage for your services. It uses the rest of the surgical fees to make interest-free loans, and to buy and sell properties at a loss. Its loans are to your wife and daughters, who use the money to buy properties from the company for less than they are worth. See what you have achieved! Your low wage as the company's employee pays very little income tax. The company loses as much in its property dealings as it gains from its surgery business, so it breaks even and pays no tax. Your wife and daughters have no income, they merely borrow to buy property, so they pay no income tax. You have converted most of your income to capital without paying income tax on it. The losers are the citizens who do pay their taxes.

The dynamics of regulation

All those simple frauds are now unlawful. But the folk who misuse company powers are endlessly inventive. As fast as simple misbehavior is outlawed they develop more complicated misbehavior, and government has to respond with more complicated regulations. You need to study that process of challenge and response as it has unfolded over time, to grasp three fundamentals of business organization.

- Though companies are privately owned and managed, government creates their institutional form and powers, and is held responsible if too many of them misuse their powers.

- It takes continuing responsive and inventive government activity to keep companies efficient and socially acceptable, i.e. safe for people to invest in and deal with.

- The law gives the companies themselves valuable

powers to discipline each other, and their employees. And the tasks keep changing. For example there is currently a growing volume of computer crime for which the law, the police and the companies concerned are not at all well prepared. And that is only one of half a dozen developments, noted later in this chapter, which are creating new regulatory problems for private enterprises in the twenty-first century.

Deregulation Because government regulation of business is now quite pervasive, and often irksome to those concerned, there is pressure to reduce it. Campaigns for deregulation give new importance to the history of regulation. It is rarely prudent to repeal laws without first finding out why they were introduced, and how people used to behave without them. But as times change some old rules can go without reviving the sins they were introduced to prevent; and plenty of regulations need to be revised, updated, simplified.

Economists and business regulation It is to get you to grasp the dynamic, unending nature of that task, and also its importance, that you are now offered some history. There is quite a lot of it, but you can read it quickly; there is no need to memorize the dates and details. What matters is to grasp the dynamic nature of these unavoidable relations between business and government. You learned earlier that what you study may be changing as you study it. Similarly for government: the corporate behavior which it regulates is constantly changing, both from other causes and in response to its regulation.

BRITISH EXPERIENCE

Company law and regulation have developed somewhat differently in different countries. We will begin with some British history, then notice some European and American differences.

CHARTERED COMPANIES

In Britain, corporate identity began with the church, then with medieval local government. The tradesmen and property owners of a town would get a borough charter from the king, usually in exchange for money or political support. The charter created a town corporation with powers to own property, tax people, regulate business and provide local services. Borough corporations and tradesmen's guilds developed, between them, quite extensive regulation of medieval trade and industry. They were public/private hybrids: private enterprisers

using public power, providing both business protection and public services.

When British merchants came to need protection overseas, the hybrid institution was adapted for the purpose. Merchant companies were created by royal charter. They were given monopolies of British trade in particular commodities or particular regions. The companies were expected to tax and discipline their members on government's behalf, in exchange for whatever naval and commercial protection their charters promised them. Most companies were not traders themselves; their members traded individually, without joint stock or limited liability. The biggest of them, the East India Company, came to govern – and to help its members to plunder – much of India.

The south sea bubble The South Sea Company

was chartered in 1711. In exchange for lending money to the British government it got a monopoly of English trade with Spain's American colonies. Since Spain severely restricted the British share of the trade, that was no big deal. But in 1720 the Company pulled off a very big deal. It induced the government to extend the Company's monopoly to English trade throughout the south seas. In return the Company undertook to pay the government £7m. cash, and to take over Britain's national debt at a reduced rate of interest. Taking over the national debt meant that the government compelled holders of its bonds to sell them to the Company. Some were paid in cash, most were paid in South Sea Company shares. In future the government would pay the interest on its debt to the Company, and the Company would pay dividends to its shareholders.

With a secure income from the government's interest payments, the Company proceeded to extend its south sea trade with modest success. But the £7m. it paid for its new monopoly, and its audacity in taking over the national debt, convinced a great many people that it must have fabulous prospects. Eager buyers bid up its shares tenfold, from their issue price of £100 to more than £1,000 a share. Other promoters took advantage of the speculative fever to launch other enterprises, some over-optimistic, many fraudulent. A thousand subscribers were found for one new company formed 'for carrying on an undertaking of great advantage, but nobody to know what it is'.

Because sham companies were diverting investors from its own share sales, the South Sea Company prosecuted some of them. That had a double effect. The shams were exposed in court. But so was the real value of the South Sea Company's own assets and prospects. The speculative bubble burst, the sham companies collapsed, South Sea shares fell from £1,050 to £135, and thousands of investors were ruined.

One *not* ruined was Robert Walpole, a Member of Parliament. He had bought South Sea shares, sold them before the crash, and made a fortune. But he had opposed the handing over of the national debt in the first place, he was an able financial manager, and he became Chancellor of the Exchequer (i.e. the chief financial officer of the government) to clean up the mess. The shareholders got a third of the face value of their South Sea shares. The government re-financed its debt at lower interest than ever. (The taxpayers thus did quite well out of the bubble.) And Parliament passed the Bubble Act, to prevent the formation of joint stock companies except by Royal Charter or Act of Parliament after proper scrutiny by government.

For a hundred years the Bubble Act did help to discourage sham companies. But it also blocked useful ones. The eighteenth century saw increasing need for joint stock organization to mobilize capital for big enterprises. There were business developments in shipping, slave trading and colonial plantations. There were technical advances in farming, mining, textile industries, water-powered and then steam-powered machinery, and canal and road building. Parliament passed special Acts to incorporate canal and road companies, because they had to be given compulsory powers to buy their routes. But, remembering the bubble, the government was reluctant to incorporate other enterprises. Entrepreneurs responded by evading the law. They used loopholes in the Bubble Act to develop elaborate kinds of partnership. In effect they created joint stock companies by private contract, without incorporation. That worked after a fashion, but had serious disadvantages. The enterprises could not sue or be sued, only their individual partners could. In principle all the shareholders had unlimited liability for their enterprises' debts. In practice it could be hard for creditors to find out who they were, then to sue them all individually, then to collect from them. That effectively – though illegally – limited their liability.

Summary Company promoters had ruined thousands of people in the bubble. Government responded with the Bubble Act and other measures to hinder the creation of joint stock companies. Business responded by developing cumbersome kinds of partnership with a dishonest and unreliable kind of limited liability. It was with that poor institutional equipment that Britain had to work its first industrial revolution, the steam revolution. That was one of a number of disadvantages (noticed earlier in Chapter 11) in the public and private management of that revolution.

CREATION OF THE MODERN COMPANY

Old and new industries grew unsteadily, with some spectacular successes and many failures, through the first half of the nineteenth century. Railways, steamships, machine and tool making, the mechanized mass production of textiles, and property development in the growing cities could all have benefited from better forms of joint stock organization.

In 1825 a speculative boom and slump led to the repeal of the Bubble Act, and between 1844 and 1862 a series of Acts at last put together the elements of the modern company. New companies with joint stock and limited liability could be incorporated simply by registering them with the government's new Registrar of Companies. They must render him regular annual accounts, which would be public. Enterprises with more than 25 shareholders, or whose shares could be sold without the unanimous consent of all the shareholders, were compelled to register as companies. Others could if they wanted to. There were alternative forms for private companies, and for non-profit companies.

The growth of regulation

The politicians and public servants who designed the new private capitalist institution kept changing their minds about the safeguards it might need. Each new element of it (such as joint stock, or limited liability) was commonly introduced by a special-purpose Act; then a year or so later the general Companies Act was amended to incorporate the new element. A number of safeguards were included in the special-purpose Acts but then dropped in the revision of the general Act. Thus companies were made subject to the law of bankruptcy – then exempted from it. Limited liability was at first confined to companies whose owners took a fair share of the risks by contributing substantial share capital; then that safeguard was dropped, to allow 'five pound companies' whose owners took no risks at all. (Instead of contributing capital themselves they raised it all by borrowing, or getting goods on credit.) The first joint stock Act made companies begin by registering for a trial period; then that requirement was dropped. Companies' returns to the Registrar had at first to be audited by auditors approved by the Registrar; then both halves of that requirement were dropped, so that until 1900 accounts did not have to be audited at all, and if they were, the auditors did not need any official approval.

While some safeguards were dropped, others were steadily increased. Besides new safeties and efficiencies the new company powers also allowed some new ways of cheating shareholders and creditors. Some of the misbehavior was lawful, so the law had to be extended to ban it. Some was unlawful but easy to commit in practice, so more regulation was needed to make it harder to get away with. Some of the frauds were deliberate. Others were merely defensive – firms did badly by bad luck or bad management, then directors responded improperly by looking after their own interests at the expense of others. Either way, government had to respond by elaborating the regulations. The first Joint Stock Companies Act of 1844 was comparatively short and simple. After eighteen years of frauds and countermeasures the Joint Stock Companies Act of 1862 had two hundred and twelve Sections and three Schedules. The Act continued to grow through the next century.

Business people fretted at the growth of regulation. But they themselves demanded a good deal of it. Directly, the honest wanted to be protected from the dishonest. Indirectly, they wanted to keep the new company powers effective. If directors could cheat shareholders, share capital would become difficult to raise. If limited liability allowed companies to cheat creditors, the honest as well as the dishonest would find it hard to get credit.

Both those reasons – to protect victims from fraud, and to maintain honest companies' credit – prompted an 1857 Act to make directors' frauds crimes. Until then, as long as they did not personally lie to their victims with intent to defraud, their frauds were not crimes – it was left to the victims to sue for their money if they could, which they often could not. For introducing criminal penalties the Attorney General of the day offered two reasons. First, 'delinquencies ... were so frequent and so gigantic'. Second, the miscreants were too clever to tell positive lies. They relied on concealment, misleading financial accounts, and the victims' tendency to jump to false conclusions. Parliament needed to outlaw 'that extensive system of fraud which was produced through the medium of false representations, coupled with acts to give a colour to those representations such as fraudulent statements of the affairs of a company, the payment of dividends out of fictitious capital, or other wrongful acts which went to the perpetration of great cheats.' Attracting new capital by paying dividends out of old capital was a common trick. New investors were impressed by a record of big dividends, and there was still nothing necessarily unlawful in 'declaring large dividends in order to deceive the public, at the very time that those who declared the dividend knew that the capital was all gone'.

The victims of fraud suffered, and honest business suffered. In 1857 one Member of Parliament instanced a number of frauds by directors of joint stock banks. One English, one Irish, one Indian, and one Australian bank had lately failed. Banks did not yet have limited liability, so their shareholders as well as their depositors and creditors took risks. The Australian Banking Company for example had been floated in 1844 with a nominal capital of £400,000; but of the shares offered, most had failed to find buyers.

> The Company never raised more than £40,000. The Directors however at once proceeded to trade on a large scale; borrowed more than £300,000 on debentures, and misappropriated the whole of the money.

Process was instituted in the Court of Chancery, which ... called upon the unfortunate shareholders in the Company to pay upwards of half a million of money. Such cases frequently occurring ... produced the painful impression ... that there was in this country ... an absence, to a lamentable degree, of commercial integrity. Of course, those were exceptional cases; for, as a rule, the commercial classes of England were composed of men of high respectability and great integrity, but unfortunately the public could not discern those who were from those who were not, and thus a stigma was cast [on honest and dishonest alike].

– House of Commons, 21 May 1857

Parliament continued to elaborate the law. So did judges. Judgments in leading cases obliged directors to maintain their companies' capital, with complicated definitions and exceptions to distinguish honest from dishonest losses of capital. (But directors who wanted to shed capital could often find circuitous ways through the complexities.) The courts said that companies could only do the kinds of business specified in their constitutions. (But companies responded by writing very wide powers into their constitutions.) The courts tried (but generally failed) to protect minority shareholders from unfair treatment by majorities. The Companies Acts aimed to protect shareholders and creditors chiefly by keeping them fully informed; company business should be public. But the courts weakened that by deciding that anything a company wrote into the small print of its returns to the Registrar of Companies could count as sufficiently published to everyone else as well.

The essentials of the modern company – joint stock, limited liability, and simple incorporation by the government's Registrar of Companies – were consolidated in the Companies Act of 1862. Detailed additions and elaborations followed, in response to changing business practice, and to misbehavior by companies or their officers, or traders in their shares. Two world wars brought temporary controls on the raising and use of capital, as part of the war organization of industry. Through much of the twentieth century governments reviewed and re-enacted the Companies Acts every twenty years or so. There were many additions and amendments to the law, but until the 1970s most of them were minor.

A British 'mess'   In the 1970s the lawmakers began to respond to some important changes in business organization and behavior: takeovers, more international activity, more corporate tax avoidance. At the same time Britain joined the European Economic Community and

began to revise its company law to comply with Community requirements, which were themselves growing and changing. The Community requirements and the changing business conditions prompted a rapid increase in the quantity and complexity of British company law – and in its inefficiency, some critics thought. Here one eminent critic cites another –

> [L.C.B.Gower has said] that English companies legislation was 'both in form and in substance in a far worse mess than it has been at any time this century.' Our present situation can be demonstrated ... by looking at the three successive editions of Butterworth's *Company Law Handbook*, which ... collects all the company law enactments between one set of covers. The first edition, that of 1978, contains the 'mess' to which Professor Gower referred at the time he was speaking. It is about one inch thick, and weighs a pound and three quarters on the kitchen scales. ... Shortly after that time, the passing of the Companies Act 1980 led Messrs. Butterworths to publish a second edition. This one is one and a half inches thick, and two and a quarter pounds. An ever greater 'mess' ... But matters did not stop there. In 1981 came another Companies Act, and so there had to be a further new edition; and now the book is nearly two and a quarter inches thick, and weighs three and a quarter pounds. Were this trend to continue (and it is not a wholly fanciful idea, for there are a couple of dozen more Eurodirectives on their way, which sooner or later will end up as law), we could well have by the year 2000 an eight-pound monster Companies Act running to something like 3000 pages!

> *– L.S.Sealy, Company Law and Commercial Reality*
> (1984) p.56

Professor Sealy regrets that so much of the development of the law has been by addition, and lists some of the nineteenth century rules which might well be simplified or done without. But however disordered they have become, many of the complexities are there for good reasons. Repealing them would not liberate more efficient production, it would more often reopen the opportunities for fraud or mismanagement which the rules were introduced to prevent. The bit-by-bit accumulation of rules over time reflects the varieties of corporate misbehavior from which investors, honest firms, consumers and the general public want the law to protect them. When economists tell you that the tangle of public regulation is preventing the efficient allocation and use of economic resources, remember three things: (1) what most of the regulation is actually preventing; (2) how much of the regulation is demanded by business itself, to protect honest business owners and managers and creditors; and (3) how a belief in neoclassical theory can blind people to the realities of business life.

European differences

This Economics text can't describe the company law of a dozen or more European countries. But two differences from the British history are worth noticing.

Most European countries have avoided the abuse of limited liability by '£5 companies', i.e. companies whose owners and directors invest next to nothing in them, and thus shift all their risks onto the people who lend them money or sell them goods on credit. French, German and other Europeans have long required companies to have substantial share capital of their own before they can borrow or get credit from others. So 'risk-free risk-taking', i.e. risking suppliers' and lenders' money rather than your own, has been less common in continental Europe than in English-speaking countries.

Led by Germany and Sweden, much of northern Europe has developed company structures with two boards, and with worker participation, or at least representation, in corporate policy-making. A lower board of full-time executives manages the business. An upper board, distanced from the managers, hires and fires the managers, has well-defined watch-dog duties, and may include representatives of any or all of workers, consumers and government as well as shareholders.

Independently of those legal requirements, West European industrial managers have tended to have more technical education, and perhaps more social prestige, than their British equivalents. Some studies have suggested that much of the best European talent is in productive industrial management, while its British equivalents – economists or accountants rather than engineers – are in the City of London juggling share ownership and tax obligations, or financing takeovers. Whatever the causes, West European corporate management through the second half of the twentieth century does appear to have been more competent than British, and responsible for less scandals, better industrial relations, and more technical and organizational innovation. (Though I believe that general observation is just, there are of course many individual exceptions to it on both sides of the channel.)

AMERICAN EXPERIENCE

The American story differs from the British in three particular ways. Firms have been free to incorporate in any of the States, each with its own company law. Americans have got many of their public services from private enterprises franchised and regulated by government, rather than from public enterprises. And the US Constitution has allowed judges to assume large powers against legislators and public servants. Those circumstances have combined with some strong disagreements about the merits of competition to prompt many experiments in business regulation, and much debate about its ends and means.

51 STATES, 51 HISTORIES?

When the American colonies won their freedom from Britain they adopted a federal constitution which said nothing about business corporations. Company law remains State business. Britain had created companies by Royal Charter or by Act of Parliament. The Americans melded those two into one: for half a century or so, companies were chartered by individual Acts of State legislatures. In one important respect they soon moved ahead of Britain: New York introduced limited liability in 1811, and other States followed.

Most of the early corporations were founded to build roads and bridges, docks and harbors, canals and river navigations. There were also some banks, insurance companies and universities. As public utilities, the corporations mixed private profit-seeking with public powers and obligations, and sometimes financial guarantees or tax exemptions. Their public obligations needed some protection from their private profit-seeking, especially when they were monopolies. They were public/private hybrids. In 1819 the Supreme Court introduced a basic distinction between profit-seeking corporations and those (like universities) whose primary purpose was public service. But many of the utility companies continued to take such private advantage of their public privileges that they generated a good deal of public suspicion of corporate behavior.

Through the 1830s there was a rapid growth of corporate business. The States coped with it by ceasing to create each new firm by a separate legislative Act. Instead, they passed general Acts which empowered public officers to incorporate new firms by simple registration. Though simpler, that introduced some rigidities. When each firm had been chartered by its own legislative Act, its powers and privileges could be tailored to fit its intended function. But the legislators would not trust public servants to write different conditions for different firms, so the general Acts imposed identical chartering rules (in any one State) on all corporations. The States happened to be passing those Acts during the Jacksonian years of populist democracy when there was widespread suspicion of corporations, especially big ones. So the general Corporations Acts were severely restrictive, especially of corporations' size. They limited the amount of share capital a corporation could raise, and the amount it could borrow. Growth by takeover was blocked because corporations were not allowed to own the stock (shares) of other corporations. Some States chartered them for limited terms, so they must periodically apply for renewal. Some States would only charter corporations owned by their own residents. Some restricted them to doing business within the State that chartered them. Others did not, and their creations could trade anywhere: the federal constitution had clauses which ensured that States could not exclude corporations chartered by other States.

The restrictions on size, takeover and interstate business soon irked many entrepreneurs. Through the middle and later years of the century the nation built its railroads, discovered oil, and rapidly industrialized. Railroads needed land grants, or powers to acquire their routes compulsorily, often in more than one State. Other industries, including oil, steel, sugar, whiskey and lead also wanted to organize – or some entrepreneurs wanted to organize them – on a national scale. Some of them wanted vertical integration, i.e. to own several stages of their productive processes. Railroads wanted to own their sources of coal. Oilmen wanted to own wells, refineries and retail outlets.

Big business eventually escaped the old State restraints in one or other of four main ways.

Railroads obviously needed land grants, or powers of compulsory purchase, to acquire their routes, and many of them needed to operate over several States on larger scale than most State charters would allow. So for railroads and some other utilities there was some return to 'tailored' powers as enterprises got individual, special-purpose Acts from State legislatures.

A second way around the States' chartering restraints was simply to break the law, bribing the lawmakers where necessary. John D. Rockefeller's early attempts to build a national oil enterprise were mostly illegal and were eventually undone by legal action. Rockefeller's lawyers then found a third way around the restraints by inventing a type of trust which enabled a collection of formally independent firms to be brought under a single control and management. Before long more than twenty such trusts were bringing elements of monopoly to a number of industries.

It was during the short life of those trusts that the federal government began, with the Sherman Act of 1890, to regulate corporate behavior. Twenty seven States also acted in one way or other against the trusts. The trusts soon disappeared – but 'anti-trust' has stuck ever since as the common name for policies which are either anti-monopolist and pro-competitive, or anti-big and pro-small business.

The fourth and permanent solution followed. 'If you can't beat 'em, join 'em.'

The New Jersey revolution

It occurred to some State governments that it might be sensible to legislate the forms of organization that the new industries wanted. It might also be profitable. Big corporations could afford to pay high fees for helpful charters under helpful corporation laws, and if they paid high fees other State taxes could be lower.

New Jersey was the pioneer. In 1891-2 it repealed its anti-trust law and replaced its corporations law. As further amended in 1896 the new law allowed corporations chartered in New Jersey to be as big as they liked; to operate anywhere; to be owned by residents of any part of the world; and most important, to own other corporations.

Rockefeller moved Standard Oil to the New Jersey registry. U.S.Steel was incorporated there. Others followed, including many mergers made possible by the new law. New Jersey was able to abolish most of its other taxes. Twenty years later its share of the business declined as other States competed for it, and New Jersey elected a reformist government which reduced some of the corporate privileges. Leadership passed to the State of Delaware, which offered the original New Jersey freedoms and some more besides. Delaware corporations could amend their own constitutions, which no longer need limit the types of business they could do. Pyramiding was permitted: a stockholder could control a large capital by owning 51 per cent of Holding Company A which owned 51 per cent of Holding Company B which owned 51 per cent of Holding Company C which owned 51 per cent of the actual business. (In that pyramid, 15 per cent of the stock could outvote the rest.) Corporations were allowed to issue shares of different kinds, some with voting rights and some without. For many years the

Ford family controlled the Ford Motor Company while owning less than five per cent of the stock.

Once again other States competed for the business and Delaware's share of it declined just as New Jersey's share had done. But Delaware made a triumphant comeback with a 1967 revision of its Corporations Law, a revision which responded to a change of command in the corporations themselves.

The Delaware revolution

Through the first half of the century the chartermongering states had competed to give corporations the powers and freedoms which their *owners* wanted. The promoters of firms like Standard Oil and US Steel were part-owners who identified their interests with their corporations' interests. But there came a widely-noticed change in that relation between ownership and management. By the 1950s there were still some individual owners like the Fords, but most big corporations had widespread shareholding with no dominant owners. They were directed instead by self-perpetuating groups of directors who recruited one another and managed stockholders' meetings by means of proxies and stockholders' inertia. As long as their corporations prospered they were effectively answerable to nobody except the public regulatory authorities.

Revising the branches of law which were supposed to discipline the directors themselves was the secret of Delaware's new success. Under its 1967 law stockholders could no longer propose amendments to a Delaware corporation's charter; only directors could. Directors could vote on schemes from which they themselves could derive loans, stock options, stock bonuses and other 'incentive compensations'. They could have their corporations indemnify them (i.e. repay them) for any civil or criminal penalties for misbehaving as directors. Most of those matters need not be disclosed to stockholders, the press or the public.

The Delaware rules were drafted by private corporate lawyers, and most of the State's Supreme Court judges who interpreted the laws were ex-corporate lawyers. Within seven years of the 1967 revision nearly half of America's thousand biggest corporations, including half of the hundred biggest, were chartered by Delaware. Most of the biggest hundred and many of the rest were paying their executives ten to fifteen times as much as judges or generals or State governors were paid. Critics concluded that State law had abdicated from its responsibility to regulate the corporate use of other people's money. Short of simple theft, directors could now take as much money as they liked from

their firms and the States would compete to legalize the plunder.

Conclusion State chartering was corrupted because government as well as business became competitive. States competed for revenue by writing laws to sell to corporations, rather than to regulate them. In effect, governments traded with them instead of governing them, and in that trade the corporations' mobility meant that they bargained from superior strength.

That is apt to happen wherever government is escapable. Rich countries' ships escape their national laws and taxes by registering in Panama, the Delaware of the shipping registries. Transnational corporations locate their profit centres in countries with low corporate taxes, and some countries – the Delawares of the tax evasion industry – compete to attract them. The European Economic Community is trying to avoid Delaware effects by directing its member governments to move towards an identical company law.

Some economists disagree with this perception of the problem. They welcome the interstate or transnational freedoms. With faith in the self-regulating character of market forces they think the less business is regulated, the better. If you are tempted to agree, read Charles Raw, Bruce Page and Godfrey Hodgson, *Do you sincerely want to be rich?* (1971). It tells how Investors Overseas Services (IOS) pioneered the idea that offshore ownership under *no* nation's sovereignty could increase the returns to investment by freeing it altogether from tax and regulatory restraints. Investors found too late that putting their money beyond reach of government put it where directors could steal it – hundreds of millions of it. If the US had nothing but Delaware chartering to regulate corporate uses of other people's money, directors might have similar opportunities nearer home.

Joint stock and limited liability need government. So does the management of other people's money when the owners are too many, scattered and unskilled to keep an eye on it themselves. Fortunately before Delaware finally liberated America's corporate directors the national government was already regulating a good deal of their activity.

FEDERAL REGULATION

The US Government's efforts to regulate business have been shaped by some basic facts of business development and a basic faith – backed by plenty of entrenched interest – in private enterprise. To understand the range of the regulators' purposes, it will help to begin with some of the business facts which they have faced.

From the point of view of a regulator who hopes to keep firms efficient by keeping them competitive, modern industries can be sorted out into five categories. Each has temptations to misbehave, determined chiefly by its technology and the market strength or weakness of its customers.

1. **Natural monopolies** like power and gas supply, piped water and sewerage; or canals and railroads at some times and places in their history.

   Temptations: Monopoly pricing; using market power to bully other enterprises; refusing essential services to needy customers.

   Remedies: Public ownership, or direct public regulation of profits, prices, routes, standards of service.

2. **Industries with continuously increasing economies of scale** in which big firms predominate, as monopolists or oligopolists, because the technical economies of scale allow them to under-sell and out-compete small firms. Examples: Steel, machine-making, vehicle-making, petrochemicals.

   Temptations: Monopoly pricing and other bullying or exploitive uses of market strength.

   Remedies: Anti-trust action to maintain a few firms rather than a single monopoly, and to prevent open collusion between the few. Exposure to international competition if the industry produces goods which can alternatively be imported.

3. **Industries with U-shaped costs** in which medium-sized firms do best, because the unit costs of production rise if the firm is *either* too big *or* too small. Examples: House-building, furniture-making, textiles.

   Temptations: Ideally, none – competition comes naturally. (But depending on the industry, there may be need to regulate safely, or to protect workers or small firms from harsh effects of competition.)

4. **Industries with constant unit costs** in which firms of all sizes can be efficient, so that monopoly is *unnecessary* but nevertheless *possible*. Firms can grow big by competing super-successfully, or by takeovers based on financial strength. Small firms also may create some monopolist advantages by co-operative agreement. These industries are the only ones which actually fit the original anti-trust assumptions, i.e. they can be either competitive or monopolist by choice, so public action can have some effect in preventing monopoly without impairing efficiency. Examples: book publishing, brewing, wine-making.

   Temptations: To build monopolies.
   Remedy: Prohibit monopolies.

5. **Industries with diseconomies of scale** in which small firms usually have lower unit costs than big ones. Examples: tailoring, repair services, individual arts like painting, composing, writing; and many kinds of farming. There may be some scope for cooperation, as when orchardists or dairy farmers form cooperatives to process their products for local markets. But these naturally competitive industries rarely generate much market strength; they more often want protection themselves, from unstable world markets or from monopolist buyers of their products.

Besides those five types there are also hybrids. There are industries in which some processes can be monopolized but others can't. For example big car-makers buy many components from small, highly competitive suppliers. There are industries in which consumer preferences allow big and small firms to coexist. In retailing, for example, big supermarket chains coexist with small corner stores and specialty shops.

We have no room for a general history of the US Government's efforts to regulate industries of those diverse kinds. We can merely sketch some outlines and sample some cases. As before, you need not memorize the details. The purpose is simply to grasp the nature, including the changing nature, of the necessary relations between business and government, to reinforce this chapter's theme that business is not something which government can choose to leave alone. Corporations are public/private hybrids; governments create their powers and license them, and necessarily share responsibility for their uses and misuses of other people's money. The question is not *whether* to regulate them, but *how*.

NATURAL MONOPOLIES

Public utilities – piped water, power, gas, telephone and rail services – need physical networks which it would usually be uneconomic to duplicate. Rival water pipes down every street would benefit nobody but the pipe-makers. The elements of monopoly may change with changing technology. For example telecommunications can become more competitive as they cease to depend on copper wire or fibre-optic networks. But wherever a single network is the most economical provision, there is said to be a natural monopoly.

Some American utilities are publicly owned but many are not. Where they are not, private operators typically get their monopoly rights and routes from government, and have their rates and services regulated by government. Their problems vary from industry to industry, but some of the most troublesome have been those of the railroads. They can supply our example, because their history illustrates both the problems of regulating private monopolies, and also how the elements of monopoly can change with changing technology.

American railroads were pioneered through the 1830s and 1840s, then spread their networks across the continent through the third quarter of the century. They had powerful effects on the nation's geographical expansion and economic growth. They opened the prairies and the west to white settlement and mining and agriculture by linking them to markets in the east and overseas. They brought round-the-year bulk transport to the industrial north-east whose transport links had suffered as their canals and seaways froze for months each winter. By revolutionizing the speed and cost of land transport, and by creating large new demands for earth-moving, timber, iron and steel, machinery and rolling stock, they gave great stimulus to industrialization.

For half a century state governments gave the rail revolution too much aid and too little regulation. That had ill effects of three general kinds: excessive competition, misuses of market power, and financial chicanery.

Excessive competition Too many lines were built, often too close together, too far ahead of demand. Some failed. For the available freight others competed by methods which included fraud, violence, and unfair discrimination between one customer and another. A more efficient national network could undoubtedly have been built at less cost if the planning and granting of routes had been coordinated by central government, as the public railways of France and Germany and the private railways of Britain were.

Although the railroads competed hard wherever they had competitors, most of them also served some areas where the customers had no alternatives and the railroad could exploit its monopoly.

Misuses of market power The misbehavior chiefly consisted in charging monopoly prices, and treating customers unequally. Captive customers – often farmers with no alternative transport to their markets – were charged to the limit they could pay, partly for profit and partly to subsidize lower rates on more competitive routes. Meanwhile operators would cut rates to particular customers for particular purposes: to undercut com-

petitors, to favor customers who were also stockholders in the corporation, to favor friendly editors, legislators and judges. Sometimes one monopolist could make others work for him. In 1885 when the Cincinnati & Marietta Railroad was charging 35 cents a barrel for freighting oil, to get Rockefeller's business it agreed to carry for Standard Oil at 10 cents, and also to pay Standard 25 of every 35 cents it earned by freighting for Standard's competitors. It was chiefly by coercing railroads to manipulate their rates in that way that Rockefeller destroyed or took over his competitors and built Standard Oil. American legislators and judges were slow to define railroads as 'common carriers' with obligations to carry all comers at equal rates.

Financial frauds The railroads managed to raise abundant capital – a fifth or more of all new American investment for many years – before there was much regulation of their use of it. Investors might have been more cautious if they had only had operating profits to hope for. But States and cities competed to attract lines by granting them land and cash or credit, so that investors saw prospects of public gifts as well as business earnings. The legislators and the 'robber barons' often got rich together. In central and western States which still had public land to give away, government would give mile-wide routes to the railroad promoters, who would keep what they needed for the line and sell the rest. By linking hitherto-inaccessible land to distant services and markets, the line would give the land agricultural and townsite value. Selling it at farm and town prices gave the railmen money to build the line, and often to bribe the legislators who provided the land. Altogether seven per cent of the land surface of the United States passed through the railwaymen's hands.

It was also possible to get rich by building unprofitable lines, though those who did so rarely shared the riches with the railroad stockholders. Here's how to do it if corporate behavior is not regulated. Incorporate a railroad company. Get a route, free land and some financial guarantees from State legislatures. Armed with those, raise capital by selling stock to the public. But get the line *built* by a separate construction company owned by the railroad promoters and directors, *not* the stockholders. Have the construction company overcharge the railroad corporation, taking most of its capital. When that has enriched the promoters (and any editors, legislators and judges they need to bribe), leave the railroad corporation to operate the line as best it can.

That sketch does not exaggerate. The Central Pacific Railroad was built for an estimated $58m. but paid $120m. to its construction company. The Erie Railroad investors were robbed by Jay Gould by means which included fraudulent stock issues, corrupt construction contracts, wholesale bribery of judges and legislators, and watering the stock from $17m. to $78m. ('Watering' will presently be explained.) Those were only the most extreme of many similar achievements of the robber barons of the rail-building age.

Eventually – too late to prevent the wasteful proliferation of lines – the scandals provoked some effective regulation.

Regulators' options

In 1869 Charles Francis Adams, the first effective railroad reformer, theorized about the relation between natural monopolies and government: 'competition and the cheapest possible transportation are wholly incompatible ... The single chance any given community has of obtaining the cheapest possible transportation is limited by its success in directing the largest possible volume of movement through the fewest possible channels'. A full train is more economical than two half-empty ones. Ten trains an hour on one track are more economical than five each on two tracks. So rather than oppose rail monopolies government should encourage them, and regulate them. The options were –

- public ownership, which Adams thought worked well elsewhere but (for various reasons) not in the US;

- unregulated private monopoly, likely to exploit the public unacceptably;

- private monopoly with public regulators fixing its prices or rates of profit; or

- what Adams liked to call sunshine and voluntarism.

Sunshine meant full public disclosure of the private operators' business affairs. Voluntarism actually meant a kind of coercion which the operators could not take to court. Adams' Massachusetts Railroad Commission had no coercive powers, except to elicit information. Instead of fixing the railroad operators' rates directly (which the operators could have disputed or delayed by court action) Adams would publish expert economic analyses of their performance and profits, then 'suggest' that they could afford to drop their fares or freight rates somewhat. The 'suggestion' might be accompanied by the draft of a coercive Act which the State legislature might well pass if 'voluntarism' failed to work. It was left to the operators to judge just how far their rates had better fall. (A similar regime of self-discipline for fear of unspecified penalties was developed in Russia by Lenin in the early years of Bolshevik government before the

new dictatorship had enough police to watch everybody properly. Lenin didn't call it voluntarism, he called it terror.)

In the US voluntarism did not succeed for very long. Firms began to disregard 'suggestions'. States gave their Railroad Commissions coercive powers. In 1886 the Supreme Court declared most of their powers invalid, so in 1887 a federal Interstate Commerce Commission was created with powers to give directions to railroad operators.

Troubles continued. The federal and state constitutions often made it difficult to predict what powers the judges would allow the legislators to delegate to public servants. 'More than any other single problem, this question would trouble future commissions as they battled repeatedly against restrictive judicial review. Ultimately the problem of constitutionality contributed to those endless delays that came to characterize the regulatory process in the twentieth century. Agency after agency, preoccupied with the requirements of due process, frittered away its energies on trivia, thereby minimizing its role in the formation of substantive economic policy.' (Thomas K. McCraw, *Prophets of Regulation*, 1984, 24-5).

Where enforcement did succeed, there were dilemmas about what to enforce. If the regulators decreed low transport prices, the quality of service tended to decline as the operators could not (or pretended that they could not) earn enough to finance proper maintenance and modernization. So instead of fixing prices, some regulators fixed permissible rates of profit. The rate of profit was expressed as a percentage of the capital employed. Some operators responded not by restraining their prices but by watering their stock.

(How do you 'water stock'? Suppose you raise $10m. of capital by selling ten million $1 shares, and build a railroad. The railroad does well and is soon earning $1m. profit each year. That's considered such a good return in the 1880s that your $1 shares are changing hands on the Stock Exchanges for prices around $2. The Railroad Commissioner compares your annual $1m. of profit to your registered capital of $10m., sees a profit rate of 10 per cent, and thinks it is excessive. He directs you to cut it down to 5 per cent. He hopes you will do that by cutting freight rates and passenger fares. Instead, you make a free one-for-one bonus share issue, giving stockholders a second $1 share for every $1 share they own. The market price of each share drops back to about $1, but with twice the number of shares each stockholder has the same money's worth as before. Profit is unchanged at $1m. a year. But the corporation's registered capital has doubled from $10m. to $20m., so the profit *rate*, as the Commissioner measures it, has been halved to 5 per cent by watering the capital stock.)

Angry at such a cheap trick, that Commissioner may direct you to halve the profit itself to $500,000. You doubt if his Act empowers him to do that, so you don't comply. He takes you to court. The hearings and appeals take two years and net your lawyers $1m. fees. If you win, you keep your profit rate and the Commissioner pays your legal fees. If you lose, your legal fees have halved your profits for those years without any cuts in fares or freight rates. The Commissioner asks the legislature for more effective powers. The railroad lobby tries to get local newspapers to persuade the legislators to leave things as they are ...

Despite those and other difficulties, regulators often managed to impose lower rates than the railmen would have liked. But just as what you study may be changing as you study it, so also what you regulate may be changing as you regulate it. The nineteenth century railroads were monopolists of many kinds of traffic, but the twentieth century brought competitors: cars, buses, trucks, then airlines. Railroads lost monopoly market strength and lost a lot of their custom. Many lines closed. Others were still needed for essential services to other industries – freighting bulky coal and wheat, getting city commuters to work – but could no longer pay their way. Where governments could not afford to let them close, the need to restrain their profits gave way to the need to subsidize them. There was new work for public watchdogs, to see that they did not inflate the subsidies and exploit the taxpayers. As before, there were alternatives of regulated private ownership or public ownership. As before, America stuck to regulated private ownership and most of Europe stuck to public ownership.

EXERCISE

Air transport poses similar dilemmas. One full plane can charge lower fares than two half-empty competitors can. There are also compelling safety reasons in favor of regulating the business to keep operators reasonably prosperous rather than desperately competitive. Propose a strategy for the United States. Keep it by you, and when this chapter presently introduces you to Jim Landis, compare your strategy to what you think his might be.

From the regulation of natural monopolies and the artificial monopolies created by public transport regulation, we turn now to the more general problems of unequal market strength which have occasioned America's anti-trust laws.

COMPETITIVE INDUSTRIES AND ANTI-TRUST DILEMMAS

You know how New Jersey led in offering corporate owners the business powers and freedoms they wanted. Then Delaware offered the corporations' directors the personal freedoms and wealth and secrecy that *they* wanted. In competition with those chartermongering States, no State could any longer exert much control over the behavior of corporations or their directors.

Federal regulation began with the Sherman Anti-Trust Act of 1890. In a world still ruled by the States' old restraints on corporate size, the Sherman Act was designed to prevent two things: (i) collusion between independent firms to maintain prices or define territories or otherwise avoid competition; and (ii) devices such as trusts, to bring many firms under single control. The Act was not designed to regulate monopolist behavior by a single big firm, because the States' laws still banned big firms. But the ink was scarcely dry on the Sherman Act when New Jersey led in legalizing firms of any size.

Big and small firms Big firms developed quickly in industries with appropriate economies of scale, and they posed dilemmas for anti-trust policy-makers. How could government enforce competition and ban monopoly in industries in which competition *produced* monopoly? When the big firms emerged, there were more dilemmas. It had seemed reasonable to stop small firms conspiring to charge uniform prices. But it did not seem reasonable to stop a single big firm charging uniform prices for its products. Indeed anti-trust rules could require uniform prices in some circumstances, for example to prevent predatory pricing.

(What is predatory pricing? Suppose you have a national monopoly as mousetrap supplier. A local firm tries to compete with you in one region. You drop your prices below cost in that region only, for as long as it takes to bust the newcomer. Then you put them up again. That's predatory pricing.)

What could anti-trust policy-makers do when collusive pricing by groups of small firms gave way to uniform pricing by single big firms? They could think of price control. But that contradicted their deepest beliefs about the value of market competition. The point of anti-trust action was to ensure that competing firms *disciplined each other* so that government would *not* have to tell them how to do their business.

In practice anti-trust administrators were inconsistent about cooperation between small firms. They often attacked it, but sometimes positively encouraged it. During the First World War the government had arranged a good deal of rationalization and cooperation between firms in war industries. The cooperation seemed to cut costs and improve efficiency. In some industries it also helped small firms to survive competition by big ones. On both grounds, some post-war anti-trust administrators encouraged it. Led by Louis Brandeis, some even encouraged it at some cost in efficiency and low prices: they were for small firms against big, even if the big served consumers better than the small did.

If the regulators could not do much about big firms' pricing, could they ban bigness itself? Could the law limit firms' size as the old state charters once did, or limit firms' market shares of their industries? No: to prevent more efficient firms from growing at the expense of the less efficient would hinder the competition which anti-trust aimed to encourage.

Moreover the big firms varied widely in the way they used their market strength. Through the middle decades of the twentieth century for example oligopolist pharmaceutical manufacturers charged enough for their drugs to earn 20 per cent or more per year on funds employed, while US Steel, a tariff-protected monopolist, charged enough to earn about 3 per cent. Question: why the difference? Answer: *it takes two to determine market strength*. Medicines are prescribed by doctors who don't have to pay for them. They are paid for by patients with no expertise or market strength at all, or by health insurers who can adjust their premiums to the prices of whatever the doctors prescribe. Steel on the other hand could only sell to other firms, many of them big and tough and able to interest the government in restraining steel prices for the American economy as a whole. So market weaklings paid high prices to the pharmaceutical companies, while market mammoths like Ford and General Motors and the government's defence contractors paid low prices to US Steel.

It became clear that no single anti-trust rule could deal well with the range of industries categorized earlier. Recall the categories: Natural monopolies. Industries tending to monopoly because of economies of scale. Industries with constant costs in which competition or monopoly may be open to choice. Takeovers which improve service to consumers, and takeovers which worsen it. Industries in which small firms do best, but price-cutting competition can be avoided by cooperation. And naturally competitive industries, including some in which people need to be protected from competition's harsh effects..

Divided powers When such diverse facts of business life belied the original anti-trust expectations, the policy makers responded in ways which might have worked well in countries with sovereign parliaments. The laws were amended to allow anti-trust administrators to discriminate between reasonable and unreasonable uses of market strength. Congress had given similar discretions to wartime price controllers. British and European price and rent controllers had exercised similar discretions in peacetime. But in a series of anti-trust cases, judges ruled that the US Constitution did not allow legislators to empower public servants to decide what business behavior was reasonable. If Congress created such discretions, only judges could exercise them.

Thus the attempt to be flexible struck double trouble. On the one hand judges have tried to detail some rules of 'reasonable' behavior; i.e. they have tried to reduce the flexibility which the legislators tried to create. On the other hand plenty of disagreement and uncertainty continue. Different judges in different courts have not been perfectly consistent. New business practices from time to time call for new exercises of discretion. And in trying to keep up with changing business practices and political demands, the legislators have continued to complicate the law. But the administrators can rarely apply the new rules in a straightforward way. Most new government initiatives, and responses to new business practices, have to go to court, where they take time and cost money. The Justice Department lawyers have limited budgets, and don't like to lose. So they have tended to take on small rather than big firms; local rather than national monopolies; winnable rather than risky cases; and a few exemplary cases rather than *all* instances of the kinds of misbehavior they want to discourage. The result is more like a mixture of bluff and guerilla warfare than the sure administration of a body of firm law.

Conclusion American anti-trust activity has had changing and sometimes uncertain purposes. It calls for considerable administrative discretion. In good hands both of those can be compatible with fair, effective and economical business regulation. But the judges' use of their constitutional powers has made anti-trust an indifferent method of business regulation: cumbersome, expensive, and only patchily effective.

Nevertheless the anti-trust offices have had 'sunshine' effects. Their investigations have intensified the critical scrutiny under which American corporations – even Delaware corporations – have to do their business. Unlike the state chartering offices and the public regulators of some of the utilities, they have not generally been captured by the interests they are there to discipline. Directly and indirectly their presence has almost certainly improved some corporate behavior.

But the effects are difficult to measure; and they might well have been achieved much more cheaply and effectively if state chartering had been replaced long ago by a national Office of Corporate Affairs empowered to charter and regulate the nation's corporations, with the charters depending on the firms' continuing compliance with a single body of national company law.

Objection: if one national office had to charter and monitor all of America's more-than-two-million corporations, wouldn't that be a bureaucratic nightmare? Done badly, it would be. Done well, it need not be. How to do it well? Read on, and learn from the Securities and Exchange Commission.

THE SECURITIES INDUSTRY, THE GREAT CRASH AND THE NEW DEAL

We noticed that national regulation of corporations' internal affairs might have been achieved by transferring the chartering power to the national government. In fact it was achieved by creating a national power over stock and bond trading. Rules of corporate behavior which might have been linked to the right to corporate existence (through the chartering power) were linked instead to the right to raise money from investors. Beginning with President Roosevelt's New Deal in 1933, half a dozen Acts and a new federal agency transformed US corporations from the freest to some of the most strictly regulated in the developed world.

The old order Before that revolution corporate capital was raised and stocks and bonds (collectively termed *securities*) were traded through private institutions of three kinds: banks, stock exchanges, and over-the-counter dealers. Except for criminal laws against deliberate fraud there was very little law or public supervision to assure investors that the enterprises which sought their money were genuine, or were telling the truth about their assets and prospects. Through the late nineteenth and early twentieth centuries there were many traps for unwary investors. Bond salesmen, including some who kept moving from door to door and town to town like intinerant hawkers, succeeded in peddling quite a lot of fraudulent, unpromising or overpriced securities. Serious investors – affluent people not in the business themselves who wanted to invest in other people's enterprises – needed expert protection. They got most of it from private enterprises of three kinds: investment bankers, stock exchanges, and the financial press. Each of them had their shortcomings – as follows.

Investment bankers (called merchant bankers in Europe) combined financial skills with what might now be called industrial espionage. They built reputations as good judges of corporate prospects. They advised investors; accepted their money and invested for them; underwrote new stock issues and sold them to their investor clients. Corporations which wanted their support had to open their books to them. The bankers thus set some standards of corporate behavior and (on their clients' behalf) saw that the firms they supported lived up to them.

However, many bankers made other uses of their inside knowledge. They bought and sold stock speculatively on their own account. Some induced clients to invest in firms in which they themselves had undisclosed interests. Some used their market influence to manipulate stock prices to their own advantage. Some lent money to their clients, financing as well as advising their investments. These activities could be specially dangerous because of a fault in American banking regulations: before 1933 the law made no effective distinction between investment banking and commercial banking.

(What is the difference? *Commercial* banks are the mainstreet banks which create new credit and mind your money for you: lend new money to you, accept your deposits, manage your cheque or savings accounts, let you withdraw what you want when you want it. Because their financial safety is vital to nearly every household in the land, most governments strictly regulate what they may do with their depositors' money. They can lend it back to the depositors against adequate security, called 'collateral' in the US, or invest it in mortgage loans, government bonds or other safe securities. Meanwhile *investment* banks attract funds for risk-taking investment, including stock and share issues by private enterprises; but in well-regulated systems they are not allowed to accept deposits and manage cheque and savings accounts whose safety depends on the solvency of the bank itself.)

Until 1933 American banks were hybrids, able to accept the citizens' deposits and invest them in anything from safe loans through corporate stocks to wildcat oilwells. They provided most of the credit for margin deal-

ing in securities. When stock prices crashed in 1929 and
continued to fall through the following depression years
more than 5,000 American banks closed their doors.
Most of their depositors eventually got most of their
money back with government help: a federal
Reconstruction Finance Corporation spent $3.5bn. res-
cuing more than 7,000 insolvent banks and trusts. It
would have been cheaper and better for all concerned to
have regulated the banks properly, as other countries had
long done and the US did for fifty years from the 1930s.

Stock exchanges were private enterprises. Besides
convenient marketplaces, their rules provided some
guidance to investors and some discipline for the firms
whose securities they traded. To be listed on the New
York or other leading exchanges, firms must already
have a successful business record; must publish regular
accounts; must not water their stock unduly, or discriminate between stockholders by issuing both voting and
non-voting stock. In good times the protections seemed
adequate and most listed firms complied with the
rules. But those rules were a poor substitute for public
regulation, for two reasons.

First, the rules were not backed by law, so when bad
times got firms into trouble it was comparatively easy
for them to deceive the exchanges and the public about
their affairs. The accounts they were required to publish
were not in standardized form, they did not have to be
audited, and if they were, the auditors could be anybody. Legally, many elements of the published accounts
did not even have to be true. Under pressure during the
depression, deceptions were frequent. When public regulators took over under the New Deal legislation and
forced proper accounting and disclosure, one of the first
to go to jail for misusing clients' money was the
Chairman of the New York Stock Exchange.

The second shortcoming of stock exchange regulation was that it reached less than half of the relevant
business. The exchanges could only discipline the firms
they listed, and they listed less than half of America's
corporations and transacted less than half of all stock
and bond sales. The rest of the business was done 'over
the counter': firms issued stock directly to investors,
who might sell it directly to one another; banks, brokers
and other dealers bought and sold it, or put buyers and
sellers in touch with one another. In many of those over-
the-counter transactions, regulated by little more than
the common law of theft and fraud, buyers had to look
after themselves. While that may sound like a healthy
discipline it did not really help investors who faced (for
example) dealers reporting false stock prices, firms issuing false accounts, or secretive directors with Delaware

powers telling their stockholders as little as possible.

The financial press provided many useful services
for investors, from daily stock market reports and business news to the investigative journalism which at times
exposed more business scandals than the official authorities did. But the financial press was also open to misuse. Without much law to regulate statements about
firms' affairs and prospects, it was possible for directors, bankers, brokers, journalists and others to issue
false or misleading information to manipulate stock
prices to their own advantage. Particular stocks could be
'talked down' then bought, 'talked up' then sold.

Investors or gamblers It was from themselves that
many investors most needed protection. Greed and optimism could not only lose all their money, it could lose
other people's money too. How? Before 1933 you could
buy stock 'on margin'. Give a broker $1000 and he
would buy you up to $10,000 worth of stock, lending
you the remaining $9000 then borrowing it from a bank
on the security of the purchased stock. If the price of the
stock then rose 10 per cent, you doubled your $1000. If
it fell 10 per cent, you lost your $1000. If it fell more
than 10 per cent your creditors could also begin to lose.
Many people made fortunes by margin gambling
through the speculative boom of the 1920s, and got out
in time with winnings intact. Then from September
1929 to January 1932 the index of industrial stock prices
fell from 381 to 41. Not only buyers-on-margin were
ruined. Plenty of their brokers, banks and other creditors
went down with them.

Many of the casualties illustrated a final market
problem, which you will meet in a later chapter on
capital money markets. Those markets serve both
investment and speculation. They allocate capital to
productive uses, and at the same time provide gamblers
with the world's biggest casino. One purpose of regulation should be to prevent the gambling from wrecking
the investment. There were no such restraints in the
American markets before the New Deal.

A new regime

By 1933, with nearly 25 per cent of workers unemployed, there was popular support for a radical reform of
banks, stock exchanges and corporate accountability.
There was also rising business desire for reform. In
1929 private corporations had raised about $8000m. of
capital by issuing new securities. Three years later they
either could not, or dared not, raise a twentieth of that:
$325m. in 1932, $161m. in 1933. If business wanted to
be trusted with other people's money after the experi-

ence of 1929-32, it must submit to government which investors could trust to keep it in order. President Roosevelt recognized a crisis of business confidence and presented the first reforms not as an attack on business but as a rescue operation. Though many continued to resist, many welcomed the changes, including many bankers, stockbrokers and accountants.

The Glass-Seagall Act (1933) separated commercial from investment banking and banned risky uses of mainstreet depositors' funds. The Securities Act (1933) and the Securities Exchange Act (1934) listed more than forty items of accounting procedure which must be followed, and business information which must be disclosed, by corporations issuing securities to the public. The accounting profession was doubled – and won over – by requirements of independent auditing. To police the new regime the Securities and Exchange Commission was created. Besides enforcing the new requirements of corporate accounting and disclosure, the Commission rewrote the rules of the stock exchanges, and outlawed a number of the trading practices that had been used to manipulate stock prices. The Federal Reserve Board, as the main bank regulator, was empowered to regulate margin requirements for buying stock on credit. (Instead of running as low as 10 per cent, the 'own money' requirement has since ranged between 40 and 90 percent.) The Maloney Act (1938) extended the rules for corporate accounting and disclosure to unlisted corporations and over-the-counter trading. The Public Utility Holding Company Act (1935) managed – less successfully, after a decade of resistance and court action – to stop some kinds of misbehavior by the private owners of public utilities.

Since its creation the securities and exchange regime has been widely regarded as one of the world's best. As American business prospered and expanded through the long mid-century boom it was comparatively free of major failures and scandals. Its growing army of accountants, hired to comply with the new public requirements, went on to do more than that. Their expertise helped firms to develop systems of management accounting which improved their self-knowledge and decision-making. Meanwhile the Securities and Exchange Commission, which achieved so much, itself cost very little. It employed small numbers. Business generally complied with its directives. It was rarely taken to court. It has not been captured by the industry it regulates. A succession of inquiries and reports on US regulatory agencies have all declared it to be the best of them. By almost any standard it has been a successful regulator.

What was the secret of its success? It was designed by a remarkable character. Meet Jim Landis.

How to make laws that work

James M. Landis was the learned, workaholic, intensely idealistic son of Presbyterian missionaries. He was a brilliant student at college and law school, then served apprenticeships with the great liberal jurists Louis Brandeis and Felix Frankfurter. At 28 he became Harvard's first Professor of Legislation. His subject: how to write laws which would *work*. Reformers had concentrated on *what* behavior the law should require. They ought to think just as hard about *how* to require it. They must draft statutes whose validity corporations would not challenge in court. They must create administrative powers which judges would not strike down or take over. They must design incentives to elicit good behavior from corporations which were difficult to punish.

When Landis took up the subject there had been no systematic study of the ways and means of regulating business behavior:

> Not even a catalogue of the devices for enforcement could be found, far less a knowledge of the fields in which they have been employed. The legislator must pick his weapons blindly from an armory of whose content he is unaware. The devices are numerous and their uses various. The criminal penalty, the civil penalty, the resort to the injunctive side of equity, the tripling of damage claims, the informer's share, the penalizing force of pure publicity, the license as a condition of pursuing certain conduct, the confiscation of offending property – these are the samples of the thousand and one devices that the ingenuity of many legislatures has produced. Their effectiveness to control one field and their ineffectiveness to control others, remains yet to be explored.
>
> – Landis quoted in Thomas K. McCraw, *Prophets of Regulation* (1984)

President Roosevelt borrowed Landis from Harvard to lead the group of corporate lawyers who designed the new securities and exchange regime. Its winning qualities could be summed up as precise requirements, indirect rule, and exceptionally clever 'motivation to comply'.

- *Clear requirements* The statutes specified what corporate accounts and prospectuses must disclose (including directors' pay and perquisites). The requirements were precise, and were detailed in the Acts, not by administrators whose powers could be questioned.

- **Clear powers** The Securities and Exchange Commission (SEC) was empowered to issue *stop* writs, to stop business in its tracks while it was investigated, for example to stop the sale of a new security if its prospectus was questioned. The SEC could subpoena corporate officers to *attend* to answer questions and *disclose* documents, and they could be jailed for refusing. It could then prosecute any offences it found. But it rarely had to prosecute. Through the sequence *stop, attend* and *disclose* there were opportunities for potential offenders to repent before offences were actually committed, and failing that, for injured parties alerted by the procedures to sue the offenders in civil actions. Some civil remedies included triple damages, i.e. the civil remedy included an element of criminal penalty too. That not only punished and deterred offenders, the triple damages offered an 'informer's share' to motivate injured parties to sue, thus saving the government the costs of enforcing the law by criminal prosecution.

- **Indirect rule**, sometimes called *self-regulation*. To make sure the law was obeyed, its designers might have created an army of government employees to audit every firm's books and approve every prospectus. It would have had to be a large army, unpopular as a socialist bureaucracy in free-enterprise America. Instead, Landis' regime required most surveillance of private enterprises to be done *at their own request, by other private enterprises of their own choice*. Corporate accounts and prospectuses must have their financial statements certified by independent accountants. Independent lawyers must advise on their legality. Stock exchanges or the National Association of Securities Dealers (NASD) must see that the required accounts and accountants' and lawyers' certificates were all there. All the government's Securities and Exchange Commission had to do was (i) approve the stock exchange and NASD rules, and (ii) prosecute the few offenders who were not sufficiently disciplined by the exchanges, their own lawyers and auditors, or civil actions by injured parties.

- **Motivation to comply** Lawyers, accountants, bankers and stock exchanges were given new duties, but the new duties brought new business, and new legal authority and independence in doing it. So – with individual exceptions – most of them and their professional associations welcomed the new regime. So did a great many stockbrokers, securities dealers and corporate directors.

Notice some of the fine detailing of the motivation. *Directors* welcome the new rules. Suppose they are preparing a new stock issue. Stock exchanges must require the prospectus for the stock, with specified information about the firm, to be certified by independent lawyers and accountants. That's good for the firm because it increases investors' confidence. It may also protect directors from charges of misrepresentation if the investment does not live up to the investors' expectations.

Bankers welcome the regime because it limits what they may lend to investors with stock as collateral. They won't lose customers as they might once have done by enforcing a conservative limit, because the customers now know it is the law. In return for administering this and other rules for the government, the banks get 'last resort' backing if hard times come.

Stock exchanges welcome the regime because it requires directors, auditors and lawyers to do most of the vetting of listed firms that the exchanges would otherwise have to do themselves. So they are pleased to help by checking that the required directors', lawyers' and accountants' certificates are all present in correct form and duly signed.

Accountants welcome the regime because it brings them business. It assures work both for firms' own account-keepers and for the chartered accountants (sometimes called public accountants though they are private firms) whom firms must hire as auditors. The law requires them to be independent of the firms they audit, so directors can't bully them as some used to do. Auditors generally work fearlessly and honestly because if they don't – if they are convicted of negligence by investors or the SEC – they will lose business. At the same time their clients are free to hire and fire them, so they will be obliging in all lawful ways, working as helpfully as they can, to attract and hold clients. If they perform poorly and firms sack them, the firms must hire other auditors, so the law is inescapable, but there is a remedy for bad administration of it.

Similar motives get similar service – helpful but independent – from the *law firms* whose certificates must appear on prospectuses and some other corporate documents. Notice the difference that a simple new rule can make. Previously, if a firm got into legal trouble it was seen to hire lawyers to get it out of trouble. The trouble was seen as the firm's fault; the lawyers were only judged by the skill with which they attempted the rescue. Knowledgeable observers might guess that the lawyers must have advised the firm beforehand, but they could not know what the advice had been or whether it had been taken or disregarded. Landis' rule required that advance legal advice be *taken, signed,* and *published*. Firms could no longer offer securities which their lawyers would not endorse; and law firms which got their clients into trouble would be known to have done so, and lose reputation accordingly. The new rule gave lawyers both a new motive and a new legal power to keep their clients out of trouble cheaply by advance advice, rather than getting or failing to get them out of trouble later by expensive court action.

Thus Landis 'privatized' most of the necessary scrutiny of corporate business, with just enough public supervision by the Securities and Exchange Commission (SEC) to make sure the system worked. Contrast that with the likely effects if all the auditing and legal scrutiny of private firms had to be done by public bureaucrats. Though the work might be done by much the same people at much the same cost, there would be complaints of 'excessive government growth'. Instead of treating their accountants' and lawyers' fees as ordinary business costs, firms would perceive them as taxes. And there would be resentment and political hostility every time a firm's business was delayed or mismanaged by one of the public bureaucrats.

You can see how comprehensive Landis' attention to motivation was. Besides giving directors, bankers, lawyers, accountants and stock exchanges a professional interest in the regime, 'privatizing' it motivated politicians to support it. Also judges, especially the conservative sort who had frustrated so much anti-trust and other business regulation. Landis' regime did not provoke much court action. Most of the few cases were either simple prosecutions of firms or individuals who issued false or misleading information, or civil actions between private parties, for example between investors or creditors and negligent directors or auditors. They were not ideological contests between business and government with business asking the judges to defend free enterprise by cutting down the bureaucrats' powers.

Lessons from Landis What can you learn from Landis' success? *Not* that the SEC is the only or always-best model of business regulation. *Not* that regulation should always be indirect, should always rely on private rather than public scrutineers, should never allow much discretion to public administrators. Right next door to the SEC (so to speak) the equally efficient regulation of American banking by the Federal Reserve Board for forty years from 1933 was more direct, and had wide administrative and policy-making discretions with which neither judges nor executive government interfered. Thus in dealing with aspects of the same financial business under the same US Constitution through the same half-century, the 'Fed' and the SEC succeeded with significantly different methods of regulation. More and greater differences must be expected when regulation is applied to different industries, at different times, under different systems of government, and perhaps with different political purposes in cultures with changing conceptions of acceptable business behavior.

In 1960 another President recalled Landis to see how the New Deal's regulatory agencies were performing after a quarter of a century. The Federal Reserve and the SEC were doing well enough. Most of the others were not. The Civil Aeronautics Board, the Federal Trade Commission, the Federal Power Commission and others were captured by the industries they were supposed to regulate, or bogged down in procedural delays, or both. Landis wrote a devastating report to explain how they got like that, and spent the short remainder of his life beginning to reform them. He proved to be as able at analysing bad administration as at designing good.

Landis' central achievements in the 1930s had been to tailor the regulatory laws and institutions to fit the facts of a particular time, place, industry and economic purpose, and to teach people to see business regulation as that sort of tailoring task. Recall his words: what regulators need is not a master model of business regulation but a catalogue of the 'thousand and one devices' that have been tried, the industries and conditions in which they have been tried, 'their effectiveness to control one field and their ineffectiveness to control others' – and he might have added, a dash of his own inventive genius in simplifying and economizing the regulation that business actually needed.

You are about to notice half a dozen regulatory problems which have appeared, or intensified, since Landis' time. Coping with them, nationally and internationally, may offer rewarding work to economists who approach them not as doctrinaire deregulators but in an open-minded institutional way. If you are interested, a good way to start would be to read the book in which Landis distilled his positive wisdom half a century ago: James M. Landis, *The administrative process* (1938); and then his analysis of how *not* to do it, in his *Report on regulatory agencies to the President-elect* (Washington: Government Printing Office, 1960). The next generation of regulatory problems will be different from his. But his approach to the work, tailoring the minimum necessary amount of the most effective kind of government to the particular needs and potentialities of each industry, has not been surpassed.

CHANGING PROBLEMS, CHANGING TASKS

Since Landis' time business regulation has had to adapt to, among other things, changes in –

- taxation
- technology
- transnationality
- takeover opportunities
- insider trading
- business influence on government.

Each is too complex for adequate treatment here. If you are interested, you will find specialist books about them. The following notes merely list some ways in which each can affect the task of business regulation.

TAXATION

With the growth of taxation to finance public services and income transfers, most governments now tax corporate profits. Rates of tax are usually above 25 per cent and range as high as 49 per cent. Firms respond by acting to reduce their tax liability. They may change their accounting to call some of the profit by other names. They may change the proportions of equity capital and borrowed capital that they use, because interest payments on debt are business costs but shareholders' dividends are paid from taxed profits. Transnationals may locate their head offices and operations with an eye to national tax levels. They may locate their profits in low-tax countries by adjusting the transfer prices at which they pass materials from plant to plant across national boundaries. They may pay capital to subsidiaries in tax havens and have them lend it back to parent companies in taxable countries, at rates of interest which cost the pair nothing but cut tax liability.

Besides acting to avoid corporate tax, firms may act to shelter their directors or shareholders from tax by making payments in appropriate countries; by disguising interest and dividend income as capital growth; by disguising investment as insurance; by tailoring benefits to fit loopholes in particular countries' tax laws; and so on. A growing financial services industry offers all sorts of tax-evasive methods of lending and investing, dignified with new language: honest taxpaying becomes 'needless tax exposure', tax-evasive ways of lending and investing are advertised as 'tax effective'.

People who avoid tax of course exploit their fellow citizens who pay tax. But besides that social effect there are economic effects. In efficient industries the opportunities to improve productivity tend to be marginal. Not many established industries achieve more than two or three per cent of productivity growth per year. At least in the short run, tax ingenuity has often offered bigger money gains than that. Not many tax dodges help productivity, some don't affect it, some damage it. (How damage it? Suppose that for efficiency you ought to replace a subsidiary company's ageing plant – but you don't, because its tax losses are worth more to the corporate group than the efficiency gains would be. You could cut costs by cutting executive perquisites – but you don't, because they convey tax subsidies to both the firm and the executives. Scientists discover metal deficiencies in your farm soil. You could double its productivity within a year by applying the missing trace elements. If the farm is your living you may do that – but if a rich city-dweller has bought it as a tax farm, he'll delay the cure by spreading it over ten tax years.) Wherever tax considerations override other considerations in business decisions, the productivity of the economy as a whole may suffer.

Between business and government the challenge and response continue. Tax authorities respond to the tax-evasive ingenuities by further complicating the regulations with which business must comply. That adds to both public and business costs. Because some taxes and accounting requirements are shown to hinder productivity, it becomes orthodox to try to design 'neutral' taxes which won't motivate unproductive behavior. Aware of that orthodoxy, business lobbyists do their best to persuade policy-makers and public that *all* business taxes motivate inefficiency, penalize productivity, handicap the nation's industries in international competition, etc. More than ever, it is worth applying ingenuity to designing taxes which are cheap to collect, equitable, inescapable, and don't motivate unproductive behavior.

TECHNOLOGY

Technical changes can affect industries' economies and diseconomies of scale, size of firms, and tendencies to competition or monopoly. You noticed how technological developments first created railroad monopolies then exposed them to new kinds of competition. Technical changes are now affecting telephone networks' natural monopolies, broadcasting channels, the enforceability of book and film and music copyrights. Data-processing technology is allowing revolutions in business accounting and record-keeping, in computer-aided design and manufacture, and in the information potentially available to regulatory agencies. The new data banks and processes pose new policy questions about privacy, financial security, intellectual property, and rights against government. Financial technology transforms whole fields of crime. Bank robbers used to tunnel through concrete, tie up guards, blow safes. Some still do – but meanwhile a gifted computer hacker can stay home, pick up the telephone, and program the bank's computer to open an account for him under a fictitious name and pay it a regular income.

Those and other technical advances alter the need for business regulation. Firms want legal protection for new kinds of property against new kinds of poaching. There need to be new rules about electronic financial transactions made without signatures. (But the machines which can already forge signatures may soon do it untraceably.) How should governments respond if offshore broadcasters transmit prohibited tobacco advertisements, state secrets, criminal libels, pirated music?

Technical change continually changes regulatory needs and tasks and methods.

TRANSNATIONALITY

If you ask the managers of transnational corporations what regulatory problems they create, they will tell you that most of the problems are for the corporations, not the countries in which they operate. A firm which produces in a dozen countries may have to know and obey a dozen systems of company law, factory law, labor law, environmental law, import/export regulation and exchange control. If it also sells its products in a dozen countries it may face a dozen rule-books and regulators of public health, food and drug purity, product safety, advertising and consumer protection.

Most transnationals cope with most of those problems by owning a separate company in each country. (Some countries' company laws require that.) Staffed by nationals, each operates under its national government. But (depending on the nature of the business) there may still be problems for head office. Products may need to be designed to comply with all twelve sets of requirements. Headquarters may need to know about local requirements if it is to judge the efficiency of local managers. (Are our Ruritanian costs high because of the Ruritanian regulatory requirements – or because our Ruritanian managers are extravagant?)

Meanwhile (the managers will conclude) the dozen countries whose differing rules cause such trouble may each be getting benefits of investment, employment, research and know-how which they could not generate for themselves; and they are getting those benefits from corporations which have to obey their laws at least as carefully as their own nationals do.

Critics nevertheless think transnationals pose some special regulatory problems. They list offences which transnationals have committed, openly or covertly, against national interests.

First, tax avoidance. Where national subsidiaries are wholly owned by a foreign parent company, many countries allow them the ordinary privileges of private or 'close' companies which don't offer shares to the public, so don't have to publish their accounts. Tax collectors still demand tax returns from them. But without public accounts it can be hard to check their returns. And firms operating in many countries can often show low profits in countries with high rates of company tax.

There can be Delaware effects, especially when big companies operate in small countries. Chrysler once threatened to move their British operation across the channel; British taxpayers paid them £250m. to stay. In 1988 an Australian brewer threatened to export its head office if national company tax was not cut. It was. That was an incident in two campaigns: a 'Delaware duel' for corporate patronage between Australia and New Zealand, and a campaign by some Australian transnationals to win favors by threatening capital flight.

It is sometimes easier for transnationals than for local firms to bribe local politicians or public officials.

Some transnationals have got diplomatic or military support from their home governments against governments hostile to their interests.

Those conflicts continue in talk and action about globalization. On the one hand there are 'social clauses' in recent trade treaties and international agreements, to protect some workers' rights from some effects of international competition. On the other hand the World Trade Organization and a group of globalizing governments have proposed a multilateral agreement on investment (MAI) which would enforce investors' as well as traders' rights in foreign countries, and override national rights to protect business or labor from many effects of international competition or – our next subject – from takeover.

TAKEOVERS

Takeovers happen (or fail) when one company makes a public offer to buy the shares of another. The offer is usually conditional on enough shareholders accepting it, by a specified date, to give the buyer control of the target company.

Like monopolies, takeovers can happen for good, bad or indifferent reasons and they can have good, bad or indifferent effects. That invites regulation. But as with monopolies, it is difficult to block the bad ones without also hindering the good ones. To see why, and the regulatory problems which takeovers pose, we can notice in turn why they happen, how they are financed, and the effects they can have.

Why do they happen? Here is a spectrum of reasons from better to worse:

1. *Productive purposes* With the growth of big firms in oligopolist industries, and the separation of ownership from management, firms were not always kept efficient by competition. Established firms could sometimes survive while performing moderately rather than optimizing. There was no longer a dominant owner – a restless innovator like Ford, or a dividend-hungry slave-driver like Rockefeller – to hound the managers or sack and replace them. For better performance some new competitive spur was needed. It came in the form of the corporate raider. He hunts the business world for firms with tired directors, unexploited opportunities, undervalued assets. He takes them over by offering their shareholders more than their shares are currently worth, which he can afford to do if he can make the firm more profitable than it currently is. At best, he does two services for economic efficiency. His takeovers replace worse management by better, thus improving productivity. And his mere presence, prowling around, changes the conditions in which all managers work. Firms face a new penalty for moderate performance and a new compulsion to optimize. But are all takeovers, and precautions against takeovers, as wholesome as that? No. Read on.

2. *Debatable purposes* Suppose a garment factory has employed a stable, unionized workforce for regular wages. You take it over, break the union, and cut costs by sacking the workers then re-employing three quarters of them for longer hours and lower pay as contract pieceworkers without job security or superannuation. You sell the same garments at the same prices as before, but the workers get less of the revenue and the owners get more. What you have optimized is market strength against the workforce. Whether you have *increased* the national product may depend on whether the owners spend or invest the additional profits. Whether you have *distributed* the national product better or worse, or improved or degraded the quality of national life, are questions for your values. Recall the twelve ways to do well in a mixed economy. Some ways of optimizing bring pure gains in efficiency and wealth. Some bring

gains with debatable costs. Others – creating and exploiting monopoly powers, for example – may do unmixed harm. From best to worst, any of them may be achieved by takeover or the threat of it.

3. *Bad purposes* Money can be made from the takeover game in ways which do nothing for productivity. How? Chiefly by insider trading or greenmail. Insider trading will be described later. Greenmail presumably got its name from greenback and blackmail. Here is an example from the time, not long ago, before it was widely regulated. A raider targeted a big media company. For a while he bought shares quietly as they came on the market. Then with about 10 per cent of them in hand he announced a battle for control and began buying hard and publicly, at rising prices. That is to say his regular broker began buying hard. Crowds soon joined in, buying speculatively as the price rose, and pushing it higher. Directors, friends and allies of the threatened company organized to defend it. They were soon buying hardest of all, outbidding the raider's broker, aiming to accumulate a big enough holding to deny him control. Through a week of frantic trading the share price doubled. But half way through that week the raider had secretly decided he could not win, and proceeded to sell his shares to the rescuers, anonymously through other brokers, while his regular broker continued to bid the rescuers up. When he had sold all he had he let the market know it. The share prices returned to normal. The rescuers had succeeded but lost £60m. The raider had failed but won £60m, untaxed at that time. It was difficult to see how he could have failed to win – how any greenmailer could fail to win – either one or the other: the company or the money.

Governments responded with more regulation. In most rich countries that raid would now be unlawful. Takeover bids must now offer a fixed price to all shareholders, raiders must declare their holdings day by day, and so on. But the rules are new and imperfect, and still broken or evaded by inventive operators.

How are takeovers financed? Raiders sometimes finance takeovers from their savings or by selling other assets, so that they buy the target with their own money. But that is rare. Here is a list of other ways to do it, beginning with some which all countries permit and ending with one or two which some countries now ban or restrict. For brevity we will call the raider 'he', but he or she acts for a raiding company.

1. The raider buys the target company with his own company's money.

2. The raider pays cash most of which he borrows from a bank, secured on the raiding company's assets.

3. The cash the raider borrows is to be secured on the assets of the target company if the bid succeeds. (If it does not succeed, the loan is not drawn.)

4. The raider uses a short bank loan while he finances the takeover by re-selling the target for more than he paid for it. That is likely to be by asset-stripping. Example: You target a publishing firm which also owns some city bookshops. Its scholarly old directors don't realize – or don't care – that its properties could nowadays earn more as office sites than as two-storey bookshops. You buy the company, demolish the shops, sell their stock to other booksellers, sell their sites and the publishing headquarters to office developers, and sell the publishing operation to a rival publisher. Cash from the sales repays the bank and gives you a capital profit. The assets of the old firm were worth more than the firm was worth as a going concern.

5. Instead of offering cash for the target shares the raider offers shares of his own, or a mixture of cash and shares. To succeed, the raider's share price will need to keep ahead of the target's share price through the offer period. To achieve that, there have been raiders who financed friends to sell raiders' shares to and fro between them at high prices to deceive the target's owners.

6. Instead of offering shares the raider offers bonds – 'junk bonds', Americans have learned to call many of them. The target shareholders are invited to swap shares with variable market prices and dividend earnings for bonds with fixed interest rates and capital repayment. To make the swap attractive the bonds may have to promise very high interest. They may be issued by the raiding company, or by the target company. If the raider intends (if his offer is accepted) to have the target company issue the bonds, he is asking its shareholders to believe that he can so improve its management that (say) a 10 per cent dividend can be replaced by (say) a 20 per cent interest payment. Prudent shareholders will remember the meaning of limited liability. If the target company fails to earn, the bonds may fail to pay interest or capital. At least one pioneer of junk bonds has since been jailed for his ingenuity.

Unproductive effects Fear of takeover tends to encourage short rather than long-term thinking. Conservative financial policies can expose firms to takeover. So can long-term investment policies with heavy forward investment in research, development, and land-holding for development. Why? Takeovers succeed by offering share prices based on higher dividends than firms are currently paying. To ward them off, firms may need to stick to short-term, high-dividend, non-saving policies.

Some observers suspect that as takeovers increase general business uncertainties, there may be ill effects on day-to-day efficiency as well as on long term policies. Recall Lester Thurow's summary, cited earlier, of the conditions in which high productivity goes with secure tenure and mutual trust. Firms, especially big ones, may have depended more than they realized on that mutual trust. Outside Japan, possibilities of takeover can breed pervasive anxieties about changing ownership and management – with asset-stripping, cost-cutting, job-shedding, and breaches of employees' informal expectations.

Divorces The 'taken' companies do not always improve their performance. Nor do some of the takers – the corporate conglomerates or multi-business companies which the raiders put together. Why should one head office command (say) an airline, a string of holiday hotels and a trucking company if each of them could operate more profitably as an independent firm without conglomerate overheads or interference? In the 1990s some American conglomerates began to free their takeover captives. Some Europeans followed: Britain's Imperial Chemical Industries, Switzerland's Sandoz, Portugal's Sonae, France's Chargeurs. By 1997 one study estimated that $100 billion of corporate enterprise was being broken up into smaller firms each year.

How is it done? Shareholders trade some of their shares in Universal Megacorp Inc. for some shares in the airline, some shares in the hotels and some shares in the trucking company. Each independent company is expected to do better on its own than they all did together. That expectation pushes their share prices above the price of the Megacorp shares for which they are exchanged. If the expectation is fulfilled, as it often has been, everyone does well. If it is not, those who sell the new shares promptly at their 'expectation' prices may still do well. Directors who mastermind the changes, and have share options as well as shares to sell, generally do well in one way or the other.

How can you make money *both* from the takeovers *and* from the break-up? It can happen if the takeovers replace worse management by better, and the break-up then gives the improved firms back their independence. With or without that honest kind of business success, you may make money if you merely know the changes are coming before other people do, and gamble on the changing share prices which they are likely to cause. That is one variety of insider dealing.

INSIDERS

Corporate employees and others can misuse various kinds of inside information, but the commonest are foreknowledge of business opportunities and of share price changes.

Business opportunities Two examples: (1) As a director of a big public company you are offered a promising property, or patent, or mining lease. Instead of buying it for your employer you persuade the vendor to sell it to a family company of your own. (2) You are a director of Company A and own shares in Company B. The two are competitive tenderers for a government contract. You reveal Company A's tender price to Company B which can then undercut it by a few dollars and win the contract.

Share prices can jump up and down unexpectedly as traders respond to news of mineral discoveries, new products, success or failure in getting big contracts, annual reports which reveal unexpected trading profits or losses, serious accidents, criminal prosecutions, takeover bids. Anyone who knows such facts before other traders do can make money at the others' expense, and such facts are always known to *some* insiders before they can become public. The drillers and geologists who discover the minerals, the inventors and designers of new products, the accountants who keep the books, the raiders who plan takeover bids and the bankers who arrange their lines of credit, the directors of the companies concerned and any others in the know can use their inside knowledge to buy shares certain to rise, sell shares certain to fall, or tip other traders to do so. Insiders in the 'jumpy' industries can sometimes make more money from share trading than from their company salaries or share dividends.

So why not? Why do governments now try, however unsuccessfully, to regulate the uses of inside knowledge?

A first reason is the owners' property rights. Western law treats corporate employees as servants of the owners, bound to serve the owners' interests. If employees induce owners to sell shares that are about to rise, or to buy shares that are about to fall, the servants cheat their masters as surely as if they robbed the till.

Besides being servants the insiders are often also shareholders. Then the conflict is *both* between servant

and owner *and* between one owner and another. That doesn't excuse the offence, it doubles it. The law which creates joint stock insists that equivalent shareholders get equivalent benefits.

Besides owners' objections there are also economic objections. Insiders benefit chiefly from foreknowledge of *changes* in share prices. If directors act to manipulate share prices rather than to enrich their shareholders, the companies' efficiency is likely to suffer. So may the private sector's reputation and political support.

Thus there are reasons of justice and efficiency for banning insider dealing. But it is difficult to do. Some of the offences are hard to define, many of the offenders are hard to catch. How long before a price-change does the dealing have to be, to offend? How can the law distinguish between my buying shares in my company because I have confidence in its forward planning, and buying them because I know what will be in the annual report five months from now? How close does the dealer have to be to the inside source? Suppose I don't use my inside information and my wife and daughter don't, but my son-in-law's partner's family company does? Suppose a corporate raider's merchant bank asks another merchant bank to advise its clients to buy the raider's shares, and offers to repay them any money they lose? Tipster and tippee are already lawyers' words; judges have even ruled on the rights of a tippee of a tippee.

Conclusion Share price manipulation and insider dealing can harm the efficiency and reputation of the private sector. But they are hard to catch, and their forms range from clearly harmful misbehavior to business practices which are hard to tell apart from legitimate competition and risk-taking.

POLITICAL INFLUENCE

Governments have long regulated some of the means by which business influences government. Bribing politicians is a crime, bullying them is a punishable offence against parliamentary privilege. American lobbyists must be registered and disclose the names of their clients. And there are other rules against buying political favors. But the rules don't prevent large numbers of US Congressmen from acting as lawful lobbyists for particular interests.

As the modes of influence change and climates of opinion change, the purposes and tasks of regulation change. Critics from Right and Left have expressed concern about some late twentieth century trends in corporate powers of persuasion. Notes follow about four of them: regulatory capture; public relations and think tanks; media ownership; and market coercion of some public policies. As before, there is no space to explore them in depth. Just notice that they're there, troubling some thinkers and regulators.

Capture Some regulators are said to be captured by the industries they regulate. Instead of protecting public interests they protect the industry's owners, managers, labor, or all three. They may also protect established firms from new competitors. This sort of capture is commonest where a single-purpose agency exists to regulate a single industry, and must listen to the industry's insistent persuasions without hearing much equivalent advocacy from the industry's scattered customers.

There are criminal versions of capture, when the drug squad protects the drug traffickers or the vice squad protects the paedophiles. There are corrupt versions, when the regulators accept lawful favors from lawful operators. (There is cause for concern if regulators are leaving the agency for well-paid jobs in the regulated industry.) And there are honest versions, where government appoints regulators sympathetic to the industry, or their experience leads them to adopt the industry's views, as at times in the US regulation of road haulage or civil aviation. Thus arms of government which were created to influence industry are used by industries to influence government. And it is not always wrong for government to learn from them.

The charges of capture have sometimes been true enough. But there is also plenty of successful regulation. With a century of experience now, business regulation should be, and usually can be, as independent as its designers want it to be.

Public relations Business has always advertised its products. It now also funds a growing PR industry to advertise itself. Firms and industries present wholesome images of themselves. More generally a good deal has been done to link capitalism in people's minds with freedom and enterprise and wealth and growth rather than with the greed and wage slavery and unemployment which used to darken its image. Some of the cleansing activity is done by business funding of management schools and economic think tanks – several billion dollars a year now finance independent research institutions to supply politicians, press and public with conservative economic analysis, ideology and advocacy.

Why not? Left critics complain of having no equivalent funds, except a trickle from trade unions, for research and analysis critical of business behavior. Shouldn't firms be barred from funding conservative propaganda?

First, it would be a difficult activity to regulate. Firms routinely buy professional services from lawyers, accountants, management services, market analysts. On what ground could economists be distinguished from those other consultants? Second, critics of capitalist society and corporate behavior do flourish. Consumers' organizations support *Which* and *Choice* magazines. Ralph Nader thrives. Environmentalists manage to fund plenty of research into corporate misbehavior. The rich countries' governments and universities employ many more economists than the think-tanks do. If the profession as a whole has become conservative, that can't fairly be blamed on the business funding of a fraction of it. The remedy is to confront its arguments, rather than regulate its funding. (Hence this course of study.)

Media ownership There have always been newspaper owners who hoped to influence government policies. They may now have commercial as well as political purposes, if they also own other enterprises which can use government favors. Rupert Murdoch's papers are said to have turned against an Australian government after it refused him a mineral export licence. After he bought the New York Post and it supported President Reagan's election, the US government's Export/Import Bank made Murdoch's airline a loan at a concessional rate of interest to buy Boeing aircraft. After his *Sun* and *News of the World* had supported Mrs Thatcher's election, her government decided that his offer to buy *The Times* and *Sunday Times* need not be referred to the Monopolies Commission. Critics who suspect that the favors were linked to the political support do not necessarily suspect that secret deals were done. It is enough that each party can discern the other's options. 'If you give him a fair go' an Australian Prime Minister said of Murdoch, 'he'll give you a fair go.'

Could such commercial effects be barred without harm to press freedom? Government could limit newspaper ownership, as some governments already limit the ownership of banks, to shareholders with less than five per cent of the stock each. That would bar masterful individual owners, and most takeovers. Alternatively the rules could allow single proprietors but require that they own nothing else (except perhaps government bonds or other newspapers), or no more than five per cent of the stock of anything else.

In a broader view, is it reasonable that a free country's press should all be owned by a few people with the class interests of rich capitalists?

On the one hand that may be freer than a nationalized press might be. Quite a lot of fair-minded papers and some crusading, investigative papers have flourished in private ownership. Some rich owners have radical beliefs. Some papers are owned by many small shareholders and dominated by directors and editors rather than owners. Some papers aimed at working class readers have had Left-of-centre editorial policies. Rich or not, most owners want their papers to sell and bland approval of established institutions is not usually the way to sell them. So the political effects of private ownership have not been as uniformly conservative as might have been expected.

On the other hand Left-of-centre opinions have rarely had equal space in the national press even when they had majorities at national elections, and some critics don't believe the press can ever be as diverse as it ought to be while it is owned by a rich minority. What alternative patterns of ownership might there be?

- Some papers have been owned by trusts which ensured their editorial independence.

- A European corporate structure with an upper and lower board might be developed with the upper board including some workers and watchdog directors as well as owners' representatives.

- With modern sources of takeover finance it should be possible for some papers to be bought by their employees and run as co-operatives.

- Though a government press monopoly would be intolerable, some publicly owned papers might well compete in an open market. The objections to public ownership of newspapers were conceived before radio and TV broadcasting began. Perhaps it is time to think again about newspapers in the light of the quality and independence achieved by the best public broadcasters.

Market coercion   In the past there have been occasional fears or threats of capital strike or flight. If governments threatened the interests of capital owners, for example by nationalization, the owners might stop investing (a capital strike) or shift investment abroad (capital flight).

A more continuous problem for government set in with the full deregulation of international financial dealing through the 1970s. The volume of dealing for purposes of trade and investment was soon exceeded tenfold by the volume of speculative dealing as large numbers of private dealers gambled on the movements of national rates of interest and unregulated, unstable rates of exchange between national currencies. The rates fluctuate from diverse causes. They continue to reflect the supply and demand of currencies for international trade and investment. But they also reflect dealers' gambling expectations, and their expectations of the likely effects of national economic policies, both on national prosperity and on the interests of capital owners. Governments have learned that talk of improvident policies or Left policies can cause their currencies to lose value; conservative promises can cause them to recover. Some politicians plead that their hands are tied: 'market forces' prohibit progressive policies not because the policies would not work but because the money markets will punish countries which adopt them.

In all these areas – the bribery or 'capture' of public officials, the private ownership of the media, the political uses of capital flight and market coercion – it is reasonable for government to regulate the means by which business can 'regulate' government. It may be difficult to draw the line between desirable and undesirable action: between oppressive uses of corporate power on the one hand and oppressive uses of state power on the other. But government creates the corporate powers, and just as it has to regulate their business uses it may also need to regulate some of their political uses. In some areas, especially of banking and international finance, a return to effective *economic* regulation, for which there are good economic reasons, would remove most of the opportunities for political misuse of financial power.

THEORIES OF CORPORATE HARM AND BUSINESS MORALITY

The changing tasks of regulation and the drive for deregulation have prompted debate about the basis of business law and the difficulty of regulating the behavior either of firms, or of their individual officers as they do the firms' business. One effect of the legal creation of corporate identity is that officers can often ascribe misbehavior to the firm rather than to themselves. But the firm cannot be jailed, and to fine it or close it down can seem unjust if it means that innocent shareholders lose money and innocent workers lose jobs for offences committed by directors who go free. How far should corporate identity be allowed to limit liability for civil or criminal wrongdoing?

Most people regard those as moral and practical questions. Most people in business want their own and others' business to be done lawfully. Most business can be more efficient the more willing and unforced its compliance is with legal and moral requirements.

But that last paragraph might be truer if it said 'most people outside Chicago'. There is a range of opinion about how law-abiding private enterprises ought to be, and about the best ways to encourage lawful behavior. We can indicate the range by contrasting opinions from the universities of Chicago and Sydney.

From Chicago

Ronald Coase, whose 1937 theory about transaction costs and the size of firms was outlined earlier, wrote another famous piece in 1960: 'The problem of Social Cost', *Journal of Law and Economics* Vol. 3. The problem, he argued, is what to do about 'actions of firms which have harmful effects on others'. Lawyers think of the problem as 'one in which A inflicts harm on B and what has to be decided is: how should we restrain A?' But to punish A, or prevent A from gaining by harming B, inflicts harm on A. Coase concluded that 'the real question that has to be decided is: should A be allowed to harm B or should B be allowed to harm A?'

(Pause to ask that question of some commonplace crime. Should I be allowed to harm you by burgling your house, or should you be allowed to harm me by locking me out?)

Instead of asking which party is morally or legally right, Coase asks about the comparative costs of regulating or not regulating the harmful behavior. There are legal costs: costs in lost production if offenders have to divert resources to defending themselves; more costs in lost production if lawful behavior (for example an industry with many competing firms) produces less efficiently than unlawful behavior (for example an efficient monopoly which breaks an anti-trust law).

Coase then asks which of the costs are social costs, by which he means costs which leave society poorer by reducing national output. Legal costs reduce output, because they are transaction costs rather than costs of production: if people were not negotiating and disputing as lawyers they could be producing goods of value. But breaking the law may or may not have social costs, depending on its effect on national output. Cutting production costs by (unlawfully) cutting red tape? Good. Increasing costs by (unlawful) monopoly pricing? Bad.

Where law-breaking would have social costs it should be deterred by the least-cost sanctions available. Jailing people has high social costs (both prisoner and jailer are withdrawn from the productive workforce). But fines don't necessarily have social costs, except the legal costs of imposing them, because those who collect the fines may invest the money more productively than those who pay them. Fines don't use up resources, they merely transfer them to other users.

Coase reaches two conclusions. (1) Firms can, and rationally should, decide whether to obey or break laws by comparing the financial effects of the alternatives. If they can't predict the effects exactly (for example, whether lawbreakers will be caught) they can estimate probabilities just as they do with trading or investment risks. They need to answer two questions. Will the likely gains from crime exceed the likely losses from retribution? If so, will the net gain from crime be more, or less, than the firm could alternatively earn by using the same resources lawfully? Then do whichever promises to pay best. With firms behaving in that rational way, the law and any enforcement of it should be designed to weight firms' incentives on the side of whatever behavior, lawful or not, will do most for national product.

Here's work for your watchdog. The only harm that appears to matter to Coase is harm to gross national product. If A can increase the national product by means which harm B – however unjustly, and however harmfully to B's innocent owners or workers or creditors – government should not interfere. Coase draws his examples from anti-trust administration, but he generalizes about any kind of corporate harm. Recall our commonplace example. If my company burgles your company's warehouse, the government should interfere only if your company would have used the stolen resources more productively than mine will.

The theme has since been developed and modified in other Chicagoan work. What should we think of it? Does Coase's ruthless unconcern for justice make him a monster of depravity? No, just a neoclassical extremist. Also, I think, irrational even for his own purposes, in two ways. First, it is absurd to expect that prosecutors and courts should regularly decide whether particular acts of industrial monopoly, theft, fraud, espionage and other misbehavior are doing more for national product than lawful behavior would alternatively be doing. Second, if that lawless amorality drives firms it must be expected to drive their members' pursuit of their own as well as the firms' interests: they'll rob their employers every way they safely can. Honest firms with honest workers will easily out-compete them.

Adam Smith is only the most famous of the many economists and business people who have understood that capitalist efficiency is motivated by *legitimate* self-interest – by interests shaped and qualified by culture, established morality and law. And not all the desires are for money. People also value reputation, respect, trust, affection. Meet two scholars who find that quite tough public use can be made of those more tender, less greedy ambitions.

From Sydney

From Sydney come Brent Fisse and (now at the Australian National University) John Braithwaite, authors of *The Impact of Publicity on Corporate Offenders* (New York, 1983) and *Corporations, Crime and Accountability* (Cambridge, 1993). The first brings together case studies of eighteen notorious offences (bribery, pollution, dangerous processes, mine and airline disasters, dangerous products, misleading advertising, illegal price-fixing, illegal political activity, illegal anti-union action and intimidation of employees) by some of the world's biggest corporations. The second book suggests a theory and method of corporate accountability and discipline.

Fisse and Braithwaite want both firms and their members to be accountable. Too often, criminal executives have bought freedom from personal prosecution by pleading the firm guilty and volunteering fines and restitution at its shareholders' expense; or they have protected both the firm and themselves by scapegoating some juniors and aiding their prosecution. An effective regime should be as preventive as possible. It should get the corporations themselves to apply as much as possible of the necessary discipline. And it should see that they do so – and that they *want* to do it themselves – by making criminal prosecution certain if they don't.

Accordingly the authors propose an Accountability Model. To understand it properly, read the book. Its barest essentials are these:

For its own purposes any firm needs a clear plan of its members' responsibilities, and accountability. That scheme, perhaps more fully and formally detailed than it presently is in some firms, should be available to the Companies Office (the public regulator). It should leave no doubt which officers are responsible, in their various activities, for seeing that the activities comply with Board instructions, and with the law. That should be all that most firms need do to keep their people, and their corporate behavior, in order. But when more is needed, Fisse and Braithwaite propose what they call 'pyramidal enforcement, with informal methods of control at the base of the pyramid and severe forms of criminal liability at the apex'. Public intervention in the affairs of an offending firm might typically go only as far as it needed to go through six possible stages:

1. The public authority warns, advises, persuades the firm to correct its behavior.

2. Any injured parties sue the firm to enforce their rights or recover any damages they are due for. These are civil, not criminal, actions – but where the effect is to enforce the law on the offending firm, some countries allow courts to award double or treble damages to successful litigants as a reward for law-enforcement.

3. The public office negotiates a voluntary agreement by which the firm promises an effective program of remedial or disciplinary action, and an accountability report. Private 'company doctors' – independent lawyers, accountants and management consultants – may be hired to help with the work

4. If the firm refuses to agree, or agrees but fails to fulfil the agreement, the public office seeks the same effect by compulsion, by a court order requiring the firm to do as it is told.

5. If the firm still fails to comply, the public office charges the firm and the responsible individuals with criminal offences, seeking probation, community service or fines for convicted individuals, and the same plus adverse publicity for the firm if convicted.

6. If the offences are more serious, courts may jail convicted individuals and liquidate firms. That's corporate capital punishment. (The public office may *start* with criminal charges, without any of the first four stages of negotiation or civil action, in cases of serious fraud or other deliberate felony.)

A main purpose of the last two steps is to persuade directors to take the first steps seriously, and put their affairs in order while they can still do it themselves, cheaply, and without public exposure. To serve that gentle purpose the criminal prosecutions (when the facts justify them) must be known to be inescapable. To make them so, the English-speaking countries' public authorities might need to be better financed and staffed, and their courts' procedures in corporate criminal cases might need to be brisker, than most of them are now. Rich corporations can impose long legal and administrative delays, and high court costs, on public attempts to prosecute them. So the threat of prosecution is at present two-edged: public authorities have too often accepted scandalously low financial settlements from offending firms to avoid the costs of prosecuting them. This does not mean that the Fisse/Braithwaite strategy is wrong – but to be effective it needs well-financed public law offices with a capacity for prompt court action when it is needed.

Many countries reverse the onus of proof in tax cases: taxpayers must prove the tax-collector's assessment is wrong, or pay up. There are good reasons for that. I think the same good reasons would justify the same principle for all criminal charges under Companies and Corporations Acts except those which expose individuals to jail sentences. That change might not speed the court proceedings, but it would allow the public authorities to start cases promptly without the long preparation which often delays them now. And the prospect of it might shift the balance of bargaining strength through the early, peace-making stage of the Fisse/Braithwaite scheme.

That balance is already improved by corporate directors' increasing dislike of bad publicity. Fisse and Braithwaite would further strengthen the courts' powers to order formal public criticism of bad business behavior. But that also, if it is to be done responsibly, requires well-staffed public offices to research the cases.

This is an unpromising time for such reforms. Deregulation is fashionable, business influence on government is strong in the English-speaking countries, and so is tax-resistance. All that is needed to continue the present degree of freedom for firms and their directors to misbehave is 'smaller government' with dwindling numbers of public servants available to discipline private firms' uses of the corporate powers which government creates for them. But paradoxically that also makes reform easy for a reforming government. Promising methods are available, and sufficient staff could quickly make them effective.

SUMMARY

1. Private enterprises can be run by individuals, partnerships or companies. Individual proprietors and partners are freer than the directors of firms, but without limited liability they may face bigger risks.

2. For companies, governments create the vital powers of corporate identity, joint stock and limited liability. The uses of those powers have to be regulated to protect the interests of firms' owners, workers, suppliers, customers and creditors.

3. The regulation needs to be inescapable. There are likely to be Delaware effects if firms have a choice of jurisdictions, whether between state laws within federations, between national legal systems or between tax systems.

4. As far as possible regulation should be designed to motivate honest and productive business behavior at least cost and with least loss of efficiency.

5. Nevertheless modern technology, taxation and business practice have occasioned a great elaboration of business law, and of the public institutions and private professions which exist to enforce (and evade) it.

6. You need not memorize the past history of British and American regulation. Just remember what those narratives tell you in a general way about the need for effective regulation if corporate powers are to remain usable; and about the dynamic nature of regulatory problems and tasks.

7. *Taxation* Most countries tax corporate profits and nearly all countries tax the incomes in money or kind which firms pay to their owners and directors. Elaborate accounting and other requirements have proved to be necessary – and sometimes still inadequate – to prevent corporate and individual tax avoidance by the misuse of corporate powers.

8. *Transnationality* Enterprises which operate in several countries have to comply with each country's legal requirements. The countries in which they operate can usually enforce 'inspectable' requirements of factory and product safety, labor law and environmental policy. But host countries have often found it difficult or impossible to tax transnationals effectively. And it may be difficult for small or poor countries to attract transnationals – for the income and employment they bring – but prevent the harm that some of them want to do.

9. *Technology* Technical changes often change regulatory problems and tasks.

10. *Takeovers* Some takeovers improve efficiency, some don't, some reduce it. Some have welcome social effects. Some have unwelcome effects, for example on employment, industrial relations, corporate loyalty. Such diversities make it difficult to regulate takeovers satisfactorily. But if they are not regulated, intolerable greenmail and other inequities flourish. There is a case for severely restricting debt-financed takeovers, and for banning bank lending on the security of corporate shares. Some business disillusion with takeovers and business conglomerates is prompting the current reversal of many takeovers.

11. *Insiders* Takeovers are one among a number of corporate activities which make opportunities for firms and individuals to profit by insider dealing. Like takeovers, insider dealing is very difficult to regulate satisfactorily. But if it is not regulated, insiders can both manipulate and profit from share price changes and business opportunities in ways which employers, shareholders, other dealers and the general public may find intolerable. Moreover such opportunities to profit by share trading may divert money and talent from more productive uses.

12. *Politics*   Business can influence government in proper and improper ways. The improper ways include bribery, corporate gifts to party funds, job offers to obliging politicians and public servants, the exchange of media support for commercial favors, and 'market blackmail' by capital flight and exchange speculation. All those modes of influence need to be resisted but some of them are difficult or impossible to regulate satisfactorily.

13. To motivate acceptable use of corporate powers there is at least this range of means:

   • leave the business to market forces wherever they suffice to motivate acceptable behavior.

   • act to protect or strengthen the market motivation – as when regulators ban monopoly in order to encourage competition.

   • regulate by rule with *private* enforcement – as when the law (1) specifies what corporate accounts must reveal, (2) requires that they be certified by independent auditors, and perhaps (3) rewards private investigators who prosecute corporate offenders.

   • regulate by rule with *public* enforcement – as when public servants scrutinize all tax returns.

   • regulate directly, with public servants telling firms what to do – as when the Securities and Exchange Commission orders a firm to 'stop and disclose', or the Department of Agriculture tells chemical companies what each of their poison labels must say.

   • if regulation won't work, take the business into public ownership.

   • if government management can't be trusted, distance the public managers from government – as in statutory corporations like the British Broadcasting Corporation; companies with government as majority shareholder; or enterprises owned by independent non-profit bodies, as when churches or independent trustees own schools, hostels, hospitals, etc.

14. Regulation has economic purposes and effects, so economists should contribute to its design. But many have disqualified themselves from doing the work well, either by opposing all corporate power for doctrinaire socialist reasons, or by opposing most business regulation for doctrinaire capitalist reasons – reasons based on theoretical faith in market forces rather than practical knowledge of business life.

If you believe that all regulation is bad and most of it is unnecessary, you won't try very hard to economize regulation cleverly, i.e. to design it to do most good and least harm at least cost. Regulators certainly need to understand the harm that bad regulation can do. But they also need to understand the harm that can be done to business itself, as well as to other parties, if the uses of corporate identity, joint stock and limited liability are *not* effectively regulated. They also need to consider other effects besides direct economic effects, especially the need for regulation to support the social and personal morality which business has to rely on in innumerable dealings with its owners, financiers, employees and customers, and in dealings between firm and firm.

29

Theories about firms' purposes

Do the directors of private enterprises act with the single aim of maximizing the owners' profits? Or do some of them act with other aims instead of, or as well as, that one? And whatever their purposes are, what ought they to be?

MANAGING FOR THE OWNERS

There has been argument about those questions for a century or more. To understand the argument it is convenient to return briefly to the subject of management. Books and theories about modern business management began to appear early in the twentieth century. One of the earliest, and for twenty years or more the most famous, was F. W. Taylor, *The principles of scientific management*, published in 1911. It recommended the detailed analysis of physical tasks, by various means including time-and-motion studies, to discover the most effective division of labor for each industrial process, i.e. the pattern of individual workers' tasks which would produce most output from given person-hours of work. The approach treated people as machines with measurable mental and physical capacities. Especially in manufacturing it tended to produce extreme divisions of labor. Hands were found to work fastest at continuous repetition of simple movements, so workers at an assembly line might get one component to drop into place, or three or four nuts to tighten. Managers could measure the speed of each operator; and on moving assembly lines they could control the speed at which the lines moved. 'Taylorism' tended to make work monotonous, uninteresting and tiring. Its many critics said that it dehumanized the work and the worker: scientific management amounted to scientific exploitation of labor for owners' purposes. Defenders claimed that more output per head per hour allowed higher wages.

Taylor concentrated on the physical processes of production. A generation later another rational thinker did similar service for the division of managerial tasks and responsibilities. In *General and industrial administration* (1949) Henri Fayol set out logical sequences of planning, organizing, implementing and measuring productive processes. He distilled some practical principles of hierarchic control. Lines of command and communication should be clear. Responsibilities *for what* and *to whom* should be clear. A manager should answer to one superior only. Each superior should have no more than six or seven subordinates answering to him. His authority should match his responsibilities, i.e. he should have the necessary power to do what he was required to do, no less and no more. And so on – Fayol made the control of a business enterprise look rather like the foolproof signalling and traffic-control system of a complicated railway network. Much of his and his followers' teaching is sensible, and is followed still. It *is* usually inefficient to have unclear responsibilities and lines of communication. It can be confusing for a manager to answer to more than one superior. It can be difficult for a manager to be responsible for the performance of more than six or seven subordinates. (Though that depends on the work: sales managers can control many more than seven salespersons, bishops can supervise many more than seven parishes.)

But Taylor and Fayol perceived no problems with the *purposes* of the organizations which they studied. Taylor assumed that workers sold their labor for wages or piece-rates. So did managers, if owners hired managers instead of managing for themselves. Owners simply hired others to work as required by owners for owners' purposes. Workers who produced most or at least cost could expect the best jobs. Managers who did most for owners' profits could expect the highest rewards. Fayol generalized his principles to other organizations besides private firms, but with the same assumption that employers would determine clear purposes for the enterprise, which all hands would then be required to serve.

Thus it was assumed that owners, directing the firm or hiring and firing those who did, could ensure that the owners' aims were the firm's aims.

DIRECTORS' PURPOSES

When Taylor wrote, most owners did still control their enterprises and decide what their aims should be. Many small businesses still work that way. But through the twentieth century a rising proportion of private production, now much more than half of it, came to be done by big firms in most of which the shareholders do not direct the business *and do not hire and fire the directors who do*. In practice directors recruit one another, and usually control the shareholders' meetings which formally elect them. There has been a general separation of ownership from control, called by some a 'managerial revolution'. One effect has been the increase of regulation described in Chapter 28 on business powers. Another has been to question the purposes which such 'undirected' directors ought to serve.

The separation was first widely noticed in the 1930s. In that same decade the hardships of the Great Depression prompted some business people to think about the social responsibilities of business. The Hawthorne experiments suggested that work could be motivated by other things besides money and fear. Some notable management schools were founded. And two famous books were written.

Berle and Means

In 1932, before Jim Landis began to design the modern federal regulation of American corporate business, Adolf A. Berle and Gardner C. Means' *The modern corporation and private property* appeared. It was a radical book with respectable conservative credentials: a proposal to save capitalism, not to replace it. Berle was a professor of corporate law. Means was a business economist. Their research had been proposed by a Harvard professor, financed by the Social Science Research Council of America, and directed by Columbia University's Council for Research in the Social Sciences. Their conclusions identified three alternatives open to choice in the relations between business and democratic government. I think they understood those options better than many leaders of business and government understand them now.

Their research indicated that 'perhaps two thirds of the industrial wealth of the country' was now owned by corporations without dominant individual owners. The consequent divorce of ownership from control introduces 'a new form of economic organization of society'. The change is likely to affect the interests of owners, workers and consumers. And future choices will determine whether the new corporate power 'will dominate the state or be regulated by the state or whether the two will coexist with relatively little connection. In other words, as between a political organization of society and an economic organization of society which will be the dominant form?'

They argued that the separation of ownership from control created two new forms of property:

- Owners of stocks and shares and bonds have *passive* property. They are entitled to income from their property. But they do not control it and they are not responsible for how it is used.

- Corporate directors have *active* property. They decide how to use corporate property but [in 1932] 'they have almost no duties in respect to it which can be effectively enforced'.

In whose interest will the directors manage the property they control? Berle and Means saw three broad alternatives.

1. They could choose to manage for the passive owners' benefit. But that could weaken the driving force of capitalism, the profit motive. How reliably will the profit motive drive directors who have to hand the profits they earn to passive owners who have no control over them? A critical link between self-interest and economic efficiency may be weakened.

2. Alternatively, the directors may manage for their own benefit. They can pay enough profit to the shareholders to attract capital and comply with the law, then pocket the rest themselves. That gives them a profit motive – but unless they are strictly regulated it threatens to instal 'a corporate oligarchy ... with the probability of an era of corporate plundering'.

3. But – third – Berle and Means believed that the separation of ownership from control had 'placed the community in a position to demand that the modern corporation serve not alone the owners or the [directors] but all society. This third alternative offers a wholly new concept of activity ... a program comprising fair wages, security to employees, reasonable service to the public, and stabilization of business ... It is conceivable – indeed it seems almost essential if the corporate system is to survive, – that the control of the great corporations should develop into a purely neutral technocracy, balancing a variety of claims by various groups in the community and assigning to each a portion of the income stream on the basis of public policy rather than private cupidity.'
   – *The modern corporation and private property*
   pp. vii, viii, 355-6

They finally wonder whether the corporation may become the dominant form of social organization. To the extent that it does, the laws under which business operates will be more important than ever. 'The state seeks in some aspects to regulate the corporation, while the corporation, steadily becoming more powerful, makes every effort to avoid such regulation.' The historic choice between a plundering oligarchy and a productive and sociable private sector may depend on which of them wins.

For half a century – beginning with Roosevelt's New Deal and Jim Landis' new corporate discipline – there was progress towards the democratic model. Then with the Delaware revolution in directors' powers, and the general shift of policy to the Right in the 1970s, the corporate forces began to reverse the trend. They achieved some privatization and deregulation. They began to negotiate international agreements to do away with national powers to regulate international trade, investment, ownership, credit and debt, and financial speculation and exchange. Led from the US, directors took steadily more for themselves. *Business Week* reported that in 1996 the chief executives of the biggest US firms raised their annual pay by more than half to average nearly $6m each, with the richest of them taking more than $100m.

These corporate gains were accompanied by lower investment, slower growth and increasing poverty and inequality. At the end of the century Berle and Means look as perceptive as they did when – eager to rescue productive capitalism from self-destruction in the depths of the Great Depression – they sketched the democracies' historic options seventy years ago. Today's business leaders may ridicule this attention to such an old book. But many of *them* are reaching even further into the past as they undo the reforms which the book helped to inspire, and return to older levels of plunder and inequality.

Barnard

Chester Barnard published *The functions of the executive* (1937) five years after Berle and Means' book appeared. He did not directly answer their questions about the right uses of the directors' new independence. But he offered a remarkable analysis of the way in which the questions must present themselves to the business leaders who had to answer them.

Barnard saw formal organization, including the organization of business corporations, as a mode of cooperation. 'Organization comes into being when two or more persons begin to cooperate to a common end.' If the common purpose requires that work be coordinated by the giving and taking of orders, the people cooperate in that. So even if their role includes giving orders, bosses lead rather than command. If they have authority, give orders, and the orders are obeyed, that is still by consent. Attracting and maintaining that consent – that willingness of everyone in the organization to cooperate for common purposes – is the leaders' central task.

Conventional incentives – the fear of the sack, the exchange of work for wages – also operate. But by themselves they cannot motivate reliably good performance; 'where conformance is secured by fear of penalties, what is operating is not the moral factor in the sense of the term used here, but merely negative inducements or incentives.' Especially for leaders and managers, 'Only the deep convictions that operate regardless of either specific penalties or specific rewards are the stuff of high responsibility.'

Though he stressed the cooperative element in organized work, Barnard also saw that it was shot through with actual and potential conflicts. His first originality lay in the way he related the cooperation to the conflicts and perceived, *in the relation between the two*, the main function of leadership. His second originality lay in seeing most of the conflicts as partly moral, so that to perform their necessary functions leaders need both high technical capacities and high moral capacities. They need to be clever and good, and each of the two is likely to be useless or worse without the other.

The following pages try to summarize some essentials of Barnard's reasoning. If it seems an unlikely or roundabout approach to matter-of-fact business purposes, be patient with it. It gets there in the end. I think it is perceptive and wise; but whatever you think of it, the debates which it started continue still.

(Warning: one publisher's reader thought that the text in this book was not broken up by enough headings, sub-headings, graphs, equations and tables. He feared that – unlike historians and political scientists and philosophers and students of language and literature – economics students simply shut books which offer them pages of prose without visible coffee-breaks. Here are three defiant pages of uninterrupted argument about an issue of deep importance to democratic mixed economies. Pack a tent and a full water bottle and see how you go.)

Barnard was not an academic theorist. He was an executive of the Bell Telephone Company and he claimed to base his argument on his direct experience of business life. That experience convinced him that economists since Adam Smith had over-emphasized the element of rational economic calculation in people's behavior, in business just as much as elsewhere. It was wrong to think 'that man is an "economic man" carrying a few non-economic appendages'. In real life economic and non-economic motives constantly mix. Also, motives conflict. The conflicts are not only between person and person, they are often between one motive and another within one person's mind. Barnard depicted those actual and potential conflicts in the following way.

Each of us has a number of roles in life: child and parent, spouse and lover, friend, neighbor, employee, and so on. Each of us belongs to a number of organizations: a family, a firm which employs us, perhaps a church, a political party, some clubs and associations. *Within* each of the more complex organizations, including firms, we have a number of relationships: with superiors, with subordinates, with fellow-workers, with the firm's suppliers or customers or government inspectors. For each of those relationships we tend to have a code of conduct. We know how to treat spouse and children, employers, workmates, government inspectors, and so on. The code for each relationship may be imposed on us by social rules, or by our own choice – there may be more choice about some of the codes than about others. Some of an individual's codes may be high-minded, enjoining honesty and generosity. 'Be kind to old people, don't cheat children.' Some may be the opposite. 'Strangers are fair game, never given a sucker an even break.' To emphasize how *many*, and how *different from each other* an individual's codes are, remember that scrap of male chauvinist dialogue: 'An ideal wife should be a lady in the drawing room, a miser in the kitchen, and a courtesan in the bedroom.' 'Yes, but what if she turns out to be a lady in the kitchen, a courtesan in the drawing room and a miser in the bedroom?'

Because they often conflict, we have to order the codes, consciously or unconsciously. The code that says 'strangers are fair game' may be overridden by the codes that say 'don't cheat children' and 'don't be caught doing anything financially dishonest'. Barnard's book suffers from a lack of concrete examples, but one of the few exceptions is worth quoting in full:

Mr. A, a citizen of Massachusetts, a member of the Baptist Church, having a father and mother living, and a wife and two children, is an expert machinist employed at a pump station of an important water system. For simplicity's sake, we omit further description. We impute to him several moral codes: Christian ethics, the patriotic code of the citizen, a code of family obligations, a code as an expert machinist, a code derived from the organization engaged in the operation of the water system. He is not aware of these codes. These intellectual abstractions are a part of his "system," ingrained in him by causes, forces, experiences, which he has either forgotten or on the whole never recognized. Just what they are, in fact, can at best only be approximately inferred by his actions, preferably under stress. He has no idea as to the order of importance of these codes, although, if pressed, what he might say prob-

ably would indicate that his religious code is first in importance, either because he has some intellectual comprehension of it, or because it is socially dominant. I shall hazard the guess, however, that their order of importance is as follows: his code as to the support and protection of his own children, his code of obligations to the water system, his code as a skilled artisan, his code with reference to his parents, his religious code, and his code as a citizen. For his children he will kill, steal, cheat the government, rob the church, leave the water plant at a critical time, botch a job by hurrying. If his children are not directly at stake, he will sacrifice money, health, time, comfort, convenience, jury duty, church obligations, in order to keep the water plant running; except for his children and the water plant, he cannot be induced to do a botch mechanical job – wouldn't know how; to take care of his parents, he will lie, steal, or do anything else contrary to his code as a citizen or his religious code; if his government legally orders him to violate his religious code, he will go to jail first. He is, however, a very responsible man. It not only takes extraordinary pressure to make him violate any of his codes, but when faced with such pressure he makes great effort to find some solution that is compatible with all of them; and because he makes that effort and is capable he has in the past succeeded. Since he is a very responsible man, knowing his codes you can be fairly sure of what he will do under a rather wide range of conditions.

– The functions of the executive, pp 267-8

Within any big firm Mr. A's modest number of potentially conflicting codes is multiplied many times by the number of material interests, and moral and social concerns, possessed by the people who must cooperate in the firm's work. Their individual purposes, and the codes which go with their diverse trades and professions and organizational roles, must somehow be reconciled with or subordinated to the purposes of the enterprise; and individual purposes are reconciled or subordinated most effectively if the individuals feel that they are members of the enterprise, and share its purposes. They can't simply be conned into feeling that. The common purposes must have some genuine interest, material or moral or both, for them.

So real-life business leaders face many more and tougher conflicts of code and purpose than Mr. A did.

Laws must be obeyed. Owners must get reasonable dividends. Taxes must be paid, creditors must be paid. Customers must get good service. Those are external requirements which the firm can't usually alter, and must meet if it is to survive. It must incorporate them into a set of purposes which are also able to attract the willing cooperation of the firm's managers and workers.

But interests conflict, and codes conflict. Some of the external requirements conflict. Some of the noblest of the codes conflict. (Think of Mr. A when a pump breakdown calls for quickest-possible repair, so that his commitment to serving the community conflicts with his commitment to fine workmanship.) Consider some of the conflicts of interest, belief and purpose with which real-life business executives have to cope:

The firm must pay reasonable dividends, or it may be taken over or capital-starved. But if it inflates profits and dividends (perhaps by historical cost accounting) it may erode its capital and endanger its future. Surviving now can conflict with prospering later.

Suppose that 'surviving now' means resisting a takeover. Then it is the present directors, rather than the firm, who are fighting to survive, because they will be sacked if the takeover succeeds. Should their resistance therefore be written off as self-interested? Perhaps – but they may also be trying to protect the firm's future from the increased dividend expectations *and* debt burden that the takeover will bring if it succeeds.

The firm must get good performance from its managers. If it merely honors good managers rather than paying them well, they will convict it of hypocrisy and look about for better employers. If on the other hand it pays them too much, that may cut into profits, it may inflame the wage expectations of the rank and file of workers, it may provoke journalists and Left politicians to excite public indignation at what the executives are paying each other.

The firm must give its customers good value or they may turn to its competitors. But the margins of good value may have to come out of workers' wages, owners' dividends, local employment, long-term research and investment.

When directors are choosing and placing and promoting managers they may have to balance skills and promise against loyalty and long service; cleverness against goodness; inventiveness against reliability; harsh treatment of competitors against harsh treatment of colleagues; and so on.

In deciding those and many other issues, directors cannot merely choose the best means of serving the firm's purposes. Many of the choices *affect* the purposes, if only by giving priority to one purpose over another. Can every other purpose be subordinated to the single purpose of maximizing profit? Not necessarily, because that can be self-defeating. The way an enter-

prise treats its people and customers and their codes of behavior has strong effects on morale, which in turn affects output and profit. Thus considerate directors dealing fairly with all concerned, and appearing to give owners no more than a satisficing dividend, may make higher profits over time than single-minded profit-seekers do. *The success of one purpose may depend on the success with which the other purposes are also served.*

Now comes the heart of Barnard's argument. Executives have to cope with conflicts between individuals; conflicts of interest between owners, managers, workers, customers, creditors, and community concerns; conflicts within some of those groups – between some shareholders and others, some managers and others, one labor union and another; and conflicts between the short and long term interests of some of those groups. (Recall the example of employees with conflicting short and long term interests in alternative accounting systems.) The conflicts are not only between material self-interests. They are usually also between codes of conduct. Business is full of situations in which 'Be fair', 'Be loyal' and 'Compete hard' suggest three different lines of action. Even the direct conflicts of interest tend to be embodied in conflicting codes, as each interest asserts moral principles which give justice to its claim.

Executives exist to resolve such conflicts. It is their main function. And when they face problems involving conflicting codes, they respond (Barnard says) in one of three ways.

1. Some can't decide. They can't bear to disappoint either party, they won't face the problem, they put it off, it paralyses them. These executives are no good.

2. Some make cutting decisions one way or the other, upholding one of the codes and breaking the other(s). That weakens the broken codes and upsets the people who believe in them and live by them or gain by them. Most of the codes are there for good reasons so the morale and common purpose of the enterprise are likely to suffer. These 'decisive' executives may be less bad than the indecisive ones, but they are still not good.

3. Good executives are inventive in one or both of two ways. They find a course of action which satisfies all or most of the relevant codes. Or they modify the codes themselves in ways which preserve the codes' necessary virtues but reduce their conflicts.

Let's have that again, in Barnard's words this time. When executives face problems of conflicting codes and conflicting purposes, the results of such conflicts may be of three kinds: (1) either there is paralysis of action, accompanied by emotional tension, and ending in a sense of frustration, blockade, uncertainty, or in loss of decisiveness and lack of confidence; or (2) there is conformance to one code and violation of the other, resulting in a sense of guilt, discomfort, dissatisfaction, or loss of self-respect; or (3) there is found some substitute action which satisfies immediate desire or impulse or interest, or the dictates of one code, and yet conforms to all other codes.

When the second situation of non-conformance to one code is the resolution and it is repeated often, it will have the effect of destroying that code, unless it is very powerful and is kept alive by continuing external influences.

When the resolution of the conflict is accomplished by substitution of a new action for that originally conceived, all the codes are strengthened by the experience; but such a solution frequently requires imaginative and constructive ability.

– The functions of the executive, p. 264

The imaginative and constructive ability has to be *both* technical *and* moral; as Barnard repeatedly insists, either can be disastrous without the other. That is reflected in the alternative ways of resolving conflicts, by finding policies which meet all the moral requirements, or by amending the moral requirements themselves. In amending the moral requirements themselves – the codes by which people live and work, and which define their organizational duties – there is always a fine line between honest moral reasoning on the one hand, and deceptive or cosmetic moral persuasion on the other. It is a fine line but Barnard is well aware of it, and argues always on the honest side of it.

One final effect [of good morale] is the elaboration and refinement of morals – of codes of conduct ... That it can degenerate into mere subtlety to avoid rather than to discharge obligations is apparent in all executive experience. The invention of the constructions and fictions necessary to secure the preservation of morale is a severe test of both responsibility and ability, for to be sound they must be just in the view of the executive, that is, really consonant with the morality of the whole; as well as acceptable, that is, really consonant with the morality of the part, of the individual.

– The functions of the executive, p.281

Individual and group concerns have to be reconciled with the purposes of the organization as a whole. All three have to be adaptable, the collective purposes as well as the individual and group concerns.

If Barnard had also required those concerns to be compatible with collective *national* purposes, he would have arrived at conclusions which Japanese thinkers had reached a generation earlier.

Japanese pioneers

Recall the history of Japan's industrialization. In 1868 the modernizing government took power in an orderly, homogeneous community with a developed intellectual and artistic culture and strong traditions of authority, obedience, and family and group and national solidarity. There were arts and crafts, some manual industries and a few big merchant houses. But commerce and industry had low social status and there were neither the technological nor the institutional conditions for modern steam-powered industry. The new government immediately abolished the feudal institutions and introduced Western freedoms and company law and organization; but its more difficult and more remarkable achievement was to develop a national 'will to economize', and to replace traditional values and codes of behavior by ambitions and codes appropriate to modern capitalist enterprise. Ingeniously, the leaders engaged some of the strongest of the old codes to inspire or force the reform of others. When the Emperor told people to modernize, tradition required them to obey. The traditional exclusion of the barbarians now required industrial steam and steel. Because Confucian values taught people to despise the pursuit of profit, Japanese entrepreneurs should be inspired instead, by reverence for ancestors and Emperor, to develop capitalist wealth and power for nation rather than self.

The leaders and thinkers saw themselves as persuading their people to develop Western industries but in a Japanese way. In composing their persuasions, and in designing the many firms which government created to hand over to private owners, they were incidentally developing a Japanese theory of the private firm and its proper purposes. Four examples:

Fukuzawa Yukichi (1835 – 1901) was the great educator of the new business class. He wrote books and articles and made many speeches about the need for such a class, and founded a school and university to begin its education. He believed that the samurai – the military, administrative and intellectual class – could not only turn themselves into effective business leaders, but could bring special virtues to the role, and a special capacity to cooperate with their samurai brethren in the upper ranks of government.

Shibusawa Eiichi (1840 – 1931) was an outstanding entrepreneur who established some hundreds of new enterprises. One of his purposes was to transform the image and reputation of commercial and industrial activity, whose feudal status had been low. So in the practice of his firms and in writings and speeches he insisted that business direction and management required, above all, honesty, independence, cooperative spirit and social responsibility.

Muto Sanji (1867 – 1934) whose role in the development of Japan's distinctive labor relations you met earlier, exerted his strong influence before and after the First World War.

Kawakami Hajime (1879 – 1946) was the son of a high-minded samurai. In 1917 he published a book called *Tale of Poverty*. He was concerned that the mass of low-skilled workers and their families in town and country were not getting much benefit from Japan's economic growth. The nation's rising income was going disproportionately to a rich minority. The same was happening in the leading Western countries. Their productive systems were accordingly biased to produce too many luxury goods and too few necessities. But Kawakami differed from many Western critics of the economic inequalities in three ways. He thought the trouble was partly social. The religious and civil codes of the upper class acknowledged a strong duty – the collective purposes of the nation – but did not include the material welfare of the mass of the people in those purposes. Their social superiority was a cause as well as an effect of economic inequality. So Kawakami's program had two differences from most of its Western equivalents. Instead of direct action to improve poor incomes, reform should begin by limiting high incomes. And instead of imposing that reform by force of law, he urged the high earners to do it themselves, voluntarily, for ethical and compassionate reasons. They should restrain their own incomes, and live frugally.

Could that proposal to capitalist tycoons be serious? A bad joke? Hopelessly naive? Have there not been some very rich and some corrupt Japanese leaders, then and since? Yes. But the book sold well to rich as well as poor. It had strong influence on some of the leaders of the 'Japanese miracle' after the Second World War. It appealed to the old accord between leaders in business and government, and to the mutual trust which contributed so much to the 'miracle'. In 1992, seventy five years after *A Tale of Poverty* appeared, corporate chief executives in the United States were taking an average two million dollars a year from their firms, which was about 120 times the average wage they paid their employees. Their Japanese equivalents were taking about one fifth of that money, and one fifth of that multiple of their workers' average pay – even though the accord between business and government, the lifetime employment of skilled workers and other unAmerican features of Japanese business life were by then under strong attack from many quarters of Japanese business and government.

Thus a Japanese theory of the proper purposes of private firms had considerable practical effect and lasting power, at least through its first eighty years.

A BROAD THEORY OF FIRMS' PURPOSES

When firms outgrow direct management by individual owners, one response is to hire directors to manage them on the owners' behalf. Another – shared by Berle and Means, Chester Barnard, the Japanese, and much of Western and Japanese law – lets the shareholding owners become merely one among a number of groups with whom the firms' directors must deal and whose interests they must respect.

The owners continue to be important, but with no exclusive right or power to determine the firm's purposes. Company law emphasizes their 'external' status. It allows them to see only the public financial statements, not the internal management accounts. It limits the amount of dividend they can vote themselves.

Meanwhile the directors who manage the enterprise are responsible for the firm's performance of its duties to creditors, employees, customers and the community. Owners have rights because they contribute some capital which the firm can't do without (though you have seen that owners can sometimes contribute startlingly little of the capital the firm uses). But neither can firms do without the additional capital they get from bondholders and banks, or without managers, workers, public services, and customers to buy their products. So not only owners but also managers, workers, bondholders and other creditors, customers, and local and national governments may all have legal rights, and codes of conduct, with which the firm's purposes must be compatible if it is to survive and do its productive work.

Thus a 'theory of the firm', meaning a theory about firms' purposes, was born in the West half a century after Fukuzawa and others had conceived something similar in Japan (but not exported it – there were no English translations of their works). The theory came from the Hawthorne experiments in motivating workers in 1929-1931; from Berle and Means' book in 1932;

from the New Deal reforms and especially the new business code developed by the Securities and Exchange
Commission from 1933; from Chester Barnard in 1937;
and from other Liberal and Left sources in the rich
countries in the 1930s. The new view saw the incorporated firm as company law had long seen it, as an entity
separate from its owners. It is an independent productive institution subject to a mixture of legal, social and
market disciplines. It must make some profit to survive.
But consistently with that it does, and *should*, serve the
purposes and respect the just rights and expectations of
capital owners, employees, creditors, customers, and the
society of which it is an organized part. Where the interests and moral codes of those parties conflict, the conflicts have to be resolved, and the firm's purposes
refined, by a mixture of law, bargaining, compromise
and creative policy-making of the Barnard kind. And
the policy-makers' judgment and creativity must often
be moral as well as technical.

Notice that this theory is about how firms arrive at
their purposes. It is not about what those purposes are,
because it expects them to vary from time to time and
from firm to firm. But remember the range and importance of policy choices which firms – especially big
firms – may face. Maximize or moderate or even (for
some tax purposes) minimize profit? Short, medium or
long-term profit? How to divide profit between paying
dividends and reinvesting in growth? Aim at biggest
revenue? Biggest market share? Biggest profit? Highest
rate of profit on turnover? Highest rate of profit on
funds employed? (Those five *can* all be compatible, but
rarely are.) Stability or growth? Safety or risk? Treat
employees as beavers or grasshoppers? Act neighborly
or unneighborly to the surrounding environment and
community? Use artificial and offshore tax devices, or
not? Retain unpopular Libyan, Iranian, Iraqi links, or
not? Accept tobacco advertising, alcohol advertising,
sex advertising, or not? Bribe politicians, officials,
financial journalists, competitors' employees, industrial
spies, or not?

In all those choices and more, this theory says that
firms often do, and always should, act with broad social
responsibility, and with purposes to which not only
owners but also directors, workers, customers and government may all properly contribute.

Because these questions of business purpose may
well be active political issues during your working lifetime, it may interest you to explore their implications,
and the tricky nature of some of the debates about them,
a little further. As follows.

Corporate purposes and surplus value

When this text defined private enterprises by the single
characteristic 'profit-seeking', it acknowledged how
selective and potentially misleading that definition was.
Recall the reasoning: to make profits, firms commonly
have to produce things their customers can use. They
must also pay their workers, pay their taxes, and meet
public requirements of safety and honest dealing. If
they don't serve those other purposes they won't
achieve their own purposes. So they could truthfully
be characterized as producing for customers' use, workers' sustenance, owners' profit, and public purposes
of health, safety and full employment. We have just
been relating that multi-purposed view of the firm to
Chester Barnard's ideas of moral consensus and social
responsibility.

Now focus on the potential conflicts within the
multi-purposed firm and relate them to the Marxian or
post-Keynesian idea of surplus value.

Think of a firm's directors as entrepreneurs who
must bring together a number of factors of production.
To make a profit they must get each factor as cheaply as
possible, then sell their product for as much as possible.
So at whatever are the appropriate standards of quality
they get land and machinery and materials as cheap as
they can. They get labor as cheap as they can. And to
pay for those items they get finance as cheap as they can
– sometimes equity capital comes cheaper, sometimes
debt capital does.

The effect of getting the best bargains they can, and
of managing the productive process efficiently, is to
maximize profit. Now slow down and think carefully
about one implication of that.

If it takes the whole profit to attract and hold the necessary capital, i.e. if the directors feel compelled to pay
the whole profit to the shareholders as dividends, you
may choose to see that as a case of the owners' interests
prevailing over all others. But think again: *you may
equally well see it as all the other interests prevailing*. It
is *because* the workers are getting such high wages, and
the equipment and materials cost so much, and the
bondholders are getting such high interest on the debt
capital they provided, and the customers are paying
such low prices for the product, that profits are shaved
to the level at which they will only just pay for the necessary equity capital. Each factor of production is getting its bare minimum market price, and after paying for
all the factors including the equity capital there is nothing left over. (Neoclassical economists would perceive
a perfectly competitive industry.)

Now suppose the firm manages to do better than that, so that of every million of profit that it can make, half a million will pay enough dividend to satisfy the shareholders (and thus sustain the market price of the shares, and attract any additional share capital the firm may need). That half million dividend is a factor cost: it is the price the firm pays for its equity capital. What will be done with the other half million of profit, the surplus value the firm is now able to create over and above the factor costs of production?

That surplus *may* go to the owners as extra dividend, or as capital growth if it is reinvested. That would serve the owners' purposes and fit the owners' theory of the firm.

But if others know the surplus is available it may not reach the owners. The directors may use some of it to increase their own pay and perquisites. The workers may seize the opportunity to demand and get a pay rise. The Consumers' Association may holler 'excessive pricing' and threaten to take the firm to the Monopolies Commission or the Prices and Incomes Tribunal if it doesn't hand its surplus to its customers by cutting its prices. The government may pre-empt the surplus by taking more company or sales tax, for the benefit of other taxpayers or recipients of public services.

In short, as this text argued about Marx's original theory of surplus value, the surplus value doesn't necessarily go to the capital owners. It's up for grabs. Owners, directors, workers, consumers and taxpayers may all contend for shares of it.

What determines who gets how much of it?

Neoclassics may say: factor prices determine that. If (say) the directors and workers manage to split the whole surplus between them, that should indicate a rise in the market prices of those categories of labor. (But it can't be because of changed supply or demand, since there is no change in the quantity or quality of labor demanded or supplied – so perhaps the salary and wage changes must be ascribed to 'market failure'.)

Post-Keynesians may say that the employees have used their bargaining advantages, probably based on inside foreknowledge of the firm's accounts, to contrive their bigger shares. If they can pre-empt the potential surplus into salaries and wages, the shareholders and consumer watchdogs need never know it was available.

This text says the post-Keynesians are probably right. But economists should also learn from Chester Barnard, or from everyday experience, to take seriously the conflict of codes which usually accompanies the conflict of interests. Is it right or wrong for directors and workers to pre-empt the potential surplus? That chiefly depends on the fairness or otherwise of their claims. If they have been keeping the firm afloat through hard times by working for less than the rates of pay prevailing in the industry, it may be right to bring their rewards into line at the first opportunity. But if they are already overpaid, from using the firm's market strength to exploit its suppliers and milk its customers for years past, this further surplus ought to go via price cuts to the consumers, or via taxes to relieve other taxpayers.

Those are not the only codes which may apply. If you think the society's income inequalities are too great, you may want to use the surplus to reduce them. If the firm produces household necessities the surplus might be split between raising wages (to reduce inequalities) and cutting prices (to reduce them further by increasing poor households' real purchasing power). But if the firm uses cheap labor to produce expensive fur coats or restaurant dinners you may want to keep prices high and use the surplus to pay higher wages and a luxury sales tax.

Do these paragraphs amount to idle moralizing about issues which are actually decided by impersonal market forces, or contests of naked self-interest?

No, for two reasons.

First, the codes help to determine what people try for. In many lines of business, people do not nick anything and everything that is not nailed down, regardless of others' pain and loss. Most people find good behavior more enjoyable: they prefer fair shares and honest earnings to ill-gotten gains they are hated for taking, or have to feel guilty about.

Second, when interests conflict the codes help to determine who wins. Most claims to money are backed by claims to fairness, justice, prudence, entitlement, etc., i.e. by appeals to codes of behavior. Those moral claims are not *all* dismissed by other people as self-interested and therefore invalid. People discriminate between fair and unfair claims, reasonable and unreasonable self-interests; and claims succeed or fail accordingly.

For example, strikes for higher pay rarely succeed if public opinion thinks the claims outrageous. On the other hand there is rarely any need for aggrieved workers to strike if employers can see that their claims would attract wide public sympathy.

Another example: what directors of big firms can take for themselves is not chiefly determined by a supply-and-demand market for directors' services. It is chiefly determined by official and unofficial codes of behavior. If doubling the chief executive's package and shifting half of it offshore to escape tax is perceived as opportunist plunder, there may be quite a lot that hostile labor leaders, financial journalists, abrasive TV interviewers, consumer groups, corporate regulators and politicians can do to prevent or punish such misbehavior. But they won't do it if they accept that greed is normal and acceptable. Alternatively they won't do it if they see the directors' rewards as necessary incentives, or as well-earned by good service. Moral codes do at least as much as law and 'market forces' do to determine how much the managers of other people's money can take for themselves.

As with director's rewards, so with other policies. Wage deals are based on bargaining strength but limited by judgments of what is fair and reasonable. Many monopolies abstain from optimum monopoly pricing, restrained by their own codes of behavior or by prudent respect for others' codes. Firms which provide charitable gifts, artistic or sporting patronage or other public services may not always be altruistic, but their spending responds to popular conceptions of generous, public-spirited behavior: to popular codes. And there are many other business relations which vary with the moral codes of the people concerned, or of the onlookers: the propensity (or not) to abide by the spirit as well as the letter of contracts; landlords' and tenants' ways of treating each other; workers' care or lack of care for their employers' equipment; employers' care or lack of care for their workers' occupational health; and so on. Beliefs are working parts of economic systems, and moral beliefs help to shape many corporate purposes.

Conclusions follow which you have met before in Fred Hirsch's *Social limits to growth*, in comparisons between the better mixed economies (as in north western Europe) and the worse (as in parts of South America), and elsewhere in this text. The behavior of private firms, like the behavior of other productive institutions, depends a good deal on the quality and strength in action of their members' moral codes. Those in turn depend a good deal on the codes prevailing in the surrounding culture. Efforts to improve and strengthen the codes, by law or example or persuasion, may be well worth while. Efforts to weaken the legal backing of good codes, for example by general deregulation, may harm business efficiency as well as business morality. Moral beliefs have often helped to shape corporate purposes, and *ought* to do so.

Advantages? This theory of firms' purposes has attractions of four kinds.

First, it fits many of the facts. Directors' actions *are* constrained by others' codes. Owners' powers over firms *are* limited by law, and by the practical difficulty of many shareholders trying to direct a few executives. Successful business leaders *have* often conciliated, persuaded or inspired their employees and trading partners with better effects than are sometimes achieved by ruthless, single-minded profit-seeking.

Second, as an explanation of the sources of success and failure in complex organizations the theory goes far towards explaining why the type of ownership need not determine the organization's performance; i.e. why it is that public Renault and private Fiat are so alike, and so many kinds of enterprise can work as well (or as badly) under public, private, or independent non-profit ownership.

Third, as a code of conduct for business leaders it promises a more responsible, sociable, acceptable kind of private enterprise than is likely to come from a ruthless pursuit of owners' interests alone.

Fourth, the theory suggests possibilities of market efficiency without great inequalities of wealth. Most small businesses may always run best if individuals own and manage them, but firms big enough to be beyond their owners' direct control – the big firms which now do more than half of the private sector's production – have no functional need of rich private owners. They could just as well be owned by their employees, by public or private superannuation institutions, by investment trusts, or even in some cases (like churches and universities) by nobody. Efficiency need not suffer from more equal ownership, or more public ownership. As long as directors have to attract capital in a market way, and their jobs depend on keeping their firms profitable, they can be equally well motivated whether the owners from whom they must attract their capital funds are a few rich individuals, a lot of small shareholders, employees' or consumers' trusts, or the investment officers of public or private financial institutions.

One tragedy of the current capitalist revolution in some of the ex-communist countries is that it is not this multi-purposed, socially responsible view of the private firm, but a ruthless self-seeking and profit-seeking view of it, that was recommended by strident Western voices and adopted by many captors of the liberated industries. It did not inspire super-efficient performance. In Russia it prompted more plunder than production, and halved national income within a very few years.

AN OWNERS' THEORY OF FIRMS' PURPOSES

An alternative to that broad view is the view that firms do, and should, act with the single purpose of maximizing profit for their owners.

This view concedes that firms must obey the laws, pay the going rate to labor, give the customers good value, and maintain good public relations. They may also get better performance from workers by humane management than by harsh management. But that attention to workers', consumers' and community interests is merely instrumental. It is what you have to do to make profits – and how much of it you do should depend strictly on the effect on profit. If kindness pays, be kind. If cruelty pays better, be cruel. Considerate treatment of others is a means to an end, not a code of conduct. The director's *only* code should be 'Serve the owners' interests in everything you do'. And that is usually taken to mean their selfish material interests, rather than any social or moral concerns that they may have.

Even if owners' self-interests prevail, they are likely to conflict. (Risk or safety? Income or capital growth? Income now or later? Which of the alternative methods of tax avoidance?) A theory that firms serve their owners' purposes still can't predict their dividend or growth policies reliably. But all the alternatives may maximize gains in one way or another, for some or other owners.

To *know* that firms maximize profits, must we see inside the directors' minds to know their actual purposes? These theorists say 'No'. They simply assume that the firms which make most profit are likeliest to survive, so whatever firms exist must be making what profits they can. Hence, 'firms maximize profits'.

Objections Critics object that this theory is untrue, unnecessary and perhaps immoral.

There are three main reasons for thinking it is untrue. First, in competitive industries a firm which is willing to *minimize* profit, i.e. to run on the least profit that will keep it alive, should be able to beat competitors who try to do better. As long as its profits or prospects are sufficient to attract the capital it needs, it should be able to expand its operation and its market share. Directors may well enjoy growth and a big market share more than they enjoy paying dividends to idle shareholders.

Second, business is often risky and futures are uncertain so profit is rarely the only thing that owners want. They also want safety. Owners vary and directors vary in the minimax balance of profit and risk that they want. But *any* minimax balance means foregoing some possibilities of profit, so a theory that 'firms maximize profits' is indeterminate, and experience confirms that tendencies to play safe or gamble fluctuate, with boom and slump and other conditions causing wide variations in investors' 'animal spirits'.

That is one effect of uncertainty about futures. Another – and a third reason for doubting that firms always maximize profits – is that there may be no sure relation between what firms try for and what they get. Directors often don't know how to maximize profits. Even if they know the approved methods and the statistical probabilities, it is always possible that market fluctuations, technical inventions, political changes or other causes may defeat them.

One critic of neoclassical theories of the firm long ago summed up these objections to them:

> We have grounds to doubt that businessmen try to maximize profit. They have other aims too. Even if they tried, we would be sceptical that they could: they often do not know the relevant data. Even if they tried and could, it is doubtful whether they in fact would maximize profits: where there is uncertainty actual returns diverge from expected returns. This divergence is in the nature of things. The theory which we have been criticizing assumes that businessmen should, would and could behave in a way which may be undesirable, unsuccessful and impossible.
>
> – Paul Streeten, 'The theory of profit', *Manchester School* XVII, 3, 1949

Common sense Many economists now agree that most firms seek some selection or mix of profit, growth, market share, and safety. The mix varies from firm to firm; and attitudes to risk and safety vary over time with fluctuations in business activity and confidence.

That reduces the 'theory of the firm' to a commonsense expectation that firms will generally pursue, willingly or of necessity, some mix of their owners', managers' and workers' interests. Most firms won't survive for long unless they make satisfactory profits. So they can rarely be very charitable. But partly by choice and partly from necessity (including relative bargaining strength) some firms are more considerate employers than others. Some are more ruthless and single-minded profit-seekers than others. Most of them pay as much attention to environmental, community and national needs as law, custom and political prudence require. A few do better than that and a few do worse. Overall, the general quality of corporate behavior, good or bad, depends on mixtures of individual morality, national custom and culture, market discipline as opposing interests check each other, and the elaborate legal provisions outlined in Chapter 28.

Those are commonsense expectations. They allow quite a lot of commonsense prediction of corporate behavior. But there remains enough range of choice for many firms, enough conflicts with unpredictable outcomes, and enough other uncertainties in business life, to make it unlikely that experienced common sense will be bettered by any more precise, predictive 'theory of the firm'.

There may however be scope for moral theories, i.e. for arguments about how firms *ought* to behave.

Pause for a moment to be reminded of the Greek philosopher Plato. Democrats disagree with his ideas about forms of government; but he was the first writer to argue, in a powerful and convincing way, that government is a moral activity. Questions of common purpose are central to it. Conceptions of justice ought to guide it. Man's moral nature does, and ought to, find some of its best exercise and highest expression in political life.

I think Chester Barnard deserves to be recognized as the Plato of business: the practical businessman who perceived how much of corporate and bureaucratic life consists of partly-moral problems and conflicts, partly-moral debate and partly-moral decision-making, and ought to be managed in ways which are morally as well as materially satisfying to as many as possible of the participants.

Plenty of powerful people nevertheless disagree with Barnard's view. They don't believe such morally-aware, multi-purposed management need happen, or should happen; and some of them have lately been doing quite a lot to stop it happening. As follows.

An alliance for the owners' theory

Moral codes don't necessarily recommend good behavior. Some recommend bad behavior, whether because they don't agree it is bad or because they think bad behavior is all right, or has good effects. A formidable alliance of owners, executives, accountants, economists and corporate raiders opposes Chester Barnard's view of firms as cooperative organizations whose common purposes need to be compatible with their members' individual codes of right and wrong. Instead (conservatives argue, often without realizing that it is a moral argument) firms should serve their owners' interests exclusively. Any consideration for others should be instrumental to that purpose. Directors should deal with all concerned, inside and outside the firm, by unsentimental bargaining, self-interested on both sides. Moral consensus is unlikely and anyway unnecessary.

Five or six beliefs support this theory: belief in basic human selfishness; in capital owners' property rights; in decisive tests of competence and efficiency; in the benign nature of the hidden hand in market systems; and in the power of a rigorous mathematical kind of economic science.

We could have a paragraph or two about each of those beliefs, but you have met them before so that should not be necessary. Instead, here are some reasons why those beliefs appeal to particular groups and professions.

Accountants can't do all their work by unambiguous rules. As you learned earlier, they have to exercise a good deal of judgment. As a guiding principle for their judgments they have always taught that when in doubt, owners' interests should prevail. It is basically to the owners and for their purposes that the public financial accounts of firms must be rendered. Though many accountants are hired and fired by directors and managers rather than by owners, their textbook principles tell them to regard the owners as their clients. That tends to hold even when accounts have to be kept for other people's purposes. Except in the tax-collecting departments of government, for example, tax accountants mostly regard their skill as that of minimizing owners' tax bills, or the corporate tax bills which reduce owners' after-tax returns.

Economists who think that firms should operate exclusively in their owners' interests generally have one or both of two reasons for their belief. First, a neoclassical model of a competitive private-sector-only economy says that it works best for everybody if the owners of capital and land and labor do all look for the best possible returns for the factors they contribute to production. So (the model implies) capital owners who maximize their returns, thus forcing the firms which compete for their capital to maximize their returns, do more for economic efficiency than do capital owners who allow the firms which use their funds to act with multiple purposes, making less profit than they might.

Second, economists who hanker for a rigorous deductive economic science – an 'economic physics' – need business life to be as single-purposed as possible. (Imagine physics if gravity and magnetism sometimes operated and sometimes didn't, as creatures of their animal spirits.) The behavior of firms should be more reliably predictable if they have uniform measures of profit, all try to maximize it, and subordinate any other purposes to that one.

The two beliefs are most persuasive in combination. If you believe that the economy would be most efficient and most predictable if it consisted of nothing but competitive private firms maximizing profits, you have strong reasons for *recommending* single-purposed profit-maximizing behavior. I think the reasoning is wrong.

But for its believers it is powerful. It is specially so because many believers think it is purely factual technical reasoning, not moral (or immoral) at all. Objective science appears to agree with the jailed inside-trader Ivan Boesky that 'greed is good, greed works'. Helping yourself is the best way to help others. It is a deeply satisfying self-righteous morality for selfish people, especially successful ones.

Business schools have mushroomed since Barnard's day. To have something to teach they have had to develop a library of theoretical and practical books, manuals, courses of study, and definitions and measures and justifications of good management. Some of the management theory has been better than some of the corresponding economic theory, for example about the human problems of management and the motivation of work.

As to the purposes of profit-seeking firms, some schools introduce their students to a range of theories, including Barnard's and his modern successors. Others do not. That is not necessarily from positive disbelief, it may be from another necessity, as follows. *All* management schools teach that everyone in an enterprise must be accountable to somebody: worker to foreman, foreman to plant manager, plant manager to production manager, production manager to chief executive, chief executive to board. But board to whom? You can't have managers of other people's money accountable to no one. 'Board to owner' is the only unambiguous answer. It is the only way to obey Fayol's rule that subordinates must answer to one superior only, to ensure that they don't get inconsistent instructions or incomplete supervision. People who answer to two or more masters may get contradictory instructions from them; may play them off against each other; may get away with irresponsible acts because each superior assumes the other is watching; and so on.

Besides that rational reason there are psychological reasons for wanting boards, like everyone else, to have unambiguous purposes and responsibilities. There are people who feel insecure without clear lines of authority, clear rules of behavior, clear measures of better and worse performance including objective, impersonal criteria for appointments and promotions. For such people 'morality' simply means resisting temptation, obeying the rules, knowing what is right and doing it. It does not mean doubting the rules, arguing about them, compromising with folk who follow different rules.

To such straight-up-and-down thinkers the notion that executives and boards must frequently decide between competing purposes, and do it partly on moral grounds, respecting others' purposes in arriving at their own, is a nightmare. The nightmare is fairly specific. Multiple purposes will make for constant disagreement and indecision in policy-making. And they will allow excuses for every kind of failure, with no sure measures of success. Rational management will disintegrate into evasive dialogues like this:

Owners:	Why are profits down?
Board:	Because we thought it only fair, for various good reasons, to pay our workers above the going rate.
Workers:	All very well, but your new quality control procedures are putting us under intolerable stress.
Board:	Can't help it, we must please the customers or we'll all be out of jobs.
Customers:	The goods are over-priced.
Board:	That's because we look after the ozone layer by spending twice as much as our competitors do on safe waste disposal.
Mayor:	Please do the same about the noise pollution you're inflicting on the neighborhood.
Board:	Can't afford to, it would take most of our owners' already-low profit.

Balancing, adjudicating, reconciling or creatively transcending those contending interests and codes is the heart of executive responsibility as Barnard saw it. What can keep such policy-making and management coherent? You know this text's answer. Somebody's values must: technical competence directed by some coherent set of business and social values must. But all that single-minded profit-seekers can see in such many-voiced, multi-purposed interchanges is muddle and incoherence, with multiple excuses for failure.

There may also be nuisances for winners. If business is a moral field, those who plainly win – who beat the competition, increase market share, better last year's profit, succeed in takeovers, and feel entitled to unmixed praise – may yet be nagged by moralists, and perhaps by governments, for the very achievements that maximize their returns: shedding labor, ruining competitors, unloading costs onto neighbors or government, evading tax, raising prices, taking the fruit out of the jam.

For those who want individual and corporate performance to be judged objectively by the single measure of the 'bottom line', the moral element of the human condition – the possibility that you may have to answer for winning as well as for losing – is upsetting. Hence the powerful attraction of a theory that the bottom line measures benefits for everyone else as well as for owners, because of the 'hidden hand' effects of competitive profit-seeking. That allows single-purposed management with clear tests of success and failure, and a clear conscience for winners.

Many management schools are matter-of-fact enterprises which don't aspire to the critical role or the philosophical sophistication of Harvard Business School. If a plain-brained school wants to teach management as an uncontroversial skill rather than a bewildering moral challenge, you can see why its simplest course (however deceptive) is to teach that firms should have the single purpose of maximizing their owners' returns.

Owners   A number of recent trends have tended to favor owners' interests despite the separation of ownership from control.

Directors in English-speaking countries are actually using that separation to increase their own gains faster than their owners' gains in many cases. But they invoke the owners' property rights to justify strictly selfish behavior in a broad way, and link the bonus element of their rewards to rates of profit (or sometimes growth) to show that their own gains depend on what they gain for their owners.

A rising proportion of shares are owned by institutions: insurance and superannuation funds, investment companies and trusts. They collect funds from small savers and operate them as big investors, and their investment officers are usually expert and watchful. Firms find that many small shareholders, of whom they did not have to take much notice, have been replaced or are now represented by big, expert investors who can enforce owners' requirements more effectively – but who, being directors themselves, are tolerant of rising levels of executive pay.

Finally the general shift of political opinion to the Right in many countries since the 1970s has brought some strengthening of capital owners' property rights. Owners no longer fear the nationalization of private enterprises; instead they wonder which public enterprises will be the next to be privatized. They can be more greedy and assertive than they dared to be under threat of the American New Deal in the 1930s or the British and French nationalizations of the post-war years.

Thus owners' traditional property rights, their market strength, and the orthodox theory and practice of many economists, accountants and business schools combine to encourage the belief that firms ought to be run mainly or exclusively for the benefit of the owners of the capital they use. That is a legal and moral belief. But it gets coercive force, increasingly, from the takeover industry.

Raiders   Remember how corporate raiders live by taking over or greenmailing firms which do not appear to be maximizing current returns for their owners. They are poorly managed, or humanely managed with more secure and better paid workers than a ruthless regime would need. Or they are planning well ahead, economising current dividends to finance expansion with minimal debt (and therefore sub-optimal tax avoidance). Or they have not noticed (or do not mind) that closing down and asset-stripping could yield more than the firm's net worth at its current share price.

Where takeovers succeed, they do not always benefit the old or the new owners or the long-term performance of the taken firms. They often hurt other parties, inside and outside the taken firms. And – most important – they affect many more firms than the raiders' targets.

The possibility of takeover becomes a general condition of business life in many industries. It drives directors to keep current profits, dividends and share prices as high as possible, leaving no potential short-term gains to attract raiders. It can discourage prudent long-term policies of saving, accumulating reserves, research, re-equipment and development which depend on restraining current dividends. And besides threatening firms which are less technically efficient than they could be, it can threaten any firm which treats its workers, customers, neighbors, natural environment or tax obligations any better than it absolutely has to. Thus it discourages broad views of corporate purpose and social responsibility

CONCLUSION

Berle and Means and Barnard were among the many people – on the Right as well as the Left, in business as well as in labor unions and consumers' organizations and government – who came to believe that firms could and should deal with their owners, workers, customers, neighbors and governments as fairly and cooperatively as was consistent with surviving and making satisfactory profits. That seemed to promise a reformable, responsible, acceptable kind of capitalism while continuing to ensure consumer choice, and plenty of scope for efficiency and growth to be motivated by competition in product design and development, pure productive efficiency, and market research and strategy. That moral view had a harsher version in a different understanding of the same facts, i.e. of firms' behavior when their control was separated from their ownership. By market pricing and hard bargaining without any moral considerations at all, directors could be expected to get the best deal they could for each factor of production they needed, *including the share capital and borrowed capital they needed.* They would get capital as cheaply as they could (which means that far from optimizing profits for owners, they would pay owners as little as possible for the use of their capital) just as they would get land or labor or materials as cheaply as they could. In that view, capital has no privileges over the other factors. It has no special right to any surplus value, or to dictate firms' purposes and policies. It merely gets its market price, like anything else.

But what shareholders lose, it does not necessarily follow that workers or customers or other citizens gain. In the English-speaking countries since the 1970s the biggest winners have been the corporate directors to whom the owners' lost control has passed. They have raised their own pay much faster than their workers' wages, the corporate income tax their companies pay, or any benefit their customers get from falling prices. You have just read what U.S. directors were taking in 1992. Chapters 43 and 44 on the distribution of wealth and income will report what various countries' executives were taking in 1997. Their gains are at the owners' as well as the workers' and customers' and taxpayers' expense – but the 'owners' theory' still serves as their main defence because it justifies tough treatment of all the other interests; it has a long and strong legal pedigree; and it has a quite new institutional strength. Scarcely any big company now has personal shareholders casting majority votes at its regular or exceptional meetings. Where its own directors do not have commanding numbers of proxy votes, other directors (from share-owning institutions) do. The laws about those rewards were designed to empower owners to control them. But most votes for directors' and executives' rewards are now cast by people with a direct or indirect material interest in escalating them.

Plenty of directors still nevertheless choose to use their independence to deal as fairly as they can with shareholders, workers, customers, taxpayers and environmental issues. But that also has increasing hazards in the English-speaking countries. Any policy of balancing all the relevant public and private interests has become vulnerable, in many circumstances, to takeover or the threat of it. And that reassertion of owners' rights has moral and theoretical support from many economists, accountants, business schools, and executives of the financial institutions who increasingly represent the private sector's actual owners.

Finally – repeating an earlier conclusion – common sense observes that many firms, especially small and medium-sized ones, and those whose business does not expose them to takeover, still seek varying mixtures of profit, growth, market share, risk and safety. Most firms must make satisfactory profits to survive but subject to that constraint they serve varying mixtures of their owners', directors', workers', customers' and neighbors' interests. They pay as much attention to environmental, community and national needs as law, conscience and political prudence require. And their behavior owes a good deal of its quality and morality to the prevailing culture. Quite a lot of business law still supports that culture. So there is some will and skill in business, as well as elsewhere in the democratic countries, to support the sort of reform that the new situation of corporate directors requires.

EXERCISES

1. Write as good an analysis as you can of the causes which have converged to increase the power and pay of American corporate directors through recent decades.

OR

2. What might you, or Jim Landis, or Chester Barnard advise government to do about private executive rewards in today's conditions?

3. Apart from laws to protect particular resources from particular threats (particular forests from logging, particular rivers from pollution, etc.) can you think of any more general ways to increase the importance of environmental care among the multiple purposes of company directors?

3. If a new law required that neither sex must outnumber the other by more than 2 to 1 on the board of any public company, would you expect any general changes in corporate purposes and the distribution of their benefits?

30

How firms work

Everything depends on everything else. Remember our mousetrap-maker's decision to invest in new labor-saving technology. Its success or failure would depend on competitors' investment decisions, labor union action, the persuasive effects of advertising on country folk with rising incomes, the weather and other natural conditions of mouse life, possible chemical or genetic approaches to mouse death, future rates of interest on the trap-maker's long-term investment loan, government decisions about interest rates and tariffs and regional industrial aids, and Mrs McTavish's personal and locational reasons for resisting a merger or takeover. Those are not all fixed or independent conditions; they can change as they interact with one another. And that fictitious small-business example greatly simplified the complexities of real business, especially big business.

How can you approach that simultaneous interdependence as a set of relationships to be studied one by one? Textbooks go about it in various ways. This one began with companies' legal powers and their directors' purposes. This chapter sketches how they start, some of the thngs they do, and the accounts they keep. Then there are chapters on investing, financing, paying wages, costing inputs and pricing outputs. It is possible to combine those tasks, i.e. to write a single, integrated account of what firms do, why they do it, and with what effects. That's more coherent; but it necessarily presents a finished product of economic analysis, rather than teaching you step by step how to do the analysis. It may nevertheless be a good idea for you to read such an integrated account, for two reasons. First, it can remind you how the parts of our step-by-step analysis fit together. Second, it may offer an alternative to this text's somewhat sceptical view of the sufficiency of the standard methods of analysis. An excellent short integrated account, which I strongly recommend, is Chapter 3 on 'The Behavior of Firms' in Derek Morris (ed.) *The economic system in the UK* (3rd edition, 1985).

OPPORTUNITIES

Firms are founded, or existing firms start new activities, when somebody perceives or creates a business opportunity.

There may be demand for a new product. (Seventeenth century navigators were demanding more accurate clocks before they were invented; twentieth century rock climbers were demanding lighter-but-stronger ropes before nylon was invented.)

There may be an idea for a new product which people will want when they see it. (Not many factory owners were demanding steam engines before Watt invented a workable one. Affluent dog and cat owners were not actually demanding animal psychiatry until the first pet psychiatrist advertised his services.)

There may be existing products which could be better designed or more cheaply produced. There may be products which could pay less tax and therefore sell cheaper if they were locally produced instead of imported. (McTavish can make a better mousetrap than the one we're importing, and he can make it here.)

New science may make new products possible. (Advances in biochemistry and pharmacology made antibiotics possible. Advances in physics made the revolution in electronic communication possible.)

There may be opportunities for small firms to serve big firms better than the big firms can serve themselves. (Carmakers once made their own brakes; now most buy them from specialists. On an offshore oil rig there may be more independent contractors than employees of Shell or BP.)

The spread of settlement creates business opportunities. (Each new suburb needs food, newspapers, hairdressing, car repairs.)

And so on. What sort of people seize the business opportunities?

ENTREPRENEURS

Business opportunities are not always used. A man who knows how to make shoes may go hungry while his neighbor who knows how to bake bread gets sore feet, because it doesn't occur to either of them to produce something to exchange with the other: they don't recognize or use their opportunities. (In that case nor does their government. It should get them going with business information services, or it should start public bakeries and shoe factories to employ them.)

'Entrepreneurs' is a broad term for people who start

things. In the private sector they *may* create opportunities, for example by inventing a new product or process or by persuading government to shelter a new industry with a tariff. Or they may simply *recognize* opportunities, and seize and use them.

An entrepreneur may produce something. (James Watt both invented and produced his new steam engine. Laura Ashley both designed and produced her new fabric patterns.) Or he or she may simply bring others together: perhaps an inventor with a bright idea, a production engineer sick of working for wages, and a financier looking for a promising use for some risk capital. (John D. Rockefeller was not an oil prospector or driller or refiner, but he built Standard Oil. Allen Lane did not write, design, print or even read books, but he created Penguin Books.)

Some entrepreneurs do and some don't take financial risks. If a penniless inventor and a penniless production engineer together persuade a financier to stake their new mousetrap factory, all three may see themselves as entrepreneurs.

The impulse to find or create opportunities, develop new products, organize productive resources for new purposes, and take risks or persuade others to take them – the impulse to *start* things, to *make things happen* – is unevenly distributed around the world. It does not seem to be a simple product of economic conditions; it owes at least as much to culture and social values. Recall the economic histories you read in Chapter 11. Some societies generate steady supplies of entrepreneurial energy (the US for centuries past). Some governments have taken deliberate steps to generate it (Japan after 1868). Some societies have had intense outbursts of it (Japan after 1950). Some societies don't generate much themselves but get it from immigrants or foreign-owned transnationals (Australia since its white settlement). National cultures also seem to vary in the kinds of entrepreneurs they produce.

What conditions produce entrepreneurs? Many explanations have been offered. Climate, race, religion, culture, political systems, national independence may all have contributed. So may parentage – an Irish study found that the parents of successful entrepreneurs ranged from very rich to very poor, but they were nearly all risk-takers with businesses of their own; even the poorest of them tended to have their own farms or shops rather than work for wages. Migrants are 'cultural risk-takers', and have often contributed more than their share of entrepreneurs to the countries in which they settle. But as eighteenth-century Britain and twentieth-century Japan have shown, there can also be home-grown entre-

preneurial revolutions.

Whatever it is that produces them, entrepreneurs are important. Without them economies don't grow, new firms don't start, new products are not developed.

STARTING UP

You already know how to start a public company. Get three or more directors together. Tell a lawyer what powers and purposes you want the company to have. She'll draft a constitution, or Memorandum and Articles of Association. Submit it with a fee and other formalities to the government office which registers or charters companies. Learn from your lawyer and accountant what duties go with corporate status: what directors need to know of Canada's 99-page Corporations Act, or Britain's three-and-a-half pound manual of company law, or your national equivalent. Besides any accounting you need for working purposes, learn the government's corporate accounting and reporting requirements.

Depending on the nature of your business, you may need premises. Should you build? Buy existing premises? Lease or rent space? If you buy or build, should you pay with the firm's share or debenture capital, or should you borrow on mortgage? The different ways of financing real estate have different tax effects and different cash-flow and asset effects over time. Which suits your business best may depend on other elements of your financial plan.

Similar choices have to be made about other investment. Should you buy the machinery and vehicles you need, or lease them?

If your business can be done in different ways with different mixes of machinery and labor, which mix will be best? If it can be done with different mixes of permanent employees and casual or contract workers, which mix will be best?

If you need to buy materials or made-up components, should you stockpile them to cushion your operation against suppliers' work stoppages, shortages, fluctuating prices? Or should you run on JIT (Just In Time) principles, getting suppliers to deliver each day's requirements the day before? That shifts storage problems to the suppliers. Stored inputs are as unproductive as idle labor – the money that buys and stores them before you actually need them could more profitably be out earning interest. JIT goes with INS (Interest Never Sleeps).

You already know the main ways of financing your fixed and working capital. (1) Equity capital from the sale of shares. Dividends are the price you pay for it, a price which can vary with your earnings and capacity to pay. (2) Bond or debenture borrowing, typically for fixed terms at fixed rates of interest. That's 'fixed price' capital, except for any effects which inflation may have on its real value. (3) Bank loans. They also *can* have long terms and fixed interest rates, but nowadays they usually have short terms or variable interest rates or both, so when you borrow bank money you don't know exactly what it will cost you; it depends how the market rate of interest fluctuates through the period of the loan. (4) An important option if you prosper is self-financing from the firm's earnings. That capital has no direct costs (though we will note later that it may have indirect or opportunity costs). And the more you have of it, the more you can usually attract of the other, dearer funds. That can be important if the firm is to expand.

GROWING

Suppose the firm prospers. It earns steadily. There are opportunities to expand. You face some strategic choices. They will be explored in more detail later, but some of them can be simplified as choices (i) between profit and growth, (ii) between dividend income and growth, and (iii) between safety and risk.

Profit and growth Market conditions may allow you some choice between (i) selling a steady amount at a high price to earn a good rate of return on the initial investment; or (ii) cutting prices and profits-per-unit to undercut competitors and expand sales and market share.

Suppose you choose the price-cutting option. Whether total profit rises or falls as you sell more volume at lower prices may depend on relations between your economies of scale as producer, and your customers' price preferences and price elasticity of demand. (Will they switch to your product because its price is lower? Will they buy absolutely more because the price is lower?) You may cut prices to the point at which those factors together maximize your profit. Or you may go beyond that point, and sacrifice profit to further growth. Why might you do that? You may hope to win a big market share and then hold it at higher prices. You may value volume and market share for their own sakes. (Are your executives' bonuses based on profit, on turnover, or on rate of growth?) Or you may be forcing your competitors to cut prices, profits and dividends to weaken them for takeover.

Thus profit and growth *may* be conflicting aims. But not always, as the next item shows.

Dividends and growth Suppose that market condi-

tions allow the firm to expand sales without cutting prices or profits. But to double your output you must double your plant. How to finance that? Should you (i) spend your earnings on the new plant instead of paying dividends; (ii) continue to pay good dividends to maintain the market price of your shares, and finance the expansion by issuing additional shares; or (iii) finance the expansion by borrowing? Which you decide to do may depend on a number of things: whether the firm's shares are 'closely held' by majority owners who don't want to lose control; the current bond and bank interest rates; the comparative corporate tax treatment of retained earnings and earnings paid out as dividends; and the comparative tax treatment of shareholders' dividend incomes and capital gains. There may well be conflicts between dividends now and gains later – conflicts between directors' and shareholders' interests, and between some shareholders and others.

Safety and risk There are basically two kinds of risk: those which go with the kind of business you do, and those which go with how you finance it.

Some kinds of business are more regular and reliable than others. Office buildings in sought-after central business districts can rely on finding tenants at prevailing levels of rent. As long as they're insured they're safe investments. Staging operas and publishing first novels have always been risky business. And so on – all the way from buying government bonds at one extreme to backing outsiders in horse races at the other.

There is a tendency for the costs of capital and the *possible* profits to increase with risk and reduce with safety. Business like mineral search, which gambles for high profits but risks total loss, must generally be financed with a firm's own 'loseable' money rather than with borrowed funds. Meanwhile safe business can borrow at the lowest rates, but is so attractive that it is likely to be crowded, with competition keeping prices and profit rates comparatively low.

But there are exceptions. Safe industries with great market strength may be able to combine safety with high profits. (Example: big pharmaceutical drug manufacturers.) Marginal industries – especially some enjoyable ones in which people invest to be well occupied rather than to get rich – may combine high risk with low or no profits. (Examples: riding schools, hand potteries, village craft shops.)

All those are risks that are in the nature of the business. But almost any business, whatever its intrinsic risks, can increase its risks by incautious financing, most commonly by gearing.

Gearing is a broad term for the relation between what you own and what you borrow: between a firm's equity capital plus retained earnings and reserves, and its bond or bank debt. A firm which runs on its own resources, without borrowing, is ungeared. A $10 company, i.e. one with next to no equity capital, which manages to borrow large sums from banks or bond-holders is (almost) infinitely geared. Between those extremes gearing can be expressed in percentage terms. A firm with $2m. of its own capital and $1m. of borrowed capital is geared 50 per cent; with $2m. borrowed it would be geared 100 per cent; with $8m. borrowed it would be geared 400 per cent. But it is a questionable measure, for two reasons. (1) There can be doubt about the value of the firm's own resources. Should its debt be expressed as a percentage of its nominal share capital plus retained earnings and reserves? Or as a percentage of the current market value of its shares? Or its saleable assets? (2) Some people prefer to express the debt as a fraction of the whole capital rather than a multiple of the 'owned' capital. If a firm has $2m. of own capital and $8m. of borrowed capital this text says it is geared 400 per cent, but others may say it is 80 per cent geared because it is in debt for 80 per cent of its capital.

How does gearing affect risks?

It commits a fixed amount of revenue to debt service, i.e. to interest payments and capital repayments to bond-holders and banks who have to be paid whatever the firm earns, or fails to earn. That increases the firm's and the shareholders' upward and downward risks.

For the firm the upward risk arises from the opportunity to use more capital than the firm's own. The downward risk arises from failing to earn the costs of the borrowed capital. If an ungeared firm has a bad year and loses or breaks even, it can pay no dividend and survive. If a highly geared firm loses or breaks even it must still pay its bondholders somehow: by borrowing more, selling assets or going bankrupt.

For shareholders, gearing increases risks like this:

Upward If an ungeared firm makes super profits, all the owners of its capital share them. If a highly geared firm makes super profits the bondholders and banks do not share them; they continue to get their fixed entitlements while the super profits go to the shareholders (whether as dividends or capital growth). Consider a $2m. firm geared 400 per cent. Shareholders own a fifth of its $10m. capital, bondholders own four fifths. Suppose that the bonds pay 10 per cent interest, but the firm manages to earn $2m. a year, i.e. 20 per cent on the whole capital it is using. Of that $2m. the bondholders get $800,000, 10 per cent of their $8m. investment The shareholders get the rest: $1,200,000, which is 60 per cent on their $2m. investment. If the firm had not geared up, but had merely earned 20 per cent on its $2m. of equity capital, the shareholders would have got 20 per cent, only a third of the return they got by gearing.

Downward Suppose that instead of earning $2m. the high-geared firm only manages to earn $800,000 – 8 per cent on its whole capital. To get their 10 per cent the bondholders get the lot. Shareholders get none. Compare the $160,000, 8 per cent on their investment, they would have got without gearing. Worse, what happens if the geared firm breaks even or loses, so that it can't pay its bondholders' interest? It may be able to borrow some more, though for lending to such a troubled borrower there may be very high interest. It may sell itself cheap, with capital losses for the shareholders, to new owners willing to pay its debts. Or it may go bankrupt, and when its assets are sold the bondholders must get all they are owed – interest and capital – before the shareholders get anything.

Conclusion: Gearing does not usually create significant risks of its own. What it does is increase (and with high gearing, multiply) whatever risks are already there in the nature of the particular firm and its industry.

MANAGING

Whatever their financial structures, productive firms have to be managed. That may be no great problem in a corner shop or a family farm. But how is bigger business managed? A traditional definition says that 'management is getting things done economically by other people'. It may begin by designing a system of work which is likely to have three elements:

- *A physical process:* whether the firm processes materials (a factory), information (a bank) or people (a health studio), there must be a plan and equipment for doing the necessary things in the right order.

- *A division of labor* to break the work into individual tasks.

- *A pattern of responsibilities* for taking necessary decisions, giving necessary orders and seeing that the work gets done.

Some managers chiefly coordinate: they see that the physical processes and human tasks mesh properly. Some are monitors, seeing that people work properly, products are quality-controlled, accounts are kept. Some are negotiators and trouble-shooters, negotiating agreements and resolving conflicts within the firm and with government, unions, suppliers, customers, citizen groups. Some are researchers or policy-makers, deciding the directions the firm should go, what to produce, how to price it, and so on. Some chiefly nurture the firm's human capital, arranging for training and re-training, recruiting and understanding and judging people and fitting them to tasks. (Don't appoint the dreamy character with artistic flair to keep the accounts. Don't entrust the firm's advertising to the logical thinker with the steel-trap mind and no imagination. Don't let anyone near the central computer who hasn't trained on that model.)

We noted earlier, in relation to business powers, that production which is complicated enough to need corporate organization must usually be organized in a bureaucratic way, with elements of central planning and command. But the command may not be like officers barking orders at the ranks on a parade ground. Coordination is usually achieved by some mixture of three methods, of which only the first involves much barking of orders.

- There are chains of command and responsibility, perhaps modified by elements of consultation, self-management, industrial democracy, etc.

- There are the plan of work and the standing orders which go with it. Those are impersonal rules which all ranks must obey.

- There is coordination by common purpose. Everyone is expected to know the firm's general purposes and act accordingly. Many questions can then be decided quickly as they arise, by workers or foremen or middle managers, without referring them far up the chain of command.

Getting employees from top to bottom of the hierarchy to know the firm's purposes and to share them or anyway comply with them is at the heart of the task of 'human management'. Chapter 23 on people as producers emphasized how diverse the motivation of work can be. Between employer and employee there is a basic exchange of work for wages, and in many occupations a recognized market rate for the job. But how much actual sweat and cooperation and output the wages buy can vary a good deal. Partly that is determined by conditions beyond managers' control: by national and group culture, labor laws, union strength, current levels of unemployment. But it can also vary with the nature of the work and the amount of independence or team-work that it allows. And it can vary with the style and quality of management.

No single style of management is best for all enterprises. Some managers are chiefly concerned with materials or money: machinery, material flows, financial analysis and control. Some of those tasks require precise technical skills, others call for judgments of risk, market response, weather or other uncertainties. Other managers are chiefly concerned with people: with motivating and monitoring the behavior of employees. Styles of 'human management' vary widely. Some hard work, especially unskilled work, is still done under bullying managers. More often, managers deal civilly with employees motivated by a conventional mix of financial and other sticks and carrots. Some managers appear to act with the single purpose of maximizing the firm's profits, or their own rewards. Others say that they aim at a fair balance of benefits for the firm's owners, employees and customers, and society as a whole. (Those options were explored in the last chapter.) Where the work is such that workers must cooperate with each other and teach skills to each other, managers may promise them secure jobs and rights of seniority. The necessary trust and teamwork can still coexist with different attitudes to management. In some firms all ranks see each other as members of the team. In others, a shared dislike of the managers is one source of the workers' solidarity and cooperation with one another.

Those differences arise from the nature of the industries concerned, from particular traditions or theories of management, and from the purposes of the firms' owners or directors. Managers are supposed to carry out policies chosen by directors. But in practice there is a good deal of overlap between the policy-making and managing activities – hence chief executives are commonly called Managing Directors. There is also, increasingly, a necessary link between policy-making and day-to-day managing. Broad purposes and policies have to be turned into manageable processes by detailed technical and financial planning.

PLANNING

A lot of modern industry has great technical complexity. Nobody understands every part of it, so firms have to put together and train particular combinations of skills. Technical processes must be done in correct parallel or sequence, with all necessary inputs at appropriate stages; so there is time-tabling and ordering to be done. For many of the inputs and outputs there may need to be transport, handling and storage facilities, with monitoring to control quality and prevent theft. The technical planning has to be matched by financial planning to ensure that bills can be paid when they are due, from money that has not meanwhile been lying idle.

Consider for example the comparatively simple

forward planning required for an airline to introduce new long-range aircraft for use on new long-hop routes. The firm must order new-model jumbos or airbuses three or four years ahead of delivery. Two years ahead of delivery it must agree the crafts' internal services and decor. Eighteen months ahead it must put the new craft into its forward flight schedules, having negotiated the necessary landing rights. One year ahead it must order any necessary loading and ground service gear. Three months ahead pilots and engineers must begin conversion training. Three weeks ahead will do for cabin and catering staff. At other dates along the way the firm must plan any relevant advertising, and start booking, printing and recording in-flight entertainment. For each of those components there must be parallel financial planning to indicate what money from what sources will be required and available at what dates. (If it sounds complicated, think how much more intricate the planning must be in the firm which has to bring tens of thousands of components together, in due sequence with faultless quality control, to build the aircraft.) Meanwhile to keep the rest of its business going the airline must also be providing for dozens of other, more routine, capital replacements and modifications.

Big firms can rarely do all that planning at head office. Good planning has to include good judgment about what policy-making and planning to delegate or decentralize. Divisions, branches, plants, working groups and individuals have to know their tasks. That includes knowing what kinds of obedience, consultation, choice, self-management or independence are expected of them in deciding how best to get their work done.

For technical and other reasons the amounts of decentralization and local discretion vary widely from industry to industry. But it is generally true that the more decentralized the decision-making, the more care needs to be taken to see that the decision-makers know and comply with the firm's purposes and policies and (for reasons explored in the last chapter) do so as willingly as possible. The more decision-making groups or individuals there are, the more lateral communications there may need to be. The less decentralization on the other hand, the more central planning and vertical communication there may need to be. Either way there is work for central planning offices.

Big firms' planning activities are increasingly designed to link policy-making, planning and managing tasks. Planning offices research alternative policies; turn chosen policies into working plans; then use those plans to allocate responsibilities and monitor the working

performance. Such planning systems may include all or many of these elements;

- Statements of corporate purpose.
- Strategies: directions of development, desired balances between profit and growth, dividends and growth, risk and security.
- Technical plans and timetables for intended developments, or briefs for technical divisions to do such planning.
- Financial plans and timetables for intended developments.
- Technical and financial provisions for routine capital maintenance and replacement.
- Budgets for each separately-accountable division of the firm.
- Who is to decide what, within what limits and guidelines.
- Who must be consulted or kept informed about what: a map of the internal communication system.
- Targets, performance requirements and monitoring and reporting arrangements for the firm's working units.

Those are traditional principles of bureaucratic organization, public or private. Remember that, when ideologists claim that private enterprise is naturally superior to government because market relations are naturally more efficient than bureaucracy. Private firms, public firms and government departments all need to plan and organize and manage their activities. Efficient ones do it well, inefficient ones do it badly. They also have to decide what part of their business to do themselves, what to buy in from market suppliers, and what unfinished work to pass on to other producers. Government buys its computers from private firms, who hire physicists and engineers educated in public institutions, which buy most of their computers from private firms, who can raise market capital because their banks and sharebuyers know that government will protect their interests partly by bureaucratic supervision of the firms' behavior and partly by requiring firms to hire publicly licensed private auditors in a market way. As this text keeps reminding you, *both* relations are intricate: between the public and private operators, and between bureaucratic coordination and market coordination of their productive activities.

In both sectors, a good deal of the necessary planning is expressed in financial terms. The rest of this chapter on 'how firms work' reviews the kinds of accounting that a big firm may need to do. The material is quite complicated, the professional business of accountants rather than economists. Do you need it? That depends on the kind of work you hope to do, and on your general interest in understanding what private business is like these days. If you work for big firms, or at deriving national statistics from corporate accounts, you will need proper accounting training rather than this chapter's sketch of the subject.

ACCOUNTING

Firms have long kept public financial accounts and private management accounts. In recent times tax accounting and various kinds of social accounting have also become important. So we can introduce accounting of four basic kinds.

1. **Public financial accounts** have to be kept by every public company. The *Balance Sheet* tells what the firm is worth at a particular date. The *Income Statement,* alternatively called the *Profit and Loss Statement,* tells what the firm has earned in a particular period. These are accounts of past and present facts, they don't include forward estimates; and they are called *external* accounts because they report on the firm to people external to it, or anyway external to its management: owners, potential investors, stock exchanges, tax and other public authorities, creditors, customers.

2. **Management accounting** is for *internal* use in controlling the firm's business and arriving at well-informed business decisions. It includes *planning* and *forecasting,* i.e. it deals with future as well as past and present information. It can be *private,* not for publication. It includes –

   • *investment appraisal* to decide what funds to raise, what system of production to adopt, what equipment to buy, etc.;

   • *cost analysis* to know what each part of the productive process costs, to arrive at least-cost ways of doing things, to know what quantity of a product the firm can afford to produce for sale at a given price, etc.; and

   • *control accounting* to see that systems work as planned, and that the firm is not robbed or defrauded.

3. **Tax accounting** stands for a special skill rather than a special sets of accounts. (You can go to jail for keeping alternative accounts for tax purposes.) In principle firms are taxed on the profits revealed in their public accounts. In practice their tax returns have to include a lot of additional information. Tax experts ensure that accounts comply with increasingly complicated tax regulations, and they advise firms how to arrange their business and design their accounts to minimize their tax bills.

4. **Other accounts** are kept for various public or negotiating purposes. Government statisticians require returns of numbers employed, industrial accidents and absenteeism, imports and exports, etc. When firms or industries bargain with unions, or negotiate with government over tariffs, tax laws, etc., they may need accounts which indicate their competitive situation, their capacity to pay particular wages, taxes, environmental charges or import prices, or their capacity to create employment if protected or subsidized – and so on. For these purposes their regular financial and management accounts may need to be supplemented by further research and information.

This text won't be concerned with control accounting. Later chapters will describe how firms relate their costs to their prices, and how they decide their investments. Here and now it is time to learn the principles of the first of the accounts listed above. At least once a year, every public company must publish two financial statements: a Balance Sheet which tells what the firm is worth, and an Income Statement (or Profit and Loss Account) which tells how well it is doing.

The Balance Sheet

The Balance Sheet compares what the firm *owns* with what it *owes* at a particular date, commonly the last day of the financial year. What it owns are its assets. What it owes are its liabilities. The difference between them is known as the firm's net worth, or the owners' equity. Here is a simplest-possible example:

McTavish Mousetraps plc
BALANCE SHEET
30th June, 1999

ASSETS		LIABILITIES	
Cash	£10,000	Bank loan	30,000
Stock in hand	30,000	Repayable debentures	60,000
Land	18,000		
Factory building	72,000		
Equipment	80,000	Net worth	140,000
Other assets	20,000		
	230,000	Total	230,000

The Balance Sheet matches assets on the left hand side with *claims to ownership* on the right hand side. The bank owns the 30,000 it lent. The debenture holders own the 60,000 they lent. The shareholders own the rest.

Notice the basic identity *Assets = liabilities + net worth,* or *Net worth = assets – liabilities.* If the assets were sold today and the debts paid, what's left is the net worth of the firm to its owners. Net worth is a residual: whatever has to be added to the liabilities (or subtracted from the assets) to make the total liabilities equal the total assets. The two sides of the Balance Sheet must always balance.

What if the firm owes more than it owns? On 30 June 1999 McTavish's net worth was £140,000. But during 2000 flood and fire destroy the factory and the stock in hand, which McTavish has been too mean to insure (an omission the bank and debenture holders should have made him put right). So –

McTavish Mousetraps plc
BALANCE SHEET
30th June 2000

ASSETS		LIABILITIES	
Land	£18,000	Bank loan	30,000
		Repayable debentures	60,000
		Net worth	-72,000
Total	18,000	Total	18,000

The business is insolvent. When the debentures mature and are due for repayment, or the bank demands its money back, the firm will be bankrupt. If it sells its assets it can still only pay 20 pence in the pound to its creditors. It is worth nothing to its owners.

Facts and estimates in the Balance Sheet Return to the first Balance Sheet, the solvent one. It expresses everything in money terms. It does not say 'Land 1 acre', it says 'Land £18,000'. Under 'Stock in hand' (sometimes called 'Inventory') it does not say '5 tons of wood, 500 metres of steel wire, 20,000 finished traps awaiting sale', it says 'Stock in hand £30,000'. The result, all in precise money values, looks factual. But the factory and land and stock in hand were not auctioned on 30 June 1998 to discover their actual market value. The Balance Sheet figures record either past prices, or accountants' estimates. As to how the estimates are arrived at, Company Law has rules and accountants have professional conventions. The law and conventions are there to encourage consistency as account-keepers cope with the following problems.

Historical cost or current value? Should the Balance Sheet value assets at what they cost to buy (however long ago), at what they are worth today, or at what they will cost to replace?

Historical costs can be factual. But they can also mislead. People read the Balance Sheet to know what the firm is worth. If its assets were acquired at past dates there may since have been inflation. Besides the effect of inflation on their money value, their real value or value relative to other goods may have changed. The real value of city land often rises over time. The real value of machinery falls as it wears out or is outdated.

Wouldn't it be better to state the current value of the assets? That is what owners, investors, creditors and others need to know if they want to know what the firm is worth. There are two main alternative ways of giving assets up-to-date values. *Inflation-adjusted* accounting, sometimes called *Constant purchasing power* accounting, sticks to the factual, historical costs but uses a deflator or historical index of inflation to convert the historical costs into current money value. *Current value* accounting ignores the historical costs (except where they are a genuine guide to present values) and estimates the present market value of the assets. If the firm has land, what is similar land fetching at auction this year? What would the firm's machinery and vehicles fetch in the second-hand market, and what would it cost to replace them at today's prices?

Those approaches will be described later in this chapter. One or another kind of current value accounting is recommended by most economists, many accounting theorists and teachers, and a growing number of practising accountants. But many practising accountants still resist it. They fear that it has too few links with actual, provable facts. If most Balance Sheet items are estimates rather than reports of actual transactions and prices paid, they fear that there may be too much room for deception, misrepresentation or honest mistake. Better stick to the historical facts as far as possible; and where estimates can't be avoided, make their basis clear. Then (conservative accountants argue) the users of the accounts, rather than the compilers, can make any risky or uncertain judgments that may be called for.

So there is a dilemma. Factual historical costs can be misleading guides to present values. But estimates of present value may be mistaken, unprovable, wilfully deceptive. Faced with that dilemma, most countries' accounting conventions currently encourage an uneasy mix of historical costs and current valuations in companies' public financial accounts.

The Statement of Income or Profit and Loss

Unlike Balance Sheets which report stocks at a particular moment, Income Statements report flows of activity through a particular period.

The Balance Sheet compares what a firm owns with what it owes. The difference is its net worth: a stock of value at a particular date.

The Income Statement compares what a firm earns over a period of time with what it spends to generate those earnings. The difference is its profit or loss for the period.

You've seen McTavish's Balance Sheet for 30 June 1999. See, below, his Income Statement for the year ending on that date. Like the Balance Sheet, the Income Statement is a mixture of facts and estimates, with some selectivity too. To show some of the choices which have to be made in putting an Income Statement together we can first characterize the standard 'accrual accounting' rules, then contrast two alternative approaches to measuring income: a cash accounting approach, and a current value approach of special interest to economists and economic policy-makers.

Accrual accounting The Income Statement is a public or external financial statement designed to give information about the firm to outsiders including share-holders. One of its main purposes is to measure profit, so that shareholders can see how successfully their investment is being managed, and what dividends they are entitled to. Accountants bring three general rules to bear on the task: rules of *conservatism, realized* income, and *accrued* expenses.

More harm can be done by overestimating profits than by underestimating them. So the *conservative* rule says 'When in doubt, prefer the cautious option'.

By *realized,* accountants generally mean turned into money. The second general rule says 'Count income only when it is realized.' Don't count finished goods awaiting sale. Why not? If Income Statements counted finished goods as income they would not distinguish a firm whose products were selling well from one whose products were piling up in the warehouse and not selling at all. So accountants record actual sales made within the relevant accounting period.

Having totalled the revenue for the accounting period, count only the cost of earning that revenue. The 'expense' items in the Income Statement for the year 1 July 1998 – 30 June 1999 do *not* record everything the firm paid out in that year. They record the costs of earning that year's revenue – whenever those costs were paid. Some of the materials may have been bought the year before. Some of the bills may not have been paid

McTavish Mousetraps plc
INCOME STATEMENT
for the year 1 July 1998 to 30 June 1999

$		$	$
SALES REVENUE			$225,000
Less: Materials		$30,000	
Wages		105,000	
Administrative & marketing costs		21,000	
Depreciation of building (4,000) and equipment (10,000)		14,000	
Total cost of goods sold			170,000
GROSS OPERATING PROFIT			55,000
Less: Bank interest		2,000	
Debenture interest		6,000	
Local taxes & charges		5,000	
Total interest and charges			13,000
NET INCOME BEFORE CORPORATE INCOME TAX			42,000
Less: Corporate income tax payable			13,000
NET AFTER-TAX INCOME (the legendary 'bottom line')			29,000
Less: 15% dividend paid on 100,000 £1 shares			15,000
ADDITION TO RETAINED EARNINGS			14,000

until the year after. But whenever the expenses occurred, they should be accounted in the year in which their product was sold. Using an odd old word, costs are 'accrued' to the period of revenue they generate. Hence the name 'accrual accounting'.

Accrual is understandable in principle but it has problems in practice. If the mousetraps sold this year were made of wire bought last year and wood bought the year before that, do you value the wood and wire at their past prices, or at the prices you're currently paying for wood and wire which you may not use until future years? For detailed answers you must see the Accountancy textbooks – but many of them call for judgments and estimates as well as hard facts. Accrual accounting indicates or estimates the profit income for a stated period rather than exactly measuring it.

Limitations of the public accounts Some important information does not appear on either of the public financial statements. Traditionally, they don't tell who owns the firm – its shareholder list is private; but the takeover industry has led a number of countries to require that major shareholders be listed. The statements tell very little about the firm's future intentions (though other parts of its Annual Report may speak of them). They tell what profit it has been making. But that may not be a sufficient measure of its efficiency. (It might be making more. It might be avoiding tax more ingeniously. It might be acting to increase its monopolist or other market strength. What strength it has, it might exploit more fully.) The public accounts don't indicate opportunity costs, i.e. any more profitable uses the firm might be making of its assets. They don't show the calculations on which it makes its investment decisions (though other parts of the Annual Report may do so). They don't detail the costs of each stage or component of the productive process (so that readers might be able to judge, for example, that the firm is buying its wood and wire shrewdly, but its machinery foolishly). They don't tell how much the firm's managers themselves do of that detailed cost analysis. They don't tell how securely or not the firm's accounting system informs it of any poor performance by employees, or theft or fraud by them or others. Account-keeping for all those purposes – management accounting, including cost analysis, control systems, investment appraisal – is the firm's private business. All that outsiders, including owners, are legally entitled to know about the finances of share-owned companies is contained in the Balance Sheet and Income Statement.

Is it enough? On the one hand, the elements of estimation and selection in those accounts, and the distortion of historical costs by inflation, lead experts to emphasize that 'when the future is uncertain, estimates are involved and the unit of measurement is constantly changing', it is unavoidable that 'financial accounts must always be largely a matter of convention, judgment and opinion, not a matter of certainty'. That is a widely held judgment – the two quotations are from Accountancy texts fifty years apart. On the other hand the accounts still serve most of their purposes, most of the time, well enough. In the business world the accounting conventions are well understood. Nobody is deceived by historical costs. Though outsiders can't see the firms' internal accounts, their public financial statements are all audited by independent accountants, with reputations to maintain, who *do* have access to many of the internal accounts. It follows that seriously misleading financial statements by public companies are comparatively rare.

Nevertheless historical cost accounting continues to lose friends in a world of fluctuating inflation and changing price relativities. More realistic treatment of the facts of business life would surely be better. Short notes follow on three alternatives to historical cost accounting.

Accounting on a cash basis

This is a simpler alternative to accrual accounting. Income accounts show total cash paid and received during each accounting period, and the difference between cash paid and cash received is the profit or loss for the period. Revenue is reported when it is actually received rather than when sales are made. Expenses are recorded when they are paid, rather than being 'accrued' backwards or forwards in time to connect with the particular revenue they help to earn.

This simple accounting suits activities which have regular flows of expenses and revenues, and no significant capital assets to depreciate and replace. If such enterprises do have significant assets – if they own offices, vehicles, expensive equipment – they may keep separate capital and depreciation accounts but still keep their Income accounts on a cash rather than an accrual basis.

Terminology: Notice three different uses of the word 'cash' in relation to accounting. (1) If only to prevent theft, every business keeps some account of its cash holdings and dealings. That's commonly called *cash accounting*. (2) Many firms plan and forecast their cash or quickly-cashable resources from month to month or day to day to ensure that they will have cash to meet their operational needs, while not holding idle cash which could be out earning interest. That's commonly called *cash flow* or *flow of funds* accounting. (3) Keeping financial accounts of revenues and expenses in the cash form we have just described, without accrual, is called *accounting on a cash basis.* Though convenient, this terminology is not always used. When you read of 'cash accounting' you may sometimes need to study the context to see which meaning is intended.

ACCOUNTING WITH CHANGING PRICES

Economists' needs For most purposes economists deal in current values, preferably measured by market prices. But they have to get a good deal of their information directly or indirectly from the financial accounts and statistical returns of firms which base their accounts on historical costs. For some purposes economists translate the historical costs into constant purchasing power, i.e. they simply adjust the figures for monetary inflation. For other purposes, especially when dealing with replaceable capital equipment, they substitute current replacement costs for inflation-adjusted historical costs. And for some purposes they substitute the current prices of new technology for the replacement prices of existing technology. (In 2010 it won't help the steel industry to know what it would cost to replace its worn-out 1980 equipment with new 1980-style equipment at 1980 prices adjusted for inflation. If it wants to maintain its capacity to make and sell steel it needs to know the 2010 price of replacing the old equipment with different and better 2010 equipment.)

Look at the investment tables of your country's current National Accounts. They will include a table showing the net amount of new fixed capital investment each year from (perhaps) 1960 to 2000, at the prices paid for the capital items in those years – i.e., the 1960 items at 1960 prices, the 1961 items at 1961 prices, and so on. That table will be followed by another which offers the same information at constant prices. Notes to the table will tell you *what* prices – perhaps constant 1990 prices. (The 1960 items will be adjusted by the amount of monetary inflation from 1960 to 1990; the 1961 items by the amount of inflation from 1961 to 1990; and so on. The constant-price table will also tell you the annual percentage changes in the amounts invested. In the original table, percentage figures would not have told you much, because you could not know how much of each annual rise or fall was a change in real investment and how much was price inflation.)

In the tables which record national totals of profit year by year, there may be different adjustments to the historical figures. Profit is surplus income after making due provision to maintain capital. The U.S. and some other National Accounts now base their estimates of capital maintenance on current replacement costs. To do that they have to increase the raw data – the depreciation provisions in corporate balance sheets based on historical costs – by as much as 40 per cent over and above any adjustment for inflation. Thus historical costs of replicating existing capital equipment are replaced by current costs of acquiring state-of-the-art equipment.

Similar 'translations' or replacements have to be made by economists who advise individual firms (for example) whether their accounting methods will or won't serve to maintain their net worth, or their earning capacities, or both, in the long run.

To make any of those necessary translations – i.e. to derive national accounts from corporate accounts and statistical returns, or to advise firms about the economic implications of their accounting choices – you need to know how the different kinds of accounts are kept, and especially which elements of them deal in historical costs, inflation-adjusted prices, current market prices and (if there is technical change) current replacement costs. Here follows a summary.

Alternative methods of accounting with inflation and technical change

To learn the rationale of inflation-adjusted accounting and current value accounting, begin by recalling the main shortcomings of historical cost accounting:

1. To know what a firm is worth, you need to know what its assets are worth now. Historical costs minus percentages of depreciation may be quite misleading if there is inflation, or if market conditions for those assets have changed.

2. Most people who want to know what a firm is worth want to judge its future prospects. So provisions to maintain and replace productive capital should relate to actual replacement costs, not past costs.

3. Historical cost accounting, with or without inflation adjustment, can overestimate profits. That can encourage firms to use too much of their income to pay dividends and too little to maintain and replace capital items. Maintaining historical capital value can mask declining real capital value and declining capacity to produce and earn.

Be sure you understand the third reason. Here it is in purer form: Profit earned in any period is – crudely speaking – what you gain above what you had to begin with (not counting any additions to capital by new investment). Accountants define it as 'the amount by which the value of net assets at the close of the period exceeds their value at the opening of the period'. Earnings for the period must first maintain the value of the assets by replacing any worn-out or used-up items. Only earnings above that capital-maintenance requirement should count as profit, available for dividends or new investment. Economists put the same point a little differently when they define profit as 'the maximum dividend a firm can pay during a period and remain as well off as before'.

The main alternatives to historical cost accounting are two:

- *Constant purchasing power* accounting (also called *inflation-adjusted* accounting) uses historical costs but applies a general price index to translate them into current money values.

- *Current value* accounting (also called *replacement cost* accounting) values assets and provides for their depreciation at their current replacement prices.

What difference do the accounting choices make?

If there is significant inflation and technical change, so that the nature or design as well as the prices of capital replacements keep changing, the choice of accounting system can have powerful effects. The range of potential effects was once illustrated vividly in a practical exercise by Tony Hope. For its detail, find pp.76-82 of the second edition of Bryan Carsberg and Tony Hope (eds.) *Current issues in accounting.* The exercise sets out some simple facts and figures of a small firm's activity through one year: the plant, machinery, stock in hand and cash with which it starts the year; the corresponding figures at the end of the year; the transactions during the year. On the self-same facts in each case –

	Profit £	Rate of return on end-of-year assets %
. Historical cost accounting shows –	500	13
. Constant purchasing price (or 'inflation adjusted') accounting shows –	20	5
. Replacement cost accounting, using current values, shows (losses of)	-200	-4

Which method is preferable? It depends on who you ask. As suggested in Chapter 1 of this course, owners, managers, creditors and employees of the firm may want different information about it for their different purposes; and some of them may have contradictory purposes, or may have to choose between short- and long-term purposes. Shareholders who want to sell out may want to see high current profits and share prices; long-term investors may want to see good reserves and replacement provisions and capital growth. Workers may want to use historic cost, showing high profits, in wage negotiations; but replacement cost may tell them more about their long-term job prospects. Managers may like historic cost and high profit as a basis for their managers' bonuses, but they know the value of replacement cost as a guide to the firm's future. Aware of all those and other conflicting interests and considerations, Hope and his associates conclude that 'It is, however, our view that the long-term decisions of all users of financial statements can only be improved by current cost information, whether as supplementary to, or instead of, historic cost information.'

For that exercise Tony Hope deliberately chose some extreme conditions – including fast inflation, and asset prices rising faster than inflation – to dramatize the effects of different accounting methods. But the exercise shows once again that a lot of business information can't quite be cold fact but has to be shaped by the accountants' judgment and the purposes of those who choose the accounting systems.

SUMMARY

1. Firms are founded to meet existing demands for new products; to generate new demands by offering new products; to use new science to develop new products or better ways of producing existing products; to compete with existing suppliers of existing products (as tens of thousands of new shops and small businesses do every year); to take over operations which existing firms wish to shed; to supply regular goods and services to new areas of settlement; to reduce individuals' or firms' tax payments; to facilitate crime and launder criminals' money; etc.

2. Perceiving or creating those business opportunities and responding to them is work for entrepreneurs. In public and private business their presence is important to economic vitality and growth. Some societies produce more, better or different entrepreneurs than others. The differences appear to spring from cultural and political as well as economic conditions.

3. The legal requirements for starting and running a business were sketched in the previous chapter. How firms arrive at their general purposes, how they cost and price their products and how they decide on their investments will be subjects of following chapters.

4. Firms which prosper may face choices between profit and growth, dividend income and growth, safety and risk. They choose between alternative capital structures, and decide how far (if at all) to increase their risks by gearing with borrowed funds.

5. Big firms must usually be big planners. They plan future technical operations and financial flows. They plan their internal patterns of authority, responsibility and communication. They develop means of coordinating decisions made at many levels and locations. By those means policy decisions are articulated into practical tasks for day-to-day management.

6. Styles of management vary widely with the culture, personal differences, theories of management, and the nature of the business.

7. To know what they are doing, firms may keep a range of planning, management, tax and control accounts. In addition –

8. Incorporated firms are required by law to publish financial accounts, usually including an annual Balance Sheet and Income Statement. The Balance Sheet shows what the firm's assets are worth, net of its debts, at a particular date. The Income Statement shows what revenue the firm has earned during a specified period; what it cost to earn that revenue; and consequently the profit or loss for the period.

9. The revenue shown in the Income Statement is usually factual. The costs of earning that revenue are partly factual, partly estimated, and selectively accrued to the revenue period. The stated profit or loss thus depends on elements of fact, estimation, and choice of accounting system.

10. Depreciation is accountants' language for financial provisions to replace physical capital and maintain a firm's capital value and productive capacity. The extent to which buildings, equipment and invisible assets have worn out in use usually has to be estimated rather than actually measured. Alternative methods of estimating depreciation can affect the amount of net worth and profit or loss that the published accounts show.

11. Accountants have responded to inflation and other changing values in (broadly) one of three ways. (i) *Historical cost* accounting reports actual transactions and keeps assets on the books (and depreciates them) at the prices originally paid for them, however long ago. (ii) *Constant purchasing power* or *general price level* or *inflation-adjusted* accounting uses the prices paid in actual transactions but uses a general price index to translate them into current money values. (iii) *Current value* or *replacement cost* accounting values assets, and provides for their depreciation, at their current replacement prices.

12. If there is significant inflation, if relative prices as well as the general price level are changing, and if the firm has long-lasting assets, the three methods of accounting may yield substantially different estimates of net worth, and of profit or loss. Those differences may encourage different short-term dividend policies and long-term investment policies.

13. Economists need to understand corporate accounting in order to advise firms about pricing and investment policies; in order to use statistical information from corporate accounts for national accounting and policy-making purposes; and for other purposes.

31

Costs of production : analysis

When Chapter 30 sketched how firms work, it deferred three essentials: how they deal with their costs, how they price their products, and how they decide their investments. This chapter introduces ways of analyzing firms' costs of production. The next is about labor costs, and how wage rates are determined. A third cost chapter relates firms' costs to others' costs, to the size of firms, and to tendencies to competition or monopoly.

FIRMS' COSTS

What do firms count as the costs of producing the goods they sell?

Remember the principles of accrual accounting. The costs of the goods produced this month or this year are not necessarily the costs paid this month or this year. They are the costs of producing this particular output. They may reach back in time, to the original purchase of plant and equipment. They may reach forward in time, to payments due next year for materials used this year. If the firm makes more than one product, accountants may have trouble deciding what shares of overhead costs – managers' salaries, head-office rent, and so on – should be charged to the production costs of each product. As in the firm's financial accounting, so also in its cost accounting, the costs of particular products have to be known by mixtures of fact, estimation and selection.

Remember that there may also be external costs. The firm's cost of producing a product may not be the whole cost of producing it. If the firm buys public products below cost, or gets free public services worth more than the corporate tax it pays, others are paying some of the costs of production. Notice that costs are not internal or external by nature – it simply depends on who pays them. If government starts to charge for hitherto-free services, some of the firm's external costs are internalized. Or consider what happens when workers have to work at remote sites far from home. In good times, or where there are strong unions, employers may have to pay travel and accommodation costs to get anyone to work at those sites. If a firm pays those costs they appear in the firm's accounts (and eventually in the national accounts) as costs of production. But in bad times, workers desperate for jobs may be left to pay those costs themselves. Then the firm's and the nation's accounts will show lower costs of production. In either case the costs are incurred; real resources are used and paid for to transport and board the workers. But whether those costs figure as costs of production is decided by the relative market strength of the workers and employers.

We will return, in the next chapter, to ways in which some costs of private production may be shifted onto public or household producers. Until then we will neglect those externalities and take 'total cost' to mean only firms' costs. But remember the twelve ways to do well in a mixed economy: one way to reduce firms' costs is to unload them onto others. Get government to supply more of any necessary research, professional training, waste disposal. Cut firms' retailing costs by getting the customers to serve themselves and do their own home deliveries. And so on.

COSTS IN THE SHORT RUN

The 'short run' means the life of existing plant, or the time it would take to replace it. What is the most economical way to use existing fixed capital: which way of using it will produce goods at least cost?

Begin with some simple definitions:

Total costs of a product are all the accrued costs of producing it. If you know the total cost of each level of output, i.e. the total cost of producing one unit, the total cost of producing two, ten, a hundred units, and so on, you can derive two other figures:

Average cost is total cost divided by the number of units produced.

Marginal cost is the additional cost of producing the last unit.

Don't confuse the latter two. If it costs $10 to produce 2 units and $12 to produce 3, the average cost of 3 units is $4, but the marginal cost of the third unit is $2.

Here is a simple (and fairly unlikely) schedule of costs to show the relations between total, average and marginal costs:

Quantity produced	Total cost	Average cost	Marginal cost of last unit
Units	$	$	$
0	5	-	-
1	8	8	3
2	10	5	2
3	12	4	2
4	16	4	4
5	25	5	9

Table 31.1 Total, average & marginal cost

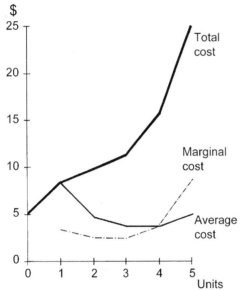

Figure 31.1 Total, average & marginal cost

For many business purposes marginal cost is a better guide than either average or total cost. The reasons for that belong in later chapters on pricing and investment, but we can preview them briefly. Read the schedule of costs in Table 31-1. Suppose that the firm can sell each unit of output for $6. Managers have to decide how many units to produce. Which kind of cost information will guide them best?

1. *Total Cost:*

3 units cost	$11 and sell for $18	Total profit	$6
4 units cost	$16 and sell for $24	Total profit	$8
5 units cost	$25 and sell for $30	Total profit	$5

2. *Average Cost:*

3 units average	$4 and sell for $6	Profit per unit:	$2
4 units average	$4 and sell for $6	Profit per unit:	$2
5 units average	$5 and sell for $6	Profit per unit:	$1

3. *Marginal Cost:*

The 3rd unit adds	$2 to costs and	$6 to revenue.	It adds $4 to profit
The 4th unit adds	$4 to costs and	$6 to revenue.	It adds $2 to profit
The 5th unit adds	$9 to costs and	$6 to revenue.	It *loses* $3.

Any one of the three should tell a manager that the biggest total profit comes from producing 4 units. But only the marginal cost tells him when he's actually losing, and how much.

Suppose that instead of deciding how much to produce, managers have to decide how to price the product. At an output of 5 units, average cost per unit is $5. A 20 per cent mark-up to sell the units for $6 each appears to yield $1 profit per unit, which is 20 per cent profit on turnover. Unless the managers also notice the marginal costs they may not notice that above 4 units a $6 price will actually lose money with each unit sold.

Next question: Why do our table and graph say that it would cost $5 to produce nothing at all? Next step in the analysis: Distinguish fixed costs from variable costs.

Fixed costs are those which can't be altered at short notice: the costs of the factory that is already built, the equipment that is already bought, the salaries of staff with fixed-term contracts. Those costs can't vary from day to day however much or little the plant produces. They are variously called sunk costs, overheads or fixed costs.

Because they can't vary, fixed costs have predictable economies of scale: the average fixed cost per unit of output declines mathematically as more units are produced. If a $1,000 machine produces 1000 mouse-traps their fixed costs are $1 each. To be more realistic, if the machine lasts ten years so that the annual allowance for its (straight line) depreciation is $100, and it produces 1,000 traps a year, their fixed cost is 10 cents each.

Variable costs At short notice the firm may be able to buy more or less raw materials, take on or lay off workers, vary its fuel bills by using more or less fuel. Those costs can vary with the quantity of output. But they may not vary evenly with variations in output. Suppose that a plant can't work at all without a certain minimum of heating, lighting and labor. There have to be half a dozen skills present – which means half a dozen workers – to produce any output. The first unit of output, if that is all the plant produces for the day, there-fore has high variable costs. But suppose that in a full eight-hour working day the plant can produce four tons – for convenience we'll call it four units – of output.

The variable costs of materials and machine fuel will be higher for four units than for one, but if the workers have to be paid for a full day whatever the day's output, the variable costs of labor will be much the same for producing four units as for producing one. So as daily output rises from one to four units, total variable costs will not rise as fast as output does. Up to four units a day, the variable unit costs diminish as output increases, much as the fixed costs do.

Now suppose there is still unsatisfied demand. The firm has orders for 6 rather than 4 units a day. It asks the workers for four daily hours of overtime. That is dear labor – overtime wages are time-and-a-half for the first two hours and double time for the next two. Fuel and material costs per unit of output are the same as before, but labor costs per unit increase. Counting only the variable costs, each additional unit costs more and increases the average unit cost of the day's output. Marginal cost now rises ahead of average costs.

Add the fixed cost and you find that, in this particular example, production has U-shaped costs. As output rises to 4 units a day, average costs per unit fall. Above 5 units they begin to rise. Like this:

Diminishing returns Figure 31.2 illustrates a basic 'law of diminishing returns' which says that if increasing quantities of one factor of production are applied with fixed quantities of other factors, there will eventually be diminishing returns to the variable factor.

The law assumes that factors of production need to be used in correct proportions. If one gardener can grow a ton of potatoes on a patch of land, two gardeners may be able to grow more on that patch, but not twice as much. Ten gardeners certainly won't get ten tons from that patch.

In that classical case the law is technical: so much dirt can grow only so many potatoes. Diminishing returns can also set in if a variable factor of production becomes not less efficient but more expensive, for example if additional labor can increase output efficiently, but has to be paid at overtime rates. So there can be diminishing returns to variable factors of production *either* because the mix of factors becomes less efficient *or* because the variable factors have rising costs.

Does it follow that producers always encounter rising costs and diminishing returns as output increases? No, for a variety of reasons, of which the commonest are these three:

1. Some producers never encounter demand for the volume of output at which diminishing returns would set in. They have level or declining costs, and level or increasing returns, up to the biggest output they can succeed in selling.

2. In many plants the fixed factors of production have exactly limited capacity. Up to that limit costs decline and there are increasing returns; beyond that limit no further output is possible. The machinery works at fixed speed, there are only twenty four hours in the day, and the maximum output can be the most efficient, with the lowest unit costs.

3. In many industries, especially those providing

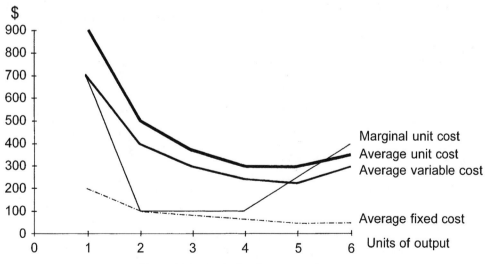

Figure 31.2 Marginal and average unit costs

professional or personal services, all the factors of production are variable. They can be increased together, in correct proportion, without limit. As long as it can find willing workers a messenger agency can employ as many messengers as its customers demand, all at the same rates of pay. If there's too much business for the telephonist to handle, more telephones and telephonists can also be hired at short notice at regular rates. So as the business grows, neither increasing nor diminishing returns need ever set in.

For those and other reasons the cost curves of different enterprises can vary widely. As output increases, average unit cost and marginal cost may rise continuously. They may fall continuously. They may run level. They may be U-shaped. They can even be bell-shaped, with costs starting low, rising as output increases, then falling as output increases further. The shape of the curve depends on the components of unit cost at the relevant levels of output: the ratio of fixed costs to variable costs, and the detailed composition and behavior of the variable costs. If output increases, will the fall in fixed cost per unit be greater or less than any increase in variable cost per unit? Theory can't tell you the answer, you need the facts of the case.

The composition of total cost and unit cost We can use another simplified example to compare three ways of producing the same product. Suppose there are (1) a modern capital-intensive plant whose machinery can be fully employed by two workers; (2) an older plant whose simpler machinery requires four workers; and (3) a back yard operation whose primitive equipment requires six workers.

Each plant can produce 10 units of output per working shift. Each can work one, two or three shifts per day, and we'll assume they are always full shifts (so output comes in batches of 10 units). But to get workers to tolerate night work the wages have to rise to time-and-a-half for an evening shift from four to midnight, and double time for a midnight-to-morning shift. Thus multiple shifts increase variable costs by increasing the wage costs per unit of output. But they reduce the fixed costs per unit, because the fixed costs per 24 hours are the same however many shifts are worked.

Question: If the three plants all want to produce as cheaply as they can, how many shifts should each of them work? Answer: That depends on the *composition* of their unit costs. To see how, compare their costs for one day's operation.

The *fixed costs* are one day's share of the capital cost of the plant: $600 per day for the modern plant, $400 for the older plant, $200 for the back yard operation.

The *variable costs* are (i) $20 of materials for each unit produced, the same for each plant and for any shift; and (ii) $100 wage cost per worker on day shift, $150 on evening shift and $200 on midnight shift.

Put those together and you will find that if the three plants work a day shift only, their total costs are the same. Divide by ten for the ten units produced, and their average unit costs are the same. That is because the higher fixed costs in the capital-intensive plant just balance the higher variable costs in the labor-intensive back yard, as you can see in the top line of the tables which follow figure 31.3. But read the second and third lines, and the graphs, to see how the plants' costs compare if they work more than one shift.

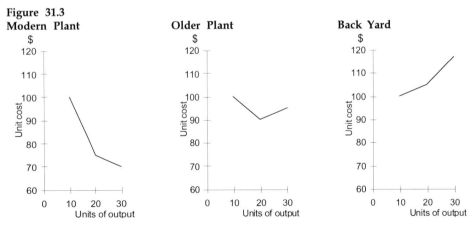

Figure 31.3 Composition of unit costs

MODERN PLANT

Shifts	Output	Fixed cost	Variable cost	Total cost	Unit cost
	units	$	$	$	$
One	10	600	400	1000	100
Two	20	600	900	1500	75
Three	30	600	1500	2100	70

OLDER PLANT

Shifts	Output	Fixed cost	Variable cost	Total cost	Unit cost
	units	$	$	$	$
One	10	400	600	1000	100
Two	20	400	1400	1800	90
Three	30	400	2400	2800	93

BACK YARD

Shifts	Output	Fixed cost	Variable cost	Total cost	Unit cost
	units	$	$	$	$
One	10	200	800	1000	100
Two	20	200	1900	2100	105
Three	30	200	3300	3500	117

Notice that the tables show total cost and unit cost at each level of output. The shifts are not separately costed: the 'two shift' line shows the total cost and unit cost for a two-shift day, the 'three shift' line shows total and unit cost for a three-shift day.

Now be sure you understand how the different composition of their costs affects the three plants' unit costs at different volumes of output.

In the modern plant, as output rises, the fall in fixed cost per unit of output is greater than the rise in wage cost per unit. So the plant has continuous economies of scale up to the limit of its capacity. This plant does best to work three shifts.

In the older plant a second shift reduces fixed costs per unit by more than it adds to wage costs. But a third shift reduces fixed costs by less than it adds to wage costs. So this plant has U-shaped costs, its unit costs falling with a second shift but rising again with a third. It does best to work two shifts. Its basic difference from the modern plant is that its variable costs are a bigger proportion of its total costs.

In the back yard, each additional shift adds more to wage costs than it cuts from fixed costs per unit of output. So beyond the ten units which one shift can produce, the back yard has continuous diseconomies of scale. It does best to work a day shift only. That is

because at every level of output, further output increases variable unit costs by more than it reduces fixed unit costs.

Notice some competitive implications. If the national culture (or industrial law, or labor unions) dictate daylight work only, the three plants may continue to share the market. But if the modern plant can work two or three shifts it can undersell the other two, and perhaps put them out of business. However, those are short-run possibilities. They may hold only as long as it takes the losing competitors to build new plants, perhaps better than the existing best plant. We need to extend this method of analysis to take account of time. But first, notice a fact of life that can complicate both static and dynamic cost analysis.

Theory and practice

Real-life costs rarely fall as perfectly as our model suggests into the 'fixed' and 'variable' categories. If 'fixed' means fixed for a period of time regardless of the volume of output, many of the variable costs are actually fixed for shorter or longer periods. Labor costs, for example: some work is done for piece rates so that the labor cost varies exactly with the volume of output, but most labor is not paid for in that way. Our simplified examples assumed that workers need only be paid for a full shift. In practice they are more likely to be entitled to a week's or a fortnight's or a month's notice. Some salaried staff have much longer contracts. Law or industrial agreements may require redundancy pay if jobs are extinguished. Thus labor costs may be fixed for varying periods. And as with people, so with plant. It may take a year or two to build and equip a factory, which may then be a fixed cost for decades. But its many components may have different lifetimes and need replacement, or be replaceable, at different intervals. It may take six months to install a new generation of heavy machinery; three months to improve working conditions by installing air conditioning; a fortnight to equip the warehouse with forklifts; a day to buy new trucks. So where our simplified examples assumed that fixed costs change rarely, and then change all at once, the reality in many lines of business is that most of both 'fixed' and 'variable' costs are actually fixed – but for periods which may range from a day or two to the long life of buildings. Cost accounting has to adapt accordingly. The principles of cost analysis are as this chapter describes them, but their application can be very complicated, depending on the nature of the business, and (as we will now see) the period of time the analysis has to cover.

COSTS OVER TIME

Our comparison of costs of production in three plants took their equipment and its costs as fixed. But suppose now that *you* own the modern capital-intensive plant, *I* own the older plant, and a *mad inventor* owns the back-yard operation. With existing equipment you can work two or three shifts and undersell us. But a year from now I will have built a plant like yours to compete equally with you. And some years later the mad inventor may break through with novel equipment which puts yours and mine out of date. Before the pace of invention over-took them, economists defined those three periods of time as the *short run*, the *long run* and the *very long run*. As follows.

The short run is the period during which a firm has some fixed costs which it cannot alter. (For example, it can't build a new plant overnight.) So if it wants to change its output it must change the proportions of the factors of production it uses. (For example it must use more labor in the existing plant by working shifts, or longer hours.)

Notice that the short run is defined as the period within which the firm can't change its fixed costs, and fixed costs are defined as those which a firm can't change in the short run. The definitions are circular. They are still useful – but the length of the short run depends entirely on technical conditions in the industry, and varies from industry to industry. A jobbing gardener's short run may be half an hour, if he can replace his fixed capital by buying a new barrow and spade at the local hardware store. A steelmaker may take three or four years to build a new plant. A poor country may be able to build and equip a modern hospital in three or four years, but may need seven to ten years to educate doctors to staff it.

The long run is the time it takes to replace the fixed factors of production which account for fixed costs (for example to replace or add to a factory or its equipment). It is thus the time it takes for a firm to increase or reduce its output without necessarily changing the proportions of its factors of production or (consequently) the propor-tions of its fixed and variable costs. It is the time it takes to install the currently-best technology and develop the skills to use it.

The very long run is defined as the time it may take to invent new technology. New technology can change any or all of the cost structures and proportions. New equip-ment may not only cost more or less than the equipment it replaces; it may also alter the proportions of fixed and variable costs at which unit costs are lowest.

Complications: There are industries in which tech-nical progress has overtaken these 'short', 'long' and 'very long' time categories. In some fields of computing, telecommunications and other high-tech industries, equipment is not only outmoded before it wears out; invention is so continuous that equipment is outmoded by the time it is built. Also, installing it may be quicker than training the skills to use it. In those conditions the old usages, which assumed that equip-ment costs were mostly fixed and wage costs variable, can work oddly: the 'fixed' costs may be more quickly changeable than the 'variable' costs, and the 'very long' run may be shorter than the 'long' run.

Mixed vintages in continuous time It does not always pay to replace equipment as soon as it is outmoded. Nor does it always pay to go on using outmoded equipment until it finally wears out. Whether and exactly when to replace it may depend on a number of things: the firm's financial resources; the price of the new equipment; the margin of advantage which the new equipment has over the old; the effects of the old and new equipment on the composition of total costs; the rate at which the new equipment can be supplied; the likely behavior of competitors; and so on. There are consequently many industries and firms in which tech-niques of different age and efficiency, with plant of different vintage, operate side by side.

When that happens, cost analyses have to calculate the cost compositions which go with each vintage at each level of output, and the vintage composition of the fixed capital as a whole. That can be complicated work. But as competitive conditions change, careful cost analysis can help firms to decide which vintages to keep operating; which to scrap, and when; which to mothball as reserve capacity for periods of peak demand; which to modernize; which to replace with the latest state-of-the-art technology.

For big firms in industries with changing technology such decisions tend to be frequent. Such a firm does not typically see itself as the operator of a single plant with three distinct planning problems in the short, the long and the very long run. Instead it is likely to have many divisions and plants and products, each with all three futures. The different divisions and plants use different kinds of technology. They have different vintage mixes. They have different time scales of 'short', 'long' and 'very long'. Their plant takes different lengths of time to replace, their skills take different lengths of time to train, so they have many different investment lead-times.

For such a firm the many particular investment problems are all significant, but time itself feels fairly continuous. Month by month and year by year every board meeting is likely to have some short run, some long run, and some very long run decisions on its agenda. The decisions may need to be related to each other, at least to show that they are financially compatible with one another, by corporate planning of the kind described earlier. They will usually require cost analyses as outlined in this chapter, and estimates of expected selling prices, quantities and revenues which will be outlined in Chapter 34. And before bringing those estimates to bear on investment decisions – the subject of Chapter 35 – they may need to consider where to locate new production.

COSTS IN DIFFERENT COUNTRIES

Just as time affects costs, so may location. The same production may have different costs in different regions or countries, for a wide variety of reasons. There may be different natural resources and raw material prices, land prices, transport costs, legal requirements, taxes. And so on. Here we will explore one factor only: the different labor costs which may arise from different wage levels.

The cost analyses earlier in this chapter held wage levels constant, so as to simplify comparisons of the capital and labor costs of using modern, older and back-yard plant, i.e. of alternative capital-intensive and labor-intensive methods of production. Labor costs varied only where different quantities of labor were employed. We will now use an opposite simplification, to compare labor costs which vary because of labor's different *price,* i.e. wage rate.

Suppose a multinational firm shifts an efficient modern plant from (say) Holland to Malaysia. Simplify by assuming that the move changes nothing except the labor cost. The same number of workers use the same skills and operate the same plant to produce, with the same efficiency, the same output for sale to the same international market. The only difference is between Dutch wages which average $20 an hour, and Malaysian wages which average $4. The Malaysian product can therefore cost less. (How much less will depend on the capital intensity of the process, i.e. the proportions of capital and labor employed.) Market conditions may then determine how the cost reduction is distributed between profit to the firm and lower prices to consumers.

Three questions:

- Why does identically productive labor come at such different prices?

- What does the difference imply for the (marginalist) theory that each factor of production is paid the value of its contribution to the value of output?

- Why doesn't every Dutch firm shift all its operations to Malaysia?

How can equally productive workers earn such different wages? Holland employs its whole paid workforce in an advanced, heavily capitalized, highly productive economy whose total output can provide high real wages. Any Dutch employer has to attract workers away from alternative jobs paying those high wages. Malaysia has a poorer, less capitalized, less productive economy. Its total output per head is about a fifth that of Holland. Wages – which are basically shares of that output – are correspondingly low. So Malaysia's comparatively few heavily capitalized, highly productive industries need only match or slightly improve on those low rates to attract the labor they want. Conclusion: the wage difference arises not from any difference between our multinational's Dutch and Malaysian workers, but from the different productivity of other Dutch and Malaysian workers, which in turn arises, directly or indirectly in large part, from differences in the quantity and productivity of Dutch and Malaysian capital.

In our example (as in the real business life of richer and poorer countries) Dutch and Malaysian workers get different pay for identical contributions to identical output. When that happens, are they both receiving the value of their contribution to output, as neoclassical theory suggests? Would they be doing so if the Malaysian-produced output sold for lower prices which exactly matched its lower labor cost? Would they be doing so, if the Dutch and Malaysian output sold at identical (Dutch) prices, so that the whole Malaysian reduction of labor cost accrued to profits? Think your way to your own conclusions.

Why don't all western firms use cheap third-world labor? Some reasons:

- Some industries cannot leave their geographical bases: mines must stay where the minerals are, farming where the soil and rainfall are, tourism where the attractions are, and so on.

- Learn a rough distinction between tradeable and non-tradeable goods and services. Non-tradeables have to be produced where they are consumed, or nearby: law and order, education, health and personal services, some perishable foods, commuter transport, your local newspaper. Tradeables are portable goods which can be transported to customers anywhere in the world. Their production can be located away from their markets, and perhaps moved from place to place – but they amount to less than half of all paid-for output, and by no means all of them are actually traded across national boundaries. Except for small free ports like Hong Kong and Singapore, few countries trade as much as a third of their output; many trade a fifth or less; the US and Japan have traded less than a tenth through most of their history. The proportion of tradeables limits the proportion of industry that could move from high-wage to low-wage countries.

- That is further limited by the proportion of moveable industries. The technical nature of production processes can determine where they can prosper and whether they can be moved about. Moveables: Some production is done by people with readily acquired skills using machinery which can be installed anywhere, and perhaps moved from place to place. Such industries (like textiles, garment-making, electrical assembly) may well be able to move from Holland to Malaysia. Immovables: Some industries use heavy and complex plant, which –

  - once built cannot be moved;

  - tends to keep up-to-date by continual piecemeal improvement rather than occasional total replacement;

  - requires a range of high skills some of which can only be developed and transmitted on the job; and

  - needs inputs from skilled suppliers, subcontractors and services which don't yet exist in less developed economies.

Such industries (for example aerospace, advanced weaponry, complex machinery-making) may only be viable in developed, high-wage economies, and once established they may not be readily movable.

Now bring together three ways that we have classified industries: as labor-intensive/capital intensive, tradeable/non-tradeable, and movable/immovable. They allow six combinations, which can be boxed thus to set you an easy exercise:

	Labor intensive	Capital intensive
Non-tradeable		
Tradeable, immovable		
Tradeable, movable		

Suppose a Dutch firm has six plants, one of each kind. Which of them might it profitably move to Malaysia? Fill in the boxes. The two plants producing non-tradeables for the Dutch market must obviously stay in Holland. So must the two immovable plants. The movable labor-intensive plant producing tradeable goods may best move to Malaysia. What about the bottom right-hand box? If the plant is heavily capital-intensive, the unit cost of its product may be reduced only a little by the lower Malaysian wages. Will that small gain be enough to outweigh the removal and setting up costs? Prudent directors may look carefully at detailed comparisons of all the relevant costs – transport and communications, land and building costs, insurance, taxes and legal requirements and so on – as well as labor costs.

Except for the different wage rates, the cost advantages mentioned so far have been determined by the nature of the industries – their movability, labor intensity, and so on. They may also be affected by characteristics of the societies. Investors thinking of establishing new industries in Holland or Malaysia need to know about more things than the wages they will have to pay. Will they find the skills, honesty and attitudes to work that they need in their workers? Is public education adequate? Water supply, waste disposal, power, road and rail links, air and sea ports? Will they be under government that treats them tolerably? Does it look to be stable government? If the industry would depend on particular policies (about trade, foreign ownership, environmental standards, forest or mineral resources) do those policies look to be stable? In short, are all the necessary household, private and public conditions for private investment present?

Where all those conditions are present, industrialization is likely to be rapid, as it has been with the 'Asian tigers'. So the better the conditions for investment in low-wage countries, the more temporary the low wages may prove to be. Western levels of national economic development will eventually bring Western wages. If the low wage costs may be shortlived it may not be worth the planning and outfit costs and perhaps social costs of uprooting industries from rich countries to move them abroad.

If there are low-wage countries in reach it may be possible to bring the cheap labor to the plant rather than taking the plant to the cheap labor. Western Europe has used varying numbers of migrant workers through the past fifty years. The host countries' citizens and labor unions would not tolerate excessive poverty or third-world wages in their midst, so the migrant workers' wages have generally been at the bottom of the host country's permanent wage structure rather than far below it. But they have often had to live without their families and without adequate housing or welfare services: i.e. many have been treated worse by the host countries' public authorities than by their employers.

Those are among the reasons why Western industry as a whole has not decamped to Africa and Asia in search of low wage costs.

Unfinished business: We have been noticing how different countries' wage levels may attract or repel investment. For that purpose we simply assumed that richer countries have higher wages and poorer countries have lower wages. But how are actual wage rates and relativities arrived at within each country? That's the business of the next chapter.

32

Costs of production: four ways to fix wages

In this chapter we will simplify factors of production to two: labor and capital. What is the relation between the cost of labor and the cost of capital? Do low wages or high wages do most to encourage capital investment, full employment and economic growth?

Productivity grows as improving knowledge is embodied in *better* capital equipment and working skills: and as saving and investment accumulate *more* equipment and skilled workers. But see, in Figure 32.1, how more and more capital and less and less labor have combined in the economic growth of the leading economies over the last century.

Notice three strands of the process:

The physical *proportions* of capital and labor change. Less labor uses more equipment to produce more output per worker and per head of population.

The *costs* of producing those factors tend to change. Improving technology increases the costs of producing satisfactory workers, who must be increasingly literate,

numerate, skilled, reliable. But the same improving technology tends to reduce the costs of producing any given item of material equipment.

The *prices* which firms have to pay for their factors of production change. As you have seen, some of the price changes reflect the changing costs of producing the factors, but others do not. Why some and not others? Simplifying, there are different answers for capital, land and labor. Capital: if the costs of producing buildings and equipment fall, competitive suppliers will usually bring their prices down. Rent: owners of land, minerals and other limited resources may respond to growing demand for them by raising their prices although they are no dearer to produce. Labor: Historically, wages had to rise with economic growth to cover the costs of supporting children through longer years of dependence and education. Above that minimum, wage changes have not usually been closely related to the costs of producing the workers.

- • – – – – Gross capital stock per capita
- • ——— Output per capita
- • - - - - - Labor input per capita
- •   Indices: 1880 = 100

Figure 32.1 Percentage growth of GDP, Gross Fixed Non-residential Capital Stock and Labor Input per Head of population, 1880-1977. Source: Angus Maddison, *Phases of Capitalist Development,* 1982, p.55, by permission of Oxford University Press.

Variable relations between capital and labor costs

In the advanced economies technical knowledge, physical capital, human skill and wage levels have tended to grow together. But they do not always do it evenly, over time or from industry to industry or country to country. In the relations between capital costs and labor costs, particularly, there is often disagreement about what causes what. Business and labor may disagree when they are negotiating wages and hours. Policy-makers may disagree when they are considering whether or not to have income policies. Economists disagree as neoclassics, post-Keynesians and Marxists ascribe wage rates to different causes. This text tells you they may each be right some of the time. Different causes operate in different conditions: relations between capital and wage costs are *variable*.

The range of variation in recent centuries can be illustrated by four simplified models: (i) a neoclassical model in which marginal costs and productivities are thought to determine investment and wage levels; (ii) a slave economy in which wages never rise however productivity or profit grow; (iii) an Australian model in which government and judges fix wage rates, which then influence patterns of investment and growth; and (iv) a Swedish model in which (from the 1930s to the 1980s) general wage levels were set by periodical negotiations between national leaders of business and labor, with labor and Left government having strong influence on them. Simplifying further, the four might be called respectively a market model, an owners' model, a government model, and a workers' model. You need to know the first in some detail because you will meet it in much economic discourse. The other three can follow in broader, simpler form.

I. A MARKET MODEL

In competitive industries, neoclassical theory models relations between capital and labor costs like this:

Labor markets in theory Producers use capital and labor. This model assumes that they can substitute some of one for some of the other if they want to. To minimize costs, they need to ensure that the last dollar they spend on equipment adds as much to output as does the last dollar they spend on labor.

Be sure you understand why theorists expect that to minimize costs, and therefore maximize profit. If those marginal productivities are *not* equal, the cost per unit of output can be reduced by substituting some of the more productive factor for some of the less productive.

Suppose that a firm finds that one more $10,000-a-year machine will add 10 units of output, and one more $20,000-a-year worker will also increase output by 10 units. Costs can clearly be cut by $10,000, without loss of output, by sacking one worker and buying one more machine.

Remember that these are marginal facts. They do not mean that you can replace all the workers by machines. Each factor is likely to have diminishing returns if it gets out of proportion with the other. If you go on replacing $20,000 workers by $10,000 machines you are likely to reach a point at which your machines are so understaffed that another machine will only add 8 units to output whereas another worker (by putting the existing machines to fuller use) would add 16. $20,000 spent on either factor would increase output by 16 units. The *marginal* productivities are equal. That is the mix with lowest unit costs.

Efficient producers accordingly substitute one factor for the other until their marginal productivities are equal. Even if they do not know they are doing it, economists may assume that they are doing it, because in competitive industries producers who do not minimize costs in that way can be undersold and put out of business by those who do. So firms which survive must be getting the mix right, whether by good luck or good management.

It follows that workers who want jobs face two limits to the amount of wage they can hope to earn. They cannot expect to earn more than the last worker hired – the marginal worker – adds to the value of the employer's output. And they cannot expect to earn more than it would cost the employers to get the same output by buying capital equipment instead.

Thus the existing technology and capital investment determine how productive workers can be, and how high their wages *can* go before hitting the limit at which capital substitutions will replace them.

Whether wages *do* rise to that limit should depend, in a pure market model, on the supply and demand for labor. If labor is scarce relative to capital, firms competing for the scarce labor will bid wages up to the capital-substitution limit. If labor is plentiful and partly unemployed, workers should in theory compete for jobs by bidding wages down. How far down? Down to the level at which some workers decide that the work and loss of leisure are not worth the money, or not for as many hours as the employers want.

Most economists concede that workers don't always 'bid wages down' in that way. They resist wage cuts, even when there is unemployment. So wage rates are 'sticky downwards'. If wages rise during booms then won't fall during slumps they are said to 'ratchet'. Some economists think that resisting wage cuts reduces the number of workers who can be employed in slack times. Other economists think it may increase the number employed, because wages are a main source of effective demand for goods, and therefore for labor. With or without such imperfections, neoclassical theory says that once workers are above the breadline and have some choice between work and leisure, the amount of labor they supply depends on the money they are offered, and their preferences for money or leisure. The higher the wage they are offered, the more people will join the workforce, and the more hours they will work. Faced with that supply curve, employers offer the wages that will get them the amount of labor they want. So (i) wage levels are determined like other prices by simple supply and demand, and (ii) if producers ever find that to get enough labor, wages would have to rise above the level at which capital substitution is cheaper, they will make the substitution, i.e. they will decide to shed workers and invest in more capital equipment instead.

Meanwhile the prices of financial and physical capital are being determined by other supply-and-demand relations (between savers and investors in the capital money market, and between producers and buyers in the capital goods markets). So – in theory – the overall costs and quantities of capital employed and labor employed are determined directly by market forces, and ultimately by the current technology and the

people's preferences for goods and leisure. (Neoclassics add that the mix may only be as efficient as the relevant markets are competitive and free from monopoly, or other market failure).

Work and wages in practice Even in countries like the US whose economic life is nearest to the neoclassical model, relations between employers and workers tend to differ from the model in two critical ways. Individual firms and workers do not behave as the model suggests. And the total supply of labor does not respond to rising or falling wages as the model suggests.

The differences are such that in my opinion relations between firms, their workers, and the labor costs of production can be understood better without the idea of a 'labor market' than with it. Work does resemble other marketable goods in some respects – I can trade you some work for some money, and there may well be a going rate for the job. But work is unlike other market goods in other respects. It is something I do for you. I have to be there to do it. I may have to concede you some power over me, to tell me what to do and how to do it. Or if I'm skilled, you may hire me to show *you*, or other workers, how to do it. And (depending on the nature of the work) you may have to trust me to do it properly when nobody is watching me. Thus we have technical relations, power relations, relations of trust or distrust, and perhaps personal and social relations, as well as our market exchange relation. We may also adjust our behavior according to how long we want our relations to continue. To single out the element of market exchange from all the rest – as if working for you was no different from selling you a loaf of bread – may not be the best way to understand *either* the whole relation between us, *or* the market relation which is part of that whole relation.

If we nevertheless continue to think of a labor 'market' it is important to know how hopelessly Figure 32.2 misrepresents that market. The reasons come presently in sections on the demand for labor and the supply of it. Meanwhile notice some of this market's general characteristics.

First, there is not one labor market, there are many. For example:–

- *Locations:* People can only work in reach of where they live, and they cannot always move house at short notice. So many labor markets are local.

- *Occupations:* Most workers need occupational skills. Even in the quite-long-run, the markets for (say) teachers, fitters, bricklayers, pilots and dentists are separate markets. There can be surplus labor in one while there is scarcity in another.

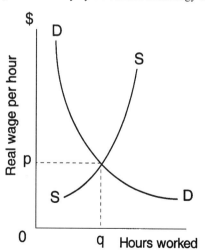

Figure 32.2. How supply (S) and demand (D) for labor are said by neoclassical texts to determine the price (p) and quantity (q) of labor employed.

- *Job requirements:* Many jobs need more than a general occupational skill. They also need personal qualities (honesty, reliability, cooperative spirit), and they need familiarity with a firm's particular organization, equipment and systems of work. Workers trained and experienced on the job have these qualifications; newcomers don't, and have to acquire them. Screening, selecting and training new recruits has costs. For jobs of this kind there are accordingly not one but two markets, as follows –

- Internal and external labor markets: A firm's internal labor market is its existing workforce. If it wants more work it can ask them for more effort or longer hours. If it wants less work it may still keep them on the payroll rather than laying them off, i.e. it may retain them in its internal labor market. The external market is all the labor the firm does not currently employ. To draw labor from that market may have advertising, screening and training costs.

Thus hiring workers can cost more than their wages. So can firing them, sometimes. Some countries make firms give redundancy pay to workers they lay off. Even without that, dismissals can have costs. If experienced workers are laid off when business is slack, it may take time and training costs to replace them when business revives. In boom conditions it may also take higher wages. The rise may have to go to existing workers as well, who might not otherwise have demanded it. Labor unions may then be able to maintain the new rates when slack times return – the ratchet effect. Thus in some industries the costs of adjusting the workforce precisely to the demand for output – i.e. the costs of a fluctuating workforce – may be greater than the cost of maintaining a stable workforce through thick and thin. Stable employment may also improve workers' morale, effort, reliability and therefore productivity. Research has found that firms often 'hoard' labor like that. Not always and everywhere, but at some times in many industries, firms which want to maximize profits may do best not to let current marginal costs and productivities determine their hiring and firing.

Those departures from the model can be intensified by uncertainty. Suppose business is slack. Firms hoard labor against the return of good times. So the decline in demand for output does not lead (as it theoretically should) to lower wages or less employment. But the slack time lasts longer than expected. Extraneous events – world commodity prices, a speculative run on the nation's currency – make financial journalists gloomy. There are forecasts that the slack time may last longer

still. The forecasts are self-fulfilling – they discourage investment. Firms can no longer afford to pay under-occupied labor, so there are big lay-offs. So with no change in the demand for output, employment falls. But for ratchet reasons, wage rates don't fall. That's *two* bad marks for the market model's predictions.

Finally, labor and capital are not often as smoothly substitutable for each other as the model requires. In some industries some of the time they are, in many others they are not. If you run a trucking firm using limit-sized trucks you can't substitute trucks for drivers or drivers for trucks. You can't use one without the other. You can't measure the marginal productivity of one without the other. Demand for trucks and drivers – for capital and labor – is *joint* demand. It is still a market demand, and it may vary with the whole price of truck-plus-driver. But the market model's two independent limits to wage levels do not apply. The capital-substitution limit does not apply. And there is no way to adjust wages to the drivers' marginal productivity independently of the cost of trucks.

To sum up: (1) There is not one labor market, there are many. (2) They can be quick to adjust to one another (to change surplus teachers into scarce waiters or postmen) or they can be slow to adjust to one another (to turn surplus waiters into teachers, or surplus classical scholars into programmers). (3) Alternative relations are possible between labor costs and capital costs. Depending on an industry's technology its demand for labor can vary either *with* its demand for capital, or *inversely* to it. The wages it can afford to pay can vary either *with* the cost of capital, or *inversely* to it.

So much for some of the peculiarities of work as a 'market commodity'. On now to the reasons why markets for real commodities – or the relations between quantity and price depicted in Figure 32.2 – are terrible guides to relations between demand, supply and price in the market for labor.

Wages and the demand for labor

In defiance of market theory, the demand for labor tends strongly to vary *with* its price, not inversely to it. Wages are high when there is full employment. Wages – especially for the least-skilled and lowest-paid – are lowest when there is least employment. The causes chiefly run from the employment to the wages, rather than the other way. Unemployment weakens the bargaining power, worsens the job security and working conditions, and lowers the pay of those still in jobs.

The lower wages do not induce employers to create more jobs. A few households may hire a little more casual help – gardening, house-cleaning, baby-sitting, minor repairs – if their own incomes rise or rates for that sort of work fall. But most business firms have no reason to take on more hands if wages decline. Only empty warehouses, or the prospect of more sales, can get them to do that, and those conditions rarely coincide with falling employment and wages. The causes tend to work the other way: unemployment lowers wages, and the lower wages do not restore the lost employment. Other causes have to do that. Since about 1980 the real wages of the lowest-paid third or so of the American workforce have declined continuously. That has brought no continuing reduction of unemployment. May it nevertheless have prevented a rise in unemployment which would otherwise have followed from other causes? Perhaps – but some recent researchers doubt it.

In *The wage curve* (1994) David G. Blanchflower and Andrew J. Oswald reported relations between wages and employment for samples totalling three and a half million workers in twelve countries. Unemployment was highest where real wages were lowest. Nowhere had falling wages been followed by rising employment or falling unemployment.

In the same year David Card and Alan B. Krueger published *Myth and measurement: The new economics of the minimum wage.* They reported an elaborate study of the effects on employment of American governments' minimum wage laws. Federal and some State laws outlaw wages below specified levels. Many economists condemn the laws, because market theory says they raise the price of labor above its equilibrium price, so employers will hire less of it, and unemployment will be higher than it would otherwise be. American facts contradict the theory. The further the wage law increases what would otherwise be the lowest wage, and the greater the number of wages that it increases, the more employment tends to *increase*, and unemployment tends to decrease. The effects are small, because the minimum wage levels are low and affect comparatively few workers. But for the five years of Card and Krueger's study, the effects are all in the same direction: raising the lowest wages either has no effect on unemployment, or reduces it. Reducing the lowest wages either has no effect on unemployment, or increases it.

Why? The best explanation, in many cases, seems to be this. Left to themselves, some proportion of American employers of low-skilled workers pay too little. That does not buy them much good service, loyal service or long service. Turnover rates are high, and may be expensive as they interrupt production, annoy customers and increase training costs. Wiser employers

pay enough to get good work, cooperative attitudes and experienced skills from workers who learn on the job and stay with it. Some economists call that the efficiency wage. When minimum income laws compel worse employers to raise their rates nearer to that efficiency wage, quality and output tend to improve, the costs of unreliable work decline, more marginal businesses survive, and some of them create more jobs as they expand. The minimum wages also reduce poverty and wage inequality.

The authors of these surveys concede that an *excessive* minimum wage might reduce employment – but they have not seen it happen. They agree that employers hire more workers when they believe they can sell more output, and cheaper labor which is also available to their competitors does not help them to do that.

Working not from surveys but by detailed study of two industries, Paola Villa reported similar conclusions in *The structuring of labour markets: A comparative analysis of the steel and construction industries in Italy* (1986). 'The price of labour – the wage rate – is incapable of performing any market clearing function: ... Quantities (employment) and prices (wages) are determined by two different sets of factors. Neither the demand for nor the supply of labour depend on wages: the demand for labour is related to the level of output that firms plan to produce'. She sees a similar independence between wage levels and the *supply* of labour. That's the other half of our subject.

Wages and the supply of labor

Begin with some apparent contradictions: In some conditions in the short run higher wages may increase the supply of labor: more people enter the workforce, some of them work longer hours. But in other conditions and in the long run rising wages *reduce* the supply. On average and with individual exceptions, the higher the wage the less paid work people are willing to do.

The reasons for the contradictory possibilities are deftly expressed in a pair of neoclassical concepts which economists of all persuasions are glad to use: price changes and income changes are said to have effects of two kinds, namely *substitution* effects and *income* effects.

Substitution effects If the price of coffee rises, some people switch to tea: dearer coffee causes them to buy more tea. People *substitute* cheaper for dearer goods to get more altogether for their money or – when some prices rise – to get as much for their money as before.

As for buyers, so for sellers. If you are selling labor

(i.e. working for a wage) and the wage rises, it means that work earns more and, as an opportunity cost, leisure costs more. That may prompt you to work longer hours, *substituting* some work for some leisure. On the other hand –

Income effects If you are a confirmed coffee addict, when the price of coffee rises your coffee purchases will take more of your income. That will reduce your real income, so you are likely to buy less of everything, including tea. Dearer coffee causes you to buy *less* tea. Conversely, if one price falls it increases your real income, and you may spend the increase on other things besides the item whose price has fallen. 'Income effects' are things people do because their real purchasing power has risen or fallen.

A worker's real income can rise because prices fall or because wages rise. In either case a common – though not universal – response is to work less. If a desired standard of living can be earned by less labor, plenty of people will labor less.

That effect is clearest in the very long run. As wage rates rose through more than a century up to the 1970s, workers reduced their daily hours of work step by step from twelve or more to seven or less. They stopped working on Saturdays, and stretched their annual holidays from a week to a month. They started earning later in life and lived longer after they retired. Look back at Figure 32.1 to see how, over time, work dwindled as wages increased.

In the shorter run, and for different groups of workers with different wants, responses may vary. Examples:

1. Some people don't want much money. When mining companies first looked for local labor in central and southern Africa the wages they paid were often the first money their hunting and subsistence-farming workers had met. The people could use a little of it, chiefly to buy hunting and farming tools, but they did not want anything else it would buy. So mineworkers would earn what they wanted in a day or two then disappear for the rest of the week. How to motivate a full week's work without legally enslaving them? Some colonial administrators introduced and enforced a poll tax. To earn enough to pay it, workers had to work a full week – the 'income effect' of the tax did the trick. Are such troubles all past history now? No. Three or four young people now can pool their unemployment doles or do a day or two of casual work a week (or both), share a pad and some rusty wheels in reach of a beach, and live happily on surf and sun, music, fast food, love, and

very little money. The *higher* the dole or the casual wage rates go, the less work they need to do. Right policy-makers want to cut the dole, hoping the 'income effect' will drive them to look for full-time work. But if there are not enough full-time jobs available? Left policy-makers may be glad that some people are *willing* to live on comparatively little, and leave the available jobs to others who need and positively want them. The labor supply curve of these groups with limited income needs is in Figure 32.3 (a) overleaf.

2. Workers on low wage rates which could never enable them to buy houses and cars may be content to work normal hours, riding buses and bikes and renting whatever housing they can afford. Suppose that wage rates then rise high enough to create the possibility of saving home purchase deposits then making mortgage and hire-purchase repayments. Eager carbuyers and homebuyers look for overtime work or second jobs to speed the process. If wages rise further to make the purchases possible without overtime, they gladly return to shorter hours. Up to a certain level substitution effects lead them to work longer hours as wages rise; beyond that level income effects prevail as higher pay allows them to work shorter hours. Their supply curve is 32-3 (b).

3. Some people work longer hours the more each hour will earn for them. Men who work at oil rigs or remote construction sites for high pay are often willing to put in very long hours: they are there to earn as much as possible as quickly as possible (perhaps to buy a house back home, perhaps to start a business, perhaps to finance a summer of sun and surf). A lone-handed truckie drives 60 or 80 hours a week, the first 40 to keep up payments on his truck. Higher rates for urgent jobs will get even more hours from him. A young exchange gambler works around the clock – when the New York Stock Exchange closes he switches his monitor to London, then Tokyo. He sleeps when the markets are slack and his labor would earn less, and works when the markets are active and his labor can earn more – i.e. the higher the 'wage', the longer the hours he will work. Except for the summer surfer (who is actually redistributing his working hours through the year, rather than increasing them) these obsessive efforts are not usually to earn more spending money. They are efforts to accumulate capital, to climb out of the wage-earning class altogether. Their labor supply curve is 32.3 (c).

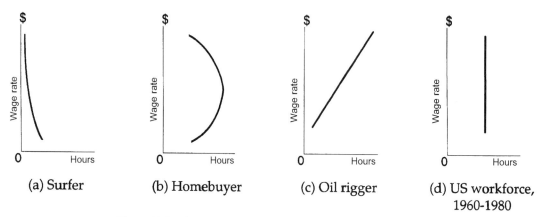

Figure 32.3 Labor supply curves of workers with different wants.

4. There remain a mass of solid citizens who work regular hours whatever the wage rates do. If they want more money they look to wage rises, promotions, better jobs, but not to longer hours. They are not all steady on a 37-hour week. They include workaholics – some artists, scholars, scientists, doctors, engineers, managers and others – who regularly work longer hours than they are paid for, for other purposes than money. But whether they are lazy or industrious, all these regular workers have it in common that their hours don't vary with their rates of pay. They have the vertical supply curve of 32-3 (d). So did a more important group: the American workforce as a whole, through the third quarter of the twentieth century. The total US labor supply appears to have ceased to respond to the total wages offered, as men earned for fewer hours and women earned for more.

But then the real wages of the lower-paid third or so of American workers reversed their upward trend and began to fall. As they fell, full-time male workers began to work longer hours. Women's demand for paid work may also increase as households try to sustain their standards of living – standards which go beyond consumption to investment in house and car ownership, children's education, and other productive physical and human capital. There may be similar effects if environmental pressures reduce real incomes and restore some more labor-intensive methods of production.

Thus the whole supply of labor tends to be determined by other causes rather than by its price. Insofar as it does respond to its price it tends to contradict traditional market theory more often than it fits it.

But notice two other kinds of market relation which do often hold between work and wages:

Inter-industry effects This chapter's review of relations between wages and labor supply is about *how much* paid work people choose to do. It is not about *what* work they choose to do. Higher wages may not motivate them to work longer hours, but may motivate them to change jobs, and may certainly influence their basic career choices. Forty hours a week for $500 beats forty hours for $400. Particular firms or industries which find themselves short of labor may well attract it by offering higher wages. History shows that above quite low levels rising wages for the workforce as a whole don't get *more* work done; but differential wages may well get *different* work done.

How effectively differential wages can shift people from job to job may sometimes depend on how willing and able they are to move house. As follows –

Inter-sector effects For a household to be as productive as it wants to be, there may need to be investment in all three sectors. Households need to be in reach of public services. They need paid jobs. And they need domestic capital at home. Between the paid jobs and the household capital there are two important relations. You already know them, but be reminded: (i) they need to be in reach of each other, and (ii) income from paid work generally has to pay for the household capital. Given those conditions, there can then be choices between working for pay and working at home.

Paid work and household work Remember Joe and Jo Weaver from our household histories? Through the first half of the nineteenth century they both went out and earned, to scratch enough to keep themselves and children alive in the bare slum they lived in. Then when growing public and private productivity allowed wages to rise high enough for one income to support a family, Joe went out and earned and Jo stayed home as housewife and revolutionized the household's productivity, mostly by hard labor. Then as household technology developed to replace some of that hard labor, Jo's daughter and granddaughter found time to go out and earn again, though for shorter daily hours and working lifetimes than their ancestors.

If you choose to see paid work as the only productive work, there may appear to have been changing, inconsistent responses to rising wages as the Weaver women first went out and earned, then stayed home for a generation or two, then went out and earned before and after their child-rearing years, then continued earning through their child-rearing years too. But their behavior is consistent and understandable as soon as you remember that household work is productive too. It also has its technological history. Household productivity often fell when country poor moved from their cottage gardens near commons and woods to live in town slums two hundred years ago. Then it rose again when higher incomes from paid work, and developing technology, provided better town housing, household equipment and housekeeping skills. Powered transport came to allow longer journeys to work. City people used that to increase their household and neighborhood space, and extend the range of things which household and other unpaid work could produce.

That household history has both income links and substitution links with paid jobs, and with relative productivities in the private and public sectors. As the Weaver women responded to changing constraints and opportunities by changing the time they allocated to paid work, household work and leisure, they were usually making the intelligent substitutions which would do most for their families' happiness, if not always their own.

Power A final objection to a market model of labor costs is that it neglects pervasive effects of market strength and bargaining power, and sometimes also political power.

Big firms, firms which command many or most of a region's jobs, and employers who employ easily replaceable unskilled workers may be able to pay low wages regardless of their workers' marginal productivity. Workers who must work or starve and so have no practical option of refusing whatever work and wages are offered, workers whose labor is easily replaceable by others, and workers with no organized capacity for collective bargaining are likely to be weak bargainers, however valuable their work may be to their employers.

Other workers can bargain from strength, to get all or most of whatever wage rates their employers can actually afford. Strong unions can sometimes do best against strong employers, if the employers have monopolist or other market strength against their customers, so that wage rises can be passed on as price rises without too much loss of business. Unions can be specially effective in slack times, preventing employers from taking advantage of unemployment by cutting wages.

Tradition, custom, and racial and gender power can also affect wages in ways which belie market theory. Until very recently women have been paid much less than men for the same work, and blacks have been paid less than whites. Their equal marginal contributions to the value of output do not get them equal wages. On the contrary the wage rates, determined by a variety of factors, determine much of the cost and market value of the output.

You will study these issues in greater depth later in chapters on the distribution of income.

Summary of objections to the market model of labor costs

Individual firms or occupations may attract workers, or entice them away from each other, by offering high wages, but the economy as a whole is different. The 'law of demand' does not apply. First, a higher price for labor will not usually get more work done in the economy as a whole. Second, the effects of changing wage levels are not always predictable: they may vary with culture, the birthrate, methods of child care, domestic productivity, and the rate of unemployment and the ease or difficulty of getting employment if you want it. Professionally speaking, the supply curve for paid labor is (i) usually vertical or backward-sloping, but (ii) historically variable.

Paola Villa, in the study cited earlier, found that the total supply of labor was as independent of its price as the total demand for it was: 'labour supply is by and large determined by demographic and social factors (though it is to some extent responsive to changes in employment opportunities).' Wage differences may help people to decide between one job and another, but people who need jobs accept the best of whatever is going. So 'the adjustment of inequalities between demand for and supply of labour do not take place through wage fluctuations. This has been supported by a large body of empirical evidence pointing out that it is not through wages but through employment opportunities that demand and supply are adjusted. In the main, employers adjust their labour force, whether upward or downward, by varying the number of workers whom they are willing to take on or to dismiss, thereby directly changing job opportunities.'

Thus 'the labour market is not a competitive market, since: (a) there is no free exchange, since there is no real choice for wage labour; (b) the employer/worker relationship is not a relation of free exchange, but a social relation exercised under constraint and specified within the labour process; (c) the price associated with the commodity – labour power – is incapable of performing any market clearing function.' (Paolo Villa, *The structuring of labour markets,* 1986, pp. 6-7)

Those are reasons why it might be better to think of work and wages, or industrial relations, or a labor system, rather than a labor market. But if you accept the 'labor market' language because it is common usage, remember the peculiarities of this market, including the tendency of both supply and demand to be independent of price in the short run, the scope for unequal bargaining and coercion, and the interrelation of paid and unpaid work.

If we now sketch three alternative methods of determining wage costs it does not mean that the alternatives avoid market processes altogether. Wage differences continue to reward skill and responsibility, and attract workers to particular jobs and occupations. But the market incentives operate under different conditions in each model.

2. AN OWNERS' MODEL

Slave states There are conditions, usually in the early stages of economic development, in which employers can keep wages down despite rising productivity. European factories in Malaysia were once an example. But what the workers lose by the wage restraint the owners do not necessarily gain. If the industry is competitive the low labor costs may simply be passed on in low consumer prices. If the low wages are widespread through the economy and are the main source of consumer spending, the effect may be permanent under-employment, with employers making less money than they might make with the same plant in a high-wage society.

However, producers may be able to keep wages down but nevertheless keep demand and prices up if they can sell their products outside the country or the economic class to which the low-wage workers belong. Wages may be kept down by market forces (as in Malaysia) or by law and physical force (as in some

racist, sexist or slave societies) while products sell to export markets or to well-off minorities at home. In all economies some goods are made by low-paid workers to sell to richer buyers, but their inequality can be increased and enforced if government restricts or abolishes the workers' bargaining capacity. Governments once banned labor unions and collective bargaining. A few dictators of Right and Left still do. For much of the twentieth century South African governments restricted the occupations and bargaining rights of black workers. British and European settlers in the Americas used private slavery, enforced by government, chiefly to grow sugar, cotton and tobacco for export to richer societies than their own. That system worked profitably for some centuries until the last of it ended scarcely a hundred years ago. None of the slave-owing regimes reformed themselves: slavery had to be abolished from British colonies by reformers in London, from the US by civil war, from the Spanish colonies by rebellion or foreign war.

All those privileged employers were exploiting special conditions, producing for export or for affluent minorities so that their low wage levels need not restrict the effective demand for their output. It is much more difficult for employers as a group to widen their profit margins by depressing wages across the economy as a whole. In modern mixed economies producing 70 or 80 per cent or more of their output for their own use, wage levels have too strong an effect on levels of demand and therefore prices and profit. There is room for *some* variation in the division of earnings between the workers' wage share and the owners' profit share, and that division may affect the division of output between spending and investment. So it is not always or necessarily futile for business and labor to contend for their respective shares by bargaining over wage levels. But the range of choice is narrow. Pushing *money* wages too high may merely cause inflation. If *real* wages go too high there may be too little profit to either motivate investment or finance it. On the other hand if owners take too much they are likely to over-invest unprofitably and shrink the consumer demand on which their sales and profits depend. Both effects may be moderated a little, the first if over-paid workers save and invest their gains and the second if over-paid owners spend luxuriously rather than investing. But in most modern mixed economies the range of wage/profit shares that are consistent with full and profitable employment of capital is quite narrow.

It may be easier to increase inequality by changing the distribution of the wage share than by reducing it. What the poorer third of US workers lose as their real wages decline is shared between their employers, consumers of their cheaper products and the rising incomes of the richest ten per cent or more of waged, salaried and self-employed workers. As the rich get richer and the poor get poorer, that may increase the casual employment of poorer unemployed by richer households, and help to keep reported US unemployment below British and European.

3. A GOVERNMENT MODEL

Australia Most Australian workers' rates of pay and hours of work and many of their working conditions have been fixed for nearly a century by judges, or by negotiated agreements which are approved by public officials and given the force of law.

At the turn of the century, following New Zealand precedents, the Australian federal and state parliaments created a national system of industrial courts, arbitrators and conciliators. Though governments designed the system and appoint the judges and conciliation commissioners, there is a sense in which it is misleading to call it a 'government model'. For most purposes the system operates independently of government, just as other courts of law do. Employers and labor unions take their business directly to the commissioners or courts who reach most of their decisions without reference to the government. Government bodies are there when they happen to be the relevant employers, and they are bound like other employers by the courts' decisions. Otherwise the only way that government can intervene in most cases is to appear as a third party to put a government view to the court. The court can take as much or as little notice of the government view as the judges think fit. Much of the system's business is done by registering and enforcing agreements negotiated by the employers and unions. Only when the two disagree – or rarely, when the judges think an agreed proposal is against justice or the national interest – is there a court case and judgment.

In 1907 a judge fixed a national minimum wage at a level calculated to keep a male worker, his wife and three children in decent comfort. A second judgment allowed no employer to pay less to adult male workers: employers who could not pay the basic wage must go out of business. Awards for more skilled and responsible jobs were expressed as margins above the basic wage, so that adjustments to the basic wage would flow through to all wages. There were soon detailed awards for most occupations in most industries, and for some decades the basic wage (and therefore all the others) were pegged to local cost-of-living indexes. Over time,

with steady economic growth interrupted by occasional depression crises, the judges' emphasis shifted somewhat from the workers' household needs to the employers' capacity to pay. Automatic cost-of-living indexation ceased and was replaced by an annual national wage case. Until some further changes in recent years, peak employers and union representatives and the government would put their views to a full court. The court would order a one-year adjustment which was then incorporated into all the detailed awards for particular occupations.

Women's wages had traditionally been far below men's and for a long time the court either neglected them or fixed them far below men's. It began to improve them during World War Two and then between 1969 and 1976 effected a staged transition first to equal pay for equal work then to equal pay for occupations judged to have equal work value.

Through the 1980s the terms of trade (how much wheat buys now much machinery, etc.) shifted against Australia and the Australian dollar lost value against other currencies. To keep business profitable and limit inflation and unemployment in those conditions the government and unions agreed to join in asking the court to reduce real wage rates. Through the decade the court did so; real wage rates were reduced by more than ten per cent altogether, with some partial compensation in tax cuts.

There is argument about how well the wage-fixing system has worked. In its favor, Australia has prospered and industrialized. Through the long post-war boom it had the world's lowest unemployment, and (together with Scandinavia and New Zealand) its lowest inequality of incomes. Its households have more household capital, more equally distributed, than most. Its wage-fixing system implemented equal pay for work of equal value in the 1970s more quickly and effectively than most countries approached it.

Critics of the system say that by reducing inequalities it weakens work incentives. Some unions have misused the strength which the system gives them, to enforce unhelpful work practices. There have been too many 'demarcation' disputes between unions competing for the right to represent particular groups of workers. None of those and other imperfections has prevented peaceful economic growth. The growth since 1950 has appeared to be comparatively slow. Australia has slipped from third or fourth to thirteenth in the league table of OECD countries' measured income per head. But that table reflects exchange rates between national currencies and neglects the unrecorded income effects of public and household capital. In Kyoko Sheridan (ed.) *The Australian economy in the Japanese mirror* (1992) Ian Castles, working from household surveys, found Australian labor more productive per hour in real terms than Japanese. The average hourly wage buys Australians about one and a half times the market goods that the average Japanese wage buys. Their household space and capital and their public cultural and recreational capital allow high household productivity. Growth of measured GNP is comparatively slow, partly because of Australian preferences for (unmeasured) household production and leisure. With relaxed lifestyles, ample space and sunshine and versatile do-it-yourself capacities, Australians appear to know what they are doing in having impartial arbitrators fix their wage rates as fairly as possible.

Some economists nevertheless theorize that the system must reduce national efficiency by distorting or replacing market wage-fixing. Our review of the relevant market forces suggests that the critics have unjustified faith in them. If you accept the judgment of Paola Villa and other researchers about what actually determines 'market' wage rates, it makes good sense to have them fixed instead by independent arbitrators with social values as well as economic efficiency in mind. The Australian system goes further in that direction than any other. It is currently under attack from the radical Right by business, political and professorial deregulators.

Summary: Australia has most wage and salary rates fixed by judges or by agreements negotiated within limits set by judges. The judges decide what weight to give – year by year and case by case – to industries' capacity to pay, to effects on inflation and unemployment, to equity between employers, employees and consumers, to equity between worker and worker, and to what it costs to share in prevailing lifestyles. The rates they fix do not limit wages: employers are free to compete for scarce labor by paying more.

Many part-time, self-employed, unemployed and retired Australians live on less than the basic adult wage. So do some sweated workers, especially women in the garment trades, who do piece-work at home for prices which courts do not regulate. But employers who need regular wage labor must pay the lawful rates or go out of business. That principle is also at the heart of our fourth wage-fixing model, pioneered in Sweden.

4. A WORKERS' MODEL

Sweden It exaggerates only a little to say that wage rates were decided by organized labor through the later stages of Sweden's spectacular modern growth to wealth, welfare and comparative wage equality.

Early in the twentieth century the Swedish labor unions and Social Democratic party decided not to try for state-owned socialism. Instead they would nourish capitalist industry and milk it, distributing its output as equally as possible through wages and welfare services.

In 1932 under stress of the Great Depression the Social Democrats won power in alliance with a radical farmers' party, and governed for 54 of the next 60 years. In 1938 leaders of business and labor negotiated the 'Pact of Saltsjobaden' under which wages were fixed for the next half-century by periodical national negotiation between them. A foreign observer described the system working at its best:

> Briefly, here's how the peace machine works: Every two (or sometimes three) years, bargaining committees from business and labor go through a ritual of meetings, public statements, expressions of despair, accusations and counteraccusations over a period of a few months; this culminates in the general outlines of a wage agreement, which is then worked out in detail by the unions and employers' organizations in each industry and further still on the local level. ... The record is so obviously too good to be true that a modicum of suspicion is excusable. Yet an effort by a suspicious investigator to uncover the truth beneath the surface amiability and mutual respect is apt to come upon a solid core of amiability and mutual respect.
>
> – David Jenkins, *Sweden: The progress machine* (1968) p.133.

We also will describe the system in the present tense, though it is past history now. In the wage negotiations labor has double strength. More than 90 per cent of workers are union members, and unions and government generally agree on the nation's economic policies, many of which the unions' economists have originated. Policies about wages and working conditions express four principles: wages should be (i) as *equal* and (ii) as *high* as possible, in return for which workers should be very (iii) *adaptable* and supported by (iv) good *welfare* services. At its best (though there have been lapses) the reasoning behind those principles is such that employers might have done just as well if wages had been fixed by labor alone:

- Wages are as *equal* as possible, with small margins between unskilled, skilled and white-collar rates. Perhaps because they are set by the unions at the workers' behest, the small margins do not seem to have harmed workers' incentives to acquire skills and responsibilities; and employers get the services of the 'labor aristocracy' at restrained rates.

- *High* wages mean as high as can be achieved by putting Sweden's resources to their most productive uses. Firms and industries which cannot pay optimum wages must make way for those who can. But wages must not be *too* high. They must not rise beyond industries' capacity to pay. (That would merely fuel inflation.) And they must leave employers enough profit share to invest in the best current technology. Two of those requirements – the elimination of less efficient industries, and labor-saving investment by the more efficient – often extinguish jobs. Hence the third principle –

- *Adaptable* workers must welcome and not resist necessary technical and economic changes. They must willingly retrain on the job or between jobs, change jobs, and move house from one place to another, as changing technology and competitive conditions require. To make that as easy and unfrightening as possible –

- *Government* should provide appropriate health, housing and educational services, parent support and day-care for children, income during re-training, and security against unemployment, including public re-training services, and employers of last resort.

The four principles support each other. With adjustments from time to time, the system worked roughly as intended for half a century. There were imperfections. When the central negotiators had arrived at non-inflationary wage levels, there were some inflationary additions in the detailed local negotiations which followed. There were welfare excesses and cuts, export and balance of payment problems, and eventually a worried decision to join the European Union. But the wage-fixing system continued to work and to apply its distinctive principles: wages were centrally negotiated, not left to market forces; they are still much more equal than unregulated local bargaining would make them; they are as high as efficient capitalist enterprise can pay; and enterprises which cannot pay them cannot survive. The success of this 'workers' model' may owe something to Swedish culture and solidarity, and to ease of negotiation and administration in a small country. But as it performed for half a century it was better for many good purposes than the comparatively free labor markets of (for example) North and South America.

What led the employers to end the central negotiations? What led the government to dismantle some of the surrounding protections of the wage policy? How did the wage system compare with Australia's 'government model' which delivers a similar degree of equality through the middle and lower range of wage incomes? We will return to the subject in chapters on national economic strategies.

CONCLUSIONS

'Labor market' is a misleading term for relations between the demand for labor, the supply of it, and its price. The whole supply of labor is not much affected by its price in the short run and has declined with rising wages in the long run. The demand for labor is determined chiefly by the amount of output which private employers think they can sell, and the services which government decides that public employers should provide.

There are *some* market effects. Wage levels may sometimes affect the amounts which exporters can sell. Wage differences help to attract workers from one job to another. Full employment with strong demand for labor tends to inflate wages. Unemployment may allow the wages of some lower-paid workers to decline. But the lower pay does not prompt many employers to hire more hands. Too high a minimum wage might in theory reduce employment, but that does not appear to have happened in practice. Historically the world's highest minimum wages (in Sweden and Australia) have for long periods accompanied the fullest employment ever recorded. And the world's *lowest* wages are nearly everywhere accompanied by its *highest* unemployment.

Unregulated (i.e. market) wages are set by mixtures of custom, balances of bargaining strength, and (in many industries) employers' experience of the wages and conditions that tend to attract and hold a stable and co-operative workforce. Those industries also tend to have labor unions. But there are industries which employ low-skilled and unskilled workers, especially women wanting part-time or piece-work, in which unregulated market forces allow quite unreasonable exploitation of 'weak' labor.

In those circumstances it is positively desirable to set wages to serve social as well as economic purposes. When communist countries tried to do that is was difficult to distinguish the wage effects from the other causes that converged to produce generally poor economic *and* social performance. Among mixed economies the Swedish and Australian principles deserve attention, and the Australian system appears (so far) to be tougher and longer-lasting, despite two or three decades of strong attack by business, conservative government and many neoclassical economists.

EXERCISE

This course of study does not usually set direct revision of the text as an exercise. (It *assumes* that you know, and do, as much of that as you need.) This is an exception. Please re-read and think about the central parts of this chapter until you understand and will remember *all* the ways in which paid work can differ from market goods, and the reasons why it does. Then think out for yourself the economic and social effects – good or bad, in your judgment – that seem likely to follow if business, government and the economists who advise them succeed in 'freeing up the labor market' as many currently wish to do.

33

Costs of production : how firms minimize their costs

This chapter is about ways in which firms can go about minimizing their costs of production, and some effects which their economizing can have on others' costs, and on society's whole costs of production.

It is easy to assume that more from less is always better: that society as a whole must benefit from lower costs of production however they are achieved. It is often so. But it ain't necessarily so. It ain't necessarily so, for example, if firms cut costs by shifting the costs onto others; by degrading the environment undesirably; by means which worsen the distribution of income; by means which increase unemployment; or by means which encourage unproductive kinds of monopoly or takeover.

Treat this chapter as a check-list of possible effects – both good and bad – of private enterprises' efforts to minimize their costs. It includes both some revision and some new material.

FACTOR COSTS AND INVESTMENT

Many investment choices are chiefly technical. Experts go shopping for value-for-money, comparing the costs and advantages of alternative business locations, building plans, types of machinery, information systems, and so on. Economists are chiefly interested in how those choices relate to two general qualities of the economy: its capital- or labor-intensity, and its tendencies to competition or monopoly (or its distribution of market strength). Here we ask how investment may be affected by factor prices, i.e. the relativities between wage rates, equipment prices, interest rates on capital funds, and so on.

Factor prices and costs

Recall our comparison of a modern plant, an older plant and a back yard operation. Neglect their raw-material costs which were the same for them all. Remember that capital cost means the cost per day of having the relevant capital equipment (not the cost of buying it in the first place). To produce 10 units of output in one day shift the modern plant had 2 workers use $600 of equipment; the older plant had 4 workers use $400 of equipment; the back yard had 6 workers use $200 of

equipment. All the workers were paid $100 a day, so the costs of producing 10 units compared like this:

	Capital $	Labor $	Total $	Unit Cost $
Modern plant	600	200	800	80
Older Plant	400	400	800	80
Back yard	200	600	800	80

Suppose wages fall to half those levels. Then –

	Capital $	Labor $	Total $	Unit Cost $
Modern plant	600	100	700	70
Older plant	400	200	600	60
Back yard	200	300	500	50

The back yard has the lowest unit costs. But if instead of halving the wage to $50 per worker we double it to $200, the capital-intensive plant does best:

	Capital $	Labor $	Total $	Unit Cost $
Modern plant	600	400	1000	100
Older plant	400	800	1200	120
Back yard	200	1200	1400	140

Now suppose that wages are $200 a day in Sweden, $100 in New Zealand and $50 in China, and those are the locations of our three plants:

	Capital $	Labor $	Total $	Unit Cost $
Sweden	600	400	1000	100
New Zealand	400	400	800	80
China	200	300	500	50

Some implications:

- The Swedes should probably get out of this business. But as technical leaders in it, they may perhaps be able to invent new, automated machinery which is *both* labor-saving *and* capital-saving, so that (say) 1 worker earning $200 can produce 10 units using equipment whose daily capital cost is only $200. With a unit cost of $40, they could then undersell the Chinese – as long as the Chinese lacked the skill to use the new machinery.

- Perhaps the New Zealanders should get out of the business too. But perhaps not. If their butter and lamb exports won't pay for all the manufactured imports they want, and if they can't employ all their population *growing* butter and lamb, they may decide to put a ban or a 60 per cent tariff on imports of this item to keep their own plant viable. Meanwhile notice why they don't buy the Swedish machinery: with $600 capital and $200 labor they would have the same costs as they do with $400 of each. They may as well keep the old $400 plant going, and all 4 workers employed, for the time being.

- If the Chinese buy Swedish machinery they will *increase* their unit costs. (Work it out and see.) Meanwhile if the world will accept their exports without trade barriers they can price them high, for high profits. With a 50 per cent mark-up they can still undercut and outsell everybody else. What might they do with that surplus value? Improve *future* Chinese incomes by investing it in Chinese industry? Improve *current* Chinese incomes by using it to cut taxes? Give it to the export workers by raising their wages? Invest it where it is received abroad, to earn a future flow of foreign exchange?

Orthodox texts graph these factor-cost relationships in various ways. For example, imagine an industry in which – in the long run, as plant is built or replaced – it is possible to make fairly smooth substitutions between capital and labor, as in our three-plant comparison. The mix of machinery and labor is likely to become less efficient at either extreme, i.e. if much capital is used with very little labor, or much labor with very little capital. Figure 33.1 graphs the technically-possible mixes to produce 10 units of output.

At A, two workers with 4 machines can produce 10 units of output. At B, four workers with 2 machines can do the same. Above A, to save one worker you have to add 4 machines. Below B, to manage with one less machine you must more than double the workforce. And so on – the curve plots the mixes which can produce *equal quantities of output*.

Now plot the mixes which could produce a given output *at equal cost*. At given factor prices these will normally lie along a straight line – steeper if labor is relatively expensive, flatter if labor is relatively cheaper. Here are isocost lines for producing 10 units (1) in Sweden where machines cost $100 a day and workers $200, and (2) in New Zealand where those factor prices are reversed with machines costing $200 a day and workers $100. See figure 33.2 on the following page.

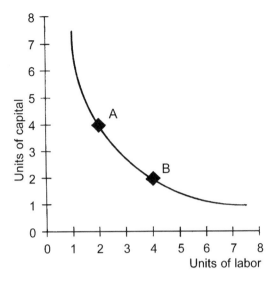

Figure 33.1   Capital/labor mixes which can produce 10 units of output per day.

Next, put those alternative factor costs together with the isoquant line which indicates the technically possible mixes of capital and labor, as in Figure 33.3.

With those factor costs the Swedes are back in competition. They do best at A, with two workers using 4 machines. The New Zealanders achieve the same total costs at B with four workers using 2 machines and earning half the Swedes' wages.

Why aren't the Chinese competing? Perhaps they have not yet developed the skills and public infrastructure which this industry requires; or they have higher priorities for their limited investment funds. Why do the machines cost the New Zealanders twice as much as they cost the Swedes? Perhaps the New Zealanders make the machines with less efficiency or economies of scale. Or perhaps the machines are all made in Sweden, but are expensive in New Zealand because investors must ship them around the world, truck them to inland locations, and fly Swedish teams out to assemble and install them.

The different mixes of capital and labor to be found in different plants, firms, industries and countries are not all determined by refined cost comparisons. They can also be affected by the age of the industry, the speed with which its technology is changing, the vintage mix of plant inherited from the past, the industrial policies and bargaining strength of labor unions, and the tariff

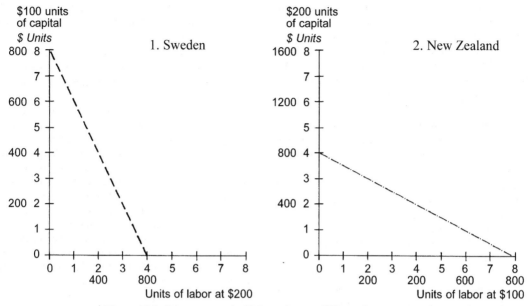

Figure 33.2 Same-cost capital/labor mixes at different factor costs.

and other policies of governments. But despite those causes of diversity, two trends tend to operate strongly, over time, in the relations between factor prices and investment patterns:

1. The uses of particular inputs to production – particular materials, types of equipment, modes of transport, etc. – change in response to changes in their relative prices.

2. In many industries, and until now in whole economic systems, productivity has grown as production has become more capital intensive. (But capital-saving inventions are beginning to change that, to derive further growth from *better* capital equipment rather than *more* capital.)

Those trends, powered by producers' efforts to produce at lower cost, are main sources of invention and economic growth. But how reliable are the trends, and how desirable for others besides the firms' owners? We can even ask 'how efficient for society' if that means meeting as much as possible of the demand that arises from existing distributions of wealth and income. Accepting that inequitable measure of efficiency (for the moment), will firms' efforts to produce goods at least cost ensure that the private sector as a whole makes the most productive use of available resources?

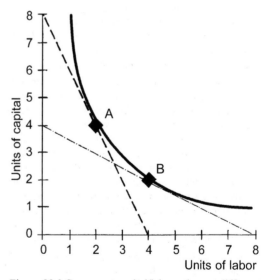

Figure 33.3 Same-cost capital/labor mixes at different factor costs

Private and social efficiency

Efficient firms produce as cheaply as they can. They make economizing choices of two kinds: (1) Whatever inputs they need, they buy each one as cheaply as they can; and (2) given the prices of those inputs, they choose the cheapest mix they can (as when Swedes use more machines and Chinese use more workers).

Overall I think that the good effects of firms' responses to factor prices greatly outweigh their ill effects. But we will notice the ill effects first, together with some things government may be able to do about them. The notes can be brief because you have met most of the items before.

How the invisible hand can err Firms' efficient responses to factor prices can be inefficient for others' purposes or for the economy as a whole in any of the following circumstances.

1. The price of a factor may not reflect the costs of producing it. Monopolists may charge too much. Public suppliers may charge too little. In either case firms buying the factor may not achieve the factor mix which would best economize the society's resources.

2. Factor costs can reflect market strength rather than the costs of producing the factor. A firm's workers may increase its costs by successful action to raise wages. The firm or its suppliers may achieve reverse effects if they succeed in cutting wages. When factor costs change for those purely redistributive reasons there is no presumption that the changes will help productivity, hinder it, or have no effect on it – it will depend on the particular facts of the case.

3. Pure 'rent' is charged for some scarce or monopolized resources. That sometimes serves to economize the use of the resources, efficiently for society. But it may also raise prices unnecessarily and redistribute wealth and income undesirably. It is anyway an unreliable mechanism; many scarce, exhaustible resources do not fetch high rents and do not get economized. For short-sighted supply-and-demand reasons, dwindling rainforests are being logged at low prices. Exhaustible natural gas is going cheap as fuel, when prudent users would conserve it for the petrochemical uses for which it is irreplaceable.

4. Firms can sometimes make factor choices which benefit them by shifting costs rather than reducing them. They unload costs onto others, collect 'external' benefits from others, or minimize tax bills. They may avoid other costs by choosing locations, materials or types of labor which reduce their liability for plant safety, workers' compensation, environmental care. Though rational for profit-seekers those choices do not necessarily improve productivity.

5. Firms may mistake their own interests and make factor choices which do not minimize their costs, and are in nobody's interest.

In any of those ways profit-seeking firms seeking to minimize their costs of production may make factor choices which are not socially desirable, or efficient for the economy as a whole. The 'invisible hand' of market forces cannot always be trusted to reconcile private and social interests. When Adam Smith conceived the metaphor he did not expect the invisible hand to work in all cases. He thought that the profit-seeking capitalist 'by pursuing his own interest, frequently promotes that of society'. Not always, just frequently. As often as the invisible hand squanders rainforests or natural gas, has children down coal mines or adults down asbestos mines, or has tendencies to monopoly, it may need correction by the visible hand of government. The visible hand may intervene for social purposes (to keep children above ground); for immediate economic efficiency (to cut monopoly prices); or for long-term justice and efficiency (to economize and share finite resources). So do some firms – for prudent or generous purposes they may act more neighborly, or pay higher wages, than they are strictly required to do.

How frequently the invisible hand gets it right Despite its imperfections the invisible hand does frequently work as Adam Smith expected. A great many factor prices do reflect the real costs of producing the factors. When they don't, their elements of rent do sometimes ration scarce resources effectively. Many wages and working conditions (the biggest factor cost for a majority of firms) represent fair exchanges between employers and employees of comparable bargaining power. In many industries most of the firms' responses to the factor prices they find in the marketplace do allocate and economize productive resources efficiently for firm and society alike.

Firms' factor choices are only one link in the chains of demand and supply which get consumers' demands served by efficient allocation and use of the available productive resources. We need not repeat yet again the reasons for the general efficiency of market mechanisms wherever they work as they should. But it is worth noticing how much of a modern economy's efficiency and growth comes from developments in the factors of production, rather than in the final goods which they produce. When you think of the marvels of modern technology you may think first of the flow of new products, especially the more recent and noticeable ones which transform daily life: videos, walkmen, CDs, computers, electronic games, electronic bank tellers and fund transfers, faxes and videophones, artificial hips and hearts, new techniques of conception and procreation. But a lot of the growth that has enriched the rich countries has come by cutting the factor costs of producing quite traditional products. A basic house costs less to build in real terms than it used to cost because instead of being hand-made on the site, 70 per cent of it is now factory-made before it reaches the site, and it reaches the site by truck and forklift rather than bullock wagon and manhandling. Cars have not changed their basic form or functions for nearly a century, but a Ford worker can earn a Ford now in half the time it once took – and the Ford may deliver twice the miles in twice the comfort it once did – because of incessant incremental improvements to the materials and components from which the car is made. Ordinary steel gave way to special steels. Some of the steel gave way to lighter alloys. Metals gave way to plastics. Carburetion was rivaled by fuel injection then both were developed into increasingly fancy, electronically modulated, lean-burn fuel feeds. Some of those came as prompt, inventive responses to the OPEC oil price rise.

Cutting the customers' factor costs Notice that in developing those fuel-saving devices which made cars cheaper to run, manufacturers were cutting their customers' factor costs rather than their own. That's common. Though producers look for better and cheaper inputs for their own operations, the initiatives often come from their customers or their suppliers. That can be for reasons of technical know-how. There are good examples in the development of plastics, and of computing. Each came as a new set of technical possibilities. The possibilities were not all obvious to the established manufacturers of houses, cars, domestic equipment and other traditional products. It was often the newcomers, expert with their new materials and mechanisms, who initiated the research and development which cut the manufacturers' costs or improved their products by substituting the new factors for the old.

That process of changing factors and factor prices and factor mixes, arrived at by innumerable inquiries and offers and choices in factor markets, is at the heart of the process of technical progress and productivity growth. The faster the inventions come, the busier the invisible hand has to be in the factor markets.

Conclusions

Orthodox texts tell you, correctly, that factor markets tend to allocate and economize productive resources more efficiently than bureaucrats could do. Some conclude that, except to correct the kinds of market failure listed above, business doesn't need government. A more realistic appreciation of the efficiency of factor markets might be this:

A modern private sector producing about half the national product, regulated as necessary by a two- or three-kilogram Companies Act enforced by some tens of thousands of auditors and public servants, and trading busily with the public and household sectors which do the other half of production, undoubtedly allocates and uses productive resources (i) more efficiently than it used to do before it shared the task with well-equipped public and household producers, and (ii) more efficiently than socialist 'command economies' without private sectors managed to do.

Meanwhile the mixed economies could sometimes improve their overall efficiency by coordinating the location of public, private and domestic investments better than they yet do. Recall from Chapter 16 how Hungary's postwar industrial development was located in reach of the existing houses of its intended workers. Now recall some more of that chapter's themes about the uses of locational planning.

RELATIONS BETWEEN PRIVATE, PUBLIC AND HOUSEHOLD COSTS

In 1961 Sydney had about 2,000,000 people, the steel town of Wollongong had 130,000 and the country town of Wagga Wagga had 20,000. Max Neutze compared some external costs of investors locating new jobs in each of the three. He found that adding one more resident would cause, per year,

940 new vehicle miles in Sydney,
435 new vehicle miles in Wollongong,
229 new vehicle miles in Wagga Wagga;

and each newcomer would cause an increase in traffic congestion to the existing residents costing

£32.4 in Sydney,
£2.0 in Wollongong,
£0.1 in Wagga Wagga.

At that time £32.4 was between two and three weeks' wages of an average worker. Neutze continued –

Thus there is a saving to the community of about £30 per year for every person who is diverted from Sydney to a centre the size of Wollongong. The saving only increases by about £2 per year if, instead of to Wollongong, he goes to a centre of about 20,000 population such as Wagga Wagga.

But only 40 per cent of the population is in the workforce so that the benefits are £76 per year per worker diverted from Sydney to Wollongong. We can go one step further if we take account of the so called 'basic industry ratio': the ratio of total employment in a region to employment in industries which do not depend on the region for their market. Primary and secondary industries are the main 'basic' industries and in 1961 they employed some 40 per cent of the workforce. In effect, when four workers are decentralized as a result of policy another six will follow to provide the local services for the firm and its employees. This is a very crude measure of the ratio but we can safely say that at least two jobs will be created in any new centre for each job in the basic industries. The benefit from diverting a job in a basic industry becomes £152 per year.

What you study may be changing as you study it – by 1990 less than 40 per cent of workers were in primary and secondary industries. There were economies as well as diseconomies of scale for many people in the big cities. But for the distribution of the particular costs of production which he was studying, Neutze was able to conclude –

> Our examination of the effect of population growth on the costs of congestion shows that there are substantial advantages in diverting growth from large, very congested, to smaller and less congested cities. Moreover these advantages are external to the locating firm or family and so will not be taken into account in making location decisions. Hence they justify encouragement of decentralization, either by location planning or by appropriate taxation and subsidy.
>
> G.M.Neutze, *Economic policy and the size of cities* (1965) 57-60.

That is one example of the wide variety of relations which can exist between the private, public and household costs of private production. To be precise, private production can have public and household costs, and it can also affect the costs of public and household production. You will continue to meet examples of both, in different contexts, as you work through this course of study. Here, in this chapter on costs of private production, is as good a place as any to set out a 'search scheme' or battery of inter-sectoral possibilities to have in your head when you analyse total costs of producing particular goods or services in any one of the three sectors. We will notice how investors may do any of the following:

• unload some of their costs of production onto others;

• affect others' costs of production;

• increase or reduce their own and others' costs together;

• disagree internally (within the firm, within the household, within the public sector) about their own costs.

Producers unload their costs onto others

Firms may shift costs of production onto others with or without shifting productive work to others. For example firms may dispose of their own wastes; some with dangerous wastes have got government to pay them for doing it; some pay others to do it; some have taxpayers finance public services to do it for them.

Farmers take their weed and pest problems to public research and advice services.

Professional researchers and authors find plenty of collecting, ordering and indexing done for them in public archives and libraries.

Parents shift costs of child-rearing onto public health, child-care and educational services.

Public services which have been free begin to charge, so that their costs are shifted from taxpayers to service users. Governments which used to bill the taxpayers for new roads, dams, pipes and wires now charge their costs to land developers and thus to the homebuyers in new suburbs.

In those cases some *costs* of production are paid by others than the producers and consumers of the product. It also happens that some productive *functions* are shifted from one sector to another, with or without an accompanying shifts of costs. Public utilities are privatized. Public services are passed to the private sector and to households when mentally defective people are 'dein-stitutionalized' to live at less public cost in private boarding houses or with kin.

Finally, some productive functions are shifted from sector to sector with a matching shift of costs. Retailers used once to make up many customers' orders and do many home deliveries. Now shoppers use their own labor and capital to serve themselves with supermarket goods and transport them home. Some people are disadvantaged by the change but majorities welcome it, and where the functions move from the private to the household sector the costs move too.

Producers affect others' costs without affecting their own

A factory expands in an old city district. Its effects increase residents' household costs of cleaning, dust-proofing and sound-proofing their houses. Its truck traffic increases public costs of maintaining roads. But its workers have short, cheap journeys to work by foot, bike or efficient public transport. Their families have equally short journeys to other jobs, schools, shops and services.

Then the expanding factory moves to a new outer-suburban industrial park. Many of its workers follow, trading old city flats and cottages for suburban houses and gardens. The industrial zoning and lower residential densities increase distances from home to work, schools, shops and services. There is less and dearer public transport, needing more public subsidy, providing no service at all on many routes. Male householders drive themselves to work. Carless, their families get to jobs, schools, shops, as best they can. Many may nevertheless welcome the move for the attractions of the house and garden and the school with grass and trees and playing fields. A decade or two later the family members may each have wheels, and be mobile again. Throughout this sequence of events the factory has not unloaded *its own* costs onto workers or taxpayers. But its behavior has altered a number of their domestic and public costs.

Misfits between the locations of private and household investment can follow from the birth, the death or the migration of particular industries. 'Company towns' in which jobs depend on a single employer are specially vulnerable. Firms invest in mining or manufacturing which depend on local natural resources: a mine, a forest, a harbor. Workers in the industry, or landlords, build houses. Government builds schools and services. Then the private employers close their works and depart. There may be many reasons for that. The ore runs out. World prices for the product fall. Its home market depended on a tariff, which is repealed. The plant is obsolete and it suits the owners to locate its replacement somewhere else. Whatever the cause, a ghost town is left with good public and household capital going to waste, or – if the people stay with their houses and public services – with obstinate structural unemployment.

All those causes have operated to some degree in turning parts of northern and western Britain into what government came to call 'depressed areas'. Is it wrong for government to use sticks and carrots to induce old employers to stay or new ones to start in those areas? Not necessarily, if it is competently done. First, it may be efficient for the industries themselves to locate there in spite of their directors' preference for golfing somewhere else. Second, it is economical to use existing houses and schools rather than leave them empty and build new ones somewhere else. What is efficient for the firm may not be what is efficient for the nation: what is efficient for the nation is to make the fullest use it can of all its capital, private, public and household.

Where economic development is slow, public and private household investment may be well coordinated by market forces, without much planning. In other conditions efficient coordination may depend on deliberate public action. However it is achieved, the coordination can have economies for all the investors concerned.

Policy conclusions

Firms do what they can to minimize their costs. Many of the things they do for that purpose also serve good social purposes: they economize resources and serve consumer preferences for the community as a whole. But there are exceptions. Most firms use public resources, sometimes economically but sometimes extravagantly. Firms may shift some of their private costs onto others. That can increase the whole cost of production if small savings for the firm impose bigger costs on others; or without increasing total costs it may distribute them inefficiently, distorting consumers' preferences; or it may distribute them unfairly, increasing inequalities of income.

So there are occasions for public action to restrain total costs of production; to distribute them more efficiently; and to distribute them more equitably, either between people now or between generations over time. Good cost-control often depends on skilful firms and some skilful government.

34

How firms price their products

Growers pricing their carrots in the local vegetable market may have only a little in common with Volvo deciding the export price of a new model, or a star barrister deciding what to charge per hour in court. Economists nevertheless try to distil some principles common to all of them, partly to guide people who have to decide on prices, and partly to relate different pricing practices to the overall behavior of economic systems.

This chapter will (i) introduce a simple theory of ideal pricing by profit-seeking firms in competitive markets; (ii) list a number of practical ways in which firms actually go about their pricing; and (iii) notice some conditions, including unequal market strength, which may determine whether the pricing practices which are best for producers are likely to be best for consumers and others too.

First, some common terms for describing various pricing conditions.

Price setters and price takers Some producers can decide how to price their products, knowing that the prices they set are likely to affect the quantities they can sell. Carmakers price their models, publishers price their books, builders decide the prices at which they tender for building contracts, and so on. These are *price setters*.

Price takers, by contrast, have to accept going prices. They produce for markets in which no one supplier can affect prevailing prices, so the question for each producer is not what price to set, but what quantity to produce at what cost for sale at the prevailing price.

Flexprice and fixprice If your carrots are not selling well from your market stall, you may be able to drop your price to a level at which they will all sell. Or if there is a shortage, you may be able to optimize your profit by raising the price to the level at which your last carrot sells to the last buyer willing to pay such a price. This is a 'flexprice' market.

But there are products which have to sell for shorter or longer periods at fixed prices. There are brand-named, widely advertised items like particular makes and models of cars, computers, refrigerators, audio and video systems, and other fixed-price items like books, records, rail and bus fares, postal and telephone charges which buyers may be reluctant to buy or retailers may

refuse to stock if the producers don't stick to their advertised prices. If demand for these 'fixprice' goods is slack, prices don't immediately fall. Instead, unsold goods pile up in warehouses. The signal to reduce output is rising stocks rather than falling prices. Similarly if demand outruns supply, prices do not rise. Instead, unfilled orders accumulate to prompt more production. If supply and demand are brought back into balance, it is by adjusting the quantities supplied, rather than the prices.

Briefly: in flexprice markets, *price* changes adjust supply and demand to each other. In fixprice markets they are adjusted by changes in the *quantity* produced. So they are sometimes called, even more briefly, p and q markets.

Notice that there can be price setters or takers in both kinds of market. A publisher prices each book in a fixprice market; a carrot-grower decides her prices in a flexprice market; they are both price setters. One farmer is a price taker in a flexprice wool market, another may be a price taker in a fixprice market if the government has fixed grain prices, or the local cannery offers fixed prices for all standard quality fruit.

This chapter will mostly focus on price setters: firms which do have to decide their products' prices. But price takers have to do much the same analysis as they decide what to produce for sale at prevailing prices. Price setters may calculate 'forwards' from their costs of production to the prices they need to charge. Price takers may calculate 'backwards' from the expected prices to decide what quantities it will pay to produce at what cost. In both types of market it remains true that products have costs of production, and selling prices. If the price is above the cost, the producer makes a profit; if the price is below the cost the producer makes a loss.

You know (from Chapter 31) why it is not always easy to decide a product's true cost. It is not always easy to know in advance the price elasticity of demand for a product. So with varying degrees of certainty about their costs and the likely demand for their products, how do price setters arrive at their prices, and price takers decide what to produce for sale at prevailing prices?

First they need to know their costs. So do you. Chapter 31 on cost analysis opened with a warning that you might need to read it more than once. Revise it now if you need to, to be sure you know what is meant by fixed and variable costs, total cost, average unit cost and marginal unit cost. Then learn a simple bit of theory:

MARGINAL COST PRICING

In certain conditions a firm will maximize profit if the marginal cost of its last unit equals the marginal revenue from selling that unit.

To grasp the principle and its limitations, consider four examples: two in which its application is simple, one in which it is less simple, and one in which it does not apply at all.

A price taker in a competitive industry Suppose you own and operate a quarry. You blast out the rock, crush it into roadmetal, and sell it at the prevailing price of $60 a ton, a price which is not affected by the amount you supply. Your plant is like the 'older plant' in Chapter 33: marginal costs of production fall as output increases up to the point at which one shift of workers is fully employed. Beyond that, overtime and other extras mean that further output has rising marginal costs. So you have U-shaped costs, a level price, and level marginal revenue. If you sell 80 tons a week at q1 there is more profit to be made by producing 20 more to make 100 (q2) altogether. But beyond that, each additional ton costs more than the revenue it earns, and reduces the week's profit. In this example, notice that marginal price equals marginal revenue: the whole price of the last ton you sell is added to your total revenue.

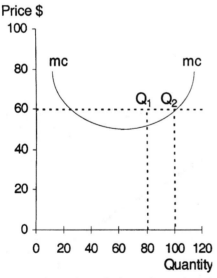

Figure 34.1 Price and marginal cost for a price taker in a competitive industry.

A flexprice price setter You have dug 100 kilos of carrots and trucked them to market. You have managed to sell 90 kilos at $2 a kilo, but it is late in the day and the last 10 kilos do not look like selling. You reckon their marginal cost of production (mostly in sweat!) is about $1 a kilo, but that cost will increase sharply if you have to truck them home then bring them back again next market day. So you drop the price to $1.50 and sell eight kilos, then find buyers for the last two at $1 each. On those last two the price equals the marginal cost of production. And – as in your quarrying business – price also equals marginal revenue: the $14 you get for the last 10 kilos is all gain.

The next example will show why we keep drawing your attention to the relation between price and marginal revenue.

A fixprice price setter You make fine furniture. Competitors cannot lawfully pirate your designs but they have good designs of their own so it is a competitive industry, and both for the industry and for each firm there is considerable price elasticity of demand. So how you price your chairs affects the quantities you can sell. As in our quarrying and carrot-growing enterprises, you are equipped to make a particular number of chairs without resorting to overtime rates or less efficient labor, so you have U-shaped costs. But your chairs are widely advertised and have to sell at their advertised prices. So the price of the last chair you sell – the marginal unit of output – has to be the price of all the chairs of that model that you sell. That fixprice requirement means that – unlike your roadmetal and carrot sales – marginal revenue may not equal price.

Marginal cost pricing when marginal revenue differs from marginal price *Definition:* Marginal revenue is the difference which selling one more unit makes to total revenue.

In a flexprice market, that may be the same as the price of the marginal unit: when you sell your last kilo of carrots for $1, the sale adds $1 to total revenue. Price equals marginal revenue.

When you sell your last ton of roadmetal at a fixprice which does not vary with the amount you sell – i.e. when the demand curve you face is horizontal – price equals marginal revenue.

But in a fixprice market in which *the price you fix will affect the quantity you can sell,* price may not equal marginal revenue, and will not do so if you face a 'normal', i.e. downsloping, demand curve. Suppose your market research suggests that the price elasticity of demand for your product is such that at a price of $600 per unit you will be able to sell 3 units, but at $500 you will sell 4. Three at $600 brings a total revenue of $1800. Four at $500 bring $2000. Though the price of the marginal fourth unit is $500 it only increases total revenue by $200, because to get that fourth sale the fixprice of the first three units *also* has to come down.

Suppose the full market analysis predicts that this product will only be acceptable on a fixprice basis, and that you can sell –

	1	unit	at	$800
or	2	units	at	$700
or	3		at	$600
or	4		at	$500
or	5		at	$400
or	6		at	$300

Add a column for total revenue at each price, and derive the marginal revenue for each additional unit -

Quantity	Unit Price $	Total Revenue $	Marginal Revenue $
1	800	00	800
2	700	1400	600
3	600	1800	400
4	500	2000	200
5	400	2000	0
6	300	1800	-200

Notice that the quantity and price columns together are the demand schedule for the product; and (by definition, with a fixprice product) the price represents the average revenue at each level of output.

Now graph the demand schedule and the marginal revenue as in Figure 34.2.

Next, bring forward the information about costs of production depicted in Figure 31.2 back on page 391. You were not to know it, but that is the cost analysis of your chair-making business. You can now compare total cost and total revenue at each price-and-output level -

Quantity	x	Total Price $	=	Total Revenue $	–	Total Cost $	=	Profit $
1	x	800	=	800	–	900	=	-100
2	x	700	=	1400	–	1000	=	400
3	x	600	=	1800	–	1050	=	750
4	x	500	=	2000	–	1200	=	800
5	x	400	=	2000	–	1500	=	500
6	x	300	=	1800	–	2000	=	-200

Four units at $500 yields most profit. Now bring together on a graph the average and marginal revenue curves from our demand schedule and the average and marginal cost curves from Figure 31.2's cost analysis –

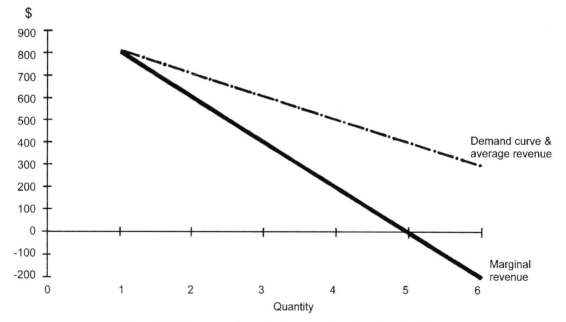

Figure 34.2 Average and marginal revenue for a fixprice price taker

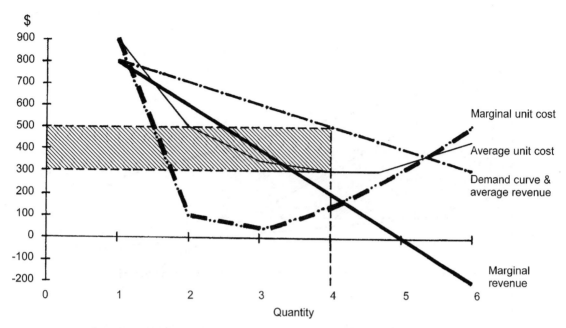

Figure 34.3: Pricing for maximum profit on a fixprice product with U-shaped costs.

The shaded area indicates the maximum profit available. The *marginal* cost and revenue curves show *where* the maximum profit will be (i.e. at an output of 4 units, where marginal cost and revenue cross); the *average* cost and revenue curves show *what* that profit will be (4 units x $200 = $800). The arithmetic of the table is the easiest way to see what the maximum profit is, and at what output. The geometry of the graph shows *why* the maximum profit is available at that output.

For a reason which will appear when we deal with monopoly pricing, the virtues of marginal cost pricing are usually illustrated, as in Figure 34.3, for products with U-shaped costs. But not all products have U-shaped costs of production. Some have continuous economies of scale: the more you produce, the cheaper they come. Books are a good example. To print a book there are fixed costs for the printing and binding machinery and for setting the type. There are then variable costs (for paper, ink, labor, etc.) which tend to be level – i..e. the same per unit – however many copies of the book you roll off. The more you print, the less fixed cost each copy has to carry, so with level variable costs and declining fixed cost, marginal cost continues to decline for as long a print run as any book is likely to need. With a normal demand curve (the lower the

fixprice, the more you can sell) marginal revenue is likely to decline more steeply than marginal cost, and for maximum profit you should stop printing where the two curves cross. Turn to Figure 34.4 for the demand/average revenue curve, the marginal revenue curve and the average and marginal cost curves, for the paperback edition of your forthcoming fascinating, violent, sexually explicit, fantastically successful first novel. Maximum profit is 500,000 x $9 = $4,500,000 at a wholesale price of $15.

(Before you start spending it, that is not your profit, it is the publishers' profit. They must be big publishers to be able to operate on this half-million scale. They dealt with you as an unknown author of a first novel. The bargaining strengths were so unequal that they got you to accept paperback royalties at 5 per cent of wholesale price. The publishers' paperback profit is $4,500,000. Your royalty is 500,000 x 75 cents = $375,000. But don't complain too bitterly. This book has established you as a best-selling author. For your next, half the publishers in town will bid against each other, the market strengths will be reversed, you will be into royalties of 10 and 15 per cent, on retail rather than wholesale price. Then there are serial rights, film rights, video royalties ...)

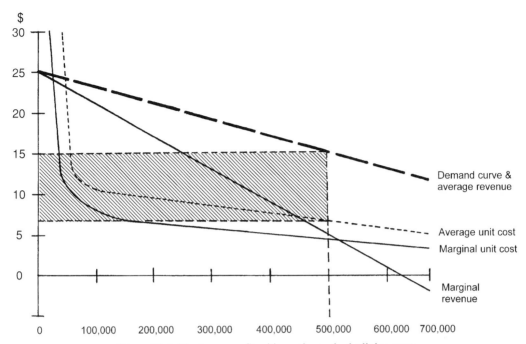

Figure 34.4: Maximum profit with continuously declining costs

Real products and costs are rarely as simple as our examples have been. Marginal analysis can be difficult, uncertain, and expensive to do. If for pricing purposes it has to be done in advance, it means that costs, revenues and the elasticity of demand for the product are not facts but forecasts. Especially for firms which produce many or frequently changing products, or flexprice products, it may not be worthwhile, or helpful at all, to require marginal analyses in advance for each product and for every change in market conditions. So as a method of deciding prices and quantities it is not much used in real business. The commonest alternative is mark-up pricing.

MARK-UP PRICING

Mark-up pricing starts with the variable cost of each unit of product, and adds two percentages: one for the fixed cost that the product should carry, and the other for profit. All three figures may have to be rough, especially for fixprice products which may have to be priced before most of them are produced. Variable costs can change with changing conditions and material prices. The share of fixed costs which each unit carries may vary with the number produced. The optimum rate of profit may depend on forecasts of the elasticity of demand. So – as with marginal analysis – mark-up prices may sometimes have to be based more on forecasts than on facts.

Whenever marginal revenue is less than price, mark-up pricing can lose money. Return to Figure 34.3 and consider producing a fifth unit for sale at the price indicated for five units on the demand/average revenue curve. It looks as if you could produce it at a marginal cost of $240 and mark it up 66 per cent to sell for $400 with $160 profit. But the marginal revenue curve for this fixprice product tells you that marginal revenue from a fifth unit will be zero, so the $240 cost of producing it will be pure loss. Even if marginal analysis cannot usefully be done in advance to set prices, it may be worth applying it to actual sales from time to time to check that the alternative price-setting methods are not concealing losses or reductions of potential profit.

All the argument so far has assumed that the price and output decisions aim at maximum short-term profit. When firms have other purposes, they may apply other pricing principles. We will look in turn at target return pricing, product package pricing, and various kinds of strategic and predatory pricing.

TARGET RETURN PRICING

A firm, especially one which makes many products and introduces many new ones, may adopt a pricing policy rather like the Swedish wage policy described earlier. Where Sweden said 'We will only have industries which can pay standard wages', a firm may say 'We will only produce products which return a standard rate of profit'. A firm may specify a minimum rate of profit on turnover, or a minimum rate of return to funds employed, and price its products to yield those rates. It may then continue to produce products which do so, but not those which do not. Such a rule for deciding which products to continue and which to discontinue may be the purpose of target return pricing. Another purpose may be to accumulate profit at a particular rate to finance a particular program of capital growth or re-equipment internally, i.e. from earnings, without borrowing or issuing new shares. A third purpose may be to set fair prices. A monopolist who does not wish – or does not dare – to exploit his monopoly for maximum profit, or a government authority which exists to regulate monopolists' prices, may do so by prescribing a particular rate of mark-up, or of return to funds employed. (More about monopoly pricing presently.)

PACKAGE PRICING

Suppose you want to export Saab cars from Sweden. Your marketing manager will tell you that Saab buyers may differ somewhat from country to country, but in English-speaking countries they want something more than the efficient transport which they could achieve more economically with a basic Ford. They want some material things – comfort, performance, gadgetry, the purest sound system on wheels. But more even than those, they want to be seen as Saab drivers: to be perceived as youngish, successful, discriminating, stylish exponents of a quietly dressed and understated excellence, shrewdly priced without the ostentatious extravagance of fat men in Mercedes – and with a whiff of danger from memories of the deadly Saab fighter planes. To project that image requires a package of qualities, one of which is price. The price must of course cover costs and yield some profit, but it must also *limit* sales (this car is for rare spirits only) and discreetly reveal the drivers' capacity to pay – or to make their firms pay – for such exquisite machinery.

There are more modest products whose prices are similarly, in one way or another, 'part of the package'. If products are difficult to judge at the point of sale (which toaster will work best, which tyre will last longest, which wine will taste best?) buyers may take price as an indicator of quality. Economic theory cannot predict when higher prices will increase rather than reduce sales; you need to understand the buyers' problems and reasoning in each case.

Another kind of package pricing may occur when buyers want not a package of qualities in one product, but a package of products. It is worth selling Barbie Dolls for next to nothing if it hooks their owners onto buying them expensive new outfits at frequent intervals. Basic model train sets, building sets, game-playing home computers, tape and CD players may be worth selling at or below cost if those who supply them also supply their add-ons. The ultimate example is drug addiction: it pays to give free heroin if it addicts new paying customers.

Some of these examples may alternatively belong under later headings as cases of strategic or exploitive pricing.

MONOPOLY PRICING

Monopolists are widely disliked because – compared with competitive producers – they are thought likely to work less efficiently, have higher costs, be less attentive to their customers' wants, produce less output, price it higher, and make excessive profits. The general merits of competition and monopoly are for other chapters. Here we deal only with how monopolists price their products.

Pricing policies vary with market conditions, the elasticity of demand for the product, and the monopolist's purposes. To indicate a range of policies we will consider (i) a profit-maximizing monopolist who must charge a fixed price to all customers; (ii) a profit-maximizing monopolist who can charge different customers different prices; and some reasons why (iii) some monopolists may choose not to maximize profit, and (iv) some may charge lower prices than competitive suppliers would charge.

A fixprice monopolist makes most profit, just as a competitive supplier does, by producing the amount at which marginal cost equals marginal revenue. Turn back to Figure 34-3, 'Pricing for maximum profit on a fixprice product with U-shaped costs'. If the demand curve represents the whole demand for a monopolist product, maximum profit will come by producing 4 units.

However, monopolies more often exist where firms have continuous economies of scale rather than U-shaped costs. With continuous economies of scale, the more a firm produces the lower its unit costs are, and the lower the price at which it can sell its products if it behaves competitively. The biggest firm in an industry can thus undersell its competitors and, if other conditions allow, drive them out of business and establish a monopoly. So the demand, revenue and cost curves of monopolies tend to be as depicted in Figure 34-4, 'Maximum profit with continuously declining costs'.

Observing where marginal cost crosses marginal revenue, a fixprice monopolist does best by selling 500,000 books at $15 each. A bigger output at a lower price can still be profitable, but the profit dwindles as output increases (because this is a fixprice product, so every reduction of price to attract additional buyers cuts the price to *all* buyers.)

Suppose that the book in question is more wholesome than your steamy novel. It is a brilliantly wise and persuasive new compendium of popular health advice. Consider how its monopolist publisher might alternatively price it:

*   **A profit maximizer** sells 500,000 copies at $15 for $4,500,000 profit.

*   **A strategist** wants to sell the book to as many readers as possible in order to maximize demand for, and profit on, this author's future books. But the firm's shareholders want a reasonable profit on every book at least comparable with competitive profit rates. The strategist settles for 800,000 copies at $8.75 for a profit of $2,600,000.

*   **A government publisher** is advised by the Minister for Health not to give the book away (which would cost too much money, and perhaps get the book taken less seriously) but to sell as many as can be sold without actual loss. That is a million at $5.

Those are fixprice options. There are different possibilities if the supplier can charge different prices to different buyers.

Flexprice monopolists Some goods and services do not have to sell at the same price to all comers. Price-setters may be able to discriminate between different groups of buyers for various reasons –

*   For some products it may be possible to sell at a high price to everyone willing to pay that price, then drop the price to attract more buyers, without annoying the first buyers enough to drive them out of the market next time around.

*   It may be possible to make small differences of quality to justify big differences in price. Airlines and opera houses charge very different prices for their best and worst seats.

*   People may accept some formal discrimination as fair, as when children or pensioners are charged different fares or admission prices.

In its usual fixprice meaning the demand curve in Figure 34.5 signifies that at $5 each you can sell a million units, at $15 you could only sell half a million, and at $25 you could only sell one. In a perfect flexprice market, by contrast, you could in principle produce a million units and proceed to sell the first for $25, the second for

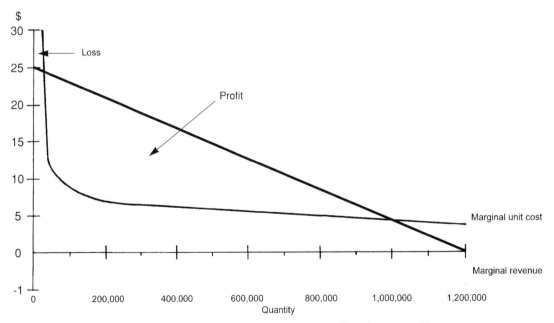

Figure 34-5 Price and profit opportunities of a flexprice monopolist

$24.99, the third for $24.98 and so on down the demand curve. In practice that would be impossible, but suppliers can often discriminate in a rougher way by 'stepping' the fixprices of successive batches of the product. Thus the publisher depicted in Figure 34-5 might sell 50,000 copies of an expensive hardback (for which the demand is not graphed in that Figure) alongside 450,000 quality paperbacks at $15, to be followed later by 400,000 cheaper pocketbooks at $7.50, and eventually 100,000 unsold remainders at $5 each. Instead of 'perfect' flexpricing there are thus four fixprice batches, with their price differences made acceptable by some differences in quality; and instead of *either* breaking even with a million copies, *or* depriving half the customers altogether by maximizing monopoly profit on half a million, the publisher can sell a million copies at a total profit well above the maximum $4,500,000 available in a strict fixprice market.

Where price discrimination is possible, monopoly pricing can usually be *either* more profitable *or* more socially sensitive and helpful (and sometimes both) than it can be in strict fixprice markets.

STRATEGIC PRICING

'Strategic' can describe almost any pricing policy with long-term purposes. Examples:

- A firm invents a new product. The development costs have been heavy. The public reception of the product is difficult to predict: it may sell to few or many buyers. If it proves popular it will take competitors a year or two to develop equivalent products, so it will have a temporary monopoly. One strategy is to exploit the monopoly by introducing the product at a high price, to recover the development costs as quickly as possible. If the market reception encourages large-scale production the price can then be lowered as costs decline and as competitive products begin to appear from firms which have yet to recover their development costs and achieve comparable economies of scale.

- A firm introduces not a new product but a new model – for example a new 'model line' of cars. The line will eventually include a basically-equipped low-powered version, higher-powered luxury versions, a convertible and a family wagon. Should the maker launch the basic model first, then (when its popularity is established) offer up-market variants at higher prices as the initial buyers of the basic model are ready to trade up to something a little better?

(This has been a common Ford and Honda strategy, for example.) Or would it be better to start by selling the top-of-the-range to the richest group of buyers to establish high prestige, then offer lower-priced versions which carry the prestige established by the market leader? (Mercedes, Rover and others have used such a strategy.) The best strategy in each case will depend on judgments – by hunch, experience or expensive market research – of the thoughts and feelings of the relevant customers.

- A firm enters a new national market with products – like cars, domestic equipment, tools of trade, pharmaceutical drugs – whose reception will depend partly on the reputation of the firm. The modern Japanese penetration of export markets is a good example. It may be prudent to spend some years (or decades) selling at low prices to attract buyers to products whose quality and durability can only be discovered by experience over time. When those qualities have been established in the customers' own experience, prices can be adjusted to yield normal profits and eventually perhaps some premium for well-earned reputation.

Those and other 'life-cycle' strategies tend to come from big, financially secure firms which can afford to forgo immediate returns for long-term purposes. Where the pricing is actually below cost, and the purpose is not only to attract or hold particular customers but also to weaken, ruin or take over particular competitors, the strategy may fairly be described as predatory.

Predatory pricing

Suppose that you are a big firm aiming at monopoly. A competitor appears, with good products at competitive prices. The competitor is a smaller, younger firm than you, with shallower financial resources. Being smaller, they own less property and equipment than you do. Being younger, they have not yet paid for it all and are as far in debt as the banks are likely to let them go. They are biting into your market, but their size and financial situation make them vulnerable. What can you do?

On products which compete with theirs you step up your advertising and drop your prices to undersell them. They must either lose sales, or lose money by competitive advertising and price-cutting. You run the prices down below cost. You have the financial resources to lose more, for longer, than they can afford to lose. If you do not need their patents or other assets you can simply drive them out of the market, or out of business altogether. If you do want what they have got (patents, designs, productive equipment, skilled staff, retail outlets) you can increase their losses and reduce their share prices until their owners accept a low-priced take-over offer. When the company is out of business or in your possession you can resume monopoly pricing and recoup your temporary losses. Besides disposing of one competitor you may well have deterred others. In many countries you will have broken the law and risked an anti-trust or trade practices prosecution. But the line between hotly competitive and anti-competitive behavior is not always easy to draw, or to prove in court. You may well get away with your misbehavior, especially if a successful takeover has left the shareholders of both firms happy.

Price-cutting is generally defined as predatory, rather than legitimately competitive or strategic, if it is (i) below cost, (ii) temporary, and (iii) designed to injure particular competitors or takeover targets, rather than merely to attract a larger share of a competitive market. What should government do about it? It is not practical for the law to ban any and all selling at a loss. There will always be firms which miscalculate their costs, or the demand for their products, or the inroads of their competitors, and find themselves with stock they cannot sell at profitable prices. It is better for both producers and consumers to sell such stock at a loss than not to sell it at all. Those and other innocent necessities make it difficult to distinguish predatory pricing from legitimate competition and business losses, and to design and enforce effective laws against it.

Dumping

'Dumping' is sometimes used to describe any low-priced sale of surplus produce, but its main use is international. Producers are said to be dumping if they sell the same product at a lower price abroad than at home, especially if they do it persistently, deliberately producing a flow of goods for the purpose. To discriminate in that way between home and foreign buyers they usually need some protection of their home market by tariff or other means, so that their home customers cannot buy the product abroad at the export price and re-import it. Firms which are hurt by dumping accordingly object to both the dumpers and the government which protects them. They may ask their own governments for reciprocal protection, perhaps by 'countervailing duties'. Those are tariffs which are designed to raise the price of imports not *above* competitive market prices but *up* to competitive market prices. They are justified if imported products are priced below cost, or are subsidized by the exporters' government.

When dumping is systematic, i.e. is not merely a disposal of an unintended surplus, why do firms do it? Why produce goods to sell at a loss, or at no profit? There may be economies of scale, predatory purposes, or effects on employment or on national balances of trade and payment. Notice them in turn:

Scale Steel, aluminium, trucks, cars and some other goods have to be produced in very large quantities to achieve maximum economies of scale. If an industry's home market is not big enough to absorb the minimum efficient quantity, the industry may cope by exporting enough to achieve the necessary scale. If it cannot do that because it cannot match the competitive prices in the export markets it may still be able to survive by dual pricing. If its home market is protected it can set a home price to sell (say) half its output at double profit, while dropping its export price to sell the other half at cost, with no profit.

By that arrangement the home consumers may appear to pay too high a price – but it may not be as high as they would pay without the dumping if the protected industry, having only its home market, had to operate on an inefficiently small scale. Suppose for example that a small country's only steelmaker has such fixed costs that if it supplies only its home demand its average cost of production is $2000 a ton. If it can double that output the cost comes down to $1400 which (allowing for transport costs) happens also to be the competitive export price. At a 10 per cent profit mark-up, if the home buyers are the only buyers they must pay $2200 a ton and (allowing for transport costs) protect their steel industry with a tariff duty of $700 a ton, i.e. 50 per cent on the international price. But if the local steelmaker can double its output by exporting half the output at cost, while maintaining an average profit of 10 per cent by doubling the mark-up on home sales to 20 per cent, the home customers can buy steel for $1680 a ton, only $180 or 12 per cent above the price at which (allowing for transport costs) they could import their steel. Government and people may well think that the national advantages of possessing a steel industry (defence, employment, skills, balance of payments) are worth a premium of 12 per cent, but not 46 per cent. The country's trading partners may tolerate a 15 per cent tariff without reprisal where they would not tolerate 50 per cent. Some countries with steelmakers of their own may impose 12 or 15 per cent of countervailing duty on our country's steel exports, but there are plenty of countries which do not make steel and are happy to buy it at 'dump' prices.

Thus dumping, in some conditions, may be advantageous for producers, the countries which protect them, and some of their export customers. But not all dumping is as defensible as that.

Employment Dumping can happen because other policies misfire. Recall the multiple purposes of Europe's Common Agricultural Policy. It was designed to improve farm productivity and enable Europe to feed itself. With limited farmable land, that could best be achieved (along with some other purposes) by maximizing output per hectare rather than per worker or per dollar invested. Rising productivity would bring rural standards of living closer to city standards, especially by improving the incomes of farmers and farm workers. It should thus reduce the drift of population to the cities where (with urban industries shedding labor) there might not be enough employment. Finally the policy should conserve the best of the traditional rural life and landscape for their own sakes and for highly valued artistic and recreational reasons. The policy-makers hoped that when the technical and economic reforms were complete, rural life could thereafter be protected and sustained by a low tariff and quite modest subsidies.

But the technical reforms over-succeeded. European agriculture developed surplus output beyond European needs. There were wine lakes, grain and butter mountains. To keep the rural population employed and reasonably rewarded the surplus had to be exported. Its labor-intensive and capital-intensive production had such costs that not much of it could profitably sell at world prices. Export prices had to be subsidized – however costly, some return for the cost of producing the surplus was better than none. Hence a paradox: instead of the farm subsidies declining as productivity improved, they had to increase to subsidize the export of the increasing surplus. By 1990 the subsidy per ton of Europe's grain exports was higher than the whole production cost per ton of Australia's (unsubsidized) grain exports. The fury of foreign farmers, the massive American countervailing subsidies and the general diplomatic stress were understandable.

But villages and landscapes which foreign tourists love as intensely as Europeans do are sustained at double cost (through export subsidies and high food prices) by the Europeans themselves. It is hard to believe (as foreign critics tend to do) that those costs are forced on unwilling majorities by nothing but the political strength of farmers who are nowhere as many as 10 per cent of the voters. Plenty of Europe's urban voters seem to know what they are doing and do it willingly enough: their taxes and food prices buy them continuing access to some of the world's most loved and celebrated countryside, and help to sustain a tourist industry from which even more town- than country-dwellers profit.

Foreign exchange If a nation's producers and consumers choose to spend more on imports than their exports can pay for, there are various ways of coping with the consequent shortage of foreign exchange. The most uncontroversially virtuous course is to increase exports by competitive means. But if the nation's would-be exporters cannot manage that (for reasons of scale, wage levels, transport or other costs, capital inadequacy, poor management), government may decide to bring their export prices down by subsidizing them. Or they may protect their home markets by tariff to allow high prices at home to finance dumping abroad, as described earlier. Both methods deserve to be called dumping and may be unfair to the foreign producers with whom the dumpers compete. But although not the best, they may not be the worst ways of coping with exchange imbalances. In effect the community which provides the subsidies taxes itself, or pays high prices, to maintain access to the imports it wants, and to provide for some of its members who would otherwise be unemployed.

The merits and demerits of other ways of coping with unbalanced trade and payments are for later chapters.

WAGE AND PROFIT SHARES

This item belongs in any one of half a dozen chapters, because it links wages, prices, profit mark-ups, and questions of market strength both between employers and workers and between producers and consumers. Here is as good a place for it as any.

The whole revenue from the sale of an economy's marketed goods and services can be divided into a wage share, consisting of all payments for labor, and a profit share, consisting of payments for the use of capital. At first sight you cannot divide a firm's revenue like that, because its selling prices have to cover other costs besides wage costs and the costs of its capital. It also pays for materials, component parts and other inputs from other firms. But each of those inputs, if you track it back, has ultimately been priced according to its wage costs and its capital costs, including profit mark-ups to pay shareholders for the use of their capital. The costs and mark-ups and pricing are likely to vary from firm to firm and from industry to industry along the way. But for the process as a whole, from raw materials to finished goods, it is in principle possible to separate the rewards to labor (the wage share) from the rewards to capital (the profit share).

Remember how complex modern production can be. Dozens of firms may have contributed materials, components or services to any finished product, each firm pricing its contribution according to its particular labor costs, capital costs, and market strength in relation to its workers, suppliers, sources of capital, and customers. The mark-ups at every stage, (including, as you will presently see, mark-ups on mark-ups) accumulate to determine the economy's total wage and profit shares.

The following simple illustration yields a 70/30 wage/profit split. Real figures tend to be within a few percentage points of those. Does that mean that most firms are marking prices up 42.8 per cent above costs, which is the mark-up that produces a 70/30 split? No. Consider a product which goes through four processes from raw material to finished product, each done by a different firm. Each firm buys material or a part-finished product, works on it, and sells it on to the next, or finally to the consumer. For simplicity, the example assumes (unrealistically) that each firm has the same wage costs and costs of capital. But their profit mark-ups vary from 5 to 15 per cent on their costs, for reasons of market strength or weakness. Here are their accounts per unit of output:

	Miner	Steelmaker	Manufacturer	Retailer
	$	$	$	$
Purchases	–	11	22.05	36.85
Costs of capital	1	1	1	1
Wages	9	9	9	9
Total Cost	10	21	32.05	46.85
Profit mark-up	10% =1	5% =1.05	15% =4.80	10% =4.68
Selling price	11	22.05	36.85	51.53

Those are the firms' accounts. Put them together and you find that of the final unit price of $51.53 the wage share is $36 and the total profit share (rent, interest and profit mark-ups for all the capital contributors) is $15.53. The wage share is roughly 70 per cent and the profit share roughly 30 per cent of the market value of output.

Notice how low profit mark-ups by firms can produce a high profit share overall. Each firm adds its mark-up to *all* costs: not only its own wage and rent and interest costs, but also the wage and profit elements in the prices it pays others for its inputs. So – for example – the miners' wages are marked up four times, and the mine-owner's profit mark-up is marked up three more times, before the finished product is priced and sold.

The wage share has varied over time and from country to country with the changing capital and labor intensity of production, and with the changing bargaining strength of the parties. Remember that each of the parties exercises market strength (or weakness) twice. Firms contend with their workers over wage rates, and they contend with their customers (and ultimately with the final buyers of finished products) over the mark-ups and prices that the market will bear. Remember also that workers and consumers are mostly the same people (or their dependants), and their material standards depend on relations between the wages they earn and the prices they pay. The current decline of wage shares in most English-speaking countries reflects a shift of bargaining strength from workers to their employers. But Japanese workers suffer similar effects from higher-than-Western prices which they pay, especially for many necessities, when they spend their higher-than-Western wages.

PUBLIC POLICY

Public influence on prices will concern you repeatedly in this course of study, especially in relation to economic structure, trade, employment, taxation and inflation. Here we merely summarize common ends and means of price policy, many of which you will deal with in more detail later.

Purposes Government may wish to influence private-sector prices, upwards or downwards, for any of a variety of reasons:

- To raise tax revenue

- To restrain inflation

- To protect particular industries – for any of the reasons noted earlier – by raising the price of the imports with which they compete

- To protect consumers, and/or the efficient allocation of resources, from ill effects of monopoly or collusive or predatory pricing

- To restrain prices, especially of necessities, when supplies are interrupted and shortages induced by war, natural disaster or other non-market causes

- To ration scarce goods, when it is thought that rationing by price would be inefficient or inequitable

- To discourage harmful processes or harmful products by raising their prices

- To conserve non-renewable resources whose use is not sufficiently discouraged by competitive pricing – for example to reduce the unnecessary use of petroleum.

Methods Government may influence private prices by:

- Import duties, quotas, prohibitions
- Export taxes or subsidies
- General or selective sales taxes, value-added taxes, taxes on pollutant products or processes
- Payroll taxes and other taxes, licence fees or charges on factors of production
- Pricing public inputs to private production
- Price surveillance and consumer protection services to encourage competitive pricing
- Price controls
- Prohibiting the existence of monopoly in potentially competitive industries
- Prohibiting monopolist or collusive pricing or restriction of output.

Most of those methods can be used well or badly with better or worse effect, and there may be disagreement about which effects are better or worse. Critics will say 'Interfering with market prices is likely to preempt the citizens' choices and distort the allocation of resources; and the possibility of getting government to do it invites self-interested lobbying and corruption.' Defenders may say 'Monopoly pricing is not efficient. It is not efficient for later generations to let the present generation squander scarce resources. It is not necessarily "undistorted" to let the producers of alcohol, tobacco and artificial energy price their addictive products for maximum consumption.' And so on – you know all sides of those arguments by now. Any public influence on private sector prices needs to be judged in context, in relation to its purposes and to any other policies which the price measures are designed to support.

35

How firms invest

Investment plans are partly technical: what buildings, machines, vehicles, materials and skills will we use to produce what quantities of what product? And they are partly financial: what will those items cost, how will we pay for them, how much will they earn? This chapter is about the economics rather than the technology. How are the economic elements of investment decisions taken?

This chapter is about some standard ways of appraising investment prospects, and deciding which of them to undertake. But there is first a question whether standard ways of appraising investment possibilities are worth having.

GIGO ?

GIGO is computertalk for Garbage In, Garbage Out: if you feed inaccurate facts or forecasts into the machine, no amount of sophisticated processing will get accurate forecasts out.

Question: Is investment planning like that? Why use exact methods of appraising alternative uses of capital if what the methods process is chiefly inexact guesswork about future costs and prices?

Answer: Directors may have any of five reasons for using formal methods of investment appraisal even though those methods must often depend on uncertain forecasting:

1. Some forecasting is reliable enough. If a property developer builds an office tower to lease to government, or a shopping centre for retailers who sign long-term leases before the investment is committed, then the costs and revenues can be forecast, and the development options compared, accurately enough.

2. Even if future costs and prices are uncertain, careful comparisons between projects based on uncertain forecasts may still be better than careless comparisons based on the same forecasts.

3. Where the directors of a firm are not bossed by a single owner or dominant leader, they may find it hard to reach agreement about intrinsically risky investment options. Established methods of expert appraisal which produce clear bottom-line ranking of alternative proposals may offer a welcome basis of agreement, even when uncertain forecasting means

that there is not much ground for confidence in the appraisals. In other words, if directors have no better grounds for agreement they may agree to use established appraisal procedures as a convenient arbitrator, or a dignified alternative to tossing a coin.

4. Investment decisions necessarily take risks with other people's futures: with owners' money, workers' jobs, directors' reputations. In case of failure or poor performance directors may want to be able to show that they took the relevant decisions in the most responsible possible way, using orthodox, widely accepted methods of investment appraisal. 'Don't blame us, blame the machine.' 'We took every known state-of-the-art precaution: nobody could have done more.'

5. Measures of past and present performance of existing investments can be used to judge and rank the performance of firms and individuals. So even if exact methods of investment appraisal have doubtful value as decision-making devices, they may still be used retrospectively for comparing the track records of different strategies or decision-makers and deciding which of them to trust next time.

Those are reasons for using standard methods of investment appraisal even when they promise no sure advantages over guesswork, hunches, astrology, or bullish entrepreneurial imagination. But as we now introduce some standard methods, remember that they are no better than the market forecasts they have to use. It was not by methods like these that Ford, Xerox, IBM, Microsoft or other famously successful investors made their way to the top – though once up there, the orthodox methods may sometimes help them to stay there.

In practice most approaches to investment decisions lie somewhere between the following two extremes:

Joe Blow, jobless, with his redundancy cheque in his pocket, sick of working for a boss, is drowning his sorrows in his local bar when he meets an old acquaintance who is celebrating *getting* a job. 'What's happening to your old mower?' (The acquaintance has been earning by contract lawn-mowing.) 'I'll flog it if I can find a sucker.' 'Whaddya want for it?' 'It's worth two hundred, so I'd accept four.' 'One.' 'Three.' 'Does the trailer come with it?' 'Yep.' 'What's the customer list like? 'There's forty. Mostly suburban lawns once a fortnight. Pulls in about four hundred a week. There's fuel, of course, and you need a stone to keep the blades sharp.' 'Two hundred, then.' 'It's yours.' Having thus perceived a business opportunity, appraised it, estimated its operating costs and returns and invested in the necessary goodwill and fixed capital, Joe is in business. Meanwhile in more expensive premises, and taking rather longer to get through the same procedures,

Mark $. Kronenthaler, Vice-President for Corporate Strategy at Delaware Megacorp, is revising the investment planning division of his corporate plan. Years ago, the plan was a 200-page book updated and reprinted annually. Now that it is on computer it can be revised daily and screen-read, E-mailed or printed-out on demand. It is thus a daily-adaptable manifest of the firm's intentions, both in aggregate, and articulated into sectional programs and targets for each of the firm's functional divisions. For the development division, the plan details current investment projects. To allow the most-advantageous financing of each of them, the machine also taps 24-hour information services on share prices, bond and bank interest rates and exchange rates in each of the world's major financial centres, and 'Delphi' distillations of the short-, medium- and long-term forecasts of general economic conditions by a dozen of the world's leading economic forecasters.

(There is mounting evidence that computerizing the accounting and planning processes, and multiplying the amount and accessibility of the information they can tap, is steadily reducing the productivity per head of Megacorp's workforce, chiefly by trebling the amount each manager believes he needs to know before each decision, and loading each productive blue-collar worker with two white-collar planners and monitors and information-shufflers. But we will ignore that problem for the moment, as Mark $. Kronenthaler has been doing for some years.)

We can leave Joe Blow's business to his common sense, and Megacorp's complexities to Kronenthaler's worldwide satellite-linked instant-access network of information and expertise. Most firms operate somewhere between those extremes. For those which apply any formal appraisal to their investment decisions, we will now outline some common approaches to (i) financing research and invention to generate investment projects, (ii) appraising the projects to decide which if any of them to undertake, and (iii) deciding how much investment altogether to undertake.

RESEARCH, INVENTION AND DEVELOPMENT

With some exceptions (for example in electronics and pharmaceuticals and market research) most of the world's scientific and social research is financed from public rather than private sources. It is done in universities, research institutions, defence establishments, hospitals, bureaux of census and statistics. Public bodies also commission and pay for some of the research that private firms do.

But discoveries need a lot of adaptation to productive purposes. Firms have to do most of that. In most industries, firms (publicly or privately owned) invent and develop most new products and new methods of production. So in many firms and industries financial provisions have to be made for 'Research and Development' (R & D), though a better label would include 'Invention' too.

Manufacturers, who do a good deal of the private sector's R & D, want answers to many particular questions of these general kinds:

- Who buys our products and our competitors' products, and why?
- Could different marketing sell more of our current products, or cut our marketing costs, or both?
- What new designs or products are our competitors developing?
- What new designs or products might we develop?
- How can we improve our productive processes, to cut costs or improve product quality?
- Is it worth hiring some 'undirected' researchers to see what they come up with?
- Could different accounting improve our managerial decisions? Our corporate control? Our tax bill?

Some of those inquiries may need no special financial provision because managers, accountants, production and marketing staff and workers can be thinking about them as they do their regular work. But most kinds of research and development have to be paid for. Firms budget for research staff and laboratories, consultant research services, the design and development of new products, patent applications or purchases, bonuses for workers who make productive suggestions, systematic market research, in-house libraries, and access to commercial information services.

Risks vary widely. Buying a proven patent, or tooling up to produce a proven product for a well-researched market, may be like any other investment with reasonably predictable returns. But the inquiring, experimental, inventive kinds of research are often too risky for that: you may not know in advance if they will yield anything of value at all. When research and development have predictable returns, or low costs relative to firms' whole budgets, they can be financed from any capital or income source. Where costs are substantial and returns unpredictable, as they are with much scientific and technical research and technical invention, they must generally be financed from 'losable' money: from retained earnings, equity capital, or government contracts or grants.

INVESTMENT CRITERIA

The core of an investment proposal is commonly a technical project accompanied by financial estimates of what it will cost and what it will earn. Most proposals have such unavoidable elements of uncertainty about future costs, prices and competitive conditions that there may not be much point in appraisals which distinguish investments likely to return 8 per cent per annum from those likely to return 8.5 or 7.5 per cent. Accountants and economists nevertheless offer methods of appraisal which make those fine distinctions, and for the reasons we listed, many firms use them. So however much GIGO they may sometimes conceal, you may need to know them if you work as an economist in the private sector, or in one of the public institutions which help to finance private research and development.

Suppose therefore that a firm has prepared a number of investment proposals. They happen to be of the independent kind, i.e. each has its own prospective costs and earnings so that it can be appraised independently of the rest of the firm's operations. How do directors and their advisers go about ranking the proposals, and deciding which if any of them to adopt? There are five common criteria. They can be short-titled (i) total return, (ii) payback time, (iii) accounting rate of return, and (iv) discounted cash flow, which can also yield (v) present value of future earnings.

Total return is the simplest, and is the criterion for many builders, property developers, and others who produce big 'one-off' items for immediate sale. It suits investments whose returns are completed within a short period. Invest $10m. (counting all overheads, costs of capital, holding charges, etc.) to build a block of offices or apartments. When it's built, sell it for $14m. If that takes two years, it's better than depositing the $10m. in the bank if the going rate of interest is 10 per cent, so that (compounding annually) your $10m. will return $12.1m. If the rate of interest were 20 per cent, and

income from moneylending were taxed at the same rate as profits from building sales, it might be better to forget the building project and lend the money for a return of $14.4m. But only if the investor has no fixed costs. If he's a builder, with trucks and cranes and skilled employees costing him money whether they're working or not, he'll do best to invest his $10m. in ways that employ them.

The questions multiply with the commoner type of investment which increases productive capacity for a long or uncertain period. The investor who buys our builder's finished office block for $14m., hoping to net (say) $1.4m. a year by leasing the offices to business tenants, starts an earning process of indefinite duration. The rents will adapt, over time, to changing conditions of demand, inflation, taxation, the desirability of the location and the obsolescence of the building. So will the costs of administering, maintaining, repairing and perhaps modernizing the building. So will the market price, i.e. the capital value, of the land and building. The further ahead they are, the less surely any of those conditions can be predicted.

How do investors appraise such indefinite prospects? The commonest methods are to try to forecast the payback period, or the annual rate of return, or the discounted cash flow.

Payback is shorthand for 'How long will it take to get our capital back, so that our gains can begin?' Estimate the initial cost of the project, then its annual running costs and revenues – and therefore net earnings – through the years ahead. At what date will the net earnings have accumulated the amount of the original investment? Alternative projects can then be ranked by their payback periods: money back in 5 years beats money back in 7. Or firms may decide on acceptable payback periods and invest only where those can be achieved.

The test is useful chiefly for comparing investments of similar kinds with similar lifetimes. With other comparisons it is sensible to forecast also what the assets will be worth, and what they will earn, *after* the payback period. A farm, a lettable office building and a passenger bus may each get the investor's money back in 10 years. After that the farm may continue to earn forever, the office building for half a century and the bus for six months. It's as well to know.

Notice that some choices have to be made in calculating a payback period. Should you count money back or real value back, i.e. should you allow for inflation? (That's similar to the question whether depreciation provisions should be based on historical cost or current value.) Many investments are not made all at once.

Capital has to be fed in over a period. In that case, how do you decide the starting date of the payback period? Is payback achieved when the annual earnings add up to the initial outlay – or do you assume that earnings are immediately reinvested and *their* earnings counted as part of the payback? In that case what rate of interest should you assume the reinvestments will earn? (You must *forecast* future market rates of interest, and *decide* whether the firm will reinvest at safe low rates or at riskier higher rates.)

In short, when the salesman from the Gold Brick Unit Trust offers to double your money in two or three or five years, be sure to find out how he's arrived at the figure.

Accounting rate of return If you buy a $100 government bond – i.e. lend money to the government – with an interest rate of 8 per cent, you will be paid $8 each year until the bond matures, when you will get your $100 of capital back. 8 per cent beats 7 per cent – between one bond and another (if their risks are equal) the rate of interest is a sufficient investment guide.

If the same revenue is not interest, but is earned by a productive investment, it is called the *accounting rate of return*. It may still be a sufficient investment guide if you are considering (say) alternative trucks or buses with the same costs and working life but with different carrying and earning capacities. Some productive investments have regular returns of that kind. But most don't, and for those which don't, it is necessary to forecast not only *what* they will earn, but also *when* they will earn it. Hence the need for the next method.

Discounted cash flow Productive investments have different patterns of earning over time. Examples:

• Machines and vehicles may earn at a regular rate for a predictable period, with some re-sale or scrap value at the end of the period.

• Office or apartment blocks may earn steady rents which rise or decline over time depending on contrary effects of locational value and building obsolescence.

• Orchards may earn nothing for five or seven years, then annual returns which increase as the trees mature, then level off for twenty or thirty years, then decline as the trees grow old, with some land value left at the end.

• A one-off pine plantation earns nothing for a generation, then a single big return at harvest.

For present purposes, neglect the uncertainties of those forecasts. Assume that each forecast is the best possible,

and you want to know which investment will make you richest. Can you do that by comparing the total return to each, or the average annual accounting rate of return to each? No. Try it, and see why not. Suppose you have $1m. to invest, and compare the two extremes: bonds and pinetrees.

• $1m. of bonds pay 8 per cent interest for 20 years then return the capital.
Total return: $1m. + ($80,000 x 20) = $2.6m.
Accounting rate of return: 8 per cent per annum.

• $1m. spent planting pines on otherwise-worthless land, to be harvested after 20 years for $2.6m.
Total return: $2.6m.
Average accounting rate of return: 8 per cent per annum.

They look identical. They are not. If your purpose is to live on the investment income, you will starve to death waiting for the pines to grow. If your purpose is to augment your capital you will reinvest each year's bond income. Assuming that you can continue to do that at 8 per cent, you should calculate the return to the bond investment not at the simple interest that the original bonds pay, but at the compound interest achieved by reinvesting. Do that, and you will find the total return is $4.66m. That beats $2.6m. from pinetrees, and over the 20 years it gives an average annual rate of return of 18.3 per cent on your original $1m., which beats 8 per cent from pine trees.

(But remember that there may be tax effects. If this is a corporate investment and the once-only pine harvest is taxed lightly or not at all as a sale of a capital asset, while the annual bond income pays company tax then shareholders' income tax, the plantation may yield more after-tax return than the bonds do.)

Internal rate of return Suppose you want to invest whatever will return $2.6m. in 20 years' time. In pinetrees that requires that you invest $1m. But what bond investment at 8 per cent of compound interest will yield $2.6m. in 20 years? Answer: $557,826.

So (rounding the figures) either $0.56m. of bonds or $1m. of pines will yield $2.6m. after 20 years. What rate of *compound* interest is each therefore earning? Answer: bonds, 8 per cent; pines, 4.9 per cent. That rate – i.e. the rate of compound interest that would yield the expected return to an investment – is called the *internal rate of return*. The effect of this method of calculation is to discount the returns from the pine harvest because they come so far in the future. The capital tied up in pinetrees could have been earning sooner, yielding income for reinvestment. Does this mean that short-term investments are always better than long-term investments with deferred returns? Not necessarily. It depends on the relevant prices and interest rates. In our example, pines would do better than bonds if lumber prices allowed the pine harvest to sell for more than $4.66m *or* if the bond interest rate were less than 4.9 per cent.

For simplicity our examples are artificial. Real investments rarely make the calculations so easy by earning *either* regular annual returns (as bonds do) or once-only returns (as pines do). If irregular returns are expected you may need to calculate each year's returns separately, and to discount each for time.

The internal rate of return can be used in any of three ways to appraise an investment. It can compare alternative investments (as we did to find that bonds at 8 per cent beat pines at 4.9). It can compare expected returns with market rates of interest, to decide whether money-lending would be a better use of capital. Or it can be used to estimate the present value of future returns, as follows.

Present value of future assets If future prices and interest rates have been forecast accurately, the $2.6m. bond payout 20 years ahead can be had by investing $560,000 now. Since $2.6m. twenty years from now can be had by investing $560,000 now, the present market value of pines which will be worth $2.6m. twenty years from now is also likely to be $560,000, because people are unlikely to pay you $1m. for something they can get for $560,000. So if you trust the forecasts and making money is your only purpose, you won't plant those pines: you won't spend $1m. now to create an asset worth only $560,000 now.

(But remember how artificial these calculations are, and how uncertain their forecasts might be. Why might you decide to plant the pines after all? (1) You might have multiple purposes: to do some reafforestation for good environmental reasons; to have woods of your own in which to hunt, or meditate, or make love in summertime. (2) The government might be encouraging reafforestation by offering a dollar-for-dollar tree-planting bounty. (3) You and your large family might

decide to plant half the pines yourselves for pleasure and recreation, over some years, thus reducing the planting cost to $500,000. (4) With the world depleting its forests you expect the price of pinewood to double or more in the next twenty years, to yield $5m. or more for your tonnage. (5) Even if pinewood prices are stable, you expect interest rates to fall so far, or the rate of inflation to rise so far, that pines will yield more than bonds. More generally, (6) unless there is fire or infestation you have a gut feeling that those pines will be there twenty years on, whatever happens to the financial system. (7) You will be handing on your housebuilding firm to your children and you want to leave them independent of the commercial timber suppliers. Pines don't have to be harvested all at once: once mature, the plantation can supply the family business for many years.)

Any of those complications may occur. But what economists and accountants commonly mean by the present value of a future asset or stream of income is the amount of money that would have to be invested now, at compound interest at current or expected interest rates, to generate the future asset or income. Because future interest rates are uncertain, and for other market reasons, that way of calculating the present value of an item may not always agree with its present market price.

We have reviewed a number of investment criteria which can be summarized in relation to our example of alternative investments in bonds and pine trees. Accepting the original forecasts of costs, prices and interest rates, and the single purpose of making money, Table 35.1, below, compares the alternatives.

Interdependence

The examples so far have been of independent investments: projects which can be appraised and compared and undertaken (or not) on their own merits alone, by relating their costs to their expected returns.

In real life some productive investments are like that but many are not. Instead of being independent operations they are parts of larger operations. It is no good relating their costs to their returns because if they are not undertaken some of their costs may still have to be

	Outlay	Average accounting rate of return	Internal rate of return	Payback	Total return	Present value
8 % Bonds	$1m.	8 %	8 %	Year 9	$4.66m.	$1m.
Pine trees	$1m.	8 %	4.9%	Year 20	$2.6m.	$0.56

Table 35.1 Five methods of investment appraisal

paid, and if they *are* undertaken they will affect returns to other investments rather than earning returns of their own. Such investments are not independent, they are interdependent.

When a girl with a paper round buys new tyres for her bike it is the whole bike, not just the new tyres, that will continue to earn for her.

When a steelmaker builds a new furnace, the investment would be worthless if the furnace stood alone in a field. The rest of the steelworks might be worth less, or nothing, without the furnace. What the furnace is worth to the firm is not what (once installed) it would be worth to anyone else; and its worth to the firm depends on returns from the whole productive process of which it is a part. Formally speaking its worth may be zero, in the sense that it may add nothing to the firm's income; but without it the income would decline, so its present value to the firm is measured by the losses it will avert rather than the gains it will generate. To appraise any investment project of that interdependent kind you need to estimate its effect on the performance of the whole firm or the whole operation of which it is part. As we will now see, that can have some theoretical difficulties.

Returns to mixtures of existing and new investment
You may be able to estimate (i) the cost of a new blast furnace, and (ii) its effect on the earnings of the steelworks as a whole. How can you take the next step of comparing that use of that much money with alternative uses of it? Be warned that you can not usually do it by comparing rates of return to the steelworks investment as a whole. To see why not, consider how you might try to compare percentage rates of return to a steelworks (i) with and (ii) without a new furnace.

It may seem simple to proceed as follows. First find the rate of return which the existing steelworks capital is earning. Then compare the rate to be expected when you add the cost of the new furnace to the existing capital value, and add the effects of the new furnace to the steelworks' expected earnings. If the furnace investment raises the rate of return on your whole capital, do it; if it lowers the rate of return, don't do it.

What's wrong with that? What's wrong is that it actually argues in a circle. You have met the objection to expressing the rate of return on fixed capital as a factual relation between independent values. Whatever it once cost to build, the market value of the physical capital now depends on what it is earning or expected to earn. So it may make sense to ask whether $10m. of bonds or $10m. of blast furnace will get the firm the biggest total income from its total capital. But it does

not make sense to ask which will give the highest percentage rate of return on the whole capital.

So how can you compare alternative additions to existing capital? You can begin by 'letting bygones be bygones'. That means that you treat past costs of present capital as sunk and irrecoverable, and its present market value as important only for purposes of raising new funds. To decide between alternative investments you simply estimate which will add most, per dollar of new investment, to the firm's future profits expressed as a discounted cash flow, or as the discounted present value of the future stream of income. (Always remembering that all these calculations are based on forecasts, with whatever degree of GIGO applies in the particular case.)

HOW MUCH TO INVEST AND HOW TO FINANCE IT

To decide how much new investment to make you can in principle do as follows. (1) Rank potential investments in order of their independent profitability or (if they are of the interdependent kind) in order of their forecast effects on the earnings of the firm as a whole. (2) Estimate the costs of the various kinds of financial capital by which new investment could be financed, i.e. retained earnings, new share capital, bank or debenture borrowing. (3) Invest up to but not beyond the point at which the last investment will earn more than the cost of the funds which finance it. As figure 35.1 represents the relation, the returns curve is stepped to represent returns to a series of investments, and the cost-of-capital curve is stepped because funds from the four possible sources are likely to have different costs.

Projects 1 and 2 are clearly worth doing and Project 4 is clearly not. Project 3 would have to be financed by a 'shandy': two thirds of its funds at 8 per cent, one point below its earning rate, and one third at 11 per cent, two points above its earning rate. Financially it is marginal, so decide it on other grounds (risk, desire for growth, interdependence with other operations, contribution to market strength and share, etc.)

You already know how the expected returns were estimated, as total return, payback, accounting rate of return, or internal rate of return. (Figure 35.1 used internal rate of return.) Now learn what may determine the market prices of capital funds from the four main sources.

Equity
Investment can be financed by creating and selling new shares. Like retained earnings, share capital doesn't have to be repaid: it's the firm's own money. Unlike retained earnings, shares do have to pay dividends, but unlike the interest payments on bank or

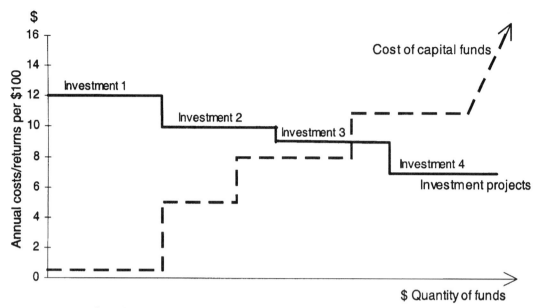

Figure 35-1 Expected returns and financial costs of four investment projects

debenture debts the amount of dividend can vary, at the directors' discretion, with the firm's capacity to pay. The amount of new share capital is limited by prudence. Existing shareholders won't want to see their stock unduly 'watered', with loss of voting strength and dividend share. They need to be convinced that funds raised by a new issue will contribute in due course to capital growth and dividend rates.

Retained earnings Firms' gross earnings first supply interest due on debts, and depreciation provisions for the replacement of existing physical capital. Those are treated as costs for most tax purposes, leaving net taxable profits to be divided between dividend payments to shareholders, and money retained for new investment or emergencies. Subject to dividend policy those retained earnings are likely to be bigger the more profitably the firm is operating. They are the cheapest investment funds, costing the firm nothing. You can accordingly label the first, zero-cost step in Table 35.1's cost-of-capital curve 'retained earnings' or as it may also be called, 'internal funds'. The amount available for investment is the firm's accumulated earnings, minus dividends paid and the financial reserve the firm decides to hold against emergencies.

Retained earnings are not only the cheapest funds, they may also reduce the cost of other funds. Firms with high earnings, substantial financial reserves and limited

debt (i.e. with low gearing) are safer borrowers than firms with less of those advantages, so what they do borrow can often be at lower rates of interest.

Debentures (or bonds) are promises to pay. Their terms vary, but they commonly promise interest payments at a specified rate for a specified term of years, then repayment of the capital. If they are secured by particular assets (which will pass to the lenders if the borrower fails to pay) the rate of interest is lower, and in most (though not all) conditions it is likely to be lower than banks' lending rates. Also, debenture-holders lend directly to the borrowing firm without paying percentages to banks or other intermediaries. Preparing a debenture issue is quite a business so it is not usually worth while for raising small sums. But it can be the cheapest and best way for established firms to borrow substantial amounts, especially if they intend to keep the funds fully employed and to pay interest only, without capital repayment, for at least the fixed term of the debentures. But lenders can get their money back at any time (with some market risk) by selling their debentures at stock exchanges.

Bank debt Banks lend more flexibly than debenture-holders, and to a wider range of borrowers. Though they may not always do so, they can allow borrowers to draw and repay funds as needed and pay interest only on the amounts in use. They lend at market rates of interest which may vary through the life of their loans – so when rates are declining they may sometimes lend more cheaply than fixed-interest debenture-holders do. Because they lend small as well as large amounts, and can investigate each borrower individually, they can lend to many small firms, partnerships and individuals who could not succeed in selling debentures on the open market. Banks can also promise credit conditionally, as debenture lenders can't: your bank may promise to lend you the funds you will need *if* you win a particular contract, buy a particular property at auction, or succeed in a particular corporate takeover.

Taxation and financial policy

Directors have to decide what dividends to pay and what earnings to retain, and as often as they want additional funds they have to decide how best to raise them. In taking those decisions, tax effects are among the considerations they have in mind – so governments should also have those effects in mind when they design their taxes.

Net profit is split between dividends to shareholders and earnings retained for use by the firm. Some countries tax the retained earnings at a lower rate, but a single rate of company tax on all net profit is more common. Retained earnings feed growth, future earnings, the balance of assets over liabilities, and therefore share prices. Shareholders thus get immediate income from dividends, or future income and capital gain from retained earnings. But although dividends and retained earnings have usually paid the same rate of company tax, shareholders may be taxed differently. Some countries tax capital gains and others don't. Some do and some don't double-tax dividends, first taxing the company's profits then taxing the shareholders on their dividend incomes. The relevant taxes can all be at different rates, and can be combined in a variety of ways.

Two extremes will illustrate the range of possibilities. Country A taxes capital gains, but exempts shareholders' dividend income from income tax to the extent that company tax has been paid on the profits from which the dividends come. That regime is called 'anti-retentive' because it motivates shareholders to take as much as possible of the profit as dividends. (They can always reinvest in the firm if it offers them new shares or debentures.) At the opposite, 'pro-retentive' extreme, Country B has no capital gains tax, it taxes all shareholders' dividends as income, and it taxes company profits at a higher rate if paid out as dividend and a lower rate if retained. Shareholders thus do best to leave the profits with the firm, and live on tax-free capital

gains. (If, having allowed for inflation, the market value of your shares grows by 10 per cent each year, and you sell 10 per cent of them each year, you effectively draw the same income as if you received a 10 per cent dividend from shares which merely maintained their capital value from year to year, without growth.)

Why do different governments run such different policies – and also policies designed to avoid biasing dividend policy in either direction?

There may be social or class reasons – for example to increase or reduce income inequalities, or to favor earned or unearned incomes. But there are also contradictory beliefs about the tax effects on national efficiency and growth. Country B's government believes its pro-retentive policies will encourage growth by motivating firms to save and invest, rather than handing profits to shareholders for consumer spending. Country A's government believes its *anti*-retentive policies will encourage growth by improving the allocation of resources. How? Firms like to invest their earnings in their own growth. That may not be the most efficient use of those resources. If shareholders are the investors (having received the firm's earnings as dividends) they will shop around for the industries and firms which offer the best returns, which some economists expect to lead to the most productive and socially desirable use of resources. (How dividend incomes are actually spent or invested varies widely – each school of thought is probably right about some and wrong about others.) There are also governments which believe that any tax influence is more likely to distort than to improve the allocation of resources, so they design taxes to be 'dividend neutral'. Beliefs are working parts of economic systems.

INVESTMENT PLANNING

Complex investment projects, with elements of interdependence, tend to demand awkward mixtures of risky guesswork and meticulous planning.

Much modern production, especially manufacturing, is done by firms which commit substantial capital to productive activities which are designed to continue indefinitely. Once into a particular line of business they are likely to be frequent or continuous investors, replacing plant as it wears out and adapting to changing conditions of demand, technology and competition. For such firms, quite a lot of investment may have *no* positive returns: it is undertaken to avoid loss, to adapt to changing tastes, to defend existing market shares against innovating competitors. Such firms face a paradox. The complexity of their operations calls for elaborate planning and coordination of their investment programs; but some 'first step' investments which commit them to new directions have risks which defy analysis. They commit large resources to lines of business from which there may be no retreat without heavy loss, but whose long-term prospects and investment needs and costs may be impossible to foretell with any certainty. Such decisions may call for broad social and historical judgment, and what economists like to call 'animal spirits', as well as or instead of the types of detailed analysis and appraisal we have been describing. But however uncertain and brave the initial commitments are, if they create complex ongoing operations they are likely also to create a need for detailed forward planning and control of investment.

These problems face most manufacturers of steel, aluminium, large machinery, ships, aircraft, vehicles, petroleum products, plastics, industrial and agricultural chemicals, soap and detergents, pharmaceutical drugs, telecommunication and computer hardware; prospectors and miners of oil and the major metals; firms which brew beer, make confectionery or process food on large scale; firms which develop air, sea, rail or road transport services on large scale; contractors equipped to build high buildings; big wholesale and retail chains; institutions which accept insurance and superannuation business with long-term financial obligations.

Such firms do sometimes make investments whose profitability can be independently assessed. But most of their investment is interdependent, and because a dozen minor replacements and developments may be in train at any one time, it is not possible to assess each one by comparing forecasts of the firm's whole performance with and without it. There are obvious needs for detailed replacements, improvements and modernizations which have to be made to keep the whole operation going, and up with its competitors. The question is not *whether* to invest but how to do it most economically: which make and model of machine or vehicle or computer to buy; whether to repair or replace worn or damaged equipment; whether to reduce, increase or reorganize particular productive capacities; whether the works canteen really needs new coffeemakers; and so on. With many of those needs the lines between 'maintenance', 'replacement' and 'investment' are hard to draw and unimportant (except for tax purposes).

Head office can't be authorizing every nut and bolt and vehicle purchase. Like other planning, a good deal of investment planning has to be decentralized. From plant managers through their maintenance engineers to their cleaners, groups and individuals have budgets,

spending guidelines, spending powers and limits. Thus the investment program of a big firm is likely to include a range of items from big, independently appraised, board-authorized projects down to guidelines and budget limits for dozens of divisional and plant managers with repair-and-maintenance responsibilities. Some of the items (repairs to keep the plant rolling) may be impossible to defer; some (replacing ageing vehicles) can be set back or brought forward within broad limits; some (additions to capacity, new products or processes) may only be undertaken if and when market conditions justify them.

It would be convenient if such investment provisions could be stable, with only minor variations from year to year, as firms' other costs tend to be. It is so for some firms and some industries – but not for many. It is commoner to have widely fluctuating levels of investment by firms, industries and the economy as a whole. The fluctuations are important elements in business cycles and in the complex causation of levels of employment, inflation and growth. Those large scale effects are for study later. Here, as you study how firms invest, it is important to learn *what prompts them* to vary their levels of investment, over time, as drastically as many of them do.

WHY DOES INVESTMENT FLUCTUATE?

A firm may vary its quantity of investment, over time, for any of the following reasons.

Lumpy capital Much productive building and equipment comes in the form of large items whose purchase can't be spread over the years. (They may be *paid for* over time, but must be *acquired* all at once.) A self-employed truckie has to buy a truck once in a while, with very little investment betweentimes. A steelmaker builds a new mill now and then, but not every year. A shipowner buys a new ship as often as he needs one.

Innovation If a popular new product is invented, there may be sudden large investment as industry equips itself to produce it. If a new and better process of producing established products is invented, there may be sudden, large-scale re-equipment.

Expectations Firms may invest in those innovations as soon as they are invented. But if there are risks – as to the demand for the new product or the advantages of the new process – investors may be cautious, and wait for buoyant times. Lumpy additions and replacements to established industries – new factories, mines, buildings, ships, vehicles, heavy machinery – are also likely to be undertaken when demand is expected to be strong. Such expectations sometimes rest on hard facts of economic or population growth or dependable government policies. But they often rest partly or wholly on expectations of boom and slump, and of customers' and competitors' likely responses to boom and slump. So firms tend to invest *when others are investing:* that is when they expect strong demand from high employment and plenty of both consumers' and investors' spending. Besides reading about those conditions in the financial press they may experience them in strong demand for their own products, with rising output and sales and dwindling stocks in the warehouse. That is when it seems safest to invest to increase capacity, or to take advantage of high earnings to replace ageing plant, vehicles, etc.

As strong consumer demand increases demand for capital goods too, it is easy to see why booms overheat. Now notice a reason why the investment response may be out of proportion to the changes in demand which stimulate it.

Acceleration and deceleration   As investment responds to changes in demand and current output, it can intensify boom-and-slump oscillations in the following way.

Suppose that a firm is meeting a steady demand for its output, which is therefore the same from year to year. The routine repair and replacement of equipment is also steady, there being no lumpy replacements. (Perhaps a transport firm replaces a fifth of its vehicles every year, a manufacturer using machinery of many vintages replaces one vintage every year, a sheep farmer replaces

a twentieth of his fences and replants a tenth of his pasture every year.) Since they are merely maintaining their capital, not increasing it, *net* investment is nil, and *gross* investment (on repair and replacement) is steady from year to year.

Then comes a boom. Demand increases, output can't keep up with it, the forward prospects look good, and the firm decides to increase its capacity. Besides the usual replacements it buys additional land or equipment so that there is a net increase of capital. Gross investment accordingly increases in that year. The increased capacity suffices to meet the increased demand, so in the following year there are the usual replacements but no further addition, i.e. no net investment. Next year the boom ends, demand declines, the recent increase of capital is no longer needed. This year the firm retires the usual quantity of old equipment *without* replacement. With no new and no replacement equipment there is a fall in gross investment.

Take the transport firm as example. It owns 20 trucks and replaces 4 of them each year at a net cost of $250,000 each. When the boom raises demand and revenue from the usual $2,500,000 to $3,000,000, the firm buys 4 extra trucks to take its fleet to 24. When the boom ends it retires 4 trucks as usual, but without replacement, thus returning to a fleet of 20. For simplicity, suppose there's no inflation. Table the changes in revenue and net and gross investment over three stable years, then a brisk boom and slump. Then compare the *percentage* changes in revenue and in investment, from year to year.

	Sales revenue	No. of trucks	Investment Net $	Gross $	% Change in Revenue %	% Change in Investment %
Years 1,2,3,	2,500,000	20	0	1,000,000	0	0
Year 4	3,000,000	24	1,000,000	2,000,000	+20	+100
Year 5	3,000,000	24	0	1,000,000	0	-50
Year 6	2,500,000	20	0	0	-16	-100
Year 7	2,500,000	20	0	1,000,000	0	+n

Table 36-1 Investment as accelerator and decelerator of aggregate demand: one firm's contribution.

To dramatize the acceleration, graph the revenue and investment quantities and percentages –

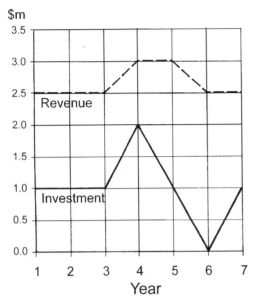
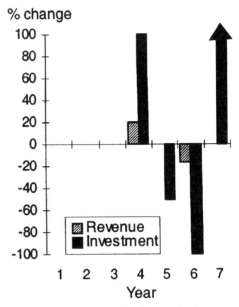

Figure 35.2 Investment as accelerator and decelerator of aggregate demand: one firm's contribution.

Our transport firm may not care about – or be able to avoid – the effect of its investment behavior on the economy as a whole – though it suffers like others from the fluctuations. The accelerative mechanism is not the only cause of booms and slumps but it is quite an important one. Remember how and why it works when you come to study the whole economy's fluctuations and government's efforts to smooth them.

SUMMARY

For revision, check that you understand, at least in principle, each of the things that a firm may need to do or forecast or take into account when considering whether to invest in producing a new product:

- Market research to identify opportunities for new products
- The likely elasticity of demand for the product
- Any likely competition to supply the demand
- Research and development of the product and method of producing it
- Lead time of the investment
- Estimated costs of production at relevant volumes of output

- Interdependence of costs and returns with those of the firm's other operations.
- Estimated returns to the investment, calculated as appropriate -
  - total return
  - payback
  - accounting rate of return
  - discounted cash flow
  - present value of future assets
- Strategic considerations of tax exposure, market share, market strength, reputation-building, political acceptability, etc.
- Available financial capital and its likely costs -
  - retained earnings
  - asset sales
  - bank debt
  - bond debt
  - share capital
    –whose availability and costs may be affected by –
- The firm's past and current profits

- The value and composition of its existing capital and debt
- Its provisions for depreciation and debt service
- Current and expected rates of interest
- The expected behavior of the business cycle
- Present and expected government policies which may affect the investment
- The directors' purposes, temperaments and attitudes to risk.

Especially the last item. Half the others – the half that are forecasts – have to be guesswork. It's unlikely that anyone will get them all right, and one or two wrong ones are enough to wreck the calculation as a whole. Most big, innovative investment owes as much to confidence as to calculation: confidence not so much in the calculations as in other investors' confidence and will to invest and keep the economy moving. The classical account of the unavoidable uncertainty of most long-term productive investment is Chapter 12 of J. M. Keynes' *General theory of employment interest and money* (1936). It's easy reading, and it treats the solemn costing and accounting procedures described in this chapter as cargo cult: routines which investors go through to propitiate the gods and solicit good luck for their next leap in the dark.

36

What private enterprises need from government :
A shortest summary

To sustain the private sector of a modern mixed economy,

GOVERNMENT MUST

- Defend the country and maintain law and order.

- Define and protect many property rights, creating and registering some of them individually (patent, copyright, land titles).

- Create the corporate powers of joint stock, limited liability and corporate identity.

- Regulate the use of those powers. Directors' behavior, and firms' treatment of one another and of their workers, shareholders, debtors, creditors, customers, insurers, neighbors and government must be regulated reliably enough to make it safe for people – especially rich people – to confide their money to be managed by strangers over whose management they have usually no personal control.

- Regulate the acquisition and uses of market strength between capital and labor, buyer and seller, firm and firm. For that purpose –

- Ban or discourage the development of avoidable monopolies, or regulate the uses of monopolist strength, or both. But at the same time –

- Regulate competition. (You may compete by offering lower prices, better quality and smarter marketing, but not by oppressing your workers, deceiving your customers, sabotaging your competitors' plant, defaming their products, intimidating their retailers, or selling dangerous goods of your own.)

- Provide commercial law and courts.

- Regulate bankruptcy, probate, intestacy, etc.

- Regulate safety at work, the safety of some products, and the packaging and truthful description of many products.

- Supply power, water, sewerage, waste disposal, roads, rails, air and sea ports and traffic control, public transport, telecommunications and other necessary services, whether by having public enterprises produce those goods and services, or by buying them from private producers for public supply, or by franchising and regulating private suppliers of them.

- In planning those necessary provisions, governments unavoidably influence the layout and form of settlement, especially in cities and towns. Along with public and household productivity and quality of life, the efficiency of the private sector can gain or lose much from the skill and purpose with which the public planning is done.

- Ration, allocate and regulate broadcasting frequencies.

- Educate the workforce and the parents who create and bring it up.

- Finance most pure and much applied research.

- Create money, design the financial system, decide how and with what economic and social purposes to manage it, and decide what if anything government should do about the allocation and price of credit, and conflicts of interest between competitors for credit and between lenders and borrowers.

- Determine, and where necessary negotiate, conditions of trade and exchange between the national economy and the rest of the world, and decide on the national contribution, if any, to the development of the international government of trade and exchange.

- Decide the amount and incidence of taxation, and collect it.

GOVERNMENT MAY

- Influence, in various ways, the distribution of productive activity between the private, public, independent non-profit, and household sectors of the economy.

- Influence the proportions of home and foreign ownership of the private sector.

- Supply inputs to private production more cheaply or reliably than (in some countries in some circumstances) the private sector can produce them for itself: for example energy, steel, rail transport, urban land, some kinds of venture capital and export/import credit, and financial arrangements to enable hard-up households to buy more and better housing from the private sector than they could otherwise do.

- Decide what the wage-fixing system shall be, and (if appropriate) manage or regulate it.

- License and certify some professional skills and rights to practise.

- Moderate employees' demands for wages, sickness and accident insurance, redundancy payments and superannuation by providing adequate public pensions and superannuation, sickness and accident insurance, and retraining arrangements.

GOVERNMENT CANNOT HELP

the fact that its necessary activities have many direct and indirect effects on –

- The supply of money and credit, and thus –

- The allocation of financial capital between the public, private and household sectors, between industries and between regions.

- Levels of investment and employment.

- The amount and composition of effective consumer demand.

- The rate of inflation.

- The distribution of wealth and income.

Since government can't help influencing business in so many ways, it is desirable that its macroeconomic policies be as coherent and competent and well-intended as possible. But the private sector is not necessarily served best by 'pro-business' policies which advantage its owners, executives and richer professionals rather than the majority of its working members. The current increase of its internal inequalities and insecurities almost certainly hinders more than it helps its performance.

CONCLUSIONS

It is wrong to think of the private sector as a self-sufficient economic system in which government can freely choose whether or not to 'intervene'. There is a double sense in which every modern market economy is a mixed economy whose public elements are as necessary as its private elements are. The products of the public and private sectors are equally necessary; and most of

them are joint products rather than being independently produced. Every private process needs appropriate government and public services, and every public activity uses many private products and services. Their daily interdependence is intricate, and vital to them both.

A productive and socially acceptable private sector depends, among other conditions, on good government. That much is clear in our past and present experience – in the world that we know. In the future that we can only imagine, the mixed economies face formidable new tasks. There is mounting evidence that continuing growth with increasing poverty, inequality and insecurity is not the way to greater happiness even among the rich in the rich countries. And the world needs radical environmental reform, including some deliberate restraint of the rich countries' output and consumption. That calls for new solutions to the problems of full and fairly shared employment in developed economies without indefinitely continuing economic growth, but with continuing scientific and technical progress. It is unimaginable that tolerable solutions to those problems can be delivered by competitive private enterprise operating globally under increasingly impotent government, as recommended in recent times by the OECD and the Washington consensus.

The coexistence of political and business freedom with good economic behavior has always depended on thoughtful government.. The precious achievement of Western democracy at its best has been to make coercive government – most of the time, for most of the people – a background protection for moral and social principles which the citizens have made their own, and mostly live by. A mass of useful, productive, well-conducted business continues in that way. But it is in danger now from three sources. Deregulation has liberated some nasty operators and some unproductive ways of making money. They change for the worse the temptations, the terms of competition and the resources available to productive business. And leading economists who are supposed to be our experts in the subject recommend the changes, explicitly including the return to more poverty, greater inequality, and fewer and poorer public services both to the private sector and to the people's welfare.

I think that majorities will return to their senses. When they do, they will want economists who understand what sort of economic government is needed, and how to make it as effective but unoppressive as possible. You want to be the next Jim Landis or Maynard Keynes? That's our next subject.

PUBLIC ENTERPRISES

37

Public growth

Public production grew faster than private in the richer countries through most of the twentieth century. Here are three chapters about it: one on the reasons for its growth, one on keeping public enterprises efficient, and one on what they need from government.

In *Public Employment in Western Nations* (1985) Richard Rose compared the growth of public employment through the last century and a half as a proportion of the paid workforce in six countries –

	Mid 19th century	Pre 1939	1951	1981
Britain	2	11	27	31
France	5	9	17	33
Germany	7	13	14	26
Italy	2	8	11	24
Sweden	(7)	(9)	15	38
USA		8	17	18

Table 38.1 Percentage of the paid workforce in public employment (rounded to the nearest percentage point)

Through most of the last half century public investment has averaged between 15 and 19 per cent of all investment, and between 4 and 5 per cent of gross domestic product. What do the public producers produce? Very roughly speaking –

- A quarter of public output is 'pure' public goods: defence, law and order, roads and bridges, etc.
- A quarter is market goods which are sold to other producers and the public: water, power, mail and telecommunications, public transport, etc.
- Half is individual services given free or far below cost to their users: health, education and welfare services, etc.

A slightly different classification groups the products according to their main uses, rather than the terms on which the users get them –

- Government: defence, law and order, tax-collection, legislation and administration, etc.
- Economic services: water and sewerage, power, roads and bridges, public transport, posts and telecommunications, coal and steel production, etc.
- Social services: health, education and welfare services (most of which also serve economic purposes, directly or indirectly).

For half a century now the first two – government and economic services – have tended to employ a constant proportion of the workforce. Most of the growth of public employment, which has maintained or increased total employment while the private proportion of employment declined, has been in the social services. Of the expansion of health, education and welfare services in the 30 years from 1960 to 1990, it has been estimated that about one third was due to population changes and the extension of benefits to greater numbers of people, and two thirds was due to increases in the real value of the benefits.

Those proportions of government, economic services and social services are proportions of numbers employed, not output. Private production and public economic services get most benefit from the continuing advance of technology: their productivity and output grow though their numbers of workers do not. Most of the health, education and welfare services, by contrast, are personal services in which technological progress does not save much labor, and may even increase the demand for it, as in medical care. So the expansion of these services has steadily increased their share of both public and total employment.

CAUSES OF GROWTH

In debates about the desirable 'mix' of the mixed economy it is important to understand the reasons for the growth of the modern public sector and for the changing proportions of its components. Richard Rose argues correctly that the history can't be sufficiently explained by a few general causes. It differs from country to country and needs to be understood program by program – education expands for one set of reasons, health services for other reasons, aerospace activities for other reasons again, and so on; they are not all driven by some single engine of public sector growth. But some of the causes of growth and change can be grouped under the broad headings of (1) scientific and technological progress, (2) discretionary spending of rising income, and (3) changing principles of social justice. We will survey them in that order.

Technology

Scientific and technological advances affect economic life in a variety of ways –

- They allow the development of new *products* and the improvement of old ones.

- They allow the development of better *methods of production* with lower costs.

- They may change *modes* of production, if they allow things previously hand-made at home to be factory-made, or if they transform household equipment to allow wider household choices between buying ready-made goods and producing them at home.

- By revolutionizing transport they transform the world's settlement, productive and trading possibilities. It becomes practicable to make steel, machinery, paper, chemicals, clothing, foodstuffs and other manufactured goods thousands of miles away from the sources of their raw materials, their customers, or both. There is a double effect: private enterprises have wider locational options, but at the same time governments can, if they wish, have greater influence on their countries' choice of industries and economic structure.

Those developments have affected public production in a variety of ways –

- Established public industries face new compulsions and technical possibilities, especially in defence. Developments in metallurgy, chemistry, ballistics, steam and internal combustion engines and powered flight revolutionize weaponry and warfare. Already in the eighteenth and nineteenth centuries old monar-

chies with little previous interest in scientific or economic development came to realize that to continue to win wars, which was a condition of existence for many of them, they must industrialize their countries. In nineteenth century France, Germany and Japan gifted public servants studied how to do it. Much nineteenth century European and Japanese public education, road and rail and harbor building, public and private steel production and public industrial research had military as well as economic motivation. In the twentieth century the British government bought into the oil business to secure naval fuel. Jet engines, radar and remote sensing were developed initially for war. US military procurement paid for aeronautical research and development which advanced civil as well as military aircraft production. Atomic bombs begat atomic power stations and medical isotopes. Rocketry developed for military purposes provided satellite communication systems with profitable commercial uses. And so on.

- Private industries develop new products which can't be produced, or can't be used, without additional public services. Cars need roads and bridges. Heavy road transport needs stronger roads and bridges. Land, sea and air transport need public navigational aids and traffic controls. As cities grow by private investors' and households' market choices they need more public infrastructure. The preventive and curative possibilities of modern medicine can't be generally available without public hospitals and public control of air and water quality. Many new private skills require elements of public education. Much technological progress depends on public scientific research and education. The more 'high-tech' the private sector's new products and processes are, the more public inputs they tend to require.

So if the public sector did no more than meet the private sector's demand for public goods and services, it would still have maintained or increased its share of economic activity through the twentieth century.

Shopping choices

As economic growth brings rising income, basic food and shelter and other necessities of life take a diminishing proportion of income. There is a growing surplus for discretionary spending. People have to decide what to do with it. Enterprising producers tempt them with new products. However widely their choices differ – individually and from society to society – three tendencies are common in varying degrees in all developed economies:

- People *invest* some part of their rising income in their housing, domestic equipment, car or other domestic capital.
- Some of what they *spend* they choose to spend on tax-financed public goods.
- Some of what they choose to spend on market goods creates some *derived demand* for public goods (as noted earlier – roads for their cars, public inputs to the production of the market goods they buy, and so on).

The household investment usually has public elements. People pay privately for more private and neighborhood space, and they pay collectively for the extra infrastructure and network services that their spreading cities demand.

Other public production increases as people spend more collectively on better health, education, culture and recreation. Besides better schools they have governments build and operate universities, libraries, museums, art galleries and art schools, national theatres and drama schools, subsidized orchestras and music schools. They dedicate national and local parks, lay out playing fields, build public stadiums, tennis centres, golf courses, swimming pools. Through public programs, and the effects of tougher regulation on the prices of some private goods, they buy environmental safety and quality for themselves and their successors. They pay to conserve historic buildings, appealing villages, beautiful town precincts and streetscapes. And so on.

Of course not everyone agrees with every item of public investment and spending. Some of the educational and cultural provisions may be decided chiefly by and for the benefit of elites. Some citizens campaign for the tennis centre, others for the swimming centre. But there is no necessary contradiction or necessary inefficiency in a system which combines some competition for public benefits with a broad agreement that there should be public provision for a wide diversity of tastes and interests, most of them possessed by minorities.

Social justice

Some of the rising *quantity* of income may be used to improve the *distribution* of income.

Economic growth since the industrial revolution has greatly increased output per head. In most Western countries it has been accompanied by the development of democracy, so that everyone has some say in

deciding what to do with the increased output. The mass of working people, with some help from well-off reformers and sympathizers, have responded by voting themselves more public benefits than they used to get when there was less output and they had less influence over government.

Public action to improve the distribution of income and other good things has taken three general forms:

- public goods and services: health, education and welfare services, especially for people who could not otherwise afford them;
- action to reorganize the productive system itself to improve the way it distributes benefits – by contriving full employment, fair wages and prices and rents, safe working conditions, accessible housing finance, etc.; and
- public income transfers: age pensions, income for the unemployed and disabled, child allowances, etc.

These are subjects for later chapters on the distribution of wealth and income. Here we merely list them among the causes of the growth of public enterprise. But notice that even where the main public purpose is to improve the distribution of income, different strategies for doing so can produce public sectors of different size and different composition. The link may be obvious where governments try for different patterns of distribution – if Swedes want flatter equalities and therefore bigger redistributions than Americans do, they may well provide more income transfers and public services than Americans do. But even where the desired distributions are similar, the strategies may differ. The differences tend to be between working at the primary distribution of income, and at redistribution. Some governments have put most effort into getting the private sector to deliver a good distribution of wages, working conditions and occupational superannuation, backed up by national policies for full employment, cheap land and housing and accessible housing finance. To the extent that those policies succeed there should be less need for public income transfers and welfare services. Comparatively good equalities may thus be achieved with comparatively small proportions of national income passing through public hands.

A bigger public sector may or may not indicate different distributional aims. If the sector is big because the public owns a big share of public utilities and heavy industry for the purpose of further improving the distribution of income, there may still be comparatively small proportions of income transfer and welfare services. But a different strategy may leave the primary distribution of wages, working conditions, employment and housing to market forces, and aim to transform the resulting distribution by large public redistributions of income and welfare services. Thus – as noted in some earlier chapters – the size of the public sector does not necessarily correlate closely with the degree of real inequality, and public sectors of similar size (as measured by the total public budget or the total numbers employed) may have different purposes, and different proportions of productive investment, welfare services, regulatory activity and income redistribution.

AN END TO PUBLIC GROWTH?

Since the 1970s there has been pressure to reverse the growth of public services in many Western countries. Causes of the U-turn were sketched under 'Right Turn' in Chapter 11. They included rising welfare costs with the onset of unemployment, and rising tax resistance.

Tax revenue is a main part of the effective demand for public goods and services. But as the relative costs of labor-intensive services rise, a *constant* level of public service costs a *rising* proportion of national income, and level of taxation. (You saw that graphically illustrated in William Baumol's diagram back in Chapter 13.) It follows that if public taxing and spending cannot increase, public services have to shrink. But majorities in countries growing steadily richer don't usually want worse services, they want steady or better ones.

Those contradictions pose what has been called 'the fiscal crisis of the modern state'. Governments are responding with two kinds of action. They cut or degrade services. Or they privatize them. The policies tend to be presented dishonestly. Their authors pretend that cutting public services makes them more efficient, and that privatizing them reduces the need for taxation. Both pretences are usually false, for reasons explained in the next chapter.

SUMMARY AND A REMINDER

The functions of public enterprises have been listed and classified in various ways in this course of study. This is a suitable place to bring the lists together for purposes of revision, and to consolidate your understanding of the roles the public sector plays in modern mixed economies, and the reasons for its growth:

- Public enterprises have grown from employing between 2 and 7 per cent to employing between 18 and 38 per cent of the paid workforce in developed mixed economies.

- Of the products of public enterprise, about a quarter are strictly public goods (law and order, roads and bridges, etc.); a quarter are market goods sold to their users (power and water supplies, public transport, etc.); and half are individual goods which are given free or nearly free to their users (public education, health and welfare services, etc.).

- Through the decades of fastest growth, and in many countries still, public investment is between 15 and 19 per cent of all investment and takes 4 or 5 per cent of gross domestic product.

- Public enterprises supply public goods; they supply intermediate goods and services to private and household producers; and they supply some market and some free goods and services directly to consumers.

- Public enterprises draw many intermediate goods and services from private enterprises and households – in extreme cases their only contribution to the public goods which they supply may be to order and pay for them.

- The last two items mean that there is continuous trade and interdependence between public, private and household producers.

Reasons for creating or acquiring particular public enterprises have included the following:

- To supply public goods.
- To supply goods which private enterprises cannot profitably supply.
- To keep dangerous trades in public control.
- To keep natural monopolies in public hands, either to socialize monopoly profits or to avoid monopoly pricing and profit.
- To do particular kinds of business more efficiently, honestly or reliably than private profit-seekers seem likely to do.
- To do market business with multiple social purposes as well as or instead of maximizing profit.
- To maintain employment, either generally or in particular regions or industries.
- To maintain reserve industrial capacities for defence or other national purposes.
- To have public control of the 'commanding heights' of the economy, i.e. of key industries such as power, transport and steel production which can support or discipline other industries with which they trade.
- To establish new industries whose early years would

be too risky for private investors, but which may be privatized when they are financially and commercially secure.

- To reduce private and increase public capital ownership for the general purpose of reducing inequalities of wealth and income.

Besides those public-spirited purposes, public initiatives may of course be supported for self-interested reasons. Depending on the prevailing state of law, culture and the political system, public enterprises may be supported for individual or corporate or party-political purposes: to trade public favors for political support, to assist particular private enterprises, to enrich individuals by corrupt means – and so on.

A reminder

Never forget how intricate the relations between the productive institutions are. Modern economic systems do not consist of a private sector in which private enterprises produce all market goods and a public sector in which public enterprises produce all public goods. The two trade with each other (and with households) incessantly – recall the example of the public, private and household inputs to British and French motoring in 1985. Most public goods are produced by similar mixtures of public, private and household activity.

Keep those relationships in mind in debates about the virtues and vices and uses of public enterprise. Public enterprises have been developed to provide some market goods directly, and to provide necessary inputs and infrastructure to private industry, as well as to meet demands for public goods and services. Similarly many public goods and services are produced by, or draw necessary inputs from, private producers. And in arguments about the modes of production, keep a clear head: what public goods we want is a different question from what public enterprises we need. What inputs and processes are required to produce particular goods is one question; who should own which of the relevant productive enterprises is another.

EXERCISES

1. The following arguments may be heard in coarser or finer form anywhere from your local bar to your country's legislature and cabinet room. Write short responses to three or four of them, giving your reasons for agreeing or disagreeing with them.

   'The private sector is the productive sector. Government spending simply diverts resources from productive investment.'

   'Economic growth has slowed in proportion as housing and government have increased their shares of resources.'

   'The more the government takes and spends, the less resources are left for efficient market allocation.'

   'Democracy will continue to be a sham as long as private capitalists command the major economic resources.'

   'Democracy becomes a sham if bureaucrats, rather than the people's market choices, decide what will be produced.'

   'You can't trust resources to politicians and bureaucrats. They're only in it for themselves.'

   'You can't trust resources to private profit-seekers. They're only in it for themselves.'

2. Feeling clever and perceptive? Repeat the exercise, for the same or different items, choosing items with which you disagree. But this time, distinguish your own real reasons for disagreeing (wherever they differ) from the reasons which you think might persuade the author of the quoted opinion to come around to your view: i.e., see if you can find a way to reason from his values to your conclusions, which may be the only way to persuade him to change his mind.

38

Public efficiency

The more public enterprise there is and the more necessary its services are, the more important it is that it be efficient. But it can be harder than you think to know exactly how efficient a public enterprise is, or to decide what sort of efficiency it should aim at. You've met such problems before. What should count as efficient? For whom? What is most efficient for an enterprise's owners may not be most efficient for other parties in the economic system, or for collective purposes for the system as a whole. (Which is more efficient, the steel monopoly which makes most profit, or the one which breaks even supplying the cheapest steel to the whole manufacturing sector?) This chapter will introduce questions about –

- conceptions of public efficiency;
- relations between the efficiency of enterprises and the efficiency of economic systems;
- how public enterprises price their products;
- some main hindrances to public efficiency; and
- how to be efficient despite the hindrances.

This course of study is in economics, not public administration or business management: why does it need a chapter on the efficiency of public enterprises? There is a double reason. Economists are often asked to assess productive efficiency, both public and private; but their ways of thinking have tended to unfit them for the task. That is partly because economic theory has been centrally concerned with *allocative* efficiency: are available resources being allocated to their most valued uses? Economists have tended, carelessly, to apply that theory to *productive* efficiency: how can the factory use the resources most efficiently, for example to make the most and best cars, with least cost and waste, from a given allocation of capital, labor and materials? That needs theory and know-how of its own, which has typically been the business of managers, process engineers, psychologists and others. The mistaken use of allocative theory – market theory – for the purpose can have ill effects on public policy and management. This chapter is here to proof you against making that mistake. Its conclusion will spell out the nature of the danger in more detail.

EFFICIENT AT WHAT, FOR WHOM?

Suppose you are asked to compare three public transport systems and report which of them is the most efficient. Careful investigation arrives at an accurate account of their costs and services. You find that only one of them makes a profit. The second one has the lowest costs, charges the lowest fares, and breaks even. The third system loses money and has to be subsidized – it takes $100 a year in taxes from every member of the community. But it gets the greatest number of people to work and play most expeditiously, it keeps the greatest number of private cars off the roads and it thus does most to economize fossil fuels and reduce pollution. Which is most efficient? Only the values which choose the criteria of efficiency, and decide which social purposes matter most, can tell you. Your own values, if you're deciding how to vote. Majority rule and collective political choices, if you're working as a public servant or consultant.

I am going to advise you, in the end, that as a general rule it is sensible to presume that doing things at the lowest cost is the most efficient way to do them, unless there is positive reason to think otherwise. But the qualification is important, and so is your capacity to recognize the many positive exceptions to the 'lowest cost' rule. So it is worth while spelling out a number of common exceptions. As you work through them, remember that the purpose is not to confuse you, or persuade you that measures of public efficiency are too arbitrary or value-based to be worth having. On the contrary, the purpose is to make you a wise economizer, an effective rather than a self-defeating economizer of public resources. It is important but often difficult work, and you need to know what you are doing.

So slow down, take care, and be patient with some necessary complexities. We will first remind you of what you already know about the general concept of economic efficiency wherever it is applied; then introduce examples to illustrate its application in a range of public enterprises; then try to distil some principles of public sector efficiency.

Meanings We can explore the idea of productive efficiency in a 'Yes, but ...' way. Begin with the simplest idea – the least-cost idea – of efficiency. Yes, but notice its limitations. They suggest a need for more complex concepts. Yes, but notice *their* shortcomings. And so on.

First, efficient can mean at least cost. To set up four notional examples, think of four industries in each of which firms are competing to produce the same product –

- to make steel,
- to build the same model of house,
- to provide the same rubbish removal service, and
- to can the same tonnage of peaches.

Start with the presumption that in each case the least-cost producer, who can therefore sell the product at the lowest price and/or the highest profit, is the most efficient. If the industrial conditions are such that all the competitors in each case have to use the same inputs at the same prices, those who achieve the lowest costs must be doing so by 'pure' efficiency, i.e. by the methods which get most output from given resources with least waste of time, effort or materials. And the efficiency of the enterprise contributes directly to the efficiency of the economic system of which it is a part.

But such perfect comparisons are rare. In practice products may not be identical (lower costs may mean poorer quality), or producers don't all face the same input prices. The world's steelmakers pay a wide range of prices for their coal, iron ore and labor. Among housebuilders one may do best because he manages to pay his workers less. One rubbish remover may spend less because he uses cheap old trucks. One fruit canner may do best because she owns her business free of debt and has no interest bills or loans to repay. The builder is using cheaper labor than his competitors, the dustman is using cheaper equipment, the canner is using cheaper money; you have to discount those advantages before you can judge the pure efficiency with which they use their resources.

But a profit-seeking producer may not want to discount those advantages: low costs may look efficient however they're achieved. And it may be efficient management which gets the cheaper inputs. A good builder may serve his own and his society's interests by using and training quite a lot of apprentice labor. A rational dustman chooses cheap old rather than smart new trucks. A prudent food processor finances her cannery with equity capital rather than debt. Efficiency can apply to the choice and procurement of resources, as well as to their productive use.

But cheap inputs don't always come by clever buying. Sometimes they come by luck or misbehavior.

Some countries make the coal-miners who fuel their steelworks work longer hours in more dangerous conditions than they should. A housebuilder may cut costs by using shoddy materials or unqualified tradesmen – by the time the buyers discover what's wrong with their houses it will be too late. A rubbish contractor's defective old trucks may afflict his workers and the neighborhoods they serve with grit and dust. A cannery may be debt-free by inheritance rather than good management. Low costs don't *necessarily* signify efficient production.

There is similar ambiguity in relations between efficiency and market strength. Marketing can be done more efficiently or less efficiently. Efficient marketing may improve productive efficiency if it improves the volume of sales and economies of scale. If it builds market strength, it may encourage directors to risk more long-term investment in research and development, which may add to the efficiency of the enterprise and the economy as a whole. But market strength may also allow big producers to underpay their workers and suppliers and overprice their products, efficiently for their owners but inefficiently for everyone else.

Examples

You have met all those complexities already in studying the private sector: what is good for General Motors is not *necessarily* good for America, or even a credit to the GM directors, if there are externalities, imperfect competition, dynamic ill effects over time, or other market failures. It is still good to understand the abstract principles in their practical manifestations in steel-making, housebuilding, waste disposal, food processing and so on. For similar reasons we now introduce the distinctive problems of *public* efficiency with some practical examples:

Trams There was a time when Norway, Sweden and Australia staffed their urban light rail transport (trams or trains) like this:

- Each Swedish and Australian vehicle carried a driver only; each Norwegian vehicle also had a conductor.

- The Norwegian conductor cost more than the Swedes' and Australians' methods of collecting fares.

- Sweden paid higher wages than the other two.

The order of costs per vehicle mile therefore ran from Norway (dearest) to Australia (cheapest). The order of costs per passenger journey and per passenger mile was different because of the countries' different urban patterns:

- Australia had big sprawling cities with a low density of population. That made for long journeys, long walks from home and workplace to transport stops, infrequent schedules, and a strong preference for private motoring.

- Norway had similar problems but on smaller scale because of its pattern of medium and small-sized cities.

- Sweden's rail services were in a few densely populated cities which made for efficient public transport routes, frequent services, short distances from transport stops to home and workplace, and heavy use of the service.

Sweden therefore had the lowest costs per passenger journey and per passenger mile. Norway came next per passenger journey, Australia per passenger mile. But there were some differences in the quality and equity of the services. In Sweden and Australia some aged and handicapped people and some young children could not easily use the transport because there were no conductors to help them. That had worse effects in Australia than in Sweden – Swedish passengers tended to be as well-behaved without conductors as Norwegians with them, but Australian trains without conductors were often vandalized and sometimes dangerous at night, so others besides the physically handicapped were afraid to use them. Thus at providing transport accessible to everyone the Norwegians were most efficient and the Australians least.

If you distinguish 'efficient' (least cost) from 'effective' (for the purpose in hand) you might call the Norwegian service the least efficient but most effective. But even that least-cost judgment can vary with circumstances. Nationally, the Norwegian conductors may not have been as expensive as they seemed. Sweden and Australia had very full employment at the time, so hiring conductors might well have switched labor from other industries and reduced national output. But Norway had some unemployment, so the conductors were not necessarily depriving other industries of labor. Sacking them would put some of them on the dole (public income to the unemployed) and increase welfare costs. So whatever they cost the transport enterprise, their national cost was less than their wages.

Thus to compare the efficiency of those services you have to get the facts right, but also decide 'efficient at what'. The multiple purposes of public transport don't excuse any waste or bad work, but they do link assessments and comparisons of efficiency to value-based choices of social purpose.

Power A generation ago, producers of electricity used to advertise and market their product to sell as much of it as possible. Nowadays they are expected to devote their advertising, educational efforts, political influence and technical research to getting their customers to use as *little* power as possible. (Switch the lights off when they're not needed, insulate refrigerators better, develop more energy-efficient motors, design office buildings to make maximum use of natural light and ventilation, wear warmer clothes and use less heating in cool weather; etc.) Virtuous producers of power are urged to (i) reduce their costs of production to reduce all power-users' costs of production and everybody's cost of living; (ii) improve the energy efficiency of their method of production, to get more electricity from less fuel or water power; (iii) minimize environmental damage; and (iv) teach their customers to use as little electricity as possible. But there may be conflicts between those aims. Lower prices may encourage more wasteful use of power. Lowest-cost production (from cheap but dirty coal, for example) may do most environmental damage. Reducing public transport with a corresponding increase of private motoring won't economize energy overall. And so on – the most efficient production of electricity may not accord with the most efficient use of energy or other resources in the economy as a whole.

Wise and foolish discipline

Instead of contrasting different concepts of efficiency, consider the effects of applying a single concept of efficiency to institutions of diverse character. The following examples are based on real cases, but to dramatize the comparison we pretend that they were all the work of the same authority. Picture a provincial city, serving about a million people, which possesses an inefficient water supplier, a moderately efficient Teachers' College and an extremely efficient Art Gallery. The local government, in cost-cutting mood, advertises for an Efficiency Consultant and (to minimize costs) hires the cheapest one it can find. His simple idea of efficiency has three components: low cost, user pays, and accountability. He's tough-minded and unimpressed by subjective values or anything else that can't be objectively measured or market-valued. The government accepts and implements his advice on the first two of the three institutions he reviews.

The Water Board consists of 12 sleepy members, appointed to reward long service or political fidelity, who meet once a month over a good lunch at public expense. They confide the actual work of the enterprise to a manager, who is usually the senior engineer in the last few years of his service. The enterprise is grossly overstaffed, by members of a number of labor unions who (for example) enforce a rule that to turn a main stopcock out of business hours (a job which takes one person two or three minutes) requires an engineer, a driver to get him to the stopcock, and a security officer to open and shut all locked gates and doors; they must meet at the main maintenance yard, proceed together from there, and return there to disperse, all at penalty rates for out-of-hours work. The operation is riddled with such self-indulgent practices.

On the Consultant's advice the government abolishes the Board, recruits a competent chief executive after open advertisement, and supports him through forceful negotiations with the unions under threat of outright privatization. A thorough rationalization of tasks, including computerized accounting and billing, allows a large reduction of staff. In the future all major building and engineering works will go to competitive private tender. Instead of charging consumers a percentage of their property values, as hitherto, they pay a price per litre of water consumed. They soon consume thirty per cent less than they did, and there is no need for the new dam and aqueduct that the Board had planned. After an expensive year installing meters and making redundancy payments to departing staff the capital budget falls by two thirds and the current budget by one third. The customers pay less for water but get it on terms which encourage them to economize it. The enterprise is required to make enough profit to provide for its own capital needs. The chief executive's contract provides for his dismissal, after an independent inquiry, if the new water price ever rises faster than the Consumer Price Index. The Consultant's simple principles of lowest cost, payment by users, and accountability have proved to be quite appropriate to the nature and the fairly uncontroversial purposes of the industry.

A question: The discussion above of Scandinavian and Australian tram services may prompt you to ask whether the Water Board's staff cuts will increase the number of unemployed, and the dole costs and other social costs of unemployment. Would it be better for the enterprise to keep its full staff, at least until the economy is fully employed and there are alternative jobs for them?

Answer: No, because if government continues to employ the surplus numbers, it could employ them more productively than the Water Board does. For example they could improve its forestry or national park services.

If any thousand workers can produce *either* a water supply alone, *or* the same water supply plus other useful services, the second alternative is better. There are thus *three* alternatives: (1) No change: the public continues to pay the existing revenue for water supply alone. (2) It pays the same revenue for the same water supply plus other useful services. (3) It pays less revenue for the same water supply – but not much less, because some of the savings must go to support more unemployed.

EXERCISE

Alternative (1) is clearly the worst of the three. You are the economics editor of the local newspaper as the government deliberates between option (2) and option (3). Write a leading article which sets out the considerations in favor of each, and your reasons for recommending whichever one you think best.

With enthusiastic government support after his success with the water supply, the Efficiency Consultant goes to work at his next task.

The Teachers' College is a modest institution – undistinguished but of fair average quality – in which 130 academics and 70 other staff teach and service about 2000 students, graduating 600 each year. In reviewing it the Consultant knows that financing it from students' fees would not be politically acceptable; he must apply his principles of low cost and accountability to a tax-financed, non-market institution. He finds that the College's numbers and costs compare well enough with those of comparable institutions elsewhere. But he sees no reason why it should not match the best rather than the average, and he believes that some productivity gains must be possible in *any* non-market institution which has not been shaken up for many years. He recommends three annual cuts of 3 per cent in the College's budget, to be matched by gains in productivity without any reduction of output.

Most of the gain in productivity is to be achieved by introducing proper accountability. The teachers seem to work as they please, with no effective assessment of their performance. When taxed with this they seem to the tough-minded Consultant to be self-satisfied and evasive. They claim (truthfully) that they often examine and assess each others' students' work. They observe each others' methods. Students are quick to complain of any neglect or maltreatment. There can't be much of either (the teachers say, and their Director agrees) because the formal complaints procedure is rarely used.

The Consultant is not impressed by this self-portrait of employees who claim to need no effective supervision or assessment. He persuades the government to revise the College's charter to incorporate new rules of accountability. The College must create and staff a Teaching Competence Unit. The Unit must check the provision of prepared materials for every course. It must poll students' opinions of each course and each teacher each year. It must monitor pass and fail rates. Each staff member must answer to a supervisor, who must report to the Director, annually in writing, on the member's performance. The College's annual report to its local government must include a general summary of the performance assessments. Accrual accounting is to be introduced of (i) the total cost of each course, (ii) cost per student taking the course, and (iii) cost per student passing the course, so that government can detect unduly extravagant courses.

The main effects of the new regime have been as follows. Two unsatisfactory teachers have been moved to another branch of public service. That seems to be the only gain from the changes. Four of the best teachers have stopped teaching to staff the Teaching Competence Unit. Three satisfactory teachers have moved to the administrative staff to supply the new accounting and reporting services. The funding cuts have reduced the remaining academic staff by a further nine. Where the 2000 students had 130 teachers they now have 112. The library has fewer staff, less money for acquisitions, shuts at weekends, and the students' reading suffers. The curriculum offers a few less optional courses, classes are a little bigger, students get a little less individual attention and criticism of their work. Staff are disgusted by the ignorant diversion and waste of resources, discouraged by the funding cuts, and insulted by the government's public disrespect for their conscientious work. Their morale suffers from all that, and from some decline in their students' respect for them. But what the Consultant defines as productivity is up – the College still graduates 600 new teachers each year, at 9 per cent less cost than before.

The principles of economy and accountability were not necessarily wrong: teachers' colleges should work as economically and responsibly as they can. But the principles were applied ineptly. First, it is absurd to measure such a product in a purely quantitative way – if only the quantity and not the quality of graduates mattered, it would be cheapest to give them their degrees and teaching qualifications without any education at all. Second, the teachers were right in claiming

that quite good quality controls were already built into their working relations with each other and with their students. Quality controls which are part of the productive process are always the cheapest and often the best; where they work satisfactorily it is wasteful to duplicate or replace them by adding non-productive supervisors. It was specially unhelpful, for example, to pay for independent monitoring of course materials by transferring library staff from weekend duty and by cutting the acquisitions budget, so that the better monitoring actually reduced the materials and the students' access to them. In real terms, if you value the quality of education and the skills and satisfactions which it generates, the Consultant has caused a double decline in the College's productivity: its output has fallen both by the amount of the funding cuts and by the reduced efficiency with which the remaining funds are used.

Those ill effects were nevertheless marginal. The good sense and spirit of the teachers and students ensure that good work continues to be done in the College and in the schools which employ its graduates. For a more destructive misuse of the same simple concept of efficiency, see the next example.

The Art Gallery is an excellent one of its kind, in that its services, though expensive in total, are of good quality, are produced economically, and are used and enjoyed by an unusually high proportion of the population. The gallery has a good collection of painting and prints, sculpture, glass, china and textile arts. Its dignified old building has exhibition space for about a third of the collection, and storage and workshop space for the rest of it. From the stored material, one or two special exhibitions are mounted each year. There is usually also a visiting exhibition of some kind, and a collective or retrospective exhibition of the work of a particular artist or school, with exhibits painstakingly tracked down and borrowed for the purpose by the gallery's professional staff. Most of these short exhibitions are 'active' ones, with explanatory printed or audio-visual material and public lectures or debates on their subjects. A great many teachers bring school classes to the gallery where, by arrangement, the gallery's education officers introduce them to the exhibitions they have come to see. School visitors average 100,000 a year, which is more than half the school population of the region. A quarter of a million individual visitors bring the total to 350,000 users per year, equal to a third of the catchment population – about the same proportion as use free public libraries.

That is how the enterprise worked in the year of the Efficiency Consultant's review. The Gallery's services were provided by a staff of 30. With provision for the special exhibitions, maintenance costs and some new acquisitions each year, the annual budget was about $2,000,000. The Consultant was under continuing pressure to cut costs and find new sources of revenue. Some careless comparisons convinced him that the Art Gallery could be a rich source of both. Other provincial cities had similar galleries, many in equally imposing century-old buildings. From the published accounts of the two nearest ones the Consultant was shocked, but also inspired, to find that they cost their local governments about a third as much as the one he was reviewing. What the accounts did not tell him was that those two did nothing except house permanent exhibitions, mostly of paintings acquired between 1860 and 1914, and deteriorating under yellowing varnish ever since. No visiting exhibitions, no special exhibitions, no school visits or educational services, no public lectures or debates, and next to no new acquisitions. Most of their small staff numbers were guards and cleaners. Their published accounts did not report how many visitors they attracted. It was enough for the tough-minded Consultant to know that his employers' gallery was costing three times as much as similar institutions elsewhere, and was allowing 350,000 freeloaders to enjoy its attractions without paying. Its expensive professional staff – which comparable institutions managed to do without – talked earnestly about the educational inspiration they were providing. But as the Consultant confided to the Mayor and City Treasurer, they would, wouldn't they? Surely educational expenditure belonged with the Department of Education, not the Art Gallery.

The Gallery had quite strong public and political support, so the proposed reforms were not presented as cuts, or changes of artistic policy. They were presented as the next step in the local government's ongoing policy of switching wherever possible from taxation to market funding. The Gallery would be free to continue all the services its users were prepared to pay for. First, a general admission charge would allow a small reduction in tax funding. Then, phased in over some years to avoid trauma, the visiting and special exhibitions should be required to pay their way from admission charges and catalogue sales. Initially they need only recover additional costs, but within five years they must recover their full costs including the professional officers' salaries. Any for which there was not effective demand should cease. School classes must be accompanied and have the exhibits explained by their own teachers. The Consultant acknowledged that there was a public duty to conserve the building and as much of the collection as could be displayed. For that purpose he recommended public funding at the level of comparable galleries elsewhere. But there could scarcely be a public duty to store a lot of surplus works of art in cellars where their public owners could never see them, so future acquisitions should be financed by selling existing holdings, at least until the collection was slimmed down to one which could all be displayed.

That plan was successfully resisted and most of it was not implemented. If it had been, it must eventually have closed down most of the Gallery's activities. Visitors would never pay high enough entry fees to support the professional staff. School parties would not pay to see only the unchanging permanent collection. Most of the stored items had low market value and their sale would not finance many new purchases. When the dull gallery in a neighboring city introduced an admission charge its custom declined to 50,000 visitors a year, and it still cost $500,000 to maintain. Compare the efficiency with which that gallery and the one described above use their funds.

Each visit to the dull gallery costs the taxpayers

$$\frac{\$500,000}{50,000} = \$10.$$

Each visit to the lively gallery costs them

$$\frac{\$2,000,000}{350,000} = \$5.71.$$

On a purely quantitative basis, if the Consultant's plan had been implemented it may well have halved the Gallery's efficiency, in almost any meaning of efficiency. And if the changes to the product, i.e. to the quality of the visitors' experience, are taken into account, the damage is worse.

The citizens are entitled to decide (as they did not, in this case) that they don't wish, or can't afford, to finance such an excellent gallery. But whatever might be saved by cutting its costs in the way the Consultant proposed, the lower costs would not improve its efficiency.

A conclusion Most questions about what should count as efficient in public enterprise can be answered by a principle which is simple to state, but not always simple to apply in practice: like private enterprises, public enterprises should produce their goods and serve their purposes as economically as possible. The practical difficulties arise because enterprises may have multiple purposes, some of which may conflict with one another, and within the enterprise and its government and the public who own it there may be disagreements about its purposes and their order of importance.

Government is there to resolve such disagreements. But in doing so it tends to be under three chronic temptations. The first is to do whatever the most powerful or strident of the interested parties wants it to do. Because tax restraint is popular, the second temptation is to assume – or pretend – that costs can be cut without harm to the product. Sometimes they can, often they can't. The third temptation is to appear tough-minded and economical by relying on objective, measurable indicators of efficiency alone. That tends to mean attending to the quantity but not the quality of the product. But notice, in the Teachers' College example above, that in resisting this third temptation the government made a mistake of a fourth kind. Without assessing the quality of the service or understanding its existing quality controls, the government imposed additional, inappropriate quality controls whose costs actually reduced the quality of the service.

Thus public producers with multiple or disagreed purposes may not have simple, objective, incontestable measures of efficiency. But rather than pretend the difficulties don't exist, it is best to face them and cope with them as conscientiously as possible, always relating the tests of efficiency to the purposes of the enterprise, however complex they may be.

PUBLIC / PRIVATE COMPARISONS

Comparisons with private enterprises doing similar work can help public efficiency in at least two ways. They may help governments to decide in which sector particular activities belong. And they may help public enterprises to be efficient and to know how efficient they are. The comparisons may still have the difficulties which go with having to decide 'efficient at what, for whom?' There may also be questions about which costs to count.

Costs of production Many of the reported comparisons have been of the costs of public and private municipal services such as water supply, power supply and rubbish removal. Others have been of commercial competitors, for example public and private airlines and steel and coal producers. Most of the American comparisons show private enterprises with lower costs or higher profits, or both, than their public equivalents. The European (including British) studies tend to differ from the American ones in two respects. They find the two sectors more alike in their cost levels. And because they take the trouble to control their comparisons for other factors, and to look for the detailed causes of cost differences, a number of them have found that other factors have more effect on costs than the type of ownership does: for example the scale of operation, the degree of monopoly or competition, the prices which the enterprises have to pay for their labor and materials, and other characteristics of the particular industries studied. And the comparative efficiencies are not necessarily fixed. They change. For example British coal and steel producers have been privately owned then publicly owned then privately owned again in recent times. In public ownership they have been at one time the least profitable and soon afterwards the most profitable in western Europe.

Some activities, like those two, are capable of doing well or badly in either kind of ownership. Some, like education, scientific and social research, religion and warfare, generally do best in public or other non-profit ownership. Many others, including most farming, retailing and other small business, do best in private ownership. It depends on the nature of the industry. One British reviewer concluded that 'there seems to be no *general* ground for believing managerial efficiency is less in public firms'. But it varies from industry to industry and firm to firm. Both within each sector and between them, careful comparisons may often be useful to indicate which enterprises are most efficient, and what others might learn from them.

Those who make such comparisons need to take care to compare similar activities; allow for any relevant differences in the conditions in which they operate; and relate efficiency as strictly as possible to the purposes of the enterprise. Those are proper precautions against irrelevant or misleading comparisons. But minor differences of purpose or circumstances should not be exaggerated to excuse bad work. If careful comparisons show (for example) that private contractors can build roads and bridges and public buildings as well and more economically than public managers and employees can, private contractors should generally get the work. When similar comparisons show that the French and German railways were better planned, were built more economically, have made greater technical advances in recent times and have often given their customers better service than the private U.S. lines have done, that may support a general case for public rather than private rail development. But at the time when those networks were built, France and Germany had national governments with the necessary constitutional powers and reasonably incorruptible public servants, and the United States did not. It might be different now that the U.S. government has shown that it can lace the nation with motorways and put men on the moon. Judgments about the best roles for public and private ownership need to take into account the capacities of the governments concerned, as well as the nature of the work.

Only profitable user-paid services can be supplied alternatively by publicly owned or privately owned enterprises. There remain all the public goods and services which have to be tax-financed because they go free or below cost to their users. For some of them, combinations of public ownership and private enterprise are possible. Short title: 'contracting out'.

Outsourcing and contracting out

Private contracts to supply public services directly to the public or to departments of government are nothing new. Many governments, for example, have long got most of their building done by competitive private contractors. Many public health insurers pay private doctors to give free service to public patients. And so on. But recent decades have seen a drive to make such 'outsourcing' and 'contracting out' the preferred methods of public service wherever they will work. From rubbish collection and office and hospital cleaning through private management of public prisons, hospitals, employment services and information systems to research and advice on high policy, work which used to be done by public employees is done instead by private contractors and consultants and their private employees.

In *Contracting out government services: A review of international evidence* (1996) Graeme Hodge reviews the 129 case studies and other reports that he could find that presented empirical evidence about contracted services. What follows is a summary of his findings.

Cost efficiency and the quality of service

1. Enthusiasts for contracting out can find many cases where it has cut costs without worsening services. Opponents can find many cases where it has failed on one or both counts. On those and other issues Hodge has done his best, with the aid of sophisticated statistical methods, to arrive at fair summaries of the evidence.

2. The available studies, based on more than 20 000 measurements, show an average cost saving for the agencies concerned of between 6 and 7 per cent.

3. Different services show widely different savings. Maintenance, cleaning and rubbish collecting show the highest savings. (They are the basis of many American economists' claims for the intrinsic superiority of all private over all public enterprise.) Many other services show no significant cost savings at all.

4. Some of the accounting is misleading. It may overestimate the gains from lower costs of particular activities if higher spending on public contract managers is omitted from the accounts. It may *underestimate* the gains from particular contracts when one or a few of a set of services are contracted out, and inspire better in-house performance in some that are not contracted out.

5. Where there is in-house contracting by competing units within the public service, the cost savings have been about the same as with private contracting. Competition rather than the type of ownership seems to have been the effective factor.

6. Measures of quality have been fewer and perhaps less reliable than measures of cost. As far as they go, they show that contracting has improved the quality of some services, made no difference to some, and worsened some. The average quality of public and contracted services seems to have been much the same. But how far that averages the quality of less competent and more competent investigations rather than the changing quality of the contracted services themselves is hard to judge. Hodge found 'that studies undertaken more recently had much smaller effect sizes, around one seventh, compared to earlier studies. More sophisticated studies, where controls for many more variables were present, also yielded effect sizes around one half of simpler studies.' (p.vi)

Economic efficiency

7. One average effect of contracting out is to abolish a quarter of the jobs concerned. At most countries' current levels of unemployment the consequent increase of dole and welfare costs is likely to equal or exceed the contracting agencies' savings. So the overall effect on the government budget may often be neutral. But costs may shift from some budgets to others, as when central governments have to spend as much on the public costs of unemployment as local governments save on cleaning streets and collecting rubbish.

Social costs

8. The social costs are chiefly the effects of unemployment on workers and their families. There may also

be some anxious loss of job security and family security for those who keep their jobs.

Honest government

9. Contracting services, especially those whose quality is hard to measure, adds to the government activities which are open to corruption. Without actual bribery, contracts can go to political supporters or contributors to party funds, and can expose politicians and public servants to undue business influence.

10. There is some loss of democratic responsibility when politicians can describe public service shortcomings as the responsibility of private contractors, and conceal their extent and some of their causes as 'commercial-in-confidence'.

11. The quality of some services is intrinsically difficult to monitor or measure. That can allow some profit-seeking contractors to provide poorer service than they should: cheapening the service can worsen it. But where contracts for human services go to churches and other charitable enterprises, the newcomers' motivation, and their capacity to attract voluntary as well as paid workers, may sometimes deliver *better* services, at less cost, than the displaced public servants did. (There's no end to the ironies and complexities in this business. Both the volunteers, and the distressed people who receive the services, may include some of the public servants disemployed by out-sourcing the services.)

12. Hodge distinguishes government itself from the 'production services' which may be suitable for outsourcing. 'Public governance functions are typically not well understood within the private sector. It is therefore understandable, but of some concern, that a newly appointed [Commissioner for Local Government] commented that his job was to "take the government out of local government"! Contracts require precise specification of deliverable services. Governance, on the other hand, requires a willingness to lead whilst resolving political and community conflict through the use of more subtle and less simple notions such as democracy, fairness, openness and due process. A blind insistence on contracts for all local government functions implies a blindness to governance itself.' (p.56)

Conclusions

Contracting out should be confined to services in which it does not degrade public services or civil rights.

While significant unemployment continues, savings in contracted services are likely to be partly or wholly matched by increased public costs of unemployment and welfare provisions. There would be a better case for cost-cutting contracts in conditions of full employment, or if surplus public servants were transferred to other public employment rather than disemployed.

Without full employment or public re-employment, most of any agencies' savings are at the expense of the incomes and family security of the poorest workers. Graeme Hodge finds that they are disproportionately 'women, part-time workers and blacks', and that they and their children 'bear the brunt of contracting reforms' whether or not the reforms reduce public costs. He also finds that the impact of contracting on employment is widely recognised in the literature, but because of the commercial concerns of the researchers 'it is in the main not treated as a social issue of any real concern. The municipality taking its governance role seriously will not succumb to this temptation, but will be able to attempt a balance in the likely drop in employment numbers with the likely economic gains to the community.' But thoughtful Graeme Hodge is not simply recommending a 'balance' between making the disemployed women and other losers poorer and making the taxpayers and other winners richer. How might minimum pain win maximum gain? He remembers how few contracts (and job losses) it has sometimes taken to stimulate better performance from the regular services. 'The value of giving all work groups the strategic message that comtracting means competition and that it is a priority to reassess the service one provides, is significant. It does not require all services to be contracted. Apparently, opening up a small proportion of services can sufficiently influence others to pursue major gains.'

So far this chapter has been asking what efficiency should mean in the public sector. Whatever it should mean, how may it be achieved?

SOURCES OF PUBLIC EFFICIENCY

You have been encouraged to keep in mind simultaneously two different approaches to public efficiency. One is the complex approach which insists that the very meaning of efficiency must often vary with the diverse and sometimes disagreed purposes of public enterprises: there is not really much similarity between the efficiency of (say) an efficient kindergarten, an efficient steelworks and an efficient parole service. People who are professionally concerned with public efficiency (as you may be) should never forget these complexities.

But there is also good sense in the simple approach which insists that whatever its proper purposes are, a public enterprise should serve them as well and economically as it can. If your kindergarten is losing money and children, it won't do to snarl that you are not running a steel mill or a parole service, so the parents' and auditors' notions of efficiency don't apply.

Without ever forgetting the complexities, return now to the simple approach. For whatever its purposes are, a public enterprise's efficiency is likely to depend on (1) the external conditions in which it operates; (2) the nature and purposes of the work it does; (3) the quality of its staff and management; (4) how it exploits the special advantages of public ownership; and (5) how it copes with the special disadvantages of public ownership. We will deal with those elements of the subject in that order.

EXTERNAL CONDITIONS

Public and private enterprises depend in much the same ways on the society in which they operate. Their potential efficiency is likely to be limited by –

- the level of development of the economy as a whole, and of any particular industries on which the enterprise depends: how well, promptly and cheaply can the economy supply the services, materials and components that the enterprise needs as inputs?

- the education, skills, experience, honesty, attitudes to work, and cooperative capacities of the available workers

- the strength or weakness of the people whom the enterprise serves: are they in a position to demand and get good service, and make trouble for the enterprise or its government if they don't get it? (Depending on the nature of the enterprise, that may be a matter of market strength, political strength or public influence.)

- the wisdom, honesty and efficiency of the branches of government which own, direct, regulate or use the services of the enterprise

- sufficient funds

- the monopolist or competitive or non-commercial nature of the enterprise, and where relevant, the strength of any competitors, or the presence or absence of comparable activities with which the enterprise's costs and efficiency can readily be compared.

In practice, in reviews of the efficiency of particular public enterprises, most of those external conditions can be taken for granted: they are the standing conditions in which all enterprises must operate in the society, so they

allow fair comparisons between enterprise and enterprise. But we will presently notice that that may not be true of the external conditions which are determined by government, especially the funding available to public enterprises, the wisdom or unwisdom of the politicians and public servants with whom the enterprises have to deal, and the prevailing theoretical beliefs of those officials.

THE NATURE OF THE WORK

How to keep an enterprise efficient must of course depend on the nature of the work it does.

Some activities need continuous strict control and exact accounting. That is true of much money-handling by banks, tax-collectors, pay offices, pension offices, retail check-outs.

Some activities need elaborate coordination. There may be questions about how to achieve it efficiently at least cost and with least harm to morale. Must it be done by central planning and command, or can operational units arrange it by negotiating with each other in something of a market way? Different principles may well apply to coordinating (say) international air traffic control, a general hospital and a national festival of arts. The means must depend on the nature of the work.

Some activities have problems of accountability. If schools and universities are publicly funded, what is the best way of ensuring that their funds are used for their intended purposes? Some governments simply trust the motivation of the teachers, students, school children's parents, the institutions' governing bodies, and a vigilant press. Some exercise light or heavy government control over the institutions. Some leave them alone but want to know a lot about their operations in order to judge what share of available funds each institution should receive. There may be conflicts between accountability and efficiency: remember the wasteful transfer of staff from teaching to account-keeping in our teachers' college example. There may be problems of expertise and freedom: does 'accounting to the taxpayers for the use of their funds' mean that politicians and public servants should tell the institutions what should be researched and taught? There are other problems of freedom and accountability when government has to allocate broadcasting channels and frequencies. If licenses go to the applicants who promise the best performance – the best-researched news and current affairs programs, the most fearless political analysis, the most wholesome children's programs – what should be done to encourage them to keep their promises? And should it be done by politicians (biased?), by public servants (inexpert?), by independent commissioners (chosen on what criteria, by whom?). In all these and other cases the alternative means of accountability have financial costs, but 'least cost' cannot be the only consideration in deciding which alternative to choose.

Enterprises vary widely in their proportions of teamwork and solitary or independent work. The solitary jobs vary from inventive and creative (artists, designers, inventors, many researchers) to jobs that need strict quality control and compliance with rules (safety inspectors, railway signalmen, auditors, data-gatherers for statistical services). Other solitary jobs need special kinds of perception, wisdom, moral commitment. Quite different institutional arrangements and approaches to motivation, quality control and accountability may be needed to get the best work at least cost from (say) a public doctor, pilot, judge, meter-reader, analytical chemist, graphic designer, speech-writer, and broadcaster to children. And those individuals may also vary in the extent to which they are self-driven to do their best, or respond more to material sticks and carrots.

We need not labor this theme any longer. In the public and private sectors alike, the best ways to keep work efficient vary widely with the nature of the work.

EFFICIENT MANAGEMENT

Good management also varies with the nature of the work.

There are thousands of books about management, and many of them tell you that it can't be learned from books alone, it takes hands-on experience too. This chapter won't make a manager of you. On the contrary, as its conclusion will declare, it is here to warn you of what economists commonly do *not* know about efficient management. In the course of your career you may have to review the performance of public enterprises and services. If you understand how complex the elements of efficient performance are, and how they may vary with the nature of the work, you won't make the simple-minded mistakes the efficiency expert made in our teachers' college and art gallery examples. Lowest cost is not always best. Competition and uncertainty about the future do not always encourage the best performance. The best work is rarely motivated by a single stick (fear of the sack) and a single carrot (desire for more pay).

More generally, efficient performance may depend partly on the external conditions of competition and access to resources on which economists' training encourages them to focus, and on the external supervi-

sion and accountability on which public servants tend to focus in their dealings with the public enterprises which answer to them as public 'owners'. But it also depends, especially for its positive qualities, on internal factors: the skill and experience of the managers and workers, their cooperative spirit or lack of it, their commitment (or lack of it) to their public purposes, their attitudes to their clients or customers: qualities which have sometimes been more harmed than helped by heavy-handed external intervention, as in our teachers' college example.

The last point is true for most people, whether they work independently or in teams: in the public sector as elsewhere, work has a range of actual and potential motivation. Some people in some occupations are self-driven to do their best: employers must merely avoid frustrating them. Many people respond to what they find: a good enterprise doing interesting work under good management can engage their enthusiasm, but bad management, bad company, hostile clients or customers or other disillusioning experience can turn them off. Some work is intrinsically dull or unpleasant, and has to be motivated chiefly by the workers' need for employment and pay – though the quality of the management and the human relations at work can still have significant effects on morale and performance.

Some cynics and some idealists argue about the relative power of the material incentives of pay and promotion, and the intrinsic attractions of the work and the human relations at work, as if they were alternative incentives. In practice sustained good work is rarely motivated by the desire for pay alone, *or* by the attraction of the work alone, *or* by duty or generosity alone. Each tends to have most force when the others are also present: when people have the compound satisfaction of doing good work in good company, in a good cause, with good pay and prospects.

A check-list Here is a short list of some ingredients of good public management. Learn and remember it, as an antidote to the economists' occupational shortcomings described in the next section. Also remember that the importance of each item will vary with the nature of the work.

First, public managers do most of the things that private managers do:

- keep the purposes of the enterprise as clear, and as widely shared, as possible

- see that the work to be done is arranged (whether by managers or by those who do it) into efficient, accountable, coordinated individual tasks

- attract and hold good people throughout the organization

- arrange for their training and retraining

- make career paths for them

- do everything possible to engage their proud, generous, sociable and cooperative propensities, and their joy in good work, as well as their desires for pay and promotion

- devolve working arrangements and quality controls, as far as the nature of the work allows, to those doing the work

- think how to economize the non-productive labor of supervising, accounting and coordinating

- try to design methods of quality control and accountability which keep workers' minds on the job, and do not switch their attention from perfecting the work to boosting the quantitative indicators of quality, pleasing the supervisors, getting credit for others' output, etc.

- specially remember this, because you won't hear it from many of the experts: in many occupations, conditions which elicit the best work also unavoidably allow some bad work, and conditions which prevent any bad work can also prevent or discourage some of the best work. Decide which matters most (with artists and inventors on the one hand, and traffic controllers and dentists on the other) and manage accordingly, defying bureaucrats who want to apply the same rules to all occupations

- judge what the enterprise itself should make and do, and what it should buy in from others or contract out to others

- judge which suppliers and contractors to keep continuously employed (for economies of scale and continuous employment of resources, familiarity with the work, and low transaction costs), and which to discipline by frequent competitive tendering and shopping around (to keep prices down and attract competitive bidders, and to get supplies and services which the enterprise wants only occasionally or in fluctuating quantities, rather than continuously).

Besides those tasks which they have in common with many private managers, public managers may have special responsibilities for their enterprises' multiple and sometimes disagreed purposes, and for their relations with the legislators, and the politicians and public servants of the government departments, who represent their public owners.

Public enterprises are typically created by legislative Acts. The Acts usually indicate their purposes in broad terms only. The enterprises may get some further direction, year by year, from the government. But the detailed working purposes and priorities still require plenty of detailed decisions, and recommendations to government, from the boards and executives of the enterprises. Many such enterprises have been deliberately set up and empowered to operate at arms length from government. 'At arms length' commonly means that the enterprises accept their strategies and often their financial resources from government, but are free from political intervention in their hiring and firing, trading and contracting decisions, and day-to-day management. Where that relation exists it is usually because it is helpful to both parties: the managers want coherent control of their business, and the politicians don't want electors or lobbyists to pester them for business favors, or to blame them for every business loss or misjudgment.

Questions about the purpose and political direction of the enterprise need not give much trouble to enterprises like water supply whose purposes are relatively simple and widely agreed. But they can loom large in the management of more complex activities with multiple and disagreed purposes, which affect conflicting interests and ideals in the communities they serve. Education, health and hospital services, housing, public transport, telecommunications, town and country planning, law and order and welfare services are among the activities whose managers have to cope with strains within and between the governments which own them, the public they serve, and their own workers whose morale can do a good deal to determine how well the enterprise satisfies the other two.

Recall, from Chapter 31, Chester Barnard's understanding of executive management as, chiefly, creative reconciliation of conflicting interests and codes of behavior within the organization. Re-read it if you need to. As you do, think how public ownership and multiple, partly-disagreed purposes might further complicate the executive task. The performance of such tasks cannot usually be judged satisfactorily by a few objective measures of costs and output alone, or improved by the measures which such tests suggest. Just as the directors and managers of such enterprises need moral and political wisdom as well as technical skills, so does anyone who has to hire and fire them and assess their performance.

How public enterprises price their products

This course of study can't hope to illustrate all the varieties of wisdom which public directors and managers may need if society is to have efficient kindergartens, efficient steelworks, efficient art galleries, efficient prisons, and so on. But as one way of sampling the diversity, we can see how variously public producers price their products.

Those which sell their services in a market way apply a variety of principles to their pricing. We will list high, normal, split, break-even and low prices. 'Normal' means the price a competitive private enterprise might charge, whether by marginal cost pricing, mark-up pricing or other means designed to yield a moderate profit. 'High' means any pricing, including monopoly pricing, above that. 'Low' means below that, yielding no profit or a loss.

After listing a number of respectable principles we add a few disreputable ones which nobody should defend, but which are undoubtedly employed by some politicians and enterprise managers.

High prices may be set –

- *to discourage use of a product.* Some countries have created public monopolies of liquor or tobacco sales, or certain kinds of gambling. Where those industries are private, many countries raise their prices by sales-taxing them. Either way, the high prices usually have two purposes: to discourage too much use of the products, and to raise money from voluntary contributors – nobody is compelled to pay because nobody is compelled to drink or smoke or gamble.
- *to protect a fragile resource.* If a tourist resort, a wilderness park or an attractive landscape for holiday houses would be spoiled for all its users by too much use, public owners may ration it by one means or another. They usually do it by physical restraints or quotas: for example by planning controls on the numbers of houses or hotels that may be built, by keeping wilderness parks free of roads, by limiting the number of daily admissions, and so on. But they *can* do it as private developers might, by raising land prices, hotel prices, road tolls and park entry fees to the levels at which few enough visitors are attracted.
- *to raise revenue.* Public monopolies can charge high prices to raise revenue for government. Most of them don't: it's politically unpopular. Those which do are commonly the ones which can be high-priced for other, more acceptable, reasons, like those listed above. But they are exceptions. When public service prices are higher than an equivalent private service

would charge, it is usually because the service is being produced inefficiently at high cost, rather than because of a policy of pricing for a high profit.

Our dry economist observes: 'Whether the high prices of liquor and tobacco are contrived by taxation or pricing policy, they are regrettable. Consumers should decide their spending preferences without having government bias their options by fiddling the prices. There may be a case for a general sales tax as a source of government revenue, but it should be levied at the same rate on every product so as not to bias consumers' choices and the allocation of resources. However, there may be exceptions where there are market failures. If there are externalities, for example if processes or products pollute the atmosphere, it may be right to add their social costs to their private costs by pricing them to yield not only the cost of their production, but also the cost of preventing or cleaning up the pollution they cause. If it is desired to slow the consumption of fossil fuels in order to leave more for future generations, it may be better to do it by raising prices than by issuing ration books – market choices at the higher prices may ration the resources more efficiently than government could do by having bureaucrats decide what shares should go to which people and firms.' There is a contrary argument in favor of administrative rationing. You will meet it presently in the discussion of deliberate low pricing.

Normal prices are commonly set for public supplies of power, gas, water and sewerage, postage, telecommunications and some other public services. Most of the price-setters' reasons are the same as the dry economist's reasons: pricing at cost plus a moderate profit keeps everyone aware of the real costs of the resources they use and the products they choose, encourages rational decisions, and discourages freeloading.

Normal prices set to yield normal rates of profit may be good for fairness as well as efficiency in industries such as land, sea or air transport in which public and private enterprises compete and it is desirable that the competition continue.

Split prices, i.e. different prices to different customers, or at different times, for identical goods, are set for a number of reasons.

Half fares and concession tickets. There are social reasons for charging children, pensioners and some others concession prices on public transport and for admission to many entertainments. Plenty of private as well as public enterprises do it. There are sometimes commercial reasons – if you want adults to pay to watch movies or football matches it may pay to addict them as children – but the main reasons are social and customary.

Peak load pricing. There is fluctuating demand through the day, the week or the year for power, commuter transport and some other services. To meet the peak demand, suppliers have to create capacity which stands idle, not earning, between peaks. Besides capital investment there are also labor problems. It may not be easy to find willing part-time and split-shift bus and train drivers, so employers may have to support idle workers as well as machines through the off-peak periods.

The services could operate more efficiently with lower unit costs and prices if the demand could be smoothed – if people did not all travel to work and school at the same time, cook their dinners at the same time, and heat and cool their offices and houses in the same seasons. Higher prices at peak hours and lower prices at other times may encourage people to change their timetables, though not many can. Those who continue to contribute to peak demand can be made to pay for creating the peak capacity, and others need not pay for it. The distributional effects of such split pricing are mixed: on the one hand most adults who have to travel to work at peak hours are employed and can afford full fares, while many of the off-peak travellers are housewives, pensioners or unemployed, poorer than the peak-hour travellers. On the other hand poor people want heating and hot dinners, and to get their children to school, at much the same times as richer people want those things, and peak load pricing may increase some poorer citizens' costs of living.

Wholesale and retail prices. Public and private enterprises alike may have wholesale as well as retail customers, and prices. Bulk buyers of electric power can be supplied at lower unit cost than retail customers can, so they are sometimes supplied at wholesale prices. Some suppliers on the other hand charge the same unit prices to all comers, using the profit on their bulk sales to restrain the price to all customers. It is then a philosophical question whether their pricing does or does not belong under our next heading.

Cross subsidies The reverse of split pricing happens when suppliers charge the same price for items with different costs. What should price-setters do when an identical service costs more to deliver to some customers than to others? Suppose it costs $10 to connect a city apartment to the nearest power or telephone line, $100 to connect a suburban house, and $1000 to connect a farm. Should the three households

pay those amounts to be connected? Or should they pay the same prices because they are getting the same service? Most governments do a bit of both in their market services.

Cross subsidies are often from town to country customers. Especially in sparsely settled regions, farmers and others whose occupations compel them to live far from town are thought to be disadvantaged by their isolation. Many of them happen also to have low or insecure incomes and could not afford to pay for long runs of pipes and wires. But without power and telecommunications – and therefore access to emergency services – they would return to the lonely, uncomfortable and dangerous living conditions of earlier centuries. So most governments offer them basic public services at level prices, which mean that city customers pay a little more than their services cost, and country customers pay less than theirs cost.

Our dry economist opposes most subsidies, including cross subsidies. 'They will lead some users to demand more of the service, and others to demand less, than they would if they faced prices related to true costs. Moreover most subsidies have one of two purposes of which one is anti-social and the other is mistaken. They go to groups who have special political influence and use it to vote advantages for themselves. Or – more respectably – they are designed to correct undesirable distributions of income. But if it is desired to alter the distribution of income it is usually better to do it directly, by transferring income. Everyone can then spend their incomes efficiently, with prices related to costs of production and nobody's options distorted by concealed cross subsidies.'

There is a counter-argument to that. It belongs later, in chapters about the distribution of income. Briefly, income transfers have administrative costs. Many involve intrusive means tests. And they don't always reach the women or children they are meant for. Wherever the desired effects can be achieved instead by appropriate provision and pricing of public goods and services, that may be a cheaper, freer and happier way to do it. Depending on the circumstances it may not affect the allocation of resources. It may improve it by correcting a maldistribution of spending power. Or if it reduces efficiency that may be an acceptable cost of its positive benefits.

Low prices We will deal in turn with strategic pricing, subsidized prices and a practice which should perhaps be called deterrent pricing.

Strategic pricing When you met this term earlier it meant strategic for the firm setting the prices. Here it means strategic for the national or regional economy, and refers to the reasons why some public suppliers of power, steel, freight handling and transport, and urban land and housing, price their products differently from the way in which profit-seeking private suppliers would price them.

These industries produce chiefly intermediate goods, i.e. inputs to other industries. Their selling prices are therefore other industries' costs, and in Chapter 34 you saw what successive profit mark-ups on a chain of productive processes can do to the prices of final goods. Some industries are thought to have strategic importance because they sell their products to others who use them to produce a wide range and large quantity of finished goods, sometimes including exports to very competitive markets. Power, steel and freight handling are examples. They are supplied by natural monopolies or other big enterprises with considerable market strength. Some of them are necessarily under government authority, whoever owns them, because they need government authority to acquire rights and routes for their pipes, wires, rails or raw materials. They happen also to be industries which – at least outside America – can do equally well (or badly) in public or private ownership. Because of the effects on others if they misuse their market strength, governments commonly restrain their prices by formal or informal controls, or by public ownership.

Public power suppliers and steelmakers can usually make profits if they want to. The question is whether they ought to. One line of behavior which will usually satisfy most of those concerned, except perhaps our dry economist, is this: the enterprise should operate efficiently enough to pay its way and keep its plant up to date while selling its products at prices at or below those of its international equivalents or competitors; any further efficiency beyond that should be applied to lowering its prices to cut its customers' costs of production, rather than to paying a profit income to its public owners.

A dry economist may want the prices to be high enough to pay a normal rate of profit. You can predict his reasons. He wants the prices to include the same profit margin as do the prices of all the alternative products which are available to the customers; only then will the prices signal the relative costs of the alternatives accurately, and the 'hidden hand' guide the customers to the choices most efficient for the economy as a whole, as dry economists define efficiency.

Against that argument the price-setters may defend their break-even, no-profit pricing for a number of reasons. Before you read them you may care to cover the following text while you see how much of the reasoning you can predict.

- Nobody wants to leave the pricing to supply-and-demand market forces; even the dry economist doesn't want these enterprises to restrict output and exploit their market strength with optimum monopoly pricing. Once it is decided to choose prices to benefit the customers rather than the enterprise itself, they may as well be the lowest prices that can be achieved without loss.

- The main allocative function of the rate of profit is to attract capital to the enterprise. But that is true only of private enterprises. Public owners can choose to invest capital and forgo any return from it if that will benefit the economy as a whole, or elements of it that they value more highly than they value the profits forgone. The citizens gain more than they lose by financing low-priced educational and health services at a heavy loss. For similar reasons they may well gain more than they lose by break-even pricing of power and steel.

- There is however a difference between the elasticity of demand for steel and for power.

  If steel is cheap, firms may buy more to increase their output, but they don't buy more to use it wastefully.

  If power is cheap, some users *do* use it wastefully, and don't invest as much as they should in power-saving technology. Many economists, including many environmental economists, argue for restraining the use of energy by raising its price. But that may do unnecessary harm to output and employment by raising the costs of marginal firms and pricing them out of business, or out of some of their markets. A policy which restrains the use of power *without* raising its price (for example by education, persuasion, public technical research and assistance, and either some rationing or some split-pricing to differentiate necessary from unnecessary uses) may attract wider support and less resistance and be easier to introduce on effective scale. It may therefore achieve *both* more output and employment *and* better environmental care than attempts at rationing by price are likely to do.

- Strategic pricing of urban land, housing and housing finance by public suppliers and banks can assist household productivity (and happiness) by increasing the proportion of households which can get the use of adequate domestic capital. Low-priced land and credit for homebuyers, and break-even rents for public housing, not only help the productivity of those they house; their competitive effects should restrain prices and rents at the lower end of the private market also. Low public pricing can thus improve young and poor households' options in both sectors. And whatever force the theoretical objections to break-even pricing may have in other markets, they have none in housing and housing finance markets. As argued in Chapters 25 and 26 these are defective capital markets which need public correction if they are to allocate resources most productively.

A conclusion: In some strategic public industries there may be a case for break-even pricing. The enterprises should usually avoid losing taxpayers' money. But if they are efficient enough to earn profits by normal pricing it may be better not to earn them, but to pass the benefit instead, via low prices, to their customer industries.

Subsidized prices Some necessary public services cannot break even however hard they try: the price elasticity of demand for them by their intended users is such that their demand cannot support a profitable supply. A leading example is public passenger transport.

In cities with unrestricted private motoring it is rarely possible to run round-the-clock or dawn-to-midnight public transport at reasonable frequency on all routes at fares which all the desired customers are able and willing to pay, and make a profit. The poorer people are, the more dependent on public transport they tend to be, and not only for their own purposes. It enables them to be economically productive: to look for work, to get to work, and to be as mobile, as workers, as may be economically desirable. Most affluent societies subsidize the service. The quality and quantity of service, the fare levels, and consequently the size of the subsidy, are questions for political judgment.

Deterrent prices This list began with high prices to deter over-use of liquor and tobacco. Low deterrent prices are sometimes set for services which the society would be willing to provide free, but which may be abused or over-used if free. Example: A city government experiments with free public transport, to encourage more commuters to leave their cars at home. Some young people respond by making a recreation of free riding: unemployed youths and truants from school ride about all day and make nuisances of themselves to drivers and other passengers. The authorities can't put children off at stops far from home. They decide that fares are their only effective means of discipline. They can't face giving free rides to adults who earn, while demanding fares from children who don't, so they revert to charging low fares for all.

Bad pricing practices Public and private enterprises alike can make pricing *mistakes*. The commonest causes are faulty cost accounting, and misjudgments of the customers' willingness to pay, i.e. of the price elasticity of demand. They can be avoided by better accounting and better market research. But they are not the subject of this section, which is about wrong pricing *principles*. Like the respectable pricing principles listed above, the merits and demerits of some of those which follow may be disagreed, especially where the purposes of the enterprises are disagreed. I think the following are bad practices, but you can judge for yourself.

- Enterprises charge too much for their products because they operate inefficiently with high costs (or they continue to operate inefficiently because they find they can get away with charging high prices). The inefficiency may come from bad management, or from lazy or wasteful work practices enforced by misuses of union power, or because governments don't capitalize their enterprises properly so they have to operate with inadequate or out-of-date plant.

- Enterprises charge too little for their products because governments forbid price increases which they fear would make them unpopular. The enterprises may then operate less efficiently because of a shortage of revenue and resources; or if their losses are made up by government they may lose the discipline that goes with having to pay their way, and switch their attention from trying to stay efficient to trying to wheedle more subsidy from government.

- Some lines are hard to draw. Governments sometimes offer special deals including cut-price public services to attract particular investors to particular regions. There is nothing necessarily wrong with that as long as the inducements are limited, and effective. But jealous voices ask why all firms can't have what a favored few get, and some governments have allowed effective inducements to a few to develop into rights to below-cost services for whole classes of business customers who need no such subsidies to stay in business.

- For friendly, frightened or corrupt reasons enterprises provide free or cut-price services to their own directors and employees, to relevant politicians, to firms which bribe them, or to other favored groups.

(Private enterprises also sin in this way, sometimes on grander scale.)

Summary Many public enterprises exist to serve multiple purposes. Some of the purposes, and the relative importance of the purposes, are likely to be disagreed. It follows that there cannot always be agreed, objective measures of the efficiency with which a public enterprise is serving its purpose(s) and pricing its products.

There are good reasons for normal pricing for normal profit in many circumstances. But it may be right for public enterprises to depart from normal pricing if they are supplying –

- strategic goods (whose prices enter with some multiplier effect into the prices of other goods)
- goods whose production need not reward its owner/investors with a profit because the public is willing to invest in producing them without profit
- necessary goods (like health services, education, public transport) whose users cannot all afford to pay normal prices for them
- unnecessary goods (like gambling) which can be high-priced rather than taxed, for revenue purposes, if public monopolists supply them
- goods supplied at high prices to classes of rich, at low prices to classes of poor, or at subsidized prices to some or all of their users, for the purpose of improving the distribution of real income.

Any of those pricing devices can be misused or misapplied. But they all can be used wisely with good effect: none of them need be outlawed as necessarily ineffective for its particular purpose, or necessarily harmful to the allocative or productive efficiency of the economy as a whole.

Exploiting the advantages of public ownership

In public as in private enterprise, the ingredients of efficiency have to vary with the nature of the work – with the differences between kindergarten, steel mill, art gallery and prison. With each of those, moreover, the potentialities may vary with the culture and human resources of particular societies. So there cannot be a simple summary of what it takes to keep public enterprises efficient. Instead, we can conclude with reminders of some general advantages of public ownership which enterprises can often exploit, and some common hazards of public ownership which they must take care to avoid or minimize.

Where public enterprises have their governments'

support, their advantages can include –

- the capacity to operate with multiple purposes, for example with balanced economic, social and environmental purposes, and with concern for their workers', their customers', and the taxpayers' interests
- strength for the long haul: the financial capacity to plan far ahead, invest far ahead of returns, invest in expensive research and development
- access to cheaper credit than private enterprises can get, because government is the safest borrower from private lenders, and can if necessary raise even cheaper funds from its central bank
- a capacity to take greater risks than most private enterprises dare take
- in some activities, a better-than-average capacity to attract people strongly and generously committed to the beneficent purposes of the enterprise; and where that fails,
- decisive external control of directors' rewards, and in public business enterprises a powerful capacity to resist unreasonable demands by organized labor.

Some of those capacities can of course be misused, and therefore reappear below among the *hazards* of public ownership. But their misuse in some enterprises does not reduce their value when used well by others.

Coping with the disadvantages of public ownership

Some troubles afflict public and private enterprises alike. They can each suffer from incompetence, fraud, bad management, bad forecasting, bad weather, dishonest or obstreperous customers. The following list is confined to hazards which are peculiar to public enterprises, or with which they find it specially hard to cope.

- Unnecessary or inefficient public enterprises are not automatically put out of business by losing money, as private enterprises are. Government needs to have the means, and the will, to detect them and to reform or sell or close them down. It is not hard to do: since the 1980s many Western governments have been if anything too destructive of their enterprises.
- About three quarters of all public enterprises and departments of government do not sell their goods or services in a market way, so there is no competitive market discipline of their costs, their working efficiency or their attention and response to their clients'

or customers' wants. Other means are therefore needed to keep them lean, efficient and responsive. Some enterprises can be designed and staffed so that the problem doesn't arise: staff positively enjoy serving their customers well and economically. Where more discipline is needed, the means may include staff training; thorough audit; periodical investigation by independent consultants; comparisons with the costs and performance of comparable private enterprises; and systems of corporate planning, target-setting, monitoring and accountability very like those employed by many big private enterprises.

- There is more than one way for public services to go wrong in their relations with their customers or clients. They may neglect them. They may be mean or oppressive to them. They may work too hard *for* their clients when they ought to be representing the taxpayers' interests and the government's policies instead of, or equally with, their clients' interests. Some subordinate the taxpayers' and the clients' interests to their own, and design their services chiefly to yield satisfying roles and rewards for themselves. Some think they know what's good for their clients better than the clients do. That is not always wrong. Some doctors, teachers and others may know what's best for their clients. Some proportion of people in other professions don't, and are oppressive or unduly permissive or simply unhelpful to the people they deal with. The designers of bad public housing towers and estates were perhaps extreme examples: they never consulted their intended tenants, and were contemptuous of what they believed their preferences to be, though in most cases the tenants wanted better-designed housing which would cost less in money, land and social suffering than the kind the authorities forced on them.

The society's culture, the skill and goodwill of the staff and the nature of the work are sometimes enough to ensure good relations with the public. Where they are not, a range of devices for non-market 'consumer sovereignty' have been developed -

- staff training and supervision
- quality controls built into the division of labor and the working relations of staff members with each other and with clients
- independent surveys of clients' experience and opinions of the service they get
- effective, well advertised and unfrightening opportu-

nities for complaints about the service
- effective protections for clients' legal rights
- citizens' access to their legislators
- a critical press, and press, radio and television consumer protection services
- public and customer representatives on the boards of public enterprises.

Those devices can protect and strengthen the effects of a well-developed 'culture of service' and respect for efficiency in the public sector; but they can't replace those qualities. Maintaining those qualities by suitable balances of inspiration and material incentive, and self-direction and external discipline, is the most important and in some activities the most difficult of all the tasks of public managers. Many public enterprises have managed to maintain high standards. There should be more study and imitation of how the best of them do it.

Some poor performance by public enterprises in recent times has been caused more by government policy towards them than by the enterprises themselves. That hazard of the public sector – that, like the private sector but in different ways, it may suffer from bad government – is the subject of the following chapter. Before that, our study of public efficiency now concludes with two troublesome professional problems. First, are some particular features of public enterprise alternatively advantages or disadvantages, depending on what politicians and enterprise managers make of them? Second, do some economists' theoretical beliefs make it specially hard for them to understand public efficiency?

Is the main advantage of public enterprise also its main disadvantage?

Public enterprises are able to serve multiple purposes, rather than single-minded profit-seeking. Does that freedom help or hinder their efficiency? We could easily find examples of experts who disagree about that. But there is one expert who appears at first sight to have changed his mind about it. A comparison of his two judgments offers a practical exercise in those questions of 'efficient at what, and for whom' with which this chapter opened.

Twenty years after the postwar nationalization of a number of British industries Richard Pryke compared their performance with that of the country's leading private industries and some comparable foreign industries, and reported the results in *Public Enterprise in Practice: the British experience of nationalisation over two decades* (1971). His thorough statistical work indicated that most of the nationalized industries had performed better than in their previous private owner-ship. They compared reasonably well with foreign equivalents, except where (as in the U.S.) the foreign country was more efficient overall than Britain, in public and private enterprise alike. And they compared well with Britain's private sector. Ranked by their growth of productivity from 1948 to 1968 the national-ized industries averaged better than the private manufacturing sector. In the decade 1958-1968 five of Britain's ten best performers were public industries.

Ten years later in *The nationalized industries: poli-cies and performance since 1968* Pryke reported on the decade 1968-1978, which included five years of diffi-cult economic conditions after the end of the long postwar boom and the first OPEC oil-price shock in 1973. Four public industries – electricity, airlines, telecommunications and gas – took advantage of new technology to continue to make large gains (from 68 to 126 per cent) in productivity. Railways and road freight services had smaller productivity gains. In five public industries productivity per worker actually fell (by from 2 to 17 per cent) as the volume of business declined faster than the numbers employed did. Where perfor-mance declined, Pryke ascribed the change to one or more of four general causes:

- World economic conditions had deteriorated, national economic growth slowed, and with the end of the long boom no amount of good management could have continued the boom performance.

- Government responded to rising unemployment and inflation by making a number of public industries subordinate their least-cost commercial principles to other economic and social purposes. Some had to continue over-staffing to maintain employment. Some had to 'buy British' though their competitors were doing better by buying American equipment. Some had to fight inflation by pricing their products below cost. Government subsidized them to do that, so – no longer compelled to pay their way – they lost some of their former market discipline and motiva-tion.

- With rising unemployment some labor unions resisted improvements in productivity which entailed shedding staff.

- Under those strains the quality of management and morale deteriorated. Pryke wrote of 'the demoralisa-tion' of the public industries.

The last judgment was a bit hard, after finding that four of the industries were doing as well as ever. Pryke's main concern was with the other six. In the first book he had warned that government should not lightly interfere with the public industries' commercial policies, and that there might be conflict between the aspirations 'to meet the needs of the consumer at the lowest possible price' and 'to act as model employers and in general to maxi-mize the welfare of the nation'. Ten years later he judged that the warning had been justified. To meet local needs, to sustain some threatened private indus-tries, to placate militant labor unions, and to restrain rising unemployment and inflation, government had imposed a number of 'national interest' policies on its enterprises. Programs to close losing rail and bus services were halted. British Steel was massively modernized and re-equipped – but not allowed to close old plants which the new ones were intended to replace. The airlines were made to buy uncompetitive British aircraft. The Coal Board was prevented from closing uneconomic pits. And price controls prevented public industries from raising their real prices, even when trading at a loss. Most of these loss-making policies were accompanied by government subsidies to the industries concerned.

That could all be seen as an appropriate response to changing circumstances. In adverse economic condi-tions the public industries could forgo profit and act to support private industry, maintain employment, restrain inflation and help the trade balance. That flexible, multi-purpose capacity was surely a main purpose of public ownership? Perhaps it was – but the capacity could be used well or badly. Pryke thought it had been used badly, for three main reasons.

First, the original instructions to the nationalized industries had included their multiple purposes: to be efficient, to be model employers, to serve national inter-ests. What demoralized some of them was having those judgments fractured by sudden, single-purposed government interventions. The 1970s governments (three of them in succession) did not replace the indus-tries' coherent strategies with other coherent strategies. They imposed bits and pieces of contradictory policies which left the strategies incoherent.

Second, nationalization raised expectations. Consumers expected low prices, workers expected secure jobs and good wages. Where enterprises could not afford those benefits in declining regions or indus-tries, government was expected to subsidize them.

Third, that problem was compounded by the large scale and the nationwide responsibilities of the new owners:

The fact that the nationalised undertakings are so

large and are in public ownership converts what would otherwise be a collection of local difficulties and decisions into a national problem about which pressure groups and trade unions become concerned and politicians adopt policies. Corner shops have been quietly closing for years, but if retailing had been nationalised there would have been a great outcry some years ago when it became known that the Shops Board had a ten-year plan to close many of its uneconomic outlets, and the process would probably have been slowed down. If the Coal Board did not exist and the railways had not been nationalised the problems of closing down loss-making pits and withdrawing unprofitable rail services would be less formidable ...

– The nationalised industries (1981) p.262

Pryke hedged his criticism in a number of ways. Public steelmaking, carmaking and some other activities were still more efficient than they had been when privately owned. Government intervention in declining industries was as common in other countries, and in private industries, as in the nationalized industries: it was not necessarily an effect of public ownership. Most of what Pryke regarded as mistakes were made within a single decade and he already saw signs that the government and the enterprises were learning from the mistakes and returning to better behavior. And although Pryke believed that public ownership had contributed to the poor British performance through the 1970s, he also believed that it need not have done so. Public enterprise does not necessarily perform worse than private. Better policies were available.

If Pryke's criticism was justified, does that mean that it was wrong to use the public industries as 'instruments of economic and social policy' – or was the effort merely mismanaged? Or was it not even mismanaged – was Pryke wrong to focus on its ill effects alone, without also investigating its good effects? We can't now quantify the likely good effects, but we can guess at some of them. Overstaffing the public industries did help as many of the workers as would otherwise have been unemployed. By reducing unemployment it also reduced dole and welfare costs to the taxpayers, perhaps by more than the industrial subsidies cost them. (Pryke did not attempt that calculation.) Though the British passenger aircraft of the 1950s and 1960s were not fully competitive their design and production maintained a highly skilled industry which might otherwise have been lost, but which survived to join with other European producers in the competitive Airbus enterprise. It may also have economized Britain's scarce

dollars. The loss-making local bus and train services did help their passengers, some of whom might have led harder or duller lives without them. The price controls helped to restrain inflation.

Pryke wanted policies to be based on cost-benefit analyses of their likely effects on the citizens in all their guises as shareholders in the public industries, as consumers and as employees. But in practice he tended to focus on only two of the citizens' interests: as consumers they wanted low prices, and as shareholders and taxpayers they wanted their public industries to pay their way. Though he mentioned their interests as employees in general terms, he disregarded that interest in most of his case studies, or identified good wages and working conditions as costs rather than benefits, especially if they were won by union action. And – perhaps because they are difficult to measure with certainty – he gave no credit to the public industries' effects on levels of employment, rates of inflation, welfare costs or the balance of payments of the economy as a whole. But those affect the citizens' interests as surely as consumer prices and the costs of industrial subsidies do, and analysis of the performance of public industries should not neglect them.

A conclusion The ability to balance a number of purposes, and adapt them to changing conditions, is a valuable quality of public enterprises. It is not wrong in principle to use them for national economic and social purposes. But the policy direction and management need to be done competently, and may need special care for morale where market enterprises accustomed to paying their way are asked to forgo available profits or competitive advantages.

Now notice a final hazard which should have special interest for you because as an economist you may be in danger of becoming part of it.

IS NEOCLASSICAL THEORY BAD FOR PUBLIC EFFICIENCY?

Neoclassical theory makes it difficult to understand productive efficiency in any of the three sectors of the mixed economy, and specially difficult to know how public enterprises can be efficient. Because bad advice to governments on this subject is common and often harmful, I hope that you will take the trouble to understand the nature of the difficulty, whatever conclusions you then draw about it.

Common sense and practical experience can of course save people from making the mistakes which the theory encourages. So may the theory itself in its fully developed and rigorous form. But in the elementary form of it which tends to be most widely known and persuasive, the difficulty is as follows.

The basic neoclassical model of the economic system has these characteristics:

- It models the private sector only.

- It expects the economy to work efficiently only to the extent that it consists of single-purposed profit-seeking firms, in market relations with their suppliers and customers, and competing incessantly with each other for the available resources and the customers' spending.

- The model purports to show how the economy would work with the greatest possible efficiency. Where real life differs from the model, the theory says it is the life that is defective: it speaks of market failure, not model failure.

- Competition to attract the customers' spending and the resources with which to meet the customers' demands ensures that the available resources find their best uses – i.e. it ensures *allocative* efficiency.

- Competition ensures that the firms which produce most efficiently survive and the less efficient are eliminated by takeover or business failure – i.e. it ensures *productive* efficiency.

Now notice a critical effect of those beliefs. Theorists are led to believe that they can know *which* firms are efficient without any need to know *how they manage to be efficient*. The theory simply says that firms which survive in competitive industries must be the most efficient. If you ask why they are efficient, i.e. what causes them to be efficient, the theory tells you that competition is what causes them to be efficient.

Now bring that together with two earlier items. First, recall the composition of public output. About a quarter of it is 'pure' public goods like roads and bridges. About half is individual goods like education and health services which government gives free or far below cost to their individual users. Only a quarter consists of goods like power or public transport which are sold to their users in a market way, and even in that market sector many of the public suppliers are monopolists or oligopolists rather than competitive enterprises. Thus very little public production complies with the ideal of competitive market discipline.

Now recall the argument of Chapters 2 and 3 about selective causal explanation. Of all the conditions which may have to be present for a firm to be efficient – a good work culture, competent and well-motivated workers, good management, necessary public infrastructure, and

so on – this theory, in the little it has to say about productive efficiency, directs your attention to one cause only, and one which is external to the firm: its situation in competitive industry. And it only tells you of two relations between that condition as a cause, and efficient production as its effect: (i) competition *motivates* firms to try to be efficient, and (ii) it *eliminates* those which fail to be efficient. The theory does not tell you what Firm A does which makes it efficient, or what Firm B does or fails to do which makes it inefficient, or why competition appears to have such different effects on the two of them. But it implies that as an economic analyst and policy-maker those are things you do not need to know.

If taxed with this, theorists tend to say that *how* to be efficient is the business of other disciplines: management, accounting, the technology of the relevant industry, and so on. Economists can't know everything, and it is sufficient for their purposes that they have theorized the hidden hand: the reasons why we can assume that firms which compete successfully are not only efficient for their own purposes, but are at the same time optimizing the use of the society's economic resources to meet its citizens' demands.

That division of labor seems sensible – of course economists can't know everything. But it is easy for them to fall into the habit of treating the causes which they do study as more important than those which they don't. Believing that competition is the main cause of efficient enterprise is doubly unfortunate. First, it is not always true. In real life competition is not always or necessarily the most important influence on enterprises' performance; and when it is, it does not always improve performance. (For example you have met the reasons why monopolist or oligopolist market strength enables some firms to plan farther ahead, do more research and take more risks than more competitive firms can afford to do. And those are advantages which many public enterprises share.)

Second, if programs of action are designed by people who focus on only one source of efficiency and don't believe they need investigate any of the other necessary conditions for efficiency, the programs may well do more harm than good. That is specially likely if those concerned make another mistake which a focus on competition encourages, namely a logical slide, perhaps unconscious, from a theory about firms to a belief about people. It goes like this: If competition makes firms efficient it must be by making their members efficient. How is that done? Competitive firms are motivated to be efficient by knowing that the more efficient will make profits and survive and the less efficient will not. Neoclassical theory makes no distinction between firms and individuals as economic units: workers sell labor just as firms sell products. It seems to follow (though logically it does not) that workers will respond to the same sticks and carrots, i.e. that they will work best, and managers will manage best, if they are in constant competition with one another, insecurely employed, knowing that the more successful competitors will get the pay and promotion and the less efficient will get the sack.

In real life there are some occupations in which competitive individuals do best, but there are many more in which co-operators do best, and in many of them job security is a necessary condition of the fullest and best co-operation. Most of the relevant psychological, sociological and management literature endorses the common sense which says that the more competitive a firm wants to be (or an army unit, an Olympic rowing eight, an America's Cup crew, a champion football team), the more co-operative and mutually trustful its members need to be.

There are also creative individuals who perform better with job security than without it, better without routine quality controls than with them, better when their whole attention can be on the task without worrying about their conditions of employment. Especially in literature, science and the arts, some of the most valuable work of creation or discovery is unorthodox enough to be denied resources by orthodox authorities, or condemned by peer review, or takes long enough to get the creator sacked before it is done, or entails such risks that it can only be done in occupations which understand the false starts and failures that normally precede payable discoveries.

Now confront these diverse facts of life with the occupational temptations of neoclassical theorists, and it is easy to see why so many of them find it hard to believe that any public enterprise can be efficient, and why the advice they give on the subject is so often harmful. They see that the public enterprises which supply public rather than market goods have no competitors. Most of those which produce services to individuals give them away without any market discipline. And most of those which do market their products

are monopolists who presumably face the temptations which private monopolists face, but without the positive profit-seeking incentive to keep their costs down. So advice about public efficiency which is based on a theoretical focus on competition as the main source of efficiency is often along these lines –

- An economic system is likely to be more efficient the more of its production is private and the less is public. Privatization is accordingly the best and often the only way to produce efficient public services.

When strongly held this belief tends to discourage efforts to make either sector more efficient. Competition is thought to be all it takes to keep the private sector efficient, it doesn't need government interference. Lack of competition is thought to make public inefficiency incurable. *So reformist energy should not be wasted in trying to improve either sector.* It should simply concentrate on shifting activity from the incurably inefficient sector to the inevitably efficient sector.

Where privatization is not practicable, neoclassical theory seems to many of its believers to imply that the best way to improve public performance is to subject it to discipline as like as possible to competitive market discipline. That may be done by a variety of means -

- Expose public enterprises to private competition.

- Make public enterprises compete with one another.

- Finance as many public services as possible on a user-pays basis.

- Have independent monitors (preferably private management consultants) compare public enterprises' costs with those of comparable private enterprises.

- Have monitors compare public enterprises' actual or notional returns to funds employed with average private sector returns, or with interest rates as indicators of the current price of capital.

- End job security throughout the public sector. Subject employees to continuous or periodical assessment. Replace unsatisfactory performers. Fill vacancies by open advertisement, on merit not seniority. For top appointments seek executives from the private sector.

EXERCISE

A summary and conclusion to this section can be written by you.

Either

1. Write an essay about the relations between the 'external' work incentives of pay, promotion and the sack and 'internal' incentives of commitment to the enterprise's purpose, the interest of the work, the workers' degrees of independence and control over their time and tasks, their working and learning relations with one another, and so on. Discuss at least two contrasting kinds of public employment (for example a racetrack totalisator and an art school, or a tax office and a general hospital) which you think demand different balances between the two kinds of incentive.

Or

2. For each of the seven dotted items at the conclusion of this chapter, beginning with the advice to privatize, suggest one public enterprise which you think would benefit from the proposed action, and one which would not. Give your reasons.

39

What public enterprises need from government

In this chapter 'government' will usually mean the elected government, the politicians who as ministers and legislators ultimately determine what public departments and enterprises there will be, and decide how to direct their policies.

How to organize the work of government is the subject of a vast library of law, political science, public administration and other disciplines. This chapter will spare a page or two to remind you of the breadth and importance of the subject. But its main business is with two particular subjects: (i) the design of the public institutions and business enterprises which operate with some degree of independence outside the civil service bureaucracy, and (ii) the 'capital temptations', especially the temptation to privatize, which those institutions offer to government.

CIVIL SERVICES

One after another through the eighteenth and nineteenth centuries Western countries and Japan developed modern civil services to staff the central government of their homelands and overseas empires. The officials were typically well educated, recruited and promoted on merit, securely tenured in the service, and subject to formal and informal rules of honesty, confidentiality, impartiality, and accountability.

Within these services the commonest form of organization is bureaucracy. The work of government is distributed to functional departments. Within each department there is a structure of jobs, each with defined tasks, and powers and responsibilities appropriate to the tasks. The jobs are linked by chains of command and of lateral coordination. There is thus a structure of government which can be depicted on a wall-chart, showing the division of labor by which the work of government is to be done, and which officials will be responsible to which others for coordinating it and seeing that it *is* done. That chart is independent of the people who happen to occupy the offices: it is meant to ensure that the work will be properly done by any competent personnel who occupy the offices.

Bureaucracy is grey with words like 'personnel'. It is traditionally unpopular – tens of millions of people watch continuing repeats of *Yes Minister*. Bureaucracy is nevertheless one of the great social inventions. It offers the least inefficient way of organizing, coordinating and where necessary commanding large-scale complicated enterprises, public and private alike. It is the organizational form of all big business, so it is odd that business people should accuse it of ruining government. For all its faults, it comes nearer than any alternative form of organization to keeping the day-to-day work of government honest, impartial, accountable and predictable, qualities without which government may be corrupt, ineffective or oppressive.

Bureaucracy is appropriate wherever government wants strict control of its money and uniform treatment of its citizens. For example all taxpayers, all pensioners, all accused persons, all users of welfare services, all recipients of student allowances, are entitled to impartial treatment under impartial rules. It is also appropriate wherever complicated coordination is needed: for example to fight a war, to run a general hospital or a city transport system, to prepare an annual national budget and control the investment and spending which it authorizes. Its elements of permanent structure and job security provide continuous government in democracies whose ruling politicians change from time to time, sometimes bringing quite inexperienced people to power. In some periods of French and Italian democracy and British colonial democracy the public services have provided continuous government while political crises and changes of government came once or twice a year.

Bureaucrats still get a bad press much of the time, and sometimes deserve it. *Yes Minister* bites deep. Many private enterprisers and some politicians speak with habitual contempt of public servants and services. Within the discipline of economics there are 'public choice' theorists who hope to understand government by assuming that everyone concerned with it – every voter, politician and public servant – is motivated by material self-interest without concern for others' interests, or any concept of duty or public interest. I think that is as absurd as the opposite assumption that they are all selfless servants of public interests alone. But keeping government itself honest and efficient is a subject for the manuals of public administration. This chapter's main business is what government needs to do for its business enterprises, and other economic institutions which work outside the national bureaucracy with some degree of independence.

REASONS FOR OTHER FORMS OF ORGANIZATION

Many public activities are carried on outside the national bureaucracy. The reasons for giving them different forms of organization and degrees of independence may include any of the following:

Economy Some activities don't need much, or any, remote control or central coordination. It would merely waste money to subject them to layers of bureaucratic control and reporting and accounting. It would often also worsen rather than improve their performance.

Efficiency Most business enterprises, public or private, need coherent management capable of quick decisions and quick and flexible response to changing conditions. They must not be subject to detailed direction or intervention by outsiders likely to be over-cautious, slow to respond, and inexpert in the business. And they must not have their management broken up and distributed to numbers of different authorities. Within the central bureaucracy there may be good reasons for making departments have their estimates approved by Treasury, their expenditure monitored by a Department of Finance, their staff hired and fired by a Public Service Board, their office space allocated by a Building and Construction authority and their equipment procured for them by a Supply and Tender Office. But the many public enterprises which would be more hindered than helped by those arrangements will generally do best outside the bureaucracy, managing their own money, premises, equipment, staffing and business.

Freedom There are considerations of two kinds:

(1) Democracies don't want their ruling politicians to control the selection of teachers and researchers in schools and universities, or (within broad limits) the teachers' and researchers' values and beliefs. Similar freedoms ought to apply in public broadcasting. Where some supervision and accountability are desirable they are best supplied by other bodies such as the governing boards of schools, universities and national broadcasting corporations, rather than by bureaucrats under the ruling politicians' command.

(2) As noted earlier, uninhibited discussion of purposes and ways and means is necessary for efficiency in many enterprises. In internal policy-making and in differences of opinion with government, suppliers, customers or press and public opinion, the directors and staff of public enterprises should usually be able to speak as freely as their private sector equivalents can do. For example a school principal who is a subordinate in a national bureaucracy can't safely tell the world what she thinks is wrong with the national government's educational policies. A school principal who answers only to local government or to the school's own governing council can do so. The freedoms and constraints are mutual. A government which employs school teachers within its own bureaucracy can't usually criticize their performance or beliefs publicly without being held responsible for their shortcomings. A government which funds the schools but does not employ the teachers has more freedom to criticize the schools' policies, and defend its own against them.

Risk To do their work properly many public enterprises need to be able, where appropriate, to take reasonable risks. Risks bring some failures. Governments must be able to survive such failures, or the risks won't be taken. If each financial loss, or business mistake or misjudgment, or maltreatment of a customer, or malpractice by a director, brings a party-political attack on the government with demands that the responsible minister resign, the enterprises will have to be unduly risk-averse: unenterprising, uninventive, devoted to safety first. If they are to work well, and especially if they are to exploit their public-sector capacity to survive financial setbacks, plan far ahead and invest in projects with delayed returns, they need to be at arms length from government. Some other authority, typically a board of directors, must have primary responsibility for their performance. Government is still ultimately responsible for them and deserves to suffer if it designs them badly, appoints unsuitable directors, gives them foolish policy directions, denies them necessary capital, fails to audit them, or fails to foresee any major catastrophes that they bring on themselves. But with normal administrative and business fortunes and misfortunes it is in nearly everyone's interest that government be seen as an innocent shareholder rather than a guilty director; and that is one of the purposes of the various corporate forms which will presently be described.

So – to begin this chapter's main business – government's first duty to its enterprises is to design them. Public business tends to vary more than private business does, because it extends from market business to a wide range of non-market activities. So its organizational forms vary more than do the standard private-sector forms of partnership, private company and public company. Public sectors typically contain Companies, Statutory Corporations, Commissions, Trusts, Authorities, Foundations, Cooperatives, Associations and other creatures whose detailed constitutions vary even more than their titles do. The best structure of course depends on the nature and purposes of the work; but we will simplify the real-life diversity by sketching three main organizational forms and their relations with government.

PUBLIC COMPANIES

Remember that 'public company' doesn't usually mean government-owned. It means a company whose shares are offered for sale to the public and traded on stock exchanges. They are typically owned by private shareholders, but governments can own them. Where a public enterprise does ordinary market business, that ordinary company form may suit it best. British Petroleum, Renault Motors and the Qantas airline are examples of firms which were private enterprises until governments acquired their shares.

A government-owned company differs in three potentially important ways from other forms of public enterprise, and in one important way from most privately-owned companies:

- To sell a government department or statutory corporation into private ownership usually requires an Act of the legislature with the assent of both houses. That commonly takes some time, and not all governments control both houses. But although national rules vary, most governments can lawfully sell any shares they own, and therefore any companies they own, without reference to the legislature. So companies are easier to privatize than other kinds of public enterprise are, and privatization may be harder for opponents to block or delay. Their government owners decided (at various dates) to sell off all three of the companies named above. Only the French government failed, blocked not by parliament but by popular protest.

- Unlike other public enterprises a company is subject to the whole apparatus of company law and

regulation. This may be seen as making for fair competition where public and private enterprises compete.

- A company therefore escapes much other control by the government bureaucracy (because that could conflict with the requirements of company law and regulation). Companies can rarely be brought under public service rules of employment, or Treasury supervision of their trading and spending, and unless they want more share capital they need not be involved in the government's annual budgeting procedures. Many directors and executives like the company form, and some government bureaucrats dislike it, because of its comparative independence of the bureaucracy. Some politicians like it because they are distanced from it by law – if the directors foul up the business, the politicians can say (truthfully in the short run) that they cannot lawfully interfere with a public company operating under company law and stock exchange rules. However –

- if the government (as opposed to the various branches of its bureaucracy) really wants to take control of the companies it owns, it can do so more decisively than most private shareholders can. Not many big firms have a dominant private shareholder with no obligations to other shareholders. But a determined government as sole owner can appoint directors willing to do what it wants.

STATUTORY BODIES

Statutory institutions are created, as their name suggests, by statute, i.e. by an Act of Parliament or Congress or other legislature. Most public Corporations, Commissions, Trusts, Authorities and other public institutions are created in that way.

A statutory corporation can have whatever structure and powers the government and legislature choose to give it. A founding Act typically states the corporation's purposes in broad terms and specifies the constitution of its governing body, its powers, how and by whom its members are to be appointed, how it is to report to the government or legislature, and what power if any the government has to direct its policies.

This chapter can't map the full variety of institutions that have been created by statute. But in the design of many of them there are two features which can have specially important effects on their performance. These are the opportunities for free speech, and the provisions for direct or indirect government control of the enterprise. To illustrate, examples of three basic types of organization will suffice. They range from one extreme to the other, from the least to the greatest independence of government, and from the least to the greatest opportunities of free speech.

Commissions often empower a single Commissioner to command the organization. Some, for example Commissioners of Police, have some legal independence of government in their day-to-day work. Where the law allows some kinds of government direction but bans others it is not only to prevent the politicians from misbehaving. In societies with generally honest government it is also to protect the politicians from improper pressure from groups and individuals wanting favors. If the favors are plainly beyond their powers, politicians can hope to refuse them without too much offence to those who ask for them.

Commissions commonly have bureaucratic structure with continuous chains of command from the Commissioner downward. That may be thought to be necessary for some purposes – many people think it necessary for police purposes – but it usually follows that members of the organization won't publicly criticize their superiors' policies or performance, and the Commissioner won't publicly criticize the government. Logically it need not follow that mutual criticism is inhibited inside the organization. But it tends to follow in practice. Sole commanders don't usually encourage much criticism of themselves, or allow anyone but themselves to discuss the commission's affairs with the press or the government. The censorship can be bad for employees' and customers' and others' civil rights. It can also be bad for efficient performance, and for the government's chances of knowing exactly how well the organization is doing its work, and whether it needs support and encouragement, or some special investigation, or a change of command. If the government Minister responsible for the performance of a public enterprise with its own statutory rights can officially deal with it *only* through its chief executive, all its other staff being forbidden to speak to government or the public, the Minister can't be sure of knowing all that a Minister *should* know about the enterprise, including the quality of its chief executive.

These disadvantages can be reduced in many cases by inserting elements of group responsibility, executive accountability and free speech between the executives and the government in the form of a corporate board, as follows.

Public corporations can have whatever constitutions their statutes specify. Some are governed by boards consisting wholly or partly of their executives, and accordingly have some of the 'command' characteristics of the type of Commission just described. To avoid those disadvantages one method (I think usually the best) is to vest the corporation's powers in a board of part-time, non-executive members, all external to the corporation, appointed by the government for fixed terms. The executives are then employees of the governing body rather than members of it, and each group can properly develop its judgments of the other. This structure has much in common with the private corporate structure required by law in a number of West European countries, in which a working board of executives answers to a supervisory board of non-executives.

Where it works well – i.e. where it suits the nature of the business and where the government appoints good board members and the board appoints good executives – this structure has a number of advantages. Executives have to explain their activities, and get approval for many of them, at regular meetings with a knowledgeable board which has legal responsibility for the corporation's acts, and unlimited access to its records and activities. In most such corporations a casual observer might well suppose that boards routinely approve whatever their executives put to them. So they usually do. But because they are there and attentive, and have the power to hire and fire the executives, the proposals and explanations have to be well supported and acceptable. Approval can always be delayed or refused. Boards can take their own initiatives. And boards of able people with diverse expertise can be a source of new ideas, 'lateral thinking' and collective judgments of risk. Most important of all, in many cases, is the fact that (i) the board, (ii) the executives, and (iii) the Minister or other representative of government make a trio who can talk freely to one another, and when necessary *about* one another. The 'closed chain of command' is thus broken in a critical way, without necessarily weakening the capacity for decision and action. Any member of the trio can talk with any other. A government anxious about a public corporation's performance can quite properly ask the executives about the board and the board about the executives. And board members can safely criticize government policies with which they disagree. They can do it privately, and where it matters they can do it publicly.

Question: Why a board of *part*-time, *non*-executive members?

Two answers: (1) So that they can afford to be fearless. Their board seats are not their main source of income, or in most cases career satisfaction, so they can afford to resign or risk the sack if principled behavior – or effective political tactics – require that. Government can similarly sack *them* without the personal and legal problems that go with depriving employees of their livelihood. Such resignations or dismissals can signal to the legislators, press and public that serious issues invite attention.

(2) So that the employers who must hire and fire the executives and monitor their performance are not in common employment with them. If a group of people have to appoint and promote one another, so that they compete but are also beholden to one another – as on the boards of the many private-sector companies which don't have a dominant shareholder – disinterested judgment of each others' capacity and performance can be difficult. Good judgment is easier for non-executive directors who are neither in collusion nor in competition with the executives they hire and fire. But their record as directors necessarily depends on the executives' performance, so they have every incentive to get the best executive performance they can. There is the further advantage that the executives don't have to be chosen (as many Commissioners are) by politicians or public servants with too little first-hand knowledge of the candidates and the business.

As with a Commission, a statutory corporation's Act may empower the government to direct the corporation, or it may allow restricted direction or no direction. The government's control of its public enterprises does not have to rely on ownership.

Capital ownership

Statutory corporations can be owned by nobody, and own their capital. That is the simplest, cheapest, freest form of ownership, with least administrative costs. There need be no annual general meetings, or conflicts with shareholders about rates of dividend. How valuable those freedoms can be is illustrated by the later history of Britain's nationalized industries. Some of their Acts were eventually amended to allow the government to draw revenue from them. The official and academic studies of those industries are nearly unanimous in reporting that their performance deterio-

rated whenever government used its power not to demand a steady revenue, but to vary its demands according to its short-term budget needs, or its efforts to fine-tune the level of activity in the economy as a whole. Those purposes don't necessarily accord with efficient long-term planning of complex processes of investment and production within the public enterprises. The industries did better as independent self-owners.

An alternative to having public enterprises own their capital is to have them borrow some or all of it.

Public debt (1) The Australian government tried to ensure a stable public income when it created Telecom as a statutory corporation to take over the country's telecommunications. The balance of the assets over the liabilities that the new corporation inherited, i.e. the net value of its capital, was declared to be a perpetual loan from government, at a fixed rate of interest. The interest was the only revenue that government could demand from the corporation. That arrangement was thought at the time to have the following advantages over enterprise-owned or share-owned capital.

Interest for the use of capital seems a reasonable way for government to draw revenue from a public enterprise. For the enterprise, it has the advantage of being a predictable obligation which allows confident forward planning, and prevents the unexpected 'revenue raids' which British governments had begun to make on their nationalized enterprises. For the government, debt has one virtuous and one deceptive advantage. It keeps the enterprise directors aware that capital has a price and needs to be economized. And the interest payments appear in the corporation's accounts as debt service, i.e. as a cost, not a profit payment. The corporation can appear to be pricing its services to break even without profit, and the government can take its revenue without appearing to do any unpopular taxing or profiteering.

Those seemed to be prudent far-sighted thoughts. But they proved to be the long-term thoughts of short-term thinkers. Ten years of high and fluctuating inflation halved the real value of Telecom's notional capital and its annual interest payment. Feeling cheated, government legislated the first of a succession of reconstructions of its financial relations with the enterprise. In a general way, debt capital can be as awkward for public enterprises as it has often been for private enterprises.

Public debt (2) Those objections would not apply

to a type of public debt proposed by some Canadian, American and New Zealand economists. Calling it the Sovereign scheme, they would have most public infrastructure financed by national central banks. Currently in Western countries more than 90 per cent of new money is created as interest-bearing credit by private banks. There is nothing necessary about that proportion. In wartime most of any new money is created by the public central banks. The Sovereign proposal is that infrastructure investment be financed by low-interest or no-interest loans by national central banks. That would require three kinds of discipline. Government and its central bank must agree the principles on which such cheap money should be rationed. The loan conditions, including repayment in most cases, must be enforced, to see that politicians don't spend the loans as they are currently spending other public capital. The capital obligations could be indexed to a general deflator, to ensure repayment of the real value borrowed. And to avoid contributing to inflation the central bank may need to make a corresponding cut in the quantity of credit it allows the private banks to create. Since most of the infrastructure is for free or user-paid use by private enterprises and households, neither business nor voters should rationally object to the scheme (though some certainly will). We will return to the subject in chapters on financial systems and policies.

Private debt Public enterprises may borrow from private lenders for many temporary purposes, but they should not need to borrow permanent capital. Private enterprises 'gear up', i.e. add debt capital to their equity capital, for various reasons: they can't attract enough share capital (many small businesses can't attract *any*); or their owners don't want to share control or capital gains with more shareholders; or debt has tax advantages for them. None of those considerations need apply to public enterprises. In the long run the citizens collectively do best by investing their own rather than borrowed money. Governments should generally finance their enterprises from taxation or other revenue, or by loans from the public central bank.

INDEPENDENT INSTITUTIONS

At an opposite extreme from public service departments, or commissions under direct government command, are some institutions which governments finance without any formal control of them at all.

There have always been public non-profit institutions – churches, charities, universities and others – which have done their work independently of government. In modern times, as the demand for some of their services grew beyond their self-financing capacity, some governments have chosen to finance them to expand, rather than replacing them by public services. For more than a century British national and local governments have financed some independent schools and some church schools as well as government-owned schools. When governments began to finance universities, some (like the French) developed national systems of university employment and management. Others (including the British) financed the existing universities without taking over their government. Government intervened from time to time to reform them, but left them still as independent self-governing institutions. When more universities were needed government created new ones with similar independence, though they were by then almost entirely government financed. If a particular government wanted more influence over them, as in the 1980s, it was achieved by attaching conditions to the universities' funding rather than by centralizing their government.

If necessary services have to be financed by the taxpayers, why aren't they supplied by government enterprises? Why pay to have them supplied by institutions which the government does not own or control? It is usually because the independent institutions can do the work better, or cheaper, or both. Some reasons:

Capital The independent institution (church, university, school, nursing home, hostel) may have physical capital (land, buildings, furniture and equipment) which government would otherwise have to buy. It may be able to attract capital gifts and bequests which government could not attract.

Labor Churches, nursing homes, urban doss-houses, meals-on-wheels, St. John's Ambulance, Lions, Rotarians and other charities may be able to enlist some voluntary labor and some low-paid or part-paid labor which a government employer could not attract, or could not employ under the government's industrial policies and public service conditions. Many churches and charities are able to stitch together the paid and unpaid labor of differently placed and differently motivated workers without provoking conflicts between the professionals and the volunteers. (Sometimes the volunteers are off-duty, after-hours professionals, who would never do such overtime for their primary employers or for government.)

Are the volunteers unfairly exploited as cheap labor? Or do they get welcome scope for generous, caring and sociable strands of their natures which neither government nor private-sector employers can offer them? (Your human perceptions must judge in each case.) Some charitable enterprises certainly have more capacity than most government or private enterprises have to exploit the full motivational possibilities of the three-sector mixed economy.

Quality The independents may be better at the work than government enterprises would be. Some churches run better hostels and hospices than either public servants or private profit-seekers would run. For some purposes independent leadership – sometimes unpaid – can be more inspired and inspiring than the available public servants might be. At some tasks the available voluntary workers may be more patient and sympathetic than the available paid workers would be. Some branches of education, the arts, and caring services to young, old or handicapped people may be done better, as well as more economically, by independent organizations than by government organizations.

Accountability In many public activities, those who do the work should be accountable to the citizens whose taxes finance it. Those who provide the money control its use. But although that is a common kind of accountability it is not always the best. Other arrangements, including some elements of trust, may work better where the quality rather than the quantity of the service concerned is what matters, and is hard for distant, inexpert authorities to judge. Some churches, charities, research centres, national academies of arts and sciences can be trusted with grants-in-aid, leaving any necessary scrutiny to their own governing bodies and auditors, and the press and the public.

Next subject: many of the government's public enterprises may also do best at arm's length from the governments which create and fund them.

POWER OVER POLICY

Here are two extreme views of the proper relations between the government and the public sector of a national economy:

- *A radical politician* believes that the people elect their government to command the public sector. The only purpose of public ownership is to impose public policies where private market outcomes would be unsatisfactory. Within the law, government's power over its public enterprises should be

total and direct.

- *A cynical enterprise manager* does not want self-interested politicians interfering in his business, or naive politicians telling him how to run it. Just as private firms have to be registered and comply with the law, so do public enterprises have to comply with their founding Acts, render annual reports, and so on. That does not entitle Ministers or public servants to interfere with the day-to-day management of either of them – they can no more tell public enterprises how to do their business than they can tell private firms how to do theirs. The founding Acts of most public enterprises specify their general purposes. If government wants changes in public economic activity it should ask its enterprise managers to assess their practicality, and leave their implementation to the enterprises concerned. Public enterprises' constitutions should accordingly set them at arms length from government, protected by law from impulsive, short-sighted or self-interested political interference.

Partly, they both exaggerate. Most relations between governments and their enterprises are somewhere between those extremes. But chiefly, the relations vary with the nature of the work. Politicians don't want the same control over (say) individual gas bills or telephone connexions as over (say) the rates of income tax or welfare pensions.

We can't hope to list all the various policy-making arrangements which have existed, or might work best, between governments and their various enterprises. Among other things the best arrangements must often depend partly on the local facts of the case, as this text never tires of reminding you. But if you ever have to consider particular cases, *some* general principles are worth keeping in mind:

Government should have sufficient control of whatever it will be held responsible for. It should generally not have power over anything which it does not wish to be held responsible for. If political or public service leaders don't want to be pestered by every citizen who wants a building contract, a public housing tenancy, a pension, a telephone connexion or a local bus stop shifted, they do best to have the law forbid them to influence such details.

When legislators creating a statutory corporation want it to comply with government policy, but be free from detailed or improper political interference, a common device is to have the founding Act require that any government instructions to the enterprise be public, and reported to the legislature. In my experience this is an effective measure, but not because anyone normally complies with it. If there is reasonable accord between the enterprise and the relevant department of government they discuss policy freely, each listening respectfully to the other. Government Ministers learn the ethics and practicalities of the business. As long as what they want the enterprise to do is practical and proper, the enterprise complies. But if there is strong disagreement, or the enterprise directors think the political requests are not practical or not proper, they can refuse to comply unless they get a formal public order. If the politicians think the order would do them credit, they make it. If not, not. Thus the rule imposes some democratic discipline on both parties: if they disagree, what is done is what the press and public are most likely to approve, or at least to accept as a legitimate policy choice.

There is however one area of policy to which very little of the above can apply in practice. Enterprises which get their money from government, rather than from their trading revenue, generally have to take what they're given. In the past they only had to fear tax-cutting, cost-cutting constraints. But they may now face the sale and lease-back of their assets, or full privatization.

CAPITAL TEMPTATIONS

Recall the processes which converged to squeeze government budgets, especially in the English-speaking countries, in the 1970s. Through the long mid-century boom, with full employment, economic growth, and rising revenue to spend, the rich democracies had extended their educational and health and welfare commitments. Then a number of developments made those commitments more expensive than had been expected. Rising unemployment increased public welfare costs. People lived longer, using more health and welfare services. Science devised more expensive ways of prolonging life. Scientific and technological advances increased the need for education as they revolutionized productivity in agriculture, manufacturing and some service industries, shedding labor and raising wage levels. The rising wage levels spread to all occupations, including those whose productivity could not be much increased by the new technology. A lot of those labor-intensive occupations are in the public sector. Their costs rose relative to other indus-

tries' costs. To maintain the services, taxes would have to take a rising proportion of national income and therefore – directly or indirectly – of individual incomes.

Honest governments linked the tax increases to the welfare increases and defended both or skimped both. When Swedes decided their welfare provisions were excessive they drastically cut them. Japan did not try to solve its welfare problems by cutting its investment in necessary infrastructure and economic services. Nor, with only minor exceptions, did the rest of Scandinavia, Germany, the Netherlands, France, Italy or the Asian tigers. Only Anglo-Saxon politicians took to kidding their electors that they could have both rising welfare provisions and fixed or falling taxation. Impossible? In the long run yes, but in the short run no: those two could be reconciled for a decade or so – i.e. for two or three elections and terms of office – by raiding the capital budget. First, public capital maintenance and new investment were reduced to allow some switch of regular revenue from capital to current use. Next, saleable public enterprises were privatized, and the cash from the sales spent. Finally governments began to sell bits of their own physical capital and lease them back again.

Economically, most of those changes were improvident. They ran down the physical capital of necessary services. They threatened heavier taxation later, when catch-up investment and maintenance would be needed. They had a double effect on national saving. Government reduced its own saving when it switched regular revenue from investment to current spending. The sales of public assets switched some private investment funds from creating new productive capacity to buying existing capacity from government. When government used the cash from those sales to replace taxation it effectively handed it to the taxpayers, who spent the usual 70 or 80 per cent of it on consumption rather than investment. Thus both public and private resources were switched from saving to spending, from investment to consumption.

(Be careful: all these shifts were tendencies to which there were exceptions. Some of the Japanese and other privatizations did not reduce the net volume of public investment, and were done more for reasons of efficiency than tax-saving. Some of what the national accounts classify as consumer spending was on consumer durables, i.e. household investment; those funds were switched from one kind of investment to another, rather than to consumption. It is a plausible rather than a provable assumption that the funds which purchased the privatized industries would otherwise have financed new productive capacity. Nevertheless there is not much doubt that the net effect of all three capital-spending activities was some national dissaving, reducing what would otherwise have been higher levels of new public and private investment.)

Many European and Asian democracies have resisted most of these capital temptations. So have the Anglo-Saxon democracies through many phases of their modern history, as their educational and scientific and cultural achievements, and many great public works, make clear. From the strands of improvidence in some of the policies of the last quarter of the twentieth century we need not conclude that better government is impossible. So it is fair to ask who led it astray through that quarter-century.

Driving forces Recall Chapter 11's account of the Right turn through those years. As the long boom ended, economic growth slowed, unemployment returned, inflation accelerated. Keynesian big government was failing to keep some of its social democratic promises. But growth had meanwhile made most people better off, reduced the proportion of blue-collar workers, and increased the proportion of comparatively satisfied people with middle incomes and – perhaps – conservative interests and opinions.

The opponents of the social democratic program seized the opportunity to step up the attack on it. Under pressure, a quartet of forces welcomed – or were driven to accept – the program of privatization:

•   Many business people welcomed it for the low-priced assets and business opportunities it offered them.

•   Some public business managers welcomed it for the greater independence and higher pay it offered them.

•   Politicians in the English-speaking countries made tax capping and cutting a main means of competition for votes and office.

•   Many neoclassical economists in business, government, the universities and the financial press recommended privatization.

With such insistent expert advice from the business, political and professional elite there appeared to be rising tax-resistance among voters. Except in some American states the appearance may have been decep-

tive. Some American, Australian and other elections continued to be won by parties offering marginally more taxation than their opponents. When polls asked people what levels of service *and tax to pay for it* they favored, majorities often supported existing and sometimes higher levels. But the English-speaking countries' politicians persistently divorced discussion of taxes from discussion of the services they financed. Taxes? They could be contained by continuous improvements of public efficiency, and the reduction of public debt. Service quality? It could be improved by the same improvements of public efficiency, or by privatization or contracting out. Those were false pretences, more often than not.

Economists' responsibility   Independent economists in the universities, think-tanks and financial press should have warned business and government leaders, the political parties' rank and file and the public about the privatizers' false tax promises and the possible effects of their capital spending on employment, total investment, future taxation, and the distribution of income and public services. Some economists did so but most did not. Many applauded the sales and helped to plan and market them. That expert legitimation of the program was powerfully influential in attracting disinterested politicians', public servants' and press support for it, and public tolerance of it. Much of the economists' support seems to have been prompted by general attitudes to public and private enterprise, and to political and market forces – attitudes derived more from neoclassical theory than from either the logical implications or the actual effects of privatization.

As an economist you will need to understand government's capital opportunities and temptations better than many of those experts did. Here is a list of questions to ask and possibilities to keep in mind when considering transfers from sector to sector. When government buys a private enterprise or sells a public one, assets change hands for money. So in each case -

•   Where does the money come from, and what might it otherwise have financed?

•   Who gets the money, and what are they likely to do with it?

•   Is the change likely to increase or reduce total investment and productive capacity in the economy as a whole?

•   Is the change likely to increase or reduce future need for taxation?

Answers reflect some general probabilities, but vary with local conditions and policies. So the questions need to be asked and answered for each particular case. Changes in either direction tend to be controversial. Nationalizers or privatizers tend to ask one set of questions, and their opponents another set. But whatever their propagandist purposes, they all do well to understand the likely effects of their policies. So whichever side you incline to, try to keep all the following possibilities in mind.

NATIONALIZATION

When the British government bought the nation's railways, coal mines and steelmakers from their private owners between 1945 and 1951, it had unusually favorable financial conditions. War had justified high progressive income tax, which the government was slow to reduce through those first six years of peace. War had also justified a change in the usual method of managing the supply of money. Instead of private banks creating new money in the form of interest-bearing loans (you will learn about it in later chapters) the Bank of England created most of it for the government at low or zero interest. Price and wage controls made for low inflation, and there was some public restraint of private rates of interest, so if government did borrow from private lenders it could do so at low interest. There was also an inflow of American aid, part loan and part gift.

Government was thus able to buy and re-equip the industries, and considerably improve their performance, without adding much to its own debt or future interest bill. The whole purchase price went to private capital owners who were likely to re-invest it. To the extent that they did so they increased private investment without increasing private debt. That helped the private sector at a time when it needed massive capital replacement and re-equipment. Together the two sectors kept the economy fully employed, and the welfare costs of unemployment low.

Is nationalization always as useful to both sectors and the taxpayers as those British acquisitions were? Not necessarily. It depends in each case on the cost of the funds which buy the industries; the effects on their efficiency and profitability; effects on inequalities, on employment, on welfare costs; effects on the balance of foreign trade and payments; and so on. Judgments have to rest on case studies. It is true that average-efficient industries can usually earn more in public ownership than it costs to service any public debt

incurred to buy them. But it does not follow that the citizens would benefit by buying the whole private sector into public ownership. Many other considerations apply.

PRIVATIZATION

Selling public services to private owners is claimed to make the services, and the economy as a whole, more efficient; to help balance the government's budget; and to reduce the need for taxes by reducing public debt. How well privatization serves those and other purposes varies with circumstances. Here is a list of contrary effects which have been observed in some or all cases. Some of them can be avoided by prudent government. Where they can't be avoided, prudent government should probably not privatize. You know a number of the items already, but it is useful to have a consolidated 'warning list', so here it is.

Efficiency

1. Remember that some activities tend to go best in public ownership, some tend to go best in private ownership, and many have done equally well or badly in either. Many recent privatizations have been of activities which can go well in either sector. Why privatize them? It may be done for other reasons than efficiency. Or it may be justified by the capacities of public and private management in particular countries at particular times.

2. Where technical changes make it cost-efficient to sack big numbers of traditionally secure public employees, some governments privatize the services to avoid wielding the axe themselves. But selling inefficiently over-staffed enterprises tends to reduce the prices they will fetch, so -

3. Governments aiming to privatize inefficient services have often reformed them first to get higher prices for them. There is then no need to privatize them to improve their efficiency – but governments still do so because they actually have other purposes than that. British and Australian governments have deliberately made some services less efficient in order to get higher prices for them. How do you do that? Give them legal rights to monopoly, and to charge higher prices than they charged as public enterprises. The private buyers of Australia's very efficient blood and serum services were given (by contract and Act of Parliament in 1994) a ten-year monopoly of blood services, to be

supplied at twice their previous price, which was already a profitable one, though less than half the prevailing world price.

4. Remember that criteria of efficiency have to be chosen, and the choices reflect values and social purposes as well as technical considerations. Services efficient for some purposes may not be efficient for others. A public service which is required to serve a number of purposes may serve them efficiently. (For example it may be required to charge the lowest prices consistent with breaking even; to serve customers at remote locations; to cross-subsidize from some richer to some poorer customers; to buy home-produced rather than imported inputs in order to maintain employment or the balance of payments.) After privatization it may be freed from some of those obligations so that it can cut some costs, raise some prices, and operate profitably. The public and then the private operations may be equally efficient for their different purposes. (But that argument does not excuse enterprises which are inefficient for *their own* purposes. Some public services have certainly been inefficient at some or all of their multiple duties. Some private enterprises have been nationalized because they went broke.)

Balanced budgets

5. In the short term, selling assets helps governments to balance their budgets. This is because they publish simple cash-flow budgets which balance all the money they receive against all the money they pay out. The accounts do not distinguish capital from income or investment from current spending. (Private directors who published accounts like that would go to jail.) Governments which use the proceeds of asset sales to balance their budgets are usually dissaving, i.e. reducing total investment. They spend capital, or – as item 7 will explain – they let the taxpayers spend it.

Debts and taxes Privatizers often promise to cut taxes by using the capital proceeds of privatization for the capital purpose of reducing public debt, which in turn will reduce the annual interest bill which has to be paid from taxation. There is one absolute and one conditional objection to this argument:

6. The capitalists who buy public industries or services always want higher returns than they could get by lending money to the government free of

risk. The prices they are willing to pay for the public assets reflect that. Example: A lender may lend government $20m at 5 per cent interest per year, for a safe income of $1m a year and his $20m back at the end of the loan. But to buy a market enterprise with full trading and share-price risks, investors commonly want the possibility of a much higher rate of return. (Economists call it the 'equity premium'.) For the chance of $1m a year a share-buyer may offer only $10m, hoping for a risky return of 10 per cent in income and capital gain. So if government is paid $10m for a business which earns a million a year, and repays $10m. of debt which costs only half a million a year in interest, it has halved the taxpayers' income from the business and doubled the corresponding need for taxation. In practice the tax effect has usually been worse than that. Remember that *real* interest – the actual purchasing power that borrowers pay lenders for the use of their capital – is the difference between the rate of interest the borrowers pay, and the rate at which inflation shrinks the value of the capital which the borrowers eventually repay. Through the third quarter of the twentieth century the rate of inflation was close on the heels of the rate of interest and sometimes ahead of it, so that the real rate of interest on safe lending to government in many rich democracies averaged about one per cent. Borrowing thus cost government and its taxpayers much less than the borrowed funds could earn for them when invested in profitable user-paid public services. So selling those services could cost the taxpayers even more than the above example suggested. One critic has estimated that the net profits of Britain's public business enterprises, if they had been retained in public ownership, would have greatly exceeded the £3 billion annual saving of real interest that could have been achieved by using the sale proceeds to repay debt. And those and other such estimates assume that the proceeds *were* used to repay debt. But they rarely were. Read on.

7. The commonest use of the proceeds of privatization has not been to repay debt. It has been to cut taxes or put off increasing them. That conveys the capital proceeds of the sales to the taxpayers. Individual uses of the money vary, but on average they spend about 70 per cent of it on consumption goods and perhaps 10 per cent on household investment goods. So total national investment is likely to be

less by 70 per cent or so of the proceeds of the sales. (Likely rather than certain, as explained earlier.)

The British case Some of the tax effects can now be observed rather than estimated. Through the 1980s the sale of British public enterprises and services financed big tax cuts. None of the responsible politicians warned that the cuts must be temporary, and they may have helped to get the government re-elected in 1987 and 1992. But by 1993 the capital windfall was spent. There was nothing profitable left to sell. The public earnings were gone. One year into its last five-year term of office the Conservative government faced a budget deficit of 8 per cent of Gross Domestic Product, nearly three times the proposed limit for a full member of the European Union. In 1993 it therefore announced the biggest peacetime tax increase in British history: £17 billion a year, as the permanent cost of the ten-year spending spree. Most of that is an annual income transfer from all the taxpayers to the minority who own shares in the privatized industries and services. The evidence does not suggest that the losers are getting much of it back in better or cheaper services. Selling profitable public enterprises necessarily increases the long-term need for taxation, and unless there are compensating changes it increases inequalities of wealth and income.

Foreign exchange

8. Countries short of foreign exchange can go through a similar cycle of quick gain then permanent loss. If foreigners buy their public enterprises and pay for them with foreign funds, the payments are windfalls of foreign exchange. Thereafter the balance is worse by the amount of profit the new owners export, and perhaps by a tendency for the industries to import more inputs than the public owners did. There may not even be an opening windfall if instead of bringing foreign funds the foreign buyers raise most of their purchase money from lenders in the privatizing country.

Acceptable privatization Opponents of the general privatization of profitable public activities usually make some exceptions -

9. Ex-communist countries are right to privatize many of their industries.

10. It sometimes takes public action to create private enterprises. When Japan was short of

private entrepreneurs, public servants created many firms to pass to private owners when they were established and viable. In modern cities, new suburbs can't attract local shops until there are enough residents to make enough business for them. Life can meanwhile be hard for the pioneers, especially women at home with children. Some public developers build neighborhood shops and subsidize them until they are profitable enough to sell to private owners.

11. Governments sometimes rescue failing industries by acquiring them, re-financing and reforming them, then selling them back to more competent private owners.

Other disagreements Some social-democrats fear privatization in a more general way as part of the Rightward shift from government to market (as its friends say) or from democratic government to private corporate government (as its critics say). Specifically -

12. Critics expect privatization to -

- raise some consumer prices

- increase unemployment, and therefore public welfare costs, as private owners shed labor

- reduce job security

- stop government supporting the private sector, especially its export and import-replacing industries, with low-priced or subsidized transport services and other public inputs

- increase inequalities of wealth and income

- reduce the citizens' and their government's democratic capacity to influence the national economy for their collective economic and social purposes.

Many privatizers agree that privatization will indeed have those effects, which however they welcome because they believe that they will -

- subject the services to profit-seeking, market-disciplined management which will make them more efficient

- relate prices more efficiently to costs of production

- economize labor, price it flexibly, work it harder and improve everybody's incentives

- increase business and taxpayers' pressure to cut excessive welfare provisions, especially those which hinder the downward movement of wages

- reduce government interference with the efficient market allocation of resources.

There are also moderate and pragmatic people on both sides of the argument and on the middle ground between. Examples –

13. Some 'dry' economists agree that efficient performance depends more on the quality of management, and on other conditions including the presence or absence of competition, than on the type of ownership. If good government, or competition, or the threat of privatization can keep a public service efficient there may be no need to privatize it.

14. Some social democrats who want an effective and influential public sector for many economic and social purposes see a need to economize public ownership *because* its necessary uses are so many and important. Government should not disperse its attention, or strain public tolerance, by owning anything it does not need to own or doing anything it does not need to do. Remember how effectively Jim Landis economized public power and employ-ment, and business tolerance, in his design of the Securities and Exchange Commission which regulates American corporate behavior.

15. There will always be opportunities for bad government of the public sector (though vigilant political, press and public opposition can reduce the opportunities). There are also opportunities for bad government of the private and household sectors. For good overall economic performance all three sectors need to perform well, and to do so all three need appropriate government and public services. If people want good performance by a well-designed public sector there is no escape, by privatization or any other means, from the need for good government. 'Public choice' theories which imply that good government is impossible, or that least government is always best, are plainly false, but if they are believed they are destructive because they discourage people from striving for better rather than worse public business policy and management.

Part Five

THE DISTRIBUTIVE INSTITUTIONS

- *MARKETS*
- *THE DISTRIBUTION OF WEALTH AND INCOME*

40

Market theory

Here begin a number of chapters on main causes which determine what actual goods and services the private sector of a mixed economy produces, and how they are distributed to its members.

You've met much of the analysis already, but some important parts of it are yet to come. We are about to pass from the component parts of the mixed economy to questions about its structure and performance as a whole. You have studied how people arrive at their wants and preferences, and how those wants are met: how households and private and public producers are organized, get their capital, meet their costs, and price their products. In one respect the analysis is incomplete. In the private sector it is from their markets that producers receive many of the signals which tell them what quantities of which products they can hope to sell at what prices. But how do those markets actually work – how exactly do demand, supply and price interact with each other, and with the market strength of producers, dealers and consumers, to determine what gets produced? And how well do they do it – how efficiently do the market processes match output to the people's demands, and how well do they satisfy *your* ideas of fair distribution?

That's the business of three market chapters. The first one reminds you how demand, supply and prices may be related in a competitive private sector as modelled in neoclassical theory. Chapter 41 then lists conditions which can cause real markets to differ from ideal models and from each other. Chapter 42 offers examples: what is similar and what is different in the markets for farm products, city land, clothing, cars, and legal and medical services.

What consumers can demand depends on what they can spend, so four chapters follow on the distribution of wealth and income, in both the meanings of 'distribution': the pattern of shares that people get, and the processes which determine what each of them gets. The distribution of spending power not only determines how much of the whole output of goods each consumer can buy. It also helps to determine *what* goods are produced. A sudden change in the distribution of spending power would allow *some* change in the distribution of goods and services to consumers, but its full effect could not follow until the productive institutions had adapted to a different pattern of demand to produce a different array of goods. Never forget that the 'efficient markets' and 'efficient allocation of productive resources' of neoclassical theory do *not* stand for what you or I might judge to be an ideally efficient use of those resources. At best, to the extent that the markets work efficiently, producers supply the effective demands that arise from the distribution of spending power. That use of the available resources can only be as good, socially speaking, as you believe the distribution of spending power to be. Thus the two divisions of this Part Five – on markets, and on the distribution of wealth and income – belong together.

SUPPLY AND DEMAND

This chapter outlines relations between demand, supply and price as they are modelled in neoclassical theory. That is not always the best way to understand them. But you will meet the neoclassical language so often that you need to know and understand it.

Back to carrots. Imagine a village whose whole vegetable supply changes hands directly from growers to consumers at market stalls in the village square. The local shoppers have different individual wants, and amounts to spend, but as a population the whole quantity of carrots they will buy depends on (among other things) the price they have to pay. Similarly, individual growers have different costs and profit requirements but as a group the whole quantity they will supply depends on (among other things) the price they can get. What quantities buyers will demand and growers will supply at any particular price is represented on the most famous of all economists' graphs. You met a demand curve for carrots back in Chapter 22. Here it meets a supply curve:

Price per bushel	Quantity demanded (bushels)	Quantity supplied (bushels)
$10	100	400
8	120	360
6	150	300
4	200	200
2	300	50

Table 40.1 Demand and supply schedule for carrots

The demand curve DD shows what quantity the customers will buy at each price. The supply curve SS shows what quantity the growers will supply at each price.

Equilibrium

At a price of $6 there will be an unsold surplus of 150 bushels. Growers will drop the price far enough to sell the surplus. At a price of $2 there will be a shortage of 250 bushels. Customers competing for the scarce supply will bid the price up. Only at a price of $4 will the supply match the demand, and the market clear, with no carrots left and (at that price) no frustrated buyers. That's the equilibrium price (E).

When high prices deter some of the customers, what do they do? Most of them buy other, lower-priced vegetables. That may bid those low prices up a bit, while the declining demand for carrots prompts their growers to switch to growing whatever the customers are now preferring. Thus market signals and buyers' and sellers' responses nudge the prices and quantities of the various vegetables towards a general market equilibrium. Recall the relevant bits of utility theory, indifference theory and the theory of marginal cost pricing. A general market equilibrium has a set of prices at which –

- supply matches demand for each vegetable
- the satisfaction which customers get from their last dollar's worth of each vegetable equals the satisfaction they get from their last dollar's worth of each other vegetable that they buy
- growers sell each vegetable at marginal cost price, so that
- the last dollar they spend on growing carrots will bring the same return as the last dollar they spend on growing parsnips, etc.

By those means the available land, labor and capital are

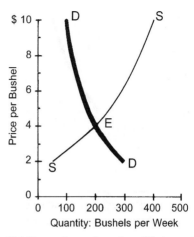

Figure 40.1 Demand, supply and equilibrium price for carrots

put to the uses which most efficiently satisfy the customers' preferences.

Time

Those market adjustments take time. To attract more carrots this week, buyers may have to offer prices high enough to divert and truck carrots from distant markets. To attract more next season by inducing the local growers to switch some land from potatoes (which use land more efficiently than carrots do) the price may have to rise, but not so far. If the rise in demand is part of a general swing from meat to vegetables it may take the growers some years to decide that the swing is permanent and to buy and convert pasture land for vegetable growing. When they have done so the new carrot price may be much the same as it was before the change in demand began. Theorists accordingly need three supply curves.

S1-S1 is this week's supply curve: it shows what prices would attract what supply of carrots this week. S2-S2 shows the likely supply curve next season, assuming that growers guess right during the planting season about the demand six months ahead. S3-S3 is the long-term supply curve: what the growers will eventually supply, at what prices, when they have had time to adjust their land and equipment to any changes in demand.

(But estimating demand six months ahead, because production decisions have to be made six months ahead, may not be easy. You will return to the time-lag problem in the following chapter under the heading of 'lead times'.)

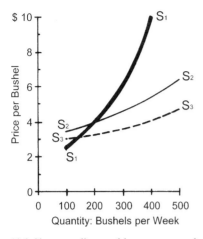

Figure 40.2 Short, medium and long-term supply curves

Perfect competition

Economists define an industry as perfectly competitive only if it produces an undifferentiated product (like wheat or some minerals), it is easy for new producers to enter the industry and start up, and there are so many producers and they are all so small that they are all price takers: nothing any one of them can do can by itself have any significant effect on prices. That excludes undifferentiated products like cement or steel which have big economies of scale and heavy capital requirements so that they tend to be oligopolies, difficult for newcomers to enter. It excludes all products which have elements of monopoly: city land, patented or trade-marked products, products differentiated by model, style or brand image. A few raw farm products and minerals are almost the only products to qualify: most competition, however vigorous and efficient, is 'imperfect' by this definition.

But however rare perfect competition is, one feature of it is common enough. There are many industries in which some or all producers are price takers, not price setters. They face market prices which their own output cannot affect. So when they have done their best to produce efficiently at minimum cost, their market options are confined to deciding how much to produce. They must have U-shaped costs, i.e. there must be some volume of output above which their unit costs will increase, or they would not be price takers in a competitive industry. (You know why *un*limited economies of scale would enable bigger firms to undercut and outsell smaller ones, and could lead to monopoly.) So although the demand curve for the industry as a whole may slope like our demand curve for carrots, for each individual producer it is horizontal: whatever quantity he supplies, the price won't change. So an individual producer's supply and

demand curves in a perfectly competitive industry, or in any industry in which the firm concerned can't influence prices, are likely to be like this:

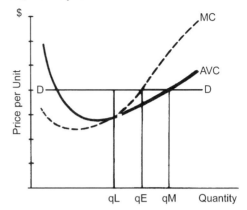

Fig. 40.3 Equilibrium for a price-taker

Revise chapter 34 if you need reminding why the firm should sell the quantity at which price equals marginal cost (MC on the graph) and not average cost (AVC). The fixed price is the firm's equilibrium price only at E, i.e. when the firm produces quantity qE. Producing either less (qL) or more (qM) will reduce total profit.

How do you know? With a price which this producer's output can't affect, the horizontal demand line (D-D) shows the price, and the marginal revenue whatever the firm's output. When marginal cost is below marginal revenue, as at qL, there is more profit to be made by increasing output. When marginal cost equals marginal revenue, at qE, to increase output any further will increase costs more than revenue. Movement either way from the equilibrium quantity will reduce profit.

Is there no way for this producer to increase output and market share profitably? It can only be done by cutting costs further, and thus shifting the firm's supply curve to the right as you will now be reminded.

CHANGING CONDITIONS OF SUPPLY AND DEMAND

Buyers' incomes and preferences can change. Producers' costs can change. When they do, demand and supply change for reasons other than price. Recall the difference between what theorists call a movement along a demand or supply curve and a shift of the curve. One means a price change caused by a quantity change or a quantity change caused by a price change; the other means a change caused by anything else. If people simply grow fonder of carrots and want to eat more of them, theorists shift the demand curve to the right –

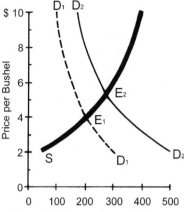

Figure 40.4 Demand curve for carrots

Price per bushel	D1 Former demand (bushels)	D2 New demand (bushels)
$10	100	160
8	120	200
6	150	250
4	200	330
2	300	500

Table 40.2 Demand schedules for carrots

S-S is the unchanged supply curve. D1-D1 is our old demand curve. D2-D2 is the new demand curve. To induce the growers to supply the extra carrots they want, the buyers have had to bid the price up from the old equilibrium at $4 (E1) to the new equilibrium (E2) at which 270 bushels change hands each week at $5.70 a bushel.

The new price may well be temporary, to induce the local growers to plant more carrots, and to attract more distant suppliers while the local crop grows. When it matures, if the new volume of output uses the same technology and has the same unit costs as before, producers competing for shares of the market can be expected to bid the price down to its former level of $4 (at which the equilibrium volume will rise further, to

330 bushels). Only if the increased volume entails permanently higher costs – perhaps from using inferior land – need the initial rise in price be permanent. If the increased volume allows new economies of scale the increased demand may even result in a lower price than before. There's an example later in this chapter.

Meanwhile some gene engineers have joined with horticultural researchers to produce a supercarrot which grows bigger and quicker for given inputs of land, labor and fertilizer. The farmers' unit costs fall. Competing with each other for market shares, they drop their prices and increase their output until they are again pricing their product at marginal cost. Here are old and new supply schedules, graphed onto our old and new demand curves.

Price per bushel	S1 Supply of carrots (bushels)	S2 Supply of supercarrots (bushels)
$10	400	600
8	360	500
6	300	400
4	200	330
2	50	20

Table 40.3 Supply schedules for old and new carrots

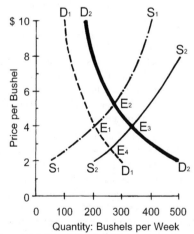

Figure 40.5 Supply and demand curves for carrots before and after changes in tastes and technology

Market responses to changing conditions

Each curve on the last graph shows what quantities buyers would buy and suppliers would sell, depending on the price, at a particular time. But we can imagine a history of successive changes which would prompt a theorist to put all four curves together, as we just did, on one graph:

1. There was once an equilibrium where the old demand curve (D1-D1) crossed the supply curve for old carrots (S1-S1) at E1. At that equilibrium 200 bushels sold each week at $4 a bushel, grossing $800 for the growers.

2. Health education persuaded people to include more carrots in their diet, so at any price they demanded more carrots than before. The demand curve shifted to the right. As D2-D2 it now crossed the supply curve (S1-S1) at E2. At that equilibrium 270 bushels sold at $5.70 to gross $1539.

3. The development of the supercarrots (by public researchers at no cost to the growers) cut the growers' unit costs and shifted the supply curve to the right, to S2-S2. Since the buyers learned how healthy carrots were they had always been *willing* (as indicated on their new demand curve D2-D2) to buy 330 bushels a week if the price were $4, and now they were *able* to do so because (as indicated by the growers' new supply curve) 330 bushels was the volume at which their marginal unit cost and price would be $4. At this third equilibrium (at E3) 330 bushels at $4 grossed $1320. (What can you deduce from the fact that, while volume has increased, gross revenue has fallen from $1539 to $1320? If you can't deduce that the demand for carrots must be inelastic, and confirm it by reference to the demand curve or schedule, you need to revise Chapter 23 on the elasticity of demand. If instead of a lot of growers competing for shares of the market the carrots were all supplied by a ruthless and unregulated monopolist, he would have kept the volume down to the E2 figure or lowered it further, and let the supercarrot's lower costs yield him a monopoly profit.)

4. A couple of years of high carrot intake and people become bored with them. (Oat bran displaces them as the miracle health food.) Buyers revert to their earlier preferences, as represented by the old D1-D1 demand curve. They still eat more carrots than they used to do because the supercarrot has brought prices down. The old D1-D1 demand curve crosses the new S2-S2 supply curve at E4, an equilibrium at which 260 bushels sell at $2.40 a bushel to gross $624. Compared with the $800 a week the growers used to make by pro-

ducing fewer carrots at higher unit cost before these changes began, they have no cause to bless the supercarrot! But everyone else can bless it – both the carrot-eaters who get more carrots for less money, so have more to spend on other goods, and the producers of those other goods who can expand to meet increased demand. Even the carrot-growers may be as well or better off, depending what use they find for the land they switch from carrot-growing.

DIVERSE CONDITIONS OF SUPPLY AND DEMAND

There are different patterns of *demand* for different goods and services, and not all industries have the *supply* conditions represented by the upsloping supply curve we have used so far, because not many industries have costs which rise with rising output. Individual firms may have U-shaped costs, which rise if output exceeds a certain optimum, but for whole industries costs which stay level or fall with rising output are commoner.

The common textbook 'cross' with a down-sloping demand curve crossing an upsloping supply curve may fairly represent conditions in the very short term: an increase of demand may push prices up for as long as it takes producers to increase their capacity, as in the four-phased response above. But in many industries a two- or three-phased response, with a delayed price increase or no increase at all, is more likely:

1. Producers, wholesalers and retailers meet the increased demand by running down their stored stocks, without price changes.

2. If new productive capacity is on stream by the time the warehouses are empty, the new demand continues to be met at unchanged prices (or lower prices if there are new productive efficiencies). If new capacity is *not* ready, prices may rise to ration the existing output or to attract imports.

3. When new capacity *is* on stream, if unit costs are as they used to be, prices should return to their former levels. They may fall further if there are new economies of scale, or if capacity has been increased by adding plant of a new, more efficient vintage.

We can finally notice and graph some other patterns that may arise from different elasticities of demand or supply in particular markets.

Constant costs There are many industries which use the factors of production in much the same proportions as the whole economy does, and have achieved all available economies of scale. Assuming that they are competitive and price their products at marginal cost, they can normally expand production without any change in price. Output depends on how much is demanded at the constant price. If output changes it must be for some reason other than price, so theorists must record a shift *of* the demand curve, not a movement *along* it.

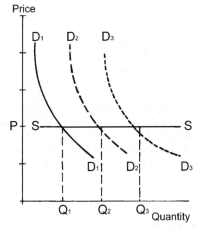

Figure. 40.6 Constant cost supply (S) with shifting demand (D1, D2, D3)

Limited supply Some goods come in quantities which can't be increased, or not beyond some finite limit, whatever the demand for them – unique works of art, unique city locations, positional goods. If more or richer people compete for shares of them, the price goes up. Because it is a price change caused by something other than a change in quantity, theorists call it a shift *of* the demand curve, not a movement *along* it.

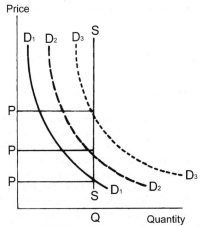

Figure. 40.7 Constant-quantity supply (S) with shifting demand (D1, D2, D3)

Income effects on supply When studying work and wages you learned that, whatever some workaholic individuals may do, whole populations tend to work less as wage rates rise. If (against my advice) you think of employment as a 'labor market' you see an unusual market relation between supply and price. The higher the price, the *less* the producers will supply; the lower the price, the *more* they may have to supply to earn enough to pay for what they regard as the basic necessities of life. So in conditions of full employment, or in industries using scarce skills, an increase in the demand for labor may raise its price but (consequently) *reduce* the supply of it.

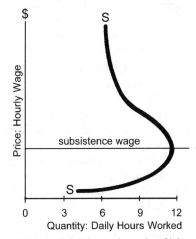

Figure. 40.8 Price and supply of labor

We say 'may' reduce the supply because the effect is not theoretically predictable. Remember the indeterminate relation between the income effect and the substitution effect: as wage rates rise you may seek *more* work because each hour of it buys you more goods and services – or you may seek *less* work because less will now earn the income you need and at the same time allow you more leisure.

You can think of other cases in which, because of the same income effect, higher prices may reduce rather than increase the quantity supplied. Examples: A subsistence farmer has to sell some of his output to pay his rent and buy things he can't grow. The higher the price he can get for his crop, the less he need sell and the better he can feed his family. His neighbor has to sell some of her land to reduce her debts in a bad season. She can sell less land the higher the price she can get per acre. For similar reasons an aristocrat living by selling his inherited art treasures may sell fewer the higher their prices rise.

Declining costs If economies of scale are available, and more demand can attract more supply without delay

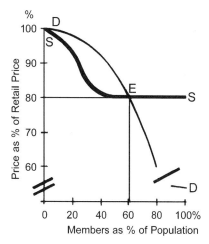

Figure. 40.9 Supply and demand for cooperative
membership and goods

or temporary shortages, supply and demand curves may both slope downward. Illustrated above are the demand and supply curves for membership in, and purchases from, a local consumers' co-operative. The bigger their bulk purchases are, the bigger the discounts they get, and the lower their prices to their members, up to the point at which the members are paying 80 per cent of retail prices – that's as far as bulk discounts can go. Some people will join the co-op for the company, without any financial advantages; because of the company, a few snobs won't join whatever the financial advantages are. On the graph the price axis represents the price of a week's membership plus a week's supply of co-op groceries as a percentage of the retail price of the same groceries. The quantity axis represents the percentage of the population who join. The supply curve shows that maximum discounts come when 40 per cent are members. Beyond that, more membership will not drop the discounted prices any further.

Rising demand You remember some circumstances in which demand may increase as prices rise. It can happen if buyers regard price as an index of quality. It can happen with some prestige goods, if big spenders want to be seen to own the most expensive car, or clothes, or van Gogh, on the market. It can happen with inferior or 'Giffen' goods. Figure 40.10 illustrates demand for margarine by a poor family who must have three pounds of spread per week but have only $6 to spend on it. They prefer butter which is steady at $3 a pound – but buy only as much butter as the price of margarine allows.

Depending on the price of margarine, the family will spend $6 a week on:

3 lb of margarine @ $2

OR

2 lb of margarine @ $1.50 and
1 lb of butter @ $3

OR

1.5 lb of margarine @ $1 and
1.5 lb of butter @ $3

Margarine does not have diseconomies of scale that could explain its price changes as effects of falling demand, so we must assume the changes in price and quantity did not cause one another. Theorists accordingly show shifts *of*, not *along*, the supply curve. (Perhaps the price fell because the butter lobby persuaded the government to remove the sales tax they had previously, mistakenly, persuaded it to impose on margarine.)

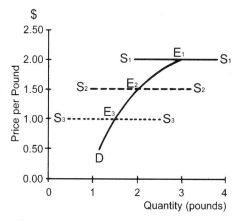

Figure 40.10 Demand and supply of margarine

Expectations There is a more general and more important reason why a rising price may increase demand. If people see a new price not just as higher but as *rising* they may buy more now, whether to avoid buying at a higher price later, or in hope of re-selling at a higher price later. Similarly suppliers may sell more if they perceive a lower price as a *falling* price. As guides to buyers' and sellers' behavior the demand and supply curves are defective because they are timeless. 'In principle', Paul Streeten writes, 'for every point on the demand curve there should be a third dimension, showing how much is demanded at this price now for different past histories of this price.'

EFFICIENCY IN THEORY

Before we digressed to survey some market diversities, we left market forces keeping the local vegetable market in equilibrium. Now stand back and imagine the same forces at work in the whole market sector of the economy, allocating resources so that consumers get equal satisfaction from the last dollars they spend on food, clothes, housing, motoring, golf, windsurfing, stamp-collecting and whatever. People sell their factors of production – the capital and capacity for work that they happen to possess – as advantageously as they can. They decide their balances between work and leisure, and between spending and saving. Firms compete for the factors they need to meet the consumers' demands. Those who survive the competition are the most efficient producers. Thus without anyone planning it the hidden hand ensures both the most efficient allocation of resources and their most productive use, to meet the people's individual demands.

Some markets work like that and some don't, as the theorists themselves agree, and as the following chapters will illustrate. But remember that however perfectly the markets work, you don't have to regard them as efficient if you don't think the distribution of income is efficient. Inequalities of spending power can be inefficient, as well as socially objectionable: society is not making the most satisfying use of its material resources if the last dollar of a millionaire's spending adds less to his joy than spending that dollar would add to the joy of (say) the poorest mother of the hungriest child in the society. If you believe in the diminishing marginal utility of goods to their consumers, as most economists rightly do, I think it makes equal sense – as a moral judgment, as a factual observation, and to keep your theory consistent – to believe also in the diminishing marginal utility of income. At their best, market allocation and competition between producers can have the great freedom and efficiency claimed for them, but there are some important functions which they cannot perform.

41

Market practice

In their practical working, markets differ from each other for reasons of four general kinds: the nature of the goods, the processes which produce them, the relative strength of buyers and sellers, and some special characteristics of speculative, gambling or confidence markets. Treat this chapter as a checklist of questions to ask when you want to understand how and why a particular market works as it does or is likely to work in future.

THE NATURE OF THE GOODS

The differences between carrots, personal computers, Hockney paintings and bus rides can affect the way they are marketed, especially the relative strength of their sellers and buyers and their capacity to respond quickly to market signals. When approaching a market new to you, notice at least these qualities of the goods:

How durable are the goods – between the extremes of cut flowers and Roman bronzes? Can they survive long periods in suppliers' warehouses? Are they cheap or dear to store?

How portable are they – between farmland and diamonds? That may be a physical question: land and most buildings are immovable; the buyers and sellers of most personal services have to be present together. Or it may be an economic question: transporting the goods may be too expensive, or they are not good enough or cheap enough to compete in foreign markets. Remember how changing transport technology allowed a few multinationals to replace thousands of village brewers of beer. Steamships and refrigeration allowed New Zealanders to grow meat for British dinner tables.

How 'transparent' are the goods to their buyers? Most shoppers can judge the quality of fruit and vegetables. Scarcely any can see for themselves what is in computer software or pharmaceutical drugs. Some goods which the buyers can't judge at the point of sale, including medicines and software, are reliably labelled because both law and commercial prudence require them to be. Some have to rely on law because the commercial incentives are unreliable: nobody can see a finished building's foundations, or where the reinforcements are in its concrete parts, and its builders may be long gone by the time structural faults show, so most countries require expert public inspection of building work in progress. Some goods and services may always have faults invisible to their buyers: used cars, commercial religions, financial advice. There are also markets in which the buyers are the experts and the sellers are the suckers, as when ordinary folk sell their antiques, rare books, coin or stamp collections to professional dealers.

What degree of monopoly, if any, is dictated by the nature of the product? Are there close substitutes for it? How distinct is it from its competitors? How legally protected and how important to the buyers are brand and model identities, patents and copyrights and suppliers' reputations? It is useful to distinguish two sources of monopoly. One is simply ownership: almost any product can be monopolized if one supplier manages to own all the sources and producers of it. 'Mr Thorn once cornered corn, and that ain't hay', the song says; one might imaginably own all the carrot-growing land in reach of the local market; but such monopolies don't arise from the nature of the goods.

Nor do 'contestable' monopolies, when a single supplier (the village main street's only cafe?) must behave like a competitor because others *could* open up and contest her market. But the nature or legal status of goods or services *can* create elements of monopoly. They do so, for example, wherever there are patents, copyrights or legally protected brand names and trademarks. This sort of monopoly can coexist with any amount of the other sort: if there are twenty brands of bath soap on the market they may be produced by twenty competing firms, or by a few oligopolists producing half a dozen brands each, or by a single monopolist who produces them all. Looking only to the kind of monopoly that arises from the nature of the goods, we can sketch a range from full natural monopoly to a complete lack of it:

Piped water is a natural monopoly.

Aircraft, cars, computers, TV and radio receivers, sound systems, books, recorded music and other saleable works of art are examples of goods which have a unique brand and model identity or performance right or copyright. Most of them are at the same time competitive goods. Competition between unique, partly-different goods (makes of car, brands of soap) is customarily called monopolistic competition.

Some goods come either way, brand-named or anonymous. Pharmaceutical drugs include brand-named proprietary lines (you can buy Panadol or Disprin from the owners of those brand names) and generic supplies of the same drugs sold under their chemical names, usually at lower prices (you can buy paracetamol or aspirin from any number of suppliers).

There are a great many products which are usually traded, especially in wholesale markets, without brand-named 'product differentiation': most minerals, metals, farm produce, building materials, paper, glass. In retail markets there are many products, especially of the cheap utilitarian kind, whose makers' or brand names have little or no significance for their buyers: cheap clothing, furnishing materials, curtain rings, can openers, doormats: things buyers can judge for themselves by sight and touch.

The nature of the product together with the prevailing technology will usually determine how the product is produced. That in turn will help to determine the market strength of its producers.

THE PRODUCTIVE PROCESS

You might reasonably have objected to the first item on that last list, that it's the dams and pipes – the mode of delivery – rather than the nature of water that makes piped water a natural monopoly. The technology which chiefly determines the most economical way to produce a particular product may have a number of market effects. Together with other conditions of production it may determine –

- the scale of production
- the size of firms engaged in it
- the length of any productive and market chains: (i) how many distinct productive processes are there from raw material to finished product; (ii) are they done by the same or by different firms, and consequently (iii) how many market transactions are there between raw material and final sale?
- lead times, i.e. how long it takes producers (for technological reasons) to respond to market demands to increase output or change products
- the degrees and kinds of monopoly and competition in the industry
- the relative market strength of buyers and sellers along the market chains.

Scale You know what is meant by economies and diseconomies of scale: poems are best written one at a time by independent individuals; steel is made most economically on a large scale by big firms; piped water can usually be delivered more economically by a monopoly than by competing suppliers. If there are continuous economies of scale up to the whole volume of demand, so that any bigger firm can undersell any smaller one, there is likely – unless government prevents it – to be a monopoly with some or all of the opportunities for good and bad market behavior described in the sections on monopoly pricing back in Chapters 34 and 38.

Nevertheless in studying markets you will find that although large scale, large firms, monopoly or oligopoly, and abuses of market strength do often go together, they don't *always* or *necessarily* go together. One purpose of this present analysis is to alert you to particular conditions in which scale and size do or do not make for market strength, and for market efficiency or inefficiency. As examples in advance, to suggest the care with which you need to explore relations between market size, strength and behavior:

- Big multinational airlines, carmakers or producers of household soaps and detergents may compete vigorously while your village newsagent, plumber and hairdresser have virtual monopolies.

- Buyers as well as sellers vary in strength. Recall our comparison of the buyers of steel and pharmaceutical drugs. Medicines sell to inexpert individuals, some of them frightened and vulnerable, many of them advised by doctors whose own incomes are not affected by the cost of the drugs they prescribe: drugs which under some countries' health schemes are paid for by insurers who will tend to do better the more the society spends on medical services. Steel, by contrast, sells to tough, expert customers like carmarkers, shipbuilders, civil engineers and building contractors who will all do better the lower their costs are. Though the drug companies are no bigger or more oligopolistic than the steelmakers, they are able to build bigger mark-ups into their prices and earn higher returns to funds invested than most steelmakers can.

- Remember why 'most competitive' is not always 'most efficient', especially in capital-intensive industries with long investment lead times. Strong firms may be able to invest in more research and product development, plan further ahead and take more risks than perfectly competitive firms can do if they must always be shaving their margins for short-term survival, and handing all their earnings as dividends to their shareholders to ward off takeovers. There may also be dangers of capital inefficiency if there is *too much* competition in industries with expensive capital but easy entry: for example half a dozen airlines, heavily indebted and competing with half-empty planes, may do worse and charge higher fares than (say) two lines restricting their capacity as collusive oligopolists, keeping their fares down to deter new competitors, and running nearly full.

Market strength The nature of a product and the best way to produce it with the available resources usually determine the possible economies of scale. Where the economies are such as to make large firms *potentially* the most efficient, there may be as much monopoly or oligopoly as law and government policy allow. It is prudent to say potentially the most efficient, because of the alternative uses that can be made of monopolist and oligopolist market strength. It may be used to restrict output, raise prices, and get labor and raw materials or other inputs at lower prices than would prevail in competitive markets. The gains achieved by those means may be used to inflate profits, owners' dividends and directors' pay, or to allow performance less efficient than competitive conditions would encourage. But the same market strength may alternatively be used to achieve all possible efficiencies and economies of scale, and to pay fairer wages, charge lower prices, plan further ahead, do more research and product development and maintain more prudent financial policies than smaller firms in more competitive conditions with fewer economies of scale could manage to do.

Those are possible uses and effects of the market strength that can *result* from large size. But market strength can also be a *purpose* of large size. When it is, i.e. when firms grow for the main purpose of increasing their market strength, there can be conflicts between size and efficiency, for example if growing firms meet diseconomies of scale.

Sometimes the conflicts can be resolved. Just as an individual can own a number of companies, so can a company. Conglomerates – groups of companies which own each other or are owned by a holding company – may sometimes keep each company at its efficient size while deriving added market strength for some kinds of concerted action by the group as a whole.

Where excessive size reduces productive efficiency it may still pay owners and sometimes employees if (i) it creates enough market strength to allow monopolist, oligopolist or collusive pricing which increases revenue by more than the excessive size increases costs, or (ii) it enables the firm to cut some costs by more than it increases other costs, for example if the firm saves more by using its market strength to get cheaper labor and inputs than its excessive size costs it in operational inefficiency and administrative tophamper.

HOW STRONG ARE THE BUYERS?

We already noted contrasting relations between buyers and sellers of steel and medicines. So far we have focused on the strength of the sellers. But wherever there is imperfect competition and therefore some advantage to be gained from market strength, what chiefly determines any advantage is the *relative* strength of buyers and sellers. Deals between equally powerful monopolists, or between equally powerless neighbors exchanging home-grown apples for home-grown pears, may well arrive at the same prices as they would in perfectly competitive markets, because they bargain from equal strength or equal weakness.

Among firms, buyers tend to be strong or weak for much the same reasons as sellers are. To assess a firm's strength as a buyer you may ask how big it is, and what market share it has. Is it the only buyer of the relevant product? (Economists call such a monopolist buyer a monopsonist.) Is it one of only a few buyers, and if so, do they collude to keep prices down? What alternative sources of supply are there, if any, if the regular suppliers bargain too hard?

We can simplify by classifying all buyers and sellers as either strong or weak. Here are the four possible market relations with an example of each. As you read, try to think of two or three other examples of each.

Strong seller, strong buyer:
Power supplier selling to aluminium smelter.

Strong seller, weak buyer:
Monopolist public landlord letting a house to an unemployed lone parent.

Weak seller, strong buyer:
Orchardists selling yellow cling peaches (which are only for canning) to the only cannery in town.

Weak seller, weak buyer:
Orchardists selling white peaches direct to consumers in the local fruit market.

Now notice an oddity on that list. The single mum is *too* weak for any landlord to extract much rent from her. This landlord happens not to be a profit-seeker: by political decision her rent is 17.5 per cent of her income. Private landlords would take more than half her income, as they do to many poor tenants in her town. But they still net only about six per cent per year on their investments. For strong sellers to exploit their strength by charging higher-than-competitive prices, the buyers, however weak, have to have the necessary money to spend.

Now take the analysis a further step. The prices which strong sellers can get depend not only on how strong the buyers are and how much money they have to spend. They also depend on *whose* money the buyers are spending and for whose benefit they are spending it. Once again there are in practice four patterns. In order of the volume of spending in a rich economy, (i) buyers spend their own money for their own benefit; (ii) buyers spend others' money for those others' benefit; (iii) buyers spend others' money for their own benefit; and (iv) buyers spend others' money for the sellers' benefit. As we go through them, notice that in two of the four cases (though they don't account for much of the whole volume of buying and selling) sellers may do better the *stronger* the buyers are.

- **Buyers spend their own money for their own benefit** This accounts for much more than half of the number and value of all transactions. It includes almost all retail sales of goods and services and almost all buying by self-employed producers and small businesses run by their owners. Though most of the buyers have little or no individual market strength they can exert some collective strength in many markets through professional associations, independent consumer associations like the publishers of *Which* and *Choice*, and above all through government.

- **Buyers spend others' money for those others' benefit** This is most business buying by share-owned enterprises, public enterprises and government. Most of the buyers are competent and look for some optimum balance of low price and low transaction cost. On the one hand people buying for firms or government may not be as personally keen for good deals as they are when they shop for themselves and their households. On the other hand there is less scope for the impulse buying and self-indulgence which retail shoppers can allow themselves if they feel like it. People buying for their employers are usually rule-bound and accountable. Many of them will suffer if they waste their employers' money. Some of them will rise high if they spend it skilfully to the employers' advantage. With some exceptions noted below, business buying tends to comply most reliably with economists' models of rational choice and maximization. There have been some spectacular exceptions in the public sector but, partly in response to them, modern standards of management, audit and accountability are reducing the opportunities for extravagant public buying in most developed democracies.

- **Buyers spend others' money for their own benefit** Here belong directors in the public and private sectors as they order their own working conditions and perquisites. First observe the hard bargaining mode of the executive when he buys industrial land, builds and equips factories and negotiates discounts from the public utilities by threatening to take the factory offshore. Then compare his eager spending when he buys central city land and commissions a head office building, buys fashionable art to adorn the executive suite, hesitates between a Merc and a Jag and a BMW as his company car, and wonders whether the next group executive conference would go best in Geneva, the Bahamas or Aspen, Colorado. Others besides executives can play the game: some white-collar unions have established that their members can only be employed in air-conditioned offices in reach of subsidized child care, and can drive or be driven only in air-conditioned cars of specified size and horsepower. Some of that spending may serve corporate as well as individual interests: grand corporate headquarters may inspire confidence and attract business, workers may perform best in controlled temperatures. But wherever the spending goes beyond genuine corporate purposes, sellers are likely to find soft, extravagant buyers. The mark-up on luxury cars, most of which are (fictitiously) business-owned, can be much higher than the mark-ups can be on cars whose users pay for them from their own taxed incomes.

- **Buyers spend for the sellers' benefit** Buyers pay higher-than-necessary prices for sellers' benefit for one of three general reasons: for profit; for collective purposes of full employment, trade balance, equitable distribution of income, charity, etc.; or for corrupt gain. As follows –

(1) *For profit:* It is sometimes prudent for firms to pay their suppliers or contractors more than the lowest available competitive price. Firms may do that to keep regular contractors in business through slumps or other misfortunes so that their skills will still be available when good times return. They may do it to get a desirable new supplier established. They may do it to save transaction costs, if it would cost $100,000 to search the market and negotiate a more competitive deal which might save $50,000. If a building contractor, desperate for work in bad times, tenders an unduly low price for a project, the low price may bankrupt him before the work is completed, or it may drive him to cut corners by using unsatisfactory methods,

materials or labor to the disadvantage of the building's eventual owners. A firm which receives such a tender may reject it, but if it is from a builder known to be honest and competent it may be best to accept it but volunteer a higher price.

(2) *For collective purposes:* Other chapters deal with public efforts to reduce boom and slump, unemployment, inflation, foreign trade and payment deficits, welfare costs and inequalities of wealth and income. We need not list all those policies here, but some of them have the direct or indirect effect that buyers pay higher prices than might otherwise prevail, and sellers and their employees are among those who benefit. There are also charitable and welfare policies: government users and charitable private buyers pay uncompetitive prices for the products of sheltered workshops, because that is both cheaper and socially better than keeping handicapped people idle on the dole.

(3) *For corrupt gain:* Bribe public or corporate buyers to buy your firm's product for more than it's worth, or in preference to competitors' products. You may do it for the benefit of your firm, which may reward you for doing it. Or if you want to progress from corporate corruption to individual crime, arrange with an accomplice that your firm will sell for $9m goods which his firm will buy for $10m, leaving both firms' books in good order for audit, and the missing million in your Caribbean bank account. The biggest operations of the first kind have probably been in defence contracts and – at various phases of its history – Middle Eastern oil. But it happens on small scale too, whenever the company secretary slips the office cleaning contract to a less-than-competitive friend or relative. (But don't assume that corrupt deals are necessarily uncompetitive or inefficient. Plenty of government buyers in some ill-governed countries have bought their governments the best available goods at the best available prices, but have required bribes to do it.)

PRODUCTION CHAINS

We are listing conditions which may affect the bargaining strength of buyers and sellers, and consequently the prices at which they deal, and the effect of their market relations on the allocation of resources and the efficiency of production. The next step is to study a relation between two of those conditions: between the length of productive chains, and the market strength of the producers who constitute the chains.

A simple way to begin is to turn back to Chapter 34, to a productive chain in which a miner sells iron ore to a steelmaker who sells steel to a manufacturer who sells finished goods to a retailer who sells them to households. Each producer has costs. Each arrives at his selling price by adding a profit mark-up to his costs. The *price* which each charges is a *cost* to the next producer in the chain.

Notice two features of the chain. First, different producers have different market strength so they are able to get away with different mark-ups: the miner adds 10 per cent to his costs, the steelmaker adds 5 per cent, the manufacturer can add 15 per cent because he has elements of monopoly: he produces patented products with respected brand names and faithful customers. He uses a mixture of his own and others' market strength to get cheap steel – most users of steel are tough buyers with alternative international sources – then he uses his own element of monopolist strength for two purposes. It enables him to charge a higher mark-up than the other producers in the chain can do. And it enables him to restrain the retailer's mark-up: he advertises his brand-named products nationally, with suggested prices. Retailers can charge less if they like, but won't get much trade if they charge more. Thus the manufacturer keeps the retail price down to attract as much demand as possible, and also takes a disproportionate share of the total profit generated along the chain from raw material to the final buyers. Market strength can be used against other producers as well as against consumers.

Conclusion: You can't conclude much about wage and profit shares, allocative efficiency, or degrees of monopoly and the consequent opportunities for inefficient production, from analysing the market forces at any single stage of complex production. If the retail marketing of a product is perfectly competitive, i.e. if any number of retailers are competing to shave their costs and undercut each others' prices, that doesn't prove that the relevant industry is a perfectly competitive one. Elements of monopoly, with high prices or slack performance or both or neither, may occur at any point of the productive chain, and their effects may compound along the chain to the final buyers. Moreover 'chain' is too simple a metaphor for a great deal of modern production. Recall the number of industries which have to contribute to the manufacture of a motor car. Carmakers don't only need steel, as our simple chain suggested. They also need copper, aluminium, rubber, glass, plastics, paint, cable, machine tools and robotics, software and programming, and fabricated components from many independent suppliers, who in turn may need metals, chemicals, machine tools and so on. We should change the metaphor and think of production *networks.*

LEAD TIMES

So much for the patterns of market strength that may be found in productive networks. Their efficiency as a whole may also depend on the time it takes each producer in the network, and the network as a whole, to respond to changing demands. Suppose that retailers sell out of a particular product, have waiting lists of unsatisfied customers, and decide that there is a real increase in demand – the demand curve has shifted to the right, their economists tell them. At the same time the manufacturers' market researchers decide that the product needs some changes: there is some new technology that should be built into it, and buyers would like to choose from a wider range of styles and colors. To meet those demands, how far back into the productive network do there need to be reorganizations or new investments? Given the technology of production, what is the minimum time it must take to make the necessary changes and get the new models, in increased quantities, into the shops?

'Lead time' means the time it takes to vary output from existing plant, to create new capacity, or to start new firms or industries. The times may be affected by financial or other conditions, but normally are set by the prevailing technology. While her current crop of carrots lasts, a farmer can dig different quantities each day in response to yesterday's market signals. To increase the crop takes six months, and market conditions may change between planting and harvesting. A steel mill built in response to buoyant demand in 1988 may come on stream in time for the depressed demand of 1992. A paper maker who plants a commercial forest has to gamble on the technology and market conditions thirty or forty years ahead.

Buyers also have lead times. Airline timetables are committed a year ahead; new routes may require international negotiations before they are committed; new aircraft types require re-training of flight and maintenance crews; so orders for new aircraft may have to be committed years before delivery.

Lead times can make for market inefficiencies in three main ways. There may be misfits between buyers' and producers' lead times. Today's supplies may have been prompted by past market conditions which have since changed. Producers planning their future output in response to present market conditions may not know how other producers are responding. And where those three conditions coincide, they can cause big trouble.

Compound uncertainties of supply If industries with significant lead times also have large numbers of competitive producers, the effects of misjudging future demand can be compounded by effects of uncoordinated supply. A farmer wondering what crops to plant and what beasts to breed for sale six or eighteen months ahead has to guess three things: what the demand for each product will be *then*, what quantities other farmers are planting or breeding *now*, and what the weather will do between now and then. The second is often the hardest question: what are other farmers deciding to do? Suppose you got a good price for your wheat this year and you guess the demand for wheat will be much the same next year. Do you plant the amount you grew this year, assuming everyone else will do that too? Or do you plant less, assuming that this year's good price will induce a glut next year? Or do you plant more, assuming that others will plant less because they think this year's good price will induce a glut next year? Even if every farmer predicts next year's demand correctly, they can still produce a glut or a famine by guessing wrong about each others' reasoning.

SPECULATIVE MARKETS

An economists' dictionary defines speculation as the practice of buying goods to re-sell later, or selling goods and buying them back later, in hope of making a profit if prices or exchange rates have meanwhile changed. A broader meaning includes the element of gambling or guesswork in any production or trading decisions that are based on forward expectations.

Is speculative dealing useful, useless, or positively harmful in its general economic effects? In the two most important speculative markets, namely futures trading and insurance, there is a range of activity from one extreme to the other: from useful activities which help to stabilize prices and reduce risks, to opposite effects which increase risks and price fluctuations and motivate unproductive kinds of profit-seeking with unnecessary social and economic costs.

Speculative dealers buy now hoping to sell at higher prices later, or sell now hoping to buy at lower prices later. They perform useful functions for some seasonal industries. Most grains, for example, are harvested once or twice a year. When they are, there's a glut, with low prices. Over the following months the price rises to cover storage costs, and it may rise further for supply-and-demand reasons as supplies dwindle. Dealers who buy at harvest time (thus raising prices a little then) and sell later in the seasonal cycle (thus assuring supplies and lowering prices a little then, when there might otherwise be shortages) perform the useful function of smoothing the market and reducing the seasonal fluctuations of supply and price.

As for seasonal fluctuations, so for other business

cycles. The biggest speculative markets are in corporate shares, national currencies, and land. Speculators buy land at low prices during slumps to sell at higher prices during booms. They buy shares when the share market is low and sell them during the next boom or 'bull run'. Banks and other fund managers gamble incessantly on changing rates of exchange between national currencies. There is big money to win and lose. After the US deregulated its exchange in 1973 the West European currencies rose about 30 per cent against the dollar then returned nearly to their former level. In 1997-8 panicky Western speculators attacked a number of East Asian economies with very damaging effects. Between those dates they had twice brought Mexico near to national bankruptcy. Gamblers of various kinds now do more than 90 per cent of all international exchange transactions – less than 10 per cent serve the needs of trade, investment, debt service, travel or income transfer. You will study how and why later in this course.

Futures markets don't require you to own the goods you deal in, except perhaps momentarily. I contract now to sell you a thousand tons of wheat each month throughout next year at prices specified now. I don't own any wheat. I'll buy it the day I sell it to you, or perhaps not even then: I may let you buy it, and collect from you, or pay you, any difference between the market price you have to pay and the price fixed in our contract. I'm in this deal because I expect the market prices to be below the prices we've fixed. Why are *you* in it? You may be a gambler too, expecting higher market prices than I expect. But it is more likely that you want to *avoid* risks. Maybe you're a flour miller who sells flour to wholesalers ready packed for retail under established brand names. You have long-term fixed-price contracts with the wholesalers and you want an assured supply of wheat at prices compatible with those in your wholesale contracts. What you buy from me is really insurance: you pay me for relieving you of risk. That's a useful, stabilizing service. So is much traditional insurance. But by no means all of it, as you will presently see.

INSURANCE

Insurance is a service for which there are demands, supplies and prices so it might earn a note here as a market commodity. But it also affects the market risks and prices of many other goods and services; it affects the distribution of wealth and income; some forms of it can smooth otherwise-unstable prices, usefully; and economists' treatment of it seems to contradict a philosophical principle in which many of them believe. So there are a

number of places in this course where it might equally well be introduced. Here is as good as any.

Some disasters can smash households' security and happiness. If a breadwinner dies, a house burns down or is robbed or vandalized, a car accident exposes a driver to big damage claims, people's emotional distress can be compounded by bankruptcy. If doctors, architects, builders and other professional people are sued for negligence they can be ruined if they *can* pay and their victims can be ruined if they can't. Firms insure for the same reason as households do, against risks of fire, accident, theft, actions for damages, and other misfortunes.

Fortunately disasters are rare. If their costs are shared by all the people at risk they are low. If they are shared by big enough numbers they also tend to be predictable: from past experience actuaries can estimate the likely total of future claims, and the premium rates (i.e. the price of insurance to the clients) which will bring enough revenue to meet the likely total of claims. As long as insurance companies have honest, prudent and skilful directors they can usually perform their risk-sharing service for their clients without much risk to themselves.

The individual clients pay small rates for big cover – but if they avoid disaster, as a high proportion do, they lose quite a lot over their lifetimes. Insurers have to collect enough revenue to pay their own wages and running costs as well as their clients' claims. So is insurance unproductive: a loss we put up with for safety and peace of mind? No, it brings economic gain. Theorists explain –

> Where does the gain come from? It arises from the law of diminishing marginal utility – which makes the satisfaction from wins less important than the privation from losses. This law of diminishing marginal utility tells us that a steady income, equitably divided among individuals instead of arbitrarily apportioned between the lucky and unlucky people whose houses did or did not burn down, is economically advantageous.
>
> – Paul A. Samuelson & William D. Nordhaus,
> *Economics* (13th ed., 1989), p.499

Though I believe the quoted passage is exactly right, it should interest your watchdog. It comes from the best of all textbooks in the neoclassical / Keynesian tradition. In the first edition (1948) a footnote warns that economists disagree about interpersonal comparisons of utility. By the sixth edition (1964) two footnotes elaborate the methodological lesson. By the thirteenth edition, cited above, the misgivings have disappeared. But in all editions, other pages still give positive, value-free scientific status to Pareto efficiency, and to no other concept of efficiency. You remember Pareto efficiency: if an economy cannot increase anyone's income without reducing someone else's, it has that privileged efficiency regardless of how equally or unequally, justly or unjustly the incomes are distributed. Samuelson himself strongly prefers equitable to inequitable distribution of income, but he describes that as a moral or religious preference – a faith or a feeling, not a fact. But here, where it rightly

justifies insurance as both individually and collectively advantageous, the different value of a marginal dollar to rich and poor people is allowed to be scientifically observable without any need of moral or religious sentiment. This passage does not merely assert that for each individual, losses hurt more than gains please. It says that an economy with less random inequality will therefore yield its people a larger total of satisfaction than will one with the same income worse distributed.

EXERCISE

Amend the last sentence of the quoted passage, changing only the cause of the people's unequal luck:

'This law of diminishing marginal utility tells us that a steady income, equitably divided among individuals instead of arbitrarily apportioned between the lucky and unlucky people born with richer or poorer endowments, is economically advantageous.'

Question: How much of neoclassical theory would have to be changed to make the whole of it consistent with that principle?

Back to insurance. Like economic theory, it can have moral hazards. You can over-insure your property, burn it down yourself, and hope to collect. That's known in the trade as honest fraud. Dishonest fraud is when you insure a warehouse full of valuables, remove the valuables one night, then claim for them after burning the warehouse next day. The crime is difficult to detect, or to connect with you. Business arson is said to be a professional occupation in the US: while you are elsewhere with an unbreakable alibi, experts burn your place for you. (Who does it hurt? Insurance companies learn to include it in their risks and therefore in their prices. Their business clients have to add the increased cost to *their* prices. Insurance fraud robs all shoppers rather than the insurance companies.)

Those are familiar hazards. But other hazards have more effect on the market strength and behavior of buyers and sellers in some service markets. These effects occur when (i) buyers are spending neither their own nor their firms' money but insurance companies' money, and more strongly when (ii) it is in the insurance companies' interest to encourage more rather than less spending at higher rather than lower prices. You will meet one example later in a comparison of the costs of medical services in countries with public and private medical insurance. A second example, smaller in scale but worse in principle, occurs where, as in the US, doctors and other professionals are insured against damage suits arising from their own negligence, and lawyers are allowed to take payment by results. Together those practices have allowed a rapid growth of gold-digging litigation. Some

law firms charge contingent fees. If they think you have a case against a negligent doctor, dentist, accountant, investment adviser, your children's school, or the good Samaritan who stopped to help you after an accident but wasn't expert at first aid, the firm will sue the target's insurance company on your behalf at no cost to you if they lose, and for half the loot (proportions vary) if they win. Some aggressive firms don't wait for you to come to them, they seek you out and suggest causes of action you didn't know you had. If a lawyer offers you this service, what can you lose? What is formally an action between you and your doctor (or whoever) is really between a risk-taking lawyer and a risk-taking insurer. In some American professions such gold-digging actions are now so many and expensive that the price of their professional insurance is two or three times what it was a generation ago, and what it still costs in countries which don't allow their lawyers to work for contingent fees.

In medicine those are not the only costs. Many of the gold-digging actions are against doctors who, observing particular symptoms, do not order all imaginable Xrays, scans, blood counts, path tests and other investigative procedures. Some of those can harm the patient. Which of them are worth their risks is for clinical judgment in each case. Where an Xray is ninety nine per cent unlikely to reveal anything helpful it may often be best not to inflict it on the patient. But if the hundredth patient is likely to sue for negligence and damage the doctor's reputation, while ninety nine who suffer unnecessary radiation are not, doctors may be driven to Xray them all.

Besides potential harm to health, applying all possible tests to all patients is expensive. So the gold-digging industry raises the premiums of health insurance as well as professional insurance, and inflates the whole cost of health services.

Some of the harm is done by the principles which some judges have chosen to apply. (British and European judges have generally been more tolerant of honest professional misjudgments, and intolerant of obvious gold-digging.) But for our purposes, notice the American market conditions. About four fifths of medical spending is ordered by doctors rather than patients. In most cases they are spending neither their own nor their patients' money, but insurance money. They have an interest in spending it if the prescribing doctor also supplies the service. Each insurance company may resist claims if it can, but collectively the insurers do better the bigger the volume of spending. In one critical respect the lawyers are unregulated, and since their contingent briefs are mostly against affluent professionals and insurance companies they don't attract much popular disapproval or demand for regulation.

It is worth remembering this example for general methodological reasons. The harm described above does not occur as a simple total of the harm done by each of the contributing conditions. The combination of three conditions makes each of them more harmful than it would otherwise be. It is not true that private health insurance does x harm, professional insurance does y harm, contingent legal fees do z harm, so together they will do x + y + z harm. Each would do no harm, or less or different harm, without the others. Scientifically it can't be true to say 'A causes x, ceteris paribus' if (misreading the Latin) you mean that A exerts a steady causal force which may only be blocked or diverted by other causal forces. A, B and C in this example are people – doctors, lawyers, insurers –who choose to act in one way in some conditions and choose to act in other ways in other conditions. So you can't know what A will try to cause in all circumstances. You can only know what A causes in these particular conditions or those particular conditions. A and B, each wholesome in other conditions, may be harmful if C is present, though C is similarly harmless if A and B are not present. People *behave differently* in different circumstances. They may be greedy at the casino, fair-minded at work, generous at home. And they can respond inventively to new opportunities, such as a combination of professional insurance, contingent legal fees, and elected judges desiring re-election.

SUMMARY

This chapter has listed some main conditions which determine how fairly and efficiently particular markets work. They can be summarized in a set of questions to have in mind when you investigate a market whose working you want to understand in order to know how best to manage or regulate or free it. As follows –

The nature of the product

- How durable or perishable is it?
- How easy or difficult to store?
- How cheap or dear to transport?
- What home or foreign trade regulations apply to it?
- In the light of the last four answers, is it nationally speaking a tradeable product (wheat, steel) or non-tradeable (public transport, hospital services)?
- Is the product homogeneous (like wheat or steel of particular type and quality) or can it be differentiated to allow monopolistic competition (between brands of soap, models of car, etc.)?
- How readily can buyers judge its nature and quality before they buy it? If they need expert help, what public or private information is available to them? (Sellers may need help too, if they are wholesalers or retailers rather than the producers of hard-to-judge goods. Some quite complicated law determines which links in the supply chain, from producer to retailer, can be sued by buyers who have been sold faulty goods.)
- What regulation (for example of quality, safety, labelling) does the nature of the product attract?

The method of production

- How long and/or complex is the network of producers who contribute to production of the product?
- What market strength do the different contributors have and for what purposes do any strong ones commonly use their strength?
- Are there any lead times which reduce the speed or accuracy with which suppliers can respond to changing demands?
- How well informed can producers be of other producers' production decisions at the start of their lead time, and of the likely demand at the end of the lead time, i.e. when their products reach the market? If there are failures of communication (as between farmers) which can reduce the accuracy with which suppliers can respond to demand, are there any

public or cooperative arrangements to improve the information or regulate the supply?

- Do suppliers' lead times fit or misfit with any buyers' lead times, and with what effect?

- What economies and diseconomies of scale does the available technology offer to producers? What pattern of large or small firms, and of monopoly or oligopoly or competition, would those economies tend to produce?

- Has any degree of 'unnecessary' monopoly or oligopoly – i.e. any which is not justified by economies of scale – been established by the purchase and takeover of firms, or by other predatory strategies, or by monopolist ownership of necessary natural resources? If so, what uses are made of the market strength?

- What regulation, for example of safety, industrial relations or environmental care, does the method of production attract?

- Are the suppliers affected by any anti-trust or fair-trading regulation?

Pricing and marketing

- Repeating an earlier question: is the product homogeneous, or is there differentiation and competition between brands, models, etc.?

- Does the product sell in fixprice or flexprice markets? How do the suppliers price it? Are there elements of monopoly pricing anywhere in the pattern of producers, wholesalers and retailers?

- How much advertising is made worthwhile for the producers by the nature of the product, the degree and kind of differentiation and competition, and the elasticity of demand for it? How much if any do advertising and marketing costs add to its price?

- Is the marketing affected by any public consumer protection or price control?

The buyers

- Where does the product lie along a spectrum from necessities of life to trivial or luxurious indulgences? What alternatives to it are available to buyers?

- How susceptible to advertising are the buyers thought to be?

- How well can they judge the quality and value of the product for themselves? If they need help, what expert help is available and how many of them use it?

- Does their buying depend on credit and if so, how much is available to them?

- How much money do they have to spend on this product or its competitors?

- Whose money do they spend?

- For whose benefit do they spend it?

- What market strength do they have, and what use do they usually make of it?

Those conditions are likely to affect the buyers' income elasticity of demand and the price elasticity of demand. If market records are available from which the past elasticities can be estimated, estimate them – but remember that most statements about actual elasticities are estimates rather than hard facts. (Remember why? If not, revise Chapter 22.)

The use of this set of questions

Estimates of elasticity based on records of past prices, quantities traded and buyers' incomes are one basis on which future behavior may be forecast. Answers to some of our summary set of questions can provide another basis. Each method deserves more confidence if it is supported by the other. You can then know both what the measured elasticities appear to be, and what conditions appear to make them so and might change to make them different. Recall another early lesson: economists who use more of the ways of knowing something may know it better than those who trust fewer ways of knowing it.

A lot of the questions in the set ask about monopoly, differences in market strength, mismatched lead times, buyers over-spending other people's money, and so on – all causes of market failure if you regard perfect competition and self-adjusting equilibrium as the only kind of market success. The questions are not meant to suggest that the market sector of a well-governed democracy is a morass of exploitation and inefficiency. In most of the sector most of the time, market relations have great freedom, economy and efficiency. But what they don't have is much of the uniformity that is too easily suggested by a simple theory of self-adjusting demand and supply. Wholesale buyers of steel have different concerns from retail buyers of cosmetics. Antique dealers don't have to sell their stock at any price within days of getting it, as greengrocers have to. Used-car dealers, currency dealers and insurance brokers do their business on partly different principles. Nurserymen decide what seedlings to offer for sale, the government decides what is allowed to be sold as butter, bankers often decide which developers can build which office buildings and which companies can offer to buy which other companies. The questions in our set don't suggest that forces of supply, demand and competition don't operate in all those markets; they equip you to discover *how* they work in *each* market.

They may also equip you to be a better judge of market efficiency than pure theory could make you. Can markets be efficient, as some theories suggest, only where there is perfect competition between many firms, all of them price takers, with easy entry for new firms and plenty of alternative goods available to the buyers? Are elements of market strength always used to raise prices and reduce efficiency? Not necessarily. If the strong sellers sell to equally strong buyers, if they have compatible lead times, if each firm knows what the others are doing and they can all judge the quality of the goods, and if their industry is one in which bad behavior is likely to attract hostile attention from media and government – as for example when miners sell to steelmakers who sell to carmakers – they may well produce and trade as efficiently as any carrot grower. Meanwhile the perfectly competitive carrot market – in which many sellers face many buyers, there are plenty of alternatives to carrots, and sellers and buyers are equally able to judge the quality of the goods – may be in trouble from the weather, the growers' lead times and their ignorance of each others' production decisions and planting programs.

Why is it important that you understand such differences? First, for business reasons. Any marketing manager knows that wholesaling steel and retailing cosmetics call for partly different skills and types of market analysis. Second, market analysts like other economists should be alert for signs that what they study may be changing as they study it, and perhaps outmoding bits of their theory and method; and our question-set can help to keep them alert (though it also may need to change with the times). Third is a reason you have met before and will meet again. All industries and markets need some government, if only to define everyone's rights and protect them from crime. They tend to need more complex regulation, for their own purposes as well as society's, as their technology and organization become more complex with economic growth. The more complex the regulation has to be, and the more frequent amendment it needs in response to changing conditions, the more those who design the regulatory systems need to know exactly how the relevant industries and markets work, and would be likely to work under alternative kinds of regulation.

This is not a particularly socialist or 'interventionist' belief. Even if what you want is minimum regulation and maximum market freedom, it is vital to know what you can safely deregulate without self-defeating effects. (Deregulating the US Savings and Loans institutions without some elementary understanding of their managers' morals and market opportunities cost the nation's taxpayers an estimated \$450 billion.) Simple principles – 'one-liners' – rarely work without detailed local knowledge, and care in their application. Examples: 'Distrust capitalists: regulate every business power they can possibly abuse.' 'Distrust protection: the only efficient trade is free trade.' 'Distrust government: deregulate everything short of armed robbery.' Those may look like mutually contradictory opinions but they share the same disastrous fault of substituting simple one-liners for sufficient understanding of the activities concerned. Perhaps more than anyone else, those who most want to 'trust the market' need each market to have the particular amount and kind of government with which that market works best.

Hence our set of questions. It may pay to learn and remember them, as this chapter's concluding exercise. Keep them in mind as you now consider half a dozen examples.

42

Market examples

This chapter compares markets for beef, town land, clothing, cars, and medical and legal services. It compares examples only. It doesn't survey all known ways of marketing those goods. It won't equip you to understand your local market for any of them: that is likely to take local knowledge as well as text-book principles. These examples are to rub in the lesson that market forces can work differently for different goods, or for the same goods in different circumstances. To understand them properly you will often need (i) to understand some common relations between supply, demand and price; (ii) to ask and answer some or all of the questions in the set which you just learned for the purpose; and (iii) to be alert for any other features of the goods, the buyers, the sellers, the culture or law or other local conditions, that may cause particular markets to differ from text-book expectations.

BEEF

Some tribes in the highlands of Papua New Guinea customarily ate the brains of their dead. That transmitted the slow virus of the 'laughing disease' which killed some of each generation. When some British and European producers began to mince up old cattle and add them to the vegetable diet of living cattle, the cannibalism had a similar effect. Wherever the BSE virus originated, that was how the 'mad cow disease' came to be transmitted from one beast to another. Since then the beef business in the afflicted regions has been changing too quickly for a slow-changing text-book to keep up with it. But this chapter is here not to make you expert in any of its subjects, but to illustrate how differently markets for different products work in different technical and cultural and institutional conditions. So the beef market is one of two which are sketched as they worked up to the 1980s. (The other, for different reasons, will be the United Kingdom market for medical services.)

The nature of the product

Beef, once killed, used to go bad very quickly. It is now durable, storable, transportable and tradeable for limited periods: some weeks for fresh meat, some months chilled, a year or two canned. But it can't be stored for long enough to smooth fluctuations of over- and under-production. Once produced it does not last as long as the

lead time for increasing or reducing output. If you keep it alive it is expensive to feed, gets tougher and cheaper, and is soon too old for affluent populations to want to eat it. If you kill it, it needs to be eaten long before much change can be made in the size of herds.

Though it varies in type and quality it is homogeneous enough to prevent much product differentiation or patenting or brand naming (though genetic engineering and the creation of property rights to new species may change that).

Production chains vary widely. An African herdsman may kill an animal under a tree and hack off the bits his customers want. An American calf may have several specialist owners in succession from birth to death, then several more between the slaughterhouse and the dinner table. In most developed countries cattlemen breed the animals, raise them on pasture land, fatten some of them with grain feed. Abattoirs turn them into beef. Some of the beef goes to other producers for canning or other processing. Some goes directly or through wholesalers to the retailers who sell it to households. The costs and prices along the way vary with the technology. In advanced economies the cattlemen may get 60-65 per cent of the retail price, the processors 10-15 and the retailers 25. The more specialized routes from ranch to dinner table, which pass the product through most hands and most transactions, are often the most efficient: in 1980 the US produced 21 per cent of the world's beef from 9 per cent of its cattle, and Europe produced 22 per cent of the beef from 11 per cent of the cattle. (The comparison is less simple than it seems because most of the US cattle were bred for beef only, many of the European cattle were also dairy producers, and besides those two functions some of the third world's cattle were also pulling plows and wagons or carrying loads on their backs. And some which were too old to work or breed or be eaten were kept alive for compassionate or religious reasons.)

Scale Above a modest farm size there are no great economies or diseconomies of scale for the cattle owners. So there is no technical need for big holdings, but no technical hindrance to them either. In North and South America and Australia there are small producers but also many big holdings, accumulated by purchase or by getting privileged land grants or leases from government when the land was first seized from its indigenous people. There can be vertical integration: Vesteys once owned a production chain from ranches in the southern hemisphere to retail shops in Britain; McDonalds own chains from ranch to hamburger. But big holdings, even with vertical integration, don't make monopoly pricing possible. Some local processors have local monopolies, but nationally and internationally beef remains a competitive industry of price takers, in which no one producer can have any effect on prices. But collective action, usually through government, can and does affect prices.

Regulation has developed for five main reasons. There are environmental reasons of increasing importance: a lot of valuable forest is being felled to extend cattle pasture; cattle can erode and degrade the land on which they're pastured; grain-feeding them is thought by some critics to be a needlessly inefficient way of turning grain into food. Meat can carry health risks which its consumers can't detect, so its hygienic processing is regulated. Transaction costs for many of the suppliers can be saved – dealers can buy and sell by telephone without inspecting each batch of meat – if the labelling of grades and qualities of meat are reliably regulated, as in many countries they are. In countries which export or import beef, governments may value employment in the industry and its contribution to their balance of trade and payments; the major exporting and importing countries regulate the trade with quotas negotiated between governments, with or without tariffs. If left to itself the industry's lead times can make it chronically unstable, so many governments try to stabilize the supply by various means. Regulation for those purposes necessarily affects producers' and consumers' interests and may have some producers' bias where cattlemen are many with many votes (as in parts of Europe) or relatively few and rich and politically influential (as in the US, Australia and Argentina).

Demand

Most of the final buyers of beef are households or individuals spending their own money for their own benefit. Exceptions such as expense-account restaurant meals are too few to affect the market much. So are the sales of some slaughterhouse by-products for use in glue, fertilizer, etc. The sale of hides for leather brings bigger revenue, but rarely enough to affect the number of animals slaughtered for beef.

A number of processors and dealers may buy the product in turn as it moves along the production chain from ranch to retailer. Most are expert and know exactly the quality and value of what they buy. All are spending their own or their firms' money for their own or their firms' profit-seeking purposes.

Some of the money may be borrowed. Many cattlemen use credit, and in most countries with big cattle numbers they can borrow on the security of live cattle. To do that they must often also insure the cattle so their credit tends to be expensive. Costs of credit, added to feed and other costs, help to make it unprofitable to keep a stock of beef cows without breeding from them through years when the market is over-supplied. The need to slaughter and sell any stock that is not currently earning intensifies the cyclical instability which will presently be described. That instability can make the allocation of resources inefficient. But the facts of scale and motivation from beginning to end of the production chain keep the industry highly competitive.

The demand for beef varies widely from country to country. Among affluent countries it seems to vary with culture more than with income. Argentinians eat an average 90 kilograms a year. When Japanese were averaging 5 kilos a year in 1980 they were paying $34 per kilo for the best cuts, while for the same best cuts the carnivorous Argentinians paid less than $3. Adjusted for purchasing power, with prices expressed in hours of work at average wages, Japanese still had to work six times as long as Argentinians did to pay for a kilo of beef. Other developed countries spread between those extremes in their prices and consumption.

Except in Japan the demand is relatively inelastic: between 0.5 and 0.7 if you remember how price elasticity is measured. There is slight cross elasticity: in the US it is thought to take a 10 per cent rise in the price of pigs to cause a 1 per cent rise in the consumption of beef. Preference for beef seems to be fairly obstinate. The low elasticity of demand means that high prices don't reduce consumption proportionately, low prices don't increase it proportionately, and changes in supply can cause disproportionate changes in price.

What chiefly destabilizes the supply and prices in many developed countries, led by the US, is an effect of the producers' lead times, follows.

The cattle cycle

Calves are born nine months after they're conceived. They are ready to become beef at ages between 15 months and 3 years. Heifers can conceive at 15 months or more so they are at least two years old when they deliver their first calf. It is then up to two months before their first opportunity to conceive again.

Consider what those lead times do to a decision to increase output. Suppose you have 1000 cows. For simplicity we'll assume you never lose any beasts by accident or disease. Your cows produce about 500 male calves and 500 heifers each season. You keep enough heifers (say 200) to replace the oldest cows, and send the rest of the heifers to slaughter with the males. Thus (not counting the old cows who sell for other uses than human consumption) your steady output of beef is 800 beasts a year: 500 males and 300 females.

Then a shortage occurs and prices rise. You decide to increase your output. (So do lots of other producers, for the same reason.) How can you increase beef output? You can slaughter some of the younger brood cows straight away – but that will *reduce* future output. What you have to do is withhold next season's heifers from slaughter and breed from them instead. Two years after they're born, when they join the brood cows instead of going to slaughter, that year's beef output will be down from 800 to 500 beasts. But two years after *that*, with your brood cows up to 1300 (200 replacements + 300 additions), you will have 1300 new calves each year. You save 200 of them to replace old cows and send 1100 to market. That's 37.5 per cent more than the 800 you were sending four years ago, 120 per cent more than the 500 you sent while you were slaughtering no heifers at all. Since the decision to increase output the lead time to do so has been 9 months gestation + 15 or 20 months maturing heifers to breed + 9 months gestation + 15 months or more maturing the next generation of calves for slaughter. That's a minimum of 4 years with intensive farming and feeding in Europe or North America, or 5 or 6 years if extensive farming leaves the herds on open pasture without winter shelter or grain feeding in Australia or South America. And through part of that time there has been some further reduction of supply and increase of prices, with further decisions to increase output, and more heifers therefore switched from beef to breeding, to produce an eventual *over*-supply.

Four or five years after the first decision to increase supply it does at last increase as the expanded herds resume sending all their heifers (except for necessary replacements) to market. If only a third of the producers have behaved as in our example, national beef supply will first have fallen about 12.5 per cent for a couple of years, then risen 25 per cent to a level 10 or 12 per cent above its original level. Demand is relatively inelastic, so adding 10 or 20 per cent to the supply drives prices down more than proportionately. Producers can see that the low prices will continue if the augmented herds continue to breed at full capacity. So they decide to

reduce output – and once again the first effect of that decision is perverse. To reduce output they market *all* the current crop of heifers to avoid replacing the old cows who are leaving the herd. If that doesn't cut the numbers fast enough they may also slaughter some of the breeding cows. Both those steps *increase* the beef surplus and drive its price down further, prompting more action of the same kind. Not all the cuts are based on deliberate estimates of future demand. Some ranchers leave the business altogether. Some are strapped for cash from the low prices and have to cut their herds further than they would like to. Three or four years after the first decisions to reduce output the herds have been reduced. The beef supply then declines further than most individual producers intended. There is shortage. Prices rise, slowly at first, then faster as producers respond to the rising prices (and worsen the shortage) by withholding heifers from slaughter to build up their breeding stock – and the cycle is on its way round again.

Why does this folly go on and on? Supply and demand are in equilibrium twice during each cycle as the growing or dwindling supply is momentarily at the equilibrium quantity. Having reached equilibrium why doesn't the supply stay there? Because the calves are already alive whose numbers will presently take the beef supply above or below the equilibrium quantity.

Why don't speculators smooth the market as they do for grain and some other commodities, by buying stock when it is over-supplied and cheap, to re-sell when it is under-supplied and dearer? Because cattle deteriorate with age and cost too much to feed.

There are some national differences. Supply is affected by weather. Demand is affected by the level of employment and prosperity, by the prices of alternative meats, by changing tastes and dietary beliefs. In Europe it is much more common to use the same breeds of cattle for beef and dairy produce, so the steady dairy business helps to stabilize cattle numbers and the supply of beef. But in the US there have been ten cycles, each of 10 or 12 years, since recording began in the 1880s.

The US is the biggest beef trader in the world. It exports some, and imports about a third of all internationally traded beef. So the American cattle cycle extends, a little less strongly, to America's beef suppliers and export competitors in South America and Australia. The cycle is well understood by all concerned. It is not too hard for producers to forecast the course of the cycle and therefore the general level of prices to be expected two or four or six years ahead. Nearly everyone – producers, processors and consumers – would be better off in the long run if the supply were stabilized and the market kept in equilibrium. So why doesn't it happen?

There appear to be a number of reasons. An equilibrium level of supply is not very likely to arise from thousands of individual producers' estimates of (i) what the ideal equilibrium supply will be four years on, and (ii) what share of it each producer should try for. Even if there were good information so that each knew what numbers the others were breeding, they might not agree about their shares of the market; and each one could expect that increasing his market share would gain him more than he would lose from the negligible effect of his individual over-production on prices. There is no pure market solution to the inefficiency of the cycle: unhindered market forces are what create it.

The problem invites a cooperative or governmental solution. Stabilization schemes exist for other farm products in the US and other countries: why not for American cattle? Why does the country which by most tests is the industry's most efficient producer continue knowingly, for a century, to be its worst allocator of resources? Producers, and many economists, fear that production quotas based on past output would protect inefficient producers, prevent efficient producers from expanding, and prevent newcomers from entering the industry. Those objections have less force if the quotas are tradeable, i.e. if you can buy and sell rights to raise cattle. But that also can be troublesome if courts then decide that a property has been created which government can't take away without full compensation, so that once created, the quotas can't be adjusted to changing market conditions to perform their stabilizing functions properly, and the industry can never be *de*regulated without government buying back the quota rights at market value. Nevertheless many stabilization schemes avoid those hazards and work well enough in other industries and other countries. Perhaps the cattle cycle is allowed to continue because of a general Texan distrust of the federal government and the use it might make of power over the industry.

The industry does support government regulation of foreigners. There are import quotas for beef from each of the countries which sell it to the US. The quotas are supposed to be used counter-cyclically. When US production is plentiful and prices are low, imports should be reduced. When home-grown beef is scarce and prices are high, imports should be increased. But in practice the government has to consider its relations with friends and allies, as well as the beef industry, when it judges how much harm it can afford to do to Argentinian or Australian producers. Some of them are more important

to their national economies and more influential with their governments than Texan ranchers are with theirs. Even when the quotas are set as the US producers want them to be, they have not so far done much to smooth the market fluctuations.

If you want to know more about beef markets before the new disease complicated them, a good short book is James R. Simpson and Donald E. Farris, *The World's Beef Business* (1982).

Other farm products

The American beef market is an extreme illustration of a problem which afflicts many farm product markets. To summarize, its three ingredients are –

- lead times which impose time lags between production decisions and outcomes, so that supply typically responds to past rather present market conditions

- uncertainty, because producers don't know each others' production decisions or what the consequent total supply will be; and

- further uncertainties about the weather and other natural causes, and their effect on output.

The effects of unpredicted or uncontrolled under- and over-production have made life harsh, uncertain and sometimes ruinous for a great many people. Though many farming families enjoy and defend their way of life, modern surveys tend to report them as less happy, on average, than people in most other occupations, especially in the Americas, Australia and South Africa where extensive farming can isolate them from each other and from daily town or village life. Besides solitude, farm life has two particular economic hazards. Over much of the world, for climatic or market reasons, farm incomes are unreliable. There are bad years of loss, privation and debt. The debt often outlasts the troubles that created it. Second, most of the troubles are not the farmers' fault. There is little or nothing that skill, prudence or hard work can do to prevent them: virtuous behavior is periodically not rewarded but kicked in the teeth. And when that happens, bankers and governments, plump in their secure city jobs, often seem to the farmers to be wilfully unhelpful.

What can make farm life more tolerable than that? At least four things can, of which three are economic.

First, be rich enough. Own enough land to graze enough sheep or beef cattle to earn enough in good years to see you through the bad years – and if necessary, right around the cattle cycle – without resort to debt. And in the seasons of the year when the beasts graze without much human help you may have time for hunting, shooting, fishing and some flyaway holidays.

Second, especially if you farm on more modest scale, have a producers' cooperative or a good government run a market stabilization scheme for your products. The world now has schemes of many kinds, and much expertise in their design and management. None of them is perfectly satisfactory, but many of them are better for producers and consumers than either the American cattle cycle or the few remaining areas of the developed world where grain or wool are grown without any stabilizing arrangements.

Third, farm almost anything on any viable scale in France's Dordogne, Australia's Monaro, the Yorkshire Dales, or some other incomparable landscape. Parts of this earth are so beautiful that almost any outdoor work they offer can be a joy. If the beauty is chiefly in the land and what it grows, farmers may enjoy its blessings most intensely the year round.

Fourth, farm in a settled way for a reliable local market with local custom or a long-term contract as the market stabilizer. That probably rules out raising beef cattle, sheep or grain – no producers can escape the effects of their unstable international markets. So produce fruit, vegetables, milk or free-range eggs for a local market, farming with up-to-date chemistry and equipment but using the land for its traditional purposes, as you know the other suppliers of that market are doing. Or get a long-term contract to grow fruit for a well-established cannery, or vegetables for a snap-freezing enterprise with a secure national market for its popular brand-named products. Time-lags between planting and harvesting need not matter if the production decisions follow the same rotations year after year, and the demand is steady.

Farming like that, for strictly local markets, does continue in a stable way here and there. Demand is maintained in country districts as declining numbers of farm workers are replaced by rising numbers of commuters from town. The farmers may even have some natural insurance against bad weather, because demand for most farm produce is less than unit-elastic. If supply declines in bad seasons, prices rise more than proportionately so farm profits may rise. Bumper years are not so good: besides the hard work of handling bigger crops, income may fall because of a disproportionate fall in prices. (But you may be able to buy young pigs or cattle to fatten on surplus fruit and vegetables.) The scope for such traditional, naturally protected farming tends to shrink with every further improvement of transport, refrigeration and controlled-atmosphere storage. Fresh strawberries and cut flowers are flown from hemi-sphere to hemisphere these days, and what used to be captive village customers can drive themselves to distant supermarkets, or shop in the cities to which they commute. But the richer and more sophisticated the customers become, the more many of them may *like* to buy good fresh local produce. So find a good orchard or vineyard or herb garden in reach of a popular market town, or contract with a dependable canner or snap-freezer, and you may be able to farm for modest but fairly regular rewards, without anxiety.

As the commuting population grows and the expanding suburbs approach, the time may come to sell the farm for suburban development. But when? Will you do best to sell as soon as the suburban use of the land will earn more than the farm does? Not necessarily. Urban land markets are our next subject.

TOWN LAND

You may doubt that land is a product – it was there before any human producers were. But *town* land in developed economies is a product of three distinct processes.

- It has been surveyed, subdivided, piped, wired, paved, powered, lit, and supplied with many public and private services.

- Besides those visible improvements it probably also has land-use rules which regulate (at very least) the floor area, height and permissible uses of buildings that may be put on it.

- Much of its value arises from where it is and what lies around it: from the access which its occupier has to workers and customers for her business, or to education, jobs, shopping and recreation for members of her family. Thus the value of an owner's land derives chiefly from the presence, and the past and present activities, of the rest of the city's population. Its value grows as the city grows, without its owner doing anything to improve it. For that unearned gain in land value which an owner gets from urban growth and other people's investments the usual word is 'betterment'.

You know a different word for that betterment. It is an externality: a benefit (or loss) which you derive from other people's transactions to which you yourself are not a party. In neoclassical theory, externalities signify market failure: someone is gaining or losing something otherwise than by their own efforts or fair exchange, and the people who *are* making the exchanges are not capturing all the benefits or paying all the costs of their transactions. Since Henry George introduced the idea in

Progress and Poverty in 1879 some reformers have wanted to capture the betterment for the public by taxing the whole of it, but no government has yet been convinced that it could be done consistently with an efficient market for land. Meanwhile open marketing may often be an efficient way to allocate urban land between people competing for its use, but it is not necessarily a fair way – what sellers sell and buyers buy is chiefly other people's externalities, plus rights of use created and limited by government.

Land with regulated uses

What purposes are served by planning, zoning and regulating the uses of urban land?

In city centres it may limit the density of office and shopping and other activities so as to limit traffic and pedestrian congestion, public transport overload, fire risk and other effects of overcrowding. It may protect people from the shadowing and wind acceleration which tall buildings can cause. It may be designed to shape handsome, well-proportioned streets and townscapes. That can be done in a variety of ways but nearly all the best examples were privately or publicly *planned*. London's best squares were created by private developers so rich that they could design and build whole precincts at once. Paris has regular building heights and styles along its beautiful boulevards because a dictatorial government seized and demolished tens of thousands of properties, built the boulevards, then sold the land that lined them to private developers with strict control of what they must build on it. Washington achieves a similar scale and continuous 'walling' of its street-scapes, with less uniformity of style, by a simple height limit: no building is allowed to be higher than the base of the Capitol dome. Some critics think London's business centre would look and work better if a similar rule had limited its modern rebuilding to the height of the base of the dome of St Paul's.

Elsewhere in cities and towns, zoning and other regulation usually have some or all of the following purposes –

- to segregate incompatible activities, for example to keep housing away from noisy or noxious industries

- to regulate environmental behavior and standards

- to conserve the general character of a street, neighborhood or town so that those who buy into it continue to get what they paid for: they won't find their peaceful house and garden overlooked by high flats, or their children endangered by activities which pour dangerous traffic into their once-quiet street

- to restrain some land prices: if residential and industrial land are zoned to exclude more profitable commercial uses, commercial buyers won't bid up the prices that residents and industrial investors have to pay for their land

- to locate activities in efficient relation to each other: a highway network, a public transport system and a land-use plan can be designed to encourage work, shopping, schools and the denser kinds of housing to cluster at the public transport junctions. Some governments also require that buyers of new urban land build on it straight away, to make full use of new public and private services so that those services can pay their way.

There are critics of the zoning and regulation of the uses of urban land. Their main objections:

- It makes opportunities for corruption.

- Residential areas are sometimes zoned to exclude shops, services, jobs, and meeting places which could make their life more interesting and efficient.

- Zoning can be used to segregate rich from poor housing (or white from black) to the poor's disadvantage.

- Regulating what people may do with their land reduces their freedom.

- Regulating land uses reduces the efficiency with which land is allocated and used.

The first three of those are objections to bad planning rather than to the principle of planning. The fourth objection has some force. But most zoning is demanded and supported by majorities, who think their secure enjoyment of their property and neighborhood is more valuable than freedom to use their land for un-neighborly purposes.

To the fifth objection – that market forces would work better without land-use regulation – there is no simple answer. But there is a complicated answer, and it is the main subject of this section on urban land markets. You can forget about regulation for a few pages now, as we explore the 'pure' market forces which are at work – or would be if there were no regulation in urban land markets.

First, who are the buyers, whose money do they spend, and in whose interest do they spend it?

Owners, lenders, users Except at the suburban outskirts, most town land sells with buildings on it. What is traded is thus a joint product with a single price, even if the land and the buildings can be separately valued.

Most 'real estate' or 'real property' (land with or

without building on it) is bought with some credit, commonly with a mortgage loan which entitles the lender to take the property if the loan is not repaid.

Buildings may be occupied and used by members of their owners' households, by their owners' employees, by tenants and tenants' employees, by the customers of services which are located in the buildings, i.e. by people other than the owners.

So if you ask how efficient land markets are – efficient at what, and for whom? – remember that their operation can affect the interests of –

- owners, of whom some do and some don't live or work on their properties
- the lenders who finance the owners
- tenants
- owners' or tenants' employees
- customers of business carried on at the property
- members of owners' and tenants' households
- neighbors and others affected by the use of the property.

We can consider in turn the buyers of real estate for housing, for shops and factories, for offices, and for changing uses as cities grow and change.

Housing

The efficiency of housing markets depends heavily on the credit available to the buyers. Recall (from Chapter 25) the reasons why household productivity is likely to be highest in total and most helpfully distributed if access to household capital, space and equipment is distributed somewhat more equally than money income. That usually takes some public action: perhaps credit from public savings banks and cooperative building societies for low-income home-buyers, and some public housing or rent subsidies for low-income tenants. If there is inflation there may also be some need for low-start or capital-indexed mortgage loans. If any of those aids need subsidies they can be rationed, for example in loans of limited size to people of limited means or to buy or build houses of limited value.

When there has to be rationing, applying it through the credit market is comparatively unoppressive and leaves the housing market free. That is a profoundly valuable freedom. Buyers spend their own money, or loans which they must repay, so they have the usual shopper's incentive to economize. They can shop around for the house they want, which also means the land, location, neighborhood character, schools and services, and access to kin, friends, employment, and what-

ever else they want. Experts might sometimes be able to judge one or two of those things for them better than they could themselves, but nobody can judge them all and weigh their relative value to particular households as well as those households can do – and have a right to do.

If the credit conditions are right, do such markets have any serious hazards for the buyers?

- The supply conditions need to be right. (If they're not, public action may be able to improve them, as suggested in Chapter 26 on housing policies.)
- There can be conflicting interests within households as to the best house to buy.
- Homebuyers are often inexperienced because they don't buy houses often. Expert advice about such things as structural soundness is usually available. For impulsive purchasers, some countries have 'cooling off' periods which allow buyers a few days to cancel contracts they regret. Some also require builders to insure new houses so that buyers can be compensated for any faults that appear after the builders have disappeared.
- Transaction costs vary. Buying a house can cost several times as much in time and professional fees in Britain as similar transactions cost in countries which have efficient public land-title registers.
- Households may grieve if they buy into quiet neighborhoods which are then invaded by disagreeable new highways or industries.

But with all those faults, housing markets still work better for most individual and social purposes than any alternative way of allocating the same resources would do. And if the mortgage-lending and town-planning conditions are helpful, housing markets can generally be extremely efficient.

Shops and factories

Efficient markets for commercial and industrial land often have the character of private markets within a public frame. City plans define a range of commercial and industrial zones. Within them there's a free market. If the planning is competent it can be at least as valuable to the commercial and industrial investors as to the public.

Most shops do best to cluster, to allow one-stop shopping for all kinds of goods. Neighborhood, district, town and metropolitan centres accommodate the clusters. If they share the centres with public services, professional services, hotels and cafes and entertainments, so much the better. The more those activities concentrate in a pattern of centres at public transport stops and junctions, the easier it may become to get their workers and customers to leave their cars at home for environmental reasons, and the easier it is for public transport to pay its way. But it can be very difficult for large numbers of commercial investors, perhaps with developers competing to establish shopping centres at rival locations, to achieve a good pattern of centres with the transport links and public services that they need. The land marketing and the outcomes can be more efficient if public planners define and zone the pattern of centres, and assure them of their necessary public services, early in the process of development.

Just as shops do well to cluster, so do many industries. Increasingly, manufacturing is done by big firms surrounded by smaller contractors and component suppliers. They cluster in particular regions and districts, if not always in single industrial zones. They are cooperative as well as competitive. Besides trading goods and services with each other and deriving advantages of scale from each other's presence they also exchange important non-market benefits – you'll meet them when you study national industrial structures and policies. It would be difficult for central planners to decide the best location for every firm. Firms are the best judges of the land and location they need. Having to pay for it encourages them to economize land. The directors and executives who buy the land generally choose it for the firm's profit-seeking purposes (though an occasional exception is noted below). Thus nearly everything about the buyers of industrial land suggests that a market is the best way to allocate it.

There remain three hazards, all of which can be reduced by public action. The risk of inadequate communication between interdependent firms is less if government establishes a suitable pattern of industrial zones with good services and road, rail and telecommunications within and between the zones. Second, the zoning reduces the danger that industrial development will be obstructed by residents, local governments or environmental protection authorities. Third, there are sometimes conflicts both within firms and within society about the regional location of industries. Some of the new industries setting up in the south of England might do better with the cheap land and willing workers of the under-employed north – but the firms' executives locate them in the south because they like to live there. Government can't prevent that, but it can offer contrary inducements: tax breaks, cheap services and other inducements to attract investment to regions which

need it.

Thus wherever the zoning can be competent and honestly administered, and can be in place before development begins, commercial and industrial land are likely to be allocated best by open marketing within defined zones. That is efficient for the investors, and it protects people everywhere else in the city both from unwanted invasions and from price competition for their land. Where shops, factories, housing, educational and recreational users can't bid for each other's land, prices tend to be lower in most of the zones. Developers who believe otherwise are usually standing in a commercial zone looking longingly at the cheaper land in a neighboring residential area. They suspect that zoning has made the commercial land dearer. In fact its main effect may have been to keep the residential land cheaper. But the zoning may *not* be worth having if corrupt administration allows land to be bought cheap, re-zoned, then sold dear. If more money can be made by manipulating the zoning than by using the land, the zoning may not help the market's efficiency.

(Some theorists expect zoning to reduce efficiency by restricting everyone's choices, and to raise prices by restricting the land available for each kind of use. But experience suggests that zoning usually increases efficiency by reducing uncertainty. It allows surer, less risky choices of location. It reduces the kinds of anxious or speculative withholding of land that occur when owners can't yet know what will prove to be the highest-paying use of their land. And it restrains prices for the reasons just explained. More about this soon, when we consider land in the path of urban growth.)

Redevelopment of built-up land

The private markets within public frames are not hard to contrive as cities grow, if the planning can be in place in time to guide the growth. There are tougher problems when built-up cities need to change their existing patterns of commercial and industrial location. The commonest causes of that are technical change and rising income. Old factories move out to new zones with room for mechanized assembly lines and workers' car parks. Residents desert the old city slums for new house-and-garden suburbs. As more households get cars and shop assistants get higher wages it becomes economical to shift most everyday shopping from corner shops in walking distance of their customers to drive-in, serve-yourself supermarkets. Land has to be found for the new factories and shopping centres, and big car parks around both. The factories can usually find vacant land at the city's outskirts. But the shopping centres have to convert land already in urban use. The workable sites are often covered with suburban houses, some of them much loved by their occupants. Some of the occupants are also shrewd, and guess that the last ones to sell to the developer will get the highest prices – so some hold out. To restrain those prices, shrewd developers conceal their intentions as long as they can, while anonymous agents buy up as many of the houses as they can. But concealing the plan from the residents also conceals it from any other developers who may be busy doing the same thing elsewhere in the district. If more than one centre is built where there is only custom for one nobody will make much money and – except at the closing-down sales – the customers won't be as well served as they could be at one efficient centre. But if, to avoid that, rival developers withdraw and have to sell their acquisitions quickly to repay their highly-geared debts, some may go bankrupt and some may take their creditors down with them.

There were many conflicts like that in English-speaking cities as the new shopping pattern was inserted into their old fabric through (roughly) the third quarter of the twentieth century. The new shopping is efficient, though there are environmental objections to the motoring it generates. But the processes by which the new shopping sites were contested, decided, acquired and cleared were often far from efficient for their developers or anyone else. Unaided market processes can't do it efficiently. If government chooses and zones the sites then leaves developers to compete to buy them there are often expensive delays as shrewd owners hold out for high prices. There may also be resentment at the prices they get: why should some households but not others be enriched by the stroke of a government planner's pen? But there are other objections if government gives private developers powers of compulsory purchase.

To convert land from one use to another in those circumstances it may be best to replace the market process altogether. Public planners can plan the new pattern, buy the sites as fairly as possible but compulsorily where necessary, then convey them to developers by competitive tender. The conditions of tender can require the new centres to have other good things besides shops. Such public action can be cruelly oppressive to some of the people who must move, or it can be done with care, and practical help to its victims. It will always be resented by some, but it may well hurt fewer people, and convert the land at less cost, than private market processes have sometimes done.

Office buildings

Dealers in office land and buildings extend our market sample in a number of ways. Some office buildings are commissioned by able people spending their firms' money for their firms' profit by providing offices well designed to meet the needs of the people who will work in them. That's at one end of the spectrum of buyers. At the other end are some office developers who use other people's money, don't own the land beforehand, won't own the finished building any longer than they can help, may not need to pay much attention to the interests of the people who will work in the building, and will do quite nicely for themselves even if their firms go bankrupt and take some of their creditors with them. We will briefly imagine one case at the virtuous end of the spectrum and some halfway along it, then report a real-life horror story from the other end.

(1) Investment officers of an insurance company, after careful market research, judge that their city's growing numbers of lawyers, public accountants, stockbrokers and other professional people who need central-city locations will soon need some more office space. The market researchers sample potential tenants and elicit their detailed needs and rent-paying capacities. Planners find the best balance of low price and good location among the available sites. Architects eager for business design the building with careful attention to the potential tenants' wants, and also to the company's desire to put up a civilized building that will improve the streetscape (and the company's reputation) and comply with all planning and environmental requirements. None of those commissioning or designing the building will work in it, but the better it suits its tenants and adorns the city the quicker it will fill, the higher its rents can be, and the more profit it will earn for its owners. There are no significant conflicts of interest, and the market transactions which get the building built and tenanted are all efficient.

(2) Market processes which suffice to supply a city with the office buildings that it needs can still be imperfectly efficient for a variety of reasons. Corporate directors may locate their headquarters to suit themselves rather than their shareholders' interests. To hoist their headquarters high into the sky they may fill the building below them with more of the firm's routine activities than necessary, i.e. with work that could well be done at cheaper locations elsewhere, with advantage to the city's and sometimes the office workers' transport problems. They may add levels of off-street car parking which contribute to further traffic congestion and high-

way building. The buildings themselves can have better or worse environmental effects, and market forces are not necessarily on the better side. Some middle-sized US cities suffer from a kind of giantism, with big office towers standing out of vacant land and car parks, laced with highway spaghetti, where there used once to be sociable town centres. Government and market forces share the responsibility for most of these shortcomings, where they occur. They don't occur everywhere. Mixtures of local tradition and public planning have given many cities the modern offices they need without spoiling the quality or prosperity of their city life.

(3) *A horror story* Through the 1980s many western cities, led by New York and London, had grossly wasteful booms in office building and associated debt. In the ten years of the 1970s American property developers borrowed altogether $300 billion. In the three years 1986-88 they borrowed twice that amount and built far ahead of demand. By 1991 more than 60 US cities had between 10 and 20 per cent of their offices empty. Their market rents and prices had fallen between 10 and 40 per cent below their 1985 peak. Since a lot of the loans that built them had been for 100 per cent of what they were expected to be worth at 1985 values, a lot of their owners and their owners' bankers were insolvent. London had five times the empty office space in 1991 that it had in 1989. At Canary Wharf in dockland it had the biggest office building in the Western world empty, with its Canadian-based multinational developer insolvent with debts above $12 billion. A number of Japanese, French, Spanish, Italian, Dutch and Belgian cities had similar troubles. The Economist of 15 June 1991 looked back –

> While the buildings were going up, they were a marvel. Completed, they were a nightmare. Empty factories and offices produce no income; interest goes unpaid; the banks themselves begin to suffer. Collateral that is unused and, in the short term, unsellable is no collateral at all. Once property assets lose value, bankers have to rein in their lending to everybody, not just to those cursed property men. Tighter credit tips economies into recession, and in recession nobody expands into new offices and factories. So the pain gets a further twist. Economies are first boosted by construction, then bashed by it.

Developers, banks, local planning authorities and national financial policies all contributed to the disaster. But the horror story is not here to discredit private developers and banks: they produce many of the best buildings. Nor is it here to discredit governments, which

have produced the Paris boulevards and other good urban things. The reasons for including this case study in your education are a familiar trio:

1. Ownership does not determine enterprises' efficiency: public and private enterprises can each be anywhere from excellent to terrible, depending on the skill and purpose with which they are directed and where necessary watched and regulated.

2. Most markets need appropriate government if they are to operate efficiently, and in the 1980s office markets were not getting it.

3. You can't always understand complex market forces by studying the market relations one by one then adding up their separate effects. Some of them operate differently in different company. In this horror story the mistakes in the real estate market could not have been made if the money market had been efficient. The bankers would not have made the mistakes they did if the real estate operators had been efficient. Neither would have made such mistakes if their government regulators had known their business.

Lessons *The Economist* based some policy proposals on the British and American experience. Government should set standards of skill and financial strength for developers. It should set standards of quality for office buildings. It should issue only enough building permits to meet the estimated demand for office space. And those permits should go by auction to approved developers. Competitive tender might be better because it encourages the competitors to offer civic benefits as well as money for their development rights. But whatever you think of those particular proposals, the need for some better regulation seems inescapable. Without intelligent government, capital markets and real estate markets, especially in conjunction with each other, can too easily do serious harm to city life and prosperity.

LAND IN THE PATH OF URBAN GROWTH

This account of land markets began with the nature of already-developed city and suburban land. Now turn the clock back and consider 'the nature of the product' before urban development begins. We are only marginally concerned with the land's nature as farmland, wasteland, forest or whatever. What we need to know are the qualities which affect (i) its potential urban uses, and (ii) its owners' behavior as the time for urban development approaches.

- Physical qualities of land can affect its urban uses. Rocky land may be expensive to sewer. Steep land may be expensive for roadbuilding and housing, impossible for factories, ideal for forest parks. Wetlands may need expensive engineering to fit them to build on. And so on.

- Land lasts. Unless it is degraded by misuse its value does not decline with age, and usually increases with urban growth.

- Land can offer direct, non-financial benefits to its occupiers over and above its financial value to them. Besides earning from its use they may also enjoy living on it. Suppose that two identical farms lie in the path of suburban growth. Their market value as farms is equal, their (higher) market value as suburban development land is equal. Developers want to buy one or both of them. One belongs to an absentee owner whose only interest is in its financial returns. The other belongs to the family who farm it, love it, and value its proximity to town schools and jobs for growing children. Which will sell soonest or at the going market price for such land? The absentee calculates only the alternative use of the price he can get now, and the price he might get by holding on for a while. The owner-occupiers consider all that, *and also* the value they put on their lifestyle and locational advantages. Those non-financial benefits will vary from one owner-occupier to another, with effect on the dates and prices at which they will be willing to sell. (Theorists will say that their time preferences and discount rates vary.)

- Uncommitted land is like money in that it has option value: it keeps options open for its owner. That can have special value where the best-paying future uses of any piece of land will change over time as the city grows, sometimes predictably and sometimes not, depending on the local circumstances; and – most important –

- committing land to one use now may rule out a higher-paying use later. Whether it does so depends on (i) the speed of urban development, and (ii) how long the first use takes to repay the capital invested in it. It may also depend, though less often, on (iii) what the first use does to the character of its location. (If the first use is a slaughterhouse which attracts tanneries and fertilizer firms to locate around it, the second use of the site won't be for a hotel or apartment block.)

Focus on (i) and (ii) in the last item. How can investment in a first use of the land rule out a higher-paying use later? Why isn't the first investment regarded as 'sunk costs' which should be written off when a better

use of the site becomes possible? Work it out over (say) a ten-year period of fast city growth:

Year 1

Your block of vacant land and your neighbor's similar block are each worth $20,000. The current highest-paying use of such a block is to build an $80,000 house on it. Together with the land value that makes a property worth $100,000, which will net an annual rent of $5000. You build it and start earning 5 per cent per year on your capital, plus whatever increase of land value comes with future city growth. Your neighbor decides to wait and see what future opportunities there may be. She grows enough market vegetables on her block to pay the rates on it.

Year 5

Five years of city growth has made the location more desirable, increased the land price to $50,000 a block, and created some demand for apartments. Your neighbor builds $250,000 of apartments to make a property worth $300,000, which nets her $24,000 rent a year, an 8 per cent return on her capital. Why don't you build such a block? Here's why: At present land prices your house is worth $130,000, so any developer wanting to buy an apartment site will prefer your neighbor's vacant block for $50,000. And if you yourself demolish your house and replace it with $250,000 worth of apartments, they will have cost you $55,000 more than the same investment cost your neighbor: the $80,000 worth of house you destroyed minus the $25,000 of rent it earned you in the five years you had it. Your neighbor nets $24,000 = 8 per cent per year on her $300,000 capital. You would net the same $24,000 on an outlay of $380,000, i.e. 6.3 per cent. If you want to build apartments you'd do better to keep your house and build the apartments on $50,000 worth of vacant land elsewhere. You would then net $30,000 annually on a total outlay of $400,000, a rate of return of 7.5 per cent. (No, there has not been a calculating error; the net house rent has risen from $5000 to $6000 with city growth.)

Thus building the house in Year 1 has ruled out a better-paying use in Year 5. But hang on – who knows what the next five years of city growth may bring?

Year 10

The city has grown further, land values have risen further. The neighborhood needs a three-star hotel. Hotels have to be fussy about their locations, and although there is still vacant land here and there, none of it is suitable. Something must be demolished

– and your house at (now) $150,000 is cheaper than your neighbor's apartments at (now) $350,000. On your block a hotelier will build $1,850,000 worth of hotel which will net him $200,000 a year, i.e. 10 per cent on his total $2m. outlay, the highest rate of return that any block in the neighborhood has yet earned.

Building her best-use apartments in Year 5 has blocked your neighbor's chances of getting the new best-use rate from Year 10. Building *your* best-use house in Year 1 has won you the best-use opportunity in Year 10, though you probably didn't guess that at the time.

Or did you? It can make quite a difference, as follows.

Market effects of uncertainty

In some circumstances those leapfrogging values and opportunities are reasonably predictable, in other circumstances they are not. Theory and experience suggest that the more uncertain they are, the more likely it is that the urban development will be scattered and inefficient.

Why?

Consider some expanding suburban sprawl of an unplanned, unregulated kind. It is difficult to know where the next patches of development will be, what the highest-paying land uses will be, where they will be, or when they will become profitable. There is likely to be a good deal of disagreement about future prospects and therefore about present prices. In those circumstances some owners sell or develop their land as soon as there is any urban demand for it, some raise their asking-prices above what most developers will pay, some farm on for a while, withholding their land from the market. Wondering who will sell next, and when, further increases the uncertainty. So – as the most important point of this analysis – development is scattered and 'gappy'. Uncertainty thus reduces the efficiency and raises the costs of development in a number of ways:

- It restricts the initial supply and raises the price of land for urban development.
- It delays, or increases the cost and reduces the early use of, the necessary roads and bridges and pipes and wires.
- Scattered development is harder to serve efficiently with local shops and other commercial services.

Market effects of development planning

Those market failures can be corrected by public action. The action can be designed to *replace* market processes or it can be designed to *improve* them. The best planning often does a little of the first and a lot of the second. Its main means are land-use planning, public investment and public land dealing.

Planning and public investment With appropriate research and consultation government publishes a development and land-use plan, and an intended sequence of public works. Landowners and developers can see where the main transport routes and services, water and power services, schools and public parks and playing fields and golf courses – and waste disposal and sewage treatment works – will go, and in what sequence they will be developed. And they can see where they can build houses, neighborhood shops, town shopping and business centres, light and heavy industries.

That reduces uncertainties. Nobody need withhold land from development to wait and see what general kind of use may turn out to be its best use. And knowing what its eventual use or its likely sequence of uses will be, owners can choose intermediate uses which allow, rather than ruling out, replacement by higher-paying uses later.

But some uncertainties continue. Owners may choose to develop their land at dates which don't fit the intended sequence of development. Owners of strategic sites intended for shopping centres, fuel and service stations, or dense housing around the centres, may exploit the monopoly rights the plan has given them to over-price their land or delay its development. Government may acquire those sites by compulsory purchase and develop them by public enterprise, thus *replacing* market processes; or it may do some land dealing to *repair* the market process.

Public land dealing A public agent may acquire the strategic sites and re-sell them by auction or tender to developers willing to develop them in accord with the plan. That still leaves the main housing and industrial developments to depend on the dates at which the rural owners choose to sell their properties. A radical alternative is for the public agent to acquire *all* the land well in advance of urban development, and sell or lease it to private users as and when it is required, on conditions that get it promptly developed. It was by one or other of those means that the Paris boulevards, British New Towns, much of modern Stockholm, central Melbourne and Adelaide have been developed. Public dealers can provide land for any mixture of public and private development. The private land provisions are at prices established by competitive auction or tender. Democracies can't seize private land as ruthlessly as the French government did to clear the way for the boulevards. It would be oppressive to acquire compulsorily land occupied by many owners, some with strong attachment to their farms and homesteads. But the method has worked well where the public already owned the land or could buy it – often without compulsion – from large landholders without too much personal attachment to it.

Critics call such methods socialist. In fact socialist regimes never allocated land in that way. That style of public dealing frees the market to function in an efficient competitive way without uncertainty or monopolist or speculative withholding.

If you want to know more about the theory and practice of the markets which pass land from country to town use, and from one town use to another, try to find the works of G. Max Neutze from which this section's analysis is drawn: *The price of land and land-use planning*, Paris: OECD (1973), has been reproduced or summarized in four other publications: T. Bendixson (ed.) *The management of urban growth*, Paris: OECD (1977); 'Urban Land Policy in Five Western Countries' in *Journal of Social Policy* 4 (1975) 225-42; J.C. McMaster and G.R.Webb (eds) *Australian Urban Economics: A Reader*, Sydney: ANZ Book Co. (1987); and 'The supply of land for a particular use' in *Urban Studies* 24 (1987) 379-388.

CLOTHING

Clothes are here because this chapter needs an example of a cruelly efficient market. Meet the rag trade.

The nature of the product Most clothing lasts well if it's not worn. You can store it, transport it, trade it around the world. Nearly every human needs some. Besides warming and protecting you it is often also self-expressive, signalling who you are or would like to be. That can include how respectable or civilized you are. When Sydney was an eighteenth century convict settlement in a wilderness it was notorious for its rum consumption – but a modern researcher has discovered that for every pound spent on alcohol in the first forty years of the colony, ten were spent on clothing.

The buyers spend their own money, or credit they will have to repay, on clothes for themselves or others in their family. They wear some clothes until they wear out. They may discard some as they tire of them, or as fashions change. In affluent societies the shops offer them very wide choices. Most of them know what they like and are competent judges of what they buy. They're efficient buyers.

Some of the suppliers work to keep the fashions changing, partly as a way of competing for custom and partly to boost demand by getting people to buy new clothes before their old ones have worn out. The influence is mostly persuasive – people don't have to buy anything they don't like. But it may be partly coercive – some people think that their jobs or social life compel them to keep in fashion. Do the suppliers' influence on the buyers' demands make this an inefficient market? Perhaps the coercive effects do but the persuasive effects don't. It depends on your respect for 'revealed preferences' regardless of how they are formed, and your notion of efficiency. But given the shoppers' preferences, most of them are efficient buyers who know what they are doing.

The suppliers are hotly competitive. Production chains supply the clothing industry with its silk, woollen, cotton, linen, plastic and other cloth and thread, and its machinery. There are some big firms in the plastics and machine-making industries. But most of the inputs to the clothing industry come from competitive suppliers and are traded in international markets. And a very wide range of garments are made by workers operating sewing machines which can work as well in big factories, small workshops or contract workers' homes. There may be economies of scale in buying materials, design and cutting, and marketing. Some firms establish popular products and brand names. But the biggest firms compete hotly with each other and are open to competition from operators on much smaller scale.

Most clothes are retailed as efficiently as they are produced. Traditional department stores and fashionable boutiques may operate with high mark-ups (and frequent sales) but masses of low-priced alternatives are available from supermarkets. Advertising and fashion magazines drench the market with information. In the industry as a whole efficient buyers deal with efficient and hotly competitive suppliers.

Regulation Some aspects of the industry attract some regulation. Wool, cotton and flax production may have some protection or price stabilization. General laws about truthful labelling and safety may apply: you must not sell skin-irritant underwear or (in some countries) inflammable children's clothes or night-clothes. Patents, trade names and design copyrights are protected. Tariffs protect some countries' clothiers from import competition. But in most respects clothing is one of the freest, least regulated industries.

Workers' pay Much of the industry's cost efficiency comes from its treatment of its workers. In most countries at most times they have been among the hardest worked and lowest paid workers. That doesn't always improve the employers' profit shares. Through the middle and lower-priced areas of the market it chiefly keeps costs and prices down and benefits the customers. Two causes contribute to that: technology, and gender bias. A woman operating a sewing machine is still the dominant technology in garment-making. There are therefore few economies of scale, because she can do the work as well in a factory, a workshop, or at home.

Why women? Except for some men's tailoring, making and mending clothes was traditionally a task for women. They are probably better at it, more nimble and patient than men. Clothiers preferred them because they were traditionally paid less than men. Some of them welcomed the work because they could do it at home, as in earlier centuries they used to spin yarn at home, while keeping house and minding children. That made them available to the clothing industry, but also dependent on it, because there were not many other ways they could earn at home. So they were weak bargainers against the clothiers who offered them work.

Keep in mind that possibility of doing the same work either in a factory or on contract at home. Now recall Coase's theory of the firm:

> All the individual contributions to production have to be coordinated. The necessary relations between them can be organized within firms. Or they can be market relations, for example when firms buy materials, components or services from individuals or other firms. Coordinating activities within the firm by telling each individual what to do has management costs. Searching the market and negotiating purchases and contracts has costs. Efficient firms compare the costs and do each bit of necessary coordination by whichever method costs least.

A distinctive feature of garment-making by women with sewing machines is that the transaction costs of those alternatives *tend to be much the same*. It costs about as much to put the work out on individual contracts as it costs to organize it in a factory. Even the incentives and discipline can be similar if wage workers within the firm and contract workers outside it are both paid piece rates, i.e. they are paid for the number of garments made or buttonholes sewn rather than the number of hours worked.

Coase was theorizing about transaction costs. But the alternative methods of coordination can also affect labor costs, even though work done within the firm and the same work done on contract use the same skills. The costs can differ if the bargaining strengths differ.

Factory workers can know each other, organize, bargain collectively, and if necessary strike. It is usually much harder for contract workers to do so. But be careful what conclusions you draw about their likely rates of pay. The weakness of one group can weaken the other. The wage workers may be able to use their organized strength effectively only if their employers can't do without them, i.e. if the garments can only be made on their machines in their factories. But in the rag trade there are often *two* alternatives. The technology may allow employers to switch to contract work by unorganized workers. And because the technology has no great economies of scale, much of the work is organized by small, hotly competitive firms. They are easily put out of business if they can't meet delivery dates and competitive prices; and because there is worldwide garment trade, a labor union can rarely discipline all the competing employers. So even though the wage workers in the garment industry have often enough been union members, they have still not been able to bargain very hard because (i) they can too easily price their employers out of business, or (ii) their employers can switch some at least of their work to contract workers who are unorganized and often unorganizable.

Many economists see that as an unusually efficient labor market. Together with efficient garment markets it keeps most of us well clothed with wide and wonderful market choices, including plenty at low prices. One reason for that is the low income that the industry manages to pay to its armies of women workers. What social objections might there be to that? You may think it is unfair to women. Regardless of gender you may think it unfair that any industry should be able to pay its workers less than other industries do for work of similar skill and difficulty. You may also remember Robert Lane's accumulation of evidence, in *The Market Experience* (1991), to the effect that the experience of work has more effect on most people's personal growth and happiness than their material consumption does, as long as they're above the breadline. If we were all garment workers we might well want to trade some of our clothing options for better conditions of work. Lane's central argument is that where there is undesirable exploitation of labor the underlying cause is more often consumer sovereignty than employers' greed. Moreover sovereignty is a misleading word for it. It is not a sovereignty of some citizens over others, because most citizens are both workers and consumers. It is a sovereignty of their shopping choices over the working choices open to them. Built into the market sector of the mixed economy are forces which determine that your shopping choices shall shape and constrain your work options, even if you would prefer an opposite bias, i.e. if you would prefer a world of satisfying work opportunities, with whatever consumption options were consistent with that.

There have been many efforts by unions and governments to improve garment workers' pay and conditions of work, and to extend the improvements to contract workers as well as wage workers. They have had varying success, and sometimes mixed effects. Many western democracies have lately been increasing the costs of employing wage workers in all industries. There are payroll taxes, workers' compensation insurance, employers' contributions to employees' superannuation funds and child care. Those all increase clothiers' incentives to avoid the new charges by shifting as much garment-making as possible to contract work at home, or to be done by low-paid, unorganized, unprotected women's labor in less developed countries. That's not all bad: the western contract workers and the Asian workers want the work and would be worse off without it. Internationalizing the industry may reduce some international inequalities. But it remains true that the industry's current technology allows its workers to be more harshly exploited than most. When you come across theoretically efficient, fully competitive markets, such as clothing markets and their associated labor markets, you may want to explore how fairly they work, and how the benefits of their efficiency are distributed between employers, workers, and the buyers of the products.

CARS

It is partly because there are such large numbers of small producers that clothing is a hotly competitive industry, and tends to pay poor wages. For contrast, take a quick look at car-making. Its main producers are few, big and oligopolistic. They have considerable market strength in dealing with their suppliers, retailers and employees. They compete hard. But despite their strength and competitiveness, most of them pay better wages than most garment-makers do.

There is plenty of common knowledge about car markets. Sketch your own analysis, beginning with 'the nature of the product', if you want to. This short note merely lists three contrasts with the clothing industry. It is here to suggest caution in generalizing about markets for manufactured goods, which actually vary widely. The contrasts are in (i) relations between the size of firms, competition, and market strength, (ii) the presence of a group of buyers able to spend their firms'

money on themselves, and (iii) environmental reasons for increasing regulation of the industry.

The size of firms, competition and market strength Carmakers tend to fit Coase's theory of the firm. For economies of scale they have to be big, but the economies of scale don't apply to the whole productive process, only to parts of it. So most carmakers don't want to manage any more of the production than it pays them to manage. They know which parts they do best themselves, and which parts it is cheaper to buy from other firms. They tend to do between a third and a half of the work themselves. Most do some research and do their own engineering design and development, though they may buy patents – and sometimes whole engine designs – from others. Some of them get others (usually Italian) to design and style their car bodies. Makers of steel, plastics, cable, furnishing fabric, paint and other materials compete to supply them. Many other firms, including many small ones, compete to make components for them. Railways, transport firms and independent truckers compete to deliver their products to retailers. Retailers compete for franchises to sell and service their cars. Thus the competition between carmarkers is by no means the only competition in the industry, and some of the competitors are quite small firms. So why are most automotive workers paid more than most of the rag trade's workers even where their levels of skill are comparable? Scarcely any of the automotive work can be done at home. It has to be done in factories or workshops with substantial capital equipment. Most of it has traditionally been done by men, and much of it requires them to cooperate in teams. So most of the industry's workers are easy to find, have some feeling of solidarity, and willingly organize. They have long been organized in democratic countries, and their unions bargain effectively for more pay than most garment-makers earn.

The industry nevertheless suggests an addition to Coase's theory. He saw firms determining their shares of the productive process by comparing the *transaction* costs of managing work within the firm, and alternatively buying products from others. Especially in Japan but in varying degrees in other countries the carmakers also compare the *labor* costs of the alternatives. The fact that small, competitive component makers are weak bargainers against big carmakers can make them relatively strong bargainers against their workers: 'If you push wages too high you'll price us out of the Toyota contract, and out of business.' Not all unions can enforce identical pay and conditions on all employers. Some of the trades concerned (for example electrical workers, furniture makers, transport workers) are not covered by the powerful automotive unions, but might be if the carmakers were their employers. So small, less secure suppliers and contractors may be able to get more work for less pay than the carmakers themselves can, and this encourages the carmakers to limit their own shares of the productive process. Nevertheless the conditions indicated earlier apply across a good deal of the industry in most carmaking countries, and help to explain the differences between carmaking and garment-making wages.

The buyers In developed countries the relations between incomes and car prices allow most people who want cars to buy them, new or second hand. Many of the buyers need credit, but cars are reasonably durable, insurable, identifiable, and recoverable by unpaid creditors, so plenty of credit is available. The producers and retailers of the cars are hotly competitive. So individuals who buy and pay for their own cars do so in an efficient market.

There are two other groups of buyers. First, employers buy cars – often fleets of cars – for their employees to use in the course of their work (as cab drivers, couriers, commercial travellers, etc.). They tend to buy suitable, economical vehicles, at prices hard-bargained by well-informed buyers and sellers. This bit of the market is also efficient.

The third group are the buyers of most luxury cars. Some rich individuals buy high-priced cars with their own money. But many more have their employers buy cars for their private use. Those who don't have employers – lawyers, doctors, star actors or musicians – often form fictitious companies to own or lease their cars. Most of these deals have elements of tax avoidance, varying with the detail of national tax laws. When a firm leases expensive cars for its managers the lease rents count as business costs and reduce taxable profits and corporate income tax. In many countries the recipients don't pay personal income tax on them, though they are part of their 'reward package'. Because other taxpayers supply the lost taxes it is reasonable to see those taxpayers as contributing part of the price of the cars. The firm contributes part. Depending on the national tax laws, the users do or don't contribute a part. It is this group, the only group who can (i) choose their cars and (ii) get others to pay for them, who constitute most of the market demand for high-priced luxury cars.

If you ignore the element of tax avoidance, you may take one or other of two alternative views of the employers' contributions to these purchases. (1) They are no more reprehensible than any other elements of

the big pay packages. If a firm pays its chief executive a million dollars a year, what does it matter whether the last hundred thousand comes by cheque or on wheels? This bit of the market is as efficient as any other. Alternatively (2) most luxury cars are produced, or are as luxurious and expensive as they are, only because one group of buyers can make other people pay for their cars. That makes it an inefficient and also inequitable sector of the market.

Environmental policy Considered as environmental hazards, clothes and cars are at opposite extremes. But the mild regulation of clothing may offer lessons for the more radical regulation which the car business faces.

Car exhausts are a major source of local and global pollution. New cars are already required to use unleaded fuel and to trap some of the pollutants from their exhausts. Governments may soon want to reduce their size and power, their numbers and their hours of use. They may want to switch some or all of them to electric power. They already talk of reorganizing cities to encourage more pedestrian, bike, wheelchair and public transport.

Some reformers, including many economists, want to effect those changes as far as possible by manipulating people's incentives. That might be done by taxing cars according to their size, power, fuel type, or pollutant emissions, by taxing their fuels, by taxing or pricing city parking, and by tolls on main roads and city entries.

Other reformers think regulation would be more effective and equitable than 'rationing by price'. Automotive technology happens to make it comparatively easy to specify the permitted size, power, engine and fuel type of new cars, to enforce such rules, and to write them into international agreements. It is also possible to ration fuel and city parking.

You were reminded earlier of what happened when society decided to stop using slaves, or to stop sending children down coalmines, or to stop drowning sailors in unsafe ships. The offending practices were not differentially taxed or priced, they were banned. In those cases the people needing protection were minorities and the bans were imposed by partly-disinterested majorities. With car exhausts everyone is a potential victim, so there are even stronger incentives to regulate rather than merely tax the damage. (Majorities are also motorists, which may complicate the politics, but the reasons for regulation are the same.)

Lessons from the clothing market? Inflammable nighties and children's clothes are not differentially taxed, they're banned. The rich as well as the poor are prevented from incinerating their little ones. That does not reduce the efficiency of clothing production or markets. Similarly, banning specified types of fuel or types and sizes of engine can leave car markets as efficient as ever.

DOCTORS

Elsewhere in this book I question whether employing people or contracting for their services should be understood as a labor 'market', as if work is a commodity bought and sold like carrots. In some respects the market model fits: workers exchange services for money. In some respects it does not: employers engage people to act in their interest as their agents. That may be a trivial quality of the relation if you hire someone to wash your car or tighten nuts on an assembly line. It is a more important quality if you hire someone to fight for you, negotiate for you, manage others for you, paint a portrait or ghost an autobiography for you – or be your doctor. Those relations still have market elements: you pay for something you want. They also have non-market elements: you trust people to act ethically, and to act in your interest even in matters you don't understand and can't judge. The following pages use market language where it seems to fit and not where it does not. But even where it does, it may not be the neoclassical model that fits. Designing medical services on neoclassical assumptions can be a mistake. This section will conclude with some reasons for that.

References to Britain's national health service will be to the system as it was through its first forty years. There have since been some changes, but the original principles related market and non-market incentives to each other in ways which are specially interesting to compare with more expensive socialist arrangements in Sweden and more expensive capitalist arrangements in the United States. So the old model is here for an educational purpose.

The nature of the product Most people buy the advice and services collectively described as health care not for their own sakes but as means to keeping healthy. A few people do enjoy the medical and nursing processes – the care – but most patients want to be done with them and back to health as quickly as possible. Health is not a commodity. The commodity is health care, and most people's demand for it is a derived demand. (The demand for health can also be seen as a derived demand – people want it in order to be able to enjoy other things.)

The need for health care is irregular. Most of the time you don't have better health the more health care you buy: the healthier you are, the less care you need.

Medical science keeps elaborating the product, developing increasingly expensive diagnostic and curative equipment and procedures. Most of the developed democracies committed themselves forty or fifty years ago to making the best health care available to all their members regardless of their individual capacity to pay. It now costs more than it did then to keep that promise – absolutely more, and up to two or three times the proportion of national income.

The buyers In most rich countries patients initiate about a fifth of medical services and pay for less than a fifth of them (measured by prices). Doctors initiate the remaining four fifths as they prescribe drugs, Xrays, scans and path tests and send patients to specialists and hospitals. They also influence the patients' own initiatives as they advise them when – i.e. with what symptoms or preventive purposes —they should visit their doctors.

Thus the outstanding peculiarity of medical 'markets' is that the suppliers determine the supply and also most of the demand. That was different (and still is in most poor countries) when doctors could only order treatments which the patients could pay for. But in rich countries now most patients pay only a fraction, or none, of their doctors' bills.

The patients are thus the users but not the buyers of medical services. There are no buyers in the usual meaning of people who both choose and pay for the goods they want. The suppliers do much of the choosing. Most of the paying is done by governments, by public or independent non-profit insurance institutions, or by profit-seeking insurance companies. It matters which, as you will see.

Who pays?

- *Government may pay*, if it employs salaried doctors and gives their services free to their patients, as in British public hospitals. For economizing, tax-cutting reasons politicians tend to pay the doctors as little as they can, as far as may be consistent with attracting enough of them, and with prevailing ideas of wage justice.

- *Government-owned insurance institutions* may pay the doctors' bills, or specified amounts of them, while the doctors remain self-employed, as in Canada, Australia and (effectively) in general practice in Britain. The institutions are commonly financed from taxation, though some fraction of income tax may be nominated as an insurance contribution.

As with salaried doctors, government usually pays as little as it can. As a monopsonist (monopoly buyer) of most of the doctors' services it is a strong bargainer. In Britain and for most purposes in Canada the fee scales are set after negotiation with the doctors' association, though not always with its agreement. British and Canadian doctors must then accept the scheduled rates. A similar system in Australia allows doctors to collect the scheduled fee from the public system then charge the patients supplementary fees. Fewer than half of the doctors charge such fees.

- *Independent non-profit insurance institutions*, financed by their members and sometimes by employers' contributions, may pay specified amounts of the doctors' bills. Blue Cross and Blue Shield do so in the US. They have no formal power, and not much market power, to restrain the fees they help to pay. Where such institutions are founded and directed by doctors, a main purpose may be to enable patients to pay *without* much market restraint of the fees.

- *Profit-seeking insurance companies* divide the US market with Blue Cross and Blue Shield. Competition for customers motivates them to restrain their premium rates; but that may be achieved by other means than restraining the doctors' fees. Some achieve it by insuring healthy customers with as few as possible of the old or infirm. They can't and don't do much to restrain doctors' fees.

- *Health Maintenance Organizations*, often abbreviated as HMOs, combine insurance with medical service. You pay them a fixed fee like an insurance premium and they undertake to supply whatever medical and hospital service you may need. As private enterprises they are nowhere the dominant providers of health care, so what they pay their doctors is likely to be determined in a market way by what comparable doctors in the society are earning. But they may exert *some* downward pressure on those rates.

In all these systems the doctors are ultimately paid by the people they serve, whether they pay as patients, as insurance contributors or as taxpayers. But to see how like or unlike markets the systems are, the important thing to notice is the extent to which the prices do not determine the demand for the product, and are not determined by it.

Incentives

However they're paid, doctors are paid to do their best for their patients, and generally do so. Financial incentives may influence *what* work they do, but rarely how well they do it. The conscientious performance is driven by professional duty and commitment, but it is reinforced by the conditions of work. The division of labor in medical services means that patients, nurses, pharmacists and other paramedicals, family doctors and specialists observe each others' work and its effects. Among the doctors there is mutual observation and advice between practice partners, general practitioners and specialists, seniors and juniors in teaching-hospital teams. Thus the nature and organization of the work provides built-in quality controls without resort to much external accountability or special financial incentives. What the financial arrangements chiefly affect are the doctors' incomes and the society's overall medical costs.

There are three common bases of payment for doctors.

- *Fee for service* Doctors are paid so much for each visit, each consultation, each therapeutic procedure. They may therefore earn more the more patients they see, the more procedures they do, the faster they do them, or the more they charge for each. But it is commonly only the family doctors who must attract their work and income from inexpert patients. The rest, who include the more expensive performers of the more difficult diagnoses and procedures, get their work from other doctors, who usually see its results. That discourages any hasty or inadequate work that 'fee-for-service' might otherwise motivate. But it does not necessarily discourage over-servicing.

- *Capitation* The doctor is paid a fee (commonly a fee per year) for each patient on her list, and gives whatever service the patient needs. When family doctors are paid this way, as in the British health service in its original form, it is for their own work only: any specialist or other services the patients need are paid for separately. When capitation is paid to Health Maintenance Organizations, the HMOs undertake to provide or pay others to provide all the services the patients need.

  Capitation has potential incentive effects of three kinds. It can encourage as much competition as fee-for-service can: doctors' incomes are determined by the number of patients they can attract and keep satisfied. They have no incentive to over-service their patients. And they have strong reason to keep them healthy by preventive care and education.

- *Salary* or sessional payments. Doctors are paid a wage like anyone else. A common variation is to pay by the hour or (say) the three-hour session, for example when specialists work for part of their time in public hospitals or clinics. The terms of employment may specify the general kind and amount of work which a salaried doctor must do. What she then has to do merely to keep her job may depend more on her employer's purposes than her own. If her employer is public she has much the same reasons as a 'capitation' doctor does to keep her patients healthy, and not to over-service them. But some private profit-seeking health centres which offer a wide range of services want their doctors to order as many profitable tests and procedures as possible, and have them all done by branches of the firm. Some have been known to sack doctors who don't generate enough business in that way, i.e. who don't order their patients to be over-serviced. If an insurer is paying fees-for-service to that sort of profit-seeking employer of salaried doctors, there are poor incentives for either good or economical doctoring, however conscientiously the unnecessary procedures are carried out.

ALTERNATIVE SYSTEMS

Health care is a service which civilized countries promise to all their members regardless of their capacity to pay. Among those who supply it are the doctors. Most of them work with high ethical standards and commitment to their patients' interests however they are paid. But how they are paid can still affect their peace of mind, some aspects of their performance, their patients' interests, and the overall cost of their services. They are paid by patients, by insurers, by government, or by all three. They are paid on a basis of fees for service, capitation, salary or sessional fees, or some of each. As usual, you can't always predict the effect of any one of those arrangements unless you know its context. For example fee-for-service can have different effects with public insurance, private insurance, and no insurance. Salaried service can work differently with profit-seeking and non-profit-seeking employers. And so on. That makes it hard to judge the merits of each method of employment or payment considered by itself. You need to compare whole systems for delivering and paying for medical care. Here are much-simplified sketches of the American, Canadian and British systems as they were during the 1980s, with the Canadian system in deliber-

ate contrast to the American, and the British not yet moving to imitate some market features of the American.

USA

Government manages Medicare, a contributory health insurance scheme chiefly for the elderly. Federal and State governments fund Medicaid, a non-contributory scheme for poor people. About 15 per cent of Americans have no health insurance. The rest are insured by Blue Cross or Blue Shield (non-profit), by profit-seeking insurance corporations, or by Health Maintenance Organizations. None of the insurers pays the whole of a doctor's fee. Patients pay directly for about a third of all health care, including a little more than a third of doctors' fees. Most doctors are paid fees-for-service for most of their work. With many competing insurers there is no monopolist public insurer to bargain hard about their fee levels.

The fees, already high, have risen further as an effect of some legal developments which you met in the previous chapter. American judges have defined as negligent a range of clinical decisions which other countries' judges tend to treat as honest misjudgments, or reasonable choices between alternative risks. American lawyers in some jurisdictions are allowed to charge contingent fees. Those who do so will represent you at their own risk. The growth of gold-digging litigation raises medical costs in two ways. Doctors have to insure against the costs of such cases. The premiums keep rising with the rising volume of litigation, and doctors' fees rise accordingly. And many of them now order more diagnostic and precautionary tests and procedures. Those all have to be paid for, and some of them expose patients to unjustified risk or discomfort.

A large majority of Americans have access to excellent medical and hospital care, among the world's best. Their costs are the world's highest. That is to be expected in the society with the highest incomes, but their costs are disproportionately higher, taking a high proportion of their high incomes. OECD figures for 1985 showed American doctors earning 7.07 times US gross domestic product per person, Canadian doctors earning 5.58 times Canadian GDP per person, British doctors earning 3.68 times British GDP per person. Health care as a whole has since risen to cost about 14 per cent of US income, compared with about 8 per cent of British income.

It is hard to judge how efficiently the high US costs are spent, because the real product – health – is produced by other conditions besides health care. But

Americans are not the healthiest or longest-lived people in the world. The people of at least fifteen countries, all of which spend absolutely and proportionately less on health care, enjoy longer life. Explanations for the apparent American inefficiency include the extent of family breakdown and violence in American life; the unequal distribution of income, housing and other material conditions; the unequal distribution of health care; and the extravagant ways of paying for it.

Canada

Canada's national health insurance system is comprehensive, covering all the people and all the health services. Provincial governments manage it and join with the national government in funding it, mostly from taxation. Patients contribute, but not much. The public insurer monopolizes the business: private health insurance is banned. Because the system is simple its administrative costs are low: about 3 per cent of health care costs, compared with the American insurers' 15 per cent.

The Canadian insurer pays for the health services but does not deliver any of them. They remain independent. The hospitals are owned by various institutions, mostly non-profit. The doctors charge fees-for-service, with some salaried or sessionally paid work in hospitals. Standard fees are negotiated between the profession and the public insurer, and it is unlawful to charge more. Partly to make the system acceptable to the doctors and partly because of proximity to the highly paid US profession, the insurers agree to quite high rates. Through most of the history of the system they have also financed the hospitals generously. Canadians live two or three years longer than Americans, at about three quarters of the cost in health care.

Britain

For about forty years from its foundation in 1948 the National Health Service could be described as follows.

The service is mostly financed from taxation. Patients have to pay various fractions of the cost of medicines, spectacles, dentistry and some other items, but medical and hospital services are paid for by the government and free to patients. Health care as a whole costs (in equivalent purchasing power) about 40 per cent of what it costs in the US. Part of the economy comes from underfinancing the hospitals. The rest comes chiefly from effects of the service conditions on doctors' pay and doctors' and patients' incentives.

Private practice with payment by fees-for-service is open to any doctors and patients who want it. Most of the patients who want it insure with independent non-profit insurers. Within the national service all three methods of payment are in use. Basically, family doctors are paid capitation with some supplementary fees for some services, and specialists and hospital staff doctors are salaried. There are elements of competition and of secure tenure. Doctors compete for membership and partnership in general practices. Practices compete for patients and are paid capitation for the numbers they attract. Specialists compete for salaried specialist jobs when vacancies occur. Once employed or in practice, most of them have secure tenure subject to good behavior. The capitation fees, supplementary fees-for-service, and salary structures are fixed by national tribunals.

Since the service began, its arrangements have been modified many times, sometimes to save public money, sometimes to refine the doctors' and patients' incentives. For some services which family doctors can alternatively do themselves or refer to specialists, capitation may encourage the use of specialists. To reduce that expensive bias a little but not too much, some fees for service are available to the family doctors. When compulsory 'apprenticeships' were introduced for general practitioners, doctors who took pupils earned supplements. So do those who continue to make their own night visits. Other supplements reward seniority, higher qualifications, service in some difficult districts, and specified standards of preventive medicine. As it became harder for doctors to afford the capital costs of the premises which the best practice was coming to require, the government began to build and lease (to those who wanted them) health centres in which doctors could practise under the same roof with paramedical and welfare services.

There is some light external discipline. There are tribunals to which patients can complain about their doctors. They can also change their family doctors, so there is some each of administrative and market discipline. Doctors and patients with no contrary incentives sometimes choose expensive treatments where cheaper ones would do, or (from ignorance) worse treatments where better ones are available. So the Health Service monitors some statistics of its members' practices, and may question any that look questionable, medically or financially.

Through all the fine tuning, and bargaining over pay and conditions, the basic incentive principles persist. Specialists who get their work from other doctors are salaried. They also get their appointments and promotions from local committees chiefly of other doctors. Doctors who get their work directly from the public, so have to be chosen by patients rather than by other doctors, are paid chiefly for the number of patients they care for rather than the number of things they do or prescribe for them. Incentive considerations are delicately balanced in that arrangement. It leaves doctors and patients free to choose one another, while encouraging doctors to accept plenty of patients. Because patients get free care a few are inclined to demand too much of it. If the government were paying fees for each service, doctors might be tempted to comply. Besides removing that temptation, capitation encourages preventive care: both parties benefit if doctors teach patients to keep healthy.

Over time, there has been some increase of bureaucracy. There are re-training requirements, age limits, restrictions on part-time doctoring, specified standards of preventive medicine. Some of the changes may not be worth their costs. They irritate doctors who were doing all the right things without them, and they have significant accounting costs.

But those changes are marginal. The basic incentive arrangements survive. They tend to be negative, in that they avoid encouraging bad practice, or interfering with the doctors' clinical independence. They offer little in the way of positive sticks and carrots or bureaucratic accountability. The system relies heavily – and successfully – on the doctors' professional commitment and mutual quality controls. If ever those conditions don't suffice, the means of detecting and correcting the trouble are as good or better than elsewhere. Hot competition for entry to good medical schools fills the profession with able people who like the work, rather than with people primarily interested in maximizing income. Britain gets very good medical service at very low cost. Its hospitals need more resources before the same can be said for its health care as a whole.

Postscript: I leave the above account as it was first written after my last experience of the service in 1985. But through the 1980s the government introduced a number of more competitive and market-like elements into the service. The changes aim at better service at less cost, but seem likely to be counter-productive. They increase bureaucracy, administrative costs, and the need for more detailed and pervasive regulation and account-keeping. Time will tell whether the quality or the equity of the service suffer, but its cost and some of its inefficiencies are already increasing. Mistaken theory, rather than common sense, seems to have driven the attempt to make the British medical service, one of the-world's best, more like the American, which is the most extravagant and one of the most inequitable in the OECD.

MEDICAL CARE AND MARKET THEORY

A market model of the supply and demand for medical care is a poor ideal for obvious social and humanitarian reasons. You may think that medical protection from disease and avoidable death should be a citizen's right, like legal protection from theft and violence, rather than a market commodity which poor people can't afford. Besides that moral reason there is also a prudent one: a society is likely to be less productive, and most of its members somewhat poorer, if it doesn't look after the health of its workers and those who produce them and bring them up.

A market model is also inappropriate for theoretical reasons. Neither the buyers nor the sellers of medical services can be relied on to act with the economizing self-interest assumed by market theory. Much of the buyers' demand is determined by the sellers. If there are ever too many sellers they don't necessarily comply with market theory by lowering their prices competitively; they have just as often maintained their incomes by *raising* their prices, or over-servicing. Most of the services are things the buyers dislike, and buy only as much as they're told to. The buyers are rarely spending their own money. Medical needs are so unpredictable and potentially expensive that if there is no public insurance, most rational buyers in rich countries insure privately. Once insured they have little or no financial incentive to increase or reduce their demands. A mass of research has found that making them pay a part of each doctor's bill makes little difference to that, except to deter some poor people from demanding the care they need. But if insurance weakens market discipline, the effects of that are moderated by some other misfits between market theory and medical practice. The buyers don't usually want any more care than the suppliers tell them they need. And although insurance may tempt fee-for-service doctors to sell more services than patients need, some facts of medical practice limit their opportunities to profit by doing so. Most of any additional services which may be ordered by a patient's doctor (diagnostic tests, specialist advice, drugs) are supplied by others: the doctor who orders them is not the one who is paid for them. Famously, one of the services is best when it's not paid for at all. If you have time to read a classic of social science and market theory, Richard Titmuss in *The Gift Relationship* (1971) will explain why donated blood is better than marketed blood, for more reasons than its lower price.

Systems of health care are likely to vary with the culture and political and administrative capacities of different countries. But one conclusion from the rich countries' diverse experience up to now is that such systems should as far as possible be designed to –

- free clinical judgments from financial constraints or temptations
- provide mutual quality controls
- deliver the service to everyone regardless of income
- pay the doctors just enough to attract and retain enough doctors of high quality
- have them selected, appointed and promoted by knowledgeable peers; and
- economize the taxpayers' money; while
- leaving doctors, patients and non-profit insurers to engage in private fee-paying practice if they wish.

No free market could achieve all that. Nor has it ever been achieved by a wholly bureaucratic service with its doctors hired and directed by public service superiors. What chiefly determines the cost and quality and equity of systems of health care is not their crude quantities of market and non-market relations. It is the skill, understanding and local knowledge with which the various incentive devices are chosen for particular purposes and related to each other to check, support or supplement each other within the system as a whole. But in guiding the design of systems for delivering and paying for doctors' services, neoclassical market theory does seem to be almost uncannily misleading.

This short account has omitted two troublesome aspects of its subject. Much of the statistical information is imperfect and difficult to interpret; and that is specially true of the international comparisons. To know more of the subject and its technical difficulties – and to sample the sort of work you would face as a health-care economist – you can read the following: *Measuring health care* (OECD, 1987); *Financing and delivering health care* (OECD, 1987); Alistair McGuire, John Henderson and Gavin Mooney, *The economics of health care* (1988); and Alistair McGuire, Paul Fenn and Ken Mayhew (eds.) *Providing health care: The economics of alternative systems of finance and delivery* (1991).

LAWYERS

Like health services, legal services are not desired for their own sake but as means to other goods. As with health services, people generally want only the legal services they actually need. But there are critical exceptions. Legal ingenuity can sometimes frustrate the lawmakers' intentions in anti-social ways, avoiding taxes and evading regulations. And people can gamble by

suing each other for damages. If legal services were free, as many health services are, life could become a crazy casino in which betting cost nothing, losing cost nothing, and winning paid. That potential misuse of legal services creates baffling difficulties for reformers. Democracies promise their citizens equal civil rights. The promise is hollow if they don't have equal power to assert and defend their rights. But if equal rights for rich and poor means free legal services for some or all of them, it will be open to the free users to be no-risk gamblers in that crazy casino.

You don't believe it? Want an example? Suppose you drop out of college and find work as a dance hostess. On the way to work one night, after the couple of gins you need as anaesthetic in that occupation, you step in front of a passing car and it smashes your legs. The ambulance is half an hour coming, the emergency surgery mends your legs but can't wholly restore one knee joint, and you lose your job. You sue the car driver, his insurer, his service garage for leaving his car with faulty brakes, the workers' compensation insurer because you were on your way to work, the distiller for failing to print the alcohol content of the gin on its label, the local government for failing to line the road with a safety rail and warning notices, the St John's ambulance crew for being tardy, the non-profit charity which organizes their voluntary service, the tired surgeon who found that your knee was not wholly repairable, the provincial government and the hospital board who employed her, the national government for underfunding the health services so that surgeons have to work when tired – also for paying you the unemployment dole rather than the higher allowance for disabled workers – and your employer who declines to go on employing a dance hostess with a gammy leg. Meanwhile you are being sued for damages by the car driver, his insurer, and a passing cyclist who had his own accident because his attention was diverted by yours. And the local government is prosecuting you for unlawful jay-walking.

You'll lose most of those phony actions but you might fluke one or two; and the losses will cost you nothing if the taxpayers are financing your legal services to make sure that, although comparatively poor, you are as well able as the richest citizen or corporation is to assert and defend your rights.

Thus despite their similarities, the markets for doctors' and lawyers' services have some critical differences.

The buyers

Many individual clients know well enough what legal services they need, use them for their own or their families' benefit, and pay for them with their own money. Wherever the fees are reasonable and the professional ethics and self-regulation are dependable, it tends to be an efficient service which does not need much public regulation. Serious market failures, and policy questions, come (1) when the suppliers of legal services can influence the demand because (as with medical services) the buyers can't judge for themselves what service they need; (2) when people can't afford to pay for the legal services they need; and (3) when plaintiffs – citizens who initiate civil actions – can pay for legal services with other people's money.

Suppliers' influence on demand Clients can't always know what their legal options are and what action will serve their interests best. The more they depend on their lawyers' advice, the more the lawyers can influence the demand for their services. Lawyers advise clients what action to demand. As the action proceeds, they have to decide from day to day how to conduct it – how to respond to opponents' moves, what research to do, what conferences with witnesses and others are necessary, and so on. Unethical lawyers can sometimes supply unnecessarily expensive services. (The sins are not always one-sided – there are celebrated cases of lawyers spinning out the defence of bank robbers until they have earned all the loot.)

Buyers' capacity to pay Most of the worst inequities of legal systems don't arise from professional misbehavior, they arise from the dilemma described above. It is wrong that people's access to justice should depend on how much money they have. But it might be worse if they could sue and be sued freely, without legal costs, in a risk-free casino.

The inequities don't all arise from inequalities. There are many conflicts between equally poor people. Some poor parents can't afford to take their custody battles to court. Some poor children can't afford to dispute their parents' wills. Some poor pensioners can't afford legal action to quieten noisy neighbors. Scarcely any poor people can afford actions for defamation, although slanders may cause as much distress to them as to anyone else.

But there are also conflicts between unequals. If richer parties can afford better legal services, that may give them unfair advantages. Where judgments are open to appeal, richer parties may keep appealing until poorer opponents run out of money and surrender.

Unequal capacities to pay can also work unfairly against the rich. Poor people are rarely worth suing for damages. Some poor wrongdoers trade on that, to harm and cheat richer people with impunity.

Most of these injustices are allowed to persist for good rather than bad reasons. In legal conflicts it is in clients' interest to let their lawyers respond flexibly to events, i.e. to let the suppliers decide the demand for their services. Free legal service in civil cases would be unsafe because of the casino effect. Appeals are permitted because it is fair that they should be. People need to be deterred from taking unnecessary or mischievous legal action, and having to pay legal costs is good discipline.

Buyers spending other people's money Politicians and public servants order legal services for which the government pays. Company directors order services for which their firms pay. Some industries and professions can insure against some kinds of legal action, and can thus have some of their legal costs, and any damages they have to pay, paid by insurers. The public and private officials are usually serving their institutions' proper purposes and the insured parties are usually acting honestly. But there are exceptions.

It is chiefly from corporate directors spending their firms' money that leading lawyers get their high fees. Those are very high indeed now in English-speaking countries: many times what those countries' Chief Justices are paid, for example. That increases the difficulty of delivering equal justice to unequally paid citizens. And it raises the costs and perhaps reduces the quality of the public legal services. Corporate directors are hard bargainers for their firms in most of their business. Why do they pay their lawyers so much?

Defenders of the high rates see them as normal market prices for a scarce and highly valued resource. At any lower price there would be excess demand for the leaders of the profession. So the leaders raise their prices to the level at which they are offered the amount of work they want, i.e. to the equilibrium price at which supply equals demand. It's an efficient market.

Your watchdog may have three misgivings about that.

First, assume that leading lawyers do earn competitive market prices, and that their skills are so scarce, and so much more effective than those of the second rank of lawyers, that they are worth the prices which firms pay them. That can only be true if they achieve better results: if they win more cases or contrive more other advantages for their clients than cheaper lawyers do. If that is so, the system of justice can't be impartial. Richer contenders can buy advantages over poorer ones as surely as if they could bribe the judges. If so, there are profound ethical and political objections to tolerating an efficient market for legal services.

But how effective is their margin of talent? Outside the United States, most important corporate cases are tried without juries. Advocates argue before judges. The judges have been leading advocates. They could argue either side of most of the cases they hear with equal skill. The heart of their skill is the ability to see through any advocacy to their own understanding and judgment of the cases they try. It seems unlikely that the skill deserts them when they move from the bar to the bench, or that marginal differences between the skill of the advocates they hear have much to do with their judgments.

A third misgiving about the 'efficient market' explanation is that the directors who pay the top prices may be concerned with other things besides value-for-money for their firms. For example it is hard to judge the quality of legal services: all lawyers, including the best, lose some cases and have some of their advice belied by unexpected judgments or other developments. When things go wrong, directors can defend their own conduct if they have confided the business to acknowledged leaders of the profession. And lawyers help to design and conceal the directors' clever, tax-evasive reward packages – so perhaps there are elements of gratitude, and cameraderie.

Policies

What follows is the merest sketch of some of the measures by which democracies try to reduce the unjust effects of legal costs. Its only purpose is to rub in the message that markets differ, and need different kinds of government.

Legal aid in criminal cases Almost all criminal trials are initiated by salaried public lawyers or police. Those officers may suffer from too much or too little zeal or too few resources, but there is not much danger of frivolous or unnecessary prosecutions: there's no casino. The problems for public decision are (1) how to ensure fair trial for people who can't afford the costs of a proper defence, and (2) who should pay the defence costs of people who are tried and acquitted.

Most countries offer a free defence to accused people who can show that they are too poor to pay for their own. Methods vary. Many countries began with the first of the following but now rely on one or both of the second and third:

- Lawyers, through their professional association, offer a free service. Each does a quota of free work, or contributes to a fund which pays those who do the work.
- Government employs salaried lawyers to do the work.
- A public legal aid office pays private practitioners to do the work.

The standard of service commonly varies with the gravity of the crime. Beginners defend drunk drivers, more experienced lawyers take more difficult cases, leaders of the profession defend people accused of murder. Everybody poor enough to pass the means test gets a defender. There may be discrimination about appeals: if the public officers think there is no plausible ground for an appeal they may not finance one. Only to that extent is there any pre-judgment of cases.

There remain two common sources of injustice.

Means tests for free legal aid are often strict, with asset as well as income tests. Home-owners or households with savings may not be helped, and many have lost their houses and savings defending family members. (The goods they lose may sometimes of course be ill-gotten.)

Second, people who don't qualify for legal aid and who are acquitted are rarely repaid their defence costs. Officially they are innocent, so why don't governments reimburse them? There may be two reasons. The sufferers are not a popular or influential group. And there is some unspoken belief that most people who are accused and acquitted are not innocent, they're villains who managed to beat the rap and should at least pay the costs of beating it.

Dilemmas in civil cases Civil actions are between citizen and citizen. Government is not the prosecutor as it is in criminal cases, but it still has a role: it makes the laws, provides the courts, compels the parties and witnesses to appear, and helps to enforce the judgments. When people (or firms or other institutions) damage each others' property, business, earning capacity, reputation or health, don't pay their debts, break contracts or conditions of employment, dispute about divorce, matrimonial property or the custody of children, can't agree what sort of fence to build between their back yards, or fall out over anything else about which there is some relevant law to which they can resort, then one of the disputants, rather than a public prosecutor, has to take the dispute to court. Business and social life depend heavily on this access to impartial adjudication and law enforcement between citizen and citizen. The more reliable it is known to be, the better people are likely to behave and the less resort to law there need be. But anyone who can't afford to sue, or to defend themselves if sued, is vulnerable to many kinds of ill treatment, and is an unequal citizen.

Here are the worst dilemmas between one injustice and another. People, firms and other institutions sue each other for the best and worst of reasons, and plenty of doubtful reasons in between. There are bullying, predatory and nuisance litigants who should not be suing at all. And there are conflicts between respectable citizens which should desirably be resolved without going to court. Easy legal aid can encourage legal action in conflicts of every kind. But the lack of it can deprive poor people of a basic civil right.

For some at least of the poorest people there has been better legal aid in the past than there is now. English statutes passed in the fifteenth and sixteenth centuries and not repealed until 1883 allowed litigants who could pass a means test to come to court as paupers. Courts waived their court fees and supplied them with free counsellors – often the best, because they were the ones who could afford to do without fees. In the fifteenth century the paupers' access ran all the way to the King's Council, where lawyers who refused them free service could be sacked. Henry VI ordered that –

> The Clarke of the Councell shall be sworne, that each day of sitting he shall cause the Bills of the poorest Suitors to be first read, and answered, so neare as he can aske, or inquire. And the King's Sergeant to be sworne to give Councell without fee, to such as shal be accepted for poore, upon paine to be discharged of their Offices.
>
> – from William Lambarde, *Archion, or, a Comentary upon the High Courts of Justice in England* (1591), pp. 173-4 of the 1635 edition; reference by courtesy of Tim Stretton.

Our concern is with the economics of this dilemma. The rest of this chapter reviews (i) some institutional encouragements to questionable legal action; (ii) some kinds of selective legal aid in civil cases; and (iii) some cheaper alternatives to court action. We begin with the growing tendency to sue anyone who gives you unsatisfactory service.

Professional negligence Depending on your country's law and practice you may be able to get damages – often paid by insurers – for unsatisfactory services you receive from doctors, lawyers, auditors, teachers, and other professionals. Until recent times those services were subject to market rather than legal discipline as long as the people worked with fair average care and erred only by honest misjudgment. Poor performers were expected to lose business rather than lose damage suits. Big damages, and speculative gold-digging actions to get them, are a recent and chiefly American development. Three conditions encourage them: the use of juries in civil cases; American judges' views of strict professional responsibility; and lawyers' rights to charge contingent fees.

Juries American courts have many civil cases decided, and the amount of any damages assessed, by juries. French courts have no juries in civil cases. Between those extremes other countries have juries for civil actions of some kinds but not others, or only when one of the parties demands a jury; or they allow juries to decide the cases but judges to decide the amount of any damages. Juries tend to award higher damages, and much less consistent or predictable damages, than judges do. And because of the different tactics and advocacy which juries attract, jury trials take longer and cost more.

Judges have exerted different influence in different countries. Two broad differences between US and British judges have significant economic effects.

A British judge's view: When you engage professionals, you are entitled to expect them to do their honest best. As long as they do that, you have no cause of action if their services prove to have been inadequate or mistaken. If the doctor available at an accident happens to be inexperienced, she can't help that and should not be held responsible for any effects of her inexperience. The most expert professionals have to make judgments between alternative risks, and should not be punished when they guess wrong. The least expert of those who are qualified and licensed to practice should not be punished for being less expert than the profession's leaders. Actions for professional negligence should only succeed if there is culpable carelessness or malpractice. Sufferers should normally look for help to the public health and welfare services rather than to private damages.

An American judge's view: The reason why professional people have to be publicly certified as qualified to practise is that their clients have to trust them. The clients are entitled to state-of-the-art service from them. A professional should know if she can't offer that standard of service in particular cases and should refer those cases to others who can. People who suffer harm from sub-standard professional service should be compensated. If there is conflict between justice for the client and justice for the professional (as when an inexperienced doctor does her inadequate best at an accident site) the compensation should be provided by insurance.

Insurance is also needed when professionals have to pay damages they cannot afford to pay. Conclusion: Liability should be strict, and the professionals should be required to insure against it.

Individual British and American judges may well disagree with those views. But they reflect the national practices. Together with the role of juries in the US, they account for doctors' insurance premiums being three or four times higher in the US. The legal costs of actions for negligence also tend to be higher. But for some of the people who sue the professionals, the costs and risks are lower in the US – as follows.

Contingent fees   Many American courts allow lawyers who appear before them to charge their clients contingent fees. In most courts which allow this arrangement, the judge has to know and approve the terms. As this chapter is written, contingent fees are forbidden in Britain and most Commonwealth countries. But the prevailing deregulatory mood has brought proposals to permit them. Because they seem to offer a market solution to a social injustice, some economists support the lawyers who want to introduce them. So you may find it useful to arrive at your own judgment of their merits.

In favor: Contingent fees enable poor people to sue for damages who could not otherwise afford to do so. But although they sue without risk to themselves if they lose, there is little or no casino effect – no long-odds gambling or mischievous waste of courts' and defendants' time. That is because lawyers who accept contingent fees will only take cases which offer a reasonable chance of winning substantial damages. Thus a market discipline ensures that people get free service only when experts think they have reasonable grounds for action.

Against contingent fees it is argued, first, that they may have unfair effects. They provide free legal service for plaintiffs (people who sue), but not for defendants because a successful defence doesn't bring in any money to pay lawyers' fees. So they may bias trials in favor of plaintiffs. Supporters of contingent fees insist that people only get free service against defendants who have enough money or insurance to pay big damages, and can well afford to pay their own lawyers. Critics complain that there is no free service for plaintiffs who want the court to control defendants' behavior (reduce noise or pollution, reverse an unfair dismissal, respect a patent or copyright, surrender custody of children, cease harassing the plaintiff) rather than award damages from which lawyers can take contingent fees. (Supporters think free service for needy clients in some cases is better than none.)

Actions for negligence do at least, in most cases, seek damages for people suffering some genuine harm. That is not always true of the most corrupt misuse of contingency fees, the blackmail or shakedown action – as follows.

Strike suit is its common name. Here's one way to do it. You're a lawyer in a state whose courts permit contingency fees, and don't usually order losers in civil actions to pay winners' legal costs. Pick a vulnerable corporation in some sensitive line of business. Find a citizen prepared, for a share of any gains, to allege that he suffers harm from the firm's activities. In his name, sue the firm – for environmental misbehavior, being a nuisance to its neighbors, endangering your client's children, misleading advertising, selling products with inadequate warnings about their possible misuse, or some other somewhat vague offence. Ask a court to order the target firm to disclose documents which in fact won't help your case much, but will give embarrassing information to the firm's competitors or public regulators. You and the firm both know that you have no real case, and if they fight the case they'll win it. But there will be legal costs, other losses, bad publicity and some waste of executive time. Together those will cost more than the sum for which you indicate that your client will settle. So they pay you to drop the case and leave them alone.

Class actions are a better American invention. Large numbers of people can suffer from a harmful product or activity. Examples have included the drug thalidomide, the Dalkon contraceptive, some breast implants. If each sufferer must independently win an action for damages against whoever is responsible for the harm, justice won't be done, because the courts won't have enough time and many of the sufferers won't have enough money or know-how to take the necessary legal action. US lawyers and courts have pioneered the class action by which a single case can establish the rights of all sufferers from the same cause, without necessarily identifying them all at the time of the action. Class actions are simplest when they seek to control a defendant's behavior, for example to reduce pollution or withdraw a dangerous product from the market: such judgments are easy to enforce. When judgments establish rights to damages for numbers of people, there can be continuing problems in identifying those who are genuinely entitled to payments.

A class action can be initiated and paid for by an individual or institution – for example by Friends of the Earth in environmental cases, the Automobile Association in cases about faulty cars, and so on. But they can also be initiated by lawyers, usually relying on contingent fees. For a class action which wins many millions of dollars to be distributed to large numbers of entitled people, the lawyers' contingent fee can be large.

Trade unions and professional associations provide their members with some legal services. Where the aid covers liabilities as well as legal costs it works like insurance, but usually with surer discipline. Union and association officers are not anxious for more legal work or for higher membership fees to pay for it. Some journalists' and other unions compel their members' employers to meet legal costs and liabilities which they incur in the course of their work. Some organizations pay legal costs but not any damages awarded. And they all confine their aid to conflicts which relate to their members' work.

Another way of reducing legal costs is to reduce the need for lawyers. Three examples:

Para-legal services Some business traditionally done by lawyers can be done in routine cases by non-lawyers with appropriate skills. Except in difficult cases, tax agents and advisers don't need to be lawyers. Non-lawyers can prepare, prove and execute wills; transfer property titles; advise people about their relations with administrative and welfare offices; advise people how to represent themselves in uncontested divorces; see that suppliers comply with consumer-protection laws; and so on.

Conciliation and arbitration may be provided by lawyers, local government officers, marriage guidance counsellors, property valuers and other experts. Where they fail to negotiate agreement, the parties may still agree in advance to abide by arbitration as a quicker, cheaper, less divisive solution than going to court. Public conciliators and arbitrators may charge for their services but may exempt bona fide customers who are too poor to pay.

Inquisitorial justice doesn't get you burned at the stake these days, it's a technical term for an alternative to *adversarial* justice. Traditional court practice – adversarial practice – has at least three lawyers in court: an advocate for each party, and a neutral judge. In some inquisitorial systems the parties speak for themselves; judges do any questioning they think necessary, decide how the law applies to the facts they find, and judge accordingly. Some countries run Small Claims Courts on this principle. They typically charge fees, but needy people judged to be bona fide rather than mischievous litigants may be excused the fees. Disadvantages: People without their own legal advisers may get less expert help in knowing their rights and obligations, deciding whether to go to court, and preparing their cases. And in court there may be no expert critics of any mistakes or bias by the judges. Advantages: Inquisitorial proceedings can usually be cheaper and shorter, and sometimes less stressful, than in adversarial courts.

Reminders

This quick review of six industries' markets has not equipped you to analyse or operate competently in beef, land, clothing or car markets or medical or legal services: it has been much too sketchy for that. Its purpose has been to hammer away at the familiar theme that you will often need local knowledge *as well as theory*; changing behavior may mean that you may sometimes need *new and different* theory; and you must learn to recognize *when* you need more than standard theoretical expectations, to understand economic behavior. Depending on the nature of the industry you may need to know something about its technology and production chains, its lead times, its institutional organization, its sources of capital and credit, its patterns of market strength and weakness, its cultural context, and – especially – the beliefs and motivation of the people who produce, sell, buy and use its products.

Summary and exercise

The best revision at this stage, and a useful exercise, is as follows. Turn back to the summary at the end of the previous chapter. Learn that set of questions. Then answer each question in the set (as far as seems relevant) for each of the markets sketched in this present chapter.

43

The composition and distribution of wealth

Pause here, for a page or two about the design of the rest of this course of study. It began with mousetraps and methodology: what you can know about economic behavior, the best ways of knowing it, and the necessary role of your values (or someone's) in analysing it. Then some history and theory of economic growth, with warnings that what you study may be changing as you study it. Then the structure of the rich democracies' mixed economies, with alternative selections of their essentials as modelled by neoclassical, post-Keynesian and institutional theorists.

Next came the more detailed analysis of mixed economies' institutions through which you are working now. So far it has followed a simple construction. Chapters 19 to 42 have described how tastes and preferences are formed and how they shape demands for goods and services; how production is organized to meet the demands; and how supply and demand interact, with varying efficiency in different markets, to determine what gets produced.

That is still an incomplete account of the processes which determine what is produced. There are other causes at work besides those mentioned in those chapters.

- Demand is determined by spending capacity as well as by tastes and preferences: you need to know how wealth and income are distributed, including how the levels of employment and unemployment are determined.

- Wealth, income, credit, investment and spending may all be affected by inflation: you need to understand how.

- Investment, trade and the distribution of wealth and income are affected by national financial systems and the skill and purpose with which governments manage them.

- What goods countries produce for themselves and what they get by trade, and the pattern of employment and the distribution of income which they consequently have, are affected by government policies as well as by home and foreign productive capacities – and many of the productive capacities are also affected by government policies.

You can see my problem. To describe these *simultaneous* interrelations in a *sequent* way, one chapter at a time, is not nearly as simple as it was to order the previous twenty four chapters to describe first demand, then supply, then their mutual effects where they meet in the marketplace.

To illustrate the problem, suppose that a government contrives a wage freeze. That may (1) increase profits in some industries. (2) It may restrict the growth of other industries by preventing aggressive, high-wage recruiting. (3) It may help to restrain cost-push inflation. (4) By restraining purchasing power it may threaten to slow the growth of demand. (5) That may prompt government to encourage spending by increasing some welfare allowances (which it would not do, for fear of demand-pull inflation, if there were no wage freeze). So the wage freeze has to be described five times in those five contexts. That amount of repetition can be boring and confusing for you, the reader. Wouldn't it suffice to have a single description of a wage-freeze and all its likely effects? Perhaps – but should it come in a chapter on methods of wage-fixing, or in a chapter on inflation, or in chapters on the determinants of profits, saving and investment – or where else?

With those difficulties any structure and sequence of chapters must have shortcomings. The structure which follows is chosen chiefly to be as short and unrepetitive as possible; to focus on present and potential problems (of equality, stability, full employment, environmental reform); and in relation to those problems, to focus on the options for public policy. To avoid even more complications I will offer the best analyses I can without much discussion of alternative views. Your watchdog should be experienced enough by now to guess what other theorists might make of the problems, and to notice what values, social purposes and technical judgments have selected and shaped the work.

What's to come

First our study of demand, production and distribution is completed with chapters on –

- the distribution of wealth
- the distribution of property income
            earned income
            home-made income
            transferred income
- taxation.

Then in the first seven chapters of Part Six –

- international trade and national economic structure, i.e. what countries export, what they import and what they produce for themselves
- financial systems: money and credit
            financial institutions
            capital markets
            inflation; and
- employment.

Those elements of economic systems are then drawn together with others dealt with earlier, to consider whole economies at work directed by alternative strategies:

- an open economy in a global world economy
- a Right and a Left strategy for the European Union
- a free-trading social-democratic strategy
- a more protected, self-sufficient social-democratic strategy
- alternative strategies for equipping ex-communist countries with private sectors.

However orderly that sequence of subjects may look, it is still true that 'everything depends on everything else' and there will be unavoidable repetitions, and references back and forth from chapter to chapter. Be as patient as you can with them. This is a difficult but most important part of this course of study.

WEALTH

Wealth is a loose term for things which people use to produce goods and services, or which they enjoy directly, without consuming them in the process. It includes land and natural resources, and produced goods which are used to produce other goods. (If they're consumed in the process, as for example fuel or components are,

they're called intermediate goods. If they survive the process, as factories or machine-tools or workers' skills do, they're capital.) Where income is usually measured as a flow (so much per week or per year), wealth is a stock, measured at a particular date.

Distribution

The distribution of wealth is another broad phrase which can mean –

- its *composition*: the proportions which an economy has of land and other natural resources, and of produced capital such as roads and bridges, factories and equipment, houses and cars, and culture and human capital
- its *location*: the geographical distribution of the various kinds of wealth between nations, regions, cities, neighborhoods and households
- *sector* shares: the distribution of the various kinds of wealth between the public, private and household sectors
- its *ownership*, especially the distribution of individual private wealth. This is the commonest meaning of 'the distribution of wealth'.

Measurement

Though some components of wealth can be measured and valued, the whole amount and value of wealth are difficult to measure for a number of reasons. Wealth includes natural resources, capital goods, rights to income, patents and copyrights. Its owners include governments, independent institutions, share-owned corporations, artful tax-evasive trusts, families and individuals. Some wealth is used to produce output for sale, and income for its owners. Some (for example public infrastructure) is used to produce output and income for people other than its owners. Some (especially housing) is used to produce income in kind rather than in money. Some (for example jewelry and works of art) is enjoyed directly rather than being used to produce anything else.

How should such diverse things be valued? Some of them have measurable costs of production. Some (such as land) do not. Some have current market prices and some (such as public roads) do not. Should the produced items be valued at what they originally cost to produce, adjusted upward for inflation and downward for depreciation since they were produced? Or at what it would cost to produce them now? Or at what they would fetch if sold? Or at their value to their owners as going concerns? Those are likely to be four different figures.

In practice the market value of business capital is usually related to the rate of profit that can be earned by its use. Rather than the capital commanding a rate of return, the flow of profit is likely to determine the value of the capital. Its value may rise or fall with the rate of profit. So it may change if wage and profit shares change. It may change if the prevailing rate of interest changes. Thus a fixed quantity of private capital goods may represent different amounts of wealth at different moments in history, or at different phases of the business cycle.

Public capital goods present other difficulties. The produced capital in public ownership has had costs of production, but some are long past: what have their costs of production to do with the present value of Greek temples or mediaeval cathedrals or other 'priceless' heritage? Or seventeenth and eighteenth century canals still in use? Current income can also be unhelpful as a basis on which to estimate capital value. Some public assets earn income, others don't. Some do, but for others rather than for their public owners. Roads and bridges and much other public capital are used freely by private and household producers. But there is no way of measuring how much of the value of private and household output and income should be ascribed to the public capital they use. (One result is that the contribution of private and household capital to private and household output is overstated in orthodox accounting, because they are given credit for capital services which are partly provided, without charge, by public capital. Another result is that the public capital which they use cannot be valued by reference to its contribution to output and income.)

Some wealth consists of rights to money rather than ownership of capital goods. Increasingly, capital is owned by superannuation funds. Their individual members may own nothing but pension rights, but the effect is much the same as if they owned individual shares of the fund capital, so most surveys of wealth treat them as if they do. From the pensioners' point of view a public age pension is a similar right to income – but most surveys of wealth leave it out, perhaps because the pension will come as income transferred from other taxpayers, rather than as the investment income from a capital fund.

Land and the buildings on it have become a nightmare for valuers of wealth. Their market prices fluctuate with under- and over-supply and with booms and slumps. During a glut, more and better housing can have less market value than less and worse housing had during a housing shortage. The Japanese government tries to keep an account of Japan's total wealth. In 1991 at the peak of a wild boom in city land prices – prices established by a very few sales to imprudent buyers financed by imprudent banks – Tokyo city's real estate appeared to be worth as much as all the real estate in the United States.

There are problems in valuing many natural resources. What are mineral reserves worth? What is the value of forests which could yield timber then farmland, but may be protected by environmental policy because they nourish some threatened species and supply some of the world's oxygen?

Hardest of all to value is human capital: the people's innate and acquired productive capacities. What human capital can produce and earn depends on the presence of other capital too, and the cost of producing human capital – i.e. skilful people – varies widely with housing costs and parents' and teachers' incomes in richer and poorer countries. An Indian Nobel Prize winner may be as productive and valuable as his American equivalent, but he has cost a lot less to bring up and educate.

The working relations between different kinds of wealth present a final difficulty. Many natural resources are worthless without some produced capital to farm them, or mine and process them. The value of the natural resources and the produced capital applied to them may vary widely with the quality of the human capital in charge of them. That means that the different ingredients of national wealth can't simply be valued independently of each other, then added up to arrive at the total value of national wealth. The value of each varies with the presence and value of the others.

Faced with those difficulties of choice and measurement, most national accounts record values for produced capital, but don't try to value wealth as a whole. They commonly value private capital and household capital at market prices; public capital at factor cost, i.e. at its cost of production; pension rights if they are funded but not if they are not; and money and other financial assets at face value, subject to some precautions. Information gathered at different times may need adjustment for inflation. Rights to money at future dates may be discounted for time. And where values are expressed in different currencies, estimates of the comparative purchasing power of the currencies may be preferred to the prevailing exchange rates between them. But in all these items national practices vary. If you have occasion to use accounts of wealth, take care to read what they have to say about the principles on which they are compiled.

Components of wealth

Briefly at the beginning of this chapter four kinds of wealth were listed: natural resources; produced material capital; culture and knowledge; and human capital. This section explores some working relations between them. First, brief reminders about each of them

Natural resources have commonly been treated as free goods (air and water) or as ordinary property (land and minerals). But there is growing environmental awareness of a common interest in the conservation of non-renewable resources. Should the extraction and sale of minerals continue to count as production yielding income – or should different accounting recognize it not as a productive use of capital but as a dissaving *consumption* of capital? Similar questions apply to farming which depletes the soil, and industries which impose pollutant costs on others.

Produced material capital has been dealt with already, in many contexts. Here you need only be reminded that there need to be complementary proportions of the types of capital: enough roads for the number of cars, enough treatment works to treat the output of household and industrial wastes, and so on. That can often be represented (as earlier in this text) as a need for complementary quantities of public, private and household investment. But some of the functional items can exist under alternative types of ownership (there can be public or private power suppliers, landlord-owned or household-owned housing, publicly or privately owned airlines, and so on). So in order to judge how efficient the composition of a nation's wealth is, or what social purposes it is likely to serve best, you need to know its functional composition as well as its pattern of ownership.

Disembodied knowledge and culture get a heading of their own because they are both material and human capital. They are human capital to the extent that people know things, have skills, have moral and aesthetic beliefs and regular habits of behavior. But not all knowledge and culture are humanly embodied like that, i.e. held in mind and memory and transmitted by speech or example. There is also disembodied knowledge, which exists as an item of produced material capital, and can exist without anybody knowing it. Law, literature and scientific knowledge are in print in the world's libraries and increasingly available on the net. So is a great deal of information about past and present social, political, moral and religious thought and practice. Works of art survive in public and private collections, and printed and pictorial representations of

them abound. More than thirty thousand symphonies composed before 1820 survived in manuscript in libraries and private collections through a century in which scarcely any of them were performed, or known, or part of anyone's human capital. But with demand transformed by recording and broadcasting technology, some of that forgotten capital is coming back into use, and into mind. Photography and film and sound recording are accumulating vivid, replicable records of life and art from the nineteenth century onward. Computerized, interlinked catalogues make it possible to search that store of disembodied knowledge from anywhere in the world, and bring any part of it back into mind, and into use, when required. Humans used to know only what they and their face-to-face associates could remember, with literate minorities supplementing memory from whatever books their local libraries held. Now every developed society has access to a world 'memory bank' of more history, art, science and general knowledge than any society could keep in its members' heads; and every satellite photograph, individual DNA analysis or forgotten baroque flute concerto is available to any member who wants it for business or pleasure.

Human capital troubles economists. It consists of natural gifts and acquired knowledge, skill, experience and capacity to work. As a first confusion it is thus a form of capital which is also a quality of labor. It is obviously productive, and necessary to the productive use of other capital – but it can't be defined, measured or connected with its products as rigorously as some other capital can. It is possible to treat the cost of a person's upbringing and education as investment, and the person's earnings as the return to the investment. But at each step of that calculation there are arbitrary choices and guesses about what causes what. Which costs of upbringing should you count? Should you impute a wage for parents' unpaid services? How should you cost the work experience and training-on-the-job which contribute to human capital? Many researchers treat earned income as the return to the investment. Why not the value of the worker's output, which may be much the same in some cases but very different in others? (I happen to know a private orthopaedic surgeon in the US and a public orthopaedic surgeon in Italy. They have much the same human capital and do the same amount of the same work. One is paid six or seven times as much as the other. But that is a fact about their countries' distributions of income, not about their productivity. Their identical *real* output is the capacity for life and work and enjoyment which they restore to the injured people whose joints they mend.) Using earnings as the measure of output also misses the productive effects which parents' human capital may have on the upbringing of their children. It misses any unpriced returns which come in the form of busier uses of household capital and free public capital. It can therefore bias educational policy to serve employers' needs rather than household productivity and individual enjoyment of life and art and learning.

Should you conclude that little can be known about the productivity of human capital: about the links between what made you what you are, and the things that you can consequently do? No: it is an ordinary case of multi-purposed activity with multiple effects, not all of which can be measured or priced or independently predicted. So it is not surprising that the amounts spent on health and education don't exactly determine the amount of earned income, either individually or nationally. You can nevertheless know some negatives. Work through the table of occupations of a developed economy. There are a great many jobs which can't be done without high levels of general education or vocational training or both. It seems likely, though difficult to prove, that general education also contributes to inventiveness, adaptability and capacity to keep on learning.

The composition of national wealth

Geography, history and choice A lot of the proportions and complementarity of capital resources are common to all systems at similar stages of development. But some of the proportions vary from country to country. They may differ because of different geography, climate, natural resources. They may differ because modernization and growth came at different dates with different prevailing technology; for example cities built before the motor car tend to be denser than those built since (though there are exceptions, notably in East Asia). The phrase 'distribution of wealth' need not only refer to the pattern of ownership. It can also refer to what there is to own, i.e. to the functional composition and the locational distribution of a nation's resources.

Why do those qualities matter? They may affect economic efficiency, or social equity. If a society's housing capital consists chiefly of mansions and hovels, then regardless of who owns the houses their inhabitants will be unequally housed. If half a city's schools are spacious and well equipped and half are crowded old asphalt slums, even a revolutionary population with perfectly equal incomes could not give its children equal

education without a lot of rebuilding. And so on. The effects of unequal *ownership* of wealth get plenty of attention. But remember that its *composition* can also have distributional and equitable effects. Three simple comparisons, two of them already familiar, will illustrate the point.

Norway / Sweden Recall our comparison of Norwegian and Swedish housing policies. Norwegian households average (along with the Swiss) the biggest houses, and the highest proportion with private gardens, in continental Europe. As Sweden modernized through the third quarter of the twentieth century, it was Social Democratic policy to house as many town-dwellers as possible in rented apartments. In the 1970s a general preference for houses with gardens forced the government to reverse the proportions of apartments and houses being built. But by then the existing housing stock was such that Swedes faced a generation or more of sharp housing inequalities between those who could get houses and gardens and those who could not. Meanwhile Norwegians, though financially poorer than Swedes, have more equal shares of bigger, more popular, and more productive housing.

Japan / Australia At first sight Japan's and Australia's housing arrangements compare much as Sweden's and Norway's do. Compared with Tokyo, Sydney has twice the proportion of detached houses. Their allotments average four times the size. New Sydney dwellings of all types average more than twice the floor area of new Tokyo dwellings. But the differences are not confined to housing forms, as they tend to be in Norway and Sweden. They are part of a more general difference between the composition of Australian and Japanese wealth. Japan's wealth is much more heavily concentrated in industrial and commercial capital and their necessary public infrastructure. Besides the differences in housing and private garden space per head there are striking differences in the public provisions for home and neighborhood life and recreation. Per million of population Sydney in the 1980s had twenty times Tokyo's area of park and playground; ten times as many playing fields; five times as many tennis courts; and many more facilities for games played chiefly by women. It also had a wider range of public services to home life and recreation.

(We will later notice similar discrepancies between recorded income and real income. National accounts compared at market exchange rates show Japan third or fourth and Australia fourteenth or fifteenth on the OECD table of income per head. But the work it takes to earn the incomes, and what the incomes will buy at local market prices, show Australians to be richer than Japanese in market goods as well as in home-made goods and in leisure. Relations between wages and prices are a main basis of 'The Penn World Table (Mark 5): An expanded set of international comparisons, 1950-1988' (*Quarterly Journal of Economics*, May 1991) in which Robert Summers and Alan Heston ranked Australia seventh and Japan thirteenth in real income in 1988.)

Japan's postwar concentration on industrial recovery and development was understandable. It achieved a miracle of fast industrial growth. But to achieve that growth I doubt if it was necessary to be so mean with the material provisions for life away from work. And some of the deliberate bias in the composition of Japan's wealth is likely to be permanent. Once built, the dense fabric of the cities is difficult, slow and expensive to replace. The bias which is imposed on Japanese life by the composition of the national wealth is not so much a class bias as a bias in favor of paid work, its products and its financial rewards, and against home life, household productivity, leisure, and versatile recreation. By limiting potential productivity outside paid employment, it necessarily limits total productivity.

Those judgments may well be criticized as expressing Australian rather than Japanese valuations of the provisions for home life and recreation. But the Japanese government does not entirely disagree with them. Since the 1970s its published *Visions* of national development have proposed shifts of national purpose and investment toward improving the material conditions of home and neighborhood life.

The comparisons above are based on statistical publications of the Japanese and Australian governments which are surveyed and summarized by Ian Castles in 'Living standards in Sydney and Japanese cities – A comparison' in Kyoko Sheridan (ed.) *The Australian economy in the Japanese mirror* (1992).

Cowboys and Indians When Europeans took North America from the Indian people, when they took Australia from the Aboriginal people, and when they took Israel from the Palestinian people, they brought some capital goods with them. Some of them also brought money with which they could buy and import more capital goods. But neither the purchasing power nor the capital goods would have enabled the Indians, Aborigines or Palestinians to develop the productivity and economic growth which the invaders developed. What they lacked was the immigrants' human capital: the science, arts, skills and productive know-how learned in more complex cultures and more advanced economic systems. In each case the natural resources were the same for the old and new populations, but the newcomers knew more uses for them. Some of the capital goods which the newcomers brought could be used by the old societies. Guns and hand tools improved their economic capacities. But they could not learn to *make* guns, bullets or steel tools, or more advanced capital goods, as the immigrants eventually did, without first acquiring the appropriate human capital. Not even complete scientific and technological libraries – all the West's knowledge in 'disembodied' form – could have helped them much, without the capacity to understand and apply it.

But however difficult it was to develop that human capital, it was not impossible. When Japan faced a similar threat of Western conquest, its leaders quickly decided that continuing independence depended on developing military strength. That depended on matching the West's industrial development. That in turn depended on, among other things, matching the West's human capital. Through the first decades of modernization the government sent thousands of potential experts and managers to study abroad, and invited many hundreds of Western experts to work and teach in Japan. The enlightened Samurai Fukuzawa Yukichi devoted his working life, and Keio University which he founded, to developing the will and philosophy as well as the working skills of a Japanese business class.

The national effort was successful. That was at least partly the work of human capital which the 'old' Japanese society possessed but Amerindian, Aboriginal and Palestinian society did not. Pre-modern Japan had a considerable literary and artistic culture, a self-conscious governing class educated and destined to rule, strong feelings of national unity, and a national system of government. That society produced some leaders able to understand the general nature of the West's military and economic achievement, and the human capacities at the heart of the achievement. They set about developing somewhat different, but equally productive, human capital in Japan. A century later much of eastern Asia is on the same path.

We now turn from the composition of national wealth to the distribution of individual wealth: who gets rich, and how.

THE DISTRIBUTION OF PRIVATE WEALTH

Measurement Besides the general difficulty of measuring and valuing all wealth, there is special difficulty with private wealth because of some owners' efforts to hide it. Owner-occupied farms and houses are easily counted. But most other individual wealth is owned by 10 per cent or less of the population, and many of them don't want you to know – especially they don't want the government to know – what they own. (The better it is known, the easier it is to tax.) All researchers who publish estimates of the amount and distribution of private wealth warn that the information on which their estimates are based is likely to understate the amount of private wealth, the inequality of its distribution, and the wealth of some of the richest owners.

Rich people have managed to exclude questions about wealth from most regular national census inquiries. That leaves probate and income tax returns as the main sources of information. But some rich people avoid death duties by concealing, exporting or entrusting their wealth or giving it away before they die, so that it does not appear in probate investigation of their wills. Some items which don't earn income – for example jewelry and works of art – are easy to conceal. So the records of estates at death are incomplete and perhaps misleading. So also with income tax returns. Taxpayers are not always required to specify or value the capital from which they draw income and most countries do not require them to declare the value of their houses, furniture and equipment, cars, jewelry, works of art and other wealth not currently earning money income. Some of them understate the income they are supposed to declare. So once again the amount and inequality of personal wealth are likely to be underestimated.

Representations of inequality When investigators have discovered what they can about the distribution of personal wealth, they have various ways of representing the inequalities which they find. They may contrast the extremes. For example the official estimates for Britain in 1979 showed that a quarter of a million people owned more than £100,000 each, when that represented about 16 years of the median wage or 23 years of the lowest full-time adult wage. Nearly half the people owned next to nothing classifiable as 'marketable wealth'. The official sources don't name individuals. Press estimates have put the wealth of the Duke of Westminster's family at between £300 and £800

million, i.e. between 45,000 and 125,000 years of the median British wage at the time. The difference between those guesstimates reflects the difficulty of knowing what the very rich own, and deciding how to value it.

Those accounts are twenty years out of date because in 1979 a Conservative government stopped publishing information about British wealth. Before it was abolished the Royal Commission on the Distribution of Income and Wealth commissioned a study of the distribution of wealth in a number of developed countries. The difficulties of discovering who owns what, and of doing it by methods which would allow reliable comparison of national patterns of inequality, led the author to devote most of his text to explaining why he did not publish comparative tables for most of the countries studied, because they would be so unreliable. (If the subject interests you, read that excellent account of it: Alan Harrison, *The distribution of wealth in ten countries*, a background paper to Report No. 7 of the Royal Commission, London: HMSO 1979.) One of the few comparisons he did print, with warnings of its uncertainty, showed the richest 1 per cent of adults owning 25.8 per cent of US wealth and 32 per cent of British wealth, and the richest 5 per cent owning 45.3 (US) and 57.2 per cent (Britain).

Table 43.1 summarizes some British capital inequalities as estimated from income tax returns at that time. Table 43.2 uses estate data (of wealth at death) to estimate changes in the distribution of wealth over the preceding sixty years. Both report 'marketable wealth'. That does not include pension rights. If you calculate the amount of capital which would notionally yield the pension incomes to which people are entitled, it makes a big difference to both the amount of private wealth and its distribution. The calculations require some arbitrary assumptions about earning rates, interest rates and discount rates. On the Inland Revenue statisticians' assumptions, the effects of including occupational pension rights and state pension rights in 1979 would have been as shown in Table 43.3.

Range of net wealth	Percentage of adult population
0 - £5,000	63
5001 - 15,000	22
15,001 - 50,000	12
50,001 - 100,000	1.4
over 100,000	0.6

Percentage of adult population	Percentage of wealth
1	24
2	32
5	45
10	59

Table 43.1 Estimated distribution of personal marketable wealth in Britain in 1979
– from UK Inland Revenue Statistics, 1981, Table 4.8. The 1979 figures were the last available in that form, since the Thatcher government stopped publishing estimates of the distribution of wealth.

Year	Top 1%	Top 5%	Top 10%	Top 20%
1923	60.9	82.0	89.1	94.2
1938	55.0	76.9	85.0	91.2
1961	36.5	60.8	72.1	83.6
1971	28.8	53.0	68.3	84.8
1981	22.5	46.0	62.8	82.5

Table 43.2 Shares in total British Private Wealth, 1923-1981
Estimates for England and Wales 1923-38, and for Great Britain 1961-81 from A.B. Atkinson, J.P.F. Gordon and Alan Harrison, 'Trends in the shares of top wealth-holders in Britain, 1923-1981', *Oxford Bulletin of Economics and Statistics*, 51, 3 (1989), Table 1.

Percentage of adult population	% of wealth without pension	Occupational pension included	Occupational and state pension included
1	24	20	13
5	45	38	27
10	59	51	37
Total wealth (£ billion)	460	550	816

Table 43.3 Percentage of Total Wealth with and without pension rights
– from UK *Inland Revenue Statistics*, 1981, Tables 4.8, 4.9, 4.10

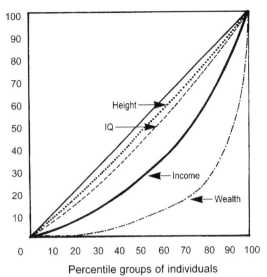

Fig. 43.1 Distribution of British adults' height, IQ,
income & wealth, 1979 – adapted from A.B. Atkinson,
The economics of inequality, 2nd ed. (1983)
pp. 17, 161.

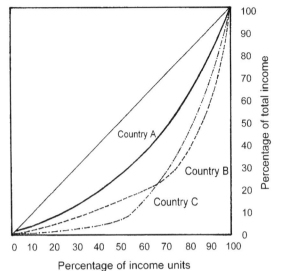

Figure 43.2 Distribution of wealth in three imaginary
countries

The statisticians add that – on some assumptions – if
pension rights are counted, that reduces the Gini coefficient of British capital inequality from 0.74 to 0.48.
What is a Gini coefficient? To know that, you first need
to know what a Lorenz curve is.

Lorenz curves are designed to depict, and compare,
degrees of inequality. The curve plots a cumulative percentage of a total asset against a cumulative percentage
of its owners. If they all own equal shares, the percentage of owners will always equal the percentage of the
asset that they own: half the owners together own half
the asset, 90 per cent of them own 90 per cent of it, and
so on. That is represented by the straight line, known
as the line of equality, in Figure 43.1. The four curves
represent the distribution of height, Intelligence
Quotient, income and wealth among British adults in
1979. No doubt the author of that graph included the
first two to suggest that the distributions of income and
wealth are not simply pro rata rewards for strength or
intelligence. The further to the right of the line of
equality a curve strays, the greater the inequality it
depicts. The wealth curve shows, as the table did, that
90 per cent of the people make do with 41 per cent
of the wealth, 99 per cent have 76 per cent of it, the
richest 1 per cent have 24 per cent of it. Wealth is
distributed about twice as unequally as income, which is

distributed many times more unequally than height
or IQ.

Any curve to the right of any other indicates greater
inequality. But be careful. First, greater inequality is not
necessarily worse inequality. Second, Lorenz curves
can cross, leaving you to judge for yourself which distribution of 'the same amount' of inequality is worse.
Figure 43.2 illustrates.

Country A is clearly more equal than either of
the others. But which of B and C is the more unequal?
B's poor do better than C's, but its rich are fewer and
individually richer than C's. There is fairer sharing
within C's middle and upper classes, but C's poor
are the poorest in the three countries. Only your values
can tell you which of those distributions should
be regarded as more unequal, and which is more
undesirable. And those judgments should if possible
be based on more information than the Lorenz curves
tell you. For example (1) How fair or exploitive are each
country's rich as employers? How productively or
not do they invest their wealth? How selfishly, co-oper-
atively or compassionately do they use whatever
political influence they have? (2) What actual physical
and social conditions do the poor experience in the societies concerned, and how temporary or permanent does
each person's poverty tend to be?

Gini coefficient is a summary measure of inequality derived from a Lorenz curve. It gives the area between the Lorenz curve and the line of equality as a proportion of the whole area under the line of equality:

i.e. the Gini coefficient =

$$\frac{\text{Area between Lorenz curve and line of equality}}{\text{Total area below the line of equality}}$$

For a society with a single owner the coefficient is 1, for a perfectly equal distribution it is 0. In between, the bigger the fraction the greater the inequality. The authors of our Table 43.3 calculated that for the distribution of marketable wealth in Britain in 1979 the Gini coefficient was 0.74; if occupational pensions were included the coefficient was 0.66 or 0.72, depending on the method of calculation; and if state pensions were also included it was 0.48 or 0.53.

Notice that Gini coefficients may tell you even less than Lorenz curves do. For example they could not distinguish the different patterns of inequality in Country B and Country C as the Lorenz curves do in Figure 43.2.

Pen's parade You need to know about Lorenz curves and Gini coefficients because they appear in economists' writing. But for some purposes they are unsatisfactory. Only economists understand them, so they're no use for communicating with anyone else. And they don't give much direct impression of the scale of our inequalities. Plain statements often serve better, by comparing what the richest 1 or 10 or 20 per cent own or earn with what the poorest 10 or 20 or 50 per cent do. For a more memorable device, try Pen's Parade. Though it is an image, it has to be described in words and the image merely imagined, because no page or screen is big enough to depict it. The Dutch economist Pen designed it for incomes but it can represent the distribution of wealth even more vividly.

Imagine a parade in which the population marches in single file past an inspection point. They march in order of wealth, starting with the poorest; and their height corresponds to their wealth. Those with average wealth are of average height. Others are shorter or taller in proportion as they have less or more wealth than average. The parade begins with some quite tall people walking upside down: business men with greater debts than assets so that they have big negative wealth. The upside-downers' height diminishes as smaller and smaller net debtors pass. They are followed by a great many people walking upright but toy-sized because they own next to nothing beyond their clothes and some pots and pans and furniture. The marchers grow taller as car owners, home owners, small business owners and life-long

savers come by. Three quarters of the people have passed by before the average wealth owner with the average adult height of 5 feet 7 inches arrives. Heights begin to rise more quickly. When 90 per cent of the people have passed they're up to 50 feet. Last of all, shooing in the stragglers, comes the Duke of Westminster, somewhere between 35 and 90 miles high depending on how his wealth is estimated. (But in an international parade he would scarcely reach the knees of Bill Gates of Microsoft.)

SOURCES OF PRIVATE WEALTH

Property is older than writing, so for want of evidence its origins are obscure. When history becomes clearer three or four thousand years ago government and property rights already exist. Nomadic hunters and gatherers tend to claim any rights to their territory and hunting grounds collectively. Much of the settled peasant agriculture of neolithic Europe and Asia seems to have had peaceful, informal, somewhat democratic village government, and customary rights to private and common land. Where life depended more on pasture or organized irrigation, or where different economies or excessive numbers competed for scarce land, government tended to be established and maintained by mixtures of force and religious sanctions and in those societies much individual property ownership seems to have come by conquest, private force or government favor. The first rich humans may have got their wealth because they were the ablest individuals at the time. But that meant the ablest fighters, priests or courtiers more often than it meant the most productive farmers, craftsmen or merchants.

Classical Athens drew heavy tribute from its island empire. As Rome conquered new provinces its army officers could often take what land they wanted. When a Norman duke conquered England his captains replaced most of the land-owning aristocracy. The feudalization of Europe and Russia saw a great transfer of ownership and customary rights from a free peasantry to a military aristocracy; and when some centuries later the serfs were given back their freedom, not many of them were given back their ancestors' land. When Cromwell reconquered Ireland he gave most of it to English owners. Through the same century the English who were taking North America from its Indians were parcelling it out to one another more democratically. When the English took Australia from its Aborigines military governors began by granting, selling or leasing it to their officers, free settlers and ex-convicts in a variety of ways. The founders of Israel took a lot of property from

Palestinians. The communist regimes took most property into public ownership. Their successors are giving, lending, selling and stealing it back into patterns of private ownership shaped by quick-changing government policies in the biggest fire-sale in history.

That and other history may not be directly relevant to the processes which determine the distribution of wealth in modern democracies with developed mixed economies. But it is a reminder of the public origins of private property: both of the institution of ownership, and of much of its original distribution to individuals. The institution of property and the lawful ways of acquiring and trading it are under continuing influence through law, taxation and economic policy. Before discussing what that public influence ought to aim at, we first review the other main influences on the creation and distribution of private wealth –

- inheritance and marriage
- the further growth of existing wealth
- life-cycle effects as people earn, save, borrow, buy houses, and support their retirement
- crime and gambling
- art, science and invention
- business success.

Marriage, inheritance and other gifts to kin
Recent British surveys find that roughly a third of the very rich made it all themselves; a third inherited some wealth and increased it substantially; a third inherited all or most of what they have. Among the American superrich there is a little less inheritance and a little more self-help; and American fortunes tend to disperse more quickly.

The British/American differences appear to have a number of causes. A higher proportion of Americans make new fortunes. More of them leave money to charitable foundations. They usually leave equal shares to their children, many of whom marry people with no money. Fewer British make new fortunes. Those who do give less to charity. Until recently they tended to leave more to sons than to daughters, and sometimes more to eldest sons. And those children married other rich more often than their American equivalents did.

Those estimates are as rough as other estimates of personal wealth are, and they only relate to the very rich: the richest 1 per cent in many of the surveys. American wealth as a whole is less concentrated than British, primarily because of the wider spread of farm and home ownership in the US.

Both countries' capital inequalities diminished

through most of the twentieth century, but family arrangements may have exaggerated the trend a little. From 1923 to 1972 the proportion of English wealth owned by the richest 1 per cent, as estimated from estates at death, fell by nearly half (from 61 to 32 per cent) while the proportion owned by the richest 5 per cent fell by only a third (from 82 to 56 per cent). But there was some dispersion of ownership within families for tax reasons. The share of the richest 1 per cent of families may not have fallen as far as the share of the richest 1 per cent of individuals did.

With the Right turn and the increase of income inequality through the last quarter of the century it is hard to know whether the dispersion of wealth was also reversed. There are big new fortunes, fast-growing executive rewards and some downward shift of taxation from richer to poorer taxpayers. But rising numbers of middle-income and some lower-income families have superannuation and are inheriting some housing capital, so the proportion of people with *some* capital has continued to grow.

Accumulation of existing wealth   Among active entrepreneurs, some inheritance has been important to a third or a half of new fortunes. That may suggest that inheritance speeds up the concentration of wealth. But many of those entrepreneurs took big risks, and their gains may be offset by the losses of other risk-taking inheritors.

Passive inheritors who keep their wealth in safe property or shares may earn a real return of 5 or 6 per cent before tax and 3 or 4 per cent after tax. If left to accumulate, that will double or treble in value over (say) the thirty years between one generation's death and the next. People with higher incomes tend to save higher proportions of them. By itself that tendency would increase the inequality of inherited wealth, with the richest getting richer fastest. But with passive inheritors there are often countervailing tendencies. Some live on the income instead of accumulating it. Some spend or lose capital – a yacht, a string of gallopers or a third spouse can disperse wealth quite briskly. The more children there are, the less each may inherit. So even in Britain, if no new fortunes were made, wealth might spread downward, and its inequality diminish, over time.

If inheritance and other family transfers thus account for no more than half or so of the present ownership and inequality of wealth, what determines the other half, the self-helping half? We will notice in turn saving by wage and salary earners; home-buying; various kinds of plunder and contrivance; creative achievements in science, industry and the arts; and various kinds of business success.

Earning and saving How much of the ownership of wealth is achieved by people saving and investing some of their wage or salary income through their working lives?

Incentives to save The rate at which people save has varied widely with time and place. One can speculate about the notice they take of any incentives to save, but their behavior varies so much even in the face of constant incentives that it can't be explained by any reliable general theory. For example people do not regularly save more when offered high interest on their savings, and less when interest rates are low. Though there is some tendency among the very rich to save more the higher the income, some national populations have saved *less* as their incomes rose with economic growth.

Examples:

Swedes saved hard until the 1960s then abruptly proceeded to save much less. Perhaps the completion of their very generous system of public welfare, including pensions geared to individual earning rates, removed the need to save for old age. Perhaps the arrival of TV helped to persuade hard-working, hard-saving people to relax and spend.

The highest national rate of saving in recent times was by the Japanese through their decades of very fast growth, when as much as 30 per cent of income was saved and invested, mostly in private industry and its necessary public infrastructure. There were special incentives. With severely war-damaged cities and industries, people worked with fierce resolve to rebuild their economy. Without public provisions for old age, and with a majority of workers without corporate welfare entitlements, people saved for old age. Government provided an easy-to-use post office savings bank and paid tax-free interest on its deposits. The home market was effectively protected from the import of most consumer goods and – despite competition among them – many Japanese firms established high pricing and profit rates, and saved hard to finance heavy investment from retained earnings.

Contrast the Australians through the same years. They saved to buy their houses and cars, but not much for other purposes. They were long accustomed to a means-tested old age pension. They had stable full employment, a public income and workers' compensation for any unemployed, and public health services – so there was little need to save for emergencies or old age. They saved at less than half the Japanese rate, and imported foreign savings to finance a fifth or more of their moderate rate of investment.

Very high earnings A few salary earners and self-employed people earn enough to live well and also save up significant wealth. They include corporate executives and some leading lawyers, accountants, doctors and other professionals. What distinguishes them from the mass of lower-paid people in similar occupations? On the one hand many of them work hard and productively and have got to the top in open competition. On the other hand equally productive leaders in science, government and public enterprises earn much less. What makes the difference? In both sectors the top rewards are fixed by people spending other people's money, and likely to do better themselves the more they pay to other leaders. But democratic governments have so far restrained public leaders' rewards. In the private sector the top pay is much higher, and there is no regular relation between high pay and productive performance – some of the highest pay has been taken from ailing or failing enterprises. Those who want regulation or tougher taxation of private rewards can point to plenty of bad examples. Those who want present freedoms to continue can point to plenty of very able executives taking very high pay.

Home purchase Look back at Chapter 26 on the difference which home ownership can make to households' net worth over household life. Spendable income after tax and housing costs may be 20 per cent higher. Net worth over household life may be 40 per cent higher. People may retire with wealth worth three years or more of income. Where 70 per cent of households own their houses, the owners include about 85 per cent of those retiring. Home purchase is one of the two main causes of the reduction of capital inequality in the twentieth century. The other is superannuation.

Superannuation Funded superannuation turns savings into a form of wealth. State pensions don't, but they have one similar effect. Taxpayers finance others' pensions through their earning years, then in their turn receive pensions which they can reasonably regard as a return of their earlier savings. Most age pensions and occupational superannuation are twentieth century creations. Table 43.3 showed their effect on British wealth in 1979. The estimated value of private wealth was increased from £460 billion to £550 billion by superannuation, and to £816 billion if state pension rights were counted as wealth. A rough guess would give about 40 per cent of that 'pension wealth' to people who had no other wealth, and about 40 per cent to people who owned their houses but not much else.

The next chapter will compare investment in the form of funded superannuation with income transfers in the form of tax-financed pensions as sources of income for the mass of retired people who don't have unearned incomes from wealth of their own. Which method to use –or what mixture of the two – is an important political choice with implications for many other areas of economic policy.

Crime Some estimates of criminal income in the US put it as high as 10 per cent of national income. That is nearly half as much as total investment income, and it is a source of new wealth as criminal gains are invested in lawful enterprises. The estimates are uncheckable, and must include many low incomes from petty crime. Incomes big enough to accumulate wealth come chiefly from fraud and embezzlement, corrupt procurement of defence and other public contracts, arson, tax fraud, prohibited drugs, some unlawful ways of profiting from gambling and prostitution, kidnapping and other extortion and protection rackets, computer hacking, and occasional big robberies.

Gambling Most gamblers lose (or there would be no bookies or casinos) but some win. Fortunes have been made on horses, at cards, in lotteries and football pools. Gambling passes money from hand to hand without adding any value: does that make it economically unimportant? No: it can have at least four effects of interest to economists. It is an industry which employs resources to produce services its customers want. It redistributes income and sometimes wealth. It addicts some people, and when it addicts poor people it can increase poverty, crime, and public health and welfare costs. There can also be economic effects, many of them bad, when the gambling is on future share prices, land prices, interest rates or international exchange rates. Those are subjects of other chapters.

ART, SCIENCE AND INVENTION

Artists Picasso left paintings valued at a billion dollars or more. That was unusual. For reasons noted presently, few painters or sculptors have accumulated as much as one million. But some writers and scores of musicians and film actors are self-made multi-millionaires. The differences partly reflect the demand for different arts. But they also arise from the techniques of reproduction. If you want to make a million from art, choose an art whose technology allows you to (i) create disembodied capital which can go on earning in your absence, and (ii) mass-produce acceptable copies of your works for mass sale. In those respects the arts fall

into three main groups: those which earn by human capital only, those which can earn by either or both of human capital and disembodied capital, and those whose only output is of disembodied capital.

For ballet dancers, stage actors and some others their human capital is their only capital. Live performances are what the customers want to see. Filmed ballet and stage plays are only minor sources of revenue. There is a sort of replication in the capacity of a live play or ballet to be seen by an audience of a thousand or two. Stage performers may thus earn more than live performers like psychoanalysts or prostitutes who must usually earn from only one customer at a time. But the replication ends when the live performance does: there are no incomes for absent stage actors, dancers, jugglers or circus acrobats.

Second, there are arts which earn by live performance but can also be recorded and reproduced in forms which the customers find acceptable enough to buy in big quantities. Music is the main one.

Third, there are arts in which there is little or no live performance. The audience wants the work of art without the artist, who can consequently sun herself on the Riviera while the royalties roll in. Books and films are the main earners, because they can be satisfactorily reproduced to meet any amount of market demand. Paintings and sculptures are also disembodied capital in that they can be enjoyed over and over in the artists' absence. But they can't be satisfactorily copied for mass sale. The customers won't pay much for photographs of them, and there is not yet any mechanical way to lay paint onto a thousand canvases exactly as van Gogh laid it on the original. Picasso could make so much money only by painting some thousands of pictures for which the buyers, including hundreds of museum directors spending other people's money, would pay very high prices.

Scientists could reasonably claim to be the worst paid workers, in relation to the value of their output, in modern times. Most of the great growth of productivity which has extended comfortable conditions of life from minorities to whole populations has been built on their discoveries. But not many of them have shared in the personal wealth which their work made possible. Most of the few exceptions have got rich by turning themselves into inventors and entrepreneurs. When James Watt had perfected his steam engine as a university employee he left the public sector and got rich as a private manufacturer. Two centuries later when computing scientists discover something payable some of them leave their universities to earn rich rewards in Silicon

Valley. But much larger numbers in other branches of science work on as salaried employees of universities and research institutes, or private firms in whose profits they don't share.

Inventors have not all been big gainers from their inventions, but they have generally done better than scientists. Fortunes were made by a number of the inventors and improvers of steam, internal combustion and electric engines; electric light; industrial chemistry and metallurgy; telegraphy and telephony; sound recording and reproduction; radio; powered flight; the revolutions in computing and telecommunications; and so on. But there have been wide variations in the division of gains between the inventors themselves and the financial and industrial developers of their products. Increasingly, invention comes from teams. It is not only hard to apportion credit to individual team members; in most industries it is hard to get teams together, and equipped and financed, except as employees of public or private enterprises which may pay them good wages and sometimes bonuses, but rarely big profit shares. Once again the spectacular exceptions tend to be inventors who manage to be their own entrepreneurs, and part-owners of the enterprises which produce and market their creations. They belong in the following section as business successes, as well as in this one as inventors.

BUSINESS SUCCESS

How firms do business was the subject of earlier chapters. This section deals with it only as a source of personal wealth.

Many firms grow by saving and re-investing their earnings. So do many existing personal fortunes. A few new personal fortunes come in that way, for example to writers and musicians. But most new fortunes from business are not made in that way. They come more quickly by a process of capital revaluation best described by Lester Thurow in *Generating inequality: Mechanisms of distribution in the US economy* (1975). Make time, if you can, to read that short clear book: only one of its themes is summarized in the following explanation of the business sources of unequal wealth.

Real capital and financial capital

Real capital means capital goods: buildings, machinery and so on: the physical means of production. Not much of the money to buy capital goods comes from the stock exchanges which Thurow calls the financial capital market. Some of it may come from there when a growing firm first 'goes public' and sells shares to the public. But after that, firms mostly finance their purchases of

capital goods from their own earnings or from loans repaid from their earnings. They don't issue more shares each time they need new vehicles or machinery or buildings. At the time of his study Thurow found that retained earnings were financing 99 per cent of US firms' capital spending.

Money spent on capital goods brings different rates of return in different firms and in different industries. In 1972 US pharmaceutical drug manufacturers were earning at three times the rate earned by metal producers. Within the car industry General Motors earned at twice Chrysler's rate. Suppose you are a passive investor looking to buy a portfolio of shares to yield an unearned income. Why would you buy steel shares paying 6 per cent if pharmaceuticals were paying 18 per cent? Or Chrysler shares paying 8 per cent if General Motors were paying 18? You wouldn't, and neither would anyone else. What happens is that buyers compete for the high-paying shares, bidding their prices up, and sell off the low-paying shares, pushing their prices down, until the rates of return *to the share prices* (not to the firms' capital goods outlays) are about equal. The firms and their shares are thus valued in the financial marketplace not by what they have invested in capital goods, but by what they earn. In Thurow's words the financial markets 'capitalize away the differences in real rates of return'.

Example: Suppose that the average dividend income from shares of firms with comparable levels of risk is 10 per cent of the share price, i.e. shares bought at market price yield 10 per cent per annum. A firm with $1m worth of capital goods earning $300,000 a year (30 per cent) will be valued at $3m, and its shares (if there are one million of them) will sell for $3 each, because at that price the shares will return 10 per cent which is the current average and expected yield. A second firm has $6m of capital goods but earns the same $300,000 a year, i.e. 5 per cent on its capital outlay. This firm also will be valued at $3m, to return the going rate of 10 per cent. If it has six million shares, they'll be priced at 50 cents each. Thus the market has taken firms earning respectively 30 per cent and 5 per cent on their original $1 shares and their real capital investments, and equalized their returns to new sharebuyers by pricing their shares at $3 and 50 cents respectively. Original buyers who paid $1 for their shares when the companies first went public have respectively trebled their money or halved it if they sell now.

That example shows share prices and rates of return adapting to firms' different performance while the average return to all shares in the market remains stable.

Now see what happens if that average rate changes. Suppose that a severe depression drops the average rate of return to 5 per cent. If the two companies in our example halve their earnings and dividends as others are doing, i.e. if they move with the market average, their share prices may not change. Buyers who formerly got 10 per cent on those $3 and 50 cent shares will now accept 5 per cent, because that is as good as they will get from any other shares. But suppose that our two companies manage to defy the depression and continue to earn at their old rates, i.e. at 30 per cent and 5 per cent on their capital outlays. So they still pay the same $300,000 dividend that they formerly did. Buyers competing for their shares will bid their prices up until the return to the share price is down to the new 5 per cent average. The $3 shares double to $6, the 50 cent shares double to $1. If the first company's original buyers at $1 a share sell now, they get six times their money back. If the second company's original buyers do the same, they break even.

A further possibility: suppose the firm earning 30 per cent on its real capital and paying a 10 per cent dividend on its share price expects to do better still. Investing retained earnings, it will soon be earning 30 per cent on more real capital and paying higher dividends. Its share price will rise in expectation of rising income – which will temporarily *reduce* its dividend as a return to the share price. Similarly if the firm earning 5 per cent on its real capital is expected to do even worse in future, perhaps because its market is shrinking or its mineral reserves are running out, its share price will fall – so that for the time being its dividend will represent an above-average return to its share price.

All the above are theoretical expectations in an imaginary world in which share-owning is the only source of unearned income. Real life is more complicated. Share prices vary not only with their earning rates but also with risk, with tax and other government policies, with the rate of interest at which sharebuyers could lend their money if they sold their shares, and with other market conditions. But subject to those modifications, they behave as described above, and the commonest way to get rich quickly is to get possession of shares in the first company in our example before the public discovers its high earning rate and bids its shares up from $1 to $3, $6 or (with future expectations in mind) higher still. In Thurow's terms 'one must create or select a situation in which an above-average rate of return is about to be capitalized'.

Create or *select* point to winners of two kinds. Inventors and entrepreneurs create such situations if

they succeed in starting firms with above-average rates of return to real investment. Others – share-buyers hunting the market for such opportunities – must try to guess which firms have above-average prospects which have not yet been capitalized. We will consider those active and passive wealth-seekers in turn.

Inventors and entrepreneurs

Not all inventors and entrepreneurs succeed. But of those who do, Ross Perot's early business career exactly illustrates the process which Thurow describes.

A Texan born in 1930, Perot became an ace salesman for IBM in the early years of general computerization. He presently perceived a business opportunity. The early computers were by modern standards heavy and expensive. Some firms which owned them did not use their full capacity. Many firms which could benefit from them could not afford to buy them. To bring the two together, Perot left IBM in 1962 and formed a private company, Electronic Data Systems. The firm arranged for the non-owners to lease spare computer time from the owners, and it wrote the programs the non-owners would need. It was a good idea, Perot was an effective manager, business boomed, and the firm progressed to owning many of the computers which it leased, and to giving a wide range of computing advice and services. After six years, needing capital for rapid expansion, the firm became a public corporation. It sold shares for $16.50. Within two years they were changing hands for $150. One reason for the expansion was the national creation of Medicare and Medicaid. Perot supplied information-processing systems to a great deal of the vast new federal, state and private medical insurance business. (Remember how interdependent the public and private sectors are.) Perot did not accumulate wealth at the rate at which he could save from his annual profits. When his firm went public after six years his share of it made him a multimillionaire. Two years later the share value had multiplied ninefold. He later sold his shares to General Motors. They paid him in General Motors shares, which they presently bought back from him for $700m.

Not all innovators do as well as that. But of those who make business fortunes at all, most do make them in that quick way, when the earning capacities which they create are capitalized into the market value of the shares which they own. If the innovators are the founders of their firms, as Perot was, they are likely to have acquired shares for nothing or at their original issue price, before outsiders discovered the firms' earning potential and bid up their share prices.

Most of those outsiders are passive investors. They buy and sell shares without managing the resources which they own. How some of *them* get rich is Thurow's second theme. But first, notice some theoretical implications of his practical observations.

Implications for economic theory Thurow was concerned to disprove some neoclassical theory. Recall, from Chapter 18, how a simple neoclassical model depicts the allocation of productive capital resources. Owners of the resources offer them in capital markets for productive use. Producers bid for them. The theory assumes that in an efficient economy the producers who can use the resources most productively are those who can use them most profitably, and therefore bid highest for their use. (They can offer the highest dividend rate on the shares they sell, pay the highest interest for the money they borrow, pay most for the land and physical resources they need, and so on.) If the markets are efficient, the competition for resources should have the effect of equalizing the return to capital in all industries, with differences only for levels of risk. If steelmaking is a low earner and pharmaceuticals a high earner, capital resources should flow from steelmaking to drug-making until the lessened competition in steel and the intensified competition in drugs equalize their pricing policies and rates of return. So says the theory.

Thurow, and parts of this present text, remind you why that does not happen always or fully to *real productive resources* –

- Steel mills can't be made over to produce drugs.

- Steelmakers don't sell their mills and re-invest in drug laboratories and factories.

- Human capital, especially in highly skilled industries, is not easily or quickly re-skilled; and even where it might be, many of the executives and experts who command the industries like the skills they have and the industries they're in, and don't want to change.

- Different industries have different power to repel newcomers – different financial and market strength, patent and monopoly rights, command of their retail outlets, established reputations and brand names and customer fidelity, and hence different capacities to defeat new competitors by takeover, predatory pricing, exclusion from retail outlets, or other means.

- Different industries sell to buyers with different bargaining strength. Recall the difference between selling steel to bridge builders and carmakers backed by governments determined to keep steel cheap for international competitive reasons, and selling life-saving drugs, whose quality control is critically important but invisible to the users, to anxious patients advised by doctors both of whom know that medical insurers will pay for the drugs.

- A final reason why real capital markets don't operate to equalize rates of return to real resources is that they don't have to. The financial markets, through their effects on share prices, equalize returns to owners *without* equalizing returns to real investment. So for most of the owners – the passive investors who own most of the shares in most joint-stock companies – there is no market incentive to equalize the returns to real resources.

Read Thurow's *Generating inequality* if this summary has not made clear how different rates of return to funds invested by different firms and industries are transformed by the share markets into similar rates of return to the owners of the firms. Owners' gains are not all the same over time. They change as firms' individual performance and earning rates change. But at any moment in time, everyone's corporate wealth as the share market values it tends to be earning similar rates of return with differences only for different expectations of risk.

That being so, how do some shareholders get richer than others?

Passive investors

First, some refinement of the analysis so far. The *average* rate of return to share owners is the same as the *average* rate of return to firms' real investments. It could scarcely be otherwise – there's only so much profit earned, so there's only that much profit to pay out in dividends or invest in capital growth. The average is derived from a wide spread of real rates of return (from 6 per cent to 18.5 per cent in one sample year). Financial markets adjust the share prices so that all shares with similar risks yield similar rates of return to their market value.

The proviso 'with similar risks' is important. Estimates of risk vary widely between firms and between industries. Shares in a morning newspaper, or an electric supply company, each with a local monopoly of its market, may have negligible risks. Industries which suffer severely in periodical recessions, or which are overloaded with debt, or vulnerable to sudden fashion changes, have high risks. In theory, share prices adjust to equalize the probability of earning the market average rate of return. Low returns with low risk can yield the same most-probable income as high returns with high risk, though one has wider possibilities than the other of rising above or falling below the average. When the financial pages of your newspaper show share prices with widely different rates of return at their last dividend payment, they may nevertheless offer similar probabilities of future returns. The argument so far has over-simplified in suggesting that all share prices adjust to offer the same rates of return. In fact they achieve similar *probabilities* of return by offering actual returns geared to levels of risk: high immediate returns where there are high risks of loss; average returns where there are low risks or symmetrical risks (i.e. equal chances of gains or losses); below-average returns where earnings are expected to increase. The averaging only produces equal present rates of return where there are thought to be equal levels of risk. (Some analysts say 'within each risk class'.)

But when people buy shares they can't *know* what the risks and returns will be, they can only estimate them. What the financial markets equalize are *expected* returns within classes of *estimated* risk. The expectations and estimates are based on what traders know about the relevant firms and industries. Law and stock exchange practice ensure that all the available information is available to all traders, and in practice share prices adapt quickly to new information about firms and their prospects. The prices are arrived at by interaction between buyers and sellers of whom many are expert and equally well informed. As an individual investor it is unlikely that you can guess any better, given the same information. It takes time and money to acquire the information and estimate its implications, so you may be better off without it. Since the information and a range of expert traders' judgments based on it have been capitalized into the share prices, any portfolio of shares at current prices promises the same return as any other. So unless you have secret information unknown to other traders, you might as well choose your portfolio by drawing names from a hat.

But life does not always fulfil expectations. Shares which seem to promise the same when you buy them perform differently after you buy them. And as in other lotteries, there is an asymmetry in your chances of gain and loss. You can only lose as much as you invest. But there's no limit to the amount a few lucky winners can win.

Suppose you had money to invest in 1968 when Perot floated Electronic Data Systems. There were dozens of small new electronics firms in the market. Most of them were founded and managed by people quite clever enough to make fortunes if others didn't beat them to the business. In the event some of them went broke (you lost your money), some of them developed solid lines of business (you earned the average market return), and Perot achieved spectacular growth (with dividends and capital gains you multiplied your money by ten in two years). Did that mean that Perot was ten times as clever as his competitors? No: quite small margins of skill or luck or inside running could beat them to the first Medicare contracts, and whoever won those was in a strong position to win many more. With many clever firms competing for that and other business, the punters who bought Perot's shares rather than shares in other enterprises which looked equally promising at the time were really luckier, rather than cleverer.

When you find you're suddenly rich, what do you do? Most people become prudent and diversify their portfolios. They buy a variety of shares, and other kinds of property. From then on, their wealth usually earns and accumulates at the average market rate.

Luck or skill? This account of the origins of business fortunes is curiously named the 'random walk' explanation. Obviously there are exceptions to it. Just as some artists and writers make fortunes by rapid earning rather than by capitalizing expected earnings, so do the owners of some firms. Some sharebuyers make fortunes not by luck but by insider trading. That means using inside knowledge, not available to other traders, about firms' discoveries or intentions. It's unlawful, but hard to detect. Some traders spread false or misleading information to manipulate prices. Finally as some traders do consistently better than others it is hard not to believe that there is some skill as well as luck at work. But the evidence against the skill explanation and in favor of the luck explanation is formidable. There have been many surveys of the performance of professional fund managers: the expert investors who decide the share buying and selling of life insurers, mutual funds and other financial institutions. Many of them spend a great deal of time and money in getting and assessing market information. Some of them do better than others, sometimes over long periods. But as far as the surveys show, none of them has ever managed to earn better than the market average rate of return, or better than a random selection of shares would be likely to earn. No fund manager has managed to develop decision rules about when to buy and sell which yield better than average returns. And no individual seems to have made more than one new business fortune, as could be expected if pure skill could do it. (Some people have made two fortunes, but at least one of the two has been by fast earning in one of the arts where skill *does* count, rather than by capital gains as a share owner.)

Conclusions Stock exchanges are for the most part secondary markets. As a way of raising funds, issuing new shares is a method which most firms use rarely. They raise funds in that way when they first go public, and thereafter sometimes for big acquisitions. Those share issues can be vitally important. But most of the time firms finance their capital needs from their earnings, or by loans serviced and repaid from earnings. The stock exchange is therefore chiefly a second-hand market. More than 99 per cent of transactions merely pass shares from one passive owner to another. Those transactions don't allocate any capital. The secondary market has to exist at all only because if people could not sell their shares they would never buy them in the first place – firms could not sell the new share issues which attract some capital at critical points in their creation and growth. The joint stock/limited liability company could not exist in its present form to perform its vital productive role. As a secondary market the stock exchange thus performs –

- a necessary though indirect function in inducing investment in the few new share issues that most public companies make;

- a useful function for individuals and institutions who want to earn by having their wealth managed by strangers under public regulation; and

- a useless function as a gambling casino.

It is from the unnecessary third function that many – some observers think most – of any big new business fortunes come.

SUMMARY

Measurement Wealth is difficult to value. Some of it has no market value, or has unstable value. Some of it has no costs of production, or has costs too long past to be relevant. Much of it has different value if valued by its cost of production, its market price or its contribution to production. Its contribution to production may be difficult to estimate. Some public capital is used by public and private and household producers and contributes unmeasured amounts to the productivity of all three. Some public output and most household output is not measured or priced or recorded in national accounts.

Individual wealth also has problems of valuation, and some of it is concealed. Estimates of its inequality can be summarily represented by Lorenz curves, Gini coefficients, Pen's parade, or tables showing what proportions of private wealth are owned by what percentages of the population.

The composition of wealth The pattern of capital that a society has is important. Its functional composition, its geographical distribution and its ownership can all affect what the economy can produce, who gets what shares of it, and the range of choice the consumers have. A society with plentiful industrial and commercial capital, and matching public infrastructure, but with minimal household capital and public recreational capital cannot offer its people the same styles and qualities of life as a society with a different functional balance. Societies with similar *quantities* of household capital may have different patterns of household equality and productivity if different equalities and inequalities have been built into the physical housing stock, and if different patterns of public and private investment give their people different working and recreational opportunities.

The composition of real capital is like the division of labor, in that it is highly interdependent. Many natural resources can't be used without some produced capital operated by people with appropriate human capital and with access to 'disembodied' scientific capital. A deficiency of any one of the four components can reduce the productivity and therefore the value of the other three. Much of the necessary complementarity is achieved by market processes; but most of the public capital, and many households' access to housing capital, depend on past and present public policies.

Who has it? The distribution of personal wealth has historical and political as well as market causes. In all mixed economies it is extremely unequal, much more unequal than income. Inequalities of wealth were reduced through the first three quarters or so of the twentieth century. Rising proportions of people with middle and lower incomes have come to own houses, land, cars, household equipment, and superannuation rights. Rising proportions – three quarters or more in some countries – are now inheriting some housing or other wealth. Thus inequalities were reduced by masses of people acquiring some wealth rather than by the very rich losing any. But some of the very rich are now increasing their holdings at rates which may mean that capital inequalities are declining more slowly, or increasing again.

How do you get it? With some national variations, about a third of big fortunes are inherited. About a third come by multiplying some initial inheritance. About a third, or as many as half in the US, are made from nothing. Those self-made fortunes come by success in some of the arts, sports and professions; by crime and unproductive contrivance; by gambling; by successful invention and entrepreneurial activity; and (among the business fortunes) by the share-price capitalization of the high earning capacities of particular firms, usually new firms. That quick way to wealth typically rewards luck as well as skill and daring.

Once made or inherited, personal fortunes grow or shrink or are divided up by the net effect of a number of processes. Many fortunes earn income at average market rates of return. Because richer owners tend to save higher proportions of income, bigger fortunes tend to accumulate faster. But many fortunes disperse over time as they are divided between children, and as owners spend or lose capital, and give to charity.

EXERCISE

Here are one question for which this chapter has prepared you, and one for which it has not. If you are feeling tough and confident, or irritated by the condescending tone of this text, here is how you might treat the second question: (1) Answer it now, at least in heading-and-note form. (2) Read the rest of this chapter. Then (3) decide whether you needed the text, or could have done as well without it, and with your own social values rather than mine shaping the answers. (And perhaps also choosing the questions?)

1. Sketch briefly two patterns of national wealth, of different quantity and composition and ownership, such that the poorer country of the two might be the happier.

2. You are advising a social-democratic politician who wants to reduce inequalities of wealth as far as can be done without reducing national income and employment. She wants to know what kinds of wealth, and which methods of acquiring wealth and owning it, government can safely try to influence – for example by moving assets from public to private or from private to public ownership, by taxing or regulating particular kinds of wealth, and so on. Consider this chapter's list of ways of acquiring wealth:

- inheritance
- saving from rent, interest and dividend income
- saving from salary and wage income
- home purchase
- crime, corporate misbehavior, deceiving or corrupting government
- gambling on – horses, casino games, electronic games
                       lotteries, pools
                       share prices
                       currency exchange rates
- capital gains from rising real estate prices
- art: music, writing, acting, painting, etc.
- invention
- successful entrepreneurship, bringing a high business income or –
- capital gains from share price capitalization of firms' earning capacities

Write notes on four or more of those, saying of each –

- Is it a socially useful, or useless-but-harmless, or harmful process or activity?
- If useful, should it have public help, and if so, in what form?
- If harmful, is it preventable or reformable? If so, how?
- Could any taxation, regulation or prevention of this way to wealth reduce inequalities of wealth without reducing national income? Could any such measures reduce inequalities of wealth and *increase* national income?

WEALTH POLICIES

More complexity: many policies which affect the distribution of wealth are designed for other purposes altogether. And policies designed to influence the distribution of wealth also have other economic effects. This account of what governments do or might do about the distribution begins with a list of policies with other purposes which can affect the distribution of wealth. It then lists policies – past, present or proposed – to increase or reduce inequalities of wealth directly by increasing or reducing –

* public ownership
* independent non-profit ownership
* co-operative ownership
* collective ownership by superannuation, mutual life assurance and other institutions whose assets belong to their members

and efforts to adjust the distribution of wealth by taxation, including –

* capital tax
* capital gains tax
* capital transfer tax
* differential taxation of earned and unearned income.

You need not memorize the lists and notes. Treat them as checklists, policy-makers' catalogues to refer to as needed. A few of the notes introduce new argument which you have not met before, but most of them are mere reminders of subjects dealt with elsewhere.

Policies for other purposes which may also affect the distribution of wealth

Superannuation from contributory public or private funds extends some of the benefits of capital ownership to non-owners. Fund managers invest the members' contributions, and pay them income from the fund in their retirement. Schemes vary. Most include life insurance. Some extend pension rights to widowed spouses and dependant children. Some allow members to take their accumulated capital instead of a pension when they retire. They don't have the ordinary benefits of ownership as long as they are earning and contributing to the fund, but some schemes allow them to borrow from the fund, or pledge their superannuation rights as security for mortgage loans to buy their houses.

Housing technology and policies did more than anything else to reduce inequalities of wealth through the twentieth century, and did so by the peaceful method of 'levelling up' rather than down. The productive capacity of households' physical capital, and public and market aids to home purchase, have done most. Public rental housing reduces private landlords' wealth without directly increasing tenants' wealth, but it helps some tenants to save enough to buy houses or better household equipment than they could otherwise afford. Some public housing is for sale to its tenants by rental-purchase or on other easy terms.

Town and country planning – meaning the planning, zoning and regulation of land uses – can affect the distribution of wealth in various ways. In town it can help to determine the scope for getting rich as a property developer. Some planning policies can restrain land prices, with advantage to low-income homebuyers and small business owners. Public land development, or appropriate regulation of private development, can do a lot to equalize the amount of private land that richer and poorer households can have, and the provision of public services and recreational space and capital in richer and poorer neighborhoods. The taxation of real property (meaning land and the buildings on it) has obvious effects on the distribution of wealth. One radical dream deserves a paragraph of its own because of the passion with which its believers have kept it alive for more than a century – as follows.

Betterment Each bit of town land gets most of its value not from its owner's investment but from the activities of innumerable other investors, public and private, past and present. The value which population growth, economic growth and city growth add to the market price of land at each city location is commonly called 'betterment'. It has enriched many owners and troubled many reformers. Why should landowners get an unearned benefit – usually in untaxed capital form – from the city growth created by others?

In *Progress and Poverty* (1879) Henry George proposed that government take the whole of that betterment in tax. He thought that single tax would suffice for all the costs of government, and at the same time greatly reduce inequalities of wealth. No government has tried a single tax, but some have tried to tax betterment. In the 1940s a British commission of inquiry recommended nationalizing all country land, so that government alone would collect the betterment that arose as country land was converted to town uses in the course of urban growth. Instead of doing that, the government introduced planning laws which, in effect, nationalized development rights. Owners who wanted to change the use of their land had to get planning permission to do so, and were charged for it. From that revenue it was intended to compensate the owners who had lost their development rights. The regulation of land uses has continued, but the financial arrangements for betterment and compensation did too much harm to builders' and developers' incentives and inflated some of the land prices they were designed to restrain, and they were abandoned. Land uses are regulated nearly everywhere in developed countries, but betterment taxes are comparatively rare, except as elements of general capital or capital gains taxes.

Country land Give 'land' the broad meaning which many economists give it, to include all the land's resources of soil, natural vegetation and minerals. When considering the uses of those resources, policy-makers' main concerns should be with production, conservation and environmental care. But some land-use and resource policies also affect the distribution of wealth. Some wealth policies have environmental effects. The many links between policies about natural resources and policies about the distribution of wealth should be kept in mind when designing policies of either kind.

Big estates To reduce inequalities there have been programs to break up big estates, or big landlords' holdings of rented farms, and to parcel out the land to independent owner-farmers. From the French Revolution to the Japanese land reform of 1946 a number of these programs have succeeded, sometimes with good productive as well as social effects. Others have done less well. Such programs tend to have worked best where they transferred ownership from landlords to the farmers who already worked the land. Programs which settled newcomers on new farms have done less well, especially when the newcomers – immigrants, war veterans, city unemployed – had no farm experience. Besides underestimating the need for skill and experience, some government programs have also misjudged the amounts of land and capital (and freedom from debt) that were needed to make new farms viable. Some of the most successful conversions from big to small farms have come in a market way where big owners have done badly (sometimes by living extravagantly) and have sold their land bit by bit to small owners who have done better (partly by working harder and living frugally).

Forests nourish the atmosphere, are the habitat of some human communities and many other living species, and supply fuel and building, papermaking and other industrial materials. This chapter is concerned not with what should be done with them but only with who should own them: whose wealth they should be. Almost all proposals for their use assume that (i) some or all of the forest consumed should be replanted, and (ii) market forces don't ensure that. Thus from extreme free marketers to extreme conservers, everyone sees some scope – small or large – for public action. Given that the public wants some say in the treatment of forests, who might best own them?

Answers should probably vary with circumstances: forests should not be all private, all public or all owned by independent trusts. There are familiar arguments for and against each of those three kinds of ownership.

Forests offer a double temptation to hard-up, profit-seeking or tax-cutting owners. When felled they pay twice, once for the timber, then as cleared land for other uses. The least profitable thing to do with the cleared land in the short run is to replant it with the natural forest species. A few papermakers and others do now plant commercial forests of quick-growing trees, but their operations are tiny compared with the rate of destruction of the world's forests. So the problem is to find owners who wish, or can be induced or compelled, to conserve their forests.

Ordinary public ownership, i.e. of land not dedicated as national park, has not so far been a reliable means of conservation. Outside Europe, governments have licensed plenty of private logging of public forest. Many continue to do so. Timber is needed for many purposes. There is pressure to protect the jobs of timberworkers, who often live where there is no other employment for them. Governments sell timber, as increasingly they sell other public assets, for revenue to reduce the need for taxation, and for foreign exchange if their countries are short of that. Poor tropical countries, especially, are deep in debt to Western banks, and want the pasture and farmland which forest clearances yield for their growing populations. Without some international aid they can't be expected to forgo the revenue, the foreign exchange and the farmland which forest clearances yield in the short run.

Many private owners continue to clear forest for ordinary profit-seeking purposes. Thus left to themselves neither public nor private owners are reliably motivated to conserve the forests.

So they can't safely be left to themselves. But which of them is easier to restrain? One argument says that government has power over private owners but nobody has power over government, so private ownership is best. Government can regulate the use of private forests. If it does not own them it may have less material interest in allowing their destruction. What pressure the loggers and timberworkers may bring to bear is balanced by the increasing scientific and public pressure for forest conservation. Where the present generation's need for timber has to be balanced against future generations' need for it, and against everyone's need for good air, government is the only available policy-maker. As arbitrator or reconciler of those conflicting interests it is best that it have no direct material interest of its own (such as a politician's interest in financing tax cuts by selling capital assets).

On the other hand the strengthening scientific and public pressures are making many democratic governments – though not so far the US government – better forest conservers than they used to be. Some of them have improved the conditions, including replanting, on which loggers and chippers can buy timber from state forests. They have dedicated many more national forest and wilderness parks. For a century now the most secure conservation has been in those parks, and very strong public support would now defend them from destruction. So (depending always on the local circumstances, the existing ownership and the quality of government) a best strategy might –

- expand the area of forest and wilderness parks

- improve their defences by confiding them to conservation trusts independent of government, or at arms length from it

- reinforce their popularity by opening them to as many undestructive recreational uses as possible

- continue to improve the conditions on which timber is sold from other state forests to the point at which cutting is limited to the rate of replacement of mature growth

- require private forest owners to apply the same restraints or to sell their forests to the state

- reduce the demand for timber products, discouraging unnecessary uses of them by education, taxing, pricing and public research into alternative materials; and

- negotiate for international agreements which (i) reinforce the legal protection of national forest resources, and (ii) require the rich countries which consume most of the world's timber products and do most harm to the quality of its air to pay the poor countries to conserve their forests which now do much of the regeneration of the world's air.

The main purposes of such policies are environmental. But they would also reduce the opportunities and incentives to acquire personal wealth by destroying inherited natural forest without replacement.

Minerals are irreplaceable, unless by extraordinary scientific advances in the capacity to transform matter. Who should own mineral wealth, and what policies should govern its consumption? National laws vary. Most give landowners unlimited rights to whatever they can find beneath their land, except sometimes to subterranean water. Many allow private prospecting on public land, with the prospectors entitled to mine whatever they find. Some oil-rich dictators make little distinction between public and private ownership of mineral resources: they treat state property as their own.

Most governments tax the output of some or all minerals. Some add further taxes on exports, especially of mineral fuels. Many of the relevant laws were designed when most mineral search was by individual prospectors or landowners. There has been some but perhaps not yet enough change in the rules since most mineral search came to be done by expensive aerial and seismic remote sensing, followed by deep drilling, including super-expensive undersea drilling. It takes big money and much expertise. Most of the expertise is supplied by specialized contractors – there may be thirty or more of them at work on an offshore oil platform. Skill at mineral exploration now consists chiefly of knowing which geologists to consult, and how to engage and coordinate the specialist contractors. Public enterprises can learn to do that as well as private enterprises can. So one effect of the technical changes is that governments can search their national seas and territories, own what they find, and mine it themselves or license others to mine it. That is an option they did not have when a prospector was a bushman with a pick and shovel and a gold-washing pan, and every farmer had a minerals manual to identify the rocks on his farm.

Conclusion: Government can now determine whether a nation's mineral resources can or cannot be used to create personal fortunes, and whether earnings from their use flow chiefly to the nation's own citizens or to others. These collective choices need not affect the efficiency with which the resources are explored, and exploited or conserved.

Exhaustible resources as wealth

National and company accounts have commonly treated mining as production and its earnings as income. Environmentalists want the extraction and consumption of exhaustible resources to be seen as destruction of capital, and its earnings accounted as capital proceeds of asset sales. What policy changes might that encourage?

Rather than surveying the range of proposals to be found in academic writing and Green Party policies, what follows is a single comprehensive proposal, chosen because it links environmental policy explicitly to the distribution of wealth. Its author is more practical than utopian, having very ably governed a national central bank for twenty years. Like other environmentalists he wants an accounting reform: 'Not until our national accounts cease classifying exports of exhaustible resources as income and treat them as the sale of capital assets, reducing our national wealth and impairing our economic future, will our business managers, economists and politicians receive accurate signals about the health of our economy.' What might they do if they got the right signals, and had the support of a prudent electorate? Among a number of proposals, one relating to exhaustible resources is as follows:

Control of Exports of Exhaustible Resources

The export of exhaustible resources, being a reduction in the country's national wealth and domestic employment opportunities and the rights of future generations, should be permitted only where a substantial part of the proceeds is to be employed in the creation of other capital assets of comparable social value. Corporations wishing to export exhaustible resources such as minerals and fuels should obtain an export licence only after a social and economic impact assessment has been conducted in public by a judicial authority. The corporation should be required to submit information including estimates of prospective use of proceeds domestically and internationally to create capital assets for sustainable purposes.

To enforce this requirement a special capital asset replacement royalty or resources tax on the export of exhaustible resources should be imposed, and the proceeds allocated to a special fund for investment in sustainable enterprises. A rebate of this royalty or tax could be granted for payments by the corporation concerned into a trust fund, under its own control, for investment (in the country supplying the resources) for sustainable production, or grants to an approved institution for the conduct of scientific and technological research.

Similarly enterprises engaged in agriculture, pastoralism, forestry, fishing, or other resource uses capable of depleting the productivity of the land or seas concerned should be subject to a similar regeneration tax. The tax could be rebated to those which have submitted to an appropriate conservation authority a land use or similar plan which that authority certifies provides adequately for the effective regeneration and/or conservation of the land or waters being used. The certificate of the authority should be subject to renewal periodically after examination of the land concerned.

The main theme of the book from which this example comes concerns the likely effect of increasing scarcity on the balance of power and the distribution of wealth and income between the owners of scarce resources and the rest of society. If left to market pricing, owners can expect to take more, and workers and consumers less, of the benefits of the dwindling resources.

These trends derive from the monopoly component that scarcity creates for the bargaining power of ownership and, as J.S. Mill observed, this monopoly power cannot be prevented in a market economy but could, in theory at least, be reserved for the community's benefit. Only if this were done could we counter the long-term decline of the bargaining power of wage-earners and others, the increasing industrial and social tension and the personal disillusionment which must result from that decline.

To ensure that the monopoly power of ownership is exercised in trust for the community benefit, action could be taken to:

• reassert, and where necessary re-establish, the public ownership of the natural resources of the country, its minerals, forests, seas, soils, vegetation and wildlife

• vest title in these resources in an authority independent of corporate and political control

• empower that authority to grant licenses for the use of these resources only on terms which will ensure their conservation, regeneration and sustainable development, and which will provide a rent determined by tender in a competitive market, so as to return to the authority a major proportion of any monopoly rent the resources extract from the consumer

• empower the authority to carry out or support research programs designed to develop the potential of these resources on a sustainable basis.

The income from the sale of licences and other sources could be transferred to a separate fund for its social use and distribution. This fund could perhaps be called the Community Estate or the Common Wealth Estate. It could be empowered to use its resources to:

- help finance community-controlled facilities providing services designed to improve and diversify the community's quality of life

- support research and development designed to conserve and enrich the Estate; or

- distribute a national dividend paid equally to all citizens.

This fund could be supplemented by the proceeds of public enterprises and taxes on capital, especially death and inheritance taxes. The aim of the latter should be to transfer progressively to community ownership (perhaps in the form of non-voting shares) a substantial part of the community's corporate wealth. This could be achieved by inheritance taxes by which, above a substantial maximum, only a life interest in income from capital assets could be transferred to heirs.

While he claims that 'there is nothing inherently impractical in these proposals', the author acknowledges that

> the action required would run counter to the ideologies which dominate our political parties, the media, business leaders and trade unions, and increasingly those who determine the structure and purposes of our education systems and our centres of intellectual and cultural innovation ... Their chances of being applied are slender while the domination of those values continues and while its ideologies guide our political and economic action. However, that domination is increasingly being questioned by those who see its destructive impact on the physical and social environment in which the destiny of humankind inevitably must be worked out.
>
> – H.G. Coombs, *The return of scarcity: Strategies for an economic future* (1990) pp. 11-20

DIRECT ACTION ABOUT WEALTH

This chapter has so far been sampling ways in which the distribution of wealth can be affected by policies designed primarily for other purposes. We now turn to policies whose main purpose is to influence the distribution of wealth. Some aim to maintain or increase present inequalities of wealth, some aim to reduce them.

Policies to maintain or increase inequalities of wealth

Government creates and protects property rights, for example through property and corporation law, the law of tort, and criminal law and its enforcement. Most countries with written constitutions add some protections *against* government, to bar it from taking people's property without paying for it. That rule has not prevented the introduction of a wide range of property and income taxes. They have sometimes included death duties at rates which amount to substantial capital confiscation. Where old defences against government have proved ineffective, some new ones have been devised: one movement, successful in some American states, aims to set constitutional limits to the amount of tax that governments are allowed to raise. Meanwhile governments can enlarge the scope for private capital by privatizing public enterprises and services. They can shift taxation off wealth and income onto commodities. They can make the remaining income tax less progressive. Wealthy people tend to have an order of preference for taxation: they would have governments tax (i) commodities, preferably at a flat rate on necessaries and luxuries alike; (ii) business transactions and corporate income; (iii) personal income, preferably at flat or proportional rates rather than progressive rates; (iv) capital gains; and (v) – worst – capital itself.

Protection for rich owners also comes by neglect. Tax lawyers invent ever-new methods of tax avoidance; governments are slow to respond by updating the tax laws. Directors and executives take steadily more wealth from their corporations; government could act to restrain them, but does not – American states even compete to charter them. Corporations register in tax havens, and individuals collect their incomes there or pretend to reside there; the countries in which they actually live and operate could discipline them, but do not. Most of these non-interventions don't leave the distribution 'to the market', as their defenders claim. They merely allow rich people to benefit from laws which suit them (property law, contract law) but evade laws which don't (tax law, corporation law).

We will return to the subject at the end of the chapter, to notice some arguments in favor of these conservative policies.

Policies to reduce inequalities of wealth

Taxation Wealth taxes affect the distribution of wealth directly. Income and other taxes may affect it indirectly through their effects on people's ability and incentives to save. A short list:

- *A general wealth tax* taxes the whole value of a person's wealth. The few countries which have used it have set such low rates – 2.5 per cent or less – that most taxpayers can pay it from income without surrendering any wealth. That being so, why have it – why not simply adjust the income tax rate? It achieves three things which income tax may not achieve. (i) Assessing it informs the government about everyone's wealth. That information may be used for a number of purposes. (ii) As a supplement to income tax it has the effect of taxing unearned income at a higher rate than earned income. (That can alternatively be done by income-taxing unearned income – i.e. dividend, rent and interest income – at a higher rate than wage, salary and self-employed income.) (iii) It can act as a luxury tax, taxing forms of wealth which don't yield income: jewelry, works of art, grand houses and gardens, luxury cars.

• *Capital gains taxes* chiefly slow the rate at which the already-rich get richer. They tax the difference between what you pay for an asset, and what you get for it when you sell it. Most countries which have such taxes adjust the gains for inflation, and confine the tax to a minority of capital owners by (i) exempting owners with small amounts of capital, (ii) exempting all or most owner-occupied houses, and (iii) taxing gains only when they are realized, i.e. when the owner cashes the gain by selling the asset.

• *Capital transfer taxes* A century ago, reformers who wanted to reduce inequalities of wealth by taxing capital reasoned like this: it would be bad for entrepreneurs' and investors' incentives to take capital away from people who earn and save and invest it. It would be harsh to take it from people who inherit it once they have committed themselves to a lifestyle which their wealth will support. But those objections need not apply if capital is taxed after its owner's death and before heirs inherit it. That way, nobody loses anything they already own. Hence death duties. Some countries levied them at very high rates through the middle decades of the twentieth century.

Rich families' tax lawyers responded with evasive devices. Capital owners gave their wealth to their heirs before they died. Government responded by charging death duties on gifts made up to two (or five, or ten) years before death. Some countries tried to tax *all* capital gifts. That also could often be evaded. How do you tell a capital gift from an irregular income to a dependant? Or from an unusually large housekeeping allowance to a spouse? If you sell valuable works of art to your daughter for half what they *might* have fetched at a public auction, can the government tax as a gift what it could not possibly tax if you had accepted that price from a smart art dealer? Rich families began to create perpetual trusts

whose capital need never change hands, but would provide income to succeeding generations.

Some countries have abandoned death and gift duties. In countries which still have them they tend to work unevenly, often taxing people with moderate wealth who don't employ tax lawyers but not richer people who do. The main reasons for their comparative failure have been –

• They have proved too easy to avoid, especially by the very rich.

• They work capriciously. Accidents of birth and death determine how often a fortune changes hands, and therefore how often it is taxed. Families with similar wealth may thus be taxed very differently.

• It was a mistake to suppose that people care less about their children's fortunes than their own. Many people, especially those with quite modest wealth, care more for what they can leave to their children than for what they can spend on themselves.

Should governments give up trying to tax capital? Decide for yourself. But an annual tax on whole wealth, perhaps exempting owner-occupied houses and family farms, may be a fairer and surer way to do it.

But very few taxes are levied solely to adjust the distribution of income and wealth. Their other purposes are usually primary: to raise revenue to finance public goods and services and income transfers, to protect the environment or the balance of payments, and so on. Many of those purposes can be served by alternative taxes with different distributional effects. It is in choosing between those alternatives (rather than by designing purely distributional taxes) that most tax decisions which affect the distribution of wealth are made. We will return to the subject in chapters on the distribution of income and on taxation.

Meanwhile consider the forms of wealth that people are *allowed* to own. There's nothing holy about the present list. At different times and places people have been allowed or not allowed to own slaves, private monopolies, public utilities, farms or factories to produce alcohol or other drugs. In some early societies, and under some modern laws about indigenous people's rights, land can be owned by communities but not by individuals. So notice, next, how the permissible *forms* of private wealth can affect its whole amount and its distribution in mixed economies.

Alternatives to personal wealth

Profit-seeking individuals don't own a fixed share of a nation's wealth. The private capitalist share can be increased by privatizing public services. It can be reduced by expanding public ownership. It varies as economic growth proceeds at different speeds in the public and private sectors. It declines or is redistributed as households replace landlords as owners of their houses and farms.

Reducing the private share of wealth does not necessarily reduce individual inequalities – the richest individual may be as rich as before. But reducing the whole private share can make inequalities within it less important. The main alternatives to private capitalist ownership need not be described here, because you've met them before: in Chapters 12-17 on new directions of development; in Chapter 18 on the structure of modern mixed economies; in Chapter 25 on household capital; in Chapters 37 and 38 on public enterprises; and in parts of this chapter on superannuation. The briefest summary will suffice to remind you of the possibilities.

Public ownership Past and present practice in developed mixed economies suggests that public ownership can extend from the standard public services to include coal, oil and metal exploration and mining; steelmaking and other heavy manufacturing including the manufacture of ships, aircraft, cars and trucks; air, sea, rail and road transport; education; scientific and social research; hospitals and health services; the planning, supply and servicing of new city land; provisions for many recreations, from stadiums and entertainment centres to golf courses, tennis courts and playing fields; banking, life assurance, funded superannuation and general insurance.

With many of those there are further sector choices. Public oil prospectors and producers may use many private contractors. Public housing enterprises may use private builders. Public educators get most of their books from private publishers. And so on. (One effect is that estimating the size of the sectors requires extreme care to avoid double counting.)

Independent non-profit ownership Many services, including many which are partly or wholly financed by government, may be supplied by independent, non-profit, self-governing institutions, self-owned or owned by churches or charities. Universities, independent schools, many hospitals, some health and welfare services and many recreational facilities are owned and self-governed by non-profit, non-government institutions and associations.

Cooperative ownership Most producers' cooperatives are direct or indirect profit-seekers, doing their business for the material benefit of their members. Most consumer cooperatives exist to buy advantageously for their members. Some, such as housing or child-care or recreational cooperatives, bring other benefits too – of power, safety, sociability, mutual care – but they also bring material benefits, and often distribute them proportionately to the members' contributions. Cooperative milk processors pay each farmer for the amount of milk supplied. Wool marketing cooperatives pay each grazier for the amount of wool supplied. Consumer cooperatives give most benefit to the members who buy most goods. So cooperatives don't usually redistribute wealth or reduce inequalities among their members. But they may reduce inequalities by removing the need for other, more unequalizing, kinds of business. Most cooperatives exist to capture economies of scale for small producers. Without the cooperatives those advantages would be provided by capitalist butter factories and wool-broking firms whose owners *could* be few and rich, could perhaps exploit monopolist market strength, and could thus concentrate and unequalize some of the benefits which the cooperatives distribute to all their members.

Collective ownership This is a loose term for life assurance and superannuation institutions which are 'mutual', i.e. owned by the contributors and policy-holders and pensioners whose funds they hold and invest. In principle their members choose and employ their directors. In practice the directors tend to be a self-perpetuating group, and some of them pay themselves hefty rewards, including capital rewards.

Not all life and superannuation institutions are owned in that mutual way. Some are more like private banks: they are share-owned companies which pay dividends to their shareholders from the profits remaining after meeting their contractual obligations to their policy-holders. Depending on their patterns of share ownership, they may thus allow some concentration and accumulation of individual wealth.

In practice there may not be much difference between the benefits which the two types convey to their policy-holders. The industry is thus something of a hybrid, with both cooperative and private characteristics.

The scope for public action

Within broad limits there is thus double scope for societies to amend their inherited patterns of the different kinds of ownership, and in doing so to influence the amount and distribution of personal wealth. There are first the decisions which determine the extent of public, independent, cooperative, collective, private, and household enterprise. And within many of the non-private enterprises there are then further choices. Work can be done 'in house' by public employees using public capital, or by household members using household capital. Or it can be put out to private contractors using private labor and the usual mix of private and public capital.

As in other policy areas, the choices can rarely be single-purposed. This chapter began with policies which may affect the creation and distribution of wealth although their primary purposes concern other things: natural resources, saving and investment, provisions for old age, tax revenue. We have moved on to policies whose primary concerns include the distribution of wealth. But many of these also have multiple purposes, and should be chosen with care for their multiple effects. However keen you are to reduce inequalities of wealth, don't nationalize activities (like farming and shopkeeping) which public enterprises generally do badly. Don't ban private enterprise from activities which give valuable scope for private initiative and innovation. Don't overload government with more public enterprises than it can keep an attentive eye on, and provide with competent directors. (That capacity varies widely from country to country.) Don't tax capital in ways which discourage desirable saving and investment. If you have open financial frontiers, don't tax capital in ways which may drive it abroad. And so on – as in any other area of policy, policy-makers should do their best to estimate all the significant effects of alternative policies.

The choices which determine the amount and distribution of private wealth are made variously by government, by independent institutions, by private investors and the financial institutions which stake many of them, and by households in their saving and housing and do-it-yourself choices. There are of course conflicts, and sometimes outcomes which none of the contending parties wanted. But if a majority wants to shift the balance between private and non-private ownership of national wealth, some step-by-step change in the desired direction is usually possible.

But whether to agree with them or to be forearmed against them, it is as well to know the reasons why a great many economists, capital owners and others believe that government should not concern itself at all with the distribution of wealth, which should be none of its business.

Reasons why government should not be concerned with the distribution of wealth

In his celebrated *Second treatise of civil government* (1690) John Locke went to a lot of trouble to argue that property rights existed before government did, and that a main purpose of inventing government was to secure those rights. It followed that government had no right to interfere with them. Three centuries later, some economists of the 'public choice' school want constitutional limits to government's right to tax. Some of them want the constitution to ban any confiscation, redistribution or direct taxation of private capital. Locke wanted to protect property from plunder by either a monarch or an elected government. Public choice theorists fear the modern equivalents of both. If you assume that political behavior is motivated chiefly by individual greed, two anxieties follow. Politicians and public servants may inflate the public budget in order to take more of it for themselves. And electoral majorities who don't own much private capital may vote to take it from the minorities who do. But confiscating capital would reduce economic efficiency and output, so the majority would actually lose by it. Thus (the argument goes) limiting the majority's taxing power would serve the majority's interests, as well as everyone else's.

A purer argument for leaving the distribution of wealth to market processes is at the heart of neoclassical theory. In a perfectly competitive economy, whoever owns capital is assumed to lend or invest it for the best available combination of risk and return, which the theory assumes will indicate its most productive use. So what matters to those who don't own capital is not who does own it, but the efficiency with which it is allocated and used to produce the best possible national output and income. For that purpose market competition for the use of the available capital should produce the same allocation whoever owns it, so it is likely to allocate it more efficiently than any other method would do.

By itself that could be a two-edged argument. If it doesn't matter who owns a society's capital, it should not matter if private individuals *don't* own it. Does the theory allow the possibility that a capitalist economy could run efficiently *without* inequality of wealth if most capital was owned by public or cooperative investment trusts? Not necessarily. When the competitive model depicts owners allocating capital to its best users, it assumes that *both* parties are the most efficient of their kind. The owners need to be skilful at finding and grasping the best investment opportunities, i.e. at recognizing who will be the most productive users of their resources.

That is likeliest if capital is owned by the people whose skills as capital users acquired it in the first place. So the owners as well as the users of capital are best chosen by market processes, rather than by any institutional alternative.

In practice economists recognize many limits and exceptions to these arguments. They scarcely apply to inherited wealth. They can be faulty wherever the most profitable uses of capital are anti-social, monopolist, protected or subsidized. Plenty of neoclassical economists support anti-trust laws, capital gains taxes, death and gift taxes on inherited capital, and other public action where market processes fail to comply with the competitive model. But there remains a presumption that wherever there is no serious market failure, private ownership is likely to work best; and because most capital is put to work by others rather than consumed by its owners, inequalities of wealth matter less than inequalities of income. People's *incomes* do much to determine their welfare. But who owns *capital* matters less than who gets to use it, how efficiently, for what productive purposes.

EXERCISE

The above arguments for accepting the market distribution of wealth ought to be followed at this point by the arguments in favor of action to reduce its inequalities. This course of study tries to introduce you fairly to both (or all) sides of such controversies. But it has an acknowledged bias in favor of greater equality where possible, and if you have come this far you have been exposed to plenty of that bias. So as an exercise, *you* may now set out as many arguments as you can think of (whether or not you agree with them) in favor of public action to reduce inequalities of wealth.

44

The composition and distribution of income

This chapter reminds you of –

- reasons why incomes matter, perhaps more than wealth does
- difficulties in measuring and comparing incomes
- the main sources of incomes in money and kind
- outlines of past and present distributions of income within and between nations, and directions in which those distributions have changed and are changing
- some arguments about what determines those distributions.

The next chapter is then about policies: what governments do, or could and should do, about the distribution of income.

HOW IMPORTANT IS THE DISTRIBUTION OF INCOME?

The main subject of this course of study is the working of modern mixed economies in their developed democratic form. One of the author's beliefs declared back in Chapter 7 is that during the twentieth century the great growth of productivity in these economies took them across a critical threshold. They passed from poverty, in which the growth of output mattered more than its distribution, to affluence in which better distribution, and the quality of work and daily life, matter more than further growth of output.

Until that century most humans had to live on bare subsistence, as more than a billion still do. They produced very little surplus above what it took to keep them alive and fit to work and raise children. Most of the small surplus went to support a few rulers, landowners and tradespeople. But those were such small minorities that if they had not existed, the peasants, keeping all that they produced, would not have been much richer. Indeed they would usually have been poorer, because the minority whom the surplus supported included some whose services were needed, and eventually some who contributed to economic growth. Wherever the inequalities between rulers and ruled were not too brutally exploitive, it was reasonable to think that growth mattered more than distribution: more could be gained for more people by increasing output than by redistributing it.

But Western societies have now achieved, and East Asian societies are achieving, productivity which could give all their members the material conditions for a comfortable, secure and interesting life. There is mounting evidence (cited by Fred Hirsch in *Social limits to growth,* 1976, by Tibor Scitovsky in *The joyless economy,* 1976, and by Robert Lane in *The market experience,* 1991) that above the present average income of the Western societies, more income does not increase net happiness. (Prevailing culture persuades people that it will, but it doesn't.) Most unhappiness in these societies comes from non-economic causes, or from misuses of affluence, or from anxiety about *insecure* incomes, or from the absolute and relative poverty of the 15 or 20 per cent of their members who live in households with no paid employment and with less than half of their society's average income. Robert Lane's evidence suggests that many of them suffer as much from the lack of work as from the lack of income. These societies could plainly improve their net happiness by improving their distribution of employment and income. Distribution now matters more than growth does.

That change may be reinforced by two others. Under their current policies most Western economies have permanently higher unemployment than they used to have, and continuing economic growth is not reducing it. So some better distribution of employment would be good. And the growth of the developed economies may be about to cease or go into reverse for environmental reasons. Depending on technological developments, that change may bring less work and paid employment, or it may bring more. Either way, competition for shares is likely to be hotter, and fair distribution even more desirable, when what have to be distributed are not shares of growth, but cuts – in rates of pay, or available jobs, or both.

Of course the morality implicit in that view may not prevail. Many liberals argue from the same historical facts to an opposite conclusion. Because the rich countries can now provide adequately for their poorest members, so that nobody need suffer from hunger or cold or lack of health care, inequalities may matter less than they did: if everyone can have enough, what does it matter how much the rich have? Government should make sure that the poorest members do have enough, but as long as the welfare safety net is in place, the rest of the distribution of income can safely be left to market forces.

Whether or not they approve of that morality, some pessimists expect it to get worse. Well-off majorities appear to be more hostile to the poor minorities than they were through the mid-century decades when much of the welfare structure was developed. More voices than before are blaming the unemployed for their unemployment, and other poor for their poverty. Voting shifted to the Right, and taxation shifted downward from richer to poorer taxpayers, through the last quarter of the twentieth century while some economic growth continued. If that majority mood persists through a period when incomes must actually be cut, the strong seem likely to impose most of the cuts on the weak. So inequalities may continue to increase.

But minds and majorities have changed before, and may change again. In 1992 a President of the United States who promised to increase taxes got more votes than the one who promised not to. Two years later the same citizens returned the most reactionary Congress in sixty years. Amid such cross purposes there must be room for action and persuasion in good causes.

THE PATTERN OF INCOMES

'The distribution of income' has alternative meanings. It can mean the pattern of incomes – for example how much the manager earns and how much the laborer earns. It can mean the processes which determine the pattern, i.e. which determine whether the manager is paid two or five or ten times as much as the laborer. And it can mean the processes which determine which individuals get which of the incomes, i.e. who gets the manager's job and who gets the laborer's job. The three parts of this chapter deal with the subject in that order: first the facts of income inequality, then what determines that pattern of incomes, then what determines which people get which of the available incomes.

Measurement and comparison

Incomes are easier to measure than wealth is. Most employers and employees make truthful tax returns of what the employees are paid. Investment incomes – rent, interest and dividends – don't have the uncertain value that many of the investments themselves have. Some small business owners and self-employed people may understate their incomes, and if they use capital equipment it may be difficult to separate the investment element from the labor element of their incomes. Some casual and part-time workers understate their incomes or are not required to state them, so some of the poorest incomes may be the least known. The goods and services which households produce for themselves with their own labor are only beginning to be surveyed. But the distribution of income as conventionally measured – i.e. of money income from property, employment, self-employment and public income transfers – is altogether better known than the distribution of capital wealth.

But measuring the distribution of income still has difficulties, especially when its purpose is to measure and compare inequalities. Three awkward choices have to be made: *whose* income to count, *what* income to count, and *when* to count it.

Whose income?

Individual incomes may be a bad guide to real inequalities if they support different numbers of people. Is a lone individual earning $20,000 richer or poorer than a family supported by one income of $30,000? Some surveys record family income or household income instead of individual income. But no method is faultless. To see why, try surveying three households each with a household income of $60,000 a year. The first household has one member, who earns and spends that income. In the second, two parents each earn $30,000 and they have three children. In the third, the house and housework are shared by six young people each earning $10,000.

- If the unit of study is the person, the survey will show that of twelve people, one is rich; two earn half as much as the richest; six earn a sixth as much; and three earn nothing.

- If the unit of study is the earner, the survey will show a similar pyramid without the non-earners: three classes rather than four, with sixfold inequality.

- If the unit of study is the family, the middle incomes will disappear. The survey will show two rich family units and six poor ones, still with sixfold inequality.

- If the unit of study is the household, the survey will show an equal society.

That example is for methodological purposes only. In real life, with a continuous spread of incomes from top to bottom, the differences are not so dramatic. But they can still be significant.

What income?

Most households' intake of material goods and services includes -

- goods and services bought with cash income
- goods and services produced by the household's own labor
- public goods and services
- income in kind from employers or other private sources

They all have problems of measurement, and of fair comparison between households and between countries. As follows:

Cash   Some accounts count gross cash income. Some count net income after tax. Some, especially in studies of poverty, count income after tax and housing costs. As noted above, some count individual income and some count household income. Some, especially in studies of the distribution of income, calculate 'equivalent' household incomes by adjusting actual household income to the number of people in the household. International comparisons have special difficulties. If you compare incomes at the market exchange rate between national currencies, you get one result. If you compare what incomes will actually buy at local prices you may get a different result. If you compare 'wage prices', i.e. the hours of work required to earn the price of similar baskets of goods in different countries, the result may be different again. (There will presently be examples.) For an account of the technical problems, and of one impressive exercise to overcome them, see the article (cited in Chapter 43) by Robert Summers and Alan Heston in *The Quarterly Journal of Economics* for May, 1991.

Household production   You know the alternative ways of valuing household output at equivalent wage rates or at equivalent commercial prices, or at equivalent hours of working time, and the difficulty of deciding which household activities to count as production, which as consumption and which as neither. This text has assumed that unpaid labor produces about 40 per cent of national output in most rich democracies. That productivity depends on households' membership, their tastes and choices, their human capital, money income, household space and capital, and the public space and capital available to people producing for themselves and one another with unpaid labor. So there are wide variations around the average, between households, between neighborhoods and between countries.

(Recall the different productivity of the latest generations of the Weaver and Farmer families in the historical sketch in Chapter 24, and the differences, to which we will presently return, between household life in Japanese and Australian cities.) Differences in household productivity reduce some inequalities but increase others. Their effects are important: don't let the difficulties of measurement lead you to underrate them.

Public goods and services have the net effect of reducing poverty and inequality in all developed countries. They do it in different degrees and in different ways in different countries, and should not be neglected (as they often are) in comparisons of national patterns of inequality.

Income in kind from employment has diverse effects. Cars, business lunches and other additions to the salaries of executives, public service chiefs and politicians typically increase their incomes, reduce their income tax and increase their societies' inequalities. Where wage workers receive board and lodging, work-clothing and other non-cash benefits, those benefits may often reduce inequalities of employment income. Both those flows of non-cash income tend to be under-reported.

Income when ?

A snapshot of this week's or this year's incomes does not tell whose incomes are secure and whose are not, whose are rising or falling, whose are low because they are young or high because they are in their peak earning years. Lifetime income would be a better basis for estimates of inequality and judgments of distributive justice – but that is not a practical thought because you can only know people's lifetime incomes after they're dead. Census and survey questions can be designed to link income to sex and age and occupation to reveal the present profile of income at different stages of life. But that is not the profile of any person's or generation's income *through* their lifetime: you can't assume that today's pensioners once earned what today's peak earners do (they mostly earned less), or that today's peak earners once earned what today's youngsters do (they mostly earned less) or that today's youngsters will one day earn what today's peak earners do (that will depend on directions of technological change, economic growth or decline, policy choices, world weather ...) In the simple model of three households sketched above under 'Whose income?', six young people share one of the households. Their incomes are equal, and are society's lowest incomes. But don't conclude that they necessarily constitute an economic class in any usual meaning of class. Perhaps one earns by irregular unskilled labor and one draws an unemployment allowance. Two earn by part-time teaching while they try to succeed as freelance artists. Two draw student living allowances as they study law and medicine respectively. The unskilled pair may never do much better. The lawyer and doctor may earn lifetime incomes in their country's top 2 or 3 per cent. One artist may be a poor but happy potter all her life, the other may make millions as the lead singer of a successful group.

Conclusion: When you use accounts of the distribution of income, read the small print to know on what basis they are compiled. Make the basis clear in anything you yourself research and write on the subject.

THE DISTRIBUTION OF INCOME

However it is measured, the distribution of income in the developed democracies has these characteristics:

- Through most of the twentieth century the distribution was growing more equal.

- It is more equal than in most poor countries, not because the third-world rich are richer, but because their poor majorities are much poorer.

- The distribution in the developed democracies is still very unequal, with the richest individuals earning many hundreds of times as much as the poorest, and some unearned property incomes higher still.

- The twentieth-century progress to greater equality was reversed through the 1980s. By most measures, in most of the rich countries, inequality is now increasing.

Sources of income In the developed democracies many people have income from more than one source – for example from salary *and* investment, or from wages *and* public family allowances. There are national differences, and changes over time. But striking a rough average for Western Europe, Australia and New Zealand in the 1980s, of every 100 people it was likely that –

5	lived chiefly on	investment or self-employed income
27	lived chiefly on	wages or salaries from private employers
13	lived chiefly on	wages or salaries from public employers
25	lived chiefly on	public transfer incomes or superannuation
30	lived chiefly on	household transfer incomes, i.e. money income brought into households by some of their members and transferred to, or spent on, others.

Japan and the United States had more private wage and salary incomes and fewer public wage, salary and transfer incomes. As we noted earlier, some people also drew some non-cash income from employers. Almost all received some non-cash income in the form of free or subsidized public services. Almost all received household non-cash income in the form of goods and services produced by themselves or other household members. Very few of the employers' non-cash contributions and none of the household income transfers or non-cash income are included in the tables sampled in this section, but (where indicated) some of them do include the estimated value of public income in the form of education and health care. The basis of each item is briefly indicated, but for the full 'small print' you must go to the studies from which they are drawn: A.B. Atkinson, *The economics of inequality* (1983); publications from the Luxembourg Income Study (a study of the distribution of income in a number of countries) including Timothy Smeeding and others, *Poverty, inequality and income distribution in comparative perspective* (1990) and Peter Saunders and others, *Non-cash income, living standards, inequality and poverty: Evidence from the Luxembourg income study* (1992); and a 1997 Eurostat paper called *Income Distribution and Poverty in EU12 – 1993.*

THE COMPOSITION OF INCOME

Simple figures of money income before and after tax don't distinguish investment income, earned income and transferred income, and they don't include estimates of the value of public goods and services or other non-cash income. That is one shortcoming. Another is that changing components, some with significant social effects, may be concealed in the overall figures. Offsetting or compounding each other there may be changes in occupational structures and rates of pay; in the amount of unemployment; in length of life in retirement; in public income transfers; in the effects of indirect taxation. An aging population, or an increase in unemployment or in the number of lone parents, may increase inequality even though no wage shares or relativities have changed. Conversely, a young population with high immigration and low unemployment may be more equal because of its lack of aged and unemployed pensioners, though its wage relativities and pension rates may be no better than those of less equal countries.

Efforts have accordingly been made to disaggregate and supplement the data about money incomes. In the UK the government reduced the publication of information about wealth and income in 1980, so some of the best analyses are now out of date, but they are still worth notice as models of method. A.B. Atkinson reported a study of British incomes in 1980 which separated the effects on whole after-tax income of –

- original income, i.e. employment and investment income
- public income transfers
- public non-cash income, i.e. free education, health care, etc.
- direct and indirect taxes.

The findings are summarized in Table 44.1.

Notice, in relation to that table -

- The 11% 'net loss' by the taxpayers as a whole is the tax cost of the public services such as defence, law and order, roadbuilding, etc., which the table does not count as income-in-kind to individual households.

- Each of the five groups is represented by an average. The figure for the bottom 20% averages a narrow range of incomes. The figure for the top 20% averages incomes from about £10,000 to many millions. So the five average figures greatly understate the top-to-bottom inequality of incomes in the society as a whole.

- The bottom group average next to no wage or property income. Most of them are old, unemployed, disabled, or lone parents. Their sustenance comes almost entirely from public income transfers and public goods and services.

- There is substantial redistribution from the richer

	Bottom 20%	Next 20%	Middle 20%	Next 20%	Top 20%	All households*
Original Income	170	2705	5905	8540	14445	6350
+ cash transfers	+ 1970	+ 1320	+ 600	+ 450	+ 390	+ 1330
– direct taxes	– 5	– 420	– 1165	– 1790	– 3280	– 1330
+ benefits in kind	+ 960	+ 990	+ 1170	+ 1220	+ 1270	+ 1120
– indirect taxes	– 545	– 1020	– 1415	– 1780	– 2530	– 1460
Final income	2550	3580	5090	6640	10295	5630
Net gain or loss	+ 2380	+ 870	– 810	– 1900	– 4150	– 720
% change to original income	+ 1400%	+ 32%	– 14%	– 22%	– 29%	– 11%

* The figures may not add up exactly because of rounding.

Table 44.1 Income effects of taxes and benefits in the UK, 1980
Average per household (£ per year – households ranked by original income)
Source: *Economic Trends* January 1982, Table B

half to the poorer half of incomes, and especially from the richest 20 per cent to the poorest 20 per cent. Earlier critics had observed that richer people tend to use more free or subsidized public services than poorer people do (as Table 44.1 confirms). Some concluded that the welfare state tended to redistribute from poorer to richer; or if progressive taxation was taken into account, the net redistribution was from both ends to the middle. What those calculations left out were (1) the higher indirect as well as direct taxation that the rich pay, and (2) the fact that the primary money incomes of the poorest quarter or so of households come chiefly by public income transfer. When all those tax-and-welfare provisions are seen together, as they should be, it is clear that there is a substantial net transfer from rich to poor, with a substantial reduction of inequality. If the average British taxpayer in the top 20 per cent actually paid the taxes parliament intended in 1980, he or she contributed nearly enough to supply public income in cash and kind to two average households in the bottom 20 per cent.

- But remember that these are still *selections* from all the distributive processes that are at work, including those that determine what Table 44.1 accepts as people's 'original' incomes.   A.B. Atkinson's discussion of that Table's information ends with a correct warning: 'It is clear that cash transfers make a major difference to the distribution. At the same time, we should emphasize that the government cannot necessarily take credit for this as positive redistribution. If its actions elsewhere, say in the field of monetary policy, lead to higher unemployment, then it would seem perverse to regard the consequent increase in the payment of unemployment benefit as evidence of greater redistribution.'

– *The economics of inequality* (1983) p.84

Just as all the components of cash and non-cash income and taxation need to be brought into any accurate account of the distribution of real income, so all the direct and indirect effects of relevant public policies should ideally be considered in judging the effect of government on the distribution of income. Of course that ideal is impracticable – all such investigations have to select and limit their scope – but we should do the best we can.

The Luxembourg income study   One attempt to do better is the co-operative, multinational Luxembourg Income Study begun in 1983. Its researchers work to refine and standardize national data about the sources and distribution of income, to allow (among other things) valid international comparisons. One project has been a study of the distribution of public non-cash income, and its effect on the whole distribution of income. In the seven countries studied, public provisions for education and health care added between 13 and 22 per cent to average household income, with some net reduction of inequality.

Like the British study tabled earlier, the Luxembourg studies show what public education and health care do to reduce poverty.

POVERTY

If governments are to act to reduce poverty, they need to know how many people are poor, how poor they are, and especially which groups are poor from what causes. But as so often, investigators face difficulties of definition and measurement. Who – or what level of income – should count as poor? A long debate has followed broadly the following course.

It is not practical to define an absolute minimum necessary income. People doing different work at different ages in different climates need different diet, clothing and shelter. Food prices and house rents vary with time and place. What one family could survive on, another could not. Even if a sufficient minimum income could be known, based on prevailing food prices and rents, some people would not know what diet would get them most nourishment for their money, and might fare badly on their 'sufficient' income.

In any case many people think that hunger and cold are not the only hazards which all citizens of developed democracies should be able to avoid. Citizenship should bring economic as well as political and legal access to a common lifestyle: to acceptable standards of cleanliness, clothing and housing; to universal education and health care; to newspapers and broadcasting as sources of information and subjects of daily conversation; to some common recreations. Minimum versions of this common lifestyle test would require that everyone have the means to look for a job, a rented house and new friends without having their chances reduced by visible stigma of poverty. A maximum version would demand that there be no economic hindrance to courtship and marriage between any two members of the society.

This idea of poverty makes it a relative rather than an absolute condition. To be poor is to lack whatever your fellow citizens regard as the material necessities of civilized life. The richer the society, the higher that minimum standard is likely to be. For practical purposes of research and policy-making it has been usual to decide on a poverty line: an income below which individuals or families or households will be regarded as living in poverty. Despite its arbitrary nature, such a line can serve useful purposes. It can simplify the detailed studies which reveal which classes or groups of people have disproportionate numbers of poor. It provides a measure of the whole number or proportion of a society's people who are judged to be in poverty. That may seem an arbitrary measure, but it allows useful comparisons. Comparisons over time show how patterns of poverty are changing, and may prompt policy changes. And a common measure allows comparisons of the amount and distribution of poverty in different societies.

To allow such comparisons the researchers of the Luxembourg Income Study proceed as follows:

1. An equivalence scale is used to adjust incomes to family size and need, so that households which can afford similar material living standards are credited with similar incomes. (A single person's income is adjusted upwards, a family's income is adjusted downwards. If a bigger family with a bigger income can afford the same living standard as a smaller family with a smaller income, their adjusted incomes will be the same.)

2. When all of a society's household incomes have been adjusted and ranked, the median adjusted income for each society can be identified. Different countries have different median incomes and consequently different poverty lines.

3. The household incomes are then further adjusted by adding the public costs of the education and health care which households receive.

4. Having considered the general levels of the relevant subsistence and lifestyle costs, the Luxembourg Income Study researchers set the poverty line at half the median adjusted income. (So do the European Union's published estimates of poverty.) Households with less than that are defined as poor.

5. The percentage of poor in each national population is one measure of that country's amount of poverty.

Has your watchdog noticed an apparent inconsistency? The Luxembourg researchers relate households' whole income – their adjusted cash plus non-cash income – to a poverty line based on adjusted cash-only income. Shouldn't cash income be related to a cash measure, or whole income to a whole income measure? The researchers have their reasons. Among other things they

want to measure how much the public non-cash benefits do to reduce poverty. To do that they need to use the same poverty line to compare the numbers in poverty before and after the addition of the non-cash benefits to households' incomes.

Watchdogs should notice another effect of relating whole incomes to a cash-only poverty line. It lowers the poverty line – i.e. the definition of a minimum acceptable income – to a good deal less than the announced level of 'half the median adjusted income'. But the detailed work of the study does not encourage complacency, least of all in English-speaking countries. It reports which groups of people, in what family circumstances, at what ages and stages of life, are most in danger of poverty; and what proportion of each group are actually poor (as defined) in each of the countries studied. For an example, see Table 44.2. Among the things it shows are -

• The likeliest people to be poor are lone-parent families or other families with only one adult; aged single people; and other single people.

• Families with children get most benefit from public education. Aged people get most benefit from public health care. Single adults who are not aged get little benefit from either service, so fewer of the poor among them are rescued from poverty by those services.

• The distribution of cash income, including superannuation and public income transfers, is much better in the European than in the English-speaking countries studied.

• In the English-speaking countries many more households than in Europe are rescued from poverty by public education and health care. This is not because Europeans have worse education or health care, it is because their better cash incomes leave fewer in need of rescue.

• In the English-speaking countries in 1981, public education and health care rescued many more people from poverty in the UK than in Australia, Canada or the US. (The Australian and Canadian health services have since improved.) Does this mean that the British cash incomes were closer to the poverty line, so more of them were lifted over it by the educational and health provisions? Or does it mean that the British educational and health provisions were more valuable? This analysis does not tell you. A disadvantage of most uses of poverty lines is that they show *how many* people are poor, but not *how poor* they are: the summaries don't distinguish between incomes just below the chosen poverty line and incomes a long way below it. Causes of both the above kinds were probably at work at the time (1979-81) of this survey. British income transfers included a universal age pension and probably reached more of the people entitled to them than did the selective, means-tested pensions in North America and Australia; so more of the British poor had cash incomes not far below the poverty line. And to hoist them over it, the British health services certainly reached more of them and cost them less than their American and Australian equivalents did at that time.

- However it was measured there was most poverty in the United States, and public services there did least to reduce it.

More recent figures are available for Western Europe.

Poverty in the European Union

In 1997 Eurostat published a study of incomes in the Union's member countries four years earlier: *Income distribution and poverty in EU12 – 1993*. Its tables are based on net money income after income tax and public income transfers. The incomes are not adjusted for public education, health or other non-cash services, but they *are* adjusted, as in the Luxembourg study, for differences in the size and composition of the households which the incomes support. A poverty line for each country is set at 50 per cent of its average household-adjusted income.

In the Union as a whole about 57 million people, including 13 million children, lived in poverty in 23 million households. That represented 17 per cent of the Union's households and people and 20 per cent of its children. The best countries were Denmark with 9 per cent of its households in poverty and Belgium and Germany with 13 per cent. The worst were Portugal with 29 per cent, Greece with 24 and Britain with 23. The order of merit is different for households, individuals and children. The differences reflect family size and composition, but also the countries' different taxes and public income transfers. France, for example, is sixth-best in its proportion of poor households but second-best in its proportion of poor children. Table 44.2 lists the twelve countries in the order in which they manage to keep their children out of poverty. Bracketed figures in the second column rank their success with households.

	Percentage of children	Percentage of households	
Denmark	5	9	(1)
France	12	15	(6)
Germany	13	13	(2)
Belgium	15	13	(3)
Netherlands	16	14	(4)
Greece	19	17	(11)
Luxembourg	23	16	(5)
Italy	24	18	(7)
Spain	25	19	(8)
Portugal	27	29	(12)
Ireland	28	21	(9)
United Kingdom	32	22	(10)

Table 44.2 Proportions of children and households in poverty (as defined) in twelve European countries in 1993
Source: Eurostat – ECHP, First Wave, 1994

The national contrasts exposed in that table may chasten some policy-makers, but won't help them much. To do better they need to know which of their countries' households are in most danger of poverty. That data can be doubly helpful, indicating where more public aid might help, and where on the other hand it might be unnecessary. Table 44.3, from the Eurostat survey, shows the incidence of poverty in households of different composition. The first column tells you what percentage of each household category are in poverty (for example what percentage of old people living alone are in poverty). The second column tells you what percentage that group are of all poor households.

Household type	Percentage of this type who are poor	Percentage of all poor households
One person 65 or over	27	19
One person aged 30 – 64	15	10
One person under 30	31	7
Single parent with all children under 16	36	5
Single parent with at least one child over 16	17	4
Couple without children	13	18
Couple with 1 child under 16	11	5
Couple with 2 children under 16	14	8
Couple with 3 or more children under 16	23	5
Other households	17	6
Total		100

Table 44.3 The poor in the European Union in 1993 by household type
Source: Eurostat – ECHP, First Wave, 1994

That table is here merely as a model. What policy-makers need, and can derive from the 1994 source, is similar data for their own countries, because the European totals conceal wide national variations. Examples:

- *Single parent with all children under 16:* In 1993, 65 per cent of these households were poor in Ireland, and 53 per cent in the United Kingdom. The Danish percentage was 8.

- *Person under 30 living alone:* 42 per cent were poor in France and the Netherlands, 13 per cent in Spain and Ireland.

- *Person over 64 living alone:* 55 per cent were in poverty in Portugal, 16 per cent in Belgium and the Netherlands.

- *Couples with 3 or more children under 16:* 43 per cent were poor in Portugal, 40 per cent in the United Kingdom, 10 per cent in France and Denmark.

A lot could be done about many of the worst of those figures. But no country has succeeded in eliminating poverty altogether. Even the Scandinavians at their social-democratic best still had three or four poor people in poverty in every hundred. Why?

Obstinate poverty

Who are those three or four or five people in every hundred to whom no society seems to be able to convey as much as a third of its average income? How many of them should be seen as personal failures, how many as failures of government, how many as not failures at all?

They're a diverse lot. As many as half of them may not be poor for long. Perhaps they just lost their bread-winners (by death, illness, unemployment, desertion, imprisonment) and it takes time for any other household member to find work or some public income, which anyway may not meet their debts – debts which it was reasonable to incur when there *was* a breadwinner. Perhaps they depend on maintenance payments – unreliable, often in arrears – from an absent father. Or their small family farm barely breaks even but disqualifies them from any public transfer income. Or their small business has failed and bankrupted them. Or they're determined to get one more university degree, or learn one more art, than their government is willing to support with a student living allowance, so they live on sparse part-time earnings. All these may be competent people who will be back in jobs, new marriages, good health and sufficient income in a month or two or a year or two: plenty of poverty is temporary.

There are also people who are poor from their own

incapacity. Different upbringing, culture or public services might have equipped them better. But as things are, some people are poor because they can't or won't use the available services; because they can't get on with other household members; because they are mentally or physically handicapped in ways difficult to compensate; because they're addicted to alcohol or other drugs; because they're in hiding from the law, or creditors, or spouses, and dare not ask for pensions or welfare services.

Not all the poor show up in surveys which measure poverty by the income and services which households *receive*. People can be poor – especially the non-earning members of households can be – because of the way the income is *spent*. Drunks and gamblers have kept some households with good incomes desperately poor, by wasting their incomes. Remember that more people depend on income transfers within households than on public income transfers. Some households with adequate incomes distribute income and services quite unfairly between their members, and very little of the individual poverty which they cause appears in reports of the distribution of income or of poverty.

But who should decide who is poor?

Return to the methodological question with which this section began. Would it be better to investigate poverty without defining a poverty line?

It takes social judgment as well as factual knowledge to decide what material conditions of life should count as poor, and deserve corrective action, in an affluent society. Researchers who use poverty lines acknowledge that. But however scrupulously they acknowledge it, the summaries of their work which reach the public, typically through newspapers and other media, tend to be taken as factual accounts of poverty objectively identified and measured. A second objection is to reports which say who is poor, but not how poor they are or what their life is actually like. Such reports don't equip their readers to decide for themselves what level of income or other material conditions should be the minimum available to any and every member of society.

What might researchers do instead? Susan Richardson and Peter Travers aim to report what life is like at the bottom of the heap in ways which do equip government and public to decide what should count as poverty and attract corrective action. They survey a lot of facts about the poorest 10 and 20 per cent of households. Like other researchers they adjust incomes according to family membership and need. They add estimated values for a range of benefits besides money income: house, car, washing machine, refrigerator, television; the ability to pay debts and to raise money in emergencies; voluntary free time, i.e. the amounts and uses of time which people choose to spend away from employment; and annual holidays.

They then study much the same groups as the Luxembourg researchers do:

- households living on unskilled workers' wages
- pensioners and others with public transfer incomes
- single adults under 60
- lone parents with children
- adult couples without children
- adult couples with children

The researchers report how many of the households in the poorest 10 and 20 per cent of households belong in each of those groups; how many within each group lack any of a list of basic items: their own house, car, washing machine, refrigerator, indoor lavatory, color television, and the capacity to raise a modest amount of cash in an emergency. The same deprivation may hurt some groups more than others. Whether readers realise that may depend on the reference group with whom the deprived group is compared.

Example: Among the poorest 10 per cent of households, the likeliest to have cars are the couples with children. Does that suggest that they're well off? Instead of comparing them with their 'poor peers', compare them with the rest of society's couples with children and they prove to have only a twelfth of the average family's chance of owning a car. In a car-dependent society with poor public transport they look seriously disadvantaged. But whether that matters, and deserves public attention, should not be decided by experts choosing a poverty line. It should be everyone's business. These authors conclude that poverty is a useful concept and poverty research is worthwhile. But –

> our objection to traditional poverty lines is that they are asked to carry too heavy a burden, they confuse issues of inequality with issues of the ability to live decently, and seek a degree of precision which is greater than can be given. Our alternative measures involve the imprecision of concepts such as 'living decently'. Researchers can provide quite precise information of the kind we have gathered in this chapter, but judgments on whether this adds up to a lack of what is required to live decently are better left to citizens acting through the political process.

> – Peter Travers and Sue Richardson,
> *Living Decently: Material Well-being*
> *in Australia,* 1993, p.199

INEQUALITY WITHIN NATIONS

It is right to focus on poverty, where the distribution of income does the greatest human harm. But it should not divert attention from the whole extent of inequality. While the poorest make do on minimal income, how well do the rest do?

In *The economics of inequality* A.B. Atkinson sketched a 'Pen's Parade' of British incomes. (Remember Pen's device: the nation's people pass an observation point in one hour, beginning with the poorest; and their heights are proportional to their incomes.) First in the British parade come people walking upside down because they lost money – had negative income – in the relevant year. The first positive incomes belong to old age pensioners, just over a foot high. Then come women workers in low-paid occupations, the poorest about 2'9". The marchers' height rises slowly, with the women everywhere preceding the men in similar occupations. Sixty per cent of the parade has passed before the 5'10" marcher with the average income passes. (Remember why the average is a good deal higher than the median income.) When three quarters of the people have passed, the height is still only 7 feet. Then heights begin to rise more quickly. Police superintendents are 11 feet. Doctors average about 14 feet. Company directors range through 35 feet (in medium sized companies) to more than 200 feet at the top. In the last half minute or so come the real rich, drawing incomes from wealth: the last is ten miles high, with an income (as far as his income is known) more than fifty thousand times the income of the lowest-paid full-time worker his enterprises employ.

Writing when he did, Atkinson based that parade on 1979 figures. British inequalities increased through the following decade. Directors' and executives' pay increased faster than that of any other group. There was some increasing difference between the highest and the lowest paid in many occupations. Higher unemployment shifted more households from wage incomes to lower transfer incomes. And there was a downward shift of taxation from the highest incomes to indirect taxation of everyone's consumption.

How does the British pattern compare with the distribution of income in other rich democracies? Nations keep their accounts in different ways, and the best efforts to adjust them to allow fair comparison still leave some uncertainties. Tables 44.4 and 5 show two comparisons of income distribution, one of five countries including three outside the European Union, and one of six within the Union.

Income group	Australia	Sweden	United Kingdom	United States	West Germany
Top 20%	40.0	36.7	39.5	40.7	38.1
Next 20%	24.9	24.3	25.0	25.5	24.1
Middle 20%	18.0	17.6	18.2	17.7	17.7
Next 20%	11.7	13.2	11.4	11.3	13.1
Bottom 20%	5.4	8.3	5.9	4.7	7.0

Table 44.4 Quintile shares of money income net of income tax in five countries
Source: Peter Saunders and others, *Noncash income, living standards, inequality and poverty : Evidence from the Luxembourg Income Study*

Income decile	Denmark	Germany	France	Spain	Italy	United Kingdom
Top 10%	20	23	25	27	26	26
9	13	15	15	15	16	15
8	11	12	12	12	12	12
7	10	10	10	10	11	10
6	9	9	9	9	9	9
5	8	8	8	7	8	7
4	8	7	7	7	7	7
3	8	6	6	6	6	6
2	7	6	5	4	4	5
Bottom 10%	5	5	3	2	2	3
Gini Coefficient	0.26	0.30	0.33	0.36	0.37	0.37

Table 44.5 Decile shares of household money income net of income tax in six European countries in 1993
Source: Eurostat – ECHP, First wave, 1994. Figures rounded.

Averaging those tables, the richest 20 per cent of households average twice the average income. The poorest 20 per cent average a quarter of it. Thus the richest fifth average eight times the average income of the poorest fifth. But that misrepresents the distribution as a whole, because much greater inequalities are concealed by averaging the top 20 per cent. Even if we count earnings only and disregard incomes from wealth, we find a few executives taking two or three hundred times as much as they pay their poorest employees. Some artists and entertainers earn similar amounts.

The chief national differences (which the previous paragraph concealed by averaging them) are at the top and bottom of the scale. Both before and after receiving non-cash public goods and services, the rich countries' poor do worst in the United States, and best in north western Europe.

INEQUALITY BETWEEN NATIONS

Countries are commonly ranked as richer or poorer according to the income per head recorded in their national accounts. Except in some poor countries which include some subsistence farm income, the accounts are of money income, and incomes are compared at the market rates of exchange of the countries' currencies.

Those comparisons can have three shortcomings:

• They don't notice the distribution of income. So if (say) Denmark has the same total income as an oil-rich dictator has, the comparisons may give the impression that the Danes and the dictator's desert-dwelling subjects have the same standards of living. This can be corrected by including Gini coefficients or Pen's parades for the compared countries, or by comparing the incomes of the richest and poorest one or two or twenty per cent of their people or households.

- Rates of exchange between currencies are affected by balances of trade, investment and debt and by exchange gamblers. They don't necessarily reflect the domestic purchasing power of the currencies. This can be corrected by studies of local wages and prices and patterns of spending.

- Home-made income is not recorded in rich countries' national accounts and there are problems about shadow-pricing it in peasant countries' accounts. But it is a big component of material income and it varies widely, including between otherwise-similar economies. This can be corrected by surveying the public and household space and capital available for household use, and by sample surveys of household activity and output.

Examples illustrate how uncorrected and corrected accounts can differ.

Comparing rich with rich

Recall Ian Castles' comparison of the public and household space and capital available to households in Japanese and Australian cities. Castles also compared income per head in the two countries. National accounts compared at yen/dollar exchange rates showed Australia about ten places below Japan on the world table of national income per head. From the national accounts Castles found that Australians are more productive per hour of work: the higher Japanese income comes from working more hours per lifetime. What will the money incomes buy? Castles divided incomes by the hours worked, to discover what an hour's work would buy. He then compared the 'work price' of a Sydney basket of most-preferred consumer goods, and a Tokyo basket. To earn the price of a year's supply of what Australians consider the necessaries of life, Tokyo residents would have to work two and a half times as long as Sydney residents do: 600 hours in Tokyo, 245 in Sydney, at 1987 wages and prices. To earn the price of what Tokyo people consider basic, the difference is only a little less: Tokyo people must still work twice the hours that Sydney people would have to work to buy that basket of goods at their local prices. For other goods the differences are less, but still significant and all in Sydney's favor. Roughly speaking, an hour's work in Sydney in 1987 bought about one and a half times the market goods that an hour's work in Tokyo bought. Castles concluded that -

> the available evidence indicates that the purchasing power of earnings, as measured by the command over goods and services obtained on average by a

given amount of working time, is much greater in Sydney than in the Japanese cities ... [Through the 1980s, despite Australia's slower economic growth] Australians apparently continued to enjoy higher real consumption levels *per capita,* in respect of virtually every significant category of expenditure. This was true notwithstanding the facts that they worked fewer hours per week, took longer holidays and had shorter working lives.

> – Ian Castles, in Kyoko Sheridan (ed.) *The Australian Economy in the Japanese Mirror* (1992).

Two other exercises yielded similar results. Robert Summers' and Alan Heston's Penn World Table, cited earlier, which included wage/price calculations in its complicated scheme, put Australia seventh and Japan thirteenth on its 1988 table. In October 1991 the magazine *Money* compared standards of living in sixteen of the richest countries by allocating points for health, job opportunities, home ownership, money income and purchasing power, upward social mobility, higher education, leisure time, car ownership, low crime rates, and possession of luxury goods. Australia ran second (after the United States) and Japan seventh.

These comparisons are not here for patriotic Australian reasons. Japan and Australia happen to be the rich countries whose income figures and exchange rates misrepresent their material standards most, and in opposite directions. They illustrate the need for economists and policy-makers to relate incomes to prices, and to supplement them with surveys of people's access to public and household capital, and uses of time and space.

Comparing richer with poorer

The difference between material life in (say) Bangladesh and Switzerland is plain, and shocking, to see. But it is not easy, and perhaps not very useful, to translate the difference into notional cash. In Bangladesh money income is much less of whole income, and in that sense less important, than it is in Switzerland. Bangladesh has few and poor public non-cash goods and services for most people. So the conventional methods of measuring income show too little to keep most of the population alive, and show hundredfold differences between average incomes in the richest and poorest countries.

Bangladeshi people live chiefly on subsistence farming and some barter. Sample surveys can yield estimates of the food that is produced and consumed without entering the national accounts by being marketed. But it may still be misleading to value that output at Bangladesh prices, and (in order to compare national standards) to convert it into Swiss or US dollars at prevailing exchange rates. Exchange rates tend to be specially misleading indicators of comparative purchasing power in rich creditor countries and poor debtor countries. I.B. Kravis and others have therefore adjusted exchange rates to reflect equivalent purchasing power. There are still difficulties, because different populations eat different diets and have different price relativities between foods. Kravis does his best to adapt to those facts too. Applying his relativities to a sample of countries from rich to poor in 1980 would have indicated this spread of average real income per head, expressed as percentages of the United States average:

United States	100
United Kingdom	76
Spain	63
Mexico	30
Thailand	15
India	7

Recall the theme with which this chapter began. American and British national income could certainly be enough, if it were appropriately distributed, to give everyone comfortable material conditions of life, such

that there would be no good reason to expect that further economic growth would increase total happiness. That is far from true of India, Thailand or Mexico. Without more output many of their people must continue to be painfully poor. Economic growth, if its output were tolerably distributed, could do much for their happiness. In 1980 Spain was perhaps crossing the threshold between the one condition and the other.

Return from national averages to the individual distribution of income. National inequalities overlap: the Spanish rich earn more than the British poor, the Mexican rich earn more than the Spanish poor, the richest Indians have more than the poorest Americans. The world distribution, however it is measured, has thousandfold inequalities. Some western individuals receive hundreds of millions of dollars every year. Every day some of the poorest people in the poorest countries die of starvation, although there is a world surplus of food.

There is work there if you want to leave human society better than you found it. Contrive growth and better government in poor countries, more effective aid from rich to poor countries, better distribution within all countries. 'Expose thyself to feel what wretches feel', King Lear said, 'that thou may'st shake the superflux to them and show the heavens more just.'

WHAT DETERMINES THE PATTERN OF INCOMES?

A great many conditions and processes combine, in a modern economy, to develop and sustain its pattern of incomes and to determine who gets which of them. Each of those conditions and processes has its own history. Nobody can know the whole pattern which has produced and is now maintaining or changing the distribution. Recall the lessons with which this course of study began: causal explanations are necessarily selective. The rest of this chapter lists things which can affect the distribution of (in turn) property incomes; owner-managers' business incomes; self-employed and freelance incomes; directors' and executives' incomes; employees' salaries and wages; public transfer incomes; and household transfers, i.e. income-sharing within households.

INCOMES FROM PROPERTY

What determines how much of national income goes to the owners of capital?

Factor shares Most production requires capital and labor. What determines how the output, or the income from selling it, is divided between the capital owners

and the workers?

Whatever it is, it has been changing, in what may seem a paradoxical way. In developed economies through the twentieth century there was a steady increase in the capital/labor ratio, i.e. the amount of capital per worker. But as the proportion of capital increased, the capitalists' share of national income appears to have fallen. (Part of the appearance is real: the workers are getting a bigger share. Part of it merely reflects accounting practices, as will presently be explained.) Estimates for the UK give capital owners about half of national income before 1914; about a third between the world wars; and about a quarter since 1945. The capitalists' share has long been lower in the United States: it was about 25 per cent in 1930 and has fluctuated between 21 and 17 per cent since. What has determined those proportions and their changes over time?

First, some causes of the changes over time.

The changing distribution of wealth

When farms, houses or small business premises cease paying rent to landlords because their occupiers come to own them, national accounts show a reduction of property income. Part of the shift of ownership actually redistributes property income from landlords to occupiers, but part does simply do away with some property income. Why the split effect? Recall the difference between business output which is sold for money, and household output which is not:

- When a farm or small business stops paying rent to a landlord, it continues to produce the same output, which sells to yield the same income. The farmer or business owner now keeps that whole income, which she previously shared (through rent payments) with the landlord. National accounts show the landlord's loss of property income. Strictly speaking they should ascribe some of the farmer's income to the farmer's capital and some to her labor; but most national accounts lump the two together in a separate category of 'farm income' and treat it for most purposes as earned income. Thus a redistribution of property income may be misinterpreted as a reduction of property income.

- The effect is different when a household stops paying house rent to a landlord. The house as capital and the residents' labor together produce goods and services for the household's use. That output is not marketed, and does not provide rent for the landlord – tenant's cash income from some other source has to provide the rent. So when ownership passes from the landlord to the occupier, what gets redistributed is not property income, it is part of the household's earned income. The household now keeps all its cash income; the landlord's property right to a share of it has simply been extinguished. (Some economists and tax-collectors disagree. They argue that the household now draws in kind the same rent as the landlord drew in cash. But the household's income in kind from the use of the housing capital has not changed with the change from renting to owning. So I think it makes more sense to see that some cash income has been redistributed by allowing the household to keep all it earns, as a result of a redistribution of capital wealth.)

There can be similar effects where people work alone and are classified as 'self-employed' rather than as business proprietors. Self-employed truck drivers, tradespeople, doctors, dentists, lawyers, accountants, management consultants and others own and use increasingly elaborate equipment. But for many purposes they continue to be classified as self-employed workers rather than as business proprietors, so their incomes are included in estimates of the labor share of national income.

Public ownership Government, public enterprises and independent non-profit enterprises now do between 11 and 23 per cent of production in OECD countries, and own appropriate proportions of productive capital. Some of them sell their output and take a profit share. But many don't: they provide free (i.e. tax-financed) goods, or trade at prices to break even.

Thus a part of the large increase of capital per worker in developed economies has come in forms, and in types of ownership, which don't yield private property income as traditionally defined. In the public sector and the household sector which between them now have half or more of productive capital, and (if only for accounting reasons) in much of the farm, small business and self-employed parts of the private sector, there has been a steady increase of capital per worker while the national accounts show a decline in the private property share of national income.

Profit and wage shares in private firms The trends listed so far show rising proportions of capital in public or household ownership, or they show more of it owned by the workers who use it so that their 'property income' ceases to be distinguished from their 'labor income'. In neither case is there direct competition for income between workers and private profit-seekers. But there remains the large sector of private business in which the traditional competition for wage and profit shares continues. And in that sector also, there appears to have been some increase of the wage share through the twentieth century despite the continuing increase of the capital/labor ratio. Economists have disagreed about the causes of that shift, or about the relative importance of its various causes. One reason for disagreement has probably been that different causes have operated with different force in different industries, in different countries and at different times. Causes which have operated with some force at some times and places include these:

- Democratic government has introduced a stream of protections for workers. Even in countries which don't regulate wages directly, employers' wage costs and workers' pay per hour are increased by the regulation of hours and conditions of work. Industrial relations policies have varied over time and from country to country, but democratic government has generally done more to protect workers and improve their bargaining power than it has done to reduce their bargaining power by regulating the behavior of unions.

- The relative bargaining strength of employers and employees appears to have shifted to the workers' advantage in many industries, at least until the Right turn of the 1980s. Union organization, legalized by democratic government, did appear to strengthen labor's bargaining for hours and conditions of work, if not always for wages. Some employers also have been strengthened by growing concentration and size of firms, and in some industries by increasing degrees of monopoly. But that can have diverse effects on wage bargaining. Monopoly can increase market strength against consumers as well as against labor. It may reduce employers' resistance to wage demands, if the demands can be met by raising prices. (Marx's mistake about that was noticed back in Chapter 9.) And some of the lowest wages have been paid by small businesses in competitive industries, running on small profit margins, with no capacity to pay higher wages.

  Arguments about the wage effects of union organization tend to be indecisive because bargaining strength is hard to measure, and its effects can be difficult to isolate from effects of other causes. Unions do seem to have prevented or limited wage cuts in hard times. That can increase real wages and wage shares if prices fall further than wages, as they did in the depression of the 1930s. Labor's more positive bargaining power – its capacity to negotiate increased wage rates – appears to be stronger in good times. When there is full employment and jobs are plentiful, workers can threaten to strike without risk of losing employment altogether. Firms competing for scarce labor concede to union negotiators things which they might well concede to market conditions if there were no organized bargaining. But the fully employed conditions which allow such wage rises tend also to allow price rises, and to have more effect on inflation than on wage and profit shares. Increasingly, unionized workers and their negotiators understand those inflationary possibilities and restrain their bargaining accordingly.

- *Supply and demand* Many of the wage rises under full employment are offered by firms which want to grow, to acquire new skills, to entice workers away from other employers, or to attract more teenagers, married women or semi-retired people back into the workforce. Many of those workers are unorganized and do no collective bargaining. Those who are union members may nevertheless be enticed from job to job by wage changes which reflect market forces of supply and demand. Although general theo-

ries of supply and demand for capital and labor can't sufficiently explain the changing factor shares, they are not necessarily useless. They draw attention to market processes which operate with varying force (along with other causes) in many cases.

Besides income from profits, property income also comes as rent for real estate, and as interest on loans.

Rent has its everyday meaning here: what tenants pay to landlords for the use of land and buildings. Don't confuse it with theorists' concepts of 'economic rent' which have partly different meanings.

Rent is property income. Most of it is paid by people who don't own property to people who do. Some households, some farms and some businesses pay rent for their real estate and others (owner-occupiers) don't. So it affects both the property and the labor shares of national income, and the detailed distribution of the labor share.

The total amount of rent paid depends on real-estate prices and rent levels, and on the proportions of (i) landlord-owned real estate whose users must pay rent for it, and (ii) owner-occupied real estate which pays no rent to anyone. Those proportions changed significantly in many countries through the last century. The shift from renting to owner-occupation of farms in Britain, and of houses in nearly all developed countries, has done more than any other single cause to reduce inequalities of wealth, and it has done more than most national accounts show to reduce inequalities of income.

(Notice a difference between the way those two shifts are commonly measured. When farms, houses and other real estate pass from landlords' ownership to be owned by their occupiers, public records of wealth show both ends of the transaction: landlords with less wealth, new farm and household owners with more wealth. But most accounts of income record income before its owners begin to spend it. So the loss of spendable income by rent-payers is not recorded. Nor are their income gains if they become owner-occupiers. Some special surveys record spendable income after housing costs, but the primary tax-office accounts of income in national accounts do not. A shift of ownership from landlords to occupiers is recorded as reducing the ex-landlords' incomes without increasing the new owners' incomes. Thus the effect of the shift of ownership in reducing inequalities of wealth is fully reported, but its effect in reducing inequalities of income is understated.)

Interest is the price you pay for the use of borrowed money. The rate of interest affects the whole amount of property income, and the detailed distribution of both property and wage income, in a number of ways.

Government or its central bank commonly sets a base rate of interest – the rate paid for the safest loans – and market dealings determine the differentials, above that rate, for greater risks. Interest rate policy is an integral part of national financial policy and economic strategy. We therefore leave it to be dealt with in chapters on financial systems and national strategies, rather than in the following chapter on income policies. But whatever the broader purposes of the government's manipulation of interest rates, it does affect the distribution of income. So here, as we survey main influences on the distribution of income, it is appropriate to notice the distributional effects which interest rates can have. Of course the effects which they do have depend on other things as well as interest rates – on prevailing market conditions and on the whole strategy of which interest rate policy is a part. But with that proviso, here are some direct and indirect effects to be expected of higher or lower interest rates.

Who gains and who loses when interest rates are high?

- Owners who lend money – i.e. buy bonds and debentures or deposit money in interest-bearing accounts with banks, building societies and credit unions – get more income the higher the rate of interest They get it from business borrowers, farmer borrowers, personal borrowers, home-buyers and people who use consumer credit.

- Lenders and borrowers each include some rich and some poor. But there is an important difference between the rich lenders and the rest. Most rich lenders are net lenders: over their lifetimes they lend more than they borrow. So the higher the rate of interest, the higher their property incomes and (if they save) the faster their wealth can accumulate. Most people with below-average incomes are net borrowers. Over life they borrow more than they lend. So the higher the rate of interest, the more income they lose. And they tend to lose it when they can least afford to lose it, through the first third or so of household life when their earnings are low and they're in debt for house, car, domestic equipment and consumer credit. They lose even more in the long run if high interest excludes them from buying their houses. Recall, from Chapter 25, the effects of lifetime renting on lifetime income.

- Business owners, especially small business owners, who finance their current operations and new investment by borrowing may have their incomes reduced by high interest rates in more than one way.
  - High interest payments cream off some business earnings. That may reduce profit directly. Or it

may force price increases which depress demand, sales and profit.
- At high rates of interest firms may not be able to afford to borrow as much as they could at lower rates. So they may invest less and generate less income.

- Reduced investment may reduce employment. Workers who become unemployed lose income and spend less, with further multiplier effects on the level of activity and the distribution of income.

- As unemployment reduces labor's bargaining strength and the demand for consumer goods, there may be less inflationary pressure to raise wages and prices. But at the same time producers facing higher interest bills may have to meet them by raising their prices. High interest rates thus have both deflationary and inflationary effects. There is no theoretical way of predicting which of those two effects will prevail, or the consequent effects on the distribution of income.

In some conditions, as an element of some economic strategies, it may be desirable to set high rates of interest, usually for short periods. But in most conditions high interest increases inequalities of income directly, and the way in which it has been used as an anti-inflationary device in recent times has often increased inequalities further by increasing unemployment. Higher unemployment increases the tax cost of income transfers and welfare services to the unemployed and their families. That can increase political pressure to reduce the income transfers and welfare provisions, with some further increase of inequality.

What determines who gets property income ?

Who gets the property income follows from who has the property. Recall, from Chapter 43, the sources of private wealth. Once (and still from time to time in the twentieth century) conquest, civil war, coup d'etat, government favor. Currently -

- business success, including the quick capitalization of new flows of earnings
- individual success in some arts and entertainments whose technology allows mass reproduction
- directors' acquisition of capital from their firms
- saving from high earnings
- some superannuation schemes
- inheritance, marriage and other gifts
- the accumulation of existing wealth by capital appreciation and/or saving from property income
- gambling on share values, real estate values, foreign

exchange rates, commodity futures, lotteries and pools, casino games, horse races, etc.

• crime and corruption

EARNED INCOMES (1) SELF-EMPLOYED

No single-cause theory can sufficiently explain the distribution of the labor share of income, i.e. of income earned by work. Market conditions, institutions, training costs, bargaining strengths, employers' and clients' capacities to pay and other conditions vary too widely from country to country, industry to industry and job to job. To understand why American doctors earn twice as much as identically skilled British doctors, or why women have often been paid less than men for identical work, or why the pay differentials differ within otherwise-similar occupations, you will usually need local knowledge. Where you need theory at all, it will usually be of the kind that equips you to ask systematic questions about the local conditions. Examples follow.

Working owners run a large number and a wide variety of farms and small businesses: such a wide variety that the things which determine their incomes are too many and various to categorize here. But many of the small businesses accord quite well with neoclassical theory. The owners' and managers' purposes are identical. They are competitive operators in competitive industries with easy entry for new enterprises, and quick extinction for unsuccessful ones. Their incomes are often hard-earned, and reward skill and inventiveness and long hours of work.

Freelances Should a novelist, a portrait painter or a studio potter be classified as a small business owner, or as a self-employed professional or craftsman? The definitions don't matter. But in surveying the determinants of income, we can use 'freelance' to describe some people with special skills who don't work for a regular employer or group of clients, but sell their services or products to all comers. Recall, from your study of the sources of wealth, how different arts have different technologies of reproduction. Ballet dancers have to be there with their audiences. Painters' and sculptors' and studio potters' products can sell in their absence, but can't be satisfactorily multiplied for mass sale. Writers, musicians and film and television actors produce products which can both sell in their absence and be multiplied for mass sale. Some of those artists work for regular employers. But there are also two kinds of freelances – writers, painters and others who produce products for sale, and actors and freelance musicians who work for whoever wants them, often for a different impresario for each play or film or concert performance. Many of these freelances earn in a fairly

pure market way, selling their products or services in open competitive markets in which prices – and therefore their incomes – are determined much as in market theory.

Self-employed professionals are also freelances in principle, but in practice many of them work for a steady clientele for a regular scale of fees; they have strong professional associations; and their incomes depend on institutions and balances of market strength which vary widely from profession to profession and country to country.

At the end of chapter 41 on market practice you were offered a set of questions to ask about any market whose operation you need to understand. You can put some of those questions to self-employed professions:

• What are the lead times and training costs for entry to the profession?

• How, by whom and on what principles is entry to the profession controlled?

• Who orders the professional services, in whose interest?

• Who pays for them, with whose money?

• Which of the people concerned are profit-seekers, and what are the purposes of those who are not? Most profit-seekers also have other interests in their work. How do the various incentives fit or conflict in the profession concerned?

• What kinds of self-regulation and public regulation apply to the profession and its clients?

• What public capital or services (if any) do the professionals use?

• Do the professionals compete for clients and if so, how expert or inexpert are the clients at choosing them and judging their performance?

Common sense will add a dragnet question – 'Is there anything else in the nature of the profession or in its local circumstances that affects its members' incomes?' The answers to the whole set of questions will usually explain, for most practical purposes –

• the different earnings of the same profession in different countries

• the different average earnings of different professionals with similar training times and costs

• the diverse patterns of income inequality within the professions

• relations between professional incomes and salary and wage incomes.

Whatever the purpose of the investigation, the amount

and distribution of professional income can't be sufficiently explained by any simple theory of supply and demand, or training time and costs, or productivity. The causation is at least as complex, and variable from case to case, as the above set of questions implies.

Company directors Legally directors are their companies' employees. But in practice, in the English-speaking countries, they determine their own pay so we list them here among the self-employed.

Governments created the basic legal forms and directors' powers of joint stock companies at times when firms were smaller than many are now. Their directors were often part owners, or were hired by owners who could decide what to pay them. Some firms still work like that, with some market discipline of their directors' rewards, but many don't. Recall how competitive State chartering of US corporations has enlarged some directors' powers, including the power to decide and conceal their own rewards. Stock exchanges force them to disclose what

they take, but don't otherwise restrain them. Wherever there are no dominant shareholders, or the dominant shareholders are other corporations represented by their directors, American directors as a group, and often individually, now decide their own rewards, and have been increasing them faster than any other group has been able to do for some decades now. In Europe and the UK there are some light constraints, for example on the rate at which directors can take capital from their firms. Each country has some informal norms of what it is reasonable for them to take. But the directors chiefly set the norms, and have been steadily increasing them, though at very different rates in different countries. Many have also been relating their pay to their companies' performance – or pretending to do so. Samples:

Australia Table 44.6 compares the year's profit with the top director's salary in the fifty biggest Australian companies (including profit-seeking public corporations, but excluding some multinationals) in 1990.

Rank/Company		Profit/Loss millions $S	Top Salary ,000 $S	$ of profit per $ of salary	Rank/Company		Profit/Loss millions $S	Top Salary ,000 $S	$ of profit per $ of salary
1	Aust Wheat Board	406.9	90	4,522	26	Australia Post	58.2	170	343
2	OTC	585.5	160	3,659	27	James Hardie	131.5	390	337
3	Commonwealth Bank	783.7	220	3,562	28	Pioneer International	203.1	685	296
4	BHP	3,725.3	1,275	2,922	29	ICI Aust	120.6	430	280
5	Alcoa	1,207.2	630	1,916	30	Tubemakers	88.8	330	269
6	CSR	739.4	460	1,607	31	Lend Lease	216.0	810	267
7	Westpac	913.7	580	1,575	32	SA Brewing	145.4	550	264
8	NAB	1,323.1	840	1,575	33	NRMA Insurance	81.4	310	262
9	BTR Nylex	932.4	620	1,504	34	St George BS	71.7	280	256
10	CRA	868.4	690	1,258	35	AGL	66.0	300	220
11	Boral	519.3	430	1,208	36	Jennings	64.0	320	200
12	AMP	570.0	600	950	37	Adsteam	236.6	1,210	196
13	MIM	451.6	520	868	38	Wesfarmers	89.9	490	183
14	Pasminco	250.2	300	834	39	Burns Philp	107.2	630	170
15	Pacific Dunlop	410.4	580	708	40	Elders IXL	240.0	1,440	167
16	Brambles	334.2	500	668	41	Goodman Fielder Wattie	111.4	710	157
17	ANI	162.2	260	624	42	Metal Manufacturers	42.0	300	140
18	Comalco	297.6	480	620	43	State Bank NSW	34.8	360	97
19	WMC	371.5	610	609	44	Coca-Cola Amatil	86.1	930	93
20	Rothmans	142.4	270	527	45	FAI	31.6	470	67
21	NBH Peko	207.7	450	461	46	Leighton	35.6	830	43
22	Amcor	219.4	580	378	47	TNT	221.8	5,130	43
23	Coles Myer	555.6	1,480	375	48	News Corp	429.2	12,745	34
24	Email	121.1	350	346	49	Qantas	-17.9	300	-60
25	Mayne Nickless	166.0	480	346	50	Bond Corp	-1,655.8	2,880	-575

Table 44.6 Profits earned for each dollar paid to top Australian Chief Executives in 1990.
Compiled by A.N. Maiden from data supplied by Egan and Associates, and published in The Independent Monthly, September 1991

Egan Associates repeated the exercise six years later. We need not repeat the whole table. But private share-holders – and anyone interested in the new increase of the rich countries' inequalities – should notice a strong trend in the figures for the private sector. Through the 1990s chief executives were earning less for their share-holders and taking more for themselves:

	Year	Profit $m.	Highest executives' pay $	$ of profit per $ of chiefs' pay $	
Totals	1990	15141.8	29,220,000	518	
	1996	12020	47,248,000	225	
Averages	1990	360.5	695,000	595	
	1996	286	1,124,000	220	
Percentage Change 1990 – 1996		-21%	+39%		Total -51% Company Average -63%

Table 44.7 Profit and executive pay in 42 of the 43 biggest Australian companies, 1990 – 1996.
1996 figures are in constant 1990 dollars. Some companies were replaced by others between the two dates. There may have been some different accounting of retiring executives' benefits. News Limited is omitted from the comparison because its exceptional executive payment in 1990 would distort totals and averages for the other 42 companies.

The relation between total chief executives' pay and total profit is bad enough, but some good performers among the biggest companies mask the worse rate at which profits have declined and executive pay has risen in the smaller companies. In 1990, 8 companies earned more than $1000 per $ of chief executive pay and 6 earned less than $100. In 1996, 2 earned more than $1000 and 17 earned less than $100.

Japan and the United States In 1997 the chief executives of major Japanese companies were averaging less than fifteen times the national average wage. Equivalent US chief executives were averaging more than two hundred times the average wage and were increasing their pay at more than twice the rate of growth of the US economy or the average wage.

A conclusion To explain corporate directors' pay as an efficient market price for their services is absurd.

EARNED INCOMES (2) EMPLOYEES

Employees are many more than half of all paid workers. So a balanced survey of the distribution of income should do its best to explain what determines the distri-bution of wages. But we already did that, in Chapter 32 on four ways to fix wages. Revise it if you need to. Remember that the labor share of income has varied from as little as half to as much as four fifths of all private sector income, and its detailed distribution is determined in partly different ways in different coun-tries. No one cause and no one theory can explain the distribution at all times and places. Here, as a reminder of items you already know, is a list of things which always or sometimes have some influence on the distri-bution. To save words, salaries and wages are both called wages, or simply pay.

• **A national economy's productivity,** from its natural resources and accumulated human and phys-ical capital, determines what income it can produce and distribute to its members.

• **Occupational productivity** is different. With economic growth there are technological reasons why some occupations have rising productivity and others don't. For example steel workers do but judges don't. But that does not mean that steel workers get rich and judges don't. Competition and other pressures drop steel prices and restrain the rate at which steelmakers' wages rise. To keep up the supply of judges their wages have to keep pace with others, and taxation and rising legal fees achieve that. Steel gets cheaper and justice gets dearer, but the wages they pay may retain their old relativities. Income produced by the high productivity of some occupations tends to be distributed to all occupations.

- *The wage-setting system* which a nation adopts – i.e. which of the 'four ways to fix wages', or what mixture of those methods – affects the distribution of wages. For example the Swedish system and the Australian system both produce flatter wage distributions with higher and more reliable minimum wage rates than North or South American systems do.

- *Capital costs* and wage rates may affect each other in industries whose technology allows some marginal substitution between capital and labor. (Buy another machine or hire another worker? Buy a better machine and sack some existing workers? Avoid the need to buy expensive machinery by moving the factory to a low-wage country?) Notice that those relations can prompt some one-eyed arguments. Boss: Take a wage cut or I'll have to replace half of you by machines. Workers: The half who stay will be worth higher wages when the machines have doubled their productivity. If we don't keep pushing for wage rises you won't invest in the best available technology and there'll be no economic growth – no rising income for either of us. (Notice that these arguments don't apply, or apply differently, where labor and capital have to increase together rather than alternatively – for example in taxi-driving – or where there are no capital alternatives to labor, for example to judges' labor.)

- *Training time and cost* have some effect on occupational rates of pay. To induce people to forgo earning through years of vocational education, highly skilled occupations may need to be well paid. But the relation between training cost and occupational pay is irregular. Doctors, academics, architects with town-planning qualifications, graduate librarians, simultaneous translators and pianists need similar periods of training, but their average earnings differ widely. So do the internal inequalities which the averages conceal. (There is more difference between the incomes of the richest and poorest architects or the richest and poorest pianists than there is between the richest and poorest librarians or simulta-

neous translators.) The occupations differ in the opportunities they offer to escape from wage earning by becoming a company director, a self-employed professional or a virtuoso soloist. The occupations demand different natural talents, some rarer than others. They have different intrinsic attractions and attract different types of people. And the years of vocational education are not always chosen simply as a means to higher income later. Many students choose them as the most interesting and liberating way to spend those years of youth.

Thus other things besides wage rates induce people to endure or enjoy long years of training; and length of training is only one of the things which help to determine wage levels.

- *New occupations* may have to offer high wages to attract workers away from other occupations. If they require scarce skills, that also may raise their wages. Those opening wage levels may become established as the regular rates for the work, and persist after the scarcity has passed. (Some of the first computer programmers were recruited from school maths teachers and other established occupations. The high wages which induced them to switch have generally persisted, though the qualifications and training times are similar to those of the older occupations, and programmers are no longer scarce.)

- *The relative bargaining strength* of employers and employees may depend on -

  - the size of firms

  - how competitive or monopolistic the industry is

  - whether any competition is in non-tradeables, safe from import competition; or is in import replacement, open to import competition from which it could be protected by government; or is in export markets

  - whether any monopolist or other strength which the industry has is easier to use against labor to restrain wages, or against consumers to raise prices

  - the level of unemployment of workers with the skills the industry uses, and if the skills are scarce, the lead times for developing them.

  - the extent to which the skills are job-specific and must be developed on the job, so that firms want loyal long-serving employees

  - the extent to which the industry's workforce is union organized, how well the unions are led, and how militant, moderate or co-operative they are

- the extent to which female, black or immigrant workers are organized by the unions or excluded by them

- how united, and capable of effective national wage negotiations, the unions are

- whether the unions are linked to a major political party, and if they are, how often and for how long it governs

- the prevailing industrial law and institutions which regulate bargaining and conditions of employment

- the public, private or independent ownership of the industry

- the remembered history and prevailing culture of industrial relations, and the degrees and kinds of conflict and cooperation which those frames of mind encourage.

Professional disagreements   Those factors don't operate uniformly in all cases. Experts disagree whether some of them affect wages at all. To sample the difficulties and disagreements, consider some arguments about labor unions' effects on wages. There have been many empirical studies of the wages paid to union and non-union workers. In different countries and industries at different times they have shown differences from zero to 15 per cent, and up to 30 per cent for specially disadvantaged groups – women, recent immigrants, ethnic minorities – when they are first organized. They have also shown diverse effects of union gains on non-union wages: union gains sometimes flow on to non-union workers, but sometimes leave them further behind.

So, first, the apparent effects of union organization vary widely with time and place. And second, theorists are divided about how many of the wage effects are actually caused by union action. As with other causal explanations of social effects, knowledge of the connections often depends on counter-factual or imagined alternatives. Might a unionized industry's high wages be produced, if there were no union, by market forces: by the supply and demand for particular skills, the training costs of developing those skills, the employers' capacity to finance wage rises by raising product prices? For example there are industries which employ high proportions of workers with job-specific skills which can only be developed on the job. To attract and hold such workers and encourage them to co-operate with each other and with their employers, firms pay premium wages. Such a stable workforce also happens to be easy

to organize, and has high union membership. But that is more an effect than a cause of the other conditions. The nature of the work and the mutual interest of the employers and employees are main causes of both the high wages and the high union membership. But in different conditions unions have been organized at risk of life and limb by militant leaders, and have then achieved substantially better wages and working conditions despite violent resistance by employers. There is thus no useful general theory or rule of thumb about relations between union activity and wage levels. But the relations are often clear enough, with local knowledge, in particular cases.

EARNED INCOMES (3) CASUAL AND CONTRACT WORKERS

Casual workers do often sell their labor in conditions it is fair to call a labor market. They may get what work they can piece by piece without a permanent employer or assured income, and often without the legal rights of employed workers. They may also lack the organization, bargaining strength and mutual protections of the self-employed professions; that is why, despite some similarities, we treat them as casual rather than self-employed.

Casual earnings are typically irregular. Some go unrecorded, for tax and other reasons. So their distribution and totals are difficult to estimate for national accounting and policy-making purposes.

The amount of casual work varies with time and place. Once, wharf laborers were hired every morning. Sailors were hired for each voyage and sometimes at each port of call. Women workers in the rag trade got work to do at home when their employers had orders and not when they did not. Many building workers are still hired for each building job. Many waiters, bartenders, bedmakers and other hotel and restaurant staff are called in when there is custom and not when there is not. The US has more than other countries have of casual car-washing, window-cleaning, lawn-mowing, snow-shovelling, rubbish-clearing, laundering, childminding and other low-paid household services.

Some once-casual trades (for example wharf work) have been converted to regular employment by union and government action, to give workers better conditions and more reliable income. Some (for example some building trades) have moved the other way, from regular employment to casual or contract work. The income effects vary with circumstances. Workers usually do better in regular employment, but not invariably. In boom times when their skills are scarce, employers will sometimes pay high prices for casual and contract work more readily than they will raise the wages of permanent employees. Reasons of four general kinds may determine what work is done casually and what is done in regular employment:

- It may be determined by the nature of the work: shearers, surf lifeguards, deerhunters, fruitpickers and department-store Santa Clauses can't usually be employed all year.

- Casual or contract work may be in the mutual interest of employers and workers: many producers and actors, homeowners and housepainters, portraitists and people who want portraits, agree that independent contracting suits both parties.

- Where interests conflict, the employers may win, perhaps to keep the employment casual because that is cheaper for them; or on the other hand -

- the workers may win, perhaps to replace casual labor by regular employment with paid annual holidays, superannuation, and no dismissal without good cause.

The 'perhaps' in the last two items is necessary. Questions of casual or permanent employment and attempts to regulate casual employment can occasion significant industrial conflict and policy-making, so you should know how to investigate them. It has often been true that employers favored casual employment and workers wanted permanent employment, but the preferences and the effects on the distribution of income are not regular enough to justify a rule of thumb. An example follows.

Example: the building trades

Follow some big and some small builders through three generations. Treat the story as easy reading rather than hard learning for two reasons. It is here to illustrate the general need for local knowledge of industrial relations, not the details of the building business. And it is a compound of different national histories rather than an accurate account of any one.

1950

Big builders build big buildings – office blocks, apartment towers, shopping complexes, factories. A big builder has capital equipment (excavators, concrete mixers, cranes) and employs a permanent team of the skilled tradesmen required in big construction. In most regions a few big builders compete for the work, but competition and the volume of demand tend to adjust their numbers to the amount of available work, and they manage to keep their teams busy most of the time. Their employees belong to unions which negotiate their wage rates nationally with the builders' national association. The builders' teams are reasonably stable, and cooperative with one another. They don't love their employers much. But they feel secure, enjoy the company at work, are proud of the tough and dangerous work they do, and are not too greedy. Their incomes average close to the national median income.

Small builders mostly build houses, or repair, modernize and add to them. They get plumbing and electrical work from independent tradesmen, but employ their own teams of bricklayers, carpenters, plasterers and painters. Like the big builders they adjust their competitive tenders to get a fairly continuous flow of work, so that when the brickies are on one job the carpenters can be on another and the plasterers, tilers and painters on others. If they are temporarily short of contracts, some of them keep their teams occupied by building spec houses for sale. They tend to be more anxiously competitive than the big builders, and some of them drive their workers hard. But the teams are small, usually friendly with each other, and if they have competent employers they are fairly securely employed. They are union members and work for nationally negotiated rates.

1970

Small builders Twenty years of the long boom have revolutionized the small builders' organization. With very full employment, and skills scarce because it takes long apprenticeships to develop them, building workers do well. But those in the wage-earning trades observe that the independent contractors – plumbers, electricians and some others – are able to raise their prices a bit farther and faster than the nationally-negotiated wage rates can be pushed up. So the wage-earners have gone independent too, and now operate individually or in small groups as sub-contractors. Though their incomes have risen, building costs have not, chiefly for two reasons. With a price for each job, they are motivated to work faster than they did as wage-earners. And now that the builders have few employees of their own, they don't have to pay for any idle time between jobs, and there have been some cost-cutting technical improvements. It is an efficient industry, though anxiously competitive for the builders, who go bust more often than the workers suffer unemployment. For the workers it is also a happy industry: they are doing well, they enjoy their independence, and most of them enjoy their skills and are proud of the houses they build.

Big builders have had a similar revolution for different, chiefly technical, reasons. The plant and equipment they use has become more elaborate and expensive. There are ready-mixed concrete plants and transporters, pre-cast panel factories, very big excavators and cranes, new systems of scaffolding and formwork. No one builder can afford to own much of the new gear, because it needs to be kept in continuous use to pay for itself. So specialist firms own it, employ its operators, and work for all the building contractors as needed. Like the small builders, the big builders who compete for the prime contracts have ceased to employ big numbers themselves. They chiefly plan, organize and pay for other firms' contributions to the buildings for which they are responsible. And whichever builder submits the best tender and wins the prime contract for a big building, much the same subcontractors and workforce will actually build it. There is thus an unusual combination of competition and monopoly. There is hot competition to win the prime contract for any new building. The builders who win most contracts are those who are best at planning and dovetailing the various subcontractors' contributions, and at keeping their prices down and shaving their own profit margins. But some of the specialist subcontractors whom they must use are monopolists; they employ workers who are well placed to exploit their monopolist strength; and any one of them can hold up the whole production process. Nevertheless the monopolists and their workers can't raise their prices unreasonably, because of the investors for whom they work. Most of the firms which commission big buildings through the long boom are insurance companies or investment trusts building office buildings or shopping centres to lease to permanent tenants, or they are big firms building their head offices or other permanent premises. Thus the owners intend to occupy the buildings, or to own them permanently as sources of rental income, and they are investing their own money. If the specialist subcontractors push their tender prices too high, or if their workers wait until buildings are half built then demand unreasonable bonuses to finish them, the investors can afford to stick to their contract prices and tough it out. They are not looking to sell the buildings and they are not in debt for them. Delays and strikes cost them money but can't bankrupt them. Since it is well known that they can't be coerced into making supplementary payments, they generally get straightforward work, on time, without strife, at reasonable prices. It is an efficient industry. Many of its workers earn more than before, but that is partly an ordinary effect of economic growth and partly because they have to do

more skilful and demanding work than before.

1990

Big builders are having a rough passage through the office-building boom. What has changed is the type of investor the builders work for. The self-financing permanent investors have been replaced by speculative developers, using money borrowed from dangerously deregulated banks, to put up buildings which they hope to sell as soon as they are finished to permanent investors. That is risky, but they have nothing to lose – only other people's money to lose. They must complete their buildings, find buyers and sell quickly, because their debts are accumulating at interest rates around 15 or 20 per cent. A few months' delay can wipe out their expected profit. A year's delay can take the all-up cost of the development above the price they originally planned to sell it for; and as the glut of office space approaches, those prices are already falling.

In this risky situation the building workers see and grasp an opportunity. They are a tough lot with tough leaders. First they negotiate new rates of pay for each new project, and they push the rates up as the boom continues. Then when each project reaches the point at which its developer and financiers have spent too much to think of abandoning it, the unions find pretexts to push the rates higher. Any building site has some accidents, if only minor ones – so the unions demand additional site allowances, danger money and completion bonuses, and prepare to strike to get them. The developers cannot survive such delays. They ask their banks to finance them to pay the new rates. For fear of worse, the banks do so, i.e. they finance the developer to pay the builder to pay his subcontractors enough to pay the wage bonuses. But there are still delays, because one or other of the subcontractors refuses. For good long-term reasons he does not want to concede the new rates to his permanent employees just to speed this one project. It only takes one subcontractor to hold them all up: if the big crane or the ready-mix drivers or the fire and safety officers strike, nobody can work – but all except the few strikers must continue to be paid.

All parties begin to foresee the likely effects of the office glut. The developers certainly, the builders probably, and the banks possibly will eventually stop paying what they owe. The only sure money is what you can get now – so get it now. Over five years of boom the skilled workers' incomes average about twice the national median income. Prudent workers save up the means of setting up in other occupations when the slump comes. (Buying a truck, a repair shop, or a cab and cab licence, are popular.) These employees have done well through the 1980s not because their union organization is any stronger than it was, but because the investors they work for are more vulnerable than their predecessors were. The employees have tended to do better in proportion as the investors who generate their work have done worse.

Small builders meanwhile have mixed fortunes as demand for house-building and alteration fluctuates after the end of the long boom. When, earlier, the skilled tradesmen ceased to be builders' employees and became independent subcontractors, most of them left their unions. So the unions are doubly weakened. They are weaker bargainers because they represent minorities in their trades. And the bargains they negotiate can't be enforced because so much of the work is now priced by the competitive tendering of independent tradesmen, now underemployed and competing for work by undercutting each others' prices. Those who stay in the industry find it harder than wage-earners do to qualify for the unemployment dole when they lack work. Those who are forced out of the industry to look for work elsewhere go empty-handed or in debt, without the stake money which the big builders' employees can often take with them. In small building in slack times, many casual and contract workers do worse than most wage-earners, and people who buy new houses or alter old ones get good work at low prices. (Is that an efficient industry? How do you balance the benefits to the households who occupy the houses against the human costs for the households who supply the labor to build them?)

In this industry there have thus been times when wage and contract workers did equally well; times when contract workers did better than wage workers; and times when wage workers did better than contract workers, and sometimes better than the investors and builders who employed them. Other variations could be found in other industries. A conclusion: workers can probably get better income shares as union-organized wage earners more often than they can do better as casual or contract workers. But there are enough exceptions to make it necessary to know the facts of each case, rather than to apply a general preference for either principle.

A methodological choice

I advised you not to think of employment as a 'labor market' because that image of it prompts mistakes about how it works. This summary of earlier arguments about wage-fixing systems can end with a reminder of some main ways in which employing workers is unlike buying carrots – i.e. is unlike a normal market relation

despite the existence of demands for labor, supplies of labor, and prices for labor.

1. Most people of working age don't regard work as pain and pay as the main reason for doing it. They want the work, the human company at work, and what both do for their competence and self-respect and interest in life, at least as much as they want the pay, or the leisure which the pay finances. (That doesn't stop them looking for the best pay they can get for the sort of work they like to do.)

2. Some work is unpleasant. But of the jobs which comply with rich countries' health and safety regulations, very few are regarded by most workers as nastier than not working at all. The past history of full employment, and current surveys of unemployed people, indicate that very few – one or two per cent of the workforce at most – prefer unemployment on the dole to working, even at unpleasant jobs which pay little more than the dole.

3. High proportions of people who are rich enough to live well without earning also choose to work and earn, or sometimes to work for charities without earning. (If you doubt either poor or rich people's preference for work, revise Robert Lane, *The Market Experience,* recommended earlier.)

4. Carrots of equal quality tend to fetch the same price whoever supplies them. But over much of the labor 'market', wage rates are determined by power – class, gender or racial power – as well as, or instead of, by the supply and demand for labor. Employers have been known to buy exactly the same work at five different prices, depending on whether they employed white men, white women, black men, black women, or illegal immigrants. Discrimination can affect both the structure of wages (women's occupations are paid less than men's) and the individual distribution of income (women may be paid less than men for the same work in the same occupation). So we will return to this subject when studying which people get which incomes.

5. The supply of work does not obey the 'laws' of supply and demand. Historically, rising prices for labor have reduced the supply of it. Falling prices sometimes increase the demand for it. Remember the alternative income effects and substitution effects which help to account for this. Men were reducing their lifetime hours of paid work through most of the twentieth century (until harder times allowed some employers to reverse the trend, especially in the US

since about 1980). Since mid-century, women have been increasing their paid hours. Both sexes may be discovering the lifetime hours of paid work, leisure and retirement that they like best. The relation between labor price and total labor supply may then cease altogether, with prices merely helping to attract people to particular occupations. But those workers' preferences may not prevail in the absence of union strength or full employment. Employers have lately been increasing their market and bargaining strength. In the United States and elsewhere they are demanding and getting two or three more weekly hours from full-time workers than they did twenty years ago. The same strength has enabled them to drop the real wage rates of the lowest-paid third or so of workers. When they do that, some workers welcome longer hours, to maintain their real incomes – i.e., a lower price increases the willing supply of work, as it would not do to the supply of carrots.

6. Labor markets rarely clear. When there is strong demand for labor, its price may rise if it is not restrained by income policy. But when demand for labor declines during recessions, labor rarely lowers its price; and if it does, that is as likely to reduce the demand as to increase it. Why? Because wage cuts reduce spendable income. That reduces household spending on capital and consumer goods. Output and investment respond by declining, so employment declines. It may decline further if government responds to falling tax revenues by reducing public investment and services too. Thus in most circumstances any general wage-cutting tends to reduce demand for labor and increase unemployment. (But don't be too quick to reverse the signs – unjustified wage increases may do more to inflate prices than to increase the demand for labor.)

7. Some of those who believe that lowering labor's price will increase the demand for it do not have such general wage-cutting in mind. They expect that additional demand for labor will appear if the unemployed alone lower their labor price. Some theorists are so sure of it that they describe all unemployment as 'voluntary'.

There are ethical, theoretical and practical objections to that belief:

Ethics It cannot be right for rich societies to pay their poorest workers even less than they do now, unless that is the only effective way to reduce unemployment.

Theory There is no reason to expect that unemployed people who offer to work for less than the prevailing minimum wage will find new jobs created in response to the offer of cheap labor. They are at least as likely to displace existing workers in industries which can use quick-changing, casual or unskilled workers; or employers in those industries will use the threat of displacement to reduce the wages of their existing employees. Thus wage cuts at the bottom of the pyramid will spread some way upwards, with the downward effects on total employment and wage income sketched above. Those effects are likely to subtract more jobs than are added by any additional car-washing, lawn-mowing and domestic service that the unemployed may be able to find by offering to work for less than before.

Practice The undeveloped countries with the world's lowest wages have most of its highest unemployment (or underemployment, in peasant economies). The non-communist countries with the flattest wage distributions and the highest minimum wages – Sweden, Australia for a long period, and until recently Japan – have had the world's lowest unemployment. Some theorists nevertheless argue that the comparatively low unemployment in the US is caused by the continuing decline of unskilled and low-skilled wages. There is evidence against that belief, but the argument belongs in a later chapter on employment.

A conclusion So much practical harm has been done by the belief that work is like carrots and obeys the laws of supply and demand, so that raising its price will usually increase the supply of it and reducing its price will increase employers' demand for it, that it may be worthwhile to emphasize a main conclusion of Chapter 32 by repeating it in full. I believe that relations between employers, their employees, the labor costs of production and the distribution of wage income can be understood better without the idea of a 'labor market' than with it. Work does resemble marketable goods in some ways – I can trade you some work for some money, and there may well be a going rate for the job, or 'labor price'. But work is unlike market goods in other respects. It is something I do for you. I usually have to be there to do it. I may have to concede you some power over me, to tell me what to do and how to do it. Or if I am skilled, you may hire me to show you, or other workers, how to do it. And (depending on the nature of the work) you may have to trust me to do it properly when nobody is watching me. Thus we have technical relations, power relations, relations of trust or distrust, and perhaps personal and social relations, as well as our market exchange relations. We may also adjust our behavior according to how long we want our relations to continue. To single out the element of market exchange from all the rest – as if working for you was no different from selling you carrots – may not be the best way to understand either the whole relation between us, or the market element which is part of that whole relation.

TRANSFERRED INCOMES

What follow are short notes of things learned already, or yet to come. They are here because an account of the distribution of income would be incomplete if it omitted income transfers. Depending which transfers in money or kind you choose to count, they are between 25 and 55 per cent of all incomes. Our main discussions of them are in other chapters. Here are merely reminders.

Private transfers

This is another name for unearned property incomes in the private sector. (Most giving or sharing of income between individuals belongs later in a section on household transfers.)

Unearned income – meaning rent, interest and dividends received as 'passive' property income – has sometimes been distinguished from earned income to be taxed at higher or lower rates. But the purpose of this present note about it is philosophical or (conservative critics may think) mischievous. It is to remind you which people work for their money and which people don't. Questionable value judgments shape the common classification of incomes as (i) property incomes, (ii) earned incomes, and (iii) transferred incomes. It would be equally reasonable to combine the first and third in a single category called 'transferred incomes' or 'unearned incomes', meaning incomes for which you don't have to do paid work. Government provides transfer incomes to some groups of people, and requires private citizens to pay transfer incomes to other groups. For example family law requires parents to support their children. Property law empowers landlords to take some of their tenants' income and lenders to take some of their borrowers' income. Passive capital owners merely allow productive people to use their property. Many of them don't do any more in exchange for their incomes than old age pensioners do in exchange for their unearned incomes. Property rights and pension rights are both created by government, and entitle people to receive income without working for it.

Why quibble like this about how incomes are classified? It may be worth doing to bring concealed assumptions into the open. For example some taxpayers think of their contribution to other people's pensions as charity, and believe that income transfers to sole parents and the unemployed support sluts and layabouts who might well be moral and industrious citizens if the welfare state did not offer them regular money for doing nothing, or worse than nothing. When you meet those beliefs it is reasonable to consider alternatives to their factual and moral assumptions. Focus, for example, on who work and earn and who don't. Passive owners receive their incomes as an effect of property law. Sole parents receive them for caring for children. Most aged parents have earned and paid taxes to finance others' pensions through their working years. Most unemployed have likewise earned and contributed taxes to others' support, and will again as soon as the economy can employ them. Of the four groups only the property owners and a minority of the unemployed get their incomes without having worked for them.

None of this need deter you from believing that property is a necessary condition of economic productivity and civilized life, or that present arrangements to support the old and unemployed could be improved. But it is right to remember that all these income transfers are made by political choice.

Public transfers

Transfers to aged and invalid pensioners, unemployed, lone parents, veterans and others provide the main incomes of about 25 per cent of the people who receive money incomes in developed democracies. We could describe a range of national distributions in this descriptive chapter, then discuss their merits in the following policy chapter. But it is easier to combine the two, and public income transfers are such 'pure' policy matters that it is convenient to deal with facts and policies together in the next chapter.

Household transfers

Transfers of income in money or kind provide the main incomes of about 30 per cent of people, including almost all children.

A household's whole real income consists of -

- the money income which one or more household members receive as property income, earned income, public transfer income or from any other source
- income in kind from public services
- income in kind from the household's own output,

using household labor and household and public capital

How the money income, the household labor and the household output were shared or distributed within the household used to be left to the household, except in extreme cases of cruelty or neglect. In most pre-democratic societies the law did more to reinforce the power of the head of the household than to protect its other members from that power. In male-headed households the women's and children's rights, freedoms and shares of income depended more on affection, custom and religious belief than on law or government.

In Western societies through the nineteenth and twentieth centuries democratic government, the women's movement and economic growth have together done a good deal to change the distribution of rights and power within households. Some of the more important changes don't directly concern income: women and children have some better protection against violence, women have acquired the same rights as men to sue for divorce, and governments have begun in a few cases to enforce the long-neglected prohibition of incest, especially against fathers. But a number of the reforms do affect the distribution of wealth and income within households, and when households break up, within families. With variations from country to country –

- Married women can own property and command any income they earn, as most of them could not in earlier centuries. (Only widows could, in many countries.)

- Spouses, and sometimes children, have rights to specified shares of property, and sometimes income, when households or marriages break up.

- Spouses have a legal obligation to provide material support, including money income in some circumstances, to each other and to their children.

- Those rights to income are often unenforceable if the only way to enforce them is by civil action, i.e. by family members suing each other in court. So in some circumstances, governments intervene directly. They take neglected or maltreated children from their parents and have them cared for in public institutions or by foster parents. When absent parents fail to transfer income to the parents who care for their children, governments have sometimes helped with the legal costs and enforcement of civil actions for maintenance. But increasingly, and more effectively, governments pay the required income transfer to the carer then recover it from the absentee (if they can find him or her) when collecting income tax.

- There is better regulation than there used to be of the wages and working conditions of live-in domestic servants, who are in many ways household members whose real incomes depend on distribution within their households.

Have those measures improved the justice and humanity with which income is distributed within households? Or have some of them merely reduced the effects of increasing domestic violence, divorce, family breakdown, and child abuse and neglect? Where too little is known about the facts of family life in the past, it is hard to tell. But the new measures certainly do something to reduce the damage which would now be occurring without them. And they draw attention to an important sector of income distribution – the distribution within households – which economists and national accounts have generally ignored.

WHAT DETERMINES WHICH PEOPLE GET WHICH INCOMES?

You have been studying what determines the pattern of incomes – the different incomes of managers and laborers, skilled and unskilled, employed and unemployed. Next, what determines which people get which of the incomes? But first there is a question which belongs in both discussions.

Do unequal individual skills determine the pattern of incomes?

No. Different individual qualities may determine who get which jobs, but they rarely determine how much the different jobs pay, or the scale of any inequalities. Income is distributed more unequally than are physical strength, measured intelligence, years of education and training, or hours or intensity of work. It is often distributed more equally than individual productivity – the discoverers of atomic power, bacteria and antibiotics, digital computing, the means of genetic engineering, and others whose work created whole new industries, were paid much the same as many judges and airline pilots whose productivity remains low for technological reasons. Some freelances (writers, film directors, pop singers) may be paid according to the output they can sell. But for most wage-earners, what happens is that their individual qualities equip them to compete for jobs whose rates of pay are determined by many other things besides the individual qualities they call for. So small individual differences can occasion big differences of income. Examples:

- A firm's divisional managers compete for appointment as its chief executive. Their capacities are much the same, they might do the job equally well. But the one who gets the job earns twice as much as those who don't.

- At the other end of the same firm's wage range, some unemployed people compete for the firm's lowest-paid job. Their capacities are much the same, they could all do the job satisfactorily. The one who gets it earns twice as much as the unemployment dole which the rest receive (if they qualify for it).

- Two finance companies have equally competent boards of directors. Each board is tempted to double its own pay by big, concealed, tax-evasive superannuation benefits, which are probably lawful but certainly unethical. One group is only a shade less honorable than the other – but that small margin of venality enables them to introduce the scheme and take twice as much income as the other group does.

Thus (1) different occupations reward different skills and personal qualities, and (2) occupations vary widely in how unequally they reward the different qualities and levels of competence that they employ. Senior jumbo pilots may earn twice as much as new captains do, though they fly identical planes with identical skills. The busiest and laziest professors may earn the same though they do the same work with very different skill and success. The most successful novelists (whom not everyone thinks are the best novelists) may earn a hundred times as much as most Nobel-prize-winning novelists do.

Despite such variations, there remain a mass of wage-earning occupations with modest differentials for skill, experience and responsibility, in which the differentials serve useful incentive purposes and reward real differences of performance. Many of those occupations have been, and in some countries some still are, subject to general bias in recruitment, promotion and rates of pay on grounds of sex, race, religion or nationality. Apart from that sort of discrimination, what conditions and processes commonly determine, for most of the population, which individuals get which incomes? In general terms we can list at least the following.

Inheritance of physical, mental and temperamental qualities. Those natural endowments affect the competition for some jobs (professional basketballer, virtuoso violinist, mathematical physicist) much more than the competition for others.

Upbringing Different families endow their children with different health, psychological security, confidence or lack of it, and personal and social values and aspirations. Children's hobbies, recreations and experience of family and household life can give them particular skills, and also make them like or dislike learning and using new skills. Parents often influence the amount and kind of post-compulsory or vocational education that children want and can afford.

Education National systems vary in the equal or unequal educational chances that they offer to richer and poorer children. What chiefly matter are (1) whether there are dual systems of public and private schooling, with most students who can afford private schools attending them; (2) whether free public schools vary much in quality because of the segregation that occurs in class-structured suburbs; (3) whether universities and other tertiary institutions charge fees, and (4) whether public transfer incomes are available to students whose parents can't or won't support them through their student years.

Some occupations have job-specific educational requirements: to do the work, there are things you must learn beforehand. Other occupations use educational qualifications simply as 'sorters', to decide which competitors to admit to the occupation's entry jobs or training opportunities. Where the education has no direct relevance to the occupation's work, the rising educational qualifications are sometimes criticized as 'qualificationism' and a waste of resources. Do general educational qualifications (as opposed to job-specific knowledge) help or hinder the justice and efficiency with which occupations distribute their jobs and incomes? There is disagreement -

- *Against 'irrelevant' qualifications:* They raise educational barriers against poorer children, especially in countries in which poorer children have poorer schools, there are fees for higher education, and there are no public living allowances for students from families with low incomes. Even if such students can support themselves with part-time work they are disadvantaged in academic competition with students who can afford to give their whole time to academic work. And functionally unnecessary education has unnecessary public and private costs.

- *In favor of 'irrelevant' educational qualifications:* (1) Where people compete for entry to desirable occupations academic tests may be fairer and more efficient than the alternative methods of selection might be. Academic tests can be impersonal, proof against favoritism. A lot of research has also found them to be better than alternative methods of selection, or predictors of occupational success, even where they are unrelated to the work of the occupation concerned. (They're not very good selectors, but the alternatives are usually worse, though research has found some exceptions.) (2) As economic growth means that more people can afford more years of formal education, law and custom come to require many people to have more education than they might otherwise choose. Much of it is not vocational; it enriches the general skill and culture, and perhaps creativity, of society. And it prevents vocational requirements from crowding out too much of the time and opportunity for general education.

Career choices The higher the skills that an occupation requires, the likelier it is that its workers will spend their working lives in it. Where the skills are specific not just to the occupation but to particular firms or jobs, there is often comparatively stable employment as firms hoard the workers they have trained, and workers value the jobs which pay them more than other employers would pay them. Other occupations are riskier as changing technology or competitive conditions call for changing skills and conditions of employment. It follows that people's career choices, taken when they leave school, or earlier when they choose their school subjects, can do more than anything else to determine their lifetime incomes.

Career choices are restricted by the occupations available in the national or local economy, and by jobseekers' qualifications, and competition for limited educational and job opportunities. Many people's preferences reflect aspirations developed in family and school life, sometimes with vocational guidance. They don't all try for the highest-paying occupations open to them. As long as the income prospects look reasonable, they are not the dominant consideration in most people's career choices. The nature and interest of the work, its likely job security, the likely company at work, and for some the social value or moral satisfaction of the work, seem to be at least as important.

Performance at work Once people are in their chosen occupations, their performance may do most to determine their progress from job to job, and up the ladders of promotion and income. But for technical reasons, occupations vary widely in their promotional and competitive opportunities. In some occupations

there is not much room for better or worse performance because everyone's performance has to be perfect. Rail signallers, big crane drivers and airline pilots must simply do it right: there's no better way to do it, and any worse way kills people. If there is promotion it is probably by seniority, or by a change of occupation from exercising the skill to managing those who exercise it. Other occupations have more scope for better and worse performance, and competition for advancement. In others, performance earns rewards in a direct market way from the sales of musicians' records, writers' books, producers' films. But wherever appointments, promotions and rates of pay depend on employers' judgments – and sometimes when they depend on fellow-workers' or customers' judgments – the judgments may reflect prejudices or coercive strength instead of, or as well as, the supply and demand for labor and the quality of the candidates' performance.

Discrimination

This should have double interest for economists. Discrimination affects the efficient use of human resources and the distribution of income. And its economic effects cast doubt on some branches of economic theory, or limit their useful application.

Discrimination means treating similar people differently for improper or irrelevant reasons. It can include

- paying different people different rates for similar work

- barring some groups of people from educational opportunities and from particular occupations

- preferring some groups to others for appointments and promotions for reasons which are irrelevant to their working performance

- allowing some groups better access than others to public services

- segregating some groups from others in schools, in public transport, or in residential areas.

Slavery is the extreme kind of discrimination. Governments legalized it, and eventually abolished it. There has been official or informal discrimination against particular races, ethnic groups, religions, young people, old people, and others. But to exemplify the methods and effects of economic discrimination we will focus on discrimination against women, which is the kind that has probably affected most people in human history. And because it has important implications for theories of the labor 'market', it is worth treating at some length.

Two hundred years ago in most western countries, women with living fathers or husbands could not own property. Slave women were their masters' property. Free women were still legally bound to obey their fathers or husbands in most things that mattered. Women were obliged to have sex when their husbands wanted it, most had no effective means of contraception, and for most there was no divorce. Women were barred from the armed forces, the civil service, the universities, and the learned professions including the priesthood. In their own households they worked for their keep at child-bearing and housework or farm work. Many worked as servants in other households for little more than their keep. Those who worked at textile and clothing trades, in coal mines or in other occupations that were open to them as farm laborers, shopkeepers, cooks, waiters and cleaners, were commonly paid less than men earned for the same work.

Some women in those conditions may have lived no worse than their men did. Many peasant households shared their work, comforts and hardships – except childbirth – fairly enough. Recent research finds that some poor women in sixteenth century England – especially lone women wanting control of their property and children – had surprisingly good access to surprisingly humane courts. Middle and upper class women in seventeenth and eighteenth century England often got some education, and equal shares of inheritance with their brothers. From the eighteenth century a few did well as writers and actors, and as theorists in movements for social and political reform. But they were still subject to their husbands' authority, and barred from the universities, the professions, government, the priesthood, and most positions of any power in business. Where they were allowed to earn, their wages were commonly 60 per cent, or less, of men's.

The wage differences might be excused as fair where men's incomes supported more people than women's did – though there were enough single men, and enough working women supporting families, to make many unfair exceptions to that principle. But the discrimination had no economic justification, except for those, mostly men, who benefited from it. It was not a market effect of the supply and demand for men's and women's labor. Women were confined to poor trades, barred from better-paid alternatives, lacked some important civil rights, and accepted pay differentials which were established and enforced without regard to relative productivity. If they had living fathers or husbands they needed permission to earn, and did not own their earnings. Altogether their employment and earning opportunities were determined less by market forces than by male power reinforced by custom, (male) law and (male) religious authority.

Change came with economic growth and democratic government, but it came very slowly as long as democracy meant votes for men only. Through the nineteenth century women and children were withdrawn from some dangerous occupations. Some countries began to regulate their hours and conditions of work in some trades. Married women got the right to own property, and their own earnings. Countries which allowed civil divorce allowed it (for the first time) for women on the same grounds as for men. Outside England women were admitted to universities and some professions, though it was a long time before many of them rose high or earned very much in the professions. At the end of the nineteenth century – a century of male democracy over much of the Western world – they still averaged less than two thirds of men's pay for equivalent work. Serious economic progress began only after they achieved political equality.

Women got the legal right to vote by mistake in New Jersey in 1776 when its revolutionary constitution was carelessly worded to enfranchise 'persons'. They did not exercise it, and lost it thirty years later when the men noticed and corrected their mistake. In the second half of the nineteenth century three American States and three British colonies enfranchised women. Then in the first half of the twentieth century almost all the democracies did: Australia in 1902, Britain in 1918 and 1928, Germany in 1919, the United States in 1920, France in 1944. Through the third quarter of the century two other processes accelerated. The technical revolution in household equipment extended to all but the poorest households, making their women both more productive at home and freer to go out and earn. And the women's movement persuaded rising numbers of both sexes to revolutionize their understanding of women's productive capacities and economic rights.

With help from technology, power and ideology, reform quickened. The public services were opened to women on equal terms. They made real progress in many of the professions. Women teachers were allowed to marry without losing their jobs or tenure. There were suddenly women judges, professors, medical specialists. Significant numbers entered national politics. India, Israel, Britain, Pakistan, Norway and others elected women Prime Ministers. New laws prohibited private as well as public employers from discriminating on grounds of sex and required equal pay for work of equal value.

But although most Western democracies passed similar laws, they differed in the rates at which they actually progressed toward economic equality. To see how and why, compare the extreme cases. The United States had the most militant feminist action, and some of the earliest and toughest-looking equal opportunity laws, but has done least to equalize women's and men's pay. Australia had less political conflict and more consensual legal changes, and made the fastest progress toward equal pay and opportunity. (West European performance ranged between those two, tending more to the Australian than the American end of the spectrum.)

In the US in 1968 female earnings per hour were 66 per cent of male earnings. The constitutional amendment banning discrimination became law in 1972. Fifteen years later in 1987 the women's ratio had improved by 6 per cent (i.e. 4 percentage points) to be 70 per cent of male earnings. Why such poor compliance with the law? There is no public institution with a duty to determine what kinds of work are of equal value and to enforce equal pay for them; and through most of the private sector there are no unions to take the employers to court to have judges decide the equivalences, and enforce the Constitution.

In Australia in 1968 female earnings per hour were 63 per cent of male. In 1969 the national Conciliation and Arbitration Commission ordered equal pay for equal work and in 1972 it ordered equal pay for work of equal value, to be introduced over three years. By 1976 the women's ratio had risen by 30 per cent (19 percentage points) to 82 per cent of male earnings per hour. The remaining male advantage arises from over-award rates negotiated by the unions in predominantly male occupations, from men working more overtime at overtime rates, and from men occupying a disproportionate number of managerial and other senior jobs. Time will tell whether a 'glass ceiling' will bar women from fair shares of promotion. Few people of either sex reach the top with less than 20 or 30 years of service, and there have scarcely yet been that many years of career-building with equal opportunity. Australian women had reached most of the summits by 1990, but not yet in big numbers.

Thus in relation to men's rates of pay American women gained 6 per cent over fifteen years, and Australian women gained 30 per cent over seven. The difference was plainly caused by the countries' different wage-setting systems: in the terms you met back in Chapter 32, a market model in the US and a government model in Australia. But what does their different performance tell us about the validity of economic theories

which treat employment as a 'labor market'?

Implications for theory In a 1990 discussion paper of the Australian National University, R. Gregory and A. Daly asked 'Can economic theory explain why Australian women are so well paid relative to their US counterparts?' Answer: no, it can't. Australian employers paid the new rates without any of the effects which a market theory of labor would predict. The higher price of women's labor did not reduce the demand for it. There was no increase in female unemployment, no net loss of women's jobs to men. But there had been no market reason – no supply and demand reason – for the traditional difference between men's and women's rates in the first place. In Australia the difference had been determined by judges of the industrial court. In the US it had been determined chiefly by the superior force and bargaining power of employers and male workers, and long-established custom.

If custom, bargaining power or institutional decisions have determined such different rates of pay for work of similar value, neither the higher nor the lower rates can actually have been determined by the marginal worker's contribution to the value of output, as required by market theory. To believe that that determines wages it has always been necessary to ignore the facts of unequal pay for equal contributions to output, and the facts of custom, unequal bargaining power and legal and informal discrimination between people of different gender, race or religion.

The wages which employers have to pay may affect the prices at which they sell their products. The prices they can get for their products may determine the numbers they can employ at prevailing wage rates. But other forces have usually determined what rates prevail.

Other diversities

The above notes have drawn attention to a number of other practical variations in the individual distribution of income. Some jobs reward virtues, some reward vices. Some reward generous or cooperative behavior, some reward selfish or competitive behavior. Some reward reliable, repetitious behavior, others reward surprise and invention. In some occupations it is much easier than in others to get away with lazy, incompetent, unhelpful or dishonest behavior. In some others, service above and beyond the requirements of duty is common.

I believe this text is right to emphasize the diversity of work and wages in this way. It is right because too much economic theory has an opposite bias, assuming too much uniformity in the nature of work, in workers' attitudes to it, and in the principles on which it is rewarded. If you are ever tempted to assume, as some theories do, that most workers – from chief executives to cleaners and from ministers of religion to real-estate salesmen – are alike in that they all -

- dislike their work enough to do it only for the money,

- are paid the value of their marginal contributions to output,

- work best when they are afraid of the sack and are competing most ruthlessly with their fellow-workers for promotion,

I hope you will look around you, and at people you know well, for the real-life diversities of which only a few have been sampled in this chapter.

Nevertheless there remains a lot of common experience in a modern economy's occupations. In many developed economies the working week has arrived at the 35 or 40 hours that most full-time workers seem to like best. Some high proportion of people like their work, the human company at work, and (often) what the work achieves, better than they would like to live on the same income without working. At the same time they want the rate for the job, whatever it is, and are glad if it increases. Many serve their own interests as well as their fellow-workers' and employers' and customers' interests by cooperating willingly with all of them. The highest pay often rewards the best natural talents and acquired skills, long education and training, experience, responsibility, difficult work, and positions of power. But those high rewards tend to be determined at least as much by power, custom, ideas of justice, and institutional choice as by judgments of the earners' marginal contributions to output.

The people who have those highest capacities tend to use them for purposes of three kinds. They use them to get the top jobs. They use them in many cases to do those jobs well, which serves many interests besides their own. And varying proportions of them also use their power and skill to increase the rewards of those top jobs. To the extent that they succeed in that third purpose I should revise one simplifying assumption of this chapter: the assumption that one set of causes determines the structure of jobs and incomes, then other causes determine which individuals get which of the incomes. In fact some of the forces at work belong in both sets. The qualities which get individuals into the most powerful jobs are then used to get those jobs more income than can be explained by differences of natural talent and acquired skill, of training time and costs, or of incentives to work hard at difficult work. The qualities which get the best workers to the top then help to get

many of them more pay than necessary – more than the minimum which would sufficiently attract them to such jobs. That margin of inequality is inefficient by almost any test of efficiency. More equal pay, besides being fairer, could also be more efficient as most economists define efficiency.

SUMMARY

This is a summary of this chapter's account of forces which shape national patterns of incomes and their individual distribution.

A methodological reminder You know that causal analyses of complex social effects can't always be sure about the relative force of many of the contributing causes, or their interaction with one another. And they have to be purposeful selections from the innumerable conditions and processes which have contributed to particular effects. In this case the effects are patterns of income and their distribution to particular occupations and individuals, and the purpose is to help us to judge (1) how inevitable or not, and how desirable or not, the present distribution is, (2) how public policies affect it, and (3) whether different policies might improve it.

The amount of income is determined by, among other things –

- the available natural resources

- the accumulated stock of physical capital, and the productivity of the technology which it incorporates

- the society's human capital, and the processes by which households and educational, cultural, governmental and business institutions instil and sustain the people's productive aspirations and capacities

- the institutional arrangements and the skills with which those resources are organized and managed for productive purposes

- the quality and stability of the society's political and cultural life

- the security and economic value of the society's international relations

And we should add 'the distribution of income', because how income is distributed can have strong effects on how much of it is produced.

Property income The amount and distribution of property income is determined by, among other things –

- the composition of the society's natural and capital resources, and the proportions of them which are in private profit-seeking ownership

- the prevailing rates of return to capital: rates of profit and dividend, rates of interest and levels of rent.

Those rates of return may be affected by, among other things –

*   the supply and demand for capital and labor, and their marginal productivity, in particular industries
*   the relative market strength of producers and consumers, and the degrees and kinds of competition, which can affect price levels in particular industries
*   the relative bargaining power of employers and employees, i.e. of the owners of physical and human capital, in dividing the income which they jointly produce.

Individuals acquire property, or indirect rights to property income, by –

*   individual business success, often with quick capitalization of firms' new earning capacities
*   individual success in some arts and entertainments whose technology allows reproduction for mass markets
*   directors' acquisition of capital from their firms
*   saving from high earnings
*   saving through funded superannuation schemes
*   inheritance, marriage and other gifts
*   the accumulation of existing wealth by capital appreciation or saving from property income
*   gambling on share values, real estate values, foreign exchange rates, future commodity prices, lotteries and pools, casino games, horse races, etc.
*   corruption and crime.

Earned income is determined in partly-different ways in different occupations, and by workers in different types of employment.

*   Working capital owners include –
    *   farmers, who supply competitive markets often at fluctuating prices. Their net incomes may depend on their indebtedness, on changing world prices, on other countries' trade policies, and on whether they have any trade protection or subsidies, or collective marketing or price-stabilizing arrangements
    *   small business owners, who range from price-takers in competitive markets to monopolists or near-monopolists in very local markets
*   freelances, who range from pop millionaires to penniless craft potters

*   self-employed professionals whose incomes may vary with their individual competence and collective marketing strength, with their clients' capacity to spend public, corporate or insurance money, and with the public regulation or the self-regulation under which they work. (The differences between the professions' average individual incomes, and between their internal inequalities, can't be sufficiently explained by supply and demand, or training times and costs, or productivity.)
*   company directors determine their own pay, collectively and individually, within some legal and customary constraints, and have lately been increasing it faster than any other salaried group
*   wage-earners' rates of pay may be influenced by -
    *   the national choice of wage-fixing system
    *   the supply and demand for labor, and its marginal productivity, in particular industries
    *   the monopolist or other pricing strength of particular industries
    *   government policy, where government is the employer or owns the employer
    *   any prevailing discrimination by gender, race, religion, etc.
    *   the relative bargaining power of employers and employees
    *   negotiators' or arbitrators' decisions where wages are fixed by central negotiation or arbitration.

The more central the wage-fixing system, and the higher the proportion of all wage-earners it covers, the higher and more equal the pattern of wages tends to be. Through the third quarter of the twentieth century, countries with centrally negotiated 'high and flat' wage distributions had fuller employment than countries like the US with greater wage inequalities. Reducing the lowest wage did not get everyone employed and 'clear the labor market'. Through the fourth quarter, some of the flat distributions coincided with high unemployment. So did some of the most unequal distributions. Other things besides wage levels contribute to determining the amount of unemployment.

*   casual and part-time workers are paid more than full-time rates per hour in some occupations and less in others. There is some tendency to pay them more in higher-paid occupations (some consultant economists earn more than salaried economists do) and less in lower-paid occupations (piece-rate garment workers often earn less per piece or per hour than wage-earning garment workers do) – but there are

many exceptions. There is also great diversity in the desirability of casual and part-time employment. Many workers like it because they want to work less than full time, or to their own timetables. Many dislike it, because they want full time work and job security.

Income transfers for welfare and other purposes are determined in a variety of ways.

- Private income transfer is another way of describing the payment of dividend, rent and interest to passive owners of capital who don't have to work for their property incomes. The mixtures of market and public influence that determine the rates of rent and interest are discussed in chapters on real estate and capital markets and national financial policies.

- Public income transfers are determined in ways to be discussed in the following chapter on income policies.

- Household and family income transfers are determined in most cases by patterns of power, affection, custom and morality within families. There is some public regulation of the distribution – less while families stay together, more when they break up.

Which people get which incomes may be determined by –

- inheritance of mental and physical capacities, family values and aspirations, a family farm or business, other property

- career choices and the dates at which they are made

- how education and training are supplied and paid for, and the extent to which individuals' access to higher education and professional and trade training does or does not depend on their own or their parents' willingness and capacity to pay their educational and living costs

- the particular types of inherited and acquired ability, and behavior or misbehavior, which particular occupations and employers reward

- how well people work once they are employed

- sexual, ethnic, racial, religious or other discrimination or favoritism in recruitment and promotion

- luck

- crime and corruption.

EXERCISE

The next chapter is about income policies: what government's role should be in influencing the whole pattern and inequality of incomes; what pattern of public income transfers would be best; and how incomes can be restrained to restrain inflation. To get you into a policy-making frame of mind, turn back to the beginning of the chapter summary you just read. Go through it again, considering each dotted item under each subheading. As far as you can, ask and answer three questions of each item:

- Does it indicate a necessary or possible role for government?

- If so, what range of choice does it offer in practice to government?

- What effects (if any) on the item can be expected of present government policies, and of any alternative policies which you think are worth considering?

45

Income policies

Governments influence the distribution of income for a number of public purposes.

- *Costs of government* Government has to be paid for. Any way of financing modern big government must have strong effects on the general distribution of income.

- *Justice* At its best, government pays, regulates, transfers and taxes incomes to produce a fair and compassionate distribution of income. There is always disagreement about the most desirable distribution, so it may be more realistic to say that government aims at a tolerable distribution – one which does whatever is politically possible to reduce the worst of the pain, inequality and unfairness that can result from unregulated competition for income.

- *Efficiency* The distribution and taxation of income can affect incentives to work, spend, save and invest. So governments operate on the distribution of income in the course of their efforts to restrain inflation and contrive growth, employment, export/import balances, environmental care and other national effects.

Growth, stability and full employment in turn affect the amount and distribution of income. The distribution can also be affected by particular directions of growth, and by the particular means by which governments try to control inflation and unemployment. Thus efforts to improve the fairness of the distribution can also affect its efficiency; efforts to improve its efficiency can affect its fairness. And as you well know, ideas of efficiency and fairness are open to honest disagreement.

That is one thing that complicates the simple pursuit of a fair and efficient distribution of income. Another is the relation between public purposes and private interests. Income and tax policies affect people's fortunes very directly, and tax politics can be intense. How do the public purposes of income policies fare if people simply vote to cut taxes or shift them onto other incomes than their own?

Some 'public choice' economists depict government as a marketplace in which everyone is strictly self-interested, and politicians simply trade favors (public services, tax cuts, defence contracts) for support (votes,

campaign funds, bribes, media support). There are strong elements of that in democratic politics. But they rarely dominate, to the exclusion of shared social purposes and ideas of justice. It is significant that even the most selfish groups commonly depict their interests as public interests, and try to link them to acceptable principles of justice. It is right to be sceptical of such claims, but it is significant that they are made. Every special interest has to seek majority support, or at least tolerance, for its proposals, and disinterested majorities don't willingly support policies which strike them as unreasonable or unfair. When the conflicts are between minorities, which many are, a majority of voters are disinterested, and prone to vote for what they see as public interests, or fair principles. And for many people, those principles also distinguish the legitimate from the illegitimate among their own material interests - as Adam Smith believed that most prople do, most of the time. So in peaceful democracies the warring self-interests are quite strongly constrained by prevailing ideas of fairness and common purpose. This chapter is not unrealistic in dealing chiefly with the public purposes of income policies. It will survey in turn -

- the main kinds of property income: dividends, rent, interest, capital gain

- the main kinds of earned income: wages, self-employed and freelance earnings

- income from crime

- public income transfers in cash and kind

- the home-made, non-cash income that people produce for themselves.

For each type of income we sketch a range of policies to be found in developed democracies, plus some as yet untried alternatives, with notes on the pros and cons of each.

The advantages and disadvantages of some of the policies vary with the conditions in which they are used and the strategies of which they are part. So there is some overlap between this treatment of income policies and later discussion of national economic strategies. And where you have met the arguments before, for example about four ways to fix wages, you may need to turn back and revise them; this chapter offers only brief reminders.

A concluding summary of the chapter would thus be listing many of its themes for a third or fourth time.

Instead, it ends with reminders of the most basic and troublesome philosophical questions about desirable equalities and inequalities.

PROPERTY INCOME

Government cannot help influencing the private share of wealth, and therefore the whole quantity of property income. It influences them when it decides -

- its public investment programs
- whose physical and financial capital its public services and enterprises will use - for example will it finance its own investments with tax revenue or with borrowed funds? Borrowed from public or private banks? Will it own its buildings and vehicles or lease them from private owners?
- which public services it will privatize altogether
- what market enterprises it will own (coalmining? steelmaking? railways? airlines?) and whether it will allow private competition in those industries
- how it will help or hinder farm ownership by farmers or landlords, and home ownership by households or landlords
- what pensions or superannuation will retired people have?
- the many wage, price, industrial and other policies which influence wage and profit shares and rates of interest and rent, and therefore the amount of property income, in the private sector.

Those choices affect the amount and distribution of private wealth and property income. But remember how intricately the sectors trade with each other. Public enterprises generate some private property income when they buy inputs from private suppliers. Private enterprises generate some of their income from the use of public capital (roads, information services). Household production and consumption use public capital (roads, telephones, playing fields). So the primary ownership of enterprises does not necessarily determine who owns the financial or physical capital they use, or who draws property income from them. For example when a new hospital is needed, government may decide -

- to build it with tax revenue (which does not generate any private property income) or with loan money (which does)
- to own the building itself (which does not generate private property income) or to lease it from private

investors (which does)

- to equip it to do its own X-ray and pathological testing (which does not generate private property income) or to lease space to private providers of those services (which does)
- to equip hospital employees to clean the hospital (which does not generate private property income) or to have it cleaned by contractors using private equipment (which does).

Public investment Many of the public decisions which affect the amount of property income are taken for other reasons altogether. The last section ('Summary and reminder') of Chapter 37 listed a dozen common reasons for public investment, of which reducing private wealth and property income was only one. It was one of the reasons - though perhaps not the most important - for the British nationalizations of 1945-50 and the French nationalizations of 1936 and 1981. For the many other purposes which may prompt the creation or acquisition of public enterprises, turn back to that summary of Chapter 37.

Privatization The general purposes and merits of public and private enterprise were the subject of Part Four. Here we need only notice the effects of privatization on the distribution of income.

The ostensible reason for selling public assets and enterprises into private ownership has usually been to improve their efficiency. That has sometimes been achieved, sometimes not; and where it has, it has sometimes involved some switch of work from secure public employment to lower paid or less secure contract work, with some increase of unemployment, so that the cost reductions have been at the expense of poorer rather than richer workers. But there have also been other purposes in the minds of the groups who advocate and decide the sales. Many economists expect private owners and managers to allocate and use resources more efficiently than public enterprises do. Many business leaders and financial journalists welcome the sales for similar reasons. Executives of the enterprises (if they have encouraged rather than opposed the sales) keep their jobs and gain greater freedom of action and higher pay. And as a decisive reason for most of the sales, politicians can use the capital returns from the sales for current public spending, and thus reduce the immediate need for taxation. But if the purpose of that is to save the citizens money it is usually improvident. In the short run the citizens pay less tax than they would otherwise pay as private investment funds are diverted from financing new investment to buying existing public assets, and are then dissaved as government spends them, and the citizens spend most of their tax savings. In the long run growth and employment may suffer from that dissaving. The yearly public profits of the sold services, which allowed some permanent tax reduction, go instead as property income to the new private owners, and government has to replace them by additional permanent taxation. Even if the proceeds of the sales are used to reduce public debt, the interest savings are usually less than the lost profits, so the privatization still increases the need for taxation. There may be additional public costs if the sold services are monopolies and new public institutions have to be created to monitor and price-control them now that they are private monopolies.

Thus most privatizations spend some capital on consumption in the short run, and in the long run shift some property income from the population as a whole to the private buyers of the enterprises. If the new managers cut costs by shedding or casualizing some labor there may also be some shift of income from their workers, to be divided between the enterprises' owners, their executives and their customers. How the gains are divided may depend on competitive conditions, the new directors' ethics, and the purpose and effectiveness of any supervision of the privatized activities. And there may be higher taxes, or cuts in other public services, if labor-shedding increases unemployment and that increases the cost of welfare services and income transfers to the unemployed.

Some privatizations are nevertheless sensible. Japan has often created market enterprises in public ownership, developed them until they were established and profitable, then sold them into private ownership. Where they operate in competitive markets they may not need special public supervision; and if (as often in Japan) the proceeds of asset sales are re-invested in other public enterprises, privatization need have no ill effects (unless you think that any shift of property income from public to private owners is regrettable). Governments may have a variety of good reasons for shifting industries or enterprises from one sector to the other, as they adjust the mix of their mixed economies. But the round of privatization that began in the 1980s has too often had the short-term, improvident purposes

and the long-term ill effects described above, and few compensating benefits. That is a conclusion of much of the accumulating research into privatizing and outsourcing traditional public services.

Taxation Life - and economic analysis - would be simpler if dividends, interest and rent (the main forms of property income) were first determined in a market way, and then paid ordinary income tax. But two things wreck that simple prospect. First, those three kinds of income pay no tax if received by firms, because firms pay corporate income tax only on their profits. Second, to meet the costs of modern government and of public income transfers to a quarter or more of the population, the rates of corporate and individual income tax are now high enough to be quite important considerations for owners with capital to invest. So those and other taxes need to be designed not only to raise the necessary revenue, but also to defeat increasingly ingenious methods of tax avoidance, and to have good rather than bad effects on investors' incentives. Some of the following review of dividend, interest and rent policies is accordingly about tax policy.

DIVIDENDS

Shareholders' rewards come as dividend income, as capital gains, or sometimes as new share issues on privileged terms.

Chapter 28 about business powers was too long to summarize here. Revise it if you need to. Legal powers, bargaining strength, market conditions and public regulation together determine how the value which firms add by their productive activity is divided between their owners, directors, workers, customers, and (through taxation) public purposes. When directors have estimated a year's profit and paid company tax on it, there are broadly three ways in which the remaining profit can benefit shareholders:

1. The whole available profit can be paid as dividend. For most shareholders, that is taxable income. If the firm wants funds for further investment it must borrow at interest, or issue new shares.

2. The firm can finance its own growth by investing part of its profit, and pay the remainder as dividend. Shareholders then get part of their benefit as taxable income and part as capital gain. Many countries tax capital gains – but usually at lower rates than they tax high income, and only when the gains are realized, i.e. when the shares are sold or inherited.

3. The firm can invest all its profits, whether in its own growth or in other investments or acquisitions.

Shareholders then get their whole benefit in capital form.

Policy questions

Most successful firms finance most of their growth from their earnings (or from short-term loans repaid from earnings) and also pay moderate dividends. Should tax and other policies encourage or discourage this common practice?

In favor: The practice is simple and cheap. Self-financing avoids the need for perpetual interest payments on debentures or other permanent debts, or the costs and risks of floating new share issues to finance every new investment. Directors like self-financing because it allows confident forward planning, and independence of the capital market. Many share-holders want regular income (so want annual dividends) but also want some capital and income growth as their share of economic growth. Pragmatic economists (of the kind this course of study is designed to educate) generally approve of the practice. It suits those concerned. It helps successful firms to grow with least risk and with low-cost, interest-free capital.

Against: On the Left are some people whose overriding purpose is to reduce material inequalities. They may want all profit to pay company tax. The remainder after that can be divided between re-investment in the company, and dividends on which shareholders pay income tax, which should be at a higher rate than the rate on earned income. There should also be a capital gains tax, or (preferably) an annual tax on all forms of capital wealth.

From the Right come some economists with theoretical objections to the pragmatic strategy recommended above. They assume that capital is likely to be used more productively the more competitively it is allocated, and the less its allocation is distorted by taxation. So competition for the use of available investment funds should be enforced by law: after payment of a low company tax, all profit should have to be paid out as dividend, so that for their capital needs year by year firms must compete for funds in open capital markets (i.e. issue new shares, sell debentures, borrow from banks at ruling rates of interest.). That will prevent directors from reinvesting profits in their own firms if those funds could earn higher returns in other uses, and thus (these theorists assume) do more for national output, and ultimately for everyone's welfare. To make such a system acceptable to shareholders, a system of 'imputation' should provide that company tax paid per share should be subtracted from the income tax paid by each shareholder.

INTEREST

Here is a problem. We are surveying dividend, interest and rent policies. You know about dividends, from studying how firms work. You know about rent from studying housing policy. But interest is yet to come, in chapters on money and banking and national economic strategies, and what you need to know about it is too complicated to summarize in advance for this chapter's purposes.

So accept two bald facts. Governments influence interest rates in the course of their national economic policies. And there is strong disagreement about those policies and their effects. Here, we will merely notice some effects on the distribution of income.

Lenders and borrowers have opposite interests in the rate of interest. Over life, richer people tend to be net lenders and poorer people net borrowers. So – despite individual exceptions – it tends to be true that the higher the rate of interest, the more income passes from poorer to richer people to increase their inequalities.

Some lending is from richer to poorer, as in many home purchase loans, some loans to small business, and much consumer credit. The higher the rate of interest, the more income passes directly from poorer to richer. High interest can also increase inequality by preventing people from borrowing. When it excludes poor house-holds from housing loans, they are likely to pay more rent (over household life) than a housing loan would have cost them, even at quite high interest.

Most business lending is from rich to rich. The lenders tend to be passive owners of money, or share-holders of the banks which create most new money. Where banks are competently regulated the borrowers tend to be productive users of their credit, generating output, employment, or both. The lower the rate of interest they have to pay, the more of those good things they can generally do, and the less income they pay to the passive lenders.

Relations between interest rates and employment are not simple. They vary with other policies. Some theorists want to combat inflation and influence employment and import/export balances chiefly by interest-rate policies which in practice keep interest rates high a good deal of the time. There is some common interest between those economists and the lenders who gain directly from high rates. If strategies which include high interest rates and strategies which include low interest rates were equally effective at restraining inflation and unemployment, I would prefer the low-interest alternative because of its direct effects on the distribution of income. But for reasons argued later I do not think the high-interest strategies are very effective for their purposes. Equality and productivity can both be better served by means which include low and stable interest rates most of the time, and those low rates can –

- reduce the direct transfer of income from poorer borrowers to richer lenders

- enable more and poorer people to own their houses, and avoid parting with a quarter or more of their incomes as house rent throughout their household life

- encourage investment in firms, and investment by firms, to maintain employment.

There could be contrary effects on the distribution of income if funded superannuation became the main source of income for everyone's retirement, i.e. if property income rather than tax revenue had to finance the old age pension. It might still be best to keep interest rates low, for their good effects on investment, employment and home ownership. Superannuation funds could then be biased toward shareholding and rental property rather than interest-bearing investment, as many of them already are.

Inflation complicates these questions. The complications were anticipated earlier, in chapters on housing. They will be set out at painful length in later chapters on money and banking. To explain them a third time here would be a headache too many for both of us. Accept that when inflation prevails, it takes special public action to keep long-term credit accessible to many small businesses and low-income home-buyers, and the policy choices can affect employment and the distribution of income.

RENT

The amount and distribution of rent income follow from –

- the pattern of ownership of the types of property that can be rented – chiefly land, buildings, vehicles and some kinds of equipment

- the distribution of wealth and income, and the credit and other conditions, which determine who can and who cannot afford to buy and own the assets they use

- the market and regulatory conditions which determine the levels of rent

- the tax treatment of rental property and income.

You have met those subjects already. All you need here are some reminders. We will consider policy questions

about rent incomes from public buildings, from private commercial and industrial buildings, from farms, and from public and private rental housing.

Public buildings have traditionally been owner-occupied: governments, public enterprises, churches and universities own their land and buildings. But some cash-strapped governments have lately been questioning that principle. Public buildings can be financed by public or private savings, and they can have public or private owners. Consider the options:

- If public buildings are built with tax revenue, the taxpayers save and invest: they do some forced saving now, and have rent-free use of the building ever after. If they had not paid the relevant tax, they would probably have spent 70 or 80 per cent of the money on consumption, rather than on private saving and investment. So their public saving and investment has added to total national saving and investment.

- Public buildings can be financed by private savings if they are financed by public loans, i.e. by borrowing from private lenders. Over time the loans are then repaid, with interest, from taxation. When the loans are raised (usually by selling bonds) they do not induce people to save more. They chiefly divert private investment funds to finance public investment instead. Over time the citizens' taxes repay the loans, so there is public saving and investment in the end. But it has cost the citizens more than direct public investment would have done, because of the interest income they have paid to the private lenders.

- Many governments continue their debts, repaying one loan by raising another, without ever returning the private capital to the private sector. There is then no public saving or investment. But there is permanent interest to pay, and a permanent increase of taxation to pay it.

- There are similar financial effects if governments lease their office buildings from private owners. Private savings supply the buildings, so the citizens do not have to save to build them. But they must pay more tax to pay a permanent rental income to the private owners. As with perpetual loan finance, it costs them more over time than public saving and investment would cost them.

- Most expensive and improvident of all: Government can avoid some present taxation by selling existing public buildings (or other assets which it needs to keep on using) and leasing them back from their private buyers. It thus receives and dissaves some private capital, because the citizens spend most of their tax cuts on consumption. But they will pay permanently higher taxes to pay rent for the use of the assets they have sold. And unlike the other alternatives, this one neither adds to national investment nor leaves it as it was: it actually reduces it.

• Why do governments do it?

As argued earlier, they do it because they can use the inflow of private capital from the sales to cut taxes now (or to defer necessary tax increases). Political leaders of government and opposition outbid each others' promises of tax restraint. They do not offer honest accounting. They do not say, as they should, 'Less tax now, more tax later'. But they get public support from the interested parties, and from doctrinaire believers in the superiority of private ownership.

What can be done to defend the citizens from that deceptive alliance? Competent economists and financial journalists can do a good deal. There needs to be insistent publication of the actual tax effects, and effects on the distribution of income, of the improvident kinds of asset sales. But the appeal to long-term self-interest may not be the only, or the most effective, corrective. A good political culture should value prudence, public economy, honest accounting and dignified government. Nobody – politician, public servant, economist or journalist – should want to sell public buildings to private profit-seekers, whatever effect the sales might have on this year's consumer spending or next year's general election. Opponents of such sales should perhaps appeal as much to national pride as to financial prudence.

It can be right to rent private space for public activities in particular circumstances, for example if government has a temporary or quick-changing need for office space, if it needs a small office in a city centre, or if public services need public counters in privately owned shopping centres. But for most purposes government does best to own the buildings, vehicles and equipment that it uses, and as far as possible to finance them from revenue, or by borrowing from public banks rather than private lenders.

Business rents There are reasons of three kinds for private enterprises to rent rather than own their business premises, and thus generate rent income for landlords. They are the nature of the business, the capital resources of the business, and tax avoidance. As follows.

Occupational reasons for renting The small shops which line city streets and the malls of modern shopping centres occupy small bits of big buildings, and cannot usually own their premises. The office towers above the city shops house many occupations which need small amounts of space at central locations: lawyers who need offices in reach of public courts, accountants and corporate offices who need to be near to each other, financial agents and brokers of many kinds.

Public and private owners can be equally efficient at designing, financing and managing such buildings, and public owners have occasionally done so, especially in planned new towns and some city reconstructions after war damage. But in most circumstances, building and letting private shops and offices has traditionally been private business. The policy questions which it poses for government are questions of city planning and land-use regulation, civic style, traffic management, fire safety, and so on. They do not much affect the amount and distribution of rent income, so need not be repeated here.

Financial reasons for renting An enterprise which needs land, buildings, vehicles or heavy equipment can buy them with its own money; buy them with borrowed money; or rent them. Enterprises which do not have enough money of their own to buy what they need have two options. Those which cannot borrow enough to buy what they need can only rent. Renting commonly costs more in the long run than the other alternatives (or the landlord would not be in the business). But for many tenants and hirers it is the simplest, easiest, least-risk option in the short run.

In countries which still have some farm landlords, some farmers may be rent-paying tenants because they cannot afford to buy farms. Or it may be because landlords will not sell: they may own their estates for traditional family or class or recreational reasons, or for capital gain, or as a secure kind of long-term investment. Most tenant farmers are worse off than they would be as debt-free owner-occupiers. But they may be better off than indebted owners, especially if their landlords are more forbearing in bad seasons than banks would be, and are generous with capital improvements and maintenance. Risks can be shared more fairly without depending on landlords' generosity if the tenant share-farms, i.e. shares costs and earnings with the landowner on an agreed basis, rather than paying a fixed rent through good seasons and bad.

Other financial reasons can incline businesses to rent rather than buy their premises, especially if they would have to borrow to buy. If interest rates are unstable, so that long-term mortgage loans have unpredictable risks, long-term leases at fixed or indexed rents may be safer. If there is a surplus of the relevant accommodation, rents may fall far enough to make renting cheaper than buying for the time being.

For business premises as well as for housing, the more owner-occupation there is the less rent income there is. We will presently recall the reasons for believing that with housing, the less private renting there is, the better. But does it matter how much or little business renting there is? Some theorists argue that it does not. Given the national stock of land, buildings and equipment, it should not matter how much of that property yields rent income, and how much yields equivalent property income in the form of profit to producers who own rather than rent the property they use. How much property income comes as rent and how much as dividend does not matter: national wealth and income remain the same.

There are two objections to that argument.

First, when landlords as a class have an element of monopoly - of a nation's farmland, or a city's central office buildings - they may be able to add some rent to the costs and selling prices of the enterprises which rent their property. They then do more than merely appropriate some of the property income which owner-occupiers would alternatively gain. By raising the price of space above what owner-occupiers would have to pay for it, and thus affecting the wages their tenants can pay or the prices they charge, they appropriate some wage income from their tenants' workers or customers or both. When farm workers worked for bare subsistence, rent to farm landlords had to be added to the price of food. When city office rents rise, lawyers, accountants and other tenants increase their fees further than property prices might prompt them to do if they were owner-occupiers.

Second, not all producers who can alternatively own or rent their premises are firms which pay dividends to passive shareholders. Many are farmers, tradespeople, shopkeepers and other working owners of small enterprises. If they own their premises and other physical capital, economists may theorize that their incomes are part wages and part property income. But it all feels like hard-earned income to those who earn it; and most of them are poorer, and work harder, than the landlords to whom they would alternatively pay rent.

Altogether it seems likely - on balance, net of many exceptions - that the more rent a nation's enterprises pay to private owners, the more unequally its income will be distributed. And that increment of inequality does not improve productive incentives. Inequalities of wealth and income perpetuate themselves, without any compensating benefit, when they force producers who

would do best as owner-occupiers to pay rent instead.

Tax reasons for renting Notice a feature of most countries' company tax and income tax laws.

When producers rent capital items (land, buildings, vehicles, equipment) tax authorities treat the tenants' rent as a business cost. Tax is payable only on profit after business costs are paid. In shorthand, business rent (unlike house rent) is deductible from the tenant's taxable income.

But when producers buy capital items, the purchase price is not tax-deductible. It has to be paid for from owned or borrowed savings or from taxed income. (Interest on mortgage loans is a tax-deductible cost, but the capital repayment is not.)

That contrast can prompt producers to rent things which it would otherwise be more economical to buy. National tax laws vary, but in extreme cases firms have leased factories, offices or vehicles from dummy firms, sometimes located in foreign tax havens, which exist only to own the capital items and convey the tax advantages. Where that is possible the tax laws could be improved with advantage to productive efficiency (even dummy firms have costs) and to honest taxpayers (who must pay what the dodgers do not pay).

House rent was treated at length in chapters on housing policy. All you need here is a brief reminder. To save words, take 'housing' to mean all household space and capital equipment.

Housing is the capital with which household labor produces a third or more of all goods and services in developed economies, an output not recorded in most national accounts. To be most productive as well as to reduce inequalities of real income housing needs to be distributed more equally than money income. Unaided capital markets and housing markets cannot achieve that (and housing's output does not sell for money so cannot finance the acquisition of the housing). Public action needs to correct some and replace some of the market processes. Its main purposes should be to -

- enable households which want to buy their housing to do so

- see that there are good options of rental housing for those who rent

- keep rents as low as practicable through the mid and lower range of the market (because household productivity needs money income, after paying tax and housing costs, as well as household capital)

- achieve those things economically and with least harm to housing choice, privacy and security of tenure.

Ways of helping people to buy their housing were discussed earlier. Buyers, and their children who inherit their housing capital, tend to pay much less for their housing over household life than tenants do. The inequality is not productive. Ways of reducing it – by extending home ownership, providing public housing, restraining private rents – were listed in Chapter 26. So was a tax dilemma: should household owners be taxed on the same basis as tenants, or should both, as producers, be taxed on the same basis as are commercial owners and tenants of buildings and equipment? The most impartial policy would not tax homeowners' imputed rent; it would allow homeowners to deduct their mortgage interest payments from their taxable incomes; and it would allow tenants to subtract their rent payments from their taxable incomes. Both allowances could have upper limits to prevent abuse.

A final way to reduce the unequalizing effects of house rent is to pay public rent allowances to means-tested tenants . Their advantages and disadvantages were detailed in Chapter 26. A summary conclusion: they are an extravagant and often ineffective substitute for measures which extend home ownership and maintain good supplies of public and private housing at restrained rents. But where those provisions do exist, rent allowances are a good supplement to them, as an economical safety net for any poor households who for one reason or another cannot find suitable public housing, or afford to buy or rent private housing without help.

Tentative conclusions

Policies about property income must often have other purposes besides improving the distribution of income, and they should generally be components of general economic strategies. Until you consider those strategies, store up the following tentative conclusions. Each is rough, based on a balance of probability, net of individual exceptions, and might need to be modified in particular conditions or strategies.

Less equal distribution of income is likely in proportion as –

- profit shares are higher and wage shares lower
- interest rates are high or fluctuating
- there is less owner-occupation of farms, housing, and business and government buildings, and accordingly more rent income
- rent income is paid to private rather than public or other non-profit landlords
- property income of all kinds is received by individuals and share-owned firms, rather than by public or other non-profit owners or by superannuation, life assurance and other institutions which distribute small property incomes to large numbers of people.

More equal distribution of income is likely in proportion as –

- wage shares are higher and profit shares are lower
- interest rates are low and stable
- there is more owner-occupation of farms, housing, and business and government buildings, and accordingly less rent income
- rent income is paid to public and non-profit landlords rather than to private landlords
- property income of all kinds is received by public or non-profit owners and by superannuation funds and other institutions which distribute income to large numbers of people, rather than by individual owners or share-owned firms.

EARNED INCOME

FOUR WAYS TO FIX WAGES

An owners' model

Chapter 32 instanced slavery. That was an extreme example of the principle that wages should be set by employers alone, with workers free only to accept them or starve. Here we modify - and modernize - the principle to mean that workers must individually accept or refuse the wages offered without collective bargaining and without the option of a dependable income if unem-

Income policies should not usually be considered by themselves. They need to be judged as working parts of more general economic strategies. You will meet the strategies later. Before you do, you need to understand a range of actual and proposed income policies, what they are designed to do, and the conditions in which they are likely to succeed or fail. That is the present task. For earned incomes, we can begin with a brief reminder of the four ways to fix wages, and some of the economic purposes which each of them can serve.

ployed. Government imposes this model when it bans strike action or collective bargaining and skimps welfare for the unemployed. It was the system in most countries before democratic government legalized collective bargaining. It commonly allowed the profit share of business revenue to be as high as half, and the wage share to be as low as half, although there was much less capital per worker than there is now. (Rich democracies now have much higher capital/labor ratios, but profit shares have declined to a quarter or less.)

A modified owners' model is now the program of some business leaders, labor market economists and Right politicians. They want to lower wages, especially the lowest wages, and make more jobs more competitive, insecure, part-time or casual. In this vision, employers decide wages and conditions. Workers individually accept them, or do not earn. A steady level of unemployment, with minimal welfare, disciplines them. This was the policy advice of the OECD economists for many years - their 1995 manifesto is quoted at length in Chapter 56 of this course. (But two years later their 1997 Employment Outlook cast doubt on some main assumptions of that advice: research suggested that union activity does not usually increase unemployment or reduce economic performance, and that flexible, deregulated labor markets have not reduced unemployment or quickened growth.)

A market model

In this model the supply and demand for labor, with organized bargaining by both sides, firm by firm or industry by industry, determines most wage rates. There may be some regulation of minimum wages and conditions of work, but subject to those limits, wages are set by mixtures of custom, bargaining strength and supply and demand.

This system does not usually allow much deliberate public influence on wage and profit shares. Where market relations yield a high wage share, as they do in the United States, they also allow steep wage inequalities between high and low skills, organized and unorganized workers, men and women, whites and blacks. So the high wage share is not an unmixed blessing for labor. Where there is full employment, this system also tends to produce inflation – though through the long postwar boom which saw the world's first prolonged full employment, inflation developed more slowly than it has sometimes done since the full employment ended. (It was restrained by a number of public controls which have since been dismantled.)

A workers' model

This label is for systems in which general wage levels and conditions of employment are set in national negotiations between peak representatives of business and labor, as once for half a century in Sweden. (Where there are strong unions but they bargain independently of each other, as in Britain, this text treats it as a market model.) The Swedish negotiators were not as good at restraining inflation as they could have been. But they achieved the rich democracies' lowest wage inequalities, with a higher minimum wage and lower margins for skill than might have been achieved in a market system. And they persuaded their members that Sweden's high wage level depended on workers being cooperative with their employers, and mobile when necessary. The system thus delivered significant efficiency as well as equality. When industrial relations deteriorated late in the century, the employers ended the central negotiations. As to whether they have profited by doing so, there is disagreement.

A government model

Australian wage rates and conditions of employment are fixed by an industrial commission independent of business and labor and at arms length from government. (Its members have judges' security of tenure.) It hears employers' and employees' representatives, and sometimes representations from government. It deals with national wage levels and conditions, and also with their detailed application to every industry and occupation. It accepts and registers voluntary agreements for particular firms or industries if they comply with some general requirements - basically, that they do not treat workers worse than the commission's awards do. Two market freedoms continue. Acceptable voluntary agreements can replace the commission's awards. And employers wanting to bid for scarce labor are free to offer better pay or conditions than the awards require. (But unions are not allowed to bargain for such bonuses by striking or other obstructive behavior.)

Institutions and culture

Wage-fixing systems are important, and which system a country chooses can help or hinder other policy choices. But German experience since 1945 warns against exaggerating the importance of the systems and underrating the force of other national differences. German practice mixes elements of the British, Swedish and Australian systems, and business and labor have generally been as co-operative as in Sweden. Wages are less equal than in Sweden but more equal than in Britain or the United States. And although the big unions bargain independently of each other, as in Britain, and there is much less public power over wages than in Australia, German wage negotiation has been the least inflationary in the developed world. That achievement seems to arise from the spirit in which parties negotiate rather than from the particular institutional arrangements. German business, labor and government share historical memories of the runaway inflation in 1923, and of the class warfare during the Great Depression which helped to destroy democracy in 1933.

POVERTY AND INEQUALITY

Two questions:

Poverty   Should market forces determine who earns income and who does not, leaving government to give public incomes and welfare services to those who do not? Or should government act to prevent as much poverty as possible by contriving full employment, enforcing a decent minimum wage, enabling all households to find affordable housing? Shouldn't the economic system, rather than public handouts, be the source of material welfare for as many of the people as possible?

Inequality   Should market forces determine the range between the highest and lowest earned incomes, with government then reducing excessive inequalities by taxing the rich to finance incomes and services for the poor? Or should employers be required to pay appropriate rates in the first place, so that the primary distribution of wage and salary income is satisfactory, with necessary but not unreasonable differentials for skill, scarcity, responsibility, and so on?

Rival arguments:

Reasons why the government should look after the poor

Two neoclassical economists – one moderate, one extreme – might argue as follows:

Moderate   The market economy works best with least government interference. Government should provide necessary infrastructure and public services, then leave the private sector to get on with its productive work with as little distortion as possible. Specifically,

- Government should not try to contrive full employment. Theory says that efforts to do that are only likely to cause inflation, exchange deficit and other troubles.

- It should not enforce a minimum wage. Theory says that will increase unemployment by pricing marginal labor out of the market.

- It should not provide public housing or regulate rents or subsidize housing loans. Theory says that distorts the efficient allocation of capital resources. It should not regulate the rate of interest on housing loans. Theory says that drives funds away from housing and frustrates some of the genuine market demand for housing.

Plenty of experience contradicts those theoretical beliefs. But the theorists do concede that market forces leave some people poor. Some cannot or will not provide for their own old age. Some are incapacitated and cannot earn. The business cycle and the 'natural' rate of unemployment leave fluctuating numbers of willing workers unemployed. For compassionate reasons government should transfer income to such people. They should be given enough income to afford basic food, housing and other necessaries. The transfers should be financed from neutral taxation which does not reduce economic efficiency by distorting consumers' preferences or producers' incentives.

Extreme   The above are acceptable provisions for physically handicapped adults, and for widows and some others who had no means of saving for their old age. But most people should provide for their old age by private superannuation. The unemployed should ideally not be subsidized at all. Theory says that unemployment is voluntary: there is a clearing price for labor, and if marginal workers would accept it, employers would find it worth while to employ them. But if it is politically unacceptable to pay the unemployed nothing, any dole they are given should be (i) below the clearing price of labor, and (ii) temporary, to see involuntarily unemployed people through short periods of job search, necessary retraining, or moving house to where the jobs are.

Now compare a post-Keynesian, institutionalist alternative.

Reasons why preventing poverty is better than relieving it

Full employment, a fair minimum wage and effective housing policies have all been known to work without the ill effects predicted by mistaken theory.

Preventing poverty is not the only virtue of full employment, but it is an important one. It can provide a decent income to the maximum number of households. It provides a better experience of life than unemployment does for most people of working age who are not fully occupied with children or other unpaid work. It avoids the stigma and alienation which many unemployed people suffer, and the bullying and insecurity which some employed workers suffer when there is significant unemployment. Full employment reduces the need for taxation, it expands the tax base, and it increases the proportion of tax revenue that can provide public investment and services rather than income transfers. To have the best effects it needs to be accompanied by wage restraint and other anti-inflationary measures.

A minimum wage – by itself or as part of a general wage-fixing system – does two services. It can keep the lowest-paid earners and their households out of poverty. And it allows the incomes transferred to any remaining unemployed to be high enough to keep *them* out of poverty. (A few pages back, you read theoretical reasons why excessively low wages cannot be expected to increase employment; and in practice the countries which have enforced the highest minimum wages have had long periods of the lowest unemployment.)

Affordable housing is also important because low earners as well as unemployed can be made poor by excessive housing costs. You know the reasons why unaided housing markets and housing finance markets are intrinsically inefficient, but can readily be made more efficient without interfering with buyers', borrowers' or tenants' market freedoms. Intelligent housing policies can improve equity and productivity in a number of ways, besides preventing poverty.

The role of these policies in national economic strategies is for study later. Here, just notice the general nature of the above arguments for attacking poverty by (i) letting it happen, then relieving it by public income transfers and services, or alternatively (ii) getting the productive system to offer work, income and affordable housing options – and thus, economic independence – to as many households as possible, so that the necessary income transfers to the remaining unemployed can be as few and as high as possible.

The difference between the lowest and highest earned incomes

Many policies affect the extent of 'earned' inequality, i.e. inequality among employed and self-employed workers. Policies about taxation, superannuation, banking, health, education and housing can all do so. But here we notice some direct wage-fixing or wage-regulating policies.

The middle range of earned incomes has very similar distribution in most advanced economies. Significant differences in inequality are at the top and bottom of the distribution, or (throughout the range) in 'lateral' discrimination against women, ethnic groups or others. We will notice what different wage-fixing methods can do – or might do – about unduly low pay, unduly high pay, and unequal pay for work of equal value. Much of that merely reminds you of things you already know. Having thus surveyed some ways of reducing unnecessary inequalities we will then foreshadow some ways to increase inequalities, if that is what you want to do.

Unduly low pay   The main things than can discourage employers from offering unduly low pay, and workers from accepting it, are -

*   full employment
*   effective union organization of casual, part-time and unskilled workers
*   a sufficient dole income for the unemployed
*   a legal minimum wage

Market wage-fixing makes it difficult to restrain wages for long, for anti-inflationary and other purposes, when there is full employment. It is quite compatible with legislating a minimum wage, but the minimum tends to be difficult to enforce where it is most needed by casual and part-time workers, and by supposedly full-time workers who can readily be laid off as often as employers are short of work for them. A minimum wage can prevent some 'employed poverty', but may not help small farmers or other self-employed people who are not unemployed but are earning too little to live on. A minimum wage and high unemployment allowance may still be worth having because they do provide a decent income for the unemployed and for workers in a range of permanent low-paid jobs. And without them the market model tends to become a harsh owners' model (i.e. one in which workers have no bargaining power at all) for the poorest workers who need protection most, but are usually the most difficult to organize in unions for collective bargaining and self-defence.

The centralized wage-fixing systems – our government model and workers' model – have been most effective in practice at setting and enforcing decent minimum wages and hourly rates. Both depend on (but also encourage) high union membership, both as a basis for national wage negotiations, and to ensure that workers abide by public awards, or agreements made on their behalf. When fewer women earned, and men's attitudes to them were not as they are now, the unions often supported unequal pay. But when the democracies passed laws requiring equal pay and opportunity, countries with centralized national wage-fixing made more and faster progress toward equal pay than countries with market wage-fixing did. (Recall from Chapter 44 the dramatically different American and Australian compliance with their equal pay laws.)

Where the poorest workers – including casual and part-time workers, many of them women – are not union members, national union negotiators have nevertheless sought awards for them, or basic rates which apply to the work they do. That is partly generous, and partly to defend union members from undercutting competition. High and low motives both work to the weak bargainers' advantage. Of course the rules can still be evaded: nobody polices what your neighbors pay you to wash their car, mow their lawn, or mind their kids. But although some casual work is paid at informal market rates, the rates still tend to reflect the official national rates. As an informal baby-sitter you know what the official rate is for that sort of child care. As a casual laborer you can convert the national minimum adult wage into an hourly rate. The informal rates rarely fall as far below the legal minimum rates in Sweden or Australia as they often do in the United States.

Unduly high pay Distinguish three kinds of high earners, whom we can call 'market successes', 'pace-setters' and 'followers'.

- *Market successes* (among the highest earners) are usually freelance artists or inventors, or working owners of fast-growing new firms. Two of their qualities matter for present purposes. They earn in a genuine market way, offering products or performances which sell on their merits to customers spending their own money. And anyone who wants to imitate their success must do it in the same market way.

- *Pace setters* Company directors of big firms with no dominant individual owners determine their own pay. Doctors earn what their national hospital and medical insurance systems allow them to earn. Though the prevailing rates of pay may be called market rates you know why they are not what economists mean by market prices. They are fixed by institutional contrivance, by bargaining from unequal strength, by collusion between suppliers and the insurers who pay them – or by other departures from competitive pricing – as evidenced by the very different rates which similar buyers with similar needs and incomes pay for similar services in countries with similar GDP per head. (Recall from Chapter 41 the questions to ask if you want to explain such prices. Who order the service? For

whose benefit? Who pay? With whose money? And so on.)

- *Followers'* incomes are geared to the pace-setters' incomes, however informally or indirectly. When company directors without dominant owners increase their rewards, directors with dominant owners ask their owners to let them pay themselves at the new rates. When private executive pay goes up, politicians are persuaded to allow some increase of public executive pay. When executive pay rises, the next level of managers ask for proportionate rises. And so on: rises at the top tend to stretch the whole spire of the income pyramid. Directors and executives of big firms are the main pace-setters. Other high earners follow as and when they can: directors of smaller firms, leading lawyers and accountants who work for corporate clients, judges whose pay must not fall too far behind the leading lawyers' pay, public executives who must not fall too far behind comparable private executives, public service chiefs who must not fall too far behind the public enterprise executives whose work they monitor; then the next level of private and public managers.

If you want to regulate high earners' pay the simplest and least oppressive way to do it might be to regulate the pace-setters and leave the followers to follow as usual. But would it be worth doing? Should democracies mind how much their highest earners earn?

Consider the reasons for answering no or yes to that question.

No There is no objective ground for deciding what would be the most efficient or ethically desirable pattern of inequality, or limit to earned incomes. There would be disagreement about any arbitrary limit. So why not leave these incomes to market forces and established practice?

Salaries above three or four times the average income are very few. They are a negligible proportion of national income, or even of the highest incomes, most of which are from property. So they come at very little cost to anyone else.

High earnings by a minority allow more saving than more equal incomes would, because high earners tend to save higher proportions of income. So it is better to improve equality by levelling up the lowest incomes, not by levelling down the highest.

Recall an argument about the skill of the capital-owning class. The most successful business leaders, who get to the top by merit in tough competition, are ideal recruits to the owning class, likely to be better investors than most passive inheritors of wealth are. So the highest earners should ideally be paid enough to become substantial capital owners. It is good that directors are increasingly doing that.

Finally, it would be difficult in practice to regulate directors' rewards, and might occasion some new inefficiency and oppression. First, what principles should regulate the rewards? All the obvious alternatives are potentially unfair or economically harmful. Should directors' rewards be geared to their firms' gross assets? Net assets? Payroll? Turnover? Size and volume are poor guides to the difficulty of the directors' tasks in different industries, the skills they require, or the quality of their performance. Should they take specified proportions of annual profits? No, it is not right to pay more to directors of monopolies or lucky oil strikes than to directors of competitive firms, or risk-takers (such as inventors or mineral prospectors) who may spend long periods without profit. It is sometimes right to forgo profit while accumulating capital, developing new products or penetrating new markets – but if directors' pay depends on profits during their own tenure, they may be tempted by improvident short-term policies. (Some of the greediest already are, where their rewards are 'performance-related'.) Thus any imaginable formula seems likely to have harmful effects on some at least of the firms to which it would have to be applied.

A second ill effect is likely to be some increase of oppressive government. It already takes quite complicated law, accounting and enforcement to protect firms and the public from incompetent, dishonest or disloyal directors. Simple regulation of directors' rewards could be evaded, first by familiar means and then over time by increasingly inventive and ingenious means. As each new evasive device was detected it would need to be defined, banned, and the ban policed. Thus the regulations would become complicated and intrusive – as company law has already become, for similar reasons. Rules to prevent misbehavior by a few directors would complicate all firms' accounting, raise their costs, and reduce some more of their freedoms and efficiencies. And at the same time they would lose the use of traditional and widely used executive incentives.

Altogether if government wants directors to have less to spend it would be better to make income tax more steeply progressive on all high incomes.

On the other hand –

Yes, regulating directors' rewards might still be worth the trouble. Recall from your study of business powers in Chapter 28 –

- how directors came to decide their own rewards
- the use they have made and are making of that power
- its potential economic effects
- its effects on public efficiency and costs
- its present and potential effects on the distribution of income.

Early in the twentieth century the great capitalist J. P. Morgan allowed the chief executives of his companies to take twenty times the average pay of their workers. By mid-century thirty and forty times were commoner rates in big companies. As the century ended, leading US executives were averaging three and four hundred times their workers' rates, and increasing their own at five or ten times the rate of economic growth. One of them was taking, year after year, above twenty thousand times the national median wage.

The increasing inequality does not appear to have had good incentive effects. American trend rates of investment and economic growth remain relatively low. There has been a good deal of corporate misbehavior, which has hurt innocent parties as well as the offending directors' firms. Mergers and takeovers which made no sense for the firms concerned have allowed quick gains for the directors who contrived them. Some directors of failing firms have plundered them rather than working to rescue them. Directors of banks and of their corporate customers have each taken commissions for negotiating loans quite unlikely to be repaid. The bigger and more flexible the personal rewards can be, the more conflict there can be between directors' interests and their firms' interests, and the more of the firms' business may be managed with personal interests and very short-term considerations in mind. Tens of thousands of honorable directors resist temptations to misbehave. But they accept the rising rates of reward, and are perhaps encouraged by those rewards to resist effective regulation of them. Altogether the rising rewards seem to have increased more incentives for misbehavior than for good performance (though most of those tens of thousands of honorable directors no doubt continue their good performance).

The external effects are even more worrying.

The widening gap between the top pay in private business and the top pay in public business, government, science and education has not yet drained the non-profit sectors of all their best talent. But it is having some of that effect, and must be expected to have more over time. Nothing in the difficulty, value or productivity of the work which the sectors do justifies those unequal rewards, or a long-term shift of more of the highest talents into private business. Nor are the rising inequalities good signals or persuasions about the values which ought to prevail in developed democracies. The use which the directors are making of their unique power to decide their own rewards can fairly be accused of making their economies both less equitable and less efficient.

Recall the awkward relation between the public/private pay gap and policy-making about public and private ownership. When a public enterprise is being considered for privatization, its executives who ought to be the government's most expert source of advice know that if they recommend privatization and it happens, their rewards are likely to double. If they oppose it and it happens they are likely to be sacked. However honest their advice in those circumstances it is likely to be suspect.

There may be some similar influence on other sources of advice and opinion, though it is difficult to estimate. Through the 'follower' effect, the directors' increasing rewards encourage increases for many more of the top five or ten per cent of earners. They include most of the influential people in business, law, accountancy, the management schools and the media. They stand to gain directly or indirectly from the directors' pace-making and thus from the relative freedom from market or governmental restraint which allows the pace-making. Public opinion and democratic legislators continue to restrain politicians' and public servants' pay. Politicians would not pay judges, public enterprise executives or economic consultants more than they pay themselves if they could help it, or if they had to justify the high pay and increasing inequality as intrinsically desirable. The two pleas which justify all the public sector's highest salaries are fairness in relation to equivalent private sector jobs, and the social need to attract and retain competent leadership in the public sector against the rival attractions at the top of the private sector.

The increasing inequality at the top end of the distribution of income reverses a long trend. Through most of the history of democratic government until the 1970s, the inequalities which mattered most were declining. Whether or not you welcome a reversal of that trend and a return to steeper inequality, you should notice two things about the present movement in that direction.

First, it is not necessarily self-limiting. There tend to be market limits and corrective reactions to other excesses – to too much saving, too much spending, too much public or too much private investment. But

although there are prudent limits to the speed at which the directors can increase their rewards, there is no obvious limit to how far they can go in that direction, over time. By the time that there is better public understanding of what they are doing, and perhaps some recoil against it and some political will to check it, national governments may find that it has become difficult to check, partly because so many of the influential elite gain by it and want to continue it, and partly for global reasons to be explained presently in relation to a new strategy for increasing inequality.

Second, the process has no valid market excuses. There is nothing natural, inevitable, efficient, or intrinsic to capitalism in the directors' freedom to decide their own rewards. The people who inadvertently designed it did not intend it. Recall the history of business powers. When the original Corporations Acts were written to create the modern firm and give its directors the legal powers they needed to make it so productive, nobody thought that those powers need include a power for directors who were employees rather than owners to decide what pay they would take from their owners. It was assumed that directors would be owners, or under owners' control, so under market discipline in either case.

By the time that Berle and Means, Barnard and other writers noticed the passing of effective power from owners to directors, with directors rather than shareholders controlling the annual company meetings at which the shareholders were supposed to fix the directors' pay, the directors were powerful enough to resist reform. In the US they still are, and the States' competitive chartering policies promise to keep them so.

The freedom with pay is doubly unusual, because directors' other powers and duties have come to be regulated more elaborately than ever before. (Remember how Britain's corporate law handbook keeps getting thicker and heavier.) There are also rules about how directors' may take their rewards, and what they must disclose about them. But there is still nothing effective to prevent their incomes continuing to draw steadily further ahead of other earned incomes and of their shareholders' rates of dividend.

Summary The directors' unique power to decide how much to take from their firms has opened a dangerous gap in the market and institutional discipline of earned incomes. It is not a traditional, necessary or even intentional capitalist freedom: on the contrary it defeats a central purpose of company law, and does more harm than good to the allocation of human and other resources. It is affecting a growing number of high incomes besides the directors'. Without any democratic decision to do so, but by default, it has begun to reverse the slow reduction of inequality that has characterized democracy and economic growth for more than a century.

That is the case for regulating those rewards. How might it be done?

How? Countries with different constitutions, wage-fixing systems and ways of registering companies and regulating their behavior may have different options.

Market model In countries with 'market' wage-fixing, wages are actually fixed in various ways, from individual wage-setting to periodical agreements between unions and firms or employers' industry councils. There is no central national wage-fixing machinery which could simply add directors' pay to its responsibilities. But – except for the US – countries with market wage-fixing do also have national corporation law, and a national authority to register companies. The European Union is developing some international authority for the purpose. That national or international power could easily be extended to allow it to prescribe and enforce rules about directors' and other executives' rewards.

Advantages: The public institution already exists and is expert at corporate regulation. Adding pay limits to its responsibilities need not add much to its bureaucracy or costs.

Disadvantages: Because it must lay down the law, rather than adjudicate between employer and employee after hearing their advocates, such an authority might be thought to be arbitrary and oppressive. The difficulty of arriving at a fixed code or formula which would fit the needs of firms in every kind of industry was sketched earlier as part of the case against attempting such regulation. And if firms or industries wanted to argue for broader rules or special needs, the authority might be distrusted as judge in its own case. It is there to represent national interests and the interests of owners, workers and consumers against the directors' interests, so it might not be trusted to arbitrate fairly between those other interests and the directors'.

Labor representatives and other egalitarians want directors' pay to relate fairly to everyone else's pay. But corporate regulators are not normally concerned with wage levels or the general distribution of income. They deal almost exclusively with corporate directors, accountants and lawyers, beneficiaries of the directors' present freedoms. They are experts in corporate financial responsibility and solvency. They might naturally relate directors' pay to their firms' capacity to pay, and

to owners' interest in buying the best management they can afford. So they might not concede much to other parties' interests, or to principles of distributive justice.

Nevertheless a government which wanted those broader principles to be applied in the regulation of directors' rewards should be able to staff a division of its Department of Corporate Affairs with officers appropriately chosen and trained for the task.

Government model Most Australian wage rates (and other conditions of employment) are fixed by public commissioners with the status and independence of judges, after hearing representatives of the relevant employers and workers. In important cases they may also hear the government on matters of national interest. But they decide independently of government, for public as well as private employees. If employers and unions reach agreement without arbitration, the agreement must still be registered with the commission and comply with its rules. The commissioners hear argument about costs of living, capacities to pay, comparative wage justice, and national interests. Their jurisdiction goes beyond wage-paid work to many salaried occupations. It could easily extend to company directors, except for one difficulty. The basic principle of the system is arbitration between opposing interests, typically employers and employees. But directors employ one another. When their trade union, the National Institute of Directors, represents them before the Commission as employees, who will represent their employers? A national organization of shareholders might claim to do so. But with more than half of all shares now owned by firms, the shareholders' representatives would also include directors with directors' interests. A composite body might be created for the purpose, perhaps representing labor unions, consumers' associations and individual shareholders. But it might be better if the opposing party, at hearings about directors' pay, were the corporate regulator. The regulators exist to prevent or detect and punish every other kind of misbehavior by directors, so perhaps they could be trusted to prevent over-payment with the same zeal and expertise; and if they lacked knowledge of other wages, or concern for distributive justice and some reduction of inequality, those could be supplied by the commissioners. The commissioners are accustomed to setting minimum rates for each occupation (which can be exceeded if employers and employees agree). They would have to learn to set maximum rates for directors, with directors or their owners free to pay them less if they chose.

That might well be the best and fairest way to regulate directors' rewards. But it could not work without a national wage-fixing system of the Australian (or similar) kind.

Workers' model Sweden had a centralized national wage-fixing system of a different kind. When the national representatives of employers and labor unions met periodically to negotiate national wage scales, they could in principle have included directors' rewards in the negotiations. It is unlikely that the employers would have consented to that, and they have already withdrawn from the centralized national wage negotiations. It is conceivable that strong unions could force directors' pay onto the negotiating agenda. They might demand specified ratios between directors' and other employees' rates. But that could scarcely be done consistently for all industries and firms without central national negotiations, which directors are unlikely to take part in if their own rewards are at stake.

A directors' model would be a reasonable name for the system in the United States, where the Constitution rather than the wage-fixing system makes it difficult to imagine any practicable way to limit what directors can take from their firms. The States have the power to charter corporations and therefore to define their directors' powers. Since 1967 a few States have attracted most of the business chiefly by empowering directors to enrich themselves. Other authorities – federal and state Departments of Justice, the Stock Exchanges and the federal Securities and Exchange Commission – can act against directors for many kinds of misbehavior, but they cannot limit what the chartering States allow directors to take lawfully. Would-be reformers would have to succeed with a constitutional amendment to remove or discipline the States' chartering powers, then overcome the formidable resistance which the corporate world would offer to any effective limitation of executive rewards.

But never underestimate American intelligence and ingenuity. The directors themselves may call a prudent halt to the plunder. In 1998 the biggest individual take was $575m. Chief Executives at major companies averaged 419 times the average pay of blue-collar workers. As those workers took a 2.7 per cent pay rise, the top 350 Chief Executives averaged a 36 per cent pay rise. The Wall Street Journal's 1999 report of those items was headed 'Enough is enough'. A group called Responsible Wealth is initiating action to ask corporations to adopt fixed ratios between executives' and workers' rates. At Citigroup whose Chief Executive took $166m as the firm began laying off 10 000 workers, and at General Electric whose leader made

Business Week's list of the Chief Executives who gave shareholders the least for their money, some of the shareholders expressed concern. Next time there is a recession with a general share-price shake-out, the executive behavior may generate support for a constitutional amendment. If it does, then from the Securities and Exchange Commission or one of the great Law Schools another Jim Landis may come to complete the work that his inventive predecessor began.

INCOME FROM CRIME

Whether this subject belongs here with other paid work, or later with transferred income, is hard to say. But together with the directors' lawful plunder it perhaps offers a suitable transition between the two.

Crime has been estimated to produce or transfer as much as ten per cent of American and Italian income, lesser proportions of other rich countries' income, and perhaps larger proportions of capital and income in post-communist Russia. Nobody really knows its extent, but together with the public and private efforts to prevent and correct it, it is a big industry. What follows is not about the economics of crime, but about some efforts to reduce its effects on the distribution of income.

Is crime an equalizer?

Robin Hood is said to have robbed the rich to give to the poor. Some poor look after themselves in that way. In peasant societies with rich landowners and many landless laborers, poaching game and stealing from fowlyards and vegetable gardens was sometimes the main mode of 'welfare income transfer'. You may sympathize with modern poor who steal from richer people. But for every excusable case of that kind there are usually bigger numbers of poor who get by without stealing; poor who steal from other poor; professional thieves, receivers, frauds, embezzlers, confidence men and other tricksters who prey on people poorer than themselves; and well-off drug dealers whose addicted customers steal to pay the dealers' prices.

This section will assume that crime is bad even when it improves the distribution of income, and that its overall effect is at least as likely to worsen the distribution.

Recovering the loot

It is unlawful to benefit from your own crime. If you are convicted of murdering your rich uncle, that disqualifies you from inheriting his millions, whatever his will says. But once criminal gains are in hand for long enough to be laundered, exported or given away to kin, most of them are in practice beyond reach of traditional criminal law and police procedures. In efforts to correct that, and provoked by fortunes made in drug trafficking and other evildoing, some governments have lately created Crime Commissions with special powers. Their powers vary, but in one representative case they include these:

- The Commission is empowered to trace and recover loot which has been given to kin or associates, or knowingly laundered or traded by others.

- The 'right to silence' is suspended: the Commission's questions must be answered, even if the answers are incriminating.

- There are no juries.

- There are civil rather than criminal principles of proof. Most criminal law requires prosecutors to prove that accused persons are guilty 'beyond reasonable doubt'. But for obvious reasons of impartiality, civil actions between one citizen and another are decided on a 'balance of probability'. The Commission cannot convict or jail people, but it can confiscate their property on a balance of probability that they know it has changed hands by crime.

- For tracing assets suspected of having been gained by crime, the onus of proof is reversed, as it already is in much tax law. If the inquisitor says "I reckon you got this money from your mate who got it trafficking hash" he does not have to prove it: the onus is on you to convince the Commission that you got it lawfully.

That Commission has so far used its powers cautiously, for fear of backlash if such frightening powers were misused. But its task has proved to be easier than expected. Not many villains have resisted it. Most of them settle out of court and pay up. They have so far been middle-sized offenders; the Commission has not yet succeeded against any millionaires. Besides the loot which such Commissions have recovered there is no way of knowing how much crime they may have deterred – or whether on the other hand they have prompted big operators to develop new, more ingenious ways of laundering their gains.

Film rights?

Some convicted criminals have done well by selling interviews, articles, books, film rights and other copyright accounts of their own misbehavior. Some governments and some courts now define that as benefiting from crime and do their best to ban it. To preserve

freedom of speech they usually ban payment rather than publication: offenders can speak and write about their experience as long as they, or their kin or associates, are not paid for it. In straightforward cases that is a good principle. But it can work harshly. If a prisoner's offence has left his innocent family without means of support, he is not allowed to compensate them by selling his story. Should they be allowed as insiders to tell and sell his story? If his purpose in selling his story is to earn the means of compensating his victims, should that be allowed? Does the rule against payment discourage confessions, warnings or analyses of criminal behavior which might serve the public interest? It seems a good rule, but should perhaps be applied with some discrimination.

Victims

Criminals and their victims have tended to attract very unequal shares of official attention and resources. Big resources are devoted to catching, convicting, imprisoning and (sometimes) rehabilitating offenders. Until lately there has been very little specific public aid to victims of crime. Like anyone else they depend on the regular public health and welfare services, pensions for the disabled and unemployed, and so on. For loss of property they must rely on private insurance, or take civil legal action against those responsible if they can be found and are rich enough to be worth suing. But in practice very little criminal harm has been put right by civil action.

However, reform has begun. It varies from country to country, but if the best practices were combined they might constitute a system like this: Juvenile offenders must meet their victims, understand the harm they have done, and where practicable put it right by payment or compulsory work. Adult offenders against property return it or pay for it if that is judged to be within their means. All criminal penalties, from traffic fines upwards, carry an additional levy which finances a fund from which victims are compensated when the relevant offenders cannot pay or cannot be found and the regular public services do not sufficiently repair the criminal damage.

CORPORATE CRIME

Recall (from Chapter 28 on business powers) how corporate powers can be misused, and what lawyers from Chicago and Sydney would like to do about it.

Crimes can be committed by corporations, by their directors and employees, and by dealers in their shares.

Corporations themselves can be difficult to discipline. If they evade tax or gain or lose money by unlawful means they can be tried, convicted and fined or deregistered. But they cannot be imprisoned, and to fine them heavily or put them out of business is usually to punish shareholders innocent of the crimes committed on their behalf. You may think that is no worse than punishing innocent families by imprisoning guilty breadwinners, which the criminal courts do every day. Moreover loss from any cause, including mismanagement, is a risk investors take when, by buying shares, they confide their wealth to be managed by strangers. But courts are often tender to shareholders because an alternative discipline is available. Most crimes by corporations are also crimes by their officers. If the offending directors or employees can be punished, courts can feel easier about sparing the shareholders.

But corporate crime is not always easy to convict. The law and practice of corporate accounting have become complex. Directors can keep deliberately over-complicated and confusing books. They can distribute their activities between any number of public and private companies. They can heap losses onto some of the companies and bankrupt them, while taking profits in other companies, perhaps in foreign tax havens. To tease out their evildoing in court with enough detail and certainty to convict them 'beyond reasonable doubt' can be expensive and time-consuming, and protracted through appeals. Big offenders can often have their firms pay their legal expenses, so they can afford to push to the limit the procedural possibilities of evasion, obstruction, delay and appeal. Since the 1970s it has not been uncommon in English-speaking countries for big cases to be finally determined – or despairingly dropped – five to ten years after the events which occasioned them, sometimes with legal costs many times greater than the sums at issue in the cases.

There is thus a case for reform. The onus of proof is already reversed in many tax cases. It would save time and money, and might have good deterrent effects, if the tax law and Crime Commission rules of procedure were extended to all investigations and criminal trials of corporations, and of non-prisonable offences by their officers in the use of their corporate powers. Neither corporations nor their officers would then have rights to silence or to trial by jury if accused of offences against corporation law. At judges' discretion the onus of proof could be reversed, and judgments based on balance of probability. And the authorities would have a little more power than they have now, in most countries, to trace and recover the proceeds of crime.

Would such a regime be too oppressive? Not all business people would oppose it. Honest business has suffered a good deal, in money and reputation, from much-publicized excesses of corporate misbehavior in recent times. It might well do better with stricter rules and quicker and surer enforcement.

What of the principle that it is 'better that a hundred guilty go free than that one innocent person be imprisoned'? That should certainly continue to protect people accused of prisonable offences. But most business offences are against shareholders, employees, creditors, taxpayers, or other firms. If the injured parties sue, courts decide on the balance of probability. So they should, surely, when government rather than the injured parties asks for the judgment, under criminal rather than civil law. The onus of proof can already be reversed when the injured parties are other taxpayers: why not when they are shareholders, creditors, customers or other firms, and when law officers rather than the injured parties are the accusers? Finally, when people buy shares they accept the risks of loss from mismanagement, misbehavior by their own or other firms, or expensive legal delays and costs. Those risks could reasonably include any risks that come with quicker, cheaper justice, especially as quicker, cheaper justice seems at least as likely to help shareholders' interests as to harm them.

For a detailed scheme for the better public discipline of private corporate behavior, with least delay and least resort to criminal proceedings, revise Chapter 28's summary of the system proposed by Brent Fisse and John Braithwaite in *Corporations, Crime and Accountability* (1993).

TRANSFERRED INCOME

PHILOSOPHY

Remember why it takes value judgments as well as factual information to distinguish transferred income from other income. Government makes the property law which entitles property owners to draw unearned income from others, and it makes the tax and pension laws which entitle pensioners to draw unearned income from others. Value judgments have to decide when to lump them together as 'unearned' and when to distinguish them as 'property income' and 'transferred income'. And is a housewife's income an unearned transfer from her earning partner, or does she earn it – and produce a good deal of it – by her hard work?

Values also shape people's selective understanding of transactions which both transfer income between persons and transfer rights to income over time. To trigger your memory of that subject, here again are two paragraphs from Chapter 12 which show two ways of understanding exactly the same facts:

- First observer: I am likely to live longer than my grandparents did. Compared with them I am lucky to have a longer education before I start earning and a longer retirement after I stop. So I need to transfer more income than they did, from my earning years to my non-earning years. That is no hardship, because growing productivity means that in real terms I earn two or three times as much as they did. But transferring income over twenty and forty years is risky for individual investors, so I would be glad if a responsible public institution would do it for me, for example by taxing my earning years to provide me with free education and a student allowance when I am young and a pension when I am old.

- Second observer: The welfare burden is becoming intolerable. A declining number of productive workers are having to pay rising rates to support a steadily increasing number of unproductive pensioners. The aging population structure shows that the dependent population will continue to grow: it is already 25 per cent of all households, and the way we are going it may approach 40 per cent a generation from now. The long-suffering producers simply will not stand for it. Tax revolts are only the beginning – the real need is to dismantle most of the welfare state.

Who is right? They are both half right and half wrong. The first observer is forgetting some real redistribution from person to person. The second is forgetting the extent to which the system redistributes income over time as well as between persons. We can simplify those two views and add a third, more comprehensive, one:

1. The system spreads everyone's income over their whole life, to support them through their non-earning years.

2. That can only be done by having the earners support the non-earners, i.e. by having people accept transfers through their non-earning years and provide transfers through their earning years.

3. In the process there is usually some net transfer from person to person: some people get more than they pay over their lifetimes, some pay more than they get. In some societies that redistribution has increased inequalities – for example in pre-revolutionary France the peasants and middle class paid most of the taxes and a rich aristocracy got many of the benefits. In modern social democracies there is some net transfer from the richest 20 per cent to the poorest 20 per cent, so besides spreading everyone's income over their whole lifetimes, there is also some reduction of whole-life inequality.

So don't make the mistake of thinking of the taxpayers and the beneficiaries as different people. Some give or get more than others do, but most of the givers and receivers are the same people, giving and receiving transfers at different stages of their lives as they transfer income of their own over time, at their own wish, for their own benefit.

POLICY QUESTIONS

In all rich democracies, government transfers income to most of the people at some stages of their lives, and to 20 to 30 per cent of them at any one time. The tax and transfer patterns vary from country to country and are everywhere quite complicated: to survey them all, and debate their merits and demerits, would take a longer textbook than this one. Here we will merely list some questions of principle which underlie the policy choices. For simplicity they are presented as dilemmas: each of the alternatives they offer has intrinsic disadvantages as well as advantages. The purpose is to arm you against over-simple, one-sided arguments that welfare should all be left to the market, or should all be provided by the government, or should all be in cash, or should all take the form of free goods and services. All those principles have some awkward effects in practice, and policymakers need to mix them in various ways if they are to achieve most advantage with least disadvantage, and implement their desired principles (always likely to be disagreed) of economic efficiency and distributive justice.

We will ask in turn –

- how much income should be transferred in cash and how much in kind?

- how much in universal provisions for everyone, how much in selective provisions for those in need?

- who should pay for them, through what pattern of taxation?

Cash or kind?

How do public services compare with money income as aids to welfare and distributive justice?

The question is too general. For some needs money is best, for other needs services are best, and both may vary with local conditions. The best way to make sure that people can get good dental service is not the same in rich cities, in poor peasant societies, and in satellite space stations. Money income may also have different value in those diverse conditions. But some general advantages and disadvantages of each are worth noticing.

The case for money is summed up in the slogans 'what the poor need is money', 'money is freedom' and 'all dollars are equal'. Money is a liberator and equalizer. It enables poor people to judge their own needs and allocate their resources as freely as anybody else does, with dignity and independence.

The case against money is that it tends to be the easiest resource to lose, misuse or steal, and of all people the poorest tend to have the weakest defences against those hazards. Public cash incomes (like other cash incomes) do not go to everybody, they usually go to one member of each household. That does not necessarily distribute free choices or anything else to the other members. Schools educate children; dental services protect their teeth; libraries lend them books to read; summer camps give them holidays; playgrounds and hobby workshops give them space and company and creative scope; counsellors widen their choices and chances of jobs; alert health and welfare officers may protect a few of them from ignorant or corrupt or violent parents. If the state withdraws those services and distributes cash to parents instead, not all the parents will spend the cash on dentistry, books, holidays – or anything else for their dependents, in some households – though some may spend it on things they need more than they need those services. No one combination of cash income and services can be best for every member of every household. But it does not necessarily do most for freedom and individual independence to give the most vulnerable people nothing but shark-bait in shark-infested seas – nothing but money in societies with drunk, drugged and violent partners and fathers, and with money-lenders and debt-collectors, landlords who keep rents up to capacities to pay, old folk's homes and hospitals which do likewise, alluring advertisers, hire-purchase offers you can't refuse – and any number of bars, betting shops, poker machines, video games, commercial religions, over-priced tranquillizers and other addictive attractions.

But services also have their problems. If the model of money-only welfare is the shark-infested sea, the model of service-only welfare is the nursing home which takes the widow's whole pension then treats her however the management thinks best. Sensible solutions lie somewhere between, in thoughtfully detailed mixtures of money and services – differing only in detail from the mixtures of private income and public services which everybody demands in a modern society.

A final reason for offering both money and services is that they can complement each other and increase each other's practical value. People need some income in order to use some of the services. They need some income in order to make the most productive use of their household space and capital. Affordable housing affects spendable income: the spendable proportion of any cash income is greater to the extent that there are aids to home ownership, or low-rented public housing, or (where necessary) controls on private rents. Housing conditions also affect other services. It can be difficult to deliver public income reliably to homeless people. Homeless or insecurely housed people can find it hard to make the best use of schools and some other services. Sheltered housing and sheltered workshops for physically and mentally handicapped people, and meals on wheels and visiting nursing for frail people, reduce the need for more expensive institutional care, and at the same time give handicapped people more privacy and independence, and enable them to use other services, and to make good use of their money incomes.

Deciding to provide mutually helpful cash income and services may resolve one policy question but it opens others: to which people, in what amounts, and on what terms should the cash and services go? Meet the toughest of all welfare dilemmas, first in a simple old version, then in a more experienced and complicated version.

Universal or selective?

Before there was much experience of the actual working of modern welfare services or much research into their effects, it was common to see many of the policy problems as aspects of a single dilemma. Should welfare provisions be available to all? If so, they might be unduly expensive and still do comparatively little to improve equalities. Alternatively, should welfare provisions economize resources and improve equalities by going only to those in real need? That would involve means-testing those needy people; it would stigmatize them; and it would often condemn them to using segregated, second-class services – for example, queueing at public medical clinics while most people went by appointment to private doctors.

Who was right? Each principle promised some advantages and some disadvantages.

Universalists wanted most public provisions to go on the same terms to everyone – the same schools should be open to everyone, the same health services to all families, the same pensions to everyone of pensionable age, and so on. Such universal provisions help to unify society and rid it of class distinctions because they treat everyone alike and do not stigmatize anyone as incompetent or a public burden. Because they are for rich and influential people as well as for poor and powerless people, there will be plenty of pressure from their influential users to see that they are good services, so the poor will not be fobbed off with second class services as they often are when their services are different from those the rest of the people use. Universal provisions can easily be designed to improve equalities. Free services to everyone reach poor people who could not otherwise afford them. Pensions and other allowances can be taxable, so that well-off people who get them will pay a good deal back in tax. To reduce overall inequality it is only necessary to finance the services and allowances from progressive taxes – capital taxes, luxury taxes, progressive income tax. There may be conflict about the distribution of the tax burden, but there should at the same time be a wide willingness to pay the necessary level of tax by one means or other, because the benefits are available to all taxpayers and all voters.

Selectivists meanwhile argued that in the real world there were limited resources for welfare and they should surely go to the people in most need. Universal provisions would cost so much that they would usually have to be provided at mean levels, and even then some of them would transfer resources in the wrong direction, from poorer taxpayers to richer beneficiaries. To reduce hardship and improve equalities, welfare provisions should usually be financed from progressive taxation and directed only to people in proven need.

What is wrong with that simple understanding of the dilemma?

Complexities

In practice scarcely any 'universal' benefits are for everybody. They are for particular groups of people and like selective benefits they have tests of eligibility. Suppose, for example, that there are transferred incomes

for full-time students, for workers who are judged to be medically unfit to work, and for people over sixty with less than a specified income. Each is a limited group of people. Each recipient has to prove eligibility. It is possible to get each allowance by cheating. Does it help to call the first two 'universal' and the third 'selective'? In fact they are all selective; the formal classification 'selective' merely distinguishes those which happen to include low income among their criteria of selection.

As with selectivity, so with equality. Selective benefits often do more to reduce inequalities than universal services do. Some universal services – for example, free university education – may do more to increase inequality than to reduce it. Others – for example free health care – tend on balance to reduce it. A universal health service which charged fees but exempted people of limited means would reduce inequality further – but it would also defeat our classification by being both universal and selective. And so on. Instead of simply deciding whether particular benefits should be universal or selective, policy-makers face quite complicated problems in the design and delivery of welfare incomes and services. The problems are of three general kinds, to do with entitlement, delivery, and effects on other aspects of the recipients' lives. We will notice them in that order, then offer some reasons why economists need to know something about them.

Entitlement   Transferred incomes and public services can be provided on any of the following conditions:

- Services (like some health services) can be free to everyone.

- Services (like some cities' public housing) can be available to anyone at economic rents or prices, and at lower rates or free to people of limited means.

- Where there are means tests, they can be applied to individuals, couples, families or households. Recall our example of three households with identical numbers and incomes who would fare very differently under individual, family or household income-counting.

- Where there are user-paid fees they can be set to cover the costs of the service wholly (as with some public housing) or partly (as with some public health services).

- Cash allowances (for old age, disability, unemployment, full-time study, parenting, and so on) can go to all entitled persons as tax-free income; or to all entitled persons as taxable income; or selectively to means-tested persons or families or households only (and again, taxed or untaxed, and means-tested on any of the individual, family or household bases listed above).

Delivery Reliable delivery is an important consideration in the design of transferred incomes and welfare services. They must reach the people they are intended for. They must not go to others. But there is tension between those two requirements. It is often impossible to meet both. Arrangements which ensure that a benefit reaches everyone entitled to it tend to make it possible for some unentitled people to get it too. But strict rules and procedures which exclude those others also in practice exclude some who are entitled – often some of the poorest who need the benefit most.

As to which alternative is best, there tend to be occupational biases. Treasury officers, Auditors-General, a critical press and (I am sorry to say) many economists want strict accountability which allows no taxpayer's dollar to go astray. People who are poor themselves or can remember what it is like, and social workers and others who deal face to face with the people for whom the benefits are intended, tend to want to make sure that the benefits reach everyone entitled to them, even if that means they reach a few others too. They may also be more discriminating judges of any 'leakage' that occurs. For example if some smart lad collects half a dozen unemployment allowances under half a dozen false names, that is bad. If a hard-up household continues to pay a rebated rent to its public landlord when a strictly accurate means test would increase the rent a little, that is not so bad. When a widow continues to draw an age pension which is subject to an asset test as well as an income test, by concealing the fact that she owns a cottage in which, rent-free, her daughter is lone-parenting three children whose father has deserted them, that may be positively good. When the rules defeat their own purposes, some rule-breaking can be sensible.

One reason why accurate delivery may be difficult is this: whether or not benefits are offered selectively, many of them are used selectively. Some of the people who need them most may not be able to get them, or know how to get them. Some of the people who need them least may be the most skilful at getting the biggest possible share of them. (Some free health and child-care services have had both shortcomings.) Those who fail to get benefits intended for them may include very young people; homeless people; country people who live too far from the relevant offices or services; newcomers to town; immigrants who need foreign-language information services; illegal immigrants and other offenders

who are not sure how safely they can approach any public services; illiterate people; mentally handicapped people; people who are frightened of violent spouses or kin; people who are just a bit ill-informed, muddled or diffident. Seeking out and helping such people has costs, which public authorities are often reluctant to pay. (I once saw a government economist commissioned to search for reports of research into the number of people who might benefit from public housing but did not know it was available to them, or how to apply for it. So ingrained was an opposite habit of mind that she returned with a survey of research into the numbers in public housing who were getting benefits they were not entitled to.)

More philosophy: How should you value and compare the efficiency which ensures that only the intended people get public benefits with the efficiency which ensures that all the intended people get them? How much inefficiency at one of those tasks is a tolerable cost of how much efficiency at the other? It goes without saying that any change which improves both at once is welcome. But where the dilemma persists, as it does to some degree with almost all selective services and income transfers, how far should law-makers and administrators lean toward the one inefficiency or the other? You will decide in the light of your values, and it may often be wise to decide differently for different services. I offer an opinion not about what the bias should be but about how and by whom such questions should be decided. They should be decided by people who in their own experience or by attentive consultation have known a fair sample of the people for whom the benefits are intended, the hardships or inequalities they are meant to reduce, and the detailed, day-by-day ease or difficulty of delivering the benefits as the legislators intend. Even more here than in other fields of their work, economists should do their best to understand the whole human experience from which theories abstract selected elements only.

Poverty traps Here are the worst dilemmas of all. Means-tested provisions usually have two inseparable effects. One: the benefit has to diminish or cease as the need diminishes. Two: that means that if the recipients earn more, as they and the legislators want them to do, their earnings must either be confiscated or taxed at high rates. Worse still, if people are getting more than one means-tested benefit, they may be punished by being positively fined for earning any income by their own efforts.

How can that happen? Consider how a thoroughly selective welfare system might treat (for example) a supporting mother with one child. Suppose it gives her a supporting parent's allowance of $200 a week, means-tested to fall 50 cents for every dollar she manages to earn (so she still has some incentive to earn). Suppose that another branch of government pays her a means-tested child allowance of $40, reducing 50 cents for every dollar earned. A different level of government lets her an apartment worth $80 a week, but rebates her rent to $50, with a means-test which will reduce the rebate and increase the rent 25 cents for every dollar she earns (so that her rent cannot rise above 25 per cent of her income).

Now suppose that she gets part-time work minding other children along with her own, earns $80 a week and is honest enough to disclose it to all her means-testers. From her public allowances and rent rebate she will lose $40 + $40 + 20 = $100, and be $20 poorer for having worked at all. That is tough, but worse is possible. If the authorities were using cut-off means-tests rather than tapered ones – i.e. if they cut her benefits by a dollar for every dollar she earned – earning $80 could reduce her benefits by $150 and cost her a net $70, and more if she had more children. The example exaggerates, because real authorities are rarely so drastic or uncoordinated, but it illustrates the nature of the notorious poverty trap which afflicts most means-tested welfare provisions to greater or less degree, and can make some of the poorest earners pay (in effect) higher rates of income tax on their earnings than the very richest earners pay.

The dilemma cannot really be avoided, though its effects may be moderated in various ways. Here are two theoretical proposals and one practical response to the dilemma. The first two are here chiefly to make clear why no country has adopted them.

A *universal income* The only way to avoid the dilemma altogether would be to pay a sufficient public income to everyone from the poorest to the richest, and let them also earn and keep whatever they could above that income. Services should then be supplied free to all or at the same prices to all. A lot of money would have to be paid to the citizens, and much more than half of it repaid as tax. The tax rates would have to be high, and to have much effect in reducing inequality they would need to be steeply progressive. It would be simpler not to pay the large part of the public income which would have to be taxed back – but that would create an incentive problem, as follows:

A *guaranteed minimum income* Government decides on a sufficient minimum income and guarantees it to every adult (or household, with adjustment for household numbers and composition). Everyone, rich or poor, makes an income tax return. Those who have more than the minimum income pay income tax. Those who have less receive 'positive tax' to bring their income up to the guaranteed minimum. As above, services are then supplied free to all, or at the same prices to all. The minor trouble with this scheme is that it would be difficult to administer – for many people with variable incomes it might not be easy to relate weekly income supplements to an annual income assessment. The major trouble is that there would be no financial incentive to earn at all unless you earned more than the guaranteed minimum; and once above that minimum the lowest earners would pay the highest rates of tax, in the sense that someone who earned (say) $440 a week when the guaranteed minimum was $400 would gain only $40 – 10 per cent of the wage – for her week's work, and in effect pay 90 per cent of her earnings in tax.

Practical *compromises* Developed countries respond to the dilemma by mixing a number of methods. The mixtures differ from country to country but their main elements are three:

- *Free benefits:* Some incomes and services are financed from taxation and supplied free to everyone. They may include primary, secondary and in some countries tertiary education; health services; child allowances.

- *Contributory, income-linked benefits:* Compulsory superannuation schemes take contributions from employees, employers and often government, to finance pensions whose amounts are linked to the pensioners' contributions. This may seem to make the productive system provide the welfare, and it avoids poverty traps and some other problems. But the governments' contributions are from taxation and the employers' contributions are a form of taxation, and there have to be tax-based, means-tested pensions for people who have not been contributing members of the schemes, so the system is really a hybrid which combines elements of self-help and public assistance.

- *Means-tested benefits:* The means-testing can vary with the nature of the service, the users' needs, and the policy-makers' preference for one horn or other of the means-testing dilemma. For pensions and unemployment allowances, tapered means tests are common. A pensioner can earn up to a first limit without loss of pension. Up to a second limit the pension is reduced by half the amount earned.

Beyond that, the pension is reduced by the whole amount earned. Housing allowances and rent rebates are usually tapered more gently, to keep housing costs below a specific percentage of income. Other services have other rules. Some mix their principles: Britain introduced a universal, tax-financed old age pension, then supplemented it with additional, means-tested allowances for people who depended on the pension alone.

Economists' contribution to welfare policy

This part-chapter on public income transfers and services has emphasized the difficulties which their designers face. Its main purpose is to draw attention to a likely professional bias of which economists should be aware when they work in this field.

Public income transfers in cash and kind are the main income of about a quarter of the people, and they contribute to the incomes of many more, in affluent societies. They are a big proportion of the public budget and the tax bill. So they are subject to much scrutiny and many pressures as politicians compete to convince their electors that they are meeting the welfare needs humanely but economically. The policy-making and debates about it call for plenty of economic analysis. Economists are the appropriate experts to do the analysis, and they have contributed valuably to the development of modern welfare systems. In recent times some of them have also been among the systems' toughest critics.

But the professional education of economists has meanwhile become very demanding. One thing it has come to demand in many English-speaking universities (but not in the US) is the whole of the student's time, so that economics – commonly neoclassical economics – is the only thing that economists study through their university years. That can narrow the mind and blinker the eyesight considerably. The non-economic aspects of life and government, and the non-economic effects of economic policies, tend to go unnoticed or under-valued, or be consigned (with much the same effect) to other disciplines. The more rigorous and mathematical the economists' education becomes, the more their expertise may tempt those who work at welfare policies to focus only on the 'pure economics' of income transfers in cash and kind: the distribution of measurable income before and after the transfers, and the effects of the transfers on patterns of inequality, the allocation of resources, and financial incentives to work.

Rigorous analysis of that kind can find apparent inef-

ficiencies and anomalies in most welfare systems. For example some transfers are from poorer to richer people because richer people use more free services than poorer people do. Many tenants of public housing are better off than poorer people on the waiting lists for public housing are. Public tenants get more help than private tenants do; and with tapered means tests, some public allowances can increase inequalities within the poorest class, between one poor household and another. Rigorous economists understandably itch to rationalize such anomalies: Income transfers should be precisely targetted. Benefits should cease as soon as entitlement does. Allowances to the unemployed should be lower than the lowest wage offering in the labor market. If public housing tenants get jobs, they should be evicted to make way for poorer folk without jobs. Inequalities will be reduced most effectively if most services are user-paid rather than free, with means-tested exceptions only for the poorest users.

But such strict policies can have ill effects. Some of them involve the dilemmas and poverty traps described above. Some require humiliating means tests which drive away some of the people they are meant to help. Some are self-defeating in other ways – for example, a main purpose of public housing is defeated if tenants have to move out as soon as their housing has helped them to prosper.

There is no escape from the awkward fact that income transfers and welfare services must often serve multiple purposes and always have multiple effects. Designing them requires expertise but it also requires social judgment of a broad, all-things-considered kind. Experts can learn to think in that way, but it can be hard if their professional training discourages it, and if their working life does not keep them in touch with the people and problems that their policies concern.

The most influential designer of twentieth century welfare systems was probably William Beveridge, whose 1942 report on Social Insurance and Allied Services was a main basis of welfare policy in post-war Britain. Beveridge was educated in maths and classics and law. Then he worked in welfare services for London's poor and unemployed. He was fifty one when he took his degree in economics, and he experienced twelve more years of depression and war before he wrote his famous report. That is a hard act to follow these days. As a twenty-first century economist you may have to make it your own business, rather than relying on your formal education, to broaden your reading and experience and sympathies.

HOME-MADE INCOME

Besides what they earn and buy, people also produce goods and services for themselves and each other. The output of their unpaid labor is more than a third of all output. It varies from person to person, from household to household and from country to country. It has much more effect on the amount and distribution of income than conventional national accounts and economic theories reveal. Recall, from our sketch of centuries of household history, the terrible difference between the things the latest generations of Weavers and Farmers were equipped do for themselves and their kin.

Do-it-yourself output varies with -

• the time available for it

• households' human capital: their members' will and skill at working for themselves and each other

• households' private space and capital

• the public space and capital available for people to use. (Recall Ian Castles' comparison of the public recreational provisions in Japanese and Australian cities)

• households' money income

• household choices between buying finished consumption goods and services, and producing for themselves.

All but the first and last of those factors are affected by government. The policy questions were dealt with in Chapters 25 and 26 on household resources and governments' housing policies. Revise them if you need to. To relate them to this review of income policies, here's an even shorter summary of Chapter 27's short summary of the subject.

HOUSEHOLD CAPITAL

Houses, private land and their equipment are a main part of the capital for household production. Within the limits imposed by their money incomes, households generally know best what housing they want. They should have full market freedom to shop around for what they want: the type of house, the location, the tenure as owners or tenants, and the proportion of their money income they spend on their housing. Settled households are generally better off over household life as owners than as tenants of their houses. Owners also have more control over the equipment of their houses, and alterations or additions to them.

But if left to themselves the housing and housing finance markets tend to operate with gross market failure.

If housing is productive capital (as this text insists it is) there is no market link between households' capacity to get it and their capacity to use it productively. In practice market forces tend to distribute it so that its ownership and its household output increase inequalities between the poorest quarter or so of households and the rest. When landlords can outbid marginal homebuyers for the available houses and housing finance, that usually gets the households less or worse housing than they could afford as buyers. And over household life it reduces their spendable income, which in turn, especially in poorer households, reduces the productive use they can make of their household capital.

If on the other hand you choose to treat housing as an aid to consumption, and you think it is natural that richer people can afford to buy more of it, then the market failure is even worse. Reversing the most basic condition of market efficiency, the quality and quantity of the item is inverse to its price for many of the customers. That is because over household life the better options cost less (to homebuyers) and the poorer options cost more (to tenants).

Thus if it is left to itself market competition cannot be relied on to allocate capital resources efficiently between housing and other investment. It cannot allocate housing capital most productively between household and household. And it will not stop landlord investors preempting housing whose users would rather buy it themselves, and could use it more productively if they could do so.

Chapter 26 listed detailed policies and strategies by which government can correct those failures and give households access to affordable houses through efficient land, housing and money markets, while preserving market freedoms and market discipline, and supplying good forms of public housing for those who need or prefer them.

PUBLIC CAPITAL

Some communities are much better equipped than others with public goods which their citizens can use to increase their material incomes, their skills and recreations and their enjoyment of life. Those goods include –

• community centres, arts and craft centres, libraries, museums

• schools with playing fields, courts, pools etc.

• public parks and gardens, playing fields, courts, pools, etc.

- good public transport
- networks of safe bicycle tracks
- easy exit from towns to accessible countrysides. (Depending on the climate and terrain that may mean pedestrian ways through the English countryside, forest ski-tracks around Norwegian cities, footpaths through the New England woods or the Australian bush; and wilderness, conservation and recreational parks, and unpolluted lakes and rivers and beaches wherever the geography allows.)

There are no records of the use of many of those facilities. Even where the numbers of school children, library users or museum visitors are known, their benefits do not appear as income in national accounts. But they can make a great difference to the quality of life, especially as they increase people's skills and capacities for both productive activity and the sheer enjoyment of life – as follows.

HUMAN CAPITAL

Education enriches human capital. That effect has been much studied and theorized by economists and educators. But they tend to focus on the economic effects which appear in national accounts rather than those which do not. So from time to time there is pressure from economic rationalists to concentrate publicly financed education more exclusively on developing employable skills. Law, medicine, engineering, accountancy and the employable branches of science are seen as more productive than literature, history, philosophy and the arts. But use your imagination and consult your experience. Compare a society with community centres, arts and craft centres, libraries and museums, and the other kinds of public capital for free private use that were listed in the previous section, with one which lacks those things. People in the well-equipped society can make more uses of their leisure time and their human potentialities. They are materially richer. They can develop more interests and skills. They transmit some of those particular interests and skills to their children. More generally, they are likely to give their children a more active and productive approach to life than they could do if – for lack of public and private capital – most of their recreation had to be passive or commercial: watching sport, watching TV, playing electronic games. Life offers them more in the way of non-cash income. And they may well be more productive as workers in the regular economy, because they are active and resourceful and accustomed to self-motivated learning and doing.

A conclusion

Most of the policies which improve the amount and distribution of home-made income are not called income policies. They are elements of financial policy, housing policy, education policy, arts policy, transport policy, environmental policy. Most of those concern activities which have public capital and running costs, but no money returns or precisely valued outputs. So it is all too easy for tax-cutters to see them as the least productive, least needed and most subsidized of the activities which taxpayers finance – and the first to cut.

A lot of the public and private activities which develop skilful, resourceful, productive people are of that vulnerable kind. The human capital which they help to develop is the main source of all productivity – public and private, paid and unpaid, recorded and unrecorded. Thoughtful economists should not call unpaid household work 'consumption', or public investment for household use 'public spending', or household capital 'consumer durables'. The household sector is as productive as the other sectors, and it is also a necessary condition of their productivity.

Remember to think

This chapter has summarized a range of public policies which can affect the distribution of income. Rather than summarize the summary to help you remember it, we can end with a provocation to think about it. Why does the democratic pursuit of greater equality – a simple enough ideal – present such problems of choice between conflicting values? I will recommend a book which poses a dozen penetrating questions about those choices. But in case you want simpler provocations, here are three:

1. Which inequalities should we try to reduce? Inequalities of money income? Whole real income? Opportunity? Capacity? Well-being? Freedom – and if so, which freedoms? To make any one of those more equal must usually make one or more of the others less equal.

2. If some unequal incomes are necessary as incentives and rewards, how unequal do they need to be? Forgetting inequalities of wealth for the moment, should the lowest earners get a third of the average income? Half? Three quarters? Should the highest earners get twice the average? Twenty times? Two hundred times? Twenty thousand times? The rich democracies have examples of chief executive pay, in multimillion dollar enterprises, at each of those four levels, with no discernible relation between the

scale of inequality and the quality of performance. What kind of reasoning would help you to decide the best scale of inequality, for example in arriving at poverty lines, public income transfers, rates of progressive income tax, proposals to regulate executive pay?

3. Given a pattern of incentives and rewards, who should get which of the unequal incomes? Should handicapped workers earn less than others in the same occupation, because they produce less – or the same because they work as hard and under greater difficulties? How should surgeons and anaesthetists split the fees for the operations they do? Should artists' and performers' pay vary with the technology that allows some but not others to earn in their absence, and by mass replication of their books or films or discs? Should executives of pharmaceutical companies which manufacture life-saving drugs earn less or more than the scientists who discover and develop the drugs? Should underground coalminers earn more or less than university professors? (In my country, I think rightly, the 'government model' of wage-fixing has them paid about the same.)

If you have time and spirit for a thorough exploration of the complexities that underlie simple ideals of equality, read Amartya Sen, *Inequality Reexamined* (1992). Read it for the light it sheds on its subject, but also to watch one of the world's most intelligent economists bring all his political, moral and philosophical capacities to bear on a profound economic problem.

46

Taxation

Where should income transfers come from? Whose incomes should supply them?

Remember the double purpose of transferring income over time and between people. You need to transfer some income from your earning years to your non-earning years. You do it by transferring income to others while you earn, and receiving it from others while you are not earning. But there are two reasons why what you give and what you receive over your lifetime may not balance. First, conditions change through your lifetime. There may be more earners to support fewer non-earners when you are young, and fewer earners to support more non-earners when you are old. But over the same period economic growth may have increased the earners' capacity to pay; medical and other welfare costs may have risen; opinions may have changed about the right amount of income to pay to aged or unemployed non-earners; and so on. So even if the only purpose of the transfers was to spread everyone's income over their lifetime, it is likely that there would be some net transfers from person to person, as over their lifetimes some people gave more than they received and others received more than they gave.

But that is not the only purpose of the transfers. Government also uses them to redistribute income, mostly from richer to poorer people, for compassionate and equitable reasons. So some transfers relate what people give to what they get, for example in contributory superannuation schemes. But many transfers don't do that. Instead, they take income from people who can afford to pay and give it to people who need it, as 'capacity to pay' and 'need' are defined in prevailing beliefs about distributive justice.

Tax policy is about how much money to take, on what basis, from which people. Of course tax revenue finances many other public activities besides income transfers. But taxation is best studied as a whole, and now is a convenient time to do it. (For simplicity this chapter deals only with the tax sources of public funds. It neglects the trading profits of public enterprises and any money or credit that government may create for itself or derive from other sources.)

TAX PRINCIPLES

Principles of taxation can be classified in a number of ways. We can begin by distinguishing squalid principles from respectable ones.

Squalid tax policies (in my opinion) are those which politicians design for their own short-term political advantage, on the assumption that the taxpayers are only interested in their short-term financial advantages. Instead of choosing the most prudent, efficient and equitable tax policies, they do whatever may get them re-elected by voters as selfish and short-sighted as themselves. If you are that sort of politician, your tax tactics may include these:

- Tax the classes or groups likely to vote against you more heavily than you tax your supporters.

- More sophisticated and treacherous: Tax both your committed opponents and your faithful supporters more heavily than you tax the groups in which opinion polls find most swinging voters.

- The rich have most influence but the rest of the people have most votes. So here is what you do. Publish steeply progressive rates of income tax for the media to tell the masses about, but with lots of exemptions in the small print that only lawyers read. Tax luxury cars and hotel rooms heavily, but let the rich have their firms pay for their cars and hotel suites as business costs.

- When you can cut taxation, cut the most acutely-felt taxes, especially income tax and property tax on the family home.

- When you have to increase taxation, increase the taxes that are easiest to conceal from the people who pay them, or hardest to blame on the government responsible for them. Prefer indirect taxes which business will collect for you through higher prices to direct taxes which the voters themselves must pay to the government.

- Company tax, payroll tax and other taxes on business activity rather than on goods call for careful judgments of political advantage. On the one hand the mass of voters may not connect those taxes with the prices they pay for the goods they buy. On the other hand the business enemies of such taxes have great influence and may be your main source of party funds.

- Be improvident. Cut taxes to attract votes at the next election, although you know that the cuts will defer necessary public investment, cut some public services, increase public debt, and necessitate future tax increases.

- Be more improvident. Spend capital. Privatize public services. Even where you can't privatize the services you can sell their assets. Sell public office buildings, library and museum and other buildings, the fleet of government cars, and lease them back for public use. Use the capital proceeds for current spending, to allow tax cuts now. When the capital is all spent, taxes will need to be higher than before to pay the lease rents. But that will be some other politicians' problem.

- Tell lies. Make enticing tax promises before elections, and break them afterwards.

That sort of leadership can degrade the citizens' as well as the politicians' behavior. If leaders keep telling voters that it is natural and rational to vote selfishly, whether their interests are legitimate or not, fair or unfair, then some at least of the people will be persuaded to go further in that direction than they would otherwise do.

Respectable taxation must still cope with pervasive conflicts of interest. People may always dislike taxes, and be tempted by opportunities to pay less than their fair share of them. But democratic voters also support plenty of taxation which they regard as necessary and fair rather than personally advantageous to them. There is of course some human tendency to confuse the two: to perceive as fair the principles that happen to favor your interests. Politicians have to decide how far to appeal to people's individual self-interest, to their collective interest in financing the public services they want, and to their compassion and ideas of fairness. The big political winners have not always been those who appeal to the worst rather than the best of voters' natures. Elected governments get a great deal of their support from voters whose self-interest is moderated by fair-minded, prudent and generous considerations. Public choice economists who assume that individual self-interest alone motivates political behavior have again and again proved to be mistaken.

The rest of this review will stick to respectable tax principles appropriate for politicians who want to hold

office by governing well rather than by more squalid means. But however virtuous, they can't assume that the citizens are all angels. However it is moderated, self-interested dislike of taxation is always present. Notice, now, a reason why it may pose special problems of political leadership.

Freeloading illusions and the demand for public goods

One theme links work published a generation ago by three leading economists: Paul Samuelson's 'Pure Theory of Public Expenditure' (1954), John Kenneth Galbraith's *The Affluent Society* (1958) and Anthony Downs' 'Why the Government Budget is Too Small in a Democracy' (1960). They perceived that the nature of public goods invites attempts at freeloading. People try to pay less than their fair shares of the cost of the goods they get. In practice that gets them less goods than they want, less than they would buy and willingly pay for in an efficient market.

The reasoning is as follows. When you shop for market goods, there is no lawful way to get them without paying for them. But you can't buy public goods in that individual way. They are public goods precisely because you can't be made to pay for exactly what you individually get. So you have to order public goods collectively, through government; and you have to vote for taxes or other revenue to pay for them. That tempts some people to hope that they can pay less than their share, and it allows disagreement about what distribution of taxation would be fairest. In practice it also allows some separation of the politics which decide what the public sector should provide, and the politics of taxation. So there is some latitude for people to oppose the taxes they themselves will pay, hoping to shift some of the burden onto other taxpayers. But with big numbers doing that, a common effect is to limit total tax to less than the cost of the public goods the majority want. And the effective demand for public goods is not what majorities decide they want; as in other markets, it is the amount they will pay for. So the people get less public goods than they want: less than they would choose to buy if they were available as market goods.

You can understand that trouble in a number of ways. It is a market failure, a shortcoming of democracy, a failure of leadership. Those views of it are not necessarily incompatible, they just focus on different strands of causation. Try them in turn:

A market failure The efficient market for private goods and the defective market for public goods may together lead consumers to distribute their spending inefficiently, buying more private goods and less public goods than they would choose if both markets were efficient.

A democratic failure Significant numbers of voters are incoherent, unethical, incompetent, or all three. Incoherent because they don't match their demands for public goods with appropriate tax provisions. Unethical because some of the incoherence is caused by their attempts to get the goods without paying for them. Incompetent in thinking they can get away with that.

A failure of leadership Though true, that last explanation is unreasonable. The mass of electors can't do the demanding technical work required to compose the public budget. That is government's business. If you're a political leader competing for the votes of tax-averse electors, you have – broadly speaking – three options:

- Squalor: You can try to entice the electors with the temptations and deceptions sketched earlier.

- Honest service: You can match your spending to your revenue by one or another kind of good house-keeping, without mortgaging the future. Cut welfare and public services to fit the taxation which majorities will tolerate, or deliver the promised welfare and services and impose the necessary taxation. In either case be honest about what you are doing and take the political consequences. You won't always lose.

- Leadership: Educate, inspire and lead your country with a coherent program of good government financed by sufficient taxation. That is not an impractical dream, it is what the most successful twentieth-century governments of both Right and Left have done. Of course the best of them have still had opponents and internal disagreements. But secure majorities and sufficient consensus have supported more principled democratic governments than purely opportunist ones.

For the second and third of those styles of government you will need to know the respectable principles of taxation which we will now review.

TAX INCIDENCE

First some definitions. The incidence of a tax means where its burden falls, i.e. who finally pays it and has less capital or income as a result of paying it. That is sometimes the people from whom the government collects the tax, and sometimes others. The following terms help to categorize the incidence of particular taxes, and of tax systems as a whole.

Direct, indirect Personal income and property taxes are direct: those who pay them are those who lose by them. Indirect taxes are paid wholly or partly by other people than those from whom the government collects the tax. Taxes on goods and services – tariff, excise, sales and value-added taxes – are collected from traders but are mostly paid (through higher prices) by the consumers of the goods. But that can be hard to measure. It is difficult to be sure about the incidence of some taxes, for reasons you will meet presently.

Progressive, proportional, regressive These refer to the effects of taxation on the distribution of wealth and income. If a tax takes a higher percentage of higher incomes and a lower percentage of lower incomes, it is progressive. If it takes the same percentage of all incomes, it is proportional. If it takes a higher percentage of low incomes and a lower percentage as incomes rise, it is regressive. Progressive taxation reduces inequalities. Regressive taxation increases them. Proportional taxation doesn't alter the mathematical inequalities (the richest income is still the same multiple of the poorest) but it may make the inequalities harder for some to bear: taking (say) half a poor household's income may do more harm to its health and happiness than taking half its income may do to a rich household. Also remember that a regressive tax may finance a progressive distribution of benefits, and vice versa. For example free university education is generally regressive, because it goes disproportionately to people from well-off households who will themselves earn above-average incomes. But if the education is financed by progressive taxation the net effect of the taxes and benefits may be less, or not at all, regressive.

Discriminate taxes apply different rates of tax to different goods and services, different assets, or different sources of income. For example it is common to discriminate between -

- capital and income. You pay income tax on earned and unearned income, but not on the money you get by selling your house, car or other capital assets. (But there are exceptions. If you make your living by buying and selling houses or other assets, the tax collector will define you as a professional dealer, and your profits as taxable income.)

- assets. Taxes on capital assets may be at different rates for different assets. Examples: (1) The property taxes (often called 'rates') which provide most local government revenue in many countries may tax houses and commercial property at different rates. (2) If government puts unusual restrictions on your property it may compensate you through the tax system. For example if your property is in a national park, or has been declared to be an item of national heritage, you may not be allowed to demolish or alter it. Government may compensate you by exempting the property from property tax.

- sources of income. Some governments apply different rates of tax to earned and unearned income, or to income earned at home and income earned abroad. Some countries exempt shareholders' dividends from personal income tax up to the amount of corporate income tax that the relevant company has paid.

- sources of goods. Tariffs tax imports but not home-country products. If a tariff is retaliatory, i.e. if its purpose is to offset another country's export subsidies, the tariff may be applied at different rates to imports from different countries.

- goods and services. Taxes on goods and services (excise taxes, wholesale taxes, sales taxes, value added taxes) are often at different rates for different goods and services. For example most goods and services may pay a standard rate of tax, but 'merit' goods and services (education, health services, basic foods) may be exempt from tax, and 'demerit' goods (alcohol, tobacco) may pay high rates of tax. Some luxury goods may also pay high rates, as a means of making indirect taxes progressive.

Who pays?

Besides the direct and indirect taxes defined earlier, it is customary to add a third category of business taxes, chiefly company tax and payroll tax, because it can be hard to know who ultimately pays them. Here are notes on the incidence of the three types of tax.

Direct taxes Personal income tax comes from the incomes of the people who pay it, though the loss may be shared by others in their households. The same is true of taxes on owner-occupied houses and other household capital. Taxes on other capital and on capital gains are direct when individuals pay them. But rich individuals may 'incorporate' themselves, by registering companies to own their wealth and receive much of their income. Depending on their countries' tax laws, this can allow various kinds of tax avoidance.

Indirect taxes on goods and services are collected at various stages of the production and distribution of the goods.

- *Tariffs* are levied on goods entering the country.

- *Excise* taxes are paid by the producers of the taxed goods.

Tariff and excise taxes are normally added to the prices of the taxed goods and passed on to all their users including their business users. So besides taxing the final consumers of the taxed item, they also tax consumers of other items whose costs of production are increased by the tax. Tariff or excise are the usual methods of taxing petrol, for example. The increased price of petrol increases farmers' costs, and the transport costs of many other goods and services. So you pay some petrol tax when you buy bread or woollen socks or airline tickets as well as when you buy petrol for your car.

- Value Added Tax (VAT) is levied on the value added at each stage of production. The farmer pays the VAT rate on her output. The food processor pays VAT on the difference between what he pays the farmer (and her other suppliers) and what he charges the wholesaler. The wholesaler and the retailer each pay VAT on the difference between what they pay for their goods and what they get when re-selling them.

- Sales Taxes are usually levied on the final retail sale of finished goods. Unlike tariffs or excise or wholesale taxes or VAT, that confines the tax to the final users of the taxed goods. When the goods are exported so that their final sales are beyond the producing country's jurisdiction, the tax may not be paid at all in the producing country. That can help exporters to keep their prices internationally competitive. And it may avoid unfair double taxation if the goods do pay tariff or sales tax in the countries which import them.

Business taxes can be direct, for example if they reduce a small business owner's income as directly as income tax does. They can reduce owners' incomes a little less directly if they reduce the dividends which companies pay to their shareholders. They can be as indirect as taxes on goods and services if those who pay them can pass them on in higher prices to their customers. It is hard to know who ultimately pays some business taxes, because estimates depend on guessing what the prices and volumes of business would be without the taxes. So business taxes get a heading of their own here, between direct and indirect taxes.

Firms pay the government charter fees or registration fees for their corporate powers. Depending on the business they do, they may pay many other fees, charges, stamp duties, resource rents. Here you need only notice company tax and payroll tax, which are the biggest business taxes in most developed countries.

Company tax (or corporate income tax) is levied on firms' annual profits. It is usually a fixed percentage of taxable profit, so between companies it is a proportional tax. But socially it is a progressive tax, because shareholders average richer than the rest of the population.

But is the tax paid by the shareholders? Think of a competitive industry in which most firms' annual profits are equal to about 9 per cent of the market value of their share capital. If the company tax rate is 33.3 per cent of profits the tax takes 3 of those 9 percentage points, leaving 6 to go to the shareholders as dividend. (For simplicity we're ignoring any undistributed profit held for re-investment.) The firms are pricing their products to yield that 9 per cent return to the firm and 6 per cent to its owners.

What if the company tax were repealed? Would firms maintain their prices and increase their dividends by half to 9 per cent? If so, the shareholders are currently paying the company tax. Or would competition drive the firms to drop their prices to a level which would yield 6 per cent profit and the usual 6 per cent dividend? If they would do that, the shareholders are not paying company tax. The firms' pricing policies are passing the tax on to their customers.

That is called 'shifting the tax forward', meaning on to the following stage of production or distribution. Taxes may also be shifted 'back', if producers can respond to taxation by cutting the prices they pay for inputs, the wages they pay their workers, or the number of workers they employ. Whether they can do so may depend on the methods of production, market conditions and bargaining strengths.

Thus it can be argued that who finally pays company tax depends on what the relevant wages, prices and dividends would be without the tax. That is likely to vary with market conditions. There is still a reasonable presumption that company tax usually costs shareholders more than it costs anyone else. But in practice firms rarely pay company tax at anything like the specified rate. The rate has commonly been between a third and a half of taxable profit, but the amount collected in most countries is below 15 per cent of actual profit. Most of the shortfall is lawful. Business has persuaded government to allow increasingly generous deductions from taxable profits. There are allowances for depreciation, research and development, undistributed profit, new investment, losses by associated firms – and tax lawyers' fees.

There has been less watering down of the second main business tax, as follows.

Payroll tax is levied on employers, usually as a percentage rate on their whole wage bill. Some countries exempt small employers, or charge them lower rates. Some countries make employees contribute to the tax. Some countries treat the tax as ordinary revenue. Others link it to contributory health insurance and superannuation so that it is more like an insurance premium than a tax. The employer's share is a simple addition to costs of production and usually to product prices. So consumers pay most of it. In some industries the tax may cut the number of workers that employers can afford to employ. If that increases the numbers unemployed, other losses follow. The government loses income tax from the lost incomes, and indirect taxes from the reduced consumer spending. The higher unemployment may increase some public welfare costs. So government may have to increase some taxes, cut some services, or borrow more. But none of these ill effects need follow if there is full employment.

So much for the people who actually pay the various types of tax. Next, how do different taxes affect the functioning of the economy?

EFFICIENCY

Remember that economic efficiency is debatable: efficient at what, by what criteria, for whose purposes? This section links the main types of tax to economic effects on which judgments of their efficiency may be based.

Taxes themselves can be efficient or inefficient, and they can affect the efficiency with which resources are allocated and used, work is motivated, and consumers' preferences are served. We'll look at those items in turn.

Efficient taxes A tax is efficient if it is hard to evade and cheap to collect. Of every $100 of the intended revenue, a very efficient tax might net $95, losing $3 to evasion and $2 in collection costs. A very inefficient tax might net only half, losing $30 to evasion, $10 in collection costs and $10 to the legal costs of court actions and appeals. Most taxes perform somewhere between those extremes. Examples: (1) Company tax may be a good tax for other reasons, but it is an inefficient one: much expensive legal work goes to trying to avoid it and checking and auditing it, and there is a good deal of lawful avoidance of it, as noted above. (2) Personal income tax is collected very efficiently from wages and salaries. Employers collect most of it for the government, by means which add very little to the book-keeping they have to do to pay their employees. Collection from property incomes and self-employed incomes tends to be less efficient.

Besides the public costs of collecting a tax there are

usually private costs of paying it, and these should be part of any assessment of tax efficiency. Company tax requires firms and some self-employed individuals to pay for more book-keeping and legal advice than they would otherwise need. An excise tax on the other hand, especially if it is levied on the physical quantity rather than the value of petrol or alcohol or tobacco produced, costs producers very little more than the tax itself: what the tax collector needs to see are records which the producers must keep for their own purposes.

Some of the public costs of collecting taxes and the private costs of paying them or trying to minimize them belong under the next heading as bad allocations or uses of resources.

The allocation and use of resources Governments now spend, invest or transfer between a third and a half of national income. What they do with it has big effects on economic performance. But where they take it from is also important. Besides its effects on the distribution of wealth and income, the pattern of taxation can influence for better or worse –

- investors' preferences, for example between investing at home or abroad, and between investing for dividend, rent or fixed-interest income

- consumer preferences and the amount and composition of demand

- the allocation of resources to meet the demand

- the location and organization of production.

We will trace those effects of goods and services taxes, then business taxes, then taxes on personal wealth and income.

INDIRECT TAXES

When considering particular taxes on goods or services, start with two questions. (1) Is the primary purpose of the tax to raise revenue, or is it to achieve some other economic or social effect? (Call them 'revenue' taxes and 'economic' taxes for short.) (2) How elastic is the demand for the taxed item?

For analytical purposes those questions frame four categories: (1) revenue taxes on goods in inelastic demand; (2) revenue taxes on goods in elastic demand; (3) economic taxes on goods in inelastic demand; (4) economic taxes on goods in elastic demand.

Of course real taxes often have more than one purpose. Revenue taxes may be designed to have economic and social effects as well. Taxes imposed for economic purposes may have their rates set with revenue in mind. But where revenue taxes have no specific economic or social purposes they should generally do as little as possible to distort market preferences and allocations. With that in mind, consider examples of the four types:

Revenue tax / Inelastic demand In the days when ruling classes really ruled and made the lower classes supply most of the public revenue, taxes on salt were common. The demand was inelastic. Everyone wanted some and for most purposes there were no substitutes for it. It was produced in comparatively few places, by methods impossible to conceal, so the tax was hard to evade. Salt was a preservative, so its price had a minor effect on some other food prices. Except for that, taxing it did not alter other market prices or preferences. It was regressive and much resented, but it was an efficient tax for its purpose.

In modern times alcohol and tobacco have been taxed, until recently, chiefly for revenue. Demand was fairly inelastic up to quite high rates of tax, so increasing the rate increased total revenue. Nobody had to drink or smoke, and as slightly disreputable practices it was acceptable to tax them quite heavily. But the main purpose of that was not originally to discourage their use: they were merely a defensible source of revenue. But times and medical knowledge have changed. We may still tax liquor chiefly for the revenue, but tobacco tax is seen increasingly as a social tax reinforced by rising numbers of other restrictions on smoking.

Revenue tax / Elastic demand Many revenue taxes these days are levied on goods and services for which demand is fairly elastic because there are many substitutes for them. Taxing one will switch some demand to others.

Question: how can you tax elastically demanded goods for revenue, in a neutral way which does not distort relative prices and preferences? Answer: by taxing all such goods, and at the same rate. That is the principle of VAT and general sales taxes. Most of them still discriminate in broad ways where there are specific social purposes. Basic foods, winter warmth, education and health services may not be taxed at all. Tobacco and alcohol, some environmentally harmful goods and some luxury goods may be taxed at higher rates. But the mass of discretionary goods bought by the mass of people with low and middle incomes are all taxed at a common rate so as not to alter their relative attractions and affordability.

Economic tax / Inelastic demand If the social purpose is to reduce the use of undesirable goods or services for which the demand is inelastic, taxation is probably the wrong way to go about it. Inelastic demand means that using taxes to raise prices won't reduce consumption much. Education, rationing or regulation are likely to be more effective in such cases. Government may still tax the offending goods. But that won't serve a social purpose, except perhaps to punish sinners. It merely treats the items, like drink or gambling, as sources of public revenue.

Economic tax / Elastic demand Here belong taxes which do reduce demand for the taxed goods:

- *tariffs* which protect producers by raising the price of competing imports. The purpose(s) may be to maintain employment, the balance of payments, the diversity of national skills and occupations, the income of the protected owners and workers

- *pollution taxes,* which induce producers to switch to cleaner methods

- *resource taxes* which raise prices and reduce demand for minerals, natural forest timber or other exhaustible resources.

If environmental taxes meet inelastic responses (the pollution continues, the forest-clearing continues, undiminished by the new taxes) then the pollution tax may be used to finance a public clean-up, and the logging tax may finance public replanting of the cleared forests. In our formal classification that may make them revenue taxes rather than economic or social taxes, because they finance public action rather than influencing market behavior. But the purpose and effect are much the same.

Our four categories merely draw attention to some economic effects of indirect taxes. In practice many taxes serve more than one purpose. Taxes on luxury goods – furs, expensive cars, Scotch whisky – are examples. They tax the rich, but paying is voluntary – nobody is forced to buy those luxuries – so the taxes are not felt to be as oppressive as high rates of income tax. The elasticity of demand for the luxuries matters for revenue purposes. Whether it matters for other purposes may depend on which purposes the legislators have in mind. If they want to reduce consumption of fur, petrol and alcohol, the more elastic the demand the more effective the tax will be. If they want to reduce inequalities, the elasticity may matter less. If the demand is inelastic, high rates of tax will reduce financial inequalities. If it is elastic, other inequalities may be reduced if the taxes induce the rich to spend less, invest more (creating employment) and live less ostentatiously, sharing more of the common lifestyle.

BUSINESS TAXES

Recall the uncertainty about the incidence of some business taxes. Because it is hard to know which people ultimately pay what shares of them, it can be hard to estimate their effects on economic performance. That leaves room for ideological disagreements which go beyond differences of social purpose to disregard what is known about responses to taxation. The following notes on the two main business taxes, and a third possible one, stick to the more careful and realistic arguments of Left and Right on the subject.

Corporate income tax (or company tax) is a tax on corporate profit. Most countries tax some of it again as personal income when shareholders receive it as dividend. Some critics think that double taxation is not only unfair but also doubly inefficient. First, company tax is an inefficient tax for reasons noted earlier. Firms have to employ tax lawyers, do more expensive accounting than they would need without the tax requirements, check every business decision for its tax effects, and perhaps maintain offshore registration and profit centres for tax reasons. So the tax forces higher costs on them before they even pay the tax. Those costs may be assumed to raise their product prices. They may therefore reduce demand and reduce economies of scale, profit and growth. Second, the double tax may reduce firms' access to share capital. If dividend income is double taxed but interest and rent are not, passive investors may prefer to lend money or buy rental property rather than buy shares. That may limit firms' growth or force them to borrow more than is efficient for them.

Would it therefore be more efficient to free producers from these unproductive costs by abolishing company tax? Governments have some pragmatic and some more principled reasons for not doing that. The company tax is nearly always less than the tax rate suggests, because of the concessions and tax avoidance mentioned earlier. The double taxation is progressive, because shareholders are a rich minority. Moreover the downward shift of most countries' taxation from richer to poorer since the 1980s leaves company tax and income tax together taking less tax from most shareholders than they paid through the long boom in the third quarter of the century, when their rates of tax were plainly not restricting investment or growth.

Governments which continue to double-tax distributed company profits, once as company tax and then as shareholders' income tax, may do it for the revenue, and because it is progressive. But it can also be argued that it is not really double taxation, because company tax buys real advantages for shareholders: the use of corporate powers, lower risks with limited liability, and public regulation and policing of firms' obligations to their shareholders.

Payroll tax Considering only employers' contributions to payroll tax, what are its effects on employment and on what gets produced?

Remember how technical progress, and economic growth based on it, increase the productivity of some industries and occupations more than others. Capital-intensive manufactured goods get cheaper, labor-intensive goods and services get dearer. Payroll taxes increase that effect when it might be better to offset it. Payroll tax discourages employment at a time when unemployment is obstinately increasing. And technological change is increasing the amount of education needed by young people, and the amount of health and housekeeping care required by old people. Those are already the most expensive of the labor-intensive services, and they strain public tolerance because they mostly have to be paid for by earners' taxes and insurance contributions, but supplied to non-earners. With growth and technical change increasing the need for those services, increasing their relative costs, and increasing public resistance to the tax bill, a tax which further increases those costs may not be a good idea.

The effect of the tax can be limited by exempting public services from paying it. But payroll tax still raises the price of many necessary private services, and of many of the inputs which public services use. In developed countries a tax on capital intensification might make more sense. We will return to the problem in later chapters.

DIRECT TAXES

Most direct taxes on personal wealth and income are efficient taxes and sources of revenue. History shows them to have had very little effect on economic behavior or efficiency, though some of them may sometimes influence the location of investment.

Chapter 43 described the main taxes on capital wealth. Other chapters have dealt more particularly with taxes on land and buildings. All you need here are brief reminders

Capital gains are generally taxed at a flat rate which does not discriminate between different forms of wealth, except (commonly) to exempt gains from owner-occupied houses. The main economic effect of the tax is corrective. There are various ways in which firms can deliver property income to their owners as

capital gain rather than dividend income, to reduce the owners' income tax. So for fairness, and to discourage tax devices which may reduce productive efficiency, capital gains tax was introduced.

Death duties (under various names) taxed inheritance in many countries. When people learned to evade them by giving their property away before they died, gift duties were introduced to prevent the evasions. But they can now be evaded, especially on big fortunes, by perpetual trusts, holdings in foreign countries, and other devices. A number of countries have abolished them, partly because they became so unfairly inefficient, and partly under pressure to reduce the taxation of the rich.

A general wealth tax, levied every year at a low rate, is a fairer and more effective way to tax personal wealth. The few countries which have such a tax have been well served by it. It does not seem to have had any ill effects on economic performance. Swedish capitalists, for example, paid rates up to 2.5 per cent of their personal wealth each year through the decades when they established themselves among Europe's most successful manufacturers and exporters.

Property taxes are a main source of revenue for local government in many countries. They are usually levied on the value of land either with or without the buildings on it. Those alternatives have the economic and distributional effects outlined earlier. Taxing unimproved value, i.e. the value of the land alone, tends to encourage building investment and increase inequality. Taxing improved value may sometimes discourage investment but tends to reduce inequality.

Income tax Taxing personal income is comparatively simple. Most developed countries tax it in much the same way. In most, it is the biggest single tax. In some it yields more than half of all revenue. It is the best tax on almost all grounds. It is an efficient tax, cheap to collect and hard to evade (except by the very rich, and on some self-employed and property incomes). It offers an effective method of adjusting the distribution of income if that is desired. Except on the evasive rich the tax is usually progressive. Enough income for basic needs is untaxed. Above that the rate of tax rises with the amount of the taxpayer's income. It can also vary with household needs and responsibilities. The top marginal rate has ranged from 95 per cent in wartime Britain down to 30 per cent in the US since the 1980s. Economically the tax is neutral: it has little or no effect on work incentives, investment or the allocation of scarce resources.

Don't believe the many self-interested voices which tell you that progressive income tax does stifle effort. You know the reasons why, once people are above the breadline and in their chosen occupations, their rates of pay and tax don't have much effect on how hard they work. The few who work longer hours if their rate of pay rises tend to be balanced by a few others who respond by working less.

Rates of tax and their effect on income don't appear to affect investment either. The US saved and invested much the same proportion of national income in 1930 and 1960, though taxation had meanwhile become higher and more progressive. When taxation became lower and less progressive through the 1980s, the proportion of income saved and invested declined. As always, other factors were at work. But steeper personal taxation of the rich does not appear to reduce investment. It may even encourage it, if it prompts firms to retain and reinvest more profit and pay less out as income-taxable dividend.

Thus progressive income tax is an efficient revenue tax. By shifting some income from richer to poorer people it may shift some demand from luxury goods to other goods. But it does no harm to the market efficiency with which resources are allocated and goods are produced to meet the pattern of demand.

So why is such a good tax so unpopular?

Is it because it is the biggest tax you pay, and you see it go from every pay cheque, so it is the tax that hurts the most? Or is it because the influential rich keep persuading you – in their interest and against yours – to want a further shift from progressive income tax to regressive indirect taxes?

We will return to the subject when we presently discuss tax politics.

EQUITY

This section can be brief, not because its subject is not important, but because you already know its themes. (If you need to, revise Chapter 7's account of the role of values in economic analysis and in students' relations with their teachers.)

There are three or four widely accepted principles of fair taxation. They are not always compatible with one another, and it is not always best to judge the fairness of particular taxes in isolation: what matters most is the social effect of the whole structure of taxes and their economic effects, including the goods and services and income transfers that they finance. For that whole effect, and also for the fairness of particular taxes, these criteria are commonly recommended:

- **Capacity to pay** Taxes should come from people who can pay them without undue hardship. Thus most income taxes exempt enough of each taxpayer's income to pay for basic necessities of life.

- **Benefit** On a user-pays principle, the people likely to benefit most from public services should contribute most of their costs. Thus people with most property and income to protect should pay most property and income tax. Truckers who make road-building expensive should pay most road tax. Graduates of Australian universities pay a graduates' tax. But the principle does not extend to making age pensioners pay most tax because they get most benefit from public health services. When 'benefit' and 'capacity to pay' conflict, capacity to pay usually prevails.

- **Horizontal equity** People in similar circumstances should be treated alike. People with similar incomes and needs should pay the same income tax; people with houses of the same value should pay the same property tax.

- **Vertical equity** The tax system should correct unfair or unproductive inequalities of wealth and income.

- **Discriminate equity** Many taxes allow various concessions and exceptions. The first few thousand dollars of anyone's income – enough to pay for basic food and shelter – are exempt from income tax. Business is given tax incentives to invest, to conduct research and develop new products, to invest in depressed areas or enterprise zones, to employ handicapped people, and so on. Most of the concessions reflect one or other of the tax principles we've listed: capacity to pay, incentives for productive behavior, protection from foreign competition. But some have wholly or mainly equitable purposes. Gifts to charity are subtracted from the giver's taxable income, even if the gifts are in kind or from capital and did not come from taxable income. Governments which once taxed earned income at a lower rate than unearned income did so partly at least because working is more arduous – and virtuous – than loafing. Besides discriminate tax gifts there are also penalties. If you are caught evading tax, most countries tax you double the amount you tried to evade. These discriminations are partly for incentive purposes. But in many people's minds they are also just. Generosity should be encouraged, greed and deception should be punished.

Those are questions of social value and purpose. As always, you have to arrive at your judgment in the light of your values, or those of the people you choose to work for and the systems of thought you learn to trust. The better your technical work, the better your understanding of the behavior concerned and the greater your ethical concern, the better your judgment can be. Don't be persuaded that ethics and judgments of value are purely arbitrary, or merely rationalize self-interests. Your moral sense and your understanding of economic realities can respond to each other and refine each other in many fruitful ways.

But do policy-makers always work in that high-minded, disinterested way? Of course not. And they are often worse than they seem, as self-interested contenders deceive themselves or try to deceive others with false pretences of public spirit and ethical concern. But don't join the cynics. Self-seekers would not pretend so hard to be fair-minded and public-spirited if there were not genuine ethical concerns in the minds of the people they want to persuade. Most policies are designed to attract support both from people whose interests they serve and from others who think them fair and in the public interest. In politics you need to be sensitive to both. And there is nothing wrong or necessarily impractical in being disinterested and fairminded yourself, and encouraging others where you can.

POLITICS

From time to time this text reminds you of the play of good, bad and muddled intentions to be found in political life. Because taxes can cause such pain, debates about them can be fierce. Buckle your seatbelts again for a bumpy ride through the turbulence as a crowd of lobbyists jostle for opportunities to tell the national Treasurer or Chancellor of the Exchequer what they think his tax policies ought to be. Treat what follows as easy reading – the details don't matter just now. You will be asked to re-read parts of it for an exercise at the end of the chapter.

We sample the delegations from business, labor, public service and the Greens. We pretend that each delegation has three members – a statesmanlike one, an average one, and either a ruthless self-seeker or an impractical dreamer. (They don't all appear in that order.) There is a similar trio of advisers to the Treasurer. This is an unreal literary device, but it is to remind you of three real characteristics of political life. First, there is a wide range of self-interested, disinterested and public-spirited purposes at work in different people's minds, and often within individual minds.

Second, people base their preferences and policies on a range of true, half-true, sometimes-true and wholly false beliefs about the economy, including the effects of taxation on economic behavior. Third, the public reasons which politicians give to attract support for their policies range from their real reasons through cosmetic rhetoric to threats and enticements deliberately designed to deceive.

But what follows is not meant to induce confusion or cynicism. It is to remind you yet again that monomotivational theories about people's behavior are nearly always wrong. In all political roles – among voters, politicians, public servants, economic advisers – there are some honorable and effective exponents of good government. If you want to be one of them, don't let cynics or monomotivational theorists persuade you not to try.

Business

The President of the national Chamber of Commerce and Manufactures is a prudent and fairminded man. He wants to keep business efficient and socially responsible and therefore respected and politically secure. He thinks that the onset of structural unemployment makes payroll tax a bad tax. But if business wants it abolished, business must expect to replace most of the lost revenue. So he proposes that government (1) abolish payroll tax, and replace it by (2) a modest increase in the rate of company tax, moderated by introducing (3) a system of imputation, to subtract paid-up company tax from shareholders' income tax. Also (4) an increase in fuel tax, which will raise some business costs and consumer prices but from which (5) exporters should be allowed rebates, so as not to disadvantage them in their foreign markets. His proposals attract quite wide support. Labor welcomes the payroll and company tax proposals, and the fact that the proposals don't reduce total revenue. The greens welcome the higher fuel tax. The welfare branches of the public service welcome a proposal from business that would not shift much taxation from richer to poorer taxpayers. And the Treasurer welcomes truthful advice about the impact of the various taxes on business and employment. The imputation proposal is self-interested, but it has been proposed candidly as a way to soften the blow of an increase in company tax, without any false claims about its likely effect on saving, investment or employment.

The second business representative is a reasonably public-spirited citizen who tends (like many others, often unconsciously) to identify his own and his industry's interest with the public interest. He wants to abolish payroll tax and some other taxes on industry because, he says, the private sector is the productive sector and it is crazy to tax it at all. He would also reduce the top rate of income tax, to reward enterprise and stimulate investment. (Cutting income tax is unlikely to have those effects, but he believes it will.) He sees the need for public health, welfare and educational services and doesn't want to skimp them. So to replace the revenue lost from business and income taxes he proposes a retail sales tax on everything except basic food and some other necessities.

The third business voice is there only as an observer. He is a leader-writer and columnist for one of the nastier tabloid newspapers. If you believe what he writes (he doesn't) he would abolish all taxes on business, halve the income tax, and not replace the lost revenue. All we need (he writes) is to stop the public servants and unemployed – is there a difference? – guzzling public money through their mostly-idle hours. Halve the dole to get the layabout unemployed to work for realistic wages. Abolish the sluts' charter (he means the sole parent's living allowance) so the girls won't get pregnant and if they do, the boys can't expect the taxpayers to finance their bastards' upbringing. Halve the number of public servants, abolish their tenure, privatize lots of their functions, put business managers in charge of those that remain, and we'll not only get less and better government at half the cost, we'll free our industries from the deadweight burden and crippling red tape that have held them back for half a century. (Nourishing his readers' resentful fantasies is his bread and butter.)

Labor

The Secretary of the national Labor Council also wants to abolish payroll tax because it encourages employers to hire fewer hands and work them longer hours. Personally she would like to replace the lost revenue by restoring more progressive rates of income tax. But her Council fears that would be so effectively resisted that it might well reduce total revenue. They actually want to increase revenue, to finance new training and employment schemes, to restore a prudent level of public infrastructure investment, and to increase public support for full-time mothers. So she argues for a small proportional increase of income tax, a higher fuel tax, and a sales tax at three rates: zero on necessities of life, a standard rate on most discretionary goods, a higher rate on tobacco and luxury goods.

She dislikes the proposals (and also the propositions) of the labor lobbyist, a lecherous drunk who is here chiefly for the expense-account week away from home.

He runs a warehousing union famous for two achievements: the number of unsolved robberies and insurance fires of the goods they handle, and the number of their members living on compensation for stress, bad backs and lung diseases from allegedly passive smoking. He stays sober enough one day to advise the Treasurer that he ought to (1) shift taxation off middle incomes, (2) introduce full self-assessment of income tax, and (3) double the premiums which employers are required to pay to the worker's compensation insurer, a franchised monopolist with some corruptible assessors.

The third in the labor group is the party stalwart who has edited the Labor Voice for the last forty years as its circulation declined from a hundred thousand to ten thousand. The paper's news pages are truthful but selective: they report news creditable to workers or discreditable to employers. The opinion pages don't demand a proletarian uprising but they do depict most private capital ownership as exploitive and public ownership as a better alternative. When workers unite, that is solidarity. When employers unite, that is monopoly or conspiracy. The wage share is always too low, the profit share is always too high. On tax policy the paper stands for steeply progressive income tax and death duties; sales taxes on luxury goods and services; tariffs wherever they protect jobs; and jail for rich tax evaders. Except for the last item that is a tax regime which worked well enough in many countries through the long boom; and the paper's one-eyed view of the business world does express a consistent desire for greater equality. But it misjudges both some political and some economic possibilities, and it often spoils its own case by exaggeration and one-sided selections of evidence. A Treasurer who wants more egalitarian taxation will probably look for advisers who understand the modern economic system and its owners and workers better than this old warrior does.

Public service

There are contradictory voices. The Secretary of the Public Service Union and the retiring head of the Department of Welfare want to increase taxes, but for different reasons. The head of the new Office of Public Management wants to cut the need for taxation by cutting the public services, in more than one meaning of 'cut'.

The union is represented by its youngest-ever secretary. She is a lawyer and statistician who made her name as an enforcer of the equal opportunity laws. Now as an advocate for the service as a whole she brings her statistical skill to bear on the widening gap between public and private sector pay, home and foreign pay, and past and present pay, for work of equivalent value. As for pay, so also for workloads and productivity. Nurses are tending more patients than they did, teachers have more students and class hours, clerks determine more welfare entitlements. For some there are also foreign comparisons to show that their pay and conditions are falling behind OECD leaders.

Every graph and table supports the public servants' case for improved pay, tenure and conditions of work on grounds of comparative wage justice. How to finance it? More stats show how, for twenty years past, self-employed professionals have been earning a rising share of national income but paying a declining share of income tax, while salaried workers have contributed a rising share of tax from a declining share of income. The union secretary proposes legal and administrative changes which would increase tax collection from the self-employed by enough to finance her public service proposals.

This officer's research and presentation are faultless. The action she proposes would correct a real tax inequity and help the public services to improve morale and retain more of their best talents, with advantage to the society as a whole. The trouble is that directly, especially as the media will report it, it will appear to benefit public servants alone. The headlines write themselves – FAT CATS WANT MORE.

Compare the proposals of her older, wiser, more compassionate colleague.

The welfare chief reached the top of the service by what was in her time an unusual route. She joined as a graduate forty years ago and left five years later to marry a family doctor. They brought up five children, one sadly handicapped. In her forties she returned to study, qualified as a social worker, ran a voluntary welfare agency, then beat the competition for an advertised job as Women's Adviser to the head of government. With a term of that as her political education she moved to the Department of Welfare and spent ten years quietly feminizing it – for the clients' sake, at least as much as for equal opportunity.

She knows better than to argue for welfare reforms in a submission on taxation: she merely refers to other reports on the rising demand for income transfers and welfare services. Her tax proposals begin with two which would reduce revenue. Tax exemption for gifts to charity should be extended to a wider range of independent welfare services, and there should be tax concessions for people who meet specified standards in running supervised boarding houses and sheltered

workshops for handicapped people. For revenue she supports the usual egalitarian case for more progressive income tax, and sales tax on some luxury goods. Her distinctive proposal is one which is designed to reduce unemployment by giving employers an incentive to ration work. Payroll tax should be not abolished but shifted. It should not be levied on wages paid for the first thirty five hours of each worker's week. Above that it should be levied at a high enough rate for the overtime wage plus payroll tax to cost employers twice as much as it would cost to get the same work done by hiring more hands.

The new Director of the Office of Public Management is thirty eight. He has first class honours in economics from a strictly neoclassical school, a Master of Business Administration degree from a private US university and ten years with a transnational management consultant before he was head-hunted into the public service. Public choice theory rather than management theory shapes his view of public servants' motives: the view that only greed and insecurity are likely to get a passable performance from most of them. He has already impressed conservative politicians with some ruthless bureaucratic cost-cutting. "Tax cutter, toe-cutter, corner-cutter", one of his victims calls him.

He advises the Treasurer that there is five-fold scope for tax reduction. First, public service numbers and costs are already being reduced by deregulation and privatization. Second, work incentives and the efficiency of the labor market can be improved by cutting the unemployment dole to bare subsistence level. Third, the consequent freedoms will improve the efficiency and entrepreneurial spirit of the private sector, so that faster economic growth will expand the tax base, i.e. the asset values and output sales and income flows on which taxes are levied. That will allow lower rates of tax. Fourth, the lower rates of tax will free resources for productive use as consumers have more to save or spend and more investment funds are available to producers. Fifth, the tax cuts can be designed to further improve entrepreneurial incentives. For best effects, cut company tax, capital gains tax and the top rate of income tax.

Together (the toe-cutter predicts) these measures will initiate a dynamic process in which tax cuts pay for themselves – so that, over time, any given revenue can be raised with steadily declining rates of tax. The Treasurer can confidently cut his forward tax provisions not only by the amount of his intended spending cuts, but additionally by five per cent a year for the next five years, down to seventy five per cent of the level indicated by his spending intentions. (Though the submission does not say so, this is a more rigorous and thoroughgoing application of the tax principles introduced in the US in the 1980s by President Reagan.)

Green

Conservationist thoughts about taxation are represented by a Deep Ecologist, an environmental economist and a political scientist.

The member of the Deep Ecology Movement (DEM) is from a rural commune where she divides her time between meditation and vegetable gardening. Tax policy is not important to DEM – what humanity needs is to recover its lost capacity to live without money income. But if the movement is asked for advice about taxation, it is as follows.

While the unsustainable urban industrial society continues, its tax arrangements are its own affair. But it could help the parallel development of sustainable modes of life by two tax measures. There should be a general tax exemption for individuals and communities who live by hand labor using no fossil fuel, network power, powered machinery or vehicles, or agricultural chemicals. And in the continuing industrial society, manufactured solar panels and heating systems, windmills, bicycles, and equipment for producing methane power should be exempt from sales taxes.

The young woman from DEM is a figure of fun to most other delegates, and her program does not attract much support. But she deserves respect as a committed campaigner for a gentler world, who lives what she believes.

The second Green is an economist from the neoclassical mainstream of environmental economics. His main concerns are pollution and the ill effects of urban sprawl. He sees both as market failures. To fix them without loss of market efficiency they should be corrected wherever possible by market methods. The main market method is to use discriminate taxation to adjust prices to include relevant external costs.

In this economist's view, urban and suburban sprawl consume productive agricultural land, divert other productive resources into needlessly elaborate housing, and stimulate other excessive consumption. They also generate too much inefficient and pollutant urban transport. More compact, economical and sustainable cities should be encouraged by taxing:

- the unimproved value of urban land
- income used to pay mortgage interest on home purchases

- the imputed rent of owner-occupied houses
- private car registration
- gasoline and diesel fuel.

Industrial and commercial pollution can be attacked by using taxes and charges to internalize their external costs. 'Making the polluter pay' in that way actually makes the consumers of pollutant products pay. The products' higher prices reduce demand for them. The tax revenue can finance corrective action. Producers who develop less pollutant products or processes pay less tax and remain competitive even if their cleaner methods cost more. Market forces continue to allocate the available resources and reward their most efficient users. Thus pollution is reduced without the bureaucratic inefficiencies of administrative rationing or public ownership.

Where price alone is ineffective and more direct control is needed, it is still possible to avoid public ownership or public rationing of individual producers. Government can create rights to whatever it decides is a tolerable total of specified types of pollution, then auction the rights. Buyers can re-sell – the rights are tradeable. In an efficient market they will go to the producers with the most efficient output/pollution ratios, so that for given bads (pollution) society will get maximum output of goods.

A good deal of that economist's advice is anathema to the third Green. He is a political scientist with some experience in government. Instead of proposing particular taxes his submission sets out principles on which a social-democratic government should decide which environmental problems are best approached by-

- public ownership of the relevant resources or processes
- public regulation of private pollution or resource use
- scientific and technological research
- public education
- pricing or other market methods.

Decisions about the approach in each case, and about tax design where tax action is appropriate, should balance and where possible reconcile -

- technical judgment of the action which will be most effective in the particular case
- ethical judgments: some evils should be open to individual and business choices, but others should not. For example CFC spray-cans or lead-painted toys should not be taxed, they should be banned.
- equitable judgments: scarce resources and the costs

of environmental care should be fairly shared between present people and between present and future generations

- political judgments about what policies are practicable and therefore worth trying for.

Taxing and pricing approaches should be used where they will work better than other methods of control, and not where they won't. They should have no necessary priority.

The treasurer's advisers

The Treasurer's Assistant Minister wants a revolution in the government's political strategy. The ruling party is a century-old social democratic party. An equally old-established conservative party constitutes the parliamentary opposition. The Assistant Minister wants the government to follow the British and New Zealand and Australian Labor Parties by shifting sharply to the Right to preempt the opposition's conservative policies. He favors the tax advice of the toe-cutter from the Office of Public Management (whom he helped to appoint), plus some selective tax cuts to sweeten the responses of the newspaper and TV proprietors.

The second adviser is the Party secretary and campaign manager. He knows the winning and losing margins in every electorate in the country. He knows the sources of all the big donations to party funds. He knows the results of all recent opinion polls, including the private polls that the party commissions in marginal electorates. He knows that four fifths of the citizens will vote as usual for their traditional party allegiances. He suggests finely-targeted tax cuts to benefit the groups which include most swinging voters in most marginal electorates. If the lost revenue needs to be replaced it should come from the rich and the poor, i.e. from the regular supporters of the two parties in their safest electorates.

The third adviser is the government's new Women's Adviser. She believes the time has come to shift the political direction of the women's movement. Women should lead a broad attack on the squalid politics of recent years, including the vote-buying tactics of the party secretary. Instead of self-interested lobbying, the movement should inspire women to vote for high-principled government. That need cost them nothing – like the workers a century ago, there is no conflict between principled government and women's quest for equality. This adviser suspects that plenty of men would also vote for genuinely principled government, as they have voted in the past for principled government of both Left and Right, for example for the leadership of Roosevelt, Churchill, Attlee, DeGaulle, Adenauer, Brandt and Thatcher. She herself wants the principles to be social-democratic, so she supports the welfare chief's tax program: progressive income and sales taxes, tariff protection where necessary, and tax support for new approaches to full employment.

She is specially critical of attempts to buy swinging votes with targeted public spending and tax concessions. That tactic surrenders government to the self-interest of the meanest, least public-spirited citizens. It disgusts many fair-minded citizens. Even if the party merely wants to win at any cost, she argues, it will do better to appeal to the swinging voters who can not be bought: the people who want high-principled government; workers who understand the need for some policies helpful to business; business people who support good conditions of employment; professional people who vote for generous welfare for the old and poor and would give a good deal to restore full employment; the many men who have voted for every step of the new deal for women. She tells the Treasurer that high-principled social-democratic government might actually be the smartest political trick of all.

EXERCISE

1. Return to (1) the first business voice (The President of the Chamber of Commerce and Manufacturers); (2) the third Public Service voice (the toe-cutter); and (3) the second Green voice (the environmental economist). Assess their economic expertise: how well does each of them understand how the economic system actually works, or can be made to work?

2. You are that Treasurer. Decide and explain your tax policy.

Part Six

ECONOMIC STRATEGY

- *ENDS AND MEANS*
- *NATIONAL STRATEGIES*

47

The parts and the whole

Now and then on a journey through difficult country it is good to rest on a high pass and look back at the route you've travelled, and forward to what lies ahead. Now is a good time to do that, as you pass from the details of the productive and distributive institutions to study processes which affect the performance of the economy as a whole.

Begin with a shortest-ever summary of the analyses (so far) of the mixed economies of the developed democracies. Like the rest of this chapter it condenses a complicated mass of material, too densely to learn it if this were your first sight of it. But it is material you already know, so treat it as easy reading to check that you do know it, and how its parts fit together in the working of national economies.

The story so far:

PRODUCTIVITY

How much a society can produce depends on –

- its natural resources
- its physical capital, i.e. its accumulated ploughland and pasture, plant and animal stock, farm buildings and equipment, houses, factories, shops, power and water systems, communication networks, land and sea and air transport – and so on
- its intellectual capital: chiefly the science and art, history, philosophy and other thought and information accessible in its libraries and scientific institutions and museums
- its institutional capital: parliament, government, law and courts; schools and universities, churches and charities, clubs and societies; hundreds of thousands of firms with legal identities and constitutions, and with millions of current contracts governing their relations with each other; millions of households with legal and customary rights and obligations
- its human capital: the knowledge, skills, creativity, competitive and co-operative qualities and attitudes to work and recreation built into the people by their upbringing, education, culture and social and working experience.

WANTS

People's material wants are determined by the effects and interactions of –

- innate instincts, appetites, needs for food and shelter
- the goods and services which they know about, or can imagine
- family, educational, cultural, fashionable influences on their wants and preferences
- producers' persuasive marketing and advertising
- moral, legal, governmental and ideological encouragement of some wants, and discouragement or prohibition of others
- free individual preferences and choices, influenced or uninfluenced by any of the above.

SPENDING POWER

In the market sector of the economy, effective demands are offers to pay. Which wants of which people become effective demands depends on the distribution of wealth, income and credit.

Wealth is distributed by –

- inheritance, marriage
- active business success
- passive investment of owned or borrowed wealth
- other people's externalities, as when economic growth and city growth multiply the value of land
- rewards for technical and artistic creativity and sporting success
- saving from income
- lawful plunder, as when directors take big capital rewards from firms they direct
- crime.

There is also wealth in public or independent non-profit ownership: wealth in mineral, forest and other natural resources, in public buildings and infrastructure, in publicly owned industries, in churches, schools, universities and other cultural institutions.

Income More than half of all primary (non-transferred) income comes from employment, paid as described in Chapter 32 on four ways to fix wages. Other sources of income are –

- property income: dividends, interest and rent from capital ownership
- active business success
- self-employed earning by professional and trades people, artists and entertainers, writers, sporting professionals
- crime.

Transferred incomes in cash and kind come as –

- public income transfers and welfare services
- household and family income transfers and services.

People produce a third or more of all material goods and services for themselves and one another by their own unpaid labor, using household capital and some public capital for the purpose.

Credit The capacity to invest or spend other people's money depends on the financial system. Financial institutions organize people's wealth and savings for other people and firms to use. They also create and destroy spending power as they expand and contract credit. The quantity and distribution both of effective demand and of producers' capacity to meet the demand are thus strongly influenced by the structure and behavior of the public and private financial institutions. Their powers are ultimately determined by government.

With wealth, income and credit distributed, people decide what to do with their spending money.

Individual and household choices

Households range from single persons, through family households with no serious conflicts about their work and spending, to households between whose members there is inequality, conflict, violence and exploitation.

Choices of products, of modes of production, and of activities However the household choices are arrived at, they can be simplified as being of two kinds:

- What goods and services do we want?
- How do we want them to be supplied? As public goods, as market goods, or by our own labor?

It actually oversimplifies to see the products as ends and the modes of production as means. First, people sometimes value the work as much as the product – the gardening as much as the flowers, the painting as much as the pictures, the child care for the carer's joy as well as the child's up-bringing. Second, modes of production are sometimes chosen for their by-products as well as their products: some people prefer public or private or house-

hold production for other reasons besides their productive efficiency or pleasure.

For some goods there is no choice about the mode of production. The government doesn't make bicycles and households can't afford the equipment to make them, so households which want them must buy them (or at least their factory-made components) as market goods. But plenty of food, shelter, transport, recreation, furniture and decorating can alternatively be bought ready-made from market suppliers, or grown, constructed, assembled or performed by the household's own labor, usually with some capital and materials bought from the market sector. So household choices determine spending on household capital (house, car, equipment), on intermediate goods (fuel, raw food, paint, furnishing and clothing materials, seeds and fertilizers) and on consumable goods (sweets and drinks, restaurant meals, broadcast entertainment). Public and private producers respond by generating demands for capital and intermediate goods and raw materials as they equip themselves to supply the household demands.

Thus demands for public and market goods express household choices, or at least preferences between the goods the producers offer, within the limits the households have to spend. The choices tend to become wider and freer with economic growth.

Household choices also call for political action.

Political choices

Political decisions have to determine –

- what public goods will be supplied
- by which modes of production (i.e. by public or private producers) they will be produced
- by what taxation, user charges, borrowing or other means they will be paid for
- on what terms they will be available to all or some of the public.

Political choices also affect the available range of goods and services as they shape the regulation of the private sector, and any national border controls on the import and export of people, goods and money.

THE PRODUCTIVE INSTITUTIONS

Households

Mostly by unpaid labor, household members produce a third or more of a developed economy's material goods and services. They contribute a great deal to the quality of the people they bring up and to the society's human capital. For those purposes they need –

- money income from public or private employment, from property, or by income transfer
- access to private shops, services, press, entertainment, etc.
- access to public services: schools, hospitals, utilities, transport, telecommunications, etc.
- household capital: house, furniture, equipment, vehicles.

Household capital is about 40 per cent of all productive capital and is used to produce about the same percentage of goods and services. It averages about the same productivity as other capital does. But its housing component averages about twice the working life of other capital, so is supplied by a lower rate of investment than other capital (on average) requires. Its output is in kind rather than money, so it can't finance its own acquisition. It follows that unaided market processes can't allocate capital funds most productively either between housing and other uses or between household and household. Some public management or regulation of the relevant markets is required.

Private enterprises

Private enterprises produce about half of a developed economy's goods and services, including many of the capital and intermediate goods used by households and public enterprises.

Modern production requires complex division of labor, specialization of skills, and coordination of productive processes. The coordination is done partly by planning and organization and partly by market exchange. The comparative cost and efficiency of those two methods of coordination vary widely from one industry to another. Where large-scale bureaucratic organization works best, there are big firms. Where exchange works best, there are self-employed trades and professions. And there are intricate mixtures of the two – for example as some self-employed individuals and small firms sell a wide range of ideas and services to big firms, whose products are advertised, transported and retailed by another range of medium-sized and small firms and self-employed individuals. Private enterprise owes a lot of its freedom and efficiency to this capacity to use whatever mixtures of organization and market exchange work best in each case.

We need not summarize Part Four's detailed chapters on firms and how they work. As a more general reminder, recall some tensions within the private sector which pose policy problems for government. There are tensions between freedom and regulation, between com-petition and cooperation, between private and public interests, between self-interest and morality. In that order:

Freedom and order Government creates the powers – the corporate identity, joint stock, limited liability and directors' powers – which enable the firm to be such an effective organizer of production. But the powers are so dangerous that their use has to be strictly policed. That is partly to protect workers', consumers' and public interests. But a great deal of the regulation is for the firms' own benefit. Without reliable policing they could not expect owners to trust them with equity capital, or banks to lend to them. Nor could they trust all the other firms they deal with, or protect themselves from dishonest directors or employees, or from unfair and unproductive kinds of competition. So there is tension between directors' freedom of action, which is one main source of firms' efficiency, and the pervasive regulation which is another main source of it.

Competition and cooperation Workers compete for jobs and promotion. Firms compete for business. But firms need their workers to cooperate with one another and with the firm's purposes. There can be tension between the competitive and cooperative imperatives at a number of levels.

Some firms have anxious workers competing with each other for jobs and promotion because managers think that keeps everyone on their toes and working their hardest. Other firms, including some of the worlds' best, get better work and quality control and cooperation from workers with secure jobs and dependable rights and expectations. Should firms be free to decide what security to offer their workers – or should employers' and workers' duties to each other be regulated by law?

Other questions about competition arise at the level of the firm and the industry. In some industries competition works in a text-book way to keep firms efficient and to allocate resources to their best uses. But there are important exceptions. Too much competition between airlines or bus companies may have them all running below capacity, with higher unit costs and fares than could be achieved by fewer, stronger fleets running nearer to capacity. Strong operators with some cash to spare and the long term in mind might also spend more on safety than hard-pressed, cost-cutting competitors could afford to spend. In industries in which long-term planning, research and product development are desirable, price-cutting competition can leave too little margin for those purposes. In industries whose competition compels harsh wage-cutting and other maltreatment of workers, you may judge that the consumers' marginal gains are not worth the workers' financial and personal suffering.

At national level, free-trading exposure to changing forces of international competition can stimulate national enterprise in some circumstances. In other circumstances it can damage a country's economic structure, employment, income distribution and balance of payments. (Following chapters will explain how and why.)

At all those levels, competition can be alternatively a valuable or a destructive force. Freeing it or restraining it is a subject of public policy. Case by case, the policymaking calls for local knowledge, cool analysis and practical judgment, rather than an exclusive faith in either market or government.

Private and public interests Self-interest motivates plenty of efficient and socially useful performance, and tends to do it reliably. Don't knock it! But there has always been some room for conflict between private and public interests, and the conflicts are currently increasing for a number of reasons:

- International financial freedoms and communication technology have made opportunities for some new kinds of business misbehavior.

- In the ex-communist world capitalist industry is being established by inexperienced people in anarchic conditions, with opportunities for bad behavior both by the new enterprises and by Westerners joining them or dealing with them.

- Most important: mounting resource and environmental problems in an over-populated, industrializing world create many new conflicts of interest between producers and environmental reformers, between producers and governments, between nations and between generations.

The environmental conflicts create many new difficulties, but also new scope, for governments.

Self-interest and morality Remember both of Adam Smith's books – the *Theory of Moral Sentiments* as well as the *Wealth of Nations*. He believed that the self-interests which propel the hidden hand of market forces were conceived and restrained within a prevailing morality. The morality arises from human nature and culture, i.e. from outside the economic system which it helps to civilize. Except for a criminal minority, most normally self-interested people pursue quite a limited range of advantages for themselves: job, pay, promotion, household possessions and so on. They don't *want* to cheat, steal, defraud or exploit one another. And much of what they seek they seek for others besides themselves –

for family, friends, neighborhood, church, nation or other collectives. However self-interested, what they pursue are what their nature and culture have taught them to see as their *proper* and *legitimate* interests: advantages which they can enjoy with good conscience and social approval.

Some of those social and moral self-restraints have been strengthened by twentieth-century material sufficiency, social experience and democratic government. But other self-restraints have been weakened – perhaps by the decline of Western religion, by affluence, by the 1960s liberation of a more assertive self. Some social restraints are weakened by the growing size and impersonality of big firms and big bureaucracy. In the private sector the separation of corporate ownership from control exposes directors to new temptations. Most of all, perhaps, the restraints have been eroded by the 'sideways' growth of capitalism, i.e. by the profit-seeking commercialization of more and more of the daily life which used to be the source and bearer of the necessary morality. Recall Fred Hirsch's argument (in *Social Limits to Growth*, 1976) that business becomes less efficient and has rising costs the more the moral and customary restraints of Adam Smith's vision have to be replaced by fine-print contracts, legal scrutiny, court action, internal and external auditing, private security and public regulation. As more of life is commercialized, less of it remains to moralize commerce. One expensive remedy for that is already quite well-developed: for a century now, democratic governments have been driven to regulate more and more of business activity. If it can't be disciplined by self-restraint and social custom, it has to be disciplined by law and government – however expensive, annoying and sometimes oppressive that may prove to be.

These general problems reach government in the practical form of an incessant flow of demands for detailed decisions of many kinds: about aids to the private sector, restraints on it, amendments to its legal and institutional basis, and so on. But the quality and effect of governments' responses to those needs and conflicts depend a good deal on prevailing political and economic beliefs – so those beliefs have practical importance.

Public enterprises

National and local governments, their public enterprises, and independent non-profit enterprises like churches and charities and universities, produce between 10 and 15 per cent of material goods and services in developed mixed economies. Governments have to decide –

- what goods and services the public sector should supply, on what terms

- which of them should be produced by public or independent producers, and which the public suppliers should buy from private producers; and

- the institutional forms of the public producers: government departments, statutory corporations, publicly owned companies, etc.

Public production needs to be as efficient and economical as possible. Some of the tests of that are the same for public and private producers, but some are not. Public enterprises which have a number of purposes need to be efficient for each of those purposes. Questions of priority, balance and conflict between their purposes can make special difficulties both for public managers and for directors and governments who have to judge their efficiency. Recall our example of Swedish, Norwegian and Australian tram and train services, each the most efficient at one element of the task, none uncontroversially best for all purposes.

Insofar as performance can be compared, experience suggests that –

- different countries have different capacities to run efficient public enterprises

- some industries (textiles, clothing and footwear, furniture, many design services and personal services, most advertising and retailing, much entertainment) go best in private ownership

- some industries (education, religion, scientific and social research, hospitals, justice) go best in public or other non-profit ownership

- many industries (especially such heavy industries as coal and metal mining, steelmaking, ship-building, aircraft manufacture, car-making, public utilities, rail, sea and air transport) can go well or badly in either kind of ownership

- the performance of industries in the last group often depends more on other conditions than on the type of ownership.

Environmental problems, inflation, rising unemployment and some worrying technological possibilities are expanding the range of activity which government must try to influence by regulation, public ownership or other means. That expanding role is not necessarily inconsistent with some privatization: the more government *must* do, the wiser it may be to shed functions that it need not do. But a lot of current privatization has the improvident purpose of cutting taxation in the short run by spending public capital. Western Europe and Japan have lately done better than the English-speaking countries in maintaining democratic support for sufficient levels of taxation and public investment and services. We will return to the subject in chapters on national economic strategies.

MARKETS

When household, private and public producers are getting the trade and services they need from each other and from government, the private sector should be able to do its half or so of production and distribution as efficiently as market theorists expect.

Private enterprise and market relations are at the heart of the mixed economy's productivity. Their freedom and efficiency are precious, however unwelcome the inequalities they cause. But their performance varies with circumstances and from industry to industry. To understand markets properly you need to study them one by one, with at least as much attention to local market practice as to general market theory. Remember the questions Chapter 41 taught you to ask. For example

The nature of the product

- How durable or perishable is the product? How cheap to store and transport? How tradeable?

- Is it homogeneous, or can it be differentiated to allow competition between brands?

- Can buyers readily judge its quality? If not, what help can they get?

- What regulation (quality, safety, truthful labelling and advertising) does the product attract?

The methods of production

- How long and complex is the production chain? What market strength do the contributors have and how do they use it?

- Do the lead times allow suppliers to respond efficiently to changes in demand? Do the buyers' lead times fit or misfit with the producers' lead times?

- Can producers predict others' production decisions in time to adjust their own? If not, are there any public or cooperative information services or controls?

- What economies of scale (or takeovers, protective tariffs or other causes) have developed what pattern of large or small firms, monopoly or oligopoly or competition?

- What regulation does the method of production attract?

Pricing and marketing

- Price taker or maker? Fixprice or flexprice? Mark-up or other pricing?

- Are there elements of monopoly pricing at any stage of the production chain?

- What advertising is worth while?

- What taxes, consumer protection, price control or other public rules apply?

The buyers

- How price-elastic and income-elastic is the demand? How responsive to advertising? What alternative products are there?

- How expert are the buyers? If they need help, do they get it?

- Do the buyers need credit? If so, how freely can they get it?

- Whose money are they spending?

- In whose interest are they spending it?

- What market strength do they have, and what use do they usually make of it?

WHAT SORT OF THEORY?

Each heading in this summary chapter stands for quite complicated processes. Those processes don't operate in simple sequence, like links in a causal chain. Many of them act and react on one another. Some of them, especially some elements of human choice and conflict, are not always predictable, or their predictability can vary with circumstances.

Modern productivity depends on complicated division and skilling of labor and coordination of productive processes. The coordination is achieved –

- partly by bureaucratic planning and command – working best where there is most cooperation and consent – within firms, within other organizations, and within government

- partly by market exchanges between individuals, firms and other institutions

- partly by voluntary cooperation, as in households, voluntary associations, partnerships and some other small businesses.

Similarly, the mixed economy makes productive use of diverse purposes and incentives: desires for money, for power, for satisfying work, for good social relations at work, for scientific and artistic and inventive achievement, for reforming the neighborhood or the nation or

the world – or for security and a quiet life. I do not believe that such diversely motivated organization and activity can be best understood by modelling just one of its incentives (money and what it will buy) and just one of its modes of coordination (market exchange), and treating all the others as exceptions or correctives to those two. The real-life diversity of motives and modes makes rigorous mathematical modelling of economic processes unpromising for many purposes, though useful for some.

Many economic activities are nevertheless steady most of the time. Producers know their markets, consumers can rely on their suppliers. Most people can go to bed confident that tomorrow's food, shelter, transport, work and opportunities for shopping and recreation will be much the same as yesterday's. But it is always possible that actions which disturb any part of that settled system will send ripples through more of it than the actors intend.

Suppose for example that science, technology and business together introduce some new products. As a result, some spending shifts. Some jobs are lost, some others are created. Some skills are outmoded, some new ones are needed, so jobs in the training schools change. Some regulations are outmoded by the new products and revised (or, regrettably, not revised). Foreigners get into the act. Some of them export competing products. Some try to take over the new producers. Under pressure, government changes some trade rules. More spending shifts, more jobs are lost or created ... and so on. Each of those changes may follow from the first inventive change – but each is itself a new disturbance of the system, with potential effects and side effects of its own.

This is the complex system, with some stable and some unstable elements, some self-adjusting market mechanisms and some tendencies to unemployment and inflation, some conflicts and some consensus, some mathematical certainties and some human free will, which economists must try to understand, and in which governments must perform their economic functions.

Hence this further reminder of a by-now-familiar principle of this course of study. Theories which purport to tell you how all mixed economies work have limited uses. To understand particular systems you more often need theory which suggests how they *may* be working: what the alternative possibilities are. To find which known possibilities or new mutations are at work, you need appropriate sets of questions to ask and (by investigation) answer. That, rather than any single axiomatic model, is the equipment you most often need when analysing economic activity for particular purposes at particular times. The reminder is here because you are about to switch from studying component parts of economic systems (firms, markets, public services and so on) to studying some aspects of their performance as whole systems. The same open-minded, investigative approach will apply.

THE PARTS AND THE WHOLE

Our microeconomic chapters have described, among other things, a great many economic functions of the public sector: providing roads and bridges, power and water, transport and telecommunications, business powers and regulations, schools and hospitals, housing aids, environmental care, income transfers, welfare services and so on.

Is it enough that government performs each of those functions well and economically?

No, it is not enough.

Why not?

The mixed economy has a contradiction at its heart. Decentralized decision-making – by households, firms, and agencies of government – is the main source of its freedom and efficiency. But it is also the main source of its malfunctions, as unintended aggregate effects of all those independent decisions run the economy into booms, slumps, inflation, unemployment and environmental degradation. So besides all its detailed tasks, government must do its best to –

- coordinate its own activities so that their combined effect is to reduce rather than increase the economy's instabilities; and

- add some stabilizing management of the economy as a whole.

So we now study the problems of maintaining full employment with low inflation within national economies, and workable balances of trade and exchange between them.

You know some reasons why *market* activity does not automatically employ all available resources, or keep prices stable without inflation. Similarly (though for different reasons) the *public* sector's many activities don't necessarily help full employment or stable prices. At different times public and market demand together may ask too much or too little of the country's productive capacities. Their totals may rise and fall to cause boom and slump and varying rates of inflation and unemployment. They may also inflate some industries while leaving others under-employed. And not all unemployed resources can switch to other uses: you can't quickly turn disused factories into hospitals, or unemployed coalminers into nurses.

So national government must try to orchestrate its own activities, and influence the levels of activity in the productive sectors, to keep the economy as a whole stable and fully employed. For that purpose its own productive activities, its services to the private and household sectors and its government of those sectors should ideally be integrated in a coherent economic strategy. But that is hard, for a number of reasons. No population will ever agree about all the aims of such a strategy, so policy-makers are likely to be under conflicting pressures. There is usually also some disagreement within and between the departments of government. And even when the ends and means are decided in principle, government is now so complicated that it can be difficult to coordinate its many activities in a coherent way.

This chapter sketches some main elements of the problem. The next seven explore aspects of it: 48 a country's economic structure; 49 its trade with the rest of the world; 50 and 51 its financial system; 52 inflation; 53 employment and unemployment; and 54 some global problems in the interrelations between economic structure, trade, banking, currency exchange and employment. Five chapters then present representative strategies – some better than others – for countries with different resources and dominant purposes.

So we return now to the working of the economy as a whole. To think about that, it is necessary to select and simplify. You have already met three selective simplifications: a neoclassical model of the economic system, a post-Keynesian / post-Marxist model, and a three-sector institutional approach. Each of them depicted a circular flow of money financing the production and distribution of goods and services. It is time now to see why the flows of money, employment, production and consumption are not so smooth in practice. We can start with the flow of money.

THE FLOW OF FUNDS

Imagine a perfect circular flow. Employers pay people wages for their labor, and rent and interest and dividends for the use of their capital. The people return the money when they use it to buy the employers' products. Thus the money circulates to and fro between producers and consumers to finance a steady flow of the jobs people want, the goods they want and the property income some of them want – all at stable prices, with full employment.

If the flow was as simple as that there would be less work – and easier work – for economists. Of course it is not as simple as that. Some of the funds pass through many hands, for example where there are long production chains. The public goods have to be paid for by taxes: for that and other reasons government handles a third or more of the flow. People lend and borrow and need safe keeping for their money, so banks handle a lot of the flow. All the handlers have opportunities to divert funds from the simple circulation imagined above. Two of them – banks and government – can increase or reduce the whole amount of money in circulation. Producers and consumers can change the total buying power of the flow in three ways. They can circulate it quicker or slower, so that each dollar finances more or fewer transactions per year. They can vary the amount of work and goods the flow will finance by raising or lowering wages and prices. And they can import and export goods, which moves money to and from some other countries' circular flows. The flow can also vary as people borrow, lend or invest abroad.

Most of those are independent decisions. Their unintended aggregate effects can affect total demand, price levels and employment.

In more detail, here are some of the options open to different groups as they handle their shares of the flow of funds:

Borrowing and lending may not disturb the flow much if it merely transfers purchasing power from some people to others. But it can have other effects if the business is done with banks or with foreigners – as follows.

Banks lend what they've borrowed. They also affect the whole flow of funds by increasing or reducing credit. (A later chapter will explain how.)

Foreigners who borrow your money may or may not take it out of your national economy. (They may borrow from you in order to invest in your country.) Foreigners who lend or invest their own money in your country add to the money circulating there when they do it – but they may then reduce the flow in future years if they take home their dividends or loan interest and repayments.

Foreigners who sell you their exports take money out of your system. It may return to the extent that foreigners buy your exports. But your decisions to buy foreign goods, and foreigners' decisions to buy your goods, are independent of each other and there is no immediate

reason why they should balance. (We will consider later whether market exchange rates between national currencies are likely to bring your imports and exports into balance.)

Government can increase or reduce the money in circulation as it taxes and spends, and as it regulates the banks' creation of credit.

Spending and investing (First, a note about the words. 'Spending' sometimes includes investing, because you can spend on consumer goods or capital goods. Alternatively it contrasts spending (on consumer goods) with investing (in capital goods). You can usually tell which meaning is intended from the context. Sometimes the usage is ideological – as with writers who contrast 'private investment' with 'government spending' even when the two are investing in similar capital goods.)

Households and public and private enterprises divide their outlays between spending and investing. Spending on consumer goods increases demand for them now. Investing in capital goods maintains or increases the capacity to produce in future. But too much of either can reduce future income and employment. Why? If we spend and consume too much and (therefore) invest too little now, there will be less productive capacity and probably less employment – and therefore less income – later. If we spend too little and invest too much now we will create excess productive capacity. Output will run ahead of demand. As warehouses fill with unsold goods, output may be cut back to less than current demand. As workers are put off and lose income there may be multiplier effects as their purchasing power declines and reduces demand.

Saving and investing may simply switch some demand from consumer goods to capital goods. But it doesn't always do that, for two reasons.

First, people have to save up for some purchases, especially to buy capital goods. They cut their consumer spending years before they spend the consequent savings on a house or car. Similarly firms which invest retained profits don't always do it straight away. They may accumulate reserves for future use. Thus even where the savers and investors are the same people, the year's investment may not equal the year's saving. If it falls short of the year's saving, total demand is reduced. Depending on other conditions, that may reduce employment.

Second, many of the savers and investors are different people. I save money and bank it. Your firm may borrow it and invest it. The decisions are independent of each other. So are the bank decisions – banks may lend more than they borrow or less than they borrow. Once again there are chances for innumerable independent decisions about spending, saving, lending and investing to produce more demand, or less demand, than producers can supply.

Thus rational individual decisions can produce misfitting totals. As noted earlier, they can also produce misfits in the *composition* of demand and supply. Even if the total value of demand matches the total value of the goods which producers are capable of supplying, it can still happen that strong demand on some industries inflates their prices while declining demand for other products leaves other industries under-employed.

Market forces eventually correct many of those misfits. But they may not do it quickly enough to prevent some inflation and some unemployment. And they often overdo the correction, over-compensating for one imbalance to run the economy into an opposite imbalance. Meet the business cycle.

THE BUSINESS CYCLE

The private sector of a mixed economy has a built-in tendency to periodical boom and slump. Total activity rises, peaks, declines, then recovers and repeats the cycle. It is customary to call the phases of the cycle boom, downturn, recession and recovery. In that order, what drives the change from each phase to the next?

Boom

There is buoyant demand for goods. Producers respond by increasing their productive capacity. They buy more machinery and intermediate goods (fuel, packaging and other inputs to production), hire more hands, pay for more overtime. Employment, wage income, spending and total demand are high. As demand outruns productive capacity, prices rise, so there is some demand-pull inflation. As firms pay overtime rates and compete for scarce labor, wages rise, and as they compete for scarce raw materials, material prices rise. So there is also cost-push inflation. The boom is over-heated.

Downturn

Government may respond to the inflation by cutting its own spending and restraining private spending and investing in various ways. But even if it doesn't, private market responses will end the boom. When producers have equipped themselves to meet the boom level of demand, they cut investment back to the level required to maintain productive capacity rather than increase it. The

falling demand for capital goods reduces total demand. Falling employment in the industries which produce capital goods reduces total wage income and consumer spending. That further reduces total demand.

As private investment declines, so does household investment. Workers whose incomes come from the capital goods industries lose income and have to cut their spending. The easiest way to do that is to defer any unnecessary investment. For the time being, run the old car, fridge, washing machine and audio and video gear as long as they will still work. Put off house repairs or extensions. This reduces demand for a further range of capital goods, including those that other texts call consumer durables.

Multipliers are at work. Job losses which reduce workers' income in some industries reduce their spending on the products of other industries. Those industries respond with cuts in output and employment, which in turn bring a further decline in total employment, income and demand.

Some producers are slow to respond to falling sales. That's good in the short run as their demand for materials and labor holds up. But unsold output accumulates in producers' and wholesalers' warehouses and on retailers' shelves. (Economists' collective name for all such intermediate and finished goods awaiting use or sale is 'inventory'.)

To empty those warehouses, by allowing the declining demand to catch up with the oversupply, the next market response has to be to cut output of the relevant industries to a level *below* the level of demand. That brings a further fall in total employment, wage income, consumer spending and demand. The economy is in recession.

Recession

Production is below current consumption until the accumulated inventory is sold and the warehouses are empty. To empty them there is some price-cutting competition. New output is hard to sell. Marginal firms and over-indebted firms go out of business. There is high unemployment, with the miserable human effects as well as the lost production and increased inequality that unemployment brings.

Government comes under contrary pressures. It needs to spend more as more unemployed workers need income transfers and their households need more welfare services. But there is less revenue as the tax base contracts, i.e. as people earn less taxable income and buy less taxable goods and services. Some governments gladly go into deficit, spending more than they collect, as an appropriate way of supporting the population's income and spending power. Others insist on balancing their budgets, commonly by cutting public spending and investment as revenue declines. That usually deepens and prolongs the recession. We will return to those policy questions later. Here, notice that even if government does nothing, private market responses to the recession are likely to end it and begin a recovery sooner or later – as follows.

Recovery

With producers producing less than the consumers are buying, the warehouses eventually empty. To bring output back up to the level of demand, producers buy more inputs and take on more hands. The multiplier goes to work. The new hands spend their new wages, and demand begins to recover. As it recovers, producers buy *more* inputs and hire *more* hands whose spending adds more demand – and so on.

Investment also picks up. Merely to maintain existing output, producers eventually have to replace old machines, vehicles and other capital items as they wear out. With business slack, banks are happy to give them credit for the purpose. And as demand revives and firms invest to expand their capacity, three other things may encourage them to expand output *ahead of* rising demand.

- **Experience** Executives expect demand to continue growing through this phase of the business cycle. It will do that more surely, the more firms expand output ahead of it (because of the effect of the extra material-buying and employment on total demand). When the financial press assures them that 'confidence is reviving', confidence revives. That's not silly sheep-like behavior. Confident expansion will only swell demand significantly if plenty of producers share the confidence and contribute to the expansion – so each needs the assurance that plenty of others are expanding too.

- **Costs and prices** Through the first year or two of recovery some firms enjoy a specially helpful relation between their costs and their selling prices. These are firms in industries whose main costs tend to be fixed in advance. They may have forward contracts for their material supplies, and wage agreements for a

year or two with their unions. If both were negotiated during a downturn or recession they may be at restrained prices and wage rates. Meanwhile the firms' product prices may be free to respond more quickly to the return of rising demand. So there can be bigger mark-ups and profit margins for a time, until the material contracts and wage deals have to be renegotiated in boom conditions. So firms are encouraged to produce all they can while the going is good. That may require some investment to expand productive capacity. For the effect of *that* on total demand and recovery, meet the accelerator.

- **Acceleration** Distinguish the whole amount of capital goods in use from the rate of investment. The *rate* is the amount spent each year (or other time period) to maintain, increase or replace the stock of capital. It is that rate – i.e. the year's demand for new capital goods – that contributes to total demand. It tends to be a much more variable component of total demand than the consumer spending and government spending that make up the rest of the demand. The consumer demand and some of the investment demand are related, and it is in that relation that the 'accelerator' occurs. You met it briefly when you studied how firms invest. Here is a reminder.

To see how the accelerator works, imagine that you run a small transport firm. You own five trucks, work them hard, and replace the oldest one each year. As a business-cycle boom approaches you expect demand to increase by 15 per cent. Instead of buying one truck that year, you buy two – one replacement plus one addition. *A 15 per cent increase in demand has doubled your rate of investment.* Next year demand grows another 3 or 4 per cent. You buy one replacement truck. Demand has continued to grow but *a decline in its rate of growth has cut your rate of investment in half.* Next year (with the boom over and the downturn heading toward recession) demand declines 20 per cent. You retire one truck and don't replace it. *A 20 per cent decline in demand has cut your rate of investment 100 per cent, to zero.* (There are lay-offs at the truck factory and its material and component suppliers. As the laid-off workers lose income and cut their spending, total demand falls further – and so on.) Figure 47.1 graphs it.

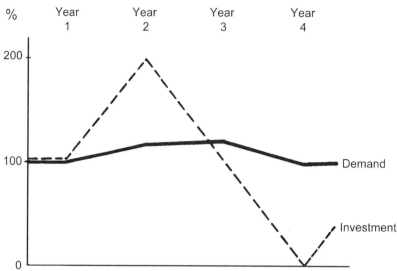

Figure 47.1 The Accelerator at work: rates of change in the demand for one firm's services, and the firm's demand for investment goods.

Through the recovery phase of the cycle, those processes drive the economy into boom. In due course producers have finished expanding their productive capacity, and reduced their rate of investment. There is some over-production, and warehouses fill up. Some costs of production rise too high. There is some inflation, and perhaps some government action to restrain credit and consumer demand. So the downturn begins, and round the cycle we go again.

Economic growth often continues throughout the cycle, merely slowing through the recessions. That can still allow big fluctuations in employment. Remember how much current economic growth is 'jobless growth' as technical improvements increase the productivity of the existing workforce. If annual economic growth declines from (say) 4 per cent in boom to 1 per cent in recession, that can take unemployment from 3 to 6 per cent or from 9 to 12 per cent of the workforce, despite some continuing positive growth of output.

Stabilizers

This account has exaggerated the force of the business cycle by focussing only on what changes. There is plenty that does not change. Life and work, earning and spending continue comparatively undisturbed for eight or nine people out of ten. The cyclical processes affect some industries more than others, and some scarcely at all. Some demands are more income-elastic than others. As income varies, people may spend more or less on new clothes, holiday travel, eating out, new cars and other

household equipment. There is much less variation in the demand for basic food, medical care, education, power and water and sewerage, commuter transport.

Besides government efforts to moderate the cycle there are also some counter-cyclical market effects. When jobs are scarce, demand for education may rise a little as young people opt for more years at school. Industries with long investment lead-times may continue their investment programs throughout the cycle. Some may slow them through booms when prices for land and capital goods rise, and quicken them through recessions when those prices decline. In the household sector, well-off people are often better-off through recessions when plenty of low-paid casual labor is available. They may spend more than usual on casual gardening, window-cleaning and other domestic work, and also on house repairs and extensions.

HISTORICAL CHANGE

Economic growth and cyclical fluctuations are rarely the only changes at work. Recall, from chapters on the mixed economies' new directions of development, how many other changes may be tangling with those two.

External causes There are economic effects of shocks: wars, bad weather, political upsets, OPEC price changes. There may be both cyclical and long-term changes in the world prices of fuels, metal ores, grains, beef, wool and other tradeable commodities. Trading countries' opportunities and terms of trade may be affected by the rapid rise of new competitors and new markets in East Asia; by the collapse of the communist economies and new investment opportunities in their territories; by civil wars and forced migrations; by changing international agreements about international trade and financial exchange.

Technological changes can be labor-saving, capital-saving, or both. Labor-saving technology has brought half a century or more of jobless growth in agriculture and many industries. Capital-saving technology (which yields output from a cheaper stock of capital than before) can reduce employment in the capital-goods industries as well as the consumer-goods industries.

Economic growth can affect stability and employment in a number of ways. Rising income increases the proportion of spending, saving and household investment that is discretionary, so demand is less regular and predictable than before. For half a century or so, jobless growth in farming and heavy industry was balanced by the growth of labor-intensive services, including new tax-financed public services. But the demand for some services may now be satisfied. The demand for some is limited by tax resistance which limits government's capacity to finance public services. Some services provide less employment as they are penetrated by labor-saving and capital-saving technology (as in banking, exchange dealing, stock exchange transactions, libraries and other information processors and retrievers). Levels of employment may thus be affected in a number of ways at once by the joint effects of growth and technical change.

Environmental stress Humans are using up some finite resources, failing to renew some renewable ones, polluting air and sea and land, and dangerously multiplying their numbers. Much of the damage is done directly or indirectly by economic activity. Most environmental reform changes some economic activity. Some of it does so without cost, but most of it increases costs or reduces output, and changes the distribution of wealth, income or employment. The changes are not always for the worse. Some environmental reform could imaginably be designed to restore full employment, ration scarce resources equitably, and reduce inequalities. But it is a divisive area of policy. Even where there is consensus about the environmental aims of reform, there is still likely to be conflict about the distribution of its costs and benefits.

Some environmental reform lets market activity continue under different rules. Some replaces market processes (as when government bans or rations or takes over some uses of some resources). Some reform is in the behavior of the citizens as they waste less, and avoid pollutant products; but much of the necessary reform has to be designed and implemented by government. Some of it brings some permanent increase of public control. And besides prompting policies whose primary purposes are environmental, the new concerns are modifying a lot of traditional policies about health, education, transport, city planning, building design, tourism and recreation, and so on.

A genuinely sustainable world economy would require more radical economic changes than have yet been attempted. Whether by collective choice or by neglect, we face big changes in economic life, and some increase of government's necessary role in it.

Economic maturity? Environmental compulsion may give practical force to the notion of 'enough' which has so far been no more than an unworldly vision, routinely scorned as depending on an unlikely change in human nature. (You know the sort of thing –we would be vegetarian, have women rule, cooperate instead of competing, let a frugal material life sustain a richer spiritual, intellectual, artistic and compassionate life together.)

Instead of deriding the vision, *intelligent* realists could actually improve its chances. Consider:

Most individual, competitive, ambitious interests are pursued through individual lifetimes. People seek desirable occupations, work satisfaction, income, promotion, business success, wealth, power. They exercise individual preferences for risk or security, leadership or a quiet life, absorbing work or absorbing recreations. None of those facts of life necessarily depend on continuing economic growth. Competing to earn more, rise to the top, become a star, enjoy a well-endowed retirement can be as absorbing in a stable aconomy as in a growing one. Those ambitions already operate as forcefully in periods of negative growth as in booms. A no-growth economy could well be driven by the same mixed motives as drive us now. Most past regimes have been unavoidably hard on many of their people, for lack of productivity. The rich democracies have the first chance in history to provide all their members with *both* enough to sustain a happy life *and* substantial competitive inequalities. Thought about mature steady-state economies may be useful after all.

Compound effects

Keep all those sources of potential instability in mind, with the problems they may pose for government.

The business cycle continues. Its effects mix with effects of sudden shocks and long-term structural and historical changes. Separately and together they affect aggregates of income, saving, investment, employment and inflation.

Meanwhile public enterprises and government departments are performing their many necessary economic functions. Besides those detailed functions, it is desirable that the public activities as a whole should do more good than harm to the economy's performance as a whole. To achieve that, government must be good at diagnosing the regular and irregular forces at work in the economy. It must coordinate its own numerous economic activities. And the coordinated activity must be flexible, to adapt to the changing effects of the other forces at work.

As we noted earlier, that's far from easy. It is our next subject.

MACROECONOMICS AND MICROECONOMICS?

The component parts of a national economic system are often called the microeconomy, and the system as a whole the macroeconomy. Hence the science of microeconomics and macroeconomics, and government's concern with microeconomic and macroeconomic policy. They are convenient labels. Why is this text avoiding them? Two reasons:

First, most macroeconomic policies operate on component parts of the system, just as microeconomic policies do. They are said to concern the economy as a whole because they aim to influence the whole amount of employment, the rates of growth and inflation and the balance of payments of the economy as a whole. But most things that governments do for those purposes have the form of microeconomic adjustments to particular components of the system. They may act to re-train or re-employ the unemployed, to restrain wages, to encourage or discourage investment, to regulate banks or foreign trade or foreign exchange. Those activities are macroeconomic only in the intention to influence some total of activity *as well as* the detailed activity which they directly influence.

Second, most microeconomic policies also have macroeconomic effects, and most macroeconomic policies also have microeconomic effects. Policy makers should do their best to be aware of both, and think about *all* the effects their policies are likely to have.

For example you may consider introducing a more generous (microeconomic) welfare policy, but decide that it might increase the (macroeconomic) rate of infla-

tion. Or you may consider cutting the (microeconomic) tariff which protects an inefficient industry. You may be willing to accept a consequent (macroeconomic) increase of unemployment – but you may change your mind after calculating that the increase of imports would also worsen the country's (macroeconomic) balance of payments.

Similarly, macroeconomic policies should be chosen with their micro as well as their macro effects in mind. To boost total demand during a recession (a macro aim) you may decide to give people more to spend by cutting taxes. Macroeconomic calculations will tell you how much tax to cut. But how should the benefit be distributed? To increase or to reduce after-tax inequalities? To leave more money in the pockets of people who will spend most of it, or people who will save most of it, or firms who will invest most of it? Buy capital goods or buy consumer goods with it? Spend mostly on national products, or spend disproportionately on imports? These microeconomic decisions about the detailed incidence of the tax cuts have both microeconomic effects on the pattern of industries and the distribution of income, and macroeconomic effects on employment and the balance of payments.

Those are the reasons why for most purposes this text uses some different terms. What government tries to do or abstains from doing about the structure and performance of the economy as a whole will usually be called economic strategy. Much of the strategic activity consists of coordinating the government's many detailed policies to see that, besides their primary effects on particular industries or markets or income distributions (or whatever), their effects on national totals of demand and supply will also be desirable. There is nothing new about that activity: national Treasurers spend most of their time telling their cabinet colleagues that they can't spend more on rocketry or child care without either increasing taxes or spending less on something else. But the language of 'strategy' and 'coordination' may encourage more coherent policy-making than language which distinguishes 'macro' from 'micro' policies as if they were independent of each other. It is merely a verbal preference – if you prefer the more familiar language, by all means use it (as this text does now and then.)

As policy-makers go about their strategic work, where do they look for – and how do they organize – the information that they need? Meet the national accounts, and some efforts to model them for forecasting purposes.

INFORMATION SERVICES

For policy-makers to know what they're doing they need to know a lot about the world in which they operate.

That is as true for business as for government. Many business decisions depend on judgments about the likely behavior of the business cycle, rates of interest, rates of inflation, exchange rates, fuel and commodity prices, changes of government policy. Small businesses may rely on the financial press for most of their guesswork. Bigger firms, and the financial press, may do some of their own investigation. They may consult independent researchers and forecasters, and their bankers and stockbrokers. But all those operators depend heavily on public statistical services and national accounts.

Public policy-makers also depend on them. They need to know current levels of economic activity: of employment and unemployment, wages and prices, rates of inflation, rates of growth. They need to know their national economic structure and how it is changing. They must be able to calculate what rate of any tax will yield what amount of revenue, and what effects particular taxes may have on prices, incentives, spendable income, likely spending and saving. Government must be able to cost its own activities and investment projects. It must estimate what they will add to demands on private suppliers of capital and intermediate goods, and what income and employment effects those demands may have. As it plans action to influence consumer demand, or private investment, or the balance of payments, it must estimate the relevant quantities: *how much* change in a tax rate, *how much* budget surplus or deficit, *how much* expansion or contraction of bank credit, *how much* restraint of imports or assistance to exports, will have the desired effect? It must often also estimate *how long* public actions will take to have their effects. How quickly will a tax cut increase spending? Exhaust existing stocks of goods? Prompt new investment? How long before new investment can increase output? Will additional consumer spending inflate prices before new capacity can deliver new output to match the new spending? If so, should producers be given investment incentives now with a promise of tax cuts and expanded credit for consumers later? How much later?

Most of those are compound questions: they ask both about quantities which can be observed and measured, and about causal relations which may be uncertain or variable, and disagreed by experts. This chapter samples the two kinds of information. First, the mostly-factual national accounts. Then the more controversial econo-metric models by which some economists try to integrate the quantities into models which simulate the causal processes at work in particular national economies. Both are complicated subjects. You must go to the national accounts themselves, and to the models themselves, to understand them properly. What follow here are simple outlines of the kinds of information that they are designed to provide.

NATIONAL ACCOUNTS

Government and its public enterprises keep accounts of their own operations. They gather a great deal of information about the rest of the economy. They supply themselves and the private and household sectors with many statistical and information services. But 'the National Accounts' customarily means the accounts of national income and its main components which governments publish periodically: consolidated accounts annually, and many of their components quarterly and monthly. Those official accounts of total national output and income, and of growth, employment and unemployment, inflation, and the import and export and other components of the balance of payments, are the subject of this section.

Recall the flow of funds in a national economy. Households buy goods and services from producers. The producers use the money to pay for the factors of production – the land, capital funds and labor – that they use, most of which are owned and supplied to them by individuals. Private producers get market prices for their goods, some public producers are paid from taxes, but the effect is the same: goods and services flow one way through the economy, money to pay for them circulates the other way.

The real income of a national society is the amount of goods and services that its people produce, and consume or trade for imports or add to their stock of capital, in the course of a year. Orthodox accounting notices only what is paid for, omitting the output of household and voluntary work. For the income that they do notice, the national accounts have three measures. One measures *income:* the total the population earns in a year. One measures *output:* the total value of goods and services produced. One measures *expenditure:* the total spent on finished goods (with some adjustment for the value of work in progress and goods awaiting sale). With minor accounting variations they arrive at the same figure. They are three measures of the same activity.

'Finished' goods is to avoid double counting. From raw material to finished goods (by which these accountants mean final sale) the work in progress may be sold many times – from miners to steelmakers to carmakers to retailers to car buyers, or from farmers to millers to wholesalers to bakers to retailers to your breakfast table. There are also many sales which add nothing to output, as people sell possessions to each other. If you add up all the sale prices you get a total far above the value of the year's output of finished goods. So the national account-keepers count only the value added at each stage: each producer's revenue minus what that producer has paid to buy goods from other producers. The difference between the two is the value added. It is added by the producer (who takes profit income) and the workers (who take wage income). So nationally, the value added by all producers equals the amount spent on final goods, and it equals the total income of those who produced the goods.

In principle, that is the national income. In practice it is subject to some adjustments to avoid errors, and some warnings to avoid misunderstanding its meaning. Including these:

- Plenty of non-earners get shares of the income. But if they get it by public income transfer (from taxation) or by household transfer (from a breadwinner) those are assumed to be transfers from producers' incomes which have already been counted. The transfers don't alter total national income; adding them would be double-counting; so they're not counted into national income, however carefully they may be counted for welfare and equitable purposes.

- Household work, output and in-kind contributions to income are not counted. Nor is the output of unpaid labor using public capital (transport by family car on public roads; recreation in public parks). Those omissions encourage the illusion that housing investment is unproductive. They can distort comparisons between national standards of living and between class standards of living. If one country has better public capital and household capital than another, it is likely to have margins of output and income which the accounts don't reveal. A society which distributes household space and capital more equally than money income is likely to have a more equal distribution of real income than the accounts show. Less equal household space and capital may mean less equal distribution of income than the accounts show. It may also mean less total income, if some richer households underemploy their household capital while some poorer households are not equipped to produce what they would like to produce with their household time and labor.

- You may think passive property incomes – rent, interest, profit to passive shareholders – are also unearned. But the accounts treat them as income earned by contributing capital to production. Profit, moreover, is treated as a residual: the revenue remaining after producers have paid all their bills. That accounting principle ensures that at any rate of profit, national income equals the value of national output.

- 'Domestic' and 'National' income differ by incorporating the relevant international activities into the 'National' figures, i.e. the effects of export, import, and property income earned from or paid to foreigners.

- 'Gross' and 'Net' output and income differ chiefly by discounting the annual loss of physical capital by depreciation or 'capital consumption'.

- For some purposes the accounts need to be in real terms. So where necessary there are duplicate accounts. 'Current value' accounts record the actual wages and prices paid at the time. 'Constant value' accounts use a deflator to adjust the values to the money value of a base year. That allows the accountants to measure the amount of inflation, and to eliminate it from the measurement of real output, income and growth. If (say) the current-value account shows that national income grew by 5 per cent last year but the constant-value account shows that it grew by 2 per cent, you know that there were 2 per cent more goods and services than were produced in the previous year, and a 3 per cent inflation of the currency.

Return now to the national accounts of income, output and expenditure. Here – in principle, in the simplest possible summary – is how they are put together:

Income *Add up* the national totals of the following:

- Wages and salaries (employment income)
- Private fees and charges (self-employment income)
- Dividends, rent, interest, and public enterprise profits (property income)

  Subtract stock appreciation (price increases of existing assets).

The result is **Gross Domestic Product** at factor cost. If you adjust it for net property income from foreigners or paid to foreigners, the result is Gross **National** Product at factor cost.

Output Use the same information to arrive at the factor cost (the capital and wage costs) of the output of all industries and services including government. The result is again **Gross Domestic Product** at factor cost. To turn it into **Gross National Product** adjust it, as before, for foreign property income. To turn the result into **Net National Income**, *subtract* the year's depreciation and wearing out of capital goods (sometimes called 'capital consumption').

Expenditure *Add up* the following:

- Consumers' expenditure

- Investment, i.e. public and private expenditure on capital goods

- Government expenditure on current costs (excluding investment)

- *Adjust* for the year's change in the value of stock in hand and work in progress

The result is **Gross Domestic Product** at market prices. To turn it into **Gross National Product**, adjust it for net gain or loss from exports, imports and foreign income, and for taxes on goods and services.

STRATEGIC INFORMATION

Accounts in those forms help to analyse current economic activity, to measure rates of growth and inflation, and (if used with care) to compare one national economy with another. But we leave those uses aside to consider how the national accounts can help governments as strategic policy-makers and managers of their mixed economies.

The commonest simplification of the structure of the national account is

$$Y = C + I + G + X - M$$

where Y is Income, C is Consumption, I is Investment, G is current Government spending, X is eXport sales, M is iMport purchases.

Its form matches the main strategic alternatives of a government which wants to contrive full employment with low inflation and balanced foreign payments. Government can influence *Consumption* by adjusting taxes to adjust consumers' after-tax income and spending, or the quantity of goods they get for their money. It can influence *Investment* by adjusting public investment and by influencing the rate of interest and the amount of credit which are available to the private and household sectors. It can influence *Government's* current spending by adjusting the public goods and services it provides. It can influence the *Balance of Payments* by regulating

trade, regulating foreign borrowing and lending, regulating the uses of available foreign exchange, or encouraging export and import-replacing industries.

In each of those alternatives, government acts to influence an aggregate: total consumer spending, total investment, total government spending, the net balance of payments. In each case there are many alternative ways of influencing the total. Some of the alternatives may be more effective than others at that primary task of influencing the total. They also differ by operating on different components of the relevant total. So besides their effect on the total, the policy choices can't help having other social and economic effects. In orthodox language, macroeconomic measures also have microeconomic effects. The micro effects can be as important as the macro effects, and they often influence the choice of macro measures.

An example: Suppose you are your country's Treasurer when the economy faces an excessive boom. You want to restrain the boom in order to restrain its likely effects on inflation and the balance of payments. You may choose to operate on each of C and I and G and X and M. We could go through the many alternative ways of operating on each of them, noticing the microeconomic effects of each alternative. But one example will do. Consider C. What can you do to restrain the demand for consumer goods?

You can increase income tax. For the fullest and quickest effect, hit the poorest taxpayers, because they spend most of their income, mostly on consumer goods. (Or so some rich advisers tell you. They're forgetting that the poor spend much higher proportions of income on rent than the rich do.) Anyway, hitting the poorest taxpayers would be unfair. Hitting all the taxpayers might be political suicide. You should probably hit the richest, who can afford some loss. But they're the most influential, and can do most political damage per head. And they save and invest more than the poor do, so for a given cut in consumer spending you may need to take a bigger total of tax, because some of the tax will reduce saving and investment rather than spending. But for your strategic purpose you want to restrain I as well as C, so why not? Furthermore the rich spend more proportionally on imports than the poor do, and you also want to restrain M. A single microeconomic measure can thus restrain consumption and investment and imports. It can also offset to some extent the rate at which executives are increasing each others' rewards, and improve the distribution of wealth and income. The virtuous head of your public service department recommends a moderate increase in the top rate of income tax. But your political colleagues can't face the backlash from the press and the financial markets, and ban any increase of income tax.

You can alternatively reduce consumer demand by taxing goods and services. After-tax income and spending will be unchanged, but the spending will buy less goods, and put less pressure on producers, as the new taxes raise the price of consumer goods. The higher prices will fuel the inflation you want to prevent. But the politicians are still adamant against increasing income tax, so you look for ways of making price increases more tolerable. Tax some goods but not others, for example. A carbon tax on coal-burning would be good for the environment and attract green votes. But your country happens to mine coal, import oil, and export manufactured goods to hotly competitive and price-elastic markets. A tax on coal will raise the home prices of power and manufactured goods and thus fuel inflation. It will increase exporters' costs of production and may reduce export sales and revenue. Users who can switch to oil will do so. That will increase the import bill. Lower X and higher M will thus worsen the country's balance of payments.

You eventually settle for a further increase in the taxes on tobacco, alcohol, and some luxury goods including expensive cars. (Your country only makes cheap cars so the new car tax is a disguised tariff.) None of those goods will lose many sales because the demand for them is fairly inelastic, but their higher prices will reduce spending on other things.

The purpose of that example is to make four points:

(1) Government can rarely operate on any one of C, I, G, X or M without also affecting the others. It can't arrive at a desired strategic effect by simply adding the effect of a consumption tax on consumption + the effect of an investment allowance on investment + the effect of a new public program on public spending + the effect of a tariff on imports and the effect of an export subsidy on exports. Each is likely to alter the effects of some of the others. Strategies need to be coherent, and to be judged as a whole.

(2) Political, social and distributional effects may be as important as the primary strategic effects, and may – sometimes rightly, sometimes wrongly, sometimes scandalously – influence the choice of strategic means.

(3) To know what they're doing, policy-makers need a great deal of detailed as well as aggregate information. Read the above example again and notice how the policy options, to be effective, would need to be based on detailed knowledge of current flows of money and goods, and the likely quantitative relations between the policy measures and their direct and indirect effects.

(4) People with different private interests and public purposes may sometimes need different information to arrive at their preferred policies. So there can be conflicts about the best use to make of the statistical services' resources. Three examples:

- Many national accounts have an unhelpful way of aggregating C. They lump together spending on consumption goods and on household capital goods (car, furniture, household equipment, etc.). They do that because the output of household capital doesn't sell for money; orthodox economists don't count output that doesn't sell for money; so they count household purchase of capital goods as consumption rather than investment. Why does that matter to economic analysts and policy-makers? It matters because the amount that households spend on consumption goods and the amount that they invest in capital goods are determined by partly different forces. Spending for consumption tends to vary with disposable income. Spending on capital goods varies partly with income and partly with the available credit and rate of interest. So for analysts who want to calculate the relation of C and I to the conditions which determine each of them, and for strategists who want to influence those aggregates, it would help if household investment was included in aggregate I, or in an I category of its own. But that would contradict economists' traditional way of defining investment, production and consumption. It would acknowledge that households produce as well as consume, and that the private sector produces only half (or so) of the material output of an advanced mixed economy. If that were reflected in policy it should advance the interests of poorer households, of many women, and of people who want to reduce inequalities. (That it *should* do so doesn't guarantee that it *would* do so, of course. But it would equip battlers for those causes with better and more persuasive information.)

- When the Thatcher government took office in Britain in 1979 it intended to increase some inequalities of wealth and income, for incentive and other reasons. It also intended to reduce the cost of government. Both purposes were served when it abolished the permanent Royal Commission on the Distribution of Wealth and Income. That Commission had monitored and reported on distributions between individuals, households, cities and regions, and between people with different inheritance, educational qualifications, occupations, and so on. Without that flow of information the increase of inequality became harder to measure, and it would now be harder to correct it as effectively and accurately as a reforming government might wish.

- In Chapter 49 you will find Paul Chapman's account of a protected key industry in South Australia. It attracted unprotected subsidiaries. The key industry and its subsidiaries together spread technical, scale and other advantages to a further circle of firms in an expanding cluster. Chapman was able to base his analysis on unusually good information. To service its long-standing and complicated tariff policies the Australian government had developed a manufacturing census. That was a record of all manufacturing activity based on compulsory periodical returns by all manufacturing firms. The State government of Chapman's region offered various aids to attract manufacturing investment, and kept detailed records of their use. As both an aid to and a check on the public activities, an independent academic constructed detailed input-output tables of the region's industries. From those sources Chapman could detail his analysis very accurately. A change of national strategy has since brought a commitment to free trade. The new leaders of the national government think they *need not* know the detailed composition of the private sector because they *should not* try to influence it. They also want to reduce the cost of government. So the manufacturing census has been replaced by occasional sample surveys, and resources to keep the input/output tables up to date have dried up. If a future government wants to judge which industries could now serve as key industries, and wants to get them established, it will need to rebuild appropriate information services.

As in other walks of life, what people need to know depends – at least in part – on what they want to do.

MACROECONOMETRIC MODELS

The national accounts tell you *what* is happening: how much output, investment, consumption, employment, inflation, import and export. But they are not designed to tell you *why* it is happening, or how a government might make some of it happen differently. To know that, you usually need to know (or estimate, or guess) four more things: (1) what causes what; (2) *how much* change in particular factors will cause given changes in others; (3) how long those changes are likely to take; and (4) what other forces may disturb those causal processes. Suppose for example that (1) a wage rise usually causes prices to

rise. To turn that into useable information you may need to estimate (2) by what percentage prices will rise after each percentage point of wage increase; (3) how long, if at all, the price changes will lag behind the wage changes; and (4) whether changes have the same effect on prices in all circumstances, and if not, what other forces may alter the effect.

One approach to those tasks is to construct a mathematical model of all the forces you believe are at work in your national economic system, separating or aggregating them as you think best. You base the model on your practical and theoretical beliefs about what causes what. You feed in the relevant quantities from the national accounts. You can then try a number of exercises:

1. Start the model with the quantities prevailing ten years ago. Run it up to the present. See if the quantities it arrives at, year by year, agree with the national accounts for those years. If they don't, you may blame external circumstances, or amend the causal structure of the model.

2. During that past period there were some changes of government policy. You want to know what actual effects those changes caused. So you duplicate the run: run the model through the same period from the same initial year, but leave the original policy settings unchanged. You thus create a precise imagined alternative to what actually happened. You may conclude that any differences between the imagined history and the actual history were caused by the policy changes.

3. You're an investor, or you're a bank officer gambling on future rates of interest and exchange. Your fortunes depend on how well or badly you forecast the future behavior of the economy. You start the model from now. You feed in present public policies, any changes of policy you expect, and any changes you expect in the world economy. You run the model into the future and bet on its forecasts.

4. You advise a government which wants to contrive the fullest employment it can without causing excessive inflation or exchange deficit and foreign debt. You run the model into the future with many alternative policies to discover what level of employment is achievable under those constraints, and what public action is most likely to achieve it.

Assessing the models Why haven't such models resolved disagreements about how economic systems work, and about the best policies for governing them? The short answer is 'because of the complexity and uncertainty of human economic behavior'. The forces at work in an advanced economy are so many that national econometric models have up to a thousand equations. Some of the forces behave consistently enough to be worth modelling. Others don't. The ways in which the irregulars disturb the regulars are at the heart of the modellers' problems. Students of the models will find that the forces can be sorted into three rather than two groups: (1) regular forces which can usefully be modelled; (2) external or irregular forces which can't usefully be modelled; and (3) forces about whose status modellers disagree.

(1) *Regular* There are causal processes which are determined fairly reliably within the national economic system. Those are worth modelling. But some regular conditions and causal processes look so dependable that modellers can safely neglect them. (Parents continue to bring up their children, forests continue to perpetuate themselves and to purify the air, law enforcement continues to limit the flow of theft.) If historical changes alter those stable facts of life, an economic model which does not include them won't know what is disturbing the relations which it *does* model. Remember the selective nature of *all* causal explanation. A modeller can only model a *selection* of the causal forces at work, and a *selection* of the necessary conditions for them to work as they do. So any model is vulnerable to changes in its taken-for-granted, unmodelled assumptions.

(2) *External* There are forces which the model itself can't predict. That may be because they are by nature too irregular. (Examples: Changes of government policy; seasons of bad weather; earthquakes.) Or it may be because they originate outside the national system. (Examples: World commodity prices; foreign governments' behavior, foreign inventions.) The model can't tell its user what external forces of that kind to expect. The user has to tell the model what external forces to expect. It is an important difference, so you must learn the modellers' clumsy words for it. Forces whose behavior the model can explain are called endogenous, meaning that they are generated within the modelled elements of the system. Forces the model can't explain or predict are called exogenous, meaning that they are generated outside the system-as-modelled. Some of those unpredictable forces actually originate within the system, in the form of decisions by actors in the system. But they are still called exogenous because the element of free will means that they are not reliably determined by the forces which the model-builder chooses to define and model as constituting the system. They are things people do to the system.

Sometimes the endogenous/exogenous distinction is

factual. Foreign prices are exogenous to your national system. Your own manufacturers' prices are endogenous, because they tend to be determined by local costs of production plus a mark-up, both of which can be modelled. But sometimes the difference between internal and external causes is the subject of disagreement between modellers. Those disputed forces are our third group.

(3) *Disagreed* When modellers disagree about the internal or external origin of some of the forces at work in the national economy, the disagreements may be methodological, or moral, or technical. There are methodological questions about what it is convenient to include in the model. There are moral questions – which you met in Part One of this course – about what it is reasonable to expect of people in particular circumstances. For example, when workers respond to rising prices by demanding higher wages, are they making responsible choices – or are they merely transmitting inflationary pressures over which they have no real control and for which they should not be held responsible? Modellers can dispute whether such actions are endogenous (determined by the relevant price changes) or exogenous (injected into the market processes by workers' free choices or uses of union power). Third, there are technical disagreements about what causes what, for example as to whether particular causes have particular effects, or whether particular effects have causes within the system or outside it.

You have met plenty of disagreements of that kind. Suppose there are workers who can't find jobs. A Keynesian modeller observes that the jobs are not there because the economic system is not generating them. The unemployment is endogenous, caused by the way the system is working. But a neoclassical modeller may believe that employers would create jobs for the unemployed if they were willing to work for low enough wages. Since they won't do that, they're unemployed by their own wish, or by public policy if government has imposed a legal minimum wage. Those decisions are made *outside* the set of relations that the neoclassic defines as constituting the market system, they're not determined by the system – so they're exogenous, and the model-user has to tell the model about them. Having been told their nature and quantities, the model can then forecast their effects.

But the Keynesian modeller disputes that characterization of the disagreement. She may agree that the neoclassic's social morality is regrettable, but she insists that it has nothing to do with this particular disagreement. If the unemployed offer to work for less than the lowest current wage, that is likely to lower more wages than their own. Employers will replace existing employees by cheaper ones, or cut their wages by threatening to replace them. That will reduce total wage income, spending, effective demand, and therefore investment and employment. Instead of reducing unemployment the wage cut is likely to increase it. This is not a moral disagreement about the unemployed workers' greed or sloth or responsibility for their own fortunes. It is a technical disagreement about what causes what in the economic system.

Summary Inaccurate forecasting does not necessarily discredit a model. It may have been misused, or misinformed about exogenous forces at work on the economy.

If the model is used to measure the effects of particular policies, the conclusions can be no more reliable than the imagined alternatives against which the effects are measured. Differences between that alternative and the actual course of events are always likely to have other causes besides the policies in question. So the analytical use of such models can be as inconclusive as their forecasting use.

Besides those theoretical difficulties there are many purely practical difficulties in the accounting and modelling of national economic activity. There are gaps, inaccuracies and time-lags in the information on which the accounts are based. Some of the forces at work in and on national economies are likely to be changing, and the modellers may be slow to detect and adapt to the changes. The difficulties have increased since financial deregulation exposed national systems to greater internal mischief and external disturbance.

For all those reasons the macroeconometric models are difficult to assess – or to assess to everyone's satisfaction. Rival models incorporating different causal patterns have survived for decades, often delivering different analyses and forecasts. Their owners excuse their shortcomings in the various ways indicated above. Nevertheless some can be seen to have performed better than others. That may be due to the skill with which they have been used, and the quality of the information fed into them, as well as the design of the models. Models of this kind should not be written off as useless. Some of the best forecasters use them and some of the best forecasters don't. Both have to do a great deal of quantitative work, and whether to develop a model for the purpose may be best understood as an individual choice of method. Each method has a range of users from reasonably successful to very unsuccessful.

Of the half-dozen models of the British economy which have stayed in use for twenty years or more, we can briefly compare two which represent opposite extremes of the range, both in their theoretical structure and in the success of their users' forecasts.

A Liverpool model

Economists at the University of Liverpool developed a model on principles sometimes called 'new classical'. The model emphasizes the force and efficiency of market processes, and the impotence of government to improve on them. It makes spending depend on net worth, i.e. on wealth as well as income. It assumes that all markets clear. That includes labor markets. Most unemployment is voluntary, and would cease if the unemployed lowered their labor price to the level at which it would pay producers to employ them. Business decisions are shaped by rational expectations, which are the expectations indicated by this model. As the model was developed through the 1980s those expectations included the following.

The money supply determines the rate of inflation.

If the government expands the money supply by fiscal means – by spending more than it takes in revenue – the only long-term effect is on the rate of inflation.

If the government expands the money supply by monetary means – by reducing the rate of interest and inducing an expansion of bank credit – the only long-term effect is on the rate of inflation.

Thus neither fiscal nor monetary policy can have any but fleeting effects on employment. The only way government can influence the amount of unemployment is by adjusting taxation or the dole to adjust people's incentives to work and the prices they will accept for their labor.

Forecasts made with the help of this model through the 1980s were generally the least accurate of the model-based forecasts.

A Cambridge Model

The Cambridge Economic Policy Group led by Wynne Godley developed this model in the 1970s and has since been adapting it to changing condidions.

The model focuses on relations between stocks and flows in the British economy: the relation between inventory stocks and the flow of production, and the relation between private financial assets and the flow of private spending.

Those relations are 'exogenous' to the model: they are determined by people's norms and habits. Producers decide what inventory stocks they need to carry at any volume of output. That varies from industry to industry, for example with the length of time it takes to turn raw materials into finished goods for final sale. But in a particular country at a particular stage of development there is a national average relation of inventory to output. You can model that relation, then predict the flow if you know the size of the stock. Similarly there are national tendencies to spend and save steady proportions of disposable income so there tend to be steady relations between the stock of financial assets and the flows of income and spending. Those relations vary with time and place, and change with structural changes in the economy, but they are commonly steady enough for short- and medium-term modelling.

The Cambridge model has four distinctive features.

Fiscal policy – the government's taxing and spending – is the main determinant of changes in national employment and output. But to be effective, especially in achieving high employment, fiscal policy needs to be supported by appropriate monetary policy and national trade performance.

Monetary policy needs to conform with fiscal policy or actively support it. It can't replace it as a main determinant of the level of activity.

Trade performance, with or without active trade policy, needs to ensure that export earnings equal or exceed payment for imports. A first reason for that is that an excess of imports over exports reduces national income, output and employment, and occasions a continuous and eventually insupportable growth of foreign debt. A second reason (to be explained presently) is a likely effect of an exchange deficit on the inflation of the national currency.

Inflation arises in a variety of ways from competing claims to income. It may be influenced by levels of demand for goods and labor, by rates of interest, by the ease or difficulty of getting credit, by taxation, by prices in world markets. If a persistent exchange deficit depreciates the national currency, import prices rise, wage rates follow, and together they raise the money costs of production and the selling prices of nationally produced goods.

The force with which competing claims to income are pressed arises from political and social and historical as well as economic conditions. "We very much doubt", the designers of the model say, "whether any purely economic theory can 'explain' the rate of inflation or indeed whether it is fruitful to seek any general explanation". It follows that "inflation cannot be controlled directly by monetary policy. If it accelerates whenever there is a high pressure of demand, there will be a conflict between full employment and price stability which could only be resolved by political and institutional means." (-Wynne Godley and Francis Cripps,

Macroeconomics, 1983, pp.215, 305 in the Fontana edition.)

The Cambridge model is a model of the British economy through the last quarter of the twentieth century. The model has been adjusted with experience, and with changes in the economy's structure and international environment. Characterizing it in a sentence, its designers say (on p.17 of the book cited above) "we make a 'monetarist' financial system (based on the behaviour of stocks of money, financial assets and debts) drive a 'Keynesian' flow system based on the response of expenditure to income."

In a few more sentences:

People are observed to divide their income in fairly regular proportions between spending on goods and services, and maintaining their stock of money or other financial assets. Spending is thus determined fairly reliably by income. Within the limit imposed by the nation's productive capacity, the volume of disposable, after-tax income is determined by government's taxing and spending. It can expand national income and expenditure by borrowing from banks to finance a budget deficit.

Producers meet any increased demand for goods from their inventory stocks. If those diminish, they replenish them by increasing output. Bank credit expands to finance the increase.

The supply of credit is thus determined by the demand for it by creditworthy borrowers, including government. Government may regulate the banks to keep their activity in that relation to the demand for it; but their role is chiefly a passive, responsive one.

In principle government can set its fiscal policies to keep the nation fully employed. In practice that is subject to three main constraints. (1) The fiscal policies need to be based on good forecasting, and to be well judged. (2) Government's monetary policies must fit with its fiscal policies. (3) The nation's exports must pay for its imports. If that doesn't happen naturally it needs to be contrived. That may be attempted by devaluing the currency, together with an incomes policy to restrain the inflationary effects of the devaluation. Or (better) it can be done by some direct control of imports. That can also be inflationary (for example if it is achieved by tariffs). But there are other ways of reducing the volume of imports which do not raise their prices.

Wynne Godley was a consultant forecaster for the British Treasury. When the Thatcher government took office in 1979 its monetarist leaders did not trust his Keynesian leanings and dismissed him. Twelve years later the continuing Conservative government invited him back, because his forecasts had meanwhile been consistently better than theirs.

It would be hard to know how much that forecasting success owes to the qualities of the model, how much to information of other kinds from other sources, and how much to the experienced skill with which Godley uses all his resources. He himself insists that such models should not be treated as black boxes or trusted unconditionally. Small changes in the behavior they model, or small errors in the information fed into them, can yield big forecasting errors; their users should always keep a sceptical eye on their output. Modelling should supplement but not replace other methods, especially direct study of the beliefs and intentions of investors, bankers, wage bargainers and other economic actors. And the models must be kept up to date with the changing structure and behavior of the economic systems which they model. 'Few laws of economics', Godley says, 'will hold good across decades or between countries.' Some combination of that pragmatism, the qualities of their model, and their broader social and historical understanding may explain the comparative success of the Cambridge group's forecasting.

Two other purposes

First, this sketch of information services has focused on those on which macroeconomic policies are based. But remember that the national accounts serve many other purposes. The large aggregates we have been dealing with are broken down into a great many components, to meet the needs of public departments, private firms, labor unions, journalists, researchers and others interested in the detailed structure of the national economy and the activities of particular industries, occupations, regions, local government areas, and so on. And those public accounts can be supplemented for many purposes by market research, opinion polls, the annual reports which all companies must lodge with public offices and stock exchanges, and the research output of universities, think-tanks, investigative journalists and other interested and disinterested searchers.

You can't know everything. Like other resources, time and information have to be economized. Finding the sources you need for this week's work will often be all you have time for. But when you can, spend a day or two in the library to find the form in which your national accounts are published, and – broadly – the range of information they provide.

Second, the account of the macroeconometric models, which you just read, is well located. This chapter makes a transition. It began with reminders of a great deal of detailed (microeconomic) work on the component parts and processes of national economic systems. You are about to study how such systems work as a whole, to generate (macroeconomic) rates of growth, rates of inflation, balances of international trade and payment, and levels of employment and unemployment. Like the mousetrap business back in Chapter One, the macro-models in this chapter give you a foresight of the work to come, with its technical and political and moral problems and disagreements.The most challenging questions are about the design of better and worse national and international strategies. As usual, 'better' and 'worse' reflect the values and the technical understanding which have shaped this course of study. And as usual, one of its aims is to equip you to replace its judgments by your own. All the following chapters review subjects of professional and public disagreement. As you work through them it will be hard not to join in the arguments, think about their application to your country's policies, and judge the balance and bias with which these chapters review them. So from now on the text offers no formal exercises.

48

Economic structure

The 'structure' of a national economy means its particular pattern of skills, industries and institutions. Together they determine what quantities of what goods and services the economy can produce, and how fully it can employ its resources, if it works at full capacity. This chapter reviews –

- reasons why structure matters
- common aims of structural policies
- the main means by which public action can influence the structure of a national economy.

Which of the means to use, for which of their possible purposes, in what national and international conditions, will then be explored in the following chapters on trade, financial systems and employment.

WHY STRUCTURE MATTERS

A country's economic structure has two kinds of strategic importance.

First, it determines what can be produced: what whole value of output and what particular pattern of goods and services. The structure does not determine what *will* be produced: just what *can* be produced, if the economy is well managed and fully employed.

Second, there are two-way relations between structure and strategy. Some economic structures give people more options than others do: more political capacity to influence the level of employment, the distribution of income, environmental quality, the directions of future development. In the short run, a country's economic structure limits its development options. For example –

- If you have no steelmaker, plastics industry or engineering skills, you can't manufacture cars without five or ten years of preparatory development.

- If you have no medical schools you must send students to foreign schools or rely on immigrant doctors.

- If your developing country's housing stock is 5 per cent grand mansions, 30 per cent comfortable villas, 40 per cent tower blocks of ageing, rather meanly designed public housing, and 25 per cent dirt-floored peasant hovels, you can't distribute housing space

and capital equitably, or give most households effective choices of housing type and tenure, or enable them to make and do as much for themselves as they would like to do. So you can't maximize household output or whole national output, and it will take a generation or more to correct the defective housing structure.

- If your agriculture has been monopolized by big state farms throughout living memory, it may take a generation to bring up and train efficient private farmers.

The *number* of policy options may not be what matters. It is possible to have (i) a structure which allows no political choices but works well, or (ii) a structure which allows a number of alternative strategies, but they are all bad ones. One good option can be better than any number of bad ones. Examples:

1. Suppose we are a free-trading country with no trade or exchange controls. Our exports comfortably pay for our imports. Government has no power over trade, or over its effects on the national economy. But we do not need political choices: as long as market forces serve us well, our strategy is to leave our economic structure to the market.

2. Some changes occur in the world economy. Foreigners invent artificial fibres and as they become popular, the demand for our wool and cotton exports is halved. So is the home demand for them, as our own consumers also switch from nationally manufactured wool and cotton clothing to imported fibre clothing. Oil (which we do not have) replaces coal (which we do) as the main transport and heating fuel, so our coal exports decline and we import more oil. Through no fault of our own – since none of our industries has fallen behind world standards of efficiency – our export earnings decline and our import bill rises.

Treaties forbid us to control imports or subsidize exports. Our export earnings will now pay for our imports only during recessions when total demand is low. But when recovery and rising employment boost wage income and consumer spending, and investment revives, the demand for imports increases faster than the export earnings do, and we face an exchange deficit. The economy has developed a structural fault: it generates more demand for imports than its export industries' foreign earnings can pay for. While that unsatisfactory structure continues, the strategic options are three:

1. Leave the adjustment to the market. For a while, importers may be able to borrow some of the foreign currency they need. That will eventually make the deficit worse, as we come to need foreign exchange to pay interest on the debt as well as to pay for our imports. Eventually the market will depreciate our exchange rate. That will mean that in our own currency, imports will cost more, and in foreign currencies our exports will cost less, so the trade imbalance may adjust as we sell more exports and buy less imports. Or it may not, depending on the price elasticity of the supply and demand for those import and export products. Meanwhile there will be some inflation as import prices rise, some unemployment, and some of our less competitive firms may go out of business before market adjustments can save them. And as long as the structural fault continues, our industries and households will be poorer from having to pay more, in real terms, for fuel and some other necessaries.

2. Have government use its power over taxation, interest rates and public spending to contrive substantial unemployment throughout the business cycle. That will restrain wage income, consumer spending and the demand for imports. But it will also restrain investment and economic growth, and increase unemployment, poverty and welfare costs.

3. Start selling assets to foreigners. Every year, sell them enough natural resources and land and office buildings and existing firms to pay for the excess of our imports over our exports. Together with borrowing from them, that will fix the balance of payments for a few years – including the next election year. But it won't be long before the outflow of rent, interest and profit to the new foreign owners puts the country into worse exchange deficit than before.

Thus with that defective national economic structure there are no good options. But over time, strategic action may be able to repair the structure. Government may be able to stimulate some better export and import-replacing industries. To do so it may need some other structural changes: perhaps a public export bank; better transport infrastructure; some rationing of foreign exchange; a wage-fixing system which could withstand the inflationary pressures of a return to full employ-

ment. Those structural changes can add to the workable strategic options, and strengthen government's capacity to choose between them.

Those are simple examples of what is meant by saying that economic structure can limit the available strategies – but over time, strategic action may be able to amend the economic structure. This chapter is about economic structure, as the first of thirteen chapters about economic strategy. So we begin with a brief reminder of the possible aims of both: i.e. the possible aims of national economic strategies, and of any structural action which the strategies may call for.

Economic strategies can rarely be planned and executed like military strategies by a single-minded high command. Governments which develop them do so under many conflicting pressures, variously self-interested and public-spirited. Some governments are supported for long periods by stable majorities and coalitions of class and group interests. Others change frequently and bob about like corks on rough water, amending their policies with every opinion poll. But most of the successful phases of modern economic growth and social progress have had the benefit of some stable elements of strategy. So we begin with a quick survey of the range of purposes which commonly compete to shape the strategies.

WEALTH AND INCOME

Economic growth to increase national wealth and income has long been a widely agreed aim of economic policy. But there is less agreement about *what* income should be maximized, how it should be distributed, and what other considerations should moderate the pursuit of economic growth. Some people want to maximize the money income that is recorded in national accounts. Some want to maximize whole real income, including what households can make and do for themselves. Some want to maximize income net of the costs of environmental care and clean-up, human and mechanical accident repair, and so on. Some want to subordinate the growth of total income, wherever necessary, to the better distribution of income.

There are similar disagreements about wealth. Some want some different distribution of wealth between individuals. Some want some different distribution of wealth between the public, private and household sectors.

EMPLOYMENT

Many people want full employment to maximize output and income, to provide the best distribution of work and income, to minimize taxation and welfare costs. Others want a 'natural' rate of unemployment which they believe avoids inflation and improves work discipline and motivation.

Some people want to expand the workforce by employing more women and older people. Others fear rising unemployment and want to ration work by getting people to retire earlier, to share incomes, to accept more part-time work. Some want to give workforce status and a wage to full-time parents, then improve their career opportunities when they return to other employment. And some want to improve the experience of paid work itself, as follows.

The balance between work and consumption

Consumer sovereignty is a central principle of market freedom and efficiency. The people's shopping choices determine what gets produced. Surely a main aim of economic policy should be to have government do as little as possible to distort consumers' options and choices.

Or should it? Recall Robert Lane's evidence, in *The Market Experience* (1991), for the value of work to the worker. Where consumer sovereignty has commonly been understood as a relation between consumers and the firms who supply them, Robert Lane focuses on the workers' experience. Thus he sees consumer sovereignty as a relation between people as consumers and *the same people* as producers. Surely neither role should have sovereign command of the other? The relation between the two should ideally be one of balance, and choice.

Think about it. Suppose you are in some unglamorous occupation. You are a cleaner, a fast-food cook, a factory worker, a bank clerk. Would you welcome more choice and control over your conditions of work? Clean, comfortable, attractive surroundings? A secure job as long as you want it and do it satisfactorily? Working with long-time friends? A say in the choice of any new recruits to your working group? Self-management wherever the nature of the work allows, with freedom to do your work in your own way as long as it is done well? Courteous, cooperative, fair employers?

Now suppose that those conditions of work would increase average costs of production, for the economy as a whole, by ten or fifteen per cent. Instead of your pay buying what it buys today, it will buy what it would buy seven or ten years ago. Living conditions were not at all bad then. If you had a choice, would you trade that margin of consumption for those sweet conditions of work?

Lane's point is that as an individual worker and consumer you don't have much choice of that kind. Most people, especially in low- and middle-income jobs, have a limited choice of jobs and even less choice about the conditions they offer. Competition drives employers to shave their costs as far as they can, and in labor-intensive industries that chiefly means their labor costs. In many industries firms don't survive by treating their workers better than their competitors do, they survive by treating their *customers* better than their competitors do, which may mean treating their workers worse than their competitors do. Nobody has much choice about that – neither workers nor consumers, neither employers nor employees. The structure and working principles of a competitive market economy *impose* consumer sovereignty on individual market choices. Your shopping choices will always tend to shape your work options more powerfully than your work choices can affect your shopping choices.

But there are also collective choices. Collective bargaining by labor unions has sometimes improved conditions of work as well as pay. Collective political action has done wonders for conditions of work. It began by banning women and children from underground mining and limiting their hours of factory work. It has gone on to revolutionize industrial health and safety. In many industries in many countries government now regulates minimum wages, standard hours of work, standards of comfort as well as safety, and annual holiday entitlements. It requires that workers be insured and compensated for injury, and compensated if sacked without cause. It requires equal opportunity and bans sexual harassment. Some of those improvements came in a market way in the course of economic growth. But many were public initiatives, and many of them extended to whole industries or categories of workers what would only have been patchy improvements if they were left to market forces.

Some of those improvements have also improved efficiencies. But many of them have increased costs of production and consumer prices. They *protect* people *from* consumer sovereignty, and restore some better balance between people's wants as workers and their wants as consumers.

Altogether there is nothing necessarily wrong with making the balance between the citizens' interests as workers and their interests as consumers a subject of strategic policy. Never forget that they are mostly the same people.

NATURAL RESOURCES

Repetitions, repetitions. Chapter 17 surveyed the options governments have for conserving their countries' natural resources. Chapter 43 reported H.G.Coombs' proposals about the ownership and use of exhaustible resources. Here we notice some implications for national economic structure. We can start with a parable. It over-simplifies its facts. It is here just to make the point that natural resources offer structural choices.

> Japan conserves most of its plentiful natural forest. Australia allows private logging of public forest, partly to export woodchips to Japan. Some Swedish forest is logged, to supply mills which make paper of very high quality for export and import-replacement.

Structural effects:

Japan conserves most of its forest. Its papermakers used to import most of the material they used. They exported enough paper – mostly newsprint – to earn the exchange which paid for their woodchip imports. They have since developed technology with which (1) recycled material is nearly half of the material they use, and (2) they make art and book paper of high quality for export. Japan now consumes more paper than it used to do. But its papermakers import a lower proportion of their materials, and export a higher proportion of their output. So they are net earners rather than spenders of foreign exchange, and Japan's forests are still well conserved.

Sweden employs timber workers. It also has a highly capitalized, highly skilled, high quality papermaking industry which earns an exchange surplus.

Australia employs timber workers. It has a few low-quality papermakers, but spends more exchange to import paper than it earns by exporting woodchips. Compared with Japan and Sweden it appears to be disposing of its forests without gaining much of the profit, exchange surplus, employment, high skill, forest conservation or national pride that they could be made to yield.

The choices are not actually as stark as that. Sweden and Australia each conserve some forest. Australia also grows commercial forest, and has barred some paper-making because it pollutes. But the parable serves its purpose: power over natural resources can be used to determine what conservation, pollution, investment, employment, skills, import replacement or export income the use of the resources may yield.

Conservation Recall Chapter 17 of this text, and Chapter 14 of Michael Jacobs' *The Green Economy* (1991). Most environmental reform involves some economic reconstruction. Here we are concerned with effects on economic structure.

Environmental reform is likely to limit and regulate the use of some exhaustible resources, including oil. It may need to regulate the use and replacement of some renewable resources, including forests and fish. It may reform and regulate some degrading or pollutant industries, including the agricultural use of chemical fertilizers, insecticides and herbicides, and farm practices which erode or degrade the soil. And reformers want to clean up or reduce the coal-fired, oil-fired and atomic production of energy, and energy-wasteful and pollutant methods of manufacturing and transport.

At the same time, reform is likely to expand other industries and services, including –

- solar, wind, tidal and geothermal energy
- soil conservation
- afforestation
- building insulation
- public passenger transport
- many kinds of waste management, disposal and recycling
- producers of capital goods for industries which have to replace wasteful or pollutant plant and equipment
- industries which may not increase output but will increase employment as they replace pollutant or high-energy methods of production with more labor-intensive methods
- environmental research, education, advocacy, consultation, monitoring, accounting, etc.

Environmental reform can put people out of work, outmode their skills, force them to move to new regions. But over time, it nearly always brings some net increase of employment, for the reasons just listed. Whether there will be less or more work in the very long run is harder to predict, especially because scientific and technological advances are hard to predict. But it seems likely that for some decades at least, if environmental reform continues at its present rate or faster, the effects on economic structure in the rich countries will include these:

The structure of industries and institutions should be capable of better environmental care and performance than now.

It should be a little easier to achieve full employment.

Most environmental reform raises costs of production and reduces output. There may be less national output and income than now.

The loss of income will mostly result from public environmental requirements. The method of reform tends to determine how the losses will be distributed. There may be significant changes in the distribution of income – changes for better or worse, depending on who wins and who loses the political battles.

Most environmental reform increases the public regulation of market activity. Some reforms replace private ownership with public, or replace market distribution with other methods of distribution. So if there is substantial environmental reform it is likely to bring some permanent expansion of the public role in the mixed economy.

THE BALANCE OF PAYMENTS

Your national economy acquires foreign currency –

- in exchange for exports, i.e. for goods and services sold to foreigners
- as profit, rent or interest earned by your investments in foreign countries
- by family income transfers, international aid or other gifts from foreigners.

Your national economy parts with foreign currency –

- to pay for imports, i.e. for goods and services you buy from foreigners
- to pay rent, interest or dividends to foreign investors in your country
- to transfer income or give aid to foreign countries.

Together those payments constitute what is known as your country's 'current account' with the rest of the world. Currency exchange for purposes of capital investment or buying and selling capital assets is usually recorded separately in a capital account. Together the current and capital accounts show whether your country is balancing its foreign receipts and payments, or accumulating a surplus or deficit.

The overall balance of payments may be comfortable and pose no policy problems. But policy questions arise if a surplus or deficit accumulates. It can be left to market forces, which may or may not correct it. It can be corrected by government action to influence the exchange rate, or to stimulate or subsidize export industries or import-replacement industries. Government may restrict imports. It may act to attract or to restrict foreign investment and ownership. It may ration the available foreign exchange to the most necessary uses.

But those different ways of influencing the balance of payments can have very different effects on consumer prices, on inflation, on employment and on industrial structure and development. So the strategic aims of trade and exchange policies tend to be more concerned with those other effects than with trade and exchange for their own sakes. And they also tend to be strongly disagreed. That is often for technical as well as social reasons. Experts disagree about what effects the alternative approaches will actually cause, as well as disagreeing about the desirability (or not) of some of the effects. You will meet the debate in later chapters.

THE BALANCE OF INCOME AND RISK

Some countries have more to fear than others do from their economic relations with the rest of the world.

Some developed countries produce most of what they use and consume. They trade comparatively little. Changes in world markets may help or hurt particular industries, but can't do much harm to the national economy as a whole. Until quite recently, for example, the US and Japan have generally traded less than ten per cent of their output, with Japan a little more vulnerable than the US because its imports include more of the fuel and raw materials on which its manufacturing depends.

Compare small, specialized economies which depend on selling high proportions of their output into hotly competitive foreign markets. Sweden exports nearly a third of its output. Belgium exports more than half. New Zealand, by contrast, has *imported* most of its manufactured goods through most of its modern history. It paid for them by exporting farm and dairy products, chiefly to a protected British market. The New Zealand economy suffered severely when Europe began to export subsidized farm surpluses, and New Zealand lost its privileged market when Britain first revolutionalized its agricultural productivity and capacity to feed itself, then joined the European Community.

Some forecasters fear new risks. Europe and the US, which export manufactured goods, are exporting increasing quantities of food as well. East Asian countries are industrializing rapidly and exporting manufactured goods. Will the world markets for food and manufactures become increasingly competitive, with new dangers for weak competitors? Might there be some advantage, even for smaller countries with fewer advantages of scale, in aiming for Japanese or American levels of self-sufficiency?

Questions of free trade and protection are for later. Here, notice that strategic aims may include a concern for the likely stability of a country's sources of employment and income. A degree of self-reliance may be worth having even if it loses some advantages of specialization and scale, and some margin of income that a more specialized, free-trading country might hope for.

Alternatively, some countries may seek safety by *surrendering* some independence, for example by joining the European Union or the North American Free Trade Area, to avoid the disadvantages of being excluded from those blocs.

Sometimes the question is not whether to trade some margin of income for some reduction of risk. It is *which* risks to prefer, in a quick-changing world in which all the strategic options have risks.

SELF GOVERNMENT

Three financial developments are affecting the scope and independence of national government, especially in small countries with vulnerable 'small' currencies.

- There is now a world-wide computerized capital market. Currencies are bought and sold and funds moved from country to country at the touch of keyboards, or as directed by automated buy-and-sell programs.

- Most Western governments have substantially deregulated foreign exchange transactions and their internal financial systems.

- The new financial freedom is defended by some powerful groups who benefit from it. It is also supported by a widely-held theoretical belief that most people will benefit more from the economic effects of free trade in money than they once did when there was extensive regulation of the trade in money.

Together those conditions allow bankers and other financial dealers to punish countries whose policies offend them. Dealers, including a country's own bankers, can quickly withdraw significant amounts of a country's liquid funds. That can depreciate its currency, depress investment and employment, force changes in interest rates, and add to inflationary pressure. And most of the financial press will blame the government and its policies for the damage, rather than blame the dangerous financial freedom or the dealers' destructive uses of it.

Increasingly, small and medium-sized democracies are threatened in that way if they try too hard to conserve their natural resources, maintain full employment, return to more progressive taxation, or reduce inequalities by other means. Many people regret the loss of national independence. But some powerful groups work to contrive it, and profit by it. Some business groups

have a general desire to reduce government's economic influence. Some local rich, keen to weaken labor unions, to restrain wages, and to cut taxation or shift it from richer to poorer taxpayers, welcome the international enforcement of regressive policies which they could not achieve by their own local influence alone.

So an increasingly important aim of economic strategy is to operate on democracy's strategic capacity: on the means of choosing and implementing deliberate economic strategies. Some contenders aim to defend and strengthen government's capacity. Others aim to weaken it.

SUMMARY

A nation's economic structure (of physical and human capital and existing industries and services) determines what quantities of what goods and services it can produce, whether and how it can balance its foreign trade and payments, and the balance of risk and security that arises from its international economic relations. The structure may also affect the ease or difficulty of achieving full employment, equitable pay and good working conditions; good conditions for bringing up children; satisfactory environmental care; and collective influence on the directions of economic development.

Government can influence national economic structure in many ways. Sector by sector –

Households The inherited stock of housing does most to determine how people can be housed, including how equally or unequally, how productively, and with what range of choice. Government influences the development and adaptation of the housing stock by its

- town and country planning policies

- building regulation

- public housing provisions

- financial policies, especially as they affect the amount, price and accessibility of credit for building and buying housing.

The public sector Most of the additional jobs to match the growth of population through the third quarter of the twentieth century were created by public enterprises and services plus the public sector's growing demand for inputs of private goods and services. A combination of technical progress and political reaction has since arrested the growth of public employment, so that in many of the advanced economies its growth no longer offsets the technological and structural unemployment which arise from other causes. To restore fuller employment, governments might –

- restore and expand labor-intensive public health, educational, cultural, welfare, police and legal services

- restore former levels of investment in public infrastructure for business, household and recreational use

- locate public employment, where practicable, in under-employed regions

- encourage, by various means, some rationing or better sharing of paid work

- design environmental policies to include labor-intensive programs of forest and soil conservation and material recycling.

The private sector Government affects the structure of private industries and employment in too many ways to list here. Besides the standard legal, educational, research and other public services to the private sector, government exerts strong influence on the sector's structure when it –

- decides what natural resources (minerals, forests, fish, wildlife) private producers can use, and on what terms

- designs and manages the national financial system

- offers special assistance, credit, tax-breaks, cut-price public services or other aids to attract foreign investors

- decides which public services, if any, are to be supplied by licensed or franchised private enterprises.

For historical, international or other reasons some countries have economic structures which cannot balance their foreign trade and payments, or which are at risk because they depend on changing or unstable world markets. Governments may be able to improve such structures by various means, some of which may also provide higher employment, reduce wage inequalities, and widen the range of skills and occupations which are open to the citizens. Policies include –

- protection of tradeable industries from import competition, by tariff, subsidy, quota or exchange control

- public import-replacement by goods which the private sector can't or won't supply: hydroelectric power to replace coal or oil imports; national shipping and airlines; etc.

- public purchases of private products from national rather than foreign producers wherever possible

- tax-breaks, easy credit or cut-price public services to private producers of exports or import replacements.

This chapter has listed some main purposes for which, and means by which, national communities can exercise collective influence over their economic structures. A number of the following chapters, beginning with the next one, consider whether, when, by which means and for what structural purposes it may be wise to exert such influence.

49

How free should trade be?

'How free should trade be?' belongs with the broader question 'What, if anything, should government do about national economic structure?'

I don't believe there should be a general answer to either question, if that means an answer which is right for all countries at all times and for all purposes. Each nation should decide what structural developments to encourage, by what means, in the light of its particular situation and resources, its existing economic structure and opportunities, and its collective purposes. This book's main discussion of the subject therefore comes later, in chapters on alternative national strategies.

However there is a widespread belief among economists that free trade is nearly always best, and that it is nearly always best to leave the structure of the private sector to be shaped by market forces. It may be best to deal with that general proposition now, while the ends and means of public influence on economic structure are fresh in mind. So first, the purposes of trade policies. Second, their ways and means.

POLICIES

Tradeable and non-tradeable goods Tradeables are whatever can be traded across national borders. Between nations, a sale of goods usually also requires an exchange of currency. The economists' definition is more financial than territorial: tradeables are goods and services that can be sold for foreign currency, non-tradeables are goods and services which normally can't. The definitions are rough, and getting rougher as transport and communications improve. A Londoner can already fly to Paris for a hair-do, get legal advice from New York by phone or fax or Email, and import cut flowers from Israel by air freight. But for practical purposes of structural analysis and policy-making it is still convenient to call personal and professional services and cut flowers non-tradeable goods.

The main *non-tradeables* include law and order, most education and health services, other personal and professional services, national and local information services, buildings, roads and bridges, local transport, water supply and sewerage, other infrastructure, and almost all retailing including the retailing of imported tradeables.

Tradeables include minerals, most farm products, most manufactured goods, books and magazines and broadcast programs and other information services of more than local interest, and tourism. Tourism is there for financial reasons. You import the tourists rather than exporting the services to them. But tourist services earn foreign exchange, so they are commonly classed as tradeables, and as exports when foreigners come and enjoy them.

There is a lot of internal trade between the tradeable and non-tradeable sectors, so they affect each others' performance in various ways. Tariffs on imported tradeables raise the costs and prices of non-tradeable industries which use imported inputs. Taxes on local non-tradeables which the tradeable industries buy as inputs can raise the tradeable industries' prices and reduce their export sales and their capacity to compete with imports in their home markets. So to balance a nation's foreign trade and payments can require some efficient non-tradeable as well as tradeable industries.

THE GAINS FROM TRADE

The gains from trade are mostly obvious. Here is one way to classify their sources:

Natural resources Tea, coffee, barley, rye, wheat, grapes, sugar and potatos grow best in different regions of the world. But anywhere in the world, trade will bring you drinks of tea, coffee, beer, whisky, rum, wine and vodka. They all come from regions which could not drink all they produce – but they trade a surplus for all the things *their* weather and soil *won't* produce, or can't produce economically. So also with coal, oil, iron, copper, lead, bauxite and other minerals. They are found in comparatively few places, but trade makes them available anywhere in the world.

Division of labor The more advanced and productive an economy becomes, the higher its skills tend to be, and the more those skills tend to depend on specialization. Once it progresses beyond subsistence farming every household specializes and trades. So – in varying degree

– does every town, region, nation. Big nations have more scope for internal specialization and trade, and may need less foreign trade than smaller nations do. But within limits imposed by their size and situation, nations can and do vary their degrees of specialization or self-sufficiency by deliberate structural policies.

Scale Some industries have such increasing economies of scale that world production is monopolized by a very few firms, which usually (though not invariably) means by a very few nations. Free trade would probably have seen all the world's passenger airliners produced now by Boeing in Seattle – the two surviving competitors in France and Russia each had substantial government aid or protection. (So did Boeing, at some stages of its development.) The bigger the optimum scale of particular industries, the fewer the countries in which they are likely to operate. Users elsewhere must import them and (short of monopoly) the freer the trade, the lower their prices are likely to be.

Diversity Even if there was no difference between the general range, quality and process of each nation's products, there would probably still be a good deal of trade. The French buy some German cars, the Germans buy some French cars, both buy some American cars and export some cars to America. Partly, economies of scale force each firm to produce a limited number of models – too few to satisfy the needs and tastes of all car buyers. So some of each country's demand is met by other countries' models. Partly, people just like interesting diversity, and material aids to individuality. Regardless of their efficiency it's sweet to put on a hand-printed T-shirt and drive around in a reproduction Morgan Sports or the only pink French Virage in town.

Think how life in developed countries is enriched by the trade that allows you to enjoy whatever you like best of the wide world's music, arts and crafts, books and films, textile designs and clothing styles, food and drink, and holiday travel to surf, snow or wilderness.

Growth Trade helps growth because it allows specialization and the division of labor to cross national boundaries. It is also the great transmitter of new technology. A few countries invent steam engines, electric light and power, jet flight, anti-biotics, computers – and soon all but the poorest countries buy and use them. In those poorest countries, think how life can be improved by comparatively cheap and simple imports: cotton clothing, steel ploughshares, farmers' and carpenters' hand tools, radio, paper, printing, medicines.

Harm from trade

Some of the harm is obvious. Dangerous goods, and services which offend human rights, should not be traded. Some dumping and other predatory exporting is unfair. Some trade worsens unfruitful inequalities of wealth and power – as when rich minorities in poor countries use scarce export earnings to import luxuries and oppressive weaponry instead of necessities of life or investment goods for growth.

Beyond that the list grows more controversial. Most trade improves the exporting country's income, but if it squanders its natural resources it may be improvident. Most trade improves the importing country's material standards, but in some circumstances it can increase its unemployment, exchange difficulties, foreign debt, internal inequalities. In those circumstances some public regulation of trade may improve national income, balance of payments, employment, growth, environmental care, culture and quality of life.

Remember that most trade is between firms or between branches of transnational firms. When economists say that trade 'between nations' benefits both nations, they usually mean that it increases their national incomes. It usually does, and that is usually a good thing. But (i) the gain may not be worth having if it is badly distributed within the trading countries; (ii) in *some* conditions, some kinds of trade can reduce, not increase, national income; and (iii) trade in harmful goods can do more harm than good.

But those effects are comparatively uncommon. Most trade benefits the buyers and sellers without harming anyone else. If Scotland makes better or cheaper whisky and France makes better or cheaper wine, it makes sense for them to trade. So says the theory of *competitive* advantage, which everyone can understand. But economists' theory of *comparative* advantage says that it may still be useful to trade where there is no such complementary distribution of skills: even if one country can produce *every* product more efficiently than another country can, it may still pay both of them to trade with each other. As follows.

THEORIES OF COMPARATIVE AND COMPETITIVE ADVANTAGE

The theory of comparative advantage was launched by David Ricardo in 1817 with a simple model of trade between two countries in two commodities, both of which can be produced more efficiently in one of the countries than in the other. In Joan Robinson's deft summary –

In Ricardo's example, a unit of cloth in England requires the labour of 100 men for a year; a unit of wine, 120 men. In Portugal, the same quantity of cloth is produced by 90 men, and of wine by 80. Prices in each country are proportional to labour cost. Cloth in England can be exchanged for wine at the ratio of one to five-sixths, and in Portugal at the ratio of one to one and an eighth.. It is, therefore, advantageous to England to send cloth to buy wine in Portugal and advantageous to Portugal to send wine to buy cloth in England. England then gets its wine at a lower cost by exporting cloth than it could get it by producing at home, and Portugal gets its cloth at a lower cost by exporting wine.

If the countries specialize in that way, a little more wine and cloth can be produced. But it does not necessarily follow that it will advantage them both to trade, or that the Portuguese can gain more from their one comparative advantage than from their two competitive advantages. Why will London wine importers (or cloth barterers) pay 50 per cent more than the Portuguese price for Portuguese wine? If they want it they can buy it in Porto at 80 and import it themselves. At 80, wine will buy less cloth in England than it will buy in Portugal. So Portugal will lose by trade with England. (Work it out if you need convincing. 170 Portuguese workers can produce 1 unit of wine and 1 of cloth. Trading with England at the prices the English will pay, they will get one unit of wine and nine tenths of a unit of cloth, or one unit of cloth and seven eighths of a unit of wine.)

Some trade arises from that sort of comparative advantage, but not usually for Ricardo's reasons. Most trade arises from *competitive* rather than comparative advantage: I trade what I can make cheaper or better than you can, for what you can make cheaper or better than I can. But in one form or other, modern economists have elaborated the theory of *comparative* advantage to show that if its principles are valid, they hold not just for two countries producing two commodities, but for a world in which any number of nations produce any number of commodities. And the force that will develop the industries of greatest comparative advantage in each national economy is expected to be the hidden hand: the self-interest of each investor, producer, trader and consumer. All government need do is leave them free to invest, produce, trade and consume as their interests prompt them, and refuse to protect any of them who are short-sighted enough to want protection.

That is very important policy advice. Most of the world's tariffs and other trade aids and restrictions are designed to develop particular industries, often by pro-

tecting weaker competitors from stronger ones. If the theory of comparative advantage is right, the legislators who create those controls are mostly wrong. So are the majorities who elect them. So are the farmers, manufacturers, workers and others whom they protect: they would be richer without protection, producing the same or other goods in a free-trading world. But if any of those parties are sometimes right, an embarrassing number of economists must be wrong.

So take some care with the following arguments.

LIMITATIONS OF THE THEORIES

Most theories of comparative or competitive advantage which have implied that free trade is best for all concerned in almost all circumstances have had six necessary assumptions, not all of which they have made explicit. They have assumed that –

- there is full employment
- each country's balance of payments with the rest of the world is self-adjusting, and the market adjustments cost the country less than deliberate adjustment by regulating trade or exchange would cost
- land, labor and capital are adaptable enough to switch from one industry to another; or alternatively the costs of such changes are less than the gains to be expected from them
- comparative advantages arise from a country's natural endowments, they cannot be deliberately created
- no industry or cluster of industries has continuously increasing returns to scale
- maximizing national income, as conventionally measured and regardless of its distribution, should prevail over any other purposes of economic policy.

Thus the theory *assumes* the presence of the main conditions – especially the most productive uses of available resources, full employment, and balanced international payments – which protective trade policies aim to *contrive*.

In practice each of those conditions is sometimes present, sometimes not. When present they have sometimes been produced by unaided market forces, sometimes not. Without any one of them, free trade may not have the good effects which theorists expect of it. We will focus on three of them: (i) natural advantages, (ii) full employment, and (iii) the balance of payments between national currencies. What may free trade do to countries without natural advantages, or with persistent unemployment, or with higher foreign spending than foreign earnings? In that order –

Natural and acquired advantages

Japan's economic success owes very little to natural advantages. She has poor coal, no oil or natural gas or uranium; no iron, copper, bauxite, gold or silver; comparatively little pasture or ploughland. Instead she had human, cultural and institutional resources which enabled her people to develop effective entrepreneurs, well-equipped industries, a skilful workforce, and exceptionally fast growth through some phases of her modernization. Those efforts were initiated, aided and protected by government, to produce a national economy with far-from-natural competitive advantages.

Advantages of that kind arise from accumulated physical capital, human capital and market experience, and in some industries from increasing economies of scale. With increasing economies of scale it can happen that whichever producer or national group of producers is biggest is likely to stay ahead, secure against new competitors.

In the short run in those cases it pays other countries to accept the leading producer's exports of the goods concerned because they are the only or the best available. But if a rival can protect a big enough market for long enough, or be subsidized to sell at a loss for long enough, it may catch up with the leader's skills and scale, perhaps with some further advantage from possessing newer vintages of equipment. The newcomer's country may then become richer for having protected local production than it would have been as a free trader. That may be doubly true if the protected development limits an import bill which would otherwise have swelled to unbalance the nation's total foreign trade and payments.

When the new industry has the necessary advantages of skill and scale, its protection should often cease. But not always. Suppose the industry is a much-prized, high-value-added industry in which a number of countries are competing to overtake the leaders, and in which frequent technical advances occur to alter some of the competitive conditions. That increases everyone's risks in an industry with long investment lead-times. But several contenders keep trying, so that the world as a whole develops some over-capacity. Free trade may then see most producers producing below their capacity, with losses which outweigh their potential advantages of scale. The best thing to do in those circumstances, if you can manage it, may be to supply a sufficiently large home market from a fully employed industry with

reasonable economies of scale. Protecting the market for that purpose may make the country richer than free trade in this industry would do.

May, not must. Other conditions apply. Are this industry's advantages of scale achieved by a cluster of firms sharing some common facilities but in price competition with each other – or is it a one-firm monopoly? If a monopoly, will it exploit its strength to maximize monopoly profit? The effects of that may be worse than the effects of free trade and some over-capacity. They may be worse still if the monopolist is foreign-owned and exports its profits. Free trade looks best.

But hang on – free trade might well have allowed the original leader of the industry to establish and exploit not just a national but a world monopoly. Nobody is in a position to discipline a world monopoly. But a national monopoly *which depends on protection* may be disciplined. A determined government can say 'Prices down, or protection down', and enforce it. Or if the monopolist strength is being used against the industry's workers rather than against its customers, government can say 'Wages and safety up to standard, or protection down', as Australia once did.

Conclusion   In some circumstances well-designed protection can develop more productive industries than free trade would allow to develop. In other circumstances it can't. Theory alone cannot tell you when it can or cannot. It depends on the facts of the case, including the nature of the industry and the quality of the government.

Employment

How may trade controls affect levels of employment and unemployment?

Unemployment increased through the 1980s and into the 1990s in many Western countries. Economists disagree about its causes, but in most of the countries it was accompanied by a considerable freeing of foreign trade and currency exchange, so it is hard to blame the rise in unemployment on trade restrictions. Our earlier chapters on the future of work suggested that the determinants of employment may be changing in historical ways, and may call for new trade and employment policies. We will return to that problem in chapters on employment and national strategy. Here, stay with Ricardo's model but consider the effects of its policy advice in a world in which 10 per cent or more of unemployment is common.

Suppose that England and Portugal have similar population numbers. Each uses 5 per cent of its land and labor to make its own wine and 5 per cent to make its own cloth. The Portuguese make both products more cheaply than the English do. And each country has 10 per cent of its land and labor unemployed. Then changes in transport technology open the possibility of trade between them. Portuguese winemakers employ some of Portugal's unemployed land and labor to double their output. They sell the surplus to England, which puts the English winemakers out of business altogether. The English government could defend the industry with a tariff but its members believe in free trade and like the low-priced Portuguese wine, so do not.

What does the trade do to the two countries' economic structure and incomes?

When their vines are in full production the Portuguese supply England's wine. The low Portuguese price induces the English to buy a little more wine, but mostly it frees some spending for other goods. Producing those goods increases English employment and income by 1 percentage point, with some multiplier effect so that it adds 1.5 per cent altogether to national income and employment. Meanwhile wiping out the English wine industry has reduced national employment by 5 percentage points. It is no good those unemployed making cloth instead: the English market is already supplied, and the Portuguese buy Portuguese cloth because it is cheaper. In England national spending and demand decline accordingly, and with their multiplier effects reduce national income and employment by 6.5 percentage points. The net effect of the positive and negative changes is thus to reduce English national income by 5 per cent, increase unemployment from 10 to 15 per cent, and increase inequalities between those unemployed and the rest, including the well-off wine drinkers.

In Portugal, doubling the wine industry employs half the unemployed. Their spending and its multiplier effects increase national demand and reduce unemployment by a further 2 percentage points. Portugal thus increases its income and reduces its unemployment by 7 per cent, chiefly by exporting unemployment to England.

The English government could have maintained England's former income and employment by prohibiting or taxing the import of wine. That would not have raised the existing English wine price. It might not have provoked a retaliatory tariff (as it might now) since England was not exporting anything to Portugal in this artificial model.

This has been an altogether artificial story, just as Ricardo's two-nation, two-commodity theory was. But it shows what is wrong with applying the theory of comparative advantage to trade between countries with

persistent unemployment.

Ricardo meant his model to represent a country's trade with all foreigners, not just one foreign country. Next question: if England loses its wine industry and imports wine instead, but fails to increase its cloth exports, where does it get the additional foreign money to pay for the additional imports?

The balance of payments

Return to modern times, and consider the payment difficulties of countries with unbalanced trade and foreign debts.

Countries can find themselves owing more foreign money than they earn for any number of reasons. There may be changes in the world economy. The terms of trade between raw materials and manufactured goods may change, and put exporters of one or the other into deficit. When artificial fibres become popular, wool and cotton producers may lose export earnings, and spend more on imports as their children switch to imported fibre clothing. Importing fibre-optic cable may increase the import bill while export earnings decline as the world uses less copper. Uranium and natural gas (which some countries have) replace coal (which other countries have) as main sources of electric power, so balances of trade and payment shift. They shift further as newly-industrialized countries bite into older producers' home and foreign markets, and as transnational corporations shift their production of tradeable goods from country to country.

Governments of deficit-trading and indebted countries currently hope to balance their trade and payments by one or more of six means:

- free trade
- devaluation or market depreciation of their currencies
- financial deregulation
- asset sales
- deliberate unemployment
- import or exchange controls

With rare or merely temporary exceptions the first five don't work. The sixth – the protection or improvement of the structure of the national economy by trade or exchange controls – is the most economical and effective method. But there are now powerful intellectual and business pressures, and World Trade Organization pressures, to ban it.

Because you will hear about them from all too few of your fellow-economists, it is important that you understand why the first five rarely work and the sixth has often worked. Notes on the six:

Free trade has not recently rescued a deficit-trading country from unbalanced trade or accumulating debt. There is no reason why it should. Even if the theory of comparative advantage were valid, there is no reason to expect that all countries will develop such complementary patterns of comparative advantage that unaided market forces will balance their trade. Trade and exchange are freer now than they have been for a century, and the main deficit traders of twenty years ago are deficit trading still, and deeper in debt than they were.

Devaluation or depreciation of deficit traders' currencies (devaluation by government, or depreciation by market forces of supply and demand) was once expected to expand demand for those countries' exports and depress demand for their imports until their trade and payments balanced and their exchange rates consequently stabilized.

When you import goods, the foreign producers usually want to be paid in their own currency (because that is what they have to use to pay most of their production costs). So to buy foreign goods you must usually acquire foreign money. You buy it from a bank, which has acquired it by selling your currency to foreigners who want to buy your exports. If your population wants more foreign money than foreigners want of your money, the market price of your money is likely to decline, for ordinary supply-and-demand reasons. Each of your pounds (or whatever) buys fewer dollars, francs or escudos than it did. So your money buys less foreign goods. The foreign producers get the same prices as they formerly did, but you pay a higher price than you formerly did, because your money has depreciated. On those facts was built one of the most widely accepted but disastrously mistaken theories of modern times. It predicted this:

As your currency depreciates, the prices of all your imports rise, so your people will buy less of them. The prices which foreigners pay for your exports fall, so foreigners will buy more of them. With a declining import bill and rising export earnings, your exchange deficit decreases. It is the deficit which causes the market depreciation of your currency, so market forces can be expected to depreciate your currency to the level at which your export earnings balance your import spending, and your country is in exchange equilibrium with the world. Reciprocally, surplus countries' currencies will rise in value, so that their citizens buy more imports and foreigners buy less of their exports, until they also are in

exchange equilibrium with the rest of the world.

Instead of that, what actually happened was this:

Market rates of exchange have prevailed since 1972. The currencies of countries with exchange surpluses have risen in value – but instead of decreasing, their surpluses have *increased.* The currencies of countries with exchange deficits have lost value – but instead of decreasing, their deficits have *increased.* (The only partial exception was the US through the 1980s. The US dollar appreciated about 30 per cent up to 1985, then depreciated about 30 per cent through the following years – but the US exchange deficit continued to grow through both phases.) Through the first free-market decades the chief surplus countries – Japan, Germany, Switzerland, the Netherlands, Belgium, Taiwan and South Korea – had appreciating currencies and increasing surpluses, and the chief deficit countries besides the US – the UK, Canada, France and Italy – had depreciating currencies and increasing deficits. (For the figures, and theoretical debates about them, see J. S. L. McCombie and A. P. Thirlwall, *Economic growth and the balance of payments constraints*, 1994.) Then in 1997-8 the free trade in money and credit allowed drastic market depreciation of the South Korean, Malaysian, and Indonesian currencies for speculative reasons which had little to do with their trade in goods.

Why did life so often contradict such a plausible theory? A list of causes follows. The first two – economic structure, and elasticities – were probably the most important in most of the countries concerned.

Economic structure A deficit country is usually in deficit because it has a defective economic structure: its economy generates demand for more tradeable goods than its structure of industries can supply either by its own output or by producing enough saleable exports to pay for the demanded imports.

The country's stock of capital, skill and economic institutions has developed slowly over time. It may have *some* idle capacity in some industries. But suppose that a fall in the exchange rate does increase the foreign demand for a wide variety of exports. It is unlikely that there will happen to be idle capacity in many of those industries. Nor may there be idle capacity to replace many of the imports whose prices are raised by the falling exchange rate. To take advantage of those new opportunities the country needs to change some of its economic structure. Depending on the particular market opportunities it must expand existing industries or start new ones. Other deficit countries may be trying to do the same, so there may be competition to beat.

The new developments may need some public as well as private investment. Some of them may need public protection to get established. Some of them may have long investment lead times. The investors may face unusual risks if the market opportunity is created by an unnatural exchange rate arising from an exchange deficit. What if new developments succeed in eliminating the deficit, and the exchange rate returns nearer to parity of purchasing power?

Conclusion: a persistent exchange deficit is certainly a good reason for acting to correct the country's structure of industries. But the necessary reconstruction may well not come as an unaided private investors' response to a depreciating currency. Public action may also be needed.

Another way to describe this structural trouble is to say that the price elasticity of supply may not be enough, in enough of the industries concerned, to respond to a currency depreciation by eliminating the trade deficit which causes the depreciation. Thus this item can reappear briefly in the next, under a different name.

Elasticities One condition for national surpluses and deficits to adjust as the theory predicts is that there should happen to be helpful relations between –

- the price elasticity of supply of your country's tradeable products
- the price elasticity of foreign demand for your country's exports
- the price elasticity of your country's demand for imports
- the income elasticity of your country's demand for imports

Each of those depends on different conditions. No market mechanism adjusts them to each other. If they are helpfully rather than unhelpfully related, that's luck, not the hidden hand.

We just dealt with the elasticity of *supply*, which may not be positive enough to correct any national deficits as the theory requires.

The export and import *demands* may have any of a number of patterns of elasticity.

Suppose, first, that they are both price-inelastic. (Foreign steelmakers want only so much of your coal and ores; foreign manufacturers want only so many of the components they buy from you; cheaper fuel, or cheaper components, won't enable them to sell many more of their finished goods. So depreciating your cur-

rency may not much increase their demand for your exports.)

Similarly, your country's importers of fuel, manufacturing components, heavy machinery, or tropical products, may have fairly inelastic demand for those necessary items, and may continue to buy what they need despite rising prices. And despite rising prices some of your rich citizens may buy much the same quantities of Scotch whisky, French perfume and Italian jewellery and cause their firms to provide them with much the same German cars. Suppose, for example, that all the elasticities average 0.5:

- If exchange depreciation cuts the price foreigners must pay for your exports by 20 per cent, but that only induces them to buy 10 per cent more goods, your earnings of foreign currency don't rise, they fall 10 per cent.

- If depreciation raises import prices 20 per cent in your own currency, but reduces the quantity imported by only 10 per cent, that cuts your spending of foreign currency by 10 per cent.

Together the two effects of the depreciation have had little or no effect on your exchange deficit.

If both demands are price-elastic, they may together reduce the deficit. Different elasticities for imports and exports have different effects again. And if the demand for exports is price-inelastic but the demand for imports is strongly income-elastic, you may be driven to fear full employment and growth, and act to limit them, because they increase your exchange deficit disproportionately. That has slowed some rich countries' growth. It may trouble poor countries which trade raw material exports for manufactured imports. Wherever the industrial countries' demand for the relevant raw materials is less income-elastic than the poor countries' demand for manufactured goods, free trade is likely to increase the inequality between them. For a generation now, deficit-trading countries have had more unlucky than lucky patterns of price and income elasticity.

Risk Unstable rates of exchange can make investment in tradeable industries riskier, especially in industries with long investment lead-times and with foreign competitors in their home and export markets. How confidently can you plant vines if you can't guess what the exchange rate may be when the wine begins to flow seven years ahead, or through the ten further years it will then take to repay your investment? Or duplicate an engine plant and car assembly line which will take seven years to pay-back?

Export-import price links Exporters import some of their inputs. (Wheat exporters use imported tractors, fuel, fertilisers. Export docks import their cranes. Publishers export books printed on imported paper by imported machines.) In a country with a depreciating currency, rising import prices increase some export costs and prices and thus limit the benefit that export industries derive from the depreciating exchange rate.

Inflation Rising import prices contribute to inflation directly, then indirectly if they prompt higher wage demands.

Allocation of resources When foreign currency is scarce its price is driven up by competing demands for it. Some of the bidders want to import necessary consumer goods, some want to import luxuries. Some want cheaper and some want more expensive items of household equipment. Some want items of public or private capital, some of which are more productive or desirable than others. (Anaesthetic machines or gambling machines? Buses and ambulances or private limousines? Equipment which home country producers could supply, or equipment which they could not? And some bidders want exchange for expensive foreign holidays, or nest-eggs in Swiss banks.) Some of the desired imports would benefit richer people, some would benefit poorer people, some would benefit nearly everyone. Some would contribute to economic growth, others would not. As a method of allocation – of deciding which bidders get the exchange they want and which go without – rationing by price does not ensure that scarce exchange goes to the most productive uses, or to the most equitable uses, or to the uses that will do most to correct an exchange deficit.

A concealed subsidy The line between 'market solutions' and 'protective subsidies' is blurred when a currency depreciation increases a country's exports by establishing an unnatural exchange rate, i.e. one which does not equate the currencies' purchasing power over goods and services. Exports which thrive on an unnatural rate of exchange are subsidized by the exporters' fellow citizens, through the higher import prices they pay, as surely as if the exports were subsidized from tax revenue by the government. But WTO and other authorities bless this 'market solution' to a trade imbalance while condemning other export subsidies or import tariffs.

Financial deregulation is among the business – the complicated business – of the next two chapters. Until you have worked through them, take this note on trust. The deregulation of the 1970s and 1980s has allowed deficit countries to finance their exchange and trade deficits by borrowing foreign funds much more freely than they could do before.

A lot of footloose capital now moves about the world, often for unproductive purposes: to avoid taxation, to find the highest interest rates, to gamble on changing rates of exchange and rates of inflation. If banks in deficit countries within the OECD pay high enough interest, they can borrow any amount of it.

Why do the lenders lend so freely?

First, because they are allowed to. Private international lending and borrowing of capital funds was restricted to a few approved purposes by most OECD governments until it was freed, step by step, through the last quarter of the century.

Second, lending to Western banks has no 'capital' risk – no risk that you won't get your money back. The banks have informal but reliable government guarantees. (The American and Japanese governments have bailed out some of the world's biggest banks, and many small ones.)

Those and other effects of the financial deregulation compel deficit countries to keep their rates of interest comparatively high. Paying high interest on increasing amounts of debt can continue to increase the debt even if the trade in goods comes into balance. In both the creditor and the debtor countries, the high interest rates tend to depress the quantity and quality of new investment and economic growth, and help to maintain unemployment.

Conclusion: Deregulating the international exchanges of money and credit has not brought a market correction of unbalanced international trade and payments. Its net effect has probably been to worsen the imbalances.

Asset sales Some countries finance some of their exchange deficit by spending capital. They sell existing assets to foreign buyers: private assets like land, office buildings, shopping centres, hotels, tourist resorts, newspapers, broadcasters, firms in many industries; public assets like gas, power and water utilities, public transport systems, hospitals.

The sales bring in foreign capital funds. Until they are all spent they may be used to buy imports, to reduce foreign borrowing or to repay foreign debt. But most foreign buyers buy assets which can earn them more than the rate of interest, and most of them want to return their profits to their own countries. So in the long run the sales increase the debtor countries' need for foreign currency, and leave their balance of payments worse than before.

(Notice that there may be better effects of foreign ownership if instead of taking over existing sources of profit the foreigners make new investments. The increase of national output and employment may then do more good than the harm done by the outflow of profit. That is specially likely if some of the output of the new investment is exported to earn foreign exchange. The case against selling existing assets to foreigners is not necessarily a case against accepting new productive foreign investment.)

Thus capital movements can both increase and correct exchange deficits. But some of the gains are temporary, and most of the losses are long-term.

Gains: Avoiding an overall exchange deficit by borrowing, selling assets to foreigners and attracting foreign investment allows a country to go on importing what its producers and consumers want to import, and to do it without necessarily depreciating the currency and raising import prices. Some foreign takeovers of local firms may bring better management, new export links, or access to new technology. New direct investment by foreigners may add to aggregate demand, employment and growth. Those are gains if local enterprise would not otherwise have supplied the same improvements.

Losses: Selling income-earning assets to foreigners or borrowing from them increase the future need for foreign exchange by the amount of profit, rent, interest and debt-repayment that foreign owners will take out of the country. Those outflows are added to the annual import bill. If there is an underlying trade deficit they are likely to reduce the funds available for buying imports unless the borrowing and asset sales continue – and continue to increase the current account deficit which the capital transactions are masking. If at length that deficit has to be corrected by a big depreciation of the currency – or if it forces a depreciation which *fails* to correct the deficit because the elasticities of supply and demand are unhelpful – the ill effects on employment, growth and inflation are likely to be severe.

Deliberate unemployment One way to restrain imports is to restrain the demand for them. One way to do that is to restrain total demand by keeping the national economy under-employed. Less investment means less import of foreign equipment or materials. Less employment means less wage income and less consumer spending, including spending on imports.

As a way of limiting imports, limiting total demand is wastefully inefficient, because a lot of useful production and consumption of home-produced tradeable and non-tradeable goods gets restrained too. The proportions vary according to the share of imports in total spending, but in almost all countries the unnecessary loss of home-produced output and income is greater – often several times greater – than the desired reduction of the import bill. (To measure those proportions you need to measure not the whole proportion of imports in total demand, but the *marginal* propensity to demand imports. Those figures can differ, as in the Australian example below.)

Remember that one purpose of the historic Right turn in the English-speaking countries' economic policies was to let significant unemployment weaken labor's bargaining power. Business leaders and others wanted that to cut the labor share and increase the profit share of income. Governments and others wanted it to restrain wage-push inflation and perhaps encourage investment. In some deficit-trading countries it got further support as a way to cut imports to improve the balance of payments.

An Australian example: When the Right turn began in earnest in 1984 about 18 per cent of all demand was met by imports. The marginal demand for imports was higher: about 30 cents in each additional dollar of spending. The government announced (1) a staged reduction of tariff protection, and (2) a financial deregulation which would allow unlimited private borrowing of foreign money. At that time Australia's public and private foreign debt was about $350 per head of population. Ten years later it passed $10 000 per head. It was growing at an average rate of 6 per cent of GDP per year at a time when GDP was growing an average 2 per cent a year. The non-debt foreign payments sometimes balanced. That was partly from some export growth and some improvident asset sales. But it was partly also from the depressing effect on total demand and import demand of persistent unemployment: 8 per cent of registered unemployment plus perhaps 4 per cent or more of unregistered unemployment and underemployment.

Through the long boom, tariff protection and strict control of foreign borrowing had accompanied full employment, economic growth at 4 per cent a year, balanced trade and payments, and eventually rising inflation. The Right liberation of trade and exchange did serve some of its Right purposes, to weaken labor, increase the profit share and end inflation. But its effects on foreign debt and the balance of payments were financially quite improvident, and they will add to the difficulty of any return to full employment.

Unreliable ways of balancing trade and payments: a summary

If unbalanced trade and payments are left to be corrected by their market effects on rates of exchange, or by international lending and borrowing and asset sales, no great harm may follow if the adjustments can be small and slow. It may well be efficient to let them happen.

But if the imbalances and the necessary corrections are large, sudden, or frequent, and the market corrections are not effective, there can be harm of the kinds just described. There is nothing in the nature of technical progress and capitalist economic development to ensure that international deficits and surpluses will not develop. They can happen if nations have different rates and directions of technological advance. They can happen if new competitors bite into the national market shares which underlie existing balances of trade and payments. They can happen if protected industries lose their protection and can't survive without it. They have happened when long-regulated financial systems were deregulated and allowed new flows of international credit, investment and exchange gambling. Those market misfortunes are not self-adjusting. They make the case for positive structural policies.

It can make sense to import foreign capital for productive uses. Beyond that, a country should ideally import only what its foreign earnings can pay for at a natural rate of exchange related to purchasing power. It should do so by means which don't raise prices, don't accumulate imprudent levels of foreign debt, don't force or subsidize the sale of assets to foreign owners, and don't force any unwilling surrender of national power over economic policy.

The best way for that to happen is in an ordinary market way. But although balanced trade and payments can develop in a market way, so can imbalances. They have often done so, and still do. Where they persist, they can force market corrections through adverse exchange rates, or through borrowing and asset sales which increase the current deficit in the long run. It is worth comparing those ill effects with the effects of structural policies which may include export aids, import restrictions, and some rationing of available foreign exchange. Collective title: *protection.*

PROTECTION

The following are circumstances in which some protection may be justified.

Infant industries

Some industries add more value per worker or per acre or per dollar of investment than others do. To be rich and fully employed, a developing country usually needs some manufacturing, including some advanced manufacturing. It needs to process some at least of its natural resources, rather than neglecting them or exporting them raw. If the people want to open their economy to imports they must export some goods, and also produce enough tradeables for themselves, to limit the demand for imports to the volume their exports can pay for.

Industries which need to accumulate much physical and human capital, including know-how which can only be learned by working experience, and industries which need advantages of scale, can't usually start up in a new country and succeed against imports from established competitors who already have those advantages. Many economists, including some free-traders, agree that developing countries, or developed countries with persistent exchange deficits, may (1) rightly want to develop some industries of that kind, and (2) need to protect them until they have developed competitive skills and scale.

Continuing protection

Suppose such an infant industry becomes reasonably efficient but not low-priced enough to be internationally competitive. That may happen because the home market is too small to allow full economies of scale. It may happen because the nation's government or its labor unions won't let its workers be worked as long or paid as little as the competitors' workers are. It may happen with less excuse: the new firms are simply not as good as their foreign competitors, and not likely to become as good.

When that happens it may often be right to give notice that the protection will be tapered to zero over a few years, so that the industry must improve or dwindle, and perhaps close down. But can it ever be right to continue to protect such industries? It may be, in any of the following circumstances.

- The labor protection, or the environmental requirements, or the product quality or safety requirements, which raise the home producers' prices above the importers' prices may be regarded by the democracy as more valuable than the price advantages of cheaper imports.

- There may be no likely market for anything that the industry's land or labor might alternatively produce. If there is already persistent unemployment, there may be no reason to expect that adding more unemployment will attract investors to employ the disemployed resources, or consumers to buy their products. So –

- allowing a marginally inefficient industry to be displaced by imports may leave some or all of its resources unemployed and leave the country poorer; and –

- the consequent imbalance of import spending and export earning may depreciate the currency far enough to cost consumers more, through the higher price of all their imports, than they were losing to the marginally higher prices of the protected industry.

If those ill effects follow, it may not be easy to repair the damage by restoring the protection. The industries' resources may have dispersed or rusted from disuse. The importers who displaced them may have replaced their distributors, marketing arrangements and established brands. Investors may have learned to distrust the government's protective policies. It might take another decade or two of high infant-industry protection and prices before it becomes possible to return to the lower protection and prices which suffice to sustain the industry once it is re-established. And there will meanwhile have been human as well as economic costs of unemployment and dislocation.

That is an unnecessary shock to inflict on an industry worth keeping. But similar competitive shocks arise in the ordinary course of political and technical change. As follows.

Rates of change

Two forces are currently speeding the rate at which competitive conditions change in some manufacturing industries. Political changes in ex-communist and ex-colonial countries are breaking down old industrial centres and developing new ones at quite a fast rate. And technical progress is now rapid in a number of advanced, high-value-added industries, including for example computing, information processing and transmission, computer-aided design, and automated and robotic manufacture of an increasing range of more traditional goods.

These changes make competitive opportunities. Some countries' firms and governments use them more effectively than others do. Japan begins to export cheaper television sets than the US can make. US producers export better computers than others can make. Also better passenger aircraft, until European producers and government cooperate to rival them. Asian tigers succeed in exporting a range of household electrical goods. China exports cheaper clothes than anyone else can. Some of the new competition comes from the old multinationals shifting some operations from (say) England to Malaysia.

Free traders theorize that capital and labor which lose employment from these changes should switch to whatever become their countries' next industries of greatest comparative advantage. But the capital and labor disemployed from declining industries may not be switchable to alternative industries. New industries may have to recruit new capital and skills, while the middle-aged and older workers from the declining industries see out their lives unemployed. The more advanced industries are, in many cases, the less switchable their resources are. And the longer the intervening period of unemployment and re-equipment, the likelier it is that competitive conditions may change again before the new producers are on stream. Experience suggests that new industries will often need some public help. If the public help could alternatively have restored the efficiency and competitive capacity of the old industries, that might have been better policy. Remember that many advantages, especially in manufacturing, are not natural endowments like mineral deposits or favorable weather; they are created. They are typically created by private or public enterprise with some government aid, and sometimes protection. Many comparative advantages are qualities which nations *choose to develop* rather than merely *discover they have*.

In a world in which competitive conditions keep changing, nations can lose industries not because their products are no longer wanted but because foreign competitors put them out of business. It is often right that that should happen, partly to replace dearer goods by cheaper or better imports, and partly to maintain the competitive discipline which contributes to everyone's efficiency. But in some circumstances the costs of losing the existing industry are higher than the costs of conserving it. Some continuing public aid or protection for mature industries may be justified –

- if it allows the industries time and profit margins with which to modernize and re-equip themselves; especially –

- if the protection is conditional on the modernization

- if the industries contribute to maintaining levels of employment and exchange balance which the economy could not maintain without them

- if the nation already has unemployed resources available to investors able and willing to employ them (so that there is no need to extinguish one industry in order to start or expand another).

Theorists tend to think of a single transition from an inefficient use of resources by one industry to a more efficient use of them by another. Even if the transition has costs, the change pays in the end. But for an increasing number of industries, a persisting rate of change may cause a continuous rate of capital waste and labor unemployment. Among the causes of waste and unemployment may be a misfit between the rate of technical change and the industries' investment lead-times and payback periods. It may take some years of research and development to produce each new vintage of products and productive equipment and organization. So it can happen that before a new vintage is installed and producing for market the next technical advance has been made, the next vintage is being developed, and it will come on stream before the preceding vintage has had time to repay its development costs. Prices have to rise as payback periods are shortened to insure against the risks of this 'vintage leapfrog'.

Where the new vintage includes a new product which clearly obsolesces the old one, there may be no way to avoid losses on the old vintage. There is no way to protect copper wire from optical fibre, or vinyl records from CDs. But where the technical advance is in the manufacturing process rather than the product, so that its competitive effect is merely to reduce the costs and prices, it *may* pay to work existing vintages longer, and defer replacing them. It may pay consumers as well as producers if it avoids the need for higher prices to cover shorter payback periods and other competitive shocks. And as the next item explains, protecting one industry may improve and expand some unprotected industries as well.

Key industries and clusters

Some industries convey both market and non-market advantages to other industries. A key industry which needs protection to survive may enable other industries to expand on their market merits without protection. The positive income gain from the surrounding industries in the cluster may be greater – sometimes much greater – than the cost of protecting the key industry. A case study can offer an example and some relevant theory. Here is Paul Chapman's summary of his study of a regional cluster of industries generated and sustained by a protected carmaking industry.

[In] South Australia the importance of such a leading sector is clearly seen. The direct impact on local employment and income of the presence of two multi-

national car plants is not of prime importance. The indirect, spin-off effects are. The presence of the motor vehicle manufacturers has (along with past policies of assistance) fostered the development of a range of components suppliers. Many do not specialize solely in motor vehicle parts but produce a range of other goods from clothes lines and mowers to washing machines and airconditioning parts. These supplying industries now cluster about the motor vehicle manufacturers in an array which intersects with other industries. Behind them is a further rim of linked industries supplying to these suppliers. Associated with *them* is a range of other industries producing other consumer durables and like products. In short, the motor vehicle industry is a lynch-pin. It is a focal point within the web of inter-industry relationships described by the industrial structure of [the region].

Because of their size, firms supplying to the multinational car-makers can secure a base-load of demand through which they can attain higher output levels, justify higher investment (in equipment, training and infrastructure) and thereby reap greater economies of scale over the long term. The motor vehicle manufacturers benefit, through the market, in lower prices. The component suppliers also benefit via higher margins. And other industries, consuming products also made by component suppliers, also benefit. They receive a benefit created by the motor vehicle manufacturers but external to and uncaptured by them. Moreover, the manufacturers have brought to Adelaide new production technologies and techniques. Uptake of them (or their derivatives) is encouraged in, sometimes demanded of, component suppliers. Again, there are benefits for the motor vehicle manufacturers but also for the suppliers and for their other customers.

This process can be repeated up and down the production chain and along other production chains linked to it. ... Many of the important effects so transmitted are unpriced by the market as they are external to the individual firm ...When, as with the motor vehicle industry, the core of a cluster of linked firms is sufficiently large, it can help create the conditions for competitiveness in a large number of other industries. This is so, regardless of whether the core industry is assistance-dependent. Competitiveness and growth is a self-reinforcing process and policy should aim to strengthen the positive tendencies. This is an opportunity. Failure to do so, combined with external shocks such as tariff removal, can readily create self-reinforcing decline.

Chapman reminds you of a neglected principle of market efficiency:

> Firms are not simply independent and competitive; they are also inter-dependent and co-operative. If firms are physically close (or at least within a single currency area) and their activities are linked they can be greatly advantaged. They can trade in a stable medium of exchange; they can respond to each other more quickly and cheaply; they are able to coordinate co-operative activities more easily, setting standards, creating industry fora and information networks; they can piggy-back on each other into export markets; they can lobby governments more effectively; they are more able to attract other, linked industries to the region creating a new round of benefits. These advantages of proximity exist both horizontally and vertically. They account for the phenomenon of clustering and highlight a key aspect of competitiveness.

Protecting some key industries within such clusters may generate more investment, growth, employment and income than it loses to the higher prices of the protected products. 'The industrial structure is a matter for government intervention because it involves interactions which are external to the market and individual firms. The market alone would build a structure which combines only those industries which link together in ways advantageous to individual firms. This will be an industry structure less competitive (and either smaller or more assistance-dependent) than one which is organized by forces in addition to the market.' But Chapman concludes with a proper warning that the interdependences vary with time and circumstances. To be effective, public intervention needs to be well researched and well judged. Theory may tell you what to look for, but it doesn't predict what you will find, or reduce the need for local knowledge:

> Finally, the obvious: Industries differ in their ability to create beneficial linkage effects. The quantity and quality of linkage effects from the motor vehicle industry is different to that of biotechnology or breadmaking. Once we recognize the different potential roles of different industries within a given economy the importance of selective and discriminating intervention is established.
> – from Paul Chapman, 'Towards an Industry Policy' in J. Carroll and R. Manne (eds) *Shutdown* (1992).

PURPOSES OTHER THAN INCOME

Trade may be regulated for purposes which take precedence over maximizing national income. Conservation,

equality, culture and national independence are examples. In that order –

Conservation Most environmental regulation is of the extraction, use, consumption and waste disposal of resources, rather than the trade in them. When national governments do regulate trade for environmental reasons it is sometimes to conserve resources for their own use, sometimes to prevent their use, and sometimes to influence other nations' behavior. Some countries ban or limit the export or import of whale products, sealskins or fur to limit the rate at which those creatures are slaughtered. Some countries with uranium deposits limit their mining at home and their use abroad because both are thought to be dangerous. Some countries limit the export of their minerals, forest timber or other exhaustible resources, for their own or for international purposes.

Some environmental restraints protect future income but many of them reduce present income, for what majorities regard as good reasons.

Equality This item connects with the employment item in the previous list. Some countries act collectively to raise their lowest wages, and improve their worst working conditions, above the levels which might otherwise prevail. In industries affected by the regulations, costs and product prices may be higher than they would otherwise be. (May, not must – better wages and conditions may elicit more efficient work.) In non-tradeable industries those requirements don't necessarily reduce national income. Depending on other conditions they may reduce it or increase it or neither; they chiefly affect its distribution. But the higher costs may expose tradeable industries to increased competition from countries whose workers don't enjoy the same protection. (That can include rich as well as poor countries. Some US exporters of farm and orchard products give their workers lower pay and worse conditions than the European or Australian governments of their export markets would allow.) A tariff or subsidy which matches and protects the 'regulated' increment of labor costs may raise or lower national income, depending on (i) the direct upward or downward effects which better wages and conditions have on labor productivity; (ii) the income gains which would be available from cheaper imports; and (iii) the income losses if resources put out of use by cheaper imports are not usefully re-employed. Without local knowledge, theory can't tell you which of those effects will outweigh the others.

Culture One French and one Australian example:

In the seventh round of GATT negotiations (1987 – 94) the French government fought even more tenaciously, and successfully, for the right to cultural protection than for their famous agricultural protection. Why do they need protection? Can't French people be trusted to prefer their own movies and broadcast entertainment to American imports? Perhaps they can – but their commercial broadcasters can't. America's vast home and foreign English-language market allows such economies of scale that whatever American commercial entertainments cost to make, they can be replicated and sold at much lower prices than the French have to charge for productions with similar costs. The French government stonewalled to the end – and a minute or two before the end, the US government conceded that national governments could retain control of the passage of cultural goods across their frontiers.

The cultural principle joined with the cluster principle in an Australian example. The Australian market is too small to support much feature and documentary film-making, unless it has enough international flavor to sell well outside Australia. So for many years commercial telecasters were required to have their advertisements made in Australia. That gave Australian film-makers a base-load of work, and economies of scale, which made distinctly Australian feature and documentary film-making and television drama much more viable. American TV ads would have been cheaper, with advantage to national income if the Australian film-makers could be employed in other industries – but Australian culture would have lost some more of its distinct character. A free-trading government has since ended the protection. TV ads for many multinational products are now made in the US, more Australian film-makers now work there, and the national output is (depending on your tastes) culturally poorer.

But notice that in other circumstances it can be free trade rather than protection that gives local producers advantages of scale in their local markets. Many Australian book-publishers are owned by English-language multinationals which distribute more imported books than Australian books in Australia. The volume of imports supports warehousing, marketing and distributive services on a scale, and with economies, which the Australian books alone could not achieve. The Australian books share those advantages.

Risk Different countries, or the same country at different times in different economic circumstances, may opt for different balances of risk and present income. And a desired balance of risk and income may be achieved by different policies in different circumstances.

Comparatively self-sufficient economies, trading less than 10 per cent of their output (as the US and Japan did until recently) and importing comparatively few of the goods that they could produce for themselves, may well have less to fear than more trade-dependent countries do from changing technology, prices and competitive conditions in world markets. That degree of self-sufficiency comes easiest to big economies because their internal markets are big enough to allow full economies of scale in most industries. Small national economies offer fewer economies of scale, and some of them have less range and quantity of natural resources. For them, degrees of trade dependence or self-sufficiency may be open to choice. To maintain a Japanese or US degree of self-sufficiency they may have to protect quite a lot of their industries. That may reduce the specialization and economies of scale, and consequently the income, that they might achieve by trading more freely and letting market forces determine a less self-sufficient, more trade-dependent structure of industries for them. But in a quick-changing, increasingly competitive world economy, some bias toward self-sufficiency, at some cost in present income, may be a reasonable strategy for a country whose income is already comfortable. It may preserve future income from shocks, and give present people peace of mind and expectations of secure employment.

But in other circumstances a small country's least-risk course may be to join a giant – the European Community, the North American Free Trade Area – and surrender national trade and structural controls altogether.

Sovereignty Economic systems face political as well as market risks. Compulsory free trade in goods, money and capital ownership can sharply reduce a nation's capacity for self-government. Some of our strategy chapters will explore those possibilities. Here, a preview.

Remember how the chartering power of American States has led some of them to compete in biasing company law first in favor of corporate owners, and then in favor of directors. States also bias other laws in favor of business as they compete with each other to attract and hold private investment. In one summary –

the history of the United States is replete with examples of the migration of business enterprises from the states with the highest taxes and greatest amount of regulation to the states providing a "more favorable climate for private enterprise"...

Not surprisingly, business concerns have not been content with merely taking advantage of differences favorable to them that already exist between states. They have been vigorous and unrelenting in playing off one state against another in order to achieve the lowest taxation and the least regulation. The state with the fewest occupational health and safety rules, the poorest workers' compensation laws; the state with the fewest restrictions against polluting air, land and water; the state most noted for its open-shop prejudices and for its willingness to make tax concessions and provide elaborate access roads and other associated infrastructure; such is the state that attracts new or relocating businesses ... Thus a Wisconsin manufacturer may say "Treat us as favorably as will Alabama or we are moving there."

If the whole world is declared a free-trade area, the inevitable trend will be for business to migrate to where there is the least unwanted exercise of national sovereignty. What enticing vistas are open to business if they have not only the option of playing off the partial sovereignty of Michigan against that of Georgia, but the full sovereignty of the United States against that of Mexico or South Korea or any other country in the world!...

A transnational corporation would like to be free to make those product components most likely to result in pollution under the sovereignty enacting the fewest environmental protections laws; make those components that are most labor-intensive under the sovereignty where there are the fewest occupational health and safety rules and labor is cheapest; make subassemblies in another place and final assemblies in yet another; then juggle the accounting so that profits are shown to occur under the sovereignty where profits are least taxed. [Thus] the making of the entire world into a free trade zone would provide the best opportunities for limiting, subverting and escaping national sovereignties.

– William Hixson, 'The shady side of free trade',
Economic Reform, May 1994.

Hixson quotes Keynes' conclusion: "Let goods be homespun whenever it is reasonably and conveniently possible, and, above all, let finance be primarily national ...The phenomenon known as 'the flight of capital' should be ruled out." Not many industries are big enough and mobile enough to force national governments to compete for their favors. But in the industries which do have that character, a nation which wants to determine its own labor, environment and tax policies may need to produce as much as possible for itself. That may sacrifice advantages of scale, and export opportunities.

Such resolute independence might well reduce present income – though not by much if it allowed secure full employment. But sovereign self-government may prove to be worth its costs, both for economic and for other reasons. And reasons of both kinds may have increasing force as the world moves towards one world economy without a world government.

WAYS AND MEANS

Suppose government does want to influence the structure of the private tradeable sector, i.e. the producers who must compete with foreign producers in their home and export markets. The methods of influence are of three general kinds. Government can help its national producers to be more competitive. It can regulate foreign competitors' access to its national market. And it can negotiate with foreign governments or international authorities about the international rules and national policies under which its own producers and their foreign competitors have to trade. We can list government's available means of aid, trade management and diplomacy in that order.

AID

Standard services Tradeable producers are helped, as all producers are, by the means described in Chapter 36: standard public infrastructure and services, provided as public goods or at low prices.

Credit Besides the ordinary services of the financial system, special-purpose banks can provide producers and exporters with credit on terms and for purposes and with risks that are not acceptable to the regular commercial banks.

Marketing Many farm products are produced by large numbers of small, financially weak producers, and sell on unstable world markets. Government can provide handling and marketing institutions, or it can support producers' cooperatives which do so. For some other goods, government can provide trade centres and tourist bureaux in export markets to help its country's exporters.

Subsidies Government can subsidize exports directly, by paying exporters a percentage of their production costs or a bounty related to their export earnings.

If that breaks international rules, it may be possible to subsidize the whole output of the relevant industry, not just its exports. Besides competing in export markets, that may help it to compete with imports in its home market. Both gains can help employment and the national balance of payments. (But subsidies financed from taxation may reduce demand for other goods, and employment in other industries. That may still be worth while for a country with a serious exchange deficit.) If subsidies still break the rules, it may be possible to get the rules changed. (You will presently learn that GATT, the General Agreement on Tariffs and Trade signed by most of the world's governments and administered by the World Trade Organization (WTO), exempts some products from its trading rules.)

If you can't change the rules and don't dare break them, you may be able to conceal the subsidies by shifting them back along the production chain: help the producers to get cheap land, fertilizer, fuel, rented factories, rail-freight rates. (These are politely called 'pre-competitive' aids.) Or simply have public banks lend the producers money then after a decent interval write off their debts. (This is not a list of aids which governments *ought* to provide, it is a list of aids which they can, and some do, provide. If you work for the World Trade Organization it's a hit-list of tricks you should detect and punish.)

Taxation   Raise revenue in ways which don't increase the costs or prices of the tradeables your country produces. Don't tax its tradeables, or non-tradeable inputs which they use. Collect low company tax and no payroll tax. Taxes on income and personal wealth are best because they don't raise costs of production. Tax-financed age and disability pensions are better than making employers finance compulsory superannuation or disability insurance.

Those are the tax principles which will keep tradeable output most competitive. But that aim of course competes with others in shaping tax policy, and it may not have high priority in countries with comfortable trade and exchange balances.

Hindering tradeable producers   Government can hinder instead of helping its country's tradeable industries. It may do so for good reasons if other purposes have priority. (See the first item below.) Or for bad reasons, to favor politically powerful groups. (See the second item below.) Or by mistake or incompetence. (The third item below.) Examples:

- Wage-fixing systems, safety requirements, environmental requirements and other civilizing measures may raise costs of production above some foreign competitors' costs.

- Obliging the influential rich by shifting taxation off high incomes onto goods and services raises the price of tradeables and may reduce the sale of exports. Goods exported may be exempt from tax, but their non-tradeable inputs can't usually be, and indirect taxes may increase wage pressures. So export costs and prices may rise even if the exports themselves are untaxed.

- Collecting excise taxes from national producers without taxing competing imports puts the national producers under a competitive disadvantage.

- Company tax, payroll tax, compulsory superannuation, disability and workers' compensation insurance, which national producers have to pay but some foreign competitors may not, may give the foreigners a competitive advantage.

- Environmental policies may restrict the extraction, use and export of coal, uranium, forest timber or other resources.

- Revenue measures (excise taxes, mineral royalties, export licence fees) may increase the export prices and reduce the export prospects of coal, oil, mineral ores, forest timber or other commodities.

TRADE

The commonest way to influence national economic structure is to help particular industries to develop or survive by protecting them from foreign competition in the national market. The main means are tariffs, import quotas, and public control of the private uses of foreign exchange. We will presently compare their merits, but there are first some advantages which they all share:

They reduce the demand for foreign currency as well as for foreign goods, so they need not affect exchange rates.

They can be selective in a double sense. First, they can discriminate between more desirable and less desirable imports: for example between necessities and luxuries, between capital goods and consumption goods, between things the country can produce for itself and things it can't.

Second, many of the restrictions raise the prices of the imports which they restrict, but they don't raise any other import prices. A market depreciation of a country's exchange rate raises the price of *all* its imports: necessities as well as luxuries, capital as well as consumer goods, imported inputs to the country's exports, goods which the country can't produce for itself as well as those it can. A selective tariff can limit imports to the volume the country's foreign earnings can pay for at a natural exchange rate, while raising the prices of the tariffed items alone. German cars, French wines, Scotch whisky and Italian suits can pay a high tariff and be rationed by price, while productive machinery, industrial materials, public transport vehicles, medicines and hospital equipment and tea and coffee can enter tax-free at competitive prices.

Tariffs have these advantages:

- They raise revenue. The extra price which the citizens pay for the imports returns to them by relieving them of other taxation. (It may also reduce other costs if it reduces unemployment, but that is common to all the methods of restraining imports.)

- People who want the imported goods badly enough to pay their higher prices can still get them. Though the inflow of foreign goods may diminish, some are still available as standards of comparison for the protected home-produced goods.

- Government can bargain with the industries and labor unions which benefit from the tariffs. Investors must keep their technology and management up to date and workers must cooperate with reasonable wage restraint and helpful work practices if they want the protection to continue, and the rates of tariff can be set to give national producers some advantage only if they discipline their costs by those means.

Subsidies were listed earlier as positive aids to producers. Here notice an argument, usually between free traders and protectionists, about the relative merits of tariffs and subsidies.

For subsidies: First, they don't raise any prices, or contribute to inflation. Second, tariffs raise revenue but subsidies spend it. Subsidies are therefore less popular with politicians and taxpayers. As public spending they have to be reviewed and authorized by national budget legislation every year. So they are among the targets of governments looking for spending cuts. They thus keep the costs of protection in sight and under yearly review.

For tariffs: The political insecurity of subsidies is not a good thing, it is a bad thing. If advantages for particular industries are to serve their purpose, investors have to have confidence in them. Because tariffs are easy to continue, you can usually trust governments which promise to continue them. Because subsidies are in danger from every budget review and every electoral promise to cut taxes, they are rightly distrusted by investors in industries with long lead-times and big cap-

ital commitments. So dollar for dollar, the tax cost of subsidy is likely to generate less of the desired investment than the price cost of a tariff will generate.

Quotas Government can license the import or export of particular products and limit the quantities imported or exported.

Import quotas, like tariffs, are designed to ration the use of scarce foreign exchange, or to protect national producers from competing imports. They have often been introduced for emergency reasons in wartime or to cope with postwar reconstruction. In those circumstances they are normally accompanied by effective price controls, the quotas are based on previous market shares, and they work well enough. Permanent quotas in peacetime are more troublesome. Permanent price controls are unsatisfactory if changing technology is changing the products and their costs. Fixed market shares can rule out desirable competition. In those circumstances shares of the quotas are usually auctioned periodically with or without contractual price controls. The price controls are likely to be less effective than they can be in wartime.

Some quotas distribute rights not between rival importers but between rival foreign suppliers. Thus the US decides how much beef its importers may buy from each of a number of foreign countries. The total quota is there to protect the US beef producers. The national shares of it are apportioned for diplomatic and equitable reasons rather than for market purposes.

Exchange controls Government can choose to regulate its citizens' uses of the foreign money that the country's exports and foreign investments earn. The power can be used to regulate imports and the export of funds to lend, spend or invest abroad. It can thus influence economic structure by helping the development of some industries and hindering others.

In some circumstances exchange controls may have a treble advantage over alternative methods of trade control. They need not raise average prices (they merely replace some scarcities by others) so they are less inflationary than tariffs can be. They don't spend public funds (so they are better than subsidies). And they can often avoid breaking trade treaties (so they are better than controls which do break rules). They were used effectively when Japan was rebuilding its economy after the Second World War. The country was desperately short of foreign exchange, and forbidden by treaty to use tariff or other direct trade controls. So exchange control was used to confine foreign spending to necessary fuel and raw materials, and capital goods for the industries which could do most for manufacturing development. (The control ceased as the economy grew and export earnings increased.)

Exchange is scarce when a country's demand for imports, plus any outflow of money to foreign investors and creditors, exceed its export and investment earnings from foreigners. If imports therefore have to be rationed, market forces will not necessarily direct the scarce funds to their best uses. If competing importers have to bid for shares of the available exchange they will raise its price. That means they will lower their national currency's exchange rate with foreign currencies, so that the price of all imports will rise and the volume of imports will fall. The highest bidders, who get the foreign exchange, may not be poor people wanting necessary food or clothing. They may not be manufacturers wanting productive capital equipment and raw materials. (Those can't bid too high if they are producing for competitive markets.) The winners may well include importers of luxury cars, furniture, clothing, jewellery, food and drink; firms and individuals exporting capital or gambling on exchange rates; money launderers of criminal or tax-evasive gains; and rich people wanting expensive foreign holidays. In those circumstances exchange control can impose more economical, productive and humane priorities than market allocation will achieve.

At times in the last half century, for example, Western governments have used exchange controls to enforce spending priorities for –

- necessary fuel, food, raw materials that the home country can't produce
- capital goods
- foreign investment and spending to promote export sales
- foreign travel for approved business purposes
- payments for family support and public and private foreign aid.

There have been bans on other imports, on capital export and on exchange gambling; and exchange for holiday travel has been rationed.

Exchange controls can work well enough when the purpose is to exclude some imports altogether. But like quotas, they may be difficult to allocate fairly if the purpose is to reduce rather than block imports. For that purpose tariffs are generally better.

Exchange controls can also be used, alone or with other controls, to restrict investment, lending or borrowing in foreign countries, and to regulate foreign investment and ownership in the home country.

Public procurement means public buying. The public sector is a big customer of the private sector. Government can direct its departments and enterprises to buy home-produced rather than imported products, either whenever home products are available, or whenever the price difference between home and foreign products is within specified limits.

Persuasion Government, other patriots, and private producers with import competitors, can campaign to persuade people to prefer home products to imports – to 'Buy British' (or whatever) whenever they reasonably can, for patriotic reasons, or compassionate reasons (to employ the nation's unemployed), or self-interested reasons (to restrain taxes by reducing the welfare bill).

Dirty tricks Suppose its treaties commit the government to free trade. It can nevertheless insist that (i) some dangerous imports such as firearms and hard drugs are prohibited, and (ii) its National Accounts are required to record what is imported. For those two reasons all importers are required to submit detailed accounts of their imports. To make sure that they do, they must detail each cargo and get a licence for it before they land it. For imports which the government favors, the licences are issued promptly. For imports it doesn't favor, the licences come with such unpredictable and sometimes long and expensive delays that importers give up trying.

That's always a dirty trick. There is another regulatory device whose respectability can sometimes be harder to judge. In their home markets governments rightly administer many quality controls. Products must be safe to use. Their labels must tell buyers many things they are entitled to know – the ingredients in processed food and drink; the flammability and laundering characteristics of clothing; the strength of cordage and fishing lines; the use-by dates of perishable products; and so on. These rules rightly apply impartially to home products and imports. But the regulators can cheat. With some products it is not too hard to find harmless differences between the home-produced and imported goods. Observing them, regulators can write rules with which the imports don't comply. (Their salt content is a shade too high. Cane sugar is required in this product but the imports use beet sugar. Ingredients are specified in imperial measures where the regulations specify metric (or vice versa) – or they are set out as quantities where the regulations require percentages (or vice versa). By the time the foreign producers change the labels on the next batch of goods there have been further refinements of the regulations, with prior notice to the home producers.)

Such tricks are often hard to beat by legal action. Retaliation may work – but that is only available if the offending country happens to be exporting vulnerable goods to the victim countries, and if their governments are as unscrupulous as the offender's. The effective preventive is honest government all round.

NTB stands for Non-Tariff Barrier. It's a collective term for quotas, exchange controls on imports, procurement preferences, and other ways – including dirty tricks – of hindering imports. The current GATT agreement wants them all abolished or converted to tariff barriers.

DIPLOMACY

National governments engage in various kinds of trade negotiation. There are worldwide agreements about the rules which should govern international trade. There are bilateral agreements or agreements between small groups of countries about their trade with each other, or the outcomes they will jointly try for in negotiations about the general international rules. And there is a mass of detailed negotiation about particular items – for example about the fairness or legality with which particular governments are enforcing particular rules (or not enforcing them, or misinterpreting them, or engaging in dirty tricks).

GATT, WTO, MAI　The General Agreement on Tariffs and Trade was first signed by a majority of national governments in 1947, and has since been renegotiated and amended eight times. It is now administered by the World Trade Organization (WTO). It makes general rules for international trade, provides machinery for negotiating and interpreting the rules, and offers some information services and other aids to trade. Its rules are complex and issue from tortuous negotiations between consensual and conflicting interests. They have progressed in two general directions. They have reduced discrimination: how a nation trades with any nation should be how it trades with every nation. Whatever tariffs or other barriers it applies should apply to all comers. Second, they have reduced trade barriers and moved some way towards a free-trading world. Recent rounds of negotiation have extended the rules from direct trade barriers to other hindrances to trade, such as trade-related exchange controls. And exceptions to the rules have been made for developing countries. For example, they may be allowed temporary increases of tariff or other trade barriers if they have serious exchange deficits.

Through the last years of the 1990s, governments of some leading countries and economists of the OECD joined, with some strong business support, in trying to negotiate a Multilateral Agreement on Investment (MAI). As originally proposed, it would empower investors to invest, or buy existing property and firms, in any member country, without restraint by any government. It would entitle them to damages from national governments whose changes of law disadvantaged them. It would further reduce the democracies' capacity to influence their economic structures, balances of payment and levels of employment. It would drastically reduce their power to defend themselves against exchange gambling, capital flight, and financial intimidation. The proposal has provoked widespread opposition, much of it led from Canada. As this goes to press, the resistance seems to have frightened enough governments to halt the negotiations for the time being.

Free traders welcome the progress toward freer trade and international investment and ownership. Critics have many misgivings about it. Most of them are the business of later chapters. But here, notice two very general ones. First, although more than a hundred nations sign the GATT agreements, very few of them have much influence over the terms. Europe, the United States and Japan effectively make most of the rules. Second, those few are economic winners. The size and wealth that make them dominant bargainers also make them, in many but not all industries, free traders. Countries with big population numbers, the best accumulation of physical and human capital and the most advanced and advancing technology have many trading advantages. New technology gives them periods of effective monopoly in some industries. Their size allows them to combine maximum specialization with maximum economies and other advantages of scale. Other countries – poorer countries, technological followers, small countries with advanced economies but fewer advantages of scale – may do well to retain more independent control of the passage of goods, money, credit and business ownership across their borders.

Unfinished business　So far, this discussion of trade policy has an obvious bias. It has focused on conditions in which free trade does not work as theorized. It has compared import and exchange controls with alternative means by which an indebted, deficit-trading country may hope to reform its economic structure to earn enough foreign currency to pay for the imports for which it generates demand. The comparison is incomplete without reminders of (i) the merits of free trade where it works, and (ii) some political and administrative problems of protection.

THE ONUS OF PROOF

This chapter is giving more space to the national conditions which may justify industrial aid or protection than to the conditions for free trade. That is partly because the conditions for free trade can be more broadly and simply specified. But it is also because I think most Economics textbooks overstate and overgeneralize the case for free trade, so there is some need to redress the balance by emphasizing the national conditions which may justify protective policies. But in redressing that balance this chapter should not be taken as recommending general protection. If an economy needs protection at all, the protection should be economized. It should discriminate. Defensive protection should be applied only where and when it is needed, and at the lowest rates that will work. Creative protection should only be applied when it promises substantial gains which will clearly exceed its costs. Wherever free trade works, free trade is best. Besides its economic benefits, its has other advantages:

Administrative costs Free trade is cheapest for all parties. Where government offers subsidies they commonly have to be the subject of investigations which cost business and government time and money. Tariffs have to be designed, administered, enforced and their effects monitored. Traders have to supply prescribed information about their goods, and with *ad valorem* tariffs the value of the goods may need elaborate accounting, and be open to dispute, sometimes in court. Thus there are costs in time and money for both parties, and sometimes also for third parties trying to attract similar protection for *their* products.

Misbehavior Most regulations create opportunities for disputed, quarrelsome or unlawful behavior by both sides. Businesses can profit by cutting corners, misrepresenting costs and values, smuggling. Officials can be slow, obstructive or corrupt in the exercise of their powers. Every offence or irritation on either side can worsen relations for the next encounter, and worsen the general regard which business and government have for each other. (But free trade can also be misused in various ways.)

The burden of government The last point, above, has wider application than to trade regulation. The necessary role of government in modern mixed economies is large, complex, and needs to be adaptable to changing conditions. Keeping the whole coherent and all the parts efficient is hard enough, without adding any unnecessary complexities. Am I contradicting this text's emphasis on the amount and quality of government that

a modern economy needs? No. The size and difficulty of the task already provoke what are often destructive campaigns to 'roll back the state' and reduce government's capacity to perform its necessary functions. Its defenders should be as unwilling as its critics to make its task harder by loading it with *un*necessary functions.

For those and other practical reasons, proposals for new industrial aids and trade controls should be subject to some discount for administrative cost, complexity and nuisance; and even then, should rarely be adopted for small or uncertain margins of gain. Free trade is best wherever its effects are tolerable. And where they are not, the onus should be on protectionists to show that they are not.

And also – just as important – to show that government could do better. A final factor which weakens any general theory of free trade or protection is the variable capacity of governments. What some governments can be trusted to do, others cannot. As follows.

THE QUALITY OF GOVERNMENT

Some governments do and others don't come under degrading pressures in arriving at their policies for trade and economic structure. And some are better than others at resisting such pressures.

Policy-makers must usually cope with pressures of three general kinds:

1. Good government calls for a national strategy with coherent purposes and a coherent set of trade and structural policies.

2. Many sectional economic interests may be affected by the policies and try to influence them: owners, managers and labor unions in particular industries; consumers' representatives; taxpayers' representatives; representatives of particular regions and regional and local governments. Some of what they contribute is knowledgeable and valuable to the policy-makers, some is understandably biased, some may be positively deceptive. And some may be accompanied by financial or political threats or inducements.

3. Political parties and their factions and individual members may have conflicting political interests in trade policy. Besides broad divisions between left and right, or men and women, or growth and conservation, some groups may represent particular economic interests; some may need the support of particular regions or swinging electorates; some may

have interested financial backers; some may want to discredit particular opponents; some may be deft headline-hunters; and so on.

In a country blessed with reasonably good government and political culture those conflicts are not too hard to resolve. Leaders plan, propose, consult, conciliate, persuade, negotiate, or fight and win on enough of the issues in (2) and (3) to arrive at national purposes and policies under (1) which have the virtues, and the public and press and parliamentary support, to prevail.

In that process, some of the self-interested contenders get the protection they want, and others don't. In a good system and culture, those who get what they want do so because what they want accords with a national strategy which attracts enough of both interested and disinterested support to get adopted, and then performs well enough to retain support and continue its good work.

Some other accounts of that process tell it differently. Like this, for example:

Industries get protected by bringing concentrated threats, persuasions and temptations to bear on politicians. They have experts prepare their cases. They contribute to party funds and hire individual legislators as lobbyists. They threaten to close down or move to Mexico, then have the press tell the people that the rusting factories and queues of unemployed are the politicians' fault. Their self-seeking campaign is not effectively resisted, because the consumers who will lose by paying protected prices will each suffer only marginally, and they are not organized or strongly represented in the corridors of power; so that concentrated pressure of a selfish few overcomes the diffuse resistance of the many. Besides inflating the protected industries' profits, the tariffs do two other kinds of harm. They distort the national economic structure, retaining industries of less competitive advantage whose resources ought to be switched to industries of greater competitive advantage. And because such rich pickings are available, they are sought by many more firms and industries than actually achieve them. Why invest in the latest vintage of equipment when for a fraction of the price you can buy enough tariff to protect the old plant and keep it going? The considerable campaign costs in time and money of all the unsuccessful contenders for protection must be added to the social costs of the tariffs which the successful contenders achieve.

Why such different accounts? I think there are three main reasons. The first account reports both the self-interests and the public concerns of the contenders. The second account reports only the self-interests. (One

consequence is that it fails to explain why so many contenders for protection *don't* get it.)

Next, the first account assumes that there can be good and bad uses of economic protection, and under good government the policy-makers' task is to sort better from worse. The second account assumes (and often explicitly insists) that *all* protection reduces national income and is therefore bad. It follows that most protection must be corrupt. (Not just honestly mistaken? No: it is unlikely that the business and political leaders who negotiate it, who have climbed to the top of their hotly competitive professions, are innocents who don't know their business.)

Finally, the first account was written with West European, East Asian and Australian as well as American history in mind. Most accounts of the second kind are written by Americans, including many public choice economists, who generalize from some periods of US trade policy. So the two accounts differ because they are about partly-different subjects. The non-American countries have not all had good government and a good political culture at all times. But no historian of Scandinavian, German, French or Japanese trade policies, or some periods of British and Australian policy, could accept the American generalizations as sufficient accounts of those countries' policy-making processes.

They are not wholly convincing about American policy either, at the end of a half-century which has seen big *reductions* of American protection, and some powerful mobilization of public opinion for purposes of conservation and consumer protection. But to the extent that business lobbies do have more influence over American than over European legislators, some historical and institutional factors help to explain the difference.

Many European public servants have – or fancy that they have – more links with aristocracy, with labor, or with an intellectual elite than with business. Their public services have long histories. Most of them were founded by autocratic monarchs, partly as counterweights to democracy, and have not entirely lost their patrician aspirations. Their leaders see themselves as competent, philosophically and historically educated, securely tenured, and with few exceptions incorruptible. Although the principles of trade policy are usually decided by politicians, their public servants are often their main advisers, and many countries confide the detailing and administration of trade and industry policies to public service commissions at arms length from government. Between them the politicians and public servants can make theoretical mistakes and practical misjudgments, but for all their imperfections it is absurd to see most of them as venal agents of the private interests with whom they deal, or to see their policies as achieving none of their professed public purposes.

There is plenty of honest government like that in the US too. But coherent, high-principled 'government from above', subject only to majority approval at election time, is made more difficult by some American institutions. The states' chartering powers and other powers which affect business allow a good deal of the behavior described by William Hixson in the paper quoted earlier, as states compete to attract charter revenue and investment. That accustoms people to the idea that business can properly dicker with government for favors. Trade policy is federal rather than state business. But Congress exercises quite detailed control of it; the government does not command a disciplined party majority in the legislature; and the legislators can accept payment as lobbyists for industrial and commercial associations. More than half the members accept such fees, some of them on terms which would count as bribery in other democracies. So the institutions and the political culture together allow more detailed private influence over trade and industry policies than is usually possible elsewhere.

There are other qualities – including speed of action, effectiveness, and generosity – in which American government is often superior to European. The point of this argument is not to decide which is best. It is to remind you that the quality and the particular capacities of democratic government vary – from task to task, from time to time, and from country to country. And some of their policy options vary accordingly.

Conclusions

1. Most trade policy, like much other policy, issues from elements of short-term self-interest, long-term prudence, and disinterested public concern. You will rarely understand it or do well at it unless you keep each of those elements in mind.

2. Good political systems and cultures are those in which the public concerns tend to prevail, so that the private interests which accord with good public purposes do better than private interests which don't.

3. You may accept your country's political system and culture, and act within their limitations. But there is also fun and justice to be gained by working at the same time, in any way you can, to improve the quality of government and its contribution to economic life.

SUMMARY

Some trade controls increase national income. Some controls reduce national income, without compensating benefits. And some controls reduce income but have other effects which are judged to be more valuable than the lost margins of income. In that order –

Controls which may increase national income

Import controls, or public aids to export or import-replacing industries, may increase national income if they enable the national economy –

- to employ resources which unaided market forces would not employ

- to balance foreign payments which would otherwise be balanced by worse means, for example by improvident asset sales and debt, and/or market depreciation of the national currency, which would eventually cost more income than the trade controls will cost

- to stabilize market expectations for investors in industries of actual or potential advantage which have long investment lead-times but quick-changing international competitive risks

- to enable an industry to achieve critical or increasing economies of scale

- to protect key industries whose linkages and externalities enable clusters of other, including unprotected, industries to develop economies of scale, technological advances, cooperative research and development, new export links, etc.

Undesirable controls which may reduce national income

- Tariffs which protect less efficient industries whose resources would otherwise be employed by more efficient industries. ('Would'. 'Could' is not enough, especially in an economy with persisting unemployment.)

- Tariffs justified by any of the good reasons listed above and below, but levied at unjustified rates.

- Tariffs which protect industries which don't need protection, but use it to raise their prices and profit margins.

Desirable controls which may reduce national income

Protective measures which reduce national income may nevertheless attract majority support if they –

- improve environmental care and conservation

- defer income, for example from exhaustible resources, for purposes of fair dealing with future generations

- reduce inequities and inequalities in the distribution of earned income
- reduce undesired risk, by maintaining more secure national income, or more secure conditions of employment in some industries, than an open economy could expect to do in a quick-changing and increasingly competitive world economy
- protect valued elements of national culture
- block or discourage the import of harmful products.

In practice, of course, judgment is not always as easy as those neat lists suggest. At the time when policies are decided, future conditions may be uncertain. If potential gains and losses from a new measure need to be compared, the likely quantities may be hard to estimate. If qualities rather than quantities have to be compared, there can be other problems. How much peace of mind is worth how much reduction of income? How much freedom of speech is worth how much imported video violence, including incitements to maltreat women, children or other vulnerable people?

And so on. You were promised no more formal exercises. Here is an informal one, especially for any undiscovered novelists among you –

EXERCISE

As a junior public servant you help to design and justify a new tariff to protect an infant industry of great promise. Soon after it passes the legislature but before it has the necessary assent of the Head of State you stumble on hard evidence that one group of politicians exacted a high price for their votes from the industry representatives: bribes, brothel services, five-star Bahaman holidays. If you expose the deal the offenders will be jailed, the Head of State will veto the Tariff Act, and after a scandal like that nobody will dare to reintroduce it. That tariff is important. The quality of government is important. Your marriage is important, and it is troubled by too much debt. What do you do?

50

Money and banking : national

This chapter will describe –

- modern money and credit
- how they are created
- the functions of banks and other financial institutions
- why they need *prudential* regulation to keep them solvent and protect their customers
- why they need *economic* regulation to influence employment, inflation, the balance of payments, the allocation of resources and the distribution of wealth and income
- alternative ways of supplying mixed economies with the money they need.

Even more than other chapters, this one needs an opening warning. National financial systems differ widely, and have lately been changing quite radically. England has four main-street commercial banks, the US has more than fifteen thousand. Britain has one Central Bank to supervise them, the US has twelve. Some countries allow their banks to act also as stockbrokers, insurers, land agents; others don't. Some countries' banks are influential shareholders of some of the firms which bank with them, others stay at arms length from their customers. There have been clear differences between the functions of commercial banks, savings banks, building societies, credit unions, life insurers and other financial institutions; but in many countries the distinctions are blurring as the institutions' functions overlap. There has lately been a lot of deregulation – and wide disagreement about its merits and its effects. So this book can't describe your national system; each country needs its national texts.

There are still some basic functions which all national systems perform. Banks mind your money for you. They put it to work by lending it at interest to business, government, homebuyers and consumers – and when you need it, to you. They ease transactions by providing cheque and credit card and electronic fund transfers. And they create money, and help to keep the supply of it up to the need created by population and economic growth.

Begin with the creation of money. Recall its circular

flow in a modern economy. As goods pass from producers to consumers, money flows the other way to pay for them. The producers return it to the consumers as wages for their labor and as rent, interest and dividends for the use of their capital. So (with many complexities) round and round it goes. The amount of money needs to increase as the population and the economy grow. How is the stuff created in the first place? How is the supply of it increased or reduced? Meet two ways of doing it, one public and one private.

PUBLIC BANK MONEY

Each country has a Central Bank or Reserve Bank. It may be publicly or privately owned, but its powers are created and its functions defined by government. It acts as banker to the government and to other banks, and in most countries it regulates other banks. It has three ways of creating money:

- It (or the government Mint) can mint coins and print banknotes. It sells most of them to the commercial banks.
- It can open a bank account on which government writes cheques, which other banks accept. Each cheque creates new money, i.e. money that is not transferred from anyone else.
- It can create credit for government or for other banks by opening accounts from which they may draw loan money which pays interest and (depending on the terms of the loan) may have to be repaid.

All three methods create new money and put it into circulation. The public power to create money has been widely used in wartime. One school of thought believes that a good deal of public investment should always be financed by creating money. The reasons are as follows:

Government has – broadly – three sources of funds. It can tax the citizens. It can borrow from them. Or it can create money. Taxation is the proper source for most of the *current costs* of government, and for transferring income from some citizens to others. But – depending on the circumstances – any of the three sources can finance public *investments* –

- Financing investment *from taxation* is a straightforward way of saving. It shifts some spending, and some production, from private capital and consumer goods to public capital goods, for the people's future benefit.

- Financing public investment by *borrowing private funds* shifts some of the available investment funds from the private to the public sector, or increases the amount of new money that the private banks create.

- *Creating new money* to finance public investment avoids either taxing the citizens, or paying interest to some of them.

The second option costs most of the citizens more, because through their taxes and public service charges they have to pay interest on public debts to private lenders. Most debt is owed to a well-off minority, so public debt tends to increase inequalities of wealth and income. For reasons of economy and equity, an intelligent democracy should surely *create* rather than *borrow* whatever public investment funds it needs beyond what it is right to provide by taxation.

So why don't we do it, except occasionally in wartime? It is partly because the private creation of money is older than democracy, and its institutions were rich and powerful before democracies began trying to reform them. Although money now gets its legal status and public confidence from government, most of it is still privately created. As follows.

PRIVATE BANK MONEY

Centuries ago, gold and other metal coins were the main kind of European money. They were easy to steal, so rich people often lodged their gold in goldsmiths' strongrooms. The goldsmiths – or bankers, as they eventually became – gave the depositors receipts for the gold held for them. Those notes came to be traded as substitutes for the gold they represented: you could make payments with them, and those who received them could exchange them for gold at the banks which issued them, or, as the system developed, at other banks which would then settle with the banks which issued them. Thus were banknotes born.

While the bank held your gold, it could earn interest by lending it to other people – or more likely by lending them similar notes, entitling the bearer to gold on demand. Those notes circulated as money, because people who used them were confident that they could convert them to gold if they wanted to.

A *multiplier* thus set in. Call it a *bank* multiplier, to distinguish it from the *income* multiplier which operates to turn an initial increase in spending into a bigger increase in income and output. The goldsmith-bankers soon realized that they could fairly safely lend more than they had, because it was unlikely that many note-holders would want to turn their notes into gold at one time. A bank which stored $1000 of your gold coins might lend notes for $1000 to each of three borrowers – or as time went by and bankers grew bolder, to five or ten borrowers. The bank trusted that (1) most of the borrowers would pay regular interest and repay the $1000 when it was due, and (2) no more than one in five or ten of the noteholders would ever actually demand gold for their notes.

Bit by bit confidence in gold was supplemented – and in the end, replaced – by confidence in the bankers. They were not expected to back every note with gold, they were merely trusted to hold sufficient reserves to meet the likely demand for gold. When paper money came to be based on faith rather than gold it became *fiduciary* money, or if government authorized it, *fiat* money.

Now jump to modern times. Banks' reserves are now regulated by law, and bank-notes are backed by the government. Suppose the reserve requirement is 10 per cent. That means that a bank must hold $10 in reserve for every $90 it lends.

Here is how the bank multiplier works now. Somebody deposits $100 000 in a bank. Another customer offers that bank a hitherto debt-free asset – her house, her farm – as security, and if the bank trusts her capacity to repay, it lends her $90 000. She spends it, perhaps on investment goods, and most of the people who receive it bank it. The banks which accept it need only reserve 10 per cent of it and they can lend the rest – to borrowers who spend it, passing it to people who deposit it in their banks, which in turn lend some of it, and so on. In principle the multiplier might multiply a new loan by nine. In practice it is never as powerful as that, because quite a lot of the new money escapes from the banks. Some borrowers send money abroad. Most of them keep some in cash, which leaves less in their bank deposits. A lot is paid to government – as taxes, public service charges, or to buy government bonds or Treasury bills – and because government does not bank with the commercial banks, any money it receives is lost to them. And the banks do not always lend as much as their deposits and reserves would allow them to lend, because they can't always find enough borrowers whom they regard as sound. (We will presently notice that bank loans are unlike other market commodities: they are not available to any and every customer who offers to pay the going rate of interest for them.) But despite those and other limitations the multiplier does work, and can expand the amount of money in a national economy, adding spending power for some without taking any from others.

Hence a paradox: when critics complain that private banks create money out of nothing, that is not true of the banks one by one: each can only lend money that it owns, or that has been lent to it or deposited with it. But it is true of the banks collectively: as the money which each lends is deposited in other banks and lent again, the bank multiplier can increase the whole sum at the citizens' disposal: the total they own plus the total they have borrowed. The multiplier can also work in reverse, if depositors lose income, deposit less and borrow less, or if they repay more of their bank debts than the banks can find new borrowers for.

Back to the goldsmith-bankers. You can see how some of them got rich, lending rights to the same gold to several borrowers, each of whom would repay the loan with interest. Taking risks like that, you can also see why some of them went broke, and their depositors with them. But more important than either of those effects, you can see *how growing economic systems created the rising quantities of money that they needed.* In those days they also created it by mining gold and silver and turning some of the metal into coins. But to whatever coin they minted, they could add credit and paper money by means of the bank multiplier.

If faith in a bank faltered, its depositors and note-holders would hurry in and demand gold, each hoping to collect before the gold reserve ran out. That's how banks failed. Those that failed were not necessarily *insolvent:* they may well have been owed, by their borrowers, more than they owed their depositors and noteholders. But they were *illiquid,* an ugly word which means they were short of cash. They could not call in all their loans at once, in gold, to pay gold to their depositors and noteholders.

> (Liquidity refers to the speed and certainty with which assets can be turned into cash. Coin and bank-notes are absolutely liquid – they're already cash. A steel mill is not very liquid: you don't know how long it may take to sell it, or what you will get for it. There is a spectrum of liquidity from cash, through cheque accounts at banks, and bonds or other financial assets which can be sold within an hour or a day, to assets which may take weeks or months or years to turn into cash, and whose cash value may not be certain until they are sold.)

Creating money in that way is known as *fractional reserve banking.* A recent change in the rules requires 'adequate capital' rather than 'reserve', but the principle is similar. Notice three things about the system as it was first developed by private banks:

- The value of the money depended on confidence in the banks.

- *All* additions to the supply of money, except by mining and minting gold, were created in the form of interest-bearing debt.

- The money went only to borrowers the bankers believed they could trust: people or firms who could earn the means of repaying the loans, who were honest enough to repay them, and (in many cases) who pledged property which the banks could seize and sell if the borrowers failed to repay.

We will now review some implications of each of those qualities.

Confidence   Too many things could go wrong. Perfectly honest and prudent banks could fail if rumors prompted noteholders to panic, cash their notes and exhaust the banks' reserves.

Incompetent or unlucky bankers could fail by making too many bad loans to borrowers who could not or would not repay.

Dishonest bankers could too easily steal from their depositors. Or they could conceal big losses, safe from detection as long as they kept their customers' confidence.

Competition could be dangerous to bank safety. How do banks compete for business? Among other ways, they can do it by offering higher interest to depositors, by lending at lower interest, and by lending to riskier borrowers than their competitors do. Each of those means can reduce the banks' safety and increase depositors' and noteholders' risks. Experienced business people may know that, and prefer to deal with the more conservative banks. But when banks compete for the custom of inexperienced people or risky borrowers, bad banking can beat good. That in turn can drive the good bankers to shave their reserves and safety margins in order to survive.

Safety   Thus to become a *safe* source of money and banking services, the private banks needed help from government. They needed regulation and auditing to keep each other honest and to let their customers know if they were solvent and holding adequate reserves. And they needed an emergency source of ready cash for any bank which suffered a panic 'run' and could not immediately meet all its customers' demands for cash.

Step by step through the last two centuries, governments have acted to meet those needs. But in acting to make banking safer for all concerned, they have created institutions and rules which also allow them to influence the banks' policies for other purposes, for example to determine how much credit they can create and on what terms. Rules to ensure the banks' safety are called *prudential*. Measures to influence their activities for other purposes – to encourage investment, increase employment, restrain inflation, balance foreign payments, and so on – are called *economic* regulation. But whatever their original intentions, a lot of the regulations actually serve both purposes. That is an important fact which some governments have failed to understand. We will presently notice how some recent financial deregulation, intended only to free the banks from *economic* control, has allowed them to behave imprudently in ways which have damaged their *safety* (and consequently their economic performance too, in some cases).

But first, two lists: the main means of prudential regulation, then the range and variety of economic regulations that national governments have applied to their financial systems at one time or another.

Prudential regulation

Government licenses private banks. It requires that they be audited, publish regular accounts, and submit to supervision by the Central Bank. It specifies the kinds of business that banks may and may not do. It specifies a minimum proportion of their funds that they must hold in reserve or as capital, and the forms in which they may hold it. Notes and coins, deposits in the Central Bank and saleable government bonds and Treasury notes are the main forms. (Treasury notes are short-term loans to government.)

The Central Bank acts as lender of last resort to the commercial banks. If there is a run on a bank and its customers withdraw so much money that its reserve is exhausted, the Central Bank will lend it whatever is necessary to meet its customers' demands. In doing that the Central Bank is not giving anything away. The commercial bank is in trouble from being illiquid, not insolvent. As its borrowers repay their loans it will repay the Reserve loan and rebuild its own reserve. But the fact that the lender of last resort is known to be there, and to represent the government, is usually enough to maintain confidence and prevent runs on the banks. As long as the facility is there it rarely has to be used.

Banks can of course fail more seriously and become insolvent, owing more than they can expect to recover from their borrowers. That usually comes of making too

many imprudent loans to borrowers who can't repay them. Some countries' Central Banks are empowered to close any insolvent bank or force its sale to solvent owners.

Economic regulation

The powers which are used to keep banks safe and solvent can also be used for other purposes, for example to influence rates of interest, and the total supply of money and credit. Through those effects, governments can influence rates of investment, of employment and unemployment, and of inflation. They can influence the distribution of wealth and income. And the powers can be extended to influence the balance of payments and the rates of exchange with other national currencies. Any prudential legislation is likely to have some economic effects, beyond merely keeping the banks safe. And the regulations can be extended to serve a range of economic purposes. Thus there is considerable overlap between between prudential regulation and economic regulation.

Governments regulate banks and other financial institutions for a wide range of economic and social purposes. The main ways of doing it include action to influence -

- rates of interest
- the quantities and directions of lending
- the amounts which banks may borrow, on what terms, from what sources
- the operations of other financial institutions, including savings banks, building societies, credit unions, and insurance and superannuation institutions
- rates of exchange with foreign currencies, rights to buy or borrow foreign funds, and what people are allowed to do with any foreign funds that they earn or buy or borrow.

Interest rates Loans with different risks, with different administrative costs and for different periods of time commonly pay different rates of interest. Some loans are at fixed rates. Others pay rates which vary with prevailing market rates through the period of the loans, so that neither lender nor borrower knows in advance what the whole interest bill will be.

Most money markets have some base rates to which the other rates are roughly related. A common base rate is the rate currently paid on loans to government. As that rate rises or falls, so do the higher rates for risk, for shorter or longer terms, and so on. Here we will disregard differentials for risk, etc., and focus on the behavior of the whole set of rates over time.

The rate of interest is the price of credit – the price you pay for the use of borrowed money. There are some market relations between the demand and supply and price of credit, but they are different from the relations between the demand and supply and price of most market goods. If the rate of interest rises, the demand for credit tends to decline, as with other goods. *But so does the supply.* Unlike most other goods, a low price tends to *increase* the supply and a high price tends to *reduce* it. Why? Because prudent bankers only lend to borrowers who are likely to repay. The lower the rate of interest, the more borrowers can afford to pay it. The more of those sound borrowers there are, the more the banks are usually willing to lend. So as the price of credit declines, the demand and supply of it may increase together if they are free to behave in a market way.

That difference between money markets and most markets for goods is critically important. Some geometry may help to plant it firmly in your memory. Figure 50.1 compares relations between demand, supply and price in the markets for carrots and for credit:

That relation has been common in normal times, but not reliably so. There have been occasional wild credit-fuelled booms in property or share prices, when the demand, supply and price of creditt soared togther then collapsed together. Neither in normal nor in wild times does the credit market show much respect for market theory.

Credit rationing   At any rate of interest there are always some borrowers whom the lenders won't trust. At any rate of interest, bank officers ration credit to those they regard as the safest borrowers at that rate. The demand for credit is *conditioned* by its price, but most credit is actually *allocated* by administrative decision, whether by the Governor of the Reserve Bank or by the loans officer of your local bank or building society. So (1) there is no market-clearing price: no rate of interest at which the supply matches the demand. The price of credit cannot perform the equilibrating function that it performs in efficient goods markets. And (2) there is no market alternative to administrative allocation of loans. The practical alternatives, and the policy questions, are about *who* should allocate credit, and *who* should decide the guidelines under which they do it.

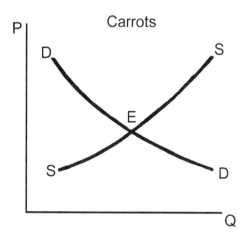
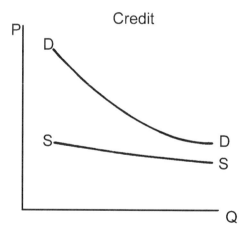

Figure 50.1 Supply and demand for carrots and for credit

There can be an equilibrium rate in another sense. In particular national conditions there may be a rate of interest which allows full employment if the other conditions allow it. By its effect on investment, that rate contributes to an equilibrium between the supply of jobs and the demand for them. But market forces of supply and demand can't be trusted to arrive at that rate. It will usually need to be contrived by government. Reasons follow.

Interest and employment Most new corporate investment is financed from the relevant firms' earnings. Some is financed by selling shares. But a varying proportion is financed with borrowed funds, and that is specially true of housing and small business investment, land development, office building and some other investment in real estate, and some of the working capital of big firms. That range of investment, and consequently of employment, tends to be sensitive to the rate of interest. New equipment which can earn 10 per cent of its cost per year is worth buying with a loan at 5 per cent interest, but not with a loan at 12.5 per cent. Each additional point of interest rules out some more borrowers. Low interest does not necessarily *cause* high employment but it *allows* it if other conditions are favorable, because of the margin of investment that it allows. And high interest tends to *limit* employment by reducing the amount of debt-financed investment.

Draw those elements of the business together and you arrive at this reasoning:

- The level and stability of the rate of interest tend to limit the amount and kind of new investment. They do so by confining credit to industries and firms whose rates of return to new investment exceed the rate of interest.

- At any time there is a set of interest rates which would allow enough investment to produce full employment if other conditions were also favorable. Call that set a full employment interest rate.

- The supply and demand for credit don't determine its price (i.e. the interest rate) in a normal market way. Even if they did, there is no reason to expect that they would arrive at a full employment interest rate.

- Nor can the forces which actually do determine rates of interest be expected to arrive at a full employment rate. Rates of interest commonly arise from 'the interaction of such factors as monetary policy, conventions employed in financial markets and the confidence in those conventions. There is no reason

to expect that those factors will combine so as to determine a long-term rate of interest which will generate a demand price for capital goods and a resultant rate of investment that will ensure full employment.' There is even less reason now that – as the next chapter will describe – countries with trade and exchange deficits balance their payments by borrowing foreign funds and have to keep their interest rates high enough to attract those funds.

- Conclusion: In a world of bank money, an efficient and stable rate of interest must be imposed by government 'as an integral part of monetary and macroeconomic policy; it does not arise spontaneously.'

Complex evidence and argument support those conclusions, which are critical of some prevailing theory and policies. To explore the debate, read Colin Rogers, *Money, Interest and Capital* (1989), from which the above quotations and conclusions come.

Interest and productivity A most important effect of the rate of interest is on the *composition* of the demand for credit. The lower the rate of interest is, the more applicants for loans there usually are. No bank lends to all the applicants. Bank officers decide *which* of them to lend to. The lower the rate of interest, the more safe options and the more productive options the lending officers have. As the rate rises there tend to be fewer willing borrowers, including fewer safe borrowers and fewer productive borrowers. This is the most basic and troublesome principle of money marketing, so it is worth spelling it out in some detail. Below are eight categories of capital borrowers, i.e. borrowers for purposes other than consumer credit. They're in a rough order – rough because there would be many individual exceptions. They're in *positive* order of likely productivity, but *inverse* order of the rate of interest they are willing or able to pay.

1. Price-takers in competitive industries, who can't mark up their prices to pay high interest. (You're a manufacturer, house-builder, trucker, or other hot competitor. You can earn 5 or 6 per cent return, with some risk, on your working capital or on the price of capital goods to expand your capacity. So it is worth borrowing at up to 3 per cent real interest but not beyond. And you must be able to rely on the rate staying low as long as you're in debt.)

2. Marginal homebuyers whose incomes can service the necessary mortgage loans only at a low rate of interest.

3. Enterprises which are usually profitable because they're monopolist, oligopolist or unusually efficient or inventive. Their rates of profit may enable them to pay any rate of interest – but those profits also enable them to finance themselves from their earnings without much need to borrow, so they generally avoid paying high interest.

4. First-home buyers with average or better incomes.

5. Investors expecting some continuing capital gain as well as income.

6. Developers using borrowed money to create assets (such as office or apartment blocks) whose rents could not service their debt – but the developers hope to sell the assets quickly to permanent owners investing their own money.

7. Firms attempting debt-financed takeovers, or buying and selling assets for quick capital gains.

8. Financial speculators gambling on future rates of inflation, interest and exchange; and other enterprises dealing in forward markets to reduce their risks from those instabilities.

There are important exceptions to the inverse relation between price and productivity. Some of the most fertile lending is to productive enterprises experimenting with promising but untried products or markets or methods of production. The rates of interest rightly match the estimated risks. But promising ventures of that kind are comparatively few, and most of the providers of 'venture capital' finance such innovators by buying some of their shares rather than by lending money to them. So they don't attract much of the flow of credit. For most of that flow it remains true that the lower the prevailing rates of interest, the more productive borrowers the banks can find, especially from the first two groups listed above.

Altogether it is a complicated market with many exceptions to those group descriptions. There are likely to be *some* borrowers from most of the groups at *any* level of interest. Nevertheless the net effect is as described: the higher the base rate of interest before adjustments for costs and risks, the fewer the safe borrowers and productive borrowers, and the less productive the banks' lending decisions and the overall allocation of resources are likely to be. Any theory that the capital market can get funds used most productively by allocating them to the borrowers who can pay highest for them is simply false. Despite the individual exceptions, competent lenders can usually allocate their funds more productively the *lower* the rate of interest is.

Influence or regulation? Governments wishing to influence the whole volume of credit may try to do it in one of two indirect ways. They may vary the capital reserves which the banks are required to hold, to influence the amount they are allowed to lend. Or they may vary the rate of interest the government offers to pay for the money it borrows, expecting private interest rates to adjust to that base rate and thus to influence the volume of lending. Neither will necessarily produce a rate of interest which allows national resources to be fully employed. And neither can discriminate, except in the crudest way, between better and worse uses of credit.

Hence the resort to direct regulation of interest rates. Governments at various times have regulated the rates of interest which may be paid on bank deposits, and on a range of loans including loans to government, housing loans, hire-purchase and credit-card accounts. Typically, regulators fix the rates at which financial institutions can borrow or the rates at which they can lend, rather than both. Fixing the rates at which they can borrow prevents them from inflating interest rates by out-bidding one another for available funds. Fixing the rates at which they can lend has a similar effect because it imposes a market limit on the rates at which they can afford to borrow. They can still compete by offering different types of service, or by cutting their operating costs to reduce the margin between the rates at which they borrow and lend. (They call that margin the 'spread'.) A common regulation used to prohibit banks from paying *any* interest on demand deposits, i.e. on cheque accounts which allow depositors to withdraw cash at any time without notice.

If they are competently designed and administered (as they have often been) such direct controls can have a number of advantages.

Quantities and uses of credit In practice no economy has just one flow of credit. Other institutions besides banks borrow and lend money. Government cannot hope to regulate interest on every kind of credit. But if it regulates some flows but not others, lenders may switch funds from the regulated to the unregulated sectors. So to regulate interest rates effectively, government may also need to regulate some of the quantities and directions of lending. And that may be desirable for other reasons besides regulating rates of interest. To cope with those problems the following methods have worked satisfactorily at some times and places. You're already familiar with the first two.

- *Public bank money* Public banks can create credit, or new debt-free money, for public purposes.

- **Private bank money** Government limits the amount of private bank credit by specifying the capital reserves the banks must hold, and their permissible capital/lending ratios. The Central Bank may also demand special deposits from the banks, which don't count as reserves, and thus further limit their lending.

- **Quantities and directions of lending** Central banks can ask or direct private banks to vary their lending for particular purposes. For example they may be asked to vary upward or downward, by some small percentage, their current lending for agriculture, for industry, for housing, for consumer credit, or for other specified purposes. The requests are for general categories of lending, not for favors for particular borrowers.

- **Portfolio requirements** are rules which have often been applied to savings banks, building societies, life insurers and other financial institutions. They could in principle be applied to commercial banks, though in practice it might take a long time for established banks to bring their lending into line with the requirements. Under such rules, it could be a condition of holding a banking licence that at least (say) 20 per cent of the bank's lending should be to government, and 20 per cent should be for housing, at specified rates of interest. The rest of their lending could remain as free as it is now, to serve all the competitive purposes it serves now. If savings banks, building societies, credit unions and life insurers are also subject to appropriate portfolio requirements, there may then be controlled rates of interest in some sectors of the money market without driving funds away to the uncontrolled sectors – provided that there are also effective boundary controls.

- **Boundary controls** Many countries, through much of the twentieth century, regulated their people's access to foreign exchange, and their uses of it. Banks were licensed to lend and borrow in the national currency only. They could deal in foreign exchange only for approved purposes, which rarely included borrowing or lending foreign currency. You remember the trading and balance-of-payment purposes of those regulations. They also had the effect of maintaining a boundary around the national financial system, so that banks and others could not evade internal regulations by borrowing, lending or investing abroad.

We will notice other means of influencing the performance of the financial system, while allowing desirable diversity and competition, when we presently deal with other financial institutions. But before leaving the commercial banks, take time to decide what you think in a general way about the system which has private profit-seeking banks create most of the new money that a growing mixed economy needs, and create nearly all of it in the form of interest-bearing debt to private banks.

ADVANTAGES AND DISADVANTAGES OF FRACTIONAL RESERVE BANKING

Having private banks create credit backed only by fractional reserves strikes many critics as an absurd way to supply a growing and changing economic system with the money it needs. Why do we persist with such an odd practice?

Advantages

- It works. It can and does expand the amount of money and credit as the economy grows.

- We need banks to mind our money, provide cheque and other services, and accept our savings and lend them usefully to those who want loans. That work keeps bank officers in touch with the day-to-day demand for credit, and should make them the best judges of the soundness (or otherwise) of would-be borrowers. So it may be efficient and economical to have them also adjust the supply of money and credit to the demand for them, rather than have some other institution do it.

- The system's pluralism has some advantages. No one can be denied credit by a single refusal. Borrowers can shop around. Banks can specialize, or develop specialized departments, skilled in lending to particular industries. And borrowers who can't get credit on their business merits can't try to get it by applying political pressure, as they might do if government-owned banks were the main source of credit.

- The system has some elements of efficient motivation. Applicants for loans are expertly assessed by bank officers motivated to judge credit risks as accurately as they can. The rate of interest does treble duty. It deters borrowers from borrowing more than they believe they can profitably use and repay. It pays the banks' working costs. And it provides profits from which banks can expand their reserves, either directly from undistributed profit or by paying their owners dividends which attract new shareholding capital.

Disadvantages

- Relations between the supply, demand and price of credit are not those of an efficient market as economists understand efficient markets. There is no market mechanism to determine what the base or average rate of interest should be, or what total amount of credit is created at any time. The cost of producing credit varies very little with the amount produced, and the supply curve for credit is unlike the supply curve for most market commodities. High interest may depress demand for credit but does not necessarily increase the supply of it. Banks don't sell credit like shops sell butter, to everyone willing to pay its price. Competent banks lend only to sound borrowers, and those tend to be fewer the higher the rate of interest is. Where low interest prevails and attracts high demand, supply also tends to be high because there are more sound borrowers. It follows that relations between total demand, total supply and price tend to be socially inefficient. Banks have sometimes expanded credit during booms and contracted it during recessions, intensifying the business cycle's fluctuations instead of smoothing them.

- There is no reliable market mechanism to direct the banks' lending to the most productive or socially desirable uses. You already know some of the reasons for that. Open competition for funds can't allocate them most productively between housing and other uses, or between household and household. Between industries, it is rarely true that the most productive uses are the ones which can pay the highest interest. Monopolists can often pay higher interest than competitive enterprises can. People investing for short terms for unproductive capital gains can often pay higher interest than farmers can, or manufacturers with long investment lead times needing long loans.

- Although market forces can't be relied on to determine an efficient rate of interest, trading conditions can push rates up or down, and many governments now push them up and down. The changing rates have other effects besides simple price effects. For many borrowers the stability of the rate of interest is as important as its level. *High* interest discriminates against some productive uses of credit. *Fluctuating* interest discriminates against other productive uses – for example in housing, and in competitive industries with long investment lead times. And in competitive industries with long lead times, big firms can usually

finance long-term investment from share capital or retained profits, but young or small firms often can't. So high or unstable interest rates can discriminate against young and small enterprises, regardless of their potential productivity.

- Although government can create unindebted money, it chooses to have private banks create most new money as interest-bearing debt. It then finances varying proportions of public investment by borrowing from those banks or from some of their customers.

Think about that last principle. Government rightly finances most public investment partly from taxation and partly from capital funds. It can create debt-free capital funds if it wants to. The amount needed is rarely as much, in any year, as the desirable increase in the money supply in a growing economy. So the increase of money for the economy as a whole can be made up of some public bank money for the public sector, and some private bank money for the private and household sectors. But in peacetime most governments choose, instead, to have the private sector create all the new money. Then they borrow private funds to finance public works. They must then tax their citizens to repay the debt or pay perpetual interest on it.

Alternatives

Plenty of critics, including some of the most conservative economists, have wanted to reform the system. Some of the proposals are crazy but among the sane ones are four, three of which are made up of components which have all operated successfully at one time or another in advanced mixed economies:

1. **Public and private money** Commercial banks should create the credit the private and household sectors need, as now, but public investment funds should be created by the Central Bank. Depending on other policies the funds may be created debt-free, or lent to their users (government departments, local governments, public enterprises) at low interest. There is currently some support in Canada, the United States and New Zealand for a scheme called 'Sovereign' which would have the Central Bank lend interest-free but strictly repayable funds to public investors.

2. **Separate money markets** The principle of (1) can be extended wherever government believes that particular industries or activities should have credit on better terms than commercial banks can provide. Export banks (like the Swedish one), housing banks

(like the Norwegian one), farmers' banks (like some Australian ones) and other special-purpose banks are publicly owned and their funds are augmented where necessary by the Central Bank. Meanwhile most business banking continues to be done by commercial banks, which continue to create money and credit as needed for their sector of the market.

3. **Public money, private banking** New money is created only by the Central Bank, which lends it to the private banks in quantities, and at rates of interest, determined by public policy in the light of market demand. As the money then circulates, the bank multiplier is frustrated by the Reserve Bank's management of its reserve requirements, special deposits, portfolio requirements and other means of influence. Within those constraints the commercial banks continue to compete with each other and to serve their usual customers as they do now.

4. **Wholly public banking** The banks are nationalized. Apart from that, the existing system continues. Commercial banks compete, serve their usual customers, and create new money under Central Bank guidelines as they do now. But with all banks publicly owned, they can on occasion be directed to operate with other purposes than profit. An Australian government tried to do this, but was prevented when courts decided that nationalizing private banks was unconstitutional. At the time, one leading commercial bank was owned by the national government, all the savings banks and farmers' banks were owned by State governments, and the public managers were generally honest and competent, so the change would not have been as radical as it might seem in —for example – the United States.

Wherever there is reasonably honest and competent government, any of those systems might well work better than the present system does. Later chapters will argue that the freer and more market-efficient you want industry and trade to be, the more strictly governed the financial system needs to be. Stricter government, and some shift from private bank money to public bank money, would be strongly resisted. But if you want a life as an inventive reformer battling against formidable opponents, money and banking may be your field.

So much for the way money and credit are created. Once in circulation money is repeatedly spent and saved, lent and borrowed. Those activities employ many financial institutions besides Central and commercial banks.

SAVINGS BANKS, BUILDING SOCIETIES, CREDIT UNIONS

Make a rough distinction between creating money and credit, and distributing them. Commercial banks do both. Within regulated limits they decide how much credit to create, who should get it, and on what terms. What they create is a small fraction of the whole volume of money they handle as they lend money, are repaid, lend it again, and so on; but they can and do create most additions to the whole supply of it.

If on the other hand *you* lend *me* money, you don't create any of it: it is already-existing money, and you do without it until I repay it. A range of institutions exist to organize that relation between us: to accept deposits from us, mind our money and lend it for us, without adding much to it.

(Two complexities: (1) These institutions do affect the whole supply of money and credit in marginal ways, but for simplicity we will concentrate on their distributive functions. (2) New technology, business practice and public policies have recently been giving some of these institutions some of the commercial banks' powers and freedoms, more so in some countries than in others. But we will begin with the savings institutions' original and distinctive features, which some of them still retain. We can then compare the performance of those which have been and those which have not been deregulated.)

Savings banks accept your savings, pay you interest for them, and lend them at higher interest, mostly to homebuyers or to government. In their traditional form they were not allowed to provide the cheque accounts which were the commercial banks' specialty.

Building societies do the same, but have usually lent more exclusively to homebuyers.

Most of the original savings banks and all the building societies were non-profit. They were mutual – i.e. they belonged to their depositors and distributed any profits to them – or they belonged to government, often to provincial or local government. They were founded to encourage thrift and to care for the savings of working people; to help them to buy their houses; and in the case of many of the savings banks, to finance public investment. Whether publicly owned or not, they were soon strictly regulated. The rules varied from country to country, but most governments required the institutions to –

• be chartered or registered by government

• accept regular inspection

- accept only personal deposits
- provide no cheque services
- lend only what they borrowed and (to provide reserves) not all of that
- lend only to government or on mortgage on residential or small-business property, and sometimes only to owner-occupiers, not to commercial landlords
- pay depositors no more than specified rates of interest
- insure their customers' deposits or have them guaranteed by government.

Those or similar rules kept the institutions safe, economical and serviceable to their communities. Other rules gave them some protection from commercial competition. Commercial banks were not allowed to pay interest on cheque accounts, so they could not compete for most people's savings deposits. They were allowed to pay interest on term deposits (deposits for fixed periods), but some countries limited them to lower rates than savings banks or building societies were allowed to pay on term deposits. As mutual institutions which returned any profits to their members rather than to shareholders, some countries exempted savings banks and building societies from company tax.

Risks

Institutions which use customers' deposits to finance long-term mortgage loans to homebuyers have special risks because they 'borrow short to lend long'. Lending to homebuyers is one of the safest kinds of credit, and as long as interest rates are stable it yields a steady inflow of interest and repayments. But depositors are less reliable, with demand deposits which they can withdraw at any time. In practice their average tendency to save and their total deposits are often steady for long periods. But the total can fluctuate with booms and slumps, and it can fluctuate if there are fluctuating interest rates in unregulated sectors of the money market, so that depositors withdraw their money to get better rates for it elsewhere. So without any panic 'runs' on the institutions' reserves, they are always in some danger of illiquidity: of their depositors demanding more money back than the institutions can get back at short notice from their long-term homebuyers. But through most of their history, Central Banks have not acted as lenders of last resort to these institutions, as they have done for commercial banks.

One or other of four devices has kept most of the institutions safe through most of the last fifty years.

Government-owned savings banks have automatic guarantees: government has to act, if necessary, as lender of last resort.

Whether or not government founded them, most savings banks have divided their lending between homebuyers and government. To lend to government they buy government bonds, municipal bonds, public utility bonds. Though those are for fixed terms and often for long terms, the bonds are marketable: they can be sold at any time through stock exchanges. A savings bank with a quarter or more of its loans in that form has abundant potential liquidity.

It has even more if its housing loans are at fixed rates of interest and its country has a secondary mortgage market. In a secondary mortgage market, lenders can sell their existing loans to other institutions which are not staffed to negotiate and issue home loans, but are happy to invest in them (i.e., to buy them) once they're signed and sealed and the interest and repayments are flowing in. For home lenders, a secondary market has two attractions. In bad times, if deposits are dwindling, loans can be reduced correspondingly by selling some of them. And in good times, the institution can lend more than it borrows. It can make loans then sell them, earning fees for its services. And if rates of inflation and market rates of interest decline, it may be possible to sell long-term fixed-interest loans for more than the borrowers were lent.

(Suppose that some years ago you lent a homebuyer $120 000 for 28 years at a fixed interest rate of 10 per cent. Repayments have reduced the capital debt to $100 000, and the market rate of interest has declined to 8 per cent and is not expected to rise again. At the market rate it now takes $125 000 to earn the $10 000 of annual interest that loan is paying, so you should be able to sell it for (say) $120 000, for a 20 per cent capital profit.)

Building societies typically don't lend to government and don't lend at fixed rates of interest, so they need other defences against the risks of borrowing short and lending long. The main defence is an aspect of their 'mutual' nature. In principle a building society is not a bank dealing with customers. As its name implies it is an association of people cooperating and sharing risks. It typically conducts *all* its business at prevailing market rates of interest. If deposits dwindle, the society can raise its deposit rate of interest far enough to attract enough deposits to stay liquid. And to pay the higher rate to depositors, the lending rate can also rise, on existing as well as new home loans. Because that flexibility is basic to their safety, governments which license and regulate building societies don't usually limit the rates of interest they can offer to depositors. That freedom allowed them some market advantage over banks when bank deposit rates were still regulated.

Credit unions are typically groups of people with some common bond: they work in the same occupation or for the same employer, or live in the same neighborhood. To register them, most governments require that there be such a bond. Like savings banks and building societies they accept their members' savings and lend to their members. They can lend only to their members, and most of them have not done much long-term mortgage lending. Their main business is usually consumer credit: they make unsecured personal loans. They help you buy your car, computer, audiovisual gear, refrigerator, washing machine, furniture, holidays. Many of them are small or homogenous enough for members to trust each other and get a lot of their business done by voluntary labor. Low working costs allow them to operate with the lowest 'spread' in the business between their borrowing and lending rates, so they can often offer the best terms to both depositors and borrowers. Governments register them, limit the kinds of business they are allowed to do, sometimes insure their depositors against loss, and regularly inspect their books.

Performance of the savings institutions As long as they were competently regulated, the savings institutions (savings banks, building societies and credit unions) tended on balance to be stabilizers of national financial systems. They turned household savings into safe loans through the saving and borrowing phases of household life. They were good sources of public investment funds. They usually maintained more stable flows of credit through boom and slump than the credit-creating commercial banks did. Public ownership or regulation were a necessary condition of their steady performance. There were many failures in the nineteenth century, and in the depression of 1929-31 in the US, before there was effective regulation; and there were spectacular failures wherever the institutions were deregulated in the 1980s.

But when properly regulated, the savings institutions have generally served their own customers well, and done more good than harm to their national financial systems. What they cannot do is adjust the whole supply of money to the need for it. Commercial banks do most of that in normal times. Central banks might do it better, and if they did, the commercial banks might operate as the savings institutions do, primarily as distributors rather than creators of credit.

LIFE INSURANCE

Some life insurance institutions are share-owned, profit-seeking companies. Others have the legal form of mutual-benefit associations owned by all their policy-holders, i.e. by everyone who insures with them. Life institutions offer two services. They insure you against the risk of death: pay a first premium, die next day, and your heirs are entitled to the whole capital sum for which you insured. And they accept your savings, usually as regular contributions (misleadingly called premiums) and accumulate a cash entitlement for you. The entitlement is based on the amount of your contributions plus what they would have earned at a notional rate of compound interest, minus a discount for the insurer's costs and risks. You or your heirs can take the cash as a lump sum or pension. How much you get, when, and in what form, depends on the terms of your contract (misleadingly called your policy). The insurance and saving services come in different proportions in the three basic kinds of policy that the institutions offer:

Term policies insure your life for a specified period. If you die during that period, your heirs get the sum insured. If you survive, you get nothing. Why buy insurance you're unlikely to collect? You may be young, with dependants and a big mortgage. If you die, your heirs may be in trouble. Term insurance for as long as they depend on your earnings is very cheap, because you are very likely to survive and cost the insurer nothing. Moreover you may have no choice – you may have to insure your life as a condition of the mortgage loan.

Whole life policies pay your heirs whenever you die. You may pay premiums until then. Or you pay (higher) premiums for a fixed term – commonly until your retiring age – then no more until death. Most policies can alternatively yield cash during your lifetime in one of two ways. The insurer keeps an account of your accumulating premiums and their investment earnings at some notional rate of interest. You can cancel the policy and get a proportion of that cash value back. Or you can continue the policy and borrow from the insurer, using that cash value as security.

Endowment policies are like whole-life policies except that the pay-out is at a specified date (commonly your retiring age) unless you collect by dying before then. When the policy matures you may take a capital pay-out and invest it to yield income in your retirement, or you may take your payout in the form of a life pension from the insurer. If you take the capital you can preserve it for your heirs. If you opt for a pension it is usually calculated to include capital repayment as well as investment income, so there's nothing for your heirs. Die soon, and the insurer wins. Live long, and the insurer loses.

Need these tedious details concern you? Yes, because they explain what sort of investors the life insurers are. That concerns government, and it may concern you as an economist, because they are now such big investors.

Life insurers as investors Life insurers take on very long-term liabilities. If you start a policy when you're 21, they make promises they may have to keep half a century ahead. Though distant, many of their obligations are fairly predictable. Individuals may die at any time but their *average* mortality is usually steady. So as long as there are no disastrous wars or epidemics, the insurers have quite good foreknowledge of the totals they must expect to pay out through future years.

To meet claims, the insurers have (1) current premium income, (2) investment income, and if necessary, (3) the capital reserves which yield the investment income. The proportions vary from company to company, but a representative insurer's income might be three quarters current premiums and one quarter investment income. The market value of the invested capital might be equal to five or six years' premium income.

Why such a big capital reserve? Policy-holders must have been over-charged for the company to accumulate it, i.e. they must have paid higher premiums than proved to be necessary to meet their claims. *Public* pensions are financed each year from that year's taxes: why can't private insurers finance each year's pay-out from that year's premium income? Answer: private insurers can never be certain that they won't suffer either a sudden concentration of claims (from wars, epidemics or natural disasters) or a decline in premium income. Premiums from the young contribute to the payments to the old. If old policy-holders expect their capital benefits but the next generation decides not to insure, or insures with other companies, a life insurer without capital reserves will soon be insolvent.

The nature of their risks and liabilities thus prompts the institutions to accumulate big reserves, and to invest them for reliable income and capital maintenance in the long term. They don't usually take big risks for big gains. They don't need much liquidity – they have plenty of that in their premium income. They don't usually want to invest as managers, i.e. to become

manufacturers, traders, transport suppliers; they want to be 'passive' suppliers of capital to be managed by others wherever the management takes specialized skill. (There are exceptions: insurers often have subsidiaries which manage rental property.) So they buy a lot of government bonds, municipal (local government) bonds, public utility debentures. They lend to the private sector by buying long-term corporate debentures. Many also buy equities – company shares – but passively as minority shareholders rather than as dominant owners of the firms in which they invest. They develop big rental properties: office blocks, apartment blocks, shopping centres. Some have invested in long-term land development: new suburbs, retirement villages, tourist centres. An Australian company turned a desert into farmland by transforming its soil with trace elements. Altogether they tend to be prudent, risk-averse, long-term, large-scale investors: good stabilizers of their national economies.

That's as long as they invest in their national economies. Should they be required to do that? Or should they be allowed to invest wherever they like in the world? That's one of a number of policy questions for government. But there is a prior question. How much private life insurance and superannuation does a society really want?

Alternative provisions for income in old age

Rich societies have various ways of supporting their retired citizens. Many Americans rely on private saving and investment, whether by individual saving, individual endowment insurance, or employers' pension schemes. There is a public, tax-financed pension for people with no other income, but for various reasons some millions of people who need it don't get it. For some decades Britain paid an inadequate public pension to everyone, with means-tested additions to those who depended entirely on the pension. Many people also had individual or corporate superannuation. Much of north western Europe has national superannuation for everyone, financed by employers' and employees' and taxpayers' contributions, and with benefits linked to contributions, so that higher earners retire with higher pensions.

Remember that real income for retired people (other than the goods and services they produce for themselves by their household labor) has to come from the output of those still working. Appropriately, most of their money income comes from those still earning, whether it comes (i) from taxation or (ii) from public or private insurance contributions. The significant differences between the national systems are really two. They have different effects on the distribution of income, and they finance different quantities of investment. The distributional effects are important for many social reasons: recall Chapter 12's exploration of relations between transferring rights to income over time and transferring income from person to person. But in this chapter we are chiefly concerned with the investment effects. They pose two strategic questions for government. (1) How much of the whole provision for old age should be provided by private superannuation, with its need for big reserve investment; and (2) what influence, if any, should government exert on the pattern of investment by life insurance and superannuation institutions?

How much investment? Considerations for and against private superannuation:

People, and firms which offer their employees superannuation schemes, may want to be able to choose between insurers. Competition between the insurers may help to keep them efficient and attentive to their clients' wants. So a 'big investment' strategy may be favored for reasons which have nothing to do with the investment effects. Once a big reserve is established, the insurers pay most of their outgoings from their current premium income. What they save and invest from then on is chiefly their investment income. That is still a substantial flow of saving. It tends to be expertly invested. And the type of investment tends to be useful. At times when rates of interest, rates of inflation and rates of exchange are unstable, many financial investors tend to have short horizons. In those conditions big, prudent, skilful investors with very long horizons – as the life insurers usually are – can be specially useful to the economy as a whole.

The case *against* relying on private or group superannuation for most people's retirement is that there are better and perhaps more popular methods. A number of north west European countries have national systems of public, compulsory, contributory, income-linked social security. Basic benefits also extend to people who can't contribute (because of unemployment, incapacity, recent immigration or other causes). People with higher incomes pay bigger contributions and draw correspondingly bigger pensions. These schemes appear to achieve what the British system tried but partly failed to do: people feel they are saving for their own old age, not being taxed to provide for others.

In Britain, higher earners pay higher contributions but (being means-tested) get smaller pensions, while poorer people pay lower contributions, or none, but draw the biggest pensions. In other English-speaking

countries the public pension has always been means-tested and tax-financed, and nowadays goes to half or less than half of the aged population. So the well-off see themselves taxed to finance pensions for the poor but nothing for themselves. Whether for that or other reasons, the tax revolt and hostility to welfare provisions has gone further in a the English-speaking world than in much of Western Europe.

So the English-speaking systems look more progressive, because the richer taxpayers don't get the higher public pensions they would get in (say) the Netherlands. But because of the stronger political support for the European system, the poorest Dutch pensioners get bigger pensions than most of their English-speaking equivalents do. That arises from the choice of rates rather than the choice of systems, but – paradoxically – the less progressive distribution of benefits to the contributors in the European system seems to go with greater generosity toward those who have been too poor to contribute.

Europeans who want more superannuation than the public system provides can buy more from private life insurers. But their public system is a monopoly backed by the power to tax, so it does not need big capital reserves and need not contribute investment funds to the capital market. Governments could, of course, decide to accumulate and invest reserves, but the pension system can work without them. Like the British and other public systems, it simply transfers income from current contributors to current pensioners.

What kinds of investment? Whatever the amount of private and mutual life insurance and superannuation, they need some prudential regulation to protect their policy-holders. There has often also been some economic regulation of their patterns of investment. The rules have changed from time to time and they differ from country to country, but their commonest concerns have been with foreign investment, with housing finance, and with loans to government and public utilities.

How far should the institutions be required to invest at home, or allowed to invest abroad?

Should the institutions be required to lend to government? Do the institutions' investments in rental housing, or their lending to homebuyers, need regulation?

Each of those activities has been regulated, and in some cases deregulated, by some governments at some times. Some reasons follow.

Foreign investment by financial institutions tends to attract public attention in countries which are short of investment and employment or short of foreign exchange, or both.

Some countries have banned foreign investment and lending by financial institutions. Some have imposed quotas: foreign assets must not exceed a specified percentage of total assets. (That can be awkward to administer if unstable exchange rates keep changing the relative values of the home and foreign assets.) Such restrictions on foreign lending and investment have been useful and effective where exchange was scarce and the home demand for investment was high. But if the institutions have long been free to invest abroad they may have accumulated foreign assets which yield more income each year than they now invest abroad each year, so there is a net gain of foreign exchange. And the investment is not always passive: British insurers have done a lot of insurance business in other countries. Freedom to lend and invest anywhere in the world is a sensible policy for winners, i.e. for countries which for the time being have surplus savings and foreign exchange – for example Britain in the nineteenth century, the United States after the Second World War, Japan now. But for those with exchange difficulties, or positive uses for their savings, boundary controls are appropriate.

Long-term government bonds used to be good investments for institutions with predictable long-term obligations. Besides central government bonds, American insurance institutions buy a lot of municipal and public utility bonds. To encourage that, the federal government exempts interest on those bonds from federal tax. Australian life insurers lived for many decades with a 30/20 rule: a tax exemption conditional on their lending at least 30 per cent of their funds to government and 20 per cent for housing, both at interest rates regulated by government. But long-term bonds became risky and less attractive with the onset of fluctuating inflation.

Lending for housing, or owning it, fits the life insurers' long-term obligations. It has adapted to inflation better than long term bonds have, by developing mortgage loans with variable interest rates. Insurance companies can lend to homebuyers. They can lend to buyers or developers of rental apartment blocks. They can own such blocks themselves. Many of them used to do a good deal of all three. Through recent decades they have retreated from making individual mortgage loans to homebuyers. To lend (say) $10 million in a hundred loans to homebuyers is troublesome and expensive compared with lending it on one mortgage loan to an apartment-block or office-building developer. And

interest rates on home lending have been lower than on other mortgage lending, sometimes for market reasons and sometimes by regulation. Some governments have found other ways of interesting institutional investors in housing. As Europe rebuilt its cities through the long post-war boom some governments offered tax concessions, subsidies or joint ventures to institutional investors financing apartment housing.

You remember why unaided market forces can't be expected to allocate capital efficiently between public investment, housing investment and other uses. Don't accept the belief that public influence on the allocation must reduce its efficiency or its social benefits. Competent government can improve both, and often has, while leaving the lenders and investors all desirable market freedoms.

OTHER FINANCIAL INSTITUTIONS

There have long been _merchant banks_ which do a variety of banking, negotiating and advisory services for business. London has _discount houses_ which act in various ways as intermediaries between the British Treasury, the Bank of England and the commercial banks. Since the deregulation of national and international financial systems there has been a great increase of financial trusts, brokers and advisers who offer to invest your money for you, or advise you how to invest it, in return for some of it.

There is also a proliferation of special financial markets. Most of them are secondary or futures markets. In _secondary markets_ you buy and sell existing financial rights or contracts. You've long been able to buy and sell company shares and debentures and government bonds on the stock market. In many countries you can now buy or sell existing mortgage loans, existing commercial debts of various kinds, existing term deposits with banks.

Forward markets let you gamble on future asset values or interest rates, much as future markets in commodities like grain or minerals let you gamble on their future market prices. There are forward markets in Treasury Bills and government bonds, mortgage loans and other financial assets whose market value and interest rates vary with market conditions. Options (in the jargon of these markets) are contracts to buy or sell shares or other property at predetermined prices at future dates. A _call option_ is an option to buy. You will exercise it, when the time comes, if the asset is by then worth more than your option price. A _put option_ is an option to sell. You will exercise it if the market price of the asset is worth less than the option price.

The forward markets are used by speculators. They are also used by traders who want to *reduce* the risks they face from changing prices, rates of interest, rates of inflation or rates of exchange. Forward trading has become busier and more complex with the end of international exchange controls, so we will deal with it more fully in the next chapter.

Whether or not the non-bank institutions and the secondary credit markets are useful to individual owners and dealers, and whether or not they improve the overall allocation of capital and credit, they have a collective ill effect. Together they make public regulation of national financial systems less accurate and effective than it could otherwise be. The main creators of money and credit are the commercial banks. But many of the other institutions do also expand or contract credit, intentionally or not, in the course of distributing and retailing it.

And some of them can be used to bypass the regulation of the commercial banks and international exchanges. So the traditional regulation of the commercial banks, and of the foreign exchanges, are less sure and effective than they once were.

Since the 1970s two political trends have made them *much* less effective than they were. One is the substantial deregulation of the commercial banks. The other is the vast growth, and the deregulation, of foreign exchange transactions. Those two are our next subjects. They are closely related, because national and international deregulation have radical effects on each other. This chapter continues the national story. The following chapter follows the parallel history of the international exchanges. There has to be frequent cross-reference from each to the other, and some repetition, because of their interaction with each other.

FINANCIAL DEREGULATION

Financial systems were deregulated step by step, over half a century, from the first easing of wartime controls in the 1940s. But for many governments the main change of mood, from confident financial regulation to a new faith in market forces (or in some cases, a reluctant surrender to them) began in the 1970s. Here is a brief review of some causes which converged to bring that change of mind.

Anticipating the next chapter, you need to know that a regime of fixed exchange rates between national currencies, and fairly strict regulation of international capital movements, had broken down by 1971. National governments resumed individual control of their exchange rates for varying periods, then 'floated' them to be determined in the market. Most of the rich countries had opened their boundaries to the free movement and exchange of capital funds by 1990.

Why did Western governments respond to the breakdown of the international financial controls, and to the onset of stagflation in their national economies, by deregulating their financial systems?

The long postwar boom had been good: high investment, full employment, fast growth, low interest rates and stable exchange rates, low inflation, generous new health and welfare services, a steady reduction of inequality. Some people concluded that the mixed economy was prospering naturally and no longer needed its earlier public controls. Many people had seen the controls as temporary, occasioned by war and postwar recovery, no longer needed now that the world was back to normal. It seemed *better* than normal to many

working people who for the first time had secure well-paid jobs, comfortable housing, cars, reliable welfare services – and increasingly conservative opinions. Seen from below, capitalism looked better than it used to look from below. Business voices recovered some of the respect and influence they had lost through the disastrous depression between the wars.

But by 1970 the long boom had stalled. Stagflation – the simultaneous increase of unemployment and inflation – was new and unexpected. Many people thought it discredited the public controls which had failed to prevent it – or had even caused it, some conservative economists said.

Those shifts of opinion made it easier to argue for freer enterprise, smaller government, lower taxation and more faith in market forces. Some interested parties were ready to seize the opportunity. Many rich and well-off people had always opposed the big government, high taxation and generous welfare that characterized the long boom. Bankers and capital owners could hope to be freer and richer the less they were regulated. Many employers disliked the bargaining strength which labor had with full employment, and with welfare incomes available to the unemployed. When stagflation discredited the theory of managed full employment, neoclassical economists who had never accepted Keynesian theory regained their former influence. Private money financed a large number of private research centres – 'think tanks' – to develop and propagate arguments for privatizing the public sector, deregulating the private sector and reducing the taxation of the rich. It was as if the appearance of flaws in the postwar economic system prompted the rich and conservative forces in society to recover their nerve and turn from defence to counter-attack, to 'roll back the state' and reverse the trend to greater equality. Social democrats still hoped to repair the full-employment policies and move ahead to even greater security and equality. But from the 1980s, the winners in many of the advanced countries' elections were now leaders (including leaders of some labor and social-democratic parties) who proceeded to dismantle a good deal of the social-democratic government of the economy, rather than try to repair it.

Politicians had some professional reasons for welcoming a change of direction. They faced difficult, easily criticized decisions about exchange rates now that they were again responsible for them. National and international financial regulations were becoming harder to design and enforce as they were evaded by ingenious new legal and technological means. The freer the currency traders became, the more effectively they could intimidate any government which tried to regain some control of them. Governments were also blamed for the growth of unemployment and inflation. One way or another, politicians could imagine that deregulation might reduce their troubles. If the market theorists were right, deregulation would allow market forces to balance the foreign exchanges and restore full employment. If the theorists were wrong, a deregulated world might at least blame market forces, rather than politicians, for its stagflation and exchange deficits.

In those conditions, as part of the general shift of economic policies to the Right, national and international financial systems were extensively deregulated through the 1970s and 1980s. Different governments took different steps at different dates. Internationally there were crises, conferences, some cooperative action by Central Banks, and occasional attempts to apply the brakes or restore some of the lost controls. But the overall effect was a substantial freeing of the national and international activities of banks and other financial institutions, including new kinds of institutions which were created to exploit the new freedoms.

LOST CONTROLS

You don't need to learn the step-by-step history of deregulation through the 1970s and 1980s. But it is very important to know (1) which controls were removed, (2) how capital owners, banks and other financial institutions have used the new freedom, and (3) how much of the new activity is unproductive or anti-productive, not

because people are wilfully misbehaving, but because defective market rules make such behavior lawful and rational for them.

The main changes have been as follows.

Fractional reserves   Since 1988 in many OECD countries the amount of credit which commercial banks are allowed to create is no longer limited by the reserves they hold. It is limited instead by rules of 'risk-weighted capital adequacy', which supplement reserve requirements in some countries but replace them in most countries.

Risk-weighted capital adequacy   works like this. Central banks require commercial banks to hold capital of their own equal to a specified percentage of the amount they lend. It is commonly 5 per cent, so for each dollar a bank owns, it can lend twenty. But its loans are rated for risk, so the safer they are, the more a given amount of capital allows a bank to lend, up to the twenty-fold limit. The risk categories vary from country to country, but in a representative system banks may be required to own capital equal to –

- 8 per cent of loans to business, to individuals, and to all borrowers in countries outside the OECD (i.e. in developing countries and ex-communist countries)

- 4 per cent of loans secured on residential property, and loans to public enterprises within the OECD

Loans to governments within the OECD are regarded as so safe they require no capital backing. It follows that – up to the limit of twenty times its capital – a bank can lend more the more it lends to government and on house mortgages, and the less it lends to business or the riskier class of foreigners. A bank with $5m capital has a top lending limit of $100m, because of the 5 per cent rule. But whether it can lend the whole $100m depends on its choice of borrowers. Disregarding the intermediate class of risk for the moment, $5m of capital allows it to lend –

- $100m if all its loans are to government

- $100m if no more than $62.5m is lent to business and the rest to government.   (Its $5m capital is the required 8 per cent of the $62.5m lent to business.)

- $62.5m if all its loans are to business.

- totals between $62.5m and $100m, depending on the proportions of full-risk, half-risk and no-risk loans.

Suppose a bank with $5m capital has lent its permitted limit of $62.5m to business. If it has more deposits, it can create up to $37.5m more credit as long as it lends it to government. Critics focus on distributional and other effects of that. With the new incentive, private banks now buy many more government bonds than they used to buy. (Canadian banks increased their holdings from $3.7 billion to $32.1 billion in the first six years of the new rules, for example.They were helped by their government abolishing the reserve requirement altogether.) To the extent that private banks have displaced public banks as bondholders, taxpayers are paying interest to private financiers for public funds which would be interest-free if the bonds were taken up (as more of them used to be) by public banks whose profits return to their government owners. That's a distributional complaint. There is also some fear that the new rules may deter economic innovation and growth by biasing banks against lending to business, especially small or risky business.

Interest rates Central banks still exert strong influence on rates of interest, but no longer by regulating them directly. They fix the rates paid on government bonds, Treasury notes and commercial banks' deposits with the Central Bank. Private banks mostly accept those as the current base rates, and add their margins for costs and risks accordingly. But there have been changes in the purposes for which the public authorities influence the rates, and in the constraints within which they do it. Since the international movement of capital funds was freed, national interest rates have become important in influencing where footloose funds go, and where they go affects national balances of payment. Three purposes for which governments may influence interest rates – to encourage investment and employment, to restrain inflation, and to attract capital funds to balance international payments – are often now in conflict, harmfully to one or more of the three purposes.

The distribution of credit Except for the broad categories of risk in the capital adequacy rules, governments in most English-speaking and most Central and South American countries no longer regulate or directly influence the way in which commercial banks distribute their lending to particular industries or types of borrower. Where special-purpose public banks already existed (for example for farming, for housing, for export/import credit) many of them continue, especially in continental Europe; but new ones are not created, as needs arise, as readily as they once were.

Savings banks – public, mutual or private – are an old-established type of special-purpose bank. They continue their special roles in Britain, France, Japan and elsewhere. They have usually been limited by law to (1) lending the deposits they could attract from individual depositors, without bulk-borrowing from other financial institutions, and (2) lending to government, or for housing, and sometimes for farming. In practice those economic restraints served also as quite effective prudential controls – but it was easy not to notice that. In the 1980s the US government and some Australian State governments called off the lending restrictions without providing adequate new prudential controls. The US Savings and Loan institutions quickly lost about $450 billion. Some of the Australian institutions lost on a similar scale per head of their State populations. Governments rescued the depositors, and taxpayers are still paying the costs of doing so.

Other financial institutions Some countries used to require insurance and superannuation institutions to keep all or most of their assets in their own country, and to lend specified proportions of their funds to government and for housing at regulated rates of interest. Most of those controls have ceased.

Hire-purchase companies, and other institutions which borrow in order to lend, are regulated prudentially for safety and sometimes for consumer protection. So are a range of property trusts and investment trusts which manage funds on behalf of their owners.

Foreign exchange Most Western governments used to control their currencies' exchange rates, and regulate the import and export of capital funds. They no longer do so. In most advanced economies now, anyone with money can change it freely into any other convertible currency. The international uses of this freedom are the next chapter's business, but its most important effect is to weaken the internal government of national financial systems. Government can't regulate interest rates effectively if that can drive funds out of the country to find better rates elsewhere. Portfolio requirements (that institutions lend specified proportions of their funds to particular industries or types of borrower) don't serve their national purposes if the required lending can be abroad, or if the rules can be avoided altogether by moving funds abroad.

Open frontiers don't only weaken government's powers. They also weaken market disciplines. If private banks can borrow any amount of money from foreigners, and private owners can sell any amount of income-earning assets to foreigners, market forces cannot stop a country spending more on imports than its exports earn. As debts to foreigners increase, and foreigners own more of the nation's assets, less and less of current foreign earnings will be available to pay for imports because more and more will be preempted to pay interest, rent and dividends to foreigners. Market discipline won't bite until the creditors begin to doubt the debtor country's capacity to earn enough exchange to service its foreign debts. But then it may bite deep into the national standard of living. These effects of free trade in money are a main subject of the next chapter.

SUMMARY OF THE NEW FINANCIAL FREEDOMS

If you own a million American or Canadian or Australian dollars now, what can you do with them?

Individuals As an active individual investor you can use the money to start a business, buy a business, or expand a business you already own.

As a simple property investor you can buy real estate – offices, shops, warehouses, houses – and live on the rents. As a more ambitious property investor you can use your million as a deposit on a mortgage loan of two or three millions, buy three or four millions' worth of property, and use the rents to pay the bank interest. You thus 'gear up' or 'leverage' your million.

As a passive investor who doesn't want the bother of maintaining real estate and collecting rents, you can buy stocks and shares or deposit your money in an interest-bearing term account at your bank. Buy a portfolio of bonds, debentures and equities (shares) with a suitable balance of income and risk, and live on the interest and dividends through the years to come.

With either real estate or stocks and shares you can also hope for some capital gains if the market prices of your assets increase over time.

Those alternatives may not be the ways to earn most from your million, or to earn fastest. The market prices of many assets keep changing. If you're smart and lucky, you may be able to make more by frequent trading. Buy things whose prices you expect to rise. Sell them after they've risen. Sell things whose prices you expect to fall, and buy them back after they've fallen. Kerry Packer sold a television network to Alan Bond for $800 million and bought it back two years later for $300 million. You can also trade on the increasingly complicated forward markets that were sketched earlier, and are described more fully in the next chapter.

Depending how you invest your million, its earnings may pay company and payroll taxes, capital gains tax, income tax and – eventually – gift tax, inheritance tax or capital transfer tax. What can you do about that if you're the type who likes to enjoy an advanced economy's public goods without paying for your share of them? Export your fortune. Invest it in a tax haven. Or leave the fortune where it is but export the ownership of it. For example, create a family trust in Switzerland, where there is less income tax. The trust becomes the owner and investor of your million. As a perpetual trust it pays no inheritance or gift or capital transfer taxes. Whether you pay tax on the income or capital gain which the trust pays to you may depend on your country's tax law or your lawyer's ingenuity. But you can escape almost any other country's income tax by living in Switzerland, or by arranging to sleep less than 183 nights in any one country in any tax year, so that no government can claim you as a resident taxpayer.

For our present purpose the methods of tax evasion don't matter. What matters is that for some decades from 1940 your government did not let you export capital funds for your own advantage without due care for effects on the national economy as a whole. Now it does allow individuals, firms and financial institutions to do that. Institutions do a lot more of it than individuals do.

Institutions Banks still offer most of their traditional services. They mind your money, make your payments, help your accounting, pay interest on any money you deposit with them for a fixed term. They lend to individuals, households, firms, and finance a wide range of consumer credit and payment services. And by expanding credit, they keep the supply of money up to the need for it.

There has been some growth of other finncial institutions, especially intermediaries who offer to do your lending or investing for you. Finance companies, investment companies, investment trusts and property trusts of various kinds borrow money in order to invest it. Banks in some countries, led by the US, will invest funds for you. Some of them give unusual credit to fund managers of whom they approve. If you confide your million to a 'hedge fund' in a country which allows such activity, the bank may gear it up with ten or more further millions, rather than the two or three they might lend you as an individual borrower. The ten millions it lends are secured on the stocks and shares which the fund manager buys. Most of the dividend and interest income goes to pay bank interest on the ten millions advanced. Most of your gains or losses come from re-selling the capital assets. If you have to sell at a time when their market prices have declined 10 per cent, you lose your million. Why take such a risk? Because if share prices *rise* 10 per cent, as they have often done, you can pick your time to sell and *double* your million. This sort of gearing has much the same effect as the 'buying on margin' which fuelled the great share-price boom and then crash of the 1920s.

The following chapter will deal with the deregulation of exchanges and movements of capital funds between national currencies. That interacts with the internal deregulation of national financial systems to allow a number of new activities, and economic and political effects. The new freedom allows new kinds of gambling, mostly unproductive. It shifts some power from governments to private banks. And it reduces both the capacity of *government* to maintain investment and full employment, and the capacity of *market forces* to generate investment and full employment and to balance international trade and payments.

National sovereignty

By signing the latest revision of the General Agreement on Tariffs and Trade (GATT) and joining the World Trade Organization (WTO) each participating government of a developed country has given up the right to limit imports to what the country's foreign earnings can pay for. It has given up the right to ration available foreign exchange and direct it to its best uses. Governments of countries with trade or exchange deficits can no longer prevent private banks from borrowing foreign funds to finance a continuing increase of imports, exchange deficit and foreign debt.

Notice how both regulation and deregulation encourage the continuing increase of private international debt. Economic deregulation allows the banks to do it. But continuing prudential regulation makes it safe for foreign banks to lend to them. Their home government's 'lender of last resort' guarantee is an informal but effective government guarantee of their debts. It was designed to rescue them from illiquidity, which can afflict any bank. But in practice though not in law it has come to protect them from insolvency too, i.e. from the consequences of incompetent banking. However badly American banks behave, the US government and taxpayers rescue them. That final security weakens the other prudential controls over directors who know their banks won't be allowed to fail however badly they misuse their powers and resources.

These effects will be clearer as future chapters deal with governments' means of balancing foreign exchange, restraining inflation and influencing investment and employment. Deregulating the banks' national and international activities affects all those public capacities. Tracing its effects in each of them in turn involves some repetition. Put up with it. These are new economic institutions and practices. The world has no precedent or previous working experience of an international system of –

- pure fiat money
- privately created,
- publicly guaranteed, and
- inadequately regulated.

People are making new uses of the new system. You need to understand them well, for practical and theoretical reasons. Practical, to equip you to operate or advise in a modern economy. Theoretical, to alert you to the need to replace existing theory wherever the practice which it models has changed – or perhaps *ought* to be changed.

Two items are deferred. National and international problems of deregulated banking are summarized together at the end of the next chapter. And Chapter 52 on inflation includes discussion of some special problems of borrowing and lending when there is inflation. This chapter could have included that item, but it is difficult enough already.

51

Money and banking : international

Managing a nation's money is complicated by trade and exchange with other countries. Chapter 49 described some financial problems that arise where there is unbalanced trade. Besides affecting rates of exchange between currencies, unbalanced trade can also complicate a country's internal task of managing its supply of money. And just as trade in goods can complicate that task, so can trade in money.

Unregulated exchange between national currencies has lately worsened the allocation of productive resources, for reasons which this chapter will set out. It has also weakened governments' means of influencing their national financial systems, and (consequently) the structure and the rates of investment, growth and unemployment in their national economies.

This chapter focuses on reasons for those ill effects, and more generally on the problems and the possible ways of managing relations between national financial systems. First, a short history of the last half-century's efforts to manage them. Then some analysis of the changing forces which affect the international exchanges. Then reasons why the major powers, who created then dismantled one international financial regime through the third quarter of the twentieth century, now need to negotiate another.

HISTORY

The following condensed and simplified history is still quite complicated. You may not enjoy it, or remember much of its detail. But it is here, and important for your purposes, because –

- prevailing theories tell you that an unregulated world capital market will allocate capital resources most productively
- this text's theory will explain why it can't and won't do that; and
- twentieth-century experience offers the best tests of those rival predictions, and the rival policies which they recommend.

So follow the story as well as you can, and return to it – or read some fuller histories – as often as you need to.

Depressions, dictators and wars

After the First World War there were short sharp depressions in a number of countries. One of them helped a Fascist dictator to power in Italy, and ten years later he started a war in Abyssinia. The Great Depression began in 1929 and put a quarter or more of the workforce out of work throughout the developed world. Public aid for the unemployed was minimal in those days. Many banks and firms failed. To defend the jobs and businesses that remained, some governments resorted to high tariff barriers, and some governments devalued currencies whose exchange rates had been steady for generations. In Germany the Nazis had attracted negligible support as long as the economy functioned tolerably, but with a third of workers unemployed they achieved power in 1933. The war and genocide which they started killed twenty or thirty million people. It left the British and European economies battered and exhausted.

Thus the generation of people who had known those horrors had good reason to want better economic performance, and they had no reason to expect it from unaided market forces. Market forces had fuelled the financial extravagance of the 1920s, then the record depression of the 1930s. In contrast to that, the war organization of industry in 1939-45, with price control and extensive rationing, had given democratic governments large economic powers which they had used quite effectively. In Britain and Europe war had generated strong community spirit, and majority support for progressive economic and social reform. It had generated confidence in the economic capacities of government. And there was widespread agreement with the argument of Keynes' *General Theory of Employment Interest and Money* (1936) that some quite moderate public action should be able to maintain permanent full employment.

That would require, among other things, a more stable and cooperative system of international trade and exchange than had existed between the wars. In 1944, at Bretton Woods in the United States, an international conference began to negotiate the terms of a new international financial regime.

The regulation of international financial exchanges

The United States was the most powerful nation, and the least damaged by the war. It had the most advanced economy. It had a trade surplus with the rest of the world, it was a net creditor, and (compared with the rest of the world) it had abundant investment funds. As a winner on all fronts its negotiators wanted free trade in goods and free movement of money at stable rates of exchange. That is standard winners' policy. It had been British policy and practice when Britain was the technical leader a century earlier.

The US negotiators got about half of what they wanted. The half they did not get was free trade in goods. They proposed that an International Trade Organization be created with power to break down national trade barriers and move the world step by step, compulsorily, toward full free trade. Britain, and others desperately short of foreign exchange, including poor countries hoping to develop, refused to surrender the power to regulate their imports. (It was not so long since the US itself had industrialized behind a high protective tariff.) Three years of negotiation yielded the weaker General Agreement on Tariffs and Trade (GATT) in 1947. It incorporated many agreed tariff reductions. It outlawed national discrimination: a country's tariff could tax mousetraps differently from can-openers, but it must tax all imported mousetraps alike, and all can-openers alike, whatever countries they came from. But GATT did not create a power to force further tariff reductions, and it did not effectively stop the use of quotas, exchange restrictions and other non-tariff barriers to trade.

Though they failed with trade, the American negotiators succeeded with money. They got the financial regime they wanted. The Bretton Woods agreement was signed in 1944. It had four main elements:

- The US dollar was linked to a gold reserve at a fixed price.

- Other currencies' rates of exchange with the dollar (and therefore with each other) were fixed.

- The International Monetary Fund (IMF) was created to supervise those arrangements, to lend to countries with temporary exchange difficulties, and to negotiate any necessary changes to the fixed exchange rates.

- The World Bank (officially the International Bank for Reconstruction and Development) was created to finance development projects, at first in postwar Europe then chiefly in poorer developing countries.

The International Monetary Fund and the World Bank drew their funds from member nations, roughly in proportion to their national incomes. The IMF could advance foreign funds to countries in temporary exchange deficit. Keynes, as the leading British negotiator, wanted the IMF to have a matching power to draw funds *from* countries with *surplus* foreign exchange, to give it an even-handed capacity to maintain exchange equilibrium. The US, as the chief source of surplus exchange at the time, refused to give the IMF that power. Thus the British failed to get half of what *they* wanted. In the short run they got much of it in another way: through the early postwar years the US made generous dollar grants and loans to Britain and Western Europe under the Marshall Plan and other aid programs. But as a permanent arrangement, fully convertible currencies at fixed rates of exchange would not work between countries with different export capacities and import dependence, and different market strength. There must either be some means of recycling surplus exchange back to deficit countries, or some means of restricting countries' imports to their capacities to pay. Once it was in full force, the Bretton Woods regime was unlikely to work as planned.

But for more than half its life it was not in full force. The Bretton Woods agreement provided for general convertibility – people should be free to exchange any national currency for any other for purposes of trade or travel. (Governments could still control the exchange of capital funds.) But for the first fourteen years of postwar recovery and growth, convertibility was not enforced. Most countries kept public control of their citizens' access to foreign exchange. Many regulated the uses of whatever exchange their exports earned. Some restricted foreign investment and ownership within their territory. Broadly speaking, they did their best to restrict imports to what they could pay for. Their capacity to pay was determined by their export and other foreign earnings, plus any dollar reserves they had, any international aid they were given, and some cautious foreign borrowing. And most of them discriminated between more necessary and less necessary imports.

Thus what operated from the end of the war through the 1950s was a cooperative system. From Bretton Woods came fixed exchange rates and the new World Bank and International Monetary Fund, but not yet the intended market freedoms. From the United States, big financial aid to European recovery. From the British and European (and some other) governments, strict regulation and some rationing of trade and exchange. It was a coherent regime, and it worked better than any of the freer arrangements which followed it have done. (Better for productive investors, workers, consumers, economic development, and the distribution of wealth and income. Not always better for bankers, or owners of uncommitted capital funds.) Economic growth averaged better than 4 per cent a year, and trade grew even faster.

But perhaps because it was such a coherent regime, it was easy to misunderstand its success. Its national and international elements complemented and protected each other. But was it safe to assume that each element could if necessary work well on its own?

- *Could* fixed exchange rates survive if national governments stopped rationing their countries' trade and exchange and living within their means?

- Could they even survive free convertibility? Would the IMF's funds suffice to correct national exchange deficits and surpluses after American aid ended?

- Would market forces allocate capital funds to their most productive uses if governments stopped rationing foreign exchange and directing it to productive uses?

To each question the answer was NO, as it turned out. Each component of the system depended on the presence of the others.

Breakdown of the Bretton Woods regime

Through the 1950s the British, West European and Japanese economies recovered and achieved high rates of growth. They overcame postwar shortages, and were able to end their food and fuel rationing and other wartime economic controls. Europeans developed freer exchange among themselves through a European Payments Union. With American financial aid, their rising output and exports began to reduce their general shortage of dollar exchange. So as their balance of payments with North America improved and they accumulated their own gold and dollar reserves, they began to allow freer conversion of their currencies to dollars. At first that simply expanded the list of approved purposes for which private banks and firms were allowed to buy US dollars. But by 1959, led by France and Germany, the major powers were allowing general convertibility for purposes of trade and travel. There were still many national controls of the movement and exchange of capital funds. Trade was becoming freer, though still subject to many tariffs and other regulations. Most countries still regulated their people's investment abroad, and foreign ownership of some of their national assets. But there was enough convert-

ibility to meet the Bretton Woods requirements. So from 1959 the Bretton Woods regime was in full operation.

Twelve years later it broke down and was soon afterwards formally ended. Why? Basically the international system could not work satisfactorily without the national self-restraint that had accompanied it through its first decade. Some countries could produce more efficiently and trade more successfully than others. As those others relaxed their import controls, and their control over inward and outward movements of capital funds, they went into exchange deficit. In its full form the Bretton Woods system was an attempt to correct unbalanced payments –

- *without* requiring any public restraint of imports by deficit countries;

- *without* compulsory transfer of funds from surplus to deficit countries;

- *without* market adjustment of exchange rates; and

- *with as few changes as possible* to the fixed exchange rates.

That was not a coherent set of policies. As Keynes feared, it could not regulate international payments satisfactorily for long. How *could* it work between countries with different export capacities, different demands for imports, and different rates of inflation? Through the 1960s its troubles took four main forms: a shortage of IMF funds; some conflicts of national interest; some ill effects of the increasing convertibility of capital funds; and a nasty new business of gambling on likely national devaluations and forcing them to happen.

IMF Resources The IMF ran short of funds for helping countries in exchange deficit. Its resources were increased a number of times, but with increasing disagreement about the need for them and about their proper use. Some advances worked as planned: they helped the countries concerned to develop their capacities to earn the exchange they needed. Other advances failed to do that and the exchange deficits continued. In those cases, if the IMF advances were interest-bearing loans the interest payments could eventually worsen the deficits of countries which were unable to repay the borrowed capital. If the advances were gifts, why should countries in deficit be financed to live beyond their means?

National conflicts Because of some continuing trade deficits, and because national currencies were being inflated and losing purchasing power at different rates, some of the fixed exchange rates clearly had to change. Governments were generally reluctant to change them, but they were not *equally* reluctant. Surplus traders were very reluctant to *re*value their currencies (i.e. increase their exchange value): that was expected to make their exports dearer and imports cheaper, and might damage growth and employment in both the export and the import-replacing industries. Deficit traders were readier to *de*value their currencies, hoping not only to balance their payments but to do it by means which might sustain employment in their export and import-replacing industries. (You know why those effects don't always follow, but they were widely expected at the time.)

Under the Bretton Woods rules, the way to revalue or devalue a currency was to raise or lower its rate of exchange with the US dollar. When there were more devaluations than revaluations, their combined effect was to raise the exchange value of the dollar without intending to, and without US government consent. But as the master currency of the system and its only link with a reserve of gold the dollar itself could not be devalued to counter the unwanted effects of others' devaluations.

The time came when the US authorities wanted to counter those effects. Through the 1960s the US began to develop an exchange deficit. It still had a positive balance of trade. But capital movements put it into annual deficit and began to run down its reserves. Some of that happened for productive or other good reasons. Dollars left the country as US corporations invested heavily abroad. Capital was exported as foreign aid. Overseas military spending increased, especially in Vietnam. But there were also some unexpected uses of the new market freedom. Many economists (not including Keynes) expected that convertibility and freer movement of capital funds would allow better allocation of capital to its most productive uses. But they were in for some surprises.

Footloose funds The new convertibility allowed owners of capital funds to develop new ways of making money without increasing any production, or (sometimes) without producing anything at all. Examples:

- Owners moved funds abroad to avoid US taxation.

- Americans pioneered the use of bank credit to finance corporate takeovers. When the practice spread to other countries, some of it continued to be financed by US banks.

- The US authorities still limited the rate of interest that US banks were allowed to pay to their depositors. So funds flowed out of the US to find higher rates of interest elsewhere. Countries trying to balance their current exchange deficits responded by raising their interest rates to attract and retain those footloose capital funds. The higher the rate of interest, the more it depressed investment and growth.

- Gambling on exchange rates progressed from a passive guessing game to a more active, manipulative one. Rates still had to be changed officially, by government announcement, and governments tended to delay such changes as long as they could. It was not hard for speculators to know which countries were accumulating exchange deficits, and to guess which were likely to devalue their currencies before long. Having identified a target country, the gamblers would sell out of its currency as fast as they could find buyers (who often included the target country's government and central bank, trying to maintain the international acceptability of the currency). That bearish pressure tended to force an earlier or a bigger devaluation than need otherwise have happened. As soon as the relevant government *did* devalue, the gamblers could buy back the currency at its new low price, for a capital profit.

Those developments all helped the US economy to lose dollars. The breaking point came when the Bretton Woods rules forced it also to lose gold.

Gold World output, trade and money were all growing. The supply of gold was not growing at the same rate. Its fixed price might have to rise, which would in effect devalue the US dollar.

Through the 1960s the British, European and some East Asian economies were growing fast, expanding their trade, balancing their payments and accumulating dollar reserves. But with gold becoming scarcer, and the US running into exchange deficit, might those reserves be safer in gold? Under the Bretton Woods agreement the US dollar was exchangeable for gold on demand. British and Europeans began to demand gold for some of their reserves of dollars. By 1971 about a third of the US gold reserve had gone. In that year the US government decided to stop selling it.

That turned the US dollar into paper money like everyone else's. The government then devalued it by forcing European governments to revalue their currencies against the dollar. (It forced them by slapping an additional 10 per cent tariff on US imports from those countries until they revalued as requested.) In 1976 the governments formally agreed that each could manage its own exchange rate. Some governments tried, for a while, to fix their rates by regulation; then freed the rates but tried to steady them by market dealing; then freed them altogether, except for some regulation of exchanges within Europe. We'll return later to some effects of that general deregulation.

Lessons

As before in this text, you don't need to memorize that history. It is only here for the lessons that may be learned from it. They are timely, now that repentant authorities are debating how to restore some stability to the relations between the world's paper currencies.

It would not make sense to recreate the Bretton Woods system now. It was flawed in its own conditions, and some of the conditions have changed since then. But it is wise to remember how that regime worked, both to avoid repeating its mistakes, and to understand what it achieved while it lasted.

Despite its flaws, the Bretton Woods regime served the world better than it has been served by the market freedoms which replaced it. But the sources of its success, and of its eventual breakdown, are widely misunderstood. The comparative financial stability of the 1950s owed much more to national than to international government. Both contributed, but national self-discipline was necessary for the fixed exchange rates to survive.

Specifically –

* The US government recycled the world's main exchange surplus to advanced countries (and some others) which had trade deficits. It did that through its aid programs, its expanding foreign investment, and its overseas military spending and aid to allies. That greatly reduced the pressure for either official or market depreciation of the currencies of the countries with trade deficits.

* As long as shortages of foreign exchange continued, most countries restricted their imports to what they could pay for without excessive foreign borrowing.

* Private traders could not evade those controls or push the import bill above prudent limits by borrowing foreign money, because their governments did not allow them to borrow foreign money except in approved amounts for approved purposes. Through the 1950s most international borrowing was done or regulated by governments, under national or IMF or World Bank aid programs.

* Poor countries had few attractions for private lenders. To augment their export earnings they relied chiefly on aid from foreign governments and the IMF and World Bank, who tried not to put them too far into debt.

Thus among the advanced countries, fixed exchange rates were an international aid to financial relations which actually owed most of their stability to national self-discipline. That discipline allowed the fixed exchange rates to persist as long as they did. For ten or fifteen years, with various leakages and exceptions, the leading countries did their best, by public regulation, to limit their foreign spending to what they could afford. What they could afford was determined by their export and other foreign earnings, the net foreign aid they received, and prudent amounts of foreign borrowing, mostly public. So through those years the international exchanges rarely had to cope with excessive market pressure on the fixed exchange rates. Most of the time, national governments were preventing serious imbalances from arising.

The controls on capital movements were imperfect, but they were good enough to allow governments to limit internal interest rates without driving too much financial capital abroad. Stable rates of exchange could thus be accompanied by low and stable rates of interest. Those were ideal financial conditions for long-term investment and fast economic growth, which – from that and other causes – duly occurred.

That is how financial stability was achieved then. I believe that its *principle* of national self-discipline is the only one that is likely to succeed in the future, though the *methods* of self-discipline need to change with changing conditions.

But the stability could not long survive the completion of the Bretton Woods system with the introduction of full current-account convertibility from 1959. Many capital controls continued, some of them into the 1980s. But from the 1960s the controls were increasingly relaxed and by-passed.

That allowed two things which the national controls of the 1950s had not allowed:

* It allowed a small but increasing flow of capital funds to leave home in search of higher rates of return than they could earn at home. That was the beginning of the end of the low and stable interest rate that investors needed. With the US government still limiting the interest which US banks could pay their depositors, London banks began to borrow dollars from Americans at higher rates to lend back to other Americans at higher rates still.

* The same freedom allowed private market activity to put national currencies into deficit or excessive debt. Capital borrowing and lending could do that. So could the use of borrowed funds to spend too much on imports.

Options for deficit traders

This lesson is so important that it is worth reinforcing. So bear with some repetition. Recall, from Chapter 49 on trade policy, the options for a country which has a serious exchange deficit, and finds that it cannot trade its way out of trouble by improving its export or import-replacing performance. Options:

Free trade   The country can open its frontiers entirely, and hope that its industries of greatest comparative advantage will develop to export enough to achieve balanced payments and full employment.

You know the reasons why, for a country with a trade deficit in those circumstances, free trade is at least as likely to *increase* the deficit.

Devaluation   Government can devalue the country's currency, or let market forces depreciate it. Theorists may expect the consequent price changes to increase the demand for exports, and reduce the demand for imports, sufficiently to balance the country's trade and payments.

You know why that may not happen (i) if the supply and demand for traded goods are not elastic enough, (ii) if devaluation *increases* existing interest and debt obligations to foreigners, and (iii) if the activities of exchange gamblers and other exchange traders have unhelpful effects on exchange rates and interest rates.

Debt, asset sales and foreign investment   The country can balance its exchange deficit by attracting foreign capital funds. It can borrow from foreign banks, attract foreign investment, sell existing assets to foreigners.

Too much of that can eventually worsen the deficit by increasing the annual outflow of rent, interest, dividends and debt repayment to foreign owners.

Rationing   The country can live within its means. It can produce more for itself; regulate imports; limit foreign investment to useful direct investment; keep any borrowing from foreigners within prudent limits; and if necessary, ration the available foreign exchange to its most necessary and productive uses.

Rationing is the only reliable method in the long run. It is also likely to be the most productive and equitable. It was British, European and Australasian policy through the 1950s, and Japan's, South Korea's and Taiwan's throughout their decades of fast growth. Some of the necessary regulation may be badly done – but its financial effects have nowhere been as destructive as the effects of unregulated trade and debt have been, since the 1970s, in some advanced countries and in many developing countries, especially in Central and South America and Africa south of the Sahara.

Those lessons from the Bretton Woods experience suggest that the Bretton Woods regime, and the national controls which supported it, needed some re-design and strengthening. But the leading governments chose not to do that. Through the 1970s and 1980s they simply dismantled most of the public economic regulation and market management of their financial systems, and their financial relations with each other.

DEREGULATION

Different governments took the steps at different dates. There were crises, international conferences, some cooperative action by Central Banks, and occasional attempts to apply the brakes or restore some of the lost controls. But the overall effect was a substantial freeing of the national and international activities of banks and other financial institutions, including new institutions which were created to exploit the new freedoms.

The movement toward general deregulation had a dramatic prelude when the world's main oil exporters combined to offer a mass of new capital funds to the Western banks. We will look at the effects of that now, before listing the regulations that were repealed in the course of the deregulation, and the uses that were made of the new freedoms. As with the rest of this compressed history, you don't need to remember the details. What matter are the lessons to be learned from the experience.

THE OPEC FUNDS

The Organization of Petroleum Exporting Countries (OPEC) represents Venezuela, Indonesia, Iran, Iraq, Kuwait, Saudi Arabia, the United Arab Emirates, Libya, Algeria, Nigeria, Ecuador and Gabon. In the 1970s most of those were comparatively poor societies except for their oil revenues. Except for Venezuela, most of them had steep internal inequalities and were ruled by monarchs or military dictators.

OPEC quadrupled the world price of oil in 1973, and increased it again six years later. Altogether the price increased ninefold, to yield the OPEC exporters US$200 billion annually. Those countries, under those governments, could not spend or invest much of the new revenue, so they accumulated big surpluses of foreign cash. What to do with it? Who might borrow and invest it elsewhere in the world?

In the rich Western countries and Japan, dearer oil did double damage. It raised enough prices to accelerate inflation. And it helped to induce a recession. Investment fell, unemployment rose. Business demand for credit was low. For the time being those countries' producers did not want to borrow back much of the money that the OPEC countries were earning from their consumers. Remember the paradox of thrift. You can hinder economic growth if you consume too little and save too much, so that as consumers you can't keep one another fully employed as producers. When OPEC cut Western consumption by raising oil prices, but lent most of the extra profits back to the West as capital funds, it was as if they had forced the West to save too much.

In the Third World there were many countries short of oil, short of foreign exchange, short of investment funds, and in need of all three for development purposes. The new oil price put a number of them further into deficit. When recession hit the rich countries which bought most of their exports, their export earnings declined. International aid and private investment by multinationals did not supply all the foreign currency they needed, and were anyway unpopular in many developing countries because of the conditions attached to them. Most of any international borrowing for those economies had to be done by their governments, which were often hard-pressed by short-term needs. Some of them were also incompetent or corrupt. Many of them would welcome unconditional foreign loans at almost any price. But banks which lent them big sums at high interest would be unlikely to get much of their money back on time, or in full, or (in some cases) ever.

Thus when Western commercial banks were offered the flood of new OPEC money, they had three broad options:

1. They could accept only as much of it as they had safe borrowers for at the prevailing rates of interest. That would have meant refusing to accept a good deal of the money, or accepting it only into non-interest-bearing accounts.

2. They could accept it but maintain their prevailing standards of safety in lending. To do that they would have to allow the over-supply of funds to bring a sharp fall in world interest rates – so they should pay correspondingly low rates of interest on the OPEC deposits. At low interest the West would have more safe borrowers willing to borrow, and loans to the Third World would be less expensive for their borrowers and potentially more helpful.

3. As a third alternative the banks could accept all the OPEC money at the prevailing rates of interest. They would then need to lend most of it to borrowers willing to take it at those rates, plus some profit 'spread'. That meant lending to borrowers the banks had until then refused because of their higher risks. To lend such a sudden increase of funds without reducing the rate of interest significantly, at a time when the rich Western economies were sliding into recession, there might have to be *much* higher risks and lower standards of safety.

The banks chose the third option – the worst. Not all banks did, but enough of them did, led by leading US banks, to accept all the offered OPEC funds at the prevailing rates of interest. (Remember the hazards when financial intermediaries compete for market shares.)

What could they do with those deposits to earn the rate of interest they had promised to pay to the depositors?

Some of the money found productive borrowers, but a lot of it did not. In the West, especially in the English-speaking countries, it financed a lot of corporate takeovers, often loading the taken companies with excessive debt. It financed booms in share prices, city land prices, more office-building than there were tenants for. Billions of borrowed money were then lost when share prices fell dramatically one day in 1987. More were lost when the property boom collapsed two or three years later.

By then, oil funds were not the only ones at work. Japanese investors, exporting their exchange surpluses through the 1980s, were said to have lost US$300 billion to falling property, share and bond prices in the US. And home-grown American, British and other Western funds were shifting to riskier lending as deregulation allowed higher interest rates.

Some of the OPEC money was lent to communist governments in Eastern Europe and to governments or government-guaranteed borrowers in the Third World. Most of those loans were made in Western currencies. Interest and repayment had to be in those currencies. To service the debts the borrowers needed to invest the new funds profitably enough to earn the interest due on them. They needed to increase their exports to Western countries to earn more hard currency. And the loans were at quite high rates of interest, on terms which allowed the lenders to vary the rates in changing market conditions. Thus with trade risks, exchange-rate risks and interest-rate risks, the costs of servicing those debts were high and not wholly predictable.

The East European borrowers were unpopular communist governments. They should have invested their Western funds productively, often to import Western capital goods to re-equip their industries. Instead they spent a lot of the money on Western consumer goods, and on subsidizing their own consumer prices, trying to buy a few more years of tolerance from their disillusioned and resentful people. When those governments were replaced, economic reform was seriously handicapped by the new debts. Hungary, for example, had one of the best of the communist economies. Before the Western loans it was in exchange equilibrium, its exports paying for its imports. But a few years later its first elected government inherited hard-currency debt equal to a year of national income. To default might well rule out any more *money* from the West. To pay would leave no change for buying *goods* from the West – the much needed capital goods and technology that the original loans should have bought.

Many Central and South American and African borrowers used their loans differently, but just as badly. There were some successful public and private investments, especially in the few democracies. Elsewhere, too many of the investments were partly or wholly unsuccessful. Quite a lot of the money was stolen by corrupt officials or private borrowers – out of reach of the lending countries' regulators and courts there was often nothing to prevent that. Money was also spent on importing consumer goods, though not usually the mass comforts that the communist regimes imported.

Considered either as profitable banking or as private international aid, that bout of private lending from rich to poor countries has probably done more harm than good both to the banks and to many of the indebted countries. By 1985 world debt had multiplied ninefold, from about one hundred to about nine hundred billion US dollars, since the first oil price rise. Not all the loans were from OPEC funds. Footloose capital was accumulating from other sources too, especially from Japan's trading surpluses.

Mexico, owing US$97 billion, mostly to US banks, was the first to default when it suspended interest payments in 1982. If a loan ceases to pay its due interest, US law defines it as 'non-performing'. That cuts its value as an asset: nobody would willingly pay $97 billion to take over the right to try to collect Mexico's debt. That reduces the value of the assets which the banks' balance sheets can set against their liabilities to their depositors. As other defaults followed the Mexican one, a number of leading US banks would

have been insolvent, in breach of the law and out of business, if the US government and Central Bank had not forgiven and rescued them.

The defaults have continued. Some debtor countries pay all they owe, some pay some and some pay none of the due interest. The banks disguise a lot of the non-payment by rescheduling the debts, adding the unpaid interest to the capital owing. Some but by no means all of the debts have finally been written off. The debtors are under continuing pressure to pay. Some now owe, each year, more than their exports earn. That hinders their capacity to develop, and helps to keep them poor.

Ironically, the losses are not borne by the primary lenders. If the OPEC oil owners themselves had done the incompetent lending, and now faced the consequent losses, that would be appropriate market discipline. But the lending was done and the losses incurred by the Western banks, as intermediaries between the primary lenders and the final borrowers. So the losses are actually borne by other depositors in those banks, by US taxpayers, and by the consumers and taxpayers of Eastern Europe and the Third World, scarcely any of whom had any democratic control over the governments which borrowed and in many cases misused the funds.

Lessons

Does it help to ask whose fault it was?

- *Should the OPEC owners have refused to deposit their money on the terms they were offered?*

  Not if you expect them to behave in a normal market way. It was safe business for them. They were lending to the world's leading banks, which had public lender-of-last-resort promises from dependable governments, and private deposit insurance to repay their depositors if they failed. And whatever the rules said, their governments could never afford to let them fail, and would in practice rescue them from any danger of failing. All the lenders' risks were thus transferred from the owners and primary lenders of the money to the banks in the first place, to Western governments as their effective guarantors in the second place, and to the citizens of the banks' countries and the borrowers' countries in the end.

- *Should the banks have refused to accept the funds at prevailing rates of interest?*

  Some did refuse – but those willing to pay the going rates and accept the higher risks were the ones who got the funds. Why did they do it? They were competing for shares of big new business. You remember the reasons why worse competitors can

often beat better ones in competition between financial intermediaries, unless strong professional
conscience and conventions restrain them all, or
governments regulate them effectively enough.
Competition cannot be relied on to take productive
forms in an unregulated international capital market
operated chiefly by intermediaries trading other
people's money.

- *Should governments have reduced the banks' temp-*
  tations by withdrawing their public supports and
  exposing them to proper market discipline?

No, for two reasons. Market pressures would still
demand and supply private deposit insurance, which
would be more expensive without the public
supports, and would still expose the bankers to much
the same temptations. And business as a whole
would get dangerously unreliable service from paper
money created by competing private banks *without*
public backing and regulation. If the Western
governments were at fault it was for providing too
little of the additional *prudential* regulation that was
needed when they ended their *economic* regulation
of international capital movements.

It is right to blame many of the borrowing governments,
some of whom were corrupt as well as inexperienced.
But even they were accustomed to borrowers being
assessed and disciplined by lenders. Hard-pressed
politicians and public servants in Africa or South
America took what looked like expert advice: experienced New York and London bankers who offered this
flow of private international aid must surely know what
they were doing?

Conclusion A lot of the OPEC funds were misused
by owners, bankers and borrowers pursuing their interests in a straightforward self-interested way, but in a
flawed and under-regulated market. With the OPEC
funds the main flaw was the type of competition
between financial intermediaries which such a system
invites.

That is not the only intrinsic flaw in that market.
There are others. They're our next subjects. But first, a
short list of the new *international* freedoms, to supplement your earlier list (on pp. 000-00) of *internal*
national financial controls which were relaxed or
dismantled through the same years.

LOST CONTROLS

International credit Most Western governments
which used to regulate private lending to foreigners and
borrowing from foreigners no longer do so.

International ownership Countries which used to
specify which of their assets foreigners were not
allowed to own, or which new purchases foreigners
were not allowed to make, now regulate much less of
that activity. Likewise, they no longer confine their own
banks or insurance or superannuation institutions to
investing in the home country. Some countries still limit
foreign ownership of some media and cultural institutions: that's about all. Enlarging the freedom to buy and
sell foreign assets in practice enlarged the freedom to
import and export capital funds.

Exchange transactions Through the 1950s Central
Banks transacted most currency exchanges, or had
commercial banks do them as agents under Central
Bank guidelines. Private traders bought the foreign
currency they needed from Central Banks or under
Central Bank rules, and were only allowed it for
approved purposes. In most advanced economies now,
anyone with money can change it into any other
convertible currency for any purpose, without question.

Exchange rates used to be fixed, and occasionally
altered, by international agreement. For varying periods
from 1971 they were fixed by national governments.
Except for the special arrangements within the
European Union, there is no public management now.
Central banks sometimes try to stabilize particular rates
by buying and selling currencies, but they do so with
less and less success as the volume of private speculative and manipulative currency trading continues to
grow. Some developing countries and some ex-communist countries maintain official rates of exchange
alongside the market rates at which most transactions
between their currencies and Western currencies take
place. But between the main Western currencies there is
no longer any public regulation of rates of exchange.
They are market-determined, and less stable than they
used to be. The East Asian financial crisis of 1997-98
saw sudden changes ranging between 10 and 80 per cent
in the rates of exchange between some leading Western
and Asian currencies.

A WORLD CAPITAL MARKET

How does the world capital market work now, and how
does it affect national financial systems, and national
economic policies and performance?

We introduce the subject with more reminders, in the
form of a summary list of forces at work in an open
world money market. Be clear about the purpose of the
list as you read it. We are shaping up to consider how
efficient such a world capital market can be. Does the

supply of capital funds respond to the demand for them? Is the demand mostly from producers of goods and services? If so, are the most efficient producers the ones who can afford to pay the highest interest or dividends, and outbid other competitors for funds? And so on, through the classical market questions.

So we begin with a quick review of the main forces at work in the market. You're familiar with most of them, so there's not much explanation of them – just a check-list.

The demand for capital funds The traditional uses of money continue: a modern economy's division of labor and organization of production and distribution need money as a medium of exchange, a measure of value and a store of value. Productive capital is provided by switching some production from consumer goods to capital goods. That is financed partly by saving from earnings and partly by creating money in the form of bank credit.

Those are traditional processes. What is new is the greatly increased demand for capital funds for three other purposes: (1) to balance national exchange deficits, (2) to balance national budgets by spending capital (acquired by selling public assets) in place of tax revenue, and (3) to gamble on the future behavior of unstable rates of inflation, interest, and exchange. One early pioneer of offshore finance (since jailed) used to advise people who wanted to get rich not to waste time producing corn or steel or anything else, but to work only with money, making money breed money without necessarily serving any other purpose at all. Banks do that now on a big scale on the international exchanges.

The supply of funds Remember how money is created, mostly as bank credit, by thousands of banks operating under the various rules and supervision of scores of national governments and Central Banks. The quantity of money varies continuously. Borrowers draw some or all of their credits, and repay some or all of their debts, day by day. A lot of what they draw is deposited in other banks, and a bank multiplier further expands or contracts the amount in circulation. People spend what they get at varying rates. At one extreme a miser locks banknotes away in his safe. At another extreme a currency dealer hits a few computer keys in quick succession and she's acquired a million pounds (or dollars, or marks, or yen) and spent them again within seconds. Funds are traded from currency to currency. Depending whether or not the transactions are 'sterilized' by the relevant Central Banks, that may or may not affect each country's supply of its own currency. Funds

are also shifted from centre to centre. When (for example) US dollars are shifted from a deposit in a New York bank to a deposit in a bank in London or the Cayman Islands, the world supply of dollars may not change, but the US economy's working supply of them does change. Free exchange and free movement of capital funds make it harder than ever for any government to control the supply of money to its national economy.

Jurisdictions National governments regulate their countries' banks and other financial institutions. They can in principle choose to regulate business done within their territory by other countries' banks. But there can be legal conflict, for example when the US government and the UK government each claim to regulate what American banks do in Britain. And private institutions have various ways of avoiding some or all national regulation. Examples:

- *Havens* Some small countries attract foreign firms to register in and operate from their territory by promising secrecy, low taxation or other advantages. They then tax big volumes of foreign business at very low rates, and may avoid taxing their own residents at all. In effect, they sell foreigners immunity from their own countries' tax or trading laws – and increasingly, from their criminal laws. (Compare the American States which offer corporate directors special powers in exchange for high charter fees.) A lot of New York business pretends, successfully, to be done in the Cayman Islands. One British tycoon located his employees' superannuation funds in Liechtenstein where he switched them to other uses, and lost them, them out of reach of the British authorities.

- *Offshore* commonly means beyond the home juris- diction. But it *can* mean in mid-ocean, beyond *any* jurisdiction. In the 1960s an enterprise called Investors Overseas Services registered bits of itself in so many countries that it operated for some years under no effective government, and continued to do so elsewhere after the US Securities and Exchange Commission stopped it trading on the US stock exchanges. It borrowed two and a half billion dollars from unwary people to invest on their behalf. Its directors paid themselves a good deal of what they borrowed, and mismanaged a good deal of the rest, before the remains of the enterprise were rescued for more respectable management. In the 1980s the Bank of Credit and Commerce International (BCCI) became 'banker to the world's biggest criminals' and some of its biggest national secret services. It specialised in laundering dirty money. 'BCCI at one time was the seventh largest commercial bank in the world. [It had] a secret bank within a bank ... that engaged in massive fraud and bribery itself and ... moved money for other major international fraudsters, for the very biggest drug empires, for terrorist groups, for Manuel Noriega and Saddam Hussein, for Peru's Central Bank to hide a quarter of the nation's hard currency from foreign bank creditors, for covert nuclear programs, and for illegal arms sales to Iran.' To get away with so much for so long the bank bribed many officials in many countries, but also 'the bank was set up in such a way that it had no home regulator. It was effectively offshore in every country in which it operated.' The quotations are from pp. 222-4 of Brent Fisse and John Braithwaite, *Corporations, Crime and Accountability* (1993). The authors ask 'How should the international banking system and the international banking regulatory system be reformed to prevent latter-day BCCIs from springing up?' There has been no effective reform as the century ends.

Unstable rates

We now move on to the three main variables in the day-to-day operation of the financial system: the rates of inflation, interest and exchange. Each rate responds to a variety of influences.

Rates of inflation are affected by wage-fixing systems, wage-bargaining strengths and wage rates; pricing mark-ups and profit rates; the amount of credit that banks are allowed to create; the amount they choose to create; changing rates of exchange; patterns of taxation and public investment and spending; and the prevailing political culture of the time and place: the degrees of conflict and cooperation between business, labor and government; styles of political and intellectual leadership; historical memories of past inflation.

Rates of exchange are influenced by the demand and supply of particular currencies. The demand and supply reflect balances of trade, investment income and debt service, and capital investment across national boundaries. More-demanded currencies tend to rise in value, less-demanded currencies tend to depreciate. Their rates of exchange may also be affected by their purchasing power (i.e. the goods they will buy in their own territory); by the rate of interest prevailing in their national economies; by any tax advantages available to holders of the currencies; and by expectations that the

rates of exchange will rise or fall in future. Where changes are expected, speculative dealing may increase or hasten them, or both. Defensive dealing by Central Banks may reduce those gambling effects, but the volume of speculative dealing is now big enough to make such defence difficult, and expensive if it fails.

Rates of interest are affected by conventions; by bankers' interests and decisions; by government efforts to influence investment, employment, inflation and the balance of payments; by the outcomes of political and market conflicts of interest between lenders and borrowers; and more generally by prevailing beliefs about the best ways to cope with unemployment, inflation, unbalanced trade, and the business cycle.

Rates of interest don't function like the prices of other goods, to bring supply and demand into equilibrium or to ration scarce resources to their most productive uses. But they have other economic effects. They can affect the composition of the demand for credit; the allocation and uses of credit; rates of investment and employment; rates of inflation; and national exchange rates and balances of payment. Increasingly in recent decades, governments which want to influence those outcomes try to do it by influencing rates of interest. But it often happens that the different purposes they want to serve require different rates, so the policy makers face contradictions and trade-offs. Some of the conflicts are not 'in the nature of things'; they arise from particular institutional arrangements. You will meet the conflicts often as you study problems of economic strategy. Here, notice the part that an open capital market plays in creating some of them.

- Suppose that a social democratic government wants to regulate interest rates, to keep them low and stable to encourage high investment and employment, while using other means to restrain inflation and the import bill. It can't do that effectively if banks and owners of capital funds are free to respond to the low interest by exporting funds to lend them wherever in the world they can expect the highest returns.

- Suppose that the government wants to avoid that problem by insulating its national interest rate from world rates. To balance an exchange deficit, or for any other necessary purpose, its Central Bank will borrow foreign funds at foreign rates of interest, and where necessary on-lend them within the national economy at the national interest rate. Thus the interest rate which sustains investment and employment within the national economy need not be disturbed by the rates prevailing elsewhere. But as before, the low rates within the national economy won't help investment and employment if banks and fund owners can respond by exporting their funds to earn higher returns abroad.

* Suppose that, to smooth the business cycle, a government wants to restrain investment through upswings by raising the interest rate, and encourage it through downswings by lowering the rate. It may find that the rest of the world is doing much the same, so it can safely keep in step, since the business cycle tends to be world-wide. But if the country has a big exchange deficit it may have to expect some market depreciation of its currency. If lenders expect that, they will want extra interest to cover the exchange-rate risk. So the country may have to pay comparatively high interest through all phases of the cycle so that it can continue to borrow as much from foreigners as its yearly exchange deficit requires.

Those limits on governments' policy options come with open *financial* frontiers. Remember that open *trading* frontiers can have similar effects. Deficit countries would not need to borrow foreign funds if they could still balance their payments by regulating their trade in goods.

A summary of these two financial chapters will presently remind you of the effects of high rates of nominal and real interest. Here, just notice how unregulated trade in money and goods limits governments' capacity to manage their economies for the usual purposes of full employment, low inflation and desirable distributions of wealth and income.

Forward markets

When governments regulated interest and exchange rates and the export of capital funds, there was not much scope for gambling on financial uncertainties, and there was not much need to insure against them. But since deregulation has made interest rates and exchange rates unstable and imperfectly predictable, gambling offers enticing gains, and many export/import industries need to hedge their financial risks.

To follow the gambling and hedging, begin by learning two terms. 'Spot rate' means the price now, i.e. the market rate of exchange between two currencies at any particular moment. 'Forward rate' means a rate fixed now at which two dealers agree to exchange currency at a future date, whatever the spot rate may then be. Between the major currencies there are now market rates of exchange for forward transactions up to ten years ahead.

Why trade on the forward market? You may do it for either of two reasons: to gamble, or to avoid gambling. A simple example of each:

To gamble: You can gamble on a future exchange rate being different from what the market currently expects it to be. Suppose the 5-year forward rate between pounds and dollars is £100 = $150 (so £66.6 = $100). You personally guess that the pound is likely to depreciate further than that against the dollar, and that the spot rate five years from now will be more like £100 = $125 (£80 = $100). So you contract now to buy $15 000 000 for £10 000 000 5 years from now. When that time comes, if you've guessed right, any bank will lend you £10 000 000 for five minutes to allow you to buy $15 000 000, re-sell them immediately at the spot price for £12 000 000, repay the bank with interest, and take nearly £2m profit. But if you've guessed wrong and lost, banks won't lend you money to lose. So 'you' were a bad choice for this example. Very few individuals are trusted to be there with millions to lose when forward contracts mature, so very few individuals can get forward contracts. Banks and well-established firms are the main dealers on forward markets.

To avoid gambling: You're a British airline which orders a $15 000 000 aircraft from an American manufacturer who takes orders at five years' notice. The dollar price is fixed but you can't predict how many pounds you will need to buy those dollars when the time comes. So you contract for them now on the forward market, and allow £10 000 000 in your forward estimates, risk free.

Arbitrage and instability

You know why futures trading in commodities tends to stabilize their prices over time. Currency trading – trading money for money – is different. It has different effects in the short run and in the longer run; and it can stabilize relations between national currencies for periods of time, then suddenly destabilize them.

In the short run there is arbitrage. That means trading to take advantage of small discrepancies between exchange rates or between national interest rates. It tends to level the rates of return on capital funds (allowing for risks) in all the advanced economies. Where there are differences, arbitrage trading soon adjusts the rates to eliminate the differences. With the usual variations for risk, it tends to impose a single rate of real interest on all the countries concerned.

But uniformity is not the same thing as stability. Over time, speculative dealing does not always have the stabilizing effect on rates of interest or rates of exchange that futures trading usually has on commodity prices. On the contrary, it will sometimes both increase and accelerate changes which arise from other causes. Suppose, for example, that currency dealers expect that Britain's exchange deficit and rate of inflation will cause the pound to depreciate in exchange with US dollars and Japanese yen. Dealers will want to get out of the depreciating currency into the appreciating ones. They will sell enough pounds for dollars and yen to depreciate the pound further, and faster, than the original causes would have done. Once, Central Banks would defend their currencies, and sometimes one another's currencies, by buying enough of the threatened currency to maintain its exchange price. To do that, they have to spend their own foreign reserves. But that defence is less effective now that the speculators trade a bigger volume of funds than the Central Banks can match.

Forward markets have proliferated far beyond those two simple examples. To learn about them you need specialist texts. (A good introduction is Julian Walmsley, *The Foreign Exchange and Money Markets Guide,* 1992.) Here's half a page to suggest just how complicated the business has become.

There are outright contracts to buy and sell at future dates, as in the two examples above. There are swaps: they are agreements to exchange one currency for another on one future day, with a reverse exchange on a later day. That is one of a number of 'forward forward' deals: contracts, signed now, to do successive deals on successive forward dates. There are SAFES: Synthetic Agreements for Forward Exchange, and other 'derivatives', which allow you to bet on the outcomes of notional forward transactions without actually making the transactions. (In our first example above, you would not buy then sell the $15 000 000 when the contract matured, you would merely settle your notional gains or losses directly with the other party.) There are put and call options. You already met put and call options for the sale or purchase of real estate. Similarly, you can buy an option to sell or buy money at a specified price (i.e. exchange rate) at or before a specified future date. There are options to buy or sell contracts, i.e. to buy or sell existing swap or other forward contracts. There are options on options, i.e. options to buy or sell existing option contracts. There is a wide range of hedge contracts which you can sign to limit your risks on other contracts. As with the gambling and anti-gambling

examples above, most of these market 'instruments' *can* be used to reduce the risks to which exporters and importers of goods are now exposed by the unstable rates of exchange. But that is a small proportion of the market trading, just as currency exchange for purposes of trade, investment or travel is a small proportion. Estimates of the proportion of currency exchange that is now purely speculative range from above 80 to above 95 per cent.

Various theories and models have been developed for understanding the behavior of the forward money market and operating profitably in it. One example will do. Suppose you're a bank with some gambling money. Suppose that this year, German marks are expected to inflate 2 per cent, and you can lend them at 7 per cent interest. Pounds are expected to inflate 5 per cent, and you can lend them at 12 per cent. It looks better to buy and lend pounds: they offer 7 per cent real interest against 5 per cent for lending marks. But through the same year the market expects pounds to depreciate 2 per cent in exchange with marks. (The figures are crudely rounded: real dealers run them to four decimal places.) The effect of the combined *interest, inflation* and *exchange* expectations is to offer the same real yield in either currency for lending in either currency. If it were not so, arbitragists would soon make it so by trading on the spot and forward markets. So between any two currencies – and between them all, if you have the right software – you can theorize that if the market is not disturbed by unexpected events there will be determinate relations (which can be expressed in five equations) between (i) the difference between their nominal interest rates, (ii) the expected difference between their inflation rates, (iii) the expected change in their spot exchange rates, and (iv) the difference between their spot and forward exchange rates.

The theory may not help you much, because unexpected events do happen, and three of the four terms in the equations are intrinsically uncertain market forecasts. But to the extent that dealers push the rates towards those relationships, you can see how their activities deprive most national governments of much effective freedom of choice about rates of interest or quantities and directions of lending within their national economies. They dare not offer foreign lenders – or their own lenders including their own commercial banks – worse prospects than the best prospects offering elsewhere in the world. A country which gets its rate of interest out of line will be punished automatically through its exchange rate and balance of payments.

That's the most important effect of deregulating

international exchanges. Without border controls on the passage of capital funds, it is much harder for governments to control the price or uses of credit *within* their countries.

That in turn reduces their capacity to influence investment, employment and growth.

A MARKET FAILURE

Most of both the arbitrage and the speculative dealing is done by private banks. Most of it does not improve either the national or the world allocation of capital funds. Its main economic effects are three:

- It diverts funds from productive investment.

- It maintains higher rates of real interest than used to prevail under national controls. That excludes a range of productive industries from access to credit.

- It denies governments the use of a number of effective aids to investment, employment, stable money, balanced exchange, and greater equality.

Over much of the Western world, real rates of interest have increased, rates of unemployment have doubled, rates of investment have declined, trend rates of growth have halved, and a century's progress to greater equality has been reversed, since the main financial deregulation began in the 1970s. There is disagreement about what has caused those changes. Many economists argue that the slow-down would have been the same or worse without deregulation. I agree with those who believe otherwise: too-free trade into countries with persistent trade and exchange deficits, high real interest, unstable rates of interest and rates of exchange, and some diversion of capital funds from productive investment to less productive or unproductive uses, have contributed, along with other causes, to the declining performance. Financial deregulation has thus intensified the troubles it was designed to cure.

It has also strengthened the owners of capital funds, and the directors of private banks and other financial institutions, against attempts to restore effective public regulation of the finance industry – as follows.

A POLITICAL FAILURE

Reversed roles: banks now discipline governments Currency traders gamble on national rates of interest, inflation and exchange. Those rates are influenced in a number of ways by government policies. The policies are influenced by prevailing beliefs. Some of the beliefs are self-interested and some are controversial. For example, members of a social-democratic government may believe that full employment is compatible with low inflation, and is anyway more important than low inflation; that there are better weapons against inflation than a high rate of interest; that good minimum wages and welfare incomes need not cause unemployment; that import controls are the best defence (if defence is needed) against exchange deficit and excessive foreign debt; that progressive taxation is equitable and need do no harm to enterprise; and that banks need strict economic as well as prudential regulation. Currency dealers and the bank directors who employ most of them may have opposite beliefs to those. So if a government acts on those social-democratic principles, the owners and managers of uncommitted capital funds will expect to do better in countries under more permissive government. As they begin to sell out of the offending government's currency, its exchange rate declines. Bankers, business leaders and media blame the government.

So – as far as other conditions allow – national governments whose policies please bankers can expect their currencies and government bonds to be in demand at stable or rising rates of exchange. Governments whose policies threaten the pockets or the beliefs of bankers and their richer customers can expect some capital flight, a depreciating rate of exchange, and (if their trade balance is not strong) increasing exchange deficit and foreign debt. The financial press is quick to link such market activity to the relevant government actions. Politicians scan the screens to see how the markets have responded to their actions of an hour ago or a day ago. Many of them fear that significant numbers of swinging voters respect the market's judgments. Bankers' pronouncements used to be greeted sceptically. Cartoonists drew avaricious, pot-bellied men with top hats, large cigars and reactionary intentions. But when the opinions are expressed anonymously by buying or selling the national currency, they tend to be taken as objective market judgments of the government's economic competence. Governments fear them. Among other things, their market power is likely to be used against any attempt to restore effective economic regulation of financial institutions. Or if some reform is inevitable, they will press governments to have the reform designed by bankers rather than their critics.

CONCLUSION

In its present form the world capital market has two serious faults. They are faults which any open international money market seems likely to have, especially in a world which also enforces free trade in goods.

First, it is an intrinsically inefficient market because the price of credit cannot equilibrate the supply and demand for it, or ration bank lending either to its most productive or to its most socially desirable uses. Only discriminating administrative rationing by capable bank officers can do either of those things; and the officers can choose from more and better options the lower and more stable the base rate of interest is, and the less rationing by price there is. Much of the best allocation in the past has been done by bank officers lending within public guidelines, at rates of interest limited by regulation, and with foreign exchange transactions confined to purposes of trade, travel, direct investment, international aid and other publicly approved purposes, with international lending (where there is good reason for it) done chiefly by national governments and public international institutions such as the International Monetary Fund and the World Bank. But most of those principles are unworkable in an open world market.

Second, the open national boundaries which establish the world capital market deprive the participating countries of a number of their best means of influencing their national rates of investment, employment and inflation. The means which they are driven to use instead, especially the resort to high and fluctuating rates of real interest, don't merely weaken government's capacity to *manage* the economy. They also do active harm to the economy's *market* efficiency.

It may now be difficult to dismantle the world capital market or to establish effective public control of it. Chapters about alternative economic strategies will presently compare the hazards of trying to live with it with the hazards of trying to reform it. But we must first complete this review of strategic ends and means – and further complicate your understanding of economic activity as a whole – with chapters on inflation and employment.

52

Inflation

Inflation means a general rise in prices, i.e. a decline in the purchasing power of each unit of money. If it takes $1.05 now to buy what $1 bought a year ago, there has been inflation at the rate of 5 per cent per year.

But be careful how you measure it, for a number of reasons.

Measurement If national accounts show that a country produced (say) $10,000 of goods per head of population last year and $11,000 this year, how do you know whether you've had –

- 10 per cent inflation and no economic growth, or
- 10 per cent growth and no inflation, or
- price mark-ups causing real wage losses, which give the wage share 10 per cent less of national income and the profit share 10 per cent more of it, or
- what mix of the three?

You must keep accounts of the quantities of goods produced, or (in practice) the quantities of goods that $11,000 will now buy. If it will buy (say) 3 per cent more goods – more pounds of butter and cinema tickets – than $10,000 would buy a year ago, that probably indicates annual rates of 3 per cent growth and 7 per cent inflation.

Why only 'probably'? A number of things may distort your measure of the pure value or purchasing power of your national currency:

Over time, some goods change their relative prices. Steel gets cheaper but hospital care gets dearer. If people regularly spend more on hospital care than on steel, those price changes will mean that each dollar buys altogether less goods. Does that signify inflation? Not necessarily. Steel is cheaper because technical progress has improved its method of production, which now uses better machinery and less labor than it did. Hospital care is dearer because technical progress has improved the *product:* the care costs more because hospitals use more skills, equipment and materials to do more for your health than they used to do. Those changes don't signify any change in the value of money.

But while those changes are occurring, there may *also* be some inflation. Suppose that the real cost of steel has fallen 20 per cent, but its selling price has only fallen 10 per cent, and the real cost of hospital care has risen 20 per cent, but the fees for it have risen 30 per cent. Hypothesis: besides the 20 per cent changes in real costs, there also appears to have been 10 per cent inflation. That's still no more than a hypothesis until research has ruled out a number of other factors that may have affected the prices: has world steel pricing grown more competitive with lower mark-ups, have doctors doubled their fees, have gluts or scarcities altered the market prices of the fuels and raw materials the two industries use – and so on. Separating (1) changes in real costs from (2) price changes which chiefly redistribute gains and losses between one group and another, and (3) pure inflationary changes in the value of money, can be a difficult exercise. And there are other complications, as follows.

Time To compare the purchasing power of money at different dates, you need to compare the whole price of the whole national output of paid-for goods, or (commonly, in practice) a representative sample of the whole output, such as the whole price of the basket of goods that an average household buys.

Over time, national economies change the composition of their output and households change the basket of goods that they choose to buy. Suppose they buy less steel and more hospital care than they did. If you compare the whole price of the old basket of goods a year ago with the whole price of the new basket now, the difference may misrepresent any change in the value of money. But if you make a better measure of inflation by comparing the whole price of the old basket a year ago with the whole price of that same basket now that those are not the proportions of goods that people buy, the difference may misrepresent the actual change in material standards of living.

Exchange If international exchange rates change, the prices you pay for imports may go up or down. So with no change in the prices of your own products, a price index may show some inflation or deflation.

Tax changes can change prices. Prices rise if government increases indirect taxes (tariffs, sales tax, value-added tax, payroll tax), or if it shifts some taxation from income tax (which doesn't affect prices) to taxes which do affect prices.

Deflator   Account-keepers can discount price changes which arise from other causes than changes in the value of money. Some of the discounts can be measured, but others can only be estimated, so the resulting index is rough. But it is better than a simple price index at distinguishing economic growth from inflation – for example at estimating how much of a change in the money value of national product represents a change in physical output, and how much represents a change in prices. Such indexes are known as Deflators.

Consumer price index   To make a consumer price index (CPI), begin by surveying consumer spending to find what proportions of all the available goods an average household buys. Call that the basket of goods. Then survey the market prices of the goods, and calculate the total price of that basket of goods. Repeat the process periodically, and record percentage changes in the price of the basket. To compare like with like, price the same basket of goods each time, even if tastes and preferences and spending patterns are changing. If spending patterns diverge *too* far from the original basket, you must eventually change the basket to bring it back into line with actual spending. But that replaces one index by another, and the move from one to the other may not fairly represent price changes in the transitional year. To make that clear, consumer price indexes are commonly distinguished by a name or letter and a base year – for example as the 'A' series in which 1975 prices = 100, the 'B' series in which 1990 prices = 100, and so on.

A consumer price index (CPI) is likely to be a less accurate indicator of the changing value of money than a Deflator can be. Why, then, is the CPI so widely accepted as the measure of inflation for practical purposes?

A main reason is that it tells most people what they most want to know. Are their incomes keeping step with their cost of living? They may want to know that for various reasons, but especially for wage-bargaining purposes. If price changes reduce their purchasing power they may not mind how much the changes owe to inflation, or to tax changes, or to exchange rates, or to employers' profit mark-ups. *Whatever* has cut their purchasing power, they are likely to want the cut restored.

(A note on terminology: If wages and prices rise at different rates, real wages rise or fall. Some economists say that real *incomes* rise or fall. Others,

including this text, don't. Why not? Real income does include what your money income will buy, but it also includes the tax-paid services you receive from government and what you produce for yourself using household or public capital. So although a rise or fall in real wage does usually increase or reduce real income, don't forget that it is possible for some households, or some national populations, to have higher real wages but lower real incomes than others, depending on the taxes they pay, the public income and services they receive, the household and public capital they have and the uses they make of it. Real wages and real incomes *can* change in opposite directions – for example if real wages fall, but government provides more public capital for people to use; or if real wages rise, but public services are cut and public capital which people have been able to use freely is privatised or converted to 'user-pays' so that people make less use of it.)

As described above, a Consumer Price Index and a Deflator differ in principle. But the difference is often blurred in practice, in the chains of causation that cause or restrain inflation. Suppose that the government shifts some taxation from income tax to sales tax. That increases prices. It doesn't reduce the value of money, it merely transfers income from some taxpayers to others. So it won't affect a Deflator. But it will increase the Consumer Price Index. If wage-earners respond to that by demanding and getting a wage rise, then employers pass on the extra wage costs by raising consumer prices, that's genuine inflation: the value of money has declined, and the Deflator will show it. Thus a non-inflationary change can have an inflationary effect, as producers and consumers try to shift the burden of the new tax onto one another.

Costs and benefits of inflation

Inflation benefits a few people, hurts many more, and reduces general economic efficiency and equity in a number of ways.

Anxious competition for income   Wages and salaries cease to have dependable value. Unless they are linked to a price index by law or contract, they have to be renegotiated year after year to keep their purchasing power from declining at the rate of inflation.

That has many human costs and scarcely any economic benefits. Competition to maintain the real value of money incomes is not a form of competition that motivates better work.

Besides responding to inflation, the constant anxiety

and renegotiation can help to maintain or accelerate inflation. As prices rise, workers demand and get higher wages. As they do, employers raise prices again. And the competition for shares is not all between employers and employees. Workers in different industries and occupations watch their relativities and leap-frog each other in their wage bargaining. Thus with continuous opportunities to gain or lose shares of income, the first harm that inflation does is to perpetuate itself.

Efficiency There are ill effects on business and household investment. Chapter 25 had a note on the 'sloped credit' effect of inflation, and there is a full account of it later in this chapter. When lenders protect the value of the capital they lend by adding a rate of inflation to the rate of interest, that increases borrowers' repayments disproportionately through the early years of their loans. Some small firms and low-income house-holds may not be able to afford the high opening repayments on 'sloped' loans. Even if they can, they face variable rates of interest, and corresponding risks, on the long loans they need for houses, farms, business premises and equipment.

The effects tend to be worse in deregulated economic systems. When the more effective means of strategic economic management have been dismantled, govern-ments tend to respond to actual or expected inflation by contriving high rates of interest. (And if governments don't, banks do.) The high interest is meant to deter investment, and thus restrain employment, workers' wage-bargaining, and consumer spending. Those effects are meant to restrain both costs of production and effec-tive demand for it. They thus restrain prices, and inflation. The strategy often works. But the human costs of unemployment and insecurity are painful. Their economic and welfare costs are heavy. And (for reasons summarized in the previous chapter) the high interest cannot ration credit efficiently. Thus besides the direct economic harm which inflation does, it can prompt market responses and policy responses which intensify the harm.

Distribution of wealth and income Inflation affects the distribution of wealth and income in two main ways.

Assets other than money or rights to money – assets such as land, buildings, equipment, patents, jewellery, works of art – tend to maintain their value under infla-tion. As all prices rise, *their* market prices rise. They are therefore a safer store of value, for passive investors, than money in the bank or out on loan. That tends to increase the demand for assets when inflation sets in,

and the increased demand has often inflated the price of assets faster than other prices: faster than the rate of inflation. So people who own or can afford to buy substantial assets – people with wealth – tend to do better than people with nothing but income. And among income earners, stronger bargainers tend to keep their incomes up with the rate of inflation or ahead of it, and weaker bargainers tend to fall behind it, i.e. to lose some real income. Though there are exceptions, the higher earners tend to be the stronger bargainers. So both between people with wealth and people without it, and between higher and lower earners, inflation tends to increase inequalities of wealth and income.

But watch it. What you study may be changing as you study it. You heard a different story about some effects of inflation through the long mid-century boom. There was a low rate of inflation and it was not expected to persist or increase. So banks, and bond and debenture buyers, continued to lend money for long terms at fixed rates of interest. The rates were low, and many govern-ments regulated them to keep them low. Contrary to expectations, inflation continued and slowly acceler-ated. That widened the gap between nominal and real rates of interest. (Suppose you borrowed at 5 per cent interest when inflation was running at 2 per cent, and inflation increased to 6 per cent during the life of the loan. Your real rate of interest might average 1 or 2 per cent.) Thus a generation of homebuyers, farmers and small businesses got their capital on credit at very low interest, and prospered. But lenders are smarter now, and don't lend long at fixed interest. Governments have deregulated interest rates and international capital movements. Real interest rates have become high and unstable. Those new bank and government responses to inflation have ruled out, for the time being, the produc-tive and equalizing effects which inflation had for some groups a generation ago.

Aims often conflict. Divisive distributional aims, when groups contend for shares of income, conflict with their common concern for stable prices and incomes. Conflicts between groups generate conflicts with government. An example:

Suppose that in the last year wages have risen 4 per cent, and prices 8 per cent. Workers have lost (roughly) 4 per cent of their purchasing power. They demand a 4 per cent wage rise. After calculating a proper deflator, employers can show that only half the workers' loss is to inflation. The other half of the price increase comes from new taxes on consumer goods. So the employers offer a 2 per cent rise, to match the 'pure' inflation. They resist paying the new consumer tax for their employees. Why *should* they pay it? The government clearly intended the consumers to pay the tax, and so they should.

Should that end the argument? Not necessarily. If the tax is to finance public investments and services which will benefit the taxpayers, I might agree with the employers. If on the other hand the additional consumer tax is to balance a generous reduction in the top rate of income tax – i.e. if the new tax is an income transfer from poorer to richer individuals – it may be reasonable for the workers to get some of it back from the capitalists by taking a bigger wage share. That may frustrate the government's intentions, but it doesn't break the law.

But suppose that instead of relieving the rich of some income tax, the new consumption tax is to finance the abolition of payroll tax. That should increase employment, reduce consumer prices, and thus hand most of the new tax back to the worker/consumers who pay it. In *that* case, is it reasonable for workers to want 2 per cent more from their employers to pay the new tax, plus 2 per cent to compensate for inflation, plus the 2 per cent (or so) that lower consumer prices will add to their spending power?

(Ethical questions: In those last conditions, what wage rise do you think that (i) a Swedish labor economist, (ii) an Australian industrial judge and (iii) an American employer of non-union labor should try for?)

Money illusion is jargon for a psychological effect of inflation. People – especially inexpert people who don't read consumer price indexes – can mistake inflationary changes in wages and prices for real changes. If real wages are steady, but money wages are rising at the rate of inflation, the wage rises may give some people the happy impression that they're doing better every year. If the wage rises lag behind the rate of inflation, people whose real wages are falling may not notice it. Or if they do, they may not be able to resist the change as effectively as they would if they were asked to accept formal wage cuts. The poorest quarter of US wage-earners lost an average 12 per cent of their real wage income between 1980 and 1995, despite continuing growth and rising real national income. Most of the loss came from 'wage lag', very little of it from negotiated wage cuts.

As government is required to do more, it needs more revenue. Under inflation, fixed rates of income tax can yield rising real revenue. (Suppose income tax is zero on income below $10,000, 20 per cent on income between $10,001 and $30,000, 35 per cent on income between $30,001 and $50,000, and 50 per cent on income above $50,000. As money incomes rise with inflation, some incomes move up to higher income bands and tax rates each year. Without any growth of real income or any increase in tax rates, there is a steady increase of real revenue. It is called 'bracket creep'.) Depending what side you're on, you may think that a good or a bad thing: a painless way to raise necessary revenue, or an opportunity for politicians to buy votes with deceptive tax 'cuts'.

Conclusions

1. Inflation can do substantial harm to economic efficiency and equity. It can hurt many people's security and peace of mind, and prompt unproductive kinds of competitive behavior. But –

2. Some current methods of combating inflation are also harmful to economic efficiency and equity. And –

3. Those harmful methods – especially using high interest rates to restrain investment and maintain substantial unemployment – get some of their support for other reasons: for example to benefit the owners of interest-bearing funds, and to strengthen employers' bargaining and disciplinary powers against their workers.

4. Deregulation has done away with a number of better methods of restraining inflation.

The story so far: Inflation is hard to measure precisely. It can be hard to distinguish inflationary changes in the value of money from other price and income changes. But it is undoubtedly harmful and ought to be restrained as far as may be consistent with other common purposes.

Next question: What causes it?

CAUSES OF INFLATION

It is wise to distrust monocausal theories of inflation which ascribe it exclusively to the money supply, or to full employment, or to government intervention (or on the other hand to the cowardice of governments which 'won't take the tough decisions'). The only valid general explanations of the causes of inflation are of the kind offered in the next two paragraphs. And though true enough, such explanations are too broad and unspecific to be much use as guides to policy.

Most inflation is induced in one way or another by competition for shares of income. Workers contend for higher wages. Unions try to keep up with each others' wage gains. They try for gains at the expense of their employers' profit shares. They compete with themselves as consumers when their wage gains will push up the consumer prices they pay. Employers price their products for desired rates of profit. They raise wages to attract workers when labor is scarce. Investors compete with each other for credit to finance investment. Banks compete for profits and market shares by extending more credit than is prudent. Politicians compete for office by taxing less than they should, or by printing more money than they should, and by flooding the economy with money in election years. None of that behavior need be inevitable or unchangeable. It is modified for better or worse by the culture, education, historical experience and leadership that shape the beliefs and behavior of those concerned, and of electoral majorities.

But – second – inflation can also be increased or reduced by mistake. Governments, investors, banks, labor negotiators and others misjudge one another's strength and intentions, misjudge the likely effects of their own actions, misunderstand how their economy and their financial systems work. Many of the impulses listed in the previous paragraph can have greater or lesser or different effects from those their authors intend, from mistake or intrinsic uncertainty.

Useful analysis needs to be more detailed, and it often needs to be local, i.e. specific to particular times and countries. We will shortly list many kinds of action, by particular business groups, labor groups, consumers, government and others, which can contribute to inflation. Most of such actions both respond to action by others, and in turn prompt action by others. Over time, many of the groups change their policies in the light of experience and changing conditions. You can rarely understand any one of them without knowing what the others are doing or expected to do at the same time.

What is the best way to learn the details of that continuous, interactive, changing process?

There's no harm in learning difficult things twice, by different means. You're about to be offered two arrangements of much the same information. First there's a *list* of the main groups whose actions can affect the rate of inflation, and the main kinds of action open to each group. That is static analysis, for students who like tabulated information – in this case a list of the players and the roles they can play. Second, there is a *narrative* of a representative process of inflation to which all the groups contribute. It shows how interactive, continuous and often circular the causation is. It is a process in which it is pointless to look for a *single* or *main* or *originating* cause. (It may nevertheless make plenty of sense to look for particular links in the chains and cycles of causation at which government, or others,

could act to change the process for the better.)

Players

Employers   When demand is buoyant, employers may want to increase output. To do that, they may raise wages to attract workers from one another and to hold their own workers against others' offers. Unions may well encourage the competition, but it can happen without them wherever the demand for labor in particular occupations exceeds the supply.

Employers can pay higher wages without raising wage rates, if they ask for more overtime.

Employers may grant union claims for higher rates if the employers think the increases are justified, or if they fear industrial conflict, or if they value their workers' goodwill. They may grant them the more readily if they believe they can pass the additional wage costs on in higher prices.

For technical reasons some industries reduce their costs and expand their output faster than others. The gains from rising productivity are up for grabs by consumers (through lower prices), by shareholders (through higher profits) and by workers (through higher wages).   How the gains are distributed depends on competitive   conditions,   wage-fixing   methods, bargaining strength, and other facts of each case. But the industry's workers commonly do better, over time, than workers in industries whose productivity grows more slowly or not at all. There is nothing necessarily inflationary in that: workers, employers and consumers are sharing some additional output made possible by technical progress. In market theory, the workers' higher wages should attract other workers to the industry until its supply of labor exceeds its demand, and wages return to their normal relativities with other occupations. In practice workers in the more productive industries tend to retain their jobs and rates of pay, and workers in other industries then bargain for equivalent rates. If they get them, *those* gains are likely to be inflationary. (We will return to this subject presently, when reviewing labor's contributions to inflation.)

That is one case of non-inflationary behavior (distributing some productivity gains) prompting inflationary behavior (higher pay without higher productivity). Here is another: An industry is working below capacity. It is not sacking people, it is hoarding labor hoping for a revival of demand. Demand does revive. Without hiring more labor the industry works up to full capacity. That brings more revenue without a proportionate increase of costs. Nothing inflationary in that. But unions notice the higher profit share, want some of it, and demand and get a pay rise. Nothing inflationary in that, either – it is merely shifting some income from the profit to the wage share, i.e. from owners to workers. But rising wages often justify higher prices, and employers may judge that they can recover the higher wages by raising prices, to hang onto their new profit share. *That* is inflationary. Owners and workers together have increased their money rewards by more than they have increased output. Consumers get less goods for each dollar they spend. The value of money has fallen.

Employers may also fuel inflation if they increase their degree of monopoly, or other market strength, and use their strength to raise prices where there is no increase of costs. Again, that is not inflationary if all it does is transfer some income from consumers to share-holders without affecting the supply or the value of money. But the higher prices will inflate the Consumer Price Index, and that is likely to prompt workers to claim higher wages. Government may support them. Employers may have to pay them. That restores the original split between wage and profit shares, but at higher prices all round. That is inflation.

Workers' bargaining strength varies with national wage-fixing systems, market conditions, the level of unemployment, the extent of union organization, and union policies. There is a spectrum from the least to the most organized:

Market wages   Eighty per cent or more of US workers are not union members and their wages are not fixed by collective negotiations. Federal and State laws regulate some of their working conditions but not their wages (except that some states specify a minimum wage). Employers offer whatever wages will attract and hold the workers they need. This is the developed world's nearest approach to a labor market. Most of the least skilled and lowest paid workers are in this category. They can rarely apply much inflationary pressure on their own behalf. Their wages rise when market conditions prompt employers to compete for their labor. When market conditions allow employers to reduce their wages, inflation makes it easier to do that. There is no need for wage cuts, which tend to be resisted. With unchanged wage rates, real wages decline at the rate of inflation. They still decline if regular adjustments raise money wages by less than the rate of inflation.

Competitive bargaining   There are countries, including the United Kingdom, in which half or more of the workforce has at times been organized in quite strong unions which operate with a good deal of independence of each other. Their wage bargaining is with

representatives of their members' employers. They are not easily persuaded to cooperate in central national bargaining between peak representatives of all labor and all employers (as they did in Sweden). They rarely cooperate with government in national incomes policies (as they have done in Australia). They may appear to compete, as wage gains for one union prompt catch-up claims by others. Those relations are not necessarily hostile: gains for one industry tend to improve the chances for others. But that leap-frogging kind of bargaining can be strongly inflationary. There are never settled relativities. There are always unions whose last deal has been overtaken by others and who will feel unfairly disadvantaged until *they* catch up (and put others at an unfair disadvantage until they catch up, and so on). And no bargainer has to feel responsible for the national rate of inflation, or under a consequent duty of self-restraint.

Central bargaining   Where the main wage-bargaining or judicial wage-fixing has been central, as at times in Sweden, New Zealand and Australia, labor has had great bargaining strength, but also the most obvious duty of self-restraint. The strength has been used more responsibly at some times than at others. It has consistently been used to give the poorest workers better wages than they get in other countries, and to reduce wage inequalities within the ranks of labor. It has often been used prudently to restrain the rate of inflation. Nevertheless Swedish and Australian rates of inflation have sometimes exceeded the US rate. (But labor's bargaining strength and strategies were not the only cause of those differences.)

Triggers   Where workers have some bargaining strength they may intensify pressure for wage increases if –

- their real wage has fallen, for any reason

- their real wage has not kept up with a rate of real wage growth which they have come to expect

- their real wage has not kept up with the wages of other occupations which they regard as comparable to theirs

- their wage share has fallen (That need not necessarily mean that their real wage or its rate of growth has declined. It is consistent with rising real wages if profit is taking a disproportionate share of increasing revenue.)

- they make tactical wage claims when bargaining for other things (job security, conditions of work, superannuation, etc.)

- political conditions look propitious for wage gains
- political conditions prompt hostile union action on wage and other fronts.

Claims on most of those grounds have the ambiguity which characterizes most inflationary action. If a wage rise succeeds in taking some real income from others – from shareholders or taxpayers, for example – it is redistributive rather than inflationary. But if those others recover their losses by raising *their* rates or prices, the action and response together are inflationary: they inflate the currency without any direct effect on real output or incomes. (But you know why the inflation may prompt other actions which *do* harm economic performance.)

Banks Home and foreign banks can create inflationary amounts of credit, if governments let them. Too much credit for productive investors may raise wages and prices in the capital goods industries by financing more demand for capital goods than the industries can supply. Too much consumer credit can raise wages and prices by financing more demand for consumer goods and household equipment than their producers can supply. Too much credit for land developers, office builders and asset traders may inflate asset prices, and wages in the building trades. Regulation by the government or self-restraint by the nation's banks could prevent the creation of too much credit. But that may not be effective if investors, asset traders, and the non-bank institutions who provide consumer credit are allowed to borrow capital funds from foreign banks.

Inflationary over-financing often includes some imprudent lending by the banks, i.e. some lending for unduly risky or unproductive projects. But notice that the creation of too much credit does not necessarily depend on bad banking. If enough of the projects looking for credit are good ones (or would be, if there were not too many of them) quite conservative bank lending can still create too much credit in total, and finance more demand for capital and consumer goods than producers can supply. Whether the excessive credit comes from careful or careless lending, it is likely to finance an increase in inflation, and then some financial failures as some of the new office buildings, hotels and holiday resorts and some of the output of the expanded consumer-goods industries can't find customers. The problem is one of national coordination. There are no automatic market mechanisms to solve it. It is also difficult to solve it by internal coordination and regulation if government has lost the power to regulate the country's foreign trade and exchange.

Government influences the rate of inflation both by its own economic activities and by regulating and influencing activity in the private and household sectors.

Fiscal policy Government can spend more, or the same amount, or less, than it collects in taxes or other revenue, so its budget can be in deficit or balance or surplus. A deficit tends to increase the quantity of money in the economy and a surplus tends to reduce it, but those effects can vary. For example –

Government can finance a deficit (i.e. spend more than it collects) by creating new money. That increases the quantity of money in the economy. Or it can finance a deficit by borrowing. The effect of that depends on the lenders. If people lend existing funds for government to spend, the quantity of money does not change. But if banks create new money to lend to government, the quantity increases.

Similarly if government runs a budget surplus and does nothing with the surplus, that reduces the quantity of money in circulation. But there's no change in the quantity if the surplus is used to repay public debt, and is thus returned to private hands.

Do changes in the quantity of money affect the rate of inflation? Not necessarily. It depends on other conditions: on the economy's productive capacity and its full employment or under-employment, the phase of the business cycle, business expectations, and the presence or absence of effective price and income policies. But subject to those conditions, deficit budgeting in an under-employed economy tends to revive demand and output, and in an economy working at full capacity it may increase the rate of inflation if the consequent increase of spending runs ahead of the growth of output.

Monetary policy Government can try to influence the rate of inflation by influencing the quantity of money in circulation, and the price of credit, in a number of direct and indirect ways. Directly, it can -

- regulate the quantity and uses of money that banks may lend
- regulate the rate of interest on bank deposits or loans
- regulate lending to foreigners and borrowing from foreigners
- borrow for its own purposes from its reserve bank rather than from private lenders.

Alternatively it can do without those powers and confine regulation to prudential controls to keep banks honest and solvent. Its main remaining monetary weapon against inflation is then the rate of interest it pays on its own borrowings, and the effect that has on market rates of interest. High interest is expected to restrain investment, employment, wage income, spending, and (therefore) the rate of inflation. (You know the possible economic and social costs of that strategy.)

Incomes policy Remember the four ways to fix wages. Each has a role for government, and government can use its influence to increase or to reduce inflationary pressure.

Where wages are 'left to the market' they are commonly decided in three main ways. (i) Individual employers offer whatever rates will attract the labor they want. (ii) Unions bargain with employers' representatives in particular industries. (iii) Governments decide what to pay their public employees. (Some governments bargain with public service and other unions. Some governments have at times made it unlawful for public employees to belong to unions.)

Other characteristics of market wage-fixing were discussed in Chapter 32. Here we are concerned with effects on inflation. They are diverse. For example, does business competition tend to raise or restrain wages? It can do either. When business is slack, cost-cutting competition between firms tends to restrain wages. When the same firms are working to capacity and competing for market shares during a boom, they may inflate wages as they try to expand capacity by enticing workers away from each other. Monopolist employers may also vary their wage policies with their circumstances. Some use their strength to restrain wages. Others – especially if they deal with strong unions – buy industrial peace by keeping wages up to or ahead of the rate of inflation, and use their market strength against their customers instead, by raising prices.

Just as employers' and workers' tactics vary in market conditions, so does the performance of national systems which have market wage-fixing in the sense that they have no central national wage-bargaining or institutional wage-fixing. Both in the US with low union membership and industrial coverage and in the UK with strong unions in many industries, wage setting and bargaining have generally been opportunist. German employers and employees have exploited their market strength less greedily, or perhaps more prudently with the long term in mind. National culture, experience and habits of behavior can vary the effects of decentralized market-type wage-fixing.

Summary: Government can affect the rate of inflation by –

- fiscal policy (raising more revenue or less revenue

than it spends or borrows; choosing inflationary or non-inflationary taxes)

- financial policy (regulating rates of interest, the creation and uses of bank credit, and foreign lending and borrowing)

- influence over the choice and operation of the wage-fixing system and (with a suitable system) by a negotiated incomes policy

- influence over private price-setting

- persuasive leadership and public education to induce fairer, more prudent, less opportunist behavior by all concerned.

Some economists might also include anti-trust and anti-protective action against monopolist and other sources of market strength – but that strength is used in diverse ways, sometimes to increase and sometimes to reduce inflationary pressure.

PROCESSES OF INFLATION

The following narrative is an artificial one rather than an actual national history. It is put together to show how the various contributors to inflation interact with one another in processes of continuous or cyclical causation. It is repetitive, because you have just read a list of the inflationary impulses. Notice, now, how many of them are items of *responsive* behavior, prompted directly or indirectly by others' behavior. The process has no single cause or recent starting point. Wherever you break into it, you find people acting chiefly in response to other past or expected changes. We will break into it when a representative OECD economy is beginning to recover from a cyclical recession.

Consider an economically advanced Western democracy as it enters the upswing of its business cycle. Government has encouraged the recovery by reducing the interest rate, cutting some taxes and increasing its public investment program. Firms which have finally emptied their warehouses are buying more materials and hiring more hands to increase production. With more public and private wage incomes, demand revives faster than some industries can supply it, so there are higher prices as consumers compete for scarce goods, and some producers (and wholesalers and retailers) seize the opportunity to increase their mark-ups.

With strong demand and some rising prices, some industries move to expand their capital and productive capacity. Many, especially younger and smaller firms, seek bank credit to buy capital goods. The banks supply the credit. To put the new capacity to work, the firms need more workers in particular occupations.

Competing for scarce labor, some of them offer higher wages.

In industries dominated by bigger firms, output is easier to expand. The big firms can self-finance most of their needs from accumulated reserves, and they tend to hoard their skilled workforce through recessions, so they have less need than the small firms have for additional credit or labor. But as they expand output and work at full capacity, their revenues increase more than their costs do. So their profits rise, and the profit share increases, without their necessarily raising their prices.

The big unions in those big industries respond with wage claims. They have a number of reasons for seeking (and usually getting) regular wage rises. They want their wages to keep up with inflation. Technical progress tends to give their industries increasing productivity so there are regular wage claims, above and beyond the rate of inflation, for a labor share of the growth. And all those claims do best if they can be timed when demand is strong, the industries are fully employed and well able to pay, and a rising profit share justifies claims to restore the traditional labor share. On this occasion many of those unions claim, and get a good deal of what they ask for.

There are occupations in which technical progress does not have the same effect on productivity. It may have little or no effect: judges, portrait painters and jockeys don't produce much more or better output than they did a century ago. Or technical progress may improve the product without reducing its wage costs. Medical technology improves services to people's health and length of life, but it does not increase the number of patients to whom each doctor or nurse can deliver those benefits. Various technologies improve what children can learn, but don't reduce the number of teachers they need. People in these occupations notice the wage gains in industries whose technology *does* improve their revenue. They respond with wage claims based on equity (comparative wage justice) and efficiency (their occupations are socially necessary, and must offer good enough wages to attract the number and quality of recruits they need). But they care for no more patients or pupils than they did, so their wage gains count as inflationary. (Competent central wage-fixers – the Swedish national negotiators, the Australian industrial judges – have long grasped that to be both efficient and non-inflationary, wages need to be linked to *national average* gains in productivity, not to gains in the industries concerned. That can conflict with firms' interest in giving their workers productivity incentives, especially in industries whose productivity depends more on the workers' behavior than on the equipment

with which they work. So there is usually some departure, even in central wage-fixing systems, from strict non-inflationary principles.)

Many of these inflationary responses to changing conditions are predictable. So is the general progress of the business cycle, if not its actual timing or magnitude. So people anticipate: lodge wage claims because prices are *expected* to rise, raise prices because wages are *expected* to rise. And as inflation accelerates or is expected to accelerate through the upswing of the cycle, people with money in debentures or interest-bearing bank deposits (which will lose capital value at the rate of inflation) tend to withdraw it and spend it on shares, houses, land, works of art and other assets that are expected to hold their real value despite the inflation. Rising demand for those assets raises their prices, rewarding people who buy them early. Others use their money to gear up with bank credit, and build or buy assets whose prices they hope will inflate at a higher rate than the rate of interest on the debts which financed them. Competing for credit and for the available assets, they fuel the asset-price inflation from which they hope to profit. Banks finance them, borrowing abroad if necessary. One reason why banks fuel the inflation by lending to such risky customers is that they are losing better borrowers. Rising inflation, market pressures and government action are combining to force high and variable rates of interest and steeply sloped credit. Many small businesses and marginal homebuyers dare not borrow for long terms in those conditions. Rather than lend less and so earn less, some banks turn to riskier borrowers.

As demand expands, imports increase. Foreign debt, and the country's exchange deficit, increase. Inflation is a little faster than the American and Japanese rates. Together those factors make it likely that the country's exchange rate will depreciate. Anticipating that, currency gamblers sell the currency down a bit faster and farther than it would otherwise go. That increases the retail prices both of imports, and of a range of national products which use imported inputs. The Consumer Price Index and the rate of inflation rise accordingly.

From encouraging the recovery, government now moves to restrain the boom.

That's not as easy as it used to be. Things government could once do, it can no longer do. When it deregulated the banks it gave up most of its power to influence the quality, quantity and price of credit.

Quality: Government can no longer influence the uses of credit. It can't persuade the banks to lend at

Economic strategy

home rather than abroad. It can't persuade them to lend more generously for farming, manufacturing and conservation than for (say) luxury housing or consumer credit.

Quantity: It can't regulate the rate at which banks expand credit for particular purposes. For example it can't make them expand and contract consumer credit counter-cyclically.

Price: It can no longer regulate rates of interest directly or selectively. So it can't keep them low and stable for the benefit of long-term borrowers. Instead, government uses its own borrowing, and market operations by the reserve bank, to keep all interest rates high and *un*stable. They're kept high during booms to discourage investment and maintain some unemployment, and thus restrain inflation. They're lowered during recessions to revive investment and employment, but the lowest rates are still higher than the rates were through the regulated years. High and unstable interest has many destructive effects on business and household activity, but the government feels it has no choice: since deregulation, this rather clumsy, indirect and indiscriminate influence on the rate of interest is one of its few remaining weapons against inflation. (And against the annual exchange deficit in the indebted, deficit-trading country of this example.)

Also, though for different reasons, there has been some loss of taxing capacity. The legal power to tax has not changed, except in some American states which have limited it by constitutional law. But the general Rightward shift of power, economic theory, public opinion and electoral numbers has made it harder than it used to be to tax rich incomes, to tax progressively, and to introduce new taxes or increase existing ones.

There have always been pressures to reduce taxation where possible. Additional pressure comes with some modern income policies which offer unions tax cuts in exchange for wage cuts or restraints. Altogether it is harder than it used to be for governments to restrain spending and 'demand-pull' inflation during booms by increasing taxes. The fiscal alternative (also encouraged by many Right ideologists) is to reduce public investment and spending, so that less of the revenue taken by existing taxes will be put back into circulation through public servants' pay and public purchases of capital and consumer goods. Assume that in our artificial narrative the government is a little to the Right of Centre. Through the last twenty years it has made some inflationary tax changes. It has reduced taxes on high incomes and corporate profits, and replaced the lost revenue by increasing payroll tax and introducing – then

occasionally increasing – a new Value Added Tax on goods and services. Each consequent jump in the price index, the rate of inflation and most people's costs of living has endangered the government's slender electoral majority. So in the present boom there will be no more tax increases. To restrain aggregate demand, the government is reducing wage income and consumer spending by cutting public investment and services. To restrain investment it is keeping interest rates high, and selling some public enterprises to divert funds from new private investment. To get the best prices for the enterprises it sells them with monopoly rights. When their revenues decline with declining demand through the next recession, the new owners will maintain their yields by raising their prices. In recession that won't increase the rate of inflation but it will help to slow its decline.

Other factors will also slow its decline. Encouraged by some of its richer supporters and its neoclassical economic advisers, the government will decide that investment is slack because owners' and executives' incentives are inadequate. It will make further cuts in company tax, capital gains tax and the top rate of income tax. Those cuts reduce public revenue too far, at a time when recession and rising unemployment bring rising welfare costs. The government responds with further cuts to public investment and services. Those further increase unemployment and public welfare costs. In the end the government – pledged not to increase taxes – increases existing user-pays charges for health, education and information services, and extends the user-pays principle to some further services. Those charges contribute to the price index and the rate of inflation.

But despite those inflationary impulses, the rate of inflation does decline. Some firms complete the expansion they began during the boom, and stop investing. Others, especially those who have to finance long-term investment with bank credit, are deterred by the risks of high and unstable interest rates. Some non-bank funds which might have found their way to some of those investors are diverted to the safer business of buying the established monopolies which government is privatizing. Meanwhile full warehouses and falling demand lead many firms to scale down current production. Cuts in government demand for goods and building contracts reduce private employment. Cuts in public services reduce public employment. These measures combine with the cyclical market forces to reduce total income and spending to a level at which there is very little 'demand-pull' inflation. High unemployment, and the continuing conversion of wage work to contract and casual work, reduce many workers' bargaining strength and the 'cost-push' effect of wage growth. These many causes combine to reduce the rate of inflation, and some of the reduction is permanent. Through the next cyclical boom unemployment is higher and inflation is lower than they were through the previous boom.

You know the economic and social costs of restraining inflation by those means. That strategy nevertheless attracts some powerful support. High real interest, the wage-bargaining effects of high unemployment, the distributional effects of less progressive taxation, and the privatization of public services combine to increase the wealth and incomes of many owners and executives, including owners and executives of the mass media and financial press. Indirectly they also tend to increase executive pay in the public sector. Many of the policies which contribute to those unequalizing effects are proposed and supported by influential neoclassical economists. Meanwhile the blue-collared workers who are the most numerous opponents of those policies have become a minority, and a declining proportion, of the electorate.

Summary

Here is the lesson a third time as we summarize this story of inflationary influences through one business cycle in a contemporary, indebted, deficit-trading Western democracy under Right-of-Centre government:

- To help end a recession and encourage an upswing, government has –
  - reduced interest rates
  - cut some taxes
  - spent and invested more.

- More wage income and consumer spending increase demand on empty warehouses, so there is some demand-pull price-inflation.

- Firms invest to expand output, some also to expand capacity. Banks finance those who need credit by creating credit and borrowing abroad.

- Big firms working to capacity increase revenue and profit shares. For that and other reasons, strong unions seek and get wage rises. Effects of those wage costs on prices may be delayed until the downturn in the cycle has the firms again working below capacity, losing profit share, and raising prices.

- Firms with progressive technology and therefore rising productivity agree to pay higher wages. There are responsive wage claims in less productive industries. There is conflict between a national interest in

sharing out productivity gains to all workers (to enable all occupations to continue to attract appropriate talent) and the more productive industries' and workers' interest in monopolizing their productivity gains. Most practical compromises between the two interests are somewhat inflationary.

- With experience, people learn when to expect wage and price rises, and begin to anticipate them. Wage agreements assume there will be increasing costs of living. Prices are set to provide for future wage rises. Long-term loan agreements provide for variable interest rates. Thus better knowledge and forecasting of inflation can *accelerate* inflation.

- For similar reasons, expectations of financial inflation can increase demand for land and other assets, and thus inflate *their* prices. Banks finance asset price booms partly because high interest, introduced as a weapon against inflation, prevents them lending to some more productive customers.

- If inflation and other causes depreciate the national currency, dearer imports then contribute to further inflation.

When government wants to restrain inflation by restraining boom demand and investment, it lacks the powers it used to have to regulate trade, foreign exchange, the quality and quantity of bank lending, and interest rates for particular kinds of lending. It still has legal power to tax, but professional and public opinion has made it politically difficult to increase taxes. Against boom-time inflation government has to use its few remaining weapons:

- It raises interest rates in a general unselective way to deter private investment.

- It reduces its own investment and spending to reduce aggregate demand for capital and consumer goods.

- It sells public assets, which may divert some non-bank funds from new private investment (though that is rarely a main purpose of the sales).

Those measures increase unemployment, reduce wage income and thus weaken spending and demand-pull inflation. By weakening demand for labor and weakening labor's bargaining power, they reduce cost-push inflation. But they have heavy economic and social costs.

ALTERNATIVES

That narrative could be balanced by others, about countries with different resources and economic structures and policies. One story might tell how a social-democratic government, in an actual past or a possible future, creates some public controls over trade and exchange, and over the quality and quantity and some of the interest rates of bank lending; makes taxation more progressive; develops an effective incomes policy; and thus restrains inflation by means which allow fuller employment, greater equality, and better options between faster growth and better environmental performance than the current policies and practices allow. But that is the theme of two of the alternative strategies yet to be discussed. (Jump ahead to Chapters 57 and 58 if you want to explore them now.)

If you fear that only high unemployment can ever restrain inflation, learn how the democracies restrained it through the Second World War. Much of their industry was switched to war production. They had very full employment, strong demand for labor, and gross shortages of market goods. Those were classical conditions for runaway inflation, as too much spending money competed for too few goods. But the English-speaking democracies had next to no inflation. The surplus spending power was absorbed by very high and progressive income tax, and some forced or voluntary saving. Food, clothing and other essential goods were rationed and price-controlled. Formal or informal controls restrained wage inflation. Public central banks replaced the private banks as the main creators of credit.

There was public control of foreign exchange, of interest rates, and of some of the uses of bank lending. And there was next to no inflation.

People are not likely to tolerate such regimentation in peacetime. But inflationary pressures are much less, and more manageable, in peacetime. They were managed fairly effectively through the first decade or so of the long boom. Conditions have changed since then. Different measures would be required. (Our chapters on strategy will discuss some of them.) The information revolution could make some of them more automatic, efficient and unoppressive than the mid-century controls were. There would need to be some better government of international trade and exchange than there has lately been. There would need to be some revision of the general belief that markets work best with least government. But experience in both war and peace suggests that democracies with developed economies can restrain inflation without unduly restricting employment, output or efficient investment if ever they really want to.

That concludes the main themes of these three chapters on financial systems. What follows is some theory about a particular problem: the structure and management of credit when there is inflation. I think the problem deserves more attention, and perhaps reform, than it has so far attracted.

INFLATION AND SLOPED CREDIT

When there is inflation, lenders want something done to protect the real value of the capital they lend. They don't want to be repaid in inflated currency with less purchasing power than they lent. Most financial institutions try to protect them by adding the rate of inflation to the rate of interest. Since the rate of inflation can't be known in advance, banks now make most of their loans either for very short periods, or at rates of interest which the bank can vary during the term of the loan without the borrowers' consent. The remainder of this chapter discusses (1) some economic consequences of that response to inflation, and (2) alternative ways of adapting credit to inflation.

Begin by recalling what an efficient capital market should ideally do. To allocate financial resources most productively, it must be possible to lend and borrow for any length of time. For example, equity capital to manufacture household equipment won't prosper unless there is also hire-purchase credit to buy the equipment, twenty-year mortgage credit to buy the houses it equips, one-year working capital for the contractors who build

the houses, short overdrafts for their subcontractors, long-term bonds to finance the dams and power generators and pipes and wires which serve the houses – and so on. An efficient capital market is supposed to attract and reorganize and augment the available funds to supply all those credit-users according to their competitive efficiency, and in the proportions which enable them to keep each other fully employed. But it can't do that unless people can borrow at payable rates of interest for any length of time.

SLOPED CREDIT

Chapter 25 (on household capital) promised you a full explanation of the terms 'nominal interest', 'real interest' and 'sloped credit'. Here it is.

Suppose that in stable conditions you lend $1000 for ten years at 3 per cent interest per annum. You will be paid $30 interest each year for ten years. Then you will get your $1000 of capital back.

Now compare what happens when inflation is expected and financial institutions adapt to it by adjusting interest rates. If you expect 10 per cent annual inflation, you add 10 percentage points to the interest rate. So you now lend $1000 for ten years at 13 per cent interest. Call that 'nominal interest', because the first 10 per cent is not really interest at all, it is there to maintain the real value – the purchasing power – of your capital against shrinkage by inflation. Only the remaining 3 per cent is 'real interest', i.e. payment for the use of your capital. Real interest is the difference between the rate of nominal interest and the rate of inflation. It can be positive or negative – if you lend at the old nominal rate of 3 per cent, and encounter 10 per cent inflation, the rate of real interest is minus 7: the lender is paying the borrower that rate, in real terms, instead of the borrower paying the lender.

Return to our comparison of a ten-year loan at 3 per cent when there is no inflation, and a ten-year loan at 13 per cent when there is 10 per cent annual inflation. Over ten years both those loans will return the real value or purchasing power of the $1000 you lend, plus some real interest. But there is a critical difference: the second loan will return a lot of it much earlier. In the first year the loan at 3 per cent pays $30, but the loan at 13 per cent pays $130, i.e. the same $30 of real interest plus $100 *which is really an early return of capital.* That $100 of real value used to be lent for ten years. Now it is only lent for one year. Similarly the second annual payment will return some capital value which has effectively been lent for two years; and so on. The $1000 repaid in the tenth year has much less real value than the $1000 that was lent ten years before; but the lender has had the rest of his real value back earlier, in annual instalments.

The adjustment from 3 per cent to 13 per cent would make sense if the 10 per cent which represents 'capital maintenance' were added to the debt each year – which would convert this loan to a capital-indexed loan. But instead of being added to the capital debt, it is paid (as nominal interest) in cash to the lender. So it has been lent for a shorter time than the formal period of the loan.

All types of long-term lending suffer in the same way. A normal housing loan, sometimes known as a credit foncier loan, repays changing proportions of capital and interest each year, to allow the borrower to make level payments throughout the term of the loan, with no capital debt remaining at the end of the term. (Pay the same sum each month for the term of the loan, and at the end of the term you will have repaid the loan, with interest.) In stable conditions most housing loans, for terms of twenty or thirty years, repay about 2 per cent of the borrowed capital in the first year. The capital payment increases, and the interest payment on the remaining debt falls, through each year of the term. But if (say) 10 per cent for inflation has been added to the rate of interest, such a loan must repay about 12 per cent of its real capital value in its first year. *Ten* per cent of inflation has thus been allowed to increase the opening rate of capital repayment by *five hundred* per cent. Without any change in the formal term of years or the rate of real interest, most of the capital value has been lent for much shorter periods than before. There is capital repayment every year on a loan of this kind when there is no inflation. When the rate of inflation is added to the rate of nominal interest, the capital repayment is shifted sharply forward to the early years of the loan. Instead of the borrower paying level real value throughout the term of the loan, she pays level nominal value, but the real value of the payment – and its likely relation to the borrower's income and capacity to pay – declines every year at the current rate of inflation. Hence the term sloped credit.

Take time to be sure you understand this relation between the rate of inflation, the rate of nominal interest, the rate of real interest, and the effective rate of capital repayment (or to put the last item in a different way, the timing of the payments which the borrower makes to compensate the lender for the loss of his capital value by inflation). Return to the explanation and examples in Chapter 25 on housing capital, if you need to. But don't read on until the meaning and mechanism of sloped credit is clear to you.

Summary When financial institutions adjust to inflation by adding the rate of inflation to the rate of nominal interest, what they really adjust is the timing of capital repayment. As the rate of nominal interest rises above the rate of real interest, long-term loans have to make early repayments of capital. That is what is meant by sloped credit. The slope, and the early capital repayments, get steeper as rates of inflation and nominal interest rise. When this method of adapting debt to inflation prevails, there is no longer any way to lend stable amounts of real value for long terms, or with a level flow of real repayment or debt service over time.

So it is worth considering alternative ways of adapting debt to changing rates of inflation.

OPTIONS FOR CAPITAL MARKETS WHEN THERE IS INFLATION

When money values are stable, debts maintain both nominal and real value over time. When there's inflation they can't do both – 'money back' and 'real value back' are no longer the same thing.

With the onset of noticeable inflation after a period of stability, lenders and borrowers (or in practice, the institutions through which they do their lending and borrowing) face a question. Should they go on specifying their debts in the old way, in nominal money terms. ('I owe you a dollar, whatever a dollar will buy when the time comes to pay you.') If they do that, they will have to cope with inflation by increasing nominal interest rates, with the sloped credit effect.

Alternatively they can decide to specify their capital debts in real terms, by linking the amounts lent to a deflator or price index. ('Whenever I repay my debt, I'll pay you back the purchasing power that you lent me.') If they do that, it should still be possible to lend stable real value for long terms. Interest rates can then go on behaving as they did when there was no inflation. And with the usual adjustments for time and risk, longer-term uses of credit can still compete for resources with shorter-term uses. It should follow that credit can still be allocated in workable proportions to its most productive uses.

Governments, banks, building societies and other financial intermediaries can therefore respond to inflation in one of three ways:

- They can continue to offer their customers the traditional nominal terms, with fixed or variable interest rates, for all lending and borrowing.

- They can convert to offering indexed-capital terms only.

- They can offer facilities for both, and let market forces sort out the volumes of the two flows of credit.

The third (dual flow) alternative is probably the efficient one. But the first (sloped credit) alternative has prevailed, with a few special-purpose exceptions, in most national financial systems and international lending. That choice was understandable. Inflation set in, in most countries, by slow degrees. It made no obvious or dramatic moment of choice. And a change to capital-indexed lending would not have been easy. Banking and tax laws would have to be amended. A great many traditional rules and routines and forms of contract would need to be re-drafted. Staff and customers would need to be re-educated. It was very much easier to add a point or two to the rate of interest with each increase in the rate of inflation. But in choosing that easier option, banks and governments 'innovated by inertia' in quite a drastic way.

The following sections sketch some effects to be expected of the use of sloped credit: effects on the allocation of resources, on investment and employment, on the distribution of income and on the progress of inflation itself. All those elements of economic performance deteriorated from the 1970s. It is not possible to measure the separate contribution of each of the many contributing causes. They included financial deregulation, a worldwide increase in real interest rates, and the development of sloped credit. The best you can do is to understand the nature and interaction of those changes; keep them in mind together with the other, non-financial, causes of declining progress; and measure the overall changes in economic performance.

The following are some likely economic effects of sloped credit. The first item concerns some fundamentals of market efficiency. It is the most important, but I believe it has been the least noticed or understood.

The allocation of resources: theory

The industries and households which have traditionally used long-term credit have typically paid for it from steady proportions of steady, inelastic household or business incomes. When long-term loans come in 'sloped' form, with high early repayments of capital and a concave downsloping curve of real repayment over time, the workable relation between income and debt-service is often destroyed. A tradesman cannot buy a small workshop, an importer cannot buy a warehouse, a small trucker cannot buy new trucks or a depot, if the opening debt-service would now be double what older-established competitors are paying (because capital repayment now has to begin at twice the rate that used to apply).

- Established firms tend to be protected against new competitors.

- Those with access to equity capital are protected against competitors who have to borrow.

- Those who can self-finance new premises or plant are protected against those who cannot.

- Those who can adapt their cash flows to lumpy repayment requirements can borrow where others cannot.

None of those advantages necessarily goes with greater operating efficiency. People who have to depend on the traditional, workable relation between steady income and steady long-term debt service are excluded from the market by that characteristic alone. They may be able to pay the prevailing rate of real interest. They may be able to use the capital profitably if they could have it on terms which allowed a level rate of debt service and repayment. They are thus excluded for reasons which are not relevant to their efficiency or capacity to pay.

The harm is not confined to individual firms. It is likely to extend, in some degree, to the structure and division of labor in the economy as a whole. Some of the industries in the economy need long credit for producers, some need it for their customers, some need it for both, some need it for neither. Many depend on one another – plenty of cash-paying or short-borrowing industries depend on trade with long-borrowing industries, and vice versa. An efficient capital market supplies those credit needs impartially and in due proportion. But when sloped credit distorts long-term lending the efficient distribution of credit is systematically hindered. Besides their other characteristics of competitive efficiency and industrial interdependence, firms begin to be sorted out *also* by their capacity to survive in a sloped-credit world. They must be able to survive on sloped credit or without credit themselves, and live on dealings with other firms which can do the same, and on end-sales to households which can do the same.

When sloped credit became acute with the inflation of the 1970s, its uneven effects on firms and industries with different credit needs dislocated some of that efficient interdependence. It stopped the growth of home ownership. I think it contributed to stagflation and rising unemployment, and has contributed to the general 'under-achievement' of the advanced economies since. But that is hard to disentangle from the other causes of the deterioration.

Inflation itself does not necessarily make the dislocation inevitable. In principle it could be avoided by adjusting capital debts rather than interest rates to the rate of inflation wherever that improved borrowers' capacity to pay. Some 'low-start' mortgage loans have been developed to help homebuyers. But there has been no general resort to the indexation of debt.

The allocation of resources: practice

To understand the changing relations between inflation and interest rates, begin by noticing a subtle, two-way effect of the slow onset of inflation through the long boom. In many Western countries it took fifteen or twenty years, through the 1950s and 1960s, to rise from 1 or 2 per cent to 4 or 5 per cent per year. From year to year the change was unobtrusive. So at any date, people tended to regard the prevailing rate as either permanent or likely to decline. So banks continued to issue long-term mortgage loans at fixed rates of interest, firms issued long-term debentures and governments issued ten-year and twenty-year bonds at fixed rates. Those rates included allowance for the rate of inflation prevailing when the loans were made, but by the time they had run for ten or twenty years the rate of inflation had often run ahead of their fixed rates of interest, to yield some negative interest to the borrowers.

There were thus two novel effects: (1) a moderate element of sloped credit, but (2) exceptionally low real interest on long-term loans, which were important sources of long-term investment. On those, real interest was lower than it would have been without rising inflation. (An Australian example: Real interest on housing loans and government bonds averaged less than 1 per cent per annum from 1952 to 1970. Those home loans financed the expansion of home ownership from 50 per cent to 70 per cent of households, and those government bonds financed much of the servicing of the new suburbs which accommodated the new houses. Similar credit financed a lot of business expansion, new small business, and farm modernization.) The comparatively low and stable rates of nominal interest are widely recognized as having contributed to the high investment, full employment and fast growth of those decades. There has not been as much notice of the exceptionally low *real* interest costs through those years.

A new phase began with the high and fluctuating inflation of the 1970s and 1980s. Banks stopped lending for long terms at fixed interest. Lenders stopped buying long-term bonds and debentures unless they offered rates of interest well above prevailing and expected rates of inflation. Credit was steeply sloped. Rising proportions of it shifted from farming and manufacturing to commercial real estate and corporate takeovers; and some shifted from poorer homebuyers to richer homebuyers and home improvers.

As the rate of inflation declined into the 1990s, nominal interest rates followed it downward. Credit was less steeply sloped and was accessible to some of the borrowers whom the high rates had excluded. But the nominal interest rate stayed well above the rate of inflation. High *real* interest had come to stay. It was nearly everywhere twice or more than twice the real rate that had prevailed through the long boom. (In Australia it was four or five times that rate.) Credit was accordingly less helpful to productive investors. Much of it continued to go to other borrowers with other uses for it. Thus high real interest was added to the other causes of slack investment, high unemployment and slow growth.

Other effects

Sloped credit affects other things besides the allocation of resources. It is worth noticing what it can do to the rate of inflation, and to the distribution of wealth and income. In each case the effect is variable – and sometimes reversible – depending on other conditions.

Inflation Wherever a high rate of inflation was added to the rate of interest it produced a very high rate of interest. That was only nominal interest, but it had to be paid. Firms paying 10 or 15 per cent or more of interest on their working capital did not see themselves as this text depicts them, as making early repayments of capital debt. They saw their interest payments as interest payments, which are a normal cost of production. As their costs went up from that cause, so did their selling prices, if competitive conditions allowed. Sloped credit thus contributed to the inflation which was inflating the nominal interest rate and 'sloping' the credit: it had some self-perpetuating effect. But that may well have been outweighed by its deflationary effects as it joined with other causes to depress investment.

The distribution of wealth and income Sloped credit has affected the distribution of wealth and income in a number of ways, most of which are not exactly measurable.

Business borrowers pay less tax. Interest payments count as business costs for tax purposes. Repayments of borrowed capital do not. As sloped credit disguises some early return of capital as nominal interest, business borrowers show higher costs and less profit, so pay less corporate income tax than they would pay *either* with lower inflation *or* with capital-indexed debt paying real interest only.

Sloped credit tends to reduce productive investment and increase unemployment, and thus to increase the inequality of incomes.

Sloped credit has excluded substantial numbers of low-income households from housing loans and consequently from home ownership. Revise Chapter 25 if you need reminding how that can affect the distribution of wealth, and the distribution of spendable income after tax and housing costs.

Nevertheless through the 1950s and 1960s, as the practice of mortgage lending for long terms at fixed rates of interest persisted through the slow rise of inflation, households which *did* get housing loans got them at exceptionally low real interest. The real interest component of their housing cost was lower than ever before or since. In countries whose credit arrangements, housing policies and physical housing forms allowed a big 'downward' extension of home ownership to poorer households – as in the US, Norway, Australia and New Zealand – that joined with other causes of the contin-

uing reduction of inequalities of wealth.

That extension of ownership ceased when inflation took nominal interest rates above 6 or 7 per cent. When inflation was reduced and interest rates returned to 6 or 7 per cent, they concealed 4 or 5 per cent of real interest. For that and other reasons (especially higher unemployment) the return to low inflation has not brought a return to increasing home ownership. And the new rates of real interest cost homebuyers more than the old rates cost their parents and grandparents.

REFORM?

To avoid the ill effects of sloped credit, financial institutions need to offer long-term borrowing and lending on a capital-indexed basis. In a dual-flow market which offers both kinds of credit, the volumes of the traditional flow and the capital-indexed flow could be determined in a market way by the lenders' and borrowers' preferences.

Some governments already issue capital-indexed bonds. But a general development of that kind of debt is likely to need legal and tax changes, and the development of appropriate indexes. (There's work for economists.) It also entails a lot of detailed hard work for a number of professions, to design loan structures to suit the users, to amend accounting methods, and to re-write the institutional paraphernalia of forms of agreement, rule-books, repayment tables, and appropriate software.

That's finicky work for specialists. But this text, with its reformist bias, does try to alert you to political and institutional difficulties in the way of any reforms which it encourages you to consider. So it can spare a page for some traps that may await reformers of sloped credit.

Managing the transition to a dual-flow market

The main danger of introducing private capital-indexed lending is that it may enable financial institutions and other owners of capital funds to establish and perpetuate unduly high rates of real interest. Four things may help that to happen:

- **Money illusion** Many people don't distinguish the element of real interest from the inflation element of nominal interest rates. Or they distinguish them only at the moment of lending, and forget the effect of time on real interest when the rate of inflation is rising or falling while the interest rate on bonds and debentures and long-term loans is fixed. World-wide rates of 5 or 6 per cent of real interest are no more than 10 or 15 years old, and have done much economic harm through those years. But except in the most expert minds – and even in some of those – there is a collective memory of nominal interest rates ranging from 7 to 15 per cent and beyond. A rate of 4 or 5 per cent sounds like a dramatic improvement. Financial institutions will try hard to establish such rates on capital-indexed credit. Reformers should remind all the potential sufferers from such rates that 1 or 2 per cent – or in some countries, less – was the real rate through the decades of fastest growth and fullest employment in living memory. But it may well take public power, as well as persuasion, to return to such fruitful rates.

- **Capacity to pay** It is easy for all to see the difference between paying 8 or 10 or 12 per cent of nominal interest in the first year of a conventional long-term loan, and paying 3 or 4 or 5 per cent in the first year of a capital-indexed long-term loan. Borrowers, unconsciously expecting the burden of their mortgage repayments to diminish over the years, as sloped-credit mortgage loans have been doing through most of living memory, will be tempted to borrow and spend too much. That may inflate house prices and load home-buyers with too much debt. The borrowers' increased capacity to pay through the early years of repayment will encourage the lending institutions to go for high rates of interest, especially at the time of transition from one system to the other. 'You know what you could afford when interest was 8 (or 10 or 12) per cent. Just think what you can afford now it's down to 5!'

- **Expertise** When public borrowers look for expert advice about the terms they should offer to induce banks, insurance and superannuation institutions to buy their new capital-indexed bonds, much of the expert advice they can get is necessarily lender-biased. Bankers, life assurance executives and other institutional lenders must be expected to take any advantage they can of the situation. They may well ask for, and hold out for, higher real rates than they have achieved even since deregulation. It may not be easy for the public borrowers to disentangle the expert bargaining from the expert advice.

- **Pride** Except for Treasuries selling government bonds, the first borrowers are likely to be big public

or private institutions offering debentures or utility bonds. The experiment is risky and the directors will have been warned against trying it at all, by many conservative voices. They may feel, strongly, that they must not fail. So they will be tempted to make certain of succeeding by offering too much. They may do that by offering an indexed bond issue at par with a high rate of interest. Or they may offer an indexed bond for tender in circumstances which more or less compel them to accept whatever tender prices are necessary to have the whole issue taken up.

A better way to manage the transition, to exert a downward rather than an upward pressure on real interest rates, might be as follows.

In principle, decide that market forces will be allowed to determine the *volume* of the indexed debt and the *price* of the conventional debt.

In practice, offer the indexed and conventional alternatives *within* major bond or debenture issues rather than between them. Each issue might offer an indexed alternative at low interest, and a conventional alternative at a fixed rate of nominal interest, but open to tender. That allows lenders to offer to buy the bond or debenture at more or less than its face value. The borrower can then accept all offers for the indexed alternative, then 'fill up' with conventional offers at market prices.

With capital-indexed lending established in that cautious way, some banks and building societies might be moved to follow, to offer depositors a new style of inflation-proof saving, and to offer home-buyers, small business and other borrowers a flow of credit repayable from level proportions of income over long periods.

But...

There is not much chance of either governments or market forces bringing rates of interest down to an economically efficient level while uncommitted funds, including new bank credit, can be freely exchanged between national currencies, and can skip from any national rule of law to any other, at the touch of a couple of keyboards. Some of the potential benefits of a dual-flow capital market, including low real interest, would depend on national governments resuming the power to control the export of capital funds.

53

Employment

Much of this chapter reminds you of things you already know. Dealing with the rich democracies' developed economies, it brings together summaries of –

- forces which determine levels of employment and unemployment,

- main means by which governments can influence employment, and

- some reasons why the aims of employment policy have been changing, and should perhaps change further.

The last is more than usually controversial, and the following chapters on alternative economic strategies will describe different employment policies at work in different circumstances and for different group, class and national purposes.

Definitions Governments and economists define people in paid work or looking for it as the workforce. So unemployment can increase if a worker loses a job *or* if a newcomer joins the workforce and can't find a job. It can decline if an unemployed worker finds a job, *or* ceases to want a job. If she still wants a job but despairs of finding one so stops looking for one, national accounts will record her as leaving the workforce, and will (wrongly) show one less worker unemployed. Depending on relations between the numbers joining and leaving the workforce and the numbers finding and not finding jobs, employment and unemployment can (i) increase together, or (ii) decline together, or (iii) change in opposite directions as changing proportions of a steady workforce are unemployed.

CAUSES OF EMPLOYMENT AND UNEMPLOYMENT

This course of study has hammered you with warnings about the complexity of economic life, and the many problems it poses for government. Here now at the heart of the subject, and at the heart of government's economic responsibilities, is what many people see (I think rightly) as the most important issue of all. But I believe that in most countries, most of the time, it is also one of the *simplest.* Simple to understand, simple to know what ought to be done. It is not always easy to *do* what ought to be done, but the difficulty is political

rather than intellectual: strong opponents stand in the way, and there are battles to win.

Simple theory: an economy will be fully employed as long as (1) there is enough demand to buy all its output, and (2) the demand is for goods and services which it is equipped to produce, or acquire by trade.

Both conditions depend on a mix of market processes and public action. The mix varies over time, and from country to country. We begin with reminders of its main elements.

Aggregate demand

Remember that effective demand consists of buyers ready and willing to pay for the goods and services they want. Economists commonly divide them into three broad groups:

1. Households' demand for final goods, defined as goods sold for the last time.

2. Private producers' demand for capital and intermediate goods.

3. Government spending on goods and services of all kinds (not including income transfers).

For aggregate demand add the three together then add export sales to foreigners minus national spending on imports. Then recall, from earlier work in this course, the reasons why –

- unaided market forces may not generate a full-employment level of consumer demand;

- unaided market forces may not generate a full-employment level of investment demand;

- unaided market forces may not provide levels of export and import demand consistent with full employment; and –

- political commitments to free trade, privatization, small government and balanced budgets can deprive government of most of the effective capacities which it would otherwise have to contrive levels of demand, in each sector and in aggregate, which are consistent with full employment.

This chapter will remind you of those capacities. But our simple theory of full employment also assumed a slow-changing economy in which the detailed composition of demand would generally match the actual productive capacities of the economy, so that a full-employment volume of aggregate demand would indeed produce full employment. It would not be frustrated by (say) an unemployable surplus of unskilled laborers and a frustrating shortage of health services, or too many farm hands and too few programmers.

But that assumption of a detailed fit between the patterns of demand and supply is never perfectly reliable, and it is less reliable than usual at present. Six chapters of Part Two spelled out a variety of ways in which changing technology, business organization, economic beliefs and national policies have upset the detailed fit between demand and productive capacity, to produce varieties of structural, regional, transitional and other unemployment. Reminders –

Culture

National cultures help to shape people's attitudes to work and leisure, the numbers who join the paid workforce, the ages at which they join it and retire from it, their tendencies to compete and cooperate, their prevailing levels of honesty and dishonesty. Cultures also differ in the variety of individual talents and temperaments that they produce. Some produce more entrepreneurs, inventors, risk-takers and adaptable people than others do. Some give women more equal opportunities in politics and paid work than others do. It is partly for historical and cultural reasons that workers have been more mobile in some countries than in others, and that full employment has been more inflationary in some than in others. It is partly for cultural reasons that Americans do so much to help themselves: start shoestring enterprises, develop new kinds of casual work and self-employment, so that in various marginal ways they can create more paid employment with less new investment than other affluent societies do.

History

Recall the historical 'march through the sectors' as technical advances have revolutionized productivity in farming, manufacturing, transport and information processing. Output grows faster than employment. The double increase of demand for those industries' products – from rising population numbers, and from rising income and spending per head – has been supplied in many industries by static or falling numbers of workers. Through the third quarter of the twentieth century most of the loss of farming and manufacturing employment was balanced by the growth of service employment. That allowed full employment if other conditions and

policies favored it. As economic growth gave people rising income and more discretionary spending, they demanded more of many public and private services: education, health care, personal services like hairdressing and manicure, holiday hotels and motels and other tourist services, and commercial recreations. Many of those are labor-intensive, so that rising demand and output create rising employment. In some, for example medical care, technical progress has actually increased the number of jobs per customer served.

But through the fourth quarter of the century the growth of service employment has been slowed, stopped and in some cases reversed. That has happened for a number of reasons –

- Technical progress, especially in computing and communications, has increased productivity and reduced employment in some services, for example in banking and account-keeping.

- Some services have increased their efficiency in ways that reduce demand for them: a revolution in dental care and education keeps teeth healthier, and has halved the number of dentists we need.

- Some of the demand for services is sated. That is partly because consuming some of them is as labor-intensive as producing them. There are limits to the amount of hairdressing, psycho-therapy, aerobics classes or golf lessons that most people have time for.

- Technical progress and rising income have enabled households to equip themselves to do for themselves things which some of them once employed others to do. There is less domestic service and commercial laundering than there used to be. (But there are reverse effects, for example as people cook less and eat out more.)

- Many public services have cut the services they provide, the numbers they employ, or both, in the course of the Rightward shift of opinion and public policy in recent years.

Technology

The first half of Chapter 13 is this text's main account of relations between technological change and employment. Unless you remember it well, read it again now. In briefest summary:

Some technical progress is labor-saving. New equipment enables fewer workers to produce the same output as before. Its introduction may disemploy some workers.

Some technical progress is capital-saving. Cheaper capital equipment, produced by fewer workers, can be used to produce the same output as before. It may dis-employ some workers in capital goods industries.

In each case productivity rises. Product prices may fall. Some of the unspent income may increase demand for the same products. Some may expand demand for other products, and investment in producing them. Thus technical progress may increase income and sustain employment in a market way.

Or it may not. Reasons why it may not:

As the disemployed workers lose income national income declines, consumer spending declines, warehouses accumulate goods so that investment declines, unemployment spreads to other industries besides the labor-saving industries.

Or there may be available jobs, but the disemployed workers do not live in reach of them, or do not have the necessary skills and could not easily acquire them.

Cyclical unemployment

In the advanced mixed economies at their present stage of development, unemployment tends to rise and fall through the phases of an irregular but persistent business cycle. Since the 1970s in many of the countries concerned (but not in the United States) the level of unemployment at each phase of the cycle has been increasing: i.e. there has been an underlying trend to higher unemployment.

Structural unemployment

First some more definitions: Many people who change jobs take time to do it. Economists call time spent between jobs *frictional* unemployment. But if unemployed workers can't find jobs because their location or skills don't fit the location and required skills of the available jobs, that is called *regional* or *structural* unemployment. If workers can't find jobs because the economy is producing enough to meet the demand for goods and services, so that producers have no reason to take on more workers, that is called *Keynesian* unemployment if it is caused by insufficient demand, and could be cured by putting more spending money into people's pockets, whether by inspiring investors to invest more or by other means. But if more spending money would mostly be spent on imports or on goods whose output could be expanded by technical and capital improvements without hiring more workers – i.e. by jobless growth – then the unemployed are structurally unemployed: no improvement of their skills and no increase of demand for market goods will necessarily reduce the number unemployed. (We will presently see that more demand for *public* goods may employ them.)

Structural unemployment is an obstinate hindrance to full employment. Technical progress typically changes some of the skills which production requires. It may also change the organization of production. It sometimes changes industrial locations and requires workers to move house. Changes in location and in the required skills also happen in the course of national and international competition. Technical progress can thus disemploy some older workers permanently, and disemploy others while they move house or try to learn new skills.

Technical progress within the national economy can do that. So can technical progress in foreign economies, or changing rates of exchange or terms of trade with them – as follows.

Trade and exchange

Some countries' export earnings and import spending balance in a market way without difficulty. Others don't. Market processes which were once expected to balance them were never entirely reliable, and are less so now that there are no public restraints on private international lending or on the speculative activity which now drives most international exchange transactions and distorts exchange rates. A country's tradeable industries can be disemployed by successful foreign competitors, by terms of trade which change for market reasons, by distorted exchange rates, or by political action at home or abroad against protective policies on which particular industries depend. And governments which are alarmed by the growth of private foreign debt may act to depress aggregate demand as a way of restraining imports. That is one of a number of intentional uses of unemployment which deserve a heading of their own.

Deliberate unemployment

Besides its direct effects, structural unemployment can also affect employment indirectly through its effects on government policy. As the demand for labor declines in some occupations and expands in others, workers can't always move freely from the declining to the expanding occupations. The new skills may take time and further education to acquire, and some of the disemployed workers may lack the money or talent to acquire them. There can thus be unemployment in some industries and regions while there is excess demand for labor in others. In the over-heated industries, wages rise. To pay them, those industries' product prices rise. Thus (1) the economy as a whole can experience some unemployment and some inflation at the same time; and (2) governments which want to restrain inflation may respond by acting to keep the level of employment well below full employment: low enough to restrain inflationary wage and price pressures in the busy industries. The consequent level of employment in the economy as a whole – or the level at which wage and price increases in the leading industries are balanced by wage and price reductions in the lagging industries, so that the price index for the economy as a whole is stable – is called by many neoclassical economists the Natural Rate of Unemployment, or more elaborately the Non-Accelerating-Inflation Rate of Unemployment (NAIRU). It may be thought to do double service if restraining aggregate demand, employment and income also restrains excessive demand for imports. But its economic and social costs will be high, and cruel.

HOW PUBLIC ACTION CAN INFLUENCE EMPLOYMENT

The following means of influencing levels of employment and unemployment have been practised at one time or other in advanced mixed economies.

The usual warnings apply. Don't assume that each listed method will work identically in all circumstances. Particular policies are quite likely to have different political chances and different economic effects in different countries, at different times, and as components of different economic strategies. Some of the assumptions about what causes what are necessarily uncertain, and disagreed.

The items are grouped under five headings: public employment; working time; trade and industry; public taxing and spending and investment (fiscal policy); and the regulation of banks and credit (monetary policy). Four of the five are reminders of work done earlier, so they can be brief.

PUBLIC EMPLOYMENT

Government can change the size and composition of the public sector. It can change the goods and services that it buys from the private sector. Within the public sector it can influence conditions of employment. Many governments have got their public servants to accept comparatively low pay in return for secure tenure. In particular services, or in underemployed regions, they have sometimes employed more workers than necessary. Public offices and industries whose functions don't tie them to particular places have been located to meet the employment needs of particular regions. Such policies may sometimes be inefficient, but are not always so if you take a comprehensive view of their social costs and benefits.

There will always be disagreement and political conflict about the quantity and quality of public health, educational, welfare and other services that a society should finance for its members. Those services affect the distribution of wealth and income, and they compete for resources with demands for other goods and services. Recall William Baumol's demonstration of the long-term effects of differential productivity in different sectors and services. Technical progress demands a growing output of labor-intensive education and health care. Both can be cheaper with public than with private funding. Both can be more equitably distributed that way. Arms-length public funding and health insurance can leave the teachers, doctors and researchers as independent in their professional work – or more so – than private insurance or user-paid service may do. The Right turn which threatens to privatize as many as possible of these services, and unequalize access to them, is also likely to raise their prices. It will thus leave most people with less, not more, to spend on other market goods.

Relations between public and private employment Where there is full employment, a slow increase in public services need not displace the production of other goods (i) if growing productivity allows some growth in all sectors, and (ii) if some sectors' output grows by jobless or job-shedding means.

Where there is persistent *un*employment, cutting public services is likely to increase the unemployment, and the public costs of unemployment. *Increasing* public services may *reduce* unemployment and welfare costs. Depending on the government's fiscal policy it may also have a multiplier effect on private employment and the output of market goods.

Suppose for example that the tax-financed dole and other public welfare costs of an unemployed worker average $50 a day, and the average wage of marginal additions to the public workforce is $100 a day. For $50 of welfare spending the taxpayers get nothing except a good conscience. For an additional $50 to move one worker from the dole to employment, they get $100 of public goods, effectively at half price, and an even happier conscience from having reduced others' unemployment.

Employers of last resort Should government go further, and offer work to all the unemployed – useful work whose output is worth having, though perhaps worth less than it costs? Should it go further still, and offer *nothing but* low-paid work to most of the unemployed, reserving the dole for people too old or infirm for such work?

Against such a policy there are reasons of two kinds. (1) Most of the citizens would rather spend their money on other things. Replacing more-preferred market goods with less-preferred public goods looks like pure loss. (2) There are severe difficulties in confining sustenance for the unemployed to disabled people only. Judgments of disability, especially of mental or psychological incapacity, are often disputable, and the symptoms can be pretended. All the evidence says that the 'voluntary' unemployed are nowhere more than one or two in every ten of the unemployed. (I think the versions of neoclassical theory which imply that all the unemployed are unemployed because they won't work for low enough pay are simply false.) And if a few employable people refuse to work, you may accept one or other of three reasons for nevertheless paying them a living income. They may have innocent dependants who ought to be supported. Without income they may resort to crime to stay alive, or to get to prison where they will cost taxpayers eight or ten times as much as a dole costs them. You may even judge that if we can't run the economy well enough to employ all willing workers, we should *welcome* volunteers willing to accept the dole without competing to take jobs from people who want to work.

In favor of public employment for *willing* workers (without the element of compulsion) there are good reasons. Rightly managed it can increase the output of both public goods and market goods. How? Increase the dole to a working wage by deficit budgeting, without additional taxation. Employ last-resort workers to produce useful public goods. They will spend most of their wages on market goods, with some income multiplier as that addition to demand increases private employment and output. If the last-resort work is tolerable, the experience may improve the working will and skill and happiness of the otherwise-unemployed.

But be careful of this reasoning. First, it assumes that additional public employees were unemployed and would continue to be unemployed without their new public jobs. So the reasoning which subtracts the public costs of unemployment from the costs of public services can only apply to marginal changes in public employment which will employ otherwise-unemployed workers. Second, it assumes that last-resort public employment will be designed and managed well enough to do more good than harm to the experience of the people employed. That can be done, but is not always easy.

Tax resistance   Those warnings don't weaken the case for restoring efficient and desirable levels of public investment and goods and services. Remember why democracies tend to under-supply themselves with public goods. Politicians offer tax cuts with the false pretence that they will bring no loss of public goods and services. Some voters support tax cuts for themselves, thinking to enjoy the services but shift their costs onto others. And so on. But experience suggests that this explanation also is faulty. Many governments have been shifting taxation downwards from richer to poorer taxpayers. But most have not actually been reducing it. The rising public costs of unemployment, of education and of increasingly expensive medical and hospital care have been reducing the share of revenue available for other services. Except perhaps in the US, the 'tax revolt' has often been misrepresented. If people are offered tax cuts without mention of their service implications, many welcome them. But if competent polls ask them if they want to save money by running down their national infrastructure, or by increasing the stress under which nurses and teachers and air traffic controllers work, or by lengthening the queues for elective surgery at public hospitals, or by consigning the mentally ill to private boarding houses without professional care, or by leaving pensioners and unemployed and low-paid workers' families to spend a half or more of their incomes on house rent, majorities say No. In the developed world outside the US and the UK through the last twenty years, parties offering more taxation than their opponents offer have won more elections than they have lost. If the case for it is honestly presented and reported, it may well be possible to restore full employment in the English-speaking countries by restoring and improving their levels of public investment and the quantity and quality of their public services.

Crowding out?   There is strong disagreement among economists about the causal relations between public and private employment.

Some neoclassical economists believe that public investment and employment, and taxation to pay for them, preempt resources which private investors would generally use more fruitfully. So when government wants to revive investment and employment during a recession, it should cut public investment, employment and services, and taxation to pay for them. That should release funds, workers and physical resources which private investors will use more productively. Part of the tax cut will give consumers money to spend on market goods which they will prefer to the public goods their taxes were buying. The rest of the tax cut – especially if it cuts company tax and tax on high incomes – will release funds for private investment.

Crowding in Critics of 'crowding out' theory argue (as this text does) that it could only apply in conditions of full employment. While there are resources which the private sector is not employing, it can't hurt to employ them. Historically the full employment of the long boom was sustained by a steady growth of public as well as private services; and since that boom and its full employment ended, increases in public investment and employment have usually *increased* private investment and employment. You've met the causal arrows before: more public employees ➜ more wage income ➜ more demand for household capital and consumer goods ➜ more private investment, employment and output to meet the demand. Also, public investors buy many inputs from private producers, so: More public investments ➜ more demand on private producers of capital and intermediate goods ➜ more private investment, employment and output to meet the demand.

On those assumptions it may well be right to restrain public investment and employment as booms approach, to avoid generating inflationary demands for more labor and goods than the economy can supply. But to revive employment in recession or to sustain it at desired levels, action which increases public investment and employment tends to increase private investment and employment too, with a multiplier effect.

TIME AT WORK and SHARES OF WORK

Governments have been acting for more than a century to restrict hours of employment. For the first hundred years that was done chiefly for the safety, health and happiness of the workers and their dependants. But north-western Europe, under-employed for the last thirty years, has been reducing working hours in efforts to reduce unemployment.

It is hard to know exactly how effective the efforts are. If you cut four hours from the working week, you do not find either every worker doing four hours overtime next week (a total failure to create more jobs), or employers hiring ten per cent more workers next year (a total success). Unemployment does usually decline. But it is never by as much as simple arithmetic would lead you to expect, and it may be hard to measure how much of the decline is from other causes. There has been much research on the question. Gerhard Bosch reviewed it in a paper (*The reduction of working time, pay and employment*) published by the United Nations in 1998. His conclusions:

The balance of opinion finds employment gains 'between 25 per cent and 70 per cent of the arithmetically possible effect'. The effects are often time-lagged, so early research tends to underestimate them.

The main enemy of success is the resort to overtime. That is likeliest when employers and workers both prefer it. Employers are reluctant to reorganize their operations to accommodate the new individual hours. Workers prefer overtime if they are low-paid and hard up, and if the cuts in time bring cuts in pay.

The main conditions for success are four:

1. **Pay** The cuts in time must not cut the workers' pay, and they must not raise the employers' unit costs. Both are usually achieved by linking the time cuts to the pay rises which come in the ordinary way with economic growth. That would have been easier through the long boom, with growth averaging above 4 per cent, than it became in the 1990s with growth averaging as low as 1 per cent. The German engineering industries nevertheless made step-by-step time cuts from 40 hours in 1985 to 35 hours in 1995. Some of the firms also got union agreement to temporary time cuts *with* pay cuts to avoid dismissing workers during recessions.

2. **Reorganization** Employers must be willing, where necessary, to reorganize their operations and shift schedules to fit the new individual hours. That may require that the workers be flexible about their hours. The hours in those German industries are now specified per year rather than per day or per week.

3. **Skill** may be scarce enough to compel overtime by the skilled workers, especially when time cuts bring new recruits to the workforce and there are more but shorter shifts. In one report of similar time cuts in comparable industries there was less recruitment and more overtime in Britain where 64 per cent of employees had no formal vocational qualifications, and more recruitment and less overtime in Germany where only 26 per cent had none.

4. **Social security** Systems of insurance and superannuation affect the incentives of employers and employed. American employers pay insurance per worker: the fewer workers, the lower the cost, however many hours each worker works. That encourages overtime. Better systems insure the workers per hour worked, so are neutral between long hours, short hours and part-time work. European systems of public social security and superannuation free firms from some obligations, and reduce the pressure on their employees to save for their retirement, or to

stay in work for as many years as possible. More workers now retire voluntarily between 55 and 65 in north-west Europe than in other advanced economies.

Notice that in working shorter hours and fewer years of life those Europeans are not 'freeloading on the taxpayers'. They *are* the taxpayers. Through their earning years they pay higher taxes than their English-speaking equivalents do. Thus they choose to transfer more income from their earning years to their non-earning years, and they do it more reliably and at less administrative cost, than do most people who have to rely on private saving and superannuation. (Chapter 12 explained how changing proportions of younger and older people can put some strain on such a system. Chapter 56 will note that the system is currently in some danger from Europe's Maastricht rules, its Central Bank and its OECD economists.)

Shares of work and shares of income

Work-sharing both helps and is helped by other equalities.

As an alternative to unemployment it spreads earned income to more households and reduces income inequalities within the workforce.

But paradoxically, it is easiest to achieve where incomes are already least unequal. It is where pay scales were flattest, and the minimum wage was highest, that work-sharing by means of shorter working time has been most acceptable. So has part-time work. And where hours are now shortest is where workers are most willing to cut them further.

These wholesome tendencies have direct and indirect causes. In the more equal systems the lowest-paid workers are better off, and less desperate for more income. They owe that to union and government policies of equality, which they support. And over time, that encourages a culture of solidarity and mutual support. By contrast the lowest-paid American workers are poorer. Bosch found the lowest-paid ten per cent of German workers averaged 2.2 times the wage which their American equivalents earned. And for less than half the German wage the Americans were doing 12 per cent more hours of work. The Americans needed all the overtime they could get. And living poorer and less protected in a more unequal and competitive system, they learn to look after themselves individually as best they can.

 But be careful how you generalize from that comparison. American inequalities and business bargaining strength may make deliberate work-sharing unlikely in the United States. But the greater equality which helps it along in Europe does not necessarily do so in other circumstances. In Japan a different culture couples relatively flat pay with *long* hours of work. But there has traditionally been some work-sharing within firms, as they do their best to keep a stable workforce through cyclical ups and downs. If they ever see a need to cut their formal hours, other qualities of their culture may well shape distinctive Japanese ways of doing it.

Don't dismiss this subject, as many 'labor market' economists do, either as unimportant or as wrong-headed government interference with market efficiency. For more than a century, the benefits of rising productivity have been divided between higher pay, shorter working hours, and fewer earning years per year of life. All three changes have owed as much to collective decisions as to market choices, and there is no good reason why the public control or the reduction of hours should necessarily stop now. Longer life, population numbers and severe new environmental constraints are already compelling some revision of the present practices. It is very important that full or fairly shared employment should be among the purposes of any changes.

TRADE AND INDUSTRY POLICY

Trade policy and industry policy make opportunities for positive and negative aids to full and stable employment.

Direct aids Recall, from chapters on economic structure and trade, the range of things government can do to develop new industries and expand, strengthen or protect existing industries. It can –

- start new industries as public enterprises
- offer land, services, specialized banking and credit, information, research and education to assist private development
- encourage and protect the national production of tradeables by tariff, subsidy or other means
- when foreign exchange is scarce, direct it to productive developmental uses which (among other benefits) create employment.

Indirect aids Employment suffers if government allows or contrives significant unemployment as a main way of limiting demand for imports and thus limiting an exchange deficit and foreign debt. So it is probably a condition of a return to full employment that governments rebuild and improve the better ways of controlling imports and balancing foreign payments. (From chapters on trade policy and economic structure you know what those methods are, and what further improvement some of them might need.)

The same applies to methods of restraining inflation. If better income and wage restraints are available and effective, governments don't need to attack inflation by inducing substantial unemployment.

FISCAL POLICY

A complicated subject: the economic effects of the relation between public revenue and public spending. The effects depend on – for example – how much of the public spending is on capital goods; what output of goods and services the spending finances; what employment it creates; how much of it is spent on national products and how much on imports; how much the government borrows, on what terms, and whether from home or foreign lenders; and so on. But we will begin with a widely used simplification. Assume that the government takes a certain amount of money from the economy as revenue, and returns a certain amount as public spending. (In this simplification 'spending' includes investment, and income transfers to pensioners, unemployed, etc.) What is any difference between the two – any net increase or reduction of the money in the economy – likely to do to national levels of employment and unemployment? First, a simple Keynesian model of what to expect. (Be warned that it was developed by some of Keynes' followers but is disavowed by others.) Second, a simple monetarist objection to it. Third, a practical way to treat them both.

A budget deficit If government spends more than it takes in tax it has a budget deficit, and leaves more after-tax income in the citizens' pockets than a balanced budget would leave them.

If the deficit is brought on by government collecting the same revenue as before but spending more and employing more people than before, the effects are likely to be as described above under 'public employment': total employment should increase by the amount of the additional public employment plus some increase of other employment from the income multiplier.

Suppose that the deficit arises from changes in revenue rather than spending: government spends at the same rate and employs the same numbers as before, but runs into deficit by reducing some taxes. The citizens consequently have more after-tax income to spend. As long as (1) there are some unemployed workers and other resources, and (2) there is some stock of consumer goods in shops and warehouses to supply the immediate increase in demand, producers are likely to respond to

the rising demand by hiring more hands to increase output. As those additional workers earn and spend and increase total demand, the income multiplier sees some further workers hired.

A budget surplus As before, we can compare the likely effects of creating a surplus by raising more revenue, or by spending less. (Changes often include a bit of both, but we can consider the likely effects of each.)

Suppose the government continues to spend as before, but gains a budget surplus and cuts the citizens' spending money by increasing taxes. If that is done when there is near-full employment, and if the amount and distribution of the tax increase is well judged, the effect may be to restrain demand to the amount the economy can supply. With supply and demand in equilibrium producers should not be able to raise prices, and consumers will have no reason to bid them up. That may prevent 'demand-pull' inflation. (Other measures may be needed to prevent cost-push inflation from rising wages or other causes.)

If the tax increase and budget surplus occur when there is substantial unemployment the unemployment is likely to increase. The higher tax leaves less spending money and less demand. Warehouses accumulate unsold goods. Services are underemployed with declining custom. Employers reduce output and some of them have to reduce the numbers they employ. The dismissed workers lose income and spend less, and the multiplier brings further reductions in demand and employment.

Now compare a surplus achieved by 'slimming government'. Government collects its usual revenue but moves into surplus by spending less and employing fewer people. This is a more popular change with people who don't immediately suffer from it, because it doesn't increase anyone's taxes. In the short run it leaves most people – everyone with a job or other income – with the same after-tax income as before. The whole cut in public spending, then in household income and spending, is taken by households whose members lose public employment, or fail to get it when they look for their first jobs. The complacent majority may also suffer eventually, in various ways. Some get less or worse public goods and services. And as fewer public employees earn and spend, total demand declines and some private employers reduce output and the number of hands they employ.

Theoretical disagreements Will rising demand actually cause producers to increase their *output*, as this account has so far suggested? Or just their *prices*? The question is at the heart of the conflict between Keynesian and monetarist theory.

Producers generally expand output if they can do so profitably. There are nevertheless conditions in which they can't or won't, and in some of those cases they may respond to rising demand by raising their prices. For example –

- If demand increases at a time when some industries have limited stocks, and it takes time to increase output, they may raise prices for two reasons: to take advantage of the temporary shortage, and to finance investment to increase their capacity. With 'stagflation' this can happen in some industries when other industries are under-employed and total demand is not excessive.

- Firms producing at full capacity may not invest to increase their capacity if they expect the boom demand to be temporary. If competitive conditions allow, they may opt to increase profit from their existing output by raising prices.

- Firms which would need long-term bank credit to finance increased capacity may not risk it if interest rates are high or unpredictably variable.

- Firms may raise prices because they *expect* demand to rise, or their wage or interest costs to rise, or their input prices to rise, though none of those things has yet occurred.

There are those possibilities, and there are others. In practice they vary with circumstances. But in theory, if other conditions allow, Keynesians expect that in an under-employed economy more spending will tend to increase employment and output. With some different assumptions about those 'other conditions' monetarists expect it to increase prices. But the sensible question to ask may not be 'Is Keynesian theory or monetarist theory the correct theory?' It may be more fruitful to ask how much of which response – higher employment and output, or higher prices – is to be expected of producers and traders *in each case*. To judge that, you usually need local knowledge: the producers' circumstances, their warehouse stocks, their financial reserves, their investment lead-times, their market expectations, the prevailing rate of interest and rate of inflation, and so on.

Conclusion Use the rival theories as guides to possibilities worth looking for in each case, not as means of guessing without looking.

FINANCIAL POLICY

To indicate the range of financial policies that can affect employment we could contrast the extremes of the range: the most-controlled financial arrangements to be found in the developed democracies in the last half-century, and the least controlled. But the least-controlled are with us now. The damage they do to investment and employment, and the good they fail to do, were the subject of chapters on national and international financial policies. Chapter 54 will presently summarize the *compound* inefficiencies which arise from the *combination* of under-governed economic structure, trade, national and international banking, and employment. Here it will do to sketch an opposite extreme: the financial elements of a social democratic strategy of full employment with low inflation and balanced foreign payments.

The strategy might include enough public employment to supply the private and household sectors with the public goods and services they need; fiscal policies to maintain a full-employment level of consumer demand; trade and industry policies to encourage efficient production and balanced foreign payments; and – to restrain inflation – central wage-fixing with a social contract, price and income policies, anti-monopoly rules, and persuasive education and leadership.

Recall the financial policies which fit with that strategy and serve its purposes. They may include –

- a low and stable rate of interest in almost all circumstances, leaving the *quantities* of credit and investment to be influenced by other means, including –

- public regulation of the quantity and general directions of private bank credit

- public banks for some special industrial, export/import and housing purposes

- portfolio requirements for insurers and some other financial institutions

- public guidelines for private foreign lending, borrowing and investment to confine them to approved purposes.

If it works as intended that strategy should allow quite high employment. It is still likely to be disturbed by some continuing business-cycle fluctuations of investment and employment; by technological changes; by some structural unemployment as the skills and location of the workforce don't keep up with the changing skills and locations of the available jobs; and by external shocks from bad weather, foreign competition and changing terms of trade and rates of exchange. But – if it works as intended – that set of financial policies (together with the rest of that strategy) is likely to do as much as any financial regime can do to maintain a high and stable level of employment without crippling effects of inflation or exchange deficit.

A middle way? It is not easy for governments to take a middle way between those extremes. Many of the possible controls are effective only in combination with each other. For example government can keep interest rates low by direct regulation only if it also regulates foreign lending and borrowing. Low interest rates which help national efficiency and employment may worsen the balance of payments if there is no control of imports, or of the export of capital funds.

Many governments do still manage to operate somewhere between the 'most controlled' and 'least controlled' extremes. But they do so chiefly by hanging on to some historical rights. The GATT/WTO agreement bans new or increased trade barriers, but it does not yet compel countries to reduce existing trade controls, except by agreement. So governments retain some established controls, though as time passes they may not be those which changing conditions require. And some governments break some of the GATT rules, whether because they are strong enough to get away with it, or they can tolerate the GATT penalties, or other traders forgive them.

Those exceptions reduce some of the harm that vulnerable countries suffer from international exposure. But while current national and international financial freedoms continue, it will continue to be hard for any national economy to achieve full employment together with low inflation, balanced foreign payments, and an efficient allocation of productive resources.

A QUESTION DEFERRED

We're about to summarize the contents of this chapter: the means by which governments can influence levels of employment and unemployment. But for a government wanting to use them, each of those means poses problems of quantity and timing. Suppose for example that you want to increase employment by (say) one per cent:

- *how much* budget deficit
- *how much* increase of tariff or subsidy on *which* tradeable goods
- *how much* increase of bank credit
- *what* rate of interest

would be right for the purpose? If some of each, *how much* of each? How long does each take to have its full effect? How may they interact, for example to increase or reduce each others' multiplier effects? How can the responsible public officials get the quantities and timing right?

Here, two answers. First, the work is complicated. It depends on there being good statistical services, as sketched in Chapter 47. At best it is far from perfect and subject to many uncertainties. Second, it is work for which this text does not prepare you. You need some advanced study, and working experience in your national system.

SUMMARY

To influence employment in the short run a government can only use the instruments which it has: the powers and institutions, and the political commitments and constraints, that exist at the time. In the longer run it can think of changing the instruments and constraints: changing laws and regulations, creating or reforming or dismantling institutions, persuading electors (or being persuaded by them) to change some of the social purposes or technical understanding that underlie prevailing policies and affect the support for them.

How government can influence employment

If it has the necessary powers, institutions and political support, or if it can develop them, a government can hope to do any or all of the following:

- It can adjust the amount and composition and locations of public employment. It can create useful work for groups the private sector can't profitably employ.

- Its fiscal (taxing and spending) policy can expand or contract after-tax income, the demand for household capital and consumer goods, and the number of workers employed by the producers of some of those goods. Employment may be affected by taxing (or not taxing) payrolls, fuel, materials and other producers' costs.

- It can influence investment and therefore employment by inducing private banks to expand or contract total credit, or credit for particular industries. It can take some credit-creation out of their hands and have it done by the Central Bank or other public banks.

- It can regulate or influence rates of interest. If it has other means of restraining excessive credit it can keep interest rates low enough to allow the most efficient allocation and use of bank credit.

- Its trade and industry policies can influence the amount and composition of employment. It can help or protect tradeable industries or expose them to international competition. It can thus determine how much of what the people want to consume they must produce nationally, or buy with earned rather than borrowed foreign exchange.

By those means governments should in principle be able to maintain quite high employment. In practice very few are trying to do so as the new century opens. Why not?

Why governments act to ensure some unemployment

They have three main reasons. Most of them have come to rely on some unemployment to restrain inflation. Business interests press them to maintain profit shares by using unemployment to weaken labor's bargaining strength. And indebted, deficit-trading countries have come to rely on unemployment as a main means of restraining the demand for imports and the demand for foreign loans to pay for them.

Governments are driven to resort to unemployment for those purposes because they have dismantled, or failed to develop, better means of managing those problems. So a return to full employment probably depends on first rebuilding independent means of managing inflation and the balance of trade and payments.

That might not be too hard to do if there was general support for doing it. But some powerful minorities would expect to lose by it and they already oppose attempts at it. Banks, many employers and many high earners and owners of capital funds enjoy and profit by their present freedoms, and defend them. Their defences are strengthened by 'labor market' economists who argue (I think mistakenly) that most unemployment is voluntary, and would disappear if unemployed workers would work for low enough wages. (The support is mutual. Business leaders now give billions of dollars a year of corporate funds to finance private economic 'think tanks' which help to propagate those beliefs.)

New reasons for wanting to restore full employment

During the twentieth century political and economic developments took the advanced economies across a number of thresholds, changing their patterns of work, many people's economic priorities, and the possible ends and means of employment policy. Reminders:

- **Productivity** For the first time, the advanced economies produce enough to keep all their people in material comfort and security if capital and income were suitably distributed.

- **Work** Research and experience find that work is valuable for its own sake, for the human development and social experience of the worker as well as for its output and the income it earns. For most people of working age, work can't be sufficiently replaced by unearned income: people need to be well occupied.

- **Happiness** There is mounting evidence that more national income (above a comfortable sufficiency) does not increase happiness. Improving the experience of work, the distribution of income and the security of employment (for those who want it) become more important than a further increase of income per head. (Remember that this is quite consistent with competition, career incentives and rising incomes through people's working years.)

- **Gender** Changing relations between men, women and children call for some reorganization and redistribution of employment. Some equitable reorganization of men's and women's working, earning, parenting and housekeeping options may have become more important than a further increase of income per head.

- **Conservation** Reform of the rich countries' environmental performance, and their influence on the rest of the world's environmental performance, is more important than increasing or maintaining their present income per head.

Those developments have increased both our understanding of the value of full employment, and our professional and political disagreements about it. They add to the other social purposes with which the aims of employment policy have to cooperate or compete: thus they complicate the considerations which policy-makers and their electors need to keep in mind. And they convince many people (though not all economists) that it takes positive public action to achieve any near approach to stable full employment (meaning paid work, employed or self-employed work and full or part-time work for everyone who wants any one of those variants).

At the same time there have been other developments which make full employment more difficult to achieve. Some changes in technology, consumer demand and economic structure tend to limit employment. As noticed above, some people don't want full employment because they believe that some of its effects conflict with particular interests or with general social aims which they value. And those and other developments have led many governments to dismantle powers, institutions and international arrangements which good employment policies would need to use.

As always, the policies you want will depend on your technical understanding of economic processes and possibilities, and on the values which shape the individual and collective purposes which you want the economy to serve. A range of ends and means will presently be illustrated in half a dozen alternative national economic strategies.

54

Global markets:
Interactive effects of inadequately governed economic structure, trade, banking, exchange and employment

As its subtitle suggests, this chapter draws together some conclusions of the last five. It summarizes effects of deregulation on economic structure, international trade, national and international financial systems, and employment. It focuses on their interaction with each other and their combined effects on economic performance as a whole and on the democracies' powers of self-government. And it discusses economists' contributions to those effects, and responsibility for them.

SOCIAL-DEMOCRATIC POSSIBILITIES

Common sense suggests that the high productivity of the rich democracies should now allow them to –

- prevent poverty and restrain inequalities of income
- help less developed countries to develop
- offer men and women equal opportunities, and equal pay for work of equal value
- care for children in ways which make their childhood enjoyable and help them to grow up as competent, sociable individuals, cooperative or competitive where appropriate, capable of happiness
- enable people to balance their experience of recreation, consumption and leisure with their experience of work
- care effectively for their environment
- balance their international trade and payments
- restrain inflation
- employ every worker who wants employment, and
- transfer, safely and economically, as much income as people want to transfer from their earning to their non-earning years.

Imagine the rich democracies as they might be now if the major powers had responded to the troubles of the 1970s by re-designing the Bretton Woods regime instead of dismantling it. The task might have been confided to French, Scandinavian and Japanese public servants who were still confident managers of their national economies. They might first have arranged what Keynes tried but failed to win in 1944: 'We intend' he said on Britain's behalf 'to retain control of our domestic rate of interest, so that we can keep it as low as suits our purposes, without interference from the ebb and flow of international capital movements.' Besides financial repairs we must imagine that the reformers also re-negotiated the General Agreement on Tariffs and Trade (GATT), and staffed the International Monetary Fund (IMF) and the Organization for Economic Cooperation and Development (OECD) with a new breed of economists. So at the turn of the century, imagine that capitalism is alive and well. In its relations with national and international government, five institutional practices are important:

1. Subject to international rules and arbitration to prevent unfair trading, nations (or trading blocs) liberate or regulate their trade as their particular economic structures require, with their levels of employment and balances of payment in mind.

2. International movements of capital funds are normally confined to aid programs, IMF and World Bank operations, and direct foreign investment approved by the relevant governments. The IMF is empowered to borrow at low interest from the exchange reserves of countries earning surplus exchange, chiefly to finance supplies of capital goods to developing and transitional countries. Where a country does allow its nationals to borrow foreign funds, its Central Bank normally borrows at the foreign rate and on-lends to the users at the country's internal interest rate.

3. National governments regulate their countries' interest rates with primary concern for investment, employment and productivity.

4. National governments restrain inflation by methods which rarely have to disturb interest rates. They do it by wage-fixing and income policies, by fiscal policy, by regulating the quantity and directions of bank lending, and by cooperative, educational and persuasive means.

5. The IMF and Central Banks cooperate to keep exchange rates fixed or within narrow bands, and to adjust them when necessary to purchasing power and national rates of inflation.

Such a system might be misused and evaded in various ways, for example by offshore dealing, by various kinds of hard-to-prevent misbehavior, by the internal financial strategies of transnational firms, and by people taking advantage of inept or corrupt or partisan government. But within and between most countries such a regime should allow less bad behavior, and motivate better economic performance, than happen now.

No strategy can expect unanimous support. In politics, the public service, business, the press and among the voters there will always be disagreements of at least three kinds. There are conflicts of interest, with some powerful interests pressing for strategies that favor them. There are disinterested, public-spirited disagreements about social values and the desirable purposes of an economic strategy. There are professional disagreements about what causes what in the economy, and what policies are likely to have what effects. Disagreements of each of those kinds had varying intensity and importance in different countries at different times in the twentieth century. Through the mid-century 'golden age' they were resolved, quite often well and wisely, by normal political means.. There have been periods of good government and effective economic strategy in many Western and East Asian democracies. That is not achieved by pretending that the conflicts of interest and belief are not there. Government has to deal with many of the conflicts, assist many legitimate interests, and attend to interested as well as disinterested concerns as it attracts support. But it can go about its work in coherent or incoherent ways. It can be anywhere from quite high principled to quite unprincipled. It can be guided by better or worse economic theory. I hope you will resist the various ideologies that tell you that government is much the same everywhere. (France and Jugoslavia? Scandinavia and South America? Britain or the United States in 1930, 1960 and 1999?)

DEREGULATION IN THEORY

The social-democratic vision is not absurd in supposing that in comfortably productive countries, democratic government should be able to recover the nerve and competence and invention that it has shown at its best. But it will not do that while majorities and the governments which they elect are persuaded that least government is best. While that belief prevails, here (yet again) is a summary of what to expect of the policies which it inspires.

Economic structure

History shapes national economic structures in ways too many and various, and different from case to case, to be formally modelled or theorized. A country's natural resources make some limits and opportunities. Its human capital includes its people's culture, education, productive skills and capacities for organized, cooperative, competitive and inventive behavior. Its physical capital has accumulated over time in changing conditions, some of it produced nationally, some acquired by trade, some contributed by foreign investors. How much of the physical and human capital continues in productive use may depend on changing technology, international competition, patterns of demand, and many public policies. In those processes no historical hidden hand guarantees that the growing and changing economic structures will be capable, at every stage, of providing full employment, balanced trade and payments, and financial stability. That may often take some deliberate contrivance.

Employment

How many of a country's willing workers can find paid work at any time depends on many conditions.

There can be misfits between the available jobs and the available skills, or between their locations. If productive capacities do match the detailed pattern of demand there can still be too little investment and consumer spending, so too little aggregate demand, to employ the whole workforce. That can arise from a variety of causes:

- There can be circular causation as unemployment restrains total income, which restrains demand for consumer goods and investment goods, which restrains demand for labor and causes continuing unemployment.

- The unemployment may arise from market causes in the first place, for example if new labor-saving technology cuts employment in some industries, which in turn cuts aggregate income and spending, and so cuts employment in other industries too.

- Fluctuating stocks of unsold goods, prompting investment multipliers and accelerators and decelerators, can propel business cycles of boom and slump with fluctuating unemployment.

- Government may create or maintain unemployment if it sheds labor from its public services, or if the relation between its volumes of taxing and spending restrains after-tax income and aggregate demand below full-employment levels, or if it depresses investment by setting high rates of interest.

- Government may contrive unemployment deliberately for any of a number of reasons. It may hope to restrain inflation by restraining total spending, by depressing investment, by weakening labor's wage-bargaining strength.

- Government may also want unemployment to depress wages in order to restrain the production costs of exports and import-replacements; to encourage investment by increasing profit shares; to increase wage and salary inequalities for incentive or class or other reasons. Many of these efforts are mistaken for their own purposes, but prevailing beliefs authorize them.

Trade

Some countries' export earnings and import costs balance in a market way without difficulty. Others don't: their citizens want to buy more imports than their exports and other foreign earnings can pay for. Recall the alternatives which those deficit traders face. Free traders hope that competition will develop all countries' industries of greatest comparative advantage, which will have the effect of balancing their trade and payments. Failing that, they hope that a deficit-trading country's demand for foreign exchange to pay for an excess of imports will have the supply-and-demand effect of depreciating its national currency to the level at which higher demand for (cheaper) exports balances lower demand for (dearer) imports. Those processes do sometimes happen, but you know why neither of them can be relied on. The first theory assumes full employment, and has other flaws. The second assumes that all the relevant elasticities of international supply and demand are positive, and that exchange rates are not affected by other factors. With unhelpful elasticities (which are quite common) a depreciating exchange rate more often worsens the troubles of a deficit-trading and indebted country. For free traders that leaves only two improvident short-term devices. A country can pay for an excess of imports, and service its foreign debts, by selling assets to foreigners. When the saleable assets have all gone the annual deficit is likely to be *bigger* by the outflow of profit to foreign owners. Annual deficits can still be financed by borrowing foreign funds if foreigners are willing to lend them. That rarely happens in an unaided market way, but it can happen if the government does

the borrowing or (as happens now) if it guarantees the private banks who do it. The debt becomes self-expanding if its interest payments have to be financed by further borrowing, as is likely in any deficit-trading country, and nearly certain (as Adam Smith warned)) if the rate of interest which the indebted country has to pay is higher than its rate of economic growth.

All those free-trading remedies are unreliable. Except for one British devaluation none of them has lately brought a deficit-trading or deeply indebted country back into balance.

The measures which do work are boundary controls. Government can tax imports, aid the home production of tradeable goods, limit foreign ownership to useful direct investment, limit borrowing of foreign funds to prudent quantities and approved purposes, and if necessary ration the available foreign exchange to its most necessary and productive uses. But all those measures are barred where there are international commitments to free international trade, credit and exchange of capital funds.

Money and credit

Though governments and their Central (Reserve) banks can create money and credit, most additions to the supply of it are currently made by commercial banks, in the form of interest-bearing loans to their customers and to governments. Though governments have at times told the banks how much new credit they could create, and for what general kinds of use, they now influence the amount of credit chiefly by varying the base rate of interest.

You remember why the price of credit (its rate of interest), the demand for it and the supply of it are not related as price and demand and supply are related in most goods markets. With exceptions (for example in some credit-fuelled property or share-price booms) it tends to happen that –

- the demand and supply of credit both decline as the price rises, and both increase as it falls

- the higher the price, the lower the productivity with which much of the credit is likely to be used – so that

- profitability to the supplier tends to be inverse to the productivity of the use.

Left to itself, an unregulated money market is accordingly not just inefficient, it is actively anti-efficient. As long as the world is supplied with money and credit by many nations –

- each with a national fiat currency,

- many with unbalanced trade and debt service,

- barred by GATT from introducing any new or higher barriers to trade, and
- with unregulated private credit and exchange between currencies,

it is likely to have these tendencies:

- Rates of interest will be adjusted for risk, including exchange risk, to yield a similar expected rate of return to lending in all the participating countries.
- The underlying rate of real interest will vary through the business cycle but is likely to be high through all phases of the cycle, for a number of reasons:
- Open frontiers make it difficult for national governments to regulate the volume of credit in a counter-cyclical way, or to restrain inflation, except by manipulating the rate of interest.
- Open trade compels countries with trade deficits to balance their payments by asset sales or foreign borrowing. Borrowing compels them to match the best rates of return available in the world market, plus some addition for exchange risk if their exchange deficits are expected to depreciate their currencies. And regardless of its trade balance, any country which tries to enforce an internal rate of interest below the prevailing international rate faces damaging capital flight and depreciation of its currency.
- Speculative currency trading strengthens bankers' political influence, which they tend to use in ways which keep rates of interest unregulated, and high.

On balance, with exceptions, high interest tends to shift lending –

- from long term to short term lending, or to long loans with variable rates of interest which increase borrowers risks
- to consumer credit rather than productive investment
- to asset-trading for capital gain rather than to productive investment
- to housing investment by households with incomes in the upper rather than the lower half of incomes, so that the home-owning proportion of the population may decline, and so may the average and total productivity of household investment.

Winners Compared with a regime of low and stable interest rates, a regime of high and variable rates is likely to give greater advantage to –

- owners of capital funds, including –
- members of funded superannuation schemes, and
- big, well-established firms which can finance most

of their capital needs from retained earnings as many new competitors cannot.

Losers are likely to include –

- small, new or otherwise hard-up firms which depend on credit for most of their investment and working capital
- firms, especially new small firms, wanting new share capital. (Shares are harder to sell when fund owners have the alternative of lending at high interest.)
- firms in very competitive industries; new entrants to industries dominated by well-established self-financing firms; firms with long investment lead-times who need to borrow investment funds
- farmers who need credit
- all households who need credit to buy housing and household equipment; but the biggest losers over household life are likely to be poorer households who are excluded from home ownership altogether, or for long periods of their household life.

Thus when high interest rates are used to restrain inflation and to restrain demand for imports, they do so by restraining investment, by substituting some less productive for some more productive investment, by inducing some unemployment, and thus by restraining economic growth. They also tend to increase inequalities. There are alternative strategies which don't necessarily have those ill effects. But most alternative ways of restraining imports are illegal under current GATT rules, and some of the alternative ways of restraining inflation are not effective if funds can be freely lent and borrowed abroad to avoid direct credit controls by national governments. The same freedom gives bankers and fund managers punitive power over national economies, so the deregulation which allows the ill effects makes reform difficult for individual countries, except perhaps the US – but the interests which currently prevail in the US, and through the 'Washington consensus' in the International Monetary Fund and the World Trade Organization, have led the deregulation, and are its chief defenders and enforcers.

That concludes this summary of what this course of study would lead you to expect when governments stop regulating trade, credit, capital exchange and asset sales between national economies, and use high and variable rates of interest and some deliberate unemployment to restrain inflation and wage shares. In deficit-trading and indebted countries, the same high interest and deliberate unemployment become the main means of balancing trade and payments. When they fail at that, they are continued in efforts to limit foreign debt and avert devaluation.

We will presently recall the kind of neoclassical theory which recommended that strategy and still predicts good effects of it. But first, the theory and the strategy have now had a world trial for a quarter of a century. How have the participating economies performed through those years?

DEREGULATION IN PRACTICE

In *Global Finance at Risk: The case for international regulation* (NY: The New Press, 2000) John Eatwell and Lance Taylor offer the best summary account I know of the deteriorating performance of most of the leading economies since the 1970s, and the reasons (which overlap and extend this text's reasons) for believing that less and worse government has been a main cause of the deterioration. In an earlier paper, *International Capital Liberalisation: The Record* (a working paper of the Center for Economic Policy Research at the New School for Social Research, New York 1996) Eatwell responded to five claims by a neoclassical author (who need not be named) that 'financial liberalisation has delivered huge benefits'. The claims:

1. 'A free capital market ensures that savings are directed to the most productive investments without regard for national boundaries. Capital can flow from capital-rich developed countries to opportunity-rich emerging economies.'

2. 'Increased competition has created a more efficient financial system, offering better opportunities for savers as well as lower costs for borrowers.'

3. 'Fancy new instruments such as derivatives (futures, swaps and options) help firms to manage financial risk more effectively.'

4. 'The long-run result should be higher investment and growth.'

5. 'Government's loss of powers is reason to cheer, not fear: all that is being lost is the power to pursue damaging policies and practice economic deception by letting inflation rip.'

In that order –

I Is there more productive investment, and has capital flowed from richer to poorer countries?

No. First, the hugely enlarged gross flows from country to country flow to and fro, with comparatively little increase of net capital transfer. The gamblers want assets which they can quit at short notice as they bet on

fluctuating rates of exchange, interest and return. So they finance very little enduring investment.

Second, much the biggest net flow is to the US. In the last year of Eatwell's study the net transfer to the United States was $119 billion. Ten years of deregulation had converted it from the world's biggest creditor to its biggest debtor. The net transfer to all the non-oil-exporting countries was $38 billion, and most of it was lent for short terms, or it bought saleable properties or shares in existing firms, rather than financing new productive investment.

2 Are there better opportunities for savers and lower costs for borrowers?

For savers, yes. Through the same years there has been a big shift of individual savings into institutional management. The institutional investors have increased their foreign holdings. But they have cut the average time for which they hold their foreign assets to less than half the individual investors' average. The institutions compete for funds by advertising high short-term returns, of which they get more from gambling on changing exchange rates and asset values than from returns to productive enterprise.

Their operations join with the deregulation of national interest rates to increase the volatility of exchange rates, and to keep rates of interest high. Average real rates of interest in France, Germany, UK and US moved from 1.7 per cent in 1956-73 to 5.1 per cent in 1981-93. So there are both higher costs and higher risks for borrowers, with some increase of inequality and some decline of the productivity of new investment. By any of the standard measures of economic performance the new strategy has worsened it.

3 Do derivatives help firms to manage financial risk?

Yes and no, because in Eatwell's words 'Liberalisation and fluctuating exchange rates have created many of the risks which derivatives are designed to hedge.' Also 'The growth of derivatives markets may increase systemic risk, both because the very complexity of some derivative instruments and hedging strategies creates severe informational problems for both management and regulators, and because derivatives trading may increase exposure to liquidity crises.'(p. 20)

4 Has the result been higher investment and growth?

No. Since deregulation there has been less investment and much slower growth. (The spectacular exceptions through the 1980s were the East Asian countries which continued the strong public direction of their development, and quite fast growth.) From the 1960s to the 1980s, growth in the six leading Western economies fell from rates between 2.3 and 9 per cent to rates between 1.1 and 3 per cent. Except in the US unemployment increased, and except in Japan and East Asia inequalities increased. (A burst of faster US growth late in the 1990s has come with no significant change in the rates of investment or unemployment. That may reward new capital-saving technology which allows faster growth without any increase of either employment or financial investment. It owes nothing to financial deregulation.)

5 *Do freer market forces discipline public economic policies usefully?*

This is a more complicated question. In one meaning, the answers to the previous questions answer it: economic performance has been generally worse, whether from the intrinsic inefficiencies of the freed market forces or from worse responses of governments to those forces. But Eatwell takes the claim as meaning that as financial penalties deter governments from intervening in the economy, market forces are freer to operate as efficiently as neoclassical theory predicts that they will. They are certainly freer. But to claim that they are operating with enhanced allocative and productive efficiency is absurd, in the light of the deterioration of investment, employment, growth, financial stability and (for many citizens) social and individual security.

Conclusion Rather than freedom allowing economic life to conform to theory, the relevant theory has had a practical trial which it does not deserve to survive. Nor do the misbehavior and worse performance, which are rational profit-seekers' responses to their new freedoms, deserve to continue.

ECONOMISTS' RESPONSIBILITY

How much of the blame should economists bear for the cruelties and inefficiencies which have followed the Right turn?

Sixteen pages (111-126) of Chapter 11 sketched the history of the long boom and then the Right turn in the leading Western economies through the third and fourth quarters of the twentieth century. Those pages were billed as easy reading. But if you have time, it might pay to read them now more thoughtfully, as you try to judge the importance of economists' contributions to the complex processes which produced such a drastic change in economic and social policy.

In case you don't have time, here's a bare reminder. There were twenty five years of fast growth and full employment – the 'golden age of capitalism'. Those

years also saw the great expansion of higher education and public health and welfare services and income transfers of the modern welfare state. Unwary governments began to dismantle some of their economic controls, thinking they were no longer needed. Some effects of that, and some effects of fast technological change, brought some unemployment. Dismantling the international financial regime brought more unemployment. A number of causes converged to increase some national rates of inflation. Growth slowed. Rising unemployment increased welfare costs. That combination of malfunctions, dubbed 'stagflation', began to discredit the Keynesian theory and policies which had prevailed through the golden age. (That was partly unfair: some of the malfunctions came from *dropping* the Keynesian policies.) Politically, the permanent opponents of the social-democratic regime took advantage of its troubles to step up their attack on it. They attracted new support. Technical progress and economic growth had shifted numbers from blue-collar to white-collar employment. In every class there were people better paid and employed than their parents had been, more content and conservative. There were also people distressed by the inflation and unemployment, and wanting a change. Thus the success of the social-democratic program, as well as its new troubles, helped to reduce political support for it.

There was nevertheless a striking difference between the English-speaking countries' responses and the continental European responses to the troubles. In the US, UK, Canada, Australia and New Zealand, majorities were encouraged by their business and political leaders to look for tax cuts, to blame the rising unemployment on the unemployed and 'too much welfare', and to liberate business from 'too much government'. West European governments and majorities held more closely, and for longer, to their social-democratic aspirations and social programs. Many of them had more comprehensive, income-linked social security and superannuation than the English-speakers had. Happy with that better way of spreading income from their earning to their non-earning years they continued to pass about 45 per cent of national income through public hands. Most of them were also slower to privatize public enterprises and utilities, and to dismantle their national economic controls. Thus in north-western Europe there was much less Rightward shift in politics, no significant reduction (except in Sweden) of the new welfare services, and little or no increase of poverty and inequality. But strikingly, the decline of economic growth was just as bad in those countries, under continuing social-democratic government, as it was in the English-speaking world. Some levels of unemployment were worse.

How could that be so? Deregulating international finance was probably the most powerful cause, but there were also others. I think (unfashionably) that there were early elements of a troublesome economic maturity. Consumer demand ran increasingly to goods and services whose production could be expanded by jobless growth. New labor-intensive services had grown fast enough through the golden age to keep that generation fully employed. But some of those services were now sufficiently staffed and doing everything expected of them, and with new technology some were themselves shedding labor. One intelligent response to that misfit between the demand for goods and services and the demand for employment is to maintain full employment by sharing whatever employment there is. Japanese firms have long done some of that. Some European governments began to do it in the 1980s by regulating and reducing working time, but they don't yet do nearly enough of it to match the need for it. And it has become more difficult to do. Cuts in working time – whether daily or weekly or yearly, or over the working lifetime – are easier when fast growth of productivity makes it possible to cut people's working time without cutting their incomes. But through the period when north-west European unemployment increased, economic growth slowed from above 4 per cent to as low as 1 per cent. Meanwhile the English-speaking countries were reducing necessary public services in order to switch revenue to maintain their (meaner) income transfers *without* European levels of taxation. With rising numbers of aged and unemployed people and lone parents drawing public incomes, each dollar of tax in both the European and the English-speaking countries now finances less employment than it did.

Those developments may well have made it harder to maintain full employment. But financial deregulation was meanwhile doing double damage. Directly, it slows growth and intensifies the technological and structural troubles. And it deprives national governments of the capacity to counter those ill effects.

Open frontiers prevent effective management of the quantities, uses or interest rates of credit within any country. They allow bankers and the owners and managers of capital funds to introduce high and unstable rates of interest. Those are soon compounded by the fluctuating rates of exchange that the speculative activities help to cause. These are not effects of the managers' wickedness or 'moral hazard'. They are the rational response of profit-seeking bankers and fund man-agers to their new opportunities. They compete by max-imizing the short-term returns which chiefly attract deposits. The highest short-term returns come from high interest, and capital gains from the changing asset values offered by rates of exchange which keep changing as the speculators gamble on them. But the high interest rates and volatile exchange rates increase the risks and cut both the amount and the potential productivity of new productive investment which the funds finance. The open frontiers also make it harder to tax companies or wealthy individuals. They allow reprisals against countries which try to continue or restore boundary controls. And for deficit-trading and indebted countries, the financial difficulties are compounded by the continuing pressure to liberate trade.

Professional authority Many interested parties contributed to the Right turn. But it is hard to believe that they could have succeeded politically without strong support from the prevailing school of economic theory and education. Real winners from the change of direction were comparatively few. They needed persuasive theory, simple enough for the mass media to propagate and the public to grasp, but backed by expert authority, to link their interests to majority interests and thus to politicians' interests. The simple versions of the theory were distilled from its full professional version, by which plenty of leaders of the change of direction were genuinely persuaded. It is hard not to see the neo-classical theory as, at least, a necessary condition of the change of political direction. Many losers from the Right turn were persuaded by mistaken self-interest to vote for it. A sad number of social-democrats, whether or not self-interested, were persuaded that it was economically necessary. In England TINA and FIF ('There Is No Alternative' and 'Fix Inflation First') were winning slogans at successive elections. Altogether it is hard to acquit the theory, and the expert profession who gave it authority, of considerable responsibility for the political Right turn and its economic consequences.

But it is hard for disbelievers to understand how such theory could be believed by the economists themselves: by so many of the people, most of them decent, intelligent, well-intentioned men, who led the profession through those years, and lead it still at the turn of the century.

Neoclassical imagination

Recall two fundamentals of social science. Social life is so complex that all analysts of it have to select and simplify. And to know what causes what in that complexity, they have to know or guess or imagine what would have been different if particular causes had been absent, or different.

Neoclassical theory does both those tasks for its users, if they allow it to. It selects the important elements of the economy, identifies and names the forces worth noticing, and models their operation. And it supplies the imagined alternatives or counter-factuals which indicate what is causing what, and what would change if any of the operative causes changed.

The theory models a self-adjusting system driven by every participant's interest in self-enrichment. Given law and order and some necessary public infrastructure, that single incentive shapes and drives a system of production and market exchange whose 'hidden hand' can allocate the available resources to the most efficient producers of the most desired goods and services, keep capital and labor fully employed, and distribute the income and output to the participants in shares which reflect the value of each one's contribution to production. Back in Chapter 18 you read these essentials of the model:

> People have productive endowments. They own land, physical capital, money to lend or invest; and they can learn skills, and work.
>
> In workplace and marketplace people trade what they *have* for what they *want*. They trade their land for rent, their capital for interest or dividends, their labor for wages. Then they trade the money they've earned for the goods and services they want to buy.
>
> Firms compete in factor markets to attract the capital, land and labor they need. They compete to use those means of production most efficiently, inventively, productively. They compete in goods-and-services markets to sell their products to consumers. The firms which produce most efficiently, using factors of given value to produce goods of greatest value, are the ones which survive.
>
> People thus express their individual preferences, and make the best of their individual endowments, in a double way. They get the best combination of risk and return for their land and capital, or sell their labor where they can get the work, wages, hours and conditions that suit them best. Then they spend their earnings on the basket of goods and services that suits them best.
>
> Thus the amount and detailed composition of a society's material output are determined jointly by the people's preferences as producers and as consumers. Collectively or individually, they can't *get* more than they *give*. But at any current level of technology, competition should sort out the more effi-

cient from the less efficient firms so that the people get the *most possible* of what they *most want* in return for the productive contributions they are *able* and *willing* to make.

Recall, also, two features of the factor markets. In a general way, any owner of land or capital and any willing worker who can't find a buyer for his factor is expected to lower its price until it attracts someone who can use it profitably, so that all markets clear. And in the money market, the higher the rate of interest (the reward for waiting, remember) the more people save. The lower the rate, the more producers can borrow and invest. The current rate at any time is the equilibrium rate at which the money market clears. And the borrowers who can afford that rate are those who can use the credit most profitably because they can use it most productively.

This text's main discussion of the theory , with some attention to its users' defences of it, was on pp. 217-225. Read it again if you need to. Here is a bare reminder:

The basic model has no government, and apparently no need for any. It is false – simply untrue – about some essentials of the life that it does model. Its participants are driven by acquisitive self-interest alone. In life they also have other purposes. Despite its assumption about their nature, the model has them act only by fair exchange. In life some of them are also tricky, forceful, violent, if they can get away with it. The model has them save in order to earn interest. In life they mostly save for other purposes. The model has the rate of interest ration credit to its most productive borrowers. In life, high interest rules out many of the most productive uses of credit and tends to switch it to less productive uses. The model assumes that savers, and other owners of capital funds, allocate them to their highest-paying uses. In life, these days, saved funds and credit are mostly managed by bankers and other intermediaries. Current laws allow them, and rational self-interest motivates them, to use quite lot of their funds in ways which do not maximize growth or employment as the theory expects them to do.

Intelligent neoclassical economists are of course aware of many of these troubles. They acknowledge the possibility of environmental harm and other externalities. They recognize a range of market failures, by which they tend to mean failure of life to behave as their theory models it. Their common sense acknowledges the economic as well as the social need for more research and education and health care than market distributions of income enable the citizens to afford. But no common sense has prevented many of them from imagining that the most competitive, price-taking producers in the most competitive industries are the investors who can afford to borrow at the highest rates of interest. Or that bank and fund executives prefer lower, longer-term returns to higher, shorter-term returns if both are available. Or that the productivity of chief executives is growing five or ten or twenty times as fast as their firms' profits or dividends or their countries' economic growth. Living through the 1970s when many savers were getting negative real interest from their bonds and bank accounts, and were driven by that, quite rationally, to save more, neoclassics still imagined that higher interest induces more saving, and lower interest induces less.

If the economy performs well, as the theory predicts, neoclassics tend not to investigate the causes of the good performance. Those can be assumed to be as modelled by the theory. If the economy performs badly, that does need explanation. What is preventing it from performing as modelled? Which of the modelled causes of good performance are blocked, by what market failure or interference? Common answers include these –

- the labor market can't clear, because stupid workers won't work for an equilibrium wage

- the labor market won't clear, because stupid government pays the unemployed too much

- the labor market can't clear, because stupid government legislated a minimum wage above the equilibrium wage

- people are not saving enough to finance enough investment to employ the available labor because stupid government is limiting the rate of interest

- too much of what people are saving is being switched from productive industry to unproductive housing because venal politicians tax companies and dividends but buy swinging votes by not taxing the imputed rent of owner-occupied houses

- poor people are badly housed at excessive rents because stupid rent controls deter housing investment

- government's taxing and spending, which is unproductive, is crowding out productive private investment and employment.

Those are seven of the many ways in which neoclassics imagine wrongly what a particular national policy or practice is causing or preventing. Turn back a few pages for the five neoclassical claims for international deregulation cited in John Eatwell's paper. Put the two lists together and of the dozen items, two or three are debatable judgments but nine or ten assert untruths, most of

them easy to disprove by research (much of which Eatwell surveyed for his five).

The retreat from reason

As evidence accumulates that the retreat from government is not performing as advertised – and worse, that majorities are noticing, and looking thoughtful – its advertisers are switching from debating the program's merits with its critics to simply characterizing them both. The program is 'the greatest revolution in two centuries', 'the way forward', 'the future'. Never mind its details or teething troubles, what matters is that it is inevitable, irresistable, irreversible. Its leaders are the bold, the innovators, the inventors, the entrepreneurs, the history-makers. Its critics are men of yesterday, frightened of change, and impractically, impossibly, unthinkably longing to return to the 1950s as to the womb.

If you want to respond in kind, the enemies of economic government want to go back rather further, to 1930 with 30 per cent unemployed, to 1830 with the children back down the coalmines, or – most appropriately perhaps – to 1720 when the British government privatized the national debt, the South Sea Bubble collapsed it and thousands of subscribers with it, and Parliament was so shocked by the use of the business powers of joint stock, limited liability and corporate identity that it banned all three for more than a hundred years.

But arguing the real issues – in practical detail, with reference to well-researched experience, and with intelligent, detailed imagination of new possibilities – is really a better occupation for both parties.

SUMMARY

The prevailing theories of economic structure, investment, employment, trade, banking and international exchange each have some internal flaws. Each also has unreliable assumptions about the real-life conditions to be expected. And their faults are compounded if the policies they recommend are all applied together, in a general reduction of public investment and employment, and a general deregulation of trade and national and international banking and exchange.

But think ahead The economic performance of the Right-turning countries since the 1970s appears to confirm that the Right theories are wrong But it may be important to distinguish alternative reasons for that conclusion. Was the Right strategy the originating cause of the poorer performance? Or did involuntary historical changes bring troubles to which neither Left nor Right responded appropriately at the time? And if so, what sort of social-democratic response might be worth trying now?

North Western Europe adopted very little of the Right strategy, and avoided most of its ill effects on poverty, inequality and insecurity. But its unemployment is the highest in the rich world. Why? John Eatwell and Lance Taylor notice that financial deregulation was the one policy change common to both the Right-turning and the continuing social democratic regimes. So may it be a main cause of the poor performance of both? The direct and indirect effects of high and unstable interest rates, unstable exchange rates, and the switch of capital funds from long-term investment to short-term asset trading and exchange gambling all give force to Eatwell's suggestion.

That explanation is quite compatible with another that you have met in this text. Technical changes continue to bring jobless growth and falling prices in manufacturing industries and some computerised services. You know why rising productivity and pay in those industries causes rising pay and prices for labor-intensive human services too. That may depress private demand for those services. Demand for some of them may be satisfied, and non-expandable. For public education and health and welfare services it may be depressed by politicians' unwillingness to raise and spend the necessary revenue. There may thus be technological causes of changing comparative costs which make full employment harder to achieve than it was.

None of this makes the Right program look any more likely to keep its promises of growth, investment, low unemployment, or diminishing local poverty or world inequalities. But social democrats may need to reform more activities than banking and exchange, and face new as well as familiar problems of economic government, if they are to serve their purposes effectively.

Keep those possibilities in mind as the next five chapters sample some real-life strategies at work with varying success, in diverse circumstances, in countries with different capacities and collective purposes.

NATIONAL STRATEGIES

55

An open economy

Five chapters now sketch alternative national economic strategies, each coherent for its purposes.

You know by now at least four reasons why there can't be just one ideal strategy for all advanced mixed economies:

- Countries have different natural resources.

- They have accumulated different physical, institutional and human capital which give them different social and economic capacities and therefore different strategic options.

- Any strategy delivers uneven benefits to different classes and groups of people, and does more for some qualities of social life than for others. The judgments which prefer one pattern of benefits to others – and therefore one strategy to others – are always likely to be disagreed.

- Classes, groups and individuals with different interests and values compete for shares of power. As different combinations prevail, so do different strategies.

Conflict can of course make government's economic performance incoherent. Bits and pieces of policy, some incompatible with others, reshuffled before and after elections, designed to attract the support of diverse groups rather than to fit together for economic purposes, and together having effects which nobody intended, don't deserve to be dignified as a strategy. We could have easy fun satirizing those non-strategies, and recent history offers rich material for the sport. But the five sketches which follow are of coherent strategies. When governments do develop consistent national economic purposes, as many do, what policies may serve those purposes best?

Two cautions:

First, the sketches have to simplify. They have obvious reference to real countries at particular stages of their recent history: the United States, a united Europe, Sweden, Australia, Russia and China. But they don't offer faithful accounts of the economies or policies of those places. Instead they select and sometimes rearrange features of real societies to illustrate a range of national situations and purposes, and strategies appropriate to each.

Second, the five are far from a sufficient set. They are not the only coherent alternatives for advanced mixed economies in the twenty-first century. They are here to illustrate themes which have been hammered throughout this course of study. National situations and possibilities and collective purposes differ. So, therefore, should their economic strategies. Their strategies should be shaped by their particular resources, institutions, culture and collective aspirations. They should not be shaped by any universal theory and by whatever values and social purposes the theory happens to express or conceal.

AN OPEN ECONOMY

Picture a big, rich country – the richest in the world. It has a long history of industrial growth and high productivity. Its land extends from ocean to ocean and through 25 degrees of latitude from snowbound forests, across plains rich with grain and pasture, to vineyards and orange groves. Under it are industrial minerals: iron, copper, coal, oil. The resources allow a big population to produce self-sufficiently most of what it consumes. In the 10 percent or so of output and consumption that it trades, it has generally been a successful exporter with its trade and payments in balance or in surplus.

The productivity springs from an inherited and continuously renewed culture of energy, inventiveness, self-reliance, pride in skill and know-how. The skill and versatility are nourished by universal public schooling, and by state and private universities which offer undergraduate and graduate education to large numbers. The people are unusually adaptable, and mobile. They move house and change jobs and occupations more readily than most.

The nation won its independence by armed rebellion. It fought a civil war partly about the individual freedom to enslave people. There has been some violence between business and labor. The murder rate is high. Nine out of ten of all firearms are said to be in private hands.

Business has been a pioneer of big organization, including transnational organization, and has often had strong influence on governments at home and abroad.

Government also has formidable organizing capacities. It organized a great public works program in the 1930s, a rapid conversion of the private sector to war production in the 1940s, atomic power and a national highway network in the 1950s, and put a man on the moon in the 1960s. But there are widely held suspicions of government as potentially oppressive, inefficient and corruptible. About half the people bother to vote.

Here then is a big, productive, freedom-loving, sometimes violent society. Its industries have long been economic winners. Their owners and directors tend to be political winners. As in Britain when Britain was the technological leader a century and a half ago, the prevailing powers are likely to want small government at home and the usual winners' policy abroad: free trade, and unhindered investment and ownership across open frontiers.

This sketch is of American society twenty or thirty years back rather than now. It is setting the scene for a question. Could the US government have found a better economic strategy than the one it actually followed through most of those thirty years? Meaning, realistically, a better winners' strategy? Not assuming any change of heart or national purpose, or any softer social conscience, or any less business influence on government?

The world in the 1970s

Imagine we're back in that decade. All over the developed world the long postwar boom has ended. But it has done its good work. Europe is back on its feet, rebuilt and paying its way. Japan is rich after its decade of miracle growth. The rich countries' new welfare standards and institutions are in place. More technical revolutions are under way in biological science, medicine, computing, telecommunications, air transport, atomic power and many manufacturing processes. Transnational firms are beginning to locate their manufacturing wherever in the world the conditions are best for it. Feminist reform, and in the US the black civil rights movement, are making progress. So is a reduction of censorship and a general liberation of personal behavior. Freedom is popular, and expanding.

But the end of the boom brings slower economic growth and rising rates of inflation and unemployment. Two oil shocks – the OPEC price rises of 1973 and 1979 – depress Western economies while at the same time generating big capital funds for which the world does not seem to have good uses. Russia is a hostile atomic power spreading communism wherever it can.

In such a world, what economic strategy promises most for America's primary purposes of military strength, economic growth, and business and personal freedom? Most for the nation, and most for the interests and ideas within it which are likely to command the government and shape its policies?

A STRATEGY

The task is to combine secure defence, economic growth, individual and business freedom, and (for those who genuinely need it) a social safety net which does as little harm as possible to work incentives and productivity.

In present (1970s) conditions the United States government may serve those purposes best by working for –

- a single free-trading world economy

- the widest possible scope at home and abroad for the US private sector

- market choices and disciplines rather than government choices and controls, wherever possible, and

- a public sector which provides necessary public services efficiently, buying them from private producers or franchising private enterprises to supply them wherever possible.

But a too-simple application of those rules of thumb can bring trouble. The strategy needs to work as a set of well-researched, continuously-updated policies well related to each other and to the activities they concern.

The government needs policies (including policies of non-intervention where appropriate) for the structure and scope of the public, private and household sectors. It needs employment and labor-market policies; welfare policies; banking and financial policies including anti-inflationary policies; and balance-of-payments policy. In each of those areas, either too much freedom or ill-chosen freedoms can be counter-productive. In some of them, the executive government or many of the legislators have obligations to particular supporters, and some of those commitments conflict with the government's public commitments or with the desirable coherence of its policies. It is troublesome to be committed *both* to free trade *and* to US beef producers, or *both* to market discipline *and* to rescuing insolvent US banks. We will notice some of those hazards as we review the main areas of policy.

As we do, don't forget that (for the duration of this chapter) you are an adviser to a government committed to those general aims. You are here to make them work, not to quarrel with them. If they prompt you to rant on about the evils of ungoverned capitalism or endangered whales you are entitled to your values but you should probably be working for some other employer – perhaps one of the governments depicted in later chapters. (Of course there may be scope for your conscience 'inside' the strategy, for example by supporting some government aims against others, or by warning that favors sought by some of the government's supporters would conflict with other elements of the strategy and make it incoherent.)

ECONOMIC STRUCTURE

This refers both to the structure of industries (what the country is equipped to produce), and to the structure of ownership (what its public, private and household sectors are equipped to produce).

The private sector

Private enterprise is what Americans do best. They have generally maximized its scope, and should continue to do so in this strategy. The main variable is the boundary between the private and public sectors. Earlier chapters of this text listed (1) activities which generally do best in the public sector, (2) activities which generally do best in the private sector, and (3) activities which can do as well in either. The US private sector should do all of (2) and (3). It should also do any of (1) that it can do satisfactorily, even if public owners might do it better. (There are reasons for that. There are other benefits besides efficient performance. Private profits need to be saved and invested, where politicians may be tempted to spend public profits for short-term tax relief, thus reducing national investment. Where technical progress allows labor-shedding or other organizational improvements private employers are often freer and more strongly motivated to make the changes and dismiss the necessary numbers. And the fewer the public sector's responsibilities, the more attention and discipline each

public agency can expect from government, press and other critics. By contrast, the market discipline of private enterprises operates however big the private sector is.)

All the market industries should be private. There need be no public ownership of coal, steel, ship-building, vehicle-building, armament or other market firms. Utility monopolies – power delivery, gas, water, sewerage, railed commuter transport – should be franchised to private operators, with competitive elements (for example in power generation) wherever practicable. All other transport – passenger and freight, by air, sea, rail, bus, truck – is private business.

And the activities which do necessarily belong in the public sector should buy in as many goods and services and components as possible from competitive private suppliers.

Free trade Back in colonial times, energetic settlers used abundant natural resources to develop a rich agricultural, merchant and maritime economy, hindered by some British restraints but helped by British protection of American shipping. National independence and the steam engine came at about the same date. Industrial development accelerated, and from the mid-nineteenth to the mid-twentieth century it was protected by high tariffs. Through that century American wages had a wide spread from highest to lowest, but they averaged the highest in the world.

As industries developed their capital, skill and scale, they needed less protection. By the 1950s few of them needed any at all. In many of them, competition within the US was such that the tariff no longer had much direct effect on mark-up prices. But it still affected costs. And in a number of heavy industries strong unions had become effective bargainers who imposed similarly high labor costs on all competing firms.

As Europe recovered from the war and East Asia industrialized, American exporters wanted freer access to some of their markets. Free trade looked promising, both for export access abroad and for labor discipline at home. The US government began negotiating for it in 1944, without much success at first. But successive rounds of GATT negotiations have made progress, and the US has drastically reduced its own protection. Now (in the 1970s) the traded proportion of US output is rising. The national economy is specializing more than it did. The private sector is more market-shaped and less government-influenced than it has been for a century.

And competition is working. In new industries, the US dominates the production of computing hardware and software. Europe and Japan make most of the world's television and sound-recording gear. In old industries, some balances are changing. Japanese cars, made in Japan, in the US and elsewhere around the Pacific, are taking a rising share of the US carmakers' home and export markets.

Those and other winners are winning with acquired rather than natural advantages. Some of the advantages came from being first in the field. Many were developed with public aid and protection. They are possessed now by big oligopolistic firms with great market strength. In their home countries those firms' skilled workers share in their gains. But the firms are strengthened against their less skilled workers and their component suppliers' workers. Free trade allows two kinds of wage competition. US producers can buy components from suppliers in low-wage countries. Or they can locate their own low-skilled operations in those countries and bring their products home duty-free. Either method reduces demand for low-skilled labor within the US. That allows some reduction of labor costs across a range of other industries, including non-tradeable goods and services. That benefits employers in those industries. It benefits other producers who buy intermediate goods and services from them. And it benefits consumers of final goods and services. That spread of benefits strengthens the winners' alliance for this strategy in a society without much care for its losers. We will return to the politics of the strategy later in this chapter.

Sector trade The private sector needs services from households and government. Some are detailed presently in policies for those sectors. But the essentials are listed here as private sector requirements. Households and government need to provide the private sector with –

- a highly educated, energetic, inventive, well-motivated elite of directors, managers and professionals

- a healthy, well-educated, willing and disciplined workforce

- sufficient and up-to-date public capital for private use: roads and bridges, sea and air and space ports, telecommunication infrastructure, stored and retrievable intellectual capital, etc.

- public research, and public aids to private research and development

- standard services to business: property law and enforcement; helpful corporate and commercial law and courts; many public information services

- diplomatic and other support for American business abroad, and for the enforcement of world trade freedoms

- a national and international financial system based primarily on private banking and credit creation and market rates of exchange

- policies to restrain inflation and to balance foreign payments with as little harm as possible to business or market efficiency

- taxation designed to encourage investment and to intensify rather than reduce productive and competitive incentives

- a labor market which reflects demand and supply rather than regulation or collective bargaining

- a safety net of welfare income transfers and services designed to motivate the unemployed to be at all times active contenders for employment.

The household sector

Most housing and household equipment are market goods. This economy is now productive enough to provide most of its households with good and affordable housing. Two thirds own their houses, and more could if they wanted to. Most of the rest can rent housing without any public assistance. Helping those who can't is best left to local government: big bureaucracies are bad suppliers of housing services. For people who are genuinely incompetent to house themselves, public rent allowances may be appropriate. The health and educational services that households need are noted later under other headings.

This strategy is built on the belief that what households chiefly need is access to efficient goods markets, an efficient housing market and an efficient labor market. Learning how to get what they want in those markets is what chiefly teaches people the skills and the spirit with which – in themselves and the children they bring up – they enjoy life, and supply the economy with an energetic, versatile, skilful and productive workforce.

The public sector

It is convenient to distinguish production from policy-making. This section is about the public supply of goods and services. Some of them (like teaching in public schools) are produced by public enterprises. Some (like most of the school books) are bought from private producers. Some (like the school buildings) are planned and designed by public agencies and built by private contractors. But however they are produced, government decides *what* to produce. That output of goods and services, ordered and financed by government, is the subject of this section. Later sections deal with government's policy-making and regulation for the other sectors and the economy as a whole.

The standard public provisions are so familiar that the briefest reminder will do. Government and independent non-profit institutions must provide or get others to provide –

- defence, police, courts of law, prisons
- most transport infrastructure: roads and bridges, sea and air and space ports; railed transport or the land and franchises to allow its private provision
- public or publicly franchised utilities: power, gas, water, sewerage, waste disposal, telecommunication networks and satellites
- most education from kindergarten to technical college and graduate school
- many public information services
- public research, and substantial public aid to private research and development.

Some of those services, especially research and education, enrich many people's lives and capacities in direct ways. How much service of that sort they are prepared to pay tax for is a matter of choice. But the services to private and household production are different, and about them, a warning is in order.

A strategic preference for private over public *methods of production* should not be confused with a preference for private over public *goods and services*. There is a strong case for having public highways built by private contractors because they are usually more efficient than salaried public builders. But that is not a reason for having less public highways and more private trucks on them, simply because highways are public goods and trucks are private goods. The public highway is essential to the private trucks' productivity and profitability. Both are essential to the efficiency of all the other industries which have to truck their goods. Those relations hold for the whole complex trade between the sectors. Less public investment won't usually make way for more private production. The two are more likely to decline together. Cutting public investment regardless of the private need for it makes a business-oriented strategy incoherent for its own purposes.

Similarly, tax-paid research and education are essential to private production and profit and a technologically advanced and inventive economy. And so on – a coherent strategy must try to get the public/private proportions right for its purposes, not bias them in one direction or the other.

But drumming that message into the reluctant heads of a winners' alliance in an individualist, tax-hating society is not easy for the conservative politicians who lead such alliances. The few who try it are in constant danger from their many rivals who don't. It is all too easy to slide from championing private efficiency to cutting the tax-paid public provisions on which, among other conditions, the private efficiency depends. Tax-cutting is *immediately* appealing. It takes longer for aging public capital and declining services to depress private performance; and when they do, conservative and business ideologists may be slow to acknowledge that 'slimming government' had anything to do with it.

A private enterprise strategy can thus defeat itself if it goes too far – if it insists on minimizing tax and public investment and services as a matter of principle, instead of relating them accurately to the private sector's actual need for public capital and services. We will return to the problem when considering the politics of this winners' alliance.

EMPLOYMENT

The level of employment To keep unemployment within reasonable upper and lower limits, the strategy allows two kinds of public action. Some manipulation of the rate of interest is useful to restrain inflation in booms and to encourage investment in recessions. But interest rate adjustments can be difficult or ineffective in a national economy that is wide open to the world money market. For that reason (and also for trade-related reasons) government needs a power to regulate the lending, borrowing and exchange of capital funds across its frontiers, as explained in a following section on financial policy.

The labor market must be freed to function efficiently. Among the existing practices and regulations are many that were introduced long ago when the economy was both poorer and more protected than it is now. In those days there were still some intolerable working conditions and some starvation wages, so some regulation was justified. Some of it still is – for example fire safety is as important as ever. But changed conditions have made two kinds of regulation unnecessary or harmful.

First, economic growth has brought levels of productivity and income at which wage rates can safely be left to the market. Some relativities may change, but no-one in employment need starve.

Second, we now have full free trade, and industrial development in the third world. A third or so of the workers in our advanced economy are unskilled or low-skilled, and they are now exposed to competition from their lower-paid equivalents in Asia and South America. There is direct competition in tradeable industries. As wages fall and unemployment rises in those industries, competition for low-skilled jobs depresses wages in non-tradeable industries too. Our workers should not be handicapped in this new competition for jobs, any more than their employers should be handicapped in their competition for markets. But the competition can be severely handicapped by minimum wage laws; by wage principles established in the past by collective bargaining behind protective tariffs; or by rules which require unreasonably comfortable (as opposed to merely safe) workplaces and working conditions. A general deregulation of the labor market must allow both employers and employed in the advanced countries' less-skilled industries to respond effectively to the new competition they face. Only so can reasonable levels of unskilled employment and total employment be maintained in a rich free-trading country in the new world conditions.

Unemployment There are three reasons why unemployed people of working age should have strong incentives to look for work and accept any they are offered. First, that helps to ensure that the numbers unemployed and the public cost of supporting them are not inflated by voluntary unemployment, i.e. by people who refuse to work for market wage rates. Second, it is generally good for the unemployed themselves, whose spirit and skills and behavior tend to deteriorate if they are idle for long. Third, it disciplines those still in employment if they know that there are active competitors for their jobs. That discipline restrains wage costs and inflationary pressures.

Accordingly a public unemployment dole will be consistent with the rest of this strategy if it –

- pays substantially less than the lowest available market wage
- is work tested, meaning (i) applicants must show that they continue to seek work and accept any they are offered, and (ii) they must undertake any course of education, training or voluntary service that the dole office requires
- may be terminated after 18 months at the discretion of the dole office.

WELFARE

Welfare incomes and services should continue to be provided wherever possible as private goods, privately produced, and financed by private saving, insurance and superannuation. Public provision should be residual, providing only what the private sector cannot provide, even where (as with health services) public provisions could be more efficient. This does not make the strategy as a whole incoherent for its own purposes. It merely means that among its purposes some other values and interests prevail over considerations of cost and efficiency, and poor people's welfare.

Accordingly the health services should continue to be privately provided and financed by private insurance, with public provisions only for some of the old and poor. Housing also is market business, except for some public rent subsidies to the few households who can't otherwise afford shelter. Home ownership is in reach of about two thirds of American households if they want it. It might not be desirable for the rest, who include a lot of the low-skilled labor whose employment is increasingly flexible: they can't take on long mortgage or lease obligations, and need to be free to move house from one job to the next. There is no need for public housing. The market provides a wide range of private rental options: apartment buildings in the old cities, modest houses in many suburbs, transportable units and caravan parks at the outskirts of most towns.

FINANCIAL POLICIES

Two difficulties remain. The policies described so far are popular with nearly everyone in the winners' alliance. As long as the alliance continues to win elections those policies are likely to hold. But the strategy needs two further policies which are acutely disliked by some groups within the alliance. For the free-trading strategy to serve its purposes effectively, government must keep some public control of the financial system. And it must raise enough tax to finance the public investment and services that the private sector needs. Some of its most powerful supporters will try hard to block those policies. If they succeed, and the economy has to operate with uncontrolled banking and exchange, and with insufficient public revenue, the strategy will be incoherent, and likely to run the country – including some of its winners – into bad trouble.

The balance of payments

Recall, from Chapters 48-51 on economic structure and trade and financial policy, the reasons why unaided market forces don't necessarily operate to balance national trade or payments. Imbalances develop. Some countries earn more foreign money than they spend. Others spend more than they earn and balance their payments by borrowing the difference from the surplus countries. Left to themselves market forces are at least as likely to increase those surpluses and deficits as to reduce them, as long as the surplus countries have willing lenders.

In the 1970s freer trade is opening US markets at home and abroad to increasing competition of three kinds. The rebuilt economies of Europe, and the new industrial economies of Japan and the other Asian tigers, are expanding their exports of high-tech products. Developing countries in South America and elsewhere are exporting rising quantities of goods produced by low-skilled, low-paid workers. And a technical revolution in European agriculture is turning Europe into a substantial exporter of food. All three – but especially foreign cars, microelectronics, telecommunications, chemicals, heavy machinery and food – are biting into US home and foreign markets.

Time will tell whether US producers respond in kind, raising their high-tech and labor-saving investment and their research and development investment to match the new competitors. But they are a little less likely to do so if –

- rising imports can be financed by borrowing foreign funds

- low-skilled industries in the US keep trying to compete by cutting wages, rather than by higher labor-saving investment

- public investment declines, under conservative business and political pressure, so that (i) the necessary public services to private industry fall behind the world's best, and (ii) total demand for private goods and services declines as the public sector's demand for them declines, and public employment and wage income decline.

So what can government do to keep the strategy coherent for the purposes of the winners' alliance?

Remember that free trade is at the heart of the strategy, and that its main purposes are –

- to keep consumers happy with low import prices

- to keep imported fuel, materials and components cheap for US producers

- to discipline US labor and lower some US wage rates by exposing them, directly and indirectly, to low-wage foreign competition

- to allow US transnational firms to distribute their operations to the countries in which each operation goes best, while allowing free traffic between the foreign operations, the US operations and the US market.

But in the 1970s the lost protection and the rising foreign competition threaten to put the US into trade deficit. Without sacrificing the advantages expected from free trade, the strategy needs some safeguards. It needs to include whatever it can of export aids and import restraints which don't break the free-trading rules. Some effective ways of serving those purposes are ruled out of this strategy for obvious business, political or ideological reasons. For example the business members of the winners' alliance are not likely to tolerate a return to direct regulation of the quantity and uses of bank lending. The least unpopular financial restraint is probably to impose public controls on *some* types only of *foreign* transactions only, thus leaving the nation's internal financial business as free as before. As follows.

International credit A national government can bar its people and financial institutions from exporting capital funds, and from borrowing foreign funds, except for approved purposes. It can corral its own foreign borrowing by limiting the types of bonds it issues and banning their sale to foreigners. It can thus require its nationals to buy rather than borrow the foreign funds they need to pay for imports or to pay interest on existing foreign debt. Those controls need not be too oppressive. Foreign exchange – the sale or exchange of one currency for another-- can be as free as before for most purposes of trade, travel and approved direct investment. Exchange rates can be market rates. Most banking and other financial business within the national economy can be as free as before.

These controls aim to strengthen rather than replace market disciplines. If trade has to be paid for by exchange of currencies rather than by borrowing, the orthodox exchange discipline through market adjustment of exchange rates has more chance to work. Poor countries can't import more goods than their export earnings will pay for if nobody will risk lending to them. Rich countries can contrive the same discipline for themselves if they prevent their people and financial institutions from borrowing foreign funds.

That policy might also bring other gains. With less foreign lending and borrowing there is less need for internationally competitive interest rates. Government is freer to set rates for internal macroeconomic purposes. And over time, somewhat lower rates offer some gains in efficiency and growth. (The gains won't be great, because rates which were low enough and stable enough to do most for efficiency and growth would need to be accompanied by direct controls on the quantity of bank lending, to avoid inflation and other troubles – but those controls would not be acceptable to the dominant forces in the winners' alliance.)

Conclusion: To serve its own purposes effectively this strategy needs to include public regulation of foreign lending and borrowing.

Taxation

A second difficulty for this winners' strategy is to get the winners to pay enough tax to finance their strategy. Revenue is needed to finance more than the traditional functions of government. The winners need all the public infrastructure and the efficient, up-to-the-minute services that are needed by tradeable industries facing increasingly efficient foreign competitors in their home and foreign markets. Whether they like it or not, they need the public sector's contribution to employment. A technically advancing, job-shedding private sector cannot expect to employ everyone dismissed by a shrinking, job-shedding public sector. Winners may not worry about the sufferings of insecure or unemployed workers, but they do need to worry about the welfare costs of insecurity and unemployment, including the cost of public incomes and welfare services to the poor and their families, and the costs of enforcing law and order on insecure and unemployed workers to whom the winners' strategy promises no relief or improvement. Those costs must be expected to rise. This is the first generation of poor Americans since the abolition of slavery to whom the future promises no improvement.

The winners are perpetually tempted to pay too little tax and finance too little government for their own purposes. And they are tempted to shift taxation downward to poorer taxpayers. But the losers whose votes they don't need can't supply enough revenue by themselves, so the shift also has to hit middle-income people whose support the winners need, but can most easily lose. So a third temptation is to make as much as possible of the tax as unnoticeable as possible.

For most economic purposes income tax, the most noticeable tax of all, is still the best tax if people will tolerate it. If they won't, the next option is a broad tax on goods and services; but people notice and resent its effect on prices. So payroll tax is tempting. It raises prices just as surely as a tax on goods and services does; but many people see it as a tax on business and seem not to notice its effect on the prices they pay. It is unpopular with business, but not as unpopular as company or income tax. In some conditions it can stimulate labor-saving investment. But wherever that is not technically possible, payroll tax is a bad tax. It penalizes labor-intensive industries, which tend to have the lowest productivity, and to be most vulnerable to foreign wage competition. And it motivates employers to replace full-time taxable workers with part-time, casual, contract and other insecure labor that can evade the tax. But for government, it is tempting, because so few voters think it is unjust, or notice its effects on their costs of living.

Altogether, tax policy tests the leadership of a winners' alliance for an open economy. The strategy is likely to do best and last longest if statesmanlike leaders can manage –

- to raise enough revenue to finance the necessary public elements of the strategy;
- to raise it by means which cause the least hindrance or distortion to market forces; and
- to attract the widest support, both self-interested and disinterested, by getting their own class to contribute a substantial share of the revenue.

POLITICS

First, a reminder of the general kinds of appeal that a political program can have, and the kinds of support it can hope to attract.

To succeed politically, an economic program needs to enlist three kinds of support. Nobody governs for long without *some* support of each kind, though the proportions can vary widely.

First, the strategy must strike enough people as technically competent: as a workable program based on a right understanding of the working of the economy

Second, it must serve the interests of enough voters and influential people and institutions. That includes material self-interests, but also less selfish concerns with particular social problems, arts, recreations, charities, occupations, ethnic groups, regions. We can call all those personal concerns 'interests'.

And the strategy must strike as many people as possible as good rather than evil: as offering good government in pursuit of socially desirable aims.

Those are not strict distinctions. The three kinds of thought overlap, and influence each other. Beliefs about what is possible influence judgments about what is good. Self-interests colour beliefs about what is possible and what is good. Support may be strongest when the three coincide, i.e. when people see particular policies as technically competent, personally profitable and socially desirable. But for most people those judgments have some independence of each other, especially because many of the questions at issue in the media, in daily conversation and at election time don't touch their particular interests at all. Cynics think people's principles reflect nothing but their material interests, but there is widespread and well-researched evidence that the cynics are often wrong. Many people vote, regardless of their material interests or against them, for moral, social, religious or other principles, or from traditional fidelity to parties, institutions, race, class or nation.

In short, people vote for practicable policies; for their personal interests; and for moral, social and other principles. Sensible politicians attract all they can of each kind of support. Now see how some of each is attracted by the open economy strategy.

The interests served by the strategy are clear enough. It should improve the material prospects of most capital owners; most mid to high earners; and business owners, directors and executives who want freedom to run their firms with least public regulation, to trade and invest anywhere in the world, and to determine their own rewards. The free-trading strategy expands those business freedoms, and strengthens business immediately against its less skilled labor and eventually perhaps against all labor. Both the freedom to locate operations away from home, and the need to placate the global currency dealers, tend to strengthen business power in a general way against national governments.

The strategy will hurt protected industries which can't survive free trade. (But some people in those industries may support the policy unselfishly. Some may trust Ricardo's theory and expect free trade to enrich them in the end. Some may welcome the policy because it weakens labor.) It is against the interest of many public servants. (But there may be rewards for those who lead in downsizing and privatizing the services.) And it is against the interests of most of the poorer half or so of Americans. (But some of them may not blame their troubles in the government. Some may chiefly blame the foreign competition. Some may be persuaded that falling wages are the only way to keep their jobs at all.)

Losers are not well served by the political system. A century ago, America's labor leaders decided not to try for a class-based or labor-based political party. They expected to do better by opportunist bargaining with parties which could not take their support for granted. Since then, blue-collared numbers and union membership have dwindled. There are no effective losers' leaders to bargain on a national scale. Expecting little from government, less than half of the poorer half of Americans bother to vote. Some of those who do vote, vote for social, ethnic or other reasons rather than for their economic interests. Some – racist, xenophobic or otherwise resentful – vote for the populist Right, which may actually support the winners. Meanwhile more than half of the winners vote. And whoever gets elected, with whatever promises, the lack of party discipline and the division of executive and legislative powers can make *coherent* policy-making very difficult. Congress doesn't enact vital bits of the President's coherent strategy The President vetoes vital bits of Congress's coherent strategy, if Congress has one.

The social principles of the strategy need some justification, to attract the many people who like to vote in a principled way, whether or not that accords with their material interests. Among the society's winners are the learned professions, artists and intellectuals, and socially concerned business people, many of whom would hate to see themselves as selfish materialists wilfully increasing American inequalities. Their professional, intellectual and publicist influence is quite important. So are the attitudes of the lowest paid and commonly the most dissatisfied and critical of the graduate professions: journalists, teachers, welfare workers and academic social scientists. Some people in all those groups want policies as equitable and socially cohesive as possible. Some winners who don't care much about those qualities nevertheless know that they attract votes. So the social philosophy which justifies the strategy is quite important both to those who believe it and to some of those who don't.

Moral and social justification of the strategy comes in various forms. The two which are probably the most influential are respectively economic and historical.

The economic philosophy relies on the familiar 'dry' neoclassical belief that the freer the economy is the more efficient it will be, the faster it will grow, the bigger the national income will be, so that (given the prevailing pattern of inequality) the more there will be for everyone. Moreover (the argument runs) the freer the economy is, the more efficient the labor market will be, and the more exactly wages will reflect the marginal productivity of each worker. There is surely nothing morally wrong with paying people what they're worth: what they actually contribute to output?

For minimizing aid to the unemployed there are alternative justifications. Hard-line economists insist that most unemployment is voluntary: there is always work for people willing to work for the market price of their labor. People who concede that the amount of unemployment is caused by other factors and not by the unemployed themselves may still have two reasons for keeping any public sustenance for the unemployed at a mean level. It is important for the whole economy, and for the discipline of those who do have jobs, that the unemployed should keep trying to get whatever jobs are going. And even if the quantity of unemployment is not their fault, their *individual* unemployment *is* their own fault in most cases. An efficient labor market allows employers to prefer better workers to worse. The ones they don't hire are usually the least skilled, or least cooperative, or least honest. The taxpayers don't owe much income or sympathy to the five or ten per cent whom the market has thus identified as the worst workers.

That's a practical justification for some increase of inequality. It can be reinforced by a historical case for it.

Productivity rose through the two centuries from the 1760s to the 1960s. The welfare transfers and services have mostly come in the twentieth century. Now in the 1970s the work is done. A safe and comfortable standard of living is available to all. Anyone left in serious poverty is there by their own fault. It is entirely reasonable for the well-off, productive classes to say to the poorest third 'For a century we've been giving you more than you earned, more than your productive contribution was worth. We gave it to save you from hunger and cold and ignorance and ill-health, and to enable you to join in our common lifestyle. To do that for you, we have taken less than we earned, less than our fair market share of the growth we did so much to engineer. But you have now got enough: a basic standard of living from which you can compete on equal terms for any more you want. The hand-outs will continue for those who need them, but they won't increase. From now on the fruits of further economic growth are for us – and of course for any of you – who *earn* them.'

COSTS AND RISKS OF THE STRATEGY

It is time to notice likely shortcomings in the strategy, from its supporters' point of view. What follow are (1) some predictable economic and social costs; (2) further risks if the strategy is applied incompletely or incoherently; and (3) what actually happened in the United States, with hindsight from thirty years on.

Costs

High interest National and international financial freedoms promise quite high rates of interest at all times, and limit the range within which national governments can manipulate the rates for counter-cyclical purposes. They rule out any deliberate regime of low interest within the national economy. High interest imposes a number of costs:

- dearer housing for more than half of all households (i.e. for all those who can't buy houses without borrowing) as home-buyers and landlord-investors pay high interest for long periods

- depressed investment and some reduced efficiency in the private sector

- some reduction of invention and competition as high interest makes it harder for small firms and new firms depending on bank credit to compete with bigger, older firms which have share capital, some self-financing from earnings, and less need to borrow.

- higher costs of public investment if it is financed by borrowing, and higher interest payments on existing public debt. Both require higher taxation, or (more likely these days) less public investment and services because existing tax revenue has first to finance higher interest payments.

- less public demand for private goods and services as public investment and services are reduced.

Business and professional costs Corporate directors and executives exploit the new Delaware charters to take more each year from their firms, increasing their rewards at several times the rate of economic growth. Their corporate lawyers keep pace with them, and other lawyers whose clients can afford it keep pace with *them*. Privately provided and insured medical and hospital services to privately insured patients cost up to twice what similar services cost in countries which provide or insure the services publicly. But the entrenched winners resist reform, and impose those costs on the pretext that private enterprise is always more efficient than public.

(But notice my value judgement which chooses to call those rising incomes 'costs'. They can just as well be seen as changed distributions of income. So can the higher interest rates which transfer more income from borrowers to the owners of capital funds. One main purpose of the winners' alliance and strategy is to increase their share of national income. But it may still be true that their rising share is of a lower national income than other policies would allow.)

Social and personal costs are hard to predict because (in the 1970s) there is no living memory of rich and poor incomes diverging, and inequalities increasing, in a continuous or permanent way in rich countries. (Even at its worst, the depression of the 1930s was seen as temporary.) For many workers the new strategy reverses a century of progress to both higher income and greater equality, during which nearly every American household, however hard up, had well-justified hopes of better things to come. The losers from the new strategy are better educated, and better informed through many more media, than their forbears were. Who can tell how they will respond to direct third-world competition, to declining job-security, and to declining real wages helped down by corresponding cuts in the dole and welfare services? What will they think to do when deprived of the hopes that sustained the American Dream?

Those are open questions, because workers in developed modern economies have never before faced such permanent reverses. There is already evidence of the high importance of secure employment to people's personal development, character, competence and happiness. Work and the company at work are valuable for their own sake as well as for the income they earn. For most people no dole, however generous, can sufficiently replace income earned by interesting work in good company. But there is less evidence about the comparative importance of the work and the security respectively. How much personal value will work continue to have if it is insecure? If permanent full-time work gives way to temporary, part-time, contract work? Done at home alone by some workers; requiring others to move house often as they move from job to job? That is harder to predict.

Risks

Predictable The interests which drive the strategy, and the persuasions which attract wider support for it, express strong antipathy to taxation, to public spending, and to public regulation of business. There is a risk that those interests and attitudes will prevail too crudely and extremely. If they do, they may manage to block unpopular but necessary elements of the strategy, leaving it incoherent. The strongest temptations are to have government provide –

- too little of the public investment and up-to-date infrastructure and services that are necessary to the private sector's efficiency, and the tradeable industries' international competitiveness

- too little taxation to pay even for that inadequate level of public provision; and

- too little of the *necessary* public regulation of business, especially of banking and private international lending and borrowing.

Those are risks for the winners themselves. There are of course risks for losers too, and for values which matter to winners and losers alike. A free-trading global economy not only reduces government power over business. It also increases some kinds of business power over government. Some national governments already compete for mobile investment, just as some American States do, by means which hurt their taxpayers or their workers or their environmental conditions. Some concessions to transnational firms hurt local firms. Some social and environmental costs trouble as many winners as losers.

In an open global economy, if the freedoms to trade and lend and borrow are enforced, other freedoms must be restricted. Democracies won't retain much freedom of choice about the ownership and use of their natural resources, their cultural heritage or their influential media, or about tax policy, interest rates, wage-fixing, levels of employment or other determinants of the distribution of income. Even if well-off people continue to do well when public policies are decided by corporate boards and other 'market forces' rather than by government, some of the winners may nevertheless regret the loss of sovereign independence and self-government. Many more will regret it if the promised economic goods are *not* delivered.

Unpredictable Times are changing. With new forces at work in the economy *and* new freedoms, there may be surprises. When existing patterns of regulation are radically changed or repealed, operators may find unforeseen opportunities for anti-social behavior. When credit is easier to create, may unwelcome new uses for it appear? When banks and business can freely borrow foreign funds, what may that do to the national money supply? The balance of payments? When they can freely lend and invest abroad, how much capital will they export? How much employment? Will other investors replace the lost jobs and output at home? What if they don't?

Conservative philosophers from Edmund Burke in the eighteenth century to Karl Popper in the twentieth have warned reformers to do nothing irreversible. If big changes seem desirable, they should be made step by step, with each step designed to be reversible if it has unexpected ill effects. But zealous reformers, perhaps expecting only a few years in power, may positively want to make the new freedoms irreversible. If they manage to establish global free trade, exchange, investment and capital movement – a global 'level playing field' – they themselves may be surprised by some of the inventive uses that are made of those freedoms.

HINDSIGHT

Remember that this has not so far been a history of real American policy. The open-economy strategy explored in this chapter is a fiction: my notion of a coherent strategy that might imaginably have been adopted in the

1970s. It is a winners' strategy in a double sense. It aims to advance the interests of winners within the economy, and also the interests of the United States as a winning nation – a dominant military power and a successful competitor, transnational investor and trader earning an exchange surplus in the world economy.

The strategy is a fiction, and so is the picture of a winners' alliance with a single mind and agreed purposes. In reality there are many conflicts of interest between business groups, and there are many well-off individuals who do not support policies to enrich their own class or increase American inequalities. Nevertheless the concerns which notionally shaped the strategy were strong among those who supported President Reagan and contributed to his policy-making through the 1980s. So we can continue to pretend that such a strategy was conceived in the 1970s. But we now return from fiction to fact, with thirty years' hindsight, to see how far actual United States policy did or did not follow that notional strategy, and with what consequences.

SUCCESSES

Some of the aims were achieved. For ten or fifteen years, until the protectionist backlash in the 1990s, trade was freer. The US negotiators bargained hard for the further trade liberalization achieved in the Uruguay round of GATT negotiations, and for the creation of the World Trade Organization (WTO). They negotiated the North American Free Trade Area (NAFTA) with Canada and Mexico. Within the US there was some radical deregulation of business, including air transport and banking. Only one worker in nine is now in a labor union. Foreign policy has dictated some periods of heavy defence spending, but other government spending has been restrained, many welfare benefits have been reduced, and taxation has been both reduced and shifted downwards from richer to poorer taxpayers.

Those main elements of the strategy have thus been implemented, and some of its main purposes have been well served. There has been a continuous increase of inequality. More than half of the below-average male wage incomes in the US have fallen in real terms, i.e. they will buy less goods than they would buy twenty years ago, and the rest have increased very little. Low-waged women have done a little better, but have still got less than their share of economic growth. Most skilled wages in the upper half of incomes have kept pace with growth, and most salaries and executive and property incomes have outstripped it. The top 20 per cent have taken more than their pro-rata share of growth, the top 10 per cent much more, the top 5 and 2 per cent more

still. (Information and analysis for the first decades of the strategy are collected in J.H. Bergstrand and others, *The changing distribution of income in an open U.S. economy*, 1994)

At the same time there has been a clear improvement in the numbers employed, and in the relation between unemployment and inflation. The rate of unemployment, currently about 5 per cent, is (after Norway) the lowest in the OECD, where many countries have double the US rate and the worst have rates up to 20 per cent of the workforce. But despite its fuller employment, the US has comparatively low inflation. That results partly from the weakening of labor's market situation and bargaining power, and thus indirectly from the competitive effects of freer trade.

That follows from the strategy. But the good employment and inflation figures also owe something to mistakes and failures in implementing the strategy, as follows.

Too little tax

Remember the three temptations for strategists intent on freer enterprise and smaller government? Through the 1980s the Reagan administration fell for all three. It raised too little tax to pay for the necessary functions of government. It cut public investment below the level necessary for full private and national efficiency. And it gave dangerous new freedoms, at home and abroad, to America's banks and other financial operators.

I suspect the government cut taxes quite irresponsibly, to enrich its supporters and attract votes, without caring what economic harm might follow. Of course it did not admit any such thing. It pretended to believe that lower rates of tax, especially on rich incomes, would liberate such extra investment and growth that total revenue would actually increase. The theory was absurd. As the tax rates fell, the revenue fell. Undeterred, the government kept the rates down and ran massive budget deficits year after year. That left more money in the citizens' pockets. For various reasons (noticed presently) that did not stimulate much increase of private investment. The government continued to make too little public investment. So most of the extra spending was on household equipment and consumer goods and services. That maintained comparatively high (though still less than full) employment. Why didn't it also speed up inflation, as it might once have done?

One contributing cause was the high rate of payroll tax, employed for political rather than economic reasons. Once established, it ceases to be inflationary; and in the US it drives employers to replace full-time taxable workers, wherever they can, by the casual, part-time, contract or illegal labor that escape the tax. That weakens labor and makes it easier to reduce its rates of pay, especially where it is exposed to low-paid foreign competition. The import competition has also disciplined some prices. And quite high interest rates have been maintained to restrain excessive investment and consumer credit, and to borrow foreign funds to pay for the new excess of imports over export earnings. All these forces converge to allow comparatively low unemployment to coexist with comparatively low inflation.

If that were the whole story, the winners could be well satisfied with their winning strategy. But the government also fell for the temptation to invest too little, and the temptation to deregulate too much.

Too little investment

Summing up a number of studies of the competitive decline of the US economy through the 1980s, David Aschauer concluded that

> the reduction of public investment spending in the United States over the past twenty-five years played a central role in a number of our long-term ills. If the United States had continued to invest in public capital after 1970 at the rate maintained for the previous two decades, we could have benefited in the following ways:
>
> • Our chronically low rate of productivity growth could have been up to 50 per cent higher – 2.1 per cent per year, rather than the actual rate of 1.4 per cent;
>
> • Private investment in plant and equipment could have increased from the sluggish historical rate of 3.1 percent, to 3.7 percent of the capital stock …
>
> Not only has productivity growth fallen over time in the United States, it has been low for the past three decades relative to our major international competitors. For example, from 1965 to 1985, Japan and West Germany achieved labor productivity growth rates in excess of 3 and 2 percent per year respectively. One reflection of our low productivity growth, when coupled with persistently high consumption growth, is the yawning trade deficit and the switch, during the 1980s, from our nation's position as the world's largest creditor to the world's largest debtor.

– David A. Aschauer, 'Infrastructure: America's Third Deficit', *Challenge* 34, 2, March/April 1991.

Too little government

The dive from largest creditor to largest debtor had a number of causes. Freer trade exposed more tradeable industries to competition, and the foreign competitors were increasingly efficient. Within the US economy there was some loss of competitive edge. Some of that followed from neglecting the public infrastructure and services, as described by Aschauer. Some may have come from increasing inequality: some disaffection of poorer workers, and some tendency of executives, with their Delaware charters, to plunder their companies. And there were two ill effects of the step-by-step deregulation of the financial system. It reduced the efficiency with which credit was allocated within the national economy. And it weakened both the public discipline and the market discipline which might otherwise have checked the growth of imports. You met those financial themes in earlier chapters. Brief reminders follow, to complete this review of the open economy strategy.

Thousands of private Savings and Loan banks, publicly regulated and guaranteed, had long performed the useful function of accepting personal savings and lending them on mortgage to home buyers and other local property owners. They were suddenly given most of the borrowing and lending freedoms of the commercial banks. Their managers used the new opportunities exuberantly, incompetently, often corruptly. Within five years a majority of them were insolvent. Their management was taken over by the national government which had guaranteed their depositors. US taxpayers had to provide about $450 billion to meet their losses.

The national government also guaranteed many private pension funds, without sufficiently policing their management. Many misused their new freedom to lend and invest abroad, and had to be rescued by government.

Most Life Insurance institutions were guaranteed by State governments. By the 1990s five of the biggest were insolvent, were under State management and were costing State taxpayers.

Most of those institutions failed because too many of their borrowers failed. As they switched more of their lending to finance speculative land dealing, corporate takeovers, financial gambling and other unproductive activities, the borrowers' failures caused the lenders' failures. Among the ultimate losers were the US industries which might have made productive use of longer credit at lower rates of interest, if those had been available.

There were, finally, the ramifying effects of dismantling the boundary around the national financial system.

The long postwar boom had seen comparatively full employment, fast growth and low inflation. One condition of that achievement was national control of private international lending, borrowing and exchange of capital funds. Together with other controls that confined most savings and bank credit to productive uses. Within the national economy, regulation and market forces interacted to allow low rates of real interest, which in turn allowed efficient allocation of credit.

But with freedom to export capital funds, those who owned or could create funds could induce international competition for them. They could hunt the world for the highest returns: the highest rates of interest for given levels of risk; capital gains from fluctuating property and share prices; gambling gains from changing national rates of interest and rates of exchange; and offshore tax evasion.

In the first flush of freedom some bankers proved to be bad judges of the new risks. Through the 1970s many of them assumed that 'there is no country risk', meaning no country whose government won't ensure that its foreign debts are paid. They lent freely to governments and government-guaranteed projects in the third world, then had to be bailed out by their own government as their hard-up borrowers defaulted.

Nobody – neither friends nor enemies of the deregulation – foresaw how the new freedoms would compound each other. Nobody predicted the volume of pure gambling that would develop in a world with (i) private international lending, borrowing and exchange of capital funds, (ii) at volatile market rates of exchange, (iii) between countries with different and changing rates of interest, (iv) growing trade and exchange surpluses or deficits, and (v) private banks empowered to create credit on the basis of risk-rated capital adequacy, which included (vi) power to create credit for foreign governments within the OECD, up to generous limits, without any reserve backing at all. Gambling, or hedging honest business against others' gambling, was soon the purpose of nine out of ten exchange transactions. Exchange rates came to respond to gamblers' rather than traders' and investors' market demands for the traded currencies.

Not everyone fell for the new temptations. At home, plenty of sensible banking continued. But when capital funds could escape national regulation by moving abroad, regulation at home had to be relaxed to avoid driving funds abroad. That worsened the conditions for sensible banking. When savings and credit were no longer kept at home by boundary rules, they had to be kept at home by competitive rates of interest. As the rates rose, you know why they ruled out some of the most productive uses of credit. Lenders faced riskier and less productive options, which in turn justified the higher interest rates. Private investment in the US declined, especially the creation of new productive capacity by credit-dependent firms. Thus all the intrinsic inefficiencies of private money markets with public guarantees but inadequate public regulation came into play.

Too much debt

A final effect of the open financial boundary was on America's balance of payments. The inefficiencies, just noticed, depressed investment and slowed the growth of America's output. But the government's deficit budgeting left Americans with plenty to spend on household capital and consumer goods. The volume of that household demand was enough *both* to sustain comparatively high employment in the US *and* to attract an increasing flow if imports. But a rising proportion of the foreign currency to pay for the imports was not earned by US exports. So it had to be borrowed. American banks borrowed from foreign banks. Foreigners bought US government and utility bonds. For a time, high US interest rates kept the exchange value of the dollar high. When the rate of interest was lowered and the rate of exchange declined after 1985, the expected market discipline did not happen. The lower dollar did not create enough extra demand for exports. It did not sufficiently reduce demand for imports. The trade deficit continued. The borrowing continued. The debt increased. The annual interest bill increased because the debt did. And despite all that, the dollar soon returned to its former high value. Thus in one important respect the incoherence of the winners' policies turned the American economy from a national winner into a national loser.

In the next decade the debt continued to grow. Early in the 1990s an eminent American economist considered what must happen if the foreign lenders lost faith and stopped lending:

> Eventually, the rest of the world will be unwilling to lend the necessary sums. Nations will refuse to lend because the risks of not being repaid by the Americans in currencies of equal value to those that were lent is too high, or because the sums that must be lent require them to save more than they are willing to save – they wish to consume their income rather than lend it to Americans. When this happens, the structure of world trade must undergo a dramatic shift.

At American productivity levels, it requires about 2.5 million full-time workers to produce $100 billion worth of exportable goods and services. Since the rest of the world has been running a $100 billion trade surplus with the United States, at least 2.5 million workers in the rest of the world owe their jobs to that trade surplus – more if the export surpluses are in countries with productivity levels below those of the United States. When the lending stops, the trade surplus stops (Americans have no funds to buy foreign goods), and the jobs associated with those exports stop.

But that is just the beginning of the problems in the rest of the world. Without foreign lending, America must run a trade surplus to earn the funds necessary to pay interest on its accumulated debts. If the lending stops when these debts are $3,000 billion, then America must have a trade surplus of $300 billion to earn the funds necessary to meets its interest obligations, assuming a 10 percent interest rate. A $300 billion American trade surplus means a $300 billion trade deficit in the rest of the world. As $300 billion in American exports displace $300 billion of local production, the rest of the world loses another 7.5 million jobs – making a total of 10 million jobs. The required changes in the structure of world trade, and hence national production, are certain to be large, and may be sudden.

In the United States the restructuring is even more profound. ... With a trade deficit, Americans get to consume an extra $100 billion worth of goods they didn't produce. When the lending stops, they lose that $100 billion addition to their consumption, but since they have to start paying interest rather than borrowing the funds to pay interest, there is a further necessary subtraction from their consumption. The $300 billion in interest payments owed to the rest of the world must now be taken away from it (in the past it was borrowed from foreigners and given to foreigners) and given to the foreigners that own those debts. Total American consumption tumbles by $400 billion.

Foreign borrowing is essentially a way to raise present incomes at the cost of lowering future incomes – the greater the addition today, the greater the subtraction tomorrow.

– Lester Thurow, *Head to Head: The coming economic battle among Japan, Europe and America*, 1992; pp 233-4 of the 1994 edition.

But don't be carried away. This is still a rich, inventive, productive country. Most of its debt to foreigners is in

US dollars, with the foreigners bearing the exchange risks. Its government is already adjusting its trade policies: still pressing free trade on its export markets but restoring various kinds of protection to a number of American industries. A coherent economic and social strategy could certainly rescue it before it faces a Mexican bankruptcy. That might be a winners' strategy of the kind sketched in this chapter, managing by one inventive means or another to have foreign creditors and the poorest American workers bear a good deal of the cost of American recovery. Or it might be in the protectionist, liberal Democratic tradition of Roosevelt's New Deal or the Kennedy/Johnson reforms. But it needs to be a coherent strategy that pays its way and governs its own, as recent American economic policies have failed to do.

SUMMARY

Considered as a winners' strategy for what was until the 1980s a winning economy, United States economic policies since the 1970s have –

- sufficiently financed and equipped the world's most powerful military capacity
- achieved a steady increase of inequality, with specially big gains for business leaders, gains above the national rate of growth for most of the necessary supporters of the strategy, and falling real income and job security for half or more of the lower half of earners; and
- combined comparatively low unemployment with comparatively low inflation.

But –

- American productivity, national income and competitive capacity have grown more slowly than they could have done; and
- foreign debts have been accumulated which may not be serviced for much longer without some painful reduction of American consumption.

However –

- if a crunch comes, a disproportionate share of the hardships will probably be borne by losers rather than winners in the economies of the US and its trading partners.

Not all the causes of the above troubles were under American control. But those for which the US government was partly or wholly responsible included –

- freer trade at a time of declining competitive strength
- too little public investment

- buoyant aggregate demand sustained by too little taxation rather than by sufficient public investment
- too little public research and aid to private research and development
- imprudent deregulation of banks and financial institutions within the United States
- imprudent deregulation of foreign lending, borrowing and exchange of capital funds by American banks and financial institutions.

Better policies than those six were possible. They could have produced a faster-growing, more competitive, more sustainable US economy, with more defensible gains for the richer half or so of Americans, and with a little less harm to the incomes and spirits of the poorer half.

Instead, what happened was roughly this: The actual economic policies were incoherent in a number of ways. They assumed the US would continue to be a surplus trader, able to get net benefit from freer trade. But they included tax, infrastructure and financial policies which reduced the economy's rate of growth and its competitive efficiency. Together with Asian and European developments which avoided some of those mistakes, that turned the US into a deficit trader with rising foreign debt. A winners' strategy in a winning economy might have been sustainable. A winners' strategy of continuously increasing inequality within a losing economy with continuously increasing foreign debt may have to face the painful readjustments forecast by Lester Thurow. But eight years on from that forecast the essentials of the strategy were still in place and at work.

A GLOBAL ECONOMY

So much for the open economy as a national strategy. How does it look as a global strategy? Could there imaginably be a humane and efficient world economy without a world government? Meaning a single economy with no internal boundaries, or national power to hinder free trade in goods and money?

Two centuries ago some fruitful private/public cooperation between James Watt and the University of Glasgow gave the world the first effective steam engine. For lack of appropriate industrial and business law, the first half-century saw dreadful rates of physical illness and business failure in the new steam-driven industries. Since then, through successive technological and institutional advances, there has been a steady step-by-step, trial-and-error development of the intricate law and government and the extensive public production that were found to be necessary conditions of increasing productivity. Like the private sector's developing organization and activities, the public activities must often adapt to changing conditions. But it is quite unlikely that the system can suddenly manage with radically less government or public infrastructure and services. If you ever fancy that it could, reflect on the financial deregulation of 1970-1986. Go back and read the deregulators' confident forecasts of stronger investment, faster growth and surer market equilibrium. Then compare the actual outcomes: sluggish investment; halved rates of growth; higher unemployment in most countries; rising inequality in the developed countries; growing international imbalances of trade, exchange and self-accelerating debt; and ninety per cent or more of exchange transactions devoted to gambling with no productive or trading purpose at all.

Those are effects of ungoverned or ill-governed relations between national economies. How far might it be possible to provide the necessary international government by agreement between sovereign nations, rather than by a sovereign world government? There are working federations in the United States, Germany, Canada, Australia. They manage – but their federal authorities are sovereign in their particular spheres of action. Might a *subordinate* federal authority supply adequate economic government if its powers depended on the continuing agreement of twenty or more sovereign national governments with many conflicting interests? Europe is trying that, whether as a permanent arrangement or as a step toward union under a sovereign government. What are the prospects of coherent economic strategy under such a regime? That's our next question.

56

A federal economy

Most of these chapters about economic strategy are about national governments' management of their national economies. This one is about the special economic difficulties of governments which have inadequate or divided powers. Any federation, or central government with divided powers, can have such problems. Remember the American effects when fifty one States compete to charter the nation's private firms, or when President and Congress try to run incompatible economic policies. The difficulties tend to be greatest where the central government is weakest. The extreme case is the European Union, so it supplies this chapter's example.

THE EUROPEAN EXPERIMENT

Sixteen national governments, and soon perhaps twenty or more, are trying to do something which is new in both political and economic history. As to just what they are trying to do, there is disagreement. Here are three of the ways in which different parties might characterize the experiment:

- Europe has spent half a century establishing a customs union. The member countries trade freely with each other, while a common tariff protects their industries against the rest of the world.

- European governments have agreed to establish a single European economy. They agree its governing rules and its economic strategy and policies. Each government then applies those rules and policies within its territory. Economic union is thus achieved by voluntary cooperation between the governments of nations which in other respects remain as independent as before.

- The European Community is developing, step by step, into one nation like the United States of America and other federations. Like the unification of Germany in the nineteenth century, the process began with economic unification. As in the early years of the American, Canadian and Australian federations, the central government began with limited powers. But as happened in those other federations, the powers of the central European government are being expanded as experience reveals the need for more coherent government of the unified economy.

The name of the enterprise has changed from European Coal and Steel Community to European Economic Community to European Community to European Union. Officially the Community continues to do the main economic business of the Union of which it is now a part, so in practice 'Community' and 'Union' serve as alternative names for it.

Changing purposes

Besides being disagreed at any moment, the prevailing purposes of the Community change over time.

The Community was conceived during and after the Second World War. Its founders wanted to speed economic recovery after the war, but above all they wanted to make the peace permanent. Europe's national governments had been the world's worst warmakers for centuries. An economic union would make the national communities depend on one another and share many interests and institutions. That would make war between them less likely than in the past. And it would unify and strengthen them against any future aggression by communist Russia.

Twenty years later the cold war continued, but with less fear of hot war. Other troubles threatened. The long postwar boom ended. America scaled down its services to Europe's recovery, and stopped acting as the unofficial central banker to the international financial system. Japan had become a major economic power, other Asian tigers were following suit, and their products were penetrating Europe's home and foreign markets. In those conditions the European Community became more concerned with its competitive economic performance in an increasingly competitive world.

Twenty more years saw the excesses and scandals of the 1980s. Power and opinion shifted to the Right. Inflation came under better control, but there were frightening increases of unemployment and international debt. The ex-communist countries' first attempts to convert to capitalism were sharply reducing their already low output and income, making them poorer rather than richer. In Europe people worried about the obstinate increase of unemployment, and the technological and structural changes which seemed to be causing it. The governments within the European Community had been required to give up, step by step, the main national powers they had previously used to maintain employment. So as unemployment grew, rising numbers of people in old capitalist Europe as well as in ex-communist Europe were getting poorer rather than richer. (Western Europe had the world's most generous income transfers to the unemployed, but the new unemployed were still poorer than they had been as earners.) Freer trade and freer banking were not delivering the goods expected of them. What could the Community's limited central powers and cumbersome policy-making procedures do about these novel problems?

Changing powers

The powers of the Community, and of its member nations' governments, are best understood historically. It is worth taking time to read more of the history than there is room for here. Try Loukas Tsoukalis, *The new European economy: The politics and economics of integration*, (second edition 1993), and – for interesting argument about the Community's effect on its member countries – Alan S. Milward, *The European rescue of the nation state* (1992). There is a more neoclassical and hopeful view of the Community's economic prospects, with more detailed information about its institutions and policies, in D.M. Harrison, *The organisation of Europe: The development of a continental market order* (1995).

Economic integration began with two initiatives in the 1940s. When the United States government provided massive Marshall Aid to help finance Europe's postwar recovery, it pressed the Europeans to develop the Organization for Economic Cooperation and Development, and the European Payments Union. And French and Belgian initiatives drew six governments – of France, Germany, Belgium, Holland, Luxembourg and Italy – into the Treaty of Paris which in 1951 established the European Coal and Steel Community. Its central purpose was to integrate the French and German steel industries under an international High Authority. That had peace-keeping as well as economic purposes. It unified the French and German steel industries. It gave Belgian and Italian steelmakers some protection from them, under a regime of regulated competition.

This first step towards integration was not inspired by ideas of free trade between nations, or small government within them. These were the years when Keynesian governments were developing their means of influencing levels of aggregate demand, investment and employment. They were all short of foreign exchange. Whatever foreign funds their exports earned, or Marshall Aid lent or gave them, they directed to the most necessary and productive imports. That entailed barring other imports, which they did. The exchange control also prevented any flight of capital funds abroad. That boundary control enabled governments to control interest rates at home. That allowed efficient market allocation of credit for investment, and for some years most governments also regulated the general directions of lending and investment to direct them to their most necessary and productive uses. Most of the controls were of general kinds of use. (Perhaps 'Lend more to farmers, manufacturers, exporters; less to property developers or consumer credit; nothing for share-buying'.) Within the permitted categories, and at restricted rates of interest, market competition could flourish.

Besides coping with postwar shortages, the controls on lending and borrowing and on foreign exchange were thus necessary conditions of other Keynesian policies. Keep in mind how coherent and necessary to each other those controls were, as you see some of them dismantled and others divided between Community and national governments through the following decades.

By 1957 the long boom was in full swing. Europe's exports and import-replacing industries were recovering. The shortage of American dollar exchange was over. People who saw the public controls as temporary means of coping with postwar shortages thought they could now be dismantled. Purer Keynesians did not. Some of both inspired the Treaty of Rome, in which the six who had signed the Treaty of Paris extended the scope, and amended some of the purposes, of their cooperation. They did now look forward to freer trade and exchange, and eventually to a single 'common market'. But progress in that direction should still be cautious: step by step, with unanimous agreement on each step. And there were a number of reservations for particular industries and national interests, and for the Common Agricultural Policy.

If national governments lost the power to regulate trade or exchange within Europe, the Community might need some central powers to cope with the effects of freedom. But in the Treaty of Rome there was –

• no provision for industrial policy – i.e. for influencing the pattern of industries that should develop in Europe, or whereabouts in Europe they should develop

- no provision for coordinating national macroeconomic policies – i.e. the taxing, public spending, credit and interest rate policies by which levels of investment and employment might be influenced

- very little provision for any redistribution of income or public services from richer to poorer countries or regions.

Thus most of the old and new economic functions of government stayed with the national governments, though there was reason to doubt that they could perform those functions properly if they surrendered their right to regulate trade and exchange.

Progress 1970 – 1992

While the long boom continued through the 1960s the integration of the six economies made good progress. There was a steady reduction of tariffs and other trade barriers between the member countries. Their trade with each other grew faster than their trade with the outside world, and faster than their fast rate of economic growth. They attracted strong investment from their own and American investors.

It is hard to know how much the buoyant growth owed to the freer trade. The two probably helped each other. The freer trade and bigger market allowed economies of scale and attracted investment; and the fast growth and full employment allowed politicians to reduce the trade barriers without fear of serious business failure or structural unemployment.

Any pains of adjusting to freer trade were also being gentled by two other activities of government. National governments were acting as confident Keynesian managers of full employment. And they were creating the welfare state. These years saw the completion of the main public health and welfare services, regular income for the unemployed, national systems of income-linked superannuation, and public aid to low-priced housing. There were thus safety nets, and while the long boom lasted there were usually other jobs, for workers who lost their jobs to freer trade.

Thus governments reduced their control of international economic activity and increased their influence within their national economies. The Community meanwhile created a fairly powerless European Parliament, and a Court of Justice, and continued to develop the Commission which served as its central bureaucracy. But the national governments, each with a power of veto, continued to determine most of what the community's bureaucrats could and could not do.

There were further steps forward before the good times ended. The Community developed its own tax resources: customs duties, agricultural levies and a percentage of each member country's Value Added Tax. It began to plan a European Monetary Union. It introduced direct election to the European Parliament and gave it a small role in the Community's policy-making. Britain, Ireland and Denmark were admitted to membership.

But the long boom ended and the climate changed. From the late 1960s and sharply from 1973 the member countries began to suffer declining investment, slower growth, some loss of markets to new competitors, faster inflation, and rising unemployment. The Community soon had higher unemployment than the rest of Europe and the rest of the developed world.

Those stresses partly hindered and partly hastened the process of integration. There was complicated, sometimes despairing, conflict and manoeuvring about the Community's form and future through the 1970s. There was some increase of overt and covert protection, inside and outside the Community. Some national and class inequalities increased, between the employed and the unemployed and between the richer and poorer member countries. So there was conflict about redistributive policies, or the lack of them. The Community had a Regional Fund and a Social Fund for redistributive purposes, but both were tiny compared with the redistributive flows within the member countries, and the inequalities between their average incomes. They looked meaner still as the poorer countries – Greece, Spain and Portugal – got rid of their dictators, elected democratic governments, and asked to join the Community.

Through the 1980s various factors combined to revive the member governments' interest in some further integration of their economies. The general shift of opinion to the Right reduced trust in government and increased trust in market forces. It also saw more restrictive monetary and fiscal policies which slowed inflation and increased unemployment. From 1985 investment revived, growth accelerated, Europe's competitive performance improved. It looked easier to adjust national economies to a further cut in protection. And four or five years of cyclical boom coincided with five years of strong leadership of the European Commission, the Community's central public service.

In 1985 the Community decided in principle to achieve a single market, with no internal barriers to trade, by 1992, and to create a single currency, with a Central Bank to manage it, by 1999.

The single market was not just a matter of removing the last remaining tariffs and trade quotas. There were also innumerable NTBs – Non-Tariff Barriers. Every country had a great accumulation of detailed economic rules and regulations. Many of them, intentionally or not, had the effect of excluding foreign goods. Could they all be replaced by single European commercial, environmental and consumer-protection codes? No – with the cumbersome Community policy-making procedures it might well take forever to agree such codes. With the Rightward shift of opinion and the new faith in deregulation, an alternative principle was adopted. It was called mutual recognition. Over a wide range of subjects, each government agreed to accept the sovereign acts of all the others. What could lawfully be made and sold in one member country could be sold in all member countries. Most federations have such rules. (Texas accepts whatever it is lawful to fish out of the waters of Maine. Tasmania accepts whatever it is lawful to manufacture in New South Wales.)

That further integration required some increase of Community powers – some political as well as economic changes. They were agreed in the Single European Act in 1986 and the Treaty of Maastricht in 1992. Formally, the single market came into force punctually from the last day of 1992. In practice its details continued to be perfected for some time after that.

European government now

Here follow short descriptions of the Community's main institutions and policy-making procedures, at the stage when the single market has been substantially achieved. This sort of institutional description is boring, but it matters. The economic strategies open to choice by united Europe are severely limited by the division of powers between the Community and its member countries' national governments. In distributing powers between them some powers have been weakened and some have been lost altogether. Before considering what the new regime should do, it is important to grasp what its institutions do and don't enable it to do.

The European Council is the heads of government of the member countries. It commonly meets twice a year. Rather than doing anything itself, it gives general directions to the Community's other institutions: what possibilities to explore, what strategies to aim at, what political limits to observe.

The Council of Ministers is the Community's effective law-maker, and it is where the national interests of the member nations – or of their governments –

are most directly represented. Members are appointed by their national governments. Each is served by a personal political staff. The Council meets twice or more each month. All its law-making business comes to it from the Commission (described below). It exercises its power in four main ways, by issuing –

- *Regulations* These are law throughout the Community. They don't have to be confirmed or enacted by national parliaments. If they conflict with national laws, they prevail over those laws.

- *Directives* tell national governments to act for specific purposes to achieve specified results, but leave it to the national governments to decide how to go about it. Some may pass acts of Parliament, some may use existing executive powers. Some may tailor their action to avoid conflict with existing national laws or practices.

- *Decisions* give instructions to particular governments, firms or individuals. Where necessary they override national laws or policies.

- *Recommendations and Opinions* are what their names imply. They may persuade or inform people but they don't bind anyone.

The uses of all those powers are limited by the treaties which created them. Some are also subject to national veto, though most business is now done by weighted majority voting. (Bigger countries' votes count for more.)

The European Commission is the Community's central bureaucracy. It has about fifteen thousand public servants, in more than twenty departments, mostly located in Brussels. It alone is allowed to prepare legislation and propose it to the Council of Ministers. Anyone can ask it to consider new proposals, and it is heavily lobbied by business and regional and other interests; but it decides how much or little notice to take of the suggestions it receives, and most of its initiatives are its own.

Besides preparing business for the Council of Ministers it has various administrative and regulatory powers. Some are powers to implement decisions of the Council of Ministers, or to see that others do. Some are regulatory functions delegated to it by the Council of Ministers.

The Commissioners are appointed for five-year terms by the national governments. But unlike the Ministers at the Council of Ministers, Commissioners are *not* supposed to be national representatives or answerable to national governments. They, and the bureaucracy which they command, are supposed to act independently on behalf of the Community as a whole.

The European Parliament is directly elected by the voters of all the member countries. It is the Community's only directly democratic institution. Unlike other parliaments it is not the main law-maker, but it has a limited role in the Council of Ministers' law-making. It has been likened to a weak upper house in a national parliament: an absolute majority in the Parliament can delay or block proposals by the Council of Ministers, or suggest amendments to them.

The European Court of Justice decides disputes about the interpretation of Community law, and disputes between Community and national authorities. Some of its decisions have been important. For example it introduced the principle of 'mutual recognition' when it decided that Germany could not ban the import of alcoholic drinks which it was lawful to produce and sell in France.

The legislative process varies according to the nature and importance of the business and the extent of agreement or disagreement about it. A representative regulation or directive must usually go through all or most of the following processes. Don't memorize them: they're only here to illustrate the general complexity of the Community's law-making procedures.

Whether on its own initiative, or at some other party's suggestion, a unit within the Commission generates a proposal. To become a law or directive, the proposal must usually be submitted to expert investigation by consultants outside the Commission; opened to consultation with firms, organizations or governments whose interests it may affect; discussed with relevant departments of member nations' governments; submitted to debate, and unanimous or majority decision, at a full meeting of the Commission; submitted to the Parliament for a first reading; examined by a parliamentary committee; simultaneously submitted to the Economic and Social Council of the Community, an advisory body representing employers, employees, consumers, farmers and some others; submitted to the Council of Ministers, one of whose committees allots the proposal a place in the queue of business awaiting the Council's attention; considered by a working group of specialists, one from each member country; subjected to a majority vote by them; passed for discussion and decision to the Council of Ministers; if no sufficient majority, returned to the Commission to explore the possibility of a compromise proposal; if provisionally passed by the Council of Ministers, returned to the

Parliament for a second hearing and a recommendation according to one or other of the decision-making contributions allowed to the Parliament by the Treaty; returned to the Council of Ministers for decision by majority if in agreement with the Parliament, or by unanimous decision if in disagreement with the Parliament; and if finally adopted returned to the Commission to be acted on by the Commission, by other agencies of the Community, or by appropriate national governments, as the business requires. (All you need remember about the 246 words of that sentence is that they still greatly shorten and simplify the actual legislative process.)

Economic powers

How are functions of government (as far as they concern the economy) distributed between the Community and the national governments?

The treaties distribute the powers of government chiefly by defining the Community's powers.

There are provisions of three general kinds. There are things the Community *must* do. It must unify the currency, create the Central Bank, enforce the rules for free trade and fair competition within the single market.

There are things the Community is not empowered to do. It cannot dictate the member countries' constitutions or electoral laws, or their government budgets.

Third, there are a lot of things which the Community *may* do, or may *help* with, or may *contribute* to. Over that range of activity the Treaty of Maastricht requires what it calls subsidiarity: 'the Community shall take action, in accordance with the principle of subsidiarity, only if and in so far as the objectives of the proposed action cannot be sufficiently achieved by the Member States and can, therefore, ... be better achieved by the Community.' Decisions should be taken as close as possible to the people they will affect.

Though the treaty doesn't say so, that is an ancient principle of Catholic political theory, reasserted by a reforming Pope in the nineteenth century. Action should be taken by the most local government that can act effectively for the purpose. Sounds simple? Only if it is clear how the objectives can best be achieved. In practice economists disagree about how to achieve most of the main objectives of economic policy: growth, full employment, low inflation, equitable distribution of income. For particular purposes some monetarists want to use one set of powers; some Keynesians want to use another set; others want to use yet other powers; some market theorists want to improve efficiency by reducing or dismantling some governing powers, or banning their use. The chosen policies influence the creation and distribution of powers; the pattern of available powers then limits the policy options. It is a two-way relation, complicated by national and theoretical disagreements.

For example the national governments agreed to create a single European currency, and a European Central Bank to manage it with considerable independence of either the Community or the national governments. The Treaty of Maastricht accordingly created the powers which the Bank assumed in 1999. By signing the Treaty the national governments agreed to hand over their monetary powers to the Bank. But they have not been willing to hand over their main taxing, investing and spending powers to the Community. Keynesian and other critics don't like that division of powers. They don't believe that coherent management of employment and inflation and economic development will be possible with national governments deciding taxation and public investment and spending, a different government (the Community) deciding trade and competition policy, and a third authority (the Bank) regulating the creation and exchange and some of the uses of money. The bankers, neoclassical economists and others who designed that division of powers don't agree. They think inflation will be restrained best by monetary means, plus a simple rule that governments balance their budgets; and they expect unregulated trade, financial and labor markets to maintain fuller employment than more active public management could do.

The list of activities on which the Community *may* act (subject to the principle of subsidiarity, and the national representatives' votes in the Community's institutions) includes research and technological development; European networks for transport, energy and telecommunications; tourism; education and public health; conservation of national culture; and a list of citizens' rights agreed in a Social Charter in 1989. They include rights to free speech, association and movement, equal opportunity, and other social protections. The Treaty of Maastricht includes a summary list of the activities in which the Community must or may take part. If you would like to see it now, it is on page 792 of this chapter.

Summary

We are about to compare two possible economic strategies for Europe. The first one assumes that powers are distributed as under the Treaty of Maastricht:

The Community makes trade and competition policy. For those purposes it regulates business or has governments adopt common or harmonized codes of corporate law and practice. More patchily, it also acts to encourage common environmental policies.

The Community raises revenue, chiefly from Value Added Tax and external tariffs. About half the revenue finances the Common Agricultural Policy. Some of the rest provides structural funds which distribute resources to poorer nations and regions in the Community. But the Community's budget is only about one and a half per cent of Europe's income and two and a half per cent of Europe's public revenue, and its structural funds distribute less than a tenth of the amount redistributed by national governments.

In short, the Community can require free trade and fair competition within Europe, and subject to World Trade Organisation rules it can give Europe's economy some protection from the rest of the world. It confides monetary policy to a Central Bank. But except for an upper limit imposed by the Treaty it cannot control the amount of revenue the national governments raise, or how they invest or spend or transfer most of it. It has no power over incomes policy. Whether you believe that division of powers allows coherent public management of growth, employment, inflation or environmental care depends on what you think causes what in modern mixed economies. The designers of our first strategy think those powers will do. The designers of the second strategy don't.

A NEOCLASSICAL STRATEGY

What is neoclassical about this strategy is its faith in market forces and its reasons for recommending further deregulation. But its cruel social proposals, for example for old, sick or unemployed people, are not specifically neoclassical, and some neoclassical economists will disagree with them.

Except for some summary passages in square brackets the strategy is reprinted from a 1995 publication of the Organisation for Economic Co-operation and Development (OECD). It is addressed to all OECD countries, but its program of small government makes it workable with limited central-government powers, so we can read it as an OECD strategy for the European Community. It comes from the world's leading independent centre of economic thought and advice, so in addition to its European interest it is a good example of some predominant economic beliefs of the 1990s.

The chapter is called CHALLENGES AND POLICY PRIORITIES. After an optimistic opening about short-term economic prospects, it proceeds to its strategic concerns as follows.

MEDIUM-TERM CHALLENGES

[Beyond the short term,] many issues will have to be confronted in the coming years to ensure that high economic growth with sustained increases in employment and productivity is achieved ... and that rising living standards and increased prosperity are shared, both across countries and among individuals within countries.

Sustained increases in employment and permanent reductions in unemployment are essential, since they would contribute both to the growth of output by reducing the waste of human resources which is now occurring, and to the reduction of the social distress which high and prolonged unemployment causes. ...

More rapid increases in productivity growth will require: open competitive markets, which put producers under continuous pressures to improve efficiency and to innovate; high levels of research and development and of new investment which embodies new technologies and ensures that they are adequately diffused; and a more highly skilled labor force. The adverse effects on particular groups or individuals of the rapid changes sometimes associated with competitive markets and technological advances can be addressed by enhancing OECD societies' capacity to adapt constructively, rather than attempting to slow the pace of change. In the final analysis, the productivity improvements which competitive processes and technological advance generate are the main source of rising living standards. They will also provide the means for increased support for the displaced and the excluded, and in particular for programmes to help re-integrate them.

Further productivity growth and an efficient allocation of the world's real resources will also depend on the free movement of financial resources. The challenge here is to maximise the benefits of globalised and liberalised financial markets while ensuring that any associated costs are minimised. In recent years, these markets have at times experienced large and unexpected pressures, often leading to abrupt movements in exchange rates and long-term interest rates. In many cases, pressures have reflected a justified loss of market confidence in macroeconomic policies and prospects. However, once a loss of confidence has occurred, the timing and magnitude of the market reactions cannot be fully attributed to changes in underlying economic conditions. The large short-term swings which sometimes result can destabilise domestic economic conditions and aggravate financial fragility. As well, prolonged misalignments of currencies can lead to large movements in trade balances and give rise to tensions in international trade and payments systems, which may contribute to protectionist pressures.

Strengthening the open multilateral rules-based trading system, and bringing international investment into a similar framework, will boost growth by raising productivity through better allocation of resources across sectors and countries, and thus contribute to continued increases in living standards. ...

MACROECONOMIC POLICY REQUIREMENTS

Achieving and maintaining a stable macroeconomic environment will provide a supportive backdrop for sustained growth. The gains made in lowering inflation must be preserved. A difficult but vital task will be to reduce high public deficits and debt-to-GDP ratios, particularly in view of the expected increase in fiscal burdens associated with ageing populations.

[Detailed analysis and advice follow, about the short- and medium-term monetary policies of a number of countries.]

In the present macroeconomic situation, the requirements of non-inflationary growth point to the need for monetary policy to moderate demand where margins of spare capacity have virtually disappeared or substantially narrowed, while it should support a recovery of activity where such margins remain large and there is little risk of inflation ...

Over the longer term, it is necessary to strengthen further the credibility of commitments to non-inflationary monetary policy in order to lower interest rate premia for inflation and inflation uncertainty, as well as provide a favourable backdrop for decisions about current resource allocation and new investment. This would improve productivity performance and help reduce the extent of financial market volatility. There are a number of measures which would contribute positively in this regard, all of which are desirable in their own right. Considerable progress has been made in many countries in terms of emphasis on inflation control when formulating monetary policy objectives, the ambitiousness of these objectives and transparency in communicating them to the public. ... Greater autonomy for central banks in their operations is also enhancing institutional pressure for maintaining price stability in a number of countries – for example in some EU countries and New Zealand. Further progress in these areas would help central banks to build successful track records and contribute to the development of public support on which these commitments ultimately depend.

Fiscal consolidation continues to have a key role to play. Chronic budget deficits and rising debt-to-GDP ratios in many countries suggest widespread unsustainability of present fiscal policies ...Reducing deficits can be expected to raise national saving, which would help ease upward pressures on interest rates, to finance increased investment and to promote sustainable growth in the medium term. It will also allow greater room for manoeuvre and help underpin the credibility of official commitments to price stability. In view of medium-term pressures from pension commitments and health care programmes, which will rise as populations age, it is all the more critical to address fiscal imbalances as soon as possible.

Since the scope for increasing taxation in many countries is limited by political resistance and the increased economic distortions that higher taxes imply, the main burden of adjustment will have to fall on expenditure. Some more specific policy recommendations, which differ from country to country, are presented in the General Assessment chapter

of this publication. More generally, recent experience in a number of countries indicates that the adjustments which deficit reduction will require are easiest for the economy to absorb if action is taken during an upswing in activity, even though pressure to act may then be less. Governments should, therefore, seize the opportunity which the current situation offers, in order to avoid much more difficult conditions when the expansion slows. Action to reduce spending may be most effective where budgetary processes combine credible and binding limits on expenditure with efforts to improve the efficiency of public activities. Beyond this, it is necessary to achieve reductions in social exclusion and marginalisation, and an equitable distribution of income, both among those currently alive and between current and future generations. Such achievements will be important factors in obtaining and maintaining broad political support for the actions required in all areas, in particular action to bring about significant improvements in budget positions.

KEY STRUCTURAL REFORM ISSUES

Reforms to reduce structural rigidities in both labour and product markets would make wage and price formation more responsive to market conditions and speed the adjustment to changing price signals, enhancing the ability of economies to adjust to changes such as shifts in demand patterns or technological advances. At the moment, rigidities in labour and product markets have the effect of channelling pressures that arise in these markets into more flexible sectors of the economy, in particular financial markets. More flexible labour and product markets will also contribute to the job creation which is necessary to reduce long-term unemployment. Improved job creation performance will assist in creating the climate necessary to address problems of marginalisation and exclusion. In these ways, the favourable impact of structural reforms on productivity and the social costs of adapting to change would increase the credibility of stable monetary and fiscal policies.

Financial markets in OECD countries are now all essentially liberalised. The potential benefits of liberalised financial markets are substantial, and include: allowing savers greater protection against inflation; facilitating portfolio diversification both within countries and internationally; providing access to financing often lacking in the past; enlarging the scope for the end users of capital to make productive investment in activities that are judged to yield the highest return over the longer term; increasing the operating efficiency of financial institutions and reducing intermediation margins; and encouraging innovative methods of risk management. To maximise these benefits it is essential that market participants be subject to the disciplines which markets impose as well as having access to the rewards they offer to ensure that they prudently balance risk-taking and the search for high returns. In particular, care must be taken to avoid a situation (often described as "moral hazard") in which participants' investment or financing decisions or government policies are distorted by the perception that they are effectively guaranteed against risk or are underwritten by domestic taxpayers or the international community.

The volatility which financial markets have displayed has led to suggestions that the process of deregulation should be reversed or that measures, such as transaction taxes. should be introduced to "slow" financial markets. In view of the adverse economic effects caused by the distortions associated with much of past regulation, reversing the trend towards liberalisation is not a solution, and in any case is unlikely to be feasible. To be effective, transaction taxes and regulations would have to be applied virtually worldwide, which would require a degree of international co-ordination that is probably not achievable. A large pool of funds to stabilise excessive currency movements has also been suggested, but it would create moral hazard problems on the part of both private sector market participants and governments, undermining healthy market discipline on their behaviour and policies.

OECD governments cannot, however, be complacent about financial market behaviour. The full benefits of liberalised markets will be realised only if the necessary information is available for market participants to make decisions wisely and for the relevant authorities to assess ... risks. ...There is also scope for improving prudential supervision of financial institutions and markets, as well as for ensuring adequate consumer protection and continued vigorous competition in the financial system.

The current expansion in the OECD area has the potential to mature into a phase of durable growth of employment and incomes in a stable, non-inflationary environment. Ensuring this desirable outcome, however, will require policy initiatives across the full range of actions outlined above. Exploiting to the full the mutually-reinforcing effects of good macro-economic policies and good structural policies is crucial to achieving the objective of rising and equitably distributed global living standards.

© OECD 1995, *Economic Outlook* 57, pp. xi-xvi.
reproduced by permission of the OECD

How to balance public revenue and spending is suggested later in the publication. If there must be higher taxes, let them be indirect; but it will be better not to increase them at all. Government should balance its budget by spending less. It can do that by increasing public sector efficiency, privatizing more public services, reducing public subsidies to private industry and agriculture, and buying whatever it needs from more competitive suppliers. And 'a fundamental reassessment of social transfers is required ... Welfare systems could be better targeted to individuals in need if eligibility requirements were tighter; work-testing of the unemployed and the disabled was more effective; means-testing was more effective; programme coordination was improved; and integration of benefit and tax systems was better.' As more old people need to be supported, the pension age can be raised to make more of them support themselves; people's contributions to their pension funds can be increased; pensions can be reduced; and people can be given fewer and cheaper kinds of health care (pp 12,15).

SUMMARY

Translated into plain language that program seems to say, for Europe:

Free the markets even further. Besides internal free trade, abolish the Community's external tariff and trade freely with the rest of the world. Do nothing for firms put out of business, people put out of work, or people who lose their savings because of the new freedoms. Just deregulate faster. But there needs to be more and better research, development, education and training.

Cut most worker and consumer protection. Governments must repeal any minimum wage regulation and ban collective bargaining. Though the wording is vague, it seems to imply that governments should also stop most regulation of product quality, safety or standardization. (Or they must do whatever else is meant by 'reducing structural rigidities in both labour and product markets' in order to 'make wage and price formation more responsive to market conditions and speed the adjustment to changing price signals'.)

Do not regulate or tax the movement or the uses of capital funds, though their movement and uses are acknowledged to produce jumpy exchange rates and interest rates, and also unemployment, unbalanced exchange, and international debt. Trust the fund-owners and bankers to invest their capital wherever in the world it will be most productive in the long run. Just be sure that they take their own risks. Don't rescue insolvent banks. Let them fail, and bring down their depositors and creditors with them. Nevertheless governments should somehow give bank customers better consumer protection.

Control inflation and smooth the business cycle by two means only. A Central Bank, independent of government, must move interest rates up and down as needed to encourage or discourage investment. And governments must balance their budgets. Balanced budgets will allow people and institutions to save more, which will free more funds for investment and economic growth.

Besides balanced budgets, the strategy calls for more research, education and training. Most of that additional spending will have to be public. At the same time rising numbers of old people will be wanting more public help. Don't give it to them. Governments must balance their budgets by spending less, not taxing more. They can raise the pension age, cut the pension rate, and lower the asset and income levels which disqualify people from the pension. By similar means they can reduce the numbers of unemployed and invalid people and lone parents who are entitled to public incomes, and reduce those incomes too.

Disagreements

If you believe that strategy would have cruel and unfair effects, don't assume that its authors think so too. They expect that the recommended policies will cause the fastest growth that is possible to achieve and the fullest employment that is compatible with low inflation; and will do more good for most of the poorest people than can be done by any other strategy.

Not all the supporters of the strategy share those expectations. Some of them want the banking and business freedoms and the lowered wages and taxes and welfare hand-outs, and think the costs for some are worth the gains for others. There are even some who think the strategy might hinder more than it would help national efficiency and growth, but still welcome it for their own reasons. With those cynics you may have moral disagreements. But many supporters of the strategy do believe its authors' forecasts. If they expected it to slow growth and intensify poverty they would have moral and social as well as technical objections to it. So either a moral or a technical critique of the strategy may do well to focus on its technical qualities and its likely material effects.

With its single currency and Central Bank, Europe now has the capacity to implement this OECD strategy. Suppose that it does so. I could offer an estimate of the main economic and social effects that the strategy is likely to have, and an opinion of its value. But there are three reasons why it will be better if you do that. You can do some useful revision. You can exercise your professional skill and judgment. And you can demonstrate your independence of this text's persuasions. So –

EXERCISE

Revise (if you need to) Chapters 49 of this text on trade policy, 50 and 51 on money and banking, 53 on employment, and 36's summary of what private enterprises need from government. Find the *Cambridge Journal of Economics* 1994, No. 18, pp. 571-585 and read Ross MacKay's article on 'Automatic stabilisers, European union and national unity'. Then re-read the summary of the OECD strategy printed above, or (better) find a library copy of *OECD Economics Outlook* 57 and read the full account of the strategy on pp. 1-42. Then compare (1) the main effects the OECD authors expect their strategy to have; (2) the main effects that a reading of this text and Ross MacKay's article would encourage you to expect; and (3) your own estimate and judgment of the likely effects, with the reasoning that leads you to your conclusions.

A SOCIAL-DEMOCRATIC STRATEGY

In 1990 the socialist members of the European parliament commissioned a policy paper from the consultant Association for Applied Research in the European Community. A four-nation team – Gerhard Leithauser, Francois de Lavergne, Terry Ward and Enrico Wolleb – wrote the report and called it *Policies for balanced development in an integrating Community*. They offer a coherent social-democratic strategy for the European Community. Their central purpose is to prevent the net increase of unemployment and inequality that must follow if Europe's economy is united under too little government. Their solution is to make Europe's government more like the government of existing federations in the USA, Canada, Germany and Australia. Here follows a summary of their reasoning and their main proposals.

A STRATEGIC CHOICE

Europe's economic integration can alternatively increase or reduce economic stability, growth, employment, equality, and environmental care. If it has too little government it is likely to do net harm on all those fronts, except perhaps the restraint of inflation. But that does not justify dismantling the Community and returning to purely national government. With appropriate governing powers and policies a united Europe could be a force for good. That is what social-democrats should work for.

Aims

The European Community should aim to –

- maintain steady economic growth
- distribute the growth between countries and regions better than unaided market forces might do
- reduce inequalities within European countries, between European countries, and between Europe and its immediate neighbors in Africa and the Middle East
- improve national, European and world standards of environmental care
- use the strength of a united Europe to negotiate and establish a better world system of trade, finance and exchange.

POLICIES

Money

Europe should have a single currency, managed by a European central bank, as already planned. But its management should differ from current plans in three respects:

- The Central Bank should not manage Europe's money and credit with the single purpose of restraining inflation. Its commission should require it to act with a balanced concern to restrain inflation, to allow full employment, and to see that funds are available for investment in the poorer as well as the richer regions of the Community.

- The bank should be insulated from direct political interference, as planned. But it must be democratically accountable. Four times a year it should report to the European Parliament and be cross-examined by a parliamentary committee, just as the Governor of the Federal Reserve answers to Congress in the United States.

- The Community's taxing and public spending need to be coordinated with its monetary policy. That coordination must be arranged by the Community and national governments, not by the bank which decides monetary policy. For a number of reasons, the report says emphatically, 'budgetary policy should on no account be under the control of Central Bankers'. Experience suggests that they would use such control with a single-minded determination to restrain inflation, too little care for full employment and growth, and no care at all for welfare or for individual, class or regional inequalities.

Budget policy for growth and employment

With open frontiers between them, and monetary policy out of their hands, the national governments' budgets can't have the full effects they used to have on their countries' rates of development and employment. Some macroeconomic causes and effects are now Europe-wide. Some means of macroeconomic influence no longer exist at all. To rebuild a capacity to influence total demand and the amount and location of investment, and to see that each nation contributes its fair share of total revenue, there needs to be coordination between the Community budget, the national budgets, and the Central Bank's monetary policy.

Some coordination can be achieved by arriving at rules for the national budgets: for example at agreed patterns of taxation, ratios of public debt to national income, levels of public investment, and so on. The nations' resources and incomes vary so widely that there must usually be provisions for suspending or varying the rules in particular cases. And the rules should certainly not require that budgets always balance. There should be a presumption that total

Community revenue should balance current spending over time. But national budgets will need to vary around that norm, or depart from it, for at least five reasons: to smooth the cycle of boom and slump; to cope with heavy burdens of inherited debt; to finance investment; to bias investment in favor of less developed regions; and to make the equalization grants from richer to poorer regions that are made in all existing federations.

Wherever coordination can't be achieved by rules because it has to adapt to changing conditions, it must be achieved by some combination of central government power and negotiation between national representatives at the Council of Ministers and other Community institutions. The social-democratic strategists want some transfer of power from the national governments to the European Parliament, Council, and Council of Ministers. But with a few exceptions (noted presently) they don't specify their constitutional proposals in detail. Instead they focus on the spirit and purposes which they believe should shape the policy-making. In all the policy-makers' deliberations, development and employment and welfare and equity should have equal weight with financial stability. (Hence the ban on any bankers' control of budget policy.)

Budget policies to reduce inequalities

In their 1990 report, Leithauser and his colleagues predicted that trade and monetary union without a corresponding development of central government 'is likely on balance to widen disparities in income, growth and unemployment across the Community, so exacerbating regional problems'.

The single market and currency would increase the wealth and power of the richer countries. That must be countered by transferring capital and income to the poorer countries, and developing their productive capacities. To do that, stronger central government – i.e. Community government – is needed. Without it, the poorer countries who lose more than they gain from economic union may obstruct further steps toward full unification, or leave the Community altogether.

There must therefore be a stronger central government with a substantial budget which would draw revenue disproportionately from the richer regions and invest and spend it disproportionately in the poorer regions. There must also be a system of cash grants from the richer national governments to the poorer ones. Budget policy would thus 'redistribute income

towards the poorer regions and help to secure more equal access to employment and social services, but at the same time aim to strengthen the productive potential of weaker areas.'

There is nothing revolutionary in these proposals. 'The present [1990] scale of the Community budget, at only just over 1 per cent of GDP, is far too small to perform the function of redistribution and promoting balanced development which the budget serves in existing federations and unitary states. In all such countries, variations in income and economic activity are automatically compensated by the fiscal system – either through the setting of uniform rates of tax and levels of social benefit or through extensive transfers. Poorer regions therefore receive proportionately more from and pay less to the federal budget than richer regions do.

'For the Community to stand any chance of achieving its regional objectives requires an expansion of the Community budget to fund comparable levels of transfer as in existing federations and unitary states. This does not mean that public expenditure in the Community as a whole needs to be any larger than at present, but that there should be a transfer of responsibility for certain functions from national to Community level.

'Responsibility for much of regional structural and environmental policy, areas which are genuinely of common interest and concern, should be transferred from the national to the Community level. There is also a case for centralising parts of the social welfare system, such as the payment of minimum levels of unemployment benefit ...'

Four main ways of reducing regional and individual inequalities are proposed. The first two relate to investment. The third concerns the cost and quality of public services. The fourth redistributes individual income:

- The Community already has the European Investment Bank and a number of development funds. They are to finance public and private investment in the poorer regions. The principle is right, but to have much effect those funds need to be several times bigger than they currently are.

- Competition policy should be modified to allow public aids and incentives to private investment in the poorer regions: tax concessions, helpful infrastructure and services, technical and professional help, special credit. Most of such aids should be financed by the Community rather than the national governments. The poorer countries should not have to compete for private investment by foregoing revenue, or by shifting taxation off business onto their poorer citizens, or by starving their social services to finance special services to business. If the Community is the only source of regional investment incentives, business won't be able to play off the national governments against each other to the disadvantage of their citizens.

• There should be automatic equalization grants from richer to poorer governments, as in other federations. The grant formula should be designed to move each country's public revenue per head a little nearer to the Community average: enough to reduce inequalities, but not enough to weaken productive incentives or drive the richer countries out of the Community. Governments which make grants decide how to finance them. Governments which receive them decide how to spend them. They don't call for any transfer of functions from nation to Community. All the Community has to do is decide the formula on which the grants are calculated, and transmit them from the givers to the receivers.

• Some functions *are* transferred to the Community, to be financed from Community taxation or borrowing and delivered by Community institutions, or by national governments acting as agents of the Community.

An example which mixes more than one of those methods is the proposal for a minimum unemployment allowance. An equal allowance for richer and poorer countries would be impractical. A rate that was reasonable for unemployed Germans or Scandinavians would be well above the prevailing wage for low-skilled work in Greece or Portugal. So it is proposed that the Community provide a Europe-wide unemployment allowance at the rate appropriate in its poorest regions. Financed from direct, progressive Community taxation, that draws more revenue per head from richer than from poorer countries. The Community pays the allowance to the national governments for whatever number of unemployed they have. Each government decides the full rate that should apply in its country. It pays that rate, supplementing the basic rate from its own revenue. Rich countries' taxpayers thus pay twice. Their Community taxes contribute to the basic allowance for every nation's unemployed. Their national taxes finance higher rates for their own unemployed.

Will that work? Won't unemployed Greeks ride their roller blades to Germany and claim the German unemployment allowance? Won't *employed* Greeks leave their jobs and do the same, when the German dole for not working is higher than their Greek wage for working? It is to cope with those delicate problems that 'home affairs', which include migration, are among the subjects which are reserved from the Community's economic regime to be dealt with by other means. If Europe introduced a system of basic plus supplementary unemployment pay it would probably link the supplement to the wage the worker earned when last employed. To get German unemployment pay, you must first (say) have earned a German wage for at least a year, or lived in Germany for at least five years.

There are similar problems of equal provision for people in unequally productive economies over a wide range of social policies. How *could* you equalize Greek and German access to education, health and welfare services, parenting and caring allowances, invalid and age pensions? The authors of the Maastricht Treaty deliberately provided for solutions like the one proposed above for unemployment pay. Where the Community is responsible for a service, it dare not discriminate between Greek and German. But it dare not, either, offer German rates of unemployment pay in Greece or Greek rates in Germany. So the Treaty empowers the Community not to take over but to 'contribute to' a range of social, educational, health and welfare services. It can thus help the poorer countries' services without preventing the richer ones from providing themselves with better services.

Most of the proposed social and redistributive policies are condemned by the OECD strategists. They think market forces will reconstruct and stabilize the poorer countries' economies and quicken the economic growth of Europe as a whole, and government intervention will hinder rather than help them. That hopeful market faith was attacked forty years ago by (among others) three eminent economists: Gunnar Myrdal in *Economic theory and under-developed regions* (1957), Albert Hirschman in *The strategy of economic development* (1958), and Paul Streeten in *Economic integration: Aspects and problems* (1961). Myrdal explored ways in which unaided market forces can go into reverse and intensify regional backwardness and unemployment, rather than correcting them. Streeten predicted the economic problems of an under-governed European union, and linked them to the theoretical mistakes which prevented the founders

Economic strategy

of the union from foreseeing them, and prevent today's OECD economists from understanding them. Hirschman noticed how public as well as market institutions can act as automatic stabilizers. Stable public health, educational and other services limit the effects of the business cycle on total employment. Unemployment pay helps to stabilize both the level and the local distribution of consumer demand. Once established, those services respond automatically to changing economic conditions without further political action, and they contribute to economic stability and growth as well as to social justice. The more automatic the public responses to unemployment are, the more they may also contribute to political peace and stability. Tax and welfare methods are best: recession automatically increases the transfer of income from richer to poorer regions and individuals, without any need for further political argument. That's surer than equalization grants from government to government are if the governments can wrangle about them every year. So grants also work best if they are assessed automatically by an established formula. Of course there can still be political efforts to change the formula or the rate of unemployment pay; but as stabilizers they can work automatically if left alone.

Thus the social democrats have theoretical and practical grounds for believing their strategy could do more for both efficiency and equity than unaided market forces are likely to do. We will return to the subject presently when comparing the OECD strategy with this social-democratic one.

International aid

The Community should direct most of its international aid to its immediate neighbors. Geography and history combine to make North Africa and the Middle East Europe's natural trading partners. In the short run those neighbors need generous financial and technological aids to development. In the long run their economic growth will benefit Europe as well as themselves. Similarly with the ex-communist countries of Eastern Europe. They are a natural market for Europe, but they need financial aid to reduce their foreign debts and enable them to pay for the productive technology that their recovery and development require.

But aid to Africa, the Middle East and Eastern Europe must be additional to continuing aid to Portugal, Greece and other Community members. Altogether the proposals for more international aid and bigger equalization grants and welfare contributions to the Community's poorer regions are inconsis-

tent with these strategists' desire to redistribute taxation without increasing it. Their strategy would certainly require some higher taxation of the richer member countries.

International influence

Europe will soon have the world's biggest unified economy, with the strength to deal as an equal, or as a leader, with the US and Japan. The huge new American debt to Japan weakens both those economies, and attracts a lot of their diplomatic and policy-making energy. It is also evidence of the folly of the financial deregulation that allowed it to occur. A social-democratic Europe which is the biggest trader and the most balanced trader of the big three, and which has traditions of strong public economic management, should be able to lead the world in rebuilding effective cooperative systems of international trade, credit and exchange: systems capable of stabilizing instead of destabilizing rates of exchange, and correcting national surpluses and deficits 'rather than reinforcing them as so often in the recent past'. In negotiating new rules of the game, a social-democratic Europe may also develop ways to 'manage the activities of transnational companies so that they are compatible with wider economic, social and environmental objectives'.

SUMMARY

This strategy calls for some strengthening of the Community's central governing and policy-making institutions. Most of the necessary changes would be permissible under the terms of the Treaty of Maastricht if they could attract the necessary national votes. Something which it would be reasonable to call a federal government could then:

- exert strong influence on the amount and progressive pattern of both Community and national taxation
- set limits to national budget deficits (with separate accounting of public investment) and adjust the limits year by year to any cyclical fluctuations of unemployment and inflation
- coordinate monetary, tax, public investment and regional policies to influence levels of demand and investment in ways designed to smooth the business cycle, maintain near-full employment, restrain inflation, conserve the environment, and accelerate sustainable development of the Community's poorer regions and national neighbors.

Until the differences between the productivity of the richest and poorest countries are reduced, it is impractical to equalize welfare services and pension rates throughout Europe. Instead, the Community should finance uniform minimum standards everywhere, and leave national governments to supplement them from national revenue as appropriate. But for economic as well as social reasons it should be possible to raise the poorer countries' health and educational standards rather faster than their pension rates and other services.

International aid can concentrate on developing Europe's traditional trading partners, for mutual benefit. And with the political and economic strength it derives from its new unity, Europe should take the lead in rebuilding stable international systems of trade and exchange, designed to serve productive and environmental purposes rather than gambling and unequalizing purposes.

Altogether, this is not a very ambitious social-democratic strategy. It accepts the vision of European unity, and the weak central government which seems to be a condition of achieving that unity. But it could serve its social democratic purposes more effectively in at least two ways which would not necessarily break the Community's constitutional rules.

First, it could make much bolder use of public employment. Public enterprises are not allowed to compete unfairly in private markets, but there are no other rules against them Three good purposes could be served if the Community encouraged its member governments to be more active employers. Some environmental work – reafforestation, long-term large-scale experiments in soil reclamation, various kinds of waste management and reprocessing, specialized environmental information services – may be done best by public agencies. The social and equalizing purposes of the strategy can benefit from expanded health, educational, housing and welfare services. And expanding those services reduces unemployment, some of which was created by cutting public employment in the first place. The Community's rules don't prevent its member nations from taxing themselves to finance improvements to their environmental, social and intellectual services, and they don't prevent the Community from helping to finance those services in its poorer regions.

A second possibility is of a bolder monetary policy. The 1990 strategy paper wants the Central Bank to care about employment and social equity as well as inflation. But it does not question the manipulation of interest rates as the Bank's main means of action. Nothing in the Community's formal rules would actually prevent the Bank from developing a coherent strategy of (i) boundary controls on capital movements into and out of the Community, allowing (ii) regulated, and generally low, interest rates, protected from inflation by (iii) quantitative controls on bank credit. If competently managed, such a regime could allow better reconciliation of growth, full employment, stable money and less inequality than are possible when public influence is on interest rates alone.

Third, the Treaty of Maastricht limited the percentage of national income that national governments may pass through public hands, by forbidding any government to increase its present percentage. If this threatens the major systems of income transfer between people's earning and their non-earning years within each country, whether by cutting them as the OECD recommends or by privatizing them, it is to be hoped that the treaty provision can be re-negotiated before it forces changes for the worse to a system which has the quadruple virtues of security, equity, economic and administrative efficiency, and strong democratic support.

But even without those improvements (which might well be politically difficult) the strategy is still a coherent one. Its economic elements are compatible, and capable of serving its social democratic purposes. If the strategy can't work, it is likely to be for political rather than economic reasons. There would be strong opposition to introducing it. There would be the usual possibility of insufficiently competent management of it. And there are the special dangers of weak and divided policy-making that are built into the Community's constitution.

Any European strategy faces some of those hazards. This chapter now concludes by comparing (1) the different uses which the OECD and the social democratic strategists want to make of the powers available under the Treaty of Maastricht, and (2) their different chances of attracting the political support their strategies would need.

Table 56.1 **ACTIVITIES OF THE COMMUNITY**

The Community MAY		The Community MUST
	The elimination of customs duties and restrictions on trade between the member states	A
	a common commercial policy	B
	an internal market characterised by the abolition of obstacles to the free movement of goods, persons, services and capital	C
	measures concerning the entry and movement of persons in the internal market	D
E	a common policy in the sphere of agriculture and fisheries	E
F	a common policy in the sphere of transport	F
	a system ensuring that competition in the internal market is not distorted	G
H	the approximation of national laws required by the functioning of the common market	H
I	a policy in the social sphere comprising a European Social Fund	
J	the strengthening of economic and social cohesion	
K	a policy in the sphere of the environment	
L	the strengthening of the conpetitiveness of Community industry	L
M	the promotion of research and technological development	M
N	encouragement for trans-European networks	N
O	a contribution to the attainment of a high level of health protection	
P	a contribution to education and training and 'flowering of the cultures of the Member States'	
Q	a policy in the sphere of development co-operation	
R	the association of overseas countries and territories	
S	a contribution to the strengthening of consumer protection	
T	measures in the spheres of energy, civil protection and tourism	

THE STRATEGIES COMPARED

Power

Article G3 of the Maastricht Treaty lists in broad terms the activities in which the Community's central institutions may or must take part.

Where the Community *may* act, its actions and policies are subject to unanimous or majority voting by the national representatives in the European Council or Council of Ministers.

The functions which the Community *must* perform are specified by the treaty, and so are the policies to be followed in those areas of action. They are mostly negative. The Community must prevent the national governments from acting to restrain trade or competition. Notice two qualities of that policing role. It is cheap, not requiring much taxation. And it is the traditional policy for winners. It guarantees access to the world's biggest single goods, investment and money market to the lenders, investors, producers and traders of the surplus-trading countries. It strips the less successful performers of the usual means of balancing their trade and exchange, limiting their foreign debt, and contriving full employment. (Of course the winners, and the OECD theorists, predict that free-trading exposure will allow market forces to do more for the losers' trade and balance of payments and employment than government action could succeed in doing.)

The activities which the Community *may* develop tend to have opposite qualities to the activities which they *must* develop. The optional activities can't be developed without unanimous or weighted majority support. Their purpose is to transfer resources from richer to poorer countries, so in budget terms they look expensive. And they are policies for losers, designed to reform Community taxation in the poorer countries' favor, speed up their development, and give them better education, health and welfare services than they could yet afford from their own resources alone.

See for yourself. The activities listed in Table 56.1 are ordered and 'lettered' as in the Treaty, but I have duplicated some of the letters. The compulsory Community functions and policies, on which the OECD strategies chiefly rely, are lettered – appropriately – on the Right. The discretionary and redistributive activities (which the Social Democratic strategists want to develop) are lettered on the Left. Compulsory activities which the Social Democrats also welcome are lettered (here though not in the Treaty) on both sides.

Politics

Summaries have to simplify. This one is going to simplify people as – economically – winners, middle ranks, and losers. 'Winners' and 'losers' have both national and individual meanings. Europe has national winners and losers: rich Germany, France, Belgium, poor Greece, Portugal, Ireland. And each country has its winners and losers: winning minorities of business owners and managers, successful artists and professionals, and so on, and losing minorities of insecure low-paid workers, unemployed people including many in middle age and the middle class, widowed and deserted lone parents, age pensioners without any income or property of their own. All the countries also have majorities on middle incomes, variously happy or unhappy with their work and earnings. When people of all those classes vote, they have in mind varying proportions of national interest, class or individual interest, technical understanding or misunderstanding of how their societies work, and disinterested social and moral concerns. It is obviously misleading to simplify their politics by grouping them crudely as winners, losers and middle classes, but for brevity that is what most of this short summary is going to do.

Small countries, which include the poorest countries in the Community, have one political advantage. National votes in the Community's institutions are weighted. Germany, France, Italy and Britain have 10 votes each; Spain 8; Belgium, Greece, the Netherlands and Portugal 5; Austria and Sweden 4; Denmark and Ireland 3; Luxembourg 2. The votes are related to population, but not proportionally: Luxembourg has much less than 20 per cent, Ireland and Denmark less than 30 per cent, of Germany's or France's or Britain's population. Some decisions have to be unanimous. Most of them require a majority of just over 70 per cent. So any three of the biggest countries, or any two with one or two smaller allies, can block legislation. But the six biggest together, with about three quarters of the Community's population, cannot force legislation through if the smaller countries unite against them.

Winners in the individual or class sense – successful people in all the member countries – may benefit from another feature of the Community's institutions. Effective power is with appointed rather than elected people. Some are Commission bureaucrats. Others are politicians who have been elected to their national parliaments, but they are appointed to the Council of Ministers or other Community authorities by their national governments. They owe their Community power and prospects to those national governments, rather than to the European electors whose fortunes their policies affect. Though there have been historical exceptions, elites tend to do more for their own individual and class interests and less for other people's if they don't answer democratically to the people they govern. If this European elite is to adopt an egalitarian social democratic strategy, it may have to be more from personal social commitment than from democratic compulsion. And if they are *not* committed to improving equalities, they can simply do what the Treaty commands them to do, i.e. free the single market and keep it free, while making as little use as possible of the optional social and redistributive and developmental powers which the Treaty offers them. Together those policies will tend to serve the immediate material interests of both kinds of winners: the most productive national economies, and many of the richer people in all the member countries including the poorer ones.

With those options, notice what the Community has actually done through recent years. It has established the single market, the first (optional) stage of the single currency, and the Central Bank. It has not tried to encourage or coordinate the macroeconomic budget policies the social democrats would like. And it has developed some but not others of its social and redistributive and developmental options. It has negotiated a Social Charter of citizens' rights, given legal form to some of them, and required member nations to comply with them. And it has created the European Investment Bank and a number of social and developmental funds whose main purpose is to transfer resources to the poorer countries. Some of the funds have more than doubled during the 1990s, but as noted earlier they are still too small to have much effect.

Politically, the European Council and the Council of Ministers are unlikely to act quite as cruelly as the OECD paper recommends. What was quoted earlier was that paper's summary. Its full text urges governments to dismantle a lot of the twentieth century's welfare arrangements, including almost all labor rights and protections, and any possibility of living tolerably on unemployment pay. Those are economists' proposals. The Community's politicians have more compassion and political sense. They may well continue on their present track and –

- perfect the single market and monetary unity;
- ask the national governments to balance their budgets, look after their own social problems and inequalities, and leave macroeconomic policy to

market forces and the Central Bank;

- help to finance activities E and N on the Maastricht list, i.e. the development of European transport and communication networks; and
- continue the Community's redistributive institutions but continue to give them comparatively little money.

That is still a winners' strategy. It promises low inflation achieved chiefly by high interest and unemployment; declining union strength, good labor discipline and rising inequalities of salary and wage income; high rates of 'rentier' income; and high rates of profit in much big business, though the high interest hurts small business. The strategy's politics look solid if the winners are hard-hearted and stick together. The richer countries which would be net losers of any transferred resources have between them more than twice the number of votes needed to block any redistribution they don't want. Moreover they can help their own poor directly from their national taxes more cheaply than by financing Community funds which go also to the poorer countries' poor. For that reason some poor as well as rich and middle voters in the rich countries may vote against any more expensive social democratic strategy.

Remember the contemporary conditions which help to attract support for a winners' strategy. There is the historical shift of numbers from blue-collared majorities to white-collared majorities, with fewer dissatisfied and more satisfied voters. Where the third quarter of the century saw welfare services developed by political alliances of middle and poor against rich, the fourth quarter has seen more alliances of middle and rich against poor – or at least against giving the poor any more than they already get.

It is harder to elicit compassion for foreigners than for compatriots. Western countries which cheerfully spend 10 per cent or more of national income on their own welfare services and incomes don't give as much as 1 per cent to the world's real poor. If rich British won't give 1 per cent to starving Bangladeshis, are they likely to give 4 or 5 percent to quite well-fed Greeks and Portuguese? Among Western losers there has been some replacement of class resentment by national or racial resentment, and even resentment of their own unemployed. Social-democratic parties are in trouble if many of their traditional working-class supporters come to distrust them for being soft on foreigners or blacks or 'welfare parasites'.

Finally there are the economic theories which prevail in the OECD offices, the World Bank until 1997, the

International Monetary Fund, most Central Banks, most national Treasuries, much academic teaching of economics and most of the financial press. Despite detailed disagreements those authorities broadly agree in telling the world that the winners' strategy is right: its theory is true, it will work as predicted, and however harsh some of its effects they are probably the best achievable, including for the poorest countries and the poorest people. What social democrats want governments to do instead would (the winning theorists say) distort the economy, reduce its efficiency, cause higher inflation, and leave most people poorer than they are now.

In such conditions what hope is there that the European Community will adopt a social-democratic strategy and make it work? What would it take?

There would have to be some change in prevailing economic beliefs. That might be prompted by the poor performance of the present strategy. It is breaking many of its theoretical promises to winners as well as losers. Growth is comparatively slow. Unemployment is permanently high. For the first time in more than a century inequalities are increasing. There are ill effects of high interest and fluctuating exchange rates. There is too much unproductive gambling on capital markets. Some of the mounting international debt that is crippling some countries outside the Community is threatening to trouble some of its member countries.

The Community must also fear the effects of disappointing the hopes of its newer and poorer members. They may leave the Community, or dump their old and unemployed across their open borders, or trigger ethnic and nationalist conflicts. So the dominant countries may be moved to increase their aid as the price of keeping their big market together.

More far-sighted winners may look to the long-term benefits for winners if ever Europe is developed and rich all over, with buoyant demand as its economy provides good incomes and services to all its people. And the potential benefits of developing the poorer national economies are moral as well as material. Both those qualities may attract support from some winners. An important element in the original development of welfare states was the presence of committed reformers within the middle and upper classes. They have never entirely disappeared. There are signs that their commitment and their numbers are reviving, in the current spate of reproachful writing about excessively selfish individualism, the financial scandals of the 1980s, the increase of unemployment and inequality, the homeless people sleeping on the streets. There is a new communitarian branch of social philosophy. And there are professional reappraisals of the long mid-century boom. Under strong national government and cooperative regulation of international trade and exchange there were two or three decades of fast growth, full employment, low inflation and increasing equality – 'the golden age of capitalism'.

The ideas and many of the institutions which shaped that boom are still alive in Europe, though out of fashion and out of power. There are long traditions of confident economic government, serious political philosophy, and social-democratic theory and practice. The middle-class parties of the liberal and Christian Right have been more concerned with generous welfare, industrial cooperation and social cohesion than their English-speaking equivalents have lately become. The social democratic parties, many with good relations with the green and feminist forces, are also electable and fit to govern. If they return to power in the big member countries and in the institutions of the European Community, they might imaginably succeed in strengthening the Community's governing powers and shifting its policies in green, feminist, egalitarian, post-Keynesian directions.

But the national hindrances, the class hindrances, the institutional hindrances and the intellectual hindrances to progress in that direction look formidable – and any one of the four is capable of blocking the progress.

The worst hindrances may be the strength of national feelings, and the 'entrenched weakness' of the Community's central powers. The next two chapters consider social-democratic strategies which may be workable in countries whose national feelings *support* confident central government of their economies, rather than opposing it or dividing its powers.

57

Free-trading independence

Can social democratic strategies survive in a global economy?

The United States economy is increasingly open to the global economy and the requirements of the North American Free Trade Area (NAFTA). Public influence over the European countries' economies is divided between their national governments and the authorities of the European Union. In neither case can economic policy be as coherent as it could be a generation ago. With those examples we now contrast two independent countries which ran distinctive social-democratic strategies through much of the twentieth century, and could perhaps do so again, but would now have to cope with a more difficult world economy.

Sweden and Australia are resource-rich countries with small populations. What they tried to do through much of the twentieth century could be summarized like this:

Sweden For half a century from 1932 Social Democratic governments did their best to –

- leave productive industry in private Swedish ownership and support it with good public infrastructure and with helpful financial, trade, labor and housing policies, including –

- free trade

- strict public control of the financial system of public and private banks

- central wage-bargaining between peak organizations of employers and labor

- Keynesian policies plus labor training and placement programs for the full employment of a skilful, adaptable, mobile workforce

- an inclusive rather than residual welfare system, with public services and income-related transfer income for *all* unemployed, retired, infirm and other dependent people, not just the poor.

In a sentence: competitive free-trading capitalism, with well-paid cooperative labor, and generous welfare for all.

Australia was a resource-rich country exporting mainly farm products and minerals when early in the twentieth century a liberal/labor coalition introduced 'new protection'. 'New' meant that besides attracting

manufacturing investment, tariffs should also enable government to enforce fair wages and working conditions. Reinforced later by Keynesian and welfare policies, the strategy had these main components:

- Protected manufacturers produced a wide range of goods almost entirely for the Australian market.

- A comparatively 'high and flat' wage structure was determined by judges of national and state arbitration courts.

- A strictly controlled financial system of public and private banks ran at very low rates of real interest.

- Keynesian full employment and egalitarian wage and housing policies were the main sources of welfare and solidarity.

- Public schools, hospitals and medical insurance eventually provided nearly-free service for all who wanted it. Private schools and hospitals continued to cater for some well-off minorities. Age pensions, unemployment allowances and most other public transfer incomes were means-tested and paid at low, flat rates. The income support system could thus be called 'residual'.

In a sentence: a protected, diversely skilled and comparatively self-sufficient economy, with welfare and equalities depending more on full employment and well-equipped, resourceful households than on public income transfers.

Questions Important components of both the Swedish and the Australian strategies broke down through the last quarter of the century. To what degree did their troubles arise from –

- changes in the world economy?

- intrinsic faults in the strategies themselves?

- avoidable policy mistakes?

- successful counter-attack by business and political opponents of the strategies?

Some of all four causes were at work. These two chapters focus on the strategies themselves as alternative means to fairly similar ends, and on the internal and external difficulties they encountered. The purpose is not to have you commit a lot of Swedish or Australian history to memory. It is to extend – as far as book-learning can – your understanding of strategic problems and possibilities, and how widely they can vary with circumstances: with social, political and intellectual as well as economic circumstances. These small countries have been adventurous innovators. For half a century or so they made equity and efficiency (as this text encourages you to understand those qualities) not just compatible but actively helpful to each other – action to make them more equal also made them richer. Whether the progress could have continued with better leadership, policy-making or public education is a much disputed question. But the strategies were promising enough, and questions about their survival are important enough, to hold your attention through a couple of chapters: the Swedish strategy in this chapter, the Australian strategy in the next.

SWEDEN'S RESOURCES

Eight million Swedes occupy a country rich in forest timber, iron ore, lead, zinc, copper, uranium and hydro-electrical waterfalls. For a century from about 1870 they industrialized fast enough to have, by 1950, one of the world's richest economies. Ship-building, engineering, tool-making, vehicle-building, electrical, petrochemical and plastics industries were developed by firms which are now leading multinationals. Their original owners were few and rich. The upper class was small. Most Swedes shared cultural and religious and peasant farming traditions. For such a population, they were well educated. They had unusually strong local and national solidarity.

Until 1932 liberal/conservative governments supplied traditional small government and some early welfare provisions while private enterprises developed most of the new industries. In the depth of the world depression in 1932 the Social Democratic Party won office and governed Sweden for most of the next sixty years. The social and economic regime that developed through those years owed a good deal to private industrial efficiency, to welfare initiatives of earlier liberal governments, and to Swedish culture and social solidarity. But to see what it owed to deliberate economic strategy we will focus on the thinking and interaction of three institutions: the Social Democratic Party, the national organization of blue-collar labor unions, and the national organization of employers.

The social democratic party

The party was founded in 1889. It battled for fully democratic government and full trade union rights until

both were achieved. Then in the 1920s it took strategic decisions which set it some way apart from other European socialist parties and British and Australian labor parties.

Sweden was still a mostly rural society. Four fifths of its people lived in the country or country towns. Many of the new industries developed outside the cities. Many of their new workers still had links with their peasant homes and kin. So, first, the Social Democratic Party would try to represent all workers and peasants and low-income self-employed, not just the industrial workers who were the main support of parties of the Left elsewhere.

Second, Sweden's successful, fast-growing industries should stay in private capitalist hands. The party would not nationalize them, as most Western socialist parties still hoped to do. Equality should be improved by full employment and good wages and working conditions and welfare services.

Those purposes shaped the 'People's Home' program with which the party won office in 1932. The program included farm price supports, accident and unemployment insurance funded chiefly by the government and employers, universal health insurance, and the already-existing flat-rate pension for the old and infirm.

Full employment The party developed a cautious Keynesian approach to full employment. Swedish economists were among the first to see how easily full employment can cause inflation. There are both demand-and-supply reasons and bargaining-strength reasons for that. If people have too much to spend so that the demand for *goods* exceeds the economy's capacity to supply them, employers trying to meet the demand have to demand more *labor* than the people can supply. Competing to entice workers from each other, they may bid wages up. Even if they don't do that, fully employed workers who can't be sacked because there are no unemployed to replace them may use their muscle to force wages up to inflationary levels. In contending with employers for a bigger wage share they may also compete with one another if union leaders, pushed hard by their members, try to match or outdo other unions' wage gains. And while those pressures are at work, excessive demand for goods may enable firms to inflate their prices in pursuit of higher profits.

There are alternative approaches to this problem. Public policy or market forces may maintain enough unemployment to weaken the employers' competition for labor, the unions' bargaining strength, and the whole amount of spending money. That's hard on the unemployed, and it has the national economy producing below capacity. Alternatively government may try a voluntary or compulsory incomes policy, to limit wage growth whatever the market or bargaining strengths are. That's hard to do. British unions have usually resisted it. Swedish unions have always opposed it. So the Swedish government developed a third approach:

- Government budgets for some unemployment: fiscal and monetary policies are designed to limit the private sector's demand for labor to a little less than the workforce could supply. That restrains market pressure on wage rates.

- Instead of paying a dole to the unemployed, the public sector employs them in useful public works or training programs, but encourages them to move to any regular employment that offers. (In Marxist language, the 'reserve army of the unemployed' is paid a wage to do useful work rather than a dole to do nothing.)

- As proposed by the employers' federation, wage pressures are further restrained by having wage levels fixed by periodical agreements between the employers' and the unions' national representatives.

Why would business and labor cooperate to the extent of negotiating national wage agreements, and getting their respective members to comply with the agreements?

Labor

The blue-collar unions, which had most of the union membership in the 1950s, bargained through a central organization called (for short) LO. In 1951 it adopted the Rehn-Meidner wage strategy, named after the two economists who devised it. The strategy had three main principles and three main purposes:

Principles

- a high minimum wage
- small wage differentials and a comparatively low maximum wage
- equal pay for equal work regardless of employers' capacity to pay

Purposes

Those wage principles could expect a good deal of support from business, especially big business. That promised good industrial relations as well as serving the plan's direct purposes, which were –

- **greater income equality** for its own sake, for social justice and solidarity
- **productivity and economic growth** Firms and

industries which could not afford the minimum wage would have to improve their efficiency or go out of business. As some of them closed, capital and labor would shift to the more productive industries which could pay the national wage rates. Government training, placement and housing policies would re-train and where necessary re-locate workers moving from less-productive to more-productive jobs. The low wage differentials and relatively low maximum wages would encourage the more productive industries to expand, and allow the most productive firms good profit margins above their wage costs to help finance their expansion. Thus a socialist policy of low wage differentials encouraged capitalist profit and growth.

- **full employment with low inflation** Centrally negotiated national wage levels prevented wage/wage competition with leap-frogging wage claims by individual unions trying to match or outdo one anothers' wage gains. As less-productive firms went out of business they created a pool of available labor to meet the more-productive firms' expanding demand for it – so those efficient firms *need* not bid wages up by competing for scarce labor, and *agreed* not to do so in their national wage agreement with the unions. It should thus be possible to have a fast-growing, fully-employed economy without much cost-push inflation.

Notice three aspects of that strategy.

First, as a means of restraining inflation, a program of economic growth which allows a corresponding growth of wage incomes is easier to sell to government and to wage-earners than an incomes policy which simply calls for wage restraint. Remember that inflation can be avoided equally well by keeping wage growth down to the rate of economic growth (the basis of most incomes policies) or by getting the rate of economic growth up to the going rate of wage growth. The second was the main emphasis of the Rehn-Meidner plan, and although it worked imperfectly in practice it was more popular and effective for longer than most simple incomes policies have been.

But second, the plan had one important element of wage restraint. The principle of equal pay for equal work *regardless of employers' capacity to pay* was two edged. By raising the lowest wages it helped to shift capital and labor from less productive to more productive industries, as described above. But in those more productive industries, especially in their most efficient firms, it restrained the unions from pushing wage rates up to exploit the employers' full capacity to pay. Those firms won extra profit, and financial capital to expand, because the nation's most productive workers did *not* demand a full fair share of their growing productivity. That contrasted with bargaining behavior in most other industrial countries.

Why did the most skilled, most valued Swedish workers – the 'labor aristocrats' – show such self restraint? Partly it was the price of solidarity with the lower-paid ranks, and the bargaining strength that came with labor unity. Partly it was prudent: workers would suffer like anyone else from fast inflation, and as wage leaders the skilled trades' bargaining tended to have disproportionate effects in propelling or restraining inflation. But those self-interests did not restrain the wage leaders in most other countries. The Swedish restraint must have owed something to genuine egalitarian values and feelings of solidarity – working class solidarity and Swedish solidarity – in the skilled workers' hearts.

Third, how can resources shift from less productive industries to more productive industries if consumers don't happen to want to shift their spending accordingly? Three answers: Price changes may induce some shift to buying the better-and-cheaper products of the advancing industries. Second, many of Sweden's advanced industries are also exporters, so they can grow by exporting more. Third, in the tradeable industries free trade allows imports to replace national products wherever the nation's declining industries are producing tradeable goods – the Rehn-Meidner strategy could not work as well in protectionist Australia. But fourth, the strategy is in trouble if consumers demand increasing proportions of *non*-tradeable goods and services from labor-intensive, *less* productive industries. Which the Swedes eventually did, as every industrial society has eventually done.

When the central union body adopted the Rehn-Meidner strategy in 1951 there was still uncertainty about central wage agreements. Some unions were reluctant to hand over their bargaining powers to LO. But in 1952 the *employers* insisted on central bargaining. Like some of the union policies, that contrasted sharply with owners' and managers' policies in other industrial economies. Why was Swedish business, like Swedish labor, running a surprising line of its own?

Business

Big manufacturers had most influence in the Swedish Employers' Confederation. The nature of their innovative engineering and manufacturing work calls for a core of highly skilled, cooperative and loyal workers. As competitors in international markets, wage costs matter to them. So does steady output uninterrupted by industrial conflict. So do a stable national currency and exchange rate, so they have strong reasons for disliking inflation. In the 1950s LO, the national labor representative, controlled the only strike fund so it, rather than the individual unions, could make the most dependable no-strike agreements. A national agreement with LO could also restrain – not perfectly but better than any other arrangement could – leap-frogging demands from unions competing with each others' wage gains. Even the traditional concern for equality was acceptable to the big firms which employed disproportionate numbers of the most skilled workers, and would lose most if those 'labor aristocrats' bargained hard and independently. The Rehn-Meidner plan promised those firms an expanding supply of labor (from the decline of less productive industries, and the government's active labor policies), with the unions restraining the wage demands of their highest-valued workers.

For those reasons, and probably also a dash of Swedish solidarity, the employers opted for wage-fixing by central national agreement with LO. In 1952, a year after the unions adopted the Rehn-Meidner plan, the employers refused to negotiate on any other basis, and thus strengthened LO's hand against the few member unions who wanted to keep their bargaining freedoms. For the next thirty years periodical central agreements set national wage levels for one, two or three years ahead. The detailed distribution of those resources was then negotiated within each industry, then within firms. Though it was not originally intended, there were usually some further wage gains in those detailed negotiations. They came to be known as wage drift, and to average about half of all wage gains – the drift tended to double the gains agreed at the centre. The central negotiators learned to expect that, and allow for it as far as rank-and-file labor pressures allowed.

THE SWEDISH STRATEGY, MARK ONE

In summary, see how the parts of that 1950's national strategy are designed to fit together and nourish one another:

Sweden's efficient, competitive private manufacturing sector continues its technical progress and growth.

The private sector is served by good public infra-structure and services, including very good educational and training services.

The government's employment policies, the unions' wage policies and the employers' insistence on central wage bargaining together shift resources into the most dynamic industries a bit faster than unaided market forces might shift them, and help to restrain those indus-tries' labor costs.

That increases the proportion of the economy that is highly productive. The continuing technological progress and the structural shift into the progressive industries together keep average productivity growing in the economy as a whole.

That allows a steady increase of wage income, and the union negotiators see that the workers get it.

The growth of income allows government to expand the welfare system without much increase of tax rates. Through the long postwar boom Swedes pay about the same proportion of national income in taxes as the other rich countries.

With those continuing rewards for their solidarity, workers support their union structures and leadership, and accept moderate wage restraint if their leaders recommend it.

Together the efficient production, the fair wage share and the comparatively equal distribution of it, the productive distribution of the profit share, and the well-developed and inclusive welfare arrangements attract enough electoral support to keep the Social Democrats in government, and the strategy in place.

By and large, the strategy worked. Swedish wage incomes were the least unequal in the non-communist world. There was full employment. Industrial relations were unusually cooperative, which helped the high productivity which in turn rewarded the cooperators. Capitalist efficiency, social-democratic strategy and traditional solidarity thus nourished each other in a variety of ways. For a time, the more equal Swedes averaged almost as rich as the less equal Americans.

But parts of the strategy worked imperfectly, and parts of it soon needed to adapt to some effects of its own success.

Changing conditions

Economic growth had the self-slowing effect that it has had in all countries that have passed through the equivalent phase of growth. Rising income and discre-tionary spending increased the demand for services. Those tend to be non-tradeable, labor-intensive, with comparatively low productivity The Swedish strategy

aimed to move workers from less productive to more productive industries. But technical progress allowed a good deal of jobless growth in the most productive industries, and the movement of workers from farms and declining industries was increasingly to labor-inten-sive services rather than to capital-intensive manufacturing. Rising income also brought some reduc-tion of working hours. (Remember the difference between carrots and work. Raising the price of labor doesn't increase the supply, it more often reduces it.) Together those changes slowed the rate of growth in the economy as a whole. Many of the new services were tax-financed public services, so there was also some increase of tax. The after-tax wage that workers took home could continue to grow, but more slowly than before.

Stresses   Two effects of these changes made restraint harder for wage leaders to bear. First, as just described, the rate of economic growth began to lag behind the accustomed rate of wage growth which two generations of industrial workers had come to expect. To continue that former rate of wage growth would be inflationary. But the highest paid, most skilled workers – the wage leaders – were already accepting a slower rate of wage growth than anyone else, to reduce wage inequality and allow high profits to the most efficient firms. To ask them for a *further* margin of self-denial, despite their own high productivity and great market strength, was asking a lot of them.

Second, there was a beginning of significant wage rivalry. The white-collar workers of the growing public and private services were unionized, but their unions were not affiliated with the blue-collar LO. The public servants had their own negotiating body. Their govern-ment employer was not represented by the private sector Employers' Confederation. There were now two or three central wage negotiations instead of one.

The highest-skilled blue-collar workers – the labor aristocrats – were accustomed to being wage leaders, and to exercising self-restraint. Now rising numbers of public servants were demanding traditional white-collar margins above the blue-collar rates. They were showing less restraint, or concern for wage equality. They bargained with a government employer whose capacity to pay was not market-disciplined. As their numbers grew their employer was also interested in attracting their votes. So it was easy for the blue-collar wage leaders to suspect that the white-collar unions bargained with unfair advantages. Wage gains in either sector began to prompt matching or leap-frogging demands in the other sector; and the commitment to solidarity meant that as the wage-leaders' rates rose, lower wages rose proportionally a little more, to continue reducing wage inequalities.

Thus three elements of the strategy needed repair. Rising wage costs were hurting some of the export industries. Excessive wage increases were increasing the rate of inflation. And the new white-collar numbers were in uneasy relations with the blue-collar unions, the principle of solidarity, and the egalitarian Social Democratic Party and government.

THE STRATEGY, MARK TWO

Through the 1960s three policy initiatives were designed to adapt the Rehn-Meidner strategy to those troublesome developments. They were –

- a new formula to limit wage rises
- occasional devaluation of the Swedish currency, and
- earnings-related supplements to age pensions, unemployment allowances and some other welfare incomes.

In that order –

A wage limit The chief economists of the white– and blue-collar unions and the employers' confederation devised a formula which the three organizations agreed should limit future wage gains. The economists' initials —EFO – gave the formula its name. To keep Swedish exports competitive, wage growth in the export industries should be limited to the rate of international price inflation plus the rate of growth of productivity in Sweden's tradeable industries. Wages in the non-tradeable sector should then be limited to the same rate of growth.

Notice that the principle is still inflationary. It allows all wages to keep up with the growth of productivity in the industries whose productivity tends to grow fastest. That allows wages to rise faster than productivity in other occupations, including labor-intensive services in the non-tradeable sector where the nature of the work does not allow much increase of productivity. Nationally, that allows some inflation as average wages (and therefore prices) rise faster than average productivity. But (1) respect for wage solidarity and equal pay for equal work was a condition of union agreement to the formula, and (2) market wage-fixing has similar effects, because however low their productivity, necessary labor-intensive industries and services have to pay enough to attract the workers they need. Their rates of pay must compete with those of the most productive employers. (Remember why judges' pay keeps ahead of steelworkers' pay, despite revolutions in steelmaking productivity.) The Swedish wage negotiators were merely doing more equitably what market forces and unequal market strength do, often less equitably, in the United States.

The EFO formula did help Sweden's export industries and balance of payments; and it restrained some but by no means all the sources of wage-push inflation.

Devaluation The central wage agreements usually observed the EFO limit. But that limit allowed some inflation; and some inflationary wage drift continued as before in the detailed negotiations in industries and firms. Government responded with occasional devaluations of Sweden's currency, designed to keep Swedish exporters' prices in line with their competitors'. They were effective for that purpose: each devaluation restored or increased the demand for exports.

But devaluations can also do two kinds of harm. As foreigners come to expect them, they demand higher interest for loans to the offending country. The Swedish government minimized that damage by restricting public and private borrowing from foreigners. But it could not prevent its devaluations raising import prices. That was strongly inflationary in a free-trading country which imported up to 30 per cent of its consumption goods and capital goods, as Sweden did.

Thus some wage-push inflation continued, and devaluations to offset its effect on exports added to the inflationary pressures.

Classless welfare? A Liberal government had introduced a low, partly contributory old age pension in 1913. The 'People's Home' program with which the Social Democrats won office in 1932 replaced it with a low tax-financed pension, means-tested but called 'universal' because it did not depend on insurance contributions and was available to all Swedes who needed it.

By the 1950's some of the higher-paid blue-collar workers and many of the new white-collar workers no longer depended on the public pension. They were contributing to private superannuation, or negotiating it with their employers, or entitled to public service pensions. Politically, they might soon think of cutting taxes rather than increasing the public pension in step with economic growth. The government must then expect to lose support both among the lower-paid workers and peasants who depend on the public pension, and among the new middle class who did not. So – after years of negotiation with many interested parties – the government introduced a supplementary pension. The amount of the pension varied with the pensioner's previous earnings. It was financed by big contributions from government and employers and small contributions from the intended pensioners. All the parties to the Right of the Social Democrats opposed the scheme. On the Left, the LO leaders of the blue-collar unions supported it quite strongly, on condition that the pension funds should be under partly-public management. Step by step, more public allowances – for unemployment, sick leave and other purposes – were similarly related to individuals' earnings.

As welfare incomes were extended to all classes, so were welfare services. Everyone already used the public health and educational services. Through the 1970s more services were developed, including public child care and other services to households which enabled the highest proportion of women in Europe to go out to paid employment.

In these developments critics from the Right could see public extravagance, excessive taxation, and demoralizing hand-outs to well-off people who didn't need them and working people who might work harder without them. In the new middle-class benefits they could also see proof that Left ideals of equality had proved (as expected) to be impractical. Critics from the Left – more from outside than from inside Sweden – could see a middle-class capture of the social-democratic party and state, and a diversion of public benefits from workers and peasants to the new rulers.

Swedish defenders of the strategy had three things to say against that. First, Sweden is now rich enough and distributes its income equally enough to offer everyone a material standard of living that until lately only middle and upper classes could afford. Many poor people are still excluded from that lifestyle in other Western countries, including the richest. But Sweden now offers it to everyone who wants it, by a coherent strategy of private productivity and inclusive public welfare provisions.

Second, (Swedes were entitled to say) socialist objections to middle-class values and lifestyles were conceived when those lifestyles were for privileged minorities, and the values they nourished were selfish and exclusive. But when *everyone* can have the basic bourgeois outfit of household capital, income, education, health care and civil rights, those cease to be class privileges (just as, for example, the flush toilet ceased to be a class item when all households acquired it). They

are no longer occasions for class envy or class guilt. Even the continuing inequalities of income are like those that have always existed *within* social classes without preventing the members of those classes from sharing their class identity and experience and mutual respect, and marrying and socializing with one another. When every Swede has that membership, it ceases to be a class membership. You can turn back to the last heading in this text (Swedish readers in the 1970s might have said) and erase its question mark.

For a third socialist defence of unequal, income-related benefits, recall an earlier account of communist Hungary's public housing policies. The regime had introduced a comparatively flat wage structure, with quite small margins of pay for skill and responsibility. The country was poor, much of its housing was primitive, and most house-building was still private. Government built about ten per cent of new housing, and built to good standards. To allocate that public housing to the lowest-paid workers (as Western countries were doing) would have turned the lowest-paid into the highest-paid: a modern house, at a subsidized rent a laborer could afford, was a bigger benefit than the difference between a laborer's and a foreman's wage, or between a foreman's and a manager's wage. So although nobody said so at the time, the administrators were right to allocate the new houses to managers and foremen rather than to the poorest workers. To do otherwise would *reverse* the incentives and the social intentions of the wage structure.

A similar principle applied in Sweden when business, labor and government set out to reduce income inequalities – but not too far for public tolerance or efficient work incentives. The strategists decided what pattern of income inequality to aim at. And they decided that the means of achieving it should be (1) the Rehn-Meidner-EFO wage strategy, (2) progressive taxation, and (3) public education, health and welfare services for all. Any other public policies should comply with the intended pattern of inequality, not flatten it further. To equalize pensions and other income transfers would flatten it further than the strategists intended – further than was fair or efficient, further than some powerful groups would tolerate. (Why should people who earned themselves a higher-than-average material standard of life drop right to the bottom of the income structure on retirement? Why should their incomes fall by fifty or sixty per cent when retiring laborers' incomes fell only ten or twenty per cent?) Alternatively if flatter equalities *were* desired they should be achieved by adjusting wages, taxes and social services, not by other means.

Summary

Through the 1960s into the 1970s the main elements of the amended strategy are as follows.

- Business and labor continue to negotiate national wage levels, linking them now to the competitive situation of Sweden's export industries.
- Taxation is as progressive as the government dares to make it.
- All classes are served by free or subsidized public education, health, child care and welfare services of high quality.
- Retirement pensions and public incomes for the sick, infirm and unemployed pay between 80 and 100 per cent of individual earnings in most cases.

Unemployment is minimized by –

- fiscal policies designed to keep demand just below a full employment level, for anti-inflationary reasons
- public re-training, and when necessary housing and other aids, to workers forced to change jobs
- flexible temporary public employment for workers without regular private or public jobs

Investment, growth and the balance of payments are assisted by –

- free trade in goods
- some regulation of the quantity and uses of bank credit
- public banks and joint public/private banks for some special agricultural, industrial and export purposes
- regulation of –
  - some interest rates
  - the exchange rate
  - the uses of foreign exchange
  - the export and import of capital funds
  - foreign borrowing

Inflation is restrained – imperfectly – by the central wage negotiators and by conservative fiscal policy. Its effect on the demand for exports is offset by occasional devaluations of Sweden's currency.

The strategy worked. It achieved full employment, continuing (though slower) growth, and a further reduction of material inequalities. By 1984 the ratio of the lowest decile to the highest decile of industrial workers' wages was estimated as

    100 : 134 in Sweden
    100 : 210 in Britain
    100 : 490 in the United States

But as before, there were stresses, some from international causes, some from effects of the strategy itself. And for the first time in fifty years business and labor could not agree what to do about them.

Changing conditions

Inflation continued, from wage drift in the detailed rounds of each wage negotiation, and the involuntary inflation that tends to come with the uneven growth of productivity in different industries. There was also some wage/wage competition as the blue- and white-collar unions negotiated centrally but separately, and so did the private and public unions and employers.

Taxation Until the 1960s taxation took much the same proportion of income in Sweden as in Britain and other West European countries. But through the 1970s and 1980s the new elements of the 'Mark 2' strategy – earnings-linked pensions and allowances, child-care and other novel public services, and some expensive subsidies to lengthen the lives of declining industries – took the Swedish tax bill above all others, to 70 per cent or more of national income (depending how it was counted) by the 1980s. That doesn't mean that only 30 per cent of income was left for private spending and investment. A lot of the tax flow was merely transferring income from citizen to citizen (and sometimes back again, for example when earnings-linked allowances went to well-off people who then paid high income tax on them). But as the tax bill grew, it had two ill effects. There was mounting political resistance to the level of tax. And the resistance to high personal tax drove governments to prefer worse taxes to better ones. Tax increases on goods and services inflated prices. Higher rates of payroll tax inflated industrial costs and prices, and discouraged the unions' efforts at wage restraint. The strategy as a whole was losing some of its coherence.

Incentives Supporters as well as opponents of the generous welfare provisions began to regret some of the incentive effects of those provisions. There was a sudden decline in household saving in the 1960s as people came to depend on public superannuation and public provisions for loss of income through illness or unemployment. Absence from work rose to double the OECD average. Some observers sensed that rising affluence and the personal liberation of the 1960s brought some selfish increase of individualism and some retreat from solidarity. The reduction of inequalities continued, but it perhaps owed a bit less to social-democratic values and a bit more to class interest and organized class action than in the old days of the 'People's Home' program. Business and labor developed some tougher, less cooperative attitudes in their collective negotiations with each other, though good relations continued within many firms.

Industrial conflict In boom years there were some high profits in efficient firms which benefited from the most-skilled workers' wage restraint. Union leaders came under increasing pressure to get their members a fairer share of those industries' gains. But how to do it? The principle of solidarity meant that higher wages in the most productive industries would mean higher wages throughout the economy, with a general increase of inflation rather than of real wages. Union leaders were driven to seek benefits for their members by two other means (to be described presently).

Meanwhile employers in some of the most advanced industries were troubled by the upper wage limits imposed by solidarity. Simple mass production ('Fordism') was giving way to more frequent design

changes, more diversely styled and 'individualized' products, shorter production runs, a need for more of the workers to be their own quality-controllers – 'post-Fordism'. The work called for more trust and local responsibility, some higher skills, and more job-specific skills whose development and training employers must provide or pay for. In those conditions employers believed that they needed more freedom to use wages as means of management: for example to pay lower rates to trainees, then rising rates to keep them in the firm when much had been invested in their development. It was also time to open career paths for the best blue-collar workers to progress to white-collar and management jobs – but separate blue and white unions and wage agreements often made that difficult. Thus when the leading employers in the engineering and export industries turned against the rigidities of central wage-fixing, their main purpose was not to cut wages, but to be freer to raise some of them, and adapt them better to particular workers and tasks.

THE STRATEGY, MARK THREE

Under those pressures, unions and employers and government all revised their strategic thinking.

Neither the union leaders nor the government wanted to respond to rising pressure from the rank and file of workers by having the unions bargain harder for what could only be more inflationary wage rates. So they set out to satisfy the workers by other means. Instead of the unions pressing employers for too-high pay, government would deliver some other benefits, by law rather than bargaining. The chief benefits should be (1) better job security and working conditions, (2) a workers' voice in management, and (3) a union share in capitalist ownership. As follows -

Regulation Through the 1970s laws were passed to improve job security and occupational health and safely, and to require union representation at workplaces.

Co-determination New laws required employers to consult with workers about the organization of their work. Firms above a specified size must have worker directors on their boards.

Ownership Advised by economist Meidner, the LO unions proposed that excessive corporate profits should be transferred to 'wage-earner funds'. The funds should be managed by the labor unions and invested in Swedish industry, chiefly in equity shares, i.e. shares of ownership. The scheme was designed to solve a number of problems at once:

- It would increase the rate of national saving and investment.

- Swedish multinationals were exporting employment by locating production abroad where wage costs were lower and regulation less strict than in Sweden. Wage-earner funds would be invested within Sweden.

- Industries which derived excessive profits from their workers' wage restraint were distorting the economic structure by attracting investment away from equally productive industries which had lower rates of profit simply because they were more competitive. Creaming off the super profits would equalize rates of profit of efficient firms in the less competitive and the more competitive industries. That would encourage a more balanced and efficient market allocation of capital resources.

- Over time, the growth of the new funds could help to achieve the 'socialization of investment' which Keynes hoped would allow better macroeconomic management.

- Over time, Sweden's unusually equal distribution of earned income would be matched by collective ownership of a rising proportion of capital wealth. But the managers of the wage-earner funds, as shareholders of the firms in which they invested, need not reduce the independence or efficiency of those firms, any more than private fund managers do. Thus a new model of market socialism might combine socialist ownership and equality with capitalist freedom and efficiency.

Conflicts

Each of the proposed additions to the going strategy would break the historic Saltsjobaden Agreement of 1937 between business and labor.

- The employers and unions had agreed to fix wages and working conditions by direct bargaining rather than by inviting government to intervene. The unions' successful bid for much greater public regulation of industrial relations broke the agreement.
- The unions had agreed to 'let the managers manage'. They broke the agreement when they got the government to legislate for worker-directors, and co-determination of the organization of work, in private firms.
- The forced transfer of profits to wage-earner funds would not only break the Saltsjobaden agreement. It would also reverse the earlier decision of the Social Democratic Party to leave Swedish industry in private ownership.

Many small business owners and managers wanted to fight all three proposals. But big employers dominated the employers' confederation. They valued their good industrial relations, especially the export industries' freedom from strikes. However reluctantly, they accepted and worked with the new regulation of working conditions, the worker-directors, and the co-determination of work, which the government introduced in the 1970s. But they joined with most other employers in resisting the socialization of ownership. They fought it hard enough to put the Social Democratic Party out of office for six years. By the time it returned to office in 1982 the employers had won. Wage-earner funds were never introduced.

Meanwhile some other malfunctions of the strategy needed attention.

Separate wage-bargaining by the blue-collar and white-collar unions, and by the private and public employers, was increasing the rates of wage growth and inflation. The export industries had to be protected by more drastic devaluations. But the bargaining system still did not allow the engineering and export industries to adapt their wage and personnel arrangements to the changing technology and management of their work.

The welfare system was basically popular and politically secure, but it had been over-developed in various ways. Earnings-related allowances for sickness, absence from work and unemployment were generous enough to induce some bad behavior. Earnings-related age pensions were paid at high rates and to a rising proportion of the population as people had fewer children, earned more, and lived longer in retirement. So the tax bill increased.

It increased further as new public services were added, and as health and educational services delivered rising standards of service and developed some bureaucratic inefficiencies. (Swedish health was not much better than British, but the Swedish health services came to cost nearly twice as much per head of population as the British.)

Those troubles bred a further one. As taxation increased, so did tax resistance. Income tax was already high. Increasing taxes on goods and services raised prices and fuelled inflation. For more revenue the politicians were driven to increase payroll tax, which did not hit the voters so directly. That was bad for the coherence of the strategy as a whole. It put an increasing 'tax wedge' between what workers were paid, and what their labor cost their employers. It meant that wage restraint by the industrial unions no longer delivered the intended cost advantages to their industries, it merely left more room for the government to tax the industries without putting them out of business. Firms began to lose more to the tax wedge than they gained from what remained of the unions' wage restraint. And the self-restraint of the blue-collar wage leaders was further strained as white-collar wages moved ahead and white-collar unions bargained with less restraint or concern for wage equality than the blue-collar unions had always shown.

The Social Democratic Party's faith in its strategy was shaken. The Party lost office from 1976 to 1982 and from 1991 to 1994. It was failing to restrain rising inflation. Its economic principles went further out of fashion as prevailing economic beliefs shifted to the Right over much of the Western world.

Under those pressures, business and government began to dismantle some essentials of the 'Swedish model'.

THE END OF THE SWEDISH MODEL?

In 1983 the employers ended central wage-bargaining by refusing to take part in it. The engineering and vehicle-building employers negotiated an agreement with the metal-workers' union. Other industries followed suit. Inflation accelerated. There were more devaluations.

Government did one prudent and a number of imprudent things.

Prudently, it began to scale down the welfare benefits. Earnings-linked pensions and allowances were cut from 90 and 100 per cent of earnings to 70 or 80 per cent. Absentees and unemployed lost income altogether for the first few days away from work. And there were other changes, designed to correct the costs and incentive effects of a too-generous, too expensive system.

Like other tax-cutting governments, Swedish government shortened its horizons. It began to borrow more, and to invest less in maintaining and improving public infrastructure and the capital equipment of the public services. With those and other changes the amount of national income that passed through government's hands was brought back from about 70 to 50 per cent. But too much of the economizing was done by cutting investment in public infrastructure and public services to private industry. Besides doing some damage to work incentives, the welfare system was now sustained at the expense of necessary investment and economic services. Present spending was threatening future productivity.

Also like other governments in the 1980s, the government was persuaded to deregulate Sweden's financial system. Foreign borrowing and capital transactions were freed. Banks were freer in their creation and allocation of credit. The usual consequences followed: higher interest rates; a credit-fuelled boom, especially in property and other asset prices, followed by a slump from 1991; a general increase of debt, including private foreign debt.

By 1991 the continuing inflation called for another devaluation. Government changed hands during the year, but both parties reversed a long-standing principle of Swedish policy by deciding that inflation now mattered more than unemployment. For as long as they could, they refused to devalue the currency. They tried hard to peg it to the European Union's ECU. They defended its exchange value, and attacked inflation at home, by offering high rates of interest.

Swedish investment and export earnings declined. Growth ceased, and income fell about 8 per cent in four years. Unemployment rose from 1.5 percent in 1990 to 8 percent three years later with a further 3 or 4 per cent in emergency employment. As national income fell, so did tax revenue. At the same time government had to meet the welfare and emergency employment costs of the sudden increase of unemployment after half a century without it. Government went deep into debt just as its financial policies raised the interest rate it must pay on its debts.

Suddenly Sweden looks like the rest of Western Europe. The Social Democratic Party no longer has a coherent economic strategy. Sweden may anyway have lost the coherent powers necessary for coherent economic government by voting to join the European Union. Francis Castles, a long-time admirer of the Swedish strategy, concluded sadly in 1994 that 'Sweden will remain a civilized and humane place to live, but the mystique will have gone, and with it the claim that Sweden is the only model for successful reformist politics'.

JUDGMENTS

From economic recovery through the 1930s to the last year of full employment in 1990, the Swedish people were among the world's richest, and they enjoyed the Western world's fullest employment, its most generous welfare incomes and services, its least poverty and nearest approach to material equality. Whether or not those achievements could have continued, they were worth having while they lasted. Whether or not the collapse of the strategy was inevitable, it leaves Sweden no worse off than its neighbors, no worse off than if it had never developed the distinctive Swedish strategy. Sweden has merely rejoined the Western mainstream, to share the troubles of under-governed, under-employed economies with – now – increasing inequalities.

It is worth asking whether the strategy could have continued for longer than it did. But notice that that is different from asking whether it was a viable strategy. It is wrong to conclude, as some conservative critics do, that because it collapsed after sixty years it must never have been a viable strategy. Remember that what you study may be changing as you study it. The technology, organization and productivity of industry changed radically through those sixty years. So did the experience, education, values and capacities of the people. It is not likely that Sweden's economy needed exactly the same government in 1930, 1960 and 1990. Institutions and policies often need to adapt to changing conditions and opportunities. That doesn't only require an openness to new ideas and a willingness to change. It also takes good judgment about *what* to conserve, *what* to change, *what* new policies and institutions to try for, and how to design them to work satisfactorily and at the same time satisfy enough of the business and labor and democratic demands on them to survive.

The Swedish strategists were thoughtful, adaptable, inventive people. They detected and exploited opportunities to advance the social-democratic values they believed in. But they also had to amend the strategy in risky ways to maintain support for it and keep its political sponsors in office. Sometimes the social-democratic values and the political necessities clashed. The white collars wanted too much pay and too much welfare. The blue collars disliked them but wanted to keep up with them. The politicians misjudged what bankers would do if given a freer hand. Corporate directors of the multinationals began to listen to American instead of Swedish economists. The strategists could have done better without those pressures. Swedes may learn from the experience and do things differently another time.

What might they learn from their twentieth-century experience?

Banking has always needed careful regulation. Now that funds can circle the world at the touch of a button, it needs more, not less, regulation. Swedish governments managed their financial system well through most of the twentieth century. Deregulating it in the 1980s was a mistake.

Welfare policy presents dilemmas. A system of residual incomes and services, provided only to people who can't provide for themselves, is comparatively cheap and can be financed from tolerable taxation. But it involves divisive and humiliating means-testing, with risks of some bullies on one side of the welfare counters and some cheats on the other. Well-off majorities who don't benefit from the system may come to dislike and stigmatize those who do, and under-finance their allowances and services.

Inclusive services can be more widely popular and politically secure. They avoid stigmatizing 'welfare' and 'dependence'. But they involve a lot of churning – paying cash to many people then taxing it back to meet the cost of paying it to so many people. However desirable the final distribution of income is, and however much of the tax goes back to the taxpayers as benefits, voters are likely to feel over-taxed. Since there is also wide support for the inclusive benefits, politicians are tempted to do three undesirable things. They turn to less noticeable kinds of tax, some of which (like payroll tax) are economically harmful. They spend capital improvidently, selling public assets to finance current spending. And they are driven to give welfare spending an unreasonable priority over necessary public investment in infrastructure and economic services, as the Swedish government began to do in the 1990s.

Whatever the pattern of residual or inclusive welfare services, it is always possible to provide some of them inefficiently. As noticed earlier, Sweden's public health services cost as much as America's mostly-private services. A little of that reflects the better pay and working conditions of the lower ranks in the Swedish services, but much if it is wasteful. There are more economical and less bureaucratic models of public hospital and medical service in Britain and elsewhere.

If Sweden had not progressed from Mark One flat-rate welfare benefits to Mark Two earnings-related benefits, the Social Democratic Party might not have held office so continuously. But the rest of its strategy could have been financed from more efficient and less unpopular taxation, and might have attracted even more bipartisan support.

Wage restraint It is hard to know whether union members pressed their leaders to bargain too hard, or the leaders bargained too hard in the course of competing for union office. Either way, they did a bit too well. Slightly slower wage growth could have slowed inflation with little or no loss of wage share or the wages' purchasing power. While central bargaining continued, the degree of restraint was nevertheless quite creditable in conditions of continuous full employment.

Free trade Sweden was and is an industrial winner, a natural free trader. But recent developments have brought some increase of risk.

There are some tough new competitors in some of the export markets.

As economic growth increases and diversifies households' discretionary spending, the demand for imports increases. Sweden's manufacturing is so efficient partly because it is so concentrated and specialized; it is not equipped to compete at home with a widening range of manufactured imports. The pressure of expanding imports on the balance of payments was limited as long as foreign borrowing and some of the uses of foreign exchange were regulated. Financial controls served, as in Japan, to restrain spending on imports. Financial deregulation allowed a sudden increase of foreign borrowing and some increase of imports. The debt made it more expensive than before to protect the balance of payments by devaluing the currency. A condition of successful free trade in goods had been careful management of the trade in money. Free trade and free financial relations proved to be incompatible policies, bringing another element of incoherence into the social-democratic strategy as a whole.

COMPARISONS

Australian governments through the same half-century had similar social-democratic aspirations but some different ways of pursing them:

- residual rather than inclusive welfare
- wage-fixing by arbitration rather than collective bargaining
- industrial protection rather than free trade.

Each country did some things better and some things worse than the other. But don't conclude that a selection of the best of each would have been best for both. In their particular circumstances Australia would probably have been poorer with free trade, Sweden would probably have been poorer with protected industries. Sweden's active labor policy might not live well with Australia's housing performance. Sweden's inclusive welfare might have struck earlier and tougher tax resistance in Australia. And so on – the comparisons suggested by this chapter and the next are not meant to show which strategy was best as a whole. They are here to emphasize that different conditions call for different strategies, which may need to change as conditions change. Sweden and Australia might each have done better than they did. But neither would have done better to derive a timeless, all-purpose 'best' strategy from a standard neoclassical textbook. And each may need to think afresh about national strategy in the emerging global economy.

A paper to read

If you can make time for it, buy or get your library to buy this paper: Andrew Martin, *Wage bargaining and Swedish politics: The political implications of the end of central negotiations.* It has been available (for US$4, last heard) from its publisher, the Minda de Gunzburg Centre for European Studies, Harvard University, at 27 Kirkland Street at Cabot Way, Cambridge, Massachusetts 02138, USA; and also (at what price I don't know) from the Trade Union Institute of Economic Research, Wallingatan 38, S-111 24 Stockholm, Sweden. It is quite a difficult, detailed paper, but it is worth reading for either of two reasons. It goes to the heart of the relations between business, labor and government in the Swedish experiment, if you're interested in that. And if you're interested in becoming the kind of political economist this text encourages you to be, Andrew Martin's paper will set exemplary standards for you. Re-read it once a year until you have learned to research and write as well as that.

58

Protected independence

Recall some reasons why protection, and other ways of influencing national economic structure, can make sense for some countries in some circumstances:

- Protection may balance some countries' trade and payments more effectively and at less cost than any other way of balancing them.

- It may be needed to establish new industries.

- It may sustain desirable industries where the national market is too small to make them fully competitive with imports, and where the relevant resources would otherwise be worse employed or unemployed.

- It may sustain key industries whose presence sustains other industries without further protection.

- It may protect a home market which gives producers advantages of scale which allow them to export competitively.

- It may allow long-term financing, research and product development to firms which could not find such finance or risk such a strategy if they were in daily price competition with imports.

- National regulation of trade, or foreign exchange transactions, or both, may be necessary to policies of full employment.

- Protection can allow more job security than full exposure to the increasingly competitive and unstable global economy allows.

- Governments of open economies can sometimes be bullied into competing for investment and employment by offering the biggest subsidies, the most regressive taxation and the worst conditions of employment, safety and environmental care. One defence against that sort of blackmail is a national capacity to say 'If you want to sell it here, you must make it here'. (Or make parts of it here, or make something else here.)

- Especially in small countries, protection may enrich human capital by sustaining a greater diversity of desirable skills and occupations than free trade and unhindered foreign ownership would allow. For example –

- It may be desirable to protect elements of national culture, and the intellectual, artistic and technical occupations which serve it (and which may also contribute to international culture).

- A protected and comparatively self-sufficient economy is likely to allow more democratic choice than an open economy can allow about the balance between people's interests as consumers and their interests as producers. (Remember the strength of the evidence marshalled by Robert Lane in *The Market Experience* for the high value of job security and interesting and sociable work.)

The economic effects of protection vary with circumstances. They can vary with the policy's intentions – is it designed to serve any of the good purposes listed above, or to preserve ailing industries the country would be better without, or just to enrich a few favored manufacturers? Whatever the policy's intentions, its effects can vary with the skill with which it is designed and administered, and with foreigners' responses to it. In some circumstances protection can reduce national income, for reasons explained by free-trade theorists. In other circumstances it can increase national income, for reasons explained in Chapter 49 on trade policy. But in rich countries there are two new reasons why effects on national income need not be the only or main consideration in deciding between open and protective trade policies. They are reasons which had much less force in the poorer worlds in which classical and neoclassical theories were conceived, so they tend to be undervalued by neoclassical economists.

You've met these twentieth century reasons already. First, when a country becomes productive enough to provide everyone with a comfortable living, margins of total national income become less important than they were when majorities were cold and hungry. They become less important than the distribution if income, the kinds of work that are available, the conditions at work and the company at work, job security for those who want it, and the general balance between people's experience as producers and their experience as consumers.

Second, there are now important economic conditions which may be affected by trade policy and economic structure but which don't figure in prevailing measures of national income. They include the productivity of individual and household and community life outside the hours of paid employment. That productivity depends on human capital, some of which may need protection. It depends on the job security and banking and tax arrangements which finance investment in household space and capital. It also depends on public investment in the public space and capital which people use as they make and do things for themselves and one another by their unpaid labor. To provide household and community capital liberally, and to distribute them productively, can be easier in a protected economy than in an open one.

For all those reasons some countries, especially those which can't balance their trade and payments any other way, may do well to give some of their producers some protection. If the emerging global economy proves to be as over-competitive and unstable as some experts fear, a degree of protection may appeal even to countries which have so far done well without it. Every case is different, but we can use Australia's twentieth century experience to explore the benefits and risks of a small country's attempt to be as self-sufficient as it could be without unreasonable cost.

RESOURCES

Recall, from Chapter 11, the nineteenth-century sources of Australia's high income. Gold discoveries brought a wave of young, energetic immigrants. They found rich natural resources. They exported gold, copper, wool, wheat, meat. That paid for importing most of the manufactured goods they needed. Besides farming and mining, most of their labor went to building the physical

capital of town and country and household life. They built houses, farms, shops and workshops, roads and bridges, water supplies and sewers, ports and railways, schools and universities and hospitals, town halls and art galleries. Compared with Britain and the United States, more of their infrastructure and services were public, often because private efforts to provide them had failed. More of their houses were owned by the households who lived in them. There was less profit-seeking business, and more of it was small rather than big business. Labor was strong, with strong unions and its own political party. Private profit-seeking capitalists were comparatively weak politically. People generally did not fear government, and they expected it to provide them with a great many economic services. It could finance public investment, where necessary, by borrowing in London at a time when the London lenders were much less willing to lend to private borrowers on the other side of the world.

Those political strengths and weaknesses were important when the six colonies federated in the Commonwealth of Australia in 1901. The constitution was, for the time, unusually democratic: with some racist exceptions, all adult men and women voted for both houses of parliament. Voting was soon afterwards made compulsory. There were three main parties: a free-trading Conservative party, a protectionist Liberal party, and the Labor party. Labor governed, or shared policy-making with Liberal governments which depended on Labor support, for ten of the new nation's first fifteen years. Between them the two parties established the strategy of 'New Protection'.

AN AUSTRALIAN STRATEGY, MARK ONE

Through its first thirty five years, the strategy had three main elements: a racial immigration policy; tariff protection; and industrial arbitration and wage-fixing by judges and commissioners. All parties agreed about racial policy. The tariff and arbitration were mostly the work of Liberal/Labor cooperation. The rationale of the strategy was as follows.

Immigration

More people were needed to justify and defend possession of such a large land. In boom times there was assisted immigration, mostly from Britain. Non-white immigration was banned for two reasons, each as strongly held as the other. There were deplorable racist theories and feelings. And Labor feared the entry of

cheap labor. (Queensland sugar planters had imported indentured Pacific islanders. Other British colonies imported Indians. Chinese made their own way to the Australian goldfields. All three worked for lower wages than British, European or American immigrants would accept.)

Protection

Tariff protection had two main purposes. First, most of the country's usable land and known mineral deposits were already taken up. Who would employ another flood of immigrants? New industries were needed. Protectionists argued for more and heavier manufacturing. The fastest manufacturing growth at the time was in the protected United States, protected Germany and protected Russia. In Australia the campaign was led as much by disinterested citizens wanting more manufacturing as by existing manufacturers wanting more protection. The early national tariffs continued and adjusted former colonial tariffs. Two world wars prompted more protection (and more public investment) to develop steelmaking and other metals processing, shipbuilding, and the production of vehicles, aircraft and weapons. The depression of the 1930s prompted some higher protection to restore employment.

The strategy's second purpose, signified by the name 'New' Protection, was to allow good wages and working conditions. Immigration controls excluded cheap workers; trade controls excluded their cheap products. With that double protection, the good wages and working conditions were to be achieved by union strength and by public conciliation, arbitration and wage-fixing.

Arbitration

The Commonwealth Court of Conciliation and Arbitration was created in 1904. A first attempt to link protection to fair wages imposed a uniform tax on importers and home producers of a range of products, but exempted home producers if their wages and working conditions were judged by the court to be fair and reasonable. The High Court found that to be unconstitutional. But before it did, a famous Arbitration judge in a famous judgment set a national minimum wage. It was based on the average needs of an average employee with a wife and three children, but it became a minimum lawful wage for any adult male employee. Under

various names, enforced by other means, linked to local costs of living and keeping up with economic growth through most of its history, it has been the minimum wage for men ever since, and for women since 1973. Many more terms of employment have become subjects of court awards. Collective bargaining is allowed to arrive at better wages and conditions than the awards provide, but not at worse.

The strategy had other elements. A Commonwealth Bank and Savings Bank served some useful purposes. To the States' health, educational and welfare provisions the Commonwealth added a means-tested Old Age and Invalid pension, and a maternity allowance. The six State governments were quite adventurous public investors through the 1920s, and the Commonwealth negotiated institutional means of coordinating the seven governments' borrowing.

The strategy did a good deal of what it was designed to do. It achieved substantial private industrial development, partly by Australian initiatives and partly by British and American exporters who 'came in under the tariff' to manufacture in Australia. It fixed fair wages for male workers in union-organized industries. But arbitration did not prevent some continuing industrial strife. It did very little for women workers. Inflation was not very effectively restrained through the First World War. And – before Keynes – the strategy did not include effective means of achieving full employment. In the world depression of the 1930s trade union unemployment reached 28 per cent and total unemployment exceeded 30 per cent. The strategy needed attention. As elsewhere, the catalyst was the Second World War.

THE STRATEGY, MARK TWO

Wartime brought high taxation; rationing and price and rent controls; strict control of bank lending and interest rates; and emergency powers to direct business and labor, as about a quarter of national economic activity was switched to war production.

A group of unusually able politicians and young Keynesian bureaucrats developed those controls with bipartisan support. They began planning the postwar reconstruction of the economy and society early in the war, and continued the work through eight years of Labor government then twenty years of government by a Liberal/Country Party coalition. The coalition tried an early 'bonfire of controls'. It coincided with the Korean war and sparked 21 per cent inflation in one year. That chastened the new government. Its two leaders had grown up in country towns. They knew the effects of

drought, depression and debt. They were suspicious of bankers and city businessmen, and they developed high respect for the Keynesian public servants they inherited from the wartime Labor regime. So despite detailed disagreements the revised strategy had wide political and public support, and some able planners and administrators.

The greatest of the Keynesian public servants recorded long afterwards how in 1945 'practically the whole of the content of the wartime banking regulations including the power to call upon Banks to deposit surplus finds with the Commonwealth Bank, the control of gold and foreign exchange, bank interest rates and of bank lending and investment policies' was embodied in postwar bank legislation (H.G. Coombs, *Trial Balance*, 1981, p113). Introducing the legislation the Prime

Minister said –

> If, after the war, the trading banks' holdings of liquid reserves with the Commonwealth Bank were placed freely at their disposal they would be able by increasing their advances and purchases of securities to build up a secondary credit expansion of formidable dimensions ... The Commonwealth Bank must be given authority to immobilize the liquid reserves of the trading banks to whatever extent may be desirable. No responsible Government could afford to move forward into the postwar period without adequate means at its disposal to cope with inflationary and deflationary movements in the monetary and banking system.

Those passages are worth quoting to illustrate the confidence of economic government at that time. Coombs governed the Commonwealth Bank then the Reserve Bank with exemplary success for twenty years. For thirty five years Australia balanced its payments, with negligible foreign debt. When another Labor government deregulated the financial system in 1983, the trading banks responded with exactly the inflationary expansion of mostly-unproductive credit that Coombs and a wiser Prime Minister had predicted forty years before. They also began to run the country into serious payments deficit and self-generating foreign debt. That is what those controls had been preventing. They had not been preventing the self-restrained and ideally productive behavior of the neoclassical imagination, or anything remotely like it.

The political circumstances of the 1940s were especially helpful to the new aspirations for full employment and more generous welfare. People were happy to see many wartime powers dismantled, so they did not mind if a few were kept on to restrain inflation and sustain employment. Similarly they welcomed cuts in the wartime rates of tax, but to finance more public investment and welfare they accepted smaller cuts than would otherwise have been possible. Thus some permanent increase of government power and taxation to finance the new elements of the strategy was accepted with less resistance than it might meet now, because it came in the course of the welcome postwar *reduction* of government control and taxation.

From 1945 the main elements of the strategy were as follows.

Immigration from Britain and Europe, and from the 1970s from Asia, helped a fast increase of population from 7 millions in 1945 to 18 millions in 1999. By then a third were foreign born or children of foreign-born parents. There was very full employment for the first generation of newcomers. Many could return home if they wanted to, and quite a lot did. Most of those who stayed could buy house and land if they wanted to, and they wanted and got slightly more suburban land, on average, than Australian-born people did. Together those items may help to explain how peacefully and appreciatively a homogeneous, racist society turned into quite a colorful multicultural one.

Protection by tariff, quota and other means continued. So did industrial development, much of it foreign-owned as British, American and Dutch multinationals 'came in under the tariff'. Most of the protected production was for the Australian market only, displacing imports. Most incoming foreign capital created new productive capacity, as it was increasingly required to do.

Governments also began to protect Australian ownership in some industries. That was done at first by exchange controls, then by direct regulation. Foreigners could own only specified proportions of the shares of banks, brokers, life insurers, radio and television broadcasters, newspapers, domestic airlines, mining companies and some other resource developers. In other industries foreign investors were still encouraged to develop new enterprises, but they were restrained from taking over existing firms, or developed assets such as commercial buildings. The main purpose at the time was to retain an Australian share of ownership, and perhaps national sovereignty. Other good effects, on the balance of payments and the level of foreign debt, were not much noticed until after the controls were withdrawn and the deficit and debt ballooned.

Money and credit There was careful control of bank liquidity, lending, interest rates and foreign transactions. Savings banks had to lend specified proportions of their resources to government and for housing, at regulated rates of interest. Life insurers had to invest their funds within Australia, and a tax rule induced them also to lend specified proportions of their funds to government and for housing. The public Commonwealth Bank developed an Industrial Finance department to help private manufacturers. State banks helped farmers and some other special groups.

Housing and home ownership were aided by (1) public investment in housing for rent, for rental-purchase and for sale; (2) public lending to low-income home-buyers; (3) regulations requiring savings banks and life insurers to lend for housing; (4) public housing loans to ex-servicemen; (5) low, controlled rates of interest for housing loans from all those sources; and (6) public investment, mostly by the States, in urban services to the new suburbs, much of it financed by borrowing at very low interest.

Aggregate demand and its employment effects were influenced by adjusting direct and indirect taxes; by adjusting the permitted quantity and directions of bank lending; and sometimes by varying the rate of public investment.

Arbitration was extended to more occupations and many more conditions of employment. Wage awards continued to be related to regional costs of living (for a time automatically, then at the court's discretion) and to the national rate of economic growth. Once each year a full bench of the Arbitration Court heard argument from peak representatives of business and labor, and from the government if it asked to be heard, and set the next year's wage levels. The Court reduced the regular working week to 40 hours, with less for some occupations. Most occupations got four weeks annual leave with additional holiday pay, and provisions for sick leave. Equal pay for equal work by women was ordered in 1969, enforced very quickly, and extended soon afterwards to equal pay for work of equal value. Throughout the period judges and commissioners were also dealing with industrial disputes.

Health and education The States provided free or nearly-free public hospitals, with clinics for outpatients. The Commonwealth provided free health services to war veterans. Many well-off people paid their doctors, had private insurance to cover their costs in private hospitals, and took those costs off their taxable incomes. Outside the public hospitals and some special programs there was no general public funding of medical services until the 1970s.

The States provided free primary and secondary schools, and universities which charged fees. From the 1960s the national government funded the universities. Australians averaged less years of education per head than most Western societies, until attendance soared, partly because of high youth unemployment, late in the century.

Welfare incomes and services Age and invalid pensions continued, at lower than the best European rates. A regular unemployment allowance was introduced, also at a low rate. Households rather than individuals were means-tested for many purposes: there was a 'married rate' of age pension for couples, but unemployment pay was for one partner only, and only if neither partner was earning. Allowances for lone

parents and for people caring for old or infirm kin came comparatively late and meanly by Swedish standards.

Welfare costs were thus low by European standards. Poverty and inequality were not as bad as that would suggest, because of the effects of housing policy, fair wages, and full employment while it lasted. For many retired workers, for example, the value of their own rent-free house was as great as the difference between Australian and European pensions. And the capital value of the house helped their grandchildren's home-buying.

Coherence

Notice how the elements of the strategy hang together and support and depend on each other.

Mass immigration of people with working skills but little or no savings would create a housing crisis without the active housing policies and the public provision of suburban infrastructure and services. The housing and infrastructure policies depend on affordable long-term credit: they could not work well without the State and Commonwealth savings banks, the other credit provisions for housing and public investment, and controlled interest rates. Full employment and low interest would together be strongly inflationary (too many people would borrow too much, too much spending would chase too few goods) without public control of the quantity of bank credit, and some tax restraint of after-tax income and spending. Protection might encourage inflationary wage-bargaining by the unions if there was no independent wage arbitration. But without protection to attract investment in new industries the mass of immigrants would be harder to employ, and foreign trade and payments could not be expected to balance.

Notice also that most of the public policies do not 'replace market by government'. Government does not tell the banks which firms to lend to. It does not tell firms which bank to use. It does not decide what products will be developed. It does not tell private landlords which tenants to accept, or tell tenants which house to rent. All market activity needs some government. What this government does is adjust some of the rules and some of the public investments in order to adjust some of the market options. The adjusted options are designed to encourage full employment, but *without* encouraging the excessive interest costs, the excessive wage demands and costs, the accelerated inflation and the excessive imports and foreign debt which might otherwise be market effects of full employment in Australia's situation at that time.

Remember, just as one example, the likely effects

of holding the rate if interest below the market rate which banks would be likely to establish in an unregulated market. Low and stable rates bring into the market a bigger number and a wider range of safe borrowers. They include home-buying households who could not meet high interest charges, or risk committing themselves to variable rates of interest, from their incomes. They include new firms, and firms in price-competitive industries, who need long credit for capital outlays, but can only afford it at low interest and can only risk it at a stable rate of interest. With controlled low rates, many of those are safe and productive borrowers. Banks can lend to them, and can do so without disadvantage to themselves if they're not allowed to take higher interest from anyone else. (In an unregulated market, high and unstable interest rates limit the banks' options to the borrowers who offer to pay those rates. Some of those are less safe, some are less productive, than the best of the low-interest borrowers.) The lower the controlled rate of interest, the freer the banks are to choose from the widest range of potential borrowers, and the safer and/or more productive their lending can be. (They can still of course choose badly. But in practice most bad bank performance in recent times has been in high-interest rather than regulated-interest markets.)

So there is a lot to be said for regulating low and stable rates of interest (subject to adjustment for risk) in countries with the necessary capacity for honest and competent regulation. But *by itself*, when there is fast growth and full employment, low interest inflates the demand for credit and the banks' opportunities to provide it. It is not a safe policy unless there is *also* (1) control of the quantity of bank lending, (2) some regulation of other financial institutions, and (3) boundary controls to prevent people and banks from evading the national rules by lending and investing abroad rather than at home.

You know all that: it is only here to reinforce the lesson that economic strategies need to be coherent.

TROUBLES

Troubles arose partly from changes which were beyond Australians' power to control, and partly from shortcomings in their own performance.

Unemployment returned in the 1970s, as in most of the other developed economies. Australia did not develop the effective labor policies which continued full employment for fifteen more years in Sweden

The terms of trade – the amount of wool or wheat or iron ore that it took to buy a Volvo or a Boeing –

changed to Australia's disadvantage. Some industries lost sales to new Asian competitors. Balanced trade and payments depended more than ever on the long-standing trade and exchange controls.

There were some misuses of the tariff. Technical progress in a number of the protected industries called for heavy investment in new plant. Some Australian producers invested accordingly. Others did not – instead they and their workers' unions persuaded government to raise their levels of protection. By 1970 critics were calling Australian manufacturing 'an industrial museum'. The government's tariff increases had jobs and the balance of payments in mind. But technical backwardness was not what the New Protection was meant to protect, and it could not expect to survive for long at increasing cost to Australian consumers.

Wage arbitration helped to slow the rise of inflation, but also made it hard to reverse its upward trend. This year's gains worked their way through product prices to raise next year's price index and wage awards. In the last years of full employment inflation had reached 6 per cent. As unemployment rose through the 1970s, so did the rate of inflation, peaking at 16 per cent.

The inflation brought high nominal interest and sloped credit. Low-income households who could afford to buy houses with level credit could no longer do so, and there were rising numbers of unemployed, age pensioners and lone parents who could not do so at any rate of interest. Five per cent of the country's housing stock was public. That had been a mean supply while there were no unemployed, and it was dismally inadequate now.

In 1972 the first Labor government for 23 years took office and tried, sometimes chaotically, to do a lot of things at once. But exuberant unions bargained unusually hard for wages above the award rates. Government gave its public servants too big a wage rise. The OPEC oil price raised the prices of other products besides petrol. There was a big jump in the rate of inflation, and in the wage awards that followed. For those and other reasons the government was short-lived. The conservative coalition returned to power, and applied restraints. Unemployment and inflation were soon running level at 10 per cent. Economic growth was little more than half its long-boom average of 4 per cent. Two main elements of Australia's welfare strategy - full employment and well-distributed household capital - were failing rising numbers of people.

Once again the national strategy needed some repair.

THE STRATEGY, MARK THREE

Another Labor government was elected in 1983. It came to power at a snap election, after a sudden change of its leadership, without a very clear or complete program. But some commitments before the election and some early action promised five repairs to the national strategy.

The Accord was an agreement between the government and the Australian Council of Trade Unions to restrain wages. They agreed that recent wage gains had been excessive. They had accelerated inflation. They had depressed investment and employment by raising business costs and reducing profit shares. So the unions agreed that, for a time, wages should rise more slowly than the rate of inflation. They would thus accept some real wage cuts. In return government promised to restore the lost income by tax cuts. Both sides delivered. From that and other causes the rate of inflation fell from 10 to 2 per cent in the next ten years.

Bargained protection Industries wanting continuing protection were required to show that they were as efficient as Australian wage levels and the scale of their Australian markets would allow. On that principle three notable plans were negotiated between government and the employers and unions of protected industries.

A steel plan provided for the full modernization of the industry, and tariff reductions.

A car plan required the makers to modernize where appropriate, and also to rationalize their operations to reduce the number of producers and models. General Motors and Toyota, traditional competitors, began sharing models!

A plan for the textile, clothing and footwear industries had a different balance of purposes. It included drastic cuts to their high protection, designed to have some of their low-skilled, low-wage activities replaced by Asian competitors. That intention was reinforced by measures to improve pay and conditions in the most oppressive factories and sweatshops. There were some aids to greater efficiency, chiefly in the capital-intensive and up-market branches of the industries. But most of the positive provisions were for transitional income and retraining for the large numbers, mostly of women, who would have to leave the industries.

Health Long after similar reforms in Britain and Western Europe, comprehensive tax-funded medical and pharmaceutical insurance was begun by one Labor government in the 1970s and completed by another in the 1980s.

Housing The incoming Prime Minister in 1983 promised to finance the States to double the public housing share of the nation's houses in ten years, taking it from 5 to 10 per cent.

Level credit He also proposed to issue capital-indexed government bonds. Private experience at the time indicated that they might sell at interest rates around 3 per cent. The proposal did not mention housing, but capital-indexed bonds could well have financed the public housing program, and encouraged savings banks and building societies to offer similar long level credit to homebuyers and small businesses, including those excluded from the market by the prevailing inflation and sloped credit.

Those additions promised to fix three of the existing strategy's five main faults. They should restrain inflation more effectively. They should economize and discipline the uses of protection. They would restore the capacity of most wage-earning households to buy basic household capital early in household life when it could be most productive. But they did not promise a return to full employment (though politicians sometimes said they did), or add anything significant to the 'Mark Two' employment policies which had ceased to provide full employment for the past fifteen years.

The Accord worked. The steel and car and textile plans worked. The health scheme worked. But that was all. The government did not issue indexed bonds, and instead of funding more public housing it was soon funding less. Within a year or two of taking office, the leaders of that Labor government had decided not to repair the old strategy but to dismantle and replace it.

A nation building state changes its mind

The heading above is the subtitle of Michael Pusey's *Economic rationalism in Canberra* (1991). Read it if you want to explore the beliefs of the political and public service leaders who decided in 1983/4 to dismantle the traditional strategy, and to replace it by free trade and small government. The market forces of the global economy, rather than deliberate national choices, should shape Australia's economic structure, its employment, and its foreign trade and payments and indebtedness. Pusey deplores the change of mind and strategy. There is a more sympathetic though still worried account of it in Robert Catley, *Globalising Australian capitalism* (1996).

The traditional strategy was no longer delivering full employment, fast growth or stable prices. The leaders' decision to replace it rather than repair it was taken suddenly, between elections, without any democratic mandate. Their main reasons seem to have been as follows.

First, there were powerful intellectual persuasions. 'Dry' versions of neoclassical theory, strongly American-influenced, were prevailing in the Australian universities. They coloured most of the financial pages of the national press. Most important, they had taken over the Treasury, Finance and Prime Minister's departments of the national government as the old Keynesian chiefs retired. The new believers expected that a freer, unboundaried, less regulated economy, in an increasingly open and competitive world, would force Australian producers to be more efficient and internationally competitive. It would increase the traded proportion of national output, and that would increase national income. Any tendency to unbalanced trade or payments would be re-balanced automatically – though sometimes with painful shocks and adjustments – by the market processes imagined by the theorists of free trade. A global capital market would allocate financial capital and therefore physical resources to their most productive uses. Within the national economy market freedom, with some lower wages where necessary, would produce fuller employment than any other non-inflationary strategy could.

Michael Pusey's research leaves no doubt that the intellectual causes of the shift to the Right were very important. But there were also political considerations.

Labor governments have to fear business, press and other articulate opposition to their traditional policies. This Labor government could expect friendlier treatment the further to the Right its policies were seen to be moving. British and US governments were leading in that direction. Why not follow? If the Labor government moved as far Right as a majority of voters would tolerate, that might even push the conservative opposition *farther* Right than an Australian majority would tolerate. That tactic need not lose much of Labor's traditional support. There was no effective party to the Left of Labor for workers to turn to. The party itself was unlikely to split: it had split three times in the course of the century, and lost power for long periods each time. And it could still expect most workers' votes if it made one exception to the Right program, and continued to defend arbitration, fair wages and the Accord against an opposition keen to end union power and 'free up the labor market'.

There were other political attractions. In the short run a return to small government should allow some popular

tax-cutting. There could be further cuts if the government sold public assets and used the capital proceeds (instead of equivalent amounts of tax revenue) for its current spending. Privatizing public services would not necessarily improve the services or cut their costs, but any dissatisfaction with the services could then be deflected from the government to their private providers.

Those and other vote-catching considerations had something to do with the leaders' success in getting the rank and file of Labor politicians to accept and support the great change of direction. But they would scarcely have reversed the party's most hallowed values and policies if there had not been a coherent, widely believed and strongly supported economic theory to justify the changes, and to promise that they would benefit Labor's traditional supporters.

We are about to review some actual effects of the changes. As we do, treat it as a test of the theory. Remember what the theory promised the changes would achieve, and why. The new strategists – or anti-strategists – doubted that full employment was either possible or desirable. But if it could be achieved at all, they believed it could only be achieved by economic growth, i.e. by reducing the numbers employed to produce any given output. They believed that the private sector was the engine of growth, and government could encourage it chiefly by getting out of its way. Government must reduce public spending and employment to release resources for private sector growth. It must deregulate the private sector, privatize as much public business as possible, make incentive tax cuts especially to the highest incomes, and (as far as public tolerance and union strength allowed) reform the arbitration system to allow wage cuts where the market demanded them. Some wages must fall to restore fuller employment, some must fall to keep export prices competitive. Efficiency and growth could only come from competition. Australia must join the global economy and let market forces do the rest.

THE END OF THE AUSTRALIAN STRATEGY

Driven by those beliefs and political calculations, the government began in 1983 to reverse some main elements of the traditional strategy:

- It deregulated Australian banks and other financial institutions, and opened the country's financial boundaries to unhindered foreign lending, borrowing and exchange of capital funds.

- Instead of further bargained protection it committed

Australia to a step-by-step progress to full free trade within fifteen years.

- It steadily reduced the States' financial resources for the public investment and services for which the States were responsible. That forced them to cut their health, educational and welfare services. To replace some of the lost revenue they began to sell State assets, privatize public services, and develop State or State-licensed gambling industries, some of which had cruelly destructive social affects.

- The national government began to cut its own services and the numbers it employed, and to reduce its public servants' job security.

- It began a big program of asset sales and privatization.

- It negotiated with the State governments various forms of private, public/private and public/public competition to provide public services which had hitherto been seen as natural monopolies.

Elements of the old strategy which were not reversed were the Accord, and the means-tested 'residual' welfare provisions. Those provisions were 'better targeted', which usually meant they were provided after tougher means tests to fewer people. But some were improved, especially the system of medical insurance, and incomes and services to age pensioners, lone parents and some other of the poorest people. But the quality of many of the services deteriorated as the numbers and morale of the public servants administering them suffered steady attrition.

In 1995, after twelve years of the new regime, one critic observed that 'a country whose governments have shaped much of its economic activity, and been substantial producers themselves, is suddenly governed by parties devoted to discrediting government, reducing its scope, and getting what remains of it done as far as possible by private profit-seekers.' In the same year Australia slipped below Greece and Turkey to become the OECD country whose government taxed and invested and spent the lowest proportion of national income. In 1996 the conservative opposition won an election, replaced the Labor government, and intensified a number of its Right policies.

How far have those policies achieved what they were expected to achieve?

USES OF THE NEW FREEDOMS

The new strategy is not the subject of this chapter. Its principles belong with discussions of open rather than protected economies. But its effects cast some retrospective light on the actual working of the strategy

which it replaced. To estimate what the protective strategy did and did not achieve, it helps to know what forces were released when it was dismantled. Remember how heavily causal analyses have to depend on choices of imagined alternatives: on guessing what would otherwise have happened if particular forces had not been at work. Free traders argue that without the New Protection, or with an earlier repeal of the New Protection, Australia would have achieved more efficient production and faster economic growth. What has actually followed the repeal of the protective and financial policies suggests that without them there might well have been slower growth, more unemployment and steeper inequalities.

Like most analysis of complex social causation, the argument can't necessarily be decisive. Other changes have been occurring at home and abroad to complicate the effects of the policy changes. But in the light of what has happened to the national economy as the protective strategy has been step-by-step dismantled, it becomes very hard to believe that the protective policies and financial restraints were simply hindering what would otherwise have been a more efficient, more fully employed and faster-growing economy.

Here's a brief review:

Floating the exchange rate (i.e. leaving it to market forces, without any public control or direct influence on it) was supposed to allow market forces to stabilize it. In fact (1) the Australian dollar has fluctuated more widely than ever before, and (2) the market influences on the rate are not chiefly the demand and supply of funds for trade and investment. Nine-tenths or more of exchange transactions are now gambling on fluctuating exchange and interest rates and asset prices, and the rates of exchange are affected more by currency gamblers' expectations and by debt-service requirements than by traders' and investors' demands. This was not predicted by the deregulators. It was not the imagined alternative against which the free-trade theorists chose to 'measure' the supposed effects of the former exchange controls. But freeing the exchanges was not a sufficient cause of the new anarchy. It was one element of the more general financial deregulation.

Financial deregulation (of banks and other financial institutions, and of the permissible uses of foreign exchange) was supposed to make more funds available to Australian producers, and it was supposed to allow the capital market to allocate funds and physical resources more efficiently to their most productive uses.

In fact less funds have since been available to productive Australian investors, for a number of reasons:

- Deregulation brought a sharp increase in interest rates, excluding many productive firms and low-income households from access to long-term credit.

- Australian banks, superannuation and insurance companies used their new freedom to export a proportion of their funds – up to a third in some cases.

- Of incoming foreign funds, less than before are for permanent investment or long-term lending. More are for short-term lending, corporate takeover or asset trading for capital gain.

- The banks' new 'capital adequacy' lending limits plus the new freedom to borrow foreign funds fuelled the destructive property boom-and-bust of the 1980s.

- About half of the new jobs created through the 1980s were in property and financial services created to exploit the new financial freedoms. A high proportion of that 'bubble' employment was unproductive and much of it disappeared in the following recession.

Freer trade has been accompanied by a decline in Australian manufacturing and an increase of manufactured imports. There has also been some increase of manufactured exports, mostly to expanding Asian markets, but not enough to balance the increase of imports and debt-service.

Foreign debt Freed to borrow from foreign banks for any purpose, Australian banks began to borrow rather than buy the foreign funds which Australian importers needed. That allows imports to exceed the value of exports without any equilibrating effect on the exchange rate. By 1995 net foreign debt, mostly private, was nearly half the value of the national income. Interest payments, all borrowed, were increasing the debt by 5 or 6 per cent of national income each year, while the income grew at a trend rate of about 2 per cent.

Compound effects

Notice some interacting effects of freeing *both* the trade *and* the financial system of a country with a protected economic structure and balance of payments.

The trade freedom allows imports to increase and displace some national output. The financial freedom allows the extra imports to be bought with borrowed exchange.

To keep the foreign loans coming as the foreign debt grows, the government has to keep Australian interest rates high. With no other means of influencing the amount of credit that the banks create, high interest is also one of the government's two remaining means of restraining inflation. (Continuing cuts in public investment and services are the other. The Accord ceased with a change of government in 1996.)

High interest and cuts in public employment are now the government's main means of restraining the growth of national income So they have become its main remaining means of restraining the import bill, the exchange deficit and the growth of foreign debt: each dollar off national income takes about 30 cents off the import bill and the growth of foreign debt.

Now notice some social effects of this method of (mis)managing the national economy. Bank lending could previously be restrained by regulating its quantity. As long as there were boundary controls to prevent capital flight, the rate of interest could also be kept low. That allowed banks to allocate their limited lending to the most productive borrowers. Now that the quantity of lending can only be restrained by raising its price (the rate of interest) some of the lending has to go to less productive borrowers. The general efficiency of the economy suffers.

National spending could alternatively be restrained (to restrain inflation, imports and foreign debt) by higher taxation. The taxation (of personal income or consumption goods) could be designed to improve equalities without harming productive incentives. But with a political ban on tax increases, restraint has to be achieved instead by the combination of high interest (to restrain investment and employment) and low public investment and services (which also restrains employment). The burden of restraint is not shared as widely as it could be through taxation. Instead the losses are concentrated on the minority who are deprived of jobs by the restraint of investment and public services. (Be careful of this argument: *any* restraint of spending, including restraint by taxation, may reduce employment. But the effects are likely to be nastier and more concentrated if contriving the unemployment is the chosen means of restraining total income and spending.)

Does a majority of the Australian people welcome the new regime? It is hard to know, because since 1983 neither political party has offered them any alternative to it. When pollsters ask them whether they would like modest increases of tax or consumer prices to finance fuller employment, more secure employment, better public services and more Australian ownership of Australia's assets, 60 per cent or more say yes they would. But since 1982 they have not been offered that option, though in four of the six elections from 1982 to

1996 they elected the party offering (marginally) higher taxation and fairer wages.

RETROSPECTIVE ANALYSIS OF THE AUSTRALIAN STRATEGY

The above are among the effects of freer trade and exchange and smaller government in Australia since 1983. How might they help our causal analysis of the actual economic effects of the preceding New Protection strategy?

With due allowance for changing international circumstances, it still seems reasonable to conclude that the effects of deregulation were among the things that the New Protection was preventing. If that is so, the New Protection was *not* preventing the more efficient, fully employed, self-equilibrating market economy of neoclassical imagination. The free-traders' estimates of the costs of protection and of big government depend entirely on the validity of that imagined alternative: on the belief that with free trade and small government, that ideal would have come true. I think the present deregulated economy offers a better measure of the actual effects of the old strategy. Not a perfect or certain basis, but a better one than the neoclassical imagination offers, for estimating the effects and judging the social value of the 'Australian strategy'.

Through its best decades that strategy allowed the world's fullest employment, equal to Sweden's; economic growth averaging 4 per cent a year; more job security than now; a very slow growth of inflation from 2 to 6 per cent (except for one high year) over twenty five years; a base rate of real interest averaging below 1 per cent for forty years; a growth of home ownership from 50 to 70 per cent of households, and to 85 per cent by the time their breadwinners retired; and a continuing reduction of inequalities of wealth and income.

There were shortcomings. Health and welfare services were meaner than they could and should have been. Australia was no better than the rest of the world at maintaining full employment after the long boom ended. But even without it, the New Protection was worth continuing. It promised a more equal, self-reliant and self-governing society than exists now. Australia would retain effective influence over its economic structure and its relations with the world economy. It could balance its trade and payments. It would not be driven to an improvident sale of national assets, or be heading for a Mexican financial default. And its people could still decide collectively how to balance their interests as consumers with the interest, diversity, security and sociability of the work they do.

LESSONS ?

Should national electors and their governments try for more trade dependence, or more self-sufficiency? More foreign investment and ownership, or less? More capacity to shape the national economy by collective choice, or less?

There's no simple, principled answer that is right in all cases. The options depend, and strategic choices ought to depend, on each country's situation and economic, political and administrative capacities. The Belgian economy is so interdependent with its German and other neighbors that it would be absurd to try for self-sufficiency. The US economy has such a range of resources and industries that it could still be rich, as it has been through most of its modern history, while trading less than a tenth of its output. There is no valid general case for either maximizing or minimizing every country's trade or every country's self-sufficiency.

There has nevertheless been a strong bias in most English-speaking economists' treatment of the subject. They tend to theorize the benefits but not the costs of free trade, and the costs but not the benefits of protection; and they estimate the costs and benefits of protection quite deceptively against an imagined alternative of free-trading full employment. So to return from the Australian case study to the general issues which it illustrates, this chapter could end with a summary of the possible benefits of a deliberate degree of protected self-sufficiency for some countries in some circumstances. But you already know those arguments in general terms, and they were listed again on the opening page of this present chapter. (Revise Chapters 49 and 51 on trade and financial policy if you need to.) We will presently focus instead on three reasons why those arguments may have more force now and in future than in the past. (1) The emerging global economy has some new hazards for open national economies. (2) As countries get richer the costs of protection may matter less, so its benefits may more often outweigh its costs. (3) Satisfactory environmental care and a fair distribution of its costs may be even harder to achieve in a world economy without a world government than in a world in which national governments can still govern their national economies, and make and enforce international agreements about environmental policy.

Those are business for the final chapter of this course. Before you reach it there are two more case studies: Russia's under-governed transition from a communist command economy to a mixed economy, and China's dictatorially governed transition.

59

Ex-Communist options

Reform of the communist economies of Russia and China has taken different directions with dramatically different results.

About 1978 the Chinese government, holding fast to its dictatorial powers and ignoring Western political and economic advice, began cautious, step-by-step economic reforms. The direction of the most successful changes was not exactly capitalist or communist, but a mix of public ownership and private enterprise which the government calls a social market economy. Through its first fifteen years it averaged above 9 per cent annual growth, one of the fastest rates in the world through those years, and increased real income per head several times over.

Ten years later the Russian government, with much forceful Western advice, began a rapid revolutionary transformation to both democratic government and capitalist economy. In only five years they halved Russian income per head, with a gross increase of inequality, poverty, unemployment and crime. The USSR fell apart into ten national republics, with Russia's economic performance one of the worst of them.

There is much to be learned from those contrasting histories. But as you might expect, there is political and professional disagreement about how to explain them, and *what* to learn from them. One of the first comprehensive comparisons of the two was Peter Nolan's book *China's Rise, Russia's Fall: Politics, economics and planning in the transition from Stalinism* (1995). Two years later he distilled some conclusions into 15 pages in 'Post-Stalinist System Reform in China and Russia: Contrasts and Implications' in Philip Arestis and others (eds) *Markets, Unemployment and Economic Policy: Essays in honour of Geoff Harcourt* (1997). An account of the Russian transition with more attention to the few signs of Russian recovery is in the final chapters of Paul R. Gregory and Robert C. Stuart, *Russian and Soviet Economic Performance*, 6th edition 1998.

CHINA

The communist People's Republic of China was established in 1949 after two decades of civil war and Japanese invasion. The country was poorer than Russia had been when its communist regime began in 1917. More than three quarters of the Chinese people lived by peasant agriculture and the village trades that go with it. The new regime collectivized agriculture and developed some heavy industry in big state enterprises in a few coastal regions. From 1960 the government was in hostile relations with both the Western capitalist world and the Russian communist world. That encouraged an economic strategy of self-sufficiency. China traded very little, and its development suffered from that. It developed coal and steel and some other heavy industrial production, but it badly needed access to twentieth-century advances in Western products and productive technology. Economic development and the popularity of the regime suffered from some unproductive shocks administered by Mao Zedong's government: the Great Leap Forward in 1958-9, and the Cultural Revolution from 1966. The leaders who succeeded after Mao's death in 1976 were better innovators than he had been: just as inventive and just as dictatorial, but more perceptive, open-minded and cautious.

They began with some local farm experiments, and a limited opening of the country to trade and foreign investment. Surprisingly, the first farm experiments were so successful that they were quickly extended to most of the country; and it was their success, rather than the industrial branch of the strategy, which generated the industries which first produced enough exportable goods to make the trade liberation fruitful. Big industry, new technology and big foreign investment followed, still with inventive mixtures of private profit-seeking management with public ownership and regulation. We can look in turn at the farm and industrial developments, trade, industry, investment, and the strategic role of central and local government.

Farming

Most rural workers – the breadwinners for three quarters or more of China's population – were wage laborers on state and collective farms. They produced output for distribution by state marketing enterprises. They had little material incentive to improve their performance. What could a reforming government do about such poor-performing public enterprises? Sell them to capitalist investors? Break them up into privately owned family farms? If either of those strategies works badly it is hard to reverse, since reversal may entail a revolutionary confiscation of land, perhaps with force and bloodshed. (Stalin had starved millions to death in the forced collectivization of Russia's family farms in 1929-32.) But Western wisdom strongly recommended private farm ownership. Since their Right turn Western economists tend to link productive incentives exclusively to private ownership. (Plenty of Western land-owners, tenant farmers and share-farmers know better. Most productive industrial and service workers, managers and self-employed professionals in the advanced economies' private sectors have no ownership incentives. But Western economists can be amazingly inattentive to the facts under their noses.)

The Chinese government encouraged some local experimentation, learned from it, and arrived at a cautious strategy. In 1984 they had local councils break up their collective farms, retain ownership of the land, and divide it as equally as possible between farming families. Farm stock and machinery were distributed in a similar way until the farmers earned enough to buy their own. The family farms had to contract to supply state marketers at low fixed prices with quotas of produce based roughly on past output. That ensured basic food supplies at affordable prices to China's non-farm population. The local councils took a share of the proceeds, as their main revenue. Output above the quota belonged to the families who produced it, and they could trade it at market prices. That – the independence and family solidarity as well as the money – transformed the farmers' incentives, and they quickly transformed their performance.

Output, and the farmers' incomes, quickly increased. People ate better, were healthier, lived longer. They soon had income to spare for better clothing, furniture, housing, farm tools and carts. But who would produce those things to meet the new demands?

Town and village enterprises

There was cumulative causation. The farmers' new demands generated two other successes, first in local industries and then in foreign trade.

Hard work and improving equipment on the farms left hands to spare for other trades. Where necessary, local councils did for the other trades what they had done for farming. Where new enterprises needed land, they contracted for its use with the local council which owned it. Many got other means of production on a similar basis, then as they prospered, bought their own. They made furniture, clothing, silk products, edible oils, paper and cardboard, some home and farm equipment,

and built bigger and better houses and smaller, handier farm buildings. Housing space per head doubled within fifteen years. Thus their own efforts did a great deal to improve the quality of life of what had been a very poor peasant class.

The town and village enterprises (TVEs) were soon producing more than their local markets needed, and selling tradeable goods to the cities. Alert government noticed how many of the things they made were low-wage, labor-intensive products which richer foreigners might well buy. But to finance foreigners to buy your exports, you have to buy theirs (or buy their assets, or lend them money.) To import (without borrowing or asset sales) you must export. The government wanted foreign investment, but it did not want to sell existing assets to foreigners, or borrow much from them. But it was eager to import the advanced technology that its big state industries needed if they were to modernize and expand. The new village trades could earn the means of paying for it. Thus the careful liberalization and growth of trade through the 1980s owed as much to the low-tech successes of the farms and village trades as to the high-tech needs of the biggest industries. By 1994, ten years after the great land reform, the TVEs were employing 60 million workers.

Most of those workers were new to the work, or at least to its new organization. Town and village councils were actively interested in their success, helped them where they could, but could also call them to account and drive them quite hard. The output of local goods was visibly improving local standards of living. Revenue from the enterprises' local and export sales was split between their members and the local authority to whom they answered, from whose revenues the whole community benefited in one way or another. Both their own and their public owners' motivation was as productive as it would normally be in private enterprise. They were energetic – more so, very often, than the secure, long-serving workers of the old state enterprises. They were competing business away from many of the small state enterprises. Their shares of China's gross material production, of China's exports, and of exports from all the world's low income countries, rose at impressive rates. 'Had the export performance of a single developing country improved in such a dramatic way' Peter Nolan wrote, 'teams of Western experts would have been dispatched to understand the cause of the phenomenon. Yet there was little serious outside investigation of the reasons for the explosive export growth of this predominantly publicly-owned sector.'

Private employment was an option for many of them by then, but by no means all of them were choosing it.

Private enterprises The TVEs were owned – or used land and equipment that was owned – by town and village councils. But 'pure' private enterprises, owned by individuals, were also lawful, and there was a rapid growth of them, mostly in small business form. By the time the TVEs were employing 60 million people, about 47 million were working in private non-farm enterprises. These tended to be small, without expensive capital, their work classified as 'petty commodity production', neither agricultural nor industrial. But they contributed in many ways to local needs and to some of the export trades.

Trade

The reforming government wanted foreign trade, but kept strategic control of it. Exports were helped and subsidized, and their producers given privileged incentives, in a variety of ways. Currency exchange was managed to the exporters' advantage. Government and the export producers, rather than market demand, decided the desirable uses of the foreign currency which the exports earned. And Chinese industry was strongly protected by tariff and other means. Foreign traders and governments complained of intolerable breaches of the General Agreement on Tariffs and Trade (GATT). China was not a member. It protected its developing industries as most of the rich countries had done through their years of fast industrial development. It directed its export earnings to their most-needed uses, especially to import inputs to its industrial development, much as Japan, South Korea and Taiwan did at similar stages of development, and most of Western Europe had done through its mid-century postwar recovery. All things considered, despite plenty of cruelties, conflicts and shortcomings, the strategy has been as successful as it was for those predecessors. But it differed sharply from its East Asian exemplars in one respect. The Chinese government welcomed foreign investment, and developed a new style of joint venturing to make the best of it.

Foreign investment

The new regime passed a Law on Chinese-Foreign Joint Ventures in 1979, and worked hard from then on to attract foreign industrial investment. For twelve or thirteen years there was a modest inflow, chiefly from nearby Chinese sources in Hong Kong, Singapore and Taiwan. Then a sudden big flow, including European and American investment, much of it still transmitted

through Hong Kong, set in from 1993. The device of the joint venture had advantages for both sides: for the foreign investors, and for China's national strategy.

For China, direct foreign investment by joint venture in approved industries had these advantages:

- It brought additional capital to augment Chinese savings. This was the least of its advantages, because Chinese saving was already high.

- It paid foreign currency for the capital goods which the investors imported, thus sparing China's sparse export earnings for other uses.

- It increased China's foreign earnings as many of the joint ventures produced for export.

- It improved China's capacity to sell exports as well as to produce them, as the foreign investors taught their Chinese partners how to find and deal with their foreign markets.

- It imported advanced technology and the skills to use it, and opened both to the Chinese partners.

- It brought advanced Western methods of organization and management. Where they seemed appropriate to Chinese conditions and purposes, the Chinese partners were well placed to learn them.

- Most of the joint ventures drew inputs from many Chinese suppliers. The suppliers had to learn what was wanted and how best to produce and supply it. That made for a further diffusion of the incoming technology and know-how. That could often equip the local firms to extend the range and volume, and improve the efficiency, of their output for the national market as well.(Compare, from Chapter 49, Paul Chapman's account of industrial clusters, and of the advantages of technology, scale and skill which Australian firms derive from the presence of a Japanese carmaker.)

For the foreign investors the government protected tradeable industries by tariff and other means. Besides protection from import competition there were various other aids available to foreign investors, to joint ventures, and to producers for export. But getting the aids, sometimes the protection, and sometimes privileged access to Chinese markets, required intricate and sometimes unprintable local knowledge, and relations, sometimes corrupt, with many branches of a complicated bureaucracy. The national partners did most of that more expertly than their foreign partners could have done, and taught the foreigners in more general ways about doing business in a society and culture that were strange to them. Relations within many of the joint ventures were nevertheless easier than this account may suggest, because so many of the 'foreign' partners were overseas Chinese from Hong Kong, Taiwan, Singapore or Malaysia. There was also some simpler cooperation as Chinese firms in the surrounding countries lent money and supplied equipment to enterprises in China, then bought their output. Thus overseas Chinese firms in richer countries got some of their regular production done at lower cost because of the lower wages and the export aids available within China.

State enterprises

Progress was slower with the big old state enterprises which still provide most of the country's heavy industry. Step by cautious step their managers have been given more independence. The old command procedures told them exactly where the planned quantities of their inputs would come from and where their outputs must go, at what prices in each case. They have been allowed to shop around the non-state sector for rising proportions of their inputs and for some of their product sales. To a different extent in different industries they have become freer to determine exactly what to produce, though in most industries some mandatory planning by the central state controllers continues.

Many of the big state enterprises have been turned into joint stock companies. Selling shares has raised some home and foreign capital to help finance their modernization. Some of the big ones have been encouraged to build conglomerate groups by taking over their 'upstream' suppliers, sometimes including sources of their scientific research, or their 'downstream' customers and marketers. They then direct or negotiate relations within the group. But the big enterprises are still state controlled, with the government as majority shareholder of the 'corporatized' enterprises. Many of them have long been subsidized, typically by dual pricing. (They may buy inputs from other state enterprises at prices below production costs. They may sell some of their output to other state enterprises at fixed prices, and some to other local buyers, or for export, at market prices.) But by cautious steps the government has been bringing the dual prices closer together, and expanding the scope for genuine market pricing, through the 1990s.

The bigger the enterprises are, the less freedom they tend to have to cut the numbers they employ. That humane policy need not harm their efficiency while they grow fast enough for their output to increase as fast as their productivity does. And it may help to maintain workers' and managers' confidence in each other, and

in the system and its careful approach to change. So much social security is provided by employers and so little by anyone else that significant unemployment would have serious implications for the system as a whole, and perhaps for the government's security.

The tax system had complicated effects on the progress of reform. The big state enterprises were taxed on their profits, which were determined as much by dual pricing and other subsidies as by their working efficiency. The subsidies served some good purposes, for example in assisting exports when no better access to foreign exchange was available. But the enterprises could often gain as much by fiddling their status and entitlements as by increasing their productivity; and when they did increase it, government tended to adjust the rates to capture the gain as tax. Together with their welfare obligations to their workers, those were not the best incentives for adventurous management. (But nor were they the worst, as Western critics tend to think. Japanese managers, for example, have often been at least as careful of their employees' welfare, and benefited from as much government contrivance, while out-performing Western competitors.) In 1994 the government reformed the system of taxation and removed most of the hindrance that it offered to efficient motivation and management.

Problems The big state enterprises continued to modernize, and expand their output. But they also continued some of their inefficiencies, and their performance attracts strong Western criticism. Peter Nolan also attracts criticism, as a Western defender of the Chinese approach to economic reform. To sample his capacity to report the regime's shortcomings as well as its successes – but also some of the critics' shortcomings – here is part of his summary of the performance of the big state enterprises through the first fifteen years of the 'social market economy':

> By 1993, over 30 per cent of state enterprises were making losses, requiring the pre-emption of large amounts of public funds to keep them afloat. The ratio of losses of industrial enterprises to profits and taxes of profit-making enterprises rose from just over two per cent in 1985 to 30 per cent in 1993.
>
> Investment decision-making had become diffused without the full rigours of market discipline acting to repress capital spending. The 'soft budget constraint' upon Chinese state enterprises was facilitated by decentralisation of rights to issue credit, but without a comparable responsibility for banks' branches to account for their balance sheet performance. Moreover, the lending behaviour of the

banks' branches was heavily influenced by the local government.

Partial reform of state industry provided a ripe environment for corruption. Parallel markets provided enormous incentives for profit-seeking enterprises to direct output away from the plan. An elaborate structure of negotiation was involved in determining the proportion of output to be included in the state's mandatory plan, in deciding the share of profits to be retained by the enterprise, and in all the complex allocation of rights connected with foreign trade. These negotiations often were accompanied by bribes, and the income to be derived from them, either by units or by individuals, could be large by the standards of ordinary Chinese citizens.

State industry overall grew relatively slowly. Its share of total gross industrial output fell sharply. Market forces operated earlier and more powerfully in the non-state sector. For many observers this provided strong evidence of the relative inefficiency of the state-owned sector, and demonstrated the high cost of a 'half-way house' reform of state industry.

However, there were many offsetting results. Losses in state industry were mainly confined to sectors with special problems in the transition. In 1991, 98.9 per cent of losses in state industry came from the coal, oil, non-ferrous metals, tobacco and military sectors. Moreover, the extent of 'losses' falls greatly if the huge state enterprise outlays on housing, health, education, unemployment pay, food subsidies, etc., are removed from the balance sheet. In the west these would be the responsibility mainly of the state or the individual. Profits became an increasingly important goal for state enterprise managers. The incentives for regional governments to assist and push the enterprises under their control to raise profits also greatly increased. Prices were increasingly market-determined. Enterprises and local governments did alter their behaviour in response to the sharp change in the environment. ...

China's outstanding export performance provided a means to technologically upgrade state industry through the rapid growth of imports. China's total imports of machinery and transport equipment rose from an annual level of under US$2 billion dollars in the late 1970s to US$45 billion dollars by 1993. A large share of this new technology was directed towards the state industrial sector. China's government export incentives flew in the face of static resource efficiency considerations, but had large dynamic gains.

The rationality of the size structure of state enterprise improved. The rapid growth of the non-state sector's share of industrial output was largely at the expense of the small-scale state sector. The large-scale state-owned sector grew at roughly the same (i.e. very rapid) rate as the whole industrial sector. Indeed, the share of large scale industrial plants in total gross industrial output remained constant at around 25-26 per cent throughout the 1980s. ...

[Output per worker, and per unit of capital, grew at acceptable rates through the period.]

Conclusion China avoided the 'quick fix' approach to the reform of state enterprises. In part this was for ideological reasons. The 'Old Guard' of Chinese leaders felt that it was a betrayal of socialism to give up state ownership of industry. However, it is unconvincing to suppose that this was the only, or even the main, explanation. The same leadership had permitted the introduction of market forces into the lives of the peasantry. This was much more dangerous in terms of traditional Stalinist thinking, since the peasantry was three quarters of the population, and had supposedly backward political thoughts associated with 'petty commodity production'. It permitted too the rapid growth of competitive, profit-seeking, community-owned enterprises. It allowed rapid growth of individual business. It permitted the state industrial sector to divest itself of a large number of small enterprises, greatly reducing the share of the state's 'commanding heights' in industry. It encouraged foreign capital to invest in Chinese industry. It reversed Stalinist hostility to international trade. A more plausible explanation is that the leadership understood the dangers of 'shock therapy' privatization and wished to avoid these.

– Peter Nolan, *China's rise, Russia's fall*, 215-18

Nolan's comparison is of the Chinese and Russian economic transformations through their most decisive phases, especially through the decade from 1984 to 1994. Since then, Chinese 'gradualism' has continued. So have economic growth, the modernization of the big state enterprises, and the volume of China's international trade. But so also has an unresolved problem at the heart of the gradualist program. That program has not so far included an effective new welfare system to meet the needs created by the changing economic system. In the communist economy, government was the employer. It was not necessarily wrong to have its employers, rather than other state agencies, provide their employees with education, health service, any other welfare services and any necessary unemployment pay as well as wages. The great land reform left local government in contractual relations with the new family farms, assuming some of the welfare obligations that had belonged to the state and collective farms. The surge in productivity of all sectors of the economy, and the rising income of nearly everyone, reduced the working population's need of other aid. But the same changes brought new sources of poverty and insecurity of the kind that lead other mixed economies to run welfare 'safety nets' independent of the system of employment.

Some children leaving school could fail to find employment. Some of the new private enterprises could draw workers out of the state and town and village enterprises, but then disemploy them. Surviving members of families whose breadwinners died might find jobs or other support, or they might not. The regime recognized those and other sources of unemployment, and in 1999 estimated their numbers at 15 million of the urban workforce, or about 8 per cent of it. But a bigger source of trouble, including political trouble, was in the rising numbers of 'xiagang' workers laid off by state enterprises. Off work, but not off the books: the state employers are still restrained, in most circumstances, from actually dismissing workers they no longer need. Those numbers, especially of the least skilled workers, rose through the later years of the 1990s with technological and other changes. For workers whom they can't use but can't dismiss the state employers are still supposed to be the primary providers of housing, medical insurance and unemployment pay. But rising numbers, especially of those who are distant from the centres of government power, cannot or will not meet their welfare obligations. Han Dongfang, an exiled labor-rights activist, spoke to Western reporters in January 1999 :

> The central government has promised to provide *xiagang* workers with at least a few hundred yuan each month so that they can live, but at the provincial and local level these policies are not being implemented. People call me up and ask me how they can get their money. I tell them to take the front page of the People's Daily to the local officials and show them the words of Premier Zhu Rongji promising that all *xiagang* workers will be given money to live on. Then they ring me back and say that the officials just laughed at them and told them to go to Beijing and see Mr Zhu themselves, and get him to hand them the cash because they don't have any.

Hostile observers guess that a hundred million or more were unemployed by 1999. Whatever their numbers, they are troubling the government. Just as government acted brutally to suppress dissent and opposition in 1989 (the year of the killing in Tiananmen Square) so is the government doing ten years later, closing down critical newspapers, banning critical books, imprisoning labor organizers and campaigners for democracy. Western critics have good cause to condemn that repression. But they should perhaps suspend judgment about its economic implications. Long experience of democratic politics and popular psychology make it easy to assume that repression and reform are usually *alternatives*. If politicians try to suppress discussion of economic evils and deny that they exist, it is safe to assume that they can't think of anything better to do about them. But the brutes who sent the tanks into Tiananmen Square had not stopped thinking fruitfully about further economic reforms. They had already more than doubled the material income of the Chinese people, including the poorest of them. They were on course to the further expansion of exports, direct foreign investment and high-tech imports in the 1990s. No doubt they had self-defensive reasons for fearing popular opposition. But they knew well that economic performance was their best defence against it. They had also shown, by the personal risks that most of them had taken in opposing Mao's sudden, violent, ill-judged changes of direction, that they thought it was important both to get the reforms right, and to maintain the people's sense of security and their tolerance of the processes of change. Only time will tell, but the new repression of 1999 may have accompanied, among other things, fruitful thought and action about the problems of welfare and unemployment which provoked it.

Speaking on the tenth anniversary of Tiananmen, President Jiang Zemin declared that China would never adopt Western-style democracy. Among his reasons were probably the achievements rather than the shortcomings of economic reform in China, and the economic consequences of Russia's first years of democracy.

RUSSIA

Through the 1980s the Russian government came to the conclusion that communist government and the communist economy had been mistakes. The government should free the country from both. Democracy would give the people desirable freedom and a government attentive to their voices. For their material needs, market forces would serve better than their command economy. After some painful transition and some necessary increase of inequality a capitalist economy would quickly catch up with the Western leaders, and reward its people with higher incomes and better working and living choices.

Decisively, the main changes were completed between 1991 and 1995. Though some of the figures are uncertain, they appear to have halved Russian investment and output. They trebled the numbers in poverty, and worsened a lot of the poverty. They fragmented the health services, increased the death rate by half, and increased the crime rate by more than that. They handed control of much of Russia's big industry to a small number of individual billionaires, some of them likely to manage it badly. They put many small enterprises into criminal hands, and many out of business altogether.

Some of the designers of the strategy see those effects as necessary pain, and still expect the promised gains. Most now concede that the collapse was an _un_necessary disaster. As to whether the country can find its way back to good government and economic recovery, or whether its new patterns of ownership and disorganization are more likely to have cumulative ill effects, there is disagreement.

In the relations between what Peter Nolan calls China's rise and Russia's fall there is a sad irony. In a logical world they ought to have happened in the opposite order. Russia's disaster would be understandable as a first attempt at a first-ever transformation for which history and experience offered no guide. China's slower, surer performance would show how much its planners had learned from the Russian mistakes. But in the real world, with the good fortune of _following_ the cautious Chinese transformation, the Russian leaders learned nothing from it. They listened instead to Western economists who insisted that a vast and complex transformation to a Western-style economy could be managed with less government than any Western country needed merely to keep such an economy ticking over. Rather than try to design the new institutions or control the transition to them, they should simply dismantle the 'command' institutions and leave their replacement to market forces. And to overcome conservative communist opposition to the necessary changes, the combined democratic/capitalist revolution should be sudden and total. Where Western philosophy and Chinese experience agreed in recommending that pioneers do nothing irreversible, Western neoclassical economists urged the Russian government to _make each step_ irreversible.

As pioneers of the transformation the Chinese leaders had had two sources of practical wisdom. The negative one was their experience of Mao's destructive leaps-in-the-dark. The positive one was the continuing economic development of their Asian neighbors, much of it accomplished by Chinese political and business leaders in those countries. But the Russian leaders and their Western advisers rejected both China's experience and the lessons of Japan's, South Korea's, Taiwan's and Singapore's development. Instead they put their trust in market forces of the Western type without _either_ communist _or_ modern Western _or_ modern Asian control over them. Peter Nolan reproaches them for thinking that 'only a bureaucracy trained in sophisticated Western neoclassical economics' could manage their transition to a market economy:

> Many of the most important interventions require common sense and experience rather than a high level of economic theory. Moreover, the bureaucracy of the communist countries was not especially incompetent in technical terms, albeit that their efforts had been grossly misdirected under the command economy. The prevailing orthodoxy among the successful East Asian industrialising countries, including Japan, Taiwan and South Korea, in the early phase of their industrialisation was not neoclassical economics but rather an eclectic blend of Marxism and the economics of List and Schumpeter, which seemed much more relevant to the 'catch-up' task that these countries faced. The fact that they lacked a a high level of knowledge of Western-style theories may not have been a large handicap to intelligent intervention. It may even have been a help, since their intellectual background inclined them not to regard the economy as a simple mechanism akin to perfect competition, but rather a sphere of struggle between interest groups in which capital accumulation was at the centre of the growth process.
>
> – _China's rise, Russia's fall_ (p. 60)

Privatization

More than half of the privatization of public property and enterprises was accomplished in two years from mid 1992 to mid 1994. On 20 June 1994 the _Financial Times_ estimated that 'by the end of 1994 ... 70 per cent of state property will have been transferred to private hands and 70 per cent of workers will work in the private sector'. The report should perhaps have said 70 per cent of those still employed.

State, provincial and local public enterprises were 'corporatized' and their shares distributed by various means: by auction, by tender, by privileged allocation to insiders in government or the enterprises, or by coupon.

Coupons went on various principles to the firms' employees or to the population of local government areas. Some coupons entitled their bearers to buy shares at fixed prices, some were convertible to shares without payment. Many cash-strapped citizens were happy to sell them, and new-style entrepreneurs were ready to buy them.

Where did the entrepreneurs come from? To become an overnight millionaire, what a well-placed entrepreneur needed was a three-way alliance between himself, somebody powerful in government, and a banker. The government might allot a batch of shares to the bureaucrat in charge of a big privatization or to the current manager of the enterprise concerned. Alternatively borrowed funds might enable an adventurer to buy enough coupon shares to control shareholders' meetings: some of the new firms were effectively controlled by owners of five per cent of their shares. The share-buying might be financed by an ally who had got a bank licence with the help of the friend in government.. (Hundreds of private banks were licensed in the first two years that they were lawful.) When the entrepreneur had substantial funds he might buy some media (or bribe their proprietors, or ally with them to share the spoils) and manipulate business news and share prices in profitable ways which could have had them jailed in respectable Western countries.

Examples will illustrate three other ways to get rich – by privately exploiting publicly regulated prices, by stealing public real estate, or by Mafia operations against privatized small businesses.

> In the spring of 1992, the state price of oil was still one per cent of the world market price. Even in 1993, the average Russian oil price was only 8.3 per cent of the world market price. Managers of state companies producing oil and metals bought these commodities at the fixed state prices from "their" state enterprises through their private trading firms. They acquired export quotas and licenses through connections in the foreign trade administration and sold abroad at the world market price. The total export rents were no less than $24 billion in the peak year of 1992, or 30 per cent of GDP, as the exchange rate was very low that year. The resulting private revenues were accumulated abroad, which led to a corresponding capital flight. The beneficiaries were a small number of state enterprise managers, government officials, politicians and commodity traders.
>
> – A. Aslund, *Why has Russia's economic transformation been so arduous?* World Bank 1999, 8-9.

In November 1991 the Mayor [Popov, Mayor of Moscow] had actually signed over an entire district of the capital to a French-Russian joint venture called AKUSO, in which he and his minister for the Municipal Economy were accused of holding 40 per cent of the shares …The 'October' district covered 4 million square metres of choice real estate from the splendid Gorky Park to Gagarinsk Square, occupied by academies, monasteries, a hospital and 22,000 residents including Mikhail Gorbachev. It was worth around $30 billion, but UKOSO got it on a 99-year lease at $10 per year˙. . . Popov resigned eventually … [but] was never taken to court because, like two and a half million government office holders in the former USSR, he had official and unconditional immunity.

For small local properties and shops and services privatized by local government –

> the rules for privatisation were fluid, bent officials were easy to come by, and most Russians had no money to speak of. In a matter of weeks the mafia had the city sewn up … Where standard bribery failed in the course of the takeover, the mafia had only to apply a little force. To acquire a popular Gastronom in the capital it simply prevented the employees from bidding by locking them up for the entire afternoon. . . . In the end the Moscow properties were sold off for only 200 million rubles, whereas the city had been expecting 1.6 billion. Asked how he felt about the whole larcenous affair, the head of the city council's privatisation committee replied 'Why not? If the mafia guarantees law and order, food in the shops and washed floors then I'm all for the mafia.'
>
> – The last two items from C. Sterling, *Crime without frontiers* (1994) pp. 86-7.

Disorganization

What to do with the acquisitions in the new conditions of an under-regulated, wholly inexperienced market economy?

In a big company or a batch of related companies acquired by a new entrepreneur, the working managers may face a number of problems. The bigger and more technically advanced the enterprises, the likelier it is that they need to draw inputs – raw materials, processed materials, finished components – from many suppliers. Until yesterday (so to speak) those suppliers have been under government command to get *their* inputs from specified sources who were commanded to supply them, and to deliver centrally planned quotas of specified products to specified customers at specified prices. Until yesterday all the enterprises had workers, often a few more than they strictly needed, who had rights to their jobs and to specified wage scales and welfare benefits. With various margins for practical negotiation and discretion, that is how the command economy worked.

But suddenly, all the parties are free. In principle, nobody is commanded to supply anything to anybody, no prices are fixed, no wage rates are fixed, workers have fewer rights, there are no effective unions.

In practice there are still public interventions – to avoid dismissing too many workers, to secure supplies or low prices for a favored enterprise, to protect some firms from market operations by others, or for other national or local purposes. But many of the government interventions, like many of the new market risks, are unpredictable. Between one system and another, harassed enterprise managers say the system is 'half pregnant'.

Some efficient profit-seeking managers may be able to cut costs in standard ways: reduce the numbers employed, get more work from the remaining workers, reduce their wages, shop around for cheaper inputs and new customers, exploit any market strength to raise output prices. Those are normal market moves. But there are also other possibilities. Until yesterday many of the state firms were subsidized (perhaps to avoid unemployment, perhaps to restrain export prices, perhaps to conceal inefficiencies, perhaps to keep prices down for powerful state customers). Without subsidy, some firms are in trouble. They may switch to other products. They may shop around for customers who will pay more than the old fixed prices. They may beg public officials to restore some subsidy. Many go out of business, disemploying their workers, creating shortages of whatever they used to produce.

An entrepreneur with a group of companies is suddenly short of necessary inputs. What can he do? He can borrow to buy some of his failing suppliers for next to nothing and put them back to work. He can take their whole output instead of his former quota. That may damage other firms which also drew inputs from those suppliers. But he himself can wake up one morning to find that a flood of imports (barred or excluded by tariff until yesterday) is putting some of *his* group out of business. (In 1991, imports supplied about 5 per cent of retail sales in Moscow. In 1995 they supplied about 50 per cent.) More resort to powerful friends is indicated – for covert subsidies, gifts of public assets, tax evasion, contracts to supply government.

Meanwhile one of the contradictions in pure market theory is exposed. If self-interest alone drives the system, why should enterprise managers seek gains for their owners rather than for themselves, their workers, or their society as a whole? Recall how back in 1932 Berle and Means asked that question about a capitalist system in which ownership was separated from control, as ownership passed from the founding entrepreneurs to thousands of passive shareholders, or to institutions whose executives were not owners either. In the US, executive directors keep their enterprises profitable and plunder them. Gregory and Stuart explain what many Russian managers do:

> In this limbo environment, Russian enterprise managers developed a unique corporate culture. During the early years of transition, the corporate culture prompted managers to use the enterprise for their own benefit. The manager would sign unfavorable contracts in return for payment of a broker's commission or sales fee. Corporate assets were diverted into small businesses that the manager or close associates owned. Hard currency earnings (which were likely to be confiscated by the government) were shipped abroad into the manager's bank account.

The big entrepreneurs are often likened to the US 'robber barons' of a century earlier. But however rough or crooked those Americans' methods were, they built their firms from nothing and the talents that built them could usually manage them competently. The talents which acquired the new Russian tycoons' ready-made enterprises – and unearned fortunes – may not manage them all as productively as Rockefeller or Carnegie managed their creations.

In the particular historical circumstances that the Russian regime and its Western economists have produced, there are many quicker ways to wealth and high income than competitive profit-seeking by efficient production and marketing. Too many of the necessary conditions for competitive profit-seeking by productive means are missing. There is no established business culture of mutual trust and honest dealing. There is very little of the intricate business law and regulation which first built those efficient virtues into the Western democracies' business life and now sustain and where necessary enforce them .What little company and business law there is in Russia is quite strict about conflicts of interest. Public regulators are not allowed to share ownership or accept favors from the industries which they regulate. But the rules are widely disregarded or misused. Some despairing observers see them not as aids to discipline but as adding to the opportunities for public/private corruption.

Corruption is not the only cause of the non-enforcement. Among other causes, privatization deprived all levels of government of a main source of their revenue, most of which had come from the profits or turnover of state enterprises. Whatever taxation the new Russian parliament legislates, the government now has great difficulty collecting. The new business owners and managers are expert at evading a good deal of it. At the same time Western economists are advising the government, and the International Monetary Fund is requiring it, to live within its means without budget deficits and without borrowing from its Central Bank. So even if it did know how to govern a mixed economy effectively in the unpromising conditions which it has created, it could probably not afford the means of doing it. If it strips the welfare safety net much barer (as some Western economists recommend) it must expect electoral defeat, or worse. Thus by contract and institutional coercion as well as persuasion the 'Washington consensus' on small government helps to prevent Russia from financing the public institutions, and the public and private human capital, that its new private sector desperately needs.

Employment, investment, aggregate demand

In those circumstances, neither the failures of non-viable firms nor the efficient downsizing of successful firms are shifting much labor to more productive full-time employment. To some extent the job losses are causing what you would expect them to cause: they are reducing wage rates and full-time employment, therefore total income, therefore aggregate demand, therefore investment, therefore employment, therefore income, therefore aggregate demand … and so on down.

But the immediate effect on consumer spending is less than Western theory or experience would expect, for three reasons. First, the new capitalists and elite are big spenders. Until 1991 the highest ten per cent of Russian incomes averaged five times the lowest ten per cent. By 1995 they averaged thirteen times, and besides income some of the richest earners were also spending plundered capital.

Second, as noticed above, freer trade is admitting a flood of luxury retail goods for those new shoppers to buy. It is also admitting a lot of cheap basic goods of better quality and at lower prices than Russian producers can yet match.

Third, business earnings are much reduced. But they used to provide high investment and quite high taxation. They now provide much less of either. With the investment halved and the taxes reduced and widely evaded, much of what remains of those financial resources has been switched to salaries and dividends, and thus to consumer spending, especially by the new elite. There has been a corresponding switch of imports from investment goods to consumption goods.

Thus consumer demand does not fall as far as the fall in Russian employment and output would suggest. Income is harder to measure, but it cannot be *very* far above output. In 1996, official Russian estimates put output at 47 per cent of its pre-reform level, and still falling. The World Bank made more allowance for deliberate understatement by business, and for unreported output of the 'informal' sector, and suggested 59 per cent, still falling. Whatever the true figure of income, there is no doubt that it has been redistributed upwards, and part of the switch of demand from investment goods to consumption goods is supplied by the corresponding switch of imports, rather than by Russian producers of consumption goods. The general uncertainty and lack of confidence prevent the continuing consumer demand from prompting much new productive investment or employment in Russia.

Unemployment has increased. In Nolan's summary –

By July 1994 the number of unemployed was estimated at around 10 million, or 13 per cent of the economically active population. However, even the concept of 'unemployment' rapidly lost meaning. There was a rapidly rising 'informal' sector in which a large proportion of the 'self-employed' worked at any kind of 'business', however low the returns per hour. The explosion of these forms of informal sector 'service' activities to a large degree reflected rapidly growing poverty and drastic shrinkage of full-time employment opportunities in the formal sector. The rapid growth of the service sector, from 31 per cent of total employment in 1989 to over 50 per cent, is widely viewed as a reflection of the new vibrancy of the post-reform economy. A more accurate way to view it is to regard it as the consequence of catastrophic deindustrialization.

–'Post-Stalinist Reform in China and Russia', 154-5

The macroeconomic effects are no better. The old productive structure, biased toward heavy industry and military output, balances Russia's trade by exporting oil and gas and metals. But it does not fit well with the changed structure of home demand. But its sudden disorganization, and exposure to import competition, discourage much responsive investment. So does the shortage, outside some heavy industries, of funds for investment. The new commercial banks have no deep reserves, and they have high risks from the general disorganization and the threat of inflation. Most of their deposits have to come from business. (Households don't trust them, and put 70 per cent of their savings into the one remaining state savings bank.) The commercial banks have to fear excessive withdrawals, so can't risk lending for long terms. In 1994 about 95 per cent of their lending was short-term, much of it speculative, not much of it commercial. Of more than 2000 banks created in the 1990s many have failed or been taken over by the few which have managed to grow big. So there is double reason for the low bank lending for productive capital investment: in the prevailing disorganization there is neither much demand for it, nor much capacity to supply it.

Fear of inflation constrains what government might otherwise do to stimulate investment. Production cannot respond to the level of consumer demand as it should in an efficient market economy. Demand for investment goods has fallen so far that the continuing consumer demand does not suffice to sustain either aggregate demand, or the pattern of demand that the structure of state enterprises was developed to supply. Many of the old inter-firm trading networks are broken up. Effective market institutions, information and know-how have not yet developed new networks. So any government efforts to revive investment and employment by putting more spending money into the consumers' pockets are likely to increase demand without much answering increase of supply, and thus add inflation to the other troubles.

Summary

Peter Nolan thinks the Russian strategy of sudden simultaneous democratic and capitalist transformation was wrongly chosen: The strategists and their Western advisers could and should have learned much more from institutional know-how, from Chinese experience, from the strongly state-directed development of the non-communist Asian tigers, and from common sense. Rather than quote a conclusion in such welcome accord with this text's principles, what follows is from Paul Gregory and Robert Stuart, who share many of the orthodox beliefs which prompted the strategy, and still hope that it may succeed in the long run. But in its first six years –

> By the middle of 1997, Russia had completed more than half a decade of transition. Judged on the basis of aggregate quantitative indicators, Russia's transition had failed, as of that date, to achieve major identifiable successes. Although ... the decline of the Russian economy after 1991 may be over-stated, the Russian economy had, at best, stabilized as of 1997. At worst, its decline was continuing, albeit at a much slower pace. The output of oil and gas – a key indicator of economic performance in an economy whose comparative advantage is energy resources – was still declining, although pundits predicted that the industry would resume growth in the near future. There were few signs of the investment boom required to replace and renew the Russian economy's depleted stock of capital and outmoded technology. The flood of foreign investment that Russian authorities had hoped for had yet to materialize. The mammoth Russian economy had attracted far less foreign capital than the much smaller [ex-communist] economies of Eastern Europe.
>
> – *Russian and Soviet economic performance*,
> 6th ed., pp. 463-4

And the 'stabilized' economy of 1997 was about to have its next serious financial crash in 1998.

LESSONS?

Begin with some lessons *not* to learn: some conclusions not to draw, or generalize, from one democratic failure and one dictatorial success.

Not all democracies are bad economic developers. Not all dictatorships are successful economic developers.

Much of the best economic development has been democratically governed. At the difficult task of reconstructing ex-communist economies the Polish, Hungarian and Czech democracies have done much better than the Russian. Any number of dictatorships – communist, ex-communist and non-communist – have been dreadful economic managers.

There is plenty to be learned from the Russian and Chinese histories. Try to make time to read Peter Nolan's book. He argues at length, and convincingly, that the different performance of the two countries was not sufficiently determined by their partly different initial conditions. Each government had effective freedom to choose its policies. The Chinese chose well, the Russians badly. His 1997 paper compresses that long argument into its last few lines, which also show that he understands the necessary service of imagination to causal analysis:

> This article contains two implicit counterfactual propositions. First, the selection of different policies in Russia could have produced rapid growth of

output and a large improvement in popular living standards. Secondly, the selection of a different set of policies in China could easily have produced a political and economic disaster, with a large decline in popular living standards.

– 'Post-Stalinist system reform in China and Russia', p.162

Meanwhile this chapter ends with a theme familiar from *this* book. Given its historical situation and resources, any mixed economy needs to get its mix right, in a double sense. It needs public, private and household production in good working relations with each other. And each of them, and their relations with each other, need appropriate government. The lighter the better wherever a light hand works best, but *least* government is rarely best, any more than heaviest government is.

Russia as a test of the neoclassical imagination

The Russian government was strongly urged by the international institutions and by many Western economists to assume that private ownership and minimal government would allow, and motivate, the most efficient allocation and use of available economic resources. Those were the good effects that too much government and public ownership were thought to be preventing: the efficient system which the economists imagined would spring into being if most public enterprise was privatized and most regulation was repealed. But when some of the government *was* withdrawn, and its productive property was offered for competitive private takeover, neither the takeover nor much of the early use of the private capital was either profit-seeking or efficient as neoclassically imagined. Bigger and quicker gains are available by other, less productive means than profit-seeking. All those other means are available because of (among other conditions) too little government. A lot of them also follow from bad government. Any transition to an efficient mixed economy with a profit-seeking private sector needs more and better government than Russia has so far provided.

But where the neoclassical faith in minimal government is strong enough, it prompts a counter-productive response to almost any failure of privatization or deregulation.. The paper by Anders Aslund which was quoted back on page 989 is both despairing and self-contradictory. It has two insistent themes. First, government does nothing right, so the less of it the better. Because its members steal from its revenue, cut its revenue. Because some regulation is corruptly misused and most regulation is thought to be distorting

efficient market forces, deregulate completely. But second, ruthless new leaders must make strict laws against corruption and enforce them effectively, and they must provide effective 'safety net' income and services for the disemployed losers from the necessary economic transformation.

How to finance that inescapable but compassionate government? Aslund is specific. Where productive Europeans put about 45 per cent of national income through public hands, and Americans 28 or 30 per cent, Russia would do better to let its central and provincial and local governments handle altogether 15 or 20 per cent. That would make the economy more efficient by freeing it from regulation altogether. And it would reduce bureaucratic theft by reducing both the number of thieves and the available loot. Nowhere in its 50 pages does the paper explain how halving the judicial, police and regulatory numbers will restore lawful behavior; how halving public education and health services will improve the performance of the employed population or the safety net for the aged and unemployed; how halving public science and research will help the technological catch-up – and so on. Or how halving public revenue will avoid halving those necessary public services. Or how all that recommended destruction of necessary institutional supports and services might generate the energetic, law-abiding, productive culture that Russian business and government lack. The simple faith in 'market good, government bad' simply disables its believers from understanding the necessary relations between market and government, or how either of them works where they work well.

The Western plan for the Russian transformation was always deliberately cruel, especially to the poorest people. Its authors knew very well that 'the big bang' would disemploy millions. They did not urge a necessary increase of public revenue to finance unemployment pay and welfare. Most of them did not apparently think, or care, that a quick destruction of the whole system of employment must wreck a good deal of the health service, which was part of the system of employment. The new democracy responds understandably to the cruel failure of the strategy by electing legislators who frustrate the executive government by trying to rebuild some stability and security into the conditions of daily life – conditions which have been routine in many middle-income democracies for half a century. They are accused of trying to 'return to communism', much as social democrats who want to restore full employment in the Western democracies are accused of trying to 'turn the clock back' or 'return to socialism'. And as the new insecurities wreck the old economic system and make it less and less possible to build a new one, the neoclassical imagination that the market economy will be most efficient when least governed can only suggest further destruction along the same lines: *less* government with even less revenue, and further deregulation.

Many who defend the Russian strategy despite its terrible performance ascribe its failures entirely to the pre-existing communist corruptions. Most of them avoid comparisons with China. Those who do compare China tend to focus not on its failure to deliver the promised growth, but on its failure to comply with the neoclassical requirements of private ownership, market pricing and deregulation. As in their analyses of non-communist countries' performance, 'market failure' and 'government failure' come to mean failure to comply with the neoclassical model, rather than failure to grow or prosper or distribute income tolerably.

Russia's exposure to global markets has been no more successful than its internal reforms. The Chinese capacity to attract abundant direct foreign investment owes a great deal to government. Joint ventures have to have a majority of Chinese ownership, often public ownership. Every foreign investment has to have public approval. By 1994 China had about fifty times the direct foreign investment that Russia had. It had much less speculative, destabilizing, short-term, asset-trading 'investment' than Russia had, chiefly because China did not allow much of it.. And 'picking winners' – the discriminating industrial and investment strategy which outrages neoclassical believers – has maximized the spin-off of foreign technology and management skills to Chinese firms in a wide range of useful industries. Nolan quotes a central government report of 1994:

> We shall guide the orientation of foreign investment in accordance with the state's industrial policies, directing foreign investment towards infrastructure and basic industry construction, key projects and upgrading technology in existing enterprises, in particular towards projects to increase the export of foreign currency earning products.

The policy did not deter the foreigners. Except for some purely extractive industries (chiefly mining) most investors who commit resources to long-term productive use in foreign countries *need* effective government there, including effective public discipline of the firms they must deal with there. And they know it.

China's mixed economy

Turn back to pages 210 to 213 of Chapter 18. Consider the structure of the public, private and household sectors through the 'golden age' of West European capitalism. That structure was probably not in the minds of the Chinese leaders when they planned their careful transformation to an efficient mixed economy. But they arrived at a vision surprisingly like it. A number of heavy industries – coal, steel, railroads, power, ports and commercial waterways, airports, telephones, most passenger transport – could stay public (as they were in much of Western Europe). Import and export of goods and funds should be regulated where that was necessary for balanced payments, for the best use of available resources, or for desired directions of growth and distribution of its benefits (as in Western Europe through its postwar reconstruction and most of its long boom). A revolution in agricultural productivity in countries with limited areas of crop and pasture land should be achieved by family farming with public scientific and educational help. The farmers need not own the land they farm, they could lease it (as many do in Britain and some other parts of Europe). In business and personal services, including banking, insurance and superannuation, there was room (as in Western Europe) for a mix of private profit-seeking services, cooperative and mutual services, and public services.

There remain three substantial differences between the Chinese vision and the European, Japanese and Korean models. Until lately the leading European countries did not want too much foreign ownership of their industries and services. Depending on their national circumstances they wanted to ensure balanced payments, cultural independence, benefit of the investment funds generated within their national economies, and – where there was any threat to it – sovereign control of their economic strategies without foreign political interference. The Chinese share those general purposes, but they differ in welcoming so much foreign investment. There may be two reasons for that. They retain strong influence over the investors through their joint-venture sector, their power of approval over all foreign investments, and their general confidence as economic regulators. And they feel too big and strong in the world to be bullied by incoming transnational firms or their national governments. Examples: In Europe, the private aircraft manufacturers and the governments of several countries joined in the French Airbus enterprise to break Boeing's world monopoly. When Ford wanted a new luxury car it bought British Jaguar. But in China –

In order to gain access to the vast and rapidly growing China market, Boeing was required to assist the main Chinese aircraft manufacturer in Xian to successively establish a capacity to produce spare parts and then manufacture whole sections of aircraft, and finally to assist in the development of a capacity to produce complete aircraft within China. In order to gain the right to invest in car production in China, Ford Motor Company was required to first invest for several years in upgrading the technical capacity of the Chinese automobile spare parts industry through a sequence of joint ventures.

– China's rise, Russia's fall, pp. 187-8

Thus new industries are developed under public protection just as they were at comparable stages of American, European, Japanese and Korean development. China differs only in choosing to attract more direct foreign investment, much as (for different reasons) Australia did.

A second difference from the mid-century European structure is China's inadequate safety net for its rising numbers of unemployed and underemployed, including the *xiagang* workers whom the old state enterprises no longer need but are not allowed to deprive of their welfare rights. Ex-communist countries need to relieve their privatized enterprises of those welfare obligations. So they need to finance a corresponding development of independent public housing, health and welfare servicss. Western advisers make that difficult when they recommend unduly low and balanced budgets. The IMF imposes such limits by contract with Russia and other ex-communist countries which it assists. But none of those international pressures constrains the Chinese government. Its welfare failures are its own, and out of character with the rest of its performance. There appear to be failures both of policy, and of the enforcement of such policies as there are.

Third, the dictators have carried out an effective and (for such a poor country) a surprisingly humane transformation of national economic structure and performance. The continuing Russian failures probably strengthen the Chinese leaders' resolve to continue the dictatorship. But there appear to be increasing underemployment, welfare failures, and popular hatred of the regime. From its proven capacity to plan and carry out the great transformation, is it safe to conclude that the dictatorship itself can long survive the transformation? Increasing income and education and changing technology enable more and more of the Chinese people to know what life in the East Asian democracies is like. Somebody predicted about forty years ago that the transistor, more than anything else, would end the Russian dictatorship. May its technological successors do the same for the Chinese regime? Two questions about the Chinese leaders:

- Will they manage to restore their early balance between benefits and brutality as the Chinese people grow richer, more educated, more skilled, more aware of the attractions of life in the successful democracies? Will they continue to improve economic performance, and develop the welfare measures which ought to be part of it, and improve the quality of life of enough of the Chinese people, to make the accompanying repression restrained enough and tolerable enough for them to survive? Or will they not?

- The present leaders have not so far relied *chiefly* on repression. There is abundant evidence that they regard that as their second string, and believe that economic improvement, including for the poorest of the people, is the most important condition of their success. Suppose that they or their successors decide that the dictatorship cannot expect to survive economic growth beyond the threshold level which – with appropriate distribution – allows secure comfort for everyone. Will they then plan and manage a transition to democracy as successfully as they transformed the economy? Cautiously, experimentally, starting with local government, proving each step before risking the next, building some of the old system's strengths into the new (perhaps, for example, an honest, competent, well educated, securely tenured Confucian public service, in place before the first elected national government?)

I hope you live to see it.

60

Democracy in a global economy

In its most innocent meaning 'globalization' stands for the new physical capacity to trade goods, money and information so quickly and cheaply over such distances that the world could imaginably run as one economic system without national divisions or boundaries. If you see it like that, the question is what best to do with those capacities.

You can read this chapter as outlining three answers to that question.

The first is not so much an answer as a program of action to find the answer. It says 'Let the market answer the question. Except for necessary property and contract and criminal law, call off most economic government, and let the hidden hand of market forces determine the best use of the world's physical and human resources. That *deliberate* liberation and unification of the world economy, rather than the conditions which merely make it possible, are what deserve to be called "globalization". Globalize is an active verb, something we have to *do* if we want it to happen, rather than something which chances to have happened to us.'

A second answer accepts that meaning of the word but thinks the program is dangerous, and opposes it. This text is biased in that direction. That is partly because of the times through which it has been written, and the visible effects of the Right turn so far. It is partly from disbelief in the theory and the neoclassical imagination which predicted good effects of the program. And it reflects a concern for democracy. In its full form with adult suffrage democracy is not much older than the high productivity which first made it possible to offer every household in the advanced economies access to material comfort and security, good health and education, a wide choice of lifestyles, and equal opportunity.

National governments are so far the only effective guarantors of those good things. There is no other source of law and order, of necessary public infrastructure and services, or of democratic influence over the purposes of private business activity, or the distribution of its benefits to the half or more of humanity to whom it does not pay wages. And if democratic government is persuaded to dismantle its powers of economic management, what regime must we expect in its place? The economists of the OECD and the IMF, the negotiators of the MAI, and the global business leaders who support them, have made their intentions clear enough.

But national government or global anarchy may not be our only alternatives. Can't a global economy be civilized by global government? Lately the most powerful international institutions – the World Bank some of the time, the World Trade Organization most of the time and the International Monetary Fund all the time – have been main protagonists of the Right program, and have themselves imposed unnecessary cruelties on some of the world's poorest people. But with different direction and policies, might they yet do the good which they were created to do, and which the Bank has often done and sometimes does still? Alternatively, just as the old League of Nations created the admirable International Labor Organization and the Food and Agriculture Organization, might not the United Nations create competent and compassionate institutions to regulate a world economy on a world scale? This more hopeful view of globalization is represented at the end of this chapter by one of its best protagonists.

So in turn now: Globalization good? Globalization bad? Globalization reformable?

TOO MUCH GOVERNMENT, TOO MUCH TAX, TOO MUCH WELFARE ?

A great many active and passive supporters of the Right program, including disinterested supporters, still take its public promises and theoretical expectations seriously. As this goes to press the OECD economists do not seem to have retreated very far from their 1995 manifesto which was cited earlier on pp.782-5. For their strategy to work properly – or perhaps to work at all – they insist

that it must be applied much more rigorously than it has yet been. Trade and finance must be *entirely* freed. There must be no protection of the losers from competition and technical change. Insolvent banks and their creditors must be allowed to fail. There must be no restraint of their gambling activities. There must be no deficit budgeting to sustain demand and employment.

National governments must balance their budgets, chiefly by spending less. There must be cuts in the number of income transfers and in their amounts. Deep cuts in benefits to the unemployed must drive them to compete for work to depress the wages and bargaining strength of those in work. There should be no minimum wage law and no unnecessary consumer protection. The overriding purpose must be 'to make wage and price formation more responsive to market conditions and speed the adjustment to changing price signals'.

Politicians who accept the need for those next steps have already cut many public services and privatized or spent what public capital they can. The worst of them now prepare for serious welfare cuts by teaching the public to blame the poor for their poverty. Aged pensioners could have saved or contributed to superannuation. The unemployed are preferring welfare to work. Self-interested welfare workers are perpetuating the ills they are supposed to relieve. Idle girls are getting pregnant to attract the lone parents' allowance. Mentally disabled people, turned out of hospital and deprived of the friendships and care they had there, are blamed for drinking, for begging, for haunting the shopping centres' concourses and park benches by day, and for the squalor of the lodgings or cardboard boxes in which they sleep at night.

Pity those politicians even if you don't forgive them. The program that has trapped them promised fourfold gains. Nationally, in each advanced economy, more of the people would earn their livings. A more efficient economy would produce more output. More of the output would be for individual market choice rather than bureaucratic distribution, so people would be freer and better satisfied. And internationally, free trade in goods, money and investment would enhance every country's economic growth and cause rich and poor incomes and standards of living to converge, slowly but surely, in an increasingly equal world.

BROKEN PROMISES

You know how and why that program broke all but one of its promises. In the rich democracies the failures were not catastrophic. That was partly because no democratic government implemented the whole program, or its more ruthless elements. Outside the US, labor retained some industrial and political strength. Some honest and reasonably cooperative business culture survived in many industries. Politicians began salami–slicing welfare incomes and services, but did not yet risk big cuts. So plenty of 'business as usual' continued, especially in non–tradeable goods and services.

Nevertheless, except for reducing inflation none of the promised benefits were delivered. Net investment declined, but some continued. The average rate of growth only halved. Outside the United States unemployment jumped to eight or ten or twelve per cent, but then its increase slowed. Inside the United States it stayed around five per cent while the poorest third of workers and households grew absolutely and relatively poorer than they had been, and poorer than their equivalents were in a dozen countries less rich than the United States.

The promises to poor countries were broken more brutally. Direct foreign investment went mostly to rich countries or China. The biggest net flow of capital funds was *into* the United States, some of it from the many poor countries whose foreign interest bills exceeded their export earnings, cut their import capacities and helped to keep them poor. The promise of free–trading 'convergence' of rich and poor countries' incomes turned out to be a cruel joke. (Some will dispute that. Suppose that poor African incomes rise by $20 to $120 while US incomes rise $3000 to $23000. Average Americans gain 150 times – that's 15000% – what poor Africans gain. Inequality is increasing. But instead of actual gains, Right thinkers prefer to compare each income's percentage gain (African 20%, US 18.66%). That way, Africans appear to have gained most so the world must be more equal. Consult your values about the meaning of 'equality'.)

If the Right program *had* succeeded there would still be cause for complaint. Remember *how* the advocates of smaller government expect it to improve economic performance. With freer trade, fast technological change, more mobile investment and deregulated labor markets (i.e. less public or union protection for the weaker ranks of labor) the theorists expect –

- hotter competition between firms
- steeper inequalities between the highest and lowest rates of pay
- hotter competition for jobs and less security in many of them
- more contract work, piece-work, shift work, part-time and variable-time work.

Workers are expected to be more productive because they will be more competitive, less cooperative with one another, less secure, more anxious, and more unequally paid. The qualities of work which have been found to do most for human development and happiness – and often for productivity too – are to be degraded. Some harmful and disagreeable conditions of employment are to be extended to more of the workforce. As the lowest paid workers and unemployed lose market income, smaller government also promises cuts in the public income transfers and free services which currently sustain those groups. Being poorer, they will be able to acquire less household capital and make less use of it to produce things for themselves. And less public investment and more user charges will give their neighborhoods less of the public space and capital that were available for free use by their parents.

So if that program *were* competent and *did* succeed you may think it would still make bad uses of economic resources. Should an affluent, pollutant society sacrifice long–term environmental prudence for faster short–term growth? Should it sacrifice full employment merely to gain higher income for some of the people still in work? Should it sacrifice qualities of fairness, security and workplace cooperation, which enrich the quality of life, for margins of affluent consumption which add little or nothing to it?

The tragedy is compounded as the retreat from government does not accelerate growth but slows it, and redistributes taxation downwards and income upwards to make the rich richer and the poor more numerous. Even for many of the winners the extra income may not be worth its personal and social costs: more competitive anxiety and insecurity at work, more crime, more conflict and squalor in the cities and the community as a whole.

If you need reminding of this text's reasons for these hostile judgments, revise Chapter 54's summary of them. Or simply memorize two of the globalizers' promises. Freedom from capital controls would see a great new flow of productive investment 'from the capital–rich developed countries to the opportunity–rich developing countries'. And with the other new freedoms it would cause rich and poor countries' incomes and standards of living to 'converge' in an increasingly equal world. Neoclassical economic theory deserves to be judged by those two promises, and by the effects of the strategy which they recommended.

Now suppose that the democracies' majorities, disillusioned, vote to change direction again. They want their rich mixed economies to deliver better environmental care, more material equality, more gender equality, more income security, safer income transfer from their earning to their non–earning years, better quality of life, and more effective aid to poor countries. How would you advise your determined new social democratic government to go about it – with due regard, of course, for your country's particular situation, resources, and economic and political capacities?

USES OF AFFLUENCE

The democracies' great twentieth–century achievement has been to become productive enough to distribute a comfortable living to all their members. There is a profoundly important relation between three effects of that triumph.

- It has revolutionized the economic capacity to deal with the traditional problems of scarcity and undue inequality.

- It creates new problems and possibilities in the relations between economic activity and the quality and happiness of life.

- Its environmental effects are dangerous enough to compel further radical changes, by choice or by disastrous default. And any effective strategy is likely to have to include some deliberate limitation of consumption.

Bad responses to all three tasks are possible, and likely if the present Right and half–Right strategies continue.

But the environmental predicament is different from the other two, in that 'steady as we go' with no change of direction is not an option. Some limits to total consumption seem inescapable. If they come by default rather than by self–restraint they may be physically and morally horrifying (disease, famine, pre–emptive genocide). And if by prudent restraint, they require the greatest restraint in the richest countries. Any deliberate permanent restraint must bring some changes to current market freedoms and distributive processes and political alliances – and to some assumptions of prevailing economic theories. Thus the frightening environmental prospects may help to break the Right ascendancy and compel new thought and action about other possibilities besides environmental care.

The few remaining pages of this course of study invite you to imagine *good* uses of those new constraints and opportunities, considered together. That may begin with some repair and replacement of the old means of coping with the old problems of scarcity and inequality.

REPAIRS

The democracies need to improve their private sectors' performance by rebuilding the intricate law and regulation, the public capital for private use and the public services which enterprises and markets need if they are to deliver their classical freedoms and efficiencies. Not much of that can be done by 'retreating to the past'. The problems of boom and slump and unbalanced trade and payments may be much as they were for an earlier generation. But the trends to increasing unemployment and poverty and inequality, to executive plunder, and to unproductive international gambling are new. So are the magnitude of the educational, health and welfare needs, the changing proportions of earning and non–earning years in the average lifetime, and the changing relation between the prices of manufactured goods and of many human services. Together those call for some shift from individual to collective spending and from earned to transferred incomes. The best responses to those problems, including the best mix of national and international action about them, are likely to vary over time and with nations' particular political and economic capacities. This course of study has tried to equip you to contribute to those judgments. And there may be fewer useful lessons from past experience, and more of your own judgment and invention, as your generation faces the new questions about the uses of affluence, complicated by new environmental and social questions about affluence itself.

RATIONING

A general perception of equality in some fundamentals, and a fair scale and distribution of continuing inequalities, is important when there has to be rationing. A consensus that the rationing is necessary and fair can maintain electoral support for it, and nourish a culture which discourages too much cheating.

There are alternative strategies. Environmentally important materials and products may be rationed directly or by discriminate pricing without any adjustment to the distribution of income. That simply leaves richer people with more to spend on unrationed, environmentally harmless goods and services.

That would not have sufficed in wartime. Rationing enforced fair sharing of scarce essentials like food, clothing and energy. But there was also a big diversion of productive capacity to war production, and some destruction of resources by the war itself. So to prevent inflation (from too much income chasing too few goods in the civilian economy) income as well as goods had to be rationed. That was done chiefly by steeply progressive income tax, price controls, and rules against increasing wage rates.

Economists, especially of the Right, have tended to recommend that any necessary peacetime rationing be done by price, or distributed by price. For example there is currently strong pressure for some price–rationing of the use of pollutant fuels. That can be done in a variety of ways. A carbon tax motivates users of coal and oil to use less of them. Alternatively a system of tradeable emission rights allows government to limit the total damage, and users to bid for shares of that total. (Government issues permits to all users who can then trade them at market prices. Or government auctions a rationed quantity of permits to competing bidders, who can then trade them.)

Are those methods of rationing as regressive as they seem at first sight? Won't raising the prices of poor people's essential heating and cooking and transport take a higher proportion of their incomes than the tax will take of most higher incomes? Some economists who are both Green and Left concede some of that effect but point to countervailing effects. American experience shows big industrial fuel users responding to carbon taxation with quicker, more effective fuel economies, and lower price increases, than were expected. From the tax revenue many poor users, notably pensioners, could in principle be compensated. Above all, poor people are the biggest beneficiaries of cleaner air. They tend to live in the most crowded, polluted, unregulated, industrialized neighborhoods. They suffer most pollution–related sickness. They can least afford air–conditioning, or to live at unpolluted addresses. They have plenty to gain from a broad social democratic strategy which does raise their fuel prices but also, by cleaner air, higher pensions and other measures, improves their health, housing, neighborhood resources, educational opportunities and after–tax incomes.

But some demands are price–inelastic. Many well–off people pay, or have their firms pay, whatever the grandest cars cost, then whatever their fuel costs. We already require car–makers to instal emission controls. Why not also limit the size and engine capacities of private cars to their functional needs as basic transport, and incidentally tame their performance?

A greening world will want economists to contribute to rationing policies, quantify and cost them, advise the people and politicians responsible for determining them, and monitor their economic effects both for environmental purposes and to contribute to judgments about compensating losers.

The distribution of paid work

The achievement of affluence opens three new questions about work.

First a debatable one. Does some of the rich world's rising unemployment signify an unprecedented kind of economic maturity? Does high productivity from capital–saving as well as labor–saving technology promise indefinite jobless growth and declining prices in the production of material goods, and declining demand for labor–intensive services as their relative prices rise or as demand for them is saturated? And have workers' hours of work diminished as far as the workers themselves want them to, so that from now on they will want more pay rather than more leisure as their share of any further growth? If so, the continuing growth of productivity threatens a continuing increase of unemployment. In short, are there new *economic* reasons for rationing working time, as Germans and some other Europeans have begun to do? And even if not, may *environmental* constraints limit employment and justify some fair sharing of it? Or might a Green regime develop enough new restorative activities, and replace some pollutant methods of production with some return to muscle power, to restore full employment?

The experience of work

With or without changes in working hours or the working lifetime, should we be thinking of ways to improve the experience of work, even at some cost which we could now well afford? Especially the dull or oppressive or unhealthy or anxiously insecure kinds of work? And the long exhausting hours of overwork that some 'lean' managers and some exploited workers are compelled to do? Should we encourage more self–management where the nature of the work allows it? More cooperative mutual quality control rather than external authoritarian quality control? More choosing of new workers by the groups with whom they will work? And anything else you can think of to make work more interesting and sociable– or just more tolerable?

Whether full employment is achieved by some rationing of work or by other means, it can get double benefit from an effective incomes policy. Whether wage and salary rates are centrally negotiated, as once in Sweden, or set by independent arbitrators as in Australia, there will need to be upper as well as lower limits to the rates to prevent inflation if full employment is restored. But inflexible limits could inhibit some useful market processes. Producers who attract rising demand need to be able to attract more workers. At

present they can usually pull them out of the pool of unemployed. With full employment they must entice them to leave other employers, commonly by offering higher pay. (That, together with excessively strong union bargaining, is the inflationary effect of full employment of which Joan Robinson, Thomas Balogh and Michal Kalecki tried but failed to convince Keynes.) In wartime, governments have reconciled full employment with zero inflation by banning wage rises and *directing* both employers and workers to the most needed tasks. That's not tolerable in peacetime. But a trio of policies might work well together. (1) Any one of the good wage–fixing systems. (2) Zero payroll tax on the normal working week, with a high tax on overtime and (3) a tax on over–award pay. That leaves employers with the necessary commercial freedom to buy the work they need. But it helps full employment by discouraging overwork. And it offers employers two ways of competing for scarce labor. If they pay too much for it, the inflationary effect of that is reduced by the tax on overpayment. And the overpayment and the tax together encourage the alternative method, which is to compete for scarce labor by offering attractive conditions of work. Depending on circumstances that might mean more secure employment, more self-management, more say in the recruitment of fellow-workers, more help with further training, less shift work, a better canteen, better child care, more accommodation of working hours to family needs. *All* employers in the busier industries might need to compete in those sociable ways, whether to attract new hands or to hold those they have. And a democracy which opts to use some of its affluence in that way, to shift the balance between producers' and consumers' benefits, may need some trade or exchange protection for its choice, and should not be prevented from applying it.

A third and most important question about rationing or re–distributing work deserves a section of its own.

Gender, childhood and work

Affluence and full democracy between them have brought new stress as well as new hope to relations between parent and parent, parents and children, paid and unpaid work, work at home and work away from home. The argument which belongs here is already in Chapter 15 on pages 173 to 180. It is hard to condense it any further, and wasteful to print it twice in the same book. Please turn back and read it in the context of this discussion of global dangers and opportunities for democracy.

There are a number of good ways, old and new, to

arrange relations between earning and parenting. The good ways should be open to parents' choice, and affluent democracies could well afford to open them all to most parents' choice. Parents should also be able, as far as their individual natures allow, to avoid the bad ways: to spare each other and their children the unfair, stressful, destructive or impoverished relations between each other, and between earning and parenting, that shortages of time and money can help to cause. Politically the necessary reforms ought to be easier than most, because the conflicts which they aim to resolve can trouble parents at every level of income.

The Right global program threatens double damage to family life. It wants intense international competition for jobs between workers stripped of most of their present protections. It wants to accept, or when necessary contrive, a 'natural' rate of unemployment. It wants low skilled and low paid workers, and rising numbers of the higher skilled and higher paid, to be easily dismissed, to change locations and move house readily, to work longer or shorter hours than they want, to have less of the income security that qualifies them for mortgage loans. From the higher skilled and higher paid ranks of professionals and managers the principles of lean management demand long hours and overwork which don't even allow much early morning or evening or weekend parenting. Likewise in the public sector. In their purchaser/provider model of public service these reformers want to spread competition and insecurity into the many public services whose employment *can* be secure because their staff needs *are* predictable. In both sectors, except for short periods of maternity leave, there are much the same disabling demands on ambitious women as on ambitious men.

The most effective resistance to the Right program has so far been in Western Europe. But some clauses of the Treaty of Maastricht (Europe's basic constitutional document) may hinder the component countries' capacity to respond to historical changes, including changes in the conditions of family life, as their people may well want to do. Some proposals to limit the proportion of national income which governments may handle have been rejected. But there are limits on public debt and on deficit budgeting, and countries which join the monetary union lose their central banking powers. Those restraints on inflation may make it harder to restore full employment, or to expand public services and income transfers. But greater danger to the democratic capacity for further reform of the uses of affluence and the conditions of family life may arise from a provision that member states of the Union must not expand their public budgets faster than their Gross Domestic Product. Demographers calculate that the ageing of population could increase the proportion of GDP handled by government by 6 or 7 percentage points in Germany and about 5 points in Belgium and Italy if present superannuation systems continue unchanged. If the people also want more medical care, education, reformed conditions of childhood and parenting, or other spending or redistributive changes in response to changing historical conditions, there can only be class reasons – inequitable reasons, winners' reasons – for continuing a rule which says 'If you want those good things you must buy them privately and unequally. You are barred from voting to buy them publicly, more equally, or (with many of them) more economically.' Turn back to p. 153 if you need reminding that even if you want *unchanged* proportions of manufactured goods and human services you must expect to shift some spending from the goods to the services as productivity improves.

Meanwhile review the various parenting possibilities sketched in Chapter 15, and any others you can think of, and reflect on the mentality of the globalizing governments and their economic advisers. They lead the first generation which could comfortably afford all those aids and opportunities for parents and children, and for women's options and equalities. But they have launched a program whose effects must block or degrade all those options for many families, and some of them for all families. Instead of a new reconciliation of men's, women's and children's conflicts of interest, the attack on big government, democratic choice, labor rights and welfare intensifies many of them. Like the rest of the attack on social democratic achievements, it is difficult to believe that it could retain its majority support if it were not for public faith that the relevant experts must surely know what they are doing, and must surely be doing it in everybody's interest.

But don't be too hard in a personal way on the economists among them, despite what this text has said about their professional roles. What they believe, and the unintended damage they do, is what their higher education taught most of them to believe and do. Treat them as bequeathing your generation some worthwhile work to do. In the rich democracies, that includes some rescue of children's upbringing. But before much of that can be done for children in the poorest countries, more of them must first be kept alive.

GLOBAL GOVERNMENT ?

What follows is not about one world government managing a world economy. It suggests what might be done by international institutions *assisting* the national governments of developing and reforming countries, and sometimes *disciplining* them, rather than subordinating or replacing them. It scarcely touches the problems of corrupt or tyrannical government, or official genocide, which some of the poorest countries suffer. The following example touches the problem of bad government only in some of the incentive measures which it proposes. Where those measures don't succeed they may have the ill effect that in rewarding good government, they deprive poor people whose rulers are already maltreating them. But that may be the least bad thing to do if, over time, it brings better government and international aid to greater numbers of people.

As you read this final section, you will meet an able economist working with humane purpose at a complicated practical problem of political economy. Notice how he goes about it. And read it all, however tediously official you may find some of its language.

A PROGRAM FOR DEVELOPING AND REFORMING COUNTRIES

In *Towards a new Bretton Woods: Alternatives for the global economy* (1994) Stuart Holland proposes international financial arrangements for developing countries and reforming (ex–communist) countries. With his permission his summary of the program is presently quoted in full. His introduction to it recognizes 'that diverse problems for different economic systems need to be addressed and resolved through greater diversity in ideas and policies, rather than constrained by a single paradigm of structural adjustment and gains from trade, or a single model of governance.' Under past policies of the relevant international institutions 'one of the main features of structural adjustment ... has been the degree to which its costs in too many cases have been borne by the poorest people in the poorer countries, and especially by children. Getting exchange rates and prices right too often has wronged the poor, without the intended gains of export–led growth or trickle–down in their favour.'

Having reasoned its way to the need for a new regime, the book proposes specific institutional responsibilities for assessing the amount and kind of aid and exchange that would enable each developing and reforming country to meet specified basic needs; what foreign funds they would need for investment in envi-

ronmental programs and further development; and where the funds should come from and on what conditions. The responsibilities of the International Monetary Fund and other 'Washington' institutions are to be checked and balanced by roles for United Nations institutions whose membership and purposes reflect their more direct representation of developing countries and their poorer people. The financial targets are in 1994 values so may need adjustment.

In Stuart Holland's summary:

1. The United Nations Regional Economic Commissions, in association with the United Nations Development Programme (UNDP) and the United Nations International Children's Emergency Fund (UNICEF), should determine the **Development Expenditure** levels in individual countries which would ensure that minimum standards could be achieved in nutrition, housing, sanitation, health care, education and basic social services, with an interim target of raising such expenditures to $1200 per head, and a longer-term target of $2000 per head. The candidate countries would mainly be developing countries. Higher imports by the developing countries on the basis of agreed criteria for increased social expenditure should be designated **Development Deficits**.

2. The new Development Expenditure targets should be incorporated into a global recovery programme determined by the G7 [Group of seven leading governments] or its reformed equivalent resulting from widened membership on either a national or regional basis. Finance for the programmes should be through increased official development assistance, with generation of counterpart funds by local governments. The expenditures – reinforced by **Environmental Programmes** for both the developing and reforming economies – would in turn promote and sustain the global recovery programme.

3. The International Monetary Fund (IMF) should disaggregate such a recovery of mutual import and export trade by main regions of the world economy, with target import levels for the reforming and developing countries. Development Deficits would be itemised by the Fund in an annual report on **Social expenditure, trade and payments** of the countries concerned. The Regional Economic Commissions of the UN also should jointly undertake an independent assessment of such target trade levels and their

impact on the different regions and countries of the global economy.

4. The IMF should then determine the **Balance of Payments** support necessary to sustain the currencies of individual developing and reforming economies on the basis of such Development Deficits, and relate this to the restructuring of debt.

5. **Social conditionality** should be imposed on the implementation of the social expenditure programmes which give rise to Development Deficits. The UN Regional Economic Commissions jointly with the Regional Development Banks would have joint responsibility for monitoring the implementation of the specific programmes, with the penalty of reduction or non-continuation obtaining for those governments which did not implement them.

6. **Financial conditionality** could still be imposed by the IMF on governments which failed to meet performance targets in areas other than those of the social expenditure and environmental programmes agreed with the developing and reforming economies. But the targets themselves should be set in a manner which assists rather than obstructs adjustment to new paths for development. In this context the Fund should be obliged to take account of parameters such as those proposed in the United Nations Economic Commission for Africa (UNECA) report on an alternative framework to structural adjustment programmes. Further, countries should be able to appeal against alleged breach of such parameters to an independent body representing the wider framework of the UN agencies and some member countries.

7. Investment finance for both social development and environmental programmes for the developing countries and reforming economies should include elements of Keynes' original intention for his Bancor unit, i.e. be related to the potential growth of world trade, income and taxable personal and corporate revenue accruing from the Global Recovery Programme for mutual import and export trade between all economies. Such finance should not imply a formal increase of IMF quotas or Special Drawing Rights, but should constitute a new **International Development Facility** (IDF). The rate of interest on drawings from the IDF should be indexed in terms of the income per head in purchasing power parity terms of the borrowers.

8. This facility should be backed through subscription by governments of the OECD countries to a new **International Development Bond** (IDB) which should fulfil Keynes' recommendation on the recycling of surpluses in international trade. In practice, at present, Japan is – and is likely to continue to be – the main surplus country, and one of the main potential subscribers to the IDB. But the US and the European Union also should undertake to be major subscribers. Lending in the main to creditworthy countries, the IDB should be expected to earn a market rate of interest. It could be administered by an **International Investment Trust**.

9. The International Development Bonds should constitute a main source for the finance of Environmental Programmes in the reforming economies. Developing countries should be able to draw on the International Development Facility for investment concerning social programmes. Serious consideration also should be given to the establishment of new **Regional Monetary Funds**. With the existing UN Regional Development Banks, and in line with the European Bank for Reconstruction and Development and the new European Investment Fund, these should be entitled to undertake their own bond issues. Regional Monetary Funds not only could ensure more pluralism and response to local development needs than a single International Monetary Fund, but also could offer advantages in higher local quotas on a regional basis for subscribers than may prove to be the case with a reform of the quota share of the IMF.

10. **Payments Clearance Unions** should be encouraged on a regional basis in order to reduce the need for countries in specific regions to settle their accounts in hard currency other than at the end of given financial years. In the case of the reforming and developing countries it can be anticipated that many member countries of such unions would remain in deficit in hard currency terms even on an annual basis. In such a case they should be entitled to apply for IDF or IDB borrowings. The index of the rate of interest on borrowings from the IDF, in such cases, would be related both to the PPP [purchasing power parity] income per head of the countries concerned, and also to their performance record in repayment.

– Stuart Holland, *Towards a New Bretton Woods*,
Spokesman 1994 pp. 31-4

Notice (hoping he will forgive the impertinence) the

range of things which that author keeps in mind. He knows the institutions, the kinds of people who staff them (different kinds in Washington, in the UN Plaza in New York, in central Africa or central Asia). He understands a good deal of what moves those different people in those different worlds. He knows many of the helpful and unhelpful conditions in which his new institutions must operate, and by what sort of people they must be staffed if they are to work effectively for the benefits he has in mind for the people he wants to help. He understands as well as anyone and better than most what causes what in the economy in which he lives and the others in which he also researches and works. Where safety and clean water supplies and some joy in life for poor Africans might benefit from boringly detailed exercises in institutional design, he doesn't mind how long they take. He uses simple language, or technical or mathematical language, or (elsewhere in the book) quietly deadly language, according to the task. That includes flat bureaucratic language where it is best for bureaucratic purposes, or deft for political purposes. He knows, for example, but does not name, but does not need to, the professional incompetence and the approximate number of millions of children dying and women despairing, through recent years, in what the value-free members of our profession call 'structural adjustment'. He doesn't rant against them, as that last sentence did, or make unnecessary enemies, as it may do. He does whatever works best for the people he's doing it for. He's good tough company to remember, as you farewell this course.

On your way, now. Go well.

Index